8/05

8/05

World Literature
and Its Times

VOLUME **7**

Italian
Literature and
Its Times

World Literature and Its Times

Profiles of Notable Literary Works and the
Historical Events That Influenced Them

Joyce Moss

THOMSON

GALE

Detroit • New York • San Francisco • San Diego • New Haven, Conn. • Waterville, Maine • London • Munich

THOMSON ™

GALE

World Literature and Its Times
Profiles of Notable Literary Works and the Historical Events That Influenced Them
Volume 7: Italian Literature and Its Times

Joyce Moss, Editor

Product Manager
Meggin Condino

Editorial
Sara Constantakis, Michael L. LaBlanc,
Gillian Leonard, Ira Mark Milne

Permissions
Margaret Abendroth, Kim Smilay

Imaging and Multimedia
Lezlie Light, Michael Logusz, Dan Newell,
Christine O'Bryan

Image Acquisition
Denay Wilding

Manufacturing
Rhonda Dover

Library of Congress Cataloging-in-Publication Data

Moss, Joyce, 1951-
    Italian literature and its times / Joyce Moss.
        p. cm. -- (World literature and its times ; v. 7)
    Includes bibliographical references and index.
    ISBN 0-7876-3725-4 (hardcover : alk. paper)
    1. Italian literature--History and criticism. 2. Literature and history--Italy.
I. Title.
    PQ4038.M67 2005
    850.9'358--dc22

                                    2005015914

Printed in the United States of America
10 9 8 7 6 5 4 3 2 1

Contents

General Preface

The world at the dawn of the twenty-first century is a shrinking sphere. Innovative modes of transmission make communication from one continent to another virtually instantaneous, quickening the development of an increasingly global society, heightening the urgency of the need for mutual understanding. At the foundation of *World Literature and Its Times* is the belief that within a people's literature are keys to their perspectives, their emotions, and the formative events that have brought them to the present point.

As manifested in their literary works, societies experience phenomena that are in some respects universal and in other respects tied to time and place. Italo Calvino's *The Path to the Spiders' Nest,* a novel set in Italy during the Second World War, and Samuel Beckett's *Waiting for Godot,* a play set at an unspecified time and place but reflective of events in World War II France, both draw on popular Resistance movements to the Nazi war effort. Yet while they reflect the same phenomenon, a close look at the two works and the related historical developments reveals differences that are indeed tied to time and place. In much the same way, Rosario Feré's "The Youngest Doll," a short story set in mid-twentieth-century Puerto Rico, and Furugh Farrukhzad's "The Mechanical Doll," a poem set in mid-twentieth-century Iran, both concern the limitations placed on the female population of their respective societies. While even the titles suggest a similarity, in this case too an informed reading of the two works reveals illuminating differences.

World Literature and Its Times regards both fiction and nonfiction as rich mediums for recognizing the differences as well as the similarities among people and societies. In its view, full understanding of a literary work demands attention to events and attitudes of the period in which it takes place and of the one in which it is written. The series therefore examines novels, short stories, biographies, essays, speeches, poems, and plays by contextualizing a given work within these two periods. Each volume covers some 50 literary works that span a mix of centuries and genres. The literary work itself takes center stage, with its contents determining which issues—social, political, psychological, economic, or cultural—are covered. The entry on a literary work discusses the relevant issues apart from the work, making connections to it when merited and allowing for comparisons between the literary and the historical realities. Close attention is given to the work as well, in the interest of extracting historical understandings from it.

Of course, the function of literature is not necessarily to represent history accurately. Nevertheless, the images and ideas promoted by a powerful literary work—be it Marco Polo's narrative *The Travels of Marco Polo* (set in China and Southeast Asia), José Hernandez's poem *The Gaucho Martín Fierro* (set in Argentina), Isak Dinesen's memoir *Out of Africa* (Kenya), or William Shakespeare's play *Macbeth* (Scotland)—leave impressions commonly taken to be historical. In taking literature as fact, one risks acquiring a mistaken notion of history. The gaucho of Argentina is a case in point, having inspired poetry by non-gauchos whose verse conveys a highly romanticized image of these cowboylike nomads, albeit one that includes some realistic details. To adjust for such discrepancies, this series distinguishes between fact and its literary reworkings.

On the other hand, literary works can broaden our understanding of history. They are able to convey more than the cut-and-dried record by portraying events in a way that captures the fears and challenges of a period or that draws attention to groups of people who are generally left out of standard histories. Many of the literary works covered in this series—from Miguel de Cervantes's *Don Quixote* (Spain) to Nelson Mandela's "The Rivonia Trial Speech" (South Africa)—draw attention to elements of society that have been neglected in standard histories. This is well illustrated by writings about women in wartime, from Laura Esquivel's *Like Water for Chocolate* (Mexico) to Isak Dinesen's *Out of Africa* (Kenya), Elizabeth Bowen's *The Heat of the Day* (Britain), Hanan al-Shaykh's *The Story of Zahra* (Lebanon), and Elsa Morante's *History: A Novel* (Italy). As illustrated by these works, literature in various societies engages in a vigorous dialog with mainstream texts, offering alternative perspectives. In fact, many of the works covered in this series feature characters and ideas that counter deeply ingrained stereotypes, from Friar Bartolomé de las Casas's *A Short Account of the Destruction of the Indies* (mid-1500s Latin America) to Mongo Beti's *Mission to Kala* (mid-1900s Cameroon Republic).

Even nonfiction must be anchored in its place and time to derive its full value. José Ortega y Gasset's set of essays *Meditations on Quixote* concerns itself with the search for Spanish identity in light of recent imperial losses and in relation to a European philosophy of the day. Primo Levi's *Survival in Auschwitz* is the memoir of a victim of Fascist anti-Semitism in Italy, trying to process his experience as a survivor of the Holocaust. A third entry, on Frantz Fanon's *The Wretched of the Earth* (about the merits of violence), considers his views as an outgrowth of the ravages in colonial Algeria.

The task of reconstructing the historical context of a literary work can be problematic. An author may present events out of chronological order, as Mexico's Carlos Fuentes does in *The Death of Artemio Cruz.* Or a work may feature a legendary character that defies attempts to fit her or him into a strict time slot. The heroic queen in *The Arabian Nights,* who puts a stop to her king's

execution of an unfortunate series of wives, is one such character. In the first case, *World Literature and Its Times* unscrambles the plot, providing a linear rendering of events and associated historical developments. In the second, the series profiles customs and background information particular to the culture at the times the epic is set and written, arming the reader with details that inform the hero's adventures. The approach sheds light on the relationship between fact and fiction, both of which are shown to provide insight into a people and their epic heritage. As always, the approach is taken with a warm appreciation for the beauty of a literary work independent of the related historical facts, but also in the belief that ultimate regard is shown for that work by placing it in the context of pertinent events.

Beyond this underlying belief, the *World Literature and Its Times* series is founded on the notion that a command of world literature bolsters knowledge of the writings produced by one's own society. Long before the present century, writers from different locations influenced one another through trends and strategies in their literatures. In our postcolonial age, such cross-fertilization has quickened. Latin American literature, having been influenced by Spanish trends, among others, itself influences Chinese writers of today. Likewise, Italy's and Africa's literary traditions have affected and been affected by France's, and the same relationship holds true for the writings of Spain and Germany, and of India and Great Britain. The degree of such literary intermixture promises only to multiply given our increasingly global society. In the process, world literatures and their landmark texts gain even greater significance, attaining the potential to promote understanding not only of others, but also of ourselves.

The Selection of Literary Works

The works covered in *World Literature and Its Times 7: Italian Literature and Its Times* have been carefully selected by professors in the field at the universities listed in the Acknowledgements. Keeping the literature-history connection in mind, the team chose titles for inclusion based on a combination of factors: how frequently a literary work is studied, how closely it is tied to pivotal events in the past or present, and how strong and enduring its appeal has been to readers in and out of the society that produced it. Attention has been paid to literary works that have met with critical and/or popular acclaim, from the inception of Italian literature in the thirteenth century to the present. There has also been a careful effort to represent female as well as male authors, to cover a mix of genres, and to treat literary works that depict the experiences of different regions of the country and elements of the population, including recent immigrants from, for example, Africa. The literary works were furthermore limited to those that have been already translated into English. There are, of course, many more valuable works of Italian literature than one could include in the volume. The inclusion of the selected list of works at the expense of these others has been made with the above-detailed concerns in mind.

Format and Arrangement of Entries

The volumes in *World Literature and Its Times* are arranged geographically. Within each volume, the collection is arranged alphabetically by title of the literary work. The setting of a literary work appears at the beginning of the entry. Each entry is organized as follows:

1. **Introduction**—provides identifying information in three parts:

   The literary work—specifies the genre of a work, the place and time period in which it is set, when it was written and/or first published, and when it was first translated into English; also provided is the title of the work in its original language.

   Synopsis—summarizes the storyline or contents of the work.

   Introductory paragraph—introduces the literary work in relation to the author's life.

2. **Events in History at the Time the Literary Work Takes Place**—describes social and political events that relate to the plot or contents of the literary work. The section may discuss background information as well as relevant events during the period in which the work is set. The subsections in this section vary, depending on the particular literary work. In general, the section takes a deductive approach, starting with events in history and telescoping inward to events in the literary work.

3. **The Literary Work in Focus**—summarizes the plot or contents of the literary work in detail, describes how it illuminates history, and identifies sources used to generate the work and the literary context sur-

rounding it. The section begins with a detailed plot or contents summary, followed by a subsection on an aspect of the work that illuminates our understanding of events or attitudes of the period. This subsection takes an inductive approach, starting with the literary work and broadening outward to events in history. A third subsection specifies sources that inspired elements of the work and discusses its literary context, or relation to other works.

4. **Events in History at the Time the Literary Work Was Written**—describes social, political, and/or literary events in the author's lifetime that relate to the plot or contents of a work. Also discussed in this section are the reviews or reception accorded the literary work.

5. **For More Information**—provides a list of all sources that have been cited in the entry as well as sources for further reading about the issues or personalities that have been highlighted in the entry.

   If a literary work is set and written in the same time period, sections 2 and 4 of the entry on that work ("Events in History at the Time the Literary Work Takes Place" and "Events in History at the Time the Literary Work Was Written") are combined into the single section "Events in History at the Time of the Literary Work."

Additional Features

Relevant primary-source material appears where appropriate in the text and in sidebars. Other sidebars provide historical details that amplify issues raised in the text and anecdotes that promote understanding of the temporal context. At the front of the volume is a set of timelines that presents a historical overview of the society or societies featured in a volume. The timelines are correlated to the literary works treated in the volume. Timelines also appear within entries to summarize intricate periods of history. Finally, historically relevant illustrations enrich and further clarify information in the entries.

Comments and Suggestions

Your comments on this series and suggestions for future editions are welcome. Please write: Editors, *World Literature and Its Times,* Thomson Gale, 27500 Drake Road, Farmington Hills, Michigan 48331-3535.

Acknowledgments

World Literature and Its Times 7: Italian Literature and Its Times is a collaborative effort that evolved through a series of stages, each monitored by experts in the fields of Italian literature and history. Deep appreciation is extended to Professor Barbara Zecchi of the University of Massachusetts at Amherst for her invaluable guidance at every stage of the development, from the selection of literary works to the review of entries, illustrations, and front matter. A special note of gratitude is also extended to Professors Geoffrey Symcox of the University of California at Los Angles and Claudio Fogu at the University of California at Santa Barbara for their monitoring of the accuracy of historical details throughout the volume.

Professor with expertise in particular authors and literary works reviewed the manuscripts of the selected entries. The editors express appreciation to the following professors for their examination of the entries to insure accuracy and completeness of the information conveyed.

Andrea Baldi, Rutgers University, Department of Italian

Franco Betti, University of California at Los Angeles, Department of Italian

Susanna Ferlito, University of Minnesota, French and Italian Department

Claudio Fogu, University of California at Santa Barbara, Department of French and Italian

Stephanie Jed, University of California at San Diego, Department of Italian Studies

Carol Lazzaro-Weis, University of Missouri-Columbia, Department of Romance Languages and Literatures

Edwin McCann, University of Southern California, School of Philosophy

Karen Pinkus, University of Southern California, Departments of French and Italian and Comparative Literature

Lucia Re, University of California at Los Angeles, Department of Italian

Franco Ricci, University of Ottawa, Modern Languages and Literatures

Margaret F. Rosenthal, University of Southern California, Department of French and Italian

Risa Sodi, Yale University, Italian Department

Geoffrey Symcox, University of California at Los Angeles, Department of History

Barbara Zecchi, University of Massachusetts at Amherst, Department of Languages, Literatures, and Cultures

For their painstaking research and composition, the editors thank the writers whose names appear at the close of the entries they contributed. A complete listing follows:

Robert D. Aguirre, Professor, Wayne State University

Loredana Anderson-Tirro, Senior Language Lecturer, New York University

Sarah Annunziato, Ph.D. candidate, Gilman Fellow, Johns Hopkins University

Acknowledgments

Andrea Baldi, Associate Professor, Rutgers University

Amy Boylan, Visiting Assistant Professor, Colorado College

Carlo Celli, Associate Professor, Bowling Green State University

Gary Cestaro, Associate Professor, DePaul University

Elena Coda, Assistant Professor, Purdue University

Terri DeYoung, Associate Professor, University of Washington at Seattle

Jacqualine Dyess, Lecturer, University of North Texas

Flora Ghezzo, Assistant Professor, Columbia University

Nicoleta Ghisas, Ph.D. candidate, Johns Hopkins University

Martin Griffin, Lecturer, Pomona College

Margherita Heyer-Caput, Associate Professor, University of California at Davis

Rebecca Hopkins, Ph.D. candidate, University of California at Los Angeles

Martha King, Lecturer, University of Maryland—European Division

Pamela S. Loy, Ph.D., University of California at Santa Barbara; professional writer

Diane R. Mannone, M.A. candidate, California State University at Dominguez Hills

Paolo Matteucci, Ph.D. candidate, University of Southern California

Jorge Minguell, Ph.D. candidate, Johns Hopkins University

Valerie Mirshak, Ph.D. candidate, Johns Hopkins University

Letizia Modena, Ph.D. candidate, Johns Hopkins University

Maria Laura Mosco, Ph.D. candidate, University of Toronto

Arndt Niebisch, Ph.D. candidate, Johns Hopkins University

Courtney K. Quaintance, Ph.D. candidate, University of Chicago

David D. Roberts, Albert Berry Saye Professor of History, University of Georgia

Federica Santini, Lecturer, University of California at Los Angeles

Tiziana Serafini, Ph.D. candidate, University of California at Los Angeles

Risa Sodi, Senior Lecturer and Italian Language Program Director, Yale University

Elissa Tognozzi, Lecturer/Director of Italian Language Studies, University of California at Los Angeles

Cristina Villa, Ph.D. candidate, University of California at Los Angeles

Colin Wells, M.A., Oxford University; professional writer

Petra Wirth, Adjunct Lecturer, University of Arizona

Laura Wittman, Assistant Professor, Stanford University

A final note of gratitude is extended to Michael L. LaBlanc of Thomson Gale for his careful editing and co-ordination of copy and illustrations, and to Anne Leach, who indexed the volume with great sensitivity to readers and subject matter. Lastly the editors thank Lisa Granados, Danielle Price, Lorraine Valestuk, and Monica Riordan for their skillful execution of the editing, proofreading, and word processing.

Introduction

"My Italy" chants a despairing Petrarch in a poem that he penned some 500 years before Italy became a unified nation. Then the area was just a collection of separate regions with a common memory. Resounding from Tuscany, his lament invoked a single name for the already long-disunited regions—*Italia*—an ancient appellation for territory that once formed the heart of the Roman Empire and that roughly corresponds to Italy today. Remarkably, for 1400 years, from the fall of the Roman Empire in 476 C.E. to unification in 1861, the regions remained separate yet conceived elements of a national identity. Fundamental to this achievement was a common literary language in a land of multiple dialects.

Italy's is a history of dramatic extremes. Its regions continually sought to recapture the cultural and political heights scaled by the Roman Empire even as they suffered invasions and domination by outsiders. After the Empire's definitive fall as a result of the Ostrogoth invasion in 476, the area succumbed to centuries of devastating warfare, including battles between the Goths and the Byzantine Empire, and invasions from the north by the Lombards, a semi-nomadic people who conquered the northern and central Italian Peninsula in 569. The Lombards mostly respected local custom, even assimilating with the surrounding populace, but they never conquered the whole territory. The Byzantines remained in Sicily, in much of the South, and in Venice, while the popes kept Rome and its environs under

Church control. *Italia* fell subject to a fragmented existence that would ensue for centuries. In the North, the Lombards established somewhat centralized political structures on the foundation of those left by the Romans, and a degree of stability ensued. Meanwhile, the Arabs began to conquer the far less stable South in 827. Under Arab rule, Sicily in particular prospered for a time. New technical and cultural inventions were introduced, and Palermo became a vibrant intellectual and artistic center.

From his vantage point in the country's center, the pope kept a worried eye on the Arab threat, responding to both it and renewed Lombard expansion by calling in the Franks to defend papal interests. The Frankish leader, Charlemagne, went on to claim the northern peninsula, attaching it to his empire, and becoming an absentee ruler, a common role in the northern and central regions.

All of the fragmentation and absentee rule helped render northern and central Italy ripe for the growth of independent urban centers in the tenth and eleventh centuries. These regions saw the rise of the communes, self-governing, republican cities, ruled not by foreigners but by influential families of insiders, with a role for representative councils and popular assemblies. The communes faded in the thirteenth and fourteenth centuries as large cities incorporated smaller ones—Milan swept Pavia into its fold; Venice conquered Padua. Some of the prominent cities grew into states, which often fell under the sway of local notables who turned despotic. By the end of the fourteenth century, a still fragmented Italy boasted five major states—the Duchy of Milan, the Republic of Venice, the Republic of Florence, the Papal States, and the Kingdom of Naples—with large stretches of land falling outside their domain. It was in one of these outside areas that literature in an Italian vernacular was born.

Sicily had by this time passed from Arab rule to Norman (French) domination, then to Aragonese (Spanish) rule. The Normans had isolated the Italian South from foreign contact, stymieing trade while the North engaged in it, turning into the more prosperous region. The two regions developed along separate, interdependent paths, with the agrarian South furnishing raw materials (wool, grain, etc.) to an increasingly urban and commercial North. When the Normans had the South re-instate the feudal system, which had been dying out in the North, they only widened the regional gap, which still plagues Italy today. On the other hand, for a glorious half century, a Norman descendant, Frederick II (1194-1250), ruled Sicily in intellectual style, his court at Palermo drawing an energetic circle of writers and thinkers from the immediate vicinity, from the North, and from other European lands, giving rise to the first poets to write in an Italian vernacular. Called the Sicilian School, their verse centered on refined love. It is these early-thirteenth-century Sicilian poets whom scholars credit with the start of the Italian literary tradition. Some 20-odd court poets established a common literary language based on the Sicilian dialect with a few Tuscan and French influences. Their activities greatly affected the next step forward in the emergence of a distinctly Italian literature, the poets of the *dolce stil novo* (sweet new style), represented in this volume by Guido Guinizzelli and Guido Cavalcanti.

Guinizzelli and Cavalcanti brought fresh direction to love poetry, writing in their own vernaculars (the dialects of Bologna and Florence, respectively). Soon after, in the early fourteenth century, Dante Alighieri codified a literary language based on the Italian vernaculars, blending together elements from various dialects (mainly Tuscan and Sicilian) in his *Divine Comedy*, a multifaceted poem on earthly and spiritual matters that far exceeded its predecessors in style and content. Dante is credited not only with establishing a standardized literary language but also with setting a new standard for a literature preoccupied at once with the local and universal,

with fleeting Italian events and perennial religious/philosophical concerns. From then on, Italy developed a cultural preoccupation with recalling and sorting out its historical experiences through literature. Writers produced works about timely experiences, from the first crusade (*Jerusalem Delivered*), to the bubonic plague (*The Betrothed*), domination by Napoleon Bonaparte (*The Last Letters of Jacopo Ortis*), Unification (*The Leopard*), Fascism (*The Conformist*), and late-twentieth-century immigration (*Moor Harlequin's 22 Misfortunes*). Also they generated poems, novels, plays, epistles, and essays that treated intimate, timeless human questions and emotions. The two preoccupations resulted in a mix of the universal and the particular worthy of Dante, as shown by a listing of some of the issues that resurface across the seven centuries of Italian literature and suggest other elements (beyond language) of a national identity:

The power of love (sacred and profane) Guinizzelli's and Cavalcanti's *Stil Novo* Poetry (late 1200s); Stampa's *Rime* (1554); D'Annunzio's *Child of Pleasure* (1889); De Céspedes's *The Secret* (1952)

Gender relations, feminism and sexuality Franco's *Poems in Terze Rime* (1575); Goldoni's *Mirandolina, or The Mistress of the Inn* (1753); Aleramo's *A Woman* (1906)

Political and social behavior Castiglione's *The Book of the Courtier* (1528); Machiavelli's *The Prince* (1532); Moravia's *The Conformist* (1957); Martinelli's *Moor Harlequin's 22 Misfortunes* (1993)

Resistance and protest (priests, foreigners, Fascists) Manzoni's *The Betrothed* (1840), Gramsci's *Letters from Prison* (1947); Fo's *We Won't Pay! We Won't Pay!* (1974); Calvino's *The Path to the Spider's Nest* (1947)

The relationship between art and life Cellini's *My Life* (1728); Boccaccio's *The Decameron* (1349-51); Pirandello's *Six Characters in Search of an Author* (1921); Banti's *Artemisia* (1947)

The Church, the Inquisition, and religion Tasso's *Jerusalem Delivered* (1560-81); Levi's *Survival in Auschwitz* (1947); Eco's *The Name of the Rose* (1980); Maraini's *The Silent Duchess* (1990)

Self-scrutiny and the search for meaning Svevo's *Zeno's Conscience* (1923); Croce's *History as the Story of Liberty* (1938); Leopardi's *Canti* (1845); Ungaretti's *Life of a Man* (1916-1970)

South versus North/Southern life Verga's *House by the Medlar Tree* (1881); Deledda's *Ashes* (1904); Camillieri's *Excursion to Tindari* (2000)

Patriotism and heroism/Unification Ariosto's *Orlando Furioso* (1516); Foscolo's *The Last Letters of Jacopo Ortis* (1802); Collodi's *The Adventures of Pinocchio* (1882-83); Tomasi di Lampedusa's *The Leopard* (1958)

Literature as documentation Polo's *The Travels of Marco Polo* (1299); Vico's *New Science* (1744); Casanova's *The Duel* (1780); *Morante's History: A Novel* (1974)

Innovations in language and form Dante's *The Divine Comedy* (1315); Marinetti's *The Futurist Manifesto* (1909); Ungaretti's *Life of a Man* (1916-1970); *The Poetry of Eugenio Montale* (1925, 1939, 1956); Gadda's *Acquainted with Grief* (1963)

The age-old issue of Italian political life comes to the fore in Machiavelli's *The Prince*, written during the Renaissance. *Italia,* this country that was not yet a country, led the European way in the rebirth of classical thought during the late fourteenth century, "rediscovering" artistic and philosophic treasures of antiquity, which the Byzantines had been preserving in the East. The efforts of Petrarch and a few other Italians touched off the humanist movement, which reoriented the worldview in the West. Though deeply Christian, the early humanists shifted intellectual enquiry away from theology, which had dominated medieval thinking, to the works of ancient Greece and Rome. The quest was for guidance from the ancient works on how to live an active, fully engaged life rather than one steeped in contemplation, as had been espoused in the Middle Ages. Also the humanists sought to recover a linguistic elegance in Latin expression, which the medieval writers appeared to have lost. Humanism stressed grammar, rhetoric, moral philosophy, history, and poetry, as well as faith in human potential and will. The focus gave rise to innovative artistic and scientific works in the fifteenth, sixteenth, and seventeenth centuries, commissioned to enhance the status of a family or city and appreciated as wondrous human creations in themselves. Individual Italians reached new artistic heights, designing the world's largest dome (Brunelleschi, 1434), sculpting a *David* (Michelangelo, 1501-1504) in marble and a *Persus* (Cellini, 1545-54) in bronze, painting the *Mona Lisa* (Da Vinci, 1503-06), and writing epic poetry such as Ariosto's *Or-*

lando Furioso (1516) or a revolutionary essay like Galileo's *Dialogue Concerning the Two Chief World Systems* (1632), which, to the horror of Church censors, argued that the solar system was sun- and not earth-centered. Galileo was forced to recant.

From the early 1500s to the mid-1800s, Spain, Austria, France and then again Austria dominated various parts of the peninsula. Italians were at first heartened by the French Revolution and Napoleon's subsequent 1796 invasion of their territory, then crushed by the disappointments of his rule, his fall in 1814, and the Restoration of Austrian control over key parts of the North (Lombardy and Venetia). All the turmoil nurtured an intense patriotism, aided and abetted by literary works that prompted interest in a unified Italy and that addressed the unhappy developments. Italian literature entered its Romantic age, which featured poetry and fiction that took a self-critical look at events of the present and past (Foscolo's *The Last Letters of Jacopo Ortis,* Leopardi's *Canti,* Manzoni's *Betrothed*).

After the fall of Napoleon, Italy entered into the long process of unification known as the Risorgimento. Progressing in fits and starts, it lasted for more than half a century, from 1815 to 1871. But only in the final decade did Italy actually become a unified kingdom, when a major northern state, the Kingdom of Piedmont-Sardinia, annexed six other states—Lombardy-Venetia, the Duchy of Parma, the Duchy of Modena, the Grand Duchy of Tuscany, the Papal States, and the Kingdom of the Two Sicilies (Sicily and the southern mainland)—to form the Kingdom of Italy. The infant nation became a constitutional monarchy under Piedmont-Sardinia's King Victor Emmanuel II, and there began a difficult synthesis of political, social, and cultural life in the long-disunited regions. Key was the reconstruction of a common past that all of the newly incorporated Italians could point to with pride, a task for the infant nation's intellectuals. Rising to the occasion, Francesco De Sanctis published a *History of Italian Literature* (1870), which presented Unification as an event long foreshadowed in the works of such cultural heroes as Dante, Petrarch, Machiavelli, Leopardi, and Manzoni.

The language question resurfaced. While literary Italian, based on the Florentine dialect used by Dante, Petrarch, and Boccaccio, had been formally established in the sixteenth century, there was no common spoken language. Dialects were still the primary mode of communication. Manzoni, author of *The Betrothed*, lobbied for the Florentine dialect of his day to serve as the basis of the national language, and indeed it became the official spoken language, but dialects persisted, entering print and visual media (as Sicilian dialect does in *Excursion to Tindari*).

Besides constructing a common language and cultural history, the nation's founders set out to instill general values into the citizenry, especially the youth, a primary goal of Carlo Collodi's *Pinocchio* (1881). Others despaired over the failed promise of female liberation from the domestic sphere (*Teresa* [1886]), over the stubbornly persistent divide between life in the North and South (*The Leopard* [1958]), and over political corruption and organized crime in Italian life (*Excursion to Tindari* [2000]). Still others struggled to free the land from its ancient Roman legacy and past glories enough to establish a modern presence. In *The Founding and Manifesto of Futurism* (1909), F. T. Marinetti rejects tradition and introduces a new genre—the manifesto—touching off a movement that spread beyond Italy's borders, exhibiting the same penchant for innovation that his literary forbears demonstrated. Taken far more seriously, Italy's leading thinker of the day, Benedetto Croce, wrote essays that were likewise heeded beyond Italian borders. Italy meanwhile participated in global developments: the labor movement, feminism, socialism, nationalism, empire building, and a world war.

In the post-World War I era, Italy became a polarized society. Conflict erupted between Bolshevik-style revolutionaries and Fascists led by Benito Mussolini, with the conflict being resolved in his favor. From 1922 to 1943, Mussolini ruled Italy, his Fascist government developing into a dictatorial regime that kept a tighthold on power through censorship, violence, and propaganda. Writers with anti-Fascist sympathies were imprisoned (Antonio Gramsci, Cesare Pavese) or forced into hiding (Alberto Moravia and Elsa Morante). After the *ventennio nero*—"black twenty years" under Mussolini–the nation strove to overcome its humiliation by hailing the anti-Fascist Resistance movement as quintessentially Italian in its defiance of tyranny. Modern writers stepped in to furnish a corrective, with novels like *The Path to the Spiders' Nests* by Italo Calvino, whose stylistic innovations and exposure of the less praiseworthy aspects of the Resistance upheld the tradition of honest scrutiny found in Dante's poetry and in Manzoni's fiction.

Soon female writers stepped in to furnish a different corrective (Maraini's *The Silent Duchess*, Deledda's *Ashes*, and Morante's *History: A Novel*), setting out to balance *his*-story (the story of the dominant male writer) with tales of their own. The Italian literary continuum became more representative of the medley of voices in real life, expanding even further to encompass some of the land's most recent immigrants, as in *Moor Harlequin's 22 Misfortunes* (1993). A testimony to the existence and dynamism of an Italian literary continuum, this Marco Martinelli play is an update of a comic scenario by Carlo Goldoni (c. 1738). While the later play is adjusted to accommodate end-of-the-twentieth-century realities, both works center on an unwelcome stranger in a culture in flux, an *Italia* undergoing transformation—with the help of its literature.

Chronology of Relevant Events

Italian Literature and Its Times

MEDIEVAL ITALY AND THE DAWN OF HUMANISM

From the eleventh century onward, Italian cities in the northern and central parts of the peninsula acquired increased independence. They developed their own artistic and political spheres, forming communes—communities with republican governments controlled by influential families. Several of these communes evolved into powerful centers of banking and foreign trade, but not without conflict. All the urban growth gave rise to political feuds—most notably, a rift between the Guelphs (party of the pope) and the Ghibellines (party of the emperor)—which led to wars between cities and invasions by foreign powers. Religious controversies flared too, leading to a major schism when the pope moved from Rome to Avignon (in what is now France), where the papacy remained for most of the fourteenth century (1305–1376). Meanwhile, southern Italy and Sicily suffered repeated invasion and conquest by foreign powers, among them, the Normans from France and the Aragonese from Spain. The political strife was compounded by natural disasters, most devastatingly the mid-fourteenth century bubonic plague, which was followed by economic depression and peasant rebellions. Yet the period also gave rise to unifying factors: a common literary language (derived from the Tuscan dialect of Italian), a revival of classical literature and art, and the dawn of the intellectual movement called humanism, all of which presaged the magnificent cultural flowering to come.

	Historical Events	Related Literary Works in *WLAIT 7*
1000–1100	Church reforms establish papal supremacy; conflicts arise between Pope Gregory VII and Holy Roman Emperor Henry IV, laying groundwork for later claims to papal temporal power	
1080s–1300	Rise of independent communes—notably the maritime republics of Amalfi, Pisa, Genoa, and Venice, and the cities of Florence, Milan, Ferrara, and Siena	
1025–1091	Normans conquer Sicily and southern Italy, ousting Saracens (Arabs), who had invaded during the ninth century	

Historical Events	Related Literary Works in *WLAIT 7*
1076 Pope Gregory VII excommunicates Holy Roman Emperor Henry IV for insisting on lay investiture, or assignment of Church position by a lay person	
1095–1099 First crusade to retake the Holy Land from the Saracens results in the Christian conquest of Jerusalem	*Jerusalem Delivered* by Torquato Tasso
1130 Roger II crowned King of Sicily, Calabria, and Apulia	
1176 Battle of Legnano: having formed the Lombard League, joint forces of the northern communes fend off German Emperor Frederick I of Hohenstaufen, maintain their independence	
1183 Peace of Constance confirms the autonomy of Italian cities	
1194 German emperor Henry VI conquers southern Italy and Sicily	
c. 1200s– 1300s Flowering of Florence and northern and central communes; struggles between Guelphs (pope's supporters) and Ghibellines (emperor's supporters) results in many Florentines being expelled	
1204 Venetians sack Constantinople, ultimately gaining three–eighths of the Eastern city	
1220–1250 Frederick II Hohenstaufen, half Norman but born and bred in southern Italy, rules the South, presiding over a brilliant court; court life gives rise to Sicilian school of poetry, originators of Italian lyric poetry	
1229 Pope Gregory IX founds the Inquisition, the tribunal to suppress deviation from the teachings of the Roman Catholic Church	
1258–1266 King Manfred, son of Frederick II, rules Sicily and the South	
1265–1266 Charles of Anjou becomes king of Naples and Sicily after his forces defeat Manfred at Battle of Benevento; his dynasty consolidates influence of French aristocratic culture in southern Italy	
1271–1295 Marco Polo, his father, and his uncle set off for the court of Kublai Khan in China, where they remain for more than 20 years	*The Travels of Marco Polo* by Marco Polo
1280–1300s Development of the *dolce stil novo* (sweet new style) of Italian lyric poetry; Tuscan vernacular begins to gain currency as a literary language	*Stil Novo Poetry* by Guido Guinizzelli and Guido Cavalcanti
1282 Charles of Anjou loses Sicily to Aragonese invasion; Angevins retain control of southern Italian mainland	
1290s Conflicts between Black and White Guelph factions in Florence	
1295 Visconti family assumes power in Milan	
1301 White Guelphs exiled from Florence, including Dante Alighieri	
1305 Papacy moves from Rome to Avignon	
1306 Giotto di Bondone paints frescoes in Arena Chapel in Padua	
1309–1343 Robert of Anjou rules as King of Naples	
1310–1313 Dante shows allegiance to new Holy Roman Emperor, Henry VII of Luxembourg; Henry dies suddenly; Dante abandons hopes of returning to Florence	*The Divine Comedy* by Dante Alighieri
1333 Petrarch rediscovers text by ancient Latin writer Cicero, *Pro Archia,* which refers to poetry and related subjects (e.g., history) as *studia humanitatis,* preferring them to physics or logic and giving rise to new intellectual movement known as humanism	
1348 The Black Death ravages Europe, claiming about a third of the population	*Decameron* by Giovanni Boccaccio; *The Canzoniere* by Francesco Petrarch

1350s–1400s	Spread of humanist movement bolsters interest among Italians in classical ideas and creative works; cities of Florence, Venice, and Milan grow into states	
1376–1380	St. Catherine of Siena works for peace between Italian cities and the papacy, tries to restore unity of the Church, dictates letters that help make her "first Italian women writer"	
1378	Ciompi revolt in Florence; the beginning of the Great Schism, in which two popes are elected, one at Rome, the other at Avignon	

RENAISSANCE ITALY

Many fifteenth-century Italian writers used the term *Renaissance,* meaning "rebirth," to distinguish their age from the preceding, medieval era. But the Renaissance actually spans more than one century, though scholars disagree over even its approximate boundaries. While many date the Renaissance from the 1380s to the 1520s, a number argue that culturally it reaches to the end of the sixteenth century. Either way, the age was one in which literature, history, philosophy, and science flourished and individuals produced stunning works of art. While intellectuals focused on rediscovering and the art and literature of classical Greece and Rome, the Italian communities suffered economic recession. A number of families and cities prospered nonetheless, and some of the cities grew into states: Florence, Milan, Venice, Genoa, the Kingdom of Naples, and the Papal States (territories surrounding Rome). At first, Florence, under the Medici family, emerged as the center of the Renaissance, but by the early sixteenth century, the nexus had shifted to Rome. This urban competition characterizes an era that, while blessed with extraordinary cultural achievements, was also fraught with political rivalry, corruption, and violence. The late fifteenth century saw the onset of invasions by foreign powers—most notably, France and Spain. From 1494 to 1559 these invasions cost all the above-named states except for Venice their political independence, and they lost much cultural freedom too. The Roman Catholic Church expanded its authority by way of the Inquisition and the Counter-Reformation movements. Yet despite these forces, Italians produced some daringly bold artistic and literary works throughout the Renaissance era.

1397	Founding of Medici banking network in Florence	
1400s	Italian states continue to enjoy close business, diplomatic, and cultural ties with Byzantine or Eastern Greek society, whose scholars teach Greek to Italians and introduce them to Greek works unknown to the West	
1405	Venetian conquest of Padua and Verona	
1406	Florence acquires Pisa	
1409	Attempt to solve problem of two popes (at Rome and Avignon) leads to election of third pope; Great Schism continues, with three popes ruling simulatneously	
1417	Great Schism resolved at the Council of Constance	
c. 1430	Donatello sculpts his bronze *David,* the first large scale free–standing nude statue of the Renaissance	
1442	Alfonso V recognized as king of Naples	
1453	Constantinople falls to Ottoman Turks	
1454	Peace of Lodi: formation of the Italian League, stabilizing relations between the warring Italian states	

	Historical Events	Related Literary Works in *WLAIT 7*
1462–1492	Lorenzo de' Medici is the effective ruler of Florence	
1460s	Appearance of first books printed in Italy	
1478	The Pazzi Conspiracy against the Medici of Florence claims life of Giuliano de' Medici and results in rioting, bloodshed, and punishment of culprits	
c. 1478–1482	Botticelli paints *Primavera* and *Birth of Venus,* works often regarded as related to the poetry of Poliziano	*Stanzas on the Tournament* by Angelo Poliziano
1484	Marsilio Facino publishes Plato's dialogues in Latin, including *De amore,* which becomes central to Renaissance discussions on love	
1486	Pico della Mirandola writes *An Oration on the Diginity of Man,* famous for picturing Adam/mortal man as a being who is free to move up or down the ladder of creation	
1494	Charles VIII of France invades Italian peninsula; Medici are expelled from Florence	
1494–1512	Republican rule in Florence; Dominican monk Savanarola leads moral crusade there, denounces Rome's temporal power, dying at hands of angry Florentines (1498)	*The Prince* by Niccolò Machiavelli
1494–1559	Age of Invasions: foreign forces enter Italy to lead factions, seize power and territories; France and Spain vie for dominance in Italy	*Orlando Furioso* by Lodovico Ariosto
1495–1506	Leonardo da Vinci paints *The Last Supper* and *Mona Lisa*	
1496–1501	Reign of King Frederick of Naples, who is forced into exile after French forces invade Naples	*Arcadia* by Jacopo Sannazaro
early to mid–1500s	Salon society (homes serving as artistic and musical centers) flourishes in Venice.	*Rime* by Gaspara Stampa; *Poems in Terze Rima* by Veronica Franco
1503–1513	Julius II is pope; Rome becomes center of Renaissance	
1504	Michelangelo completes his sculpture of *David*	
1505–1509	Michelangelo paints Sistine Chapel ceiling	
1507	Baldesar Castiglione assigned to the court of Urbino	*The Book of the Courtier* by Baldesar Castiglione
1520	Pope Leo X excommunicates Martin Luther	
c. 1520–1600	Mannerist period: new generation of artists rebel against Renaissance classical restrictions, favor, for example, elongated, unnatural, and elegant forms	
1520s–1700s	Counter-Reformation restores greater power and authority to the Catholic Church	
1527	Army of Charles V of Spain sacks Rome; the Church and Inquisition develop a stronger foothold in Italian states	*My Life* by Benvenuto Cellini
1535–1706	Spanish govern duchy of Milan	
c. 1538	Titian paints *Venus of Urbino*	
1542	Pope Paul III establishes the Roman Inquisition	
1545–1547	The Council of Trent convenes for the first of three sessions to define Catholic doctrine; second (1551–1552) and third (1562–1563) sessions held over the next 20 years	
1556	Philip II becomes ruler of Spanish empire, which includes kingdoms in Italy, Spain, the Low Countries, and the New World	
1559	Treaty of Cateau–Cambrésis affirms Spanish control over Italy; Emanuel Philibert of Savoy restored to throne	
1565	Tintoretto paints *Crucifixion*	
1571	Battle of Lepanto: Holy League of Western Powers defeats Turkish fleet	

Historical Events	Related Literary Works in *WLAIT 7*
1573 Turks capture Cyprus from Venice	
1575 Venice suffers severe outbreak of bubonic plague that claims a third of the city's population	
1582 Pope Gregory XIII introduces the Gregorian calendar	
1598 Jacopo Peri composes *Dafne*, the first opera	
c. 1600 Caravaggio produces his masterful cycle of paintings on Saint Matthew's life	
1600 The philosopher Giordano Bruno is executed by the Inquisition	

FROM THE BAROQUE PERIOD TO THE NAPOLEONIC INVASION

Several Italian states experienced a decline in the seventeenth century, the first half of which was one of the most troubled periods in Italian history. The region suffered the plague, economic recession, and military conflict. European invaders continued to vie for Italian territory, which became a bone of contention in several continental wars. The Spanish dominated the peninsula, ruling Milan, Sardinia, Naples, Sicily, and part of Tuscany, and exerting indirect control elsewhere. Local government was in the hands of the nobility (just 1 percent of the population). Later in the eighteenth century Austria held sway in northern Italy while the Spanish Bourbons ruled the South. There were attempts at reform, but they met with only limited success. The French Revolution and Napoleon Bonaparte's subsequent invasion of the Italian peninsula at the end of the eighteenth century inspired hopes of independence from outside powers, which were soon dashed. Meanwhile, scientific discoveries like those by Italy's Galileo Galilei and the European philosophical movement known as the Enlightenment began to change how Italians saw themselves and the world. Artists and intellectuals of the Baroque period questioned authority, rejecting old ways, favoring experiment and personal experience, which led to a renewed interest in European travel and the creation of some innovative artistic works.

1590s–1610 Caravaggio invokes new realistic style of painting, using dramatic contrast of light and shadow; style gains followers	*Artemisia* by Anna Banti
1600s–1790s Venice enters lengthy period of political and economic decline; the city becomes notorious for decadence, pleasure-seeking, and immorality but remains culturally vital, contributing greatly to Italian theater, painting, and music	*The Duel* by Giacomo Casanova; *Mirandolina, or The Mistress of the Inn* by Carlo Goldoni
1605–1606 Judicial dispute between papacy and Venice results in papal interdict against the latter	
1610 Galileo Galilei publishes *Sidereal Messenger*, announcing discovery of first four moons of Jupiter with his telescope	
1618–1648 Northern Italy becomes directly involved in Thirty Years' War between France and Spain	
1622–1625 Gian Lorenzo Bernini sculpts *Apollo and Daphne*	
1623 Giambattista Marino publishes *Adonis*, the chief Italian baroque literary work	*Adonis* by Giambattista Marino
1630 Severe outbreak of plague in Lombardy and Milan	*The Betrothed* by Alessandro Manzoni
1632–1633 Galileo's *Dialogue Concerning the Two Chief World Systems* introduces revolutionary ideas on science and cosmology; placed under house arrest by the Inquisition, Galileo is forced to recant	

Historical Events	Related Literary Works in *WLAIT 7*
1647 Revolt of Masaniello (Naples)	
1655 Massacre of religious disciples known as Waldenesians in Piedmont	
1700s– 1790s Enlightenment, a philosophical movement emphasizing people's ability to govern themselves and reason independently of divine revelation, takes hold in Europe; historians Voltaire, Edward Gibbon, and Giambattista Vico refine their discipline, weigh sources in pursuit of objectivity	*The Silent Duchess* by Dacia Maraini; *The New Science of Giambattista Vico* by Giambattista Vico
1701–1714 War of the Spanish Succession: Italian possessions of Spanish Habsburg ultimately pass to Austrian Habsburgs	
1725 Italian musician Antonio Lucio Vivaldi composes *The Four Seasons*	
1729 Corsica revolts against Genoa	
1733–1738 War of the Polish Succession: Charles of Bourbon conquers Naples and Sicily	
1740–1748 War of the Austrian Succession: French invade Piedmont but are ultimately defeated by Austrian-Piedmontese forces	
1748–1796 Period of relative peace and acceptance of Austrian rule, which includes progressive legislation	
1759–1773 Jesuits begin to be expelled throughout Europe	
1763 Severe famine, especially in Naples, Rome, and Florence	
1768 Genoa cedes Corsica to France	
1773 Pope Clement XIV suppresses the Jesuit order	
1780s– 1820s Neoclassical movement in Italian literature gradually yields to Romanticism	*Myrrha* by Vittorio Alfieri; *The Canti* (Songs) by Giacomo Leopardi
1789 French Revolution spreads republican sympathies across Europe	
1792 Pro–Revolution Jacobin movement spreads to the Italian states	
1794–1795 Repression and dispersal of Jacobins in the Italian states	
1796–1815 Napoleon invades northern Italy, defeats Austrians, establishes Cisalpine Republic in Milan	
1797 Napoleon signs Treaty of Campoformio, ceding Venice to Austria and ending Venetian hopes of independence	*The Last Letters of Jacopo Ortis* by Ugo Foscolo
1799–1800 French armies defeated in Italy by Austro-Russian invasion	
1800 Napoleon returns to Italy, defeats Austrian army at Marengo	
1802 Napoleon establishes Italian Republic, which becomes Kingdom of Italy under his rule in 1805	
1806 French armies conquer Naples; French domination extends to most of northern and central Italy	
1814 Napoleonic regime falls; old rulers return	

RESTORATION AND RISORGIMENTO

After Napoleon's final defeat at Waterloo, the victor nations attempted to restore the pre-war political situation in Europe. Italy was once again divided into territories governed by Austria and Spain. Nationalist sentiment was growing, however. In the early nineteenth century, secret societies formed, intending first to rid their country of its foreign rulers and then to achieve unity and independence as a nation. The process of unification, known as Risorgimento, gained momentum first under Giuseppe Mazzini and then under Victor Emmanuel II; Camille Benso, Count of Cavour; and Giuseppe Garibaldi. At last in 1861, after two wars of independence, unification was achieved, and the Kingdom of Italy proclaimed with Victor Emmanuel as monarch. Meanwhile, the new nation faced the daunting task of unifying a populace tied to separate regions with disparate dialects and historical experiences. In subsequent decades, Italy strove to forge a common language, educational system, and more. The North outpaced the South in industrial development, which only aggravated perceptions of the South as backwards. Meanwhile, with an eye on the rest of Europe, Italy began to implement social reforms and boost economic productivity in order to take a respectable place among the modern nations of the West.

1806–1808	New laws (e.g., division of the common lands) dismantle feudal practices in the South
1814–1815	Napoleon is overthrown; Congress of Vienna grants Lombardy-Venetia to Austria; Bourbons regain control of Naples, form alliance with Austria, the power that dominates peninsula; only state to retain large measure of independence is Piedmont, under Victor Emmanuel I
1815	Final defeat of Napoleon at Waterloo; Holy Alliance formed by Emperor Francis I of Austria, Frederick William of Prussia, and Tsar Alexander I of Russia, beginning the Restoration, a reactionary era in Europe
1816	Reorganization of Italian states; Naples and Sicily are reunited into the Kingdom of the Two Sicilies under Ferdinand I
1820–1821	Revolution in Naples; Palermo, Sicily, declares its independence from Naples; Holy Alliance sanctions suppression of revolution; Austria intervenes against revolutionary government in Naples
1820s–1830s	Italian nationalist sentiment grows, secret societies dedicated to ousting foreign rulers develop throughout Italian peninsula
1821	Spanish constitution proclaimed in Piedmont; King Victor Emmanuel I abdicates; Charles Albert becomes regent
1831	Founded abroad by Giuseppe Mazzini, Young Italy movement strives to turn Italy into a unified republic established by the people; insurrections in Italy
1831–1861	The Risorgimento, a unification and independence movement, gathers momentum under Victor Emmanuel II (king of Piedmont), Count Cavour (prime minister), and Giuseppe Garibaldi (revolutionary republican general)
1832–1833	Failed insurrection by Young Italy movement; Mazzini flees to Switzerland
1842	Giuseppe Verdi composes opera *Nabucco*, centered partly on theme of nationhood
1843	Vincenzo Gioberti publishes *Del primato morale e civile delgi Italiani* (Of the Moral and Civil Primacy of the Italians), calling on Pope Pius IX to lead the *risorgimento* (means "resurgence") of the Italian nation
1847–1848	Liberal wind sweeps peninsula: King Ferdinand grants a constitution in Kingdom of Two Sicilies; Charles Albert concedes to a constitution in Piedmont; Pope Pius IX reforms censorship in the Papal States
1848–1849	Uprisings in Palermo, Lombardy, Venice, Naples, and Rome; Piedmont fights Austria in first War of Independence but loses; Mazzini and Garibaldi lead insurrection in Rome, drive out pope and organize Roman Republic but are later defeated by French forces; Bourbon kings retake Naples and Sicily; only Piedmont retains a constitution

Historical Events	Related Literary Works in *WLAIT 7*
1853 Uprising in Milan	
1855 Piedmont joins Anglo–French alliance against Russia in Crimea—at peace talks, possible independence and unification of Italy is discussed by Piedmont, England, and France	
1856 Austrian forces withdraw from the Italian region of Romagna but retain garrisons in Bologna and Ancona	
1859 Second War of Independence results in northern Italian states being incorporated into the Kingdom of Sardinia	
1859–1861 The Casati law requires local authorities to provide elementary schools and teachers	
1860 Garibaldi marches on Sicily, crosses to mainland and advances as far as Naples; Kingdom of Sardinia annexes central Italian states	*The Leopard* by Giuseppe Tomasi di Lampedusa
1864 Anna Maria Mozzoni publishes *Women and Her Social Relationships,* helps initiate women's movement in Italy	*A Woman* by Sibilla Aleramo
1861 First Italian parliament meets in Turin and establishes the Kingdom of Italy with Victor Emmanuel II of Piedmont as king	
1861–1876 The conservative right dominates the political scene	
1864–1870 Florence serves as the national capital	
1865 New Civil Code of 1865 makes husband head of the household in newborn Italy, obligates wife to recognize his authority	
1866 Secret alliance made between Italy and Prussia against Austria in Austro–Prussian War; Austria cedes Venice to Napoleon III of France, who cedes it to Italy	
1870 Italian troops occupy Rome, achieve further unification; Pius IX denounces occupation, excommunicates Victor Emmanuel; parliament transfers capital to Rome; end of papacy's temporal power	
1871 Francesco De Sanctis writes first history of Italian literature—*Storia della letteratura italiana*	
1871–1880s Rome, new Italian capital, gains 80,000 people, undergoes vigorous development	*Child of Pleasure* by Gabriele D'Annunzio
1876–1887 Left-wing government comes to power with Prime Minister Agostino Depretis, who implements limited social reforms, including compulsory education and extension of the voting franchise	
1878 Death of King Victor Emmanuel II, succession of Umberto I to Italian throne	
1870s– 1880s Intellectuals conduct studies on life in southern Italy, highlighting differences between the North and South; primary education becomes compulsory (1888), but law is often ignored; South perceived as backward, North as obligated to civilize it	*Ashes* by Grazia Deledda; *The House by the Medlar Tree* by Giovanni Verga
1880s– 1900s Italian political leaders show increasing concern for educating the lower class and creating model citizens; middle-class women begin entering the workforce	*The Adventures of Pinocchio* by Carlo Collodi; *Teresa* by Neera
1885–1890 Italian troops land in Eritrea in East Africa; Italy creates a protectorate in Somalia, makes Eritrea an official Italian colony	
1887–1891 Francesco Crispi becomes prime minister, initiates some domestic reforms and adopts ruinous foreign policies	
1891 Pope Leo XIII's encyclical *Rerum novarum* affirms the belief that women are made for domestic duties	
1892 Socialist party is founded	

Historical Events	Related Literary Works in *WLAIT 7*
1893–1896 Second Crispi government; unrest in Sicily; Crispi government dissolves workers' associations in Sicily	
1896 Italian army suffers defeat by Abyssinians (Ethiopians) at Adua; 5,000 Italian soldiers killed; Ethiopia declares independence	
1896–1900 Giacomo Puccini composes his major operas, *La Bohème* and *Tosca*	
1898 Rioting in Milan and elsewhere to protest cost of food; 80 killed and 450 wounded in official count of casualties in Milan	
1899 Founding of Fiat automobiles in Turin; government under Luigi Pelloux limits freedom of press and rights of people to assemble and go on strike	

FROM GIOLITTI TO THE FIRST WORLD WAR

After the unpopular King Umberto I was assassinated by anarchists, his son took the throne as Victor Emmanuel III. The new king's liberal prime minister, Giovanni Giolitti, became the dominant figure in Italian politics, implementing moderate social reforms, encouraging labor unions, and extending the voting franchise. Under Giolitti, foreign trade doubled, wages increased, and the standard of living improved. But this general condition is somewhat deceptive. While Italy underwent remarkable industrial growth from 1901–1914, most of the people still labored in agriculture and failed to benefit from the economic boom. The age brought with it an emphasis on materialism, and intellectuals objected, turning to new philosophical and psychological ideas. Meanwhile, Italian workers were organized into labor unions and conducted strikes, clashing with the police; between 1900 and 1904, violent strikes killed or wounded more than 200, and additional casualties followed. A view circulated that violence was necessary to achieve change, a notion embraced by the Futurist movement. Rejecting the past, its followers championed progress, technology, and conflict with a vehemence that helped propel Italy into the First World War. In the end, this war proved disastrous for the country. A victor, Italy scored some territorial gains but less than the country hoped for, and its military defeats were staggering. An estimated 680,000 Italians perished in the First World War.

Historical Events	Related Literary Works in *WLAIT 7*
1900 King Umberto I of Savoy is assassinated by anarchists; Victor Emmanuel III accedes to the throne	
1900–1901 In German, Sigmund Freud publishes *The Interpretation of Dreams* and the abridged *On Dreams,* inaugurating psychoanalysis	*Zeno's Conscience* by Italo Svevo
1901–1914 Giovanni Giolitti dominates Italian politics	
1904 General strike	
1908–1916 Founding of *La Voce,* an influential Florentine journal that discusses new European philosophies	*Ghìsola* by Federigo Tozzi
1909 From Paris, Italians launch Futurism movement, which celebrates experimentation, technology, and aggressive action; Guglielmo Marconi develops wireless telegraph, becomes one of two winners of Nobel Prize in Physics	*The Founding and Manifesto of Futurism* by Filippo Tommaso Marinetti
1911 Giolitti expands voting franchise to include all men; Italy declares war on Ottoman Empire and annexes Libya	
1912 Benito Mussolini becomes editor of Socialist Party newspaper *Avanti!;* Italy renews Triple Alliance with Austria and Germany; peace with Turkey ends Libyan War	

	Historical Events	Related Literary Works in *WLAIT 7*
1913	Giolitti makes Gentiloni Pact—provides Catholic support in elections to candidates who oppose divorce and socialism but favor the priesthood and private education; pact alienates Giolitti from leftists	
1914	Giolitti resigns, is replaced by Antonio Salandra; First World War breaks out; Mussolini is expelled from Socialist Party for advocating intervention in World War I; he launches *Il Popolo d'Italia,* a newspaper dedicated to war and revolution	
1915	Italy signs Pact of London and enters World War I on the side of Britain and France against Austria and Germany	
1917	Italians suffer crushing defeat at Caporetto; 300,000 Italian soldiers are taken prisoner	*Life of a Man* by Giuseppe Ungaretti
1918	Italian army forces Austrians to retreat at Vittorio Veneto; First World War ends	
1919	Italy gains less than it hopes for at World War I peace conference—wins Trent, South Tyrol, and Istria, not Dalmatia or Italian part of Fiume; Trieste becomes part of Italy	

FASCIST ITALY AND THE SECOND WORLD WAR

In the years after World War I, Italy faced severe economic depression. Heavy wartime casualties, ineffective government, socialist insurrection, and widespread dissatisfaction with the terms of the peace treaty only exacerbated the country's problems. Out of this environment arose the Fascist movement, led by Benito Mussolini. In its initial phase, Fascism attracted former soldiers, disgruntled intellectuals, small landowners, workers, and peasants. The movement changed over time, growing openly violent and repressive, stifling strikes and labor unions. Gathering momentum, the Fascists marched on Rome in 1922, a bold move that propelled Mussolini into the position of prime minister and then dictator. Mussolini formed an alliance with the Nazi Germany's Adolf Hitler, and when civil war broke out in Spain in the mid-1930s, both Germany and Italy sent troops to support the future Spanish dictator Francisco Franco. World War II followed, with Italy entering into the global conflict as an Axis power on the side of Germany. The invasion by enemy Allied troops of Sicily in 1943 spelled the end of Mussolini's regime. Supported by Hitler's troops, he formed a breakaway republic in northern Italy, which led to an Italian civil war during the last two years of the global war. In 1945 Mussolini and his mistress, Claretta Petacci, were captured and executed by Italian partisans. The joint efforts of Allied and partisan forces won back territory he had seized, and the war ended, leaving a maimed population to recover from years of crippling destruction and loss.

1918–1922	Italy struggles with crippling economic depression; Socialists dominate parts of central Italy	
1919	Gabriele D'Annunzio seizes Fiume, an act disavowed by the Italian government; formation of first Fasci di Combattimento (fascist paramilitary groups) by Benito Mussolini; formation of Italian Popular Party, first Catholic political party	
1919–1922	Fascist squads employ violence, beat up Socialist union members in Central Italy, after which laborers go back to work; Fascists seen as restoring law and order	
1920–1922	Railway and postal workers go on strike; Fascists break strikes, continue to use strong-arm tactics—commit murders, seize towns and occupy official offices	
1921	Fascist Party is officially founded; Communist Party is founded; mass rally of 40,000 Fascists in Naples, October 24	

Historical Events		Related Literary Works in *WLAIT 7*
1922	To pressure king Victor Emmanuel III into giving them key role in government, Fascists march on Rome (October 27–28) while Mussolini awaits reaction in Milan; king makes him the Italian prime minister	
1922–1943	Entire Italian nation under Fascist rule; civil liberties and opposing political parties are gradually suppressed; government attempts to control social and cultural spheres; opposition movement develops	*Six Characters in Search of an Author* by Luigi Pirandello
1924	Reformist socialist deputy Giacomo Matteotti is murdered by Fascists; non–Fascist deputies quit parliament in protest	
1925	Mussolini assumes responsibility for Fascist violence, begins to turn his regime into a dictatorship	
1926–1927	Regime debates role of the Fascist artist, discusses relationship between politics and art in order to enlist intellectuals in regime	*The Conformist* by Alberto Moravia; *History as the Story of Liberty* by Benedetto Croce; *Life of a Man* by Giuseppe Ungaretti; The Poetry of Eugenio Montale
1927	Communist leader Antonio Gramsci is imprisoned by special Fascist tribunal	*Letters from Prison* by Antonio Gramsci
1929	Lateran Pacts reconcile papacy and Fascist state of Italy	
1930s	Papal encyclical Casti connubi (1930) is strongly against women working outside the home; campaign waged to boost population; intellectuals grow increasingly disenchanted with Fascism	*Acquainted with Grief* by Carlo Emilio Gadda; *The Moon and the Bonfires* by Cesare Pavese
1935	Italy invades Ethiopia; the League of Nations condemns Italy, imposes sanctions	
1936	Italy forms federation of Italian East Africa, including Eritrea, Italian Somaliland, and Italian–speaking parts of Ethiopia	
1936–1939	Mussolini speaks of a Rome-Berlin Axis; like Hitler, sends his country's troops into Spanish Civil War on side of General Francisco Franco and the Nationalists	
1937	Italy withdraws from League of Nations	
1938	Fascist government introduces anti–Semitic racial laws, leading to 1938–45 persecution of homosexuals and Jews in Italy	*History: A Novel* by Elsa Morante
1939	Pact of Steel: Italy forms military alliance with Nazi Germany	
1940	Italy enters the Second World War on the side of Germany	The Poetry of Eugenio Montale
1940–1943	Italian soldiers wage North African and Russian campaigns	
1943–1945	King Victor Emmanuel III signs secret armistice (1943) with Allies (Great Britain, France, Russia, the United States); Mussolini is overthrown; king appoints Pietro Badoglio to head government; Nazis rescue Mussolini, make him puppet ruler of breakaway republic in northern Italy (Republic of Salò); civil war ensues; 250,000 Italians join the Resistance movement; Nazis deport anti-Fascists and Jews to concentration camps	*Survival in Auschwitz* by Primo Levi
1944–1945	Supported by partisan actions in Resistance movement, Allies liberate parts of Fascist Italy; partisans capture and execute Mussolini; Second World War ends	*The Path to the Spiders' Nests* by Italo Calvino

THE REPUBLIC OF ITALY

In 1946 Italy voted in favor of abolishing the monarchy and becoming a republic. King Umberto II abdicated, and a new era began. Two years later the Christian Democrats won Italy's first postwar parliamentary election. Meanwhile, Italy struggled to recover from its Fascist experience as well as the ravages of the World War II and the civil war it entailed. The country struggled to rebuild its economy, greatly aided in this endeavor by financial aid from the U.S. Marshall Plan. In the 1960s, an export boom brought about an "economic miracle"; industry increased, and enterprise flourished. But new problems surfaced: overcrowded schools, labor unrest, periods of economic decline, widespread political corruption, and terrorism. The number of immigrants from Africa and Eastern Europe increased rapidly, and regional patriotism returned with renewed vigor. In the 1990s, southern Italy saw a resurgence of organized crime. While causes that had earlier taken root, such as the women's movement, gained new political force, the country struggled not to make itself, as it had during the Risorgimento, but to remake itself in politics, economic and social life, and the related cultural sphere of art and literature.

	Historical Events	Related Literary Works in *WLAIT 7*
1945	Italian women gain the right to vote	
1946	Italy becomes a republic	
1947	World War II peace treaty is signed—Italy loses all colonies except Somalia, which is retained on a ten-year trusteeship basis	
1948	New constitution goes into effect; Article 37 prescribes equal pay for equal work, but women continue to earn less than men; Christian Democrats (DC) win first parliamentary elections in Italy, beginning several decades of political dominance	*The Secret* by Alba de Céspedes
1948–1952	Italy receives monetary assistance from U.S. Marshall Plan on condition that the Communist Party is ousted from government	
1949	Italy joins North Atlantic Treaty Organization	
1957	Italy enters European Economic Community	
1958	General Elections; DC (42 percent) and PCI (23 percent) are the two main parties; state–licensed brothels are closed	
1958–1963	Rapid economic development transforms Italy into a modern industrial state	
1960s	Sicilian mafia (Cosa Nostra) gets involved in drug trade; women go on strike for equal pay; clothing industry (1960) accepts principle of equal pay	
1968	Abolition of law that made adultery a crime for women, condoned punishment of the unfaithful wife	
1968–1972	Student and worker unrest; after 100 years of centralized government, Italy empowers regions, gives each elected council rights to pass laws in such areas as public works and social welfare within national framework	
1970	Italy legalizes divorce	
1971	Nursery school law provides free nursery education	
1972	Abolition of law that forbids circulation of birth–control information	
1974	Protest against divorce law leads to 1974 referendum—voters retain divorce law; consumer prices soar; inflation rises to record height; economic recession	*We Won't Pay! We Won't Pay!* by Dario Fo
1975	Family Law is updated—dowries are abolished, a wife gains right to retain her maiden name, decide equally with husband where to live; poet and filmmaker Pier Paolo Pasolini is killed outside of Rome	
late 1970s	Terrorism (bombings, kidnapping, murder) escalates to 2,000 incidents a year; Aldo Moro, president of Christian Democrat Party, is kidnapped and killed by Red Brigades; abortion is legalized	*The Name of the Rose* by Umberto Eco

Historical Events		Related Literary Works in *WLAIT 7*
1980s–1990s	Economic prosperity; Italy becomes seventh economic power in the world	
1981	Italian Communist Party repudiates Soviet model	
1983–1987	Socialist government under Bettino Craxi	
1984	Right–wing terrorist attack at train station near Bologna kills over 80, injures 200	
1987	Nearly 500 alleged Mafiosi are tried in Palermo courts	
1991–1994	"Clean Hands" inquiry, a judicial inquiry into political corruption, leads to the arrest of prominent politicians and dissolution of political parties that ruled the "first republic" of Italy; communist party begins to call itself Partito Democratico della Sinistra (PDS; Democratic Party of the Left); hardliners split to form Rifondazione Comunista (Communist Refoundation Party)	
1991–2003	Immigrant population more than doubles from c. 800,000 to 2.6 million	*Moor Harlequin's 22 Misfortunes* by Marco Martinelli
1992	Mafia murders Judge Giovanni Falcone (planner of campaign against organized crime) and his colleague Paolo Borsellino	*Excursion to Tindari* by Andrea Camilleri
1994	Wealthy media mogul Silvio Berlusconi founds center–right political movement, Forza Italia, and becomes prime minister	
1996	Romano Prodi, leader of the center–left coalition Ulivo, wins elections; PDS and Rifondazione Comunista are part of government	
1998	Italy gains admission to European Union; Prodi's government falls; Massimo D'Alema becomes new prime minister, is the first ex–communist to lead a Republican government in Italy	
2001	Berlusconi and his center–right coalition, Casa della Libertà, are elected to power	

Contents by Title

Contents by Title

Contents by Author

Contents by Author

Image Credits

Alfieri, Conte Vittorio, drawing. The Library of Congress.—Alighieri, Dante, photograph.—Ambrogini, Angelo, engraving. The Library of Congress.—Amilcar poster, lithograph by Paolo Garretto, 1929, Art Deco, photograph. © Swim Ink 2, LLC/Corbis. Reproduced by permission.—Auschwitz concentration camp entrance, photograph. © Bettmann/Corbis. Reproduced by permission.—Boccaccio, Giovanni, engraving. The Library of Congress.—Bologna University, engraving. Hulton Getty/Liaison Agency. Reproduced by permission.—Calvino, Italo, photograph. © Jerry Bauer. Reproduced by permission.—Casanova, Giocomo Jacopo, engraving. The Library of Congress.—Castiglione, Baldassare, illustration. The Library of Congress.—Cavalcanti, Guido, engraving. The Library of Congress.—Holy Roman Emperor Charles V with his hunting dog, photograph. © Gianni Dagli Orti/Corbis. Reproduced by permission.—Cellini, Benvenuto (foreground), photograph. © Chris Heller/Corbis. Reproduced by permission.—Collodi, Carlo, photograph.—Croce, Benedetto, photograph. Italian Cultural Institute.—D'Annunzio, Gabriele, photograph. The Library of Congress.—*Dante and Virgil with the Condemned Souls in Eternal Ice,* from Dante's *Divine Comedy,* 15th century manuscript, painting. Archivo Iconographico, S.A./Corbis. Reproduced by permission.—*The Decameron,* written by Giovanni Boccaccio, painting by Botticelli, photograph. © Archivo Iconografica, S.A./Corbis. Reproduced by permission.—Depiction of the death of Roland, photograph. © Bettmann/Corbis. Reproduced by permission.—Deledda, Grazia, photograph. © Corbis. Reproduced by permission.—Drawing of Lodovico Ariosto, photograph. © Michael Nicholson/Corbis. Reproduced by permission.—Drawing of Casanova's duel with Ksawery Branicki, c. 1750, photograph. Mary Evans Picture Library. Reproduced by permission.—Eco, Umberto, photograph. © Peter Turnley/Corbis. Reproduced by permission.—Ethiopian natives give fascist salute as Italian troops march through Aksum, Ethiopia, photograph. AP/Wide World Photos. Reproduced by permission.—Fasces, a pair of axes side-by-side, symbolized the power and authority of ancient Rome. The fasces were later adopted by Italian dictator Benito Mussolini, photograph. The Granger Collection, New York. Reproduced by permission.—Fo, Dario, photograph. © Jerry Bauer. Reproduced by permission.—Foscolo, Ugo, drawing. The Granger Collection, New York. Reproduced by permission.—Francis I visiting the studio of Benvenuto Cellini in Rome, photograph. © Archivo Iconografico, S.A./Corbis. Reproduced by permission.—*The French Army Enters Venice,* print by Philip de Bay of mounted and dismounted troops marching through the streets of Venice during the early 1800s, photograph. © Historical Picture Archive/Corbis. Reproduced by permission.—Freud, Sigmund, photograph. © Bettmann/Corbis. Reproduced by permission.—Garibaldi, Giuseppe, print.—Gentileschi, Artemisia, self-portrait, oil on canvas, photograph. The Granger Collection,

New York. Reproduced by permission.—*Gerusalemme Liberata,* title page and engraving. Written by Torquato Tasso. Picture Vision. Reproduced by permission.—Giacomo Leopardi's signature, photograph. © Neri Grazia/Corbis Sygma. Reproduced by permission.—Goldoni, Carlo, engraving.—Gramsci, Antonio (likeness on banner), photograph. © Pizzoli Alberto/Corbis Sygma. Reproduced by permission.—Guicciardini, Francesco, wood engraving. The Library of Congress.—Hitler, Adolf, and Benito Mussolini, Munich, 1940, photograph. National Archives and Records Administration.—Italian resistance fighters with rifles slung over their shoulders, photograph. © Hulton-Deutsch Collection/Corbis. Reproduced by permission.—Italian troops and refugees traveling in wagons at the Isonzo Front in northeastern Italy during World War I, photograph. Hulton/Archive/Getty. Reproduced by permission.—The Jewish Ghetto in Rome, photograph. © Araldo de Luca/Corbis. Reproduced by permission.—Leopardi, Conte Giacomo, engraving. The Library of Congress.—Levi, Primo, photograph. © Jerry Bauer. Reproduced by permission.—Line of men standing in a street giving Fascist salute to the Italian royal family and their guests, photograph. © Hulton-Deutsch Collection/Corbis. Reproduced by permission.—Long line of sheep on a Sicilian road, photograph. © Roger Wood/Corbis. Reproduced by permission.—Machiavelli, Niccolo, portrait. Photograph by Time Life Pictures/Mansell/Time Life Pictures/Getty Images. Reproduced by permission.—Manuscript folio from Book of Poems, 14th century, by Guido Cavalcanti.—Manuscript illumination of education in a monastery from a facsimile of the Manesse (Manessa) Codex, German manuscript, 1305-1340, photograph. © Gianni Dagli Orti/Corbis. Reproduced by permission.—Manzoni, Alessandro, engraving. The Library of Congress.—Maraini, Dacia, photograph. © Viittoriano Rastelli/Corbis. Reproduced by permission.—Marinetti, Filippo Tommaso, photograph. © Alinari Archives/Corbis. Reproduced by permission.—Moravia, Alberto, photograph. © Jerry Bauer. Reproduced by permission.—Mussino, Attilio, illustrator. From an illustration in Pinocchio, by C. Collodi. Translated from the Italian by Carol Della Chiesa. Macmillan, 1969.—Mussolini addresses 50,000 Fascist followers in Turin, Italy, photograph. Hulton Archive/Getty Images. Reproduced by permission.—Mussolini, Benito, photograph. AP/Wide World Photos. Reproduced by permission.—Napoleon on horseback leading his troops over

the St. Bernard pass to begin his invasion of Italy, painting by Jacques-Louis David, c. 1801, photograph. © Archivo Iconografico, S.A./Corbis. Reproduced by permission.—Nuraghe Su Nuraxi, Barumini, Sardinia, Iron Age hill fort, c. 1500 B.C., photograph. © Gianni Dagli Orti/Corbis. Reproduced by permission.—Old Sicilian woman standing in a doorway, photograph. © Philip Gould/Corbis. Reproduced by permission.—Palazzo Ducale in Urbino, Italy, exterior view, 15th-century Italian palace overlooking its courtyard, photograph. © Angelo Hornak/Corbis. Reproduced by permission.—Petrarch, Francesco, engraving. Corbis-Bettmann. Reproduced by permission.—*Philosphiae Naturalis Principia Mathematica,* 1687, by Sir Isaac Newton.—Piazza San Marco in Venice (*Mirandolina*), painting by Hermann David Salomon Carrodi, photograph. © Araldo de Luca/Corbis. Reproduced by permission.—*Pietro Aretino,* print by Marcantonio Raimondi, c. 1517-1520, photograph. © Historical Picture Archive/Corbis. Reproduced by permission.—Pirandello, Luigi, photograph. AP/Wide World Photos. Reproduced by permission.—Polo, Marco, engraving. Corbis-Bettmann. Reproduced by permission.—Polo, Marco, illustration. © Bettmann/Corbis. Reproduced by permission.—*Procession in Piazza San Marco* (detail), painting by Gentile Bellini, oil and tempera on canvas, 1496, photograph. © David Lees/Corbis. Reproduced by permission.—"Resistenza Contro La Mafia" banner hanging from a fence atop a stone wall, photograph. © Martinez Paz Ricardo/Corbis. Reproduced by permission.—Rialto Bridge over the Grand Canal in Venice, Italy, painting by Canaletto (a.k.a. Giovanni Antonio Canal), oil on canvas. photograph. The Granger Collection, New York. Reproduced by permission.—Sannazaro, Jacopo, drawing by Nicolas de Larmessin (1638-1694), photograph. Mary Evans Picture Library. Reproduced by permission.—Skeletal remains of Italian soldiers strewn over a World War I battlefield along with rotted clothing and equipment, photograph. © Alinari Archives/Corbis. Reproduced by permission.—Statue of Clio, the Muse of History, photograph. © Corbis. Reproduced by permission.—Tasso, Torquato, photograph. © Bettmann/Corbis. Reproduced by permission.—Tasso, Torquato, writing a poem for two women at the Court of Ferrara, photograph. © Bettmann/Corbis. Reproduced by permission.—Ungaretti, Giuseppe, Rome, 1961, photograph by Mario Torrisi. AP/Wide World Photos. Reproduced by permission.—Venus and Adonis, marble sculpture by Antonio Canova (1757-1822), photo-graph. © Mimmo Jodice/Corbis. Reproduced by permission.—Verga, Giovanni, painting by Amedeo Bianchi. Reprinted by permission of Grant & Cutler Ltd.—Woman sitting at sewing machine with several students standing near her, others seated, photograph. © Alinari Archives/ Corbis. Reproduced by permission.—Young woman with dark hair looks down at an Olivetti typewriter that she is assembling, photograph. © Hulton-Deutsch Collection/Corbis. Reproduced by permission.

Acquainted with Grief

by

Carlo Emilio Gadda

THE LITERARY WORK

A novel set in Maradagàl, an imaginary South American country, between 1925 and 1933; published in Italian in installments in 1938-41 and as the novel *La cognizione del dolore* in 1963, in expanded form in English in 1969 and Italian in 1970.

SYNOPSIS

An isolated and impoverished nobleman is locked into a bitter, tumultuous, and lyrical relationship with his mother and middle-class society.

Engineer Carlo Emilio Gadda (1893-1973) is one of twentieth-century Italy's most innovative and eccentric writers. He was born in Milan into a middle-class family with distant ties to the aristocracy. His mother was a schoolteacher; his father, an industrialist. In 1899 the family built an expensive house in Longone in the province of Como, near Milan. The house, together with other financial obligations, subjected young Gadda to deprivations that he never forgot. In 1915, after a difficult childhood and adolescence, Gadda joined the army. That same year Italy entered World War I, and Gadda fought at the front, where he was captured during the disastrous defeat in Caporetto. After being held captive in Germany, Gadda returned to Milan. On learning that his brother Enrico had died in a military plane crash, Gadda suffered psychologically. He managed to graduate in electrical engineering and went to work in Argentina in the early 1920s. When he returned to Milan, Gadda taught math and physics and immersed himself in the study of philosophy. From the 1920s onward, he combined writing with his other activities, publishing his first volume of essays, *La Madonna dei filosofi* (The Madonna of the Philosophers) in 1931. His mother died in 1936, after which Gadda sold the family house in Longone and began writing *Acquainted with Grief*. Finally, in 1940, Gadda quit engineering altogether and moved to Florence, where he wrote and became an active member of the city's literary circles. Completed during World War II, *Acquainted with Grief* fictionalizes some of the author's biographical and ideological traumas; its protagonist, Gonzalo, is often regarded as Gadda's alter ego. By turns tragic and hilarious, *Acquainted with Grief* is a journey through the chaotic mental world of a man unable to integrate himself into his family or his society.

Events in History at the Time the Novel Takes Place

World War I and its impact on Gadda. *Acquainted with Grief* takes place after World War I in an imaginary South American country that, according to several hints in the novel, represents Italy, especially Lombardy, the northern region whose capital is Milan. Gadda himself was experiencing an emotional breakdown at the time the fictional events take place. According to his *War and Prison Diary*, he entered World War I confident that he would find order, action, and self-fulfillment in military life. He also looked to the war for national regeneration. Instead he experienced disaster. The Italian defeat at Caporetto, where the Austrians took nearly 300,000 prisoners, was the result of gross military mismanagement. The debacle led to Gadda's imprisonment in concentration camps and woke him abruptly from some longstanding illusions. He concluded that "unpreparedness, errors, stupidity and cynicism move the levers of a machine that he envisioned as perfect" and that supreme chaos, rather than rationality, propels human events (Ferrero, p. 30; trans. L. Modena). *Acquainted with Grief* alludes to war as a playground on which unreliable strategists scrape battalions over hills as if they were striking matches to light them, a reflection, no doubt, of Gadda's own military experience (Gadda, *Acquainted with Grief*, p. 13). The loss of his brother in the war weighed heavily on Gadda's heart too. "Enrico," he wrote, "you weren't my brother, but rather the best and dearest part of me. I don't know how to go about living" (Ferrero, p. 31; trans. L. Modena).

AN EMBLEM ROOTED IN ANCIENT ROME

Mussolini's group, the Battle Fasces, was not the first to take as its emblem the fasces—a bundle of rods surrounding an ax. This same emblem was adopted a few years earlier by the Intervention Fasces, who pushed for Italy to enter the First World War. In ancient Rome, the fasces, carried by bodyguards to government officials, symbolized the power of life and death that a civil magistrate held in times of extreme danger over a group of soldiers; the soldiers were supposed to be united by absolute obedience to the magistrate until the danger subsided. Thus, the emblem stood for unity, subordination of the group to the rule of one leader, and a connection between military and civilian powers. It represented both absolute authority and supreme obedience while indicating that strength lies in unity.

The rise of Fascism. Out of the ashes of World War I rose the Fascist regime, under which Italy was governed from 1922 to nearly the end of World War II. In 1919 Benito Mussolini founded a new movement, the "Battle Fasces," adopting

as its emblem the Roman fasces—a bundle of rods around an ax. Three years later Mussolini's Fascists entered Rome. King Vittorio Emanuele III of Italy, acknowledging their power, passed control of the government to Mussolini without resistance. In 1923 the Fascists organized a paramilitary force, the Voluntary Militia for National Security (MVSN). Through the institution of the Voluntary Militia the state legitimated the preexisting paramilitary squads that violently squashed resistance to Fascism. Mussolini thereby imposed on all citizens a disciplinary political "police," whose members did not hesitate to beat people and destroy private property. Two years later the originally constitutional regime officially became a dictatorship. Between 1925 and 1928, the Fascists transformed Italy into an authoritarian state: they deprived the parliament of all authority; outlawed the Socialist and Catholic parties as well as anti-Fascist associations and labor unions; eliminated democratic elections; established the Court for the Defense of the State and the Fascist secret police; instituted the death penalty for certain political crimes; and greatly curtailed the independence of the existing courts and the media. With the Lateran Pacts (1929), the Catholic Church made official its support for the Fascist regime. The Church recognized the Italian nation and Fascist government as legitimate while the government recognized the Vatican as a state, compensated the Church financially for its loss of the Papal States during the unification of Italy, and awarded the Church special status, allowing it, for example, to operate the only non-Fascist organization (called Catholic Action) within the nation. Church support for the government would continue until the campaign of 1938 introduced race discrimination laws (which mainly affected the Italian Jews, who were prohibited from marrying Aryans, from studying or teaching in public schools, attending libraries, and so forth). The Church condemned these laws. In fact, they contradicted Mussolini's own claim a few years earlier that Italy had no racial problem. The shift illustrates the chameleon-like nature of Italian Fascism, which made it hard to grasp its true intentions. Gadda was initially ambivalent about Fascism; he saw in the new movement the possibility for social order in an Italy that had too long been mired in corruption and chaos, and also saw a pragmatic, realistic approach that he did not find in socialism. However, as he witnessed Fascism's destruction of the democratic way of life, he came to reject it entirely.

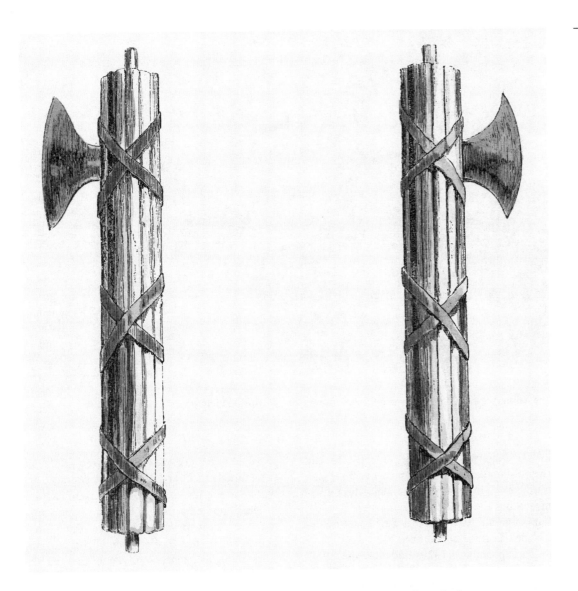

The Fasces, the ancient Roman symbol displayed by lofty civil servants (tribunes) to claim absolute
authority in times of extreme danger. Mussolini chose this symbol for his Fascist movement to signify
the subordination of civic values and principles of authority to military ones.

Italian Fascism and the intellectuals. "Everything in the state, nothing outside the state, nothing against the state"—the formula became the catch phrase of the Fascist regime, applying not just to politics but also to art and scholarship. So what was the nature of this state? Fascism set out to reconstruct Italy as a new kind of nation, in which intellectuals would take responsibility for shaping the civil and moral conscience of the land's "new man." A number of these intellectuals genuinely supported Fascism in their quest for a modern, distinctive national culture and for the moral regeneration of Italians (to be achieved, they thought, through art). They saw in Fascism an ethical force that could toughen a people who, according to Mussolini, had been "feminized"

and "disarmed" by centuries of foreign domination (Mussolini in Ben-Ghiat, p. 6).

The very meaning of *Fascism* was nebulous; Mussolini did not associate it with any definition or lofty theoretical notion, which worked to his advantage when it came to winning over the intellectuals and artists. They were drawn into the game of defining the term and manipulated through censorship and funding. A complicated system of patronage emerged, "designed to contain dissent" and bring intellectuals "into collaborative relationships with the state" (Ben-Ghiat, p. 9). Shrewdly, Mussolini paid lip service to intellectual freedom, even as he sent spies to monitor the activities of intellectuals and artists. The Academy of Italy and the Fascist National Institute of Culture (both founded

The Italian defeat at Caporetto, where the Austrians took nearly 300,000 prisoners.

in 1925) directed cultural expression. The Ministry of Popular Culture (named in 1937) exercised control over the press, cinema, theater, and music. But the excitement generated by the efforts of intellectuals to create a new culture outweighed all this state control.

Throughout the 1920s and into the 1930s, there were competing views about the role of intellectuals in society. The leading thinker, Benedetto Croce, adopted a policy of cautious yet insistent intellectual opposition to the regime but believed that intellectuals should stay out of party politics. His friend Giovanni Gentile, on the other hand, thought intellectuals should be directly engaged in the creation of the new Fascist state and acted accordingly. Still others, such as Antonio Gramsci and Piero Gobetti, defended the right (and thought it the responsibility) of the arts and sciences to object to the regime, and paid for their outspokenness with their lives. The anti-Fascist intellectual had, it seems, a few distinct options—silence, imprisonment, exile, or cautious protest (if one were as famous and celebrated in society as Croce).

Before the establishment of the Fascist regime, intellectuals debated their social responsibilities in literary journals such as *La Ronda* (1919-22). Now, under Fascism, editors asked the intellectuals to focus on style and cut all political and social commentary out of their writings. One of the journals, *Solaria* (1926-36), encouraged its writers to produce a symbolic, abstract literature in which immediate social concerns were transferred to remote places and times, a strategy that helps explain the transposition of Italian concerns to an imaginary South American country in Gadda's novel.

The rise of psychoanalysis. At the beginning of the twentieth century, Sigmund Freud published his first major work, *The Interpretation of Dreams,* which only slowly won recognition from the European medical community. Its psychiatrists remained wary of his newly developed theory of psychoanalysis, which proposes, among other ideas, that much human behavior is governed by unconscious motives, and that in adults many of these motives stem from sexual impulses shaped by long-forgotten childhood experiences. In Italy the Fascists denigrated psychoanalysis by branding it as Austrian, even Jewish, which only compounded obstacles to its acceptance and practice. The negative attitude of Italian intellectuals such as Benedetto Croce and Giovanni Gentile numbered among these obstacles. Gentile believed in the study of individual consciousness, maintaining that the unconscious could not be the object of scientific inquiry because it was "totally removed from our knowledge" (Gentile in David, p. 44; trans. L. Modena). In Croce's view, Freud's theories were not entirely without merit, but the notion of unmasking the unconscious was objectionable. It was too risky, thought Croce, to try to explain such a hidden area. Croce feared that such an examination could justify an individual's unethical choices or relieve an individual from self-control.

Freudian ideas were introduced in Italy through such studies as Dr. Edoardo Weiss's *Elements of Psychoanalysis* (1922). When the Italian medical journals finally began to acknowledge psychoanalysis and such concepts as "the unconscious" and "free association" started to gain currency, the country's psychiatric establishment directly attacked Freud's theories, dismissing them as one-sided and perverted. By the 1920s, a gulf had opened up between the practices of psychiatry and of psychoanalysis. Because there was no convincing evidence that any illnesses had been cured by Freud's method, the psychiatrists approached psychoanalysis only as a set of hypotheses, not as a science. The distance between the two disciplines would be stretched further after some Italian psychoanalysts were forced to leave their university posts because they were Jewish. Dr. Weiss, for example, had to quit his post at a psychiatric hospital in Trieste, ostensibly because he refused to support the Fascist Party.

Over time, the psychiatric community's open hostility toward psychoanalysis abated, and studies such as Dr. Enrico Morselli's *Psychoanalysis* (1926) compelled psychiatrists to take Freud's theories into account. But Gadda's encounter with psychoanalysis took place between 1926 and 1940, when many Italians still thought of Freud as a pervert and of all the ideas and studies in his field "as the devil's handiwork and almost shameful" (Gadda in Ferrero, p. 33; trans. L. Modena). Yet Gadda embraced psychoanalysis, which informs most of his writings, including *Acquainted with Grief*. He was convinced that psychoanalysis promised a new understanding of human life.

The Novel in Focus

The plot. Set in Lukones, Maradagàl (an imaginary part of South America) from 1925 to 1933, *Acquainted with Grief* has two central figures: the reclusive engineer Gonzalo Pirobutirro and his mother. She is sometimes referred to as "the Señora," mostly as just "the mother," an antithetical archetype to "the son." Aristocrats who

have fallen on hard times, the pair live together in an isolated country house known as Villa Pirobutirro. An unnecessarily large residence, surrounded by a scarcely productive plot of land, the house is above their means. The novel has little action but considerable description. Vehement outbursts, lyrical depictions, portraits of society, and speculations of every sort flesh out the skeleton of events.

The narrator begins by describing how the country is emerging from a bitter war with a bordering state. The postwar atmosphere in Maradagàl is tense, in part because of the presence of the state security apparatus, the Night Watchmen. The narrator details the nonsensical eligibility requirements to be met by those who wish to join this security apparatus, including the preference given to war veterans regardless of their ability to perform their duties. The chaotic nature of life in Lukones is further illustrated by the tale of Pedro Managones, a Night Watchman who triggers a village scandal by faking his identity and his war injury. Having ridiculed the government and the common folk, the narrator proceeds to attack the penchant for kitsch exhibited by the upper and middle classes. The focus shifts to a Doctor Higueroa. On his way to make a house call at the Pirobutirro residence, Doctor Higueróa's mind wanders. He integrates town gossip with musings and digressions in a lengthy internal discourse largely about Gonzalo that foreshadows the physician's inability to understand Gonzalo's malady. Surrounded by rumors, Gonzalo has acquired a downright "unsavory reputation" (*Acquainted*, p. 36). He is a misanthrope, a rancorous bachelor, and a slothful intellectual with no sympathy for the humble or "the wretchedness and the yellowishness of povertydom" (*Acquainted*, p. 36). In general, he is a voracious, greedy, and moody sort, and he treats his mother roughly. It becomes clear that his habits are the stuff of legend, including his manias for order and silence. But his insides are anything but silent; he harbors "torment in wanting to swim against the current of meanings and causes" (*Acquainted*, p. 49).

Doctor Higueróa is still on his way to visit Gonzalo when he encounters Battistina, a maid in the family's house. She enlightens the doctor about Gonzalo's outbursts (often over money and spending), his hatred of intruders, and the misery of his aged mother. Old and weak, his mother passes her days with a heavy heart, weighed down by two great sorrows: the loss of an undisclosed someone and the burden of living with her menacing, disturbed, and unhappy son. The narrator recounts how Gonzalo, in one of his angry fits, stomped on a framed portrait of his father. "As if from her weakness were to be born the final devotion," the mother bent to pick up the pieces (*Acquainted*, p. 62).

Once at the house, the doctor examines Gonzalo, who laments some unspecified sufferings, apparently affecting his digestion. The visit reveals no "visible sickness," yet a sudden change takes place in the appearance and behavior of Gonzalo: he gradually sinks into an "inscrutable opacity," an alarmed, anguished, desirous state in which he rejects all words of comfort (*Acquainted*, p. 69). A 50-page conversation follows between Doctor Higueróa and Gonzalo, which makes its way through the entire spectrum of Gonzalo's moods. Alternately grievous and violent, the patient mumbles about his aging mother, death, and the cemetery. Perplexed, the doctor listens to one of Gonzalo's dreams, in which his mother's ghost motionlessly appears to her son in the empty house. Gonzalo fears that something might happen to his property and his mother, given the house's isolation and the ineffectiveness of the surrounding wall. Night thieves do in fact infest the area. The *Nistitúos provinciales de vigilancia para la noche*, or Night Watchmen's organization, offers optional protection to those who pay for the service. Gonzalo, nonetheless, strongly resents the organization, maintaining that the guards are either weak or trespassers themselves.

As Gonzalo swings from mood to mood in a "succession of opposed humors," Doctor Higueróa tries to steer conversation from the irrational to the rational (*Acquainted*, p. 108). Then Pedro, a Night Watchman, approaches the house and reminds Gonzalo that he has no choice but to accept the paid protection of the Night Watchmen. According to a new law the fee is mandatory. Gonzalo objects: "What about the nonsubscribers then? . . . I want to remain free" (*Acquainted*, p. 113). Pedro utters a thinly veiled threat before he leaves, letting Gonzalo know that he will return when his mother is home. Enraged by the insolence and worried about his mother's safety, Gonzalo fantasizes about hanging the Night Watchman. His mind lingers "over the most consolatory details," but he is in fact incapable of reacting in any concrete fashion (*Acquainted*, p. 114). The narration afterwards brings to the foreground Dr. Higueróa's middle-class desire for personal prestige: the doctor shows off his command of the latest town gossip by interrupting Gonzalo's imaginative flow to share what

he claims is the definitive account of the scandal associated with Pedro.

A tale of the mother's as well as the son's loneliness, *Acquainted with Grief* then moves into the Señora's mind and heart. The mother has lost two sons: one, "her finest blood," to the war, and the other, Gonzalo, to an inexplicable malady that she, like the doctor, does not understand (*Acquainted*, p. 142). The narrator describes the moment when the mother learned that Enrico had died during a military operation, and a terrible storm forced her to take shelter in the cellar; the sky and wind seemed "to be seeking her, too, her, in the house" (*Acquainted*, p. 135). While her fear grew, "she huddled then, her eyes shut, in her final solitude," as if the hurricane had turned to ashes all she was, "a grieving spark of time," as well as all she had been, "woman, wife and mother" (*Acquainted*, p. 136).

Next, for the first time in the novel, mother and son appear together. Fearing one of his tantrums, she struggles to prepare dinner. An atmosphere of misery and silence envelops the kitchen as she anxiously awaits his insults directed at the house, of which she is extremely proud. The mother offers her perspective on her son's lack of peace: she is finally aware, after much denial, that his deep rancor is an "obscure sickness" coming from an "inexpiable zone of shrouded verities" that his will cannot control (*Acquainted*, p. 154). The novel proceeds to portray the inner workings of Gonzalo's mind. He is saddened by their frugal meal, and angry because all of their money has been squandered on building the house. An avalanche of mental images follows: Gonzalo pictures tides of men and women, an extensive gallery of middle-class people grotesquely deformed, tawdry, hopeful, ostentatious, and confident. With bitter insight, the narration reveals Gonzalo's need to distinguish between true and false appearances. Gonzalo is aware that "nonvalid depictions were to be negated and to be rejected" (*Acquainted*, p. 170). Yet he too is attracted to the lure of appearances, torn between them and truth:

> To seize the lying kiss of Appearances, to lie with her on the straw, to breathe her breath, to drink in, down into the soul, her belch and strumpet's stench. Or instead to . . . to deny. . . . But . . . to deny vain images, most of the time, means denying oneself.
>
> (*Acquainted*, p. 171)

There follows a moment of tenderness between mother and son, broken by an unwelcome interruption. The sudden arrival of a dirty peon stirs Gonzalo's anger, prompting him to emotionally withdraw from his mother's affections and to brusquely fire the peon. Gonzalo's reaction is prompted in part by a need for his mother's exclusive attention. This same need motivates the anger Gonzalo feels a few days later when, entering the house, he finds several peasants are paying a visit to his mother. The presence of "intruders" again brings to mind the easily scalable wall surrounding the house. From the wall, the narration moves to the road and the valley beneath, then finally rests on the strokes of a distant bell tower: the original version of *Acquainted with Grief* ends here, on the image of the empty, desolate passage of time.

In the English edition and in a later Italian edition, Gadda expands the narrative. Gonzalo hears the report of a burglary meant to intimidate a neighbor who, like himself, refused to subscribe to the Night Watchmen's organization. Then a sequence of memories reinforces Gonzalo's main obsessions, particularly his lack of joy in childhood and his abhorrence of physical proximity to others. In a fit of anger, Gonzalo threatens to kill his mother and leaves. Suspicious noises lead villagers into the house, where Gonzalo's mother lies dead in her bed, her head terribly injured by an unknown aggressor. Among the murder suspects are her son, the fired peon, and a Night Watchman. Or perhaps, even, "the shadow, black and mute, which had appeared on the terrace: no telling who it was; it passed the fields and the walls like an image," like a "wicked cause operating in the absurdity of the night" (*Acquainted*, pp. 223, 237).

Alienation, society, and psychoanalysis. In the novel, Gonzalo calls for Doctor Higueróa, and a lengthy dialogue between the two ensues. After the visit, the doctor, "with a slightly mortified tone, confessed that he had discovered nothing to worry about" (*Acquainted*, p. 68). The patient-doctor dialogue manifests two characteristics of post-World War I culture in Italy: traditional medicine's inadequate response to psychological maladies and the suffocating conventions of middle-class life. On the one hand, there is the doctor's simplistic discourse and his inability to understand Gonzalo's profound alienation as something other than social awkwardness. On the other, there is Gonzalo's rush of distorted, sometimes bizarre, thoughts and perceptions. Wholly unbridgeable, the emotional and intellectual chasm that opens between the two interlocutors produces dramatic, even hilarious effects. For example, the doctor mentions a cheese man, and then the cheese of

the material world, "the world's baggage," as the novel explains it, enters the bubble of Gonzalo's imaginary universe, where it is transformed (*Acquainted*, p. 75): "He arranged them as best as he could, those wheel-like forms of cheese, in that outrageous field of nonforms: in that caravansary of impedimenta of every sort: cicadas onions clogs, hebephrenic bronzes, paleo-Celtic Josés, Battistinas faithful through the ages [taken from the name of Gonzalo's maid]" (*Acquainted*, pp. 75-76).

"GONZALO"—A NATIONAL CHARACTER

In Italian literature, "Gonzalo" has become so famous that his name alone stands for a singular kind of person. Cantankerous, solitary, wrapped in thought, mad at a world that does not meet his desires, the wounded Gonzalo-type grotesquely deforms everything he sees or thinks about. People, objects, feelings, and so forth, become the target of his unrestrained, hyper-imaginative outbursts.

Gadda immerses his reader in the Freudian concept of dreams as the privileged space where reality flows unrestrained. The dream about his mother that is central to the novel—and that entirely confounds Dr. Higueroa—brings to the surface Gonzalo's remorse and self-loathing. In the dream, his mother's ghost appears to Gonzalo, turning all of his hopes to stone, and denying him self-redemption. In the years following his own mother's death, while Gadda was writing *Acquainted with Grief*, he repeatedly shared with friends the unbearable remorse that paralyzed his life at the thought of how he treated his mother in her old age.

The narrator's contempt for physicians is clearly visible in the ridiculous criteria the doctor employs when dismissing Gonzalo's dream: "It seemed incredible to Doctor Higueróa that a man of normal height, rather tall in fact, and of such 'lofty' social station, could let himself become anchored to foolishness of this sort" (*Acquainted*, p. 82). Doctor Higueróa's lack of awareness of psychological conditions is an indictment of the medical establishment in the early twentieth century, which left people such as Gonzalo adrift in a sea of psychological torment.

The doctor's character does double-duty, allowing the novel to convey not only the resistance against psychoanalysis in Italy at the time but also the perception of its middle class as narcissistic, prejudiced, and status-conscious. It is because Gonzalo does not conform to middle-class expectations and conventions that he has fallen ill, thinks the doctor: if Gonzalo simply went out more, or accepted the Night Watchmen's protection, or dated the doctor's daughter and learned to drive, he would feel better. Always the doctor presents a stubbornly one-sided interpretation and rejects all contrary views. The narrator balances everything, however, offering a diagnosis the doctor ignores: Gonzalo may be suffering from "interpretative delirium," the tendency to elaborate on existing facts: the facts are real but the interpretation is highly individualized (*Acquainted*, p. 105). At the same time,

---

THE DAWN OF A CONSUMER CULTURE—DISPARAGED

~

Owning an automobile was the highest of all middle-class aspirations in 1930s Italy, as suggested in *Acquainted with Grief* when Doctor Higueróa pushes Gonzalo to learn how to drive. Society was becoming generally obsessed with the display of possessions, and the gap between reality and appearances grew. Gone, thought Gadda, was the old upper-class mix of wealth with productivity and ethical values (honor, honesty, efficiency). This new class devoted itself to "appearing," at the expense of "being." Some writers of the day, such as Alberto Moravia, linked material riches to spiritual poverty; others, like Gadda, resented the growing "disorder," "imbecility," self-righteousness, narcissism, and associated decline of treasured values (Gadda in Ferretti, p. 28; trans. L. Modena). In Gadda's novel, observes one scholar, Gonzalo displays four forms of resistance to middle-class materialism: an aristocratic attitude, withdrawal from society, passivity, and free use of his intellect through reading and writing.

"Gonzalo's madness is a truth which reveals the deception of the world's false truth" (Sbragia, p. 106). In other words, his sickness is as much social as it is individual. Indeed, Gadda himself commented later in life that Gonzalo's raging fury primarily reflected external reality, or "the madness of the world itself" (Sbragia, p. 109). In those years Gadda saw an upside-down world dominated by middle-class arrogance and ignorance, a mania for owning country villas and other goods whether or not one could afford

them, and a social order that had given rise to a murderous state-security system. Thus, cloaked in a fictional setting, the novel lodges a protest against Italian Fascist society. It furthermore exposes realistic complexities. If the novel ridicules the mania for owning things, it also portrays Gonzalo's attitude to ownership as no simple matter. However alienated he may be, Gonzalo strives to defend from intruders the objects of his love and hate—his mother, his personal effects, and the country estate. He is himself obsessed with personal property and possessions, his compensation perhaps for the deprivations he has suffered as a child. To his mind, his teachers' ruthlessness and his parents' coldness and stinginess (burdened as they were by the country villa) forced him to endure cold, hunger, punishments, and unforgettable humiliations.

Sources and literary context. *Acquainted with Grief* is one of the first Italian novels to use language and narrative structure to depict someone's state of mind. Italo Svevo was an important forerunner. In *Zeno's Conscience*, (1923; also in *WLAIT 7: Italian Literature and Its Times*) Svevo combined the elements of neurosis and fiction to create a novel that shunned traditional linear narrative in favor of psychoanalysis, perspectivism, and interior monologue. Gadda moved a step further by transposing the exact dynamic of Gonzalo's thoughts. His readings in psychoanalysis heavily influenced his creation of the novel. In fact, Gadda created the character of Gonzalo to arrive at his own understanding of grief.

More than anything else, however, Gadda's personal experiences inspired the novel. The memory of his brother Enrico's death in World War I haunted him for decades. Later, the death of his mother and the sale of the family's country house brought him face-to-face with years of bottled-up rancor that blighted his relations with his family and their possessions. Critics agree that Gadda thinly disguised his own family's social-climbing tendencies in Gonzalo's refusal to integrate himself into middle-class society. Likewise, Gonzalo's outbursts in the novel recall childhood deprivations experienced by Gadda himself and his lifelong attack on the bourgeois ideal of ownership. The novel also reflects an effort on Gadda's part to understand his mixed emotions after his mother's death. In doing so, he combined autobiographical and larger social elements to a degree not seen in his previous works. For example, the novel reflects his resentment against the high value placed on owning a villa, which stretched his family's means.

The novel's *Nistitúos provinciales de vigilancia para la noche*, or Night Watchmen's organization, is a veiled allusion to the Fascist National Party. This indirect reference to the dictatorship is at first almost comic. However, as the novel progresses, the violent presence of the supposedly reassuring organization acquires a darker tone, when a Night Watchman makes clear to Gonzalo that the organization's fee is mandatory. Those who do not accept the "paid protections" are the target of threats and robberies. Thus, Gadda evokes the strong-arm tactics of the Fascist leadership when it came to enrollment in the party, and refers also to its deceptive form of security.

Writers of the 1930s (for example, Alberto Moravia and Eugenio Montale) produced works that combined realism and lyricism with a strong historical and moral sense. In this literary context, Gadda was unique for his ability to depict what he saw as the excruciating tension between the person and the hostile, harmful external world. It was his belief that writers should use all the resources of language at their disposal to portray the agony of life.

Events in History at the Time the Novel Was Written

Growth of Fascism and reinvention of the Italian self. Beginning in 1935 Italy's Fascist regime openly showed its imperialist intentions by invading Ethiopia, intervening in the Spanish Civil War on the side of General Francisco Franco, and accepting the German occupation of Austria. To garner public support for military intervention abroad, Mussolini portrayed the Fascist state as the reincarnation of the Roman Empire and pushed Italians to embrace their "imperial destiny" by promoting a racial myth: Italians belonged to a higher civilization and were destined, separately and together, for greatness. Mussolini attempted to instill in the public at large the need to continually strive for new goals and resist weariness. Gadda's passive, ruminating protagonist constitutes the exact opposite of such an active, untiring personality. When in 1936 Mussolini brought Italian Fascism closer to that of Nazi Germany, similar attempts strove to instill anti-Semitism into a country where many perceived of Jews as differing in religion only. The Jews of early-twentieth-century Italy were well assimilated into the mainstream, some as highly respected academics and businessmen.

According to Fascist ideology, national greatness had to be achieved through Mussolini's leadership and through the merging of each person's will into one public, collective, and decisive identity. An enormous propaganda machine worked to create an image of Mussolini as a decisive, austere, and powerful Roman emperor: Gadda's contempt for the cult of Mussolini would manifest itself years later in *Eros e Priapo* (1967), which satirizes the larger-than-life, authoritarian masculinity of Mussolini's public image.

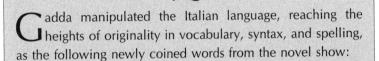

GADDA'S WORDPLAY

Gadda manipulated the Italian language, reaching the heights of originality in vocabulary, syntax, and spelling, as the following newly coined words from the novel show:

Banzavóis Supposedly a type of South American corn. In Latin, the botanic name for corn is *zea mays*. The term *Banzavóis* recalls *mays* in its *-is* ending, but the first part is from *panz vöj*, which in Gadda's home region is the dialect form of *pance vuote*, or "empty belly." The association with a rural dialect suggests that, at least in the 1930s, corn was the major—and an insufficient—source of nutrition for the poor. In other words, the *Banzavóis* is the *mays*, or corn, that fills up empty bellies.

Pitecántropi-granoturco A term meaning "the peasants," formed by combining the Italian for "corn," *granoturco*, with *pithecanthrope*, the name anthropologists give to the hominid that bridges the gap in evolutionary development between apes and humans. Gonzalo's term conjures an image of the peasants as apelike creatures, little more than anthropomorphic monkeys, because of very poor nutrition.

Manichini ossibuchivori A term that refers to "the wealthy," Gadda applies this term to the well-off because of their passion for the expensive *ossobuco*, or marrowbone. Their stomach, always too full, is caught in the act of *mantrugiare* the marrowbone: an archaic expression from the Latin *manu trusare*, "to push with the hand."

Along with the icon of national leadership, Fascists concocted an image of the ideal man— patriotic, single-minded, virile, and aggressive— able, in other words, to achieve the goals of the regime. Slogans such as "war is to man what motherhood is to woman" appeared over and over again. The future was to be guaranteed by a genuinely Fascist generation of new men, all potential heroes, fortified to endure war and suffering. In 1940, giving its men the opportunity to become new, Italy entered World War II on the side of Germany, attacking France and Greece.

Carlo Ferretti suggests that when Gadda began writing *Acquainted with Grief* he had already moved away from Fascism, as some oblique references in the novel suggest. For example, the boastful, violent official who visits Gonzalo and insists on imposing on him the paid protection of the Night Watchmen represents the ideal man of the Fascists. In contrast to the swaggering, gun-slinging ideal, Gadda's novel proposes an altogether different image. Actually in Gadda's opinion, there was no one image, no stable, unified, and decisive self, no "I"; rather man was a conglomeration of circumstantial relationships.

Reception. When the first installments of *Acquainted with Grief* appeared in the Italian literary journal *Letteratura* in 1938-41, a small group of critics enthusiastically embraced it. The majority, however, dismissed the ironic and what they saw as grotesque deformation of language and events as mere self-indulgence. Gianfranco Contini, one of the most influential critics, recognized immediately that Gadda's expressionistic pastiche was the chaotic rendering of a culture and world in crisis. But he was in the minority. The work did not reach a wide public and Gadda's name remained almost unknown. It was only after the publication of *That Awful Mess on Via Merulana* (1957; *Quer pasticciaccio brutto de via Merulana*) that the public recognized Gadda's stature and *Acquainted with Grief* was published as a book. Critics finally acknowledged the novelty and depth of the work and the novel went on to win the Prix International de Littérature in 1963. According to the critic Emilio Manzotti, one of Italy's foremost Gadda scholars, the originality and the value of *Cognizione del dolore* lie partly in the aphoristic conciseness of many of its

memorable sentences, and primarily in the "cognitive tension that drives the text, in the strenuous attempt to uncover reality, to get beyond the surface, to show the complex and bewildering constitution of reality, to radically transform the eye's usual grammar by abolishing its received clichés and stereotypes" (Manzotti, p. 325; trans. L. Modena).

—Letizia Modena

For More Information

Ben-Ghiat, Ruth. *Fascist Modernities: Italy, 1922-1945*. Berkeley: University of California Press, 2001.

Bertone, Manuela, and Robert Dombroski, eds. *Carlo Emilio Gadda: Contemporary Perspectives*. Toronto: University of Toronto Press, 1997.

Corner, Paul. "Italy 1915-1945: Politics and Society." In *The Oxford Illustrated History of Italy*. Ed. George Holmes. Oxford: Oxford University Press, 1997.

David, Michel. *Letteratura e Psicanalisi*. Milan: Mursia, 1967.

Ferrero, Ernesto. *Invito alla lettura di Carlo Emilio Gadda*. Milan: Mursia, 1972.

Ferretti, Carlo. *Ritratto di Gadda*. Bari, Italy: Laterza, 1987.

Gadda, Carlo Emilio. *Acquainted with Grief*. Trans. William Weaver. New York: George Braziller, 1969.

Luti, G., ed. *Storia letteraria d'Italia, Il Novecento*. Padua: Piccin Nuova Libraria, 1993.

Manzotti, Emilio. "La cognizione del dolore di Carlo Emilio Gadda." In *Letteratura italiana: Le opere*. Vol. 4, pt. 1. Torino: Einaudi, 1996.

Preti, Luigi. "Fascist Imperialism and Racism." In *The Ax Within: Italian Fascism in Action*. Ed. Roland Sarti. New York: New Viewpoints, 1974.

Sbragia, Albert. *Carlo Emilio Gadda and the Modern Macaronic*. Gainsville: University Press of Florida, 1996.

Adonis

by

Giambattista Marino

The most renowned poet of seventeenth-century Italy, Giambattista Marino, was born in Naples in 1569. Though his family attempted to force him into a career in law, he soon abandoned his studies to pursue his literary ambitions and so was expelled from his father's house. In 1596 Marino became the secretary of Matteo di Capua, Prince of Conca, and experienced for the first time the luxuries of court life. He was, however, twice imprisoned during this period: once for having seduced a rich merchant's daughter, who died attempting to have an abortion; a second time for forging documents to help a friend avoid the death penalty. After escaping prison and fleeing to Rome in 1600, Marino spent a few years traveling through Italy in the service of a nephew of Pope Clement VIII, Cardinal Aldobrandini, with whom he moved first to Ravenna and then, in 1608, to Turin. By this time Marino had published his initial volume of lyrics, *Rime* (1602), later revised and republished as *La lira* (*The Lyre*), parts 1 and 2. In Turin, at the court of Duke Carlo Emanuele I of Savoy, Marino achieved his first great literary success; in 1609 he was awarded the honorary title of Cavaliere (knight). But he acquired new enemies too, among them the duke's secretary, Gaspare Murtola, who was also a poet. Murtola attempted to shoot Marino and landed in prison for his pains. Marino's service at the duke's court ended unhappily in 1611 when, for reasons that remain unclear, he himself was sentenced to prison for over a year. In 1614 Marino published the third part of *The Lyre*, and in 1615 he finally realized his

---

> ## THE LITERARY WORK
>
> A poem set at a mythical time in Venus's palace on the island of Cyprus, Greece; published in Italian (as *Adone*) in 1623, in English in 1967.
>
> ## SYNOPSIS
>
> Adonis, a beautiful youth, arrives on the isle of Cyprus, where he and the goddess Venus fall in love. Jealous, the god Mars commits indirect murder, but Venus finds a way to immortalize her earthly lover's beauty.

---

dream of being honored at a great court. He was invited to Paris by Maria de' Medici, widow of Henry IV and mother of Louis XIII. Accepting the invitation, Marino remained in France for eight years, working fervently during his stay, publishing *Epithalami* (1616; *Epithalamia*), *La Galeria* (1619; *The Gallery*), *La Sampogna* (1620; *The Bagpipe*), and finally, in 1623, his masterpiece, *Adonis*, an ambitious poem of 40,984 lines on which he had been working since his Roman years. At this point, his precarious health convinced Marino to return to Italy, where he was received triumphantly as the greatest living Italian poet. He died in Naples in 1625, at the apex of his success, leaving behind an unfinished work, *La strage degli innocenti* (1638; *The Slaughter of the Innocent*), and his monumental *Adonis*. Though placed on the *Index Librorum Prohibitorum* (the Church's list of forbidden books), the poem would be republished at least 11 times in the next 50 years, becoming the very symbol of the baroque era.

THE TERM *BAROQUE*

The term *baroque* is believed to have originated from the Portuguese *barroco*, which denotes a pearl that is not perfectly spherical. From this literal meaning is extracted a metaphorical one, that is, something extravagant or whimsical. The term became more common in the sixteenth century, when it was used in philosophy as the label for a particularly ambiguous kind of syllogism or logical procedure. An "in barroco" syllogism consisted of a general statement followed by a specific one in the negative, and then a witty deduction produced from both the general and specific statements. For example:

General statement: All women are mortal
Specific statement in the negative: Venus is not a mortal
Deduction: Venus is not a woman

Such a conclusion, though correct (Venus is indeed not a woman, she is a goddess), shows a high grade of ambiguity. Isn't it true that Venus is the woman among women, the quintessence of femininity—ergo, the ambiguity.

The highly elaborate, artificial style of much seventeenth-century art and literature can be likened to this kind of deceitful logic. Around the middle of the eighteenth century the Italian term *barocco* began to be used deprecatingly in reference to the art of the preceding century, which became known as the Baroque period (also called the early modern period). Though the twentieth century attached new value to Baroque literature, today the term continues to carry with it some disparaging connotations. For many, it connotes a negative judgment of the rich, overly elaborate style of which Cavalier Marino was a master.

Events in History at the Time of the Poem

The poetic setting—mythical or real? The story of the mortal Adonis and his love for the immortal goddess Venus takes place in a mythical, distant world. The characters move outside regular time and space, in a magical era before history, when gods walked the earth together with mortals and almost anything was possible. A closer look at this setting, however, reveals that it is not as mythical as it appears at first blush. The poet sets the action in a version of his own world. Not only does the verse include references to historical facts and figures belonging to Marino's time, but the poet also infuses into the work many aspects of seventeenth-century Europe, with its sumptuous courts, its new scientific discoveries, and its elaborate art. The art is often referred to as *baroque* (from the Portuguese *barroco*, for "an imperfect pearl"), a term that points to the artificiality and irregularity of the works generated during the seventeenth century.

Along with artificiality came the representation of a world in constant flux. The milieu described in *Adonis* changes continuously. Its characters lack certainties and a universal truth to rely upon; instability is an important part of life, and appearance doesn't always coincide with reality. This sense of vacuous instability, which pervades much of baroque art, reflects real-life conditions at the time.

Life in seventeenth-century Europe was grim. The Thirty Years War (1618-48), which pit Austria and Spain (both under Habsburg rule) against Germany's princes, the Dutch Republic, Sweden, and France, stands out as the main conflict among many widespread struggles. In the 1590s and again in 1630, the plague turned into a raging epidemic in the Mediterranean region and, along with repeated social disorders, brought the uncertainty of human life into ever-sharper focus.

The melancholy, affliction, and insecurity of the century affected its art. Living in an unsteady universe, baroque artists were acutely aware of the despair diffused through much of their society. The sense of the writer's detachment and disengagement in much baroque literature to some degree reflects a desire of escaping grim reality, and the increasing popularity of mythological material can be attributed to the same cause. The recourse to artifice is never completely successful, however. Even the mythology contains a very realistic sense of danger and instability, as in Marino's poem, in which innocent, inexperienced Adonis obtains the favors of the most beautiful among the goddesses only to die suddenly at the very apex of his happiness.

From free thought to the birth of a new science. The conflict between Catholics and Protestants, which originated in Germany a century earlier with the Augustinian friar Martin Luther, escalated over the decades that followed. By the beginning of the seventeenth century, Luther's drive against the corruption of the Catholic Church had developed into a full-fledged movement (the Reformation) that instigated a full-fledged countermovement (the Counter Reformation) by the Catholic Church. What began as one man's drive to rid the Church of abusive practices had turned into a geopolitical conflict of powers.

Italy was divided into a number of separate states or political entities at the time, which fell under the control of either Spain (ruling more or less directly over central and southern Italy) or France (attempting to impose its hegemony in particular in the Milan area). The states became little more than pawns on the chessboard of European politics. Spanish Catholic rule, reinforced by the strict laws of the Counter Reformation, greatly affected social life in the Italian states.

The Counter Reformation attempted to restore the power of the Roman Catholic Church in the face of the challenge mounted by Protestantism, the new branch of Christianity formed by the Reformation. To restore the Church's power, the Counter Reformists adopted certain strategies: they glorified ecclesiastical authorities; disseminated an obsessive, fearful conception of sin and death; and imposed moral and intellectual dogmatism. The Church's publication in 1557 of its first list of prohibited books (the *Index Librorum Prohibitorum*) marked the end of an era of free thought for artists and intellectuals wherever the Church held sway.

At odds with such censorship, an increasing interest in science and intellectual speculation characterized the century, the first half of which saw the rise of such luminaries as the German astronomer Johannes Kepler (1571-1630), the French mathematicians René Descartes (1596-1639) and Blaise Pascal (1623-1662), and the Italian writers Tommaso Campanella (1568-1639) and Galileo Galilei (1564-1642). The latter two—the first a philosopher, the second an astronomer—were both tried by the Inquisition. Campanella was condemned to a lengthy prison sentence; Galileo was forced into a shameful abjuration of his theories to avoid being burned at the stake. Despite the obstacles, the intellectuals persisted, and regard for science grew.

New scientific discoveries opened fascinating but often shocking perspectives. For instance, the invention of the telescope generated a new way of conceiving the relation between different objects, altering forever the conception of space, enlarging it beyond extremes never considered before, as Marino reminds us in a canto of *Adonis* that celebrates Galileo and his work.

The new science was important not only in itself, but because it opened fresh perspectives on the understanding of reality. Severo Sarduy, who studied the connections between art and astronomy in the seventeenth century, noticed that Kepler's discovery about the ellipsoidal trajectory of planets around the sun altered the very concept of the position occupied by humankind in the universe. More exactly, the substitution of the ellipsis (which lacked a geometric center) for the circle constituted the first intrusion of something shifty and insecure in a universe till then closed, steady, and well regulated. Such a discovery could be connected to the lack of unity—and therefore thematic center—typical of baroque art, evident in the succession of independent episodes that comprise *Adonis*.

ADONIS APPLAUDS GALILEO'S "MARVELOUS" NEW INSTRUMENT

The time will come that with no doubt
His notes will notorious be and clear,
Thanks to a marvelous instrument,
For which what far is, closer appears
And, closing an eye, the other intent
All men will look at the lunar globe,
Making long intervals of space so short
With a little cannon and two crystals.

Through you, Galileo, was composed
The telescope, unknown to this age,
Which in one's sense of sight makes close,
Though remote, an object and enlarges it.
(Marino, *Adone*, Canto 10,
Stanzas 41-42; trans. F. Santini)

A new society, a new reality. The whole structure of European society was altered during the baroque era. People increasingly moved to large cities to escape famine and to find work, their migration turning capitals like Paris, London, Naples, and Madrid into the continent's first metropolises. The ranks of the underclass—those who survived by begging, stealing, or prostituting themselves—grew. Both the rural and urban areas had long included such an underclass, a permanently poor minority. In hard times, when harvests failed, this underclass grew as it was joined by the temporary poor—those who normally scraped by as peasants but, when there was no food or work, sank into poverty until conditions brightened again. Economic hardships exacerbated such slippages after 1590, and especially after 1620, at the end of Marino's lifetime. The underclass swelled, which helps explain why other city dwellers began to see the incoming farmers who might slip into its ranks as socially dangerous. A major shift in perceptions occurred. In the Middle Ages, in keeping with Christian teaching, the poor had been regarded as sacred; now they started to be viewed as a threat. The difference between beggar and bandit or beggar and thief narrowed in the eyes of the upper classes.

CYPRUS AND CYTHERA: THE MYTH OF VENUS

The cult of the Greek goddess Aphrodite (called Venus by the Romans) attracted a widespread following in the lands influenced by the Greeks. According to mythology, Aphrodite was born when Uranus (the Sky), desirous of uniting himself with Gaea (the Earth), was assailed by Chronos (Time), who emasculated him. Uranus's genitals fell into the sea and, covered by foam (in Greek, *afrós*), generated Aphrodite, the goddess "born from foam." Pushed by gentle winds, the beautiful, naked maiden floated, first to the island of Cythera in the Ionian Sea and then to the island of Cyprus (the two islands would turn into main locations for the cult of the goddess). In Marino's poem, mythology and history intermingle: Venus resides in a mysterious palace on the island of Cyprus, but during the season of the festivals of Cythera, occasions that indeed took place in real life, the goddess travels to the Ionian Sea to participate.

This change in perception had artistic consequences. Social outcasts began to have a greater effect on creative renderings produced in the cities. Artists found themselves in touch with a more diversified social reality, which found its way into their works. Commoners rather than aristocrats appeared more frequently as protagonists of poetry and paintings. In the poetry of Marino and his followers, the starry-eyed, blonde châtelaines (mistresses of castles) who had dominated courtly love literature are often overshadowed by exotic, non-aristocratic beauties, like the raggedy "beautiful beggar" in a sonnet by Claudio Achillini, a poet who was incredibly popular in his day (though he was later singled out as the main example of baroque bad taste) and who

greatly admired Marino. In *Adonis*, even blonde Venus appears disguised as a gypsy; with her curly black tresses, she reads Adonis's palm.

Baroque artists tended to include in their works all the shades of the complex reality in which they lived. In doing so, they often transformed even the most bitter issues (death, poverty, human decay, folly) by attributing to them a lightness and beauty they in reality did not have. Achillini's raggedy beggar, for instance, is so transfigured by the poet that the shoeless waif becomes a heavenly creature whose cascade of golden hair is far richer than real gold. She takes on the persona of a starlet, and the artist himself becomes the creator of a shimmering world, more fascinating and mysterious than the real one. It follows, according to this view, that nature and art operate on parallel tracks of existence; both result from the effort of a skilled wit—God's in the first case, the artist's in the second one.

The superiority of art to reality was a favorite theme of Marino, who often remarked how life as represented in paintings could be better (more beautiful and even more natural) than everyday existence. Through this medium, both poet and audience could see the world in a different light; in the midst of the often gloomy situations in which they lived, they could perceive another world made of wordplay and ingenious creations.

The Poem in Focus

Contents overview. *Adonis* is divided into 20 cantos, each comprised of a variable number of octaves (stanzas of eight rhymed lines). Every canto opens with a brief allegory of its contents and a four-line synopsis, attributed to two friends of Marino, Lorenzo Sanvitale and Luigi Scoto respectively. Since its first appearance, the work has always been accompanied by a dedication to Maria de' Medici, the regent of France and Marino's patron, and by an introduction in French by J. Chapelain. The events narrated in the poem transpire over one year, of which 22 days are referred to specifically. The story takes place entirely on Cyprus, with two exceptions: Venus and Adonis's visit to the heavens (Canto 10), and Venus's trip to the island of Cythera by the Peloponnesian Peninsula (Canto 17).

The story itself is a recounting of the tragic love between Venus, the Roman goddess of love, and a mortal youth, Adonis. Many minor events and subplots are included, with a number of elaborate descriptive passages making the narration extremely complicated. The work is perhaps most

Venus and Adonis. Marble sculpture (1789–94) by Antonio Canova.

accurately described as a series of loosely related fables and episodes, for it has no unitary structure. Schematically the plot unfolds as follows:

Contents summary. *Canto 1.* Cupid, forever a child, has been spanked by his mother Venus, and resolves to avenge himself by making her fall in love with a young mortal, Adonis. With the help of Neptune, god of the sea, Cupid conjures a storm and Adonis's ship lands on the shores of Cyprus, where Adonis meets the shepherd Clizio.

Canto 2. The canto describes Cupid's palace. A long digression follows, in which Clizio recounts the myth of the Trojan prince Paris, who chose Venus as the most beautiful among the goddesses. In Marino's version, each of the three most admired goddesses (maternal Juno, virginal Athena, and sensuous Venus) tries to convince Paris of her su-

periority. Venus, extremely self-assured, requests the golden apple, symbol of beauty, in no uncertain (and not in particularly appealing) terms:

> If the apple for which we are combating,
> Insensate as it is, could feel and sense,
> You would see it flying hastily to me,
> Nor would it be in your power to retain it.
> Since it cannot draw closer itself, I demand it:
> I am the one and only worthy of its
> possession.
> Whichever gift my gorgeousness receives,
> It is not but an owed tribute to love.
> (Marino, *Adone*, Canto 2, Stanza 105;
> trans. F. Santini)

Canto 3. Venus, wounded by Cupid's arrow, sees the sleeping Adonis, falls in love with him, and awakens him with a kiss. Adonis attempts to flee but, seeing Venus, is immediately enamored. In this canto appears one of the best-known passages of *Adonis*, perhaps the most representative of Marino's witty imagery and elaborate style. In it, Venus praises a rose with a long series of similes and metaphors that lasts for over 50 lines. Among other images, the red rose is called a "queen surrounded by an army of thorns," a "gem of spring," a "cup made of rubies," and a "sun on Earth," while the sun is "a rose in the sky" (*Adone*, Canto 3, Stanzas 155-61; trans. F. Santini).

Canto 4. Cupid narrates the story of his love for Psyche.

Canto 5. Adonis visits Cupid's palace, where the messenger god, Mercury, narrates to him six famous stories about the encounters of mortal youths and deities, some of which are related to hunting and its dangers.

Cantos 6-8. Adonis finally enters Venus's palace and visits its five gardens, each of which represents one of the five human senses (sight, smell, hearing, taste, and touch). In these three cantos, Adonis is prepared for a full sensual awakening, which culminates in the sexual union of the two lovers in Canto 8.

Canto 9. The lovers approach an area of Venus's garden where they meet a fisherman, Fileno, who narrates the history of his life (the fisherman is said to represent Marino himself). Next they see the Fountain of Apollo (god, among other things, of poetry), and listen to a competition among poetic swans. The art of many famous poets is admired in the process, as are the families who sponsored them, including the Medici.

Cantos 10-11. Adonis, Venus, and Mercury visit the heavens, where they admire the Grotto of Nature, the Island of Dreams, the Palace of Art, and—in the heaven of Venus—the Garden of Beauty. Here are the spirits of the most famous and beautiful ladies who ever existed (this is the occasion for a eulogy of Maria de' Medici). At the end of Canto 11, Mercury draws a horoscope for Adonis and prophesies his early death. The three then return to Cyprus.

Canto 12. Mars, the god associated with war, and Venus's primary lover, arrives on the island, so Venus urges Adonis to flee. During his flight, Adonis meets a sorceress, Falsirena (literally means "fake-mermaid"), who attempts both naturally and magically to win Adonis's love. When she fails (Adonis can resist, thanks to a magical ring and Mercury's advice), she imprisons the handsome mortal.

Canto 13. After languishing in prison all winter, Adonis, transformed into a parrot by a magic love potion, escapes and returns to Venus's garden, where he sadly witnesses the love of Venus and Mars. Mercury helps Adonis regain his human form, while Falsirena, enraged at having been spurned, plots to recapture him.

Canto 14. Adonis keeps fleeing Falsirena. He dresses up as a girl to avoid being recognized and falls into the hands of bandits. Saved by one of Falsirena's helpers, Adonis again escapes.

Canto 15. Adonis encounters Venus in disguise as a gypsy. She appears as an exotic, dark-haired beauty like those Marino must have often encountered in his native Naples. The couple returns to the palace, where they amuse themselves playing various games, including chess.

Canto 16. After winning a three-day male beauty contest (a long description of the candidates is included), Adonis is crowned king of Cyprus.

Canto 17. Venus must leave Cyprus to take part in the festival of Cythera: once again, she and her earthly lover are separated. During her trip, Venus hears another prophecy of Adonis's death.

Canto 18. Falsirena advises one of Venus's maids to reveal to Mars the presence of Adonis on the island. While Adonis is hunting, Mars (with the help of Diana, goddess of hunting) bewitches a female boar that, after falling in love with Adonis, tries to embrace him and kills him. Venus and Cupid grieve, Venus's maid commits suicide in guilt, and the boar pleads for a pardon, which is granted.

Canto 19. Four deities visit Venus and tell six tragic stories of love and death. After the funeral rites for her fallen lover, Venus immortalizes Adonis by transforming his heart into a flower, the anemone.

Canto 20. In honor of Adonis, Venus organizes sumptuous funeral games in which both mortals and gods participate. The pageant of participants is representative of the powers that reign respectively in the heavens and on Earth. A long tribute to the French king Louis XIII concludes the poem, counterbalancing the dedication to his mother, Maria, which opened it.

Art and diplomacy. Toward the end of Canto 9, Marino presents a satirical attack on one of his main enemies, the poet Tommaso Stigliani (1573-1651), whom he represents as an owl, a creature hardly comparable to the melodious "poetic swans" symbolizing famous poets of the past and present. After the publication of *Adonis*, Stigliani would reciprocate with harsh criticism, accusing it of obscenity in his own poem "Occhiale." (It remains unclear if Stigliani was involved in the placement of *Adonis* on the *Index* after Marino's death.)

This escalation of literary rivalries into personal attacks reflects an atmosphere in which intellectuals were generally more subject to attack in the Baroque era. Due to the strict policies of the Counter Reformation, they experienced increasing pressure to conform to prevailing ideas. The restrictive atmosphere of the age is perhaps best reflected in the way the Jesuits, with their very orthodox curriculum, dominated public instruction in the Catholic world. In such an environment, intellectuals looked more often to the courts of nobles for welfare and support. But those who attained court patronage paid a price in literary and personal freedom; beholden to the noble or sovereign, they had to refrain from offending the hand that fed them. Also they had to refrain from offending the Church, as Galileo's experience shows. In 1633 Galileo fell afoul of the growing climate of orthodoxy in the region when he supported Copernicus's revolutionary idea that the earth revolves around the sun. Though an eminent scholar who had enlisted the Medici for his patrons, he still was tried and condemned by the papal Inquisition. How cautious, then, less eminent scholars needed to be!

Upon entering a court, an artist became part of a delicately organized sphere, complete with rules of behavior, an endless round of formal functions, and magnificent entertainments: it was a dangerous world in which an individual's fortune could be made or destroyed in a moment and envy gave rise to assorted intrigues. The abysmally desperate condition of the newly poor contrasted strongly with the richness of life at court, but that very life, though admired, often hid humiliations and compromises, as suggested by the tribute Marino pays to his royal patrons in *Adonis*.

Praising sovereigns within a literary work could require a complex balance of diplomacy. In *Adonis*, Marino maximizes his praise for Maria de' Medici, to whom he owes his invitation to court, and for her son Louis XIII, who became king during the poet's years in Paris and whose disfavor could have caused Marino's ruin. (Marino's task was certainly made harder, and highly dangerous, by the many disagreements of the two sovereigns over political matters.)

Aside from the king and his mother, several other historical figures (e.g., Dante Alighieri) are mentioned or included as characters in the poem, along with many historical, political, and social events from Marino's time (for instance, recurring references to the wars between France and Spain). The juxtaposition of mythology and historical material from Marino's age, of course, gives rise to anachronisms. The reader, fascinated by the shimmery surface of the things described, tends to forget that a chessboard (Canto 15) or a telescopic looking glass (Canto 10) could hardly exist in a time in which they had not yet been invented.

At the same time, the mythological setting allows Marino to express his opinions in a safe manner. For instance, when in Canto 6 he enumerates the best painters of his time (e.g., Caravaggio) while not mentioning the ancient masters, his choice makes evident the poet's preference for modern art over classical.

MARINO ON SERVING AT THE COURT OF FRANCE

"I am a servant, there is no doubt of that, but I cannot be ashamed of my servitude, since I serve one of the greatest kings in the world, and I must add that there are many princes, who would consider it a glory to serve in such a manner. A pension of two thousand gold écus, not to count the gifts, and to be free from any courtly obligation, are very honorable conditions, and there are cardinals in Rome who don't have as much."

(Marino, *Lettere*, p. 93; trans. F. Santini)

Furthermore, the very setting of the poem, a peaceful, faraway island, rather than a battlefield—as it is with *Adonis*'s predecessors, Ariosto and Tasso's works—is Marino's way of diplomatically supporting the desire of his patron, Maria de' Medici, for a peace agreement between France and Spain. The fact that in the introduction to the poem, Chapelain referred to it as a "poem of peace," shows that Marino's choice to support Maria's political views had been correctly interpreted and understood at the time *Adonis* was published.

Sources and literary context. The love affair between Venus and Adonis is one of the stories narrated in Ovid's *Metamorphoses*, a 15-part collection of mythic and legendary tales in verse. Many authors of the late Renaissance, in keeping with the popularity of mythological subjects in Europe at the end of the sixteenth century, enlarged and embellished Ovid's brief account (which consists of little more than 100 lines).

In his version of the Adonis story, Marino not only enlarges the episode (to more than 40,000 lines), but also changes its original purpose. While for Ovid the core of the fable was represented by Adonis's metamorphosis into a flower after his death, Marino minimizes that part of the narration to focus, instead, on the sensual awakening of young Adonis.

HISTORICAL ELEMENTS INFUSED INTO *ADONIS*

Historical Events

Cantos 1, 9, 10, 19: Polemics against courtly life

Canto 10: The French wars under Henry IV; the rule of Maria de' Medici and Louis XIII

Cantos 10, 15: Antigovernment polemics

Canto 14: Antimilitary polemic

Canto 15: History of Cyprus

Canto 20: Religious wars between France and Spain

Historical People

Canto 2: Catalog of beautiful ladies (including a lengthy passage on Maria de' Medici)

Canto 6: Catalog of painters (e.g., Caravaggio, who in the words of Marino could create a "falsity that surpasses reality")

Canto 9: Marino as the fisherman Fileno; catalog of noble families who sponsored the arts; catalog of poets (e.g., Dante, Petrarch, Ariosto, Tasso)

Canto 10: Galileo Galilei

Canto 12: Catalog of war captains (among them are ancient heroes such as Alexander, Caesar, and Hannibal, and more modern ones like Alessandro Farnese and Francesco Bona)

Canto 20: Catalog of valiant gentlemen; Louis XIII

(Pozzi in Marino, *Adonis*, pp. 64-74)

In addition to Ovid's story, Marino drew on many other sources for the corpus of the poem, from classical ones (a range of Greek Alexandrine poets and of Latin authors, primarily Claudian), to medieval Italian writers (particularly Petrarch), to contemporary poets, especially Torquato Tasso, author of the famed **Jerusalem Delivered** (also in *WLAIT 7: Italian Literature and Its Times*). The garden of Venus in *Adonis* is strongly reminiscent of Armida's garden in *Jerusalem Delivered*.

Identifying the many sources from which Marino drew his material preoccupied readers when the poem first appeared. Some contempo-

raries even accused Marino of plagiarism (including, of course, his archenemy Stigliani). Marino answered his detractors with blatant self-assurance, claiming one's right to consider the literature of the past as an immense storehouse of words and imagery, available for the taking. In a letter to the poet Claudio Achillini, he stated:

> Since I started my literary studies, I learnt to read holding a hook, and pulling up to my benefit all that I found good, noting it in my archive to be used when the time would come, and indeed this is the fruit you collect from reading books.
>
> (Marino, *Lettere*, p. 150; trans. F. Santini)

Publication and reception. As early as 1605, Marino described the contents of *Adonis* in a letter to a painter, whom he asked to draw some images for his soon-to-be-published poem. He next mentioned *Adonis* in 1614, when he stated in another letter that he was ready to travel to France, where he would publish his works, especially *Adonis*. (Publishing in France would allow the author to avoid the strict Inquisition censorship to which books published in Italy were subject.) By then, Marino's Venetian printer, Ciotti, was expecting a final version of the poem (in 12 cantos), which the poet felt confident would be a success, since his friends were completely enchanted by it. He nevertheless delayed publication for eight years, during which he embellished and enlarged the poem till it reached its final size.

When, in 1623, *Adonis* was finally published, the curiosity regarding Marino's latest work was so great both in France and in Italy that its impact was enormous. The book sold extremely well in France, where it was received with great admiration at the court of Louis XIII. In Italy, the poem was read and admired even before being sold in shops, and it reportedly aroused general enthusiasm. Despite such a favorable reception, Marino encountered problems after his triumphant return to Italy in the summer of 1623: *Adonis* was at risk of being put on the *Index* (as it would be in 1627, two years after the poet's death). A number of detractors, who considered the work obscene and vain, dampened Marino's success. Thankfully, the poem's admirers largely outnumbered its detractors, even in Marino's day.

The ability of the Neapolitan poet as a crafter of verses and a creator of witty metaphors, together with the stylistic complexity and the vastness of the material covered in the poem, succeeded in achieving exactly that *maraviglia*, that marvel, which was then considered, in the words of Marino himself, the main aim of poetry. In the decades after Marino's death, the number of poets who imitated his elaborate style and imagery was so large, that even now Italian baroque poetry is referred to as "Marinismo" ("Marinism").

Adonis's huge success came to a halt at the beginning of the eighteenth century, when the baroque style was denigrated as tasteless and exaggerated. Only in the twentieth century was the work reevaluated and appreciated for what the poem is: a work at times overly developed and artificial, and at times truly enchanting.

—Federica Santini

For More Information

Cherchi, Paolo. *La metamorfosi dell'Adone*. Ravenna, Italy: Longo, 1996.

Guardiani, Francesco, ed. *The Sense of Marino: Literature, Fine Arts and Music of the Italian Baroque*. New York: Legas, 1994.

Marino, Giambattista. *Adone*. Ed. G. Pozzi. Milan: Adelphi, 1988.

———. *Adonis*. Trans. H. Martin Priest. Ithaca, New York: Cornell University Press, 1967.

———. *Lettere*. In *Opere scelte di Giambattista Marino e dei Marinisti*. Ed. G. Getto. Torino: Unione Tipografico-Editrice Torinese, 1962.

Mirollo, James Vincent. *The Poet of the Marvelous: Giambattista Marino*. New York: Columbia University Press, 1963.

Ovid. *Metamorphoses*. Ed. M. Forey. Trans. A. Golding. Baltimore, Md.: Johns Hopkins University Press, 2002.

Sarduy, Severo. *Ensayos generales sobre el Barroco*. México: Fondo de Cultura Económica, 1987.

Scaglione, Aldo, and G. E. Viola, eds. *The Image of the Baroque*. New York: P. Lang, 1995.

Shakespeare, William. *Venus and Adonis*. In *The Poems: Venus and Adonis, The Rape of Lucrece, The Phoenix and the Turtle, The Passionate Pilgrim, A Lover's Complaint*. Ed. J. Roe. Cambridge, England: Cambridge University Press, 1992.

The Adventures of Pinocchio

by
Carlo Collodi

Carlo Collodi was born Carlo Lorenzini in Florence, Italy, in 1826. Both of his parents were servants, his father a cook for the Ginori—an aristocratic Florentine family—and his mother a seamstress. Young Carlo received his elementary schooling in his mother's country village; he showed such intellectual promise, however, that the nobleman of the house, Marchese Ginori, sent him to a Tuscan seminary in Colle Val d'Elsa for five years. Having no vocation for the church, Collodi completed his education with some priests in Tuscany, then found employment as a journalist and a civil servant. He meanwhile became involved in Italy's national unification movement and fought with the Tuscan army in the 1848 war of independence from Austria. With his brother and two friends, Carlo founded and contributed to a short-lived satirical newspaper, *Il lampione* (The Lamppost), then became editor for a new theatrical journal (*La scaramuccia*). At age 30 he adopted the pseudonym Carlo Collodi, joining his given name to that of his mother's native village. Collodi's vast literary output included newspaper articles, plays, novels, memoirs, and—most famously—children's books. His first children's book, *Giannettino* (1877; Little Johnny) was a reworking of an earlier educational bestseller called *Giannetto* (by Luigi Alessandro Parravicini) about a boy's journey around Italy. Adding innovative touches, Collodi introduced a more natural writing style and realistic characterization of Giannettino, making him a naughty, lively boy rather than a prim paragon. In 1881

THE LITERARY WORK

A novel set during an unspecified time in a small Italian village and various fantastic realms; published serially in Italian, first as *La storia di un burattino* in 1881, then as *Le avventure di Pinocchio* in 1882-1883; in English, in 1892.

SYNOPSIS

A willful, disobedient puppet comes to life, runs away from home, and has a series of adventures, but ultimately decides to mend his ways in hopes of becoming a human boy.

Collodi began the tale of Pinocchio for which he is best known today. Published serially from 1881 to 1883, the saga of a disobedient puppet that longs to become a real boy enchanted readers and succeeded on a didactic level too. From the late-nineteenth-century vantage point, the story offers stern but sound guidance on children's moral and intellectual education as well as a more subtle message to an Italy still in its infancy.

Events in History at the Time of the Novel

The Unification of Italy. Throughout much of Collodi's life, Italy struggled to achieve national unity and independence. French forces commanded by Napoleon Bonaparte had invaded

Carlo Collodi

Italy back in 1796, bringing the peninsula under French control until 1814. Before and after the French interlude, parts of Italy were dominated by Spain or Austria, powers that held the reins until the Unification of 1860.

Although the first war of independence (1848-49) had ended in failure and Italy remained under Austria's control, Italians continued to hope for unification, looking to Sardinia (later known as Piedmont-Sardinia) for guidance. Its king, Victor Emmanuel II (Vittorio Emanuele II), appointed Count Camillo di Cavour to the post of premier in 1852. Shrewd and capable, Cavour implemented policies that led to fiscal and military reforms, an alliance with France against Austria, and the acquisition of several important territories by Piedmont-Sardinia. In 1859 it engaged in a second war of independence against Austria, emerging victorious after a bloody battle at Magenta in northern Italy. The negotiated Peace of Villafranca proved less advantageous than Cavour had hoped; nonetheless, Sardinia acquired Lombardy, and the war itself inspired successful revolts in Tuscany, Massa Carrara, Parma, Modena, and Romagna, all of which wanted to unite with Piedmont-Sardinia.

Equally dramatic developments were taking place in southern Italy. In 1860 the charismatic Giuseppe Garibaldi amassed over 1,000 red-shirted volunteers and launched a successful military campaign against the Bourbons ruling the Kingdom of the Two Sicilies. The island of Sicily was liberated in May, after Garibaldi won a decisive victory at Calatafimi. Joined by still more volunteers, he crossed the Straits of Messina and proceeded to Naples, where he deposed the Bourbon monarchy and established a kingdom in the name of Victor Emmanuel II. Meanwhile, Victor Emmanuel had affiliated himself with the Piedmontese army, which met up with Garibaldi's forces just south of Rome. Tension as well as friendly banter ensued until Garibaldi dramatically turned over Naples and Sicily to the king.

Although Rome and Venice were yet to be acquired, a national parliament proclaimed the kingdom of Italy on March 17, 1861; Victor Emmanuel II was recognized as king, and a new constitution (the Albertine statute) was introduced. The new-formed kingdom faced a barrage of problems, especially after the sudden death of its premier, Cavour, in June 1861. Tensions existed between the prosperous industrialized North and the poorer, agricultural South, with differences in laws and traditions exacerbating those tensions. Many wondered how such chasms could ever be bridged. The formation of a national character became as tantamount an issue as the establishment of a nation. A statement made by Piedmontese novelist Massimo d'Azeglio at Unification took on heightened significance: "We have made Italy; now we must make Italians" (d'Azeglio in Killinger, p. 119). Collodi, who had volunteered for military service in both wars of independence, soon found himself involved in this struggle as well. In 1860 he had written a pamphlet in support of unification; his work for the cause continued through the somewhat unlikely means of children's literature. At once instructive and imaginative, stories like *Pinocchio* were to exert a powerful influence upon Italians.

Education in nineteenth-century Italy. As the country struggled with severe economic and social problems, liberals and moderates looked increasingly to schools as a remedy. The process of educating Italians posed difficulties, however. At mid-century, at least two-thirds of the populace still could not read or write; in parts of the rural South, the illiteracy rate approached 100 percent (Duggan, p. 154).

The Casati Law of 1859, which was extended to all of Italy in 1861, attempted to address the problem by requiring local authorities to provide elementary schools and teachers. In the two decades after Unification, the number of primary schools doubled. However, an estimated 40 to 50 percent of children never attended, partly because of the lack of financial, human, and material resources, especially in the South. Many of these schools consisted of little more than a single room, often too small for all the students who did come. Teachers themselves were poorly paid and there were few qualified applicants for teaching positions in rural areas. More often than not, local authorities turned to parish priests to serve as teachers.

To complicate the situation further, some middle-class Italians expressed reservations about popular schooling. Conservatives feared that education would transform peasants into revolutionaries. In any case, members of nearly all factions felt that when it was provided, education should encourage Italians to become good, loyal, productive citizens. This last aim took precedence over all others. A statement made by the education minister in 1886 argued that Italians should be "as far as is possible instructed, but above all, they should be honest and hard-working, an asset to their families, and devoted to their king and their country" (Duggan, p. 154). In accordance with that goal, popular education emphasized national loyalty and the work ethic. Indeed, these two values were increasingly touted in reading material for children, both instructional and recreational. Children's writers did not hesitate to portray dire consequences for lazy, disobedient youngsters. Some years later, the Italian physician Maria Montessori (1870-1952) would argue that children learned best in a loving, nurturing environment. During Collodi's lifetime, however, fear and punishment were frequent themes in didactic children's literature.

Collodi himself was a firm believer in education, at one point declaring, "Open a school, and you will close a prison" (Collodi in Person, p. 141). His novel about Pinocchio continually portrays the virtues of education and the evils of sloth. When the puppet works at his studies, he approaches his goal of becoming a real boy. When he neglects his books in favor of idle entertainments, he suffers such misfortunes as being abducted, jailed, or transformed into a donkey.

The development of children's literature in Italy. Up to the mid-eighteenth century, reading material for European children was mainly instructional in approach and often heavily didactic in tone. Primers, alphabet books, manuals on etiquette, and religious catechisms comprised the majority of books for the young. In society at large, children themselves were most often viewed as miniature but imperfect adults and passive receptacles of facts, figures, and other forms of empirical knowledge. Rejecting this view, some pivotal thinkers began to change the way people conceived of children, thanks in part to the Enlightenment, the eighteenth-century philosophical movement that emphasized rationalism. The shift had something to do with social change: the influence of the aristocracy began to diminish, while the middle class increased in size and dominance. The family unit meanwhile gained importance and so did a child's place in it. Children came to represent the future not merely of their families but of their nations.

The philosophical writings of the Englishman John Locke (1632-1704) and the Frenchman Jean-Jacques Rousseau (1712-1778) posited that children were rational beings in their own right. Locke added that children should not "be hindered from being children, nor from playing and doing as children" (Locke in Demers and Moyles, p. 77). While his conception of the child was not universally embraced, his tenets contributed to changing attitudes about education. Rousseau was similarly influential. In *Émile*, Rousseau's 1762 treatise on education, he argued that children are born naturally good but are corrupted by artificial, antagonistic institutions of society; in order for children to grow into virtuous adults, Rousseau recommended they be raised at home, preferably in the country. Parents should be closely involved in their rearing, the father serving as tutor, the mother as nurse. Nature, however, would be a child's first teacher, honing the child's perceptions and instincts, until about age 12, when the child could reason, at which point formal education was in order. Gradually, in keeping with this new philosophy, children's books became less dogmatic and austere; writers did not cease to moralize, but their tactics became less heavy-handed as the eighteenth century progressed.

Children's literature in Italy continued to be heavily didactic. Its inception in the land can be dated to a contest in 1775, sponsored by Count Bettoni, for the best 25 instructive stories for children. There followed decades of moralistic tales highlighting qualities to emulate (generosity, courage, etc.), at first without children as heroes and in stilted language. The Roman Catholic Church heavily influenced children's literature prior to Unification (1861). Indeed, several of the most prominent writers for children in the late-eighteenth century and nineteenth century were affiliated with the Church, including Father Francesco Soave (1743-1806) and the priest Giovanni Bosco (1815-1888). Their works were heavily didactic, with an emphasis on shaping the morality of the child reader. Exceptions to the grim reality of these texts did exist. Luigi Fiacchi (1754-1825), also a priest, wrote verse fables for children. And Giuseppe Taverna (1764-1850) foreswore the usual format of presenting dignified adults by using children as protagonists. Pietro Thouar (1809-1861), referred to as the founder of Italian children's literature, wrote his *Racconti per i fanciulli* (1853; Stories for Children) with a calm sensitivity to the lives of children.

THE FAIRY TALE

The oral tradition in previous centuries relied upon fairy and folk tales—for the amusement of adults. Giambattista Basile (1575-1632) produced a significant collection of these tales in his *Lo Cunto de li Cunti* (The Tale of Tales), published posthumously in 1634. Written in the dialect of Naples, the collection came to be known as *Il Pentamerone* (The Five Days) because it consists of 50 tales told over five nights. Among them are versions of many tales widely known today, including "Cinderella," "Snow White," "Puss-in-Boots," and "Hansel and Gretel." Basile's tales were translated into Italian in 1747, German in 1846, and English in 1848. The collection was followed 60 years later by Charles Perrault's famous French collection *Histoires ou Contes du temps passé: avec des moralitez* (1697). Translated into English in 1729 as *Histories, or Tales of Past Times: Told by Mother Goose*, the book contained some of the most famous tales in the Western tradition: "Little Red Ridinghood," "Bluebeard," "Puss-in-Boots," "Sleeping Beauty," and "Cinderella." These tales, with their sly morals, were certainly meant for adults. Only later were they seen as proper fare for children, in a revival that marked another important milestone in children's literature. The resurgence saw the first editions of the landmark German collections by Jakob and Wilhelm Grimm, *Kinder- und Hausmärchen* (1812; Children's and Household Tales), and the Danish collection *Eventyr, fortalte for børn* (1835; Tales, Told for Children) by Hans Christian Andersen. Once distrusted by the moralists, fantasy became another way to instruct children. Collodi himself, at his publisher's request, translated the fairy tales of Perrault and other French writers into Italian in 1876.

Morality was still the keynote, though. Luigi Alessandro Parravicini's *Giannetto* deserves special mention, because Collodi modified the title for one of his own tales. Published in 1857, but often revised and reprinted during the nineteenth century, *Giannetto* is a compendium of information about human beings and the world as seen through the eyes of young Giannetto, in, as Hawkes ironically writes, "his constant and never-thwarted growth in virtue" (Hawkes, p. 40).

In the post-Unification period, patriotism took its place alongside religion in influencing the content of books for children. Many intellectuals came to believe that educating Italians about their homeland was one way to foster a sense of cultural unity. To this end, several editors requisitioned instructional texts for the young, who represented the new country's future. Education itself, including the dissemination of shared values, was seen as a prerequisite for democracy. Collodi, having translated French fairy tales into Italian in 1876, was approached to participate. From 1877 onward, he created a series of successful, primarily instructional children's books—several were intended for use in schools—infusing humor and fun into them to hold the attention of his young readers. His approach was innovative and progressively bold. Collodi's *Giannettino* (1876; Little Johnny), a remaking of Parravicini's popular text, though refreshingly lighthearted for its day, was still "a few delightful scenes, isolated in the midst of much science" (Hawkes, p. 64). It remained for *The Adventures of Pinocchio* to break the mold, balancing lessons on overcoming sloth and selfishness—behaviors that resulted in fearsome punishments—with interludes of comedy and adventure in a way that turned the novel into Italian children's literature's first enduring work.

The Novel in Focus

Plot summary. The novel begins when Master Cherry (Mastro Ciliegia), a carpenter, tries to carve a piece of firewood into a table leg, but stops when he hears a little voice complaining that the carpenter is hurting him. Unnerved, Master Cherry gives the piece of wood to his friend Geppetto, who plans to make a puppet of it.

The resulting creation, which Geppetto names *Pinocchio*, springs to life and immediately proves to be naughty and recalcitrant. The puppet runs away and Geppetto, who gives chase, ends up in jail for his pains. Meanwhile, Pinocchio returns to Geppetto's house; the Talking Cricket on the hearth reproves him for rebelling against his "father" and warns him against the evils of becoming an idle, good-for-nothing child. Enraged, Pinocchio flings a hammer at the Cricket and kills it. A series of domestic mishaps ensue as Pinocchio tries to attend to his basic needs: there is no bread in the cottage; an attempt to cook an egg fails when a chick hatches from it and flies off; and an old man dumps water over the puppet as Pinocchio attempts to beg for food from door to door. He returns home exhausted and drenched, falls asleep with his feet on a brazier of hot coals and wakes to find that both feet have burned off. When Geppetto returns from jail, he finds Pinocchio wailing over his lost feet and his hunger pangs. Geppetto relieves the puppet's hunger with two pears he got from jail, and Pinocchio expresses remorse for his misdeeds, promising to behave in the future. Geppetto also carves Pinocchio a new pair of feet and later, to buy him a schoolbook, Geppetto sells his only jacket. Setting off for school, Pinocchio is almost immediately tempted to forego his duty by attending a puppet show. He sells his book for the price of admission; the other puppets recognize Pinocchio as one of them and he is snatched up by the puppet-master, Fire-eater, who threatens to use him as firewood for disturbing the show. Pinocchio's pleas persuade him to relent, and Fire-eater sets the puppet free, giving him a parting gift of five gold florins to support himself and his father.

Intending to return home with the money, Pinocchio is instead lured into a new series of adventures: he meets a pair of swindlers, the Fox and the Cat, who try to kill him for his gold. A beautiful Fairy with blue hair nurses him back to health in her cottage after his attackers leave him hanging by his neck in a tree. Like Geppetto and the Talking Cricket, the Fairy tries to impart moral guidance to the errant puppet:

'Good boys like to learn and to work, and you—'
  'And I instead lead an idle vagabond life the whole year through.'
  'Good boys always speak the truth—'
  'And I always tell lies.'
          (Collodi, *Pinocchio*, p. 98)

During his convalescence, Pinocchio makes a startling discovery—his nose grows whenever he tells an outrageous lie:

At this third lie his nose grew to such an extraordinary length that poor Pinocchio could not move in any direction. If he turned to one side he struck his nose against the bed or the window-panes, if he turned to the other he struck it against the walls or the door, if he raised his head a little he ran the risk of sticking it into one of the Fairy's eyes.
          (*Pinocchio*, pp. 64-65)

Geppetto and Pinocchio. Illustration by Attilio Mussino from a 1928 edition of *The Adventures of Pinocchio*.

Just as Pinocchio is about to be happily reunited with Geppetto, he again encounters the Fox and the Cat, whom he fails to recognize as his would-be murderers. This time, the swindlers dupe him out of his money. Pinocchio's attempt to seek legal redress in the topsy-turvy Booby Town results in his being imprisoned for four months. No sooner is he released than he lands into trouble once again: he is caught in a trap intended for thieves and forced to serve as a watchdog—complete with chains and warning bark—for a peasant whose chickens are being stolen by a gang of polecats. Fortunately Pinocchio traps the polecats en route to rob the henhouse, and the grateful peasant sets him free as a reward.

On returning at last to the Fairy's cottage, Pinocchio is devastated to see a headstone announcing her death from grief at his desertion. When a Pigeon arrives to tell Pinocchio that Geppetto has gone to sea in search of him, the puppet flies to the seashore on the Pigeon's back. He arrives just in time to see Geppetto and his boat disappear beneath the sea. Flinging himself into the water, Pinocchio swims out to save his father, making his way to a distant island. A passing Dolphin tells Pinocchio that his father was almost certainly swallowed by a giant Shark.

Sadly Pinocchio journeys further inland until he reaches a village of "Busy Bees," where none of the inhabitants are idle. Although the lazy Pinocchio has no desire to work for food, he finally volunteers to carry water for a woman. On reaching her house, he discovers her to be the beautiful Fairy in disguise—she has not died after all. The two are reconciled, and Pinocchio once more vows to mend his ways, this time in hopes of becoming a real boy someday. Only if he proves hard-working, honest, and obedient can this dream become a reality, warns the Fairy, who also fills Pinocchio with hope that he might somehow be reunited with Geppetto.

Thereafter, Pinocchio devotes himself to his books and becomes a good pupil, although mischievous classmates lure him from his studies with talk about a giant Shark. After this latest scrape, the Fairy, with whom Pinocchio is now living, warns him against further misbehavior. Rededicating himself to his studies and demonstrating obedience and truthfulness, the puppet is within a day of realizing his dream of becoming a real boy when his schoolmate Candlewick persuades him to run away to the school-less Toyland where everyone plays all day.

After five months in the Toyland, Candlewick and Pinocchio discover that they are turning into donkeys, like all idle children who have made asses of themselves. The wagon-driver who drove them to Toyland captures and sells them at the marketplace. Purchased by the manager of a traveling circus, Donkey Pinocchio works until he is badly lamed and his owner resells him. Pinocchio's new owner decides to drown him and make a drum out of the donkey-skin. Thankfully, the Fairy foils the new owner's plans: once Pinocchio is in the water, she sends a school of fish to eat away at the donkey-skin until he is a wooden puppet again. Escaping his owner, Pinocchio swims out to sea, where he encounters the giant Shark; it promptly swallows him.

In the Shark's belly, Pinocchio discovers Geppetto, miraculously still alive after all this time. They joyously reunite and plan to escape by walking out of the Shark's open mouth while it is sleeping. After two attempts, they make it to shore, with the help of a Tunny (Tuna) Fish that escaped the Shark's belly too. As Pinocchio and Geppetto head homeward, they encounter the Fox and the Cat, now reduced to begging in the streets. Pinocchio rejects their pleas for alms, telling them they got exactly what they deserved. He and Geppetto journey on until they reach a hut, where they ask for and are granted shelter. The hut's owner turns out to be the miraculously resurrected Talking Cricket, who tells Pinocchio

that the Fairy witnessed his being swallowed by the Shark and now believes him dead.

Geppetto and Pinocchio settle down in the hut, and Pinocchio takes on jobs to support his ailing father. He is no longer in school at this point; he works and continues to practice his reading and writing independently. During one job, he encounters Candlewick again, still a donkey and dying from overwork. After five months of hard labor, Pinocchio has earned enough to keep his father in comfort and buy himself some new clothes. On his way to market one day, he encounters a Snail who used to work for the Fairy. Learning that she has grown ill and impoverished, Pinocchio quickly gives the Snail his 40 pence to help the Fairy.

That evening Pinocchio dreams that the Fairy visits him, praises his kind heart, and forgives him for all his misdeeds. On awakening, he discovers that the hut has been transformed into a beautiful house, his 40 copper pennies—now returned to him—have changed into gold pieces, and, most miraculously, he himself has become a real boy. Geppetto, restored to health and again practicing his trade as a wood carver, tells Pinocchio that all these happy changes are the result of his good deeds. Beholding his old wooden form propped up against a chair, Pinocchio exclaims, "How ridiculous I was when I was a puppet! And how glad I am that I have become a nice little boy" (*Pinocchio*, p. 167).

Moral education of a puppet. The most striking element of Collodi's novel is Pinocchio's character. Not surprisingly, readers familiar with softer, more sentimentalized versions of the puppet-protagonist from later adaptations are often taken aback by his original persona and by the violence surrounding him. The puppet's naughtiness at the start serves two purposes—to humanize him and to emphasize the moral transformation he must undergo before he can transform physically into a real boy. Tied to its times, the story can be seen as both personally and nationally instructive.

Most obvious is the personal message to young Italians. From the outset, the virtues to which Pinocchio should aspire are made manifest, especially industriousness. When the puppet declares his intention "to eat, drink, and sleep, and to have a good time from morning till night" rather than seeking an education and a trade, the Talking Cricket, Pinocchio's first moral preceptor, issues an ominous warning that those who behave in such a fashion end up "nearly always either in hospital or in prison" (*Pinocchio*,

p. 13). The Cricket is literally flattened for his pains when Pinocchio flings a hammer at him, but his counsel proves sage. Pinocchio ignores it, only to suffer dire consequences that place him in repeated peril—imprisonment, abduction, and attempted murder.

The blue-haired Fairy offers similar moral counsel, exhorting the puppet to work hard at his studies, obey his parental figures, tell the truth, and think of others, not just himself. Echoing the Talking Cricket, she warns her recalcitrant charge that people who complain of hard work "end almost always either in prison or in the hospital. Let me tell you that every man, whether he is born rich or poor, is obliged to do something in this world—to occupy his time, to work. Woe to those who lead slothful lives" (*Pinocchio*, p. 99). Also, the Fairy holds out a possible reward to Pinocchio should he improve himself through work and education: the chance of becoming a real boy, the implication being that with diligence and obedience comes the potential for material rewards. A final set of adventures, culminating in Pinocchio's rescue of Geppetto, allows the puppet to redeem himself and show that he has taken life's lessons to heart. To support Geppetto, Pinocchio takes on work, pumping water for a peasant and crafting wicker baskets to sell. Beyond hard work, he learns the virtue of self-sacrifice: on hearing that the Fairy is ill and destitute, Pinocchio sends her the money he is saving for new clothes for himself, his generosity winning him not just her forgiveness but the humanity he covets. The Fairy, recognizing that he still is no moral paragon, chooses to reward his kind heart and honest attempts to improve himself because "boys who minister tenderly to their parents, and assist them in their misery and infirmities, are deserving of great praise and affection, even if they cannot be cited as examples of obedience and good behaviour" (*Pinocchio*, p. 166).

The message here can be extended from Italian children to a nation still in its infancy. The emphasis the story places on Pinocchio's need to develop a work ethic reflects a prevailing attitude that Collodi and fellow Italians shared—namely, that citizens should be not only honest and virtuous, but productive too. To some degree, this belief may have stemmed from a desire to see Italy—economically outstripped by other European countries—become a productive, prosperous modern nation. Italy had suffered a severe agriculture depression in the 1860s and 1870s—a grim development since 60

per cent of the people depended directly on agriculture for survival. Italian manufacturing was still struggling to establish itself; a modern factory labor force did not yet exist and the nation lagged behind others in basic industries—"At the time of unification Italy had 500,000 cotton spindles: Britain had 30 million, France 5.5 million" (Duggan, p. 151).

COLLODI'S ORIGINAL ENDING

In July of 1881, Ferdinando Martini began the weekly *Il Giornale dei Bambini* (The Children's Paper) and commissioned Collodi to write for the paper. Collodi's *Storia di un burattino* (Story of a Puppet) began in installments that year and continued weekly until November 10, 1881, at which point (the conclusion of Chapter 15) Collodi meant to end the series with Pinocchio hanging from an oak tree, "stiff and unconscious" (*Pinocchio*, p. 56). But the protest from readers was so loud that Collodi resumed his tales a few months later, under the new title *Le avventure di Pinocchio* (The Adventures of Pinocchio), and the series continued until January 1883. That February, it was published in book form. The book's serial history is evident both in its episodic nature (Pinocchio moves from one adventure to another) and the suspenseful moments that concur with the ends of chapters. As Jack Zipes argues, the original structure of *Pinocchio* refutes the optimistic tale of development that came later, since Collodi did not initially intend to transform Pinocchio into a boy. Instead, the series first had a grim end: Pinocchio, the peasant puppet gone wrong, punished for his naughtiness, seemingly with death (Zipes, "Introduction," pp. vix-vx).

In his educational text *Giannettino* (1876), Collodi mentioned the importance of increasing national production "so that Italians should not be forced to ask France, England, and Germany for so many, many goods, to pay for which, millions of lire are escaping beyond the Alps" (Collodi in Duggan, p. 155). Significantly, Pinocchio's transformation from stubborn, wooden-headed puppet to proper human boy occurs after he becomes a productive member of society. The outcome sends a message not only to Italian children but to the newborn nationality as well: Italians, having just emerged from a history replete with outside domination, ought to rely on themselves, on their own strength and that of their families rather than on outsiders or even religion, which is not mentioned in Collodi's story and can be seen as conspicuous by virtue of its absence.

Sources and literary context. According to critic Jack Zipes, *Pinocchio* forms part of the tradition of "Jack tales," oral stories common in Europe about peasant boys saved from scrapes by their own ineptitude (Zipes, "Introduction," p. xiii). Collodi also included numerous elements from folklore, such as fairies, talking animals, and magical transformations, a reflection of his experience writing and translating in this

---

THE *COMMEDIA DELL'ARTE*

A form of comic drama, the *commedia dell'arte* originated in Italy about the middle of the sixteenth century. Guilds of professional actors, portraying stock characters, performed standard scenarios in which the dialogue was largely improvised. Often the plots revolved around the intrigues of young lovers and wily servants seeking to outwit rich, tyrannical fathers. Clowns and buffoons injected broad humor into the proceedings, and the happy endings were usually a foregone conclusion. The *commedia dell'arte* spread throughout Renaissance Europe, and puppet theater ultimately inherited the tradition, with marionettes taking on the stock roles once played by living actors. Among those stock characters were Harlequin (a masked figure in variegated tights who often played the trickster), Columbine (Harlequin's equally mischievous sweetheart), Pantalone (a skinny, gullible old man), and Punchinello (a fat, humpbacked clown who became the star of England's Punch and Judy show). Critics often link Pinocchio to Harlequin.

---

genre. What most readers remember about Pinocchio are two transformations. The first is the puppet's nose, which grows longer when he tells a lie. Unusual noses are a feature of some folk and fairy tales, though Collodi created his own particularly memorable variety. The second is Pinocchio's change into a donkey, the result of his laziness. The donkey as a symbol of ignorance has a lengthy literary history, stretching back to Aesop's *Fables* (sixth century B.C.E.), Apuleius's *The Golden Ass* (second century C.E.), and Shakespeare's *A Midsummer Night's Dream* (1600).

Collodi's career as a political and satirical journalist and as a dramatist influenced the novel too. It lampoons several professions, most notably medicine and the law. Between 1853 and 1873 Collodi wrote six plays in an attempt to improve the quality of contemporary Italian theater. Although he achieved only limited success, he remained passionately interested in the theater, in the end plumbing his experience in it to invent his wooden-puppet protagonist Pinocchio. Featured in miracle plays, spectacles, and farces, puppets and marionettes had long been staples of the theater. During the Middle Ages, Italy often used them to enact biblical and epic stories, a tradition of which Collodi was probably aware.

Pinocchio's journeys, his multiple near-deaths, his sojourn in the belly of a great fish, and his ultimate rebirth into a new life recall the classical hero Odysseus and the biblical hero Jonah. In addition, Collodi drew on various elements of the Italian theatrical form known as *commedia dell'arte*, including stock situations and characters (Pinocchio's misadventures and creatures such as the wily Fox), slapstick comedy (Pinocchio's nose growing when he tells a lie), and masks and disguises (sometimes worn by the swindling duo of the Fox and the Cat).

Whimsical, exuberant, at times surprisingly violent, *The Adventures of Pinocchio* is most often categorized as a fantasy, though it set out to provide moral instruction. Critics sometimes compare Collodi's works to those of Edmondo De Amicis (*Cuore* [1886]), arguing that both authors were moved by the aspirations of a newly unified Italy. Unlike De Amicis' works, however, *The Adventures of Pinocchio* transcended national boundaries, achieving global recognition as a classic of children's literature.

At least one children's literature historian attributes Collodi's success to the heroes he created. His young characters "go about satisfying their own curiosity and desires by themselves, without the reproving parental eye upon them, as had never been the case previously" in Italian literature for young people (Hawkes, p. 71). Only when Pinocchio finds himself in a seemingly insolvable predicament does the plot develop to help him interpret the situation so he learns not to repeat it.

Reception and impact. *The Adventures of Pinocchio* was immediately successful, selling more than one million copies in Italy. Although Collodi did not live to see it, the work went on to achieve international popularity, beginning with its English translation in 1892. *The Bookman,* a

London periodical of the day, praised the novel, particularly its unusual protagonist, noting that Pinocchio "has a very distinct personality, and most winning manners even in his depraved moments. But his greatest charm is a certain inexhaustible vitality" (Person, pp. 134-35).

Pinocchio gave rise to other distinguished works in Italian children's literature. Credited with redirecting attention to the novel in Italy, the philosopher Benedetto Croce (1866-1952) wrote that Pinocchio is a tale for both adults and children because "the wood from which Pinocchio is hewn is humanity itself" (Croce in Frongia, p. 7). Of all Collodi's successors, perhaps the most notable is Luigi Bertelli (1860-1920), known also as Vamba. Like Collodi, Vamba was first and foremost a humorist. His All Italian Children Are Called Balilla (1915)—about a boy who becomes an ant—features Italian youth during Unification; his The Diary of Hurricane Johnny (1920) features a naughty child who most certainly does not want to attend school. Italo Calvino's (1923-85) first novel, Il sentiero dei nidi di ragno (1947; **The Path to the Spiders' Nest**, also in WLAIT 7: Italian Literature and Its Times) features a protagonist named Pin (an abbreviated form of Pinocchio) and a structure that is also picaresque. More generally, it is said that many contemporary Italian writers, whose works have not been translated into English, owe a debt to the darker side of Pinocchio.

The Adventures of Pinocchio has inspired numerous spin-off tales about Pinocchio and his relatives, translations, imitations, web pages, and motion pictures. Along with the Bible and Quran, Pinocchio remains one of the world's most reprinted texts. Nearly a century after Collodi's work appeared in print, critic Martha Bacon summed up its enduring appeal:

> Collodi set out, at the urging of his publishers, to write a book for Italian children which should celebrate diligence, deplore idleness, and convey the idea that man is rationally happy only through work. He sought to caution the Italian child that pleasure-seeking leads to misery and a donkey's grave. He succeeded in writing a wry, elegant, comic, and wistful book, as universal as *Pilgrim's Progress*, which it resembles in structure, as Tuscan [the language and region of such great Italian writers as Dante, Machiavelli, and Petrarch] as a terraced vineyard and antic as the commedia dell'arte, which informs it.
>
> (Bacon in Person, p. 139)

—Pamela S. Loy

For More Information

Collodi, Carlo. Pinocchio. Trans. M. A. Murray. New York: Penguin, 2002.

Demers, Patricia, and Gordon Moyles. From Instruction to Delight. Toronto: Oxford University Press, 1982.

Duggan, Christopher. A Concise History of Italy. Cambridge: Cambridge University Press, 1994.

Frongia, Terri. "Pedagogy, Aesthetics, and Humanism: The Three Muses of Italian Children's Literature Theory." The Lion and the Unicorn 19, no. 1 (1995): 50-70.

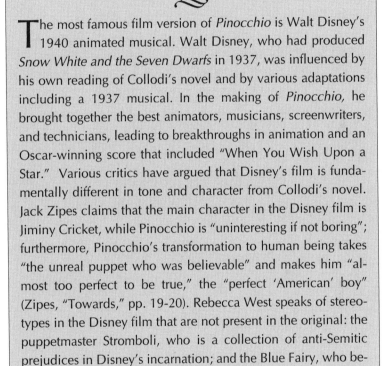

WALT DISNEY'S *PINOCCHIO*

The most famous film version of *Pinocchio* is Walt Disney's 1940 animated musical. Walt Disney, who had produced *Snow White and the Seven Dwarfs* in 1937, was influenced by his own reading of Collodi's novel and by various adaptations including a 1937 musical. In the making of *Pinocchio*, he brought together the best animators, musicians, screenwriters, and technicians, leading to breakthroughs in animation and an Oscar-winning score that included "When You Wish Upon a Star." Various critics have argued that Disney's film is fundamentally different in tone and character from Collodi's novel. Jack Zipes claims that the main character in the Disney film is Jiminy Cricket, while Pinocchio is "uninteresting if not boring"; furthermore, Pinocchio's transformation to human being takes "the unreal puppet who was believable" and makes him "almost too perfect to be true," the "perfect 'American' boy" (Zipes, "Towards," pp. 19-20). Rebecca West speaks of stereotypes in the Disney film that are not present in the original: the puppetmaster Stromboli, who is a collection of anti-Semitic prejudices in Disney's incarnation; and the Blue Fairy, who becomes "primarily decorative" (West, "Persistent Puppet").

Hawkes, Louise Restieaux. Before and After Pinocchio: A Study of Italian Children's Books. Paris: The Puppet Press, 1933.

Killinger, Charles L. The History of Italy. Westport, Conn.: Greenwood Press, 2002.

Person, James E., Jr., ed. Nineteenth-Century Literature Criticism. Vol. 54. Detroit: Gale Group, 1996.

Sahakian, Mabel Lewis, and William S. Sahakian. Rousseau as Educator. New York: Twayne, 1974.

Senick, Gerard J., ed. Children's Literature Review. Vol. 5. Detroit: Gale Research, 1983.

West, Rebecca. "The Persistent Puppet: Pinocchio's Heirs in Contemporary Fiction and Film." http://

www.fathom.com/course/72810000/session8 .html.

———. "The Real Life Adventures of Pinocchio." *University of Chicago Magazine* 95, no. 2 (December 2002). http://magazine.uchicago.edu/ 0212/features.puppet.html.

Wunderlich, Richard, and Thomas J. Morrissey. *Pinocchio Goes Postmodern*. New York: Routledge, 2002.

Zipes, Jack. Introduction to *Pinocchio: The Tale of a Puppet*, by Carlo Collodi. Trans. M. A. Murray. New York: Penguin, 1996.

———. "Towards a Theory of the Fairy-Tale Film: The Case of *Pinocchio*." *The Lion and the Unicorn* 20, no. 1 (1996): 1-24. http://muse.jhu.edu/ journal/lion and the unicorn/v020/20.1zipes .html.

Arcadia

by
Jacopo Sannazaro

Jacopo Sannazaro was born to a prominent family of Naples, Italy, in 1458. Two distinguished classical scholars, Lucio Crasso and Guiniano Maio, educated him. Young Sannazaro showed great promise as a student, pursuing his education despite the death of his father in 1462. In 1470 Sannazaro's mother moved the family to the Picentine Mountains, north of Salerno, where they could live more economically. By 1478 Sannazaro had returned to Naples, where he joined the Academy of Naples, an intellectual and cultural institution. Sannazaro probably began his pastoral novel, *Arcadia*, in the 1480s; he also acquired a friend and patron in Prince Frederick of Aragon, who acceded to the throne of Naples in 1496. When competition between France and Spain led to the invasion of Naples in 1501, King Frederick was forced to flee to France; Sannazaro voluntarily followed his king into exile. After Frederick's death in 1504, Sannazaro returned to Naples to discover that an unauthorized and incomplete edition of his *Arcadia* had been printed in 1502. He published his approved version in 1504. Sannazaro also became well known for his *Piscatorial Eclogues* (1526), which transposed the themes of the pastoral to a community of fishermen, and for his *Rime* (1530), a collection of love poems after the style of Francesco Petrarch's ***Canzionere*** (also in *WLAIT 7: Italian Literature and Its Times*). Though written in a vernacular dialect (combining Tuscan and Neapolitan elements) rather than Latin, Sannazaro's *Arcadia* is not widely read today. The work nevertheless remains historically significant

---

THE LITERARY WORK

A pastoral romance—consisting of alternating poetry and prose—set within the legendary realm of Arcadia in ancient Greece, during an unspecified time; published in Italian in 1504, in English in 1904.

SYNOPSIS

A community of shepherds in Arcadia sings, composes poetry, discusses the merits of its art, and discourses upon the ills of the world.

---

because it embodies the pastoral mode so popular during the Renaissance.

Events in History at the Time of the Romance

Naples during the 1490s. For half a century after 1442, the Aragonese royal family controlled the much-contested Kingdom of Naples. The founder of the line, Alfonso I (also known as Alfonso V of Aragon), ruled Naples until 1458, leaving the kingdom to his son Ferdinand I, who reigned from 1458 to 1494. Both monarchs were enthusiastic patrons of the arts and capable rulers. They brought stability to a kingdom that had suffered its share of dynastic struggles over the years.

That stability ended, however, when Ferdinand I died unexpectedly in 1494. His son, Alfonso,

Jacopo Sannazaro

succeeded him but, less than a year into his reign, chose to abdicate. He left the throne to his son, Ferdinand II and retired to a Benedictine monastery. Meanwhile, Charles VIII of France claimed his right to the Neapolitan throne—based on his kinship with the Angevins, a French dynasty that ruled Naples before the Aragonese annexed the kingdom. Charles invaded Naples in February 1495, with fleeting success; within a few months, his former allies, the pope and the Catholic monarchs of Spain (King Ferdinand of Aragon and Queen Isabella of Castile), joined forces against Charles. Ferdinand II, who had fled into hiding when Charles invaded, returned to Naples in July, and he expelled the French by November 1495.

In 1496, Ferdinand II died of natural causes and his uncle, Frederick, acceded to the throne of Naples. Once again, France and Spain set their sights on Naples, this time forming an alliance. Hoping to obtain protection from both countries, Frederick made overtures to Turkey, ruled by the powerful Islamic Ottomans. The gesture prompted Pope Alexander VI to excommunicate Frederick for treason against Christendom. On August 4, 1501 the pope invited the new French king, Louis XII, to take over the Kingdom of Naples; the French accepted the invitation, invading Naples. By year's end, Frederick surrendered his kingdom to France in exchange for the county of Maine (part of today's Maine-et-Loire)

and a pension of 30,000 ducats per year. The erstwhile king went into exile in France and died there in 1504. Meanwhile, France disagreed with Spain on how to apportion the kingdom of Naples; Spain ultimately forced the French to retreat in 1504, going on to rule the kingdoms of Naples and Sicily through viceroys until 1707.

Sannazaro's fortunes became tied to Frederick and the Aragonese rulers in Naples. In 1481 he joined the court retinue of the future Alfonso II. However, it was with Alfonso's scholarly younger brother Frederick that Sannazaro formed a more intimate relationship. By the time Frederick acceded to the Neapolitan throne in 1496, he and Sannazaro were close friends. It was also during these decades—the 1480s and 1490s—that Sannazaro was especially prolific, writing court entertainments, Italian lyrics, Latin elegies and epigrams, and his pastoral novel, *Arcadia*. In 1497 Frederick invited the poet to become godfather to his son; two years later, Frederick conferred upon Sannazaro the villa of Mergellina, located on the bay of Naples. When the king suffered his reversal of fortune in 1501, Sannazaro voluntarily accompanied Frederick into exile and remained with him until his death in 1504. The poet then returned to Naples. It is perhaps no coincidence that one of *Arcadia's* recurring themes is exile, since family circumstances, political upheavals, and deep personal loyalties prompted Sannazaro's departure from Naples, not once, but several times during his life.

Humanism and the Academy. From the ninth century onward, there developed the intellectual movement of humanism. Humanism's basic goal was "to put scholarship at the service of contemporary experience," to treat all aspects of existence as subjects worthy of serious study (Shinn, p. 14). Called humanists, followers of the movement explored such disciplines as language, literature, history, science, and moral philosophy. They concentrated in particular on ancient Greek and Roman texts, rediscovering and interpreting them, and adopting many of their ideas and values.

Spreading throughout Europe, the humanist movement reached its apogee during the High Renaissance (c. 1480-1520). It was an intensely intellectual movement, appealing most strongly to a small minority—the scholars, writers, artists, and architects. Altogether there were perhaps 1000 humanists in the Italian peninsula from 1420 to 1540. The movement was vigorous nonetheless; humanist circles and societies flourished in various Italian states, including Naples. One such society, Accademia Antoniana (often known simply as the Academy), was founded by Antonio Beccadelli, ambassador, secretary, and historian to the first Aragonese king, Alfonso I. Members of the Academy studied science and literature, encouraging each other's efforts in these and other fields. Naples attracted formidable minds because of the Academy—including writers Lorenzo Valla, George Trebizond, and Giovanni Pontano. After Beccadelli's death in 1471, Pontano became leader of the Academy (eventually Accademia Pontaniana). Like his predecessor, Pontano attracted many learned scholars and aspiring poets to the Academy, including young Jacopo Sannazaro, who was inducted into its society by the early 1480s. The induction ceremony required that Sannazaro adopt a Latinate name to demonstrate his devotion to the classical humanities; he chose "Actius Sincerus," possibly derived from the Latin words "acta" ("seashore") and "sincerus" ("sincere"). Thereafter, he generally used the name "Sincero" in his signatures.

Sannazaro's deep affection for the Academy and its members, especially Pontano, who was a friend, mentor, and even a father figure, manifests itself in several places in *Arcadia*. Some of its characters are deliberately modeled after members of the Academy. The revered shepherd Androgeo, at whose tomb the others gather, is a stand-in for Beccadelli, the founder of the Academy, while Meliseus—the widowed shepherd whose lamentation comprises the final eclogue—reflects Pontano after the death of his wife Adriana. This conceit, however, has a two-fold significance: while paying tribute to his friends and mentors, Sannazaro also adhered to the pastoral tradition of placing the author and his associates—thinly disguised as shepherds—in the work.

Reviving the pastoral. Humanism, as noted, revived interest in classical language and literature. Many of the early humanists tried to reconstruct elements of ancient Greece and Rome, including their original languages. By the mid-fifteen century, however, the humanists doubted whether this endeavor was possible, since the surviving ancient texts were incomplete and inconsistent. Several scholars, including Lorenzo Valla and Leon Battista Alberti, argued that the passage of time and the evolution of language itself thwarted a full recovery of the past. Therefore, while the ideas of antiquity still resonated for humanists, many believed that a new mode of literary expression was required. For several writers, that mode was the vernacular, or familiar everyday language: true, the vernacular varied by state and even by local area, but the Tuscan and Floren-

tine dialects were among the most widely known and used. Fourteenth-century writers Dante, Boccaccio, and Petrarch all composed works in the vernacular (see **The Divine Comedy**, **Decameron**, and **Canzoniere**, all also in *WLAIT 7: Italian Literature and Its Times*). During the 1480s, the young Jacopo Sannazaro followed suit in his *Arcadia*. Later in life he would reverse direction, choosing to write in Latin rather than his native Italian—a hybrid vernacular of the Tuscan and Neapolitan dialects. *Arcadia* was an experiment for Sannazaro in fusing classical tradition with the modern vernacular.

At the same time Sannazaro was attempting to revive a genre—the pastoral eclogue—which had lain dormant for many centuries. Used by the Greek poet Theocritus and, later, the Roman poet Virgil, the traditional pastoral poem was at once elaborate and conventional: a nostalgic expression of an urban poet's yearning for the peace and simplicity of a rural shepherd's life, depicted in an idealized natural setting. Conventions of the pastoral included shepherds reclining beneath trees and meditating upon their rural muse, playing upon wooden pipes, engaging in singing contests with comrades, relaying tales about their fortunes in love, engaging in rustic sports, or mourning the death of a fellow shepherd. Any resemblance of a shepherd to an authentic "dirt-poor and unlettered" rustic was entirely coincidental; often the shepherds were thinly disguised versions of the poet and his literary colleagues (Lee, p. 11).

Well-acquainted with the pastoral form, Sannazaro favored this mode partly because it was a mixture of monologue, dialogue, narrative action, philosophical rumination, and satirical observation. He also appreciated the form for its archaeological importance: the rediscovery of a genre with such a long history would lead to improved understanding of antiquity in general. Finally, he valued the pastoral for its connection to ancient language. The form stemmed from ancient roots; using it entailed a study of the structure and expression of the ancient language.

Sannazaro's experiments are most visible in the Arcadian eclogues themselves, which include several poetic forms, including *terza rima,* the *frottola,* and the *sestina.* The *sestina,* for example, consists of 11-syllable lines arranged into six stanzas of six lines, each followed by a concluding three-line verse (or envoy). Within any given stanza, the lines do not rhyme, but all the stanzas after the first one have lines that finish with the same end words as the first stanza, only in different orders. The concluding three-line verse contains all of the end words, three at the finish of its trio of lines and three inside them. In *Arcadia*, the seventh eclogue—spoken by Sannazaro's fictional counterpart, Sincero—is a *sestina*; the recurring end words are in dark print.

ARCADIA: FACT OR FANTASY?

The ancient Greek poet Theocritus (c. 310-250 B.C.E.), credited with creating the pastoral, set his *Idylls* in the remote countryside of his native Sicily. Virgil, however, transferred the pastoral setting to Arcadia—a convention followed by most subsequent imitators, including Jacopo Sannazaro and England's Sir Philip Sidney. Ancient Arcadia was a landlocked area in Peloponnese, the peninsula that formed the southern part of the mainland of Greece. Cut off by mountains from the rest of Greece, Arcadia developed a pastoral civilization, supported by the raising and herding of cattle, sheep, and goats. Of course, real shepherds did not spend their time composing poems and participating in singing contests. Rustic, poor, and unlettered, the real shepherds spent their time making sure their livestock had enough to eat and protecting their charges from wolves, foxes, and other predators. Nonetheless, the shepherd and the region became parts of a longstanding poetic conceit. To many ancient Greek and Roman poets, Arcadia came to represent a rural paradise where shepherds dwelt in peaceful simplicity, composing songs as they tended flocks, and worshipping Pan, Greek god of the forests. It is only this mythical Arcadia that concerns Sannazaro in his romance.

Like the nocturnal bird an enemy of the **sun**
weary I go among places shadowy and **black**,
while I see daylight bright upon the **earth**:
then when the world is overspread by
    evening
I am not, like other creatures, soothed by
    sleep
but then I wake to weep among the **hills**.

If ever these eyes among the groves or **hills**
(where is no splendor from the rays of the
    sun)
weary from weeping then are closed in **sleep**,
cruel visions and misapprehensions vain and
    black
sadden me so that verily I hesitate at **evening**
for fear of sleeping to stretch myself on the
    earth.

(Sannazaro, *Arcadia*, p. 75)

The Romance in Focus

Plot summary. *Arcadia* is composed of 12 prose chapters, each followed by an eclogue or poem in the pastoral mode. The plot is mainly episodic, focusing on various members of the shepherds' community in Arcadia. The melancholy recollections of the narrator Sincero—a figure based on Sannazaro himself—lends some unity to the story. A prologue and an epilogue, both in prose, frame the text. The prologue says that the poems about to be "repeated" have been roughly hewn by the shepherds of this paradise.

Chapter 1 of *Arcadia* begins with a description of a plateau on Mount Parthenius where the shepherds gather for athletic and musical contests. On one occasion, the shepherds notice the melancholy of their comrade Ergasto. In the first eclogue, another shepherd, Selvaggio, offers comfort and tries to persuade Ergasto to reveal the cause of his distress. During their dialogue, Ergasto reveals his passion for a shepherdess whom he saw washing clothes by the river; she revived him when he swooned for love of her, but she abandoned him once he regained consciousness. The mountains, woods, and Ergasto's own flock have witnessed his still unrequited love for the shepherdess. Ergasto's comrades attempt to comfort him; thereafter, they all return to their cottages for the night (Chapter 2).

Several days later, the narrator, while leading his flock to pasture, encounters the shepherd Montano. The narrator asks to join Montano and offers a handsomely carved staff if the latter will sing to pass the time. In Eclogue 2, Montano obliges; he is joined part way through his song by another shepherd, Uranio, who has been sleeping in the valley after a night of keeping the wolf away from his flock; the two shepherds begin a contest of love poetry, in praise of their respective sweethearts, lasting until the evening. The other shepherds praise the song and discuss the merits of both competitors as they walk home that night.

The next day the shepherds celebrate the feast of Pales, the goddess of shepherds. They visit her holy temple, whose door is graced with elaborate carvings of pastoral scenes. Entering the temple, the shepherds purify themselves by washing their hands in running water and leaping over fires of straw. Having performed these rites, the shepherds visit a beautiful meadow, where many shepherdesses are strolling and making garlands of flowers. The sight inspires the shepherd Galicio to sing of his love (Eclogue 3). In the next chapter, two other shepherds, Logisto and Elpino, challenge each other to a singing contest.

In Eclogue 4 the competitors each sing of the pains of love so skillfully that Selvaggio, the judge, declares that both deserve victory. The other shepherds concur, and again everyone returns home at sunset.

In Chapter 5, the oldest shepherd, Opico, leads his fellows to a place that he remembers fondly from his youth. Under his guidance, the company passes a roaring stream and ascends another mountain. On reaching the summit, they discover ten cowherds mourning at the tomb of the shepherd Androgeo. After one cowherd delivers a eulogy, the shepherd Ergasto sings a funeral lament (Eclogue 5).

In Chapter 6 another shepherd, Carino, joins the company and relates that he is looking for a lost heifer. His situation leads Serrano and Opico to bemoan, in song, the sorry condition of the world (Eclogue 6).

After Serrano and Opico have finished singing, Carino turns to the narrator, Sincero, and asks about his past and why he came to Arcadia (Chapter 7). The narrator then identifies himself as a youth from Naples from a good family, which had suffered when an unfit ruler ascended the throne. The narrator proceeds to relate the tale of his own misfortune: he fell in love with a childhood playmate and, realizing that his affections were unrequited, fled from Naples to exile in Arcadia. Homesickness and yearning for his beloved still trouble Sincero—the name by which she used to call him instead of Sannazaro—and he longs for death or a speedy reversal of his fortune. In response to Sincero's lament, Carino offers words of consolation and an elderwood pipe, with which he hopes Sincero can eventually attain poetic greatness:

> With this I trust that you, if it be not denied you by the fates, in the future will sing in loftier vein the loves of the Fauns and the Nymphs. And even as up to this point you have fruitlessly spent the beginnings of your adolescence among the simple and rustic songs of shepherds, so hereafter you will pass your fortunate young manhood among the sounding trumpets of the most famous poets of your century, not without hope of eternal fame.
>
> (*Arcadia*, pp. 74-75)

Sincero then sings of the sorrows of exile, which are alleviated by a dream-vision of "my lady (of her grace)," who gathers flowers upon the hills and exhorts him to leave his dark caverns (*Arcadia*, p. 76).

Carino continues to offer solace to Sincero and relates his own story (Chapter 8), closely paralleling the one just told. Like Sincero, Carino fell in love with a childhood companion—in his case, a girl dedicated to the goddess Diana. On discovering Carino's love for her, the girl grew troubled and parted from him without a word. Carino despaired, proclaimed his sorrows to the natural world, and planned to kill himself. The appearance of two white doves and the return of his beloved, who offered words of comfort and chaste embraces, persuaded Carino to abandon the idea of suicide. Carino exhorts Sincero to believe that he will find happiness and takes his leave.

No sooner has Carino departed than Clonico, another lovelorn shepherd, appears, looking wretched. Eugenio, Clonico's dearest friend, exhorts him to tell his troubles. When Clonico reveals that he too is crossed in love, Eugenio recommends that his friend turn to his work and his art as a cure for his malady (Eclogue 8).

The next morning Clonico wishes to visit a witch who will cure his lovesickness. However Opico persuades him to accompany the other shepherds to the temple of Pan, Greek god of the forest, whose priest, Enareto, has impressive magical powers of his own (Chapter 9). On reaching their destination, the shepherds find Enareto resting beneath a tree. The priest notices Clonico's pallor and misery. Just then a quarrel erupts between the shepherd Ofelia and a goatherd, Elenco, who had been playing his lyre to his sheep but quickly hid it when he saw the newcomers approaching. Ofelia flings insults at Elenco, who responds in kind; the two engage in a competition, singing first of their mistresses and then seeing who could deliver the most cutting insults (Eclogue 9). Montano, presiding over the contest, finds them equal in skill and declares Apollo, Greek god of music and poetry, the only victor.

In Chapter 10 the shepherds follow Enareto to a sacred grove, then to a cave with a great altar to Pan. There Enareto tells the curious shepherds how Pan's creation of reed pipes gave rise to pastoral poetry. Remembering Clonico's plight, Enareto promises to cure the shepherd's lovesickness. The rest of the company leaves. Opico requests from Selvaggio a song celebrating the present age that has brought forth such fine shepherd-poets. Just then, Selvaggio glimpses something upon a hill; it is the tomb of Massilia, Ergasto's mother, whom shepherds regarded almost as a divine sibyl, or prophetess, when she was alive. Selvaggio proposes that the company go to the tomb in memory of Massilia, who used to judge their competitions with such evenhanded grace, and the others agree.

After the shepherds pay their respects at Massilia's tomb, Selvaggio sings about the subject Onica had requested them to treat, the great poets of the present age. Fronimo joins him (Eclogue 10) and points out that the poets of the day are unappreciated. This leads Selvaggio to discourse upon the ills of poverty and worldly corruption that beset life. During their discussion, the shepherds mention the beauty of Naples, filling Sincero with nostalgia for his homeland.

In Chapter 11 Ergasto performs various funeral offices before his mother's tomb on the anniversary of her death. He then presides over a series of funeral games, granting prizes to the victors in racing, wrestling, and using a slingshot. After the games, Ergasto composes and sings his own lament for Massilia to complete her commemoration (Eclogue 11).

PAN AND SYRINX

While Enareto's long discussion on the rise of pastoral poetry appears to be Sannazaro's own invention, most readers would have been familiar with the myth of how pan-pipes were created. The half-goat Pan (god of shepherds, goatherds, and the forests) loved a water nymph, Syrinx. But she was dedicated to serving Artemis, virgin goddess of the hunt, and so did not return his passion. Trying to escape the god's attentions, Syrinx called out for divine aid and was transformed into a clump of reeds along the riverbank. The disappointed Pan noticed that the reeds made a beautiful sound when he breathed upon them. He proceeded to cut several reeds of varying length, then bound them together and turned them into a set of pipes on which he played sad songs about his lost love.

Night comes and the shepherds return to their cottages (Chapter 12). Awaking from a disturbing dream, Sincero leaves his cottage and goes for a walk through the dark countryside. On his ramblings, he meets a nymph who guides him underground through valleys and mountains until they reach the source of the earth's rivers. When they glimpse the waves of the Sebeto River, the nymph tells Sincero to continue alone and vanishes. Mystified, he follows the Sebeto to Naples; he emerges in the hills of his homeland, where he sees a weeping god surrounded by equally sorrowful nymphs. One nymph guides Sincero to

the road and cryptically informs him that his "sole Phoenix," a reference to his lost love, lies beneath the slopes of the mountain (*Arcadia*, p. 140). By this, Sincero infers that his beloved has died. Overcome with grief, he curses the hour he left Arcadia and wonders where he should go now. In time, still in Naples, Sincero adjusts. He recognizes his two shepherds, Barcinio and Summonzio, who are "widely renowned in [the area's] forest regions" (*Arcadia*, p. 141). Settling himself in the grass, Sincero listens to Barcinio and Summonzio sing of the great sorrows and lamentations of Meliseus, a noble shepherd whose beloved, Phyllis, has died (Eclogue 12). The two shepherds then ascend to Phyllis's tomb and witness Meliseus's grief firsthand.

Arcadia ends with an epilogue in which Sincero warns his *sampogna*—his shepherd's pipe—that sophisticated audiences may not be receptive to its songs. He thus enjoins it to remain in the Arcadian solitudes, where its humble beauties will be best appreciated: "Wherefore you may hold it as matter true and undoubted, that he who lives the more hidden, and the more removed from the multitude, lives better. And that man may with most truth be called blessed among mortal men who, without envy of the grandeurs of others, in modest spirit contents him with his fortune" (*Arcadia*, p. 154).

The pains of love. Despite its idyllic setting, the overall tone of *Arcadia* is more melancholy than joyous. While most of the shepherds happily sing, dance, and play rustic sports, those whom Sannazaro chooses to narrate the eclogues suffer from unrequited love, bereavement, and, in Sincero's case, a combination of lovesickness and homesickness. As one literary scholar notes, *Arcadia* is full of "episodes illustrating, for the most part, failures in human relationships, personal inadequacies, frustrated aspirations and hopes and trust deceived. . . . *Arcadia* is not a happy book" (Kidwell, p. 9). A general mood of melancholy pervades the twelve episodes, growing by the close of the poem into unrelieved despair.

The most common malady in *Arcadia* is unrequited love. More than half the eclogues deal with a shepherd's passion for a beautiful but unattainable woman, who is either unaware of or indifferent to her lover's devotion. Significantly, women seldom appear in Sannazaro's romance; the lone exception occurs in the third and fourth chapters, when the shepherds, celebrating the feast of Pales, briefly find themselves in the company of beautiful shepherdesses making flower garlands in the meadow. However, despite their purported pains of love, none of the shepherds attempt to court or speak to the shepherdesses; rather the young men appear content to gaze upon the beauty of the garland makers and sing their praises.

The idealized love portrayed in *Arcadia* reflects a widespread literary trend of the time. Although the figure of the lovesick swain had existed since antiquity, the works of Dante and, especially, Petrarch, which deal with the speaker's passion for an unattainable beloved, gave it new prominence. The beloved's very inaccessibility fuels the poet's art: "Petrarch's lover experiences torment because his beloved is distant from him. That distance requires compensation. To achieve it the lover" gives his beloved a new value, making her the central figure of his "literary pursuit. He exists not just in order to desire her, but also in order to write about her" (Kennedy, p. 38). A similar type of logic is at work in *Arcadia*, especially when shepherds describe the beauty and cruelty of their respective beloveds, as in this singing contest between Montano and Uranio as they drive their flocks to pasture:

Montano: O my lovely Phyllis,
    whiter art thou than lilies,
    more blushing than mid-April's
      mead,
    more fugitive than the roe-deer's
      speed
    or speed of timorous fawn;
    more arrogant to me
    than to great Pan was she
    who tired and overgone
    transformed her to the tremulous
      pliant reed;
    now for rewarding of my heavy
      care
    ah, to the winds outspread your
      golden hair.

Uranio: Tirrena mine,
    whose color doth outshine
    the lovely morning rose
    or purest milk—thou sweet
    flame of my heart, more fleet
    than forest does,
    or woodland fawn,
    and ah more cruel than she
    that made in Thessaly
    the primal laurel, from her limbs
      outdrawn:
    for the sole remedy of thy riven
      breast
    turn here the eyes where Love hath
      made his nest.
          (*Arcadia*, pp. 39-40)

However removed the shepherds are from their beloved, the work is an intimate one. *Ar-cadia*'s intimacy comes not from male-female relationships between characters, however, but rather in the relationship between the work and its audience. At the center of *Arcadia* are the feelings of individuals, even of lowly shepherds, if one takes the writing at face value. Pastoral poetry, concerned with such feelings, is hereby revived by Sannazaro and others "after a thousand years of neglect." It conveys values that are "by no means trivial," and speaks to his court society, suggesting that "true happiness is enjoyed by those withdrawn from turmoil and satisfied with what they have, unenvious of others' success" (Brand and Pertile, p. 161).

Sources and literary context. As was the frequent practice of writers of pastoral literature, Sannazaro drew upon his life experiences, as well as a variety of literary sources, for his *Arcadia*. Some of Sannazaro's friends from the Academy appear in the romance disguised as shepherds; in Eclogue 12, the shepherd Meliseus—depicted as grieving over his wife Phyllis—was modeled after Sannazaro's close friend Giovanni Pontano, whose wife, Adriana, had died in 1490. Pontano himself had written several poems of lamentation concerning his wife's death, including a pastoral eclogue titled *Meliseus*. Sannazaro's early biographers also claim that he based Sincero's unnamed sweetheart—for whose sake he exiles himself from his beloved Naples—on a real-life love interest. Carmosina Bonifacio was a young girl whom Sannazaro had known and loved as a child. She died at 14, while the poet was in Salerno. Later scholars, however, point out that family finances, rather than unrequited love, led to Sannazaro's removal from Naples as a boy.

Sannazaro's literary models for *Arcadia* included the writings of the Greek poet Theocritus, considered to be the originator of pastoral literature, and the Roman poet Virgil, who composed pastorals in Latin. However, Sannazaro drew not only upon bucolic works (works dealing with shepherds, herdsmen, or rural life), but also epic poems as well, such as Homer's *Iliad* and Virgil's *Aeneid*. More recent writers including Petrarch, Boccaccio, and Pontano—the latter a Sannazaro contemporary—also influenced *Arcadia*.

While adhering closely to the traditions of Greek and Roman pastorals by depicting an idealized natural landscape and shepherds singing and composing poems, Sannazaro introduced several innovations. First, he combined classical and contemporary motifs by introducing the popular figure of the sighing Petrarchan lover into classical-style pastorals. While shepherds in classical pastorals were often embroiled in love affairs (both happy and unhappy), the shepherds in Sannazaro's *Arcadia* portrayed their relationships as sources of ceaseless torment. They were hapless victims of an all-consuming passion resembling a disease or a form of madness, a

---

INFLUENCE AND IMITATION

Sir Philip Sidney's *Arcadia* shared many features with Sannazaro's *Arcadia*, including experimentation with verse forms. Both poets attempted double *sestinas,* presented in their works as love dialogues between two shepherds:

Logisto.   Shepherds, nor bird nor beast dwells in the valley
that does not know the harmony of my rhyme,
nor is there cave or grot among the rocks
that does not echo my continual plaint;
nor flower nor bush is growing in these fields
that I do not trample a thousand times a day.

Elpino.   Alas, I know not well the hour or day
that I was shut within this mountain valley;
nor ever do I recall running through the fields
free or unbound; but making complaint in rhyme
I have lived ever in flames; and with my plaint
I have moved to pity the very trees and rocks.
(Sannazaro, *Arcadia*, p. 53)

Strephon.   Ye Goat-herd gods, that love the grassy mountains,
Ye nymphs which haunt the spring in pleasant valleys,
Ye satyrs joyed with free and quiet forests,
Vouchsafe your silent ears to plaining music,
Which to my woes gives still an early morning,
And draws the dolor on till weary evening.

Klaius.   O Mercury, foregoer to the evening,
O heavenly huntress of the savage mountains,
O lovely star, entitled of the morning,
While that my voice doth fill these woeful valleys,
Vouchsafe your silent ears to plaining music,
Which oft hath *Echo* tired in secret forests.
(Sidney in Abrams, p. 502)

---

frequent Petrarchan conceit. Sannazaro also made the passion in *Arcadia* entirely heterosexual; his shepherds burn with love for cruel or indifferent shepherdesses, not for each other, as in some Greek and Roman pastorals. Finally, Sannazaro inserted poetry into his storyline and chose to

write not in Latin, but in vernacular Tuscan (with some Neapolitan variations), as had Dante, Petrarch, and Boccaccio. Thus, *Arcadia* helped to establish Tuscan dialect as a standard Italian language and contributed to the popularity of the vernacular as a means of literary expression.

Publication and impact. Although Sannazaro composed many poems during the 1480s and 1490s, he apparently preferred to circulate his work privately, rather than have it published. He may have been especially reluctant to consider the publication of *Arcadia*, which he seems to have regarded, perhaps dismissively, as a youthful effort. In 1502, a year after Sannazaro had accompanied Frederick III—former king of Naples—into exile, a pirated edition of *Arcadia*, based on an old 1489 manuscript, appeared in Venice, to the indignation of Sannazaro and his friends from the Academy. This version contained only the first ten eclogues and many textual errors and inconsistencies. To counter the pirated version, Pietro Summonte—Sannazaro's friend and the head of the Academy—published the complete *Arcadia*, apparently with Sannazaro's approval, in 1504. This version contained Eclogues 11 and 12, their accompanying prose chapters, and the epilogue "To His Sampogna."

Sannazaro's *Arcadia* enjoyed immediate success after its publication. A new edition appeared about every two years during the poet's lifetime and throughout the sixteenth century. The work inspired a renowned pastoral play, *Aminta*, by Italian writer Torquato Tasso; *Aminta* (1580), concerns a young shepherd-poet happily united with Silvia after her initial rejection. *Arcadia*'s popularity with Renaissance readers led to countless imitations in various countries and languages. One of the most famous was Sir Philip Sidney's *Arcadia*, on which the English poet worked from around 1580 to 1586, the year of his death. Sidney's sister, the Countess of Pembroke, published a version of his *Arcadia* in 1593. Sannazaro's influence on Sidney's work is easy to detect; not only does the English *Arcadia* take place in a pastoral setting similar to that in Sannazaro's romance, but each chapter ends with pastoral eclogues in which shepherds sing, dance, play rustic sports, and participate in song and poetry competitions.

—Pamela S. Loy

For More Information

Abrams, M. H., ed. *The Norton Anthology of English Literature.* Vol. 1. New York: W. W. Norton, 1986.

Brand, Peter, and Lino Pertile, eds. *The Cambridge History of Italian Literature*. Cambridge: Cambridge University Press, 1996.

Kennedy, William J. *Jacopo Sannazaro and the Uses of Pastoral*. Hanover, Conn.: University Press of New England, 1983.

Kidwell, Carol. *Sannazaro and Arcadia*. London: Gerald Duckworth, 1993.

Lee, M. Owen. *Death and Rebirth in Virgil's Arcadia*. New York: State University of New York Press, 1989.

Martines, Lauro. *Power and Imagination*. New York: Alfred A. Knopf, 1979.

Sannazaro, Jacopo. *Arcadia & Piscatorial Eclogues*. Trans. Ralph Nash. Detroit: Wayne State University Press, 1966.

Shinn, Rinn S., ed. *Italy: A Country Study*. Washington, D.C.: Foreign Area Studies, 1987.

Artemisia

by

Anna Banti

rtemisia is the second novel written by Anna Banti (literary pseudonym of Lucia Lopresti), who was born in Florence in 1895. Her parents soon moved to Rome, where Banti attended school. After she graduated from the University of Rome with a degree in art history, she married Roberto Longhi, a professor at the University. As his fame as an art historian grew, Banti felt compelled to abandon her own ambitions in that field, and acting on her husband's suggestion, began what was to become her long and successful literary career. Banti had already mastered the art of describing the forms and colors of the plastic arts and only a slight shift of emphasis was necessary to describe the mental landscapes, scenes, and faces so integral to fiction. These pictorial skills, along with her fertile imagination and lifelong interest in storytelling, coalesced into a distinctive writing style. No doubt the style was affected by her experience as an editor of a literary volume put out periodically by her husband's art journal, *Paragone*, founded in 1950. Altogether Banti produced 9 novels and 7 collections of short stories, which for the most part concern women and their struggles with societal pressures in order to lead fulfilled lives. Her finely crafted short stories, such as "Il coraggio di donne" ("The Courage of Women") and "Lavinia fuggita" ("Lavinia is Gone"), earned her lasting fame, which was only reinforced by her fictional biography of the famous artist Artemisia Gentileschi (1593-c. 1652). Banti's overt purpose in writing about this neglected painter was to restore her to her rightful place,

THE LITERARY WORK

A historical novel set in seventeenth-century Rome, Florence, Naples, France, and England, which interjects descriptions of Italy in 1944; published in Italian in 1947, in English in 1988.

SYNOPSIS

Dishonored as a young girl, Artemisia Gentileschi overcomes all obstacles to become one of the most accomplished painters of her time.

to the exalted position she once held with her contemporaries. In all likelihood Banti's own marriage to the great "Maestro" (Professor Longhi), did not live up to her hopes (as suggested by her final novel *Un grido lacerante* [1981; *A Piercing Cry*, 1996]). This marital disappointment plus a long lifetime of exclusion and challenge as a woman probably sharpened her insight, as Banti resurrected the seventeenth-century from the dusty storage rooms of art history.

Events in History at the Time the Novel Takes Place

The real-life Artemisia Gentileschi. Few facts are known about Artemisia's life. She was born in Rome in 1593 (the novel, written before the discovery of Artemisia's birth certificate, says 1597). Her father, the renowned Orazio Gentileschi, taught her the art of painting.

It is a matter of record that Orazio brought charges against the painter Agostino Tassi for the rape of Artemisia in 1611. This resulted in a trial lasting approximately three months, from March 18 to May 16, 1612. Records of this trial are to be found in the archives of the State of Rome, which Banti consulted. Taking the stand, Tassi denied ever having sexual relations with Artemisia and furthermore accused her of having slept with assorted painters and of having committed incest with her father. Artemisia, determined to prove her innocence of these charges and the truthfulness of her accusations against him, submitted to the torture of *sibille*—the ingenious practice of wrapping a cord around the fingers and then pulling it tight. It was named after the "sibyls," or ancient prophetesses, with the hope of convincing its victim to tell the truth.

TOURING THE "NEIGHBORHOOD" IN THE SEVENTEENTH CENTURY

In the 1600s, Naples, Sicily, Sardinia, and Milan were ruled by the Spanish Habsburg monarchy; Tuscany was a duchy ruled by the Medici family; Venice and Genoa were republics; and Rome and the Papal States were ruled by the pope. These separate political entities (Italy was not united until after 1860) would have made Artemisia's traveling to Florence or Rome or Genoa somewhat the same as entering France and England. The food, customs, people, and even language were almost as different in each area of the Italian peninsula as in each European country.

In her testimony, Artemisia said she resisted Tassi's advances at the time he raped her in her bedroom, and raised a knife against him after the rape but never harmed him. Later, after he promised to marry her, she agreed to have sexual relations again. From the start a female neighbor, Tuzia, facilitated his access to Artemisia. This betrayal by her father's friend and colleague, and the betrayal by a woman she considered her friend, left a lifetime scar.

> My father was a close friend of the said Agostino Tassi who, because of our friendship, began to visit our house frequently. . . . "He who wants me must give me this," meaning marry me and put a ring on my finger. . . . I told him that I was feeling ill and I thought I had a fever. He replied; "I have more of a fever than you do."

> . . . He then threw me onto the edge of the bed, pushing me with a hand on my breast, and he put a knee between my thighs. . . . I tried to scream . . . I scratched his face. . . . He said: . . . "I promise to marry you" . . . and with this promise he induced me later on to yield lovingly, many times, to his desires. . . . What I was doing with him I did only so that, as he dishonored me, he would marry me.
>
> (Artemisia Gentileschi in Garrard, pp. 414-18)

The records contain no statement of the trial's outcome, although an introduction to the proceedings and the skeptical attitude of the judge toward Tassi's testimony suggest that he was found guilty and perhaps served a prison sentence of fewer than 9 months (through the time of the trial until shortly thereafter). Tassi had also been accused of having his wife killed around the time of the rape (Artemisia had not known he was married and when she learned it, confronted him, but he always denied it). The curious reader can find the entire transcript of this infamous trial translated in Appendix B of Mary D. Garrard's study of Artemisia's artistic renderings of heroic women.

Other sketchy records of Artemisia's life confirm that she married Antonio Stiattesi and had at least one daughter with him, though in letters she mentions two daughters, one of whom was a painter. Without her husband, Artemisia accompanied her father to Florence and to the royal court in England from 1638 to around 1639. These travels are a matter of record, as are her sojourns to Naples and Genoa.

In Rome, Florence, Genoa, and London, her paintings were commissioned by church and civil dignitaries, as well as such worthies as the Grand Duke of Tuscany and the art enthusiast King Charles I of England. Artemisia's father died in England in 1639, and she returned to Naples, where she spent the last ten years of her life still painting for her various patrons. The circumstances of Artemisia's death remain unknown, but she probably died after 1651. Throughout the years, rumors of sexual promiscuity surrounded Artemisia, thanks in no small part to her unconventional life. Two satirical epitaphs, published in 1653 after her death, comment on her "as cuckolder of her husband and as temptress, reducing her extraordinary artistic life to a threadbare type of conventional misogyny" that history has since attempted to correct (Garrard, p. 137).

A woman's place. Only in very rare and exceptional cases was a woman of a certain class in the seventeenth century able to step out of the limiting role defined by society. An unmarried woman was carefully watched over by male members of her family, because her good reputation was extremely important, and the slightest taint could bring disgrace to the family and dash any hopes for a suitable marriage. Two ways of life were ordinarily possible for a young woman: the convent or matrimony (provided her family could provide an acceptable dowry). Married women, though they were considered the property of their husbands, enjoyed more freedom than single women. For a young woman like Artemisia, marriage was a way to escape her father's severe restrictions at home and to avoid the convent life he is known to have desired for her.

The honor of fathers and brothers was fiercely defended in a patriarchal society. Any man who besmirched the honor of a family's womenfolk could expect cruel retribution. In Artemisia's family, her father brought the charge of rape against his painter friend and colleague, Agostino Tassi, which led to the sensational court trial described above. This accusation was probably more in defense of the father's own honor than in consideration of the suffering visited upon his daughter. More suffering would follow for her in the form of humiliating physical examinations and the torture to which she was subjected in the course of the 1612 trial. To be sure, she endured it to redeem her own reputation, but more importantly, from the viewpoint of most patriarchs like her father, to redeem the family name.

Women received no formal education in seventeenth-century Italy, except in the wealthiest families of high social rank. The vast majority of the female population in Europe was illiterate at the time. Artemisia could not read or write when she was 18, as attested by the trial records of 1612. She became literate later, taught perhaps by her devoted brother Francesco, for she is known to have written letters in her maturity.

Only the most gifted and ambitious woman could hope to develop her talents and interests, as indeed a handful of female painters did, among them, Sofonisba Anguissola, Lavinia Fontana, and Elisabetta Siriani. However, for these artists "it appears to have been enough to be accepted professionally; to attempt an innovative artistic contribution [as Artemisia did] was unnecessary" (Garrard, p. 6). In any case, for a woman, acceptance as a serious artist came at great personal cost. According to Banti's portrayal, Artemisia had to sacrifice any sort of satisfactory family life for the sake of her art. Her husband left her when he felt superfluous; her daughter was raised in a con-

The Allegory of Painting. A self-portrait (1630) by Artemisia Gentileschi.

vent and developed little affection for her mother; her father was cool and demanding.

Caravaggio and the Caravaggisti. Michelangelo Merisi came from Caravaggio in northern Italy, hence his nickname. He went to Rome sometime between 1588 and 1592 as a very poor but extremely talented painter. This aspiring artist became famous quite early, thanks to his revolutionary use of live models and his dramatic contrasts of light and shadow, or chiaroscuro, which promoted naturalism, diverging sharply from the artificial, exaggerated, often unrealistically proportioned works of the so-called mannerist style in vogue in Rome. Caravaggio's innovative style strongly influenced a group of artists who worked in Rome, the most outstanding being Artemisia's father—Orazio Gentileschi—and Artemisia herself. Others in the group, coming from various parts of Italy as well as from Germany (Adam Elsheimer) and Flanders (Wenzel Coebergher), settled in the area where the Gentileschis lived. Orazio was a personal friend of Caravaggio, and Artemisia would have known him also. His fame spread abroad. Artists as far afield as France's Georges de la Tour and the Netherlands' Rembrandt van Rijn found the charm of Caravaggio's work irresistible.

Art historians eventually labeled as Caravaggisti these and other painters influenced by Caravaggio's innovative realism and his startling way of illuminating his subject to delineate form. Artemisia would have seen his early, astonishingly vivid and dramatic depictions of a rustic, very realistic Saint Matthew. These depictions appeared in frescoes in the Roman churches of San Luigi dei Francesi, Santa Maria del Popolo, and the Chiesa Nuova—frescoes that Caravaggio had painted when he was 23 years old.

JUDITH

The theme of Judith and Holofernes occupies a larger place in Artemisia Gentileschi's oeuvre than any other subject. In part, this may be an accident of survival, for although the artist is known to have painted more than one version of several themes—at least four Susannas, two Dianas, two Davids—many of these examples are lost or unknown to us today. But at least five autographed Judiths have been preserved, three of which are deservedly placed among Artemisia's finest works. Moreover, the theme is likely to have held personal importance for the artist, for of all the female characters that she painted, Judith was the most positive and active figure, whose heroic deed held for Artemisia the greatest potential for self-identification.

Artemisia's five Judiths depict the apocryphal legend of the Jewish widow Judith beheading King Nebuchadnezzar's general, Holofernes, in his tent to prevent his invading Bethulia. Although these paintings have been interpreted as Artemisia's symbolic punishment of the man who raped her, it was a popular subject for many male artists, such as Andrea Mantegna, Michelangelo Buonarroti, Caravaggio, and Sandro Botticelli, and it was sculpted by Donatello, whose *Judith and Holofernes* stands in the Piazza Signoria in Florence in all its gory glory.

Artemisia's father was a Caravaggista, and the influence filtered down to her. Her early reliance upon her father's model is not surprising. It was unheard of for females of the day to pursue the customary paths to artistic careers, such as training with multiple master artists, traveling, and belonging to guilds. Her apprenticeship to her father was the only way she could realize her ambition to become a professional artist. In fact, her early show of independence from him—she struck out on her own—was perhaps the most remarkable element of her budding career.

Artemisia's apprenticeship with her father probably extended from 1605 to 1610, and he spoke proudly of his pupil's work. Even her earliest paint-

ings displayed a talent rooted in a command of technical skills, informal artistic instruction in Rome, and her own dash of creativity.

Artemisia's paintings are noted for their distinctive color and masterful technique, characterized by the dramatic lighting learned from Caravaggio's works. Her heroines—Judith, Susanna, Mary Magdalene, Cleopatra, Lucretia, Esther, Saint Catherine—painted from live models, are portrayed as strong characters and are neither young beauties nor old hags, as most men traditionally painted women subjects. Many of her heroines resembled the artist herself; in fact one painting, entitled *The Allegory of Painting*, is a self-portrait.

Banti shows that the reason this talented artist was neglected after her death (and had to struggle harder than usual for her rightful place as an artist during her lifetime) was due primarily to male prejudice. Men were the art historians and they set the criteria for excellence. In general, their own biases blinded them especially to Artemisia's realistic portrayals of women. A disinterested, when not negative, opinion in relation to her work lasted until the twentieth century when it was reevaluated by people "conditioned by a consciously realized feminism to respond to and share in an art in which female protagonists behave as plausible human beings" (Garrard, p. 8).

The Novel in Focus

Plot summary. The novel opens with an explanation from the narrator-writer to the reader: she explains that her original manuscript of *Artemisia* was destroyed during the war in the spring of 1944, and that she feels impelled to preserve the memory of someone she has become perhaps "too fond" of, as well as to give vent to "personal emotions too imperious to be ignored or betrayed" (Banti, *Artemisia*, p. 2). She then recounts the few facts known about the life of her protagonist.

The story itself begins with a voice telling the writer not to cry. It sounds like the voice of a young girl, but it is actually a voice in the writer's head as she sits on a gravel path in the Boboli gardens apart from the other refugees who flee the mines that have been set off by the Germans on their way out of Florence. The writer is crying because the bridges spanning the Arno have been demolished and because the book she had written about Artemisia has been destroyed. She then realizes that the voice she hears telling her not to cry is Artemisia's as a child of ten playing on Pincio Hill in Rome. Suddenly the image shifts in the writer's mind. Now Artemisia is a young woman shut in her room, crying in anger and despair, a mental image that mixes with the actual misery before the writer's eyes of hungry crying babies in war-torn Florence. The twentieth-century writer focuses her attention on a ragamuffin child in her own day, which touches off in her mind an image of Artemisia and her childhood Roman friend, the wealthy but bedridden Cecilia Nari.

Artemisia is quickly growing into a young woman and preserving her purity worries her painter father, Orazio Gentileschi. He wants her to enter a convent but in the meantime has the neighbors keep close watch on her when he is away from home. Her father has taught her to draw and paint, and the famous painter Agostino Tassi has explained perspective to her. Artemisia still slips away to visit her ailing friend Cecilia, but less often now.

The scene then shifts to 1944, in the Palazzo Pitti, where the writer has sought shelter and where Artemisia appears before her again. The writer still mourns her lost manuscript and is amazed by her obsession with this artist from the past: "I am shocked by the impetus with which I am carried beyond the limits my memory allows me, beyond the bounds of the story" (*Artemisia*, p. 12). She continues meeting with Artemisia, now at the Forte di Belvedere above Palazzo Pitti. Her visitor from the past goes on with the story of her life in the 1600s, as Florence collapses and burns below them in 1944.

Artemisia relates how Agostino ingratiated himself by giving her lessons in perspective, how he visited her father every day in the home studio, how, when she was 14, her good friend Tuzia (a neighbor whose portrait Artemisia painted) acted as a go-between by letting Agostino in and closing the bedroom door. Admittedly Artemisia wanted to get married and Agostino gave her a ring with his promise of marriage. Artemisia, the writer now realizes, has become independent of her, even to the point of walking ahead of her. The writer is now embellishing the account of the seduction to impress Arcangela Paladini, her singer friend, who just came out of an old Duchess's bedroom at the Pitti Palace. The writer gives vent to her irritation: "But Arcangela's shadow is fragile and the [1944] refugees in the courtyard are shouting in ill temper; nothing simpler than for me to take Arcangela's place and once more force Artemisia into the harsh sincerity of the present" (*Artemisia*, p. 16).

Back under the control of the writer, Artemisia obediently recites the details the writer attached to her after reading the proceedings of the sen-

sational rape trial. The writer cautions Artemisia: "It's not important to remember what the judge thought of women; even if I wrote it, it wasn't [necessarily] true" because it originated in the author's imagination (*Artemisia*, p. 17). Artemisia resumes her account, recalling how her father's anger initiated the trial, his avoidance of her, the advice others gave her. But she wanted to confess everything in her own way. Agostino had taken her into her room and raped her; she had resisted to the point of grabbing a knife, but only succeeded in cutting her own hand. Her regret over the loss of her virginity under such circumstances will never fade completely, though it will stimulate her to compensate for the loss in an artistic way. The writer had hoped to provide some solace for Artemisia's pain, but it has come back stronger than ever.

FLORENCE UNDER FIRE

Florence escaped some of the devastation visited on other Italian cities during the Second World War, but as the retreating Germans left it toward the end of the war in the spring of 1944, they blew up all the bridges over the Arno River except the medieval Ponte Vecchio. To impede the Allies' advance over that ancient bridge, the retreating Germans destroyed the houses at either end. Banti's house on Via San Jacopo, which ran alongside the Arno, was demolished, and with it her first manuscript of *Artemisia*. Along with other homeless residents, Banti was forced to sleep in the open, in the Boboli gardens of the Pitti Palace. It is here that she envisions Artemisia, the seventeenth-century painter and protagonist of her novel.

The women banter back and forth and the writer admits that she is too close to the subject to write about it without distortion. The already violated Artemisia describes an innocent walk in the country with Tuzia and Artemisia's brother Francesco that ends with more importuning from Agostino. She feels she should be as free as a man after her disgrace, but wherever she goes there is Agostino in pursuit. One day he gives her a ring that makes her feel safer, almost like a bride.

The writer and Artemisia quarrel: Artemisia is concerned that she isn't telling the story the way it was written; the writer is tired and angry because Artemisia does not appreciate the loss of the writer's manuscript.

Artemisia then describes the attempt of her neighbor, old Stiattesi, to free Agostino from jail. If Artemisia will say he was not the first man she had experienced, or the only one (i.e., that she was not a virgin), the charges will be dropped and Agostino will marry her immediately. Artemisia follows her impulse to run home where she crawls into her bed and is assailed by disconsolate thoughts "that were too quick, too desperately concise for a brain as young as hers: 'If only the dark would last forever, no one would recognize me as a woman, such hell for me, woe to others'" (*Artemisia*, p. 24). Yet she does not hate all those involved—Agostino, the go-betweens, the false witnesses. Today she feels guilty, as guilty as her persecutors want her to feel. She resigns herself to her solitary destiny as an outcast, comforted only by her pride: she will show the world what Artemisia can do.

Returning to the present, the writer interjects further comments about this obsession of hers to revive the biography of a woman so unjustly treated. Then the narrative reverts to 1615. Agostino has been acquitted and is out of jail, thanks to his scheming friends. Artemisia, 17 years old, spends her days shut up in her house painting. Her father eats and sleeps away from home; her brothers Marco, Giulio, and the devoted Francesco come home at night after work. Sometimes Francesco draws with her—an "occupation which is like a conversation for the Gentileschi family" (*Artemisia*, p. 28). They begin talking and Francesco tells her about the painters who are in demand. To her pleasant surprise, he says he overheard words of praise for her work.

Whenever her father comes home, Artemisia does everything she can to win his approval, to prove herself worthy of his attention and love. But nothing she says or does has the desired effect. He remains cold, grim, and indifferent. One exceptional evening he comes home while she is absorbed in her drawing and shows signs of satisfaction that give her hope. That same evening, while eating their supper of soup and omelet, her father announces they will be going to Florence to work for the grand duke. He will take Artemisia with him, but she must get married first.

Again the seventeenth-century storyline is interrupted by the writer: "I will never be free of Artemisia again; she is a creditor, a stubborn, scrupulous conscience to which I grow accustomed[,] as to sleeping on the ground" (*Artemisia*, p. 33). Then she "drags" Artemisia on a walk through the Boboli gardens.

When the Pitti Palace comes in view, the writer is compelled to face up to the injustice of her en-

forced walk and lets Artemisia return to her story. The young painter packs to leave Rome, still not sure if she is supposed to go because her father has said no more about it. But finally Artemisia and her famous father are in a carriage on their way to Florence. She has married, but her husband, Antonio Stiattesi, stays behind.

In Florence her father finds Artemisia a commission to paint a panel for the ceiling in the house of Michelangelo Buonarroti, grandnephew of the famous Michelangelo. After completing the assignment, she finds her first commission on her own, to paint the portrait of a woman married to a courtier. More heartening developments follow. The duchessa, wife of the Duke of Tuscany, sends for Artemisia. Befriending her, the women at the ducal court beg her to secretly teach them to paint. Artemisia consents, teaching them as they are able to learn.

At the duchessa's request to paint an epic subject, Artemisia paints a scene of Judith beheading Holofernes. These new friends of hers like to come to the studio and watch her depict on canvas the burly, bare-chested model who poses as they gossip among themselves. They do not realize whose expression is on Judith's face—the artist's own, which she copied from the mirror. The painting itself takes shape from experiences of her past: Agostino, the knife, the four-poster bed.

> Meanwhile an immense pride swells in her breast, the awful pride of a woman who has been avenged, in whom, despite her shame, there is also room for the satisfaction of the artist who has overcome all the problems of her art and speaks the language of her father, of the pure, of the chosen.
>
> (*Artemisia*, p. 46)

She works long and tirelessly on the painting, retrieving from it her sense of worth and victory. The shame she had felt in Rome dissolves in the emotional release of painting the slaying of Holofernes. Presented at court, the picture is a success. Everyone is enthusiastic about it. With her release from shame comes a sense of sympathy or at least forgiveness for men, who are "tormented," thinks Artemisia, "by arrogance and authority" (*Artemisia*, p. 50).

Artemisia reminisces about the husband she left in Rome, about when Antonio Stiattesi was a boy collecting odds and ends to sell and trade. The Stiattesis were accustomed to following the Gentileschis wherever they moved, camping in a spare room with their four children. Artemisia had always ignored them and made fun of them just as everyone else did. But her father had chosen

Antonio to be her husband, and her thoughts now dwell on that day when he appeared in his finest clothes, along with his family, for a trip to the church. Now she is in Florence and he is in Rome; the two will not meet again for several years.

Her father praises Artemisia's painting of Judith and Holofernes. He informs her he will be going to the court in England and asks her to return to her husband in Rome. Reluctantly, the dutiful daughter complies.

The Stiattesis are living in a dank cellar. By this time, Artemisia has developed enough confidence, thanks to what she has learned from the ladies in Florence, to deal with the railings of her father-in-law. He says Antonio is supporting them all by peddling old clothes and trinkets at markets. An antidote to the misery and degradation around her is the satisfaction taken from her painting, from "all that blood of Holofernes drying on the canvas in the Palazzo Pitti. 'I painted it, and it's as if I'd killed a tyrant'" (Artemisia, p. 61).

Artemisia is happy to see her husband again and they make a bedroom out of a room once used to store grain, using a straw mattress on the floor as their bed. In time Artemisia begins to enjoy the unusual experience of living with family comforts. Antonio is kind and devoted. She finds herself beginning to love him, and yet questions the advantages of love at the cost of losing one's identity. She wonders just what passionate love is, and if it is worth the consequences: "That constant internal violence, that suppressing of one's own abilities, limits and preferences?" (Artemisia, p. 74).

In her brother Francesco's studio Artemisia begins painting her vision of the dying Cleopatra. Francesco approaches her with an offer: a Frenchman will provide her with a lovely apartment in Rome in exchange for ten large canvases a year. Feeling threatened, Artemisia's husband, Antonio, begins to bring her more luxurious gifts—a fur blanket, thick rugs, a beautiful armchair, an oil lamp for a table. She feels torn between Antonio's gifts and Francesco's insistence that she accept the apartment. After going to look at it, she tells Antonio she has a surprise. When Antonio hears that she plans to accept the Frenchman's offer, he is shattered. He follows her to her new house but, entirely out of his element, hardly finds the new environment to his liking. He feels extremely uncomfortable.

Important people begin to visit the house. Artemisia acquires patrons and her career continues to blossom, but she and Antonio grow estranged. Meanwhile, her brother keeps helping her and takes pleasure in her success when she receives new commissions. Relations with her husband deteriorate. Artemisia blames Antonio for not making himself more presentable. In spite of herself—because she still loves him and does not want to lose him—she scolds Antonio bitterly, calling him a fool and accusing him of letting her down. After her outburst Artemisia feels dizzy, and before she realizes it, Antonio has left. She fears he will never return.

The writer intervenes once again to comment on Artemisia's tears, and to report that the painter never does see Antonio again. Unbeknownst to him, Artemisia is pregnant with his child.

Francesco persuades his sister to move to Naples where she will have greater opportunities. He helps her pack, but, feeling she needs no one, she decides to go there alone. Artemisia settles in the guest quarters of the convent of the Poor Clares and is treated like a noblewoman. Friendships with the humble nuns cause her to modify her former critical opinion of women. Before this experience she had often thought, "If only I were not a woman" (Artemisia, p. 89). Now she thinks differently:

> Far better to ally herself with the sacrificed and imprisoned, participate in their veiled, momentous fate, share their feelings, their plans, their truths; secrets from which the privileged men were barred.
>
> (Artemisia, p. 89)

As she observes the Neapolitan scene from the convent balcony, she tells herself that unlike the artists of the North, she is not a landscape painter, but she can use landscape as a background for her figures.

After giving birth to her daughter, Porziella, Artemisia leaves the convent and returns to her painting and to teaching art to young painters. There is little time left for her daughter, whom she really looks at only when she needs a model for a cherub. She shrugs off the rumors that circulate about her loose behavior with men. Others criticize her for what seems to be a lack of maternal feeling, but she does not change her ways. In fact, the criticism makes her feel exceptional, like "a woman who has renounced all tenderness, all claim to feminine virtues, in order to dedicate herself solely to painting" (Artemisia, p. 94). She had chosen a solitary life, and at this point has no use for men of any sort—husband, lover, father, or brother.

The writer begins to realize she has lost Artemisia. She had been disrespectful of her memory, playing a cruel game—"the convulsive game of two shipwrecked women who do not want to abandon the hope of being saved on a barrel" (*Artemisia*, p. 109). Perhaps she lost Artemisia when she brushed so lightly over her childhood and could not save her from the tragic events of her life. Now Artemisia is exceedingly distant. The writer admits that it is beyond her powers to bring Artemisia to life after 300 years. It was a mistake to try to share with someone so long dead her own feelings of desolation aroused by the war and her frustrations caused by the exclusion of female artists from the cultural mainstream. But now she has no choice but to keep going to the end.

It is 1638 and Artemisia is busy with commissions. Sometimes she feels happy. Now 45, she has reached the height of her artistic powers and begins to think of herself as old. She must get a dowry together by selling property in Pisa so her daughter can make a good marriage. When Artemisia's father sends for her to join him in England, she makes the arduous journey all alone by carriage and boat, stopping off in Genoa, where she stays a while to paint some portraits. Once she reaches France, Artemisia lingers in Paris for a time, where people on the street seem always to be quarreling. Parisians come to see her paintings.

Artemisia's father meets her in Canterbury, England, and she is very happy to see him. She and the old and ailing Orazio live together, and she takes pleasure in being of some use to him domestically as well as artistically. Her father had been commissioned to paint by different people and Artemisia helps carry out the work. Father and daughter remain together until the awful day of his death. Grieving the loss, Artemisia wonders if any understanding soul in the future will mourn for her.

Afterwards, Artemisia heads back to Naples, the only place that ever seemed like home to her. She imagines numerous ways she herself might die—from the plague, at the hands of bandits, because of an accident. In the end, however, she dies in bed, the only way she had not considered.

A two-tiered picture of historical attitudes toward women in Italy. Banti's dialogue with Artemisia in her novel presents the struggles of a woman artist in her lifetime and the sad neglect of her work after her death, merely because she is a woman and men have been in charge of writing art history. Banti hoped to rectify the bias, even though the status of women in Italy with ambitions outside the norm had not changed much in 300 years—by the Second World War, when Banti was writing the novel.

The attempt by Italian women to gain legal rights to equality with men in education, opportunity, and pay began between Artemisia's and Banti's days, in 1864, with the publication of *La donna ei suoi rapporti sociali* (Woman and Her Social Relationships) by Anna Maria Mozzoni. There were a growing number of organizations and conventions in support of this drive for economic and social equality with men until Benito Mussolini and the Fascist Party came to power in 1922, during Banti's lifetime. Under Mussolini's 22-year regime, women were admonished to focus all their energies on striving to be exemplary wives and mothers. They should limit their work, said the Fascists, to the home or the fields, and if necessity required a woman to work outside the home, she should only fill a position subordinate to men. Education was not deemed important for females in the Fascist era, nor were women considered suitably endowed to be educators. Not until 1945, after the fall of Fascism and the establishment of a democratic government, did Italian women gain the right to vote. Before and after this milestone, women writers were largely ignored in Italy, Banti among them. Anthologies of the mid-twentieth century and later seldom included female writers, their neglect becoming an acknowledged fact. In Banti's day it was difficult for the work of a female author to attract the attention of critics, even if it was generally thought worthy of consideration.

There would be some improvement by the time Banti died in 1985, although the inequity would by no means have disappeared. Even then, she could legitimately complain about the situation for the female artist in particular and for working women in general. While late-twentieth-century Italian women had the freedom to choose careers in politics, business, and professions such as law, they were still highly underrepresented in those fields. According to one historian of the period, "the great majority of women's work was neither managerial nor professional" but service-oriented, with women being hired as "clerks, typists, secretaries, shopworkers, and so on" (Ginsborg, p. 37). Yet gender differences have been gradually narrowing: women are better educated than ever and laws of equal opportunities open up new areas of work. There has been "a spectacular rise in the female presence in some high-status professional jobs. The number of female magistrates, to take just one example, more than doubled between 1985 and 1992, increasing from 852 to 1,791" (Ginsborg, p. 35). The translation of *Artemisia* into English in the middle of this same span testifies to the increasing attention being accorded women writers as well.

Although Banti's novels and short stories, with few exceptions, focus on the barriers women face in a male-dominated society, she "hated" to be called a feminist. Her rather austere personality precluded any public demonstration of solidarity with other women for whatever worthy purpose, and certainly prevented her from taking part in any volunteer activity during the war. When she was reminded that her writings made her position seem clear, Banti defended herself by saying: "[My work] is more a form of humanism than true and proper feminism" (Petrignani, p. 106).

When the writer Grazia Livi mentioned to Banti that feminism had taken on new life in Italy after the war, Banti replied: "Feminism! Again! If you only knew how it irritates me. . . . I thought it was exhausted by now" (Livi, p. 151).

Nevertheless, Banti carried deep inside her the conviction that men were still so dominant in the Italian society of her own day that only the most talented and determined woman could hope for any success, and only after overcoming numerous obstacles put in her way by a wary establishment. Her imaginary conversations with Artemisia gave Banti the opportunity to explore the status of women in two periods of history widely separated in time, yet with enough painful similarities to make them two sisters in art.

Sources and literary context. In 1916 Banti's husband, Roberto Longhi, published an article about the seventeenth-century pair of painters, "Gentileschi padre e figlia" (Gentileschi Father and Daughter) in *L'Arte*. One can assume that this article was at least partially responsible for planting the seed in Banti's mind that would come to fruition as a novel nearly 30 years later.

Setting the outstanding precedent for historical novels in Italy was the first such work to appear, Alessandro Manzoni's **The Betrothed** (*I promessi sposi*, 1840; also in *WLAIT 7: Italian Literature and Its Times*). The novel, which fictionalized events in seventeenth-century Lombardy, became an instant Italian literary classic against which all novels—historical or not—were measured. None of its nineteenth-century successors, all written by men, achieved the status it attained in Italian literature. As Italian women began to write fiction in the mid-nineteenth century (later than their peers in England and America), they tended to produce more subjective works, writing of the pain caused by an inferior status, which they felt helpless to change.

Neera's **Teresa** (1886) and Sibilla Aleramo's **A Woman** (*Una donna*, 1906) are examples (both also in *WLAIT 7: Italian Literature and Its Times*). Banti's novel in the guise of historical fiction started a new trend in writing by Italian women. Banti drew on her own experience in writing *Artemisia*; she identified with the painter in spite of the centuries that separated them, and wanted to form a bond of mutual suffering as female

---

A QUESTION OF GENRE

One could rightly call *Artemisia* a historical novel if Banti's only purpose in writing it were to bring Artemisia's accomplishments to our attention. But this novel teems with her own concerns as a literary artist. Considering its autobiographical characteristics, one wonders how *Artemisia* should be categorized—as a historical novel, a biographical novel, or a fictionalized biography that includes large sections of autobiography?

It is admittedly a fictionalized portrait of Artemisia Gentileschi, but it is also an analysis of Banti's state of mind. Reflecting on *The Betrothed,* Alessandro Manzoni's historical novel, Banti writes that the author of such novels necessarily delves into the past (with a nearly "transcendent memory") in order to rearrange and reinterpret facts analogous to those of one's present (Banti, "La memoria storica," p. 295; trans. M. King). In other words, the thoughts of historical novelists cannot avoid being anchored in their own times. This was certainly the case when Banti wrote *Artemisia*, which aimed to both define what it meant to be a female literary artist in her own time and to reestablish a female painter in official history. As the aims are achieved, the two creative mediums converge: "In Banti's novel, art and writing are major components of the private haven where the self can break the hold of history and destiny" (Lazzaro-Weis, p. 131). In other words, the two mediums are used to liberate the self from patterns of the past and prescriptions for the future. While Banti used the form of the historical novel to help achieve this liberation, the question of *Artemisia's* genre remains open to debate.

---

artists in a world dominated by men. The writer was, in short, as anxious to tell her personal story as she was to depict the life of the neglected female painter. Thus, she juxtaposed the two different time periods, another innovative facet of her fiction.

Banti continued to write through the war years in Italy (1940-45). The first manuscript of *Artemisia,* destroyed at the end of the war, was written at least a year before; her first book of short stories was published in 1937, followed by others in 1940, 1941, and 1942. During her adult life she was entirely involved in the activity of writing and publishing. She said in an interview that she had always been a solitary character, without any need for other people (Petrignani, p. 103).

PAINTINGS BY AND OF ARTEMISIA GENTILESCHI

At Uffizi Museum in Florence
- *Judith Slaying Holofernes* (1620)
- *Saint Catherine* (1614-15)

At Palatino Gallery in the Pitti Palace in Florence
- *Madonna with Child* (1609-10)
- *Judith and the Maidservant* (1613-14)
- *Repentant Magdalene* (1617-20)

At Casa Buonarroti in Florence
- *Allegory of Inclination* (1615)

At Palazzo Cattaneo, or Cattaneo Palace, in Adorno, Genoa
- *Lucrezia* (1621)

At Pinacoteca Nazionale, or National Picture Gallery, in Bologna
- *The Portrait of a Standard-Bearer* (1610)

At the Detroit Institute of Arts
- *Judith and the Maidservant with Head of Holofernes* (1625)

At New York's Metropolitan Museum
- *Esther in the Presence of Ahasuerus* (1622-23)

After the Second World War and after Banti's pioneering novel, Italian women turned to writing historical novels as a way to understand their times and themselves and in an attempt to redress the lack of narrations about women's experience in history. Among the many works in this genre, three have had an especially strong impact on the Italian literary scene: Elsa Morante's **History** (*La storia,* 1974), Maria Bellonci's *Private Renaissance* (*Rinascimento privato,* 1985), and Dacia Maraini's **The Silent Duchess** (*La lunga vita di Marianna Ucrìa,* 1990). (See **His-**

tory and **The Silent Duchess**, also in *WLAIT 7: Italian Literature and Its Times.*)

Reception. *Artemisia* was well received by critics and readers when it appeared in 1947, and it is one of Banti's few works that has remained in print since its initial release (the other is the autobiographical novel *A Piercing Cry* (*Un grido lacerante*). Fixing on the interplay between the distant and the recent past, the important Italian critic Cesare Garboli characterized the novel as "an imaginary diary of two, an intense dialogue beyond Time and History between two women who were artists" (Garboli, p. 175; trans. M. King). Another critic of note, Emilio Cecci, regards *Artemisia* as "a myth of a woman artist whose creative power excluded her from a naive and spontaneous life; though she deeply aspired to forget her femininity she was unable to. It is a myth of the female artist, perhaps more tormented than a man's, and Banti has interpreted it with inimitable grace" (Cecchi, p. 22; trans. M. King).

—Martha King

For More Information

Arico, Santo, ed. *Contemporary Women Writers in Italy: A Modern Renaissance.* Amherst: University of Massachusetts Press, 1990.

Banti, Anna. *Artemisia.* Trans. Shirley D'Ardia Caracciolo. Lincoln: University of Nebraska Press, 1988.

——. "La memoria storica." In *Manzoni e la critica.* Ed. Lanfranco Caretti. Bari, Italy: Laterzi, 1969.

Cecchi, Emilio. "Artemisia Gentileschi." In *Di giorno in giorno.* Milan: Garzanti, 1954.

Garboli, Cesare. "Una signora a scuola da Caravaggio." *L'Espresso,* April 12, 1970, 175.

Garrard, Mary. *Artemisia: The Image of the Female Hero in Baroque Art.* Princeton: Princeton University Press, 1989.

Ginsborg, Paul. *Italy and Its Discontents: 1980-2001.* London: Allen Lane, 2001.

Lazzaro-Weis, Carol. *From Margins to Mainstream: Feminism and Fictional Modes in Italian Women's Writing, 1969-1990.* Philadelphia: University of Pennsylvania, 1993.

Livi, Grazia. *Le lettere del mio nome.* Milan: Tartaruga, 1992.

Ornella, Maria, and Gabriella Brooke, eds. *Gendering Italian Fiction: Feminist Revisions of Italian History.* Madison, N.J.: Fairleigh Dickinson University Press, 1999.

Petrignani, Sandra. *Le signore della scrittura.* Milan: Tartaruga, 1984.

Sontag, Susan. "A Double Destiny." *London Review of Books,* September 25, 2003, 6-9.

Ashes

by

Grazia Deledda

Grazia Deledda was born in 1871 in Nuoro, Sardinia, to Francesca Cambosu and Giovanni Antonio Deledda, a notary and small businessman. Deledda's early life was marked by loss. Two sisters died, one at birth and the other of trachoma at the age of six. Disgrace fell upon another sister, Beppa, when she was abandoned by her fiancé. Deledda's father died in 1892, after which one of her brothers ended up in jail for theft while another, alcoholic brother squandered the rest of the family estate. Despite these tribulations, Deledda achieved a remarkable literary career for a Sardinian woman of her day. In 1926 she became the second Italian writer to receive the Nobel Prize for Literature (after the poet Giosue Carducci in 1906) and the second female Nobel laureate in the world (after Sweden's Selma Lagerlöf in 1909). She reached these heights after schooling herself for the most part by reading classic and contemporary literature at home. Despite the emphatic disapproval of her family, who believed she should embrace only the traditional roles of wife and mother, Deledda turned to writing, publishing her first short stories, "Sulla montagna" (On the Mountain) and "Sangue Sardo" (Sardinian Blood) in 1888 at the age of 17. These were soon followed by a novel, *Stella d'Oriente* (Star of the Orient), published in 1891. Her first novel to become a critical success was *La via di male* (1896; The Evil Way). Three years later Deledda married Palmiro Madesani, an employee of the Department of Finance, with whom she moved to Rome and had two sons.

THE LITERARY WORK

A novel set in Sardinia in 1904; published in Italian (as *Cenere*) in 1904, in English in 1910.

SYNOPSIS

An illegitimate son is haunted by the memory of his mother, who abandoned him to his father. Obsessed with finding her again, he locates the "fallen" woman and resolves to care for her, with tragic results.

Deledda kept writing, producing a total of about 30 novels and more than 400 short stories, articles, poems, and theatrical works. Along with *Ashes*, her most celebrated novels include *Elias Portolu* (1903), *Canne al vento* (1913; Reeds in the Wind), *Marianna Sirca* (1915), and *La madre* (1919; The Mother). Deledda collaborated on the film adaptation of *Ashes*, featuring the famed actress Eleanora Duse, released in 1916. A decade later she won the Nobel Prize for Literature. Just before leaving to accept the award in Stockholm, Deledda learned she had breast cancer, which claimed her life in 1936. In the interim she continued to write. An unfinished fictional autobiography, *Cosima*, was published posthumously in 1937, but elements of her life permeate her other fiction too. In *Ashes*, Deledda sketches a rich portrait of the land, the individuals, and the community that make up her native Sardinia.

Grazia Deledda

Events in History at the
Time of the Novel

Uneasy Unification. In 1861, just a decade before Deledda was born, Italy became a unified kingdom. Spearheading the effort to unify its separate regions was Piedmont-Sardinia, a kingdom born in the northwest portion of the Italian peninsula that seemed thereafter to feel justified in imposing its policies on the rest of Italy. The city of Turin, in Piedmont, became Italy's capital, and it was here that the first parliament met. Partly in an effort to consolidate the fragile new nation, Piedmont extended its organizational apparatus, tariffs, business treaties, and educational and police laws to the entire nation. Northerners in general proceeded to dominate the new government. Not until the early 1900s, when *Ashes* takes place, would its civil service begin to hire many southerners. The result, at first in Naples and other parts of the southern mainland, even more so on the island of Sardinia, was a general regional mistrust of civil society.

Located southwest of the peninsula, in the Mediterranean Sea, the island of Sardinia proved to be one of the most difficult regions to assimilate into the new Italian nation. Sardinians themselves referred to the main peninsula as "the Continent," acknowledging their cultural and physical separation from the rest of Italy. Due to

the isolation of their island, which is cut off from the mainland by the Tyrrhenian Sea, the exchange of ideas between it and other regions lagged years behind areas situated on the peninsula. This did not bother the authorities of the Kingdom of Piedmont-Sardinia when it existed; its officials had treated Sardinia with indifferent tolerance. Suddenly this changed. Italy's new government actively exercised its authority on the island. Officials centralized the government administration in Sardinia and initiated a large-scale effort to "teach and modernize" the islanders, with the intent of creating a homogenous Italian identity. However, the new government failed to adequately address many of the economic and social problems unique to the island (e.g., an out-dated education system and various sanitation issues), making the integration of Sardinia into the new nation an exceedingly long and complex process.

Sardinia around 1900—economy and society. Though swept into the fold of Italy's new centralized government 30 years earlier, Sardinia continued to be plagued by economic tribulations at the turn of the twentieth century. The island's per capita earnings from 1901 to 1903 were the lowest in the nation, surpassing the poverty of the historically disadvantaged southern regions of the peninsula. One of the obstacles to economic growth was a lack of funding: the federal government typically provided less money for land improvements in Sardinia than on the mainland. There were other impediments too. Nature militated against economic success. Much of the island—around the town of Nuoro, for example—is mountainous and so not amenable to cultivation. Between 1883 and 1903, the year before the novel takes place, this was compounded by natural disaster: a phylloxera infestation destroyed large tracts of Sardinia's grape vines. Wool remained the dominant export, but the shepherds earned little profit from their herds because the under-industrialized island had to send the wool elsewhere to be manufactured. Those who processed and distributed the material were the ones who received the real profits.

Despite all these obstacles, there were some economic gains on Sardinia after Unification. The production of cheese became a major industry in the 1890s, when *pecorino sardo* (cheese from sheep's milk) grew enormously popular in the Americas. Also, olive mills (and their production of olive oil) continued to constitute an important part of the economy. Following Unification, the federal government created new jobs to construct a railroad and roads that would connect previously isolated Sardinian towns. The mining of zinc and lead also boosted the island economy. Although most Sardinians were farmers and shepherds (73.9 percent in 1880; 56.8 percent in 1921), government mines provided many male islanders with work (Sanna, p. 244).

Unfortunately, the Sardinian mining industry was not without problems. Boys 11 and older were allowed to perform tasks inside the mines. Working conditions were abysmal; the miners endured long hours at dangerous sites. The majority of the miners joined unions and participated in the national workers' movement sweeping Italy. In fact, the first national strike in Italian history had its impetus in an event that took place in Buggerru, Sardinia, in 1904. The director of the Buggerru mining site informed his laborers that the winter work schedule would be imposed at the beginning of September, which meant they would be denied their usual three-hour break from toiling in the intense afternoon heat and would have to work an extra hour each day. A crowd gathered as the miners quarreled with the director's decision. In the ensuing chaos, three workers were shot and killed by the authorities, and the news of their deaths prompted workers around the country to strike.

Strangely enough, the workers' movement never united with the struggling peasant class in Sardinia as it did elsewhere around Italy and Europe. The island had its own social profile; unlike other areas, Sardinia did not have a distinctive class system at the end of the nineteenth century. Economic obstacles, like the destruction of crops and inability to manufacture wool on the island mentioned above, meant both landowners and dependents struggled to survive. Since the small landholder did not earn much more than the peasants who worked his land or the shepherds who tended his flock, lines between classes were often blurred. Rather than distinct classes, the economic structure of Sardinia seemed to be comprised of ranks, with miniscule differences between them. From "bottom" to "top," the ranks rose from farmhand, up to artisan, small merchants and small landowners, and then, after a sizable gap, up to government employees and the military, large landowners, and finally the peak of businessmen and professionals. Most at the peak, the professors and doctors, for example, were foreigners, who moved to Sardinia from the Continent.

The problems of sanitation and education. The economic struggles of Sardinia at the turn of the twentieth century were accompanied by halting progress in public sanitation and education. Due to limited health care and unsanitary living conditions, Sardinia's mortality rate remained higher than in the rest of Italy. Three illnesses were largely responsible for deaths on the island: malaria (although an effective remedy, quinine, was discovered in 1900); trachoma, a contagious illness of the eye often causing blindness followed by death; and tuberculosis, a serious danger at the start of the twentieth century. Meanwhile, there were fewer health-care professionals on the island than on the mainland. Also the island lacked modern sewage systems. People still drew their daily water supply from rivers and streams, and drinkable water was scarce. Even cemeteries became sanitation hazards, due to the practice of burying the dead without coffins.

THE CULTURE OF BANDITRY

Sardinia has a long history of *brigantaggio*, or brigandage. Under ancient Roman rule, the island became a holding ground for convicts, political dissidents, and Jews. Many of these "offenders" were confined in a large prison in the mountains overlooking Nuoro. Others escaped and formed a resistance movement in the mountains among the ancient stone ruins called *nuraghe*. These mysterious, dome-shaped dwellings have fascinated Sardinians for centuries; like a character in *Ashes*, many think that the original inhabitants or later bandits may have buried treasures near these ruins.

Brigantaggio continued to flourish on the island, due to lack of confidence in the justice system and the absence of a strong government authority. Its age-old, intermittent bandit culture resurfaced after the Act of Closure of 1820. A set of drastic land reforms, it ended the feudal system in Sardinia, parceled out uncultivated land to what would become the new middle class, and introduced strict property regulations and taxes. The reforms led to intense conflicts among the new landowners, farmhands, and shepherds, which they set out to settle themselves. At the end of the nineteenth century, around the time of the novel, Sardinia had the second-highest homicide rate in Italy, after Sicily (Sanna, p. 245).

Another health concern was the sparse diet. For most of the island dwellers, daily meals consisted primarily of bread (or orzo, a barley-like pasta popular in mountainous regions like Nuoro),

Nuraghe Su Nuraxi, c. 1500 B.C.E., near Barumini, Sardinia. An example of the ancient *nuraghe* hill forts.

potatoes, legumes, thin soups, and cheese. Sardinians rarely ate meat, although shepherds sometimes slaughtered a sick lamb or elderly goat to celebrate for special occasions. The inhabitants of coastal fishing towns were able to supplement this modest diet with fish, but it was uncommon for people in the central regions of Sardinia to have access to this additional staple.

Education on the island was woefully inadequate and Unification did little to improve the system. The new Italian government supplied less than half the funding for education to Sardinia than to Lombardy, for instance. In 1888, primary education became compulsory for three years, but especially in the South the law was practiced more in the breach than the observance. Truancy often exceeded 80 percent in the region; certainly most Sardinians never attended school, so it is hardly surprising that their illiteracy rate was 68.3 percent in 1901 (Clark, pp. 36-37). Here as elsewhere a difficulty facing the educational system was the post-Unification linguistic shift from the local dialect to standardized Italian. Progress was slow in this regard: half the elementary schools in Sardinia still used dialect as the primary language of instruction in 1910 (Marrocu and Brigaglia, p. 49). Females were at an extra disadvantage. The extent of their education was limited; at the end of the nineteenth century, and for most girls, even later,

they could still only attend up to four years of elementary school. Female students of the early 1900s could continue beyond elementary school *if* they trained to become schoolteachers.

Despite the underdeveloped school system, Sardinia saw the burgeoning of a small intellectual class in the late 1800s. New periodicals such as *L'unione sarda* (The Sardinian Union) and *La nuova Sardegna* (The New Sardinia) found a loyal readership among these scholars. While the isolated nature of the island community had previously slowed the transfer of progressive ideas from the Continent to Sardinia, in 1882 a new rail/ferry line connecting Terranova, Sardinia, and Civitavecchia (a port northwest of Rome) facilitated the spread of such ideas. New possibilities for faster, easier travel between the island and the mainland opened another environment to the Sardinian intellectuals; some of the more serious students even availed themselves of the opportunity to study at the university in Rome. These scholars often felt torn between two worlds—the old-fashioned, cherished traditions of their roots and the urban modernity in which they immersed themselves on the Continent. In the end, intellectual success for many Sardinians around the time the novel takes place depended on a physical—and often mental—separation from their homeland.

The role of women, religion, and folklore. At the start of the twentieth century, women were not expected to venture into intellectual or professional activities outside the role of homemaker. The limited public education they received was adequate in preparing them to carry out their principal functions in Sardinian society: raising a family, tending the home, gathering herbs and figs for cooking, and cultivating the family garden. Additionally many peasant women contributed to the household income by sewing, basket weaving, harvesting olives, planting vegetables, or traveling from village to village selling fruit or eggs. In contrast to these peasant wives, middle- and upper-class women were becoming "modernized" at the turn of the century, attending high school and taking up diverse pastimes such as painting, playing musical instruments, singing, and writing.

Although the activities of Sardinian peasant women were limited at the time, they played a key social role. One of their main functions was to pass down traditional beliefs and codes of behavior through oral storytelling. In the warmer seasons, women in various Sardinian towns could be found sitting by the doorstep, gossiping about recent events in the village and telling colorful folkloric tales. Grazia Deledda provides a thorough review of Sardinian customs and folklore in *Tradizioni popolari di Sardegna* (1895, *Popular Traditions of Sardinia*), first published as a series of articles in *Rivista delle tradizioni popolari italiane* (Journal of Italian Popular Traditions) in 1894. The collection emphasizes the mix of superstition, folklore, and Catholicism that made up the religion practiced by inhabitants in her native town of Nuoro.

According to Deledda, women would kneel or sit on the floor of the church during the Holy Mass, while the men sat in the wooden pews. The congregation often prayed aloud during the Mass, sometimes saying a rosary while the priest prayed or preached. Parishioners usually prayed in the dialect spoken in Nuoro (called *Lugodoro*), although sometimes they recited parts of the Mass in Latin, a language that most of them did not actually understand. Women donated money, rings, and other jewelry to the saints, and sometimes even crawled on their knees through church when making a votive offering. Men, women, and children often made pilgrimages, especially on saints' days. At times, the most devout journeyed barefoot, and slept outside or in makeshift huts once they had reached their destination. Large bonfires were often part of the celebration, providing the pilgrims with both warmth and a place to gather and swap stories.

The majority of the inhabitants of Nuoro believed in miracles and other supernatural occurrences. It was custom for religious women to wear crosses, medallions, relics, cords, and amulets called *rezettas*. The devout also used blessed palms and wax to create holy crosses and other talismans that were then worn or hung over beds for protection. Short prayers or chants, involving remedies as well as curses, testify to the superstitious nature of many late-nineteenth-century Sardinians. Deledda devotes a full section of her book on Sardinian customs to these *berbos*, or remedies and curses; spoken mantras, they ranged from chants to keep foxes from damaging a farmer's grapes to chants aimed at causing a pregnant woman to miscarry.

The Sardinians' devotion to religion—however much infused with myth and superstition—revealed itself in the importance placed on chastity in women (though a husband's infidelity was deemed acceptable). According to Deledda, the people of Nuoro placed utmost value on female honesty and purity around the turn of the twentieth century, and few wives committed adultery. In keeping with the religious teachings of their society, Sardinians viewed chastity as one of the greatest virtues of women, and promiscuity as one of their greatest sins. But, as in other Italian regions, the young women of Sardinia began to act more liberally towards the end of the 1800s. In Deledda's words, more and more of its young women were becoming "stained by the gloomiest notoriety that can darken a woman's name"—the reference here is to the shame heaped on any woman who had sexual relations with a man outside marriage (Deledda, *Tradizioni*, p. 258; trans. V. Mirshak). For the increase in promiscuity among young women, Deledda blames both the changing times and the inability of fathers and brothers—too overwhelmed by the burdens of everyday survival—to defend the honor of a daughter or sister as actively as they had in the past.

The Novel in Focus

Plot summary. The novel begins at nightfall on St. John's Day as a 15-year-old peasant, Olì, awaits the arrival of her lover, the farmer Ananias. The young girl ventures into the fields surrounding her family's small home under the pretense of gathering flowers and herbs for the feast day. Ananias, a dreamer who fantasizes about one day discovering ancient treasure among the area's *nuraghe* (stone ruins) promises Olì they will marry once he finds his fortune. In reality, the farmer is already married. When Olì becomes pregnant as a result of the lovers' tryst, her father, a railway signalman, disowns her for having brought dishonor upon the family.

Discovering the plight of his lover, Ananias brings Olì to live with one of his distant relatives in the mountainous town of Fonni, where he then abandons her. The relative, Zia Grathia, takes the expectant mother under her wing, and baby Ananias is born shortly thereafter. Little Ananias spends his early childhood roaming the woods with Zia Grathia's son, Zuanne, who at age 11 has already become a shepherd. Every night, the two boys eagerly gather at the hearth to listen to Zia Grathia recount dark tales of her late husband's life of banditry. The widow claims that bandits aren't bad people; they are "just guys who have to express their talents" (Deledda, *Ashes*, p. 31). The bandit's old black cloak hangs prominently on a wall of the humble dwelling, presiding ominously as a lasting testament to the violent life and death of Zuanne's father.

ST. JOHN'S FEAST DAY

St. John's Day is one of four important Catholic feast days that divide the liturgical year into quarters (the others are Christmas, Lady's Day [the Annunciation], and Michaelmas). Commemorating the death of St. John the Baptist, his feast day falls on June 24, just days after the summer solstice. At the time *Ashes* was written, people from many countries celebrated St. John's Eve by gathering herbs for medicinal purposes and by building a large bonfire and burning old sacramental cloths in it. The resulting ashes were often blessed and kept for Holy Masses throughout the year. Legend warns of the danger of falling in love on St. John's Eve. In some regions, folklore claims that single women can tell whether or not they will soon marry by hanging St. John's wort over their beds on this eve; if the plant is still fresh the next morning, they will marry within a year. Another tradition directs a single woman to mark a plant in the ground on St. John's Day. The type of insect on its leaves the next day will reveal the occupation of her future husband.

When Ananias is seven years old, Olì brings him on a day-long journey to Nuoro. Before leaving their home, the mother places a pouch-shaped cloth amulet around the boy's neck, in-

structing him to always keep it close to his heart. Once they arrive in Nuoro, Olì sends him into an olive mill and directs him to state his name to the men inside. Meanwhile, the mother slips away, abandoning little Ananias to his father. While "Big Ananias" is outraged that Olì has left their son with him, his wife, Zia Tatàna, welcomes the boy into her home. Ananias grows to love his stepmother and even to understand his father, who treats him brusquely in public and kisses him goodnight when he believes him to be asleep. Together with his new friend Bustianeddu, Ananias explores the town of Nuoro and spends time at the olive mill, where at night many of the workers grow drunk, laugh, curse, and dance. The boy's new life is colored with various tragicomic characters: Efes Cau, a rich landowner ruined by alcoholism; Nanna, a friend of the family, also perpetually inebriated; Zio Pera, the elderly farmer with a penchant for young girls; Agatha, the beautiful bartender; and Rebecca, a chronic invalid who lives in abject poverty. Although Ananias thrives in his new setting, he is often haunted by the memory of his life in Fonni and of the mother who abandoned him. He dreams of some day traveling to Rome, where he believes his mother to be living. When Ananias performs well in school and speaks of his desire to study law on the Continent, Signor Carboni, a distinguished gentleman who is both the landowner for whom Ananias's father labors and the mayor of Nuoro, offers to pay for the boy's education once he has finished his elementary schooling in town. Ananias has by this time fallen in love with Carboni's daughter, Margherita. Before leaving for high school in Cagliari, the capital of Sardinia, the young man discovers that his romantic feelings are reciprocated.

While studying in Cagliari, Ananias exchanges love letters with Margherita and dreams of their future together. However, even as he pines for Margherita, as he attends the university in Rome, the young man grows ever more obsessed with finding his mother. The son is haunted by the thought that he could encounter her on the Continent and fears that she may be prostituting herself to survive. If this is the case, Ananias decides, it would be his filial duty to take Olì in and to provide her with an escape from her life of sin and poverty. However, such a course of action would surely end things between him and Margherita, who considers herself too pure to live alongside a former prostitute. Ananias himself expresses the impossibility of having both

Margherita and his fallen mother in his life when he later asks Zia Grathia, "Surely you don't think that a pure and delicate young girl can live near a fallen woman?" (*Ashes*, p. 182). So intense is the young man's fear of finding his mother and having to provide for her that he sometimes wishes to discover that she has died.

In Rome, Ananias becomes the boarder of a Sardinian woman with a mysterious past. He entertains the possibility that she could be Olì, taking momentary comfort in the thought that his mother could now be leading a respectable life renting out rooms in the city. Upon his return to Nuoro for summer vacation, Ananias sends Zia Tatàna to ask Signor Carboni's permission for an engagement between Ananias and Margherita. His benefactor blesses the union; the engagement, he says, can become official following the student's graduation.

Overjoyed, Ananias sets out to Fonni to visit Zia Grathia, the old widow in whose home he spent the first seven years of his life. Joy turns to anxiety when he learns from her that his mother has returned to Fonni, disgraced and physically ill after traveling for years with different men. The widow arranges a mother-and-son reunion, at which both become emotionally distraught. The son grows violently angry, proclaiming it his duty to care for Olì and forbidding her to leave him again. When he writes Margherita that his mother will soon be living with him, his fiancée breaks their engagement. After returning home, he follows-up on Zia Grathia's instructions to him before he left Fonni to send his cloth amulet back to his mother in a colored handkerchief if Margherita refuses him.

Upon his return to Zia Grathia's house, Ananias finds that Olì has committed suicide. Horrified at the tragic sight of his mother's slit throat, the mourning son opens the tiny sack amulet she gave him 15 years earlier. Upon discovering it to be filled with ashes, he finds a glimmer of hope: "he remembered that often there is a spark among the ashes—the beginnings of a bright, purifying flame. And he hoped. And he loved life again" (*Ashes*, p. 217).

The dilemma of maternity and self-sacrifice.
Given that *Ashes* centers on a son who suffers the sins of his mother, it is startling that the novel concludes with a complete reversal: the son is the one to ultimately destroy his mother, and a self-sacrificing mother at that. It is Olì's final selfless act that liberates Ananias socially and emotionally. The role reversal of victim and violator begins when a grown-up Ananias first finds Olì

in Fonni; almost immediately, he becomes openly hostile towards his mother. Deledda uses the image of a beastly predator to describe Ananias during this disturbing encounter. Olì is so frightened by her son's aggressive behavior that the widow Zia Grathia finds it necessary to reassure the trembling woman: "After all, he's not going to devour you; he's the flesh of your flesh" (*Ashes*, p. 191). In the end, however, Olì's son does destroy her, albeit indirectly. The news of his broken engagement fills her with a desire to protect her son: "A thirst for self-sacrifice devoured her"; she, not he, is thus devoured (*Ashes*, p. 197). Olì's need to sacrifice herself for the happiness of her son is relayed by a verb (*divorare*— "to devour") that emphasizes the instinctual, animalistic, even detrimental qualities at the base of this mother-child relationship. The language conveys a negative view of maternity as self-destructive.

Deledda was not the only woman writer in Italy to rebel against the maternity cult at the time of *Ashes*' publication. Around the turn of the twentieth-century female writers in Italy began to emphasize the equality of the sexes and to refute their limitation to the maternal role. Regina di Luanto, Anna Franchi, Carola Prosperi, and Sibilla Aleramo are women whose novels reveal a certain antagonism towards conventional ideas about motherhood in Deledda's day.

In light of its dramatic and violent conclusion, *Ashes* would seem to fall neatly into the category of works by women that denounce the traditional maternal role. Deledda, however, declares her independence from any circle of dedicated feminist writers, and her corpus as a whole reveals the ambiguity of her views on motherhood. Although *Ashes* appears to be influenced by the feminist stirrings of the era, Deledda not only claimed to be detached from these contemporary debates but also spoke of herself as belonging to the past. Whether or not the feminist thinking of her age affected Deledda's writing, the concluding images of *Ashes* reveal tremendous compassion towards women who find themselves trapped in a destructive pattern of unmitigated self-sacrifice for the benefit of their children.

Sources and literary context.
While there is no evidence that a specific event in the life of Grazia Deledda inspired *Ashes*, the author drew from her experiences growing up in Nuoro, Sardinia, when writing most of her works. The isolated mountain village, with its colorful, rustic inhabitants, serves as the novel's primary setting, although Ananias spends his young childhood

in the town of Fonni and later attends high school in Cagliari and college in Rome. This latter part of the protagonist's journey, from his native island of Sardinia to the Continent, is perhaps the closest link between the novel and the author's life. Deledda's firsthand experience of travel outside Nuoro, to Cagliari in 1899 and to Rome the following year, is most likely the source of inspiration for Ananias's journey. Although the novelist did not finally return to her native island as her protagonist does, Deledda clearly understood the cultural and emotional struggles of the Sardinian intellectual abroad, torn between the centuries-old traditions of his homeland and the progressive modernization of continental Italy.

DELEDDA'S "SECRET"

"When I began to write, was I not using those materials which were at hand? If I continued to use this material for the rest of my life it is because I knew who I was when I grew up, tied as I was to my people: and my soul was linked with theirs, and when I peered into my characters' souls it was into my own soul that I was looking and all the agonies that I have told on thousands of pages in my novels were my own suffering, my own pain, my own tears shed in my tragic adolescence. This is my secret!"

(Deledda in Balducci, p. 3)

The literary climate of Italy and of the entire European community at the time of the publication of *Ashes* was one of great change and transformation. From the mid-1800s through the beginning of the twentieth century, literary movements were in constant flux, sometimes merging into and often clashing against one another. Unlike most of the well-known European writers of her day, Deledda did not openly identify with any one literary school of thought, and it is impossible to pinpoint just one school that encompasses her entire corpus. Instead novels like *Ashes* contain elements of various literary trends, from Romanticism, to the Italian form of naturalism known as *verismo*, to the Decadent tradition. Deledda's penchant for passionate, sentimental encounters between characters, as well as their struggles with religion and tradition, is decidedly Romantic. Other aspects of *Ashes*—its

regional settings, attention to details of everyday life, and use of verisimilar dialogue—can be viewed as examples of *verismo*. At the same time, Deledda resembles writers of Italy's Decadent tradition as she delves into the subconscious struggles of her characters, often showing more sympathy for them than for the restrictive mores of her society.

Reviews. While little is known about the critical reception accorded to *Ashes* in particular, Deledda's works usually enjoyed great popularity with the reading public, whose interest only increased when she received the Nobel Prize for Literature in 1926. Her success with readers at the turn of the century was most likely due to the boom of regionalist literature in Europe, as well as Deledda's knack for depicting the universal dimension of human struggles.

Given the rapidly changing literary context of her time, Deledda's works baffled many critics, such as Arnoldo Bocelli and Eurialo De Michelis, who could not decide in which "-ism" to categorize her writing. In fact, countless reviews of her works debated the genre of her novels, without evaluating the works in total. The inability to identify her school of thought led to a reevaluation of literary criticism in general in Italy. The well-known critic Pietro Pancrazi acknowledged her monumental effect: "Italian literary criticism is in debt to Grazia Deledda" (Pancrazi in Rapisarda, p. 25; trans. A. Boylan).

Just as critics disagreed about Deledda's school of thought, they debated her prowess as a writer. Benedetto Croce and Renato Serra both found her writing "tiresome," "repetitious," and "mediocre"; at the same time, Serra believed that she should be taken seriously and admired her ability to aptly describe the travails of humanity (Soru, p. 84). Luigi Capuana, a renowned author of the *verista* tradition, lauded Deledda for presenting her readers with a realistic regional portrait of Sardinia. Attilio Momigliano compared her works to those of Leo Tolstoy and Fyodor Dostoevsky, identifying similar themes of sin and expiation in the novels of all three writers. Deledda won praise too from translators and scholars abroad: from Edmond Haguenin in France, Henrik Schück in Sweden, D. H. Lawrence in England, and Joseph Kennard in the United States. Disputes among literary critics of her day aside, perhaps most unarguably Grazia Deledda's Nobel Prize for Literature attests to the immense success that her writing achieved at home and abroad.

—Valerie Mirshak

For More Information

Amoia, Alba. *No Mothers We!: Italian Women Writers and Their Revolt Against Maternity*. New York: University Press of America, 2000.

Balducci, Carolyn. *A Self-Made Woman: Biography of Nobel-Prize-Winner Grazia Deledda*. Boston: Houghton-Mifflin, 1975.

Clark, Martin. *Modern Italy*. London: Longman, 1996.

Deledda, Grazia. *Ashes*. Trans. Jan Kozma. London: Associated University Presses, 2004.

———. *Tradizioni popolari di Sardegna*. Ed. Dolores Turchi. Rome: Newton Compton, 1995.

Levy, Carl, ed. *Italian Regionalism*. Washington, D.C.: Berg, 1996.

Marrocu, Luciano, and Manlio Brigaglia. "Società e cultura nella Sardegna di fine Ottocento: Note per una ricerca." In *Grazia Deledda nella cultura contemporanea*. Vol. 1. Nuoro, Sardinia: Consorzio per la pubblica lettura "S. Satta," 1992.

Offen, Karen. "Liberty, Equality, and Justice for Women: The Theory and Practice of Feminism in Nineteenth-Century Europe." In *Becoming Visible: Women in European History*. Boston: Houghton Mifflin, 1987.

Rapisarda, Serafina. "Grazia Deledda alla luce della critica straniera." *Procellaria: Rassegna di Varia Cultura* 16, no. 1 (1968): 25-28.

Saladino, Salvatore. *Italy from Unification to 1919: Growth and Decay of a Liberal Regime*. New York: Thomas Y. Crowell, 1970.

Sanna, Natale. "Dal 1870 alla prima guerra mondiale." In *La società in Sardegna nei secoli*. Turin: ERI, 1967.

Soru, Luigi. "Grazia Deledda e la critica." *Cenobio: Rivista Trimestrale di Cultura* 19 (1970): 83-89.

The Betrothed

by

Alessandro Manzoni

Alessandro Manzoni (1785-1873) was born in Milan to Giulia Beccaria, the free-spirited daughter of the famous criminologist, Cesare Beccaria (see **On Crimes and Punishments,** also in WLAIT 7: Italian Literature and Its Times). Officially Manzoni's father was Pietro Manzoni, Giulia's husband and a conservative who was 17 years her senior. There is much speculation that Beccaria's actual father was Giovanni Verri, a prominent liberal intellectual. In any case, Giulia eventually eloped with the well-known Milanese banker Carlo Imbonati. Alessandro experienced a rather unstable childhood of wet nurses, boarding schools, and traveling back and forth between Paris and Milan, but he adored his new father figure, Imbonati. His time in Paris, as well as the French occupation of Milan (under Napoleon Bonaparte), greatly influenced young Manzoni, providing him the opportunity to meet and study many great European cultural figures of the day. The time he spent at his paternal family's property near Lake Como also left a strong impression, as reflected in his description of the region in The Betrothed. In 1808 Manzoni married Enrichetta Blondel—the daughter of a Swiss banker and a devout, puritanical Protestant. Manzoni himself was raised with atheistic beliefs. Soon after the marriage, he and his wife converted to Catholicism. Of their ten children, eight died during Manzoni's lifetime.

Manzoni wrote poetry, fiction, plays, and treatises on language, literature, and religion. Already famous in Europe as a poet (for "March 1821"

THE LITERARY WORK

A novel set in Lombardy, northern Italy, in 1628-30; definitive version published in Italian (as *I promessi sposi*) in 1840, in English in 1844.

SYNOPSIS

An evil nobleman interferes with a couple's wedding plans; to escape his reach, the two part and go on adventures that intersect with some of the most harrowing events to occur in early-seventeenth-century Lombardy.

and "The Fifth of May"), he began to write his only novel, The Betrothed, in 1821. The first version appeared in 1828. Dissatisfied with the novel's language, which Manzoni thought was too reliant on Milanese dialect and French influences, he spent most of the next decade rewriting it in the Tuscan vernacular, and the definitive version appeared in 1840. It enjoyed such widespread popularity that the novel helped establish the Tuscan dialect as the national language that Italy so desperately needed to become a unified culture and country. When Manzoni died, he was celebrated with a state funeral honoring him as the father of the modern Italian language. Giuseppe Verdi composed a requiem for the occasion. Manzoni's masterpiece, The Betrothed, is hailed as Italy's first modern novel. A work that portrays the impact of large historical events on ordinary people, it also promotes a view of Christianity

Alessandro Manzoni

based on justice and brotherhood with the aim of influencing society at large. The novelist furthermore set out to create a sense of national sentiment that would unite Italians against their foreign rulers.

Events in History at the Time the Novel Takes Place

Spanish occupation of Milan: the political side. The French and the Spanish battled for control of the Italian Peninsula at the end of the fifteenth century. Ludivico Sforza triggered the wars by inviting the French into Italy in 1494, then lost control of the duchy of Milan to the French and ended up a prisoner in France. The struggle continued. In 1525 the Spanish ruler Charles V (part of the Habsburg dynasty) conquered Milan. Charles left the last Sforza duke (Francesco II) as nominal ruler of Milan until the duke's death in 1535, at which point the government reverted to Charles V as its overlord. Along with Naples, Sicily, and Sardinia, the duchy of Milan was incorporated into the Spanish Empire in Italy until the demise of this empire in 1707. In sum, the Spanish governed the duchy for most of two centuries (1535-1706). Many historians consider this period the nadir in social and political life in the region of Lombardy.

After the Spanish victory, relative peace descended on Milan for much of the remaining six-

teenth century. However, in the early years of the seventeenth century, disputes began to erupt again, and the region was plunged into 60 years of intermittent battle. Wars over small strategic territories broke out in northern Italy as old rivals saw a chance to take revenge on enemies or annex new land by siding with France, Spain, or Austria. When in 1628 Spain and Austria learned that there was a French-friendly duke being groomed to take over the duchy of Mantua—a territory that bordered the duchy of Milan to the southeast—the Spanish and Austrians banded together to install a duke more friendly to Spain. The partnership soon foundered, though. Austria upset the alliance when it claimed the right to choose the successor to the dukedom and then sent in 36,000 troops to seize Mantua. The problem was eventually settled in 1630 when a French duke (the duke of Nevers) was allowed to rule on the condition that he swore allegiance as a vassal of the Austrian Empire.

In 1700 Charles II, the last of the Spanish Habsburgs, died. His death, along with the fact that Spain for various reasons found it difficult to stand up militarily to other European powers, especially France, provoked a continent-wide conflict: The War of the Spanish Succession (1702-13), involving France, Austria, Spain, and England. The regions of Italy, contested territories, were parceled out to the victors. In the Treaty of Utrecht (1713), Austria acquired Lombardy and the Kingdom of Naples as part of its spoils.

Spanish occupation of Milan: the social side. With respect to the area's growth, the seventeenth century was unremarkable in contrast to the previous 50 years, during which the population had risen so precipitously (from 40,000 in 1530 to 100,000 in 1580) that Milan became Italy's second largest city after Rome. In order to both protect and sustain itself in such an environment, the Spanish government began to levy heavy taxes on its subjects, which kept the economy depressed and aggravated the divide between rich and poor. A world recession in the 1620s compounded the difficulties, destroying Italian industry. In Milan the number of silk looms—a mainstay of the Lombard economy—fell from 3,000 in 1606 to 600 in 1635 (Duggan, p. 71). Unemployment increased rapidly. There was what some historians call a "refeudalization" of society, especially in the countryside: "the reappearance of a whole array of privileges, prerogatives, abuses, and shackles . . . at the hands of the landed nobility with the result that peasant conditions experienced a slow, but continuous deterioration" (Sella, p. 63). This "refeudalization"—a term used by historians to describe this particular moment in Milanese history—had less to do with the economic system than with reinstating a rigid social hierarchy that emphasized "noble" behavior—manners, dress, titles, etiquette, and language. Milan under the Sforza family—the rulers before the Spanish—had seen a sharp distinction between the nobility and the lower classes, and this only intensified under the Spanish. With the Spanish came a sense and show of privilege as well as far heavier taxes on farmers and merchants that resulted in an even more highly stratified society. At the top were the Spanish governors and the native Milanese nobles, whom the Spanish allowed to stay in their privileged positions. The local nobility, behaving as in past centuries, in effect betrayed the poorer Milanese, treating them just as badly as the Spanish. While many lowly urbanites and farmers staved off starvation, thievery, and other hardships as best they could, the rich lived decadent lives throwing lavish parties and balls. Manzoni sought to portray this gaping inequity, which was even more pronounced in the seventeenth century than in his own nineteenth century.

Aggravating conditions in the sixteenth century was the fact that the concepts of brotherhood and equality were rarely acted upon at the time, especially in the corrupt Church, where the behavior of the clergy was oftentimes as appalling as that of crooked politicians and selfish aristocrats. In *The Betrothed*, Manzoni portrays both sides of the clergy. Brother Cristoforo, a monk, is the epitome of self-sacrifice and service to the helpless and poor while the actions of the Don Abbondio, a weak-minded local priest, show him to be a virtual accomplice of oppressive power.

A string of disasters—famine, riots and plague. Famines struck frequently in Lombardy in the first half of the seventeenth century. While hunger was the norm for commoners and life expectancy was generally low—there was a one-third infant mortality rate and only half of the population survived past the age of 20—some years were worse than others (Cavalazzi and Falchi, p. 85). A famine led to major grain riots in 1628, and then another famine a year later resulted in a 97 percent increase in the prices of bread, rice, and wine, among other perishables. There followed a devastating outbreak of the plague, carried into the region by the imperial soldiers of Austria, who passed through Lombardy on the way to fight against the duchy of Mantua. In Milan, the plague, which is the back-

Portrait of Holy Roman Emperor Charles V with his hunting dog. Painting by Titian c. 1532.

drop to so many of *The Betrothed*'s chapters, killed much of the population. According to Manzoni's sources, the disease claimed more than half the inhabitants; later sources contend that it claimed less than half (under 60,000 of a total 130,000), but the loss in any case was devastatingly high. And the epidemic spread through northern Italy, striking thousands more (1629-33). In Milan, as elsewhere, the *lazzaretto*, the hospital for those with contagious diseases, was stuffed to capacity with victims.

The Novel in Focus

Plot summary. The novel tells an essentially simple story of Renzo Tramaglino, a weaver, and Lucia Mondello, two young peasants whose marriage plans are disrupted by the feudal lord, a Spaniard named Don Rodrigo. Intertwined with the main storyline of their adventures are the tales of many other characters and a sweeping historical view of life in seventeenth-century Lombardy.

The first part of the novel takes place over four days (November 7-10, 1628) in the town where Renzo and Lucia live. Don Abbondio, a small-time parish priest, is walking through the idyllic countryside when he finds himself confronted by two thugs, called *bravi*, who work for the local feudal lord, Don Rodrigo. Don Rodrigo has been eyeing Lucia for himself. He wants to prevent her marriage and abduct her for his own pleasure—which he sees as his right since he is the local feudal lord. So, with the help of his *bravi,* he warns the priest not to marry the couple. The *bravi* manage to intimidate Don Abbondio into putting off the wedding, even though this goes against Catholic law. When Renzo realizes he is being stalled, he schemes with Lucia's mother to force the priest's hand by appealing to a clever lawyer, only to learn that the law is not set up to help poor, honest people and is as corrupt as the Spanish nobility. At this point Lucia's mother asks for help from Brother Cristoforo, a Capuchin monk. Armed with little more than his religious beliefs and sense of moral justice, the monk will turn into an effective family protector. The novel segues into a flashback on the background of the monk, who was once a wealthy merchant's son, then returns to the present to follow him as he makes plans to help Renzo and Lucia flee. In the meantime, Lucia's mother has another plan: if Renzo and Lucia can get into the house of the priest, Don Abbondio, and declare themselves husband and wife before him and two witnesses, they will in effect be married according to the laws of the Catholic Church established at the Council of Trent (before which, clandestine marriages were permitted and recognized). They accomplish half the plan, but just as the two are about to say the important words, Don Abbondio runs off through the village screaming about the dirty trick that has been played on him. At this point, it is decided that Renzo and Lucia must flee the village to escape Don Rodrigo's vengeance. Renzo goes to Milan, and Lucia takes refuge in a convent in Monza, a city about 10 miles outside Milan.

The novel's second and third sections, which unfold over a few months, treat the separate hardships of Renzo and Lucia while the two are apart. Just after Lucia and her mother arrive at the convent, the narrative shifts into a flashback about a nun at the convent whose aristocratic parents forced her to take the veil. They no longer wanted to support her financially, opting to invest their money in their eldest son's future instead. Since entering the convent, the nun, Gertrude, has received special privileges because of her noble blood. She is held in awe by the others, not just because of her nobility but also because of her beauty and her cruelty. Gertrude harbors a dark secret. While in the convent, she took a lover named Egidio, whom she would

meet secretly until one day a lay sister, a young woman who did domestic work at the convent but was not a nun, threatened to expose her. Suddenly that lay sister stopped showing up for work at the convent, the implication being that Gertrude has had her killed.

Eventually Lucia meets Gertrude. In fact, the nun feels compassion for the pure and innocent Lucia, so different from herself, but Gertrude is forced to push her compassion aside. Don Rodrigo, determined to get Lucia at any cost, asks for help from another villain, the most powerful man in the area, identified only as The Unnamed. He is a mysterious figure, feared throughout the region for his tyrannical acts. The Unnamed sets a plan in motion. He sends a message to one of his local thugs, who happens to be Gertrude's ex-lover, Egidio. Because Egidio can blackmail her by threatening to expose their love affair and the dead girl, Gertrude has to play a role in The Unnamed's plan to kidnap Lucia. Gertrude informs Lucia that she must be moved from the convent to another safe place, and as soon as the trusting Lucia steps into the street, she is snatched by some of The Unnamed's *bravi.* The kidnappers lock her in a room in The Unnamed's castle, where she anxiously awaits her doom. She is spared, however. Lucia's religious faith and inner strength help effect a profound change in The Unnamed. He dwells on her words: "God will forgive so many things, for an act of mercy!" and decides to abandon his wicked ways (Manzoni, *The Betrothed*, p. 395). Fortunately, at the moment of his conversion, Cardinal Federigo Borromeo, a real historical figure, steps into the story. The cardinal, an intellectual who believes that "no man can rightly claim superiority over his fellows, except in their service," embodies, in the novel's view, the most elevated of human qualities: compassion for all (*The Betrothed*, p. 403). The Unnamed seeks and wins an audience with the cardinal, who welcomes the wayward sheep and assures him that he still has time to right some of his wrongs. The two set out immediately to free Lucia. After The Unnamed begs her forgiveness, she starts downhill to the nearest town. A tailor and his wife take her in, and Cardinal Borromeo visits Lucia. The cardinal promises to find out about the fate of poor Renzo, who has been caught up in all the turmoil to recently hit Milan. Lucia's mother visits too, and Lucia finds a job as a maid at a nearby estate. On the surface, life improves, but Lucia made a vow while trapped in The Unnamed's castle, and it is torturing her now. She promised the Madonna to give up the relationship with Renzo if the Madonna would just let her survive and see her mother once more.

During all these tribulations, Renzo endures troubles of his own. He arrives in Milan during the bread riots, which resulted from poor harvests, brought on by a mix of bad weather, wartime destruction of the countryside, and the abandonment of fields by farmers faced with high taxes. The hungry residents, convinced that certain establishments are hoarding grain and flour, begin to riot and steal bread, then turn toward the commissioner's house. The terrified commissioner, who cares nothing for the masses, is rescued by Spanish troops. Renzo observes all this unrest with the earnestness of an innocent who knows nothing of the big city. He gets caught up in the crowd mentality, a reaction the narration disparages. After the disturbance, Renzo spends the night at an inn, where he not only has dinner but also gets drunk. His guard down, he rants about the government and the riots to a police spy and ends up incriminating himself as a provocateur. The innkeeper denounces him to the police, and the following morning Renzo is arrested. But on his way to the station, he gains the sympathy of a growing crowd and manages to escape. He heads for Bergamo, a city beyond the border of the duchy of Milan in the republic of Venice, and learns on the way that the authorities have branded him a troublemaker and fugitive. Crossing the border, he makes his way to the home of his cousin, a silk weaver like himself, then moves on because the Milanese authorities are on the chase. This makes it difficult for Cardinal Borromeo's messengers to track Renzo down.

The novel's third and fourth sections turn to larger historical developments: the economic crisis, famine, plague in Milan, and the war for control of the dukedom of Mantua—the Italian manifestation of the European-wide Thirty Years War. The Holy Roman Emperor sends in his army, mercenaries who carry plague into the region and behave savagely as they proceed through the countryside, frightening Renzo and Lucia's village: "News that the army had marched, that it was near at hand, and of its behavior all arrived together" (The Betrothed, p. 534). Lucia's mother, among others, must quit the village until the soldiers pass. She and others return to find their houses plundered, an ominous foreshadowing of things to come.

The story moves to the horrors of the plague in Milan, which falls into near anarchy under incompetent government officials. The novel discusses at length the phenomenon of the untori, or "anointers," a notion that arises out of superstition and terror. Because people do not understand how the plague spreads from one body to another, a theory develops that evildoers are purposefully passing on the disease by "anointing" benches, walls, and church columns with some contaminated oil. Many are arrested and even executed for the offense, which has no basis in reality.

In the meantime, the plague spreads to some of the novel's characters. The villain Don Rodrigo is stricken in Milan, and a servant takes him to the dreaded lazzaretto, the hospital for people with contagious diseases. The epidemic reaches Renzo in the Venetian Republic too. Strong and lucky, he survives and resolves to find Lucia. He returns to their home village to find his modest property looted and destroyed and to learn that Lucia has moved to Milan. He arrives there, only to be confronted by visions of hell-on-earth: heartbreaking scenes of children suffering, dead and dying people in the streets, corpses ignominiously carted away, people committing desperate crimes. All the while, others locked up in their own homes, perish of hunger, filth, and hysteria. Renzo discovers that Lucia has been taken to the lazzaretto. He approaches it, convinced that he cannot bear the sight of more misery, only to realize that he has not seen the worst yet. Inside Renzo finds Brother Cristoforo who has been working there for the past three months. Anxiety-ridden about the possibility of not finding her, Renzo begins to rant about taking revenge on Don Rodrigo. This earns him a harsh scolding from Father Cristoforo, who teaches Renzo a lesson in forgiveness by taking him to the bedside of the wretchedly ailing Don Rodrigo. Renzo forgives Don Rodrigo, then locates Lucia who, like her betrothed, contracted but survived the plague. Presently she is comforting the sick. Lucia reprimands Renzo for coming, since by now he knows about the vow she made. An argument ensues about the nature of the vow and God's wishes, and she sends Renzo away. Refusing to give her up, Renzo appeals to Father Cristoforo for aid and he convinces the steadfast young woman that the vow was improper. She promised to forfeit something she had no right to give up, since she was already engaged to Renzo at the time. Thereafter, Renzo and Lucia marry and move to another village where he earns a good living as a silk weaver, and the couple lead happy, normal lives, complete with many children. Looking back at what their experiences taught them, they reach a philosophical conclusion (which expresses Manzoni's own conception of Divine Providence):

> That troubles very often come because we have asked for them; but that the most prudent and innocent of conduct is not necessarily enough to keep them away; also that when they come . . . trust in God goes far to take away their sting, and makes them a useful preparation for a better life.
>
> (*The Betrothed*, p. 720)

The *puntiglio*, or "point of honor." The villain Don Rodrigo embodies what Manzoni sees as the worst qualities of seventeenth-century Milanese Spanish culture, which are tied to the male aristocrat's obsession with honor. Honor, to people of Don Rodrigo's class, meant social reputation and privilege and the right not to be insulted, denied, or humiliated in any way by anyone, in-

---

MONACA DI MONZA

The tragic story of Gertrude, the "Nun of Monza," is based on an actual person. The real Gertrude was named Marianna and she lived from 1575 to 1650. Marianna had noble parents. The daughter of Prince Don Martino De Leyva and of Lady Virginia Marino, she was a novice at the Convent of the Benedictines of Santa Margherita in Monza. Beginning in 1597, she had an affair with Giovanni Paolo Osio, and in 1607 the authorities arrested her for a murder committed in the attempt to preserve her reputation by covering up this affair. She was condemned and imprisoned until 1622 when she was liberated by Federigo Borromeo. In the novel's original manuscript, Manzoni dedicated many chapters to the plight of Gertrude but he cut much of them out in the final version because he was concerned about creating too much sympathy for such an immoral and dark person, no matter what the psychological reasons, for her misdeeds. However, she is still considered by many the book's most intriguing figure.

---

cluding people of all social strata. Honor had always played—and would continue to play—a role in European culture. It played a prominent role in Manzoni's day and manifested itself in ways diametrically opposed to the very values Manzoni was espousing in the novel. Because Don Rodrigo feels entitled to claim ownership of Lucia by virtue of his higher social status and noble blood, a sense of shame and dishonor overtakes him when she rejects him in front of his cousin,

and he reacts in a way that forces Renzo and Lucia to flee. His sense of honor leads to their separation from each other and their families, and touches off all the subsequent misadventures.

For the aristocracy of seventeenth-century Milan, one's sense of honor was intimately tied to the concept of masculinity and masculine modes of defense or retribution. In fact, dueling over points of honor became so widespread in Italy, especially in Spanish-ruled Italy, that the colonial government tried to impose laws to ban it. But since the nobles considered themselves above the law, such policies were largely ineffectual.

When Brother Cristoforo reproaches Don Rodrigo for his interference in Renzo and Lucia's marriage, Don Rodrigo suffers another insult to his pride. He is indignant, first at being denied Lucia, then at being scolded for demanding from her what he sees as rightfully his. Ironically, those whom he takes to be offenders to his honor are portrayed as far worthier than he. The novel ridicules the absurdity of such a "noble" sense of honor, intensifying the scathing depiction by drawing on historical disputes from treatises on chivalry. The Spaniards were especially famous for their ferocious allegiance to personal and family honor, and many treatises on the subject were published in Milan during the Spanish rule there. Particularly inspirational for Manzoni were two treatises on honor he goes so far as to mention in his novel. The treatises were written by two seventeenth-century Milanese aristocrats: G. B. Olevano's *Trattato nel quale co'l mezzo di cinquanta casi vien posto in atto prattico il modo di ridurre a pace ogni sorte di privata inimicitia nata per cagion d'onore* [1620; Treatise in which, through 50 examples, it will be shown how to make peace out of any type of private hostility brought on by an offense to one's honor] and Francesco Birago's *Li discorsi cavallereschi* [1628; Discourses on chivalry].

A component of *puntiglio* in these treatises is outside opinion—the gentleman, in order to retain his honor, cannot allow someone else to threaten or dishonor him, publicly or privately. Obviously, a public offense must be avenged. But the thinking was that even if the offense is committed in private, the dishonored man should not have to live with the fact that the offender carries within him the memory of the insult he delivered. Don Rodrigo conceives of what he sees as his tongue lashing from Brother Cristoforo in this way.

So obsessed is Don Rodrigo with his own honor that he does not even take into account that Cristoforo is a monk with a commitment to protect his flock, particularly the poor, who have no other defender. Brother Cristoforo, on the other hand, is a genuine man of honor, for he shows compassion even for the disease-racked Don Rodrigo. Through the two figures, the novel sets up a fundamental contrast—between the immoral, irrational behavior that pervaded much of seventeenth-century Italy and the reasoned, fraternal, honest Christian behavior of the novel's lowly heroes. While this contrast may impress the modern day reader as one that promotes stereotypes, in Italian literature Manzoni's harsh criticism and ridicule of aristocratic modes of behavior was groundbreaking.

Sources and literary context. In a foreword to the novel, Manzoni explains how the idea came to him while transcribing a seventeenth-century historical manuscript, which he decided to rewrite in modern language and turn into a novel (whose facts he would corroborate with other sources). Thus, the work introduces itself as a historical novel about characters that did exist or could have existed. Indeed, some of the most memorable characters are based on historical figures—namely, the aristocratic nun Gertrude and Cardinal Borromeo.

Not just a historical novel, *The Betrothed* is a religious work based on Manzoni's beliefs about the past, present, and ideal future state of the Catholic Church. His conception of Catholicism is often at odds with official Church positions because of his emphasis on equality and democracy. Manzoni wanted to concentrate on the original message of the Gospel in connection with social relations, particularly with respect to the poor and oppressed. This explains much of the novel's human interaction. Another influential dimension is his belief in Divine Providence—the idea that people need to entrust their lives to God rather than to humans for the eventual triumph of good over evil. A convert who was raised to place his faith not in religion but in the ability of people to reason, Manzoni embraced Catholicism in 1810. He was 25 years old at the time and became an ardent follower of the faith. While he continued to believe passionately in the Enlightenment ideals of liberty, equality, fraternity, and rational thought, he now wanted to reconcile them with the practice and hierarchy of Catholicism. What resulted was a sort of Christian democracy, a message from Manzoni that the Gospel was not just for a privileged few (priests, Church leaders, people of noble blood) but everyone, even the most humble.

The Betrothed is also a historical novel written with patriotic objectives in mind. Nineteenth-century thought attached great importance to history as a discipline. Historiography was seen as central to establishing a national identity. One of the primary exponents of the historical novel was Sir Walter Scott, whose novels circulated widely in the regions of Italy. Two of his landmark novels—*Waverly* (1814) and *Ivanhoe* (1819)—were published in Italian translation in 1821. Manzoni, who met Scott, speaks of his debt to the Scottish novelist: "If Walter Scott had not existed then I would not have had the idea to write a novel" (Ghidetti, p. 69; trans. A. Boylan).

In addition to Scott, Manzoni studied actual histories to make his details as faithful to fact as

---

FEDERIGO BORROMEO

Born in 1564 into the illustrious, aristocratic Borromeo family of Milan, Federigo (Federico) Borromeo became the cardinal and archbishop of the city. In *The Betrothed*, during the height of the plague, not knowing how the disease spreads, he gets the people of Milan to hold a religious procession to appease God's wrath, which aggravates the contagion. In fact, Borromeo was a loyal friend to the people and extremely dedicated to education. He founded the Ambrosiana, at once a seminary, a college of fine arts, and the second public library in Europe.

---

possible. He consulted the work of Giuseppe Ripamonti (1573-1643), a canon of the Santa Maria della Scala church in Milan. Under the guidance of Cardinal Federigo Borromeo, Ripamonti wrote *Storia della chiesa milanese* (The History of the Milanese Church) before serving as Milan's official chronicler and then the historiographer of the Spanish kingdom in Italy. For other details he referred to the already named Spanish treatises on honor and to a historical work on the food business: *Sul commercio de' commestibili e caro prezzo del vitto. Opera storico-teorico-popolare* (1802; On the commerce of foodstuffs and the high price of food) by the economist Melchiorre Gioia.

It was theorized that if the historical novel could be written to communicate with the general population, it would fulfill a need to teach a people about their common roots. With this in mind, Manzoni breaks new ground by featuring "unimportant" people swept up in monumental events that were usually only connected to famous people, showing how even the most humble participate in history. He furthermore champions their middle-class aspirations and portrays former peasants like Renzo, who becomes a silk weaver and an entrepreneur, as the future of the nation. The story of peasants in a small Lombard town builds to a larger view of early-seventeenth-century Lombardy and in the process slyly criticizes politics and society in nineteenth-century Italy without the risk of directly attacking

---

THE NOVEL'S DIFFERENT VERSIONS AND THE "QUESTIONE DELLA LINGUA"

~

Between 1821 and the novel's first publication in 1827, Manzoni revised his work many times, trying to strike a balance between historical information, fictional narrative, authorial intervention in the work, and character development. After the 1827 edition, however, he became dissatisfied with the novel's linguistic condition and felt that he wanted to contribute to the long-standing "questione della lingua"—the controversy over what the standard, modern literary Italian should be. The question arose because Italians, since their country was not a unified political entity, generally spoke either the dialect of their own region or the language that foreign rulers imposed on them. As a native of Milan, Manzoni at first wrote in the city's dialect mixed with many French influences. But Manzoni came to believe that the Tuscan dialect, the language of hallowed national figures such as Dante and Machiavelli, should be used in literature, in part to inspire a feeling of communal national sentiment. He therefore traveled to Florence to imbibe the dialect and set about rewriting his novel in it, or, as his famous metaphor goes, he went to "rinse his clothes in the Arno [the river that runs through the middle of Florence]." This led to a publication of the definitive edition in 1840.

---

the foreign rulers. The Austrian rulers of Manzoni's day, his novel implies, functioned much like their Spanish predecessors, especially in enlisting the allegiance of the Milanese nobility, who in effect betrayed their poorer compatriots.

Events in History at the Time the Novel Was Written

Napoleonic rule. After the Austrians won control of Milan in the War of the Spanish Succession in 1714, they ruled the city for nearly a century. The eruption in 1789 of the French Revolution terrified absolute monarchist governments all over Europe and served to embolden those who championed democracy. Republican France went on to fight a war against Austria, from which France emerged victorious. A French army led by Napoleon Bonaparte entered Milan as its liberator in May 1796, and under the Treaty of Campo Formio (October 17, 1797) Napoleon forced Austria to recognize the formation of a new Cisalpine Republic with Milan as its capital. The Cisalpine Republic was effectively under the control of Napoleon and the French. They proceeded to make some democratic changes, such as prohibiting factory owners to fire workers and changing the old monarchic street signs like "Via dei nobili" (Street of the Nobles) to more egalitarian signs like "Via dell'Uguaglianza" (Street of Equality). But the French also raised taxes, imposed obligatory military service, suppressed opposition, and did little to institute independent democratic rule. In 1799 war broke out again between France and Austria, and Austria and their Russian allies occupied Lombardy. Shortly thereafter, Napoleon led a coup that put him in control of the French state. In 1800, he led the army into Italy and defeated the Austrians and Russians, thereby securing his control over Lombardy for the remainder of his rule. In 1802 the Cisalpine Republic was enlarged and renamed the Italian Republic, but this arrangement did not last long. In 1805 Napoleon declared himself French Emperor and King of Italy, consolidating all power in his own hands. The atmosphere in Milan became ever more oppressive, censorship grew, and spies infiltrated the city streets. An era that had begun with great hope and democratic ideals deteriorated into tyranny. When Napoleon's empire finally fell in 1814, the city was relieved.

Restoration. Eight days later the Austrians returned and repossessed the city, making Milan, as well as the newly acquired Venetian Republic, part of their empire. Austrian troops, until they had their own barracks, even stayed in Manzoni's city and country houses. The period was called the Restoration, although the Austrians showed no interest in restoring the type of semi-enlightened and tolerant government they had practiced earlier. In the interim, however, Napoleon had accelerated the desire for geographical self-rule, though at this point it was still a desire for regional self-rule and the concept of national unity had not yet taken hold. Still, this era is filled with the revolutionary impulse. The Milanese, particularly the intellectuals, after having had a taste of the possibility of self-rule, kept conspiring to overthrow their oppressive rulers. Manzoni himself frequented salons where rebellion was fomented. The discovery in 1820 of one particular conspiracy sent many of Manzoni's circle into exile, silence, or prison. Manzoni was spared, however, since, though he shared many of the revolutionary sentiments, he did not directly participate in any of these clandestine affairs.

The Lombard Romantics and Unification. The idea of "cultural nationalism" surfaced among a group of intellectuals in early-nineteenth-century Milan. The writers in this loosely affiliated group, whose members shared a commitment to creating a sense of nationality among Italians through literature and art, were called the Lombard Romantics, and included Manzoni and Silvio Pellico. The group published the subversive, anti-Austrian political and literary journal *Il Conciliatore* [The Peacemaker] between 1818 and 1819. During this time, in addition to Manzoni's *The Betrothed*, which indirectly criticized Milan's current foreign rulers—the Austrians—a few other subversive works were published (e.g., Tommaso Grossi's scathing political satire the *Prineide* [1816] and Carlo Porta's series of works in dialect about the city's poor and outcast population [1812-16]). Manzoni's novel went a step further than these other works, striving to create a national modern literary language that all inhabitants of the Italian peninsula could understand and relate to, one that was not "tainted" by the localisms of his own regional dialect or by foreign (French) influences. Ideals of nationality and shared cultural heritage were diffused by this type of literature and, along with military and political action, would eventually excite enough enthusiasm, at least among the upper classes and intellectuals, to unify the country. By 1848 the Milanese had had enough of Austrian rule, so when the Austrians were concentrating on uprisings in Vienna, the people of Milan took to the streets and wrested the city free from Austrian rule. After several days of fighting, in which 350 died, the Milanese voted to be annexed to nearby Piedmont under the King of Savoy (future king of united Italy). A few months later the Austrians managed to retake Milan, and a decade of terrible repression followed. Finally, in 1859, another war broke out between the Austrians and the Savoy kingdom (Piedmont) and this time the rebels emerged victorious (in the battle of Magenta in June 1859). Afterwards, Lombardy was permanently annexed to the Savoy kingdom, which in 1861 became the Kingdom of Italy.

Reception. When the first version of *The Betrothed* was published in 1827, it was warmly welcomed by the reading public, although it met with some resistance from critics and members of the intellectual elite. They complained that a) the novel form was not a legitimate literary genre, particularly not the realist novel because it did not express lofty, abstract ideals in the style of neo-classicism, b) the language was too accessible and banal, c) Manzoni's protagonists, being humble peasants, were not dignified enough to merit readers' attention. This last factor was one of Manzoni's great innovations, and it shocked those used to caring only about the stories of people from the upper classes. However, such international writers as Goethe, Edgar Allan Poe, and Stendhal, and the influential Italian critics Niccolò Tommaseo, Silvio Pellico, and De Sanctis praised the work. About Manzoni Pietro Giordani, literary critic and ardent anti-Austrian patriot, declared: "How this helps the minds of the people —The oppressors will realize—what a profound intellect, what a powerful incentive he is who has taken so much care to appear simple, almost as if a fool. . . . Oh, why doesn't Italy have 20 books just like it!" (Viti, p. 152; trans. A. Boylan).

—Amy Boylan

For More Information

Cavalazzi, Giovanna, and Gau Falchi. *La storia di Milano*. Bologna: Zanichelli, 1989.

Duggan, Christopher. *A Concise History of Italy*. Cambridge: Cambridge University Press, 1994.

Ghidetti, Enrico. *Manzoni*. Florence: Giunti Lisciani Editori, 1995.

Manzoni, Alessandro. *The Betrothed*. London: Penguin Books, 1972.

Sella, Domenico. *Italy in the Seventeenth Century*. London: Longman, 1997.

Viti, Gorizio. *Guida ai Promessi sposi*. Florence: Felice Le Monnier, 1970.

The Book of the Courtier

by

Baldesar Castiglione

Baldesar Castiglione was born in 1478 at Casatico near Mantua, in the region of Lombardy, to an aristocratic family (his mother was related to the illustrious Gonzaga dynasty, which ruled the region). He received a traditional humanistic education in Milan, then was drawn by family connections into courtly life. At 21, Castiglione replaced his recently deceased father as a diplomat and military officer at the court of Francesco Gonzaga in Mantua. In 1504 the young courtier moved to Urbino, where he served under Guidobaldo da Montefeltro (1472-1508), holding a semi-military post and carrying out diplomatic missions to Rome and abroad. Castiglione remained at the service of the Urbino rulers until 1516, when he rejoined the Gonzaga court in Mantua. In 1524 Pope Clement VII appointed him as *nuncio* (papal ambassador) and sent him to the court of the Holy Roman Emperor, Charles V, in Madrid. In his post at the Spanish court, Castiglione witnessed the growing tension between the pope and the emperor. In 1528 while negotiating a reconciliation between the two powers, Castiglione was made Bishop of Avila. A year later he died of plague in Toledo, leaving behind his most renowned work, *The Book of the Courtier* (1528), which soon became a popular handbook for European civility. Castiglione authored other, minor writings belonging to the conventional genres of courtly literature, including the dramatic eclogue *Tirsi* (performed in 1506), a celebration of the Duchess of Urbino and her circle. He also wrote a eulogy extolling a former patron—*De vita et*

THE LITERARY WORK

A manual in the form of a dialogue set at the court of the Duke of Urbino in 1507; published in Italian (as *Libro del cortegiano*) in 1528, in English in 1561.

SYNOPSIS

Fictional conversations detail the qualities and the conduct of the perfect courtier and define his relationship with his colleagues and his prince.

gestis Guidubaldi Urbini ducis (The Life and Deeds of Guidobaldo, Duke of Urbino); the text memorializes him in idealized fashion, as an enlightened ruler endowed with moral virtues who excels as a soldier, statesman, scholar, and patron of the arts. Serving such rulers were attendants like Castiglione, whose duties might encompass both diplomatic and literary activities, and whose profession could lead to upward mobility in Renaissance society. *The Book of the Courtier* is a conduct manual for this profession.

Events in History at the Time of the Dialogue

Courts and courtiers in Renaissance Italy. According to a guide of 1603 called *Iconologia* ("Moral Emblems") by Cesare Ripa, a court was a "company of well-bred men" summoned to

Baldesar Castiglione. From the portrait by Raphael
c. 1514–15.

work for a distinguished lord, who rewarded them with protection and patronage. Structured around the ruler, the courtly entourage consisted of his family, associates, and servants, as well as writers and artists. The ruler drew from a pool of relatives and associates to staff his administration, which governed in conjunction with an ongoing state bureaucracy. Government bodies appear to have been informal, without clear boundaries between a court and the state's on-going bureaucracy. The court, however, was a world apart.

Mostly it insulated itself from the outside world. In *The Book of the Courtier*, the conversations are held among a select circle of cultivated noblemen and ladies in the magnificent halls of the Urbino palace, carefully shielded from any contact with the town. By separating himself from his citizens, a prince gained an aura of superiority, meanwhile protecting his government from civic scrutiny. The performance of courtly rituals and etiquette served to enhance the prestige and authority of his entourage, setting them apart from the general populace.

The court apparatus was formidable. In addition to household officers to serve a prince's needs, his attendants included counselors and officials who relied on the personnel of the different chanceries when performing their duties. Three main departments in the court handled ad-

ministrative business: a chancery directed by a secretary, a department of justice under a magistrate, and a treasury and financial department headed by a treasurer-accountant. At least two other key professionals served in administrative capacities: a secretary who functioned as public relations manager and a scholar who worked as historian and genealogist to commemorate and extol the ruling family's accomplishments. The secretary helped glorify his prince through written works that celebrated him or through proposals for projects to be executed by court artists. As a trusted adviser, he often oversaw government business and performed specific administrative duties as well. Secretaries and scholars at court commonly took an active role in politics. They could replace a member of their prince's aristocracy on administrative bodies or provide service as diplomats. As the prince's representatives, they helped contain the influence of local nobility. In 1516 Lodovico Alamanni, a Florentine adviser to Lorenzo de' Medici (Lorenzo il Magnifico's grandson), warned him against the nobility's aspirations for freedom from his control. To subdue this resistance to his power, Lorenzo was advised to strip the most prominent citizens of their republican aspirations, demoting them "into such courtiers as might be useful to him," and recasting them into "secretaries, agents, delegates, ambassadors" (Bertelli, p. 29).

The size of a court was not always indicative of the actual political power of the state or ruler that supported it. A larger "family" of courtiers and servants allowed for a more diversified employment of its members. The court of Federico Gonzaga, Duke of Mantua, numbered some 800 until his death in 1540, when his brother, Cardinal Ercole, curbed expenses by reducing it to 350. The entourage of lesser lords was even smaller, but still impressive. In his handbook on *De cardinalatu* (1510; The Cardinalate), Paolo Cortesi stated that a cardinal's court should comprise 60 gentlemen attendants and 80 servants. A few decades later, Cola da Benvenuto, in his manual, *Del governo della corte d'un Signore di Roma* (1543; The Government of a Roman Lord's Court), claimed that the "family" or household of a lord should number "one hundred and seven [members], with a stable of forty horses; which I deem to be very suitable, neither too large nor too small" (Cola da Benevento, p. 6; trans. A. Baldi). These officials were entrusted with the "internal organization of the palace, administration of revenue, and the application of justice in what were known as 'lesser causes'—that is, actions brought between fellow subordinates of the signore [gentleman] or between them and outsiders" (Bertelli, p. 8). No matter the size, court society strove for excellence in various pursuits, including learned and spectacular endeavors, which were considered effective propaganda tools. The prince generally reinforced his authority by holding elaborate festivals and ceremonies; showcases of his wealth and generosity, such fanfare served to fascinate his subjects and to maintain the nobility's allegiance to the prince.

The court of Urbino. In former days, lords compensated their courtiers with personal privileges; by Castiglione's day, courtiers received salaries. But often a courtier's income failed to meet his needs or expectations. At Urbino, Duke Federico da Montefeltro (ruled 1444-1482) hired Gianmario Filelfo to teach his young son Guidobaldo Latin and Greek. In May 1478 Filelfo wrote to the Marquis of Mantua asking to enter his service and maintaining that he had "a lot of expenses, with sixteen to feed": one may infer that he was unhappy with his compensation at Urbino, though the duke is said to have generally spent a great deal of money on patronage (Clough, pt. 8, p. 133). As a patron of the arts, he bestowed commissions on renowned painters and architects (Piero della Francesca, Melozzo da Forlí, and Luciano Laurana). His appreciation of oil painting even led him to commission work from prominent foreign artists (for example, the Flemish Justus of Ghent and the Spaniard Pedro Berruguete).

Federico da Montefeltro could afford to spend lavishly. He was a foremost *condottiere* (military leader) of his day, and naturally those who required his services (which included the raising of armed forces) paid handsomely. Apparently he amassed quite a fortune. He had various estates in his territory, and every town there made him an annual grant. By conservative estimates Federico's income must have run around 50,000 ducats a year, "an enormous sum, when one considers that . . . the Doge of Venice [received] 3,000 ducats a year, and the total revenues (not profits) of prosperous merchants, bishops and cardinals were rarely 20,000 ducats a year" (Clough, pt. 8, pp. 130-131). Such wealth permitted him to spare his citizens heavy taxes and to launch magnificent civic projects. His most audacious endeavor was surely the splendid Ducal Palace, designed by Luciano Laurana and Francesco di Giorgio Martini of Siena, and endowed with a library of precious manuscripts. Here, as Castiglione recounts, "at great expense, he [Federico] collected many very excellent and rare books in Greek, Latin, and Hebrew, all of which he adorned with gold and silver" (Castiglione, *The Book of the Courtier*, p. 11).

In 1482, when Federico died, his son Guidobaldo was just ten. He grew to adulthood around the same time as Castiglione. The young duke soon faced financial burdens from palace construction and maintenance, resources were becoming scarce, and, unlike his father, he could not afford generous patronage or rare library acquisitions. Guidobaldo's failure to pay the contracted wage helps explain why Castiglione was often forced to ask his mother and closest friends for loans.

Living at court could ensure nobles and scholars various advantages beyond prestige and financial rewards. The career of Pietro Bembo is a case in point. After his first stay as a guest at the

The fifteenth-century Palazzo Ducale in Urbino, Italy, where Castiglione served as a courtier.

Urbino palace in 1505, he returned in September 1506 to become one of its permanent courtiers, remaining for six years. Bembo was certainly attracted to the hospitality and the riches of the ducal library. But the main reason for joining the Montefeltro entourage rested on the close link between the Urbino court and the pope's retinue. In fact, Bembo positioned himself for a call to the papal court and hoped to be granted a benefice, or official post endowed with assets. In 1512 he transferred to Rome and was later appointed as a papal secretary. The profession of courtier had meanwhile been losing prestige. By the time Bembo was there (when *The Courtier* takes place), the Urbino court was undergoing deep transformations. Several of the people whom *The Courtier* fictionalizes had died, and the cultural prestige of Urbino had already declined.

Scarce are the testimonies on the requisites and daily lives of court ladies. Vespasiano da Bisticci, Federico da Montefeltro's biographer, claims that the duke "kept his daughters in a sep-

arate part of the house, attended by many noblewomen of respectable age and irreproachable conduct; and to these apartments there was no admittance. . . . When he visited his daughters, all those accompanying him were left outside the door" (da Bisticci, p. 107).

The Dialogue in Focus

Contents overview. In an opening letter to Don Michel de Silva—the bishop of Viseu and a Portuguese ambassador at the papal court (1515-25)—Castiglione explains that he is hastening the release of *The Book of the Courtier* because of the many unauthorized versions already being circulated. Written in February 1527, the letter announces the author's intention to commemorate the cultural and aesthetic refinement of the Urbino court, where he spent the most significant years of his life. To depict the "perfect courtier" and celebrate one facet of what was regarded as civilized life, Castiglione dramatizes parlor games held over four consecutive nights by actual members of the duke's circle, as well as esteemed figures in the pope's retinue who were staying in the Montefeltro palace en route to Rome. The author's tendency to idealize is clear. In his view, the excellence of this exclusive environment will become a monument to the Renaissance court, a disappearing political and cultural institution. As Castiglione lists the casualties among his protagonists, it becomes evident that a certain historical process has reached its peak. The ruling class in small Italian principalities has been unable to withstand the clash with major political forces, but the author captures a select group in a remarkable daily routine.

The treatise is divided into four books, each recounting an evening's fictional conversations. These discussions tackle a wide range of topics, from which emerges a model of courtly behavior. The treatise alleges that these nightly pastimes were held in March 1507, claiming that its author was absent on a mission in England. With this distortion of historical truth (Castiglione had returned to Urbino at the end of February), the writer removes himself from the dialogue, claiming that he is simply recording the memories of the participants. His documentation of these memories fulfills a request from a fellow courtier, Alfonso Ariosto, in trying to assess "what form of Courtiership most befits a gentleman living at the courts of princes" (*Courtier*, p. 2). To this end, the book presents heated debates in a non-dogmatic fashion.

Duke Guidobaldo's residence, where the conversations take place, is described as "a city in the form of a palace" and "the very abode of joyfulness" (*Courtier*, pp. 11, 12). The company is a group of diplomats, intellectuals, artists, and court ladies; Duke Guidobaldo's absence from this circle (because of ill health) allows for the expression of conflicting views.

Contents summary—Book 1. In Book 1, on behalf of the duchess, Emilia Pio asks each member of the company to suggest "some game after his own liking that we have never played" (*Courtier*, p. 14). After a series of misguided or comical proposals, Count Ludovico di Canossa agrees to lead a discussion on what constitutes a perfect courtier. He begins by addressing physical and moral qualities. Above all, a courtier is to assist and counsel his lord, thereby winning his favor. Since the courtier must serve his prince "in every reasonable thing," he should excel in the profession of arms, that is, in the military domain (*Courtier*, p. 9). Nobility and grace, says the count, are two main qualifications. Objecting to the social discrimination, Gasparo Palavicino, himself an aristocrat, says nobility should not be a prerequisite. The manual defines grace as a quality closely connected to a certain balance that is "difficult to achieve and, as it were, composed of contraries" (*Courtier*, p. 150). The definition recalls Aristotle's principle of the Golden Mean, which describes virtue as a mean between two vices—excess and deficiency; courage, for instance, is the mean between rashness and cowardice (see Aristotle, *Nicomachean Ethics*, 2.6, 1107a). Concerning a courtier's gracious attitude, Count Canossa insists on the need to avoid the appearance of affectation, or artificial behavior, by using *sprezzatura*, a term he coins to describe comportment intended "to conceal all art and make whatever is done or said appear to be without effort" (*Courtier*, p. 32).

The debate then shifts to how to speak, condemning the use of pretentious, stilted verbal expression and entering into a discussion of the *questione della lingua* (language question), a central topic in sixteenth-century Italian literary circles. The manual favors the language spoken in conversation by the well-educated at princely courts, not the unnatural language used by purists for writing. ("The power and true rule of good speech consists more in usage than in anything else," says the manual, "and it is always bad to employ words that are not in use" [*Courtier*, p. 5].) The dialogue goes on to address another recurrent controversy, about whether military abilities are more important than literary abilities or vice versa, and concludes that the courtier should be a connoisseur of the arts as well as an accomplished soldier. The discussion also sketches out the moral requirements a courtier ought to have, a subject it will return to later.

Book 2. In the second book, the disputants elaborate on the qualities of a courtier and discuss the circumstances under which he demonstrates them. The main speaker of the first part of the evening, Federico Fregoso, lays out some general rules: the courtier should display his qualities so flawlessly and naturally that he wins his lord's favor and the admiration of his peers while reducing the risk of their envy. He must adapt to changing circumstances and interpret his onlookers' reactions. Besides mastering elegant conversation, he needs to make a good impression. If he happens to handle military arms in some public show, he must "strive to be as elegant and handsome in the exercise of arms as he is adroit" (*Courtier*, pp. 72-73). He has to avoid uncouth behavior and abstain from the company of people "of low birth" (*Courtier*, p. 74). Far more crucial to his fortunes, however, is winning his lord's favor. According to Federico "the Courtier [should] devote all his thought and strength of spirit to loving and almost adoring the prince he serves above all else, devoting his every desire and habit and manner to pleasing him" (*Courtier*, p. 80). Such complete submission runs the risk of reducing his behavior to that of a "noble flatterer," especially since it is permissible to use deceit in shaping his image (*Courtier*, pp. 100-101). Returning to the subject of the moral constraints a courtier ought to observe, Federico claims that he must obey his lord "in all things profitable and honorable to him [the prince], not in those that will bring him harm and shame" (*Courtier*, pp. 85-86). The debate then shifts to more trivial matters, such as dress codes, a topic linked to first impressions in shaping one's reputation.

FEMALE COUNTERPARTS TO THE COURTIER?

Women did not begin to come into their own as public figures in Renaissance Italy until after Castiglione's lifetime (1478-1529). At the end of the sixteenth century, upper-middle-class women could enter a courtly entourage, provided they displayed some remarkable skills and had strong connections. In the mid-1580s, when, at age 11, Lavinia Guasco joined the Savoy court in Turin, she had already mastered the art of calligraphy and had received extensive training in music. The later years of the Renaissance witnessed the rise of the "virtuosa," that is a lady endowed with and recognized for outstanding artistic talents, such as singer and harpist Laura Peverara, who flourished in the 1580s. She impressed Alfonso d'Este, who recruited her as a lady-in-waiting to sing and play for his court, rewarding her with a generous dowry.

Comic relief now enters the discussion as Bernardo da Bibbiena takes charge of the proceedings, deliberating at length on "pleasantries and witticisms" (*Courtier*, p. 103). The section (chapters 43-90) classifies jokes and sets down criteria for effective and appropriate humor, supplying examples that provide the reader with a rich repertoire of repartee and playful stories.

> But, among other witticisms, those are very well turned that are made by taking the very words and sense of another man's jibe and turning them against him, piercing him with his own weapons;

as when a litigant, to whom his adversary had said in the judge's presence: "Why do you bark so?" replied at once: "Because I see a thief."
>
> (*Courtier*, pp. 115-116)

Book 3. Responding to the final words of the previous day, Book 3 sets out to describe the court lady ("donna di palazzo"), a contentious subject. The women-haters in the company, Gasparo Pallavicino and Nicolò Frigio, have already voiced their prejudices; they bitterly reject any praise of female virtues. Into the verbal fray steps Giuliano de' Medici, "the defender of women's honor" (*Courtier*, p. 142). Leading the debate, he describes the ideal female counterpart to the courtier. The court lady must "have knowledge of letters, of music, of painting, and know how to dance and how to be festive" so that she can participate in entertainments and cultivated conversations, "using witticisms and pleasantries that are becoming to her" (*Courtier*, pp. 154-55). Besides developing some of the same qualities as a courtier, she must exhibit those "that befit all [women] (such as kindness, discretion, ability to manage her husband's property and house and children, if she is married, and all qualities that are requisite in a good mother)," along with "a certain pleasing affability" (*Courtier*, p. 151). Giuliano maintains that women are endowed with a balance of qualities that differentiates them from men (rather than simply possessing a smaller amount of the same properties). To settle a dispute on "the imperfection of women," the dialogue steers into consideration of their worth. Giuliano argues that women ought to be considered as necessary as men for the preservation of the human race through procreation. After discussing some theoretical subtleties, he gives several examples of illustrious women, both ancient and modern, who proved their value. The evening ends with talk about the court lady's amorous conduct and her "knowledge of what pertains to discourse of love" (*Courtier*, p. 190). A true lady of the court must be cautious about any dalliance, or flirtation, detecting her suitors' hidden intentions. By pretending to ignore their "covert words of love," she can keep them at bay through a refined strategy of dissimulation (*Courtier*, p. 191).

Book 4. Addressing the courtier's political role and his pursuit of spiritual love, Book 4 begins with the belated reappearance of the courtier Ottaviano Fregoso. As he was scheduled to be the main speaker, his delay alters the proceedings, and the company starts dancing. This change in the ritual marks the transition to a more serious discussion of the courtier's purposes. Ottaviano (Federico's brother) criticizes the debates of the previous three nights: the previous discussions, he complains, deal with the "excellence of the courtier for his own sake" and overlook his crucial role in power relations at court (Woodhouse, p. 147). The courtier as sketched so far might appear small-minded in his devotion to a seemingly ego-centered array of accomplishments. His attempt to refine his skills could degenerate into a self-promoting exercise, whereby he attracts an unseemly attention to himself. Such behavior would interfere with his primary role as counselor to the prince. Indeed, only the pursuit of a higher aim can save the courtier from this nearly effeminate form of self-absorption, in view of its preoccupation with "frivolities and vanities" (*Courtier*, p. 210). These same concerns, however, can be nurtured to good effect if they serve to gain the prince's favor for a lofty purpose:

> Therefore, I think that the aim of the perfect Courtier, which we have not spoken of up to now, is to win for himself . . . the favor and mind of the prince whom he serves [so] that he may be able to tell him, and always tell him, the truth about everything he needs to know, without fear or risk of displeasing him.
>
> (*Courtier*, p. 210)

Charged with guiding his lord, the courtier must act as his instructor, steering him away from arrogance, helping him to avoid the traps laid by flatterers, and leading him "by the austere path of virtue" (*Courtier*, p. 213).

Next Ottaviano turns his attention to princes, discussing the moral qualities they should develop; he places high value on temperance (the control of one's instincts through reason). The ensuing discussion examines different forms of government, favoring monarchies over republics, according to a line of thinking that elevates unity over plurality. In keeping with an ethical view of courtly life, the prince must be virtuous and capable of winning his "people's love and obedience" while ensuring peace between the social classes: his aim should be "to keep his subjects in a tranquil state, and give them the blessings of mind, body and of fortune" (*Courtier*, p. 230). Besides providing a handbook on how to navigate the turbulent waters of life at court, Castiglione shows his own political shrewdness in the fiction of the dialogue, which extols as promising heirs to European thrones three princes destined to indeed become powerful rulers (Francis I, Charles V, and Henry VIII).

(Since the conversation is set in 1507, the author, writing with the benefit of hindsight, can easily pretend to predict their fortunes.)

From a discussion of politics, the conversation shifts to the form of love the courtier should cultivate. The treatise takes a fresh look at the subject, renouncing courtly rituals and earthly passions in favor of a spiritual love. The duchess gives Pietro Bembo "the burden of speaking, and of teaching the Courtier a love so happy that it brings with it neither blame nor displeasure" (*Courtier*, p. 243). Bembo shapes his argument according to the notion that "love is nothing but a certain desire to enjoy beauty," an idea from a current (the neo-Platonic) school of philosophy (*Courtier*, p. 243). With this credo in mind, the mature courtier can keep his passions in check and overpower his sensual cravings. He is free to pursue the synthesis of beauty and goodness, to seek the spiritual value of love that makes it possible for him to benefit from his beloved lady's "amorous influence" even if she is far away (*Courtier*, p. 253). Such detachment from the animalistic, corporeal world encourages his ascent to "the lofty mansion where heavenly, lovely, and true beauty dwells, which lies hidden in the innermost recesses of God" (*Courtier*, p. 257). Speaking of a holy love infused with "divine wisdom," Bembo's language "becomes not only mystic, but increasingly more Christian" (Woodhouse, p. 180). He is almost carried away by his rapture, so that Emilia Pio tugs at the folds of his robe and humorously warns him to restrain his thoughts, lest his soul should abandon his body. To their surprise, the members of the party realize that their conversation has lasted the entire night. With daylight filtering into the room, they open the windows and contemplate the rosy sunrise, in which the star of Venus still shines. Under the influence of this celestial body (symbolizing the mythical Venus Urania, goddess of heavenly love), the speakers, having promised to continue their conversation in the evening, retire to their separate quarters.

The "language question." In Book 1 of *The Courtier*, the discussion veers toward the *questione della lingua*, the "language question," at the time a highly controversial topic. In the various regions of Italy, people spoke dialects derived from Latin, but subjected to distinct linguistic influences. After the superb achievements of Dante, Petrarch, and Boccaccio in the late thirteenth and fourteenth centuries, Tuscan emerged as the predominant vernacular language, though its position was questionable in the following century.

With the revival of the classics in the 1400s, Latin gained prestige as a more refined and effective means of literary expression. By the time Castiglione wrote *The Courtier,* however, Tuscan was regaining its status as a vehicle of eloquence. Moreover, there was an effort to define a written form of vernacular able to supersede both the different variants then in use and Latin. Faced with a peninsula still fragmented into courts and literary circles with distinct dialects, scholars examined the nature of the Italian language. The search for a unifying linguistic identity gave rise to many treatises, which gravitated around a few general positions:

The classicist position: The proponents of this theory looked to the masterpieces of the great Tuscan writers of the fourteenth century for models—for prose, to Boccaccio's **Decameron** and for poetry to Petrarch's **Canzoniere.** Although these Renaissance scholars praised Dante's **Divine Comedy,** they had reservations about its use of newly coined words, foreign words, and "vulgarity" (all also in *WLAIT 7: Italian Literature and Its Times*). The most influential representative of this position was Pietro Bembo, who appears as a character in the *Book of the Courtier* and penned an influential treatise expounding his view (*Prose della volgar lingua,* 1525; [Writings in the Vernacular Language]).

The courtly language position: Troubled by the regional aspects of Tuscan, other writers recommended a vernacular linked more closely to Latin. They proposed a hybrid or mixed form for writing and speaking, defending a form of Italian they argued was already in use in the courts. This position was first articulated by Vincenzo Colli in a treatise (now lost) and by Mario Equicola (in *De natura de amore* [The Nature of Love], circa 1505-1508). *The Courtier* advocates a subtle compromise of this sort.

The naturalist position: Still other writers (such as Lodovico Martelli and Benedetto Varchi, both natives of Florence) offered further alternatives. On the one hand, these writers stressed the Florentine (or, more generally, Tuscan) roots of the fine language in the fourteenth-century masterpieces. On the other hand, these writers refused to adopt old-fashioned, bookish forms of expression, preferring their current vernacular. In some cases this meant looking beyond Florence and extolling another Tuscan dialect, that of Siena, a town endowed with a rich cultural heritage. The theorists in this camp took a naturalist approach, combining their own native usages with the language of Boccaccio and the other illustrious Tuscan writers.

In writing *The Book of the Courtier,* Castiglione used a language modeled after the one spoken in northern Italian courts, rich in Latinisms and regional expressions. Once his treatise reached Aldine Press for publication, however, the work underwent linguistic revision by Giovan Francesco Valerio, who adapted it to the style of fourteenth-century Tuscan prose. So, to a degree, the printed version of *The Courtier* misrepresents its author's linguistic intent.

Sources and literary context. Large sections of *The Courtier* can be seen as carefully wrought patchworks of quotes that rely heavily on classical precedents. However, the derivative nature of the manual should not be counted as a weakness; it reflects a common practice of the day, the reworking of ancient models in an attempt to both emulate and compete with them. Greek and Latin sources inspired ideas in *The Book of the Courtier.* In justifying his approach to creating an idealistic image of the perfect courtier, Castiglione mentions Plato and Xenophon, along with Cicero, as sources. Some notes in a 1556 edition of *The Courtier* indicate that several passages were modeled after the prologue to Cicero's *Orator* (Burke, p. 42). The dialogue format is inspired mainly by Cicero's works on rhetoric (*De oratore, Orator,* and *Brutus*) and to a lesser extent by his philosophical writings. *The Courtier* is filled with short quotes. One noteworthy example is a simile concerning the need to charm a prince "with salutary deception," "like shrewd doctors who often spread the edge of the cup with some sweet cordial when they wish to give a bitter-tasting medicine to sick and over-delicate children" (*Courtier,* p. 213). An image from Lucretius, it appears in his *De rerum natura* (1.935-942). The crucial notion of *sprezzatura* (nonchalance) is indebted to Latin precedents: Castiglione takes his warning to avoid pretense from Quintilian, who declares (in *Institutio oratoria* 1.6 and 1.40) that "nothing is more unpleasant than affectation." Drawing on Artistotle's principle of the Golden Mean—a midpoint between excess and deficiency (formulated in the *Nicomachean Ethics*)—and on his *Politics,* Castiglione makes Aristotle the dominant authority in political matters. Another deep influence on political and moral positions was Plutarch. Even the dispute on language echoes ancient precedents: Castiglione shares Cicero's view that stylistic variety expresses the diversity of writers' minds and that one should match style to content (from *De oratore*).

Castiglione drew on Italian as well as classical sources. The large section of *The Courtier* devoted to jokes borrows its theoretical principles from Cicero's *De oratore* and takes some jokes from Quintilian (*Institutio oratoria*) of ancient Rome and from later Italian jokesters, Boccaccio's *Decameron*, Poggio Bracciolini's *Facetiae*, and Giovanni Pontano's *De sermone*. The manual's detailed account of power relations is linked to a well-established literary tradition in the 1400s, discussing the perfect form of government and the ideal ruler (including works such as Giovanni Pontano's *De principe* and Filippo Beroaldo the elder's *De optimu statu et de principe*). Plato's presence, filtered through his fifteenth- and sixteenth-century Italian followers (Marsilio Ficino, Francesco Cattani da Diacceto, Mario Equicola, and Pietro Bembo) is felt in the discussions of love and beauty at the end of the conversations.

Reception. The publication of *The Book of the Courtier* was a carefully orchestrated event. It involved two of the most prestigious Italian publishing houses in the early period of printing in Italy, the Aldine press in Venice and, a few months later in 1528, the Giunti press in Florence. The work, an object of curiosity in intellectual circles even before its release, met with much success among Italians and soon spread to other parts of Europe. Between the sixteenth and the seventeenth centuries, 62 editions of *The Book of the Courtier* were published in Italy in a wide variety of formats. A short time after its release, *The Book of the Courtier* appeared in Spanish (1534) and French (1537); the English and German versions followed in 1561 and 1565, respectively. The flurry of reprints testifies to the book's widespread popularity. It contributed greatly to the spread of values and customs of the Italian Renaissance throughout Europe. *The Book of the Courtier* became an influential source for more than proper courtly behavior. Responding to a preference for maxims during the Renaissance, publishers plumbed the manual for aphorisms and precepts. In doing so, they violated Castiglione's intent, for he had used the dialogue format to discourage a one-sided concept of truth. On the other hand, the manual did more than intended, serving as a blueprint for parlor games and dramatizing lively and portraying civil

behavior in action as well as providing its readers with prescriptive information.

Legend has it that even Charles V, the King of Spain and Holy Roman Emperor—who is said to have called Castiglione "the best knight living"—trusted the counsel he found in *The Book of the Courtier,* keeping a copy of the manual at his bedside, along with Machiavelli's *The Prince* (or, ironically, the Bible, depending on the strain of the legend).

—Andrea Baldi

For More Information

Aristotle. *Aristotle: Nicomachean Ethics.* Trans. Christopher Rowe. Oxford: Oxford University Press, 2002.

Berger, Harry, Jr. *The Absence of Grace: Sprezzatura and Suspicion in Two Renaissance Courtesy Books.* Stanford: Stanford University Press, 2000.

Bertelli, Sergio, Franco Cardini, and Elvira Garbero Zorzi, eds. *The Courts of the Italian Renaissance.* New York: Facts on File, 1986.

Burke, Peter. *The Fortunes of* The Courtier: *The European Reception of Castiglione's* Cortegiano. University Park, Penn.: Pennsylvania State University Press, 1996.

Cartwright Ady, Julia. *Baldassare Castiglione, the Perfect Courtier, His Life and Letters, 1478-1529.* 2 vols. London: John Murray, 1908.

Castiglione, Baldesar. *The Book of the Courtier: The Singleton Translation.* Ed. Daniel Javitch. New York: W. W. Norton, 2002.

Clough, Cecil H. *The Duchy of Urbino in the Renaissance.* London: Variorum Reprints, 1981.

Cola, da Beneveto. *Del governo della corte d'un Signore in Roma.* Rome: Vincenzo Lucrino, 1552.

Finucci, Valeria. *The Lady Vanishes: Subjectivity and Representation in Castiglione and Ariosto.* Stanford: Stanford University Press, 1992.

Hanning, Robert W., and David Rosand, eds. *Castiglione: The Ideal and the Real in Renaissance Culture.* New Haven: Yale University Press, 1983.

Osborne, June. *Urbino: The Story of a Renaissance City.* London: Frances Lincoln, 2003.

Vespasiano, da Bisticci. *The Vespasiano Memoirs.* Trans. William George and Emily Waters. London: Routledge, 1926.

Woodhouse, John Robert. *Baldesar Castiglione. A Reassessment of* The Courtier. Edinburgh: Edinburgh University Press, 1978.

The Canti (Songs)

by

Giacomo Leopardi

Giacomo Leopardi was born in 1798 in Recanati, a very small town in the isolated, mainly rural region of Marche in central Italy. His father, the extremely conservative Count Monaldo Leopardi, was an amateur writer and scholar who spent most of his time in the family library. The administration of family life was left to Leopardi's mother, Marquise Adelaide Antici. A strict, unloving, extremely religious woman, she envied parents who lost their children in infancy, since that meant they "had flown safely to paradise, and had freed their parents from the bother of supporting them" (Leopardi, *Canti*, p. 164).

Lonely and estranged, Leopardi took some comfort in the affection of his siblings Carlo and Paolina. The future poet's education was formal and extensive; at ten he could read ancient Greek, Arabic, and several other foreign languages. In a seven-year-frenzy of study between 1811 and 1818, Leopardi extensively examined philology to theology, from classical writings by Ovid and Virgil to modern ones, including the works of the French Enlightenment. Meanwhile, his health deteriorated and his isolation increased. In 1817 he started writing a lifelong journal of sorts, the *Zibaldone*, a collection of notes, observations, projects, and quotes. The next year Leopardi wrote his first two *canzoni* ("songs," poems with a particular metrical structure), "To Italy" and "On the Proposed Monument to Dante in Florence." In the poems, he joins a classical style to contemporary political and social content. Leopardi wrote politically en-

> ### THE LITERARY WORK
>
> A collection of 41 poems whose settings range from ancient Greece to early-nineteenth-century Italy; written between 1818 and 1836, published in Italian (as "Canti") in 1845, in English in 1962.
>
> ### SYNOPSIS
>
> In one of the early poems, "Brutus," the ancient Roman opts for suicide rather than tyranny. "Remembrances" concerns the tragedy of fleeting youth. In one of Leopardi's last poems, "The Setting of the Moon," he connects human life and historical development by comparing old age with a dark, moonless night.

gaged *canzoni* and *idilli* (idylls), poems that were more personal. These included "The Infinite" (1819), "To the Moon" (1819), and "The Solitary Life" (1821). In 1824 he began planning a philosophical work in prose, the *Operette Morali* (1835). The following years saw him enter a phase of restless travel, first to Milan, then to Bologna, Florence, and Pisa. The death of one of his brothers, Luigi, called Leopardi back to Recanati for 16 months, a period in which he wrote some of his most important poems—known collectively as the *great idylls* ("The Solitary Thrush," "The Calm after the Storm," and "The Village Saturday"). In 1830 Leopardi left Recanati forever,

The Canti (Songs)

Giacomo Leopardi

returning to Florence, only to be crushed by a failed passion for one of its aristocratic ladies, Fanny Targioni-Tozzetti. Leopardi spent his last five years in Naples writing satirical works and poems. His failing health took a sudden turn for the worse and he died on June 14, 1837, leaving behind two final poems, "The Broom or The Flower of the Desert" and "The Setting of the Moon." His stature would grow thereafter, until he gained renown as Italy's major nineteenth century poet.

Events in History at the Time of the Poems

Discrepancies of the new century. Leopardi's works, though spanning human history, are deeply rooted in the political and cultural milieux of nineteenth-century Italy. Early in the century, the levels of disparity among the various Italian states drew attention. The French general Napoleon Bonaparte invaded northern Italy in 1796. In the following three years, most northern regions of the Italian peninsula were reorganized as republics under French control. The new administrative and legal unity in much of the North encouraged the sector's economic development, generating a new faith in progress and fostering dreams of unity there. The sector established a common pattern of districts and departments, adopted a uniform set of weights and measures, and introduced Napoleonic penal and other codes. But often the reforms were not put into effect, and corruption raged: "it is unbelievable," said one official in Naples, "how much employees [of the new government] steal and embezzle; the vice has passed into their blood" (Duggan, p. 94). Meanwhile, Italian patriots in the North saw all the reorganization of their section of the peninsula as an opportunity for the whole land to enter modernity. This involved fighting the old feudal forces that still prevailed in the South and in the pope's mainly rural dominions (including Leopardi's region, the Marche). New laws in 1806-08 ended some of the feudal practices, but produced disappointing results. Common lands and lands of the old ruling houses were sold largely to new middle-class landowners, who differed little from the noble class in their views and practices, with no distribution to the peasants. France received the proceeds of the sales, confirming that Napoleon intended not to liberate Italy but to carve it up for his family and use it to finance French endeavors.

In 1797, Napoleon bargained with Austria, ceding it the Italian region of Veneto. Disillusionment set in abruptly among the Italians. It worsened under Napoleon's highly despotic regime that intended to make the Italian peninsula a mere satellite of France. Italian intellectuals despaired. As in past centuries, Italy seemed to serve as a mere "pawn in the diplomatic and dynastic games of others" (Duggan, p. 93). These political events shook the belief that history produced continuous progress, a central idea on the earlier 1700s Enlightenment movement that highly valued the human ability to reason. Nevertheless Napoleonic rule in Italy (1796-1814) gave rise to more than despair. During these years the idea of national unity took root. This dream developed within a few decades into the Risorgimento, the movement for the formation of a modern, unitary Italy. This was far from apparent immediately after Napoleon's rule of Italy collapsed, though. The old rulers quickly returned to power—Victor Emmanuel I in Turin, Ferdinand III in Florence, the pope in Rome—and another outside power, Austria, dominated most of the peninsula.

The decline of the Age of Reason. The political impetus for unification was born on the heels of major developments in other spheres of human activity. At the end of the eighteenth century, a new artistic and cultural movement emerged in various parts of Europe. The new movement rejected the steadfast faith in reason and progress that marked the Enlightenment. Initiating the new movement were artists, writers, and intellectuals who felt the logical and clear processes of rational thought had failed. These processes seemed incapable of shedding enough light on a rapidly changing political and social reality, where cataclysmic events like the French Revolution (1789) shattered social and political order. The Enlightenment gave way to Romanticism, which stressed not reason but freedom and heroic action, as well as strong sentiment. A force that initially just opposed total faith in rationality grew into a movement with its own Romantic art, works that focused on "feelings and mood" rather than "reason."

The Romantics showed an interest in the most' mysterious aspects of reality. One result of this attraction to the mysterious was a change in attitude towards nature. Rather than an idyllic setting for human life, Romantics recognized nature's independent power, with its rules and cycles not necessarily corresponding to the needs and wishes of humans.

Classicism and Romanticism. An article by the Frenchwoman Madame de Staël brought the ideas of Romanticism, already popular in northern Europe, to the attention of Italian intellectuals. The article, "On the Manner and Utility of Translations" (1816), urged Italian writers to look "beyond the Alps" to developments elsewhere and familiarize themselves with the new European sensibility:

> In my opinion, Italians should start to diligently translate the most recent British and German poems, in order to show a few new things to their countrymen, who for the most part are content with ancient mythology and think that those old fables are not antiquated at all, while the rest of Europe has already abandoned and forgotten them.
>
> (Madame de Staël in Marchese, p. 66; trans. F. Santini)

The Italian response was mixed. Some writers chose to embrace Madame de Staël's advice, resolving to transform and update Italian literature. Traditionalists bristled at her harsh attack, staunchly rejecting her idea. Among the latter was Pietro Giordani, a friend and mentor of young Giacomo Leopardi. Giordani agreed that many writers used a dated style, but he felt that an over-reliance on foreign writings would destroy rather than enrich Italian literature. In Giordani's opinion, instead of becoming a part of the new European mania for novelty, Italian writers should look back to proud moments of their literary tra-

dition (to predecessors such as Dante). Leopardi joined the debate, siding with Giordani and the supporters of the "classical style." In a letter on the subject written shortly after the publication of de Staël's essay, he argued that originality could not come from studying foreign literature. Leopardi regarded the "classic" style of ancient writers as naturally superior to modern ones because of the purer conditions of antiquity, in which humans could relate more directly to nature.

ORIGINS OF "ROMANTICISM"

The term "Romanticism" derives from the English adjective "romantic," originally indicating the fantastic and adventurous nature of certain popular seventeenth-century literary works. In the following century, French philosopher Jean Jacques Rousseau (1671-1741) started using the word as a synonym for "picturesque" or "melancholic," referring to those vague, nostalgic feelings stimulated in a sensitive soul through the contemplation of barren, solitary natural landscapes. It was in Germany, though, that the term (translated into "romantik") acquired a completely positive value, emblematic of the new conception of art and literature that opposed the classical values of the Enlightenment.

In his early writings, Leopardi revealed his position by remaining more passively deferential toward classical authors, apparent in the somewhat stilted verses of one of his first songs, "To Italy." Later, he developed a very personal poetic style, reflecting a respect and knowledge of the tradition of Italian literature and a deep understanding of modernity (including Romanticism) to create a highly innovative body of work.

The Poems in Focus

Contents summary. *The Canti* includes both *canzoni*, longer poems on historical or social themes, and *idylls*, short, contemplative poems centered on more personal sensations, memories, and feelings of the writer. In an idyll, the author reduces explicit references to the outside world to a minimum.

"Brutus." Among the early *canzoni*, "Brutus," written in 1821 and first published in 1824, deals with suicide in ancient Roman society. After depicting in highly dramatic tones the scene of the battle of

Philippi (42 B.C.E.) and introducing the character of the defeated Marcus Junius Brutus, the poem presents the thoughts of Brutus himself in a monologue. His suicide is representative of the crucial moment that marks the end of the Roman Republic and the beginning of the decline of Rome. As Brutus tells it, the demise of the republic is a sign of inevitable corruption, which he predicts signifies the ruin of Rome and the whole world.

LIBERTY OR DEATH IN ANCIENT ROME

A lover of the republican form of government in ancient Rome and its associated freedom, Marcus Brutus (85?-42 B.C.E.) joined the conspiracy to kill Julius Caesar (100-44 B.C.E.). Apparently Brutus, a senator praised for his virtue, was pressured by Cassius to join the conspiracy, a resolute group of more than 60 who refused to accept Caesar's decision to remain a dictator for life. The assassins had no follow-up plan, expecting the constitution to reassert itself and republican government to return of its own accord. For five months, Brutus remained in Italy waiting, but the people's loyalty to the now-dead Caesar only intensified, shifting to his former co-consul Mark Antony and nephew Octavian. Brutus finally went into voluntary exile, where he raised an army with Cassius that was later crushed by Antony and Octavian. Deeming the republican cause lost, Brutus committed suicide by his own sword. He left behind a lofty reputation for honorable deeds and noble commitment, stirring compassion, as Leopardi's poem suggests, for centuries to come. That Brutus also stirred such compassion in his own day is evident in the ancient words of Plutarch, who observed that the victors in Rome could not stop people there from "thinking that the unjust and wicked who destroyed the just and good did not deserve to rule" (Plutarch in Clarke, p. 71).

After an era of purity and innocence, civilization is destined for decay. Brutus, though he can foretell the destiny of his world, realizes that historical development itself has caused this imminent ruin and that corruption is part of progress:

> Did gods perhaps arrange our miseries,
> Our bitter chances, our unhappy feelings,
> As drama to delight their hours of ease?
> No life of grievous guilt—
> Free in the woods a life of innocence
> Nature ordained for us
> (Leopardi, "Brutus," *Canti*, p. 30)

Now, the poem continues, that corruption has laid waste to nature's blessed kingdom, will nature blame the "dart" that is not natural but self-inflicted (a suicide) ("Brutus," *Canti*, p. 30)? As the poem portrays it, Brutus's suicide is an act of extreme heroism, a last attempt to deny the power of history by refusing to take part in future ruinous events. At the same time, the suicide is a sign of the powerlessness of even the most virtuous of individuals to oppose fate, and more generally, of the vanity of human efforts against the preordered scheme of history.

"Remembrances." During his stay in Pisa, after leaving Recanati, Leopardi composed a group of poems considered the very nucleus of his *Canti*. These works, known as the *great idylls*, center on the themes of the loss of youth, the illusory quality of happiness, and the infinite misery of the human condition. The sense of isolation, already established as one of the main topics of Leopardi's *canzoni*, is moved from history to the individual in the great idylls. The somewhat emphatic, highly dramatic tone of the *canzoni* also becomes much sweeter and more tranquil in style. Though these poems too convey a sense of desperation, they robe their subjects in serene, lyrical sadness rather than indignant or highly rhetorical cries.

One of the great idylls, "Remembrances" (1829), concerns the implacable loss of all the hopes of youth. The poem, consisting of seven long stanzas of verses in the hendecasyllable form, recalls different moments of the poet's past. A sorrowful appeal to the stars ("Beautiful stars of the Bear") leads to a recollection of the evenings young Leopardi spent gazing at the nocturnal sky from the garden of his home in Recanati:

> When, silent, sitting on the verdant turf
> I used to pass the best part of each evening
> Scanning the sky, and listening to the music
> Of distant frogs in open countryside!
> The fireflies wandered here and there by
>   hedges
> And bedded flowers . . .
> ("Remembrances," *Canti*, p. 89)

In such a setting, never-realized dreams took shape:

> . . . What enormous
> Thoughts, and what dreams came to me at
>   the sight
> Of that sea in the distance, those blue
>   mountains
> (I make them out from here) I had in mind
> To cross one day . . .
> ("Remembrances," *Canti*, p. 89)

In the following stanzas the ideas of death and loss of illusions reappear ever more forcefully until the climax, in which personal destiny symbolizes the fate of humanity:

> Fugitive days! Fast as a lightning-flash
> They're over. And what mortal can be ever
> Blind to life's blows, once he has seen the last
> Of that brief brilliant season, once his best
> Of times, his youth, has been extinguished?
>> ("Remembrances," *Canti,* p. 92)

The final stanza closes the poem with renewed tenderness through an invocation to a girl, Nerina, who died in her youth. Nerina represents the impossibility of going back to even the illusion of love:

> But you have passed on;
> Sighed for, you have passed on: and as
>> companion
> For all my fine imaginings, for all
> My tender senses, and my heart's sad beats,
> What I am left with is the harsh remembrance.
>> ("Remembrances," *Canti,* p. 93)

"The Setting of the Moon." At the end of his life, Leopardi composed two final philosophical poems, "The Broom" and "The Setting of the Moon," in which personal sorrows once again evolve into a general sense of disillusionment. This last poem contains a fusion of themes and rhythms. Within a strongly negative argument that humans have no hope of partaking in the eternity of nature is another, more vibrant perspective: the notion that a fascinating world of beauty and illusion pulsates magically, though briefly, under the surface of everyday things. Schematically, "The Setting of the Moon" unfolds as follows:

- Just as the moon sets leaving the world immersed in total obscurity, human youth fades, leaving life empty and dark. (Stanzas 1 and 2)
- Old age was imposed on humanity by the gods, who did not think that human life was already bitter enough. (Stanza 3)
- After the darkness of night, nature will reawaken to a new, shiny dawn; in contrast, humans will never be able to reawaken after the darkness of old age. (Stanza 4)

Leopardi compares human life to the night. It is beautiful and fascinating when the night is still young, its moonlight transforming and beautifying reality, becoming dark and hopeless at the end. (Such a comparison is unusual in Western literature, which normally connects life to day and death to night. On the other hand, Leopardi's choice of a nocturnal landscape is typically Ro-

mantic; the attraction to night is one of the great themes of European Romantic poetry.) The world of illusions is dominant in the first stanza, a nocturnal realm filled with moonlight:

> Over the silvered countryside and water,
> Where Zephyrus [the west wind] is breathing,
> Where many a shadow makes
> A myriad vague shapes
> A myriad illusions
> In the unrippled seas
> And branches hedges hills and villages;
>> ("The Setting of the Moon," *Canti,* p. 138)

Next, darkness triumphs over the familiar landscapes of Italy (the Alps, the Apennines, and the Tyrrenian Mountains): "The moon goes down; and drains the world of color" ("The Setting of the Moon," *Canti,* p. 138). Suddenly the world loses its shape, and the landscape, before transformed by the moonlight into a swirling vortex of silvery beams, is now enveloped by obscurity. Beauty vanishes in the very moment it has reached its greatest power. The stanza closes with the human voice of a solitary wagon-driver who, with a mournful song, bids farewell to the moon and the beauty it had created. The wagoner shows the indifference of nature to the human condition: the moon, deaf to the man's song, proceeds in its cycle, leaving him totally alone. His song signals the disappearance of the moon, but it cannot hold it back: humans, incapable of containing such beauty, are limited to just a brief perception of it.

In the second stanza, a comparison between the setting of the moon and the fading of youth is developed. Moon:night = youth:life.

Stanza 1:
"the moon goes down"
"the night is left bereft"

Stanza 2:
"our youth disappears"
"our life is . . . / abandoned and obscure"
>> ("The Setting of the Moon," *Canti,* p. 138)

Again Leopardi at once refers to the youth of individuals and all humanity, once "young" and innocent. In this poem too, a single individual becomes representative of humankind. There are no direct references to the poet, but at the end of the stanza is a "doubtful traveler," and certainly he can be thought of as Leopardi. Now alone and hopeless, the poet, whose own youth has quickly waned, faces the end of his life:

> The doubtful traveler but vainly tries
> To find some kind of purpose in his way
> Ahead; only to see

How human haunts become
Estranged from him, and he estranged from
them.
("The Setting of the Moon," *Canti*, p. 138)

However, the *canzone* constitutes more than the poet's farewell as he sits dying in the villa of Torre del Greco. The poem also serves as a concluding point in his philosophical reflections on human life. At the end of the second stanza, old age is the absence of everything that is positive: "and good will never come again" ("The Setting of the Moon," *Canti*, p. 139). Such bitterness and despair progress into the third and last stanza, in which the comparison between night and human life finally dissolves into dawn, a dawn that is impossible for the individual. This is a primordial dawn, a rebirth repeating itself identically from the beginning of times. It pervades the world with unthinkable splendor, one that completely excludes humans:

ON THE RELATION BETWEEN HUMAN YOUTH AND ANCIENT HISTORY

The *Zibaldone*, the collection of Leopardi's thoughts, contains many references to youth and old age. A particularly important entry of August 24, 1821, distinguishes between individual youth and historical youth. "Let us consider nature. Which is the age of man that was destined by nature to be the happiest? Is it perhaps old age, when human senses are visibly decaying, and one fades, wanes, weakens? It would be a contradiction for happiness, which is in other words the perfection of a human being, to be located in a time that naturally marks the decay and the corruption of that being. Therefore it is youth, the bloom of life, when the senses are the most vigorous etc., which marks the age of perfection and of a possible happiness both of humans and of all other things. Now, youth is an evident image of the ancient world, while old age represents modern times. . . . Therefore, ancient times were happier than the modern ones. The consequences of this consideration are incredibly vast" (Leopardi, *Zibaldone* 1555-1556, *Tutte le opere*; trans. F. Santini).

But human life, when once its best of times,
Its youth, has disappeared, will not again
Be tinged with any light, or other dawn,
But widowed to the end; and to the night
Which fills old age with gloom
The gods have set no limit but the tomb.
("The Setting of the Moon," *Canti*, p. 139)

The inadequate individual. In "Brutus," the hero chooses suicide to avoid participating in the corrupted destiny that awaits his country: "The times / change for the worse; we would be mad to trust / to poor posterity / the honor of high minds . . . ," declares Brutus. "Carry my corpse away! / The wind disperse my name and memory!" ("Brutus," *Canti*, p. 32).

At this stage, Leopardi was still siding with "Classicism," explaining his choice of an ancient Roman character. Yet his treatment of the subject is highly personal and emotional, in other words, closely related to Romanticism. The poem certainly does not use ancient history or mythology to escape or avoid dealing with the contemporary world. Rather, the use of classical characters allows Leopardi to depict the unchanging situation of humankind throughout time. Leopardi shows what he sees as the relentlessly negative position of individuals within history, a history both ancient and contemporary. Brutus is as much a modern man as a Roman when he faces the unbeatable forces of nature and destiny. Leopardi, who by then had already flirted with taking his own life, no doubt identified with the Roman. Like Brutus, Leopardi observed the condition of his country with dismay; it had no strong army, he noted in his poem "To Italy" (1818), a factor Napoleon had shown to be key to any land's strength. In 1819 anguish and loneliness brought Leopardi to the verge of suicide. As he wrote to one of his few friends, Pietro Giordani:

> I'm so astonished by the nothing that surrounds me, that I don't know how to find the strength to pick up my pen and answer your letter [. . .]. This is the first time that boredom not only oppresses and tires me, but also anguishes me and tears me apart like a fiery pain. I am so scared by the vanity of things, and by the condition of man, for whom all passions are dead, just as they are extinguished in my soul, that I have come to the astounding realization that my very desperation is nothing.
> (Leopardi, *Tutte le opere*, p. 1157;
> trans. F. Santini)

Leopardi's despondent outlook persisted during the writing of "Brutus" in 1821 and extended into the 1830s, which found him surrounded by a group of supportive intellectuals in Florence who were hopeful about Italy's destiny as a unified nation. Leopardi did not share their optimism; by this time, Italy's problems appeared of little consequence in light of the general condition of humanity, as he confessed to a Florentine intellectual:

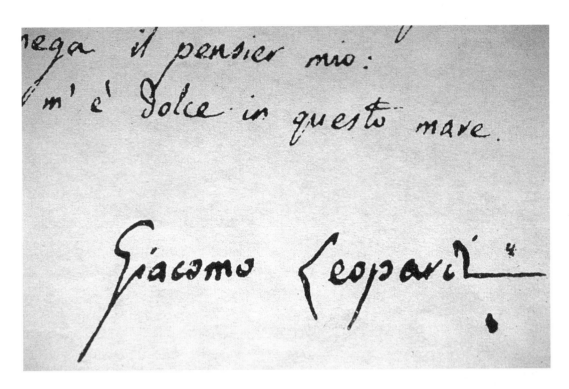

Giacomo Leopardi's signature.

In my eyes, men are just what they are in nature, that is a very tiny part of the universe, and my relations with them or their mutual relations don't interest me at all; since I'm not interested, I don't notice them if not in the most superficial of manners.

> (Leopardi, *Tutte le opere*, pp. 1242-43;
> trans. F. Santini)

Leopardi was certainly not alone in his negative outlook. Many beliefs were shattered in his era. The ideals of "liberty," "fraternity," and "equality," the basis for the French Revolution, seemed impossible to realize. The Revolution itself had turned into a great massacre, and the consequent ascent of Napoleon led, as shown, to a new authoritarian regime.

Meanwhile, the notion that there is more to value in human beings than rational thought had prompted Romantic thinkers and artists to focus on obscure aspects of the soul and on bitter themes, such as death, sorrow, and most of all the transitory quality of human life. Out of these preoccupations came the creation of dramatic anti-heroes, who, instead of adapting to circumstances, often clashed with what they saw as a world full of contradictions. They chose suicide rather than compromise, conscious of their own inadequacy in the grand scheme of reality. Brutus, as Leopardi portrays him, is one such anti-hero. A highly philosophical poem, "Brutus"

unveils the desolate condition of humanity through time, robbing even classical Rome of its illusion of purity. Little seemed to Leopardi to have changed. History, rather than progressing, as alleged by the philosophers of the Enlightenment, appeared to be falling back as a new wave of repression and absolutism gripped Europe. While in Italy a newfound sense of a national identity had begun to take root, it appeared more of a dream than a realistic objective.

Sources. Because of Leopardi's immensely vast literary knowledge, references to many writers, both ancient and modern, can be found in his works. The poet himself often noted, in the *Zibaldone*, how his usage of a certain expression coincided with that of other writers, as in *inargentate* ("silvered"), a word that did not belong to the Italian of his day, but that he nevertheless used at the beginning of "The Setting of the Moon": "Over the silvered countryside and water" (*Canti*, p. 138). Leopardi himself noted that many poets of the past had associated that word with the light of the moon, including Boccaccio (who used the adjective in one of his lesser-known works, *Ameto*) and Torquato Tasso (in Canto 18 of **Jerusalem Delivered**, also in *WLAIT 7: Italian Literature and Its Times*). Among other influential Italian poets of the past is Petrarch, whose words musically reverberate in many of Leopardi's verses. Line 48 of "The Setting of the Moon," for example ("There still remains desire, but hope has gone" [*Canti*, p. 139]), echoes line 4 of Petrarch's Sonnet 277 ("desire's alive, but all hope's dead" [Petrarch, p. 291]; trans. F. Santini).

Given Leopardi's stated preference for ancient authors of the "classical style," one would expect him to draw more from them than from modern works; in *Zibaldone*, the poet noted that:

> The eternal source of all that is great and beautiful are writers, works, examples, habits, and feelings of ancient times; and any extraordinary spirit of today feeds on antiquity.
>
> (*Zibaldone* 341 in *Tutte le opere*;
> trans. F. Santini)

Leopardi's notes reflect the deep effect on him of reading works by Virgil, Xenophon, Ceres of Callimachus, Homer, and Plato. But Leopardi's literary knowledge was not limited to ancient authors; references to authors of his times (in particular, he had dedicated great attention to the works of the French philosophers belonging to the Enlightenment movement) and echoes of modern poets can often be found in his writings. In "The Setting of the Moon," next to the lines reminiscent of Petrarch, veiled allusions can be traced to one of the works that most influenced Romantic poets throughout Europe. James Macpherson's *Fragments of Ancient Poetry* (1760) is a collection of moody, nocturnal verses translating ancient Scottish and Irish songs, which Leopardi had read in the Italian translation by Cesarotti.

Once again, in his personal and inventive use of sources, Leopardi posed himself between antiquity and modernity. He created highly innovative works that are simultaneously revolutionary in style and content, yet firmly rooted in tradition.

Reception. During Leopardi's brief life, his literary efforts, though admired by a tight circle of intellectuals and friends, were mostly ignored by the wider public. The personal isolation of the poet, his absence from vigorous centers of intellectual life including Rome and Milan, and his own preference for tradition and ancient literature over fresh approaches all contributed to the general perception of his work. He preferred to write about his personal dramas rather than to help advance the struggle for liberty begun by some other writers of his day, including his own mentor Pietro Giordani. Much of the early criticism of Leopardi's works shared this negative

opinion of the poet, whom many thought of as a skilled but dispassionate writer. Critics saw a pessimistic individual whose writing reflected his own despair and isolation. This is certainly reductive in view of the strong connections of Leopardi's work with the new climate of Romanticism and the similarity between his themes and those of the best European poets of his period, such as England's William Wordsworth. A first step in re-evaluating Leopardi came in 1947, when Cesare Luporini published "A Progressive Leopardi" ("Leopardi progressivo"). Subsequent new studies considered the poet's personal situation along with his attention to the destiny of humankind and his continuing reflections on history and progress. Today, Leopardi is viewed as a highly original writer who achieved an extremely personal fusion of "Classicism" (a reverence for the imaginative and pure literature of the classical past) and "Romanticism." He is counted as one of the most innovative and poignant poets of his time.

—Federica Santini

For More Information

Alexander, Foscarina. *The Aspiration Toward a Lost Natural Harmony in the Work of Three Italian Writers: Leopardi, Verga, and Moravia*. Lewiston, N.Y.: E. Mellen Press, 1990.

Brioschi, Franco. *La poesia senza nome: saggio su Leopardi*. Milan: il Saggiatore, 1980.

Clarke, M. L. *The Noblest Roman: Marcus Brutus and His Reputation*. London: Thames and Hudson, 1981.

De Man, Paul. *The Rhetoric of Romanticism*. New York: Columbia University Press, 1984.

Duggan, Christopher. *A Concise History of Italy*. Cambridge: Cambridge University Press, 1984.

Ficara, Giorgio. *Il punto di vista della natura*. Genova: Il melangolo, 1996.

Leopardi, Giacomo. *The Canti: With a Selection of His Prose*. Trans. J. G. Nichols. Manchester: Carcaness Press, 1994.

———. *The Letters of Leopardi 1817-1837*. Trans. Prue Shaw. Leeds: Northern University Press, 1998.

———. *Thoughts*. Trans. J. G. Nichols. London: Hesperus Press, 2002.

———. *Tutte le opere*. Ed. W. Binni. Florence: Sansoni, 1969.

Marchese, A. *Storia interestuale della letteratura italiana*. Florence: D'Anna, 1991.

Petrarch. *Canzoniere*. Ed. M. A. Camozzi. Milan: Rizzoli, 1954.

The Canzoniere

by

Francesco Petrarch

THE LITERARY WORK

A connected sequence of lyric poems set in Italy and Avignon, France, during the fourteenth century; published in Italian (as *Rerum vulgarium fragmenta* [Fragments in the Vernacular]) in 1470, in English in part c. 1557.

SYNOPSIS

A poet relates the vicissitudes of his love for an unattainable woman, a love that endures even after her death.

Born in the Tuscan city of Arezzo in 1304, Francesco Petrarca (better known as Petrarch) was the son of an exiled Florentine notary. His early years were spent in Pisa, Tuscany, and in Avignon, and Carpentras in Provence, where he was educated in grammar and rhetoric. In 1316 he began legal studies, first at Montpellier, then in Bologna. Upon the death of his father, however, Petrarch abandoned the law to pursue a Church career that would enable him to concentrate on literature and scholarship instead. He returned to Avignon and in 1330 was appointed household chaplain to Cardinal Giovanni Colonna, who remained Petrarch's patron for many years. While in Colonna's service, Petrarch purchased a house in Vaucluse on the left bank of the Sorgue River and began to compose Italian lyrics and scholarly works in Latin, including the *Africa*, an epic celebrating the military hero Scipio Africanus, and *De viris illustribus* (On Famous Men), historical biographies written in the manner of the Roman historian Livy. Petrarch eventually acquired a reputation as one of the foremost Italian humanists, members of a widespread intellectual movement inspired by classical art and classical writings on philosophy, history, science, and literature. In 1341 Petrarch was crowned poet laureate at the Campidoglio in Rome. He was at this point hard at work on the *Canzoniere* (poetic "songbook"), otherwise known as the *Rime Sparse* ("scattered rhymes"). The work is a series of erotic poems that Petrarch wrote in the Italian vernacular about his love for the mysterious beauty "Laura," whom he first encoun-

tered on April 6, 1327, at the church of St. Clare. Apparently in 1348 Laura and Cardinal Colonna both succumbed to the Black Death, the bubonic plague that was ravaging Europe. Petrarch himself escaped the plague, though he recorded these devastating personal losses in the *Canzoniere*; Laura's death, in particular, shaped the resolution of the sequence of poems. Tiring of Church politics, Petrarch left Avignon in 1353 and spent his remaining years in various Italian provinces. He continued work on the *Canzoniere*, sorting and arranging its poems, until his death in 1374. Although Petrarch was best known among contemporaries for his Latin writings, his vernacular works, especially the *Canzoniere*, are now regarded as his masterpieces. His exploration of the emotional states of love, yearning, and spiritual aspiration in this work would have a major influence on future generations of poets.

Francesco Petrarch

Events in History at the Time of the Poems

Petrarch's Laura. At the center of the *Canzoniere* is the enigmatic figure of Laura, whose beauty, chastity, and unattainableness inspired most of Petrarch's Italian poems. Several attempts have been made to identify a real-life "Laura"; at one point, she was believed to be Laura de Noves, an ancestress of the Marquis de Sade. But these attempts ultimately proved fruitless, leading some to speculate that Laura was wholly a creation of the imagination. Petrarch, however, assured at least one skeptical friend, Giacomo Colonna, that "Laura" and his passion for her were real: "I wish indeed," remarked the poet, "that you were joking about this particular subject, and that she indeed had been a fiction and not a madness" (Petrarch in Braden, p. 16).

Additional proof of Laura's existence appeared on the flyleaf of Petrarch's copy of Virgil's poetry. In the habit of writing obituaries of his friends and relatives, Petrarch apparently penned the following note about his beloved:

> Laura, illustrious through her own virtues, and long famed through my verses, first appeared to my eyes in my youth, in the year of our Lord 1327, on the sixth day of April, in the church of St. Clare in Avignon, at matins; and in the same city, also on the sixth day of April, at the

same first hour, but in the year 1348, the light of her life was withdrawn from the light of day, while I, as it chanced, was in Verona, unaware of my fate. The sad tidings reached me in Parma, in the same year, on the morning of the 19th day of May, in a letter from my Ludovicus. Her chaste and lovely form was laid to rest at vesper time, on the same day on which she died in the burial place of the Brothers minor. I am persuaded that her soul returned to the heaven from which it came, as Seneca says of Africanus.

> (Petrarca, *Canzoniere,* pp. 5-6)

Other evidence comes in the form of a portrait of Laura. Mentioned in Sonnets 77 and 78 of the *Canzoniere*, it was painted by Simone Martini of Siena but was then lost.

Poems from the *Canzoniere* describe Laura as blonde and beautiful. Beyond these details, however, little is known about her. Her social rank and marital status are never revealed in the poetry, nor is the exact nature of her relationship with Petrarch, whether they were friends, mere acquaintances, or even complete strangers. Nonetheless, Laura, or rather Petrarch's response to Laura, determined the overall shape of the *Canzoniere*. While her thoughts and emotions remain unknowable, those of her lover—from his first sight of her in Sonnet 3 to his reaction to her death from the plague in Sonnet 267—are vividly portrayed.

The courtly love tradition. The poems in the *Canzoniere* reflect the established mode of courtly love, which originated in France in the late eleventh century. As celebrated by the troubadours and poets from the Provençal region in southern France, *l'amour courtois* challenged and redefined Christian ideals of love, marriage, virtue, masculinity, and femininity. Powerful nobles, such as Eleanor of Aquitaine and Marie de Champagne, patronized these troubadours, with the result that the philosophy of courtly love soon spread throughout the courts of Europe.

According to the troubadour songs, relationships based upon the tenets of courtly love shared several attributes: the couple involved was always of noble rank; the male lover wooed his chosen lady with gifts, tokens, and songs in praise of her beauty; the lovers' passion for each other was a closely guarded secret; and finally, the lovers' romantic bond was adulterous. One or both could be married, but never to each other, and their illicit love often went unconsummated, fueled by its very lack of fulfillment.

Of the two, the male lover played the more active role in the relationship, performing deeds of valor and skill in honor of his lady. By contrast, the lady was beautiful, distant, and passive. She might reward her lover's efforts with a brief gesture of approval or affection, but for the most part, she remained on the pedestal where he had placed her. The rituals of courtship took on the significance of religious observance, with the earthly beloved replacing the heavenly goddess, or, in Christian terms, the Virgin Mary.

By the thirteenth century, the precepts of courtly love had taken firm hold in Italy. Indeed, the Provençal School influenced the development of the *dolce stil novo* ("sweet new style"), an important literary movement in thirteenth-century Florence (see **Stil Novo Poetry**, also in *WLAIT 7: Italian Literature and Its Times*). Introduced by Guido Guinizzelli, this style celebrated the spiritual and intellectual, rather than the carnal, aspects of love. The relationship between lovers was purified, becoming wholly platonic; the woman's loveliness inspired the man with a deeper comprehension of divine beauty. Dante Alighieri greatly admired the *dolce stil novo*, which influenced his writings about his enduring passion for his love, Beatrice, even after her death. Petrarch's *Canzoniere* was likewise affected; his poetry can be said to work within the *dolce stil nuovo* tradition, to which he added. Petrarch's innovation was to convey with a vivid freshness the lover's psychology—specifically, his innermost thoughts and feelings about his love, in Petrarch's case, about Laura.

The Avignon papacy. While most of the poems in the *Canzoniere* are romantic in nature, Petrarch also condemns—in a handful of sonnets—the religious politics of his time, especially those of the papal court in Avignon, the French city where Petrarch lived and worked for several years. Nor was he the only one of his contemporaries to do so.

In 1309 the papacy moved from Rome—the longtime, official center of the pontiff—to Avignon. After asserting his supremacy to all Christian rulers in a papal bull (an official proclamation), Pope Boniface VIII was assaulted by agents of King Philip IV of France, with fatal results for the 86-year-old pontiff. Fearing reprisals from Italians and anxious over rebellion and intrigue in Rome, the new pope, Clement V (r. 1305-1314), decided to establish his court at Avignon, in Provence, near the mouth of the Rhone River, a decision influenced by his friendship with Philip IV of France. Although the move was to be only temporary, Clement and six of his successors served out their terms in Avignon. This period (1309-1377) in Church history is sometimes known as the Babylonian exile, recalling the exile of the Israelites to Babylonia in the 500s B.C.E.

The Avignon papacy soon acquired a reputation for worldliness, pomp, extravagance, and corruption. Simony, the selling of official posts,

THE BLACK DEATH

The worldwide epidemic of bubonic plague known as the Black Death appears to have originated in India, the Middle East, and the Crimea around 1346. Carried by the fleas of shipboard rats, the disease traveled westward, reaching Italy in October 1347. Within days of exposure to the Black Death, hundreds lay dying, while panicked survivors spread the plague even farther when they fled. Port cities were among the first to be stricken. By January 1348 the plague had reached Genoa and Pisa, moving on in the following months to Venice and the inland cities of Tuscany. The city of Florence was especially afflicted; in the introduction to his *Decameron*, Boccaccio claimed that 100,000 Florentines succumbed to the disease. By the spring of 1348 the plague had worked its way northward to attack Spain, Germany, France, and England. The death rate was horrifying; modern historians estimate that the epidemic claimed perhaps one-third of Italy's population (Killinger, p. 67). A contemporary account, by Henry Knighton, canon of Leicester Abbey, presents a stark record of the casualties in several European lands, including France: "There died in Avignon, France in one day one thousand three hundred and twelve persons, according to an account made for the pope. At Montpellier there remained out of a hundred and fifty friars only seven. At Marseilles out of a 150 friars minor, there remained only one who could tell the others" (Knighton). Although Petrarch himself escaped the plague, Laura and Cardinal Colonna—both living in Avignon—apparently fell victim to the disease, a double tragedy commemorated in *The Canzoniere*.

became a widespread practice. Other unpopular practices included decreasing the finances of parish priests, taxing bishops heavily, selling indulgences (cancellations of earthly punishment for sins that have been forgiven), and charging heavily for all papal court services. As one historian explains it,

> Diminished by its removal from the Holy See of Rome and by being generally regarded as a tool of France, the papacy sought to make up

prestige and power in temporal terms. It concentrated on finance and the organization and centralization of every process of papal government that could bring in revenue. . . . Everything the Church had or was, from cardinal's hat to pilgrim's relic, was for sale.

(Tuchman, p. 26)

Many clerics denounced the greed and corruption of the Avignon papacy. In the 1340s Petrarch wrote, "I am living in the Babylon of the West," comparing Avignon to the biblical city of vice and corruption. He went on to condemn the habits of prelates who feasted at "licentious banquets" and rode white horses "decked in gold, fed on gold, [and] soon to be shod in gold if the Lord does not check this slavish luxury" (Petrarch in Tuchman, p. 29). His disgust found fuller expression in several sonnets, among them, Sonnet 138, which he addressed to the papal court at Avignon: "O foundry of deceits, cruel prison where good dies and evil is / created and nourished, a hell for the living: it will be a great / miracle if Christ does not finally show his anger against you" (*Canzoniere*, p. 282).

The Poems in Focus

The contents. Petrarch's *Canzoniere* consists of 366 lyric poems: 317 sonnets, 29 canzoni, 9 sestinas, 7 ballads, and 4 madrigals. At one point, a manuscript of the *Canzoniere* was divided in two parts, one, including 263 poems, headed "in vita di madonna Laura" (During the Life of Madonna Laura) and the other, including 103 poems, entitled "in morte di madonna Laura" (During the Death of Madonna Laura). Another critic divides the poems into three categories: poems about Laura, poems that attempt to reject her influence, and poems that do not concern Laura at all. In any case, the Laura-related poems vastly outnumber the political and patriotic poems. The course of Petrarch's love for Laura—from his first view of her to his acceptance of her death—dictates the structure of the *Canzoniere*. But while Petrarch idealizes his beloved—often comparing her with the evergreen laurel of poetic inspiration—theirs is not an idyllic romance: for one thing, the chaste Laura keeps the smitten Petrarch at a distance, which only inflames him further. He furthermore comes to acknowledge that erotic desire has impeded his spiritual progress towards God and divine love.

In his opening poem, Petrarch establishes that he is looking back upon his life from the perspective of many years, referring to his "first

youthful error, when / I was in part another man from what I am now" (*Canzoniere*, p. 36). He claims to regret that youthful error and to have reached a truer understanding about the transience of earthly joys: "But now I see well how for a long time I was the talk of the / crowd, for which often I am ashamed of myself within; / and of my raving shame is the fruit, and repentance, and the / clear knowledge that whatever pleases in the world is a brief dream" (*Canzoniere*, p. 36).

From that point, Petrarch goes on to tell of his passion for Laura, which dates from their first meeting on April 6, 1327, the anniversary of Christ's crucifixion, namely, Good Friday.

Poem 3

It was the day when the sun's rays turned pale with grief for his Maker when I was taken, and I did not defend myself against it for your lovely eyes, Lady, bound me.

It did not seem to me a time for being on guard against Love's blows; therefore I went confident and without fear, and so my misfortunes began in the midst of the universal woe.

Love found me altogether disarmed, and the way open through my eyes to my heart, my eyes which are now the portal and passageways of tears.

Therefore, as it seems to me, it got him no honor to strike me with an arrow in that state, and not even to show his bow to you, who were armed.

(*Canzoniere*, p. 38)

No sooner has the poet glimpsed Laura than he falls violently in love with her. Significantly, Petrarch portrays himself as a captive, even a victim, of Love and Laura's beauty, a stance that does not alter throughout the cycle of poems. Love, in the classical personification of Cupid with his bow, is portrayed as such a powerful force that Petrarch can only struggle helplessly in its toils, unable—and unwilling—to free himself.

Poem 134

Peace I do not find, and I have no wish to make war; and I fear and hope, and burn and am of ice; and I fly above the heavens and lie on the ground; and I grasp nothing and embrace all the world.

One has me in prison who neither opens nor locks, neither keeps me for his own nor unties the bonds; and Love does not kill and does not unchain me, he neither wishes me alive nor frees me from the tangle.

I see without eyes, and I have no tongue and yet cry out; and I wish to perish and I ask for help; and I hate myself and love another.

I feed on pain, weeping I laugh; equally displeasing to me are death and life. In this state am I, Lady, on account of you.

(*Canzoniere*, p. 272)

In the above sonnet Petrarch describes how his passion for Laura has put him in a frenzy of conflicting emotions; he experiences intense pain and joy in equal measure. The paradoxes set forth in each of the poem's lines may be said to reflect the contradictory nature of love itself.

Poem 267

Alas the lovely face, alas the gentle glance, alas the proud, carefree bearing! Alas the speech that made every harsh or savage mind humble and every base man valiant!

And alas the sweet smile whence came forth the dart from which now I expect death, no other good! Regal soul, worthy of empire if you had not come down among us so late:

For you I must burn, in you breathe, for I have been only yours; and if I am deprived of you, it pains me more than any other misfortune;

with hope you filled me and with desire, when I left still alive that highest pleasure, but the wind carried off the words.

(*Canzoniere*, p. 436)

Petrarch's hope of consummating his love for Laura ends with his discovery of her death on April 6, 1348, at the same hour of their first meeting 21 years earlier. Devastated, he laments the loss of his beloved, for the sake of the virtues she possessed and the disappointment of his own hopes and desires.

The remaining poems of the *Canzoniere* all deal with Petrarch's attempts to come to terms with Laura's death. Despite his grief, the poet ultimately learns to look at the experience differently. He grows glad that Laura resisted his advances in life since this proves her perfect virtue and chastity. He never doubts that her soul has attained heaven. Furthermore, as the sequence draws to a close, Petrarch's thoughts themselves turn towards spiritual love and religious devotion. As his own life nears its end, he addresses the last poem in the *Canzoniere* (Poem 366) not to a mortal woman but to the Holy Virgin, asking for grace and pardon for past error and promising to love her with even more constancy than he gave to Laura:

Kindly virgin, enemy of pride, let love of our common origin move you, have mercy on a contrite and humble heart; for if I am wont to love with such marvelous faith a bit of deciduous mortal dust, how will I love you, a noble thing?

If from my wretched and vile state I rise again at your hands, Virgin, I consecrate and cleanse in your name my thought and wit and style, my tongue and heart, my tears and my sighs. Lead me to the better crossing and accept my changed desires.

The day draws near and cannot be far, time so runs and flies, single, sole Virgin; and now conscience, now death pierces my heart; commend me to your Son, true man and true God, that He may receive my last breath in peace.

(*Canzoniere*, p. 582)

THE PETRARCHAN SONNET

Petrarch did not invent the sonnet (a 14-line lyric poem written in iambic pentameter, with an interlocking rhyme scheme). He, however, became inextricably associated with this type of poem to the point where the Italian form also became known as the Petrarchan sonnet. The Italian sonnet consists of an octave (eight lines), followed by a sestet (six lines). Usually there is a break between the two around the ninth line of the poem, sometimes known as the *volta,* or "turn": the octave sets forth a situation, while the sestet presents a twist on or response to the octave. The octave's rhyme scheme is *a-b-b-a-a-b-b-a*; the sestet's, either *c-d-e-c-d-e* or *c-d-c-c-d-c.* Other early Italian practitioners of the form were Guittone d'Arezzo, Dante Alighieri, and Guido Cavalcanti, but their sonnets were less famous than those of Petrarch.

The spread of Petrarchism. After Petrarch's death, the poems of his *Canzoniere* circulated in a variety of incarnations, not merely in their original manuscript form, but in neo-Latin and vernacular translations and musical adaptations. Petrarch had inadvertently established a tradition of love poetry that would be admired and imitated for several centuries. Appropriately known as Petrarchism, this tradition found adherents not only in Italy but in other European countries as well.

The conventions of Petrarchan love poetry included the poet's address to his chosen lady (who usually had a classical name); praise of the lady's beauty in the most extravagant terms; recurring

Bologna University, the oldest surviving university in the world. In addition to Petrarch, other alumni include Torquato Tasso, author of *Jerusalem Delivered*.

contradictory phrases and images (fire and ice, captivity and freedom); emphasis on the poet's subjective experience of the pains and pleasures of love; characterization of the lady as the poet's muse and sole source of inspiration; and finally, the promise of immortality—the lady's and the poet's—through his verse. Later generations of poets found these conventions easy to imitate; many drew heavily on the works of Petrarch for their inspiration.

More than 100 years after Petrarch's death, his influence remained powerful. In Italy works such as Giusto de Conti's *La bella mano* (1440) and Matteo Maria Boiardo's *Amorum libri* (1499) imitated Petrarch's metrical patterns and the narrative structure of his *Canzoniere* (the pattern of the poet's love for a woman). Petrarchism gained momentum in the early 1500s, however, after Pietro Bembo (1470-1547), Venetian scholar and nobleman, proposed Petrarch as the stylistic and thematic model for all Italian verse. Like Latin prose, Bembo argued, vernacular poetry could only achieve excellence through study and imitation of a master. Numerous Italian poets, including Trifon Gabriele (1470-1549), Giovanni Guidiccioni (1500-1541), and Torquato Tasso (1544-1595), subscribed to Bembo's theory and composed poetry in the Petrarchan manner, praised for its purity and simplicity.

Petrarchism also flourished in other countries, especially after the invention of the printing press. In Tudor England, which had developed a passion for all things Italian, Petrarch's works found enthusiastic disciples in Sir Thomas Wyatt (1503-1542) and Henry Howard, Earl of Surrey (1517-1547), who translated several of the Italian poet's pieces into English. Indeed, Wyatt and Surrey are credited with introducing the sonnet form to England. Several English writers even composed their own sonnet sequences; Sir Philip Sidney's *Astrophel and Stella* (1591) follows the Petrarchan model closely, depicting the poet's love for a beautiful but inaccessible woman. Other English poets sought to subvert Petrarchan conventions; for example, Edmund Spenser's *Amoretti* (1595; Little Love Poems) told the story of a successful courtship between the poet and his beloved, which ended in marriage. And in one of his more famous sonnets, written around 1609, William Shakespeare introduces a series of Petrarchan superlatives only to reject them, concluding instead, "My mistress' eyes are nothing like the sun. . . . And yet, by heaven, I think my love as rare / As any she belied with false compare" (Shakespeare in Abrams, p. 884). Petrarchism endured as a literary movement throughout Europe until the seventeenth century, though modern scholars might argue that

PETRARCH AND HIS IMITATORS

Petrarch's poems inspired many later poets in his native Italian peninsula and abroad. Two of the more famous disciples were Sir Thomas Wyatt and Henry Howard, Earl of Surrey, who are usually credited with introducing Petrarch's poems to an English audience via their translations of his work. Petrarch's Sonnet 140 from the *Canzoniere* appears below, followed by Wyatt and Howard's translations of the same poem:

> Love, who lives and reigns in my thought and keeps his principal
> seat in my heart, sometimes comes forth all in armor into my
> forehead, there camps, and there sets up his banner.
>
> She who teaches us to love and to be patient, and wishes my
> great desire, my kindled hope, to be reined in by reason, shame,
> and reverence, at our boldness is angry within herself.
>
> Wherefore Love flees terrified to my heart, abandoning his every
> enterprise, and weeps and trembles; there he hides and no more
> appears outside.
>
> What can I do, when my lord is afraid, except stay with him until
> the last hour? For he makes a good end who dies loving well.
>
> (Canzoniere, p. 284)

> The long love that in my thought doth harbor
> And in mine heart doth keep his residence,
> Into my face presseth with bold pretence
> And therein campeth, spreading his banner.
> She that me learneth to love and suffer
> And will that my trust and lust's negligence
> Be reined by reason, shame, and reverence,
> With his hardiness taketh displeasure.
> Wherewithal unto the heart's forest he fleeth,
> Leaving his enterprise with pain and cry,
> And there him hideth and not appeareth.
> What may I do when my master feareth
> But in the field with him to live and die?
> For good is the life ending faithfully.
>
> (Wyatt in Abrams, p. 463)

> Love that doth reign and live within my thought
> And build his seat within my captive breast,
> Clad in the arms wherein with me he fought,
> Oft in my face he doth his banner rest.
> But she that taught me love and suffer pain,
> My doubtful hope and eke my hot desire
> With samefast look to shadow and refrain,
> Her smiling grace converteth straight to ire.
> And coward Love, then, to the heart apace
> Taketh his flight, where he doth lurk and plain,
> His purpose lost, and dare not show his face.
> For my lord's guilt thus faultless bide I pain,
> Yet from my lord shall not my foot remove:
> Sweet is the death that taketh end by love.
>
> (Howard in Abrams, p. 474)

Petrarch's influence in Italian poetry persists to this day.

Sources and literary context. Not surprisingly, Petrarch's own life was the primary source of inspiration for the *Canzoniere*. Indeed, it seems impossible to separate the speaker in the poems from the poet himself. Petrarch's unrequited passion for Laura, his grief over her untimely death, and even his frustration over the religious politics of his day all found their way into the poetic cycle. It also refers to other historical personages with whom Petrarch was familiar—his employer Cardinal Giovanni Colonna, for example, and Benedict XII, the pope from 1334 to 1342.

While Petrarch's own experiences shaped most of the *Canzoniere,* the poet also drew upon Christian texts, like the Bible and the writings of St. Augustine, from which he extrapolated that his love for Laura, however constant, was still sinful and that his thoughts were ultimately best directed towards God. Classical myths and legends influenced the *Canzoniere* too, especially the myth of Apollo and Daphne from Ovid's *Metamorphoses*. It has been argued that Petrarch viewed his hopeless desire for Laura as a reflection of Apollo's equally fruitless pursuit of Daphne. In both instances, the ladies refuse their pursuers, wishing only to remain chaste. Daphne, praying for deliverance from her pursuer, is transformed into a laurel tree. While Laura undergoes no such transformation, Petrarch continually associates her with the laurel tree and the poetic glory and fame that the laurel came to represent.

As a work, the *Canzoniere* is generally categorized as a collection of lyric poems, figuring among the earliest in Western literature to present a sustained narrative. While working within an established tradition of courtly love poetry, Petrarch's verses were considered notable for their intensely personal perspective and their musicality.

The *Canzoniere* can also be connected to humanism, the major intellectual movement of the Italian Renaissance. Inspired by the writings of classical Greek and Roman philosophers, the humanists devoted themselves to the study of ancient literature, history, politics, moral philosophy, and science. Their primary interest was humankind and all aspects of human existence. In the *Canzoniere*, Petrarch, who is considered one of the earliest humanists, depicts one such aspect—a man's experience of unrequited love.

Impact. While the first scholarly commentaries did not appear until about 70 years after the death of Petrarch (1304-1374), there were many early admirers of the work. One Italian chronicler Filippo Villani (c. 1325-1405) praises the *Canzoniere*'s lyricism and discloses its effect on an early audience: "the musical modulations of the verses which Petrarch addressed to Laura flowed so melodiously, that even the most grave could not refrain from repeating them" (Villani in Foscolo, p. 92).

Later disciples and imitators of Petrarch's poetic style were also lavish in their commendation. In England, it was widely held that "the sweete and stately measures and stile [sic] of the Italian Poesie," as practiced by Petrarch and adopted by the English poets Wyatt and Surrey, "greatly polished our rude & homelie manner of vulgar Poesie from that it had been before" (Puttenham in D'Amico, p. 11). Elizabethan scholar and critic Gabriel Harvey (c. 1550-1631) wrote that "All posterity honour Petrarck, that was the harmony of heaven; the lyfe of Poetry; the grace of Arte; a precious tablet of rare conceits, & a curious frame of exquisite workemanship; nothing but neate Witt, and refined eloquence" (Harvey in D'Amico, p. 8).

Although Petrarchan imitation became less frequent around the seventeenth century, his influence remained powerful. In his *Essays on Petrarch* (1823), the Italian poet and novelist Ugo Foscolo (1778-1827) summed up the enduring appeal of Petrarch's works, especially the *Canzoniere*: "It is precisely because the poetry of Petrarch originally sprang from his heart that his passion never seems fictitious or cold" (Foscolo, p. 62). Like previous admirers, Foscolo also praised the verse's musicality, arguing that "the sweetness of Petrarch is enlivened with a variety, a rapidity, and a glow, which no Italian lyric has ever possessed in an equal degree" (Foscolo, p. 92).

About 150 years later, toward the end of the twentieth century, the scholar Nicholas Mann attests to the supremacy of Petrarch's love-poetry, speaking of its international flavor, since by his time the poetry had been widely imitated and translated into multiple languages (Catalan, Spanish, Portuguese, French, English, Scottish, Flemish, Dutch, German, Dalmatian, Hungarian, Polish, Russian, and Cypriot Greek). Petrarch himself was working in a language still foreign to literature, vernacular Italian. When he used it to create a fresh love-poetry, he hardly expected such widespread and long-lasting acclaim; posterity, it seems, "has judged his vernacular fragments more kindly than ever he dared openly to hope" (Mann, p. 112).

—Pamela S. Loy

For More Information

Abrams, M. H., ed. *The Norton Anthology of English Literature*. Vol. 1. New York: W. W. Norton, 1986.

Braden, Gordon. *Petrarchan Love and the Continental Renaissance*. New Haven: Yale University Press, 1999.

D'Amico, Jack, ed. *Petrarch in England*. Ravenna: Longo, 1979.

Foscolo, Ugo. *Essays on Petrarch*. London: John Murray, 1823.

Foster, Kenelm. *Petrarch: Poet and Humanist*. Edinburgh: Edinburgh University Press, 1984.

Hainsworth, Peter. *Petrarch the Poet*. London: Routledge, 1988.

Hainsworth, Peter, and David Robey, eds. *The Oxford Companion to Italian Literature*. Oxford: Oxford University Press, 2002.

Killinger, Charles. *The History of Italy*. Westport, Conn.: Greenwood Press, 2002.

Knighton, Henry. "The Impact of the Black Death." *History Magazine—The Black Death*. http://www.history-magazine.com/black.html.

Mann, Nicholas. *Petrarch*. Oxford: Oxford University Press, 1988.

Petrarca, Francesco. *Rime Sparse [Canzoniere]*. In *Petrarch's Lyric Poems*. Trans. Robert M. Durling. Cambridge: Harvard University Press, 1976.

Tuchman, Barbara W. *A Distant Mirror: The Calamitous 14th Century*. New York: Alfred A. Knopf, 1978.

The Child of Pleasure

by

Gabriele D'Annunzio

Gabriele D'Annunzio was born in Pescara, a small town in the Abruzzi region of Italy, in 1863. He went on to become a national treasure of Italy, the most celebrated (and sometimes reviled) poet, playwright, and novelist of the late nineteenth and early twentieth century. His huge body of work was read widely across all social classes, translated in many languages, and imitated in Italy and abroad. D'Annunzio came from a distinguished family of merchants and landowners but his father (who was once the mayor of Pescara) was a dissolute man. He fathered several illegitimate children, though Gabriele was legitimate, and, in the late 1880s, finally abandoned his devoted wife to live with one of his mistresses. Gabriele, who was always very attached to his mother, did not attend his father's funeral in 1893. Initially educated at home by private tutors, the boy was sent to Cicognini College at Prato—a prestigious, Jesuit-run boarding school—when he was 11 years old. He excelled at his studies, showing special prowess in Greek and Latin, and, as his own father desired, learned voice control to lose his Abruzzese accent and sound more Tuscan. At the age of 16, D'Annunzio published *Primo vere* (1879; In Early Spring), his first collection of poems. After graduating from Cicognini in 1881, where he was impeccably trained in the classics, the young writer entered the University of Rome. Instead of attending classes, however, he developed a keen interest in high society and journalism. D'Annunzio would never complete his university education, but he was a tireless reader

THE LITERARY WORK

A novel set in Rome during the 1880s; first published in Italian (as *Il Piacere*) in 1889, in English in 1898.

SYNOPSIS

The romantic entanglements of a young nobleman with a passion for art and beauty play out against the background of nineteenth-century fashionable society.

all his life, eager to absorb everything he could about literature and the arts. He began penning short fiction, society columns, and sports articles for local newspapers. He also published *Canto novo* (1882; New Song), poems inspired by his first love affair, and two collections of short stories in the realistic vein, *Terra vergine* (1884; Virgin Earth) and *San Pantaleone* (1884; Saint Pantaleone). In 1883 D'Annunzio married Maria Hardouin, Duchess of Gallese, but continued to become enmeshed in scandalous affairs with high-society women, which provided much grist for the mill of fictional stories he was to produce. His liaison with the world-renowned actress Eleonora Duse, which he fictionalized in the novel *Il Fuoco* (1900; The Flame), became mythical in Europe and the United States. In 1888 D'Annunzio suspended his journalistic career to concentrate upon writing his first novel, *Il Piacere* (1889), or *The Child of Pleasure*. Richly detailed and lushly romantic, it depicts the decadent

Gabriele D'Annunzio

atmosphere among the affluent classes of contemporary Rome at the end of the nineteenth century, a period when scandals and corruption mired the political and financial world of the recently unified nation of Italy. Highlighted is the influence of this dissolute, cynical atmosphere upon a young *aesthete,* a type of the period, who—following in the footsteps of such European writers as Charles Baudelaire and Oscar Wilde—feels that art is life and life is art. For the aesthete, narcissistic self-love and a passion for beautiful, elegant, and luxurious objects, women, and works of art eclipsed all other values (moral, religious, political, and economic). In Italy at the turn of the twentieth century, only a very small intellectual elite actually lived the life of the aesthete. D'Annunzio himself was the most visible and admired (or hated) representative. Still, the aesthete and his world symbolized a reaction against several societal traits: smug conventionalism; the practical, unartistic outlook; Catholic morality; and other middle-class or bourgeois values. Also the aesthete was plainly disenchanted with the patriotic ideals of the Italian Risorgimento, or Unification Movement. How did Italians react to such a character? He fascinated the public, who generally embraced him. D'Annunzio's fictional aesthete and the spectacle of his own real-life example afforded his audience a vicarious, escapist, and forbidden pleasure.

Rome in the 1880s. In the years following the process of national unification, formally achieved in 1860, the new Kingdom of Italy faced numerous obstacles, including a struggling economy, pronounced regional differences, a poor and predominately illiterate populace, and its own lack of status on the world stage. In addition, lacking raw materials and unable to afford machinery from abroad, Italy lagged far behind in the European industrial revolution, and soon nationalist groups began lamenting the young nation's lack of status on the world stage in the era of European imperialism. Moreover, unification was not complete in 1860. Some territories in the northeast, traditionally considered Italian, remained under Austrian occupation until 1866, and Rome continued to belong to the papacy until the Italian Kingdom conquered it by military force in 1870. After an additional decade of conflict between the Vatican and the new government, Rome was finally absorbed into a unified Italy. From 1865 to 1871 Florence had served as the Italian national capital. Rome, while still under papal rule, had existed as something of a rural backwater, unaffected by industrial development; goats still grazed in the Forum, for example. All this changed after the Italian government seized control of the weakly defended city in 1871 and made Rome the country's new capital.

Within ten years of Rome's annexation, its population had increased from 220,000 to 300,000 inhabitants (Woodhouse, p. 37). Military garrisons had been established there, as had a foreign diplomatic corps. Businessmen, entrepreneurs, speculators, and would-be politicians took up residence in Rome, while immigrant workers from the impoverished rural South also flocked to the city in search of gainful employment. Like many Italian cities of the time, Rome experienced a period of rapid expansion and development.

Roman society was undergoing a similar transformation; in an attempt to catch up with the rest of the world, Italian society in general began to model itself on that of other Western nations, such as England and France. This was especially true of the Italian aristocracy, which abandoned the near-feudal lifestyle it had led for centuries in an attempt to fit in with the values of the new regime. "The Kingdom was new, life seemed to be changed, new industries and fortunes were being built, railroads were reaching out everywhere—it was necessary to be more modern. The old traditions seemed to have been left behind and appeared dangerous to the principles of unification. Everybody was looking for foreign models to imitate" (Barzini in Rhodes, p. 26).

Italian aristocrats often chose to model their behavior on that of their English counterparts. Many began to observe a more rigid adherence to the social hierarchy; for example, servants who waited upon the family at dinner were now expected to remain silent throughout the meal, whereas they had previously been permitted to participate in the conversations if so inclined. Some emulated English lords by embarking upon such pursuits as voyages of exploration and hazardous big-game hunts, while others redecorated their ancestral palaces and turned these *palazzi* into elaborate showplaces, threw grand parties, traveled through high international society, and contracted marriages between their daughters and foreign nobles. Yet another element of the aristocracy engaged in extravagant acts like dueling and reckless gambling. "In other words, the Italian nobles for the first time set about acting the part of 'nobles'; they ceased to be patriarchal, with a place in the people's ancient way of life, in order to live a fictitious literary and choreographic existence" (Barzini in Rhodes, p. 27). It is this highly artificial milieu that inspires *The Child of Pleasure*. Indeed Rome is almost a character in the novel, brooding over the action and ensnaring its inhabitants with its beauty and its potentially corrupting sensuality: "Rome appeared, all pearly gray, spread out before him, its lines a little blurred like a faded picture, under a Claude Lorrain sky, sprinkled with ethereal clouds. . . . Under this rich autumnal light everything took on a sumptuous air. Divine Rome!" (D'Annunzio, *The Child of Pleasure*, p. 178).

The Aesthetic and Decadent Movements. During the late nineteenth century, many European intellectuals became involved in a philosophical and artistic phenomenon known as Aestheticism. Its roots could be traced back to German philosopher Immanuel Kant, who proposed in his *Critique of Aesthetic Judgement* (1790) that a disinterested contemplation of an object, without reference to reality or consideration of the object's utility or morality, represented a pure aesthetic experience. The French, however, appropriated and refined that theory during the nineteenth century, perhaps around the time that Theophile Gautier claimed that art itself lacked all utility in his 1835 preface to *Mademoiselle de Maupin* (1835). Other French thinkers, includ-

ing the authors Charles Baudelaire, Gustave Flaubert, and Stéphane Mallarmé, further developed the idea. The slogan for French Aestheticism subsequently became "*l'art pour l'art*"—art for art's sake—again emphasizing that works of art had no purpose beyond their own existence and beauty.

A related movement flourished in Italy in the late nineteenth century. Called Decadentism, it stressed the individual, the subconscious, and the instinctual, and cultivated the irrational impulse. An offshoot, the Decadent-Aesthetic Movement, focused on artificiality and art for art's sake, and showed a preference for the exotic and the refined, as well as a lack of moral scruples. As its name suggests, members of the movement associated Decadence (in an ironic, tongue-in-cheek way, for they proudly believed themselves to be not only great artists but also absolutely modern) with the artistic qualities of declining, even decaying civilizations, such as the later Roman Empire and Byzantine Greece. The typical Decadent writer employed a highly polished, elaborate style and bizarre subject matter, and rejected the natural and organic in favor of the artificial and ornate. Sometimes the writer indulged in drugs or sexual deviation "in an attempt to achieve (in a phrase echoed from the French poet Rimbaud) 'the systematic derangement of all the senses'" (Abrams, p. 8).

Both the Decadent and the Decadent-Aesthetic Movements spread beyond France to other European nations, including England and Italy. Indeed, the new Italy's eagerness to adopt foreign models inspired writers such as D'Annunzio to steep themselves in French Decadent writings and thereby redefine themselves, breaking away from the established naturalistic mode of literature that had predominated since the unification. Certainly, *The Child of Pleasure* reveals a Decadent influence in its depiction of a corrupt, decaying society which has lost its morality while retaining its beauty.

D'Annunzio and high society. D'Annunzio first came to Rome in 1881. He soon fell under the city's spell, delighting in the warmth, splendor, and stimulating atmosphere of his new surroundings. "A brilliant red gaiety glows around me," he wrote to his sweetheart Giselda Zucconi (D'Annunzio in Woodhouse, p. 37). While in Rome, D'Annunzio struck up a close friendship with Edoardo Scarfoglio, editor of the weekly newspaper *Il Capitan Francassa*, to which D'Annunzio quickly became a contributor. D'Annunzio also met Angelo Sommaruga, a young Milanese entrepreneur who

D'ANNUNZIO AND POLITICS

Despite the similarity of their experiences, D'Annunzio did not intend for everyone to identify him with the aesthete anti-hero of his novel, Andrea Sperelli. There were significant differences: Sperelli was an aristocrat, born to mingle effortlessly in high society, while D'Annunzio achieved admission to more exalted circles through talent and force of personality. Also D'Annunzio was more interested in politics than his character. In 1897 D'Annunzio was elected as a deputy to the Italian parliament. He proved, however, to be a somewhat inconsistent and unpredictable politician, and his tenure in parliament ended in 1904. Forced to flee to France in 1910 to escape his creditors, D'Annunzio returned to Italy in 1915 to protest his country's neutrality in the First World War. He published eloquent and ornate interventionist poems and articles in important newspapers such as *Il Corriere della Sera*, and became the most vociferous advocate of Italy's entrance into the war on the side of France. When Italy did in fact enter the conflict on the side of the Allies, D'Annunzio served in the Air Force, taking part in several daring and highly publicized missions over Pola, Trieste, and Vienna, for which he received decorations from France and Britain as well as Italy.

D'Annunzio achieved further fame and notoriety after the war. In 1919, outraged over the Treaty of Versailles' refusal to recognize some of Italy's territorial claims, D'Annunzio—accompanied by several thousand irregular troops—seized the town of Fiume (now Rijeka, Croatia). The occupation lasted more than a year, during which Fiume was transformed into a strange libertarian state (where free love, yoga, nudism, war games, and cocaine use were practiced). As a result, D'Annunzio became the most visible of the Italian war veterans, a rival of Mussolini himself for the charismatic leadership of the Fascist Movement. In fact, much of the revolutionary rhetoric and ritual of Fascism (including the Roman salute and the black shirt) was forged in Fiume, though Fascism absorbed none of Fiume's free-thinking, permissive, anti-practical spirit. The Fiume episode ended D'Annunzio's political career. After Italy's central government sent troops that put a stop to his occupation of Fiume, D'Annunzio was allowed to retire to a villa on Lake Garda (*Il Vittoriale degli Italiani,* now a museum). He filled the villa with war memorabilia, elegant crafts, and artwork (mostly copies) that he had collected all his life, transforming the place into an extraordinary monument to himself. When Benito Mussolini assumed control of Italy in 1922, he compensated D'Annunzio for his withdrawal from public life by arranging for a government-sponsored edition of all his works (released beginning in 1925). Although he privately expressed dislike for Mussolini, in public D'Annunzio refrained from criticizing the dictator or his regime.

introduced D'Annunzio to English literature (Sommaruga was an expert on English Romanticism) and in the next few years published D'Annunzio's next two works, *Canto Novo* (New Song) and *Terra vergine* (Virgin Earth). D'Annunzio's journalistic and poetic endeavors established him as a rising literary figure. Consequently, higher circles of Roman society began to take an increased interest in the young man.

The fascination was mutual; eager to impress his new acquaintances, D'Annunzio—who was an expert in identifying new cultural and social trends—soon adopted the dress and demeanor of a dandy. Scarfoglio noted his friend's transformation with disapproval, writing in his memoirs:

> Gabriele, who was modest, kind, ingenuous, is now becoming foppish, cunning and affected. The child-like grace, half-wild, half-timid, from

the Abruzzi has been transformed overnight into the perfumed elegance, the capering mannerisms of the dandy. He has abandoned himself to the smart crowd, from whom his artist's instincts should have fatally divided him. When the doors of the great Roman houses open, he gives himself up entirely to female blandishments. . . . Now, for six months, he has been going from one party to another, from one ball to another, from a morning's riding in the Campagna, to a supper-party of some pomaded old idiot furnished with nothing more than a set of quarterings. Gabriele never opens a book. Not one serious thought enters his head. He is a puppy-dog on a silken thread.

(Scarfoglio in Rhodes, pp. 30-31)

Despite Scarfoglio's harsh criticism, D'Annunzio continued to pursue his new lifestyle, attending glittering social functions and paying extravagant court to fashionable women. The early part of his amorous career reached a climax in 1883 when he married Maria Hardouin, the only daughter of the Duke of Gallese. Within a month of making her acquaintance, D'Annunzio severed his relationship with Giselda Zucconi, whom he had regarded as his unofficial betrothed since early 1881.

Maria's father, Jules Hardouin, had been a French army officer before his marriage to the widowed Duchess of Gallese, who obtained the permission of the pope for her new husband to assume the title of duke. After his first wife's death, Duke Giulio—as he now preferred to be styled—married Natalia Lezzani, daughter of a marquess, by whom he had two children, Luigi and Maria. It was through his acquaintance with the second duchess that D'Annunzio met the rest of the Gallese family in 1883. Nineteen-year-old Maria soon became infatuated with the up-and-coming young poet; they enjoyed secret trysts that resulted in Maria's becoming pregnant. Knowing that her parents disapproved of the romance, the couple attempted to elope but were apprehended in Florence and brought back to Rome under police escort. Given Maria's condition, the marriage was inevitable. The duke, however, refused to give his daughter a dowry or attend the small wedding ceremony in the family's private chapel; and never did he acknowledge D'Annunzio as his son-in-law or reconcile with Maria.

The newlyweds stayed for some time in the young husband's native Pescara, where Maria gave birth to their first child six months after their wedding. However, they eventually returned to Rome and D'Annunzio resumed his former way of life, which included intrigues with other women. His experiences in high society— amorous and otherwise—would form part of the backdrop for *The Child of Pleasure*.

The Novel in Focus

Plot summary. At a dinner party held by his cousin, the Marchesa d'Atelata, Andrea Sperelli, Count of Ugenta, meets the beautiful Elena Muti, the widowed Duchess of Scerni, and conceives an immediate passion for her. The attraction is mutual. They meet again at an auction, where Elena persuades Andrea to buy an elaborate clock shaped like a death's-head (human skull). The next time they meet, at a ball, Elena falls ill and departs early.

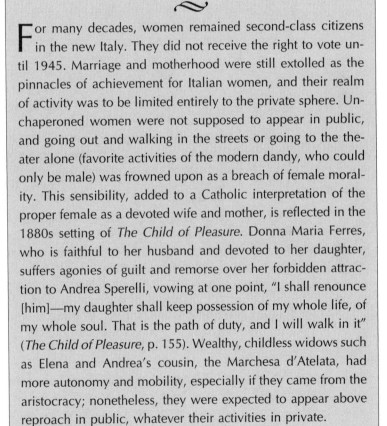

WOMEN IN POST-UNIFICATION ITALY

For many decades, women remained second-class citizens in the new Italy. They did not receive the right to vote until 1945. Marriage and motherhood were still extolled as the pinnacles of achievement for Italian women, and their realm of activity was to be limited entirely to the private sphere. Unchaperoned women were not supposed to appear in public, and going out and walking in the streets or going to the theater alone (favorite activities of the modern dandy, who could only be male) was frowned upon as a breach of female morality. This sensibility, added to a Catholic interpretation of the proper female as a devoted wife and mother, is reflected in the 1880s setting of *The Child of Pleasure*. Donna Maria Ferres, who is faithful to her husband and devoted to her daughter, suffers agonies of guilt and remorse over her forbidden attraction to Andrea Sperelli, vowing at one point, "I shall renounce [him]—my daughter shall keep possession of my whole life, of my whole soul. That is the path of duty, and I will walk in it" (*The Child of Pleasure*, p. 155). Wealthy, childless widows such as Elena and Andrea's cousin, the Marchesa d'Atelata, had more autonomy and mobility, especially if they came from the aristocracy; nonetheless, they were expected to appear above reproach in public, whatever their activities in private.

Andrea visits the ailing duchess at home and they begin a passionate affair. During this time, Andrea—an aesthete and amateur artist—creates engravings and composes poems, drawing on Elena as his muse. After several months of intense involvement, Elena abruptly breaks off the affair and leaves Rome without explanation.

Angered and bewildered by Elena's defection, Andrea throws himself into a series of casual liaisons with other society beauties, one of which results in his being seriously wounded in a duel. Accepting the Marchesa d'Atelata's invitation to recover at her villa in Schifanoja on the Adriatic Sea, Andrea experiences a spiritual renewal for a time, disdaining women and rededicating himself to art. However, he becomes attracted to another guest at the villa: Donna Maria Ferres, a Sienese friend of the Marchesa's and a Guatemalan politician's virtuous wife. Maria is likewise drawn to Andrea, which distresses her because she is determined to be a faithful wife. In her diary, Maria records her growing attraction to Andrea as they engage in long walks, horseback rides, and sightseeing expeditions. Driven at last to admit her love for Andrea, Maria nonetheless resists temptation and leaves the villa before they can consummate their passion.

Back in Rome, Andrea renews his former way of life, dabbling in art and casual affairs. He meets Elena again and learns she has entered into a marriage of convenience with Lord Humphrey Heathfield, a wealthy Englishman. While Elena swears she still loves Andrea, she also insists that they can never be together again. His vanity piqued, Andrea vows to win her back. The appearance of Donna Maria, now visiting Rome with her husband, furnishes the count with the perfect means to do so. Hoping to make Elena jealous, Andrea pays extravagant court to Maria, who once again falls under his spell and longs to redeem him from the dissolute life he has led. Despite his ulterior motives, Andrea begins to return her feelings, even fantasizing about winning both women for his own. Memories of his Roman idyll with Elena impinge upon his present wooing of Maria, until the latter's purity merges with the former's inconstancy in his mind: "Where Elena Muti had passed, there Maria Ferres passed also. Often enough, the sights they visited suggested to the poet the same eloquent effusions which Elena had once heard. Often enough, some recollections carried him away suddenly from the present and disturbed him strangely" (*The Child of Pleasure*, p. 268). For her part, Maria senses that Andrea and Elena share a history but fears to inquire as to its true nature.

As with Elena, Andrea carries out his pursuit of Maria against the backdrop of Rome's most famous and beautiful sights. The romantic triangle reaches a crisis, however, when Don Manuel, Maria's husband, is caught cheating at cards. The resulting scandal and financial ruin means his departure from Rome, and as his wife, Maria must accompany him. Meanwhile, after further struggles with her conscience, Maria has finally decided to give herself to the man she loves. Unfortunately Andrea utters his former mistress's name at the exact moment Maria yields to him:

> All at once she struggled free of his embrace, her whole form convulsed with horror, her face ghastly and distraught as if she had at that moment torn herself from the arms of Death. That name! That name!—She had heard that name!
>
> (*The Child of Pleasure*, p. 306)

Heartbroken and disillusioned, Maria leaves Rome without ever seeing Andrea again.

In the last scenes of the novel, Andrea attends the auction of Don Manuel's possessions and bids for several furnishings. Feeling oppressed and oddly sickened, he hides from a large party of visitors, which includes Elena and her new lover. Later, he returns to the auction rooms but finds them deserted. Fleeing to his own house, he walks slowly up the stairs behind the cabinet he has purchased, conscious of a sense of sterility and emptiness in his life.

The dandy, the femme fatale, and the decaying aristocracy. In a letter to his friend Francesco Paolo Michetti, D'Annunzio described *Child of Pleasure* as a study of corruption and "of many other subtleties and falsities and vain cruelties" (D'Annunzio in Kepos and DiMauro, p. 28). The corruption in the novel is inextricably linked to the Decadent sensibility that, in D'Annunzio's imagination, informs Roman high society and its denizens.

Two of the main characters, Andrea Sperelli and Elena Muti, may be said to personify the Decadent Movement. Andrea embodies the dandy. While the well-dressed man about town had been a fixture in high society throughout the centuries, Charles Baudelaire modified the popular concept of the dandy in his 1863 essay "Le Dandy." According to Baudelaire, the dandy's elegant clothes reflected something—the "aristocratic superiority of his mind"; also the dandy found his greatest pleasure in shocking others with his original appearance and opinions (Baudelaire in Beckson, p. 35). Embraced by the Decadents like Oscar Wilde, who added their own modifications, the dandy of the late nineteenth century emerged as a sophisticated man who worshipped the modern city and all things elegant, graceful, and artificial. Sincerity, industriousness, and moral energy were anathema to the dandy, who cultivated a fashionable air of idleness and languor. In *The Child of Pleasure*, Andrea Sperelli possesses many dandy-ish attributes; art may stir him to unfeigned passion, but, once ensconced in Roman high society, he readily assumes the persona of the idle young man about town. He succumbs without resistance to sensual pleasures and drifts through a series of dissolute, immoral affairs whose increasingly refined perversity is as removed as possible from the romantic and bourgeois cult of the ethical, authentic, productive, and sincere self: "By degrees, insincerity—rather towards himself than towards others—became such a habit of Andrea's mind, that finally he was incapable of being wholly sincere or of regaining dominion over himself" (*The Child of Pleasure*, p. 25).

If Andrea embodies the modern dandy and the antithesis of the productive bourgeois individual, Elena represents the *femme fatale* (fatal woman), a figure especially prominent in art and literature around the turn of the twentieth century. She undergoes many mutations through D'Annunzio's own body of work, including the novels *Il Fuoco* (1900; The Flame) and *Forse che sì forse che no* (1910; Perhaps Yes, Perhaps No). Sensual, exotic, sterile, and corrupt, the archetypal fatal woman of the turn of the century was the opposite of the model maternal bourgeois woman and an eloquent expression of male anxiety. The *femme fatale* seduced and destroyed the many men who succumbed to her deadly charms. From the beginning of D'Annunzio's novel, Elena is linked with the forces of death and destruction. On beholding her, Andrea is struck by her beauty, comparing her lips to "the mouth of the Medusa of Leonardo, that human flower of the soul rendered divine by the fires of passion and the anguish of death" (*The Child of Pleasure*, p. 8). According to the classic myth, however, Medusa was transformed into a snake-haired Gorgon, whose horrific appearance turned all beholders to stone. While Andrea's romance with Elena does not result in such a fate, their entanglement damages him nonetheless. Unable to deal with her mysterious departure from Rome, he indulges in some meaningless liaisons, one of which results in a near-fatal duel. Later, Andrea's frustrated passion for the now-married Elena causes him to destroy the sincere love that Donna Maria offers him. Meanwhile, indifferent to the havoc she has caused her former lover, Elena moves on to her next "victim," Galeazzo Secinaro, in whose company she is seen at the end of the novel.

Not only are Andrea and Elena representations of decadence, but they also embody a de-caying social order, the landed aristocracy, as seen by the middle classes. The middle classes both despised and envied this aristocracy, never ceasing to fantasize about it. D'Annunzio's novel concerns a phenomenon in late-nineteenth-century Italian society (though the novel does not explicitly portray it): the old landed aristocracy or pseudo-aristocracy (monied non-nobles who styled themselves as aristocrats) to which these characters belonged was losing importance in the social and political realms. As the aristocracy declined, the middle and professional classes became more prominent, so much so that, in 1878, Leone Carpi, author of an 1878 contemporary study of Italian society, described the middle class as "the life, the strength, and the backbone of the nation" (Carpi in Davis and Ginsborg, pp. 222-23). The Unification created new opportunities for Italians seeking to improve their status. Industry was still in its infancy, but prestigious, lucrative professions like law and medicine became more accessible to the sons of lesser professional men (notaries, chemists, surveyors) and tradesmen. New laws also insisted on mandatory primary education for all Italians, though these laws proved difficult to enforce, especially in poor, rural areas of the country. Nonetheless, the decades following the Unification witnessed a dramatic rise in power among an expanding professional elite, who increasingly replaced the aristocratic landowners in parliament and government.

As the middle classes expanded, the importance of the old landed aristocracy in Italy dwindled. The scions of the old aristocracy sought to improve their fortunes through employment in such traditional forums as the diplomatic corps, the judiciary, and the military, or by marrying other wealthy aristocrats (as Elena Muti does in *The Child of Pleasure*). Meanwhile, the new government conferred noble titles upon families and individuals who had distinguished themselves during the Unification by contributing in some way to the new country's formation. This new minor nobility, who, beyond their newly minted titles, gained no special privileges, began to merge with the professional classes, either by independent employment or marriage, ultimately narrowing the overall gap between the middle class and the aristocracy.

Sources and literary context. While not autobiographical in the strictest sense, *The Child of Pleasure* was based upon many of D'Annunzio's own experiences. Like his protagonist Andrea Sperelli, D'Annunzio had immersed himself in the glamorous and dissipated world of Roman high society during the 1880s. Also like Andrea, D'Annunzio had love affairs with numerous society beauties, several of whom furnished inspiration for his fictional characters. The sensual Elena Muti was partially inspired by two of the women with whom he was involved after his marriage: the journalist Olga Ossani (D'Annunzio called her Elena Muti in a letter he wrote her February 27, 1932) and Elvira "Barbara" Leoni (thought by some biographers to have been D'Annunzio's greatest love).

AMERICA'S ISADORA DUNCAN MEETS D'ANNUNZIO

For much of his life, D'Annunzio engaged in flirtations and casual affairs with beautiful women. According to various accounts, he was quick to become infatuated and equally quick to discard his lovers when the novelty wore off. The American dancer Isadora Duncan, who encountered D'Annunzio in France, described his effect upon women: "The lady he is talking to suddenly feels her very soul and being are lifted, as it were into an ethereal region, where she walks in company with the divine Beatrice. Above ordinary mortals, she goes about with a kind of imaginary halo. But, alas, when the caprice is over and he moves on to another lady, the halo dulls, the aureole diminishes, and she feels again of clay. She does not quite understand what has happened, but seems to be back on earth searching desperately for her transfiguration, aware that never in her whole life will she meet this kind of love again" (Duncan in Rhodes, p. 30).

Despite the semi-autobiographical slant of his novel, D'Annunzio's literary models for *The Child of Pleasure* were mainly French writers. Various critics have detected in *The Child of Pleasure* the influences of Joris Karl Huysman, Alphonse Daudet, Joséphin Péladan, Jean Lorrain, Guy de Maupassant, and Gustave Flaubert. D'Annunzio admired Flaubert especially; some of D'Annunzio's detractors (Guy Tosi, for example) charged that he had gone so far as to plagiarize certain passages from Flaubert's *L'Education sentimentale.* Literary scholar Mario Praz, a near contemporary of D'Annunzio and one of his severest critics, also detected the influence of English Romantic and Decadent writers, specifically Percy Bysshe Shelley, Lord Byron, and Algernon Charles Swinburne. D'Annunzio himself admitted, "I am the

mythical composite of all fruits, of all secret gardens—a bee that plundered freely from French flower-beds" (D'Annunzio in Jullian, p. 64). Within the context of Italian literature, *The Child of Pleasure* represents a major artistic departure for D'Annunzio, whose earlier prose work was written in the realistic vein so much in vogue during the nineteenth century. As noted, *The Child of Pleasure* is considered representative of Italian Aesthetic-Decadentism, which has often been compared with end-of-the-nineteenth-century movements in England and France. In D'Annunzio's time, *Decadentismo* carried somewhat negative connotations; Italian critic Benedetto Croce associated the phenomenon with "a morbid cultivation of insincerity and irrationality, politically cynical with respect to liberal democracy, and, ultimately, a mere outer display around an inner void" (Hainsworth and Robey, pp. 174-75). Scholars after Croce offered a political and moralistic interpretation, considering works like *The Child of Pleasure* reflections of the decaying values of a corrupt society, whose collapse led to the rise of Fascism in the early twentieth century. Even later scholars have re-evaluated D'Annunzio's work in the larger context of the evolution of modernist European culture around the turn of the twentieth century; D'Annunzio himself has been seen as a pivotal prophet of modernism. Recent scholarship regards him as representative of a generational search for new values.

Reception. When it was published in Italian in 1889, *The Child of Pleasure* received a cool reception from Italian critics, partly because of its bold subject matter, partly because of its emphasis on the aesthetic, which made it very different from the realistic novels then in vogue. However, the novel enjoyed great popular success, not least because readers delighted in discovering and dissecting the story's more scandalous and autobiographical elements. D'Annunzio would go on to gain distinction as the first writer in Italy to have a truly mass audience.

The Child of Pleasure garnered more critical success abroad, mainly in France, where it was published as *L'Enfant de volupté* in 1894. This translation was, it should be noted, not exactly the novel as written. Prepared by Jacques Hérelle in close consultation with D'Annunzio himself, it censored some of the original text, among other reasons, to suit general moral tastes in France at the end of the nineteenth century. The French translation also reordered some of the first chapters to make them more strictly chronological.

All the effort appears to have been worthwhile; French critics embraced this hand-tailored edition, curiously for the same lush sensuality the Italian critics had deplored.

D'Annunzio's novel earned guarded praise when it first appeared in England, where Arthur Symons pointed out flaws, crediting them to inexperience: "[D'Annunzio] has begun, a little uncertainly, to mould a form of his own. . . . There is still much that is conventional and unskillful in a book which, it must be remembered, was written at the age of twenty-five; but how . . . the imaginative feeling of the description of Rome struggles with the scraps of tedious conversation" (Symons in Hall, p. 128). Others complained about the writing style in such works by D'Annunzio, comparing it to "a beautiful tropical morass, filled with luxuriant vegetation . . . whose air . . . is heavy with subtle poison" (Rose in Kepos and DiMauro, p. 3). Later critics, however, showed appreciation for what *The Child of Pleasure* manages to achieve. Sergio Pacifici singles it out as D'Annunzio's most representative and probably his finest novel, sizing up the reasons for its sweeping success:

> Seldom before (or for that matter since) has another writer managed to match d'Annunzio's re-creation of the incredibly pretentious, sophisticated, and bored life of the Roman aristocracy in the 1880s. We move amidst the "beautiful people" of post-*Risorgimento* Rome; we hear their conversations about futile matters—mistresses, *objets d'art* being auctioned, the latest gossip—and we are privileged to be present as invisible observers of the gaiety of their drawing rooms and the intimacy of their bedrooms.
> (Pacifici in Kepos and DiMauro, p. 27)

—Pamela S. Loy

For More Information

Abrams, M. H. *A Glossary of Literary Terms.* New York: Holt, Rinehart and Winston, 1988.

Beckson, Karl. *London in the 1890s.* New York: W. W. Norton, 1992.

D'Annunzio, Gabriele. *The Child of Pleasure.* Trans. Georgina Harding. New York: Howard Fertig, 1990.

———. *Il Piacere: The Pleasure.* Trans. Virginia S. Caporale. Bloomington: First Books Library (Online Library), 2000.

Davis, John A., and Paul Ginsborg, eds. *Society and Politics in the Age of the Risorgimento.* Cambridge: Cambridge University Press, 1991.

Hainsworth, Peter, and David Robey, eds. *The Oxford Companion to Italian Literature.* Oxford: Oxford University Press, 2002.

Hall, Sharon K., ed. *Twentieth-Century Literary Criticism.* Vol. 6. Detroit: Gale Research, 1982.

Jullian, Philippe. *D'Annunzio.* Trans. Stephen Hardman. London: Pall Mall, 1972.

Kepos, Paula, and Laura DiMauro, eds. *Twentieth-Century Literary Criticism.* Vol. 40. Detroit: Gale Research, 1991.

Praz, Mario. *The Romantic Agony.* Trans. Angus Davidson. London: Oxford University Press, 1951.

Rhodes, Anthony. *The Poet as Superman.* London: Weidenfeld and Nicolson, 1959.

Woodhouse, John. *Gabriele D'Annunzio: Defiant Archangel.* Oxford: Clarendon Press, 1998.

The Conformist

by

Alberto Moravia

Novelist, playwright, essayist, short-story writer, travel writer, film reviewer, and activist, Alberto Pincherle (1907-90) was one of Italy's key early-twentieth-century intellectuals. His father's wealthy Roman family was Jewish. Young Alberto suffered from tuberculosis until the age of 18 and started to write early in life to combat the loneliness of his ailment. At 22, under the name Alberto Moravia, the seasoned writer published his first novel, *Gli indifferenti* (1929; The Indifferent Ones) to literary and popular acclaim. He went on to compose works critical of totalitarianism and to become active in the pacifist movement, at the same time gaining a reputation for being sexually liberal. Together these qualities made Moravia a controversial figure in Italy until his death in 1990. He became romantically involved with two female writers, Elsa Morante, whom he married and divorced, and Dacia Maraini (see **A History** and **The Silent Duchess**, also in *WLAIT 7: Italian Literature and Its Times*). Just four years before his death, Moravia married a young Spanish woman, Carmen Llera. In the postwar years, he co-founded (with Alberto Carocci) a literary journal, *Nuovi argomenti* (New Arguments), to help bridge the gap between communists and liberals in Italian culture. Moravia wrote more than a dozen novels, which can be grouped into periods. *Agostino* (1944) marks the end of his moralistic stage, featuring characters who face ethical dilemmas, while *La Romana* (1947; The Woman of Rome) marks the beginning of a decidedly Catholic period, stressing purgation and guilt. It

THE LITERARY WORK

A novel set in Italy in 1920, 1937, and 1945; published in Italian (as *Il Conformista*) in 1957, in English in 1957.

SYNOPSIS

Dispatched to Paris on an undercover mission, the protagonist must help kill his former college professor as proof of his loyalty to the Fascist regime.

is in this last period that Moravia created *Il Conformista* (1957), a novel about a society that is obsessed with sex, money, and power, and that drives the protagonist to the brink of his own destruction.

Events in History at the Time the Novel Takes Place

The rise of Fascism. The protagonist of *The Conformist*, Marcello, is a product of the Fascist regime in Italy, with all its contradictions. Gathering into its fold different political models, Fascism came to power as a revolutionary force bent on striking a third way between communism and capitalism, between socialism and democracy. The champions of this third way found themselves entering the political system of a country traumatized by the First World War and gripped by economic crisis. Fascism began with the

Alberto Moravia

the Fascist Party. The organization spoke of mounting a preventive counter-revolution against the prospect of Russian-style Bolshevik socialism in Italy. To this end, its squads attacked politicians and union and newspaper headquarters, as well as peasant and working-class activists. By 1921, the Fascist Movement had gained enough momentum to become a political party, one that, despite its newly official status, continued to use strong-arm tactics. These climaxed with a revolutionary march on Rome in October 1922. Directed by Mussolini, about 30,000 black-shirted Fascists converged on the city, and the threat of force achieved its aim. The Italian king, Victor Emmanuel III, appointed Mussolini prime minister on October 30, 1922.

Violence would continue to figure prominently in Mussolini's Fascist regime (1922-43). The regime set out to fashion a "new Italian," the tough conqueror, to this end insisting on the use of the disciplined military goose step, emotional and physical self-control, and strict conformity to Fascist organizations and policies. This new Italian was to be Catholic, apolitical, athletic, virile, unemotional, and patriotic. These were pillars of the Italian *razza* (race) upheld by the regime in the mid-1920s.

The Fascist regime. After Mussolini gained power in 1922, he organized his squad members (*squadristi*) into the Fascist Militia (Milizia Volontaria di Sicurezza Nazionale), an armed body whose members answered only to him. Mussolini, now addressed by the title *Il Duce* (the leader), also created his own extralegal government body, an assembly of Fascists (the Gran Consiglio del Fascismo); though this assembly was not officially recognized, it made the decisions that Parliament would rubber stamp. Then, in April 1924, in an election rife with manipulation and intimidation, the Fascist Party won a majority of seats in Parliament (356 out of 535). Two months later, a group of Fascists murdered Giacomo Matteotti, a Socialist deputy who in a speech in Parliament denounced the strong-arm tactics used by the Fascists in the April elections. Matteotti's murder prompted anti-Fascist lawmakers to quit Parliament, a drastic ploy to force the king to dismiss Mussolini. But the order his regime had brought to society and his own clever public relations campaign had won Mussolini the support of the middle class and of Italy's powerful elites—the Church, king, army, industry leaders, and landowners. In a speech to Parliament on January 3, 1925, *Il Duce* assumed responsibility for all that happened in Italy—including

promise of renewal after the failure of a liberal period in Italy under Giovanni Giolitti (1901-14), followed by economic-related violence in the late 1910s. A wave of strikes and riots wracked the country in 1919-20. Landlords and industrial leaders looked to Fascist paramilitary squads to defeat the gains made by the Socialists, the political representatives of the workers and peasants. Especially in rural Central Italy, a lorry full of Fascist squad members (ex-soldiers and students) "would descend on some village at night, beat up the local unionists, 'purge' them of their inequities by making them drink castor-oil, burn down the local party offices, and depart" (Clark, p. 216). Sometimes these attacks even transpired with the help of peasants who were discontented over the tight grip the Socialists had assumed over their area. The Fascist squads made violence a legitimate tactic in Italian politics.

A wave of strikes and riots coursed through Italy in 1919-20, and the Fascist paramilitary squads promised to control what no doubt seemed like mayhem. Close to 3,500 industrial strikes and 400 agricultural strikes erupted during this interlude (known as the *Biennnio Rosso* or "Red Biennium," meaning two years of bloodshed). It was in this atmosphere that Benito Mussolini founded *Fasci Italiani del Combattimento* (leagues of ex-servicemen), an organization that gave rise to paramilitary squads and evolved into

Matteotti's murder—then began to establish his full dictatorship of the country. With his leading opponents gone from Parliament, his path was clear. He lacked, though, the support of artists and intellectuals. Mussolini set about enlisting them into his regime, leaving the exact meaning of *fascism* open to interpretation. In 1926-27, the regime debated Fascist art, initiating vigorous discussions on the relationship between art and politics. The regime adopted a benchmark slogan that summarized its desire for conformity in art, as in every other aspect of Fascist life: "Everything within the State, nothing outside the State, nothing against the State."

The regime gave high priority to making itself the central authority at every level of Italian society. This process, commonly referred to as the "Fascistization of Italy," began with reforms in education, then moved to censorship of the press and the formation of Fascist-led workers' unions (corporations) that regulated work contracts. The Fascists organized separate groups for youth and for women too. In cultural affairs, Fascism took over the Dante Alighieri Society (the most prominent organization for the protection of the Italian Culture), and created corporations to which all intellectuals had to belong. The regime took control of key newspapers and of the radio and cinema industries. New legislation in 1925 introduced two repressive institutions: first, a branch of the police (named OVRA) to suppress anti-Fascist activity; second, a "Special Tribunal for the Defense of the State," empowered to use martial law for dealing with anti-Fascists. But while the Fascist regime repressed intellectuals, it also attempted to win them over by turning Italy into a patron state that gave out subsidies, grants, and prizes. The regime established a Ministry of Popular Culture that hired photographers, filmmakers, and artists for propaganda purposes. It also hired reporters, critics, and writers to censor their colleagues. Made up of some 40 employees, the ministry's book division reviewed 700 titles a month, with a heavy hand: "Books and stories were routinely confiscated, altered by the censors, or condemned to oblivion through press directives that commanded critics to ignore them" (Ben-Ghiat, p. 47).

Moravia, along with many others, was initially caught up in the excitement the regime generated. In the 1920s, he was a regular guest in the cultural circle around Margherita Sarfatti, a prominent figure in Italian art and Mussolini's mistress. Then, in 1929, Moravia published *Gli Indifferenti*, or *The Indifferent Ones*, featuring an apathetic

middle-class family, victims of the mother's selfish lover. Had this novel been published after 1933, it probably would have been censored. Moravia's later novel *La mascherata* (1941; *The Masked Ball*) met with official resistance. The regime banned any review of the book, after which Moravia published under another name, Pseudo.

THE ROSSELLI BROTHERS, SILENCED

Nello and Carlo Rosselli, cousins to Moravia, were two promising historians who, although trained by the leading historian of the Fascist regime (Gioacchino Volpe), became outspoken anti-Fascists. Carlo, who immigrated to France, founded the radical group Justice and Liberty (*Giustizia e Libertà*) in 1929. Justice and Liberty called on its members to fight for the overthrow of the Fascist dictatorship and for the victory of a free, democratic republican regime in Italy. The group attracted intellectuals in Italy and abroad. Committed to acting on his beliefs, Carlo volunteered to fight in the Spanish Civil War against the forces of Francisco Franco. He had returned from Spain and was recovering at a health resort outside Paris on June 9, 1937, when his wife, Marion, and Nello arrived for a visit. After dropping Marion at the train station, the two brothers were ambushed and killed on a deserted road by French assassins, members of a right-wing sect (the *Cagoule*) known for the hooded cape its members wore. Moravia later recalled being shaken to the core by news of their murders, "which were not discussed at home for fear of informers" (Ben-Ghiat, p. 162).

There were authors who continued to write, and even to oppose the regime, which succeeded only partly in its effort to "fascistize" society. Though some genuinely supported the regime, others merely played the game, agreeing only outwardly with Fascist authorities. Many Italians in the larger population behaved similarly, never becoming devoted to Fascism despite its propaganda. Most of those who opposed the Fascist order outright were punished. Italy's most renowned intellectual, Benedetto Croce, went so far as to write a *Manifesto of the Anti-Fascist Intellectuals* (1925), which was tolerated by the regime because of his international stature. But those who signed his manifesto were punished for it; the regime withheld grants from these intellectuals for years to come. More outspoken anti-Fascists, like the Rosselli brothers (Moravia's cousins) and Antonio Gramsci, paid for their outspokenness with imprisonment, exile, and even death (see Croce's ***History as the Story of Liberty*** and Gramsci's ***Letters from Prison,*** both also in *WLAIT 7: Italian Literature and Its Times*).

CONFORMITY AND WOMEN

As part of its propaganda campaign, the regime put out *Decaloghi* (decalogues)—lists of ideas, rules, or norms aimed at transmitting Fascist ideas in a simple, efficient manner. These decalogues, which Italians would learn by heart, served as tools of conformity. There was the Decalogue for the Young Fascist, the Decalogue for Women, the Decalogue for Cyclists, and more. Introduced in 1925, Decalogue for Women celebrated the traditional roles of wife and mother. While Fascism reinforced such roles with fervor, it also gave Italian women a new sense of themselves by having them join volunteer organizations and stressing the importance of their contribution not only to the home but also to the state.

Decalogue for Women

1. With God, she serves the *Patria* [homeland, fatherland] and the Family, and with the *Patria* and the family, mankind.
2. Don't waste your energy on laziness and emptiness; respect the Woman in yourself, the one who elevates.
3. Honor in yourself the Mother, in whom the new sons and the new workers of Italy will take bodily form.
4. For the man who loves you, be the sweet and secure companion who shares with the same tempered strength the bread of happiness and the bread of pain.
5. Remember that true love, the one that purifies, renews and saves, is the sacrificial spirit.
6. The center of your life is your house, which you will enrich with the endless wealth of your heart.
7. But if your *Patria* asks for your house and heart, give it to him; he will make rocks for bigger walls and lights for more families.
8. Work in silence, with patience, tenacity and serenity.
9. Believe in Duty as the only element of peace.
10. Consider life like a wonderful gift, which you will have to return and whose hours and days are being counted. Nurture it so it will raise you, here, not anywhere else.

(Perduca in Galeotti, p. 147; trans. J. Minguell)

Fascism loses its grip. While the 1920s witnessed the Fascist regime's consolidation, the 1930s saw the first symptoms of its decline. Though prominent individuals, like the Rosselli brothers, were silenced, socialists and communists went underground and conducted activities throughout the Fascist period. Students, workers, and intellectuals gathered to criticize the regime and circulate dissident writings (like the Rossellis' *Justice and Liberty,* a weekly journal put out by the group of the same name). Meanwhile, international events worked to alert Italians to the dangers of Fascism. The Spanish Civil War (1936-39), in which Republicans fought Francisco Franco and his Nationalists, provided radical anti-Fascists with a slogan: "Today Spain, Tomorrow Italy." The racist and expansionist doctrines of Nazi Germany provided another frightening example of Italy's possible fate.

Domestic problems also caused the regime to falter. When the children of the 1920s grew into the workers, clerks, and government ministers of the 1930s, it became impossible for the regime to tightly control the ideas fed to these Fascists as it had when they were young. To compensate for this failure, the regime tried to control adult behavior. In 1938, it outlawed shaking hands (only the Roman Salute was permissible) or wearing a hat while seated. Italians everywhere resisted such controls. Also in 1938 Mussolini introduced a set of anti-Semitic laws that drove 6,000 Jews to emigrate and alienated many of their non-Jewish countrymen and women. Even before the war, the population was divided.

In May 1940 Italy entered the Second World War on the side of Nazi Germany, with Mussolini thinking the war would end quickly and he would consolidate Italy's hold on its lands in the Mediterranean region. But he was wrong. One military disaster followed another. In the Balkans, the Italians lost a part of their colony of Albania. Their campaigns in Eritrea, Somaliland, and Ethiopia—Italy had colonial interests in all three—were disastrous. And Mussolini's aid to the Germans on the Soviet front (he sent 227,000 troops) lost him support at home, where doubts mounted about Fascist foreign policy. World War II turned into a military fiasco for Italy's troops, who struggled with old commanders, outworn strategies, and rusty weaponry that became the subject of enemy jokes. On May 13, 1943, Allied troops landed in Sicily, and soon after Mussolini fell from power. King Victor Emmanuel III signed an armistice with the Allies, and Italy split into two, southern Italy falling to the Allies, central and northern Italy to the Germans. The Germans rescued Mussolini, propped him up as leader of a breakaway Italian republic, and continued to do battle in Italy for another two years, finally losing to the joint Italian Resistance fighters and the Allied forces on April 25, 1945. By popular demand, Mussolini was executed in a public square in Milan on April 28, 1945; the date of his execution is commonly referred to as the end of Fascist Italy.

The Novel in Focus

Plot summary. In the prologue, Moravia portrays the main character, Marcello Clerici at the age of 13. Born to a wealthy Roman family, Marcello grows up in the household of a domineering, impulsive father and an absent mother. He uses objects as a substitute for contact with people and seeks approval for everything he does. At school the others ridicule and taunt him, calling him "Marcellina" because of his feminine attributes. One day after class, Lino, a chauffeur, rescues him from the hands of his schoolmates. Marcello, unaware of Lino's sexual intentions, agrees to go to the chauffeur's house in exchange for a revolver. Once there, the chauffeur represses his sexual desires and asks Marcello to leave. The following day, Lino waits for Marcello after school and lures him to the house, again with the promise of a revolver. In Lino's bedroom, where a confusing attempt to seduce Marcello occurs, the boy shoots Lino and escapes.

The action resumes in 1937, when Marcello is 30 years old. In a library, he reads an old newspaper to verify the murder of Lino—it seems that Marcello's youthful shooting of the chauffeur killed him. Because of this act, and his sexual ambivalence, Marcello becomes obsessed with normalcy. The fixation motivates him to work as a state bureaucrat and to wed the beautiful but common Giulia. At the Ministry he is asked by the secret service to infiltrate a community of Italians in exile in Paris and to provide the government with information about one of his former university professors, Edmondo Quadri. Without knowing that his superiors intend to have the professor murdered, Marcello agrees to the assignment. He will gather the information about Quadri during his own honeymoon. Before getting married, Marcello visits his parents. His mother, a drug addict, is having an affair with her chauffeur; his father, now in a mental asylum, is often delirious.

After the wedding, Marcello and Giulia leave for Paris. On their way, they stop in the unnamed village of "S," where Marcello receives detailed orders in a house of prostitutes. On the train, Giulia confesses to Marcello that she is not a vir-

Benito Mussolini, leader of the Fascist movement that seized control of Italy in October 1922.

gin and that she had an affair with the witness to their wedding, an elderly lawyer named Fenizio. Excited by the transgression, Marcello consummates the marriage on the train.

Once in Paris, they meet the doomed Quadri and his wife, Lina, a young lesbian who reminds Marcello of one of the prostitutes in "S." Marcello is immediately attracted to Lina, who, in turn, tries to seduce Giulia. After Marcello declares his feelings for Lina, and her advances on Giulia are spurned, Lina and her husband leave for the south of France and are murdered en route. Back in Italy, Marcello reads of the murders in a French newspaper and begins to suspect that Giulia knew about his mission.

The epilogue is set in 1945 after the Fascist regime has been defeated. Giulia and Marcello are back in Italy, living in Rome with their six-year-old daughter. One day during a walk Giulia confesses that she knew about his mission. Liberated, Giulia and Marcello start to make love at Villa Borghese when they are surprised by a park guard. The guard happens to be Lino, the chauffeur, who did not in fact die from Marcello's gunshot wound. Lino had married but returned to pedophilia when his wife died. At the park, Marcello realizes the fierce degree of emotional denial in his life and of conformity to authoritarian dictates, a habit that enables him to avoid personal development. The novel ends with the couple going off to their summer home and dying in the Allied bombing of Rome.

Homosexuality and Fascism. The protagonist of *The Conformist* aspires to be a model of the Fascist era—a virile bureaucrat educated by the regime who lives a pleasant middle-class life. A bureaucrat was a highly respected occupation at the time. The State safeguarded its employees in various ways, providing them secure positions in times of inflation and unemployment. As Marcello saw it, working for the government would guarantee him the stability and structure he needed to become part of normal Italian society. His assumptions about the economic wisdom of working for the State were in fact justified at the time. After the First World War and the global economic crisis of 1929, Italy weathered an unstable period. Prices fluctuated rapidly and salaries did not keep pace with prices, which led to mounting household debts and business failures that caused unemployment to soar. A government position in such troubled times brought not only social prestige but also economic security. Happily for those in search of such jobs, the Fascist bureaucracy grew exponentially. During the 1930s its work force (mostly men) doubled from 500,000 to one million employees. A strong Fascist middle class developed as the decade progressed, composed in no small part of these workers.

The second half of normalcy in Marcello's eyes is connected to the virile image of the steely tough man so strongly touted by the regime. From a very young age, Marcello feels he must hide his homosexual tendencies. He struggles to define his sexual nature in a period ill-suited to such introspection. While most societies discriminated against homosexuals in the 1930s, Fascist Italy and Nazi Germany developed distinct anti-homosexual policies. Nazi Germany saw homosexuals, like Jews, as genetic aberrations who ought to be annihilated to purify the Aryan race. In the Nazi penal code, the infamous paragraph 175 outlawed sexual relations between men. There was no such law in Italy; here sexual repression was a result of public opinion and conditioning rather than law. While homosexual relations between males was socially unacceptable, the Fascists never thought of it as a genetic aberration. Rather they saw homosexuality as a threat to the hearty, forceful Italian Race being fashioned. In the Codice Rosso (the Fascist Penal Code) of 1931, there is no mention of homosexuality. The only relevant legal measure, also of 1931, was the *Testo Unico delle Leggi di*

Pubblica Sicurezza (Unique Text of Laws for Public Security), which said any citizen who committed *attegiamento scandaloso* (scandalous behavior) towards the Italian race was a candidate for *confino* (geographical displacement) or another such measure (such as house arrest). Judges interpreted the vague law differently, using it from 1936 to 1939 to convict 90 Italian males of scandalous behavior and to dispatch them to the South. In many of these cases, the active partner was not regarded as a homosexual, only the man being penetrated, a perception that would endure for years to come. The passive partner's behavior was also regarded as anti-Italian, a widely shared perspective.

Sources. Moravia drew on a mix of personal experiences to write *The Conformist,* involving the real-life novelist Curzio Malaparte (1898-1957); Moravia's wife, the writer Elsa Morante; and the murder of the Rosselli brothers. In 1934 Moravia and Malaparte traveled together to Paris, where Malaparte introduced his friend to some of its most renowned intellectual figures of the day, including Jean Giono, Jean-Paul Fargue, and Paul Valéry. Moravia used this firsthand glimpse of modern Paris to situate part of his novel here just a few years later.

Elsa Morante provided Moravia with another important source of inspiration. Morante told her husband that once she had a male lover ("T.") who happened to be bisexual and who had a male lover in addition to her. One night Elsa's lover appeared at a party with a gun and, under the influence of alcohol, asked T. to kill him. T. did so before the whole crowd. The incident inspired the Lino-Marcello-Giulia triangle in the novel, as well as Marcello's homosexual ambivalence.

Another tragic event that shaped the basic plot of *Il Conformista* was the previously noted murder of Moravia's cousins, Nello and Carlo Rosselli in 1937. Tailed at intervals by the Fascist police and otherwise closely watched, Moravia would express his grief and anger about their death in a novel. He would write their story, but invert the perspective, telling the tale from the viewpoint of someone who contributed to their killing, stressing what he saw as the tragic elements of the incident.

Events in History at the Time the Novel Was Written

Postwar renewal? On June 2, 1946, Italy voted to abandon monarchy as its form of government and became a democratic republic. Despite the revolutionary hopes of many who had fought in the anti-Fascist Resistance, there was rampant corruption in the postwar Republic of Italy. Favors were traded, compromise became standard, and unethical behavior poisoned much of the official bureaucracy. The nation was meanwhile transfigured, due largely to the discovery of natural gas (in the Po Valley) in 1944 and some oil off Sicily, from a land populated by mostly peasants into a modern industrial nation. The face of Italy, especially North and Central Italy, underwent dramatic transformation, seemingly overnight. Southerners began a heavy migration from rural to urban Italy, but were mostly left out of the economic boom that ensued. With all these developments came new opportunities for corruption. In exchange for votes, Christian Democrats showed preference when it came to passing out contracts or jobs. Civil officials and politicians looked out for themselves, putting friends and supporters into appointed posts and into their debt. "The state bureaucracy came to resemble a medieval kingdom: a patchwork of feudal lordships," each somewhat independent and willing if necessary to "rebel against the centre" (Duggan, p. 268). Meanwhile, the masses had to do without. Not until after the release of Moravia's novel would the economic picture brighten considerably, with unemployment falling from 1,500,00 in 1957 to 500,000 in 1963.

Neorealism. In the postwar period, Italian intellectuals argued about the reasons behind the rise and fall of Italian Fascism and the role they ought to play in a society under reconstruction. Since the early twentieth century, writers and artists had been preoccupied with realistic depictions of life. Moravia himself spoke in the 1920s of the urgent need for a "true and above all convincing representation of life" (Moravia in Ben-Ghiat, p. 48). His words pointed to a tendency toward realism in the arts. In literature, realism implied an approach more than a given set of principles. The approach consisted of the impetus to become socially engaged through one's writings, an impetus that grew stronger as the 1920s and the 1930s unfolded. Different varieties of realism emerged. Some wrote in an elliptical style, setting stories in faraway places or otherwise cloaking their meaning to bypass the censors (see *Acquainted with Grief*, also in *WLAIT 7: Italian Literature and Its Times*). Others acted on the idea that authors ought to do more than register reality; they ought to write works to transform it. These writers created psychologically complex characters whose behavior was motivated by a concern for doing the ethically right thing and thought it fine to manipulate reality in ways that would help convey their moral vision. In the early 1940s, writers tended to depict human hardships of the era, using art as an agent for social liberation. Moravia, now using the pen name Pseudo to escape the censors, had by this time grown disenchanted with Fascism, as had others, who now used story to express thoughts and feelings they could not yet openly share. Such creative effort continued to be risky, but some anyway attempted to effect change through their art, feeling the kind of urgency that follows: "It is not necessary for a painter to be of one party or another, or for him to make a war or a revolution but it is necessary that when he paints, he acts in the same way as someone who does—like someone who dies for a cause" (Guttuso in Ben-Ghiat, p. 198). Artists of cinema and literature showed the same conviction. Neorealist thought influenced the era's films and novels, including *Open City* (*Roma, Città Aperta*, 1945), directed by Roberto Rossellini and **The Path to the Spiders' Nests** (*Il sentiero dei nidi di ragno*, 1947), written by Italo Calvino (also in *WLAIT 7: Italian Literature and Its Times*).

Like others in the postwar era, Moravia faced serious economic difficulties. The success of his novel *The Woman of Rome* (1947) provided some relief. But the experience of war and of Fascism left Moravia despondent about Italy's future, and postwar developments did little to lift his spirits. Seeing no real difference between the policies of the Fascists and their successors, the newly elected Christian Democrats, he regarded hopes for freedom as unrealistic, illusory. Indeed there was much cause for distress at the time; apart from all the corruption, a 1951-52 government survey determined that a quarter of the population was "poor" or "needy." Concentrating on this sector, Vittorio de Sica made the film *Umberto D.* (1952), about relations between the government and the powerless, conveying such a pessimistic view that he received a public scolding from a government official. The filmmaker apparently shared Moravia's negative outlook. In Moravia's view the postwar population would have to reflect deeply on what Italy had just endured if it was to become a fully modern state. It was to this end that he founded his journal *Nuovi Argomenti* (New Ways of Thought), which would investigate the psychological connections between the Fascist regime and the Italians. Moravia wanted also to figure out how best to create literature in postwar Italy.

Reception and impact. When *The Conformist* was published, critics faulted the work for being too simplistic with regard to Fascism. Carlo Muscetta, an influential literary critic, dismissed the main character as an idiot and said that not even Moravia seemed interested in him. Muscetta saw Marcello as a typical conspirator, someone lacking in political or psychological complexities. His review accused Moravia of adopting a snobbish tunnel vision, of mistaking a segment of the populace for the whole, and of pandering to the two opposing sides of controversial positions. In Muscetta's words, "Moravia has quite a negative concept of what he loves to call '*Italian Society,*' but which in effect is limited to certain . . . middle and petty bourgeoisie in decay"; and he furthermore tries to strike a "balance . . . between pornography and morality . . . between fascism and superficial anti-fascism" (Muscetta, pp. 322-25; trans. J. Minguell). But other readers reacted much more approvingly, finding unique, positive characters in this and other writings by Moravia. In 1970 Bernardo Bertolucci would adapt the novel to cinema, creating a film of the same name, which became one of the director's masterpieces.

—Jorge Minguell

For More Information

Ben-Ghiat, Ruth. *Fascist Modernities.* Berkeley: University of California Press, 2001.

Clark, Martin. *Modern Italy 1971-1995.* New York: Longman, 1996.

Duggan, Christopher. *A Concise History of Italy.* Cambridge: Cambridge University Press, 1984.

Dunnage, Jonathan. *Twentieth Century Italy: A Social History.* London: Longman, 2002.

Elkmann, Alain. *Life of Moravia.* Milan: Bompiani, 1990.

Galeotti, Carlo. *Mussolini ha Sempre Ragione: I Decaloghi del Fascismo.* Milan: Garzanti, 2000.

Kline, Jefferson. "The Unconformist." In *Modern European Filmmakers and the Art of Adaptation.* Ed. A. Horton and J. Magretta Horton. New York: F. Ungar, 1981.

Moravia, Alberto. *The Conformist.* Trans. Angus Davidson. New York: Straus and Young, 1951.

Muscetta, Carlo. "Il Conformista di Moravia." In *Realismo, Neorealismo, Controverismo.* Milan: Garzanti, 1976.

Peterson, Thomas E. *Alberto Moravia.* New York: Twayne, 1996.

Pillitteri, Paolo. *Il Conformista Indifferente e il Delitto Rosselli.* Milan: Edizioni Bietti, 2003.

Pugliese, Stanislao G. *Carlo Rosselli: Socialist Heretic and Antifacist Exile.* Cambridge, Mass.: Harvard University Press, 1999.

The Decameron

by

Giovanni Boccaccio

THE LITERARY WORK

A collection of 100 novellas set throughout the medieval world, recounted in Italian outside Florence during the plague of 1348; published in Italian in 1349-51, in English in 1620.

SYNOPSIS

Seven young women and three young men meet in a church in Florence during the Black Death and decide to flee the city for the countryside, where they pass the late afternoon telling stories.

Giovanni Boccaccio was probably born in 1313 in Florence. The illegitimate son of a partner in one of the city's most important banking companies, the Bardi, he began his life when Florence was well on its way to becoming the capital of international European finance. We know nothing of Boccaccio's mother, though there has been speculation that she was French. Ignoring the boy's illegitimacy, his father accepted him into the household and provided him with all the material and moral advantages due to a son of the thriving new middle class at the time. He received a first-rate grammatical education from the notable Giovanni Mazzuoli da Strada. The poet Dante Alighieri (1265-1321), a native of Florence as well, lived in exile during Boccaccio's day. Already something of a legendary presence in the Florence of Boccaccio's early childhood, he no doubt helped spark the young boy's literary imagination. But Boccaccio senior had settled on a serious career in finance for his son. In the latter part of the 1320s, father and son relocated to Naples, site of the most brilliant Italian court of the day (under the reign of a French dynasty, the Anjou) and home to an important branch of the Bardi bank. It was at this branch that the young Boccaccio began his mercantile apprenticeship. He remained in Naples for some 15 years; the period was in many ways the most exciting, formative, and happy time of his life. Because of his father's position, the young man had access to the full splendor of the Angevin court, including its regal libraries and prominent, learned guests. He appears to have abandoned his economic training early to make way for an emerging passion for literature and vocation as a writer. Although he also studied canon law at the university in the early 1330s, by the second half of that decade he was producing his own literary creations, mythological and classical romances of the type in vogue at court during his day. Many of these reflect a courtly love infatuation with Maria d'Aquino, the daughter of King Robert of Anjou, who became known as Fiammetta ("little flame") in Boccaccio's literary universe. The writer's rose-tinted youth came to an abrupt end in the 1340s: the failure of the Bardi bank forced a return to Florence where his father's subsequent death left him in charge of the family. Even more dramatically, bubonic plague struck Italy and Florence towards the end of the decade, decimating the population and wreaking havoc on what had

Giovanni Boccaccio

been a burgeoning new commercial culture. This devastating event marks the middle of Boccaccio's life and informs his most celebrated creation, the *Decameron*.

Events in History at the Time of the Novellas

Italy in the age of the *comuni*. The Italian peninsula, especially its northern and central sections, underwent a process of urbanization after the year 1000. Serving as centers of production and economic exchange, the towns of northern and central Italy heralded the rise of a new urban class of workers, artisans, and merchants—a middle class situated between the nobility and the peasantry of the land-based feudal system that had characterized Europe through much of the Middle Ages. Members of this new middle class left behind the servitude of the countryside in search of economic self-sufficiency and personal independence in the towns. By the beginning of the fourteenth century a few of these towns had emerged as pre-eminent: on the Mediterranean highway, there were the seafaring republics of Genoa and Venice; to the north, there was Milan; and in the center, Florence, the hub of thriving textile and banking industries.

Politically the map of Italy at the time shows a complexity related to all this urban develop-

ment. The northern and central towns formed miniature states, called *comuni*. Developing their own governmental structures, some strove for autonomy from the pope or from the Germanic Holy Roman Emperor in political and economic affairs. Across the middle of the Italian peninsula, from Rome to the Adriatic Sea, stretched a patchwork of small feudal entities that began to cohere under the pope. The South, including the key areas of Naples and Sicily, was another story altogether; under foreign rule in the Middle Ages, the southern region remained largely agricultural and feudal.

Already by the thirteenth century, Florence had gained widespread prestige as a financial capital and site of innovative cultural production. A thriving textile industry and a host of other commercially viable crafts gave many Florentines a standard of material comfort unusual for the day, leading to broad schooling for its youth and an extraordinary degree of literacy. Merchants could hardly get by without some basic skills in reading and writing while government posts demanded more advanced rhetorical ability. In 1252 the Florentines first minted the gold florin, which would become an international form of currency and the cornerstone of the city's dominance in European finance. From this material success and the high degree of literacy came stunning cultural achievements in art and literature that would make Florence famous throughout the Renaissance. A small group of high-minded poets elevated the courtly love tradition to a new scientific and philosophical plane, creating vernacular verse in the *dolce stil nuovo* or "sweet new style," forming a group from which Dante emerged triumphant in the early fourteenth century to create **The Divine Comedy**. In this same century the humanist scholar and poet Francesco Petrarch (1304-1374) composed his **Canzoniere** (both also in *WLAIT 7: Italian Literature and Its Times*). Together Dante, Boccaccio, and Petrarch earned the moniker "the three Florentine crowns" for giving birth to an illustrious literary tradition. Also at this time, Florence made huge strides in the visual arts, thanks to painters such as Cimabue (c. 1240-c. 1322) and Giotto (c. 1267-1337).

Florence in the thirteenth and fourteenth centuries was also a laboratory for experiments in republican democracy as the *comune* strove to devise governmental structures that would meet the needs of dynamic new social and economic realities. In the later thirteenth century, most of the towns that grew into states moved along the path to rule by a few prominent noble families, and eventually to rule by a single lord, or *signore*. Florence, however, retained the forms of popular government longer—the city was ruled by representatives of the guilds, or *arti,* officials drawn from the city's merchants and artisans. In 1293 the so-called Ordinances of Justice excluded from government office anyone—including noblemen—not enrolled in one of these guilds. During the fourteenth century, however, the government came under the control of an oligarchy of powerful families (which would be replaced in the fifteenth century by the dominance of the Medici family, completing the transition to one-man rule, or *signoria*). Actually through much of the fourteenth century, the streets of Florence witnessed civil strife as a few powerful clans vied for political dominance. All too common were eruptions of gang warfare of the sort familiar to readers of English literature from Shakespeare's *Romeo and Juliet* (set in the streets of nearby Verona where similar scenes were being played out between the Montecchi and Capuletti families). These local alliances attached to larger European powers of the Roman Catholic pope versus the Germanic emperor in various, complex ways. By the time Boccaccio was born, Florence had become a Guelph (i.e., a papal) state increasingly controlled by a handful of powerful families. Still, the dream of a truly popular government never died. In July of 1378 (three years after Boccaccio's demise), the Florentine wool workers (*ciompi*) stormed the city hall and took control of the city government. While short-lived, this proletarian revolt stands as dramatic testimony to the discontent of a people under siege for nearly a century by economic depression, medical disaster, and social chaos.

The crises of the fourteenth century. In this picture of civil strife, Florence and the other areas of Italy merely reflected Europe as a whole. In 1337, the territorial pretensions of England's King Edward III in France spawned a series of battles known as the Hundred Years War, which in truth dragged on beyond the midpoint of the following century. At roughly the same time, the popes abandoned Rome to the city's most powerful families and took up residence in Avignon in the south of France. Referred to as the Babylonian Captivity of the Papacy (1305-77), this period of the papacy in France was followed by decades of schism, during which French and Italian pretenders to the papal throne battled for recognition. Economic greed and administrative disarray at all levels plagued the Church, an easy target for social satire, as so many of the *De-*cameron's novellas prove. France and England turned to Italy—and Florence in particular—to finance the enormous costs of virtually uninterrupted warfare. England then defaulted on the loans, which by the 1340s brought the *comune's* major mercantile companies to bankruptcy.

At the same time, inefficient agricultural practices, famine, and overpopulation in the towns left fourteenth-century Italians particularly vulnerable to the onslaught of bubonic plague when it arrived in 1348. Known as the Black Death, variants of this pestilence, which was spread from rodents to humans by fleas, had already battered parts of China, India, and Syria when Genoese sailors carried it back to Italy from ports on the Black Sea. The effect was lethal, to say the least. According to most current estimates, the Italian peninsula lost half its population, while Florence itself lost at least that much. The limits of medical knowledge left people helpless to combat this unseen enemy, which people ascribed variously to misalignment of the planets, contaminated subterranean air released by earthquakes, and human immorality. Social structures collapsed as family and friends deserted one another in desperation. In the countryside, whole tracts of cultivated land were abandoned and reverted to swampland or forest. An immense human tragedy, the Black Death at least enabled surviving peasants and workers to demand better terms due to the depleted labor supply. The tragedy also catalyzed a cultural feat—the masterpiece of world literature known as the *Decameron*.

The rise of Italian literature and courtly love in the city. Creative literature in the Italian vernacular had only just begun to exist when Dante, Petrarch, and Boccaccio established the Tuscan form of Italian as the preeminent literary language by writing exceptional works in the fourteenth century. At the time, the Italian peninsula was as fragmented linguistically as it was politically. Every region and city enjoyed its own neo-Latin dialect. In his treatise on the Italian vernaculars *De vulgari eloquentia* (*On Eloquence in the Vernacular*), Dante marveled that these dialects numbered 1,000 or more. By the twelfth century, some of them were being used for literary expression. An explosion of popular spirituality struck central Italy (Tuscany and Umbria) after the year 1000, inspiring many creative works with religious themes. There were allegorical morality plays, dramatic reenactments of the Passion (the sufferings of Jesus after the Last Supper and up through his crucifixion), and hymns of praise to the Virgin, God, or creation, most famously St. Francis of Assisi's "Canticle of the Creatures." Founder of a monastic order that was to influence Italian religious life for centuries, St. Francis (1181-1226) spawned a vast vernacular literature aimed at recounting his life and transforming him into an early folk hero. This same period witnessed the writing of works by religious women, also in the vernacular dialects, who told of their mystical experiences of the divine in deeply personal, rhetorically innovative texts.

Far to the south on the island of Sicily, secretaries, notaries, and a host of other functionaries with literary pretensions at the Palermo court of the emperor Frederick II of Hohenstaufen began to invent a courtly love literature in Italian. Privileging the lyric, these poets picked up on the European vogue that had triumphed at the courts of France and Provence in the previous century to pen longing laments and pleas for mercy to distant, sometimes cruel ladies. This Sicilian School mostly dissolved after the death of Frederick in 1250, by which time another region—Tuscany and its leading city, Florence—were well on their way to cultural supremacy. Tuscan poets extended the lyric tradition with renewed stylistic and philosophical force. Dante was a prized member of this elite group. His decision to write the monumental *Divine Comedy* in his native Tuscan secured prestige for the vernacular and showed it to be as viable a literary instrument as Latin. In the following generation, Petrarch and Boccaccio cemented the Florentine vernacular's reputation as the Italian literary language *par excellence*. Throughout the Renaissance and beyond, Petrarch's psychologically complex poems to Laura would endure as the model of Italian verse stylistics, just as the elegant sentences of the *Decameron* would set the standard for Italian prose composition. Boccaccio was also influenced by the chivalric romances of the courtly tradition. By the mid-fourteenth century, however, the courtly world of lords and ladies and their highly stylized codes of conduct in love and war (to some extent already the product of literary artifice) must have seemed ever more remote to Boccaccio's middle-class readers in their new urban reality. Some stories in the *Decameron* seem to stem directly from that world, venturing back nostalgically into plagueless times. But trying to determine just how seriously to take the narrative voice at these nostalgic moments is a challenge posed by Boccaccio's text. One often senses its author-creator smiling in the margins.

The Novellas in Focus

Contents summary. The *Decameron* consists of 100 novellas and a narrative frame. Each of the novellas has its own unique, often very elaborate plot. Presented in the narrative frame is the story that leads to and allows the recounting of the novellas: the gathering in Florence of ten young men and women—Boccaccio calls them a *brigata* (brigade or troop)—their flight from the plague-infested city to the countryside, their daily activities before and after the storytelling, and their return to Florence at the end. The 100 stories are thus contained within a story, which is itself framed by a proem (or preface) and a conclusion, in which the author explains his reasons and defends his motives for writing. In the preamble to Day 4, he also intervenes to defend himself and his work against charges of immorality.

The proem. "To have compassion for those who suffer is a human quality which everyone should possess" (Boccaccio, *The Decameron*, p. 1). Like so many of the tales, Boccaccio's proem begins with a broad statement of truth, a logical premise from which it proceeds gradually to particulars, echoing an intellectual craze in Boccaccio's day for the use of Aristotelian logic. The author explains that in his impetuous youth he himself suffered from unregulated passion and was consoled by the pleasing discourses of those who took pity on him. He would now like to return the favor and come to the aid of those most in need: women in love. There follows some discussion, partly playful but grounded in historical reality, about the gender roles of upper-middle-class men and women in fourteenth-century Italian urban society. Women suffer more than men, says the proem, because they are physically, socially, and emotionally more restricted. So few outlets do they have for expression of any kind that their desires grow unbearably intense, pent up "within their delicate breasts" just as they are themselves locked into the domestic space, "the narrow confines of their bedrooms" (*The Decameron*, p. 2). Men have all sorts of possibilities for social engagement and distraction: they can walk around town, go hunting, play games, or transact business. By contrast, women must constantly do the bidding of others (fathers, brothers, husbands, mothers) while neglecting themselves.

To the enamored women, the narrator offers 100 novellas ("or fables, or parables, or histories, or whatever you wish to call them") that explore cases of happy and unhappy love and other adventures from ancient and modern times as told

From Sandro Botticelli's *Story of Nastagio degli Onesti* (1483), depicting an episode recounted in *The Decameron*.

"in ten days . . . by a worthy group [*onesta brigata*] of seven ladies and three young men who came together during the time of the plague (which just recently took so many lives)" (*The Decameron*, p. 3). (The use of "worthy" here aims to reassure readers of the *brigata*'s upstanding morals and the correctness of their behavior despite the often "dishonest" or lewd content of the tales they tell.) The proem ends with an invocation to both the Christian God and the pagan god of love, from whose bonds the writer has been liberated so that he can now attend to the pleasures of sensitive women with his writing.

The tales. The Introduction to Day 1 is by far the lengthiest as it contains the most crucial elements of the narrative frame: Boccaccio's famous description of the plague and its effects on life in Florence; the meeting of the *brigata* on a Tuesday morning in spring in the church of Santa Maria Novella; their decision to move to the country the following morning; and, once there, the establishment of the rules for their cohabitation and the organization of daily activities (including the storytelling). The Black Death is described in sometimes gruesome medical detail as Boccaccio recounts its arrival from points east and its immediately devastating effect. In Florence, the main symptom was a bulbous swelling in the groin or under the arms that spread to the rest of the body, followed by black spots, followed by death within

three days. Medicine was utterly powerless even to slow the lethal contagion, which—if we believe Boccaccio's account—could be caught instantly just by touching a victim's clothing.

According to the introduction, human reactions to the disaster fell into three broad categories that reflected prevailing schools of ancient thought: some attempted to isolate themselves from contact with the sick and to restrict their appetites and diets in the extreme (Stoics); others abandoned themselves to sensual pleasures with a devil-may-care defiance (Epicureans); still others struck a careful middle-of-the-road moderation (the Golden Mean). Whatever the strategy, nothing guaranteed survival and all were forced to fend for themselves as the laws of daily existence came undone. Many abandoned the city, their homes and property, and their loved ones (husbands, wives, brothers, sisters, even children) in a desperate attempt to survive. The result was a dissolution or an ironic reversal of social hierarchies: between humans and animals, upper class and lower class, servants and masters, men and women:

> And since the sick were abandoned by their neighbors, their parents, and their friends and there was a scarcity of servants, a practice that was previously almost unheard of spread through the city: when a woman fell sick, no matter how attractive or beautiful or noble she

might be, she did not mind having a manservant (whoever he might be, no matter how old or young he was), and she had no shame whatsoever in revealing any part of her body to him—the way she would have done to a woman—when necessity of her sickness required her to do so.

(*The Decameron*, p. 9)

Such a suspension of normative social rules prepares the reader for the *brigata*'s unorthodox decision to set up house together in the country.

The introduction goes on to detail the ways in which the customary human rituals for burial have collapsed under the weight of the enormous number of casualties, and to show how rural areas have fared little better than the urban environment. The narrator ends the introduction with a cry of lament for the pathetic state in which the beloved, once glorious city finds itself: "Oh, how many great palaces, beautiful homes, and noble dwellings, once filled with families, gentlemen, and ladies, were now emptied, down to the last servant!" (*The Decameron*, p. 12).

At this point, we cut to the inside of the church of Santa Maria Novella and zoom in on seven lovely young maidens, who are friends or relatives between the ages of 18 and 28, all noble, beautiful, and, of course, virtuous. Anticipating that some readers might object on moral grounds to their behavior, Boccaccio chooses not to reveal their true identities. He instead invents names for them suggestive of personal characteristics (drawing on his knowledge of Greek). The eldest and group leader is Pampinea ("fully developed, florid"), followed by Fiammetta (recalling Boccaccio's youthful flame), Filomena ("the nightingale" or "the beloved"), Emilia (a seductress in one of Boccaccio's earlier works), Lauretta (recalling, perhaps, Petrarch's own beloved and the lyric tradition), Neifile ("the young lover," "new to love"), and Elissa (another name for Dido in Virgil's *Aeneid,* an appellation that evokes the image of the abandoned, tragic lover).

Without question, Pampinea motivates the action and serves as moral authority for the rest. It is her idea to leave Florence, death, and gloom, for the solace of the countryside. She is careful to frame her proposal in strictly moral terms: there is no longer any reason for them to stay in the city, where there is nothing but death and destruction; all their relatives have died so they are abandoning no one; indeed, at this stage, acting to save their lives is the only moral choice. Some of her companions remark (not without a dose of self-deprecating irony) that a group of women without men can come to no good: "Men

are truly the leaders of women, and without their guidance, our actions rarely end successfully" (*The Decameron*, p. 16). Just then three young men enter the church, all relatives or suitors of the women, none under the age of 25: Panfilo ("all love"), Filostrato ("conquered by love"), and the young, sometimes mischievous Dioneo ("lustful"). Pampinea does not hesitate to seize the opportunity of male protection that fortune has presented, but Neifile, who is being courted by one of the men, recoils at the idea of going off with them, afraid that people will talk. The voice of experience, Pampinea dismisses her concerns: so long as the ladies know that their motives are correct, they should not worry about the gossip of others. Pampinea approaches the men and makes the necessary arrangements in short order. The following morning they set out.

The *brigata*'s villa sits in an Eden-like garden some two miles outside Florence. In this utterly uncorrupt natural locale, the storytellers reconstruct a new society in a sort of fantastic dream space, replete with new laws and perfectly reconstituted social relationships. The contrast to the all-too-real chaos they have left behind could hardly be more emphatic. It is precisely this contrast that gives the *Decameron* its comic flavor and colors the generally jubilant air of what follows. First, the young people, who have brought along servants, plan their days. Pampinea proposes they select a leader, a king or queen to decide how the group will pass the time and who the next day's leader will be. Pampinea is elected queen of Day 1. After frolicking in the gardens, eating, and taking an afternoon siesta, she makes another proposal: they should tell stories on the shaded lawn while waiting for the afternoon heat to dissipate. After her suggestion meets with unanimous approval, she orders Panfilo to begin the first tale, about anything he likes.

Now the 100 tales of the *Decameron* begin to unfold. The frame narrator returns briefly between tales and at the beginning and end of each day, usually just long enough to review the *brigata*'s other activities (eating, dancing, playing games, sleeping); each day closes with a song sung by someone in the group. As the title indicates, the *brigata* devotes ten days to storytelling. The action of the frame spans two full weeks (from Tuesday to Tuesday), since the group decides to abstain from storytelling on Fridays and Saturdays for religious and pragmatic reasons. On the first Sunday, they relocate to a second, equally idyllic villa. Nearby lies a stunning valley—called the "Valle delle Donne," or "Valley of Women"—where they spend Day 7.

Boccaccio delights with typical medieval gusto in ordering his material, but the order is always open to variation and exception. For example, at the end of Day 1, the *brigata* decides that each day's stories should adhere to a theme chosen by the king or queen. Dioneo convinces his companions to exempt him from the daily theme and let his tale always be the last of the day. Another exception involves Days 1 and 9, on which there are no themes:

Day	King or Queen	Theme
1	Pampinea	Stories on any subject
2	Filomena	Stories with unexpected happy endings after misfortune
3	Neifile	Stories about people who use their ingenuity to recover precious items they have lost
4	Filostrato	Love stories with unhappy endings
5	Fiammetta	Stories about lovers who attain happiness after misfortune
6	Elissa	Stories about people who escape danger or ridicule with a quick retort or witty remark
7	Dioneo	Stories about tricks wives play on their husbands
8	Lauretta	Stories about tricks people play on each other
9	Emilia	Stories on any subject
10	Panfilo	Stories about people who act with generosity or true magnificence

Day 4 stands out as the only tragic day (ruled over, appropriately, by Filostrato, "conquered by love") in this otherwise comic work.

The list of themes in itself begins to convey the richness and variety of the tales. For the reader's convenience, every story begins with a brief synopsis. Although the tales occasionally touch on ancient matters, almost all reflect Boccaccio's era and a few generations preceding—the age of courtly romance and the new middle-class urban reality. The stories span the entire European and Mediterranean world and embrace characters of every social class.

Many of the novellas engage in anticlerical parody of the Church and its corrupt representatives. The first tale of Day 1 (1.1) concerns Tuscan ser Cepparello; a walking catalogue of sin, he deceives an overly pious friar in Burgundy with a false confession on his deathbed and is transformed into a popular saint. In the very next tale (1.2), Abraham, a Jew, is urged to convert by a Christian friend. The potential convert decides to spend some time in Rome among Church officials and sees nothing but debauchery there. In an ironic reversal, he converts anyway, reasoning that Catholicism must be privileged by divine power if it has managed to thrive despite such depravity among leaders.

Several of the stories take us inside the convents and monasteries of medieval Italy where Boccaccio uses sexual farce to lampoon the less-than-chaste brothers and sisters and their hypocritical superiors. In tale 3.1, the lustful Masetto da Lamporecchio poses as an incapacitated deaf-mute to get a job as a gardener in a convent of young nuns. He eventually succeeds in making love to them all and in being welcomed as a permanent—indeed, indispensable—member of their community. In 9.2 an abbess catches one of her novices *in flagrante* with a male lover. As it turns out, the abbess herself has just been in bed with a priest and in her haste in the dark has put his pants on her head instead of her veil. She scolds the novice in front of all the other nuns, but before finishing is made to recognize her error. In the end, they learn a lesson laced with irony. All the nuns agree they need to be more discrete when taking a lover.

Sexual farce is not reserved for the clergy. Other stories play on the tension between the sexes as the many proud women who parade through the pages of the *Decameron* strive for recognition in a profoundly misogynistic society. In tale 5.10 Pietro di Vinciolo's wife is frustrated because he prefers men to women and cannot satisfy her sexually. When he discovers her with another man, she refuses to be cowed into submission and eventually the husband and wife reach an agreement that will keep them both satisfied.

Other tales affirm the value of religious faith. In tale 2.2 the merchant Rinaldo d'Asti professes his faith in San Giuliano, to whom he prays for safe lodging whenever he is on the road. This faith is sorely tested when highway bandits rob him of his money, horse, and clothing; ridicule his belief in prayer; and abandon him to the cold night. But he is rescued on the verge of doubt by a beautiful young widow who invites him inside her house, where she has prepared an evening of sensual delights for a marquis who fails to arrive. Thus, the swindled Rinaldo ends up with lodging fit for a king. The next day he recovers his stolen property and his assailants are brought to justice.

Still other tales concern the hardships dished out by fortune and life's endless adventures. In tale 2.6 Madonna Beritola loses her noble status, husband, and sons; becomes the victim of piracy on the high seas; and ends up living as a savage with two goats on a deserted island. After many years and no small number of plot twists, the family is reunited, wealthier than they could have imagined, and restored to even greater nobility.

Not all the tales turn on complex intrigues. The relatively short stories of Day 6 rely on a witty remark or one-liner, anticipating the brief narratives and punch lines of the modern joke. In 6.8, Fresco da Celatico is disgusted with his niece's haughty attitude and he lets her know it: "My girl, if you find disagreeable people as disagreeable as you say you do, I suggest for your own happiness that you never look at yourself in the mirror again" (*The Decameron,* p. 400). The tricks of Days 7 and 8 make liberal use of slapstick; they also include the only recurring set of stock characters in the tales, the pranksters Bruno and Buffalmacco and their gullible stooge Calandrino, who probably hark back to oral tradition (see *The Decameron* 8.3, 8.6, 8.9, and 9.5).

A distinct minority of stories abandons humor altogether, particularly the tragic love stories of Day 4 and to some extent the magnanimous deeds of Day 10. In tale 4.1 the doting Tancredi, prince of Salerno, grows jealous of his own daughter, murders her lover, and serves his heart to her in a golden chalice. A paragon of female eloquence, she defends her love to her father in a moving, perfectly reasoned speech. She then sprinkles the heart with poison and drinks from the chalice to join her beloved in death. The final tale of the *Decameron* (10.10) lauds the Job-like patience of the young peasant girl Griselda, whom the marquis of Saluzzo (a confirmed bachelor wary of women) takes as his bride at the urging of his courtiers. He then pretends to turn against her in order to test her loyalty. He has their two children carried off and tells Griselda he has had them murdered. He cruelly taunts her for her alleged deficiencies as a wife and in the end turns her out in nothing but a shift. She remains steadfast through it all and offers no complaint. The joyous conclusion restores her in one dramatic revelation to her now-grown children, loving husband, and noble life. Of course, such a tale puts an ironic spin on age-old chivalric values such as loyalty and suffering, testing the patience of some members in the *brigata* and, no doubt, of many of Boccaccio's readers.

Fortune, love, and human ingenuity. Critics disagree over the precise nature of the *Decameron's*
modernity. In the past some have characterized the work as a human comedy (in contrast to Dante's *Divine Comedy*) reigned over by a new, more realistic trinity: fortune, love, and human ingenuity. But we have seen that much of the *Decameron* reflects medieval culture, and while Boccaccio surely celebrates the human spirit in ways that may feel very modern, most informed readers today tend to see the work as a medieval complement—not contrast—to Dante. Boccaccio's penchant for architectural symmetry should already be apparent. The lofty theme of the final day, for instance, counterbalances the opening description of the plague and bestows a comedic movement on the whole, away from earthly concerns and towards the transcendent.

Each of the daily themes emphasizes one or another of the trio consisting of fortune, love, and human ingenuity, just as every tale plays a unique variation on these basic motifs. Shuffling human events and lives at random, the goddess Fortuna serves as an important warning that in this life things change without notice and nothing lasts forever. The much-bemoaned god of love comes to Boccaccio straight from the pantheon of medieval romance. But it is the third element of the trinity that gives the *Decameron* its unique comic flavor. Many of Boccaccio's stories showcase individuals who stand up to love or to fortune with quick thinking and strength of spirit: individuals who use their wits to get out of tough situations. Some have seen this emphasis on individualism as distinctly modern.

Conversely, some tales poke fun at an individual's lack of wits and/or dramatize a character's sometimes painful education in the ways of the world. This is the case in tale 2.5, the story of Andreuccio da Perugia, one of the most famous in Boccaccio's collection. Andreuccio sets out from his provincial town for bustling Naples to buy horses with 500 florins, no street smarts, and a rather inflated sense of himself. He foolishly flashes his money at the market and is instantly noticed by a beautiful young woman, a hustler in every sense who now has Andreuccio's cash in her designs. The young woman sends a messenger to invite Andreuccio to her home. Physically vain on top of all his other defects, Andreuccio is convinced that a romantic tryst is at hand and runs willingly to his fate in Malpertugio ("evil hole"), an infamously dark quarter of Naples. The enterprising young lady relieves him of his florins as Andreuccio takes a spectacular fall—physical and moral—from an upper-story latrine into a cistern below. The rest of the tale recounts his perilous misadventures on the streets of Naples at night and his redemption after some cronies force him into the tomb of a recently deceased archbishop, where at long last he begins to think for himself: "'These guys are making me go into the tomb to cheat me: as soon as I give them everything that's inside . . . they will take off with the goods and leave me with nothing!' . . . so . . . he took the ring from the Archbishop's finger and placed it on his own" (*The Decameron*, p. 95). Thereafter, Andreuccio returns home to Perugia, having invested his money in a ring when he had gone to Naples to buy horses. Concluding with this last detail, the story entails what we might call an "investment logic" (as do many of the novellas): at the beginning and end, the tale inventories the protagonist's net worth—in economic and/or moral currency. The story about Andreuccio is careful to say that the archbishop's ruby ring is worth *more than* 500 gold florins, the precise amount Andreuccio brought with him to buy horses. Thus, he has profited monetarily and experientially. It is especially appropriate that this bookkeeper's logic apply to a tale that in some ways commemorates the Naples of Boccaccio's youth, site of his banking apprenticeship and great love for Fiammetta (who, not coincidentally, tells the Andreuccio tale). In fact, many of the novellas reflect the new commercial culture of his day by applauding entrepreneurial spirit or, more broadly, individual effort and resourcefulness in the face of life's unpredictable challenges.

Sources and literary context. Boccaccio's *Decameron* draws on a variety of literary traditions. The Greek title itself could have been suggested to Boccaccio by a number of medieval works about the six days of creation often called *Hexameron*. While his description of the plague reflects firsthand experience, he seems in part to have relied on such descriptions by earlier writers (perhaps Lucretius and Thucydides; in the eighth century, Paulus Diaconus also supplied an account of the devastating effects of plague in his history of the Lombards). As for the tales, short, pithy narratives with a clear moral were a favorite genre of the ancient world and Latin Christian writers reworked them in a variety of forms.

While classical literature provided some inspiration, the *Decameron* is primarily indebted to the medieval world of courtly love and chivalric romance. Prose and verse romances on the difficult desires and amorous intrigues of knights and ladies had been all the rage in the courtly circles of twelfth-century France. Their popularity spread throughout Europe, becoming an important literary influence thereafter. Gracious, pleasing conversation of the sort that animates Boccaccio's collection was much prized in literary works of his day. Some popular European romances even enjoyed early Italian vernacular translations, such as the tales of King Arthur and his knights of the roundtable. As for shorter forms (closer in length to Boccaccio's own novellas), the twelfth-century French *lais* (mini courtly love narratives in verse) like those of Marie de France and the *fabliaux* (short verse narratives with a comic realism not unlike Boccaccio's own) were important precedents.

A GREEK TITLE, A MULTICULTURAL SUBTITLE

*D*ecameron means "ten days." Its etymological origin is Greek, like the names Boccaccio invents for the members of the *brigata*. Boccaccio's subtitle, "Prince Galeotto," has literary significance in the medieval world of letters. In the hugely popular British cycle of King Arthur tales, Gallehault was a knight at Arthur's court who facilitated the illicit love between Lancelot and Guinevere. In Canto 5 of Dante's *Inferno*, among those condemned for lust is Francesca da Rimini, who blames romances and their writers for causing her to commit the sin of adultery and suffer the torments of hell, branding all writers "Galeotto." Boccaccio rehabilitates the term by using it as his subtitle; giving it a positive connotation, he associates it with facilitating not adultery but the consolation of lovelorn ladies, whose suffering the work hopes to alleviate with story.

Boccaccio was not the first to compose a collection of narratives within a frame device. The Arabic *Thousand and One Nights* dates from the ninth century, with translations into Latin circulating in the twelfth century and becoming well known in the European Middle Ages. Other twelfth-century framed story collections include the Latin *Disciplina clericalis* (morally instructive tales contained within a dialogue between father and son) and Latin and vernacular versions of the *Book of the Seven Sages* (stories offered to instruct and console a young man condemned to die). While we cannot say that Boccaccio relied directly on any of these predecessors, he may very well have known versions of them all and thus none can be discounted as a possible source. Boccaccio was probably also inspired by a late-thirteenth-century Italian novella collection without a narrative frame most commonly called the *Novellino*.

Reception. The *Decameron* itself suggests how its tales should be received. A regular feature of the work is the narrator's account of the *brigata*'s reaction to the various tales. Boccaccio uses the *brigata* as a model audience (or reader). Their comments on the novella just told give readers some idea of what Boccaccio himself considered an appropriate—or at least a possible—response to that story. "The young ladies and men all laughed heartily over Andreuccio's adventures as recounted by Fiammetta" is typically brief (*The Decameron*, p. 97). Other responses are more involved: "At first, the story told by Dioneo pricked the hearts of the ladies who were listening with a bit of embarrassment . . . but then, as they looked at each other, they could hardly keep from laughing, and they smiled as they listened" (*The Decameron*, p. 42). Still other responses anticipate differences of opinion in reaction to a story: "Dioneo's tale had ended, and the ladies, some taking one side and some taking the other . . . discussed the story at great length" (*The Decameron*, p. 682).

FROM PETRARCH TO BOCCACCIO

"Your book, written in our mother tongue and published, I presume, during your early years, has fallen into my hands. . . . My hasty perusal afforded me much pleasure. If the humor is a little too free at times, this may be excused in view of the age at which you wrote, the style and language which you employ, and the frivolity of the subjects, and of the persons who are likely to read such tales. . . . Along with much that was light and amusing, I discovered some serious and edifying things as well."

(Petrarch in Robinson, pp. 191-92)

In the Introduction to Day 4, Boccaccio attempts to defend his work from the charges of critics. The placement of this attempt part way through the work, when it was only a third complete, confirms that some tales were already in circulation before he had finished writing it. He responds to charges that the work is immoral or otherwise flawed, delivering his defenses with a strong dose of irony and (false) humility that mocks his critics. If we are to believe Boccaccio, his tales inspired a firestorm of criticism, including the charge that he gets some of the stories wrong. He lays down the gauntlet—if his critics have more accurate versions, they should bring them forth. There is an Author's Conclusion at the end of Day 10 that anticipates more criticisms and responds with equal confidence. To those who object that he took too many liberties, Boccaccio responds that the nature of some of the tales requires a certain license, but that his manner of telling them is always proper. He asks his critics to consider the setting: a garden of earthly delights, not a university or church.

Boccaccio's vigorous defenses in anticipation of various criticisms might suggest that his creation met with widespread disdain. On the contrary, the *Decameron* enjoyed broad circulation and popular success almost immediately upon completion. This is not to say that the book was always embraced with enthusiasm. Particularly significant are the attitudes of the early fifteenth-century Italian humanists, initiators of the Renaissance proper, who regarded classical Latin literature as a paragon of human achievement. Paying little mind to writing in the vernacular, particularly writing so steeped in the medieval romance tradition and popular culture, the early humanists mostly looked down on the *Decameron* or refused to consider it at all. Petrarch in many ways anticipated this attitude in a famous letter he sent Boccaccio after receiving a copy of the book. In the letter, Petrarch says he has not had time to read the whole thing, occupied as he is with more serious matters. Still, he has skimmed it here and there and found much that is pleasing, if perhaps a bit frivolous. He singles out the final tale of Griselda as worthy of serious attention, then translates the story from the vernacular into Latin and sends it back to Boccaccio.

Later humanists became less rigid in their attitude to the vernacular and to the *Decameron*; in the sixteenth century Pietro Bembo in his influential *Prose della volgar lingua* (1525; Writings on the Vernacular) enshrined Petrarch as the model for Italian vernacular poetry and Boccaccio as the model for vernacular prose. Notable too is a 1573 censored edition of the *Decameron*—product of the morally prudish Counter-Reformation—that aimed to preserve Boccaccio's style while doing away with some of the bawdier content.

The *Decameron*'s impact on other writers through the centuries is extensive. Perhaps most controversial is the question of its influence on English storyteller Geoffrey Chaucer (c. 1343-1400), who wrote a work that is also a compilation of narratives in a frame device, *The Canterbury*

Tales. Critics still debate whether Chaucer read the *Decameron.* He probably had the opportunity to do so and some of his tales are close analogues to Boccaccio's. Certainly the many early printed editions and translations of Boccaccio's work into the major European languages inaugurated a rich novella tradition both within Italy and beyond. In our own day the *Decameron* has inspired writers, dancers, musicians, painters, and filmmakers. Perhaps most noteworthy is Italian film director Pier Paolo Pasolini's 1971 version of the *Decameron,* part of a trilogy that includes *The Arabian Nights* and *The Canterbury Tales.*

—Gary Cestaro

For More Information

Bergin, Thomas G. *Boccaccio.* New York: Viking Press, 1981.

Boccaccio, Giovanni. *Decameron.* Ed. Vittore Branca. Milan: Arnoldo Mondadori Editore, 1985.

———. *The Decameron.* Trans. Mark Musa and Peter Bondanella. New York: W. W. Norton, 1977.

Branca, Vittore. *Boccaccio: The Man and His Works.* Trans. Richard Monges and Dennis J. McAuliffe. New York: New York University Press, 1976.

Decameron Web: A Growing Hypermedia Archive of Materials Dedicated to Boccaccio's Masterpiece. http://www.brown.edu/Departments/Italian Studies/dweb/dweb.shtml.

McGregor, James H., ed. *Approaches to Teaching Boccaccio's Decameron.* New York: The Modern Languages Association of America, 2000.

Procacci, Giuliano. *Storia degli Italiani.* 2 vols. Rome: Editori Laterza, 1980.

Robinson, James Harvey. *Petrarch, the First Modern Scholar and Man of Letters.* New York: G. P. Putnam, 1898.

The Divine Comedy

by

Dante Alighieri

Dante Alighieri was born into the minor nobility of Florence in May or June of 1265. He claims to have been just nine years old when he first set eyes on his beloved Beatrice, who in various guises would inspire a lifetime of literary creation. As a young boy Dante probably studied with a local grammar master to gain the basics of Latin language and letters, the gateway to higher study. He later spent time in the schools of Florence that were attached to the great churches of the new monastic orders (the Franciscans and/or the Dominicans) and spent a brief period in Bologna, site of the first European university. Dante began writing courtly love lyrics in the Italian vernacular as a teenager, becoming part of an elite group of philosophically minded Tuscan poets who would elevate the genre to a *dolce stil nuovo*, or "sweet new style" (see **Stil Novo Poetry**, also in *WLAIT 7: Italian Literature and Its Times*). When Dante was about 20, he married a woman named Gemma Donati, with whom he had at least four children. Several years later, in the 1290s, he collected many of his poems and surrounded them with prose commentary to form his first book, the *Vita nuova* or "New Life," a first-person account of his youthful love for Beatrice. The work recounts the shattering effect of Beatrice's young death and the poet's difficult contemplation of human mortality, ending with Dante's vow not to write again of Beatrice until he can do so in a manner worthy of her now quasi-divine status. This last statement is often taken to announce the *Divine Comedy*, in which the poet will narrate his journey back to Beatrice

THE LITERARY WORK

A narrative poem set in the Christian afterlife of hell, purgatory, and heaven during Easter week 1300; circulated in Italian from c. 1315; published in English in 1802.

SYNOPSIS

Lost in a dark forest, Dante is rescued by the shade of the Roman poet Virgil, the first of three guides who lead Dante through hell, purgatory, and heaven. Along the way, he encounters hundreds of fictional and historical characters and constructs a deeply personal vision of the human condition and the possibility of human happiness.

in paradise. During this same period, Dante began his participation as sometime soldier and government official in Florence, which was on its way to becoming the most wealthy and powerful of those Tuscan cities that had grown into states. Dante's career as public servant culminated in the summer of 1300 with a two-month term as one of six priors; forming the city's highest executive body, they struggled to reign in factional violence between powerful Florentine families. The years 1300-02 found Dante on the losing side of the battle between the White Guelphs (his party) and Black Guelphs: at age 35, he was exiled from Florence, never to return. Little is known with certainty about his whereabouts during the exile that

Dante Alighieri

would define his last 20 years of life. He was the guest of various princes of Tuscany and northern Italy, including Guido da Polenta in Ravenna, where he succumbed to a malarial fever in 1321. His tomb remains there to this day. Cut off from active participation in Florence, a place he dearly cherished, Dante's poetic and scholarly creativity intensified. He produced two other important minor works in exile: the incomplete *Convivio (Banquet)* an encyclopedia of sorts based on several of Dante's own poems and *De vulgari eloquentia (On Eloquence in the Vernacular)*. Written in Latin, this last work surveys the history of human language from Adam and Eve to the many dialects and poets of Italy in Dante's day. The work also defends the new Italian vernacular as a scientific and poetic language that is as viable as Latin. Dante also composed a Latin treatise on government, *De Monarchia*, which advocates strict separation of church and state. He began work on the *Comedy* shortly after going into exile and labored on it through the end of his life. Written in three parts and in the vernacular, the poem engages all of ancient and medieval culture to reflect one man's experiences at a troubled time in history.

Events in History at the
Time of the Poem

Grandeur and greed in Dante's Florence. After the year 1000, the cities of northern Italy—

never entirely expunged since Roman times—began to witness a gradual rebirth. Only now the cities included a new middle class of workers, artisans and bankers. By the time Dante was born, the towns of the Tuscany region were swelling with new people and activity; during his lifetime, Florence would grow from one of a handful of prominent urban centers (Lucca, Siena, Pisa) to the wealthiest, most populous and culturally prestigious city in the region. Wool-working was the Florentines' major industry, but they had already minted the first gold florin more than a decade before Dante's birth and were destined to become the bankers of Europe during the fourteenth century. The streets in and around Dante's boyhood home were abuzz with new construction. Many of the monuments admired today—the churches of Santa Croce and Santa Maria Novella, the Duomo cathedral of Florence, Giotto's bell tower—were beginning to rise during the years leading up to his exile. We can appreciate Dante's rage at some of his fellow citizens for casting him out unjustly from an ebullient hub that must have felt in many ways like the center of a new world.

The Florentines were industrious in devising systems of governance for the new social and economic reality that was their city. In this endeavor, they strove to keep peace among themselves and to ward off undue interference from outsiders, particularly from the contending medieval powers of the pope and the Holy Roman Emperor (whose imperial realm included present-day Germany, Prussia, Hungary, Bohemia, Switzerland, and Italy). Though ultimately the Florentines failed to either keep the peace or ward off outsiders, they forged some truly innovative experiments in popular government. Central to their popular government were the trade guilds, or *arti*. An ordinance of 1293 prohibited anyone not enrolled in one of these guilds from participating in government, and around this time Dante himself joined the Guild of Doctors and Apothecaries.

Yet Dante's Florence was anything but a picture of social harmony. Wealth and power inspired bitter rivalries and a complex system of alliances among the city's leading families. They, in turn, sought support and legitimacy from an external power, the pope in Rome or the Germanic Holy Roman Emperor. Fighting between Guelphs (party of the pope) and Ghibellines (party of the emperor) had plagued the streets of Florence since early in the century; shortly after Dante's birth, however, the Florentine Ghibellines were routed for good, after which the city was solidly Guelph. This did not prevent local hostilities from reemerging in battles between White Guelphs (who wanted to keep Florence independent) and Black Guelphs (who wanted to align it with Dante's great nemesis, Pope Boniface VIII). These tensions came to a head during the summer of 1300, when Dante served as prior. In cahoots with the French king Charles of Valois, Boniface's designs on Florence became increasingly apparent. Dante was probably on his way back from Rome, having made a diplomatic attempt to appease Boniface there, when he learned that Charles and his troops had taken Florence (in late 1301). As was the custom, the triumphant Black Guelphs banished leading Whites from the city and confiscated or destroyed their property. Dante was initially sentenced to two years in exile and a heavy fine (the official charge was graft), later converted to perpetual exile on pain of death by fire. For a time, Dante held out hope of a return to Florence as he consulted with fellow exiles on strategies to retake the city. He personally felt that the rule of a single just emperor, such as Augustus in ancient Rome, would constitute the ideal political system, and he blamed the political misfortune of Italy (and consequently Florence and himself) on the lack of such a ruler. Around 1310 he pinned his hopes for political redemption on the newly elected Holy Roman Emperor, Henry VII of Luxembourg. Henry intended to leave Luxembourg and to rule his empire from Italy, but he never quite made it to Florence, and after he died suddenly in 1313, Dante appears to have given up on the dream of returning home to Florence, at least in the literal sense.

The world and the afterlife: medieval thought and belief. Medieval Christians believed that the human being was made up of a mortal body and an immortal soul. The soul survived bodily death and lived on eternally. The state of an individual soul through eternity depended on the type of life that person had led: 1) virtuous individuals gained the timeless joy of heavenly paradise; 2) those committed to a life of vice or sin suffered eternal damnation and torment in hell; 3) sinners who repented spent time in purgatory, a makeshift middle kingdom for those in a temporary holding pattern of penance and preparation for heaven. Dante's poem leads us through these realms, focusing on the state of many different human souls after death in order to teach us something about life in the here and now. His purpose, aside from flexing his powers of imagination and creative writing, is to help humans out of misery and towards happiness in this life

on earth, as he writes in a famous letter to his patron Cangrande della Scala, to whom the third part of the *Comedy* is dedicated. (Although scholars still debate the authenticity of this letter, it in any case provides a valuable key to understanding the poem.)

Other Christians before Dante had written accounts of experience in the world beyond death (*St. Patrick's Purgatory,* for example, or St. Bonaventure's *Itinerarium mentis in deum*). It is unclear if or how any of these works influenced Dante. They tend to be either popular in inspiration or highly conceptual and impressionistic; none comes close to matching the elaborate scope and realistic detail of Dante's vision. Significantly, Dante's most important predecessor in describing the world beyond the grave remains the ancient writer Virgil in his epic *Aeneid.* In book 6, the hero Aeneas, with the Sybil as his guide, ventures to the classical underworld in search of his dead father. Although Virgil (70-19 B.C.E.) lived and died before Christ, the ancient poet uses a moral standard. He invokes pagan notions of vice and virtue to invent a clear moral topography in his afterlife, with categories of human shades or spirits: those who died for love, those who took their own lives, and so forth. Virgil even designates an area where those who led wicked lives suffer unspeakable torments, as well as a zone of light and beauty where dignified souls enjoy serenity.

Dante developed intimate familiarity with the *Aeneid* and dozens of other classical and Christian texts through a combination of intense private study, instruction in the Florentine schools, and perhaps attendance at medieval universities. Certainly he was well-versed in the sorts of learning taking place at the universities of his day. Late medieval university culture was generally obsessed with new Latin translations, interpretations, and elaborate commentary on the works of the ancient Greek philosopher Aristotle (384-322 B.C.E.). For much of his natural science, ethics, and the moral organization of hell, Dante relies on Aristotle and on medieval versions of Aristotle. The university of Paris reigned supreme for the study of philosophy and theology in the thirteenth century, and Dante was well acquainted with the work and thought of Paris's most famous professor, Saint Thomas Aquinas (1225-74), a fellow Italian (Aquino is a small town in the mountainous interior of southern Italy). Thomas wrote a multivolume work in Latin (*Summa theologica*) that uses Aristotle's methods of logical deduction to reconcile Christian belief with Aristotelian ideas on topics ranging from the definition of *body* and *soul* to the structure of the universe. For centuries, Thomas's *Summa* would become the definitive reference for details of Christian doctrine.

Medieval intellectuals of the time were less directly acquainted with the other great Greek philosopher, Aristotle's teacher Plato (428-328 B.C.E.). But Dante certainly knew of and shared Plato's commitment to an invisible, unchanging realm of ideal forms and Plato's conviction that our life here on Earth is a mere and temporary shadow of these forms. Study and interpretation of Plato's concepts had continued virtually uninterrupted since ancient times in a movement known as Neoplatonism. Important Christian Neoplatonists included Saint Paul (3-64 C.E.), Saint Augustine (354-430 C.E.), and medieval mystics like Saint Bernard (1090-1153 C.E.), the final guide in upper paradise in Dante's *Comedy*. Though fiercely intellectual, these writers tended to favor intuitive vision over logical thought and to stress the futility of material achievement or human glory in this life. They thought of earthly life as dwarfed to insignificance by the eternal: the human lifespan was conceived of as a pilgrimage, a momentary detachment from the eternal that will ideally return to its origins in divine totality and goodness.

Though Dante's learning was vast, he was first and foremost a poet, because only poetry afforded him the liberty to mix and match many theological, literary, and philosophical perspectives. It may be difficult today to appreciate the supreme power of poetry in Dante's worldview. Much like their fellow citizen artisans, Dante and his colleagues were craftsmen; they plied their trade in language and thought. But for Dante, the poet or writer was uniquely charged with an additional serious moral responsibility: to ensure that his or her creations be both beautiful and instructive. In the liberal arts curriculum, poetry was included in the broad category of rhetoric, the advanced language course that taught how to shape words to dazzling effect and, most crucially, to persuade people to your cause. Ancient society had identified rhetoric mostly with public speaking, but as time passed the public forum shifted to writing, including the writing of poetry. More than philosophy or theology, poetry was rhetorical; it persuaded through beautiful artifice, speaking directly to human hearts. Poems could affect human will and thought, and so could change behavior and history in ways that philosophy, directed at the intellect, could never hope to do. Thus, poetry was a noble calling and

a grave responsibility. Dante writes the *Comedy* to present a compelling vision of the universe, to convince his fellow humans of the goodness of life and the real benefits of faith, hope, and love. His poem aims to lead (as stated plainly in the vexed letter to Cangrande) human beings out of despair and into happiness.

The Poem in Focus

Contents summary. *Inferno* 1 and 2 serve as a prologue to the entire *Divine Comedy*. At the start Dante writes of finding himself lost in a dark wood halfway along the path of "our life," beginning already to present himself as a character at once unique and representative of all humanity (Dante, *The Divine Comedy, Inferno*, canto 1, line 1). He is about to embark on an extraordinary voyage, but then again so are we, since he has decided to take his readers along for the ride. He is one among us, "in the middle" of human experience, as he puts it (*Inferno* 1.1). At the same time, the "middle" refers to his own existence. Given the average human lifespan (according to Scripture) of 70 years, the character Dante is 35, which makes it the year 1300, a time of harsh political and personal turmoil in the poet's own life. Thus, the opening lines plunge us right into the thick of adventure and a midlife crisis for both humanity and a man named Dante. The poet tells us he wants to go back and re-live the journey with us, so from the very start, we must keep in mind the poem's two Dantes: the poet Dante who uses memory to recall a past journey he claims to have taken, and the character Dante that the poet creates, the main protagonist of the poem's present action.

The first canto projects a dramatic landscape of hope and despair, the dual moral poles of the entire poem. Dante has barely escaped with his life from a night in the low, dark forest. He emerges onto a plane that slopes upward into a hill bathed in sunlight from above. The sight of the sun and the spring morning revives his spirit as he moves instinctually up the slope. But a ferocious spotted leopard intervenes to block his progress, then a lion, and finally a ravenous wolf. The beasts succeed in beating him back to the edge of the wood, that is, to despair and near death. The faint shade of Virgil appears at this moment and Dante cries out for help. Virgil presents himself as a fellow Italian, a pagan, and poet of the story of ancient Rome. Dante is awestruck before his hero, whom he calls "master" and whose *Aeneid* he professes to know by heart. Vir-

finluctucmemo affat cidiae lambatda

Chelle lagrime prima fanno groppo

"Dante and Virgil with the Condemned Souls in Eternal Ice," from Dante's *Divine Comedy*, (the ninth circle in *Inferno*). Manuscript illumination in the Biblioteca Nazionale Marciana, Venice, Italy.

gil gently chastises Dante for succumbing to the beasts and focuses on the wolf's insatiable appetite for material gain in terms that condemn the current political chaos of Italy. He mysteriously prophesizes (one of several political prophecies in the poem) the advent of "a greyhound," a savior for Italy. Identified with wisdom, love, and virtue, this savior will chase the wolf of envy back to hell. After the prophecy, Virgil returns to the present moment. Dante cannot, Virgil explains, simply climb the hill before him. If willing, Dante must follow Virgil on another journey: through the desperate screams of hell (*Inferno*), up a mountain of souls happy in their torments (*Purgatorio*), and then, with another guide more worthy than he, through the realms of the blessed (*Paradiso*). Dante agrees and the two men set out.

In *Inferno* 2, Dante is beset by doubt and questions his personal qualifications for such an unusual voyage. He invokes two important human predecessors who have glimpsed the world beyond death—one pagan, the other Christian. Virgil's hero Aeneas was chosen to descend to the underworld (*Aeneid* 6) in order to facilitate his historical mission to establish Rome. Likewise St. Paul was carried up into heaven for a blinding instant on the road to Damascus (II Corinthians 12:4) in order to spread the message of Christianity to the entire world. Now Dante is to follow a similar path but he feels unworthy. To restore his confidence, Virgil explains that his voyage is ordained from on high. His decision to rescue Dante in the dark wood was prompted by a visit from Dante's love, Beatrice, who came down from paradise at the insistence of St. Lucy and the Virgin Mary. Dante's courage is thus renewed and the voyage begins. Between them, *Inferno* 1 and 2 have set the itinerary for the entire poem, have suggested that Dante's journey is divinely sanctioned and of historical magnitude, and have let us know that for Dante the man the journey to heaven is at the same time a journey back to Beatrice.

Inferno—the bowels of the earth. The trip begins in earnest with *Inferno* 3, whose opening verses relay a now-famous inscription on the gate of hell. The dramatic last line—"Abandon all hope you who enter here"— underscores Dante's view of hell as a state of despair (*The Divine Comedy, Inferno* 3.9). Dante's *Inferno* is an inverted cone that extends below the earth's northern hemisphere (for him, the only hemisphere with land and people) to the center of the earth, which was also considered the center of the universe in Dante's day. Here lodged in ice is monstrous Lucifer, the fallen angel, source of all sin and suffering. We soon learn that this underworld unfolds in a series of nine, ever-narrower concentric circles, each with a specific class of sinners and punishment. As Dante and Virgil descend, the sins worsen and so do the punishments until the pair reaches Lucifer at the very bottom.

The first group of sinners that Dante and his guide meet are the neutrals, souls who in life refused to take sides for or against good and

thought only of themselves. They are herded into groups that are constantly being stung by large wasps, and they chase eternally after banners of various sorts. We are not yet in the first circle of hell but rather in a kind of ill-defined antechamber or vestibule. Neither heaven nor hell really wants these sinners, who were unwilling to commit to one side or the other in life. Just as the neutrals chose passive self-interest and refused to take a side in life, so in eternity they are stimulated into unceasing group action, forever chasing a partisan banner of the sort carried into battle in medieval warfare. Thus, before even entering hell proper, Dante instructs the reader in an important principle of divine justice (Dantean divine justice, that is). It is a principle about the relationship between sins and punishments, which he later calls "counter-suffering" or *contrapasso*. The reader needs always, then, to pay attention to the sometimes obvious, often subtle relationship between the sin and the punishment the poem invents for it, which can reveal much about the poet's intent in a given circle.

Circle one is Limbo, a rather special case. Christian theologians had created a marginal zone (*limbo* just means "edge" in Latin) for babies who died before receiving the ritual cleansing of baptism, thought to remove the original sin of Adam and Eve that stains all human souls by default. We find unbaptized babies in the poem's Limbo, but Dante uses the space for a much grander purpose as well: to contain virtuous pagans, morally great individuals born before Christ or outside Christ's geographical reach and so ineligible for paradise. Scores of esteemed pagan thinkers (like Plato and Aristotle) and characters from classical history and literature fill this circle. In it, there is no gruesome physical torment or thick black air, but relative light and calm, interrupted by sighs of unfulfilled longing. The pagan Virgil normally sits in this circle with an elite school of great epic poets, who momentarily invite Dante to join their club (no false modesty here!).

Dante and Virgil continue through upper hell. In circle two, a pair of famous adulterers named Paolo and Francesca are blown about in an eternal wind with other lustful sinners of their sort. Francesca claims she was an innocent victim of the inexorable god of Love as portrayed in the pages of medieval romance. Dante the character swoons in romantic sympathy as Dante the poet slyly condemns romance literature and reasserts the writer's moral responsibility. A putrid acid rain drenches the gluttons of circle three in eternal suffering. In circle four, the greedy and wasteful push huge stone weights. The angry and the sullen slap and tear at one another in the foul slime of the river Styx in circle five.

Dante and Virgil are ferried across the Styx to the great stone battlements of the city of lower hell, also called Dis. The monstrous female Furies and the infernal female Medusa (hair entwined with snakes and eyes glaring) temporarily impede their path. Relief comes from a Christ-like heavenly messenger, who descends to scatter the demons and shatter the gates with a touch of her wand: now Dante and Virgil are in lower hell.

Red-hot tombs with suspended lids cause unending misery for the heretics of circle six, those who in life stubbornly insisted that the soul dies with the body. Here we encounter the great Ghibelline general Farinata, a picture of personal majesty and misguided political obsession, who spars verbally with Dante the character from the opposing political camp, the Guelphs. Dante and Virgil spend the last two-thirds of *Inferno* moving through the bottom three circles (seven, eight, and nine), which are divided and subdivided in complex ways unlike the top six circles. Various categories of sinners who committed violence are punished in the three rounds of circle seven: 1) murderers, tyrants, bandits—those who wronged others—stew in a river of boiling blood guarded by Centaurs with bow and arrow; 2) suicides—those who committed violence against themselves—are implanted in gnarled trees fed upon by Harpies; 3) blasphemers, userers, and sodomites—those who practiced violence against God and Nature—suffer skin-scorching rain on a plain of burning sand. To get down to the next circle, Dante and Virgil take an amazing flight on the back of a terrifying winged beast with a scorpion's tail called Geryon. Circle eight consists of an inwardly sloping amphitheater named Malebolge ("Pouches of Evil"); here no fewer than ten separate varieties of fraud are punished in ten concentric mini-circles connected by spoke-like bridges, over which Dante and Virgil must pass. Pimps, flatterers, lying popes, fortune-tellers, corrupt politicians, hypocrites, thieves, con men, instigators, and counterfeiters come alive for readers in an awesome display of twisted human potential. In Malebolge, Dante and Virgil are granted an audience with the great Greek epic hero Odysseus—the Romans called him Ulysses—who suffers among the con men or false counselors of the eighth pouch. While today's world knows Odysseus from Homer's famous poem *The Odyssey,* Dante had barely encountered

Homer's works and so decided to invent a Ulysses all his own: a super-human adventurer who used his considerable intellect and rhetorical skill to convince his crew to sail beyond the proper limits of human experience into the forbidden southern hemisphere. This brazen attempt to capture, what for a medieval Christian must remain, divine knowledge necessarily ended in doom.

A great, dumb giant lowers Dante and Virgil to the icy floor of hell in the palm of his hand. Encrusted to various degrees in the rock-hard ice of circle nine are traitors, for Dante a special category of fraud. Traitors deceive people who have exceptional reason to trust them: family members, fellow citizens, guests, benefactors. In the last famous episode of *Inferno,* Ugolino, a prominent citizen of Pisa, feeds on the bloodied nape of the archbishop Ruggieri, his one-time political ally. Ugolino tells the dreadful tale of how the archbishop Ruggieri turned on Ugolino and had him locked in a tower with his little children to die of starvation. Overcome by hunger, Ugolino suggests he may have eaten the bodies of his dead offspring before succumbing to death by hunger himself. He bites into Ruggieri's neck in an act of cannibalistic revenge and blind rage.

Dante and Virgil escape hell's darkness by climbing down Lucifer's haunch through the earth's center and then up through a natural grotto to emerge at the base of a mountain in the middle of the southern hemisphere.

Purgatorio—the mountain of hope. The word *purgatory* simply describes a place to clean oneself; it came to designate the medieval Christian notion of a middle realm where souls prepared to enter paradise. Not hardened in their sinful ways and thus not condemned to eternal hell, purgatorial souls nonetheless possess significant sinful dispositions that need to be purged before the souls can go to heaven. Purgatory is a happy place because, though they suffer punishments like those in *Inferno,* the souls here are filled with hope: they will enter paradise after fulfilling their period of penance. Time is thus a major theme of purgatory—the only of Dante's three realms to exist in time, as life does on Earth (and the only of the three realms actually on earth, in the middle of the uninhabited southern hemisphere surrounded by ocean). At the end of history and time, the poem suggests, there will be just the damned and the saved, *Inferno* and *Paradiso.*

On the shore, Dante and Virgil meet the guardian of purgatory, Cato of Utica, from ancient Rome, who chose death rather than life under Caesar's tyranny. A symbol of personal liberty, Cato underscores purgatory's other great theme as Virgil informs him that Dante too is seeking liberty from all the sin that has weighed him down. Cato instructs them to cleanse themselves of *Inferno's* grime in the waves that lap the shore. Dante and Virgil go on to spend the first third of this part of the poem in a zone called "antepurgatory" (before purgatory), where they meet a variety of souls who waited until the very last moment of their lives to repent their sinful ways. As punishment for their negligence in life, they must now wait thousands of years in this purgatory-outside-purgatory before they can begin the process that will get them to heaven. So we see that a kind of *contrapasso* applies in purgatory too.

There are subtle structural similarities between *Inferno* and *Purgatorio*. Dante's purgatory is a mountain that mirrors hell's subterranean inverted cone. Just as Inferno has an upper hell before the city of Dis, so Purgatorio has an antepurgatory. When Dante and Virgil reach the gate of purgatory proper, a guardian angel inscribes Dante's forehead with seven P's (probably for the Latin "peccatum" or "sin"). The mountain rises in a series of seven concentric terraces, each of which purges one of what medieval Christians knew as the seven deadly sins. Just as hell descends from the least to the most serious sins, so purgatory rises terrace by terrace in the opposite moral direction, from the most to the least serious sin: 1) Pride, 2) Envy, 3) Wrath, 4) Sloth, 5) Avarice, 6) Gluttony, 7) Lust.

On each terrace, Dante encounters souls suffering some penance aimed at purging their particular vice: the proud, for instance, are bowed low under great slabs of rock. Each terrace also contains artistic representations of that vice along with scenes of the opposite virtue (on the first terrace, humility is praised). Especially in purgatory the poem focuses on the meaning of art and artistic representation since it is only in time and on Earth that art can be useful to represent eternity and give humans some idea of the right direction. On the upper terraces, Dante meets a series of poets, provides a history of vernacular lyric poetry in his day, and offers his understanding of the origin and function of true poetry. At the end of each terrace, an angel erases one of the P's from Dante's forehead until he is utterly free of sin at the top of the mountain.

Dante the poet chooses to place earthly paradise—the very Garden of Eden from which Adam and Eve were banished due to original sin at the beginning of human history—at the top of

his mountain of purgatory. Dante the character is initially hesitant to pass through the wall of fire that separates him from paradise until Virgil informs him that Beatrice is waiting inside. The last part of *Purgatorio* takes place inside earthly paradise, where Dante witnesses an elaborate pageant that symbolizes all of history as defined by Christian scripture. At the very center of this parade of human history is a mythical griffon (half eagle, half lion) meant to signify Christ (God and man); the creature pulls a chariot on which Beatrice—Dante's own personal savior—stands triumphant. Dante is overcome with emotion as a stern Beatrice berates him like a little child for his moral wandering. Virgil has disappeared. Dante swoons. When he comes to, he is being bathed and purified in two Edenic rivers. He then stands ready with Beatrice at his side to ascend to the heavens.

***Paradiso*—light and joy.** The character Dante is at first confused when he finds himself soaring heavenward with Beatrice. But Beatrice soon explains that it would be unnatural for Dante not to ascend now that he has been freed of all earthly vice. All elements in the universe possess a sort of innate moral gravity. Just as in Aristotle's physical universe heavy objects fall to earth and fire rises, so in Dante's moral universe individual souls fall or rise to their appropriate place. All human souls naturally harbor an inherent desire to return to their origins in divine truth, though some lose sight of this while on earth. Weighed down and waylaid by earthly concerns or attractions, they fall to infernal damnation.

Dante's *Paradiso* reflects the perpetual joy of those reunited and continually reuniting with divine light. Around the planet Earth revolves a series of translucent spheres at differing speeds. The first seven spheres, or heavens, carry the orbiting bodies for which they are named: the Moon, Mercury, Venus, the Sun, Mars, Jupiter, Saturn. The eighth heaven holds the Fixed Stars, including the zodiacal schemes and other stars against whose backdrop the remaining heavenly bodies revolve. The ninth heaven is the Primum Mobile or Prime Mover, the invisible motor for all the rest. Finally, God in his essence resides in a motionless tenth heaven of perfect superabundant light and repose that Dante calls "Empyrean." The rest of the heavens all spin—each one faster than the previous heaven—as a sign of their appetite for this ultimate fulfillment, reunion with divine essence.

In the opening cantos of *Paradiso*, Beatrice offers Dante and the reader a number of difficult doctrinal lessons to explain some basic truths about light and vision in heaven and about God's creation generally. Dante finds her staring directly at the sun and he follows suit. But his human sight cannot sustain this direct solar gaze for long and soon he averts his glance to Beatrice herself as she reflects the sunlight. Embodied humans, it seems, cannot experience divine light directly, but can sense divinity indirectly through reflections and accommodations to their inferior vision. (To Dante's mind, the whole visible universe is one such accommodation, a reflection or shadow of divine unity that points to God; also right-minded literature is a rhetorical invention that reflects divine truth in ways humans can understand.) Apparently each individual element of creation has a unique capacity to absorb and reflect divine light—some more, some less. There is immense individual diversity within perfect unity in this joyous part of the universe. Yet all can completely satisfy their separate appetites for perfect fulfillment. The divine light is shared but unlike a physical substance, whose amount diminishes when shared, divine light-energy increases when reflected to others. Beatrice explains that in its essence heavenly paradise is complete light and silence, all souls at one with God in the Empyrean. But the souls have, as it were, condescended to the limitations of human vision and understanding in a display of the nine heavens to allow Dante the character (and the readers) to experience paradise within the confines of their abilities.

To this end, Dante the poet creates for *Paradiso* categories of blessedness and a structure of graded blessedness comparable to the circles and terraces of sin in the previous two books. The first three heavens contain souls whose undeniable virtue was in some small measure marred by human defect. In the heaven of the Moon, Dante meets Piccarda Donati, sister of his great Florentine political opponent Corso Donati, and Constance of Normandy, mother of the emperor Frederick II. Both were virtuous women who entered a convent but then broke their vows due to difficult circumstances. In the heaven of Mercury are souls like the sixth-century Roman emperor Justinian, whose great service to humanity was slightly sullied by ambition for worldly fame. The lovers in the heaven of Venus were a force for good in the world, but their love was not always 100 percent pure—the biblical Rahab, whore of Babylon for a time, is but one example. Only with the fourth heaven of the Sun do we leave the shadow of earthly defect entirely behind to meet souls of total virtue. So *Paradiso* too

has a less perfect subrealm, like *Inferno*'s upper hell and *Purgatorio*'s antepurgatory.

Dante populates the heaven of the sun with his intellectual heroes, ancient wise men and medieval theologians like Saint Thomas Aquinas. Unlike the shadowy bodies of hell and purgatory, souls in paradise appear as brilliant points of light who form dynamic configurations in a concert of luminosity. Souls of the wise men configure themselves into two circular crowns that dance around Dante and Beatrice at their center. In the fifth heaven of Mars are the courageous warriors for Christ arrayed in a Greek cross. Dante here meets his great-great-grandfather Cacciaguida, who confirms Dante's historical destiny as prophet and poet. In the sixth heaven of Jupiter, just rulers spell out words of light that enjoin all rulers on earth to love justice, in many ways the theme of the entire *Divine Comedy*. One of the letters transforms into an eagle, symbol of the emperor and reminder of Dante's political convictions even at this great height. In the seventh heaven of Saturn, thinkers and mystics form a ladder reaching to the very top of paradise. In the heaven of the Fixed Stars, Dante meets the apostle-saints Peter, James, and John, who grill Dante on the three theological virtues of faith, hope, and love, his entrance exam to upper paradise. There Dante also sees Adam, the first man, and does some intense questioning of his own about the nature and origin of human language.

Dante's experience of the uppermost reaches of heaven is a metaphorical flood of overwhelming light, first a flowing river that he drinks in, then a celestial rose reflected off the convex surface of the Primum Mobile. In this rose, which quickly becomes a sort of immense amphitheatre, all of the blessed souls have their seats. Beatrice quietly takes her place among these blessed souls as the poem returns to the point promised way back at the beginning of *Inferno*.

Dante becomes aware of another presence beside him, Saint Bernard of Clairvaux, who urges him to look up and at long last to take in the source of all love and light, that is, to face God directly. Words, says the poet, fail to describe what he saw: a flashing point of light that was at the same time the image of a human face and three circles (suggesting the Trinity of Father, Son, and Holy Spirit, the central mystery of Christianity). The poet knows only that at that enraptured moment of complete joy and satisfaction, he was one with all creation, an integral piece of the divine love that moves the sun and all the stars.

History and allegory. Critics still debate the nature of the allegory in Dante's *Divine Comedy*. His medieval world used the term *allegory* to describe a text or image that contained an additional meaning beyond what was immediately apparent, what today might be called symbolism. Most common was a type called poetic allegory (or personification allegory). In poetic allegory, a person or animal simply represented an abstract category: a female figure, for example, might be called Patience or Pride. In this rather crude form of allegory, the actual person has little or no substance, but functions as a mere cipher for the concept. Dante's poem sometimes flirts with poetic allegory of this sort. The three beasts of *Inferno* 1 seem to represent three large categories of sin. But one does not know for sure. Dante the poet rarely links his elements to one clear meaning, preferring instead to leave his verse open to a range of possible meanings.

WHY "COMEDY?"

Dante called his poem a "comedy" in accordance with ancient definitions of comedy and tragedy ("divine" was added later by an early commentator). Tragedies used elevated language to treat upper-class characters in a plot that begins in great fortune and ends unhappily. By contrast, comedies treated a broader social spectrum of society (including servants and peasants), often in popular language. Like Dante's poem, they typically began in confusion and ended in happiness.

Yet Dante clearly wants his reader to take his poem as history—the literal story of a man who journeyed to a very real place beyond death. His exhaustive attention to details of every sort, the dramatic flair of his characters' encounters with real people, and the psychological complexity of his portraits persuade the reader of the poem's realism. Meanwhile, the poem's many episodes allow Dante the poet to offer instruction for living a happy life and on the good and bad effects of various mental attitudes. Dante also conveys a very specific theory of history, according to which the events of the Hebrew Bible and the ancient classical world unfolded in preparation for the coming of Christ, who gives meaning to everything before and after. Virgil came before and so is relegated to Limbo in hell, yet he is chosen as a main guide because Virgil is the poet

who captures an important segment of history for Dante, the history of the founding and destiny of Rome. Virgil neatly represents the story of the world right up to the birth of Christ, and of the limit of human virtue before this birth. Then Dante takes this story up to his own day, translating official history into very individual terms (and inviting us to do the same): hundreds of years after Christ, Dante enjoyed a personal savior named Beatrice who informed his life with meaning and led him to divine truth. The allegory can be understood on a personal level too. Whether or not one is Christian or believes in an afterlife, the *Inferno* can be understood to represent despair, an attitude the poet, in unhappy exile, finally rejects. To have no hope that life has direction or meaning is to be in hell. In the same vein, *Purgatorio* is challenge and suffering gladdened by hope. *Paradiso* affirms that human longing can end in fulfillment.

Sources and literary context. *The Divine Comedy* reflects Dante's wide acquaintance with, indeed passion for, ancient and medieval learning and literature of many kinds. Two books stand out for the sheer degree of their presence in his mind and thus in the text of the *Comedy*. The first is the Bible in the medieval Latin translation by Saint Jerome (c. 340-420), commonly known as the Vulgate. The second is Virgil's *Aeneid*, the great Latin epic that tells of the founding of Rome.

Also influential was the popular vernacular literature and Dante's contact with other Italian writers. Old French romances about the military exploits and torturous loves of knights and ladies at court like Lancelot and Guinivere circulated widely in many versions. Picking up on various traditions, Dante wrote in the vernacular and included episodes that recalled, for example, romance as well as other forms of literature. Dante's past experience as a man of letters was with fellow Italian poets like Guido Guinizelli and Guido Cavalcanti (Dante's one-time best friend), who themselves were indebted to earlier versifiers in Provence and Sicily. Dante the character meets many of these predecessors in the *Comedy*, while Dante the poet is keen within its confines to share his assessment of the romance tradition, the new vernacular poetry, his fellow practitioners, and his own (superior) place among them.

For his construction of a reality beyond death, Dante may have been influenced by other Christian poems on the afterlife, though none can rival Virgil's *Aeneid* as a source for concrete detail. In a broad sense, Dante was surely influenced by the Christian Neoplatonists, for whom all human desire pointed to an unchanging, invisible unity beyond our understanding. This is Saint Augustine's insistent message in his *Confessions*, a meditation on individual human consciousness in time and the crucial role of rhetoric in moving human hearts. For Dante's understanding and ordering of sins in *Inferno*, Aristotle's *Ethics* is fundamental. His *Purgatorio* relies on long-held notions of the seven deadly sins as well as Christian mythology of the Garden of Eden. His scheme in *Paradiso* draws on ancient and medieval astronomy along with established mystical notions of the angelic hierarchies.

Reception. Dante's *Comedy* was an enormous success from the moment it first circulated in manuscript. A tradition of interpretation and meticulous line-by-line reading of the text began immediately and has continued virtually uninterrupted to the present day. *The Divine Comedy* has generated a body of commentary second perhaps only to the Bible. The Florentines soon regretted the shabby way they had treated the now famous Dante; in the late fourteenth century, the community commissioned an aging Boccaccio, writer of the **Decameron**, to deliver public lectures on what was regarded as Dante's glorious poem (also in *WLAIT 7: Italian Literature and Its Times*).

The poem's architectural structure captured the imagination of illustrators and artists from the very start. While Dante's original appears to have vanished, dozens of manuscript versions—some illuminated with brilliant images of tormented sinners, mischievous demons, and radiant angels—have transmitted Dante's text, which was also among the most popular choices for early printers. The best-known illustrators include the painter Sandro Botticelli (1445-1510) in the Renaissance, much later in the nineteenth century, the English poet and engraver William Blake (1757-1827) and the French engraver Gustave Doré (1832-1883). A testament to Dante's powers of persuasion, Renaissance mathematicians began the tradition of calculating the exact size and shape of Dante's realms and mapping his hell, purgatory, and paradise with professional precision. The heirs to these early maps can be found in the visual supplements that accompany today's many printed and online editions of the poem.

Dante's importance for other poets and writers the world over has endured for centuries. His presence can be felt throughout the English and American tradition in the poetry of Geoffrey Chaucer, Alfred Tennyson, William Blake, and Henry Wadsworth Longfellow (an important

early translator) to the verse of a modernist like Ezra Pound or, in our own day, the Irish poet Seamus Heaney. Another modernist poet, T. S. Eliot, spelled out Dante's stature in no uncertain terms: "Dante and Shakespeare divide the modern world between them; there is no third" (Eliot, p. 225). Across seven centuries the *Divine Comedy* has inspired lines of human thought and creativity, from commentary, to mapmaking,

---

AN ARCHITECTURE OF NUMBERS

As a rhetorician and poet, Dante needed to make his creation beautiful in order to attract readers to his moral message. Medieval aesthetics identified beauty with symmetry and arithmetic harmony. For a Christian poet like Dante, the most significant numbers were three and one, a reflection of the Holy Trinity said to contain three persons (Father, Son, Holy Spirit) in one perfect divine unity. *The Divine Comedy* contains three books in one; each book contains 33 brief chapters called "cantos" plus the introductory first canto of *Inferno* for a total of 100 cantos (33 times three plus one). Dante used the classic Italian eleven-syllable line known as hendecasyllable and invented an elaborate interlocking rhyme scheme of three-verse stanzas or tercets (*aba bcb cdc . . .*), but each canto ends with an additional single verse. Thus, the number of verses in each canto is a multiple of three plus one verse, or $3x + 1$, and the total number of verses is 14,233, also a multiple of three plus one.

---

prose, poetry, drawing, music, painting, sculpture, film, television, and video. This is perhaps the surest sign of the poem's success.

—Gary P. Cestaro

For More Information

Dante Alighieri. *The Divine Comedy*. Trans. Charles S. Singleton. Princeton: Princeton University Press, 1970.

——. *The Divine Comedy of Dante Alighieri*. Ed. and trans. Robert M. Durling and Ronald L. Martinez. Oxford: Oxford University Press, 1996.

"Dante Online." Italian Dante Society in Italian and English. http://danteonline.it/italiano/home ita.asp.

"Digital Dante." Columbia University. http://dante .ilt.columbia.edu.

Eliot, T. S. *Selected Essays 1917-1932*. New York: Harcourt Brace, 1932.

Hollander, Robert. *Dante: A Life in Works*. New Haven: Yale University Press, 2001.

Jacoff, Rachel, ed. *The Cambridge Companion to Dante*. Cambridge: Cambridge University Press, 1993.

Lansing, Richard, ed. *The Dante Encyclopedia*. New York: Garland Publishing, 2000.

Taylor, Charles H., and Patricia Finley. *Images of the Journey in Dante's Divine Comedy*. New Haven: Yale University Press, 1997.

The Duel

by

Giacomo Casanova

THE LITERARY WORK

A novella set in eighteenth-century Europe (primarily in Venice and Warsaw); published in Italian (as *Il duello*) in 1780, in English in 2003.

SYNOPSIS

A misunderstanding between a rival and Casanova over his intentions toward a ballerina results in a duel to redeem Casanova's honor. Illegal in Warsaw, it takes place outside the city and wounds both duelists before one emerges victorious.

Giacomo Casanova was born April 2, 1725, in Venice to a family of stage dancers and actors, professions then considered so lowly they were often equated with pimping and prostitution. Though his mother, Zanetta Farussi, was married to Gaetano Casanova (who died when Giacomo was eight years old), there is some question as to who his biological father was—Gaetano or the patrician Michele Grimani, who took on the responsibility of rearing Giacomo. Whether out of *noblesse oblige* or paternal devotion, Grimani and his two brothers (all unwed) provided Casanova with a noble connection and thus an entrance into upper-class European society. While his mother pursued her "acting" career in various great cities of Europe, Casanova attended school in Padua, where he started to serve in the Roman Catholic Church and earned a Doctor of Law degree at the age of 17. Unsuited for the clergy, Casanova tried his hand at several other professions, becoming a soldier and a violinist before finding his true calling as a lover and court favorite. Drawing on his keen wit, charm, good looks, and noble connections, Casanova "comforted" women—and men—of the aristocracy throughout Europe and earned a living through financial schemes and government intrigues. Not surprisingly, these intrigues and his amorous adventures frequently landed him in prison or drove him into exile. In flight from one place or another throughout his life, Casanova wandered from city to city, always able to ingratiate himself with the aristocracy but never truly able to become a part of it. His final years found

him virtually unknown and in poor straits in Bohemia, taken on as librarian to Count Waldstein. Seemingly at odds with his public persona, Casanova produced a formidable body of substantial literary work throughout his adventurous life. He composed and translated histories, satirical and political pamphlets, math treatises, plays, novels, and, finally, his highly acclaimed autobiography, *The Story of My Life* (*L'histoire de ma vie*), begun in 1789 in Bohemia but never completed or published during his lifetime. He published only two original works of fiction (autobiographical adventures): the first, the story of his escape from the Leads prison in Venice and the second, *The Duel*—both also recounted in his autobiography. *The Duel* details an episode in Warsaw involving a rival who impugns Casanova's honor as

Giacomo Casanova

a man and a Venetian—a significant attack on a man who struggled his whole life for respect and honor in a highly stratified society.

Events in History at the Time of the Novella

Venice and vice. By the beginning of the eighteenth century, Venice was a republic in decline. No longer a major player in the world as master of the Adriatic and Mediterranean, the republic's power was at perhaps its weakest point in its thousand-year history. Its citizens could at least take comfort in the fact that they lived in relative peace. No longer was war being waged against the Turks (or anyone else), which gave Venetian society and culture—particularly the arts and leisure activities—a chance to flourish. Indeed Venice did flourish, thanks in large part to its status as a tourist attraction. The eighteenth century saw the rise of a phenomenon known as the Grand Tour, in which tourism in continental Europe became all the rage, with Venice as a primary destination. Aristocrats from Great Britain to Russia flocked to Venice and its neighboring states in droves to visit the remains of classical antiquity and to indulge in sensual activities. Gambling, Venice's celebrated Carnival season, theater, and prostitution made it the "sin city" of this era; its relatively relaxed moral climate and an abundance of single women in the city only added to its appeal. As John Masters describes it, "Mountebanks tumbled, harlequins pranced with dominoes, charlatans cajoled, herb doctors cried quackish cures: and everywhere there was the smell of fish, of water, of over-ripeness of history, a city of the sea, settling under the weight of past riches, vivid, beautiful, *morbida*, a queen turned courtesan" (Masters, p. 59).

A unique aspect of Venetian society was its preponderance of unmarried aristocrats. Of the 42 noble houses that now ruled the republic, 66 percent of eligible bachelors remained single in the eighteenth century for one simple reason: to conserve what remained of the family's wealth (Norwich, p. 594). The eldest son of each family was required to marry to keep the noble line going but other sons were denied marriage, in order to prevent the dispersal of wealth that no longer accumulated the way it once had, when Venice controlled all trade through the Adriatic Sea. The result of this policy was twofold: first, many noble lines went extinct because no male heirs survived; and second, the city swelled with noblemen bachelors. This new demographic produced a thriving community of courtesans and *cicisbeo* (male gigolos), who operated either openly or secretly. Unable to find suitable husbands, many aristocratic women were forced into the nunnery—women who had no calling or inclination to take the veil. This coercion led to many of the convents in Venice becoming little more than thinly disguised brothels. Aristocratic women who did manage to marry commonly took a *cicisbeo* to serve as companions while their husbands occupied themselves with their own bevy of courtesans—all of which was tolerated in a society tired of the strict morals of previous generations. A true product of this hedonistic environment, Casanova not only found his calling as a *cicisbeo extraordinaire,* but benefited from the single status of the noble Grimani brothers, who, with no children of their own to help, served throughout his life as surrogate fathers (though, as noted, Michele Grimani may have actually been his biological father).

Venetian government. The Republic of Venice had long figured among the most liberal of Catholic Europe; of the Catholic republics this one alone could claim that it never burned a heretic. Unlike other Roman Catholic political entities, this one tolerated various sects and religions: Greek Orthodox and Armenian Christian, Jewish, and Muslim. Venice was a city-state, an independent republic that was subject to no sovereign authority; it differed in this way from other former Italian city-state republics, like Florence

FREEMASONRY AND KABBALISM

Both Freemasonry and Kabbalism promised to land its practitioners in jail while the Inquisition ensued (1231-1800). An association of gentlemen, politicians, and professionals, the Freemasons formed an official union in 1717 for the purpose of bringing order, reason, and brotherhood into the world. They set out to advance the purpose of the Almighty and, with this in mind, practiced religious toleration. Anyone who believed in a supreme being could be a member. In 1738, the Freemasons were banned by the Catholic Church under pain of excommunication. Despite the ban, Masonic temples sprang up throughout Europe and the future United States. The temples became centers for socio-political networking and free thinking. Freemasonry "attracted some quacks and freaks and crooks, but its chief appeal at the time was to men of intelligence and curiosity, because it recreated a free society. Here Catholic could talk to Protestant, tradesman to aristocrat, Spaniard to German, merchant banker to master builder" (Masters, p. 80).

Kabbalah, also spelled *Cabala,* is a mystical Jewish tradition that by Casanova's day had been in existence for more than 500 years. It is based on the *Zohar,* a book of mysterious or esoteric commentary on the Torah, the first five books of the Hebrew Bible. In the Zohar are texts that one could purportedly use to prevent sickness, defeat enemies, and alter physics. The Catholic Church banned the book and the practice of its secrets. Defying the ban, and getting caught, led to charges of heresy, which was punishable by imprisonment or burning at the stake.

Casanova indulged in both Freemasonry and Kabbalism. While people studied the Kabbalah in earnest, he used it as a means to a selfish end. On the road and in prison Casanova learned some basic charlatanry based on the Kabbalah, and he used the little he knew to swindle nobles out of money, which landed him in jail on more than one occasion (including in 1755). He became a Freemason to improve his social connections. In the mid-eighteenth century, European society was flirting with the idea of democratization, a flirtation that would simmer and then boil over into the French Revolution soon after *The Duel* was released. Becoming a Freemason in his day was therefore a prudent move; it "would serve to open a thousand barred doors" (Masters, p. 81). Casanova, without money and of low birth, desperately needed this association in order to work his way up the social ladder. Ironically, then, he used a democratic form to promote an elitist aspiration.

(which had succumbed to princely rule under the Medici) or Milan (which had been conquered and absorbed into the Habsburg empire). Venice relied on a founding group of 480 patrician families, so designated in 1297, for its rule. They formed the Great Council, which, in turn, appointed the Council of Ten (in charge of internal security in the state); the ruling Doge (head of state); and the much feared Inquisitors of State, who were empowered to investigate and secretly arrest, imprison, and torture those identified as enemies of Venice. By the eighteenth century the Inquisitors still existed but were much less vigorous than they had been in past centuries, having fallen out of favor with both society and the ruling succession of Doges. The old instruments of torture served as "elegant curiosities" more than anything else, and the Inquisitors had not used their famous poison for close to a hundred years (Hibbert, p. 166). Arrests, however, were often made for both moral and legal violations, as Casanova discovered. He was jailed for immoral activities in his youth and then again in 1755, this last time without formal charge. The authorities held him for over a year, ostensibly because of occult activities (practicing Jewish mysticism, generally known as the Kabbalah) but actually the arrest may have been for spying. At any rate, he escaped and the authorities retaliated by exiling him from Venice, which led to his stay in Warsaw, the scene of the duel.

Eighteenth-century Europe. The map of Europe in the eighteenth century was an amalgam of competing colonial powers: in the west, France, Great Britain, Spain, and the Netherlands; in the southeast, the Ottoman and Habsburg empires; in the northeast, Russia and Sweden; and on the Italian peninsula, about a dozen independent states, of which Venice was one. These powers vied for economic, political, and social control, resorting to everything from war to strategic marriages to attain it. Meanwhile, political, social, and economic changes transpired, some of them emanating from a new variety of rule.

The concept of "enlightened absolutism" emerged from Frederick II of Prussia (1740-85). Absolute monarchs had long been claiming they ruled by divine right and were answerable only to the Almighty. Enlightened rulers justified their claim to absolute authority by identifying themselves as servants of the state or society, leaders charged with wiping out inequality and preserving the rights of their subjects. People started to debate the meaning of *noble*—was it an inherited quality or one earned by virtue and talent? In keeping with this debate, there was some movement across social ranks; in Italy, as in the rest of Europe, noble titles were sometimes sold. The fact that one's education, achievements, and social connections made some difference is evident from Casanova's own social rise. But society in general remained divided between the haves and have-nots. While other European leaders followed Frederick's example, "no such ruler . . . had any idea of establishing an equality of rights between middle class and nobility," much less the lower classes (Anderson, p. 126). The masses still lived under the thumb of the elite. In Eastern Europe, where *The Duel* takes place, a small minority—the 2 to 3 percent that comprised the upper class—controlled virtually all the wealth, land, and laws for the largely illiterate, agrarian majority. The nobility—enlightened or not—retained power.

Nobles dressed in finery that distinguished them from other groups. They could brandish a sword and govern. While some of their privileges were enjoyed by non-noble army officers and government officials, the nobles generally monopolized the positions of highest command. In keeping with the advent of enlightened rule, however, as the century progressed, society began to consider the negative consequences of policies invoked by the nobles. An educated few started to question the social inequities around them. Advances in science and thinkers such as Locke, Rousseau, Voltaire, Diderot, and Montesquieu helped shape a newly emergent concept of human rights and democracy. The winds of change were stirring, though not until the century's end would a real revolution occur.

Noble in name only. In general, European society was sharply divided between the nobility and the rest of the population. Theoretically the nobility consisted of greater and lesser nobles, all protected from prosecution under most laws and entitled to special privileges. By the eighteenth century, although many lesser nobles were doing well, others, especially in Eastern Europe, where *The Duel* takes place, had little to boast of except for these privileges. These nobles were virtually bankrupt. In Poland—the site of Casanova's duel—the family of the king (Stanislaus Lubomirski) owned 31 towns and 776 villages, but thousands of poor, uneducated squires had neither the material goods nor the cultural training generally associated with the class. Yet the bankrupt aristocrats refused to work, viewing such activity as not only beneath them but as a stain on their name and social rank. In a society where the appearance of nobility won a person privilege and respect but the occupation of worker did not, a person who wanted to maintain a position in society had few "acceptable" ways to earn a living. One could own land or hold a governing post, but without either, the options narrowed to almost none. A man could become a professional soldier and buy a commission; he could become a clergyman and engineer a powerful posting; or he could do what most did: secure patronage. Patrons, who were the greater nobles, paid to have lesser nobles in their debt, ready and willing to execute deeds, from conducting court intrigues to concocting revenue schemes, to providing political support and showering a patron with flattery. A man who all his life wanted to be respected by society, Casanova tried all three—soldiering, the clergy, and patronage—eventually settling on this last means of survival.

The custom of dueling. Though officially illegal, the custom of dueling remained an honorable way to settle disputes in eighteenth-century Europe. Originating in the medieval era, dueling had by this time evolved into the gentleman's way to settle disputes and questions of honor, while simultaneously proving bravery. It was widely held that God would grant victory to the duelist who was in the right. There was an understood standard of behavior with respect to dueling: "If you disagree with someone, it is your responsibility to your own word, and your opponent's to theirs, to bring it to a duel, because only when facing death against live steel is your commitment truly tested (God, of course, will grant victory to the one who is right, and what self respecting and angry nobleman would believe God wasn't with them?)" (Hodges, p. 1).

The rules of the duel were the same throughout Europe. As in Casanova's case, however, they were not always stringently followed, in large part because dueling was an illegal activity. Duels generally transpired according to the following "rules":

1. The offended party issues a challenge to the offender.
2. The offender accepts and both parties agree to meet in a timely manner—usually the same day the challenge is issued. The parties name their "seconds," or witnesses, who are to issue the weapons and ensure the fairness of the fight (in Casanova's case, he does not have a second and Branicki's—far from ensuring the fairness of the fight—tries to kill Casanova after he has injured Branicki).
3. The challenger can name the place of the duel but the challenged has the right to choose weapons. Swords can only be used if the challenger swears he is not an expert fencer. (As in Casanova's case, most duelists didn't know or trust each other so they chose other weapons, usually pistols.)
4. When using pistols, each duelist stands a fixed distance from the other and fires one shot, with the challenged firing first. If no one is killed, the duel can end at this point. However, if agreed beforehand, the duelists can reload and fire again until one or the other is killed.
5. All participants in the duel—the duelists and seconds—swear secrecy concerning the duel, both before and after it takes place.

The primary "rule" was that both participants had to be of the same class and social standing for the fight to be an honorable one. It has been said that the duelists entered into the fight to demonstrate their sense of honor rather than to win. This idea of honor demanded the foes be of the same social standing because only men of comparable status could impugn each other's reputation. It was not necessary for a noble to fight a commoner. Attacks from men of lesser ranks could be punished in court or the noble could have them beaten. But if a noble refused a direct challenge from a fellow noble, chances are he would suffer a worse fate than if he had fought. He risked be-

ing labeled a coward, publicly humiliated, and ostracized from polite society—an outcome worse than death among most of the aristocracy. So keenly does Casanova feel the loss of honor that it threatens to ruin his life. So he reaches for the remedy of the duel to restore his honor.

The Novella in Focus

Plot summary. "A man born in Venice to poor parents, without worldly goods and without any of those titles which in cities distinguish the families of note from the common people, but, by the grace of God, brought up like one destined for something different" (Casanova, *The Duel*, p. 3). So the narration—in third person—introduces us to Casanova, a would-be man "of note." At the age of 27 he has a run-in with the government of Venice and at 28 he manages to escape a penalty he is unwilling to pay. Preferring exile to imprisonment, Giacomo Casanova, now a fugitive, embarks on yet another adventure in his action-packed life.

Just escaped from the Leads, the famous political prison under the Doge's palace in Venice, Casanova sets out for France and various courts of Europe in search of patronage. He is on the run, exiled from his beloved homeland after his daring jail break, and ready to wheedle money from the nobles of Europe and Russia, as is his custom. En route to Russia, Casanova explains,

He only is certain of being employed and given a fat salary who arrives at that Court after having had the skill to introduce himself in some European court to the Russian ambassador, who, if he becomes persuaded of that person's merit, informs the Empress, who gives the order to send him to her, paying the expenses of his journey. Such a person cannot fail to succeed, because no one would be able to say that money has been thrown away on the travel expenses of someone with no ability.

(*The Duel*, p. 5)

Casanova well understands the politics of impressing the ruling nobility and puts his knowledge to good use as he tries to make his fortune in the world. Though of lowly birth, Casanova has managed, through aristocratic friends and education (in school and on the street), to elevate his status by now, and he is not about to lose any part of it.

Casanova's quest for lodging and riches eventually brings him to Warsaw, then allied with both the court of Louis XV and Russia. Armed with a letter of introduction, he is accepted into

Illustration of Casanova's duel with Ksawery Branicki, by Antoine Gaymard.

the court of Prince Adam Czartoryski, the Prince Palatine (a court position) to Russia. One night they attend a ballet that features, among others, a Venetian ballerina. Though they are compatriots, Casanova and the ballerina do not get along well. In fact, Casanova prefers the other prima ballerina in the production. Viewing this as an affront, the Venetian ballerina more or less forces Casanova to congratulate her on her performance after the show.

Unfortunately, as Casanova is paying tribute to the Venetian ballerina in her dressing room, her paramour, Ksawery Branicki, Podstoli (a court official) to the Polish Crown, enters the room. Spying Branicki, Casanova takes his leave but instead of letting him go, Branicki follows the Venetian and demands he state his intentions. Casanova, honestly uninterested in the ballerina, jokes to Branicki that he loves her but is willing to yield her to "a fine knight like you" (*The Duel*, p. 14). Outraged, Branicki calls him a Venetian coward. Casanova responds, "A Venetian coward will shortly send a brave Pole to the next world" and proceeds outside to face him *mano a mano* (hand to hand) (*The Duel, p.* 15). But Branicki does not take the bait.

Later, as Casanova is lying in bed, he cannot sleep. He turns over and over in his mind the affront, the attack on his honor. He reasons, "If to the word 'coward,' which was rude enough in itself, that man had not added the word 'Venetian,' the other might have borne the affront. But there is, I believe, no man who can stomach a word which vilifies his nation" (*The Duel*, p. 15). With that, he dashes off a letter challenging Branicki to a duel.

Branicki responds by letter, accepting the challenge and allowing Casanova to choose the weapons. Casanova picks swords but wants the duel postponed to the following day. To his surprise, Branicki shows up at his house and demands that the duel take place that afternoon. They agree to a place outside the city limits (since dueling is illegal in Warsaw) but when they arrive, Branicki switches weapons. He insists they use pistols instead of swords, fearing that Casanova may be a master fencer (which he is not). Casanova reluctantly agrees and the opponents, with Branicki's "friends" in tow, assume their positions.

The two men fire their pistols simultaneously—Branicki is struck in the ribcage, Casanova in the hand. Branicki falls to the ground and his friends immediately rush Casanova and try to finish him off. As Casanova notes, "this was an outrage, because if the Podstoli had been killed, those friends would have killed his killer" and that is against the rules of the duel. But Branicki calls his avengers off (*The Duel*, p. 41). He is rushed to a doctor, and Casanova flees the scene, fearful that Branicki will die and he will be held accountable. The Venetian holes up in a monastery where his wounds are treated.

Luckily for Casanova, Branicki survives, and, though word of the incident has spread, the king pardons both men for dueling. The Venetian resumes public life in Warsaw, now more popular than ever. However, his new fame inspires jealousy in others, who throw forth threats and circulate vicious rumors about his exile from Venice and "from almost all the countries of Europe: from one for robbing banks, from another for treachery, for theft, for infamous acts of wickedness" (*The Duel*, p. 55). Casanova says these are all lies but then adds suggestively, "do not calumnies have the same effect as accusations which are based on the truth?" (*The Duel*, p. 55). At this point, Casanova decides to again move on, promising to one day recount his lifetime of adventures, which he ultimately does. Thus ends the story, with Casanova on the road once more, searching for a new home and another opportunity to make his mark on the world.

From novella to autobiography. When Casanova penned his monumental *History of My Life,* he was writing in what is now considered "the classical age of autobiography." Jean-Jacques Rousseau, William Wordsworth, and Goethe, among many others, produced and published their monumental works during this era, recording not simply personal experiences like the one in *The Duel*, but exploring fundamental questions concerning the meaning of life. In confessions, memoirs, histories, and more, writers famous and not so famous recounted their trials and triumphs in a socially cathartic exercise that allowed readers to share in their common humanity. Then, as now, the autobiographies also afforded readers vicarious thrills, allowing them to experience the extraordinary adventures their ordinary lives would not.

Casanova's autobiography was perhaps the most daring of all, its tone set by his two preceding autobiographical novellas—*The Duel* and *History of My Flight from the Prison of the Republic of Venice*. They set the tone for an autobiography filled with the intrigue, sex, and scandal that would cement Casanova's reputation and make his name a household word.

Penned in French because the language was more widely known than Italian, Casanova's *History of My Life* reveals an adventurous man at the end of his life trying to make sense of society and his small role in it. He begins by declaring himself a Christian as well as a believer in philosophy (he was, after all, living in the Age of Reason) but then, true to his self-deprecating nature, confesses, "Despite an excellent moral foundation, the inevitable fruit of the divine principles which were rooted in my heart, I was all my life the victim of my senses" (Casanova, *History of My Life*, vol. 1, p. 27). He also states that he "had no scruples about deceiving nitwits and scoundrels and fools" and gains nothing but pleasure by recalling his amorous affairs. Though he realizes that his exploits may shock readers, he shows no remorse for any of his actions—in this memoir he is certainly not repentant! Instead he invites readers to laugh at his follies with him. "My follies are the follies of youth," he says, ". . . and if you are kind you will laugh at them with me" (*History of My Life,* vol. 1, p. 27).

The most memorable aspects of Casanova's autobiography are his seemingly unending series of amorous trysts with young girls, married women, and even boys. So matter-of-factly does he declare his desires—and the effect of them— that he clearly does not see anything immoral about his behavior. For example, while staying with a married couple, he begins an affair with the wife (as is his custom)—even pursuing her while the husband is in the same room:

> He [the husband] having gone to the table by the window—and the maid having gone to fetch some linen, I asked her [the wife] if there were any hard lumps in the calf of her leg and if the redness went up in streaks as far as her thigh; as I asked these questions it was natural that I should accompany them with my hands and my eyes; I neither felt lumps or saw redness; but the sensitive patient laughingly dropped the curtain at once, yet not without letting me reap from her lips a kiss of whose sweetness, after four days of abstinence, I sorely needed to refresh my memory. After the kiss, I licked her wound, firmly believing that my tongue would be the balm for it; but the maid's return forced me to give over this sweet remedy, which my love as doctor made me believe infallible at the moment.
>
> (*History of My Life,* vol. 1, p. 164)

Of course, Casanova was not a doctor, but he would play whatever part was required to attain his and his lovers' desires.

In the tradition of the great Italian autobiographies—from Dante's *Vita nuova* (c. 1292) to Petrarch's *Secretum* (1353) to Cellini's *Vita* (1728)—Casanova's memoirs are replete with controversy and social commentary (see Cellini's **My Life,** also in WLAIT 7: *Italian Literature and Its Times*). Casanova was not a famous artist like Cellini, or a renowned writer in his lifetime like Dante, but his autobiographical stories compel readers, perhaps precisely because he is penning the life of an extraordinary "common" man. He struggles all his life to gain honor and respect (preoccupations of Cellini as well) and distinguishes himself by unabashedly detailing the folly of the aristocracy and of his own exploits

to sustain himself within that strange community. *The Duel* sets the stage for the autobiography with respect to straight-shooting insights and observations about society and himself. For example, in St. Petersburg "he who has the air of needing nothing can easily make money, and it is not difficult there to have that air, just as it is most difficult to have it in Italy, where there is no one who supposes that a purse is full of gold until he has first seen it open" (*The Duel,* p. 6). Casanova's autobiographical stories are at once a survival guide to eighteenth-century Europe and a stinging critique of society. *The Duel* specifically describes his encounter in Warsaw with Branicki, but it clearly shows the absurdity of this custom and questions the social structure that demands such activity in order for citizens to keep their place in society. In his autobiography, he indicates his contempt for certain so-called "pious" clergymen and tells of the common practice of young girls who sleep naked with priests. He notes, tongue firmly planted in cheek, "So the charming Christina, who would turn Xenocrates himself from the path of virtue, was in the habit of sleeping undressed with the priest of her uncle, an old man, it was true, pious, very far from anything which could make the arrangement improper" (*History of My Life,* vol. 1, p. 246). Here Casanova shows a talent for witty understatement, which makes his social commentaries all the more palatable. He likewise recounts real historical events he finds ridiculous. When the queen of France declares there is no better dish than chicken fricassee (a gourmet chicken dish), for months afterward it is the only dish served by all the courts of Europe: "Every day in every house where I dined, I found chicken fricassee," writes Casanova, who does not like the dish but will not say so, "because, now that the Queen had composed a eulogy to it, they would have booed me" (*The Duel,* p. 13).

From humorous jabs to serious condemnation, Casanova critiques society and pokes fun at himself. His stories reveal a multifaceted man who both loathes and loves figures of authority, who decries and defies the morals and laws of his time yet seeks to be accepted by society. Unafraid of exposing what he sees as the hypocrisy of even "men of cloth" Casanova describes a monk he meets on the road as "a lazy lout" who "had become a monk only so that he could live without tiring his body" (*History of My Life,* vol. 1, pp. 220, 221). Every bit as scathing in his critique of himself, Casanova blames himself for being too passionate: "Having observed that I have all my life acted more on the force of feeling than from my reflections, I have concluded that my conduct has depended more on my character than on my mind . . . I have alternately found myself with too little intelligence for my character and too little character for my intelligence" (*History of My Life*, vol. 1, p. 31).

Portraying himself as part of the very fallible human race, Casanova leaves it to the reader to decide if his character is good or bad, and sees it as his duty to file this report of his life so that others may profit by it: "A member of the universe, I speak to the air and I imagine I am rendering an account of my stewardship as the majordomo does to his master, before vanishing" (*History of My Life*, vol. 1, p. 29). Ultimately he concludes that though he has acted "more on the force of feeling than from my reflections," his character is sound: "I believe that, without offending against modesty, I can apply [to] myself these words from my beloved Virgil: 'I am not such a monster; lately I saw my reflection by the shore when the sea was calm'" (*History of My Life*, vol. 1, p. 31). Indeed, through his monumental autobiography and his two preceding tales, one of the Western world's most infamous figures emerges not as a monster but as a complex, clever, and perpetually fascinating member of the human race.

Sources and literary context. *The Duel* is based on a real event in Casanova's life, which occurred just after he was exiled from Venice for escaping from the Leads prison in 1755. Scholars have verified the times and places detailed in his memoirs, including the account of the incident that inspired *The Duel*. According to biographer John Masters, the account is reasonably credible—distorted only by memory and poetic license. It differs from the account in Casanova's *History of My Life* (his memoirs) in that it is written in the third person. Otherwise, it is largely the same, as indicated by this comparison of the offense that incites Casanova to fight:

**Two Versions of "The Duel"—
The Inflammatory Spark**

From *The Duel*: "While the Venetian was going away very slowly, the Podstoli (Branicki) said in a loud voice, so that it could be heard by two officers who were not very far away: 'The Venetian coward has made the right decision in going away. I was going to send him off to f*** himself.' To these words the other, without turning round, replied: 'A Venetian coward will shortly send a brave Pole to the next world'" (*The Duel*, p. 15).

From *History of My Life*: "I had not gone four steps away from the dressing room when I heard myself honored with the title of 'Venetian coward'; I turned and said to him that outside the theatre a Venetian coward might well kill a brave Pole, and I went down the main staircase leading to the door which gives onto the street" (*History of My Life* in *The Duel*, p. 70).

Publication and reception. Published on the heels of Casanova's *The History of My Flight from the Prison of the Republic of Venice*, *The Duel* caused a sensation throughout Europe. The story of the duel was recounted in many European newspapers, including the *Vossische Zeitung* in Berlin, the *Zeitung Diarium* in Vienna, and *The Public Advertiser* in England. The tale also surfaced as a popular topic of conversation in contemporary correspondence. But by Casanova's death in 1798, the book itself had gone out of print.

BAD BEHAVIOR OR GOOD SENSE?

The last thing Casanova penned before his death was the Preface to his autobiography. In a humorous passage, he seeks to justify his often immoral behavior:

They will find that I have always loved truth so passionately that I have often resorted to lying as a way of first introducing it into the minds which were ignorant of its charms. They will not condemn me when they see me emptying my friends' purses to satisfy my whims. They were possessed by chimerical projects, and by making them hope for their success, I at the same time hoped to cure them of their folly by opening their eyes. I deceived them to make them wise; and I did not consider myself guilty, because what I did was not prompted by avarice. I was simply paying for my pleasures with money allotted to acquiring possessions which nature makes it impossible to obtain. I should consider myself guilty if I were a rich man today. I have nothing; whatever I had I squandered; and this consoles and justifies me. It was money which was to be spent on follies; I merely changed its application by making it pay for mine.

(*History of My Life*, vol. 1, p. 35)

The autobiography containing the incident— the original text of *History of My Life*—was republished in 1960 and "created a sensation in the literary world. . . . [It was] the literary event of the century" (Trask in Casanova, *History of My Life*, p. 17). Upon publication J. Rives Childs wrote in *Arts* magazine, "There is hardly an example in the history of literature of a work of the importance of the Memoirs having been withheld ... for more than 160 years" (Childs in Casanova, *History of My Life,* vol. 1, pp. 17-18). In 2003 Hesperus Press republished the novella

---

BRIEF PUBLISHING HISTORY OF THE MEMOIRS

Casanova died in 1798 before his autobiography was completed or published. The manuscript vanished until the 1820s, at which time a German publisher produced a translated version in 12 volumes, from 1822 to 1828. Offended by the graphic content, French professor Jean LaForgue produced his own heavily edited 8-volume version in 1826-38 that was published in both German and French. He altered significantly Casanova's sexual exploits as well as his attitude toward the nobility and the Church. Thereafter, the autobiography went out of print until the early twentieth century (when a 1932 translation appeared, purportedly based on a 1925 translation of the 8-volume French edition). During World War II, the text met with near destruction. Luckily, Casanova's original manuscript was discovered by United States soldiers in Germany in 1945 in the bunker of the bombed-out Brockhaus Publishing House. The original was transported to a bank in Leipzig for safekeeping and was finally reprinted in French and in English in 1960, to high acclaim. Nearly 150 years after his death, Casanova became an overnight sensation.

Casanova's *History of My Life*, in addition to being the longest literary autobiography ever written (12 volumes), is the text from which sprang the legend of Casanova as the quintessential playboy and adventurer. Examined by scholars since its publication, the autobiography has been the subject of intense debate about its truthfulness. Some doubt that Casanova even existed, opining that another writer invented the character and created "Casanova" as a *nom de plume* (pen name). However, most agree that indeed he did exist and, as a child of actors and dancers, lived larger than life "as though he were on the stage" always wanting "to be the star performer" (Kesten, p. xiv).

---

version of *The Duel*, bound together with the excerpt from Casanova's memoirs. Praised by scholars and readers, *The Spectator* called it "fascinating to read the fictional next to the factual version—each illuminating and illuminated by the other" (*The Spectator*). Tim Parks, writing for *The Guardian* says, "The remarkable thing about Casanova is that not only did he have a bewilderingly eventful life, not only was he a thinker of wide reading and great shrewdness, but he also knew how to tell a tale as well as the cleverest of novelists; knew, above all, how to wring out of it the maximum tension and irony" (Parks).

—Diane R. Mannone

For More Information

Anderson, M. S. *Historians and Eighteenth-Century Europe, 1715-1789.* Oxford: Clarendon Press, 1979.

Black, Jeremy. *Eighteenth Century Europe: 1700-1798.* New York: St. Martin's Press, 1990.

Casanova, Giacomo. *The Duel.* London: Hesperus Press, 2003.

———. *History of My Life, Vols. 1 & 2.* Trans. William Trask. Baltimore: Johns Hopkins University Press, 1997.

Frevert, Ute. *Men of Honour: A Social and Cultural History of the Duel.* Cambridge: Polity, 1995.

Hibbert, Christopher. *Venice: The Biography of a City.* New York: W. W. Norton, 1989.

Hodges, Gareth. "Duels and Honor in History." http://users.chariot.net.au/amaranth/articles/7th Sea/duelshonour.htm.

Kesten, Hermann. *Casanova.* New York: Harper & Brothers, 1955.

Masters, John. *Casanova.* New York: Bernard Geis Associates, 1969.

Norwich, John Julius. *A History of Venice.* New York: Vintage Books, 1982.

Parks, Tim. "For Dear Life." *The Guardian,* March 22, 2003. http://books.guardian.co.uk/review/story/0,12084,918487,00.htm.

The Spectator. Review of *The Duel,* by Giacomo Casanova. April 12, 2003. http://spectator.co.uk/books_section.php?issue=2003-01-04.

Wheeler, Bonnie. "The History of Dueling." Southern Methodist University. http://faculty.smc.edu/bwheeler/Ency/duels.html.

Excursion to Tindari

by

Andrea Camilleri

THE LITERARY WORK

A detective novel set in Sicily during the late 1990s; published in Italian (as *La gita a Tindari*) in 2000, in English in 2005.

SYNOPSIS

Inspector Salvo Montalbano attempts to solve two seemingly unrelated crimes: the execution-style murder of a young womanizer and the mysterious disappearance of a quiet elderly couple.

Born in 1925 in Porto Empedocle, Sicily, Andrea Camilleri held a string of jobs in television (mostly with the Italian public network RAI), film, and theater before retiring to become a full-time writer. Married with three children and four grandchildren, he currently lives in Rome. His first novel, *Il corso delle cose* (The Order of Things), was not published until 1978, and he wrote for another 15 years or so before achieving his current enormous fame. It derives almost entirely from the popularity of his crack detective Salvo Montalbano, whom Camilleri first introduced in *La forma dell'acqua* (1994; The Shape of Water). Camilleri was 69 at the time. Thereafter, he placed Montalbano at the center of several more novels, including *Il cane di terracotta* (1996; The Terra-Cotta Dog), *Il ladro di merendine* (1996; The Snack Thief), *La voce del violino* (1997; The Voice of the Violin), *La gita a Tindari* (2000; Excursion to Tindari), and *L'odore della notte* (2001; The Fragrance of the Night). Camilleri also writes historical novels set in Sicily, among them *Il birraio de Preston* (1995; The Brewer of Preston), *La concessione del telefono* (1998; The Telephone Contract), *and La mossa del cavallo* (1999; The Knight's Move). The Montalbano series, however, outstrips these in popularity, and has been adapted for Italian television and translated into German, French, Spanish, Portuguese, Greek, Japanese, Dutch, Swedish, and English, earning Camilleri accolades both at home and abroad. No doubt, the series owes much of its appeal to its richly drawn main character—Inspector Montalbano. He is well read,

passionate about good food, and driven by intuitive, sometimes mystical thought patterns. Another compelling feature is the series' loving depiction of Sicily, Camilleri's homeland and the setting for Montalbano's actions. In the author's hands, Sicily is as much a living presence as Montalbano himself. In fact, in *Excursion to Tindari*, as in the other novels from the series, one cannot imagine Montalbano apart from the land that shapes and sustains him. Although it has its share of problems, the detective takes them in stride as he finds ways to carve out a rich existence on the island.

Events in History at the Time of the Novel

The Sicilian Mafia. Few subjects in the world of crime have fascinated readers more than the

Mafia, especially since Mario Puzo's 1969 novel about the Italian American Mafia, *The Godfather*. Of course, there are some similarities between the Italian American and Sicilian Mafia organizations, but also each is intimately tied to its own historical context. The context for Camilleri's novel depends on knowledge of the Sicilian "Cosa Nostra" (as the Mafia in Italy is called), particularly of developments over the last 25 years.

The existence of Mafia groups dates from the mid-nineteenth century, but details about the organization and operation of this infamously secretive group were for years difficult to detect. The effort to describe the organization, membership, and activities of the Sicilian Cosa Nostra has been made easier by the 1000 or so defections of Sicilian Mafiosi since the mid-1980s. Camilleri refers several times in the novel to the phenomenon of the so-called *pentiti* (literally, "repentants"), who, in exchange for leniency from prosecutors, give evidence against their former associates. From these informants, we have learned that Cosa Nostra comprises a loosely knit confederation of Mafia families, about 100 in all, with a total membership of about 3,500. This appears a small number until one calculates the size of the Sicilian Mafia in per capita terms. Here, a comparison of the U.S. and Sicilian Mafias is striking: about one in 1,500 Sicilians belongs to Cosa Nostra, whereas in the United States, the figure is only one in 165,000. In addition, as opposed to the U.S. Mafia, which has little direct influence on politics and little direct involvement in the state *per se*, since its beginnings Cosa Nostra has been deeply intertwined with government. The Sicilian Mafia has in this respect been a socio-cultural force in Italy that transcends its status as a criminal organization.

Although its origins are still somewhat enveloped in mystery and uncertainty, the Sicilian mafia dates back to the Unification of the Italian peninsula under the Savoy Monarchy. In 1860 the Island of Sicily was liberated from Bourbon rule by the volunteer army of the national hero Giuseppe Garibaldi, but not all Sicilians welcomed the liberation and the promise of modernization. The very term "mafia" may have derived from an area of grottoes in which Sicilian landowners began to assemble bands of faithful *picciotti* (literally, "children," but in jargon, "mafia foot soldiers") to organize forms of resistance, first to Garibaldi and then to the representatives of the new Italian state. In essence, the Mafia constituted itself as an anti-state organization bent on preventing "northern" (modern) institutions from taking root in the Si-

cilian territory, and on defending aristocratic-rural values from the encroachment of all forms of modernization. To understand the Mafia, one needs to remember that in Italy there exists a clear distinction between the state and the government. The *state* (made up of the bureaucracy, the judiciary, and police forces) is symbolic of threatening new processes: secularization, democratization, and capitalist urbanization of the economy. Not only have these processes taken away power from rural elites; they have also eroded their cultural identity since the early nineteenth century. On the other hand, the *government* represents the powers that control and may delay such processes, and therefore have been seen as the natural allies of Cosa Nostra. Since its beginnings, then, Cosa Nostra has used its criminal activities to create an alternative economic, social, and cultural world that challenged the state, meanwhile trying to preserve pre-modern values of rural-patriarchal societies. Naturally, Cosa Nostra has evolved in time, and its criminal activities have tended to become ends in themselves. But Cosa Nostra's long-standing involvement in government affairs has granted it continuing influence on Sicilian life. This involvement has fostered increasingly pervasive forms of corruption, as is so frequently observed in histories of contemporary Italy and portrayed in Camilleri's novels. Today estimates of the economic impact of criminal organizations in Italy range from a high of 12.5 percent of the Gross Domestic Product (output of the domestic economy) to a low of 4.4 percent; even the smaller number makes the Mafia the second largest business "firm" in Italy (Ginsborg, p. 201).

As witnessed in Camilleri's novel, Cosa Nostra is a patriarchal group characterized by secrecy, discretion, elaborate codes of honor, the practice of *omertà* (silence), and a commitment to absolute loyalty to the membership. When new recruits are initiated into Cosa Nostra, they form strong "brotherhood bonds" that supersede all others, including blood ties to one's own relations (Paoli, p. 5). If called upon, the new "man of honor" must be willing to sacrifice everything for his brotherhood, even his own life. The men of honor are also instructed to deny the very existence of the group to which they belong. For Giovanni Falcone, a famous anti-Mafia prosecuting judge, the tendency of Sicilians to tight-lipped communication or a mute response (*omertà*) reached its height in Cosa Nostra (Ginsborg, p. 195). The Sicilian brotherhoods depend on their close relationship with various levels of government to influence a wide range of businesses—another difference from the U.S. Mafia, which historically relied on gambling as its principal source of revenue. Through a system of extortion backed by threats or violence (including murder), Mafia families levy a kind of "tax" on all productive activities in the area they control, such as construction, public works, and the like. They thus feed off the entire Sicilian economy while failing to produce any tangible goods.

In the 1960s, the Mafia moved into drug dealing, once forbidden by an informal moral code. The drug trade flourished as a result of the sharp demand for heroin in the United States. One Mafia boss summarized the effect: "We all became millionaires. Suddenly, within a couple of years. Thanks to drugs" (Ginsborg, p. 199). Subsequent criminal prosecutions in the United States revealed a link between the Sicilian Mafias and the Bonnano Mafia family in New York, which ran its drug operations out of pizzerias. The powerful Gambino family in New York was also involved in the transatlantic drug trade. Yet with the rise of the Colombian drug cartels in the mid-1980s and the decline of heroin as a drug of choice, the Sicilian Cosa Nostra became increasingly marginal to the international drug business and responded by moving into other rackets, employing its influence in municipal government to secure control over public contracts and extort money from building firms (Paoli, p. 10). Here again, however, external events affected the Mafia. The mid-1990s witnessed a steep decline in public investment and thus a drop in the amounts the Mafia could skim off. Also the Mafia itself came under attack when the Italian state responded to the threat of it with judicial tools that further weakened its influence in Sicilian life.

Criminal prosecution of the Mafia. In the first hundred years of its existence, the Sicilian Mafia killed only two "establishment figures," one in 1893 and another in 1909 (Dickie, p. 383). The Italian state, in turn, did not vigorously root out the Mafia in Sicily, an area of the country that continued to suffer from an attitude of benign neglect by the state. It allowed the Mafia to thrive there until an especially bloody wave of murders in 1981-83, which themselves resulted in widescale war among the Sicilian Mafia clans for control of the lucrative drug trade. It was only after these murders that the Italian state took action, directly confronting Cosa Nostra with a sophisticated array of judicial instruments. The group now had to contend with specially appointed anti-Mafia judges, crack prosecutors, investiga-

tive commissions, and undercover operations, all of which culminated in the 1987 "Maxi-trial" that handed down a set of verdicts including a total of 2665 years in prison, 19 life sentences, and the equivalent of 8.5 million U.S. dollars in fines (in 1987 figures). During this period, courageous public servants fought a pitched battle for the rule of law against a terrifying and ruthless enemy, often at the cost of their own lives. The Mafia lived up to its image, responding to increased state repression with dramatically increased and open violence. The phenomenon of the *cadaveri eccelenti* (eminent corpse) became routine in Sicily, with many of the Mafia's victims drawn from law enforcement, journalism, and politics.

In 1982 the Italian government appointed General Carlo Alberto Dalla Chiesa to be the new prefect of Palermo, the Sicilian capital. Renowned for his work in exposing Italian terrorist groups, he promised to bear down on the Mafia, but also asked for special support to take on what he knew to be a determined effort to stop him. He arrived in Sicily in April; early in August, he was still waiting for adequate support from the government; by the end of the month, he was dead, gunned down (along with his wife and bodyguard) by the Mafia as he drove to a dinner party. During the funeral, which was televised nationally, viewers witnessed an irate crowd "throwing coins at the government ministers who attended" (Dickie, p. 385).

The Italian government responded with two measures designed to hit at the heart of Mafia power. One measure made it a crime for the first time to associate with someone "for criminal purposes of a specifically Mafia nature" (Ginsborg, p. 207); the second gave judges the power to overcome bank confidentiality. Giovanni Falcone, along with Antonio Caponnetto, took on the role of leading the investigations of the principal Mafia families. So dangerous was the job that Caponnetto had to live in a heavily guarded police barracks close to his work. Their efforts, however, paid off when one of the senior Mafia bosses, Tomasso Buscetta, became a *pentito*, agreeing to cooperate with Falcone in his investigations. Buscetta's testimony was one of the principal keys to the success of the "maxi-trial" in 1986-87. With worldwide media glare illuminating the spectacle, the Italian public was now focused as never before on the problem of Mafia criminal activity in their midst. Despite pressures to lessen or overthrow the prison sentences and fines, they were upheld five years later, a ruling that broke the "chain of collusion" between the

Sign protesting Mafia violence in Sicily.

state and the Mafia for the first time (Ginsborg, p. 212). Later in the 1990s, the so-called Clean Hands investigations further weakened the Mafia by exposing the practice of rigged contract bidding. Despite these setbacks, however, the Sicilian Cosa Nostra is widely believed to be biding its time until promised investment in Southern Italy, both by the Italian government and European Union, materializes. It is thought that Cosa Nostra will then resume its efforts to skim a percentage of that investment capital. In the meantime, Cosa Nostra hopes to "exhaust law enforcement pressure and to weaken the popular anti-mafia movement," while also taking advantage of softer anti-corruption policies of the government of Sylvio Berlusconi, who was elected in 2001 (Paoli, p. 12).

The Novel in Focus

Plot summary. As the novel opens, a phone call from police headquarters interrupts Inspector Montalbano's early morning reverie, a reverie in which, with the sounds of the ocean breaking through his open window, he has drifted from images of student rebels in 1968, to thoughts of his lover, Livia, who lives in a distant town. One of his subordinates has phoned to tell him the basic facts: a 21-year-old man, Emanuele Sanfilippo, known as Nenè, has been murdered, shot

in the face while entering his apartment at Via Cavour 44. With a new case to solve, Montalbano feels his "bad mood passing," and springs into action (Camilleri, *Excursion to Tindari*, p. 6).

Slowly, Montalbano gathers clues to the murder. Nenè's apartment is filled with the latest consumer gadgets—TV, satellite dish, computer, video camera. And Nenè owns, along with a humble Fiat Punto, a glamorous sports car, an Alfa Romeo Duetto, which is discreetly stowed in the garage, perhaps to conceal ill-gotten gains. The keys to his apartment were still in the door when the police arrived at the crime scene, suggesting that the murderer called out Nenè's name, who turned around before the shots were fired. On his keychain is a key to an unknown building, a key that has, furthermore, been designed to prevent duplication.

Just as Montalbano starts piecing these clues together, a man named Davide Griffo steps forward to report that his parents, who live in the apartment building, have gone missing. The investigation now splits into parallel tracks, with as yet no link between them. In contrast to the young, high-living Nenè, the elderly Griffos have led a quiet, almost invisible life, keeping to themselves, speaking hardly a word to anyone in the building. A canvass of the apartment building yields few clues. The other residents are unanimous in their surprise at the Griffos' disappearance. Nenè's murder is less surprising. The residents treat the detectives with vivid tales of his raucous, late-night lovemaking, the sounds of which echoed from within his flat.

The plot now detours to love affairs of other kinds. First, Mimì Augello, Montalbano's close friend and right-hand man, informs his boss that he has decided, after a long bachelorhood, to marry, and that he will seek a transfer from Vigàta, the fictionalized Sicilian town in which the novel is set, to Pavia, the town where his fiancée lives. This news enrages Montalbano, who cannot accept what this means—the break-up of his team. His relationship to his men is so close (and at times secretive) that one of his superiors compares them to the Mafia. Yet Montalbano himself is romantically entangled, also at a distance, though he and Livia, unlike Augello and his lover, have reconciled themselves to their separate lives. Despite her physical absence, however, Livia is a constant presence in the novel; she not only telephones Montalbano at key moments, but also humanizes him by figuring in his dreams, memories, and desires.

The novel contrasts these love plots with Nenè's taste for pornography, the evidence for which lies in his videos, CD-ROMs, and hard drive. Catarella, another assistant to Montalbano, reports that Nenè's computer files contain a "lotta filth. Guys wit' girls, guys wit' guys, girls wit' girls, girls wit' animals" (*Excursion to Tindari*, p. 44). The computer also contains a 600-page novel written by Nenè himself, along with a series of sexually explicit letters between Nenè and one of his lovers, whom the detectives believe is a married woman, in part because the letters have been copied into the computer to make them untraceable by handwriting experts.

In the meantime, we learn that the Griffos were last seen on a bus trip for seniors to Tindari, the Sicilian tourist site that gives the novel its title. The Griffos were among three dozen or so retirees who had booked tickets with a local company for the day-long excursion to Tindari. As the bus driver tells Montalbano, most of the passengers on such trips are not interested in the sites themselves, but in spending time with other retirees; they always ask for the same driver because he is willing to make frequent stops along the way. The bus invariably makes such a stop at a café on the return journey, but on this trip an additional stop had been requested only 30 minutes from Vigàta. When Montalbano interviews some of the passengers, he learns that the Griffos

sat in the very last seat of the bus, keeping to themselves and not conversing with anyone.

Montalbano discovers that there was another key passenger on the bus, a woman named Beatrice Dileo who sold kitchenware and other related products to the other passengers along the way. Montalbano's interview with Beatrice proves useful in several ways. First, she reveals that despite the availability of better seats, the Griffos

TINDARI

Tindari, a popular destination for locals and tourists alike, was founded as a Greek colony in 396 B.C.E. by Dionysius the Elder. Its strategic location in the hills of northern Sicily enabled the Greeks to rule the waters between the nearby city of Messina and the Aeolian Islands just off the coast, but it was subsequently controlled by the Carthaginians and the Romans. The ruins of the ancient city are still visible. Along with its strategic location, Tindari's fame also rests on the venerated statue of a black Madonna.

The origin of the black Madonnas is a subject of academic debate. Some scholars argue that they derive from the Byzantine period, and others claim that their blackened appearance results from the accumulation of hundreds of years of soot. Still others hold that these statues represent pagan goddesses who have been Christianized. The Black Madonna of Tindari was first honored with a procession in 1905, and each year on her feast day (September 8), thousands of pilgrims descend on Tindari to view the Madonna.

stubbornly chose the rear seat, which was piled with boxes of merchandise, and from time to time turned around to look through the rear window. Second, when the bus arrived at Tindari, the Griffos never got off, raising the question of why they went. Third, it was Mr. Griffo who requested the bus's last stop, half an hour from Vigàta. Incidentally, Beatrice, who is stunningly beautiful, provides a possible solution to Montalbano's imminent loss of his right-hand man; at the end of the interview Augello enters the restaurant, and is as struck by Beatrice's looks as Montalbano. Desiring to thwart Augello's transfer, Montalbano leaves his weak-kneed Deputy Inspector to finish the interview with Beatrice.

Montalbano's suspicion of a possible Mafia connection to Nenè's murder grows stronger when he receives a request for an interview with Don Balduccio Sinagra, a powerful, if also aging, Mafioso who controls half the province's crime activity. On his way to Sinagra's estate Montalbano mentally reviews the long history of conflict between the Sinagras and the other prominent crime family, the Cuffaros. In his interview with Montalbano, however, Sinagra suggests, in a brief exchange exemplifying the code of *omertá*, that a ruthless younger generation of mobsters enriched by the drug trade is making the old families—and their traditional ways of resolving conflict—irrelevant: "Nowadays people don't wanna reason. . . . They shoot" (*Excursion to Tindari*, p. 113). Without saying much more than this, Sinagra conveys another key message: he wants his grandson, Japichinu, who is in hiding, to be picked up and sent to jail, in order, paradoxically, to keep him safe from the younger mobsters who will otherwise certainly kill him. Montalbano later discovers that he is to be the means to this end. But when he and his men are led by a tip to Japichinu's hideout, they find him already dead, killed, as Montalbano infers, by Sinagra's own men. Montalbano realizes Sinagra wants to make him a pawn in a generational struggle between Sinagra and his grandson, but he refuses to play the part. That is, he refuses to bring the murder to the media's attention so that Sinagra can spread propaganda about the brutal young Mafiosi. Montalbano instead sends word to Sinagra that he must bury Japichinu quietly. There will be no investigation and no media coverage.

Montalbano soon learns that the Griffos have not only disappeared but have also been murdered, mob style; they were forced to kneel down, then shot in the head. Now there are three murders to solve, Nenè and the Griffos. Hereafter, the novel shifts from one investigation to the other and back again, moving from each new clue to the next. First, Montalbano analyzes the Griffos' passbook and discovers that for two years they have received unexplained payments of 2 million lire a month (about $1,400 U.S. in 2004)—on top of their monthly pension of 3 million lire. This is a modest sum, but still unusual for retirees with no other known source of income. Second, Montalbano and Augello, following their hunch that within Nenè's extensive media collection lies another clue, find an erotic home video hidden inside a videocassette of the film *The Getaway*. The video depicts a nude woman who the inspectors believe will help them solve the murder. Augello identifies the woman, whom he has seen before, as Vanya Titulescu,

wife of Doctor Eugenio Ignazio Ingró, a famed transplant surgeon whose clients are spread across Europe. Augello further speculates that the video, with its faint sounds of waves lapping at the shore, was filmed at the Ingrós' seaside villa while the husband was away, making Professor Ingró the prime suspect in Nenè's murder. It is here that the two cases become intertwined. As Montalbano predicted, his right-hand man, Augello, and Beatrice, the beautiful saleswoman-passenger, become involved. The relationship leads to Augello's discovery that the bus driver took photographs of the pensioners, which he sold as souvenirs. When the crime lab analyzes one of the photos, it discovers a Fiat Punto through the rear window with the same license plate as Nenè's car. The ability to see this car, Montalbano realizes, is the reason the Griffos made sure to sit in the rear of the bus.

Montalbano's famed intuition then guides him toward the connection between the Griffos and Nenè. It involves a piece of rural land with a small building on it that was left to Mrs. Griffo by her sister. Montalbano finds the site and breaks down the door to the one-room building, only to discover a bare room outfitted with numerous electrical outlets and phone jacks. Montalbano guesses that Nenè was being employed by someone to use the building either for drug trafficking or internet pornography. His interest in the remote building led him to the Griffos, who had inherited it. The Griffos would be paid monthly on condition they said nothing about the deal or their inheritance of the land, even to their son. When something went wrong with the business Nenè was running, his employer concocted a plan to have both Nenè and the Griffos executed to conceal the arrangement. Nenè would feed the Griffos a story about their needing to get away for a day and then turn them over to their executioners at the excursion's next-to-last stop, not knowing that he, too, was about to be killed.

Later, however, Montalbano arrives at a different conclusion, one that brings us back to the Mafia and its pervasive presence in Sicilian life. Dr. Ingró, who is a passionate art collector, incurs a debt he cannot pay, and this comes to the attention of the mob. They offer him all the money he wants to buy paintings on condition that he supply their clients across the globe with transplants taken from donors in jails, immigrant detention centers, and the like. Ingró hires Nenè to use the internet to bring the "donors" (who will all be killed) together with the patients—one of whom happens to be the mobster Balduccio Sinagra, who needs a new kidney. This is how Nenè comes to be involved with Ingró's wife. Montalbano fits these pieces together by closely reading the novel Nenè wrote, which encrypts this scheme within the form of a science fiction story about robots and replacement parts.

The novel's conclusion finds Montalbano drawing on scenes from his favorite gangster movies to hoodwink Dr. Ingró into believing he is about to be killed (with Montalbano in the role of assassin). Just as in the movies, however, Ingró is "saved" in the nick of time by the arrival of the police (Montalbano's men, who feign not to recognize him). Ingró is so relieved to have his life spared that he unwittingly follows the script Montalbano has written for him by telling all. In one of his many thoughtful moments, Montalbano reflects that these crimes he has investigated reveal the new face of evil: "Pitiless crimes committed by anonymous people" (*Excursion to Tindari*, p. 279).

Montalbano and Sicily. The relationship between Montalbano and his beloved Sicily lies at the heart of Camilleri's popularity as a novelist. The novel's loving portrayal of the island—from its food to its unique dialect and sea-enriched geography—counteracts a longstanding negative image. Since the late nineteenth century, the Italian South has been seen as backward and the North as responsible for closing the gap, a situation described as the "southern question." The southern question, by attending to southern Italy's poverty, sharpened the focus on regional differences between the technologically advanced North and a presumably underdeveloped South. There emerged first a highly negative perception of the South as a barbaric threat to the more civilized North, and next, the conviction that it was the duty of Italy's more advanced northerners to somehow help civilize their southern compatriots.

In Camilleri's novels one does indeed find the constant presence of the Mafia—one of the key indications, according to some, of southern backwardness and clannishness. But one also finds a detective who is deeply read in classic and contemporary literature (Montalbano alludes easily to Shakespeare, Dante, Laclos, Doré, Kafka, Conrad, Pirandello, Montale). The detective is likewise familiar with European painting, music, and philosophy. A whip-smart inspector, he is funny, wise, loving, and extraordinarily responsive to the beauty of the land and sea that surrounds him. Such a portrayal counters the negative image of the South still held by many Italians.

The negative portrayal of the South is also offset by Montalbano's love for Sicily as a special place with a unique history. The novel turns on an excursion to a place unique to Sicily: Tindari, a city first established by the Greeks, then successively colonized and conquered, and now as famous for its black Madonna as for the ruined walls of the ancient city. More broadly, Montalbano finds emotional sustenance in the specific geography of Sicily, particularly its seashore and hills. At several points in the novel, frustrated by clues that seem to go nowhere, he takes a swim in the ocean, sits thinking by a favorite beach, or drives into the hills to lie down below an ancient Saracen olive tree, whose branches suggest to him the interconnected events unfolding in his investigation: "He had discovered that, in some mysterious way, the entanglement, contortion, overlapping, in short, the labyrinth of branches, almost mimetically mirrored what was happening inside his head, the intertwining hypotheses and accumulating arguments" (*Excursion to Tindari*, p. 91). The tree is also an image for the novel's densely woven fabric, its method of skipping from one plot line to another, its refusal of linear or directly causal explanations. The roots of this image go deep into the Sicilian earth and Montalbano's soul.

But perhaps Montalbano's most appealing quality is his pure zest for life, symbolized both by his complex, analytical mind (a phenomenon of all great literary detectives), but also by the delight he takes in simple, everyday enjoyments. Here, one may speak of his passion for food—surely a trait widely ascribed to Italians, but for Montalbano specifically focused on the *frutti di mare* (literally, "fruit of the sea"), the albacores, king mackerels, squids, baby octopi (*purpiteddri*), and other delicacies that Sicilians relish within hours of the fare having been pulled from the sea. From its opening scene to its very end, the novel constantly reminds the reader of the sea. Even when Montalbano is not directly looking at it, smelling it, or swimming in it, he feels the ocean in his marrow and in his stomach. When Montalbano interviews Beatrice Diello for the first time, the meeting takes place over a meal of squid ink risotto and freshly grilled sea bass. The meeting turns out to be of crucial importance to the investigation, but the novel, by examining Montalbano's thoughts during the meal, also manages to make the scene an important testimony to Montalbano's love for life as experienced in Sicily and through its fresh seafood. When Beatrice tells Montalbano that she is glad to talk but only between courses (so as not to ruin the pleasure of eating), Montalbano internally remarks how wonderful it is to meet one's twin in such matters. Later in the meal, when she refuses dessert because she wants to "keep that aftertaste of the sea," Montalbano thinks, "not just a twin, but a Siamese twin" (*Excursion to Tindari*, p. 84). In this and many other instances, the novel reminds its readers of a unique place and of the sophistication of the people who live there.

SICILIAN DIALECT

Camilleri's love for Sicily's land and culture is apparent everywhere in his novels, nowhere more so than in his use of Sicilian dialect. Among the many such usages found in *Excursion to Tindari* are "Madunnuzza santa!" (Blessed little Madonna); "Beddra Matre Santissimia!" (most holy beautiful Mother); and "sfincione" (a thick crust pizza served in Palermo). Stephen Sartarelli, who renders Camilleri's works into English, leaves many of these Sicilianisms untranslated, retaining the local color encountered by Italians from other parts of the country when they read the novel, which is written mostly in standard Italian. The localisms remind readers that Sicily in many ways retains a distinct culture evident at least in part through its dialect. A number of Sicilianisms have been translated in the English edition—for example, "I've got a heart like a lion and another like a donkey," which means, roughly, "I'm torn." As Sartarelli's appendix explains, Montalbano frequently uses such expressions to confuse non-Sicilians he encounters, particularly his superiors in the police force who want to reign in his independence.

Sources and literary context. Montalbano does not appear to be based on any historical person. Rather he belongs to a richly detailed tradition of literary detectives dating from the nineteenth- and twentieth-century stories of Sherlock Holmes and Agatha Christie. Like George Simenon's Inspector Maigret, in Belgian-French literature, Montalbano enjoys good food and has an uncanny knack for intuitively discovering the hidden threads that tie together the separate clues found in any crime. But what sets Montalbano apart is his rootedness in Sicily and his profound immersion in the great tradition of western art, literature, and philosophy—a buttress against the constant threat of death he faces in his interac-

tions with the murderous forces of Cosa Nostra. For example, when he first sees the image of a nude Vanya Titulescu captured on Nenè's videocassette, he immediately takes refuge in art as he thinks of two paintings, Leonardo Da Vinci's *Mona Lisa* and Francisco Goya's *Nude Maja*. As at other moments, he uses the world of aesthetics and literature to impose his own sensibility and notions of order on the seamy and sometimes dangerous world of crime.

Camilleri is also notable for a kind of wry, postmodern irony he takes to his subject, in which he reflects on the artifice or strategies of the detective genre itself. Late in the novel, Augello, remarking on Montalbano's vivid imagination, suggests that he should write mysteries after he retires. Montalbano replies that he could, but it would not be worth the trouble because "certain critics and tenured professors, or would-be critics and professors, consider mystery novels a minor genre," and omit them even from standard literary histories (*Excursion to Tindari*, p. 255). (An observation true in some circles but untrue in others, whose members consider detective fiction as important as the realist novel or postmodern drama.)

Reception. The popular reception of Camilleri's Montalbano series has been enthusiastic and wide ranging. As noted above, one measure of his immense popularity is the translation of his novels into several languages. But the novels are also a phenomenon in Italy. Frank Bruni, in a glowing tribute in *The New York Times*, notes that during one particularly heady summer in the 1990s, six of the bestsellers in the Italian newspaper *La Repubblica* were authored by Camilleri. *The Economist*, meanwhile, observes that although there are over 400 books on the Mafia in print in Italy, so greatly does the chief prosecutor in Palermo respect Camilleri's knowledge of Mafia ways that he uses the novels as his primary cultural guide.

Camilleri's English translator, the American poet Stephen Sartarelli, who is the recipient of many literary prizes for his own work, has rendered Camilleri's Italian into robust, idiomatic English, while also capturing the Sicilian dialect of Camilleri's characters. Especially noteworthy is Sartarelli's hilarious translation of the Sicilianisms of Agatino Catarella, one of Montalbano's lieutenants, who Montalbano, in *The Terra Cotta Dog*, described as becoming most muddled when "he got it in his head—which happened often—to speak what he called Talian" (Camilleri, *The Terra-Cotta Dog*, p. 21). Sartarelli's ability to preserve the regional flavor of Camilleri's prose is a remarkable feature of the English translations. Along with other strengths, such as the novel's playful language, reviewers praise this regional flavor in *Excursion to Tindari*. An anonymous critic in *Kirkus Reviews* notes approvingly that the novel presents Sicily "with humor and without illusions" (*Kirkus Reviews*, p. 1118).

—Robert D. Aguirre

For More Information

Bondanella, Peter, and Andrea Ciccarelli, eds. *The Cambridge Companion to the Italian Novel*. Cambridge: Cambridge University Press, 2003.

Bruni, Frank. "A Writer Who Followed His Own Clues to Fame." *The New York Times*, October 12, 2002, p. A4, col. 3.

Camilleri, Andrea. *Excursion to Tindari*. Trans. Stephen Sartarelli. New York: Penguin, 2005.

———. *The Terra-Cotta Dog*. Trans. Stephen Sartarelli. New York: Penguin, 2002.

Dickie, John. *Cosa Nostra: A History of the Sicilian Mafia*. London: Hodder & Stoughton, 2004.

The Economist. "The Mafia, Italy's Favorite Topic." *The Economist* 348, no. 8081 (August 15, 1998): 39.

The Economist. "Spirits of Invention." *The Economist* 356, no. 8189 (September 23, 2000): 103.

Ginsborg, Paul. *A History of Contemporary Italy: Society and Politics, 1943-1988*. London: Penguin, 1990.

———. *Italy and Its Discontents: 1980-2001*. London: Allen Lane, 2001.

Kirkus Reviews. Review of *Excursion to Tindari*, by Andrea Camilleri. *Kirkus Reviews* 72, no. 23 (December 1, 2004): 1118.

Moliterno, Gino, ed. *Encyclopedia of Contemporary Italian Culture*. London: Routledge, 2000.

Paoli, Letizia. *Mafia Brotherhoods: Organized Crime, Italian Style*. Oxford: Oxford University Press, 2003.

Porter, Dennis. *The Pursuit of Crime: Art and Ideology in Detective Fiction*. New Haven: Yale University Press, 1981.

The Founding and Manifesto of Futurism

by

Filippo Tommaso Marinetti

Filippo Tommaso Marinetti was born December 22, 1876, to Italian parents in Alexandria, Egypt, where his father amassed a fortune through speculation and service as a lawyer to the Egyptian ruler. At home, young Filippo spoke Italian, but he received a French education at a Jesuit school. The school ultimately expelled him because of his deep admiration for the writings of Émile Zola, which were banned by the Church. Marinetti went on to study literature in Paris, France. After receiving his baccalaureate in 1894, he studied law in Pavia and in Genoa, Italy, but then pursued a literary career. Marinetti commuted between Paris and Milan, writing, and publishing the journal *Poesia* (Poetry), which served as a forum for such other important writers of his day as France's Alfred Jarry and Germany's Arno Holz. A versatile writer as well as a publisher, Marinetti generated poetry, drama, fiction, and nonfiction. His first long work, a novel about a cruel African leader—*Mafarka the Futurist* (1909)—was banned in Italy because of the work's pornographic details. That same year, having established himself as a prominent artist and intellectual, Marinetti produced *The Founding and Manifesto of Futurism* (more commonly known as *The Futurist Manifesto*). The manifesto became the foundational document of a new artistic movement—Futurism—which called for a rejection of the past and a celebration of modern innovation and aggressive action. Living up to his precepts, Marinetti became involved in several military campaigns in the 1910s (in the Turkish-Italian war in Libya and as a war correspondent

THE LITERARY WORK

A manifesto set in the first decade of the twentieth century; published in French (as *Le Futurisme*) in 1909, in Italian and English later in 1909.

SYNOPSIS

The manifesto proclaims the program and ideology of Futurism—the first European avant-garde movement—which shuns tradition and embraces technology, war, and aggressive action.

in the Balkans). His Futurist movement meanwhile flourished, especially between 1909 and 1916, when its members declaimed their program throughout Europe. The first manifesto was followed by more than two dozen other manifestos over several decades, on everything from painting to literature, theater, marriage, fashion, cuisine, and architecture. Fusing the arts with the rest of society instead of adopting the traditional perception of them as part of a separate sphere, the Futurist movement gained for Marinetti a reputation as the "caffeine of Europe," though there were many in Italy who took him less than seriously.

Events in History at the Time of the Manifesto

Futurism and the industrial revolution. Formulated at the beginning of the twentieth century,

Filippo Tommaso Marinetti

Italian Futurism glorified industrial and technological progress. Automobiles, trains, airplanes, and all the different usages of electricity—from street lighting to telegraphy—surfaced in works of art as symbols for the advent of modern times.

Industrial development climaxed on the Italian peninsula in the first half of the nineteenth century; in the second half, the steel and coal industries were already declining but there were advances in the chemical and electrical sciences to compensate. This latter half of the century was the era of multiple inventions—from the internal combustion engine, to the gramophone, cinema, x-ray technology, and the use of electricity as a public source of light and power. People everywhere celebrated the inventions, which promised to irrevocably change daily life. Especially lauded were transport-related landmarks—the completion of the Trans-Siberian railroad in 1902, the Paris-Madrid car race of 1903, the Peking-Paris car race of 1907, all associated with a quickening of life, with the element of speed.

Communication too benefited from all the developments. The nineteenth century had seen an increase in the flow of printed news through journals and newspapers, a development greatly hastened by the invention of the rapid linotype press in 1886 (it was in fact the linotype press that would make possible the vast manifesto production of the Futurists). Along with the growth of print into mass media, came revolutionary developments in long-distance communication. In Italy, the engineer Guglielmo Marconi made wireless communication possible by inventing the Marconi antenna; already in 1901 Marconi proved that radio signals could be transmitted across the Atlantic Ocean. The invention of wireless transmission gave rise to a host of innovations in long-distance communication, including the birth of the radio, which enabled simultaneous mass communication.

The radio was not the only new machine used to broaden communication. In 1911 the liquor distiller Cinzano employed an airplane to distribute the first real "flyers" over Milan, and other enterprising entrepreneurs followed suit. The Futurists embraced first the automobile, then the airplane, as their symbol of speed. Along with combat or aggressive action, rapidity became the highest of values. Speed, combat, youth, the machine—Futurism esteemed whatever propelled humanity forward and dismissed the past as debilitating, especially in Italy, a country seen as "infested with professors, archeologists, guides, and antique dealers" (Del Antonelli, p. 79). Surrounded by all the inventions of the age, *The Futurist Manifesto* declared that time and space died yesterday; they no longer mattered. In such a world, art ought to be fused with, not separate from, society and politics—hence the writing of manifestoes on food, women, and family as well as literature, painting, and theater. It was the artists' job, the Futurists taught, to adopt a revolutionary mentality, to overcome the status quo and introduce a dream, an ideal. In order to do so, one had to defeat impediments posed by the existing social order, which explains the esteem for combat. It also explains the alignment of Futurism with other philosophies and iconoclastic movements of the day.

From positivism to heroism. In the late nineteenth century, positivism held sway in much of Europe. A philosophy formulated in France by Auguste Comte (1798-1857), positivism differed from traditional systems of thought. Instead of focusing on the essences of things, for example, it held that the only valid objects of study were facts that could be tested and the relations between such facts. The philosophy was adopted by some Italians, for example, Vilfredo Pareto (1848-1923), whose studies led him to conclude that the societies of the world should always be run by an elite. But others rejected the philosophy. In Italy, unlike much of Europe, the response to positivism was lukewarm at best. The beginning of the twentieth century even saw a reaction against it, a revival of more speculative approaches to life. Champions of this more speculative approach started the journal *La Critica* (The Critique) in 1903. Founded by idealist thinkers Benedetto Croce (1866-1952) and Giovanni Gentile (1875-1944), the journal would establish itself as the most distinguished expression of Italian philosophy for the next four decades.

Two prominent philosophers of the day who caused a stir among European intellectuals and also countered the positive approach were Germany's Friedrich Nietzsche (1844-1900) and France's Henri Louis Bergson (1859-1941). The two formulated ideas that Marinetti may or may not have read directly (probably he encountered them through the works of others—the ideas enjoyed vigorous circulation at the time). Most prominently, in his major work *Thus Spoke Zarathustra*, Nietzsche developed the concept of the "Superman." The Superman forges his own individuality, liberating himself from Western tradition and morality; he formulates his own values, basing them completely on earthly life without any anticipation of transcendence. At the core of Bergson's philosophy stands the *élan vital*, or life force, an explanation for alteration and innovation in the evolution of civilization. Bergson pits his organic conception of growth against the merely mechanical idea of progress, taking more fully into account the element of artistic creativity than his predecessors had.

Nietzsche and Bergson generated ideas that, however indirectly, probably provided impetus for the launching of the Futurist movement. Another such personality is Georges Sorel (1847-1922), a French engineer whose writings were instrumental in the formation of syndicalism, a movement that advocated sabotage, general strikes, and other forms of direct action to bring industry and government under the control of federations of labor unions. Marinetti is known to have read Sorel's political manifestoes and essays, which spoke of heroic combat as a key condition of life, necessary for the well-being of society. Rejecting reform and evolution as too mild, Sorel argued that workers had to trust their ability to fight for power, that they needed to take the initiative to shape their own future through revolutionary action. He and others like him had little faith in democracy or capitalism and dismissed the idea of joining a socialist political party. Showing a cynicism born of past experience, they decided that such a party, forced to participate in a bourgeois government, would become corrupt and could accomplish little in a sea of political parties.

Italian political disarray at the turn of the twentieth century. The political climate in Italy at the end of the nineteenth century was marked by a frequent change of conservative and liberal governments. The two most important politicians of the era were Francesco Crispi and Giovanni Giolitti, both liberals. Crispi, who became prime minister in 1887, was an eloquent, passionate patriot who fought in the mid-nineteenth-century Risorgimento for the unification of Italy. His administration instituted strong policies and reforms: the state gained new powers to regulate public health and charitable institutions; it supported the monarchy; and it established Italian colonies in northeast Africa. Financial matters led to Crispi's fall in 1891 and for a brief year, in 1892, the less progressive Giolitti came to power. He was the first major politician of the era not to have participated in the Risorgimento and throughout his career, his refusal to engage in patriotic bombast made him vulnerable to the accusation that he lacked ideals. He belonged to the Liberal Party (a moderate group). His premiership was ended by a bank scandal, and Crispi returned to power in 1893, only to lose it three years later when a catastrophic colonial expedition to Abyssinia aborted his political career.

Giolitti regained political power in 1903, opening a dialogue with the labor movement and in 1912 introducing universal male suffrage. Italy meanwhile competed with European nations for "a place in the sun," waging war against Turkey in 1911-12 and gaining Libya as a colony in the process. Yet these achievements are overshadowed by what was not done. Giolitti did not try to remedy the social injustice that was pushing the peasants and workers ever closer to revolutionary ideologies. Nor did he use state power to guarantee the privileges of the wealthy. The Giolittian system of politics was a skillful balancing act that required Giolitti to cooperate with radicals, republicans, moderate socialists, and finally Catholics in his governing coalitions. His system of politics succeeded in balancing the most powerful groups in Italy but did not secure the peace. Moreover, corruption raged during Giolitti's tenure—votes were bought and sold, electors manipulated, and elections rigged.

Sorel, among others, sought to overthrow democracy and capitalism, not, in his case, through terrorist bloodshed but by way of a general strike. For Marinetti and Futurist ideology, on the other hand, war and violence were central. The Futurists thought of these forces as tools that could be used to "clean" out the residue of outworn traditions, paving the way for new possibilities, as articulated in the Futurist manifesto "La Guerra, sola igiene del mondo" ("War, the sole hygiene of the world"). Far from a pessimistic worldview, the movement promoted the idea that humanity—through an exercise of will on the part of some forward-thinking individuals—could achieve anything.

THE NEWLY MANUFACTURED AUTOMOBILE—FRIEND OR FOE?

Although automobile production energized the Italian economy, Fiat and Lancia produced cars mainly for very rich buyers. This made the automobile drivers of Marinetti's day a popular attraction; reports about speed records and spectacular accidents filled the newspapers. Was the car a friend or foe in the eyes of the Futurists? In these early days, cars did not offer much comfort. Their combustion engines were relatively dangerous; uncontrolled explosions occurred haphazardly and often. This hardly discouraged the Futurists: it was precisely the chaotic, risky nature of the combustion engine that so attracted them. "All three attributes [of engines]—power, danger, and unreliability—are advantageous from Marinetti's viewpoint, since they permit the development of a body/machine complex founded on notions of struggle, sacrifice, feverish effort, and expenditure" (Schnapp, *Propeller Talk*, p. 161). The Futurists, despite their attraction to it, conceived of the automobile as adversary. Technology was an enemy to be bested or at least disciplined. In keeping with such ideas, the *Futurist Manifesto* used combative imagery in connection with the automobile: "I stretched out on my car like a corpse on its bier," says the narrator, "but revived at once under the steering wheel, a guillotine blade that threatened my stomach" (Marinetti, *Futurist Manifesto*, p. 40). In general, a Futurist such as Marinetti saw himself neither as just a mechanical supplement to the machine nor as a master in absolute control of it. There was an ambivalent love-hate relationship at work: on the one hand, the Futurists admired the precise mechanics of machines; on the other hand, they regarded such a mechanism as a powerful and dangerous adversary that they must try to control.

Italian economic disparity at the dawn of the twentieth century. At the turn of the twentieth century, Italy was still an agricultural country, despite its industrial progress over the past hundred years; in 1911, the majority—59 per cent of all employed adults—still worked in the countryside (Clark, p. 127). Still, the first decade of the new century saw enormous growth in the Italian economy. Between 1899 and 1907 the national income rose by nearly 38 per cent (Lyttelton, p. 18), and the North was more fully industrialized, becoming home to the typewriter manufacturing of the Olivetti company and the automobile manufacturing of Fiat, Lancia, and Alfa Romeo. These new industries contributed to a worldwide economic boom at the time, yet many in Italy benefited little from this boom.

The ability to harness hydroelectric power from the water of the Alps promoted modernization in northern Italian cities, particularly in Milan, where Marinetti lived. In 1893 Milan became the second city in the world with electric street lighting and an electric tram, innovations that encouraged urban expansion. The population in Milan soared, exceeding a half million inhabitants by 1911 (Clark, p. 164). But the economic growth was concentrated in northern Italy and in the Po Valley. The gap between the industrialized North and rural South became ever more apparent, as the economic boom bypassed the *mezzogiorno* (Italian South). Many southerners reacted by emigrating from the country to America and elsewhere. Such was the state of Italy when *The Futurist Manifesto* was written.

Italian cultural evolution by the turn of the twentieth century. The cultural landscape of Italy at the end of the nineteenth century was marked by great diversity. The Risorgimento was a period of upheaval. Establishing an economic base for Italy was regarded as more important than developing a new artistic tradition to represent the fledgling nation. Art created in the second half of the nineteenth century reflected bourgeois preferences. The dominant voices looked for their new country's cultural foundation to the previous glories of the Italian peninsula—to ancient Roman aesthetic traditions and to long-established authors such as Dante and Petrarch: "In social terms, this reliance on ancient models and ideas was important, because it invoked symbols and notions with which everybody was familiar, particularly through the ubiquitous Roman monuments and ruins which littered most Italian cities" (Beales and Biagini, p. 9). There emerged a number of intellectual groups whose members objected to this tendency, criticizing the admiration of past ideals and advocating the construction of a fresh artistic identity for Italy. Two of the most important

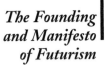

Futurism's influence touched literature, theater, marriage, fashion, cuisine, architecture, and the graphic arts, as demonstrated in this 1929 poster for an automobile, by Paolo Garretto.

art movements of the day were *scapigliatura* and *verismo*. A literary movement of the 1860s, *scapigliatura* (means "disheveled" or "unkempt") showed disdain for piety and the established values of bourgeois and upper-class culture. The movement denigrated the conservative lifestyle and praised drug use and promiscuity. The other movement, *verismo*, flourished from 1878 to 1890. Related to French naturalism, it featured writers who attempted, through precise observation and stylistic impersonality, to depict social reality, especially that of the rural South. Highlighting the inequity between North and South, *verist* writers also exposed discontent among members of the new urban working class.

Along with these movements, it must be noted that not all late-nineteenth-century writing in Italy came packaged with a prescriptive type of social consciousness. Gabriele D'Annunzio wrote "Decadent" novels that are anything but critical of their aristocratic protagonists from a moral or sociological angle. *Decadent,* a term for the literary culture of late-nineteenth-century Italy, has also been used to designate literature of the era that highlighted the insincere, politically cynical, and superficial, all part of an outer display cloaking an inner emptiness in upper-class society. To writers like D'Annunzio, this condition of emptiness was not a negative facet; rather they cele-

brated it as a sign of the aristocratic, antibourgeois lifestyle.

Within this cultural mix, the Futurist movement became another player in literary efforts to define Italy, offering the still new country a nationalistic program of strength and force that opposed classical tradition and embraced the modern. In northern cities like Genoa and Milan, says one cultural historian, "modernity was powerfully experienced as the everyday clash of cultural tradition with . . . industrial innovation. Marinetti's basic insight was that such a struggle was relentless, unpitying, and weighted in favour of the modern" (Nicholls, p. 85). Not only an artistic movement, Futurism also styled itself as a social and political force. Again, the Futurists set out to overhaul a society riven by disarray and disparity. Such a revolutionary goal, they taught, demanded a violent rejection of the past, including the overthrow of old rules and themes in favor of the modern.

The Manifesto in Focus

Contents summary. The overall intent of the manifesto is to proclaim its principles in simple, outline form for a general audience. Nonetheless, the text constitutes a complex artistic document. It includes an introductory narrative; eleven statements that compose the programmatic agenda of Futurism; and a concluding polemic against Italian society.

The introduction. At the outset, a first-person narrator, presumably Marinetti, situates himself and his companions within an exotic environment. On soft oriental rugs under lamps with "electric hearts" they discuss the night away in a narcotic, half-conscious state that teeters on the "borders of logic" (*Futurist Manifesto*, p. 39). However fantastic it seems, the setting can be understood as a concrete place (Marinetti's apartment in Milan, decorated with souvenirs from his time in Egypt). Identifying with workers operating powerful industrial machines, the narrator and his guests consider themselves the only fully awake individuals in the modern world. They think of themselves as an avant-garde contingent of humanity, as forerunners of a new era.

FUTURISM AND WOMEN

The *Futurist Manifesto* declares scorn for woman and a war on feminism. Does this mean that hatred of women was a characteristic of Futurism? It has been argued that we need to look beyond the words of the *Manifesto*. First, Marinetti repudiated his phrase "scorn for woman" as an inexact way of describing his dislike of "'the ideal woman in works of the imagination'" and also qualified his remarks in a new preface to the work in 1910 that says his real opposition is to "'the sentimental significance' attributed to women" (Marinetti in Nicholls, p. 89). Secondly, Futurism embraced social reforms (divorce, universal suffrage, equal pay) favorable to women (Nicholls, p. 88). Thirdly, though Futurism at first remained closed to women, there were notable exceptions and ultimately its policy changed. One of the exceptions was Valentine de Saint-Point (1875-1953), Marinetti's friend and lover, who wrote her own *Manifesto of the Futurist Woman* (1912), and followed it up with a second Futurist work—the *Manifesto of Lust* (1913).

Suddenly the city awakens, the noise of a morning tram interrupting the private scene. A train passes; then another sound intrudes, the roaring of "hungry cars" (*Futurist Manifesto*, p. 39). Calling for action, the narrator proclaims a new mythology, that of the machine, which will triumph over the memory of the old Western world.

But first there is work to be done—it is time now, says the narrator, to chase Death.

The Futurists jump up, leave the house, and with erotic desire approach the automobiles. ("We went up to the snorting beasts, to lay amorous hands on their torrid breasts" [*Futurist Manifesto*, p. 40].) The narrator climbs into a car and starts driving, or rather racing recklessly, down a road. Forced to stop for two bicycle riders, he loses control of his car, and it lands in a ditch full of industrial waste, with blackened mud. Bystanders haul out the car. Up it comes, but without its body or upholstery. The crowd deems it "dead," but no problem—Marinetti can revive it easily enough. Even though the car has been destroyed, he can start the engine.

The basic manifesto. Laying out the Futurist agenda, the manifesto sets forth eleven programmatic points through a succession of aphorisms.

1. We intend to sing the love of danger, the habit of energy and fearlessness.

2. Courage, audacity, and revolt will be essential elements of our poetry.

3. Up to now literature has exalted a pensive immobility, ecstasy, and sleep. We intend to exalt aggressive action. . . .

4. We say that the world's magnificence has been enriched by a new beauty; the beauty of speed. A racing car . . . is more beautiful than the *Victory of Samothrace*.

5. We want to hymn the man at the wheel, who hurls the lance of his spirit across the Earth. . . .

6. The poet must spend himself with ardor, splendor, and generosity, to swell the enthusiastic fervor of the primordial elements.

7. Except in struggle, there is no more beauty. No work without aggressive character can be a masterpiece. Poetry must be conceived as a violent attack on unknown forces. . . .

8. We stand on the last promontory of the centuries! . . . Why should we look back, when what we want is to break down the mysterious doors of the Impossible? Time and Space died yesterday. We already live in the absolute, because we have created eternal, omnipresent speed.

9. We will glorify war—the world's only hygiene—militarism, patriotism, the destructive gesture of freedom-bringers, beautiful ideas worth dying for, and scorn for woman.

10. We will destroy the museums, libraries, academies of every kind, will fight moralism, feminism, every opportunistic or utilitarian cowardice.

11. We will sing of great crowds excited by work, by pleasure, and by riot; we will sing of the multicolored, polyphonic tides of revolution in the modern capitals . . . and [of] the sleek flight of planes whose propellers . . . seem to cheer like an enthusiastic crowd.

(*Futurist Manifesto*, pp. 41-42)

First comes the love of danger and the fearlessness of Futurist men. Secondly courage and rebellion are touted as elements of Futurist poetry. The ten remaining elements echo the love of danger and denigrate traditional forms of culture, art, and memory. Central to the manifesto is Marinetti's aesthetic program, which holds that beauty was, is, and will always exist only as struggle. In battle, there is beauty, implies the manifesto when it lauds war as the only "hygiene" of the world. Speed, the fourth point, is beauty too. The modern works of engineering, a racecar, for instance, contain more splendor than the "Victory of Samothrace," a classical sculpture of the goddess Nike (victory) that was discovered just a few decades earlier (in 1863) on the Greek isle of Samothrace. The manifesto's declaration that time and space are dead suggests that the velocity of modern transport and communication has put Marinetti's era into an a-historical dimension, separating it from all other ages ("we have created eternal, omnipresent speed" [*Futurist Manifesto*, p. 41]). Incorporating the human dimension, the *Manifesto* glorifies the representative of modern society, the automobile driver, then praises the phenomena of industrialized urban life, from city crowds to electric lighting.

In the last point of the manifesto, Marinetti again praises the symbols of the modern world. He applauds the great crowds, the metropolis, the war, trains, and automobiles. Emphatically he regards these symbols as the promise for an even faster, more complex and more technological Futurist world to come.

The conclusion. The end of the manifesto addresses what it sees as an Italy entrapped in an ideology of the past, a country that seems to the writer to be in dire need of wresting itself free. He argues against the traditionalist society of Italy in 1909, characterizing it as a land governed by traditionalism in a culturally codified way. Professors, archeologists, antiquarians are *passatista* (traditionalists) to the detriment of the country; by preserving Italian traditions, they retard or countermand any orientation towards future. Museums are graveyards, and visits to these memorial sites are debilitating to modern men. One ought to visit museums only once a year and then to place a funeral wreath on paintings such

as the *Mona Lisa.* Energy must be redirected onto the present and future.

After this polemic, the narrator reflects on the future of Futurism itself. If the movement is correct in its glorification of eternal progress, the passage of years condemns it to becoming *passatistic,* or traditional too. In the future, other, younger artists will bristle against the Futurist ideals of art. The narrator gives himself and his coworkers a decade to achieve change before being replaced by younger men. He welcomes the challenge, declaring that this antagonism constitutes the true dynamic of every art. "Art, in fact, can be nothing but violence, cruelty, and injustice," or the climax of conflict (*Futurist Manifesto*, p. 43).

The manifesto closes by addressing an imaginary audience. Yelling at any possible objection, the narrator says the Futurists are not interested in it. They stand erect at the top of the world, hurling their forceful "defiance to the stars!" (*Futurist Manifesto*, p. 44).

A revolution in literature? "Courage, audacity, and revolt will be essential elements of our poetry" promises *The Futurist Manifesto.* Three years later, in the *Technical Manifesto of Futurist Literature,* the movement attempted to prescribe procedures for writers to use as tools for conducting the literary revolt and training the sensibility of modern man. Marinetti prescribed a new type of Futurist poetry, "Parole in libertà" (words in freedom), in this *Manifesto of Literature.* This

The Founding and Manifesto of Futurism

poetry abolished traditional syntax, punctuation, and parts of speech such as adjectives. The poetry featured fragmented language, which resembled a message transmitted by the telegraph. In addition to this telegraphic style, Futurist poetry employed modern varieties of typography, several fonts in different sizes, for instance. These strategies in many ways reflected contemporary experiences. On the one hand, they testified to the accelerated

One of the most prominent texts of Futurist writing was Marinetti's novel *Zang Tumb Tumb* (1914), which describes the battle of Adrianopolis in 1912. Already on the title page, Marinetti plays with the graphic dimension of the printed words *Zang Tumb Tumb* in such a way that they resemble a canon on the battlefield. The text on the cover is a complex mix of graphic design, onomatopoetic expressions, and seemingly endless rows of juxtaposed words smattered on the page without syntactic order.

Futurist poems were published in the movement's own magazines, and were also translated and printed in important literary and artistic journals all over Europe. Marinetti aimed for an international revolution of poetic language; he wrote a collection of French poems "Les mots en liberté futuristes" (1919; The Futurist Words in Freedom) explicitly to target an international audience; to be sure, the poetry provoked energetic discussions among European intellectuals. One of the most prominent critics, the German author Alfred Döblin, accused Marinetti of producing senseless juxtapositions of unrelated words. In contrast, Marinetti's poetics inspired August Stramm, a prominent German expressionistic poet, to develop his famous telegram style. A more ambivalent response came from the Dada movement, an artistic experiment with sound poems and textual collages. Founded in Zurich, Switzerland, in 1916, the Dada movement adopted poetic strategies from the Futurists but strongly opposed their commitment to violence, power, and war.

Sources and literary context. Some of Marinetti's *Futurist Manifesto* harks back to real-life experience. The car crash at the start of the manifesto recalls a key moment in Marinetti's life. Just a few months before writing the piece, Marinetti had a similar experience. On the morning of October 15, 1908, he was driving his car when a bicyclist suddenly appeared, Marinetti lost control of the vehicle, and it flipped into a ditch. The writer survived without injury.

Less obviously, *The Futurist Manifesto* was influenced by developments of the age in which it was written, but to speak about particular influences on Futurism is a controversial topic. On the one hand, Futurism absorbed major currents of its age, and on the other hand, it claimed to be born out of the absolute and thus to be without history or tradition. Some intellectuals such as Germany's Karl Vossler recognized in Futurism the end and not the beginning of an art movement: "But you [Marinetti] will surely be

---

OTHER FUTURIST MANIFESTOES

The Futurist manifestoes covered almost every aspect of life and culture. First came texts such as the *Technical Manifesto of Futurist Painting* (1910) and the *Technical Manifesto of the Futurist Sculpture* (1912), which called for innovative ways of representing dynamic forms and events. Next came the *Technical Manifesto on Futurist Literature* (1912), the *Manifesto of Futurist Architecture* (1914), and *The Futurist Cinema* (1916) as well as manifestoes on aspects of daily life, like clothing and cooking. The manifesto on Futurist fashion (1914, written by the Futurist painter Balla) called for radical new styles: "WE MUST DESTROY ALL PASSAEIST [Traditionalist] CLOTHES, and everything about them which is tight fitting, colourless, funereal, decadent, boring and unhygienic. As far as materials are concerned, we must abolish: wishy washy, pretty-pretty, gloomy, and neutral colours, along with patterns composed of lines, checks and spots. . . . WE MUST INVENT FUTURIST CLOTHES, hap-hap-hap-hap-happy clothes, daring clothes with brilliant colours and dynamic lines" (Osborn). Marinetti's attack on pasta in his manifesto of Futurist cooking (1930) is probably the baldest example of the ideology's opposition to all things traditional:

Above all we believe necessary:

a) The abolition of pastaciutta, an absurd Italian gastronomic religion. It may be that a diet of cod, roast beef and steamed pudding is beneficial to the English, cold cuts and cheese to the Dutch, and sauerkraut, smoked [salt] pork and sausages to the Germans, but pasta is not beneficial to the Italians. . . .

(Osborn)

---

communication of modern electronic media; on the other hand, they drew on modes of typesetting in everyday culture, in, for example, commercial posters and newspaper advertisements. The inclusion of facets of everyday culture became an innovative aspect of Futurist art in general.

168   WORLD LITERATURE AND ITS TIMES ∼ VOLUME 7

disappointed because it [Vossler's book] treats Futurism . . . as the final expression of a movement that starts with Romanticism" (Schnapp, *Gorilla Art*, p. 669). Indeed, the Futurist Manifesto itself alludes to prior literary traditions, such as symbolism and Decadentism, both of which it views as force*less*.

Futurism distinguished itself as the first artistic avant-garde movement. *Avant-garde*, a term that by then referred to the cultural/artistic elite, has been applied to several early-twentieth-century artistic movements, from Futurism to Dadaism, expressionism, cubism, and surrealism. Perhaps most influential on these later movements was the Futurist effort to capture elements of modern life even as it was being shaped. Italian Futurism especially influenced German expressionism. The impact on the Dada movement in Switzerland has already been noted. In France, surrealism showed the effect of Futurist techniques—the surrealist strategy of automatic writing can be traced back to Futurist concepts. Another avant-garde art movement emerged in Russia in 1912. Also called Futurism, its members quickly claimed independence from the Italian avant-garde.

Publication and reception. The Futurists, especially Marinetti, actively and eagerly informed the public about their new vision of modern life. They toured Italy and Europe, making proclamations that elicited public outrage in capital cities on the continent. These proclamations were staged events, *serate*, or evenings of public performances of Futurist art. The performers presented poems, music, pictures, and the manifestoes themselves. So belligerent was the attitude of the performers that they riled the spectators into a frenzy, which led to angry riots. Crowds threw old vegetables and entered into fistfights with the Futurists. In fact, the Futurist performances became renowned as chaotic events rather than as exhibitions of modern art, a development that the Futurist performers anticipated.

A number of Italian intellectuals welcomed the Futurist call for movement, speed, and aggressive action. Benedetto Croce, the foremost Italian literary critic of the day, was not one. His disdain for Futurism dominated the literary response in Italy. One reaction, to a *serata* at the Teatro Lirico in Milan, is particularly telling. Marinetti and his companions had by this time become laughingstocks in his hometown. There was a cartoon of the group that showed them at the police station, with an accompanying caption that read: "'I've seen them led away, just when they reached the climax. I don't know if they were taken to the jail, or directly to the madhouse'" (Berghaus, p. 49).

Given all this notoriety, it is hardly surprising that the Futurists influenced European avant-garde movements, even those that denied inspiration from or sympathies for Italian Futurism. In retrospect, 42 years after Futurism appeared, the German poet Gottfried Benn delivered a speech (*Problems of Lyric/Probleme der Lyrik* [1951]), in which he acknowledged the fundamental impact of the movement: "The founding moment of modern art in Europe was the publication of the *Futurist Manifesto* by Marinetti, which was released on February 20, 1909, in Paris by *Le Figaro*" (Benn, p. 508; trans. A. Niebisch).

—Arndt Niebisch

For More Information

Beales, Derek, and Eugenio F. Biagini. *The Risorgimento and the Unification of Italy*. New York: Longman, 2002.

Benn, Gottfried. "Probleme der Lyrik." In *Gottfried Benn: Essays und Reden*. Ed. Bruno Hillebrand. Frankfurt: Fischer Verlag, 1989.

Berghaus, Günter. *Futurism and Politics: Between Anarchist Rebellion and Fascist Reaction, 1909-1944*. Providence: Berghahn Books, 1996.

Clark, Martin. *Modern Italy 1871-1995*. New York: Longman, 1996.

Del Antonelli, Karen. "Marinetti: From Manifesto to Machine Gun: A Study of the Works of F. T. Marinetti from 1909 to 1916." PhD diss., University of California at Los Angeles, 1979.

Landes, David S. *The Unbound Prometheus: Technological Changes 1750 to the Present*. Cambridge: Cambridge University Press, 1969.

Lyttelton, Adrian, ed. *Liberal and Fascist Italy: 1900-1945*. Oxford and New York: Oxford University Press, 2002.

Marinetti, Filippo Tommaso. *Futurist Manifesto*. In *Marinetti: Selected Writings*. Ed. R. W. Flint. Trans. R. W. Flint and Arthur A. Coppotelli. New York: Farrar, Straus and Giroux, 1972.

Nicholls, Peter. *Modernisms: A Literary Guide*. Berkeley: University of California Press, 1995.

Osborn, Bob. *Futurism and the Futurists*. http://www.futurism.org.uk/futurism.htm.

Perloff, Marjorie. *The Futurist Moment: Avant-garde, Avant Guerre, and the Language of Rupture*. Chicago: University of Chicago Press, 1986.

Schnapp, T. Jeffery. "'Gorilla Art': On an Unpublished Letter from Karl Vossler to Filippo Tommaso Marinetti." *Modernism/Modernity* 9, no. 4 (2002): 667-73.

———. "Propeller Talk." *Modernism/Modernity* 1, no. 3 (1994): 153-78.

Ghìsola

by

Federigo Tozzi

THE LITERARY WORK

A novel set in Siena, Italy, in the early twentieth century; written between 1910 and 1913, published in Italian (as *Con gli occhi chiusi*) in 1919, in English in 1990.

SYNOPSIS

A naïve young man falls in love with a precocious servant girl. After much soul searching, he discovers her true nature.

Born in Siena in 1883, Federigo Tozzi grew up in an atmosphere of parental abuse, the victim of a violent father. His mother, a deeply religious and longsuffering woman, educated her son as best she could, given the opposition of her husband, only to die suddenly, leaving her 12-year-old boy under the tutelage of his father. In part to escape the oppressive atmosphere at home, Tozzi frequented the local library from the age of 15, reading literary, philosophical, and psychological texts and keeping abreast of the latest cultural trends in such journals as the *Revue Philosophique* (The Philosophical Revue). He fell in love with a young woman, Isola (thought by some to be the real-life inspiration for Ghìsola), only to find her pregnant with another man's child. Shortly before this discovery, the author had begun an epistolary exchange with another young woman (who identified herself as Annalena) in response to an ad in the local paper. While she filled an emotional void in Tozzi's life, he discontinued the letter writing after being stricken with a venereal disease that severely affected his sight. Confined to a dark room with little human contact for six months, Tozzi emerged profoundly changed. He returned to his readings in the library, made some preliminary attempts at writing, and resumed communication with Annalena, who by then had revealed herself to be Emma Palagi. Following an intense courtship marked by parental opposition on both sides, she became Tozzi's wife in 1908 after the death of his father.

A modest inheritance allowed Tozzi to devote himself to writing. During the formative years of his career (1908-1914), he produced numerous short stories, a volume of poetry, an anthology of early Sienese writers, and critical articles. He wrote his first novel, *Ghìsola*, between 1910 and 1913, though it would not be published until 1919. Economic constraints and a desire to make a name for himself prompted Tozzi to move to Rome in 1914. Here he met Luigi Pirandello, with whom he worked on the literary supplement of the Roman newspaper *Il Messaggero* (The Messenger). When Italy entered World War I, Tozzi took up service with the Central Press Office of the Red Cross, while continuing to write and frequent literary salons. He died of pneumonia at age 37, on the threshold of realizing his goal as a writer. Many of Tozzi's works were published posthumously by his wife, and his son, Glauco. For years his novel *Tre Croci* (1920; Three

Crosses) was regarded as his masterpiece, until *Ghìsola* displaced it after discoveries in the 1980s of the research that shaped its composition.

Events in History at the Time of the Novel

Shifting perspectives. The early 1900s saw conflicting intellectual currents in Italy. Positivism was a philosophical approach that came into vogue in the late nineteenth century and centered on scientific fact and evolution. An opposing current, the anti-positivist school, insisted on the value of intuition, some of its members subscribing to a philosophy known as vitalism, the belief that all living things contain a vital flux or life force that cannot be reduced to scientific or environmental factors. The quarrels between these and other approaches were argued in magazines of the early twentieth century, most prominently the anti-positivist journal *La critica* (1903-1944), put out by Benedetto Croce. Taking a stand against the positivists, Croce and his associate for a time, Giovanni Gentile, championed a new idealism in Italy, which rejected the notion that reality is determined by scientific conditions. The two instead envisioned reality as the "free self-expression of the 'spirit'" (Brand and Pertile, p. 510).

In literature, positivism took the form of an objective analysis of the relentless march of progress. Croce, for one, took issue with this view. He conceived of art as a self-sufficient phenomenon, a universal, intuitive form of knowledge that transcends the practical world. Fueling this newfound idealism were Italian translations of the works of such philosophers as Henri Bergson (French), Friedrich Nietzsche (German), and William James (American). These philosophers stressed the value of an individual's interior or emotional life and ability to impact the world.

Such attitudes inevitably influenced politics. In 1903, the same year that *La critica* began publication, anti-Socialist elements started to congregate around *Il Regno* (The Kingdom), a journal directed by Ettore Corradini. This group of intellectuals declared themselves against socialism and replaced the more traditional focus on human generosity and community with one centered on the negative human traits of greed and destruction. For these men, the origin of evil could be found in the principles of freedom and the French Revolution. A sense of nationalism, or nationhood, was promoted as a remedy for the rivalry between political classes and the la-

bor strikes then ensuing in Italy. Chief among the first adherents to *Il Regno* were Giuseppe Prezzolinni and Giovanni Papini, the future founders of *La Voce* (The Voice), a journal launched in 1908 that would set the direction of the Florentine avant-garde.

The Florentine avant-garde. *Ghìsola* places Tozzi right in step with the Florentine avant-garde represented first by the journal *Leonardo* and subsequently by *La Voce*. The founders of *Leonardo*, Giovanni Papini and Giuseppe Prezzolini, felt that modern society had opened a cultural vacuum in Italy. In 1905 Papini declared that the country suffered from a loss of spiritual vitality (Adamson, p. 90). The Leonardini (the writers associated with the journal) therefore proposed a renaissance of sorts, a secular-religious quest for new values through a modern cultural direction. This was to be one built on regional strengths, the autobiographical form, a more lyrical approach to writing, and the rejection of traditional narrative structures. They were primarily inspired by the philosophies of Nietzsche, Bergson, and James and by the new discipline of psychology emanating from France, Germany, and Austria.

Prezzolini and Papini explored these new theories on the pages of *Leonardo*. They appropriated Bergson's view of time as a lived experience or "duration" and of the value of intuition, its ability to penetrate to the heart of something and reveal its essence (Adamson, p. 71). Also inspired by William James's *The Will to Believe*, they embraced his view that reason alone cannot answer all questions. James, like Bergson, underscored the importance of the interior or emotional life, teaching that belief was fundamental to modifying reality.

Following the demise of *Leonardo* in 1907, both Papini and Prezzolini became interested in the Catholic modernist movement, which sought to persuade the Church to accept a doctrine that could incorporate science and philosophy. While both men would remain unconvinced by the movement, it nevertheless led to a personal relationship with Alessando Casati, editor of the Catholic journal *Il Rinnovamento* (Renovation), who together with philosopher-critic Benedetto Croce, would go on to finance *La Voce*.

La Voce advocated a somewhat different perspective than that proposed by the earlier *Leonardo*. Anti-positivistic, it retained a secular outlook, but it did not completely marginalize religion. Although the Vociani (the circle gathered around *La Voce*) denounced mainstream religion, they recognized its value in promoting a new spiritual direction. *La Voce* was, however, most celebrated for its attention to the relations between Italian and European cultures. Readers found information on foreign psychologists, philosophers, and writers, often with commentary by their Italian counterparts. French culture in particular, considered the world's most advanced by the *Vociani*, came in for much preferential treatment. Select issues of *La Voce* also concentrated on individual topics in order to provide readers with an in-depth view of the subject. One such high-profile topic was the sexual question, which would find particular resonance with Federigo Tozzi.

The sexual question. On February 10, 1910, *La Voce* dedicated its issue to the much-debated question of human sexuality. That same year Florence hosted a congress on sexuality. The city was also home to such journals as *Psiche* (*Psyche*), whose editor, Roberto Assagioli, became one of the first to write about Sigmund Freud in Italy. Much of the period's interest in this area was centered on women's sexual conduct and its effects on men. Opinions about women had taken a new form in the mid-1800s, after the release of Charles Darwin's *The Descent of Man* (1871), which appeared to embrace woman's inferiority to man. Women's sexual nature underwent a great deal of scrutiny and quickly became the focus of a social crusade of the era. Scientists sought to expose women as "a source of social disruption" and "degeneration" (Dijkstra, p. 3). Female wantonness was regarded as a disease, and promiscuous women stood as the symbol of society's deterioration as a whole. As a result of these perceptions, women were vilified as akin to beasts or sexual predators, intent on sapping men's vital energy.

Such animosity was further fueled by the women's movement. Through the work of early Italian feminists such as Anna Kuliscioff and Anna Maria Mozzoni, the struggle for women's emancipation gained momentum early in the twentieth century, becoming all the more pronounced after women joined workers' unions and the Socialist Party. However, the feminist demands were not well received, and they helped inspire a backlash of sorts.

The perceptions and events related to women gave rise to a flood of publications. Max Nordau, a Hungarian doctor, linked women's immorality to deterioration in his work *Degeneration* (1893). Prostitution and unrestrained sexual appetite, he claimed, were the inherited markers of female depravity. Not surprisingly, he dedicated his study to the Italian psychologist Cesare Lombroso, author of *The Female Offender* (1893), who likewise stressed the ancestral roots of the loose sexual behavior of women. Men were thus encouraged in such an atmosphere to curb a woman's sexuality with the age-old bond of marriage.

Tozzi's generation of intellectuals was especially influenced by *Sex and Character* (1903), written by Otto Weininger of Austria. Weininger's antifeminist views were taken up by Papini, who hailed *Sex and Character* as a masterpiece in the Italian newspaper, *La Stampa* (The Press) on December 31, 1912 (Adamson, p. 289n), right about the time Tozzi was writing *Ghìsola*. Weininger contended that women were intellectually and creatively inferior to men, primarily because they were devoted to sexuality and reproduction; they could never attain spiritual transcendence, being tied, as it were, to earth. Men, on the other hand, the true repositories of the intellect, fulfilled their assigned role by aspiring to spiritual transcendence. It followed that men had to fortify their willpower to meet the formidable challenge of women's sexuality.

Scholars of Italian literature generally credit Gabriele D'Annunzio with having proposed the archetype of young men grappling with women's sexuality; from 1900 to 1906 many of D'Annunzio's male protagonists were individuals who sought meaning in sensual pleasure. When a female protagonist shuns the piety deemed appropriate for a young woman and falls prey to sexual desire, as in D'Annunzio's novella *La Vergine Orsola* (The Virgin Orsola), she invariably meets with the worst kind of end.

D'Annunzio's stature as a writer and hence his paradigms naturally came to bear on other narratives. While the *Vociani* repudiate what they saw as his "feminine" style of writing, his influence was clearly felt by the entire literary milieu, including the then hopeful Tozzi.

The "will to power." Friedrich Nietzsche introduced the concept of the "superman" (*übermensch*), a daring type who continually strives for greatness and a life of creative adventure, cultivating strength and a noble, refined character. From this concept grew the idea that propelling society forward was the task of a minority of men who would be able to move beyond good and evil and impose their will on the masses. In Italy, the introduction to Nietzsche's philosophy is generally credited to Gabriele D'Annunzio's article, "La bestia elettiva" ("The Voluntary Animal"), which appeared in an 1892 issue of *Il Mattino*

(The Morning). Nietzsche's theories eventually found their way into D'Annunzio's most popular literary works, and through these to a wide swath of the population. Though misinterpreted by many, including D'Annunzio, the spread of Nietzsche's philosophy drew widespread attention to the concepts of the superman and the will to power, the drive, that is, "to enhance [one's] vitality to act on the world" (rather than reacting to it) (Solomon and Higgins, p. 16). Nietzsche's *Thus Spake Zarathustra* (1883-1885) features a prophet, Zarathustra, who speaks of destroying outmoded institutions and beliefs to make way for new ones. His words would inspire many young men of the period.

FROM *LA VOCE*

Part of a review on Otto Weininger's *Sex and Character*:

The fundamental psychological characteristic that distinguishes the typical man from woman is this: man has a soul while woman does not. . . . In not having a soul, woman has a less responsible life: her psychic matter always remains indeterminate and incapable of transforming itself into theory. In not having a theoretical framework, she is unable to judge, she does not have the zeal for truth, any participation in thought process; she lies without feeling guilty about it; she places no value on herself, and is thus vain, or desires becoming an object of appreciation by others. . . . The woman doesn't represent anything but coitus to the world. . . . Consequently she voluntarily takes on the role of a pimp for love. She wants coitus either for herself or for the preservation of the species; she is . . . instinctually a prostitute or a mother.

(Levi, p. 260; trans. L. Anderson-Tirro)

The will to power and the superman were taken up by Papini, and to a lesser extent Prezzolini, in *Leonardo* and *La Voce*. Papini proclaimed Nietzsche the philosopher of masculine power as early as 1906, and afterward called his philosophy the basis of a new morality that would undermine a Europe under the domination of Christianity and the "reign of the weak" (Adamson, pp. 89-90). Both men argued that their generation should address the lax moral atmosphere with a fresh set of values that included forcefulness, courage, and sincerity.

American psychologist and philosopher William James contributed a number of parallel arguments, providing justification for action that promised to "change the world and create truth" (Adamson, p. 76). James argued that powerful beliefs lead to the achievement of one's convictions by motivating the will to act. With this argument, he satisfied Papini's quest for a modern religion. Papini maintained somewhat differently, however, that the action itself produced belief.

Tozzi, like many of his compatriots, was fascinated by Nietzsche's *Thus Spake Zarathustra* and by James's *Principles of Psychology* (1890). His enthusiasm for their ideas was very much in step with the times, especially when it came to the debate about the role of man's will, which he would turn into the thematic thrust of *Ghìsola*. However, while Papini and his fellow avant-garde writers pressed for a modern secular religion, Tozzi adapted these new ideas to his own beliefs. He chose instead the more traditional path of Catholicism.

The Novel in Focus

Plot summary. As the novel opens, Domenico Rosi, proprietor of the Blue Fish, a restaurant in Siena, avidly counts the day's earnings. Married to Anna, an orphan of humble origins similar to his own, he is grateful that God has seen to his good fortune, a result he attributes to hard work. A volatile man given to sexual indiscretions, Domenico has fathered eight children, all of whom have died except for the last, Pietro, now almost 14 years old. A sickly, clinging child, Pietro receives scant attention from his parents, who are too involved in the comings and goings of the trattoria to follow him closely. Anna, however, does show some concern for her son's education, despite the constant opposition of her husband, who feels that Pietro's schooling is a waste of time. Domenico would prefer that his son learn the restaurant trade, and eventually take over the family business.

Following an altercation between Domenico and a client, Anna, who is given to convulsions, experiences an increase in their severity. Ordered by the doctor to spend more time away from the Blue Fish, she leaves for the family farm at Poggio a' Meli, taking Pietro with her. Here they make the acquaintance of the farm's latest arrival, Ghìsola, the 12-year-old niece of an unwed servant.

Pietro is attracted to Ghìsola, but also feels uneasy around her. The following year, shortly after his return to the farm and Ghìsola, he suffers a seizure. He grows pale and apprehensive in Ghisola's presence, and so distracted that he is unable to study. As their relationship progresses, he experiences feelings and physical sensations around her that he does not understand. Attracted by her singing, among other attributes, he becomes possessive, vying with the neighborhood boys for her attention.

Ghìsola develops into a beautiful but reckless young woman. No longer well-behaved, she disappears from Poggio a' Meli on Sundays to walk the streets of Siena. The men of the city, attracted by her unseemly conduct, follow her, making suggestive comments and unsuitable proposals. Pietro nevertheless remains captivated by her. His studies continue to deteriorate, and his parents argue about the best course of action. Anna, convinced "that her son is intelligent," manages to keep him in school despite his poor performance (Tozzi, Ghìsola, p. 53). One morning, as she prepares to seek out the parish priest for advice, she suddenly dies of a heart attack. Pietro, unable to comprehend the impact of her death feels little emotion until forced to kiss her lifeless corpse. Only then does he react, first recoiling, then denying the reality of her demise.

Anna's death marks a turning point in the plot, which now fixes on Pietro's worsening relationship with Domenico, and his search for solace and love from Ghìsola. Domenico disapproves of his son's intellectual aspirations, his disobedience, and particularly his continuing fascination with Ghìsola, whose conduct Domenico views as disgraceful. This results in severe beatings for Pietro and in Ghìsola's eventual banishment from Poggio a' Meli. When Pietro leaves home to attend technical school in Florence, he learns that she resides nearby. Unbeknownst to him, however, she has become the live-in paramour of a crockery salesman, Signor Alberto. After informing himself as to her whereabouts, and believing that she now is employed as a live-in servant, Pietro pays her a visit.

Though a sense of foreboding permeates their meeting, Pietro cannot contain his joy at once more being reunited with Ghìsola. Her declarations of love convince him of her sincerity, and he resolves to pursue the relationship. When Signor Alberto suffers bankruptcy and Ghìsola must find another means of subsistence, Pietro, believing that she has lost her position, escorts her back to Siena with some expectation that he can convince his father of his intention to marry her. Ghìsola knows full well, however, that Domenico will not accept the match. After a brief stay at Poggio a' Meli, she returns to her home in Radda to live with her sister Lucia. Pietro vis-

its her here but finds her unkempt and sullen. Appalled at her appearance, he also is disturbed by her attempts to seduce him. Barely managing to control himself, he leaves.

When Pietro finally sees Ghìsola again, she has found employment in an upscale bordello in Florence where she earns a good living. To prevent him from discovering her profession, she pays him a visit before he searches her out himself. He is delighted to see her and naively continues to believe in her wholesomeness. The couple spends a few days together, after which Pietro returns to Siena to fritter away the time under the disapproving eye of his father, who by now has given up on ever bringing his son to his senses.

One day an anonymous letter arrives, revealing Ghìsola's duplicity. Pietro immediately leaves for Florence, where he proceeds to the address indicated in the letter. As he climbs the stairs to the last floor, he encounters prostitutes plying their trade at every angle. Holed up in the lowest type of brothel, one catering to soldiers, Pietro is horrified to see Ghìsola exit from a room, filthy and barely clothed. Once in her room he can no longer deny the truth about the woman he has loved so ardently. When she turns and he sees that she is pregnant, emotion overcomes him. He falls to the floor, and on reviving discovers that he no longer loves her.

The threat of female sexuality. Pietro Rosi's struggle for control over his sexual inclinations is the primary focus of Ghìsola. While the novel has been described as a fictionalized account of Tozzi's own experience, it is also a reflection of the cultural mores of the day, particularly with respect to views on female sexuality.

One of the ways early-twentieth-century culture explained women's sexual misbehavior was by linking it to mental illness, specifically hysteria. Support for this type of explanation came from studies like The Sexual Question (1907) by Swiss sexologist, Auguste Forel (hailed by the editors of La Voce as the one whose views most reflected their own) and Psychopathia sexualis (1889; Sexual Psychopathology) by the Austrian psychologist Richard von Krafft-Ebing. At the Salpêtrière Hospital in Paris, renowned neurologist Jean-Martin Charcot conducted exhibitions of hysterical women, events that were widely publicized in Italy. Tozzi, who consulted both Forel and Krafft-Ebing when writing the novel, identifies its female protagonist as a hysteric: "Ghìsola in a burst of hysteria that made her condition even stronger, was staring at the window, ready to fling herself from it" (*Ghìsola*, p. 141). He draws on Forel's phases of female sexual development (from childhood precociousness, through the stages of female moral decline, to prostitution), and Krafft-Ebing's symptoms of hysteria (mood swings, sexual promiscuity, egotism, and delusions), then widely thought to underlie sexual promiscuity.

KRAFFT-EBING ON HYSTERIA

In hysterical women episodic forms of psychopathology take place that can last hours as well as days. These have a delirious imprint, and this delirium revolves more often than not around an axis of erotic content. . . . The clinical forms of transitory insanity that one can observe in hysterical women are: morbid passions . . . very acute mania associated with primordial, erotic deliriums, . . . states of agitation of an euphoric nature associated with a serious disturbance of the conscience, . . . forms of terrifying, hallucinatory delirium often coupled to a demoniac-maniacal core and episodic outbursts of hysterical-epileptic convulsions.

(von Krafft-Ebing, p. 315; trans. L. Anderson-Tirro)

It was commonplace to represent promiscuous women as akin to cats, snakes, or birds. Tozzi repeatedly associates Ghìsola with these creatures. Birds were the natural choice for representing the seductiveness of women given their song-like traits: "At midnight [Pietro] woke up. He heard a nightingale. . . . The call seemed a message that the bird's mate was answering in a distance. He couldn't help listening to both birds for a long time, imagining that Ghìsola was outside trying to catch them" (*Ghìsola*, p. 12). This association of the character and the nightingale is Tozzi's nod to a cultural icon of the period, the half-bird, half-woman sirens of mythology (sometimes also depicted as half-fish). Artists such as Aristide Sartorio showed more than a passing interest in these mythological seductresses, as illustrated by his painting *The Siren* [1895]. Sirens also appeared in literature of the day, in D'Annunzio's *Metrope* (1911-1912) and in Giovanni Pascoli's *I poemi conviviali* (1904; The Convivial Poems), for instance.

The novel links Ghìsola to flora as well as fauna. As symbols of nature, virtuous women were often pictured as part of a domestic flower garden with their husband as the gardener. Ghìsola however, is represented among "reddish flowers like the wild lilies," pointing to her exclusion from the cultivated gardens reserved for virtuous women (*Ghìsola*, p. 52). In the nineteenth century, the French writer Charles Baudelaire, among others, began using the flower to indicate the threat posed by women's genitalia. It is so used in *Ghìsola*, when the title character walks through Siena in the guise of a temptress: "If she was wearing a flower she had to stay away from the walls because there were plenty of men standing in doorways ready to reach out and grab at it" (*Ghìsola*, p. 51).

Pietro's struggle to overcome his fascination with Ghìsola can be seen as an example of man's struggle to rise above his physical inclinations, so bound to nature and forever at odds with spiritual transcendence. Man, not woman, was considered the true repository of the intellect. It was thus his role to strive for spiritual transcendence, a formidable challenge for which he had to fortify his willpower. The male intellect, people believed, was affected by seminal fluid. A strong will served as man's greatest defense in preventing the loss of semen, and with it, reason.

The glorification of masculinity would manifest itself in a number of ways during this period. Much of the so-called Futurist movement (see the **Futurist Manifesto**, also in *WLAIT 7: Italian Literature and Its Times*) was bursting with masculine energy, as seen by its allegiance to images of machinery, speed, and violence. An offshoot of this view was the image of a weak male character being "consumed" by the deadly female. In Tozzi's novel, Pietro Rosi is just such a male; he overcomes his attraction to Ghìsola only by intense effort.

This approach is in keeping with Tozzi's generation, who set out to reject the sensual pleasures of the human world to gain those promised by spiritual transcendence. For Tozzi, the teachings of the Catholic Church held the key, with marriage offering the only sanctioned escape. Unlike the *Vociani*, Tozzi did not embrace a "secular" spiritual quest for new values, but he was nevertheless guided by his cultural milieu to similar pronouncements.

Sources and literary context. An absence of background information has until recently resulted in an inadequate assessment of Tozzi's importance to modern Italian literature. *Ghìsola* incorporates all the compelling issues of the time. As public library records and Tozzi's private library (recently made available to scholars) indicate, he was acquainted with the works of many of the opinion shapers named above, including William James (*The Principles of Psychology*); Friedrich Nietzsche (*Thus Spake Zarathustra*); Henri Bergson (*Time and Memory, Creative Evolution*); August Forel (*The Sexual Question*); Richard von Krafft-Ebing (*Trattato di psicopatologia forense*); Cesare Lombroso (*The Criminal Man*); and Max Nordau (*Degeneration*). This newfound evidence has led to a reassessment of Tozzi's stature as a writer. He is now seen as a figure of transition. His settings mirror the regionalism associated with Naturalist writing, which focuses so intently on environment and heredity. Tozzi's heavy reliance on psychological and philosophical studies however, align him with the avant-garde. Whether or not he was influenced by the teachings of Freud remains open to debate. Though Italo Svevo's **The Confessions of Zeno** (also in *WLAIT 7: Italian Literature and Its Times*), published four years after *Ghìsola,* would garner greater recognition for Svevo's grasp of Freudian theory, research into Tozzi's cultural background is still in its early stages and may produce unanticipated results. Tozzi was certainly aware of Freud; *La Voce*'s 1910 issue included an article by Roberto Assagioli entitled *Le idée di Sigmund Freud sulla sessualità* (The Ideas of Sigmund Freud on Sexuality), and Tozzi's private copy of James's *The Principles of Psychology* cites Freud.

Tozzi wrote *Ghìsola* to promote sexual temperance, a value championed by the Catholic Church as well as by a large segment of contemporary Italian society. He portrays his character Pietro struggling against his own sexual desire, a desire he conscientiously tries to channel into marriage. Tozzi thereby sanctions this Catholic sacrament and its accompanying tenet of coitus for procreation. At the same time, he aligns himself with the prevailing sentiment of his day, which advocated sexual restraint as indispensable to spiritual transcendence. His ambivalence is symptomatic of a general dilemma of the day, whereby men grasped for a spiritual world while doubting its existence. This was Tozzi's predicament.

Stylistically, there is a breakdown of traditional temporal categories in *Ghìsola,* in the novel's many dream sequences, the weaving together of past and present, and the emphasis on the psychological and spiritual dimensions of his characters. This temporal breakdown places Tozzi among such innovative writers as Luigi Pirandello (see **Six Characters in Search of an Author**, also in *WLAIT 7: Italian Literature and Its Times*).

Reception. When *Ghìsola* was published in 1919, it received mixed reviews. The critic Ferdinando Paolieri, though he responded favorably, qualified his response: "more than a true novel, this is a great regional story" (Paolieri in Tozzi, *Carteggio*, p. 368n; trans. L. Anderson-Tirro). Other well-known writers, such as the critic Margherita Sarfatti, praised *Ghìsola* in personal notes to Tozzi, but never revealed her admiration in public writings. Those who did compliment the novel in writing, such as the critic G. A. Borgese, underscored its autobiographical component: "the autobiography is objectified with incisive precision" (Borgese, p. 25; trans. L. Anderson-Tirro). There were indications, however, that Tozzi's intent was not that of simply writing an autobiography. When the critic Pietro Pancrazi referred to the inspiration Tozzi drew from his own personal experience, Tozzi furiously wrote back: "I can write a book about a delinquent, a forger [or] a prostitute without anyone being able to attribute their moral qualities to my own personal reality" (Tozzi, *Mostra*, p. 92). These same critics would proclaim *Three Crosses*, published one year after *Ghìsola*, Tozzi's masterpiece, not realizing that it was essentially a reworking of themes already present in his earlier novel. Only Domenico Giuliotti, Tozzi's closest friend at the time of the novel's writing, would find *Three Crosses* inferior to *Ghìsola,* and would note in 1936 that the sparse attention given Tozzi had more to do with the fact that he "is not an entertaining writer. . . . For this reason he has had few readers. He is of those who delve in great depth into life's sorrow. Who are therefore disregarded by their contemporaries and are discovered at a later time" (Marchi, p. 138; trans. L. Anderson-Tirro).

—Loredana Anderson-Tirro

For More Information

Adamson, Walter. *Avant-Garde Florence: From Modernism to Fascism.* Cambridge: Harvard University Press, 1993.

Borgese, Giuseppe Antonio. *Tempo di edificare.* Milan: Fratelli Treves, 1924.

Brand, Peter, and Lino Pertile. *The Cambridge History of Italian Literature.* Cambridge: Cambridge University Press, 1996.

Dijkstra, Bram. *Evil Sisters: The Threat of Female Sexuality and the Cult of Manhood.* New York: Alfred A. Knopf, 1996.

Krafft-Ebing, Richard von. *Trattato di psicopatologia forense (Treatise of Forensic Psychopathology).* Torino: Fratelli Bocca, 1897.

Levi, Giulio. "Ottone Weininger." *La Voce* 2, no. 9 (February 10, 1910): 259-266.

Marchi, Marco. "Di Tozzi, Giuliotti e Altro." *La Rassegna della Letteratura Italiana* 8, no. 3 (September-December 1991): 138-145.

Nordau, Max. *Degeneration.* Lincoln: University of Nebraska Press, 1993.

Solomon, Robert C., and Kathleen M. Higgins. *What Nietzsche Really Said.* New York: Schocken, 2000.

Tozzi, Federigo. *Carteggio con Domenico Giuliotti.* Firenze: Vallecchi Editori, 1988.

———. *Ghìsola.* Trans. Charles Klopp. New York: Garland, 1990.

———. *Mostra di documenti.* Ed. Marco Marchi and Glauco Tozzi. Firenze: Tipogr. C. Mori, 1984.

Weininger, Otto. *Sex and Character.* New York: AMS, 1975.

History: A Novel

by

Elsa Morante

THE LITERARY WORK

A novel set mainly in Rome during and after World War II (1941-1947); published in Italian (as *La storia*) in 1974, in English in 1977.

SYNOPSIS

Divided by brief timelines of larger historical events, the chapters center on a half-Jewish Italian schoolteacher who is raped by a German soldier, and on her two sons during and after the Second World War.

Born in Rome in 1912 to Irma Poggibonsi and Francesco Lo Monaco, Elsa Morante was the second of the unmarried couple's five children. Irma, a Jewish schoolteacher, raised the children with her husband, Augusto Morante, who worked as a tutor at the Aristide Gabelli school. Both he and Morante's biological father were Catholic. Mainly self-educated, Morante left home at the age of 18 to dedicate herself to journalism. In 1936 she met Alberto Moravia, who was already a novelist of some repute. Like Morante, Moravia was part Jewish and had been baptized—facts that would greatly affect their experience in wartime Italy. Morante's relationship with Moravia brought her into contact with leading Italian intellectuals. She and Moravia married, and remained so for 22 years (1941-1963). Early in the marriage, Morante published her first novel, *House of Liars* (*Menzogna e sortilegio*, 1948), for which she received one of Italy's highest literary honors, the Viareggio Prize. Over the course of her career Morante would publish numerous articles; a poetry collection, *The World Saved by Children* (*Il mondo salvato dai ragazzini,* 1968); and three major novels: *Arturo's Island* (*L'isola di Arturo,* 1957), *History: A Novel* (*La Storia,* 1974), and *Aracoeli* (1982). Morante has been praised for "capturing in prose the rhythms of the torment of mutual dependence" (Hainsworth and Robey, p. 393). She does so in *History*, meanwhile depicting the impact of World War II on ordinary Italians, especially women, children, and Italian Jews condemned to deportation or lives in anxious hiding.

Events in History at the Time the Novel Takes Place

The Jews under Mussolini before 1938. The Jewish population of Italy had maintained a continuous presence on the peninsula for more than 21 centuries before Benito Mussolini seized power in 1922. At times on harmonious terms with their Italian rulers and compatriots, at times persecuted, Jews figured prominently in the Unification of Italy in 1861. Mussolini himself was keenly aware of this fact ("Mussolini could never forget that 4 of 7 founders of Italian nationalism were Jews" [Begnath in Bosworth, p. 343]). After Unification, the Jews assimilated into national life, attaining positions in business, education, government, and the arts, and intermarrying with the Catholic majority. Italo Svevo and Alberto Moravia, two of the nation's foremost novelists, were of Jewish descent (see *Zeno's Conscience* and *The Conformist,* also in *WLAIT 7: Italian Literature and Its Times*). These trends continued into and beyond Mussolini's ascension to power. Jews and Catholics mingled easily at the time, with mixed marriages numbering as many as one in three (Roth, p. 505). The Italian Jews, a small minority, fused thoroughly into mainstream life. Children who were Jewish attended Italian schools; musicians who were Jewish conducted orchestras; professors who were Jewish taught at key universities; and Jewish soldiers fought for the Italian homeland. Little did anyone know how abruptly all this was about to change.

ITALIAN JEWISH POPULATION

Emigration and conversion reduced the number of Italian Jews to roughly 45,000 in 1937 (0.1 percent of the Italian population). The number was further reduced to 35,000 by the fall of 1943, when circumstances conspired to divide Italy, placing the South in the hands of the Italian king and the Allied powers, and the North and center under German control. Earlier in the war, Italy had mostly ignored or enacted half-heartedly its anti-Jewish measures. One such measure expelled foreign Jews (about 10,000) and all Jews who became citizens after 1918. But many Jews stayed and with the help of the general populace managed to escape arrest. There were clergymen, officials, neighbors, and colleagues who protected Jews. "All night and throughout the day," explains one such citizen during a round-up of Jews, "the Germans moved through Rome, seizing Italians for their furnaces in the north. The Germans would like us to believe that these people are alien to us, that they belong to a different race; but we feel that they are flesh of our flesh and blood of our blood. They have always lived, fought and suffered with us" (Yahil, p. 427). Records show that for every Roman Jew caught, nine escaped. Of course, this was little comfort to the detained and deported or to those who, like Morante's protagonist, escaped the round-up but afterwards lived in constant terror of arrest.

Mussolini's stance towards the Italian Jews deteriorated over time. Early in his tenure (1922-1943), he was publicly cordial toward Italian Jewry but later, especially after his alliance with Hitler in 1936, relations foundered. The official Fascist stance changed to one of outright anti-Semitism from 1938 to 1943, followed by physical persecution and deportation from 1943 to 1945.

At first eager to solidify his hold on the country, Mussolini cultivated the support of Italian Jews along with the rest of the population. And indeed Jews figured among the initial adherents of his regime, some filling administrative or political posts, others serving in the Fascist navy of Italy. Guido Jung, an Italian Jew, served as finance minister under Mussolini, for example. On the other hand, many more Italian Jews opposed Mussolini even then, among them, General Emanuele Pugliese, one of Rome's defenders during the Fascist march and takeover of 1922.

The turning point came in 1936-37, when Fascist Italy signed a treaty of friendship with Nazi Germany (the Rome-Berlin Axis) and Mussolini visited Hitler. Afterward, Italian Fascism turned fiercely anti-Semitic and its rhetoric grew hateful. One anti-Jewish pamphlet (1936) accused the Jewish minority of putting their Judaism before Fascism and so failing to be sufficiently patriotic. Soon the Fascist media, as well as Fascist intellectuals, were promoting racism. Jews, they said, did not belong to the "Italian race"—Italians were Aryan; Jews were not. Whereas previously southern Italy had been the scapegoat for all that was "wrong" with Italy, now the blame shifted to the Jews, only less charitably. Despite the fact that Jews had been assimilating ever more fully into national life, they were suddenly described as incapable of assimilation. These attitudes laid the groundwork for the 1938 racial laws.

Fascist anti-Semitism, part 1: racial laws. Italy enacted its anti-Semitic laws in 1938. Having decided to persecute the Jews as a race, the government had to conceive a legal definition for the Jews and establish a criterion for the half Jews born of mixed marriages. The state defined a Jew as a person whose two parents were Jewish by birth, whose father was Jewish and mother foreign, or who, though only half Jewish, practiced Judaism. For children born of a mixed marriage between a Jew and a non-Jew, if at least one parent was Italian, the child was considered non-Jewish, as long as he or she demonstrated "ethical, political, and religious behavior in keeping with this non-Jewishness" (Sarfatti in Cooperman and Garvin, p. 419). The laws expelled Jews who were not Italian citizens or had just recently (beginning in 1919) become citizens. The remaining Italian Jews became subject to a host of bans and restrictions. They were forbidden to marry Aryans, to hold public office, to join the Fascist Party, to serve in Italy's armed forces, to

A street in the Jewish Ghetto in Rome, where more than 1,000 Jews were arrested and sent to concentration camps in the round-up of October 16, 1943.

own more than 50 hectares of land, to run a business with more than 100 workers, or to employ Aryan servants. Jewish students were expelled from Italian schools; Jewish professors, from Italian universities; Jewish textbooks, from Italian classrooms; Jewish names, from the textbooks. Overnight the government reclassified Jews as aliens, as members of an enemy nation. Reactions in the larger population varied. Some betrayed Jews to the authorities. Others denounced the anti-Semitic laws as immoral, helping Jewish friends and co-workers find refuge in the homes and convents of Italian Catholics. Abandoning their own quarters, a number of Italian Jews went into hiding. Others waited and watched, until the fall of 1943, perhaps to their fatal misfortune.

Fascist anti-Semitism, part 2: bodily harm. In 1943 relations between Italy and Germany collapsed. The Italian king, Victor Emmanuel III, signed an armistice with the Allies, and Mussolini fell from power. He was rescued by the Germans, then propped up as leader of a breakaway Italian republic, the Italian Social Republic (also known as the Republic of Salò), which ruled northern and central Italy, where most of the Italian Jews lived. Thereafter, Nazi Germany took charge of the Italian Jews, conducting round-ups in major cities for deportation to concentration camps in Eastern Europe. Nazi officers initiated a phase of mass arrests, moving from Trieste, to Rome, to Florence, and Bologna (a deportation that included Jews from Milan, Verona, Trieste).

A *JEW* DEFINED—NAZI GERMANY VS. ITALY

The protagonist of *History*, Ida Ramundo, is nervous about her Jewish heritage, even though just one of her parents was Jewish, which exempts her from Italy's 1938 anti-Jewish laws. Her nervousness is clearly understandable in light of Nazi Germany's earlier 1935 laws, which differed dramatically in this regard. In Fascist Italy one was either Jewish or non-Jewish; there was no category for the half-Jew. But in Nazi Germany, and most of the countries it dominated, children of mixed marriages (*Mischlinge*) were referred to derisively as Jewish offspring, and although a "full" Jew was someone with three Jewish grandparents, there were categories for half-Jews and quarter-Jews. This Nazi attitude found its way into Italy, despite its different racial laws.

In Rome, on September 26, 1943, two Jewish spokesmen were summoned to the German embassy by Major Herbert Kappler. The two were asked to raise a ransom of 50 kilograms of gold in 36 hours for 200 Jews who would otherwise be deported. When asked if the forthcoming anti-Jewish measures would also be applied to Italians of Jewish descent who had been baptized or had been born of mixed marriages, Kappler replied, "I make no differences between one Jew and another. Whether they are . . . baptized, or mixed, all those with a drop of Jewish blood are the same to me. They are all enemies" (Kappler in De Felice, p. 203).

Other raids followed. The round-up in Rome, conducted October 16, 1943, made its way through 26 neighborhoods, starting with the Jewish ghetto. Arriving at daybreak (5:30 A.M.) Theodor Dannecker and his Nazi police moved from door to door, arresting and holding 1,022 Roman Jews, releasing 237 who turned out to be non-Jews or children of mixed marriages. The 1,022 Jews were dispatched to the Auschwitz-Birkenau extermination camp in Poland, where 839 were sent directly to the gas chambers; of the remaining 183, just 17 would survive the war.

The arrests continued. Jewish prisoners were jailed in local prisons, detention centers, and transit camps. At San Sabba, near Trieste, the Fascists, and later the Nazis, ran an extermination camp for political prisoners and Jews, with a crematorium to burn the bodies of those executed or tortured to death. It was the only such camp in Italy. In general, inmates fared better in the Italian concentration camps than in other European concentration camps; Italy's inmates could live with their families and did not have to don prison garb. But conditions varied depending on the camp or prison, and most places were insufferable. Food, clothing, and blanket allotments barely kept the jailed alive at San Vittore prison in Milan. At Fossoli, in northeastern Italy, a transit camp in which the novelist Primo Levi was confined, murder and torture became common (see Levi's *Survival in Auschwitz,* also in *WLAIT 7: Italian Literature and Its Times*). Prisoners grew desperate; some committed suicide.

By December 1943 the phase of mass arrests had ended, and a new phase, focused on individual manhunts, began. Nazis and their Fascist partners seized Jews on the run or in hiding. Mussolini's breakaway republic, the Republic of Salò, had recently ordered the arrest of all Jews and the confiscation of their property, but to limited effect, since many had already emigrated, converted, or fled into hiding, and the ones easily caught had already been rounded up and deported. Nevertheless, Italians of Jewish descent became newly vulnerable, which sheds additional light on the nervousness that grips the protagonist in Morante's *History*. Excluded from arrest were Jews older than 70, Jews who were gravely ill, children of mixed marriages, and Jews who were married to non-Jews; still, the anxiety remained.

In Rome after close to eight months of anguish and terror, the city's Jews found relief: on June 5, 1944, the Allies, along with 5,000 Italian troops, took Rome; they would go on to seize more of central and northern Italy in the coming months. But the Germans held on to Trieste, and the transports bound for extermination from the nearby San Sabba camp continued, a final one leaving January 11, 1945.

Meanwhile, in the fall of 1944, the Nazi empire had started to crumble, which led to the liberation of many camps, including Auschwitz, where most of the Italian Jews (5,951 out of 6,746) had been sent (Sarfatti, p. 15). The few hundred survivors headed home to Italy to reunite with loved ones. The Italian Jews in hiding emerged to welcome back the death-camp survivors. But the community's problems were far from over. Many Italian Jews returned to find their homes destroyed, looted, or occupied by refugees. The luckiest landed jobs or resumed their former occupations. Moving to rectify official wrongs, Italy's postwar government abrogated the anti-Semitic laws, and enacted new laws to ensure the civil rights of Jews. Jewish educators regained their positions in schools; synagogues reopened; religious services resumed; and people mourned.

A memorial plaque at Portico d' Ottavia (the archway at one end of the Jewish ghetto) in Rome recalls Nazi Germany's round-up of October 16, 1943, and other Italian Jews who fell victim to atrocities in the Nazi death camps.

> Here on October 16th began the ruthless hunt for the Jews and two thousand ninety one Roman citizens were sent to a cruel death in the Nazi extermination camps, where they were joined by another six thousand Italians, victims of infamous racial hatred. The few who escaped the slaughter, the many who sympathize invoke love and peace from humanity and invoke pardon and hope from God.
>
> (SIDIC Roma)

Later estimates place the total number of Jews deported from Italy to the death camps at close to 6,800 (Picciotto Fargion in Cooperman and Garvin, p. 454). Nearly 6,000 of them perished in the camps. Another 300 or so died in Italy from massacres, murders, and similar causes. Altogether the war killed roughly one fifth of Italian Jewry, and of the four fifths that survived, many emerged alive but "physically and spiritually broken" (Guttman, p. 726).

The Novel in Focus

Plot overview. *History* unfolds in eight chapters, the first serving as an introduction and each of the rest coinciding with a year—from 1941 to 1947. At the start of each chapter is a timeline of global events, and all eight are followed by a postscript that is a timeline of events from 1948 to new wars transpiring in 1967. Before the chapters are a few literary excerpts—a few lines of poetry, prose, and scripture—that introduce the novel's focus on victims in human history (the poor, the sick, women, children, the illiterate). The first excerpt is a line taken from Peruvian poet César Vallejo: "Por el analfabeto a quien escribo [For the illiterate to whom I write]" (Morante, *History*, p. ix). Scattered through the novel are other such excerpts—nursery rhymes of deported Jewish children, a

verse by the Russian poet Marina Cvetaeva, another by the Spanish poet Miguel Hernández. The novel ends with a quote from Gramsci's **Letters from Prison** (also in *WLAIT 7: Italian Literature and Its Times*). The excerpt is an anonymous message taken from a prison wall: "All the seeds failed except one. / I don't know what it is, but it is / probably a flower and not a weed (Prisoner no. 7047 in the Penitentiary of Turin)" (*History*, p. 557).

RACE AND RAPE IN WORLD WAR II

~

Nazi Germany linked Aryans to male strength and dominance, Jews to women and weakness. The stronger group was meant to conquer the weaker, a mindset that made rape a fitting tool for Aryan men seeking to establish themselves as the master race. In the words of one historian, "it was perfectly logical within the framework of fascism that rape would be employed by the German soldier as he strove to prove himself a worthy Superman" (Brownmiller, p. 49). But in truth soldiers on all sides committed rape during the war, German soldiers in the various countries they invaded, Russian soldiers in Germany, Japanese soldiers in China (the Rape of Nanjing), Moroccan soldiers in Italy, and other Allied soldiers elsewhere. The Russians assaulted German women at the war's end, ravaging them because of their nationality, their ties to the male enemy, and their womanhood, factors that prompted many of the random rapes committed in Europe and Asia during the war. In Italy, the Moroccans behaved as they wished with the local population, the commonly ignored victims of war, the subjects of Morante's *History*. Seventeen years later, Vittorio de Sica made this last travesty the subject of his film *Two Women* (1960), about a mother and her virgin daughter who survive the war only to be gang-raped by some of the Moroccan soldiers in Italy. In real life, such incidents went unpunished. The war crimes tribunal at Nuremburg failed to prosecute Nazi rapists, and no tribunals were ever held to expose and condemn Allied rapists. There was not even an effort to publicly document sexual atrocities against women in the war, which only confirms Morante's point—that mainstream history (or *his-story*) fails to tell either *her-story* or the story of other disempowered parts of local populations.

Plot summary. The story proper begins with an epigraph:

> One January afternoon in the year 1941
> a German soldier was out walking

in the San Lorenzo district of Rome.
He knew precisely 4 words of Italian
And of the world he knew little or nothing.
His first name was Gunther.
His surname is unknown.

(*History*, p. 11)

As he wanders the San Lorenzo district, this unknown German soldier comes upon a 37-year-old widow, Ida Ramundo, whom he rapes. Gunther is portrayed not as malicious but as a desperate, sensitive youth "gripped by a ghastly, lonely melancholy, proof of his still adolescent character" (*History*, p. 15). A victim himself of especially the war, he soon dies prematurely in an air strike.

Ida's story continues. She is a woman of no exceptional intelligence or beauty with a "rather undernourished body, shapeless, the bosom withered, [and] the lower part awkwardly fattened" (*History*, pp. 17-18). A schoolteacher and the widow of Alfio Mancuso, Ida has a son, Nino. Nino is a happy, thoughtless, rebellious sort, who switches roles through the novel: from anarchist, to Fascist, partisan, and lastly *contrabbandiere* (smuggler) for the American soldiers. Ida herself is the only child of Giuseppe Ramundo and Nora Almagià, a Jewish woman from a lower-middle-class family, who made her husband and daughter swear not to divulge the secret of her "obscure *racial* background" (*History*, p. 19). In 1938, when Italy "intoned the official chorus of anti-Semitic propaganda," Nora, a widow by now, feels threatened by the order to report to the census takers and "declare publicly her fatal secret" (*History*, p. 40). She resolves to leave Cosenza, her hometown, for Palestine, "the only place where she could be received, as a fugitive Jew" (*History*, p. 43). One day in a delirious state, garbed in nothing but Giuseppe's old cloak, she heads for the sea and a few days later is found there—drowned. The account of her death includes a list of the Italian racial laws promulgated in the autumn of 1938. It becomes clear that the mother has transmitted her anxiety over her Jewish descent to Ida, who considers herself Jewish, despite her mixed blood. She worries whether she and Nino will qualify as Aryans.

In "1941" and "1942," Ida becomes pregnant as a consequence of the rape and gives birth to another son, Useppe, who has epilepsy. She survives the shame of the other schoolteachers discovering the secret of her rape, but her anxieties mount. Her fear over the possible return of the rapist—"she would go into the hall and listen, her ear to the door, afraid of hearing again that firm tread which had remained into her ears"—builds on her anxiousness over her Jewish descent (*History*, p. 72). In the midst of all this personal stress, Rome's Jewish ghetto, in which Ida does not live, assumes new importance: "almost everyday, with the pretext of having to buy some little article, without any motivation, Ida would set off for the Jewish quarter" (*History*, p. 81). Another factor that gains importance is the support she receives from female relationships. One summer afternoon Ida meets Ezeckiel, a Jewish midwife. At summer's end, when labor pains strike, Ida rushes to Ezeckiel's house where she gives birth to "a little man . . . so small he could fit comfortably into the midwife's two hands" (*History*, p. 82).

In the next chapter, "1943," the official history of the Second World War intersects more directly with the protagonists' personal stories. Still following Ida's daily comings and goings, the narrative describes how she manages to survive wartime hardships, from hunger and homelessness, to the air strikes over Rome. Also covered are the drama of incoming *sfollati* (refugees) and the deportation of the Jews to Germany. When an air raid leaves Ida homeless, she escapes to a refugee shelter at Pietralata, where she keeps to herself. On top of all her other misfortunes, she suffers an almost impossible relationship with her teenage son, Nino, who laughs at all the fear around him and cares little about the possible loss of the family property. Afraid that people in the shelter might find out she is Jewish, Ida decides to return to one of the vacant apartments in the ghetto, but then remembers that it has been emptied of people. What follows is one of the most emotional scenes in the novel. At the Tiburtino train station, Ida and her son Useppe watch the Jews embark onto the cars headed to the Auschwitz extermination camp, amidst all the disorder created by "babies' cries," "meaningless mumbles," and "ritual chanting" (*History*, p. 209).

In "1944," a 16-year-old named Carlo Vivaldi (who later turns out to be a Jew named Davide Segre) mysteriously appears at the Pietralata refugee center. Thereafter, the novel interweaves his personal saga into Ida's story. Also the novel fuses into the story the impact of the war on unsuspecting animals, from the little dog, Blitz, whose death accompanies the loss of Ida's house, to some canaries, a cat named Rossella, and another dog, an affectionate companion to Useppe named Bella.

During the final months of German occupation, the situation deteriorates and decay is apparent everywhere: in Rome where "beggars and refugees camped on the steps of the churches or below the Pope's palaces" and also at Pietralata (*History*, p. 277). Driven by a "daily imperative—find food for Useppe"—Ida becomes insensitive to outside happenings and loses any sense of shame and fear (*History*, p. 279). One morning, her heart pounding wildly, she steals some flour from a German truck packed with food.

A short chapter, "1945," explains how the Nazi genocide intensifies in Italy as the war winds down. Mussolini is caught while trying to escape in disguise as a German, and is shot to death near the Italian border. In the fall of the same year, a small remnant of surviving Jews returns from the concentration camps and Ida is a witness to the first horrifying accounts from Auschwitz.

In the postwar chapters, "1946" and "1947," the contrast between daily life and the grand sweep of history gives way to the general drama of existence and the extreme solitude prompted by the characters' separate tragedies. Without divulging anything about the hard times ahead, these chapters start happily enough: Ida and Useppe move into a new house close to Ida's school, which has announced its reopening. Digressing to focus on Davide Segre, *History* reveals the fate of his family members, who were deported in 1943 and died because of illness or extermination in the gas chambers at Auschwitz. While still in high school, Davide started to isolate himself from them and take long trips, wandering Italy like a penniless gypsy. He never finished school and refused to be sent "across the ocean like other Jewish youngsters," instead remaining in Italy and spreading propaganda for some militant anarchist (*History*, p. 348). After being caught by the Nazis, Davide renounced all political activity and found a job as an unskilled worker in a factory in the North where he met Ida's son, Nino. Davide, it becomes clear, had a combative relationship with his family, whom he regarded with contempt because of their acceptance of Fascism "since they were bourgeois" (*History*, p. 348). Now, in the postwar years, he responds to the violence perpetrated on them by committing an act of violence himself: the murder of a German soldier. His internal conflicts intensify and he begins using drugs. The promising beginning of postwar life is completely shattered by further developments: Useppe suffers from increasingly frequent epileptic attacks, and Nino dies in a truck accident. The tragic death of her elder son comes as a shock to Ida; that day "she couldn't scream, she had become mute [and] felt a lacerating sensation in the vagina" (*History*, p. 394). Only Useppe pushes her onward, giving her a reason to live.

The sense of tragedy continues into the final chapter, "19—," the dashes suggesting the mostly unrelieved repetition of wars and other destruction. One day, in a meeting at school, Ida is overcome by an unbearable sense of sickness and an urge to rush home to her six-year-old son. There, to her horror, in the dark little entrance, she discovers Useppe's dead body "arms flung out, as always in his falls" (*History*, p. 546). Refusing to comprehend the truth, Ida attempts to shout, but stops herself, thinking, "If I shout, they'll hear me, and they'll come to take him away from me"; instead she runs "wildly around her small home as the scenes of the human story (History) also [revolve]," perceiving them "as the multiple coils of an interminable murder. . . . And today the last to be murdered was her little bastard Useppe" (*History*, p. 546). At this point, the broken woman descends into mental illness, moves to a hospital, and dies an ordinary, unremarkable death on December 11, 1956, at the age of 53.

Gender and race discrimination. Morante's novel begins with Ida's rape and the account of her mother's life and tragic death. The mother and daughter are members of two marginalized groups: they are women and they are Italians of Jewish extraction. Though Morante's novel deals with more than female characters, it shows them to be "exploited and oppressed as *women*" (Boscagli, p. 169). When for the first time Useppe reads some magazines at an *edicola* (newsstand), he spots the photos of several dead partisans, which include a woman. Unlike the photos of the hanged men, which bear the inscription "Partisan," the photo featuring the woman lacks any identification. The photo furthermore shows her to be the victim of an atrocity that reduces her to the level of a slaughtered animal: "And all were males, except for a single girl . . . who had no sign and, unlike the others, was not hanged by a rope, but with a butcher's hook through her throat" (*History*, p. 315). In another incident, some Germans in search of anti-Fascist Partisans violate another mother-daughter pair. Denying any knowledge of where the partisans are, the women are forced into revealing the hiding place, then brutally raped and killed: "A couple of days later, some country people found the bodies of Mariulina and her mother massacred by bullets, shattered even in the vagina, with knife-stabs or bayonet wounds in the face, on the breasts, everywhere" (*History*, p. 263). Such savagery can be linked to what the women represented. In the eyes of the German soldiers, they likely symbolized Italy—an Italy that had betrayed Germany—and, *because they were women,* served as easy targets for vengeance and frustration. Ida herself is a target: the German soldier Gunther "rape[s] her with rage as if he wanted to murder her" (*History,* p. 59).

Ida's pain and suffering take on a new dimension with the passage of the racial laws. Because her mother baptized her into the Catholic religion, Ida manages to retain her job as a schoolteacher. Yet she is drawn toward her Jewish heritage. The more Ida becomes terrified about and obsessed with her ancestry, the more she feels attracted to the Jewish ghetto as a "nurturing and maternal space" (Re, p. 364). Meanwhile, she moves through larger Italian society (which history shows to have been rife with anti-Semitic political cartoons and remarks about Jews polluting Italy). There results an internal conflict in Ida, the agony of which is depicted in the scene featuring the deportation of Jews from Rome to Auschwitz. Accompanied by Useppe, she arrives at the train station, where the desperate cries from inside the cattle-cars take her mind back to her lost childhood innocence: "All this wretched human sound from the cars caught her in a heart-rending sweetness, because of a constant memory that didn't return to her from known time, but from some other channel: from the same place as her father's little Calabrian songs that had lulled her, or the anonymous poem of the previous night, or the little kisses that whispered *carina, carina* to her" (*History,* p. 209). She identifies with the victims even though she is not fully Jewish, a reaction that emerges as a redeeming human trait amidst all the social savagery. But this factor is not strong enough to withstand the savagery visited upon her, mostly because of gender and racial status. Violated because she is a woman, in danger of violation because she is born of a Jew, she escapes the tragic fate of the Auschwitz-bound cargo only literally. A certificate of baptism may have saved her from the cattle-cars, but circumstances conspire to wound her fatally nonetheless. The brutality inflicted on Ida because of the rape, compounded by the terror she endures because of anti-Semitism, leave her with only a fragile hold on sanity in postwar Italy. Conditions improve, but for her, as for many in real life, it is "impossible to cancel the memory of the evil years, impossible to redress the broken spirits" (Roth, p. 552). So Useppe's end drives her to a breakdown and death, one not written up in mainstream histories but statistically significant, argues the novel, nonetheless.

Sources and literary context. Italian writers of the 1970s gravitated to a traditional type of literature that resembled neo-realism, which attempted to represent social reality in a specifically Italian way. Within this climate, Morante's novel showed a return to simple storytelling in chronological order and to representational fiction. By choosing what many regarded as an outdated focus of interest for literature (the Second World War and its aftermath) Morante demonstrated not only her unconventional approach to literature, but also her ideological independence.

The influence of mainstream historical accounts on Morante's novel is obvious. Of no less importance are the writings of America's 1950s beat movement, which generated underground works that Morante read. Her friendship with the young American painter Bill Morrow no doubt also influenced her sensitivity to a spirit of uneasiness and rebellion, which then affected her development of the young characters in her novel. Finally, Morante was a passionate reader of the French writer Simone Weil's *Notes,* concerning death, war, and human relationships; her novel tackles these same issues in ways that recall Weil's writing.

Behind *History* is the legacy of the historical novel in Italian, beginning with Alessandro Manzoni's **The Betrothed** (also in *WLAIT 7: Italian Literature and Its Times*). Despite numerous differences, the two novels converge in their strategy of using everyday people as protagonists in the sweep of history. Manzoni's interest was in the portrayal of innocent victims of history and in the interplay between power and oppression. Morante seized upon this interplay and developed those elements she saw as essential: the experience, the body, the unconscious, and the everyday event. Morante too shows more marked interest in the victimization of women among the oppressed.

The 1970s gave rise to vigorous feminist activity in Italy as elsewhere in the West. In the feminist piece *Sputiamo su Hegel* (1971; Let's Spit on Hegel), Carla Lonzi spoke of the importance of elaborating on a culture of difference between men and women and of re-evaluating the female essence. The task was to create another history and an alternative culture different from the one imposed by patriarchal society. In keeping with this aim, one of Morante's goals was to create a parallel account to official history, an alternative that features ordinary people. She thus begins each chapter with a brief account of global events, contrasting history as men have conceived it with the story of a woman and her small struggle for survival. Morante furthermore set out to portray women in a way that would give them central roles and would reveal female truths, joining an array of new works giving voice to female views by women writers: Natalia Ginzburg (*You Never Must Ask Me, Family Sayings, The Little Virtues*); Oriana Fallaci (*Interview with History, A Man*); Dacia Maraini (*The Age of Malaise, Woman at War*); Rosetta Loy (*The Dust Roads of Monferrato*); and Gina Lagorio (*Tosca's Cats*).

Finally, Morante's *History* includes autobiographical elements. During the German occupation, the growing anti-Fascist reputation of Morante's husband, Alberto Moravia, caused the endangered couple to flee their Roman apartment and seek refuge among remote farming villagers in the mountains south of Rome. There Morante observed the impact of the war and may have first resolved to write an account of how history affects ordinary people struggling to survive. Also Morante's own Jewish legacy, inherited from her mother, influenced the characterization. Ida's inner conflict over her Jewish heritage recalls Morante's own internal struggles in relation to her mother's Judaism.

Events in History at the Time the Novel Was Written

Italian feminism in the 1970s. Postwar economic development saw significant changes in social roles and family life. Especially affected was the role of women, who began to enter the work force in larger numbers. Other factors, such as a delay in the age of women at marriage, and the downsizing of the Italian family contributed to the growth of a postwar Italian women's movement.

Two main trends distinguished the modern-day women's movement in Italy: individual self-awareness and a larger feminist struggle featuring groups of women who organized committees and mounted, for example, a campaign to claim wages for housework. The first trend concerned itself with a need for self-definition. Women were no longer willing to define themselves according to the expectations and perceptions of a man. Instead such women insisted on pursuing an independent variety of self-construction. DEMAU ("demystification of authority"), the first official feminist group in Italy, struggled against the authoritarian structure of society, trying to find an alternative to the patriarchal system. The same urge to unveil the myths perpetuated by men animated the Rivolta Femminile (Feminine Revolt) founded in 1970 in Rome. The Italian feminists spoke of the need for women to change their patterns of behavior and of the role of language and literature in shaping a woman's consciousness. Carla Lonzi (1931-82), one of the first Italian feminists, advocated re-education of society by adopting a new concept of sexual difference, wherein women would no longer be identified in relation to men. In Morante's *History,* the absence of such a separate identity is what leaves Ida so ill-equipped to deal with her world. She teaches and raises children, filling the sanctioned maternal role, and once childless, lacking a sufficient sense of herself, she crumbles.

By the writing of the novel, the status of the Italian woman had begun undergoing significant change, thanks in no small part to the modern feminist movement. Encouraged by Lonzi and other feminists, women demanded equality of treatment in education and by the law, as well as full access to abortion and contraception. In 1970 divorce was legalized and, in 1975, the new Family Law established gender equality, asserting that a husband has no more rights than his wife, maintaining that within a marriage, the man and the woman have the same rights and obligations.

Publication and reception. The first 100,000 copies of *History* flew off bookstore shelves. By year's end, the novel had sold an astonishing 465,000 copies. Morante had insisted on a very low price for the book, thereby making it accessible to the ordinary people it features, and, of course, this may have had something to do with the numerous sales. But the first reviews were unanimously positive too. Then a damning letter appeared in *Il Manifesto,* a leftist newspaper. Written by Nanni Balestrini, Elisabetta Rasy, Letizia Paolozzi, and Umberto Silva, the letter condemned *History* for its lack of political commitment and denounced the resignation and despair that coursed through the novel. Morante was accused of failing to represent the social class struggle and of promoting a mindset that envisions humble folk as irredeemably subordinated to and defeated by the powerful. The critics also complained that the novel lacked irony; rage and hatred toward the oppressors were missing, they said. Morante's characters observed injustice but never denounced it, resigning themselves to it.

The attacks went a step further when Natalia Ginzburg was attacked for writing an overly favorable review of *History* in which she called the novel "il più bel romanzo di questo secolo" [the most beautiful novel of the century] comparing it to the great novels of the nineteenth century (Ginzburg in Bernabò, p. 91). This praise led to more criticism. Morante was accused of trying to restore the classical novel, which promoted a repetition of the existing social order rather than revolutionary change.

To weigh this response, it is important to recall that 1974 was a year in which the Italian left (*la sinistra rivoluzionaria*) influenced various dimensions of life, including culture. In such an atmosphere, it is hardly surprising that some reviewers had such strong objections to the novel. Morante certainly could respond by pointing to the novel's focus on the larger patterns of history and their intersection with individual lives. Clearly her purpose was to expose rather than denounce: "my novel 'History' wants to be an accusation against all the fascisms of the world. And, nevertheless, an urgent and desperate question, addressed to everyone for a possibly common awakening" (Morante in Lucente, p. 240).

—Nicoleta Ghisas

For More Information

Bernabò, G. *Come leggere* La storia *di Elsa Morante*. Milan: Mursia, 1988.

Boscagli, Maurizia. "Brushing against the Grain: Elsa Morante and the *Jetztzeit* of Marginal History." In *Gendering Italian Fiction*. Ed. Maria Marotti and Gabriella Brooke. Madison, N.J.: Fairleigh Dickinson University Press, 1999.

Bosworth, R. J. B. *Mussolini*. London: Arnold, 2002.

Brownmiller, Susan. *Against Our Will: Men, Women and Rape*. New York: Simon and Schuster, 1975.

Cooperman, Bernard D., and Barbara Garvin. *The Jews of Italy: Memory and Identity*. Bethesda: University Press of Maryland, 2000.

De Felice. "Hunting down the Jews." In *Fascism, Antifascism, and the Resistance in Italy*. Lanham: Rowman and Littlefield, 2004.

Guttman, Israel. *Encyclopedia of the Holocaust*. Vol. 2. New York: Macmillan, 1990.

Hainsworth, Peter, and David Robey, eds. *The Oxford Companion to Italian Literature*. Oxford: Oxford University Press, 2002.

Lucente, Gregory L. "Scrivere o fare . . . o altro: Social Commitment and Ideologies of Representation in the Debates over Lampedusa's *Il Gattorpardo* and Morante's *La Storia*." *Italica* 61 (autumn 1984): 220-251.

Morante, Elsa. *History: A Novel*. Trans. William Weaver. New York: Alfred A. Knopf, 1977.

Re, Lucia. "Utopian Longing and the Constraints of Racial and Sexual Difference in Elsa Morante's *La storia*." *Italica* 70 (1993): 361-75.

Roth, Cecil. *The History of the Jews of Italy*. Philadelphia: Jewish Publication Society of America, 1946.

Sarfatti, Michele, ed. *Il ritorno alla vita: vicende e diritti degli ebrei in Italia dopo la seconda guerra mondiale*. Firenze: Giuntina, 1998.

SIDIC Roma. "The Jews in Italy—Before and after the World War." Service International del Documentation Judéo-Chrétienne. http://www.sidic.org/english/dossier/ghettojewishit.htm.

Yahil, Leni. *The Holocaust: The Fate of European Jewry*. New York: Oxford University Press, 1987.

History as the
Story of Liberty

by
Benedetto Croce

Benedetto Croce (1866-1952) was born into a family of wealthy landowners in Pescasseroli in the Abruzzi region of central Italy. He attended a Catholic boarding school in his youth, then, at age 17, lost his parents and his younger sister, who died in an earthquake in which he himself was injured. Afterward Croce moved to Rome to live with his father's cousin, the noted thinker and political leader Silvio Spaventa, through whom he met other major thinkers, including the philosopher Antonio Labriola. Croce briefly studied law, then abandoned it to dabble in literature and local history. But by 1893 he was ready to address the current philosophical controversies concerning the status of history as a form of knowledge. He gained European renown in 1902 for his *Aesthetic as Science of Expression and General Linguistic* (*Estetica come scienza dell'espressione e linguistica generale*), which offers a conception of creativity in language with grandiose implications for the place of humans in an ever-new world. From the *Aesthetic* he went on to produce, in 1908, the twin works *Logic as the Science of the Pure Concept*, on the theoretical side of human activity, and *Philosophy of the Practical: Economic and Ethic*, on the practical side.

When he published *History as the Story of Liberty*, Croce was one of the world's best-known intellectuals. His bi-monthly review *La critica* (*Critique*), which appeared for more than four decades after its inception in 1903, was among the most respected journals of its kind ever to be published in the Western world. Based in Naples, independently wealthy, remarkably pro-

> ## THE LITERARY WORK
>
> An extended essay pertaining to Western politics, history, and culture; published in Italian (as *La storia come pensiero e come azione*, or History as Thought and Action) in 1938, in English in 1941.
>
> ## SYNOPSIS
>
> Addressing cultural problems in Italy and the West more generally, Croce argues that a new understanding of the human relationship with history can revitalize liberal democracy.

lific, Croce became known especially for his contributions to aesthetics, literary criticism, and the philosophy of history.

With Giovanni Gentile (1875-1944) as his junior partner, Croce embarked on a broad program of cultural renewal prior to the First World War. The advent of the Fascist regime in the 1920s led each of the two thinkers to devote greater attention to politics. But the result was a dramatic split. Gentile became the most significant European intellectual to play a central role in fascism; Croce, perhaps the world's best-known anti-Fascist.

Events in History at the
Time of the Essay

The emergence of the fascist challenge. Appearing at the height of the fascist period in Italy,

Benedetto Croce

Croce's essay responds to both fascist totalitarianism and the wider challenge bound up with the making of the modern, secular society. These two forces, the specific and the broader challenge, seemed related: to many, the fascist reaction against liberal democracy suggested some deeper crisis within Western culture, though the relationship was and remains difficult to pin down.

Fascism was an Italian invention; the term itself was coined only in 1919 with the emergence of the first Fascist movement, led by Benito Mussolini (1883-1945). Growing out of Italy's experience of World War I, Fascism reacted against the liberal regime that had emerged from the Italian Risorgimento, the movement for unification and independence that produced the new Kingdom of Italy in 1861. Although by some reckonings the new Italy was on its way to modern democracy by the first decade of the twentieth century, critics worried. They found Italy's parliamentary government corrupting and ineffectual, incapable of realizing the promise of national renewal bound up with the Risorgimento itself. In light of Italy's wartime experience, many of the disaffected concluded that the old liberal ruling class was exhausted—but also that Italy was now poised to do better. Fascism was to provide a post-liberal alternative that would not only realize Italy's potential but also offer a new direction for the modern world.

Modern uncertainties and Croce's wider cultural program. During the first decade of the century, before the term *fascism* had even been coined, Croce and Gentile embarked on a broad program of cultural diagnosis and prescription, seeking to specify human possibilities and priorities in light of changing modern conditions. In the 1880s, the German philosopher Friedrich Nietzsche proclaimed the death of God, giving extreme expression to the notion that, for better or worse, Western culture would have to do without the religious underpinnings that had long sustained it. Raised a Catholic, Croce had begun losing religious faith in his late teens. Looking back years later, he observed that it had been the task of his generation to address explicitly the challenge that had gradually arisen over the past several centuries and translate the wisdom embodied in traditional religion into purely secular terms. The challenge was not so much to destroy the old, which was disintegrating on its own, but to construct anew, while salvaging as much of the old as possible. There was thus a need to translate religious categories like faith, prayer, grace, and immortality into modern secular terms. At the same time, Croce, like Nietzsche, felt that it was not only belief in a transcendent God or revealed religion that was falling away. There seemed nothing higher, nothing transcendent; thus there was no natural law specifying "values" or "rights" or "standards." Philosophy was no replacement; it could not establish cultural foundations or disclose (as G. W. F. Hegel and Karl Marx had claimed to do) the shape, direction, and goal of history.

Many believed that science offered the essential alternative to religion and philosophy. In science, they saw the key to understanding the world and humanity's place in it. Indeed, confidence in science reached its peak when positivism, the doctrine that only sense perceptions provide the basis for genuine knowledge, came into vogue during the last decades of the nineteenth century. But Croce was central to a generation coming of age in the 1890s and reacting against, or at least questioning, the cultural role of science, and especially the applicability of the natural sciences to the human world. He insisted that science, though essential in its sphere, merely offers rough-and-ready generalizations about particular, historically specific instances, in response to questions human beings have asked. It does not serve as a key to the way things really are, apart from human needs and purposes. Whatever we might learn through study of the natural world, science was being over-sold; it could not provide a cultural core.

Although he did some systematic philosophy during the first decade of the century, Croce was not a philosophical system-builder. Indeed, he sought to show why there could be no systematic philosophy above and beyond history, no set or a priori rules. He was a philosopher of openness, of freedom, of the human creativity that, he insisted, is first expressed in language itself. The flip side of any systematic philosophy was, for Croce, the endless novelty and incompleteness of the world, which is forever coming to be over time, through history. History results from free creative human response to what the world has become so far, which is itself the result of previous creative human response. So what the world becomes depends on our collective response at every moment. Though such responses may be self-serving, they may also stem from our ethical capacity, our care for the world. And we can orient ourselves for action by learning how the present world came to be through history. We can use our human abilities to arm ourselves with knowledge that prepares us to pursue potentially successful forms of action in the current moment. Although we lack overarching "values" or "principles" to guide us, we have, as humans, the capacity to judge, to understand, and to respond, based on the historically specific situations we endlessly face.

Croce, Gentile, and Fascism. The rise of Fascism forced Croce to think more explicitly about politics and led him to deepen his diagnosis and prescription. When the Fascist leader Benito Mussolini became Italian prime minister in October 1922, it was not immediately clear that a change of regime, replacing Italy's parliamentary democracy, was in the offing. Mussolini represented something new, to be sure. But perhaps it was simply the revitalization of the Italian governing class that many found necessary in light of the Italian war experience and the political uncertainty that followed the war. In the first years of Mussolini's government, before its direction was clear, Croce was among the many prominent Italians who adopted a wait-and-see attitude, based on a sense that the liberal political elite was exhausted—and that an alternative to Mussolini's rule might well prove worse. But Croce became a diehard opponent early in 1925, when it became clear that continued government by Mussolini meant the advent of a one-party dictatorship.

Meanwhile, Croce's long-time collaborator Gentile served as minister of education in Mussolini's first cabinet, then joined the Fascist Party in 1923. Gentile quickly emerged as a major Fascist ideologue and cultural power-broker, pushing for the creation of a totalitarian state, limitless in its aims, and propelled by constant mobilization and participation. Early in 1925, while forming the new Fascist National Cultural Institute, Gentile prepared a manifesto, signed by a number of Italian intellectuals, that portrayed Fascism as the political outcome of the best in contemporary Italian culture. Together with another liberal, Giovanni Amendola, Croce responded with an influential counter-manifesto disputing Gentile's claims. From then on, Croce would be central to anti-Fascism—and a bitter critic of his erstwhile partner Gentile.

Though Croce's opposition was obvious, the Fascist regime tolerated him to a degree (when typically it muzzled opponents; see *Letters from Prison*, also in *WLAIT 7: Italian Literature and Its Times*). Mussolini valued Croce as a national asset in light of his fame abroad. The one act of Fascist violence that Croce suffered, an invasion of his house by militants in 1926, provoked an international outcry. Still, although his relative freedom is striking, Croce was subject to constant police surveillance and occasional harassment. It was never clear what might befall him next.

Though the fascist regime was repressive and totalitarian in direction, its priorities evolved over time. Only during 1935-36, with the conquest of Abyssinia (Ethiopia), did it turn to overt imperialism. This venture prompted sanctions from the League of Nations. The sanctions, spearheaded by Britain and France, seemed hypocritical, even to many Italians who disliked Fascism; Britain and France, after all, were themselves major imperial powers. Among these Italians was Croce, who responded to a governmental appeal by donating his gold senatorial medal in support of the Italian cause.

But the conquest of Ethiopia was followed by further aggressiveness on the part of Mussolini's regime, including intervention in the Spanish Civil War (1936-39), on the side of the insurgent Nationalists, and ever-closer relations with Nazi Germany. After Mussolini began speaking of a Rome-Berlin axis in 1936, the two sides signed a military alliance early in 1939. Moreover, the Italian Fascist regime began adopting anti-Semitic measures for the first time in 1938. It was in this context, as Fascism came to seem ever more aggressive and brutal, that Croce wrote *History as the Story of Liberty*.

Croce's anti-Fascism. Croce continued to publish *La critica* throughout the Fascist period (1922-43), and he offered a number of books and articles with a clearly, if covertly, anti-Fascist thrust. His *A History of Italy, 1871-1915*, published in 1928, defended liberal Italy from Fascist slurs. Another one of his works, *The History of Europe in the Nineteenth Century*, published in 1932, offered a critical review of the rise, the seeming triumph, and the subsequent weakening of the liberal ideal. In closing, Croce called for liberal renewal while assuring readers that human freedom could not be extinguished. Each book enjoyed considerable commercial success in Italy.

GIOVANNI GENTILE AND THE TOTALITARIAN ALTERNATIVE

Gentile and Croce understood the modern cultural challenge in comparable terms, but Gentile felt it was possible to achieve a grandiose new mode of collective history-making by creating a totalitarian ethical state. To his way of thinking, as the state's reach became limitless, the human sense of responsibility could be nurtured and focused to enable everyone to participate. Gentile went so far as to insist that people are genuinely free *only* to the degree that they concentrate power in such a state, through which they can all act collectively. Everyone *must* participate, essentially all the time. The effort to actually create such a totalitarian state in Fascist Italy led to repressiveness, to merely superficial participation, and ultimately to defeat and ignominy.

Through sustained activity in a variety of interlocking roles, Croce became the key link within a web of exchange among anti-Fascists in and even outside Italy, including some who had gone into exile. His publications, and his ideas for post-Fascist renewal, served as rallying points. Croce, moreover, offered personal support and often generous but discreet financial help to friends and the friends of friends forced to make difficult choices under the repressive Fascist regime. In short, he was central to the moral community that sustained anti-Fascism during the long years of opposition and harassment.

With Fascist Italy facing military defeat during World War II, Croce was called upon to play a more specific political role, even to help mediate between the emerging post-Fascist Italy and the victorious allies. In that context, he sometimes seemed to suggest that Fascism had been a mere "parenthesis," an interlude stemming from a spiritual crisis that was by no means confined to Italy. In Croce's view, Italy's experience with liberal democracy had been reasonably successful; it followed that it would be possible, and sufficient, simply to reconnect with liberal traditions after the Fascist interlude. In making such arguments, Croce was at once seeking favorable treatment from the victors and denying the claim of more radical Italians that socio-economic revolution was necessary to create the conditions for genuine democracy in Italy.

But Croce had insisted again and again that a broader rethinking of the liberal tradition and modern political possibilities was essential. The problem was by no means specifically Italian; the challenge was not simply for Italy to catch up to the more successful democracies. Indispensable though it had been, the nineteenth-century liberal tradition had entailed limits and blind-spots. Croce in fact thought extending the vote to more people was progressive, and he explicitly criticized the fashionable disillusionment with parliamentary government. But he also observed that the lack of an adequate understanding of the underlying bases of liberal democracy made politics seem lackluster and unimaginative; there had followed a tendency to abandon rational approaches and reach for irrationalist and morbidly aestheticist ways to fill the apparent void. But now it was essential to gain a deeper understanding, to push beyond conventional notions of utility, individual rights, and *negative* freedom (or "freedom from") to an understanding of human freedom as positive and constructive, bound up with the human relationship to history.

The Essay in Focus

Contents summary. The title chosen for the English translation of Croce's essay, *History As the Story of Liberty*, plays up the work's anti-Fascist thrust, but is in fact taken from just one chapter. The original Italian title, *La storia come pensiero e come azione*, is easily rendered into English as "history as thought and action" and better conveys the overall thrust of the essay. Indeed, the phrase nicely sums up Croce's overall program for cultural renewal. Though his argument proceeds unsystematically, Croce sought to address the deepest cultural needs of the age as he explored the intersection of philosophy, history, and politics in this essay.

In this essay, as in earlier ones, Croce insists on a reversal of the conventional relationship between philosophy and history. In light of its historical nature, people get a handle on the world not through philosophy, as has so long been assumed, but through historical inquiry and understanding. Philosophy simply shows people how to understand and respond to history. However, because the world, through history, is constantly changing, we must often re-form such categories as materialism and democracy, or re-define such concepts as justice and utility, to come to terms with the fresh circumstances generated by history. His own philosophical categories, admits Croce, had grown from his encounter with the concrete problems of life and were subject to adjustment. Philosophy in the abstract is useless.

People need to understand their present world so they can better respond to it in action. But any present situation can only be understood by examining its genesis, how it came to be historically. (In other words, "history" can no longer be understood as the inquiry of detached, aloof scholars who objectively study the past, somehow for its own sake, shunning responsibility and struggle in the present.) Any inquiry that is genuinely historical, rather than mere antiquarianism, starts with a problem, some contemporary issue that leads the inquirer to ask how this or that present situation came to be.

So in opposition to the commonplace notion that history deals with the past *as opposed to* the present, Croce portrays historical inquiry as the key to present orientation. Even when focused on the distant past, history seeks the seeds of the next moment, the process that leads to the future, not the past on its own terms, taken as an end in itself. Thus, focusing on history does not tie us to the past, as we might first assume; it enables us to respond creatively to the present. Thus, Croce's insistence that writing history "is one way of getting rid of the weight of the past. . . . The writing of history liberates us from history" (Croce, *History as the Story of Liberty*, p. 44). To transcend Fascism, for example, it was necessary to understand how it had emerged, in light of inadequacies in the earlier liberal tradition. Mere moral rejection would not be sufficient.

But to feature this present-minded, moral-practical impetus for historical inquiry does not warrant reading present-day concerns into the past, maintains the essay. Nor does it warrant using history as a storehouse of examples to exemplify or dramatize some a priori or preconceived moral principle. Nor, finally, does it invite "party history," the serving of some political interest that turns history into mere propaganda. On the contrary, the need to act in response to the present leads to a genuine search to learn. Insofar as people inquire in this Crocean spirit, open to learning, they come up with a *true* historical account. Put differently, truth is what happens when people question the world in a certain spirit or frame of mind. Like the capacity for moral response, the capacity to search for truth, to be open to it, helps define existence.

This notion is especially hard to grasp because we tend to assume a "correspondence" theory of truth; that is, we assume that a historical account seeks to represent reality, the past as it actually happened. Croce denies the validity of any such notion in an endlessly historical world; indeed, the conventional notion of historical truth is incoherent. For one thing, the meaning of the past is constantly changing as ever more happens and the world grows. But even supposing the aim is to convey the actual experience of those living through this or that, regardless of outcomes, truth would require an inconceivable totality.

In making this argument in *History as the Story of Liberty*, Croce was relying on a point he had first made, in dramatic fashion, in a 1912 article attacking the Russian writer Leo Tolstoy's ideal of a "universal history." In his famed novel *War and Peace* (1869), Tolstoy had imagined such a total history, encompassing the lived experience of every participant in a great event. He even suggested that conventional historical accounts, being selective, amount to little more than myths. In response, Croce admitted that in some of our moods we think we would like completeness, the whole historical record laid out to us. But can we even conceive of having all our historical questions answered? When we try, we realize that there could be no end, that every answer gives rise to a new question. Skeptics might argue that unless people know everything, they know nothing. But in his 1912 article, Croce insists that they already have what they need; it is not the infinite that expands every time we touch it, but rather the finite, the concrete that is the base of our existence and the point of departure for our actions. Even if infinity or completeness was somehow within our grasp, we would still concentrate on the particular finite strand that responds to an active, living problem—and forget the rest.

On this basis, Croce sought to be reassuring in *History as the Story of Liberty*. If we are uneasy about the incompleteness and finite nature of historical understanding, it is only because we assume there is some historical "thing in itself," a fixed, completed past reality that we seek to render once and for all. In the ever-growing human world that we inhabit, there is no such thing, but that is not what we need to understand in any case. It is important to know that we seek not to reconstruct past reality, but merely to construct a *history*, some particular, finite connection or process, which affords the mode of understanding we need for response to the present. In doing so, we participate in the ongoing reconstruction of the world as it continues to develop in some finite, particular way. Insofar as we understand that we construct our histories in order to deal with some present problem, says Croce, we free ourselves from the fallacy that history is a copy or imitation of reality (*Story of Liberty*, p. 133).

By providing an orientation, historical understanding prepares us for action, but Croce reminds us that it cannot *determine* action, in the sense of specifying what people are to do, thereby relieving them of making an ethical decision (*Story of Liberty*, pp. 187-88). On the other hand, we can make such a decision rational by basing it on historical understanding.

History is "the story of liberty" because it is generated by free, creative human response to whatever has resulted from prior free, creative human response. So liberty is not merely a goal of history, Croce insisted against Hegel, but is itself the creator of history—and so the subject of every history. What people do as free human beings, when responding in their ethical mode, is overcome obstacles to free creativity and so liberate themselves to create, to go on building the world. Whether reacting against fascist censorship or economic exploitation, people are forever seeking to establish the political, social, and even economic conditions for more intense liberty.

Croce's theme of "history as action" means not only that what we do has history-making implications. To *experience* the history-making weight of what we do, recognizing that what will matter is not our subjective experience but what becomes of what we do, reinforces the ethical concern that both stimulates us to act and opens us to a true understanding of the genesis of some present situation. To experience what we do as history-making thus carries us beyond any premium on being authentic or making a personal gesture.

Not that Croce denied subjective experience; indeed, he suggested that life in this fundamentally historical world entails ever higher and more complex forms of human suffering. But rather than dwell on personal anxiety, we should embrace the vocation that seems best to suit us, do what we take to be our duty, and look to the consequences. And though some of Croce's characterizations seem to deny the masses any genuinely historical role, he insisted that we are all historical actors caught up in the same overall process, making some small contribution, as the next moment results from the interaction of all we do.

As Croce saw it, the contemporary fascists, Nazis, and communists had fundamentally misconstrued the relationship between history-making and the political sphere. In a sense, in fact, they were fleeing from the freedom and attendant responsibility that had opened up in the modern world. Croce attacked the exaltation of the state in Fascist Italy, the accent on race in Nazi Germany, and the communist insistence on what he viewed as an impossible equality. Race, he maintained, is not fixed, but historical. It offers, at best, rough classification as an aid to memory, but no basis for judgment according to value. The Nazi insistence on racial determinism denied both human freedom and the fundamental commonality of humanity.

Responding to the excesses of totalitarianism, Croce champions a new kind of liberalism, one that requires limits, humility, pluralism—and openness to the input of all individuals, even those who may fail to conform to abstract ideals of freedom, reason, or justice. Individuals need not be specially mobilized, educated, or liberated before their input counts. Though some will be more active and influential than others, all must have access, the opportunity to participate, including freedom of speech and assembly. In the same way, a plurality of political parties best serves collective history-making by enabling varied points of view to be expressed.

At the same time, Croce reacts against those anti-totalitarians who, he feels, are drawing the wrong lessons from the totalitarian challenge. The new liberalism does not require a restricted state or free-market economics; the reach of the state and the form of economic organization are empirical matters to be determined by the community, in light of historical circumstances. Indeed, Croce observes that "the absolutists of private enterprise are no less utopian than the absolutists of communism" (*Story of Liberty*, p. 244).

From within the new liberal framework, the essay explains, people must learn to operate on two levels simultaneously. They make individual commitments and act on the basis of them, seeking to influence others as they do so, but they need to recognize their limits as individuals at the same time. Indeed, they need to acknowledge that the agent, the maker of the world, is collective, encompassing everyone, and that individuals are only finite parts of it. To be sure, we all, says Croce, using the inclusive "we" that implicates himself too, sometimes imagine ourselves to be dictators of the world, putting everything aright, but in our deeper moments we recognize that though we seek to influence what happens as best we can, we would rather entrust the making of history to the interaction of all.

Croce recognized that there was something a little unnerving about the endlessly provisional world he was positing, but the challenge was precisely to conform ourselves to the dynamic nature of reality. It need not sadden us that we are constantly projected forward, that, once completed, even our finest works do not satisfy us. Though there could be no end to the struggle, let alone some utopian fulfillment, there was no warrant for despair, for loss of nerve, for generalized anxiety, for mere self-indulgence. A culture wound around "history as thought and action" affords people all they need to mesh in a positive, constructive way with the fundamentally historical world.

History, values, and personal decision. At one point in the essay Croce sought to clarify his own position by pointing out what he took to be the errors of the noted German thinkers Friedrich Meinecke and Ernst Troeltsch, with whom he had interacted periodically over the years. The two Germans worried that because we are caught up in history, we can only respond to historically specific situations on the basis of merely relative values, depending on who we are, when and where we live, and so forth. This meant, they assumed, that we are cut off from some higher, truer, stable realm of values, which we at best can glimpse, or apprehend in pale reflection.

Croce was denying any such higher realm—and thus any tension between values and history. There is nothing inadequate about being historical; we are not missing anything, are not cut off from anything, and we do not have to worry that ethical values change depending on who holds them. Thus Croce insisted, in response to Meinecke and Troeltsch, that to accept the fundamentally historical nature of the world does not undermine values but guarantees their inexhaustible vitality by making them concrete, embedded in history itself (*Story of Liberty*, pp. 83-84). Although we cannot pluck down val-

ues from on high, we reinvent justice, or the good, every time we respond morally to a new, historically specific situation. We do not *know* what to do, on the basis of some overarching value or principle, but we have the capacity to *decide* what to do. And we endlessly do so. In fact, if there is no one right way that can be specified in advance, the diverse individual moral responses of all human beings help carry the world to the next moment. Thus, Croce offers his humble, pluralistic mode of collective worldmaking as an alternative. He offers it first as an alternative to totalitarianism but also to other forms of thought and action that had already begun to tempt his contemporaries.

Especially in light of the disasters of the World War II era, traditionalists renewed the demand for what Croce saw as a nonexistent higher realm of values above history. Others agreed with Croce that there is no such realm but then assumed that we are left with nihilism, the conviction that nothing matters, that nothing can be known or communicated. Croce claimed to see beyond both such competing alternatives to a new, more hopeful orientation, based on the belief that we as individuals have the capacity to respond morally without absolute values. And insofar as our responses are guided by historical understanding of the situation to which we respond, we do not merely affirm our individual personalities but rather contribute to the ongoing making of the world in history. Herein lies the sense in which "history as thought and action" sums up Croce's cultural program. Historical understanding provides the orientation that gives our moral responses history-making weight.

Sources and literary context. As he began to grasp the terms of what seemed to be the cultural challenge facing society around the turn of the century, Croce identified especially with a predecessor from Naples, the literary historian Francesco De Sanctis (1817-1883). During a period in which Italians sought to forge a solid nation after Unification, De Sanctis had stressed the moral and civic import of cultural renewal. The committed humanistic culture championed by De Sanctis seemed to have been marginalized, almost lost altogether as the late nineteenth century progressed. Croce wanted to reconnect with De Sanctis and his mode of cultural leadership, though he understood that the challenge was now different—and deeper.

In his effort to conceive of the human situation without a transcendent or higher realm, Croce learned especially from an even earlier predecessor from Naples, Giambattista Vico (1668-1744), (see *The New Science of Giambattista Vico*, also in *WLAIT 7: Italian Literature and Its Times*). It was through Vico that Croce came to his understanding of the process through which the human world is built up over time as people continually respond creatively, in language, to a succession of novel situations. Because we have made it, said Vico, we can know the human, historical world as we cannot know the natural world, made by God, and which only God can truly know. Following Vico, Croce concluded that the knowability of the real is not a problem; thought is fully adequate to what the world is—and to what we are, to our place in the world. To be sure, our knowledge is provisional and finite; there can be no final grasp of the whole. But human knowledge is adequate to a world that is forever incomplete, a world endlessly coming to be through time, in history.

OUR COLLABORATION IN HISTORY

One learns from Croce that the world results from the sum of the actions of all who came before us, that we have fallen heir to their collective legacy. This sense of kinship stimulates each of us to do our part, to pick up and transform, through our own present action, the world bequeathed to us. As their collaborators, says Croce, we feel ourselves under obligation to use their legacy well.

Whoever opens his heart to the historical sensibility is no longer alone, but united with the life of the universe, brother and son and comrade of the spirits that formerly labored upon the earth and that live in the work that they completed, apostles and martyrs, ingenious creators of beauty and truth, decent and humble people who spread the balm of goodness and preserved human kindness; and to all of them he makes entreaty, and from them he derives support in his efforts and labors, and on their lap he aspires to rest, pouring his labor into theirs.

(Croce, "Antistoricismo," pp. 263-64; trans. D. Roberts)

Croce's early embrace of Vico decisively shaped his reading of the philosopher G. W. F. Hegel, whose thinking Croce first addressed in an essay published in 1907, and to whom he returned repeatedly throughout his career. As Croce saw it, Hegel had been on the right track in conceiving the world as historical, and even as a totality. But even as he understood the sig-

nificance of historical change up to a point, Hegel was still thinking in terms of stable essences, still supposing that the world has a structure and goal that human beings discover through historical experience. Croce, on the other hand, believed that we don't discover this structure; we *create* it. Although a kind of totality, resulting from all that has been done so far and that structures what next becomes possible in life, it is a weak and provisional totality that leaves the future open to creative human response.

With the advent of fascism, Croce responded especially to his erstwhile collaborator Gentile and his totalitarian thinking. For Croce the grandiose totalitarian mode of collective action that Gentile came to advocate rested on a misreading of human possibilities. In its place, Croce offered his own humble, pluralistic mode of collective worldmaking.

Reception and impact. Although it was ignored by the Italian press, Croce's essay quickly went into a second edition after publication in 1938. Private letters and police reports indicate the book's considerable impact. It was widely and favorably reviewed when published in English translation a few years later, in 1941. The work was also published in Spanish (1942) and in German (1944).

Into the 1940s, as the effort of post-Fascist political renewal gathered force, Croce remained broadly influential in Italy and highly respected abroad. But his thinking had always been somewhat elusive, its center of gravity hard to pin down. As discussion turned, with the imminent collapse of Fascism, to the immediate requirements for a new liberal democracy, differences in practical priorities emerged even between Croce and those like Guido Calogero and Guido De Ruggiero, who had looked to him for leadership.

By the late 1940s Croce's influence in Italy was swiftly declining as he became the target of an array of adversaries, from Marxists to Catholics to existentialist philosophers. The communist Antonio Gramsci, in his *Prison Notebooks*, critiqued Croce's overall position; his critique helped cement the erroneous notion that Croce's thought placed more weight on abstract speculation or mere understanding than on concrete action. By the time of his death in 1952, Croce was widely deemed *superato*, passé. In 1978 Raffaello Franchini, the most distinguished of the last group of Croce's followers, lamented that Croce had become taboo in the dominant circles of Italian culture. By this point Croce had largely fallen from view all over the Western world.

But together with Gentile, Croce was subject to renewed interest during the 1980s. Some began to suggest that, with his program of "history as thought and action," Croce could usefully be compared with such recent thinkers as the German Hans-Georg Gadamer and the American Richard Rorty, each of whom, like Croce, tried to specify the terms of a cultural situation in a context in which neither science nor religion nor philosophy seemed to afford the necessary orientation, and whose cultural prescriptions were similarly based on a deeper sense of the human place in history.

Though his influence was waning by the later 1940s, Croce himself found his historicist orientation more relevant than ever in light of cultural tendencies of the era. Although he understood the frustrations and fears that fed such responses, he sought to show how we can operate in a constructive spirit without lapsing back into some authoritarian claim to privilege, and without becoming crippled with anxiety over the human condition. Though each of us is only a collaborator in the flow of history, it is crucial that there is scope for us to collaborate. Through "history as thought and action" we do so in a mature, responsible way, thereby serving the future.

—David D. Roberts

For More Information

Croce, Benedetto. "Antistoricismo." In *Ultimi saggi*. Bari: Laterza, 1963.

————. *History as the Story of Liberty*. Trans. Sylvia Sprigge. London: George Allen and Unwin, 1941.

————. *My Philosophy, and Other Essays on the Moral and Political Problems of Our Time*. Trans. E. F. Carritt. London: George Allen & Unwin, 1949.

————. *Philosophy Poetry History: An Anthology of Essays*. Trans. Cecil Sprigge. London: Oxford University Press, 1966.

D'Amico, Jack, Dain A. Trafton, and Massimo Verdicchio, eds. *The Legacy of Benedetto Croce: Contemporary Critical Views*. Toronto: University of Toronto Press, 1999.

Moss, M. E. *Benedetto Croce Reconsidered: Truth and Error in Theories of Art, Literature, and History*. Hanover, N.H.: University Press of New England, 1987.

Rizi, Fabio Fernando. *Benedetto Croce and Italian Fascism*. Toronto: University of Toronto Press, 2003.

Roberts, David D. *Benedetto Croce and the Uses of Historicism*. Berkeley: University of California Press, 1987.

————. *Nothing but History: Reconstruction and Extremity after Metaphysics*. Berkeley: University of California Press, 1995.

The House by the Medlar Tree

by

Giovanni Verga

G iovanni Verga was born in 1840 in Catania, Sicily, to an upper-middle-class family of landowners. His mother, Caterina
di Mauro, was considered an intellectual—rare
for a woman in those days—and was politically
liberal. Verga's father, Giovanni Battista Verga,
descended from a noble family. Verga received
his education in a school run by Antonio Abate,
a revolutionary who fought in the 1848 uprising
in Sicily against the Bourbon monarchs (who
ruled Sicily until 1860, the year Italy achieved
formal unification). Abate instilled a patriotic,
anti-Bourbon sentiment into young Verga. At 18,
at his father's urging, he enrolled in law school
at the University of Catania. But far from concentrating wholeheartedly on law, he began to
write the historical novel *I Carbonari della montagna* (1862; *The Carbonari of the Mountain*). After presenting it to his father as evidence of his
promise as a writer, he was permitted to pursue
his calling. The following year Verga published
Sulle lagune (1863; On the Lagoons), a love story
set in Venice. He also founded the patriotic journal *Roma degli italiani* (Rome of the Italians) and
wrote for various new journals in Catania. At
about the age of 25, Verga left Sicily for Florence,
where he wrote two romance novels—*Una pec-
catrice* (1866; *A Mortal Sin*, 1995) and *Storia di
una capinera* (1872; *Sparrow*, 2002)—both highly
popular in his day. Verga next moved to Milan,
continuing to write in the same romantic-
passionate vein. In 1874, his style took a sharply
realistic turn in the short story "Nedda," a sketch
of a poor young Sicilian woman exploited by her

> **THE LITERARY WORK**
>
> A novel set in Sicily in the 1860s and 1870s;
> published in Italian (as *I Malavoglia*) in 1881,
> in English in 1890.
>
> **SYNOPSIS**
>
> The Malavoglia family struggles to remain
> faithful to its traditional values in the face of
> poverty, debt, and social upheaval.

employers. After publishing a collection of short
stories in the same vein (called *Vita dei campi*
[1880; *Life in the Country*, 2003]), he began writing a cycle of five novels depicting people who
fail in the struggle for survival because of a tragic
human error in the face of the struggle's unavoidable and cruel economic reality. The first in
this cycle was *The House by the Medlar Tree*; the
second, *Mastro-don Gesualdo* (1889; *Mastro-don
Gesualdo: A Novel*, 1979). The other three were
never completed. The two novels were written
between 1878 and 1889, during which Verga
produced his most widely acclaimed stories and
plays. He afterwards withdrew from society and
stopped writing almost completely, convinced
that literature was useless as a way to institute
change. While Verga believed in the unification
that linked Sicily to the rest of Italy, his works
portray the problems that occurred when the
central government imposed its laws and customs on Sicily, disrupting traditional Sicilian

Giovanni Verga

ways. He saw himself as an observer and a documenter of society and its victims, as shown by the unique way in which he wrote *The House by the Medlar Tree*.

Events in History at the Time of the Novel

Sicily and the Unification of Italy. In 1860, the year of Italian Unification, the island of Sicily had been under Spanish-Bourbon rule for more than a century (1730s-1860s). Earlier it had been ruled by various foreign powers, including the Arabs, the Normans, the French, and the Austrians. After the French Revolution and Napoleonic wars, there was a restoration of old boundaries and rulers over the Italian lands (1815-48). During this Age of Restoration, the idea of a united Italy began to spread through the peninsula, motivating local rebellions. In 1848, Sicily became the site of several revolutionary outbursts, prompted mainly by poverty and taxes but also by patriotic sentiment. The outbursts resulted in a break with the ruling Bourbon monarchy and in the formation of the "Sicilian Assembly," which named Ruggiero Settimo president in March 1849. Sicilian independence was short-lived, however, because the movement for national unification, led by Piedmont, could not open a second military front in the South while fighting the Austrians in the

North. Ferdinand II sent troops to sack the two major Sicilian cities of Catania and Messina. The ensuing conflict ended in May 1849, when the Sicilian Assembly surrendered to the Bourbons. A decade later, in 1859, Sicilian peasants again rose up against the Bourbons, and this time leaders on the Italian peninsula took interest, most notably the Republican patriot Giuseppe Garibaldi. Piedmont had by then already launched a second war of independence against Austria in the North; in view of this fact, Garibaldi seized on the local unrest in Sicily as an opportunity to turn a peasant revolt into a national revolution.

Garibaldi, not exactly trusting the Piedmontese government but knowing he needed its help, appealed to the king, who backed his idea for an expedition to liberate Sicily from the Bourbons. In the end Garibaldi's *Spedizione dei Mille* (Expedition of the Thousand) was highly successful. He and his army of 1,000, mainly young men with no military training, left Quarto, near Genoa, on May 6, 1860, and arrived in Marsala, Sicily five days later. The group began its march inland, taking the Sicilian town of Palermo and other towns both on Sicily and the Italian mainland, all the way up to Naples, and proclaiming Victor Emmanuel to be king of Italy, which, given Garibaldi's recent victories, now included southern Italy. Frustrations converged to the benefit of his enterprise:

> The main reason for Garibaldi's success lay in the convergence of a cluster of often negative feelings around the banner of revolution. For the peasants, Garibaldi offered the hope of a relief from suffering; for the landowners, the overthrow of the Bourbons meant an opportunity at last to secure independence from [the Kingdom of] Naples; for the provincial middle classes . . . there was the chance to seize control of local government and worst their enemies. The majority of those who took part in the revolution probably did so with little clear sense of what they were fighting for. Most had never encountered the term *Italia* before: some even imagined that 'La Talia' was the name of Victor Emmanuel's wife.
>
> (Duggan, p. 130)

While the movement for Italian independence and unity inspired great hope, it was also the source of much disillusionment in the post-Unification period, when the victors faced some difficult realities. Garibaldi's democratic ideals and his great popularity among "the people" were threatening to the king and his prime minister who, through many political machinations and much military strategy, managed to peacefully wrest power from Garibaldi and bring together all of Italy under a constitutional monarchy headed by the king of Piedmont, now of Italy, Victor Emmanuel II. To many of the new country's citizens, however, the lack of discussion about the constitution and structure of government implied that the king and prime minister felt their own region, Piedmont, had conquered all the other parts of Italy and so could impose their own terms on the new-formed country. Moreover, while many intellectuals and politicians shared the goals of unifying the territories into a country and developing a modernized Italy that could compete economically with other countries in Europe, the peasants worried about their immediate material needs. Economic growth and industrialization were having a positive impact on the standard of living for some in the North but provided no economic relief for the South. Sometimes northern prosperity even exacerbated poverty in the South, as demonstrated by new hardships portrayed in Verga's *The House by the Medlar Tree.* Among these hardships were new taxes on salt and mules (but not, notably, on cows, mostly the property of rich landowners) and the obligatory military service, which was required of young Sicilian men and deprived poor families of their most precious resource: labor. There were meanwhile few new benefits. The little government money sent to Sicily was often selfishly squandered by unscrupulous local officials on their own material comfort, bribes, or superfluous projects to please the aristocrats—a grand theater instead of road-building, for example.

The "Southern Question." Southern Italy is generally considered to consist of the areas now known as Campania, Apulia, Basilicata, Calabria, and Sicily. In the 1870s a concept called the "Southern Question" developed with respect to the area. Studies by Pasquale Villari, Leopoldo Franchetti, and Sidney Sonnino highlighted the differences between the North and the South, exposing the horrendous living conditions and exploitation of workers in the South and the indifference of most northerners to the abysmal situation their southern compatriots had to endure. However noble these intentions, the studies contributed to the perception of the South as a barbaric threat to the "more civilized" North and of the North as duty-bound to bring civilization to the "unwashed southern masses."

Before Unification, a large economic gap separated Italy's two halves. There was, of course, disparity within the North as well as between the North and South. Tuscany, in the North, for example, contended with formidable economic and agricultural problems that kept it from making the same progress as some nearby areas. But Sicily was even poorer and it still bore the traces of the feudal system, which endured well into the nineteenth century and stunted the island's economic and industrial growth. Yes, Sicilian society included some exceedingly rich aristocrats and landowning nobles, but most Sicilians were farmers, fishermen, and peasants. While northern regions like Lombardy could boast advances in industrialization, production, and agriculture, Sicily lagged far behind, as did other areas of the South. The crop yield for each hectare in the region was far below that of Lombardy, for example. The South had only a primitive banking system, and by 1860 only 60 miles of railway track. Illiteracy prevailed, totaling about 85 percent in 1881, two decades after Unification.

Sicilian woman standing in the doorway of her home.

The image of the backward South meant that even though the two halves of Italy had been formally united into one nation, the economic and social wedge between them was growing deeper. It has been asserted that the negative image of the South owes as much to the insecurities of the Italian political elite as to reality. At the time, many Italians "were haunted by a sense of their country's backwardness" (Moe, p. 2). While their civilization had paved the way during the Renaissance, in the centuries that followed, the

Italian states were overpowered politically and outpaced culturally by countries to the north. Differences between areas of the Italian peninsula had long been acknowledged, but now a new prejudice emerged. Northerners, and even some southerners, perceived of the South as primitive, ignorant, and embarrassingly destitute, and as a burden to the North. The new Italian elite was committed to participating in the march of progress in Western Europe. In the drive to make Italy more like nations to the north, the southern part of the country was branded different. "When, in the fall of 1860, a northern general reported back to Count Cavour in Piedmont about the conditions in the south, he put it quite succinctly: 'This is not Italy! This is Africa'" (Moe, p. 2).

In the years after Unification, repression and chaos pervaded Italy, brought on mainly by attempts to suppress revolts and bring people under the central rule of King Victor Emmanuel. The South caused his government the most severe problems; to quell the disturbances in Sicily, the government resorted to violence. This suppression was couched in the rhetoric of a "war against brigands," but the brigands (another negative image widely associated with Sicily) were more likely political dissenters than criminals. Many "brigands" were executed and whole towns suffered because of the government's drive to centralize authority at all costs.

The unrest was provoked by a number of perceived injustices, including the new centralized government's attempts to impose its ways on Sicily without understanding the effects. Taxes had been abolished by Garibaldi when he liberated the island, but they were immediately reinstated by the central government—which, again, was located in Piedmont—at rates based on Piedmontese standards of living. The central government also introduced obligatory military service for the first time in Sicily, which was deeply resented. In fact, the military service was "one of the principle sources of opposition to the new state" (Duggan, p. 139).

On the one hand, there was little understanding by the peasants about the meaning of a unified nation. On the other hand, the national politicians evinced a continuing indifference to the peasants' needs. Verga's novel reflects this state of affairs, as well as the fact "that the annexation of their Island to Italy meant for many Sicilians a new enslavement" (Montante, p. 48).

Sicilian family life. In *The House by the Medlar Tree* Verga portrays a time of political, economic,

and social transformation in Sicily. Progress in areas such as communication and education, while slow, was being made, which prompted the dissolution of traditional social and economic ways. There were both advances and declines, and they were transpiring all over Italy, but especially in the South and Sicily. Verga's novel portrays different attitudes toward modernization on the island. The novel depicts the erosion of both the primacy of the nuclear family (or "religion of the family," as it has often been called in Sicilian life) and the values that long bound Sicilian society together. This erosion comes with the discovery of a larger world where not all people outside the upper class have to work incessantly just to survive. For the young especially, the discovery stimulated a drive for upward mobility, a desire to leave one's birthplace in order to better one's station in life.

The image of the ideal Sicilian family can be gleaned from the proverbs, customs, and folktales documented by folklorists such as Giuseppe Pitré in the mid- to late-nineteenth century. This ideal family revolved around the married couple, which was seen as a harmonious, cooperative unit, with the husband at the helm, wielding financial and moral authority, and the wife at his beck and call—obedient, industrious, child-bearing, and nurturing. Finding a decent husband or wife for sons or daughters consumed much of a Sicilian family's time. Marriage negotiations were very complex and tenuous, depending significantly on the financial benefits that would accrue to either family and on the virtue of the potential wife. Rarely were romantic love and the opinions of the betrothed taken into consideration.

Some Sicilian Proverbs in Verga's Novel
- You can't sail a boat without a helmsman.
- You must learn to be sexton before you can be Pope.
- Do the job you know; if you don't make money, at least you'll make a living.
- Be satisfied to do what your father did, or you'll come to no good.

Upon marriage it was typically the husband's duty to provide the house and furniture; the wife's, to contribute the linens, mattresses, a loom, and accompanying equipment. Ordinarily the husband served as breadwinner, but, in poorer families, the wife, and even the children when they reached a certain age, were expected to contribute. If the wife worked outside the home, her primary duties continued to revolve around housekeeping and cooking. Verga's portrayal of the perfect housewife, Maruzza, relies heavily on her ability to make a little money selling eggs and nuts and still have the fire burning under the pot when the men come home from their daily fishing expeditions. Such a family structure, which relied heavily on rigid gender roles and division of labor, did not necessarily lack deep affection and a sense of respect between husband and wife or different generations. Verga portrays both the rigid roles and complexity of family emotions in his novel.

Neighbors played an important role in family life. The family treated them almost as if they were extended family members. A neighbor could be a positive or a negative force, based on the neighbor's goodwill or gossip. Two Sicilian proverbs capture these dual aspects: "Your true kinsman is your neighbor" and "You can hide from everyone except your neighbors" (Montante, p. 99).

The Novel in Focus

Plot summary. *The House by the Medlar Tree* takes place in Aci Trezza, a fishing village between Catania and Acireale in eastern Sicily. The title refers to the house of the Malavoglia family, whose story begins in 1863 and spans roughly 13 years.

In Chapter 1 the narrative introduces the Malavoglia family members: Master 'Ntoni, the patriarch; 'Ntoni's son, Bastiano; Bastiano's wife, Maruzza; and their five children—young 'Ntoni, Luca, Mena, Alessi, and Lia. Kept together by Master 'Ntoni, they are an extremely close-knit family, attached to their work as fishermen, known for their integrity, and firmly rooted in the traditional values of Sicilian peasant life. While Bastiano won't "even blow his nose without his father's permission," Maruzza is "a little woman who [sticks] to weaving, salting anchovies and bearing children, like the good housewife she [is]" (Verga, *The House by the Medlar Tree*, p. 8). The only potential rebel is young 'Ntoni, "a great lout of twenty . . . [who is] always getting cuffed by his grandfather, and sometimes kicked as well," says the narrator, who seems to be a local gossip, speaking in the tone and using words that any villager might (*The House by the Medlar Tree*, p. 8). Along with the family, we meet its two prized possessions—a fishing boat called *Provvidenza* (Providence) and the family home, both so prominent that they resemble actual characters.

The story proper begins with an account of the family's failed attempt to exempt young 'Ntoni from obligatory military service. The tem- porary absence of the family's oldest son is not only an emotional loss; it also brings on more economic hardships than usual. To relieve the situation, Master 'Ntoni makes an uncharacteristic business deal with an unscrupulous money-lender called Uncle Crocifisso; Master 'Ntoni buys—on credit—a load of *lupins* (beans) that he has been convinced he can sell for a profit in another town. Not only do the *lupins* turn out to be rotten, but on his voyage to the other town, Bastiano encounters a terrible storm and is lost at sea, along with the useless cargo. This tragedy is the first in a series that will bring about the family's downfall.

Before the Malavoglia family finds out about its loss, the novel introduces a long list of other villagers, who serve almost as a collective entity amounting to one character—the village itself. Women are introduced through their gossiping at the water well (about who has marriage designs on whom) and men through their talk of village business and politics on the church steps, at the barbershop, and in the tavern. Readers come to understand that there is no escape from the watchful eyes of the neighbors. It is they who eventually bring the bad news to the Malavoglias.

The family is devastated by Bastiano's death. They receive little sympathy from Uncle Crocifisso, who refuses to forgive the debt for the *lupins* under any circumstances. Master 'Ntoni, honorable to a fault, does not put up a fight even though he knows the *lupins* were rotten. Mena is doubly sad because not only has she lost her father, but also her dowry, which imperils her chances of a good marriage. However, in the works is a quick plan to marry her off to Brasi Cipolla, son of Master Cipolla, one of the richer villagers. Mena, though, has fallen in love with Alfio Mosca, a poor salesman who struggles just to feed himself.

In the meantime, the *Provvidenza* is brought up from the sea and found to be repairable, so the Malavoglia family decides it can once again go fishing. Because of his father's death, young 'Ntoni wrangles a discharge from the military.

'Ntoni's return is a joyous day for the family and is widely celebrated in the village. The young man himself comes swaggering into town after his experience of the large world (Naples). However, the following day when he has to rise before dawn and start working on Master Cipolla's boat—a job Master 'Ntoni has secured for them—young 'Ntoni is clearly displeased and gripes about the family's unfair lot in life. As the days pass, the Malavoglias take on any work they possibly can in order to feed the family and repay their debt, but they find themselves unable to make the payments. After many months, Uncle Crocifisso still has not received his money. The other villagers tell him the money would be tainted anyway because the *lupins* were rotten, but their warning fails to detour the resolute loan shark. He plans to pretend to sell the debt to another, more financially comfortable villager, Piedipapera, and thereby cleanse the money of its stigma. Thus, the two men enter into a business deal, which leads the bailiff to serve papers on the house by the medlar tree on Christmas Eve, further disgracing the Malavoglias. The family visits a lawyer who says they don't have to pay Uncle Crocifisso because the *lupins* were rotten, and although the family is momentarily relieved, Master 'Ntoni's sense of dignity reasserts itself and he realizes he must anyway pay his debt for the *lupins*. He agrees that if by Easter he cannot pay, the debtor can have the house.

To make matters worse, Luca is conscripted into the military. On the bright side, the family relaunches the *Provvidenza* among the good wishes and cruel gossip of the villagers. Young 'Ntoni begins to court one of the village girls, Barbara Zuppidda, who has also caught the attention of Don Michele, the sergeant of the customs guards. When young 'Ntoni asks for Barbara's hand, her parents say they will consent if his family does, but Master 'Ntoni declares that Mena must marry first and admonishes young 'Ntoni for not consulting with him, in traditional fashion. Young 'Ntoni is incensed and he begins to direct his frustration at his rival, Don Michele, the customs guard.

The arrangements for Mena's marriage into the rich family continue. Meanwhile, the lovelorn Alfio Mosca decides to try for work in another town and packs his things. Before he leaves, he exchanges a few words with Mena that sum up the emotional center of the novel: their ill-fated relationship and the uselessness of human emotions in the face of such harsh economic realities. Mena asks, "Why are you going to La Bicocca if there's malaria there?" And Alfio replies: "What a question! . . . And why are you marrying Brasi Cipolla, I should like to know?" (*The House by the Medlar Tree*, p. 102).

After a while the Malavoglias manage to save a little money from all their odd jobs, and their *Provvidenza* resumes its work at sea. The family seems well on its way to repaying the debt. Yet, as Mena's engagement party takes place, Uncle Crocifisso and Piedipapera plot to prepare legal papers to claim the Malavoglia house. A few days later, more bad news reaches the house by the medlar tree. Luca has been killed in the Battle of Lissa, fought against the Austrians as part of Italy's attempt to gain control of the Veneto region. This comes as a great surprise to the villagers because both the enemy and reason for battle are unknown.

Barbara Zuppidda's mother quickly breaks off her daughter's engagement to young 'Ntoni, reasoning that Luca's death now puts the entire financial burden of the Malavoglia family on 'Ntoni's shoulders. Next the family finally loses its house to Crocifisso and Piedipapera, and the Malavoglias move into a tiny hovel and become outcasts. Mena's wedding is cancelled, and, spurned in love himself, young 'Ntoni mopes. He starts hanging around the tavern, drinking, and longing for jobs that require no work, meanwhile nursing his intense hatred for Don Michele. Young 'Ntoni begins to publicly threaten his rival.

One day young 'Ntoni meets two rich travelers who speak of exotic places, which inflames him with grand ideas. He starts telling his family about the world's large cities and his dreams to travel and grow rich. Complaining ever more bitterly, 'Ntoni begins to lash out at the family; their hard work is for nothing, he says. Mena counters with the traditional Malavoglia values:

> "Leaving your own village, where even the stones know you, is worse than anything," said Mena. "It must be heartbreaking. Blessed the bird that makes its nest where it was born!"
>
> "Yes," muttered 'Ntoni, "and in the meantime, while we toil and sweat to build your nest, no doubt we'll have to go short of food. When we do manage to buy back the house by the medlar tree, we'll still have to go on wearing ourselves out from Monday to Saturday. We shall be no better off than we were before!"
>
> (*The House by the Medlar Tree*, p. 157)

Haunted by this thought, 'Ntoni withdraws from his family. He declares that he wants to change the conditions of his life, to be rich rather than poor, to "go and live in town, and do nothing, and eat macaroni and meat every day!" (*The House by the Medlar Tree*, p. 159). The family unravels further when its matriarch, Maruzza, dies of cholera during an outbreak. The outbreak, which requires people to sequester themselves indoors, hinders the family from selling its daily catch and other goods for their small income, and the Malavoglias lose half the money they had managed to save. At this point, young 'Ntoni finally musters the courage to leave, and Master 'Ntoni sells the *Provvidenza* to Uncle Crocifisso, in a deal brokered by Piedipapera. The dignified Master 'Ntoni and Alessi go to work for Master Cipolla, despite the fact that he broke off his son's marriage to Mena.

Eventually young 'Ntoni comes slinking back home from his adventures in the big world, poorer than before and ashamed to show his face in the village. Although his family welcomes him, he is ridiculed mercilessly by the gossips. He walks about the village raving, unable to reconcile why "there were people in the world who were born lucky and were able to enjoy themselves all day long without doing any work, while others were born penniless and had to spend their lives pulling wagons with their teeth" (*The House by the Medlar Tree*, p. 184). Frustrated, he returns home drunk every night and unable to work the next day, which devastates Master 'Ntoni. This kind of thing has never happened before in his hardworking family.

Gossip begins to circulate that Don Michele desires 'Ntoni's youngest sister, Lia, and Don Michele's visits to the Malavoglia girls (while the men are at sea or 'Ntoni is loafing about town) increase. One day Michele tells Mena and Lia to warn 'Ntoni not to trust some of his companions and to stay away from the lava field where smugglers anchor their boats and pretend to fish. The girls are hysterical and relay the message, but 'Ntoni, who is actually involved in smuggling, convinces himself that Don Michele is bluffing and knows nothing of his plans. In a fit, he goes to the tavern and picks a fight with Don Michele. The other customers break them up, but 'Ntoni vows to finish the job the next time they meet.

The next time they meet, however, Don Michele is intercepting 'Ntoni and his gang in the act of smuggling. Unfortunately for Don Michele, 'Ntoni stabs the customs sergeant before he can defend himself. 'Ntoni is led to the barracks to await trial while a wounded Don Michele is taken to the hospital. The scandal confers the ultimate disgrace on the Malavoglia family and, if possible, results in their being even more ostracized. The villagers gather in their usual spots to talk about the shamed family and about the positive economic ramifications of the arrests, now that the families will have fewer mouths to feed. At the trial 'Ntoni's lawyer mounts all kinds of defenses, from the darkness of the night to the lack of concrete evidence. He mentions the longstanding feud between young 'Ntoni and Don Michele and claims that a hundred witnesses have seen enough to corroborate the love affair being carried on by Don Michele and 'Ntoni's sister, Lia.

This last accusation, while partly but not entirely true, brings the final dishonor onto the family. Although the strategy wins 'Ntoni a lighter sentence, that evening, Lia, the disgraced young woman, walks out of the house and is not seen by the family again. Later the family finds out that she has become a prostitute.

At this point, Master 'Ntoni is a completely broken man, unable to work, not caring anymore about buying back the house by the medlar tree; despite the protests of his grandchildren, he has taken to living in the poorhouse, where he sits waiting for death. Alessi, on the other hand, finds work, marries, buys back the house by the medlar tree, and starts a family of his own. Mena, still unable to marry due to her sister's dishonor, resigns herself to life as a spinster.

In the novel's final pages, the remaining Malavoglia family receives a surprise visit from young 'Ntoni. Just out of jail, he has come to say his goodbyes. Having ventured beyond the boundaries of village life, he cannot reconcile the modern world with the fading traditional one, and therefore must go. He hesitates, then picks up his bundle and leaves, thinking soon the people who matter to him will be gone, after which the village day begins as usual.

Out of time. In writing this novel, Verga aimed to make the author's voice disappear, to create a work of art that seemed to create itself using the perspective, speech, and thoughts of the people about whom he was writing. To achieve his goal, he created a narrator who seems to be a village gossip, speaking in the rhythms and syntax of the Sicilian peasants, relying heavily on dialog rather than description, and incorporating Sicilian proverbs that capture the mood and mores of the island. His narrative strategies create a world outside historical time, one based on cyclical events, natural rhythms, and the isolated life of a small Sicilian village. Unlike the world outside, Verga's characters do not mark time by dates and years, but by feast days, harvests, and seasonal occurrences.

To portray a population out of touch with contemporary history, the novel depicts the events that impinge on their lives in a slightly distorted way, as these events would have seemed to the characters. When news reaches Aci Trezza that Luca Malavoglia has been killed in military service, it is vaguely described in the voice of the villagers: "there had been a battle in the direction of Trieste between our ships and those of the enemy—nobody knew who the enemy was" (*The House by the Medlar Tree*, p. 113). A confused exchange between the village men brings out how detached the villagers are from the newly created Italy, and their obsessive concern with only their own immediate affairs:

> "But all the newspapers say we've lost!"
> "Lost what!" said Uncle Crocifisso, putting his hand to his ear.
> "A battle."
> "Who lost it?"
> "I, you, everybody, the whole of Italy," said the chemist.
> "I haven't lost anything!" replied [Crocifisso], shrugging his shoulders. "It's Piedipapera's business now; let him worry about it!"
> (*The House by the Medlar Tree*, p. 111)

The informed reader understands more than the characters—that this is the Battle of Lissa in 1866 in a third War for Independence aimed at taking the Veneto region from the Austrians. Despite the fact that their Sicilian sons are being called to serve, this fight for Italian unity and independence is so far from the villagers' world that they don't even know why or against whom the battle is being fought.

This fictional unworldliness reflects a genuine one that has several historical causes. First is the lack of time or means on the part of Sicilian peasants to do anything other than attend to their urgent material needs. Sending children to school was often not a priority, since many needed their young to help work, and even when it was a priority, schools were not easily accessible. The Casati Law of 1859 required Italian children to attend elementary school to learn to read and write. But public funds were often controlled by corrupt local governments and an elite that managed to avoid complying with the law. The new schools that did appear were often understaffed with unqualified teachers who would go months without receiving their proper pay. Consequently men like 'Ntoni often learned to read during their military service, acquiring a skill that, again, proved not very useful once they resumed a village life worrying about basic survival.

Those who did read and took an interest in national events tried to inform their fellow Sicilians. On several occasions Verga has Don Franco, the pharmacist who manages to get the newspaper delivered to him from the city, interpret the news for the small group of men who gather around his shop, but he has a hard time getting anyone to listen or convincing anyone that the news matters to them. Travelers brought news too, but they were few and far between, and mostly regarded with suspicion. *The House by the Medlar Tree* takes place just before emigration became commonplace for Sicilians, so villagers could not even rely on letters home from relatives. At the time, the best way to gain knowledge of the outside world was to get drafted into the military, like young 'Ntoni and Luca. But this could be deadly, as it was for Luca, and it could make reintegrating into the rhythms of traditional life untenable, as it ultimately was for young 'Ntoni, a man alienated from both worlds since he cannot accept the archaic qualities of one nor survive without the support system of the other.

Sources and literary context. *The House by the Medlar Tree* is the first in a cycle of novels designed to present "a sort of phantasmagoria of the struggle for existence, extending from the rag picker to the cabinet minister and to the artist—taking all forms, from ambition to greed" (Verga in Cecchetti, p. ix). If the relationship between this design and naturalist writing, which emphasizes heredity and environment, seems clear, Verga is considered the primary exponent of *verismo*. An Italian literary and artistic style, *verismo* was loosely inspired by French naturalism and realism (as reflected in works by Èmile Zola, Honorè Balzac, and Gustave Flaubert, to whom Verga acknowledged a debt). The style is indebted as well to empiricism, a doctrine contending that the five senses are the only acceptable basis of human knowledge and precise thought. Empiricism demands rigorous adher-

Sicilian shepherds and their flock travel the road from Agrigento to Licata, as generations before them have.

ence to experienced reality, calling for faithful observation of situations, facts, settings, and people in order to present an "unmediated" reality, particularly in depicting feelings and the language of characters. In his preface to the novel, Verga lays out his stylistic objectives: that the novel writes itself, that it is an organism that develops without the direct participation of the author (contrary to Romantic notions of the author and his role), that the author writes from a detached, dispassionate, impersonal vantage point akin to that of a scientific observer. His descrip-

tions are conveyed through the characters' reactions and dialog, not the narrator, and herein lies his newness in Italian fiction. Usually, the characters in such a literary study portray people in the lower classes; Verga goes so far as to declare that he wants to write about those who are trampled in the great forward movement called (sometimes ironically) progress. This declaration was in itself highly original in Italian literature.

In his depictions of the tragedies of human life, Verga was affected by ideas stimulated by the scientist Charles Darwin. Verga based much of his thinking about society on the "struggle for existence," a concept Darwin applied to the animal world. Progress, in Verga's view, was a violent wave; once confronted with modern life, a person can never acquire enough material goods, and someone's success is always at the expense of someone else, so no one can really ever be declared a winner.

As noted, *The House by the Medlar Tree* infuses into the story Sicilian proverbs. Also included are customs of the island's peasants and fishermen. Verga relied heavily for these components on the writings of Giuseppe Pitré (1841-1916), a folklorist from Palermo whose work was widely read and respected during his lifetime. Especially influential was Pitré's *Proverbi siciliani, raccolti e confrontati con quelli degli altri dialetti d'Italia* (Sicilian Proverbs, Collected and Compared with Those from Other Italian Dialects), a four-volume work published in 1879-80.

Reception. *The House by the Medlar Tree* was not a popular success in its time. The writer, critic, and primary theorist of *verismo*, Luigi Capuana, praised it enthusiastically, as did a few of Verga's friends, but it was not widely reviewed. Verga was disappointed by the novel's cold reception but unswayed in his convictions, as shown in some lines from a letter to Capuana: "Luigi, I can tell you that the indifference with which the so-called 'literary public' here in Italy looks upon our efforts absolutely nauseates me" (Verga in Alexander, p. 89). Zola, whom Verga greatly admired, had promised to write an introduction to the French translation but did not, and when the novel was released in France in 1886, it met with silence there too.

In general, critics of the time disliked the pessimism and harshness of the life Verga described. They furthermore took issue with the form, dismissing the linguistic experimentations as unacceptable. The biographer Alfred Alexander notes that,

> In Verga's time . . . any acceptable Italian prose was meant to follow the tradition which Manzoni had set in *I promessi sposi* [**The Betrothed**, also in *WLAIT 7: Italian Literature and Its Times*]. Because Verga used the words that were natural to his characters, because he used a language restricted in vocabulary, frequently incorrect in syntax, and sometimes even in grammar, the critics as well as the public found it difficult to accept his innovations.
> (Alexander, p. 85)

Edoardo Scarfoglio, one of Verga's harshest critics, called the language "a boring monotony," while G. A. Cesareo faulted the novel for a "lack of a noble literary language" (Scarfoglio and Cesareo in Viti, p. 101). By the end of the nineteenth century, the work had been all but forgotten. Just two decades later, however, in 1919, Italian critics began to re-evaluate the initial harsh judgments, and Verga acquired the status of a major literary figure (thanks largely to the critics Benedetto Croce and Luigi Russo). Verga's status continued to grow thereafter, with critics and literary historians alike proclaiming him to be the "greatest Italian novelist after Manzoni" (Bergin, p. 46).

—Amy Boylan

For More Information

Alexander, Alfred. *Giovanni Verga: A Great Writer and His World.* London: Grant & Cutler, 1972.

Bergin, Thomas Goddard. *Giovanni Verga.* New Haven: Yale University Press, 1931.

Cecchetti, Giovanni. Introduction to *The House by the Medlar Tree,* by Giovanni Verga. Berkeley: University of California Press, 1983.

Duggan, Christopher. *A Concise History of Italy.* Cambridge: Cambridge University Press, 1994.

Mack Smith, Denis. *A History of Sicily: Modern Sicily After 1713.* London: Chatto & Windus, 1968.

Moe, Nelson. *The View from Vesuvius: Italian Culture and the Southern Question.* Berkeley: University of California Press, 2002.

Montante, Michela. *A Psycho-Social Study of the Sicilian People Based on Selected Characters from Verga's Novels.* Caltanissetta, Italy: Salvatore Sciascia Editore, 1976.

Verga, Giovanni. *The House by the Medlar Tree.* Trans. Eric Mosbacher. Westport, Conn.: Greenwood Press, 1953.

Viti, Gorizio. *Guida a I Malavoglia.* Florence: Felice Le Monnier, 1971.

Jerusalem Delivered (Gerusalemme Liberata)

by

Torquato Tasso

Torquato Tasso (1544-95) was born in Sorrento, Italy. At the age of 10, he was forced to literally follow in the footsteps of his father, the poet Bernardo Tasso, who moved first to Rome, then to Bergamo, Urbino, and Venice. The elder Tasso focused on writing compositions for his various patrons and writing his own epic poem, the *Amadigi* (1560, based on a Spanish chivalric romance *Amadis de Gaula* [1508]). At the age of 16, the younger Tasso had already begun a first attempt at the subject of *Jerusalem Delivered*, which he abandoned in order to focus on the *Rinaldo*, a short poem about the adventures of the legendary knight. His education began at the court of Urbino and continued at the universities of Bologna and Padova from 1560 to 1565. That same year, 1565, saw the beginning of his lifelong relationship to the Este family of Ferrara, at first as attendant to Cardinal Luigi D'Este. In 1572 Tasso passed into the service of Duke of Ferrara Alfonso II D'Este as court poet for the family. In the end, his writings would embrace nearly every genre, including plays, lyric and narrative poems, dialogues, and literary criticism. Tasso's most memorable works remain the pastoral play *Aminta* (1573), *Jerusalem Delivered*—which consumed more than two decades in the making—and its revision *Jerusalem Conquered* (*Gerusalemme Conquistata*, 1593). Despite Tasso's continuing doubts about the content and structure of the *Liberata*, the poem successfully melded together the themes of earlier romance chivalric verse with classical epic structure, meanwhile keeping pace with the

---

THE LITERARY WORK

An epic poem set in 1099 during the first crusade; written from 1560 to 1581; published in Italian (as *Gerusalemme Liberata*) in 1581, in English in 1600.

SYNOPSIS

Led by their captain, Godfrey, a group of Christian knights confront psychological and physical obstacles on their way to free the shrine of the Holy Sepulcher in Jerusalem from Muslim rule.

---

religious, Counter Reformation sensibilities of his readers.

Events in History at the Time the Poem Takes Place

The First Crusade—background. In November of 1095, Pope Urban II gave a speech at a council in Clermont, France, calling upon the knights of Christian Europe to help recapture the shrine of the Holy Sepulcher from Muslim rule. He urged the Western European knights to come to the aid of the Byzantine Church (in the East) by waging war against the Muslims. At the time, Muslim rule extended from the East into southern Spain and Sicily. Before the eleventh century, the relationship between Christians and Muslims in the Holy Land had been relatively peaceful,

Torquato Tasso

but later Christian pilgrims suffered persecution at the hands of some Muslim rulers, such as al-Hakim (985-1021?), leader of the Fatimid dynasty in Egypt, under whose rule the church of the Holy Sepulcher was destroyed in 1009-10. Internal affairs under al-Hakim were tempestuous too; he became embroiled in a conflict in Syria and in Palestine with the Seljuk Turks, who continued to expand their domains in the eastern Islamic world. Under al-Hakim's successors, the church was rebuilt. Christians resumed their pilgrimages, but Seljuk pressure grew and the conflict between Eastern powers made the journey treacherous. The conflicts preoccupying leaders in the East offered Western crusaders a perfect opportunity to proceed with their plans to reconquer the Holy Land. So in the 1090s, when the Byzantine emperor Alexius Comnenus called upon Europe to come to his aid in protecting Near Eastern Christians from Seljuk oppression, the papacy was more than willing to answer his plea. Comenus himself had no designs on Jerusalem. The emperor wanted to recapture the mercantile city of Antioch, and he in fact tried to dissuade the crusaders from pursuing their larger goal—but to no avail.

The First Crusade—its execution. Plans were made for the crusaders' departure on the day of the feast of the Assumption of the Blessed Virgin, August 15, 1096. As it turned out, the pope

got more than he bargained for when he attempted to raise a Christian army. His zealous sermons throughout Europe influenced not only the noblemen he set out to recruit, but commoners too. The commoners departed before the crusades officially got underway, mounting what became known as the People's Crusade, led by charismatic personalities such as Peter the Hermit. Although his group managed to reach Constantinople, many did not, for lack of supplies and organization. Others faltered because of their own unruliness, some of them stopping to massacre Jews in the Rhineland of Germany. After reaching Constantinople, Peter's group and others like it would join the main army of the princely crusade.

The princely crusade was another enterprise altogether. It was a diverse group, including (1) Godfrey of Bouillon and his brothers Eustace and Baldwin from France, (2) Bohemond and his nephew Tancred of Otranto in southern Italy, and (3) Count Raymond IV of Toulouse, together with the pope's legate Adhémar, Bishop of Le Puy. Despite the diversity, though, these crusaders achieved more success than their predecessors, which is hardly surprising given their training and store of supplies. These three armies, along with a fourth led by Robert of Normandy, Count Stephen of Blois, and Robert II of Flanders, left Europe and arrived in Constantinople between December 1096 and May of 1097. After convening there, they almost immediately departed for Nicaea in Asia Minor with 50,000 men—nobles, pilgrims, and other non-combatants who latched on to the group. The heavily armed garrison of Nicaea surrendered on June 19, and the crusaders once again took to the road, this time marching towards Dorylaeum, also in Asia Minor, which fell in July of the same year. By October, they had reached and laid siege to Antioch in northern Syria. The siege would go on for months. Early chroniclers blamed military reverses that were suffered by the crusaders on their lust, pointing to brothels in their camps. Apparently the Council of Princes shared the anxiety, for at Antioch, the Council "drove out the women from the army [camp] . . . lest they, stained by the defilement of dissipation, displease the Lord" (Fulcher of Chartres in Billings, p. 49). Antioch finally fell in June of 1098, and the crusaders gave it to one of their own, Bohemond, to rule.

Although the Christian forces had marched 700 miles without a single defeat, the most important leg of their journey, the reconquest of Jerusalem, loomed ahead. As they pitched their tents under the city's walls in June of 1099, they most certainly were aware of the complexity of the task before them. Jerusalem's defenses were difficult to breach, especially since the garrison's commander had ordered nearly all the water sources outside the city to be poisoned and had petitioned the Egyptians for help. It is at this juncture in the crusaders' quest that *Jerusalem Delivered* takes place. In his epic portrayal, Tasso replicates some real-life details of the task that awaited the crusaders, as well as their decision to construct siege engines (to throw projectiles) and siege towers (to help them scale the city's walls). The final attack was set for the evening of July 13 from two separate towers on the northern and southern sides of the city. After more than a day of fighting and repeated attempts to burn his siege tower, Godfrey became the first crusader to cross over from it into Jerusalem on the morning of July 15. On the same day, what was left of the Muslim forces surrendered to Tancred, who had his banner flown over the al-Aqsa mosque. A massacre followed that became legendary for its cruelty, which was documented in historical chronicles:

> Forthwith, they joyfully rushed into the city to pursue and kill the nefarious enemies. . . . Some Saracens, Arabs, and Ethiopians took refuge in the tower of David, others fled to the temples of the Lord and of Solomon. A great fight took place in the court and porch of the temples, where they were unable to escape from our gladiators. Many fled to the roof of the temple of Solomon, and were shot with arrows, so that they fell to the ground dead. In this temple almost ten thousand were killed. Indeed, if you had been there you would have seen our feet colored to our ankles with the blood of the slain. But what more shall I relate? None of them were left alive; neither women nor children were spared.
>
> (Fulcher of Chartres in Duncan and Krey)

Tasso reproduces the fierceness of the bloody final struggle for control over the holy city, relating how the crusader Raymond "came to a field all slick and smoking red, / for it was steeped in more blood hour by hour, / so that it seemed a kingdom of the dead, where Death displayed the trophies of his power" (Tasso, *Jerusalem Delivered*, p. 403). But Tasso mentions nothing of this massacre of the innocents, preferring instead to offer up his heroes as examples of pious magnanimity for his readers.

Women and the crusades. Women played a key role in the acquisition and development of the crusader states in the Holy Land. Many of the wives accompanied their husbands on the crusade while others stayed home and took charge of the governance of their husband's lands and titles (the fiefs, or estates, of vassals under his control). Those who joined their husbands in the enterprise might benefit from the feudal custom that allowed a wife to succeed her husband as ruler of a fief or kingdom, including any territory he might have won along the way.

THE CHURCH OF THE HOLY SEPULCHRE

A few centuries after the death of Jesus Christ, an edifice arose to commemorate the site at which people said he had been crucified, buried, and resurrected. The edifice, the shrine of the Holy Sepulchre, was first erected by Emperor Constantine (285?-337); originally it consisted of a trio of connected parts: a basilica-shaped building, an open-air atrium around the Golgotha, or Rock of Calvary, where Jesus is believed to have been executed, and an open-air rotunda around the remains of the cave identified as his burial place, later covered by a dome. Despite fires, a large earthquake, and the basilica's destruction and restoration, the Church retained this essential form until 1009, when the Fatimid caliph al-Hakim ordered that it be destroyed and all of its Christian symbols removed. Much of the structure surrounding Jesus's tomb was demolished, but evidence suggests that some part of it survived, and that Christians used it as the basis for a second restoration in 1012. An account by a Persian traveler confirms that by 1047 the church was fully restored. It would now remain intact until the first crusaders, the ones featured in *Jerusalem Delivered*, reached the edifice in 1099; victorious, they quickly set out to enlarge the church and connect its three parts under one roof, adding a bell tower. In 1149 the remodeled church was consecrated; it has endured in the form that the crusaders gave it to the present day.

Christian chroniclers often speak of women carrying water to the fighting men during sieges. The chroniclers also, as noted, mention camp brothels, alluding to the presence of women who catered to the crusaders' lustful cravings. These chroniclers do not, however, speak of the women participating directly in battle. However, according to some of the Muslim records there were women warriors "in men's garb and . . . prominent in the thick of the fray" amongst the crusaders who "act[ed] in the manner of those endowed with intellect although they [were] ladies" (Hillenbrand, p. 348). Though there is no mention of Muslim women participating in the first crusade, Arabic literature is filled with examples of the woman warrior, and Arabic epics feature "many leading female heroes" as well as "their male counterparts" (Kruk, p. 100). The same is true of Tasso's *Liberata*, where women feature prominently, from the captive Erminia to the Muslim warrior princess Clorinda to the Christian wife Gildippe, who fights alongside her husband Edward to the death. The appearance and eventual defeat of a warrior princess on the battlefield is not without precedent in the literary models available to Tasso. This is particularly true of his Princess Clorinda. Tasso borrows many details of her story from classical epic, from descriptions of the Amazons of Penthesilea in Homer's *Iliad* and Camilla in Virgil's *Aeneid*. In *Jerusalem Delivered*, unlike her male counterparts, who are based on actual historical figures, Clorinda is a complete fiction on Tasso's part.

The Poem in Focus

Plot summary. At the outset of the poem, the speaker recounts that it has already been six years since the crusaders left their homes. From the celestial city, God looks down upon the troops and finds most of them lost in their own cares. They have forgotten the importance of their mission of recapturing the Holy Sepulcher; only Godfrey remains full of zeal for the completion of the enterprise. Thus, God sends down the archangel Gabriel to inform Godfrey that the knight will serve as the captain of the Christian forces and that they should continue to Jerusalem without delay. Upon Peter the Hermit's suggestion, the troops then elect Godfrey captain and begin the march. On the way, they engage in several skirmishes with the enemy. Two Christian champions, Rinaldo and Tancred, first exchange blows with the Muslim troops in this fray, including their formidable warrior Argante and their warrior princess Clorinda.

From the high walls of the city, Erminia, a princess whose kingdom of Antioch has already been conquered by the crusaders, points out the strongest members of the Christian forces to the Muslim ruler of Jerusalem, Aladin. They include the young paladin Rinaldo, who is already famous for his strength and prowess in the field yet remains a boy in many respects, and Tancred, who is so lost in his thoughts, in particular his love

for the female warrior—Clorinda—whom he has just seen on the battlefield but not yet met, that he is completely distracted from the task at hand. Meanwhile, Erminia is secretly in love with Tancred from the time when she was his prisoner but tries to disguise her longing under a veil of hate for her former captor.

Satan decides that if God will sustain the crusaders, then Satan must do the same for their enemies, since the spread of Christianity diminishes his power and influence in the world of men and women. So he sends forth his legions to wreak havoc amongst the Christians in any way possible. At the same time, another enemy of the crusaders, the wizard Hydrotes, sends his niece Armida, herself a sorceress, to wreak havoc of a different sort. She enters the Christian camp in the guise of a damsel in distress, her presence further complicating the fate of the Christian forces. Armida weaves a false tale of how she has fled from the unwarranted advances of a lecherous uncle and was forewarned in a dream of her imminent death by poison should she choose to stay. Many of the knights fall prey to her charms and ten are chosen to accompany her after Godfrey refuses her plea for the aid of the whole army. She eventually imprisons all the knights who follow her, which amounts to more than the chosen ten, in an enchanted castle on the banks of the Dead Sea. Rinaldo is not with them; the competition for Armida became so fierce and spiteful that in a fit of rage he killed a crusader, Gernando, and was therefore forced to quit the camp altogether.

The Muslim warrior Argante, impatient for the battle to begin, wants to decide the fate of Jerusalem by means of a duel to the death with just one Christian champion. The Christians select Tancred to face him and after many hours of fierce blows, their fight is suspended until the following day. Erminia watches the entire scene from on high, and, fearing for Tancred's life after she envisions him calling for her help in a dream, resolves to sneak into the Christian camp. In order to easily leave the city, she steals Clorinda's armor and pretends to be the female warrior herself. When she reaches the camp, she is ambushed and forced to flee because the knights believe her to be Clorinda. Tancred awakens during the confusion and chases her too, but gets waylaid. He eventually comes upon Armida's castle and is imprisoned by the sorceress. Thus Tancred joins the ranks of the Christian champions led astray by personal desire and no longer in the service of the crusaders.

At dawn the next day, the renegade Erminia awakens to find herself in an idyllic setting far

Title page from *Gerusalemme Liberata,* 1581.

from the battlefield. She encounters some local shepherds and decides to escape the war by taking refuge among them. Back in Jerusalem, Argante is eager to resume the duel but Tancred is nowhere to be found. He taunts the Christians and even challenges Godfrey. However, the ag-

ing knight Raymond convinces the captain not to take up the challenge for he is too valuable to the camp as its leader. Shortly afterward, Raymond is chosen by lot to replace Tancred and with the help of an angel amazes both Argante and the crowd by skillfully holding his own against such an intimidating opponent. Satan's demons then come to the aid of Argante and the duel dissolves into a melee until a violent storm forces everyone to retreat.

A messenger, Charles, arrives at the Christian camp and tells of the young prince Sven of Denmark, who, on the way to help them, was defeated and killed by the Turkish sultan Soliman. The sultan, only recently ousted from his kingdom by the Christians, sought revenge. As the soul survivor of the massacre, Charles has come to pass on Sven's sword to Rinaldo, whom Sven tried to emulate as a model of the perfect knight. The crusaders are so moved by this story that when reports surface about the discovery of a headless body with Rinaldo's coat of arms, the entire camp is in doubt and anguish over the whereabouts of their champion. Incited through a dream sent by Alecto, an infernal fury of classical mythology, the Italian crusader Argillan accuses Godfrey of having murdered his compatriot Rinaldo out of envy and rallies together the other Italians to overthrow their leader. When the violent mob arrives at his tent, Godfrey prays to God for help in quelling the mutiny, and divine grace infuses him with a new regal presence, which, coupled with his harsh words, quells the strife. Argillan is imprisoned for his treason and yet another attempt at ruining the Christians' enterprise is thwarted.

That night Soliman and his forces assault the camp with the help of Clorinda and Argante. Fortunately Rinaldo has managed by this time to free Tancred and the rest of Armida's prisoners. When they return, the tide of battle turns, and the crusaders are able to hold off their rivals.

Yet another divine intervention in the form of the archangel Michael arrives to send Satan's demons back to hell so they will no longer impede the crusaders. For their part, the Christian troops make a solemn procession to the Mount of Olives, one of the places Jesus appeared to his disciples after his resurrection, to invoke God's favor in the final assault on Jerusalem. They decide to construct large wooden siege machinery in order to breach the city's defenses. Interrupted by night's arrival, they await the following day to resume their battle.

That same night, the eunuch Arsete, Clorinda's caretaker since childhood, reveals to Clorinda that she is really a Christian and recounts the tale of Clorinda's miraculous birth as a white child to the Queen of Ethiopia. He also tells her of his dream predicting her death, preceded by her conversion to Christianity, and begs her not to accompany Argante on a night raid to set fire to the Christians' wooden towers. She ignores the advice, only to find herself in a fix. After Clorinda and Argante set fire to the towers, she suddenly gets shut out of Jerusalem's gates and must face the mob of crusaders alone. At a certain point, Clorinda realizes she might be able to sneak away since she is not wearing her own armor and so is unrecognizable to her enemies. Tancred, however, pursues her, unaware that the warrior he is about to exchange blows with is the woman he loves. Tancred and Clorinda duel. The fight dramatizes the mixed themes of love and war in the poem as the virgin warrior dies at her lover's hand. Tancred only realizes what he has done once it is too late. He begins to recognize the frail voice, whose last words, infused with a "new spirit" of "faith, hope and charity," beg him to perform her baptism, which he readily does (*Jerusalem Delivered,* p. 244). It is only when he starts to perform this sacred act that he recognizes his mistake: he finally "saw her, knew her. And he could not move / or speak. / Ah, thus to see and know his love! (*Jerusalem Delivered,* p. 244). Her fate is sealed with the following moral: "rebel in life, on her such grace is poured / that she may die the handmaid of the Lord" (*Jerusalem Delivered,* p. 244). Desperate at the loss of her, Tancred slips into a despair that almost leads him to the point of suicide until Clorinda's heavenly spirit appears in a dream, assuring him of her forgiveness and promising that they would one day be reunited in the afterlife.

Their siege machinery now burnt to the ground, the crusaders go to the nearby forest of Saron for wood to rebuild the towers. Shortly before their arrival, the sorcerer Ismen, a master in the black arts, arrives to cast a spell on the forest, making evil spirits inhabit each tree. One by one the knights are bested by this forest, which reproduces images that play on each knight's deepest fears. When the task falls to Tancred, he enters a clearing with a lone cypress tree. Clorinda's voice emanates from its branches and, each time he tries to strike it, out spurts blood. The reenactment of her murder proves too much to bear, and he flees.

Just as the situation of the crusaders appears at its worst, a drought befalls them. Both men and animals languish under the heat of the unrelenting desert sun, and Godfrey's troops question his motives for pressing on when all appears lost. Again Godfrey pleads to God, and again his prayers are answered. This time the Lord declares "the new order now begins, / prosperity returns and all is well" (*Jerusalem Delivered*, p. 267). He sends Godfrey a vision in which the spirit of the crusader Hugh of Vermandois inspires him to retrieve Rinaldo from captivity in the palace of Armida. They make their way into its inner garden, after having seen all manner of monsters and sensual delights; shocked, they discover Rinaldo stripped of his valor, entwined with garlands of flowers, and transformed into Love's slave. The two crusaders show him his reflection in a magical diamond shield which reveals "himself for what he was, / how tressed with dainty touches, reeking of perfume, his hair in curls and tassels on his vest, his dangling sword effeminate at his side" (*Jerusalem Delivered*, p. 306). Mortified at this sight, Rinaldo departs immediately. Armida, full of scorn after being abandoned in such a manner, joins the Egyptian army to get revenge. When he returns to the camp, Rinaldo climbs to the Mount of Olives to seek penance and purification for his sins. He then breaks the forest's spell and declares with a smile, "Such empty fantasies. / A man's a fool to pause for things like these" (*Jerusalem Delivered*, p. 343).

Now that the forest has been vanquished, the Christians are able to reconstruct their siege machinery and proceed with their offensive on Jerusalem. They first breach the city's outer walls, at which point Aladin and Soliman take refuge in the tower of David. The Christian champion Tancred and the Muslim champion Argante step away from the battle to finally resume their duel. In the end Tancred is the victor and kills Argante, but not without suffering serious injury himself. Erminia finds him and saves his life by dint of her knowledge of natural remedies. When the Egyptian army arrives at Jerusalem's walls, the final battle commences. Soliman leaves the tower, joins the fight, and is cut down by Rinaldo, who then spies Armida. At first she tries to kill Rinaldo with a poisoned arrow, but upon finding herself unable to do so because she still loves him, Armida attempts suicide. Rinaldo stops her and convinces her to switch to his side. When Godfrey defeats Emiren, the captain of the Egyptians, both the battle and the poem come to a close as the pious Godfrey, "with devoted brow, adores the great tomb, and fulfills his vow" (*Jerusalem Delivered*, p. 413).

A new form of heroism. Like the close of the eleventh century, the late sixteenth century, during which Tasso wrote his poem, was a period of intense political and religious strife. Early in the sixteenth century (1517), the Christian community had been torn by strife that began to split the community into two branches: the Protestants (who mounted the Protestant Reformation) and the Catholics (who responded with the Counter Reformation). Along with the turmoil came a redefinition of the concept of "good works," or works worthy of the devout Christian. Apart from the traditional devotional practices of prayer and charitable acts, an individual's faith was also measured by the extent to which he or she could emulate Christ's ultimate sacrifice for the good of all Christians in everyday life. This focus on the individual, coupled with Tasso's interest in the crusades, led to his portrayal of alternative models of heroism to the typical stories of a knight's quests to save a damsel in distress or recover hidden treasures. Instead of these traditional models, Tasso's heroes are Christian and Muslim, male and female, physically strong yet psychologically weak. In fact, *Jerusalem Delivered* "redirects our understanding of heroic action to the inward and psychological [since] he raises to a new pitch the potentiality for heroism in inner action [by] invent[ing] powerful images for such heroism . . . [such as] Rinaldo's conquest of his passion for Armida, his achievement of manhood on the Mount of Olives, or the purely psychological heroic action of the enchanted forest" (Kates, p. 124).

The beginning of the poem gives away the entire plot, leaving the parts that follow to reveal what is truly important about the story. *Jerusalem Delivered* is a poem based on a past event that is unchangeable; thus, its outcome is predetermined. The significance of the first crusade as portrayed by Tasso is not so much the outcome as the journey the crusaders and Godfrey undergo as he "restore[s] his straying men to the banner of the Lord" (*Jerusalem Delivered*, p. 17). Much of why Godfrey is a suitable captain has to do with his steadfast focus on the singular goal of conquering Jerusalem. He has taken a "vow" to do so, and rescuing damsels in distress or other pursuits worthy of a typical knight's valor are unimportant by comparison.

Godfrey, however, does not succeed on his own in this poem. While Tasso describes him as the head of the Christian enterprise, the poet identifies Rinaldo as its right arm. Rinaldo embodies the earlier, classical and medieval chivalric notion of what constitutes a hero. A young knight, he possesses the physical strength and courage the mission requires, but his chivalric code of conduct interferes with the goal of freeing Jerusalem. In the end, it is the combination of these two models of heroism—one based on action and a quest for individual glory, the other on religious devotion and a singular focus on a determined objective directed at the common good—that allows the Christians to succeed. Tasso's shift in perspective anticipates many of the changes the figure of the hero would undergo with the advent of the novel as a literary form. Tasso gives his protagonists a psychological depth that allows the reader to consider them heroic not only for their acts, but also for the intentions that guide them.

Sources and literary context. Tasso studied literary theory intensely (particularly the rules of epics in Aristotle's *Poetics*). To his mind, the ideal "heroic poem" was the mixture of the best elements of the chivalric tradition of medieval romance and the classical epic tradition, which took its original inspiration from actual events. Tasso therefore turned to historical chronicles for many of the poem's details. In fact, he believed that even the marvelous must be lifelike in a poem; this, he thought, could be achieved "by attributing the presence of marvels to a supernatural power capable of producing such effects according to the shared beliefs" of his readership (Biow, p. 128). With this in mind, he drew on the Bible and on **The Divine Comedy** by Dante Alighieri (1265-1321; also in *WLAIT 7: Italian Literature and Its Times*) for a number of his marvels. At the same time, he also sought inspiration from the texts of his day on the soul, demonology, and dream interpretation. There are approximately 14 dream experiences in the *Liberata,* including visions, apparitions, and nightmares. While the dream had long been an element in epic and religiously inspired literature, Tasso adds another dimension, conveying the anxiety produced by dreams engendered by one's own fears, as demonstrated by his poem's enchanted forest.

Tasso drew on the works of his predecessors in other ways as well. No doubt, Tasso was aware of his comparison to his near contemporary Ludovico Ariosto. Although he often criticizes Ariosto's **Orlando Furioso** (also *in WLAIT 7: Italian Literature and Its Times*) for digressing from the main narrative and lacking unity of plot, he frequently uses modes of speech and imagery recalling Ariosto's story.

The most important source for the structure of his work was Aristotle's already-mentioned *Poetics,* which, after its rediscovery in 1536, became the cornerstone of discussions on literary theory throughout sixteenth-century Italy. Tasso adopted Aristotle's notion of unity of plot struc-

ture, convinced that it would bring him closer to imitating the ancient epic poems than his predecessors. Both the *Aeneid* and the *Iliad* not only inspired episodes in *Jerusalem Delivered*; Tasso used them as models when distributing themes and episodes throughout his poem.

Contemporary circumstances entered into the writing of *Jerusalem Delivered* too. By the time Tasso began composing *Jerusalem Delivered,* his patron, Alfonso II d'Este, was engaged in a struggle to preserve the power and lands of his family. In 1567, Pope Pius V published a bull banning illegitimate heirs from inheriting feudal titles in papal domains. The bull seemed to be directed at Duke Alfonso, whose title was held by papal grant and who had not produced a legitimate heir. Tasso attempts to resolve his patron's problem by weaving into *Jerusalem Delivered* the ancestry of the Este line, portraying the family as descendants of the poem's champion Rinaldo.

Events in History at the Time the Poem Was Written

Early modern Italy—political uncertainty. Whether it is described as a time of crisis or the disintegration of ideals associated with the previous century, it is obvious that some major ideological changes occurred from 1550-1600. Niccolò Machiavelli's (1469-1527) bleak predictions for Italy's future in **The Prince** (also in *WLAIT 7: Italian Literature and Its Times*) turned into reality as the stability enjoyed under powerful figures such as Lorenzo de' Medici (1449-92) became little more than a fleeting memory. Instead, two world powers, France and Spain, struggled for control over parts of the Italian peninsula and even after the peace established by the treaty of Cateau-Cambrésis in 1559 ushered in more stable times, the memory of previous invasions, such as the sack of Rome in 1527, remained fresh in the minds of the public.

In *Jerusalem Delivered,* Tasso has his speaker address his patron, Alfonso, directly, at times urging him to take up arms in a new crusade after the example of Godfrey. Tasso offers up the poem as an example for Alfonso or any of its readers or listeners: "Strive," says the speaker, "with Godfrey as your exemplar, / heed my song well and gird yourself for war" (*Jerusalem Delivered,* pp. 17-18). In the case of Alfonso the action implied is to undertake a new crusade against the Ottoman Turks. Italy was subject to frequent attacks by the Turks until at least the 1620s. Tasso's sister Cornelia narrowly escaped

Torquato Tasso, 1575, at the Court of Ferrara, where he wrote *Gerusalemme Liberata*.

capture by a band of Turkish pirates in his hometown of Sorrento, so the threat of these invaders held personal significance for him. In attempting to persuade Alfonso to do battle in the name of the Church, Tasso's poem brings together his concerns about being a worthy court poet and a good Christian.

Tasso and the Church. In addition to political turmoil, there was a troubling ideological shift in the religious institutions of Tasso's day. Although the Protestant Reformation in many ways forced the Catholic Church to codify its dogma in an effort to distinguish itself as the one true church, changes in the notion of piety and the shrinking of religious tolerance were already underway by the time Martin Luther took action that instigated the Reformation in 1517. By the late sixteenth century, the Council of Trent, which met in three sessions from 1544-63, had asserted the authority of local bishops and the parish as the center of religious life. The Council also laid the foundations for a more personal, active notion of religious faith than before. This concept was manifested in a number of ways: one consequence was the establishment of the Society of Jesus in 1540, more commonly known as the Jesuit order, which became the right hand of the Church in its missionary and educational efforts for centuries to come. A second consequence was the formation of a commission of six cardinals

by Pope Paul III in 1542, later known as the Roman Inquisition.

Tasso's own relationship to the Church was, like the rest of his life, full of conflict. His father, Bernardo, had participated in the 1522 rebellion of Naples against papal rule, which forced Bernardo into exile along with his patron. Later he grew anxiety-ridden about the relationship between his work and the Church. By the time Tasso completed *Jerusalem Delivered,* his doubts about it had grown; the response to the initial text he circulated was not entirely positive. So concerned was he about the poem's various digressions on the subject of love between the Christian knights and the Saracen women that he submitted it for review by the Holy Office of the Inquisition. It approved the work, but this gesture failed to quell his nagging doubts. Tasso grew obsessed with the unresolved conflicts both within the poem and himself.

After Tasso attacked a servant with a knife, Tasso's patron, Alfonso, sent him to the asylum of St. Ann, where he was allowed visitors and continued to write prolifically. After seven years there, Tasso had improved enough to leave. He began an itinerant existence, wandering among the Italian courts at Mantua, Bergamo, and Naples. He also began to write a number of religiously inspired works, including several madrigals, the tragedy *Torrismondo,* a poem entitled *The Creation of the*

World (*Il Mondo Creato*), and what he deemed his greatest work, *Jerusalem Conquered,* a refashioning of the earlier Jerusalem poem without any of its romance elements. Remaining religiously inspired, Tasso ultimately gained not only the approval but also the acclaim of the Church. He spent his final days in Rome, where he died before he could accept the honor of being crowned Italy's poet laureate by Pope Clement VIII.

Publication and reception. In 1580 the first 14 cantos of *Jerusalem Delivered* were published in an unauthorized version under the title *Goffredo* (Godfrey). More definitive editions followed in 1581 and 1584 after repeated revisions by both the editors and the poet himself. In 1593, after Tasso removed many of the episodes on love, a completely revised version of the poem was released under the title *Jerusalem Conquered.* This later version never achieved the popularity or success of the original, but in Tasso's view, came much closer to the classical epic model.

Jerusalem Delivered, on the other hand, was both an immediate success and a catalyst for controversy. The poem's content became part of a debate as to which of the two most accomplished modern poets, Ariosto or Tasso, was worthy of the stature afforded to ancients such as Virgil or Homer. There were many individuals, especially among the members of the nascent Academy of the Crusca in Florence who favored Ariosto's multiplicity of plot and inventiveness to Tasso's adherence to the Aristotelian principle of unity. Feeling the need to defend his strategy, in 1585 Tasso published the *Apology in Defense of the "Jerusalem Delivered."* He argued for the superiority of his epic by explaining that it rested on a concept of unity that was twofold: first it entailed Aristotle's idea of formal unity and second, the notion that political and religious unity under a single earthly ruler is preferable to the chaos that results when many individuals attempt to rule simultaneously. The earthly ruler in the poem is, of course, Godfrey, earthly head of all the crusaders as God's chosen emissary, God being the supreme ruler.

The first English translation of the *Gerusalemme Liberata* by Edward Fairfax appeared in 1600 and subsequently in 1624 under the title *Godfrey of Bulloigne.* The vast number of references to Tasso throughout this period gives an indication as to the popularity and influence of his work on English poets such as Edmund Spenser and John Milton, whose *Paradise Lost,* (1667, 1674) became but one of several Christian epics that followed in the wake of Tasso's influential epic. Many of Europe's later, nineteenth-century Romantic writers viewed Tasso as the supreme example of poetic genius. They tended, however, to compose works not on his poetry but on his biography, works like *The Lament of Tasso* by Lord Byron (1788-1824) and the play *Torquato Tasso* by Goethe (1749-1832), both of which recount Tasso's unrequited love for Leonora D'Este. On the other hand, countless artists and musicians created pieces based on some of the poem's most memorable episodes—for example, the cantata *Combattimento di Tancredi e Clorinda* (The Battle of Tancred and Clorinda) by the composer Claudio Monteverdi.

—Jacqualine Dyess

For More Information

Billings, Malcolm. *The Cross and the Crescent: A History of the Crusades.* New York: Sterling, 1990.

Biow, Douglas George. *Mirabile Dictu: Representations of the Marvelous in Medieval and Renaissance Epic.* Ann Arbor: University of Michigan Press, 1996.

Brand, Peter, and Lino Pertile, eds. *The Cambridge History of Italian Literature.* Cambridge: Cambridge University Press, 1996.

Duncan, Frederick, and August C. Krey, eds. *Gesta Francorum Jerusalem Expugnantium* [The Deeds of the Franks Who Attacked Jerusalem]. In *Parallel Source Problems in Medieval History.* New York: Harper and Brothers, 1912. http://www.fordham.edu/halsall/source/cde-jlem.html#fulcher1.

Ferguson, Margaret. *Trials of Desire: Renaissance Defenses of Desire.* New Haven: Yale University Press, 1983.

Hillenbrand, Carole. *The Crusades: Islamic Perspectives.* Edinburgh: Edinburgh University Press, 1999.

Hindley, Geoffrey. *The Crusades: A History of Armed Pilgrimage and Holy War.* New York: Carroll and Graf Publishers, 2003.

Jeffries-Martin, John. "Religion, Renewal, and Reform in the Sixteenth Century." In *Early Modern Italy: 1550-1796.* Ed. John A. Marino. Oxford: Oxford University Press, 2002.

Kates, Judith A. *Tasso and Milton: The Problem of Christian Epic.* London: Associated University Presses, 1983.

Kruk, Remke. "The Bold and the Beautiful: Women and 'Fitna' in the 'Sirat Dhat Al-Himma': The Story of Nura." In *Women in the Medieval Islamic World.* Ed. Gavin R. G. Hambley. New York: St. Martin's Press, 1998.

Riley-Smith, Jonathan, ed. *The Oxford Illustrated History of the Crusades.* Oxford: Oxford University Press, 1995.

Tasso, Torquato. *Jerusalem Delivered (Gerusalemme Liberata).* Trans. Anthony M. Esolen. Baltimore: Johns Hopkins University Press, 2000.

The Last Letters
of Jacopo Ortis

by

Ugo Foscolo

orn on the Greek isle of Zante in 1778,
Niccolò (later known as Ugo) Foscolo was
the eldest son of Andrea Foscolo, a Venetian doctor, and Diamantina Spathis, the Greek
daughter of a tailor. His father's death in 1788
plunged the mother and children into poverty,
forcing them to leave Spalato, where Andrea had
worked as director of the hospital, and return to
Zante. For a time, the children were sent to different relatives, but the family finally reunited in
Venice, where they established a home in 1792.
Ugo was educated at the school of San Cipriano
in the area of Venice known as Murano, where
he studied philosophy and literature and began
to write poetry. His talents attracted the atten-
tions of the cultured and influential Countess
Isabella Teotochi Albrizzi, who invited him to
join her literary circle, which included the poets
Ippolito Pindemonte and Melchiorre Cesarotti.
At 19, Foscolo composed his first play, *Tieste*
(*Thyestes*, 1797), which attracted the praise of
Italian dramatist Vittorio Alfieri (see Alfieri's
Myrrha, also in *WLAIT 7: Italian Literature and
Its Times*). In addition to his literary pursuits,
Foscolo engaged in political activities. He sup-
ported Napoleon Bonaparte's invasion of Italy in
1796, believing that it would lead to Venetian in-
dependence from the aristocratic families who
had essentially ruled the centuries-old republic.
After the French signed the Treaty of Campoformio, giving control of Venice to Austria in
1797, Foscolo became disillusioned and fled to
Milan, where he worked for a Milanese periodical. In 1799 Foscolo began a military career,

THE LITERARY WORK

An epistolary novel set mainly in Italy during
the late 1790s; published in Italian (as *Ultime
lettere di Jacopo Ortis*) in 1802, in English in
1817.

SYNOPSIS

Despairing of his country's future after
Napoleon's invasion and suffering because of
a doomed romance, an idealistic young man
resolves to commit suicide.

serving with the National Guard of Bologna
and Genoa. During this period, he was also
at work on *The Last Letters of Jacopo Ortis*, a
semi-autobiographical epistolary novel. Widely
praised by the Italians who first read the novel,
the work remains notable today for its portrayal
of a romantic hero struggling in vain to cope with
his nationalistic and romantic disappointments.

Events in History at the
Time of the Novel

Italy during the French Revolutionary Wars.
The Last Letters of Jacopo Ortis takes place during
the late eighteenth century, when poverty, banditry, begging, vagrancy, and other social ills
grew especially widespread in the Italian states.
Such wealth as the country possessed was mainly
concentrated in the North or in the cities, while

Ugo Foscolo

the majority of peasants in the agrarian South lived in debt and squalor. Conscious of their country's ills, many Italian intellectuals and progressives felt that only drastic change would bring about the reforms they sought in order to improve the general quality of life in their land. The radicals consequently looked with approval on the outbreak of the French Revolution in 1789. Some Italians no doubt hoped that a similar uprising might result in the formation of a national homeland in their country, which at the time consisted of separate states and principalities, some ruled by the Italian nobility, some by foreign powers.

Enthusiasm waned, however, even among radicals when the French Revolution took an increasingly bloody turn around 1792. At the same time, the kings, princes, and dukes who ruled the various Italian states became more resistant to progressive reforms. Fearing similar outbreaks within their own domains, these rulers moved to enforce censorship rules and to suppress both the Freemasons (fraternal groups pledged to humanist, secular values) and Jacobins, outspoken advocates of the Revolution who were inspired by the newborn ideals of democracy and equality.

To some extent, the rulers' fears were justified. War broke out in 1792 between France and several European nations. Italy was soon dragged into the conflict when French troops attacked the Kingdom of Piedmont-Sardinia and occupied Savoy and Nice in an attempt to expand French boundaries and protect the new republic of France from attacks by other European powers. While most of the other Italian states chose to remain neutral, a few declared war on France, joining the anti-French coalition of Austria, England, and Prussia. The Italian areas that were under Austrian control (Tuscany and Lombardy) had little choice.

In 1795 a new government was established by the French republic, and its policy towards Italian opponents, such as Piedmont-Sardinia, became more aggressive. In March 1796 a young Corsican general (and future emperor of France), Napoleon Bonaparte, took command of French troops in northern Italy and within two months, had defeated the Piedmontese, forcing their king, Vittorio Amedeo III, to sign an armistice permitting French occupation of all Piedmontese fortresses. Napoleon's army then triumphed over Austrian forces at Lodi, further strengthening France's hold over northern Italy.

Following these victories, Napoleon entered Milan, Bologna, and Verona and brought all three under French control. Overall, he encountered little resistance, especially in Milan, where a nest of Italian Jacobins had gathered. Several influential Milanese, including Francesco Melzi and Paolo Greppi, believed it was in the best interests of their state—Lombardy—to break with Austria and seek alliance with France. Taking it upon himself to redraw the political map, Napoleon turned Bologna and Ferrara (ceded to him under duress by Pope Pius VI in 1797) into the Cispadane Republic and similarly arranged for the territories of Milan and Mantua to become the Transpadane Republic. By April 1797 the two Napoleonic states had merged to form the Cisalpine Republic. A month later, Napoleon turned his attention to subduing the Venetian Republic, which had lasted for more than a millennium.

The end of the Venetian Republic. Already by the ninth century, Venice, situated amid lagoons at an oceanic crossroads, had developed itself into a commercial force. It then recognized the authority of the Byzantine Empire, whose decline in the ninth century led to Venice's own proud emergence as a self-governing city, a status it would maintain for nearly a millennium while one Italian neighbor after another suffered foreign rule. Political power in Venice was concentrated in the hands of an oligarchy of merchant families. No doubt, they felt entitled to rule, since Venice had by this time established itself as a maritime power exceeding all other Italian cities, except Genoa. Around 1300, in the face of naval threats from Genoa, Venice expanded its ruling body and made the right to participate in this Great Council hereditary. The council expanded to 1,500 members out of a total population of about 120,000. In 1310, by election, the Great Council formed a smaller Council of Ten, whose main job was to ensure internal security and order. There was also a Doge, or head of state, accompanied by six counselors who limited his power. Commoners participated in government too, filling official secretarial posts. All this organization bred civic loyalty and adherence to principles, especially to the one that insisted no single person ever monopolize power. Then, in the 1600s, Venice entered an economic slump and political decline followed. The late 1700s found small cliques of Venetians competing as usual for political power, none of them strong enough to withstand Napoleon.

During the French Revolution and Napoleon's first Italian campaigns, Venice claimed to be neutral, refusing to ally itself openly with any European power. Nonetheless, Venice's sympathies were most closely associated with those of the deposed monarchy in France; the Comte de Provence—the brother of former French king Louis XVI—applied for and was granted refuge in the Venetian Republic. For two years, the government of the Doge (the chief Venetian official) accepted the presence of the "Comte De Lille" and his family; ultimately, however, fearing Napoleon's hostility, the Venetian republic asked them to leave.

Unfortunately, the revolutionary government in France was too offended to be placated by the Comte's departure; moreover, the French were further antagonized by the fact that Austrian troops were permitted to move with impunity on Venetian soil. So incensed was Napoleon that he threatened to burn down Verona and Venice. After successfully occupying Verona in 1796, he demanded an alliance with Venice, which refused his terms and continued to cling to its neutral status. An anti-French rising in Verona in April 1797 and the sinking of a French ship by a Venetian fort on the Lido, an island sandbar outside the lagoon of Venice, led to Napoleon's declaring war on Venice in May 1797.

Although the Venetian senate issued orders for the defense of the city and preparations for a siege, the Doge and his ministers chose to accept unconditionally all of Napoleon's terms, owing in part to pro-French sympathies among the Venetian masses. Their policies of appeasement

effectively ended the 1,200-year-old Venetian Republic. In a proclamation dated May 16, 1797, Napoleon announced the end of all the traditional institutions, the recognition of the people as sovereign, and the abolition of hereditary rights held by the Venetian nobility and Great Council. French troops were deployed to maintain law and order.

Initially, some Venetians hailed the advent of the French with elation, believing that the forces of revolution would usher in a new age of liberty for their homeland. Joyful demonstrations were held in the Piazza San Marco, where a tree of liberty was planted, and the ancient Libro d'Oro, a Golden Book containing the names of the most privileged Venetian families, was burned. All prisoners were released and some towns triumphantly proclaimed their independence from the now dissolved Republic of Venice.

THE KINGDOM OF ITALY

While Foscolo's novel deals only with the two years immediately following the Treaty of Campoformio, it is worth noting that, after becoming First Consul of France in 1799, Napoleon renewed his military campaigns against Austrian forces in Italy. In 1801 the Treaty of Lunéville forced Austria to cede all of its Italian territory, with the exception of Venice, to France. By 1805, however, Venice too, along with Istria and Dalmatia, had passed into French hands, becoming part of the Kingdom of Italy, which had been established in the North, with Milan as its capital. Another French-ruled state, known as the Kingdom of Naples, existed in the South after 1806. Most of the Papal States fell under French rule in 1808-09. Until his abdication in 1814, Napoleon controlled the entire Italian peninsula, but not the islands of Sardinia and Sicily.

Five months later, however, Venetians' hopes for liberty were dashed when Napoleon signed the Treaty of Campoformio, which gave Venice and her territories in Istria and Dalmatia to Austria in exchange for the latter's Belgian provinces and the new Cisalpine Republic. After appropriating Venetian ships, gold, and works of art, the French departed on January 18, 1798; the Austrians arrived to occupy the former republic on the very same day. *The Last Letters of Jacopo Ortis* begins just days before the signing of the treaty, with Jacopo's first letter conveying the bitterness and disillusionment experienced by many Venetians at news of this betrayal by their supposed liberators: "The sacrifice of our homeland is complete. All is lost, and life remains to us—if indeed we are allowed to live—only so that we may lament our misfortunes and our shame" (Foscolo, *Letters*, p. 7).

Romanticism. The passionate tone of Foscolo's novel reflects the beginnings of a new literary movement known as Romanticism, which first swept through Europe during the late eighteenth century and became increasingly dominant in the nineteenth century. Although each country brought its own unique interpretation to the movement, universal characteristics of Romanticism included a preference for innovation over traditionalism and for subjective over objective experience, emphasis on the imagination rather than the faculty of reason, emotional reaction to one's natural surroundings, and an exaltation of the individual person, however imperfect or flawed.

These Romantic characteristics apparently manifested themselves first in Germany before taking hold elsewhere. Several modern scholars contend that Romanticism did not become a full-blown phenomenon until the post-Napoleonic years, from about 1815 to 1827. However, German works like Johann Goethe's *The Sorrows of Young Werther* (1774) were available in translation, often in French, the language of cultured society all over Europe in the 1700s. Foscolo himself read Goethe's work in translation, courtesy of his friend and lover Countess Isabella Arese. *The Last Letters of Jacopo Ortis* often evokes comparison with *The Sorrows of Young Werther*, not least because the protagonists of both novels struggle with unfulfilled romantic hopes and ultimately commit suicide. However, in his passion for the unattainable Teresa and his lingering grief over Italy's oppression, Jacopo Ortis also anticipates the Romantic hero immortalized by the British poet Lord Byron: a brooding, melancholy, often self-absorbed individual who wanders in lonely exile far from his native shore, while languishing in the grip of a forbidden passion.

The Novel in Focus

Plot summary. *The Last Letters of Jacopo Ortis* is written in the form of an epistolary novel. Most of the protagonist's letters are written to his friend Lorenzo Alderani, whom he meets periodically over the course of the novel. Other letters are addressed to Teresa, the woman Jacopo loves in vain. Occasionally notes and story frag-ments—written by Jacopo or Lorenzo—interrupt the narrative progression of the letters. Before it begins, Lorenzo informs the reader in an editorial note that Jacopo has died and that Lorenzo is publishing these letters "to raise a monument to unknown virtue, and to consecrate to the memory of my only friend those tears which now I am forbidden to shed upon his tomb" (*Letters*, p. 3).

The first letter in the novel is dated October 1797, shortly before the ratification of the Treaty of Campoformio, which will grant the Austrians control over Venice. Jacopo, an upper-class Venetian youth with strong nationalist sympathies, reveals that "[his] name is on the list of those proscribed" and so he has taken refuge in the Euganean Hills to escape persecution as a rebel (*Letters*, p. 7). Despairing of his homeland's future, Jacopo contemplates suicide rather than life under foreign rule: "Ah, how often in despair of vengeance I feel like plunging a knife into my heart to pour out all my blood amid the last shrieks of my homeland!" (*Letters*, p. 7).

While in his country retreat, Jacopo meets the cultured Signor T*** and his two daughters, the child Isabella and her older sister Teresa, who is betrothed to Odoardo, a wealthy but dull nobleman. This marital agreement has been made to ensure the family's future security as Signor T***'s own nationalist sympathies have brought him under governmental scrutiny. The family grows fond of Jacopo, who becomes enamored of the beautiful Teresa. After a bond develops between the two, Teresa confides to Jacopo that her mother disapproves of the arranged marriage between Teresa and Odoardo and has left her own husband because of it. Teresa also admits that she is unhappy and does not love her betrothed. Jacopo complains to Lorenzo, who is also acquainted with the family, about the unyielding attitude of Signor T***, who will brook no resistance to his plans: "He loves his daughter deeply, he often praises her and looks at her with pride, and yet he holds a sword over her. . . . To make it worse, he considers his wife's opposition a violation of his own authority" (*Letters*, p. 17).

When Odoardo is called away to Rome because of a relative's death, Jacopo begins spending more time at Signor T***'s villa with the family. One day, listening to Teresa play the harp and sing an ode by the Greek poetess Sappho that he has translated, he realizes that he loves the girl. Not wishing to distress her or her father by his attentions, he leaves the hills for the University of Padua in December 1797. In Padua the beautiful, dissolute wife of a nobleman attempts to seduce him but memories of Teresa impel Jacopo to decline her advances. Discontented with his surroundings, Jacopo grows bored, restless, and short-tempered; he enters into a quarrel concerning his honor and challenges his adversary to a duel, only to have the challenge refused. The university also displeases him because it is "composed of proud professors at odds with each other and dissolute students" (*Letters*, p. 29). Finally, Jacopo asks Lorenzo to sell all of his books and give the profits to his mother. By the new year, Jacopo has returned to the Euganean Hills and Teresa's side. In response to Lorenzo's criticism of his decision, Jacopo argues that "If I had to keep a constant watch on my irrepressible heart, I would always be at war with myself, and to no advantage. I shall give myself up for lost, and let what happens happen" (*Letters*, p. 31).

With Odoardo still in Rome, Jacopo and Teresa spend even more time together. Although happy in his beloved's company, Jacopo is frequently reminded of his country's plight, which plunges him into gloom. At one point, he digresses from his letters to write a romanticized account of Lauretta, a young girl he knew who lost her sweetheart Eugenio in the wars and subsequently lost her mind. Distraught, she wanders the fields, carrying a basket containing a skull, which she crowns with fresh roses. Later, learning that Lauretta has died, Jacopo feels relieved that she is at last free of her affliction.

The attachment between Jacopo and Teresa deepens. One evening in May 1798, Teresa confesses that she loves Jacopo and they exchange a single kiss. However, she also declares that they can never be together because she must obey her father. Jacopo alternately rejoices at the knowledge that his love is reciprocated and despairs that his political and economic circumstances prevent his marrying Teresa. His distress escalates when his rival finally returns from Rome; Jacopo agonizes over Teresa's impending marriage and unhappiness, despises Odoardo as complacent and commonplace, and rails against every perceived injustice, from the condition of his homeland to the necessity of Teresa marrying to please her father. The violence of his emotions eventually causes Jacopo to fall ill with a fever. Upon recovering, he yields to the entreaties of Lorenzo and Signor T*** and agrees to depart the hill country again.

In the second part of the novel, Jacopo, still mourning the loss of Teresa, wanders through northern Italy, witnessing various social problems, including poverty, regional hostilities, and political oppression. In Bologna he observes the executions of two men who committed theft out of hunger and feels disgust at the way the rich continually victimize and punish the poor. In Florence he visits the tombs of Galileo, Machiavelli, and Michelangelo; sights that exalt and at the same time depress him:

> Near these marble monuments I felt myself living again those ardent years of mine when, staying up late over the writings of great men, I imagined myself enjoying the applause of future generations. Such thoughts are too elevated for me now! They may even be mad. My intellect is blind, my limbs unsteady, and my heart corrupt, here, in its very depths.
>
> (*Letters*, p. 84)

The beauties of nature have the power to soothe Jacopo, but their solace is only temporary. In his letters, he reproaches Lorenzo for not writing more frequently and for not including more news of Teresa, even though he dreads to hear of her marriage to Odoardo. Finally, he asks Lorenzo not to speak of him to Teresa and admits that he cannot help exacerbating his own torment: "I finger my wounds where they are most grievous, and I try to ulcerate them, and I look at them as they bleed. And it seems to me that my sufferings are some expiation for my faults, and a brief comfort for the griefs of that innocent young girl" (*Letters*, p. 88).

Jacopo's embittered wanderings continue. He travels through Tuscany and Parma, feeling like an exile in his own country, especially after he is denied a passport to visit Rome because of his nationalist sympathies: "So all we Italians are political exiles and foreigners in Italy, and when we are only a short distance away from our own little bit of earth, neither intellect, nor fame, nor a blameless life protects us" (*Letters*, p. 89). Journeying instead to Milan, Jacopo witnesses further evidence of foreign rule: the general population speaks mostly French, a local bookseller does not stock Italian books, and the elderly poet Giuseppe Parini, whom Jacopo meets several times during his Milanese sojourn, has become disillusioned by the current regime and withdrawn from the struggle for a free Italy. Although Parini sympathizes with Jacopo's ardor and idealism, he sees no hope for their homeland and advises the young man to find another outlet for his passions. But torn between his despair over Italy and his hopeless love for Teresa, Jacopo feels that only death will bring him peace.

Napoleon crossing at the St. Bernard Pass. Painting by Jacques-Louis David, 1801, depicting Napolean on his way to defeat the Austrians at Marengo in northern Italy in June 1800.

In February 1799 Jacopo sets out for Nice in France, taking a route through Genoa and the Maritime Alps. While staying in the small village of Pietra Ligure, Jacopo meets a friend of Lorenzo's who has fallen on hard times. Having emigrated after the Peace of Campoformio, the former army lieutenant now finds himself unemployed with a young family to support and "[d]riven from town to town by every government, either because my poverty kept the magistrates' doors closed to me, or because no one took account of me. And those who knew me, either did not wish to know me, or turned their backs on me" (*Letters*, p. 103). Moved by the man's misfortunes, Jacopo gives him what money and clothing he can spare, and refrains from condemning him for whatever errors in judgment brought him to this pass.

Reaching the frontier at Ventimiglia, Jacopo experiences an epiphany, of sorts. Despite his torment, he decides that death in Italy, among his countrymen, is preferable to life in exile, where nobody knows or can sympathize with him. Rather than continue into France, Jacopo turns back towards Italy. In Rimini he writes to Lorenzo, inferring from the latter's silence that Teresa is now married to Odoardo. Describing himself as "incredibly peaceful," Jacopo writes that "It is better like this, because now it is all decided" (*Letters*, p. 114). In a note following this letter, Lorenzo surmises that his friend apparently decided to die and informs the reader that he has arranged Jacopo's remaining papers according to their dates.

During his last days, Jacopo sets his affairs in order. He makes a brief trip to Ravenna to visit the tomb of Dante, poet of **The Divine Comedy** (also in *WLAIT 7: Italian Literature and Its Times*). Next Jacopo returns to the Euganean Hills and, after a brief, emotionally tense encounter with Teresa and the rest of the T*** family, shuts himself up in his retreat with a Bible borrowed from the parish priest. To Lorenzo, Jacopo reveals a ten-month-old secret: while out riding, he had accidentally trampled a poor workman to death and then fled the scene. Subsequently, he had taken the man's widow and children into his household and seen to their security. Despite the family's gratitude, Jacopo remains overcome with remorse at having deprived them of a husband and father.

On a later visit to Signor T***'s villa, Jacopo tells the family he is preparing for another journey, this time to the once Venetian Islands. With the exception of Odoardo, everyone is sorry to hear of his impending departure, and a tearful Teresa gives Jacopo a miniature portrait of herself as a parting gift. Accompanied by Lorenzo, Jacopo then pays a last visit to his mother in Venice to receive her blessing. Jacopo's mother entreats her son to go on living but after he has left, she voices her fear to Lorenzo that they will never see Jacopo again.

Returning to the Euganean hills, Jacopo begins writing his last impassioned letters, one to Lorenzo enjoining him to take care of his mother, one to Teresa assuring her of his eternal love and exculpating her from all responsibility for his untimely demise. Jacopo fears interference with his plans when Lorenzo arrives unexpectedly at the country villa and witnesses his final farewell to the T*** family, but he manages to send his friend to Padua on the pretext of fetching letters from one of his former professors at the university. Late that night, Jacopo places Teresa's portrait around his neck and stabs himself fatally in the chest. His servant discovers his mortally

wounded master the next morning and rushes to the T***'s villa for help. Teresa faints on hearing the news and her father hurries to his dying friend's side; Jacopo expires within moments of the older man's arrival. Returning from Padua, Lorenzo is grief-stricken to learn of Jacopo's suicide: "That night I trudged along behind his corpse which three labourers buried on the hill of pines" (*Letters*, p. 140).

Man without a homeland. Arguably the most distinctive element in *The Last Letters of Jacopo Ortis* is the protagonist's continuing anguish over his country's fate. Exiled from his native Venice after the Austrian occupation, Jacopo wanders through Italy, brooding over its oppression by foreign powers and its inability to defend itself:

> These, O Italy, are your borders! But every day they are crossed at every point by the obstinate greed of other nations. Where are your children then? You lack nothing but the strength which comes from a common purpose. I would indeed give my unhappy life gloriously for you. But what can be done by my arm alone, and by my mere voice? Where is the ancient terror your glory inspired?
>
> (*Letters*, p. 110)

Jacopo's recognition of the sheer magnitude of his country's problems and his personal inability to solve them aggravates his gloom. "Nations devour each other," he muses, "because no single one of them could go on existing without the bodies of another. When I gaze at Italy from where I stand on these Alps, I weep and tremble, and I call for vengeance on the invaders. But my voice is lost in that murmur which is all that now survives of so many dead nations" (*Letters*, p. 111).

Jacopo's other disappointment in life—his inability to marry Teresa—likewise stems from Italy's political repression. During the late eighteenth century, unmarried Italian women still led lives defined by custom and tradition. In general, a young girl of good family was often educated in a convent school, then, upon reaching maturity, brought home to marry a man whom her father had chosen, regardless of her preferences. Teresa, in keeping with this practice, is betrothed to a wealthy nobleman chosen by her father. The arrangement causes severe strain in the family; her mother chooses to leave her father rather than condone a loveless marriage between their daughter and Odoardo.

Not only do Jacopo's nationalist sympathies and hatred of the Austrian regime prevent him from proposing marriage but Teresa's father, likewise under suspicion for "having desired true

In 1805 French forces under Napoleon enter Venice to incorporate it into the Greater French Empire.

liberty for his country, a capital crime in Italy," would be ruined if he allowed a match between Jacopo, openly condemned as a revolutionary, and his daughter (*Letters*, p. 72). Therefore, he has arranged for Teresa to marry a nobleman, whose wealth and status will afford the family some protection. Significantly, Jacopo acknowledges in his last letter to Teresa that their doomed romance is not the primary motive for his decision to commit suicide: "No, my dear young friend, you are not the cause of my death. All my desperate passions, the misfortunes of those people most necessary to my life, human crimes, the certainty of my perpetual slavery and of the perpetual infamy of my betrayed homeland—all had been decided a long time ago" (*Letters*, p. 128). Later, imagining himself called to account for his life before the throne of God, Jacopo again repeats the cry, "If you [God] had granted me a homeland, I would have spent all my intellect and blood on its behalf, and even so, my weak voice has courageously shouted out the truth" (*Letters*, p. 135).

At the time of Foscolo's novel, the notion of an Italian homeland seemed at once tantalizingly near and hopelessly distant. The ideals of the French Revolution had been largely responsible for inspiring Italians with the dream of nationhood, but when the French entered Italy in 1796, they came as an invading rather than as a liber-

ating force. However, the formation of northern and central Italy into the Kingdom of Italy in 1805 represented a landmark in modern Italian history. For the first time in centuries, northern Italy existed as a unitary state, with a centralized administration and a national civil code, even though the French were responsible for the structure and implementation of both. As one historian writes, "The Napoleonic era was one of mixed gains for Italy. Many of the old privileges and much of the administrative chaos that had so plagued pre-revolutionary governments, formally disappeared; yet the benefits were far less than they might have been" (Duggan, p. 96). Napoleon, nominally king of the newly formed state, regarded Italy as either a territory to be apportioned to relatives and allies or as a source of funds for furthering French military campaigns. He had little interest in Italy itself, nor in the cause of Italian independence.

Significantly, Italian nationalist sentiment only increased in the face of his opposition. While no organized political or intellectual movements arose to counter the forces of occupation openly—indeed, such movements would inevitably have been suppressed by the Bonapartist regime—Italian patriots found subtler ways of fighting back, namely, through art and literature. In response to Napoleon's attempt to make French the official language of the empire, many Italian writers, including Foscolo, determinedly produced important works in their native language. Meanwhile, in the South, secret societies intent on ousting foreign invaders from Italian soil became increasingly active. The most famous of these societies was the Carboneria, so called because its members—the *carbonari*—met in caves around charcoal fires. Disunity and internal conflict still plagued the regions of Italy, so years would pass before such resistance movements became sufficiently organized to be effective. Nonetheless, the dream of independence and unity took firmer hold decades before it was realized in the mid-nineteenth century.

Sources and literary context. Although *The Last Letters of Jacopo Ortis* was partly influenced by Vittorio Alfieri's tragedies and Lawrence Sterne's *The Sentimental Journey* (specifically, the section about Lauretta), the novel mainly shows a strong autobiographical influence. Foscolo's life did not, it is true, end in a dramatic suicide like that of his protagonist; nonetheless he drew heavily upon his own youthful experiences and emotions in writing his novel. Like many of his countrymen, Foscolo had hoped that the French invasion would result in an independent Italy, but his hopes were dashed when his native Venice was ceded to Austria under the Treaty of Campoformio. Foscolo reacted just as Jacopo Ortis did, by leaving Venice and fleeing to Milan to avoid political persecution.

Also like his protagonist, Foscolo proved unlucky in love. For a time he was romantically involved with his patroness Isabella Teotochi; her marriage to Giuseppe Albrizzi in 1796 so disappointed Foscolo that he suffered a decline in health and had to be sent to the Euganean Hills by his mother to recover. Later, while in Milan, Foscolo fell in love with Teresa Monti, wife of the poet Vincenzo Monti. He also became enamored of a beautiful unmarried girl, Isabella Roncioni, whom he met in Florence. Although Isabella returned Foscolo's affections, marriage between them was not possible because she was already betrothed to a suitor chosen by her family. Teresa, the unattainable beloved in Foscolo's novel, appears to be a composite of all three women whom he loved but could not have.

Foscolo's work is most readily classified as an epistolary novel, a genre that enjoyed great popularity with eighteenth-century audiences. In particular, Johann Wolfgang Goethe's *The Sorrows of Young Werther* (1774), which Foscolo had read and admired, served as a model for *The Last Letters of Jacopo Ortis*. Both works feature idealistic young men who suffer from political disillusionment and thwarted love for an unattainable woman; both works end with the protagonist's suicide. But while Werther's decline is partly attributable to the dull mediocrity of his surroundings, Jacopo's is a result of the frenzy and subsequent disappointments of the Napoleonic Wars.

GIUSEPPE PARINI

Although *The Last Letters of Jacopo Ortis* is fictional, its protagonist mentions and even encounters real-life literary figures, such as the writers Vittorio Alfieri (1749-1803) and Giuseppe Parini (1729-99). Like Foscolo, Parini recognized the need for significant social change in Italy. When the French entered Milan in 1796, Parini was among those who hoped that some of the nobler principles of the French Revolution would take root in his country. In 1797, when Napoleon established the Cisalpine Republic, with Milan as its capital, he made Parini a member of the municipal government. But the idealistic Parini soon became disenchanted with the new regime and lost his position, partly because of his liberal utterances and sympathies. According to one anecdote, Parini publicly responded to the outcry of "Long live the Republic. Death to traitors!" with "Long live the Republic. Death to no one!" (Parini in Hearder, *Italy in the Age of Risorgimento*, p. 255).

Reception and impact. Published in 1802, *The Last Letters of Jacopo Ortis* proved highly successful in and beyond Foscolo's native Italy. Its popularity spread to other parts of Western Europe, where translators rendered the novel into English, German, French, and modern Greek. Critics generally applauded the novel, one of them praising its portrayal of the effect of grief on the mind (Anonymous in Harris and Tennyson, p. 260). Other reviewers praised the vivid depiction of Italy's political woes and the difficulties faced by Italian patriots who longed to see their homeland independent and united. Andre Viesseux, writing for the *Foreign Quarterly Review* in 1832, argued that its great attraction "lies in the political structures and patriotic sentiments, in the living picture of the extraordinary epoch in which they were written, in the sarcastic exposure of the republican mimics of the time, the pungent satire on the corruptions of Italian society, the glow of indignation against injustice, hypocrisy, and oppression, from whatever quarter they came" (Viesseux in Harris and Tennyson, pp. 262-263).

Foscolo would not have disagreed with that assessment of his novel's strengths; indeed, he observed that "*Ortis* may boast of having been the first book that induced the females and the mass of readers to interest themselves in public affairs" (Foscolo in Harris and Tennyson, p. 261). When Foscolo left Italy for England, he found himself most often associated with his one early novel in his adopted country. To his embarrassment, some young English ladies even addressed him as "Ortis" (Vincent, p. 7).

More recently, *The Last Letters of Jacopo Ortis* has been considered a work of Romantic self-expression and has been singled out as Italy's first modern novel. It not only depicts its Romantic hero's feelings of rebellion and despair, notes literary historian Antonio Cippico: "What gives the greater historical importance to Foscolo's book," he continues, "is . . . the tragedy of Jacopo himself, who lives through the death of his country" (Cippico, pp. 53-54).

—Pamela S. Loy

FOSCOLO IN EXILE

Like his fictional counterpart, Foscolo became deeply disillusioned by the various foreign regimes occupying Italy. He fled Venice when Austrian forces marched into the former republic after the Treaty of Campoformio, and later, despite having served in Napoleon's Atlantic army from 1804 to 1806, he found himself frequently at odds with the Bonapartists, who from 1805 to 1814 ruled the Italian peninsula as the Kingdom of Italy in the North and the Kingdom of Naples in the South. His appointment as lecturer in eloquence at the University of Pavia came to an abrupt end when Napoleon suppressed teaching of eloquence at all Italian universities, a decision to which Foscolo's reportedly inflammatory lectures against tyranny may have contributed. After Napoleon's abdication in 1814, the Austrians regained much of their power over northern Italy. Rather than take an oath of allegiance to Austria, Foscolo went into exile, fleeing first to Switzerland, then to England, where, after a precarious existence marred by debts and ill health, he died in 1827.

For More Information

Brand, C. P. *Italy and the English Romantics*. Cambridge: Cambridge University Press, 1957.

Cambon, Glauco. *Ugo Foscolo, Poet of Exile*. Princeton: Princeton University Press, 1980.

Cippico, Antonio. *The Romantic Age in Italian Literature*. London: Philip Lee Warner, 1918.

Davis, John, ed. *Italy in the Nineteenth Century: 1796-1900*. Oxford: Oxford University Press, 2000.

Duggan, Christopher. *A Concise History of Italy*. Cambridge: Cambridge University Press, 1994.

Foscolo, Ugo. *Last Letters of Jacopo Ortis*. Trans. J. G. Nichols. London: Hesperus Press, 2002.

Harris, Laurie Lanzen, and Emily B. Tennyson. *Nineteenth- Century Literature Criticism*. Vol. 8. Detroit: Gale Research, 1985.

Hearder, Harry. *Italy: A Short History*. Cambridge: Cambridge University Press, 2001.

———. *Italy in the Age of the Risorgimento 1790-1870*. London: Longman, 1983.

Killinger, Charles. *The History of Italy*. Westport, Conn.: Greenwood Press, 2002.

Radcliffe-Umstead, Douglas. *Ugo Foscolo*. New York: Twayne Publishers, 1970.

Vincent, E. R. *Ugo Foscolo: An Italian in Regency England*. Cambridge: Cambridge University Press, 1953.

The Leopard

by

Giuseppe Tomasi di Lampedusa

Born in 1896 in Palermo, Sicily, in Italy, Giuseppe Tomasi di Lampedusa descended from a wealthy family whose ancestors gained distinction in the seventeenth century when they were named princes of Lampedusa—a small island south of Sicily. Although the family's fortune declined during the 1800s, the title remained, with Giuseppe himself gaining distinction as the last Prince of Lampedusa. Young Giuseppe was educated at home by a private tutor; from 1912 to 1914, he attended the Liceo-Ginnasio Garibaldi in Palermo, where he studied philosophy, history, and Italian. Between 1914 and 1916 Giuseppe Lampedusa studied law, first at the University of Genoa, then at the University of Rome. He served in the First World War as an officer in the Italian artillery. Captured by the Austrians, Lampedusa managed to escape from a prison camp in Hungary and to make his way back to Italy. He remained in the national army until 1921, then spent the rest of his life traveling through Europe, reading and studying world literature, and trying to recoup the family fortune.

In 1932 Lampedusa married Alessandra Wolff, a Freudian psychiatrist and the daughter of a Latvian aristocrat; the couple were frequently separated because of his familial responsibilities and her career. Alessandra nonetheless had a marked effect on her husband's future. After his family palace was bombed and looted by Allied troops during World War II, Lampedusa sunk into a deep depression for several years. His wife suggested he begin writing as a form of therapy, touching off

THE LITERARY WORK

A novel set in Sicily between 1860 and 1910; published in Italian (as *Il Gattopardo*) in 1958, in English in 1960.

SYNOPSIS

A Sicilian nobleman witnesses the emergence of modern Italy as his own way of life slowly declines.

an impressive outpouring. From 1955 until his death in 1957, Lampedusa wrote copiously, producing a historical novel, *The Leopard*, some short stories, and a collection of memoirs.

Rejected for publication during Lampedusa's lifetime, *The Leopard* was finally published posthumously in 1958. It became an immediate popular success, as well as the object of heated critical debate. Conservatives attacked it for its decadence, while leftists dismissed it as the nostalgic ramblings of a dispossessed aristocrat. Yet *The Leopard* often impressed readers because of its elaborate style and its meticulous depiction of two worlds, one in decline, the other struggling to be born.

Events in History at the Time the Novel Takes Place

Sicily during the nineteenth century—an overview. For much of its existence, the island of

Sicily, at the southernmost tip of the Italian peninsula, has been dominated by one foreign power or another. A branch of the Spanish Bourbons ruled Naples and Sicily as a single entity from the mid-eighteenth century, but the family was deposed during the Italian campaigns of Napoleon Bonaparte (1796-1814). By 1814 Napoleon had extended his dominion over most of the Italian peninsula, ruling it as a single kingdom. He was emperor of a France that had grown considerably because of his conquests, but Sardinia and Sicily escaped his grasp. In 1806 Ferdinand III, the Bourbon king at the time, fled to Sicily; that same year, the British established a garrison there, ostensibly to protect the king but also to prevent the island's valuable sulfur deposits from seizure by the French.

SECRET SOCIETIES

During the Napoleonic period (1793-1815) secret societies flourished in Italy, especially in the South. Driven underground by the police, these groups met clandestinely to spread nationalist sympathy and express solidarity against the foreign invaders. The most famous of these societies was the *carbonari* (charcoal burners), so called because they would meet in caves around charcoal fires. The *carbonari*, who belonged mostly to the lower and middle classes, continued to meet during the 1820s and 1830s, after the restoration of Austrian and Spanish rule. As a movement they had no political agenda beyond their vague desire for political reforms and their dislike of foreign tyranny; consequently, their resistance efforts remained generalized and ineffective. However, other, more ambitious groups adopted their ideals. Giuseppe Mazzini, who had joined the *carbonari* in 1827, left them to found a new society, Young Italy, in 1831 at Marseilles, France. Mazzini's movement advocated mass revolt and the use of guerrilla war tactics against foreign oppressors; the ultimate goal was to force the Austrians, the Spanish, and even the papacy out of power and to found a democratic republic. Many young Italians flocked to the cause, including Giuseppe Garibaldi and Francesco Crispi, who were to play pivotal roles in Italy's final struggle for unification.

While under British administration, Sicilians became accustomed to a greater degree of independence. William Bentinck, a British general acting as virtual governor of Sicily, convened a parliament in June 1812. The parliament's first actions were to abolish feudalism (many Sicilian nobles agreed to this in hopes of personal economic gain) and to draw up a liberal constitution. The constitution called for some innovative measures: the formation of a two-chamber parliament similar to that of the British, with a House of Peers and a House of Commons; a jury system; and the abolition of torture. While not all of the policies were adopted and some proved difficult to implement, the idea of liberal reform had at least been introduced to Sicily. This helps explain its reaction when Napoleon fell in 1814 and the Bourbons were restored to power after the Congress of Vienna (1814-15). Sicily became one of the earliest and most active centers for the recruitment of liberal patriots to the cause—first of territorial independence from foreign powers and, ultimately, of unification of the peninsula.

The new Bourbon state, again consisting of Naples and Sicily, was known as the Kingdom of the Two Sicilies. Ruling from Naples as Ferdinand I, the restored king quickly established a more centralized, autocratic regime, abolishing the Sicilian flag and freedom of the press. It soon became clear that he would never call another parliament. While some Sicilians adapted to the new order, others resented it and hostility towards the Neapolitan government mounted, especially when the European economy underwent a general slump for the next 30 years. In southern Italy peasant farmers and large landowners alike suffered from this depression, which was compounded by government policies (price controls, export licenses, restrictive corn laws) to the point where both the upper and lower classes began to contemplate armed resistance to Bourbon rule. Many began to join secret societies of liberal patriots such as the *Carboneria* and Giuseppe Mazzini's *Giovine Italia* (Young Italy).

The 1820s and 1830s witnessed several failed rebellions in the South but also the transformation of the secret societies into properly "national" forces, whose goals included the elimination of foreign rule as well as the unification of Italy. The latter phenomenon became associated with the nationalist movement for unification known as the Risorgimento (resurgence). The brewing conflict first came to a head in 1848 with a series of uprisings that started in Palermo (February) and swept through all of Italy. Although each rebellion ultimately ended in failure and the restoration of the status quo, the nationalists were not permanently crushed; some leading rebels, including Giuseppe Mazzini and Giuseppe Garibaldi, fled into exile, hoping to fight another day.

During the 1850s many Italians began to look to the Piedmont region—the northern Kingdom of Sardinia—for guidance. Governed by Victor Emmanuel II of Savoy and his formidable premier, Count Camillo di Cavour, Piedmont increasingly took the lead in the drive towards national unification. Despite the longstanding differences between the rural South and the industrialized North, Sicilians numbered among those who looked to the North. They began to feel that allying themselves with the Piedmontese would be more advantageous than continuing to chafe under Bourbon rule. The death of the ineffectual Ferdinand II in 1859 and the subsequent accession of his equally inadequate son, Francis II, further weakened the Bourbons' hold over the Kingdom of the Two Sicilies. Within a year, taking advantage of a Franco-Austrian conflict, Piedmont moved against Austria, raising the hopes of all patriots throughout the peninsula. But the main agent in this second war of independence in the South would not be the Royal Piedmontese army but volunteers led by the national hero par excellence, Giuseppe Garibaldi.

Garibaldi's Sicilian campaign. The most pivotal historical event described in *The Leopard* is Giuseppe Garibaldi's successful invasion of Sicily in 1860. Garibaldi, born in Nice in 1807, was a sailor who became a key figure of the Risorgimento. Flamboyant and charismatic, Garibaldi joined the Mazzinian secret society, Young Italy. After a series of failed nationalist insurrections, however, Garibaldi and other disciples of Mazzini were forced to flee abroad. For 12 years Garibaldi devoted himself to the cause of freedom in South America, leading patriotic revolts in Brazil and Uruguay.

In 1848 Garibaldi returned to his homeland to join the various uprisings sweeping through Italy. Sardinian and Milanese forces were attempting to overthrow Austrian rule, while Mazzini, also returned from exile, had led a successful revolt against the papacy and established a Roman Republic. Garibaldi lent both his skills as a guerrilla war leader and his volunteer army to the cause, but the two campaigns—against the Austrians and the pope—ended in failure, with the Austrians still in power and the pope restored to his position. Garibaldi, who was again forced to flee into exile, took refuge in the United States for a time and then moved on to Peru before returning to Italy.

At the end of the 1850s Garibaldi was again called into service for Italy. This time rebellion erupted in the South; in October 1859, Francesco Crispi, another Mazzini disciple, led a band of Sicilian insurgents against the Spanish Bourbons, who were weakened by the death of King Ferdinand II. Although that attempt failed, the rebels did not disband, mounting another insurrection in Palermo in April 1860 in conjunction with the Piedmontese move against Austria. When that revolt was also quelled, Crispi wrote to Garibaldi, now living quietly on the island of Caprera, north of Sardinia, and asked for his assistance. Garibaldi responded with alacrity; recruiting over a thousand volunteers (known as "Red Shirts" from the uniform they wore and that Garibaldi had adopted in his Latin American campaigns) for a daring expedition that would have brought them by boat from Genoa to Sicily to liberate the whole South from Bourbon rule. Though concerned about the liberal-republican credo of the Garibaldini, Cavour and Victor Emmanuel decided to allow the expedition to take place and got the British fleet in the Mediterranean to agree to let Garibaldi's boats pass undisturbed. Thus backed, Garibaldi set sail with his "thousand" for Sicily in May 1860.

Garibaldi's forces landed at Marsala in western Sicily. They advanced without opposition until they encountered and defeated a larger Bourbon army at Calatafimi on May 15, 1860. Proclaiming himself "dictator of Sicily," Garibaldi attracted more followers to his cause by promising land grants to all who fought for him. The Red Shirts went on to take Palermo (the Bourbon capital of Sicily) and Messina (the last Bourbon stronghold) and then crossed the Straits of Messina to the Italian mainland. From there, Garibaldi's army proceeded to Naples, defeating Bourbon troops at the River Volturno. Francis II, the new, young Bourbon king, fled to Gaeta, and the rebel forces occupied Naples. Matching the military success of the Piedmontese against Austrian forces in the North, Garibaldi had thus "liberated" the South. He now threatened to march north to free Central Italy from papal authority. At this point, however, politics took precedence over military matters.

Apprehensive over Garibaldi's astounding success, Cavour had already ordered Piedmontese troops south. He also had engineered the holding of plebiscites, in which Central Italians voted to annex their separate territories to Piedmont. The newly enlarged Piedmontese state would become the Kingdom of Italy under the Savoy monarchy. Meanwhile, in the South, Garibaldi's forces attacked a much larger Bourbon army, emerging victorious but with heavy losses. Lacking the strength to hold Naples on

Italian national hero Giuseppe Garibaldi.

Alfonso (nicknamed "The Magnanimous") created the first marquis not of royal blood. By 1621 the number of titled landowners in Sicily had more than doubled that of 60 years before; the process accelerated, resulting in the creation of 102 princedoms in Sicily by century's end, when the total population of the island was just one million (Finley, Smith, and Duggan, p. 87).

The ranks of the aristocracy continued to swell; by the end of the eighteenth century, there were 142 princes, 788 marquises, and 1,500 dukes and barons in Sicily. Ironically, despite their exalted rank, most of these nobles were quite poor, some only slightly better off than the peasants who worked their land. Within the aristocracy itself, there was considerable diversity; their members included those whose titles dated from centuries back, newcomers who had just achieved their rank, some who were cultured and cosmopolitan, and others who were illiterate, provincial, and unable to afford a grand lifestyle in the Sicilian capital of Palermo. Aristocratic temperaments and achievements were likewise varied: there were nobles who took their responsibilities as landowners seriously, treated their subjects with benevolence, and patronized the arts, and others who neglected their lands and carelessly spent huge sums of money to maintain their lavish way of life.

People elsewhere generally held the Sicilian aristocracy in low regard. During the Risorgimento—which is when *The Leopard* takes place—the British consul in Palermo described the Sicilian aristocrats as leading "idle, objectless lives" and complained that only two "of the nobles are men of fortune, none of them are men of energy, and none enjoy the public confidence" (Gilmour, p. 12). This scathing indictment is reflected to some degree in *The Leopard*: Don Fabrizio, Prince of Salina, heads an ancient family that has squandered its wealth over several generations. Don Fabrizio, himself of indolent disposition, watches "the ruin of his own class and his own inheritance without ever making, still less wanting to make, any move towards saving it" (*The Leopard*, p. 27). However, the Prince does attempt to look after his people, advising them to comply, at least ostensibly, with the changes wrought by unification.

their own or to advance on Rome, the Garibaldi forces offered no resistance when they met the Piedmontese army just south of Rome. Instead, Garibaldi acknowledged the authority of Victor Emmanuel, acquiesced to the royal demand that his forces fight under the Piedmontese, and turned over Naples and Sicily to the king in a characteristically dramatic gesture.

In *The Leopard*, Don Fabrizio's nephew, Tancredi, initially throws in his lot with Garibaldi. However, the ambitious, opportunistic young man is quick to abandon his rebel affiliations once Victor Emmanuel has taken command of the South. Tancredi explains to his uncle: "We were [Garibaldini] once and now that's over! Cavriaghi and I, thanks be to God, are officers in the regular army of His Majesty, King of Sardinia for another few months, and shortly to be of Italy. When Garibaldi's army broke up we had the choice: to go home or stay in the King's army. He and I and a lot of others went into the *real* army. We couldn't stand that rabble long, could we, Cavriaghi?" (Lampedusa, *The Leopard*, p. 123).

The Sicilian aristocracy. One idiosyncratic feature of Sicilian society is its high incidence of aristocratic titles. Landowners frequently sought and received elevation to the nobility, even purchasing their way up the ladder of noble ranking. The trend towards ennoblement seems to have begun in the fifteenth century when the Aragonese King

The Novel in Focus

Plot summary. *The Leopard,* a reference to the Salinas's ancestral coat-of-arms, consists of eight episodic chapters, most of them set in the early

1860s. The chapters detail the life and death of Don Fabrizio Corbera, Prince of Salina. Physically powerful but emotionally passive, Don Fabrizio engages in aristocratic pastimes like hunting and astronomy, presides with benign indifference over his large family, visits his mistress, and observes the changes sweeping through Italy in the wake of national unification, remaining fundamentally untouched himself.

Introduction to the Prince. The story begins in May 1860, on a typical day in Don Fabrizio's household. After the daily recital of the rosary, the Prince wanders through his Palermo palace—handsomely decorated with expensive artworks—walks in the garden with his favorite dog, Bendicò, and reflects upon the current state of the country. Although he has mostly refrained from political involvement, preferring to lead an untroubled existence in the country, Don Fabrizio senses the winds of change. Military forces have been preparing to repel invaders, and recently, a government soldier was found dead in the Prince's garden.

Despite his allegiance to the Bourbons who rule the Kingdom of the Two Sicilies, Don Fabrizio senses that their regime is crumbling, especially now that the rebel Giuseppe Garibaldi is attracting followers. The Prince's penniless but beloved nephew, Tancredi Falconeri, decides to join Garibaldi, and in a moment of indulgence, Don Fabrizio gives the young man a roll of gold pieces before the latter's departure for the hills. Although the Prince realizes that he is expected to choose a side in the brewing conflict, he questions whether revolution will truly change an ingrained way of life and ultimately opts to do nothing. As the events of the Risorgimento gain momentum, the Prince carries on as before.

Donnafugata. The second chapter takes its name from the estate and town in the Sicilian hinterlands where Don Fabrizio and his family go in August 1860. By this time, Garibaldi and his followers have triumphed over the Bourbon forces and a new king, Victor Emmanuel II, has assumed power over most of Italy. Don Fabrizio's gift to Tancredi, now a captain under Garibaldi's command, has had the unexpected benefit of making the Prince appear to be a supporter of unification. Consequently, he and his family are treated leniently by the new regime. Comfortably settled at Donnafugata, Don Fabrizio meets the nouveau-riche mayor, Don Calogero Sedàra, who has recently managed to amass a fortune, purchase a property of his own, and gain considerable local influence. Despite being slightly repelled by the mayor's origins, the Prince invites Don Calogero and his beautiful daughter, Angelica, to dine with the family.

Don Calogero arrives for dinner in ill-fitting evening clothes, but Angelica's beauty compensates for her father's gaucherie. A visiting Tancredi flirts with her, to the dismay of the Prince's own daughter, Concetta, who is in love with her dashing cousin. After Tancredi tells a naughty anecdote from his store of military adventures, Concetta snubs him at dinner and during a family visit to the Convent of the Holy Ghost the following day. Undeterred, Tancredi steals some peaches from his uncle's orchard and gains admittance to the convent under the guise of bringing a gift.

THE VOICE OF THE SOUTHERNERS?

During the earliest stages of unification, to gauge the popular opinion of annexation of a region by the Piedmont, Cavour relied upon plebiscites, which polled the individual residents of the given region. In October 1860 plebiscites were held in Naples, Sicily, Umbria, and the Marches; voters were asked to respond with "yes" or "no" to the proposal of becoming part of a new and indivisible nation, with Victor Emmanuel as their constitutional king. The final results—all of which favored unification—were recorded as follows: Sicily, 432,053 to 667; Naples, 1,302,064 to 10,312; the Marches, 133,072 to 1,212; Umbria, 99,628 to 380 (Holt, p. 255). But while Cavour, safely distant from the South, might have rejoiced at the outcome, southerners viewed it with some skepticism. Many voted for unification simply because nothing better was being offered. Also some of the elections were probably rigged, the boxes stuffed with "yes" votes by ambitious regional politicians hoping to curry favor with the new regime. In *The Leopard*, Lampedusa describes just such an occurrence. Knowing that several of his subjects voted against unification, he listens with cynicism to the recorded tally: "Voters, 515: Voting, 512; Yes, 512; No, zero" (*The Leopard*, p. 96).

The Troubles of Don Fabrizio. The action of the next chapter unfolds in October 1860, not long after the popular vote for unification. Aware of the political climate, the Prince advised his subjects to vote "yes," knowing that several would vote "no." In any case it made no difference since the mayor stuffed the ballot box with votes for unification. Meanwhile, the opportunistic Tancredi, now in

King Victor Emmanuel's Piedmontese army, seeks to recoup his family fortunes by proposing marriage to Angelica. He asks Don Fabrizio to approach Don Calogero on his behalf. Reluctantly, despite family opposition and the realization that his own daughter loves Tancredi, the Prince obliges. Throughout his interview with Don Calogero, Don Fabrizio is painfully conscious of the difference in their stations and of the knowledge that, once, the men of his proud family would have simply bedded rather than wedded girls in Angelica's position. Nonetheless, the Prince and Don Calogero come to terms, and a handsome settlement of money and property is bestowed upon the young couple.

Love at Donnafugata. The fourth chapter unfolds a month later and depicts the budding romance between Tancredi and Angelica when she visits the Salina family. Both lovers are calculating people and aware of the advantages each can gain from their future marriage; nonetheless, they enjoy some lighthearted, romantic moments together as they explore the various deserted rooms and forgotten chambers of the palace. Ironically, they are never to be as happy again once they are married. Meanwhile, Count Carlo Cavriaghi, Tancredi's friend and fellow officer, tries in vain to woo Concetta, who is still in love with Tancredi. And the Prince receives a visit from Cavaliere Aimone Chevalley di Monterzuolo, who asks him to accept a post as senator in the new Kingdom of Italy. Don Fabrizio declines on the grounds that being a relic of the old order, he would feel uncomfortable in the new. He recommends Don Calogero for the position instead, then subjects the confused Chevalley to a lengthy explanation of the nature of Sicilians, who are resistant to change, even for the better, and who would rather endure misery and squalor than acknowledge their imperfections: "In Sicily it doesn't matter about doing things well or badly; the sin which we Sicilians never forgive is simply that of 'doing' at all. We are old, Chevalley, very old . . . for two thousand five hundred years we've been a colony. I don't say that in complaint; it's our fault. But even so we're worn out and exhausted" (*The Leopard*, p. 142). Chevalley and the Prince take their leave of each other, the former disturbed, the latter depressed by the encounter.

Father Pirrone Pays a Visit. Set in February 1861, the fifth chapter deals with the Prince's chaplain, Father Pirrone, who has returned to his birthplace—the hamlet of San Cono—on the fifteenth anniversary of his father's death. While visiting his relatives, he learns that one of his nieces has become pregnant out of wedlock by the son of an estranged cousin. Thanks to some shrewd haggling on Father Pirrone's part, suitable financial terms are set up and the young couple becomes engaged. The chaplain cannot help being reminded of the arrangement between Tancredi and Angelica, which is just as calculated despite the higher status of the "lovers."

A Ball. Chapter 6 jumps ahead to November 1862 as the Salina family attends a grand party at the Palazzo Ponteleone in Palermo. Tancredi and Angelica also attend, as does Don Calogero. Despite her humble origins, Angelica is soon recognized as the most beautiful woman there. All is not well, however. Throughout the ball, Don Fabrizio feels restless and melancholy, aware that the world he knows is fading away and that he himself has grown weary of life. Having sent the rest of the family back in the carriage, he walks home alone, drawing comfort from the immutable stars in the heavens.

Death of a Prince. The seventh chapter leaps to July 1883 and Don Fabrizio's final days. Having suffered a near-fatal stroke at the end of a long journey to Palermo, the bedridden Prince reflects upon those who have predeceased him, including his pious wife, Stella, and eldest son, Paolo. His surviving kin, including Tancredi and Angelica, keep vigil at his bedside; death finally arrives in the form of a beautiful woman dressed for a railway journey.

Relics. The last chapter takes place in May 1910. By this time, Tancredi too has died, though the widowed Angelica keeps in close contact with his family. Don Fabrizio's daughters Carolina, Concetta, and Caterina, remain unmarried in the family villa, surrounded by various mementos and supposed holy relics. One day a representative of the Church visits the villa and announces that all but five of the relics in the chapel are worthless as objects of devotion, leaving the sisters disillusioned and disappointed. Concetta suffers an added blow when she learns from an old acquaintance that Tancredi may have returned her affections, but her offended pride drove him into Angelica's arms instead. Wishing to sever ties with the past, Concetta orders that the stuffed carcass of Bendicò, her father's dog, be thrown upon the rubbish heap: "A few minutes later what remained of Bendicò was flung into a corner of the yard visited every day by the dustman. During the flight down from the window its form recomposed itself for an instant; in the air there seemed to be dancing a quadruped with long whiskers, its right foreleg raised in imprecation. Then all found peace in a little heap of livid dust" (*The Leopard*, p. 210).

A family's decline. Many critics have commented that death and dying are evoked from the very first line of *The Leopard*, which is taken from the daily reading of the rosary: "Nunc et in hora mortis nostrae," meaning "Now and in the hour of our death" (*The Leopard*, p. 25). Images of death and decay permeate the novel: the mortally wounded government soldier who dies in the Prince's garden, the rabbit killed during the Prince's hunt, the Prince's own lingering demise in a hotel room, and even the stuffed corpse of the Prince's favorite dog, thrown on the rubbish heap at the end of the novel. These images underscore its major paradox: the birth of a new world necessitates the death of the old.

Don Fabrizio, Prince of Salina, represents the old, dying world, and to his credit recognizes that change is inevitable, inescapable, and, in some instances, even desirable. His family's best hope for survival hinges upon its ability to cooperate with whatever regime emerges victorious. Consequently, he offers no opposition to Garibaldi's rebel forces, persuades his subjects to vote for national unification in the plebiscite, and supports a marriage between his favorite nephew and the daughter of a ruthless, self-made man, even at his own daughter's expense.

However, the Prince does not rejoice at these changes; rather, he accepts them as a necessary evil. Contemplating the future, he reflects, "We [the aristocrats] were The Leopards and Lions; those who'll take our places will be little jackals, hyenas" (*The Leopard*, p. 148). Likewise, he is ambivalent about the new order taking shape, an order in which he senses he and his kind will play no part: "Italy was born on that sullen night at Donnafugata, born right there in that forgotten little town, just as in the sloth of Palermo or the clamor of Naples. . . . And yet this persistent disquiet of his must mean something . . . he had a feeling that something, someone, had died" (*The Leopard*, p. 97). Years later, on his deathbed, the Prince acknowledges the end of his world: "He had said that the Salina would always remain the Salina. He had been wrong. The last Salina was himself. That fellow Garibaldi, that bearded Vulcan, had won after all" (*The Leopard*, p. 190).

The semi-autobiographical element of *The Leopard* enhances the pathos of an already poignant story. Lampedusa drew not only upon his family's present but also upon its past. Although the Tomasi had been named princes of Lampedusa in 1667, their dynasty continually suffered from the threat of extinction. For several generations posterity depended upon the survival of a single child, mainly because most Tomasi opted for the religious life. Then, in 1812, the abolition of feudalism in Sicily dealt a severe financial blow to the family, which adapted to the new economic situation with only limited success. Eventually, the Tomasi had to sell off much of their land, including the island of Lampedusa itself (one of the Pelagian Islands south of Sicily purchased by the Neapolitan king Ferdinand II for 12,000 ducats in 1840), to pay their mounting debts. Continued extravagance, financial mismanagement, and inheritance squabbles further drained the coffers, and by the time the last prince was born, little remained of the Lampedusa fortune except the family estates, the most important of which—the palace at Palermo—was destroyed during World War II. Even more than his fictional hero, Giuseppe Tomasi di Lampedusa was the last of his line; his own sense of loss and displacement are reflected in the Prince, a figure who thus elicits sympathy from modern readers.

Sources and literary context. Although most of the action in *The Leopard* takes place long before his birth, Lampedusa drew largely upon his experiences as the scion of an aristocratic Sicilian family whose fortunes were in decline. Don Fabrizio Corbera, the novel's protagonist, was based mainly upon Lampedusa's great-grandfather, Don Giulio Maria Fabrizio, a distinguished amateur astronomer who discovered two asteroids (named "Palma" and "Lampedusa") and sat in the Sicilian Chamber of Peers in 1848. Other characters, such as Don Fabrizio's opportunistic nephew Tancredi, were composites of historical personages whom Lampedusa had come across in studying world literature and history. Lampedusa's memories of Sicily and his family's stately residences provide much of the atmosphere in *The Leopard*.

While Lampedusa's family history supplied the novel's subject matter, various European writers influenced its style. A voracious reader, Lampedusa admired the works of William Shakespeare, Lawrence Sterne, Leo Tolstoy, Charles Baudelaire, Marcel Proust, and Stendhal (Henri-Marie Beyle). Stendhal was a particular favorite and probably the foremost literary model for *The Leopard*. As Stendhal had done in such works as *The Charterhouse of Parma* and *The Red and the Black*, Lampedusa fused historical drama with his own personal philosophy in relation to that drama.

Events in History at the
Time the Novel Was Written

Italy after World War II. Dramatic changes took place in Italy after World War II. On April 25, 1945, a joint effort, an Allied military offensive along with a popular insurrection led by the anti-Fascist Resistance, put an end to 23 years of Fascist regime and two years of Nazi-Fascist occupation of the Italian North. Italy now faced not only the difficult task of reconstruction but also that of national reconciliation after the two years of civil war between anti-Fascist partisans and Nazi-Fascists. The division was made plain by the referendum held in 1946, in which Italian voters split down the middle, choosing by a very narrow margin to abandon the monarchy in favor of a republic.

Political parties, forbidden to exist under Fascist rule, were reestablished in Italy in the postwar period. These parties shared a new anti-Fascist militancy, but beneath the surface, there simmered divisiveness, a unique political culture tied to the Cold War competition between democracy and communism that had started to engulf Europe. Gathering strength from its wartime leadership in the Resistance movement, Italy's Communist Party emerged as one of the strongest Communist parties in the West; in Italy it rivaled the most powerful Catholic party, the Christian Democrats. For the next 40 years the Christian Democratic Party would rule alone or in coalition with other parties, never allowing the Communists a chance to dominate. Yet, it would also adopt the most advanced program of industrial nationalization and social welfare in southern Europe.

During the first postwar decade, Italy strove to rebuild its economy and take its place in modern Europe, joining the Organization for European Economic Cooperation (1948), the European Coal and Steel Community (1951), and the European Economic Community (1957). Longstanding domestic problems were tackled as well, such as land reform in the impoverished agricultural South. After 1948 state institutions were set up to oversee land redistribution. Also the government planned to provide vital services such as roads and irrigation at public expense. Two years later, it launched the Cassa per il Mezzogiorno (Fund for the South) in 1950, invest-

ing large sums of money in the region to stimulate its economy and finance public works projects. These reforms were not an unqualified success, however; some wily landowners found ways around the new distribution laws and some of the new smallholdings granted to peasant farmers suffered from poor soil. Worst of all, the Cassa's resources often fell into the hands of such criminal organizations as the Mafia, whose leaders appropriated the funds to strengthen their ties with major political parties.

Ultimately, many frustrated southerners resolved their situations by migrating to the northern cities in search of work. During the 1950s and 1960s more than 9 million Italians migrated to another part of the country. Although social and economic problems would erupt again in the late 1960s, the influx of cheap labor contributed to an economic boom in the 1950s. The decade saw Italy nearly double its industrial output, producing massive quantities of automobiles, airplanes, ships, office machines, electricity, and so forth. Between 1950 and 1958 Italy's economy expanded at an annual rate of 5.3 per cent, more than that of Great Britain, France, and the United States, and then expanded further to 6.6 per cent over the next five years (Killinger, p. 163). Although Lampedusa makes no reference to contemporary events in *The Leopard*, his writing of the novel coincided with Italy's "economic miracle." Indeed, witnessing the dramatic transformation of much of Italy while the South remained virtually unaltered may have influenced his depiction of how Don Fabrizio's fiefdom remained more or less untouched in the midst of world-changing events.

Reception. Published a year after Lampedusa's death, *The Leopard* became an enormous popular success, first in Italy, then in Europe. Critics, however, were sharply divided on the novel's merit. Carlo Bo, who wrote the novel's first review for *La Stampa*, was favorably impressed; a few years later, he recalled, "I opened [*The Leopard*] with the certainty that by the fiftieth page I would have nothing more to do with it, but it was not like that. I needed only a few pages . . . to understand that this Sicilian gentleman was a real writer" (Bo in Gilmour, p. 185). Other well-regarded literary figures in Italy were similarly enthusiastic, including Eugenio Montale, Geno Pampaloni, and Luigi Barzini.

But *The Leopard* had its detractors as well: Roman Catholics complained about the novel's pessimism; the literary left disdained the story as traditional rather than avant-garde; Marxists attacked Lampedusa's view of history; and Sicilian apologists objected to Lampedusa's portrayal of the Sicilian character as violent and irrational.

Despite its mixed critical response in Italy, *The Leopard* met with an enthusiastic reception abroad, most notably in France and England. Many critics have praised the novel for its vivid depiction of a dying social order as revealed by an insider. In the journal *Les Lettres française*, the French Marxist writer Louis Aragon called *The Leopard* "one of the great novels of this century, one of the great novels of all time" (Aragon in Pallotta, p. 370). Aragon also rejected the charge that *The Leopard* was right-wing and reactionary, contending that Lampedusa was really offering an incisive critique of the ruling class to which he had belonged. British critics were similarly enthusiastic. Roy Perrott of *The Guardian* praised the novel's "brilliant ironic sparkle" and the vividness of the characters, especially "the Prince [who] emerges as a classic picture of the man who draws his vitality from profound disillusion" (Perrott in Davison, p. 778). Finally, the reviewer from the *Times Literary Supplement* expressed astonishment that *The Leopard* was a first novel, admired Lampedusa's depiction of character and setting, and concluded, "This is a book which should be read by everyone who is interested in Italy, or in the nineteenth century, or indeed in the conduct of the human race" (*Times Literary Supplement* in Davison, p. 779).

—Pamela S. Loy

For More Information

Davison, Dorothy P., ed. *Book Review Digest*. New York: H. W. Wilson, 1961.

Duggan, Christopher. *A Concise History of Italy*. Cambridge: Cambridge University Press, 1994.

Finley, M. I., Denis Mack Smith, and Christopher Duggan. *A History of Sicily*. New York: Viking, 1987.

Gatt-Rutter, John. *Writers and Politics in Modern Italy*. New York: Holmes & Meier, 1978.

Gilmour, David. *The Last Leopard*. New York: Pantheon, 1988.

Holt, Edgar. *The Making of Italy 1815-1870*. New York: Atheneum, 1971.

Killinger, Charles L. *The History of Italy*. Westport, Conn.: Greenwood, 2002.

Pacifici, Sergio. *The Modern Italian Novel*. Carbondale: Southern Illinois University Press, 1979.

Pallotta, Augustus, ed. *Dictionary of Literary Biography*. Vol. 177. Detroit: Gale Research, 1997.

Poupard, Dennis, and James E. Person, Jr., eds. *Twentieth-Century Literary Criticism*. Vol. 13. Detroit: Gale Research Company, 1984.

Tomasi di Lampedusa, Giuseppe. *The Leopard*. Trans. Archibald Colquhon. New York: Alfred A. Knopf, 1991.

Letters
from Prison

by

Antonio Gramsci

Political thinker, philosopher, literary critic, and writer, Antonio Gramsci (1891-1937) was one of the major intellectuals in early-twentieth-century Italy. He was born into a lower-middle-class family in the rural community of Ales in southern Sardinia. In 1911, a scholarship enabled him to leave the sheltered rural area to attend university in the industrial city of Turin. There, Gramsci witnessed the living conditions of the working classes, joined the Socialist Party, and abandoned his university studies to engage in political activism. A prolific journalist, he wrote articles that influenced the political struggle of northern Italian workers, inspiring the formation of "Factory Councils" (a network of worker-led revolutionary cells that, during the general strikes of 1920, mobilized more than 50,000 workers in Turin). In 1921, Gramsci helped found the Italian Communist Party, going on to serve (1922-1923) in Moscow as an Italian delegate to the Communist International. In 1926, while serving as general secretary for the Communist Party, Gramsci was arrested and later sentenced to more than 20 years in prison for conspiratorial activity against the state, instigation of civil war, incitement to class hatred, justification of crime, and subversive propaganda. He spent more than a decade in prison, largely in solitude, during which he read extensively and produced an impressive array of writings. These include both the wide series of notes, monographs, translations, and commentaries later collected in the *Prison Notebooks* and several hundred messages (to both relatives and friends), posthumously edited un-

THE LITERARY WORK

A collection of letters written mainly to Gramsci's relatives in Italy from 1926-1937; first published in Italian (as *Lettere dal carcere*) in 1947, published in part in English in 1973, in full in 1994.

SYNOPSIS

Gramsci's letters portray the life of an anti-Fascist in prison; the letters also convey a series of personal, political, literary, and philosophical thoughts.

der the title of *Letters from Prison*. Deteriorating physically during the long confinement, Gramsci died in 1937. His life remains one of the most famous examples of repression during Italy's Fascist dictatorship, and his writings figure among the most influential in early-twentieth-century Italy. Gramsci's *Letters from Prison* is both a first-hand account of the slow murder of one of Fascism's key opponents, and an exceptional work in Italy's time-honored epistolary or letter-writing tradition.

Events in History at the Time of the Letters

From a Fascist dictatorship to the Fascist state. Gramsci was arrested in Rome in 1926 at a crucial point in the history of the Fascist

Italy's Fascist leader, Benito Mussolini, addresses the "Blackshirts," his paramilitary supporters, from an eagle-shaped podium in Turin, Italy.

regime. Conventionally, historians identify the beginning of the Fascist dictatorship with October 1922's insurrectionary March on Rome, in which some 50,000 armed Fascists helped Benito Mussolini (1883-1945) take control of the government. In the early 1920s, a time of transition in which the Fascists transformed Italy into a totalitarian state, they perpetrated violent acts against their opponents. Yet, at least nominally, the Fascist government still operated with the cooperation of different political parties, and Mussolini led with authorization from the parliament and the king. This changed dramatically in 1924.

On May 30, 1924, the Socialist Party deputy, Giacomo Matteotti, delivered a stirring speech against Fascism and its manipulation of the April 1924 elections. A few days later, Matteotti was kidnapped; his body was found a few weeks later. Everyone knew that the Fascists were behind the murder. After this episode, opposition deputies withdrew from parliament (their political protest is known as the *Secessione dell'Aventino*, or Aventine Secession) and began an intensive campaign of public denunciation of Fascist violence. But instead of restoring democratic debate, the protestors' withdrawal gave the Fascists full control of parliament. A new wave of intimidation and violence, mainly against anti-Fascists, ravaged Italy. On January 3, 1925, in a speech delivered to the Chamber of Deputies, Mussolini assumed responsibility for the violence and mayhem that was sweeping the nation. His opposition was powerless to prosecute him for any of the crimes. A few months later, a series of laws known as the *Leggi Fascistissime* ("ultra-Fascist laws") was approved. From this point onwards, the head of the government was not accountable to parliament, and only the king retained the power to revoke Mussolini's mandate. Furthermore, no law could be submitted to parliament unless previously approved by Mussolini. The "ultra-Fascist laws" marked the end of parliamentary debate as the foundation of Italian government and almost totally eliminated political dissent. Italy became a totalitarian state centered on Mussolini's personal dictatorship; formally, Mussolini governed with the authority granted him by the monarchy, but his rule was enforced and strengthened by the legal and illegal action of the Fascist militiamen. A series of laws were promulgated against the freedom of the press, while the major newspapers fell under Fascist control. In 1926, the right to strike was abolished and women were excluded from the workforce and suffrage. All other political parties were dissolved, and the Fascist National Party (PNF) became the only legitimate political party in Italy. To be eligible for public work, membership in the Fascist Party was required.

From 1926 onwards, Fascism also developed an intense program of ideological propaganda devoted to the reorganization of daily life in Italy. This process (known as the *fascistization* of Italy) involved not only the use of rigid—often cruel—police repression. It also gave rise to a massive propaganda campaign waged through para-Fascist subgroups, created to achieve various social aims.

Fascism's economic policies. The economic policy of Fascism can be roughly divided into four main phases:

(1) **The liberalism of 1922-25,** a period marked by inflation, during which the state encouraged private enterprise and weakened workers' unions and organizations. At this time, Gramsci devoted his energies to the threat to the worker's movement of emergent Fascism, which he called the "white guard of capitalism against the class origins of the proletariat" (Dombroski, p. xvii).

(2) **The protectionism of 1925-29,** when deflation benefited the big industrial concerns and the state increased customs' duties. Small and medium industries were either damaged or absorbed by bigger conglomerates, yet the middle class and its savings were safeguarded to bolster support for the regime. As repressive laws gagged the opposition, extinguished political parties, and restricted trade, Fascism launched the *ordine corporativo* ("corporative order") to combat economic depression and unemployment. This policy was conceived of as a "peaceful social revolution" to establish a "third way" between individualistic capitalism and collective socialism (such as that of Bolshevik Russia). A document called the *Carta del lavoro* (1927) held that work contracts should be regulated by associations of business owners and workers, called *corporazioni*. In the end, however, these associations fell under government control. Corporation representatives were nominated by the Fascist elite on the basis of their loyalty to the regime and workers found themselves condemned to near servitude. The new order left them without any leverage to negotiate. Among other consequences, the working class suffered lower salaries (as much as a 16 percent cut in some factories of northern Italy).

(3) **The strict state control of 1929-35,** during which the regime, in response to crisis and depression (the collapse of prices, unemployment, the reduction of import and export activity), subjected the national economy to tighter control than that of any other European country (including the Soviet Union). The state, as a shareholder of the main financial and industrial companies, promoted a large-scale series of public works—the construction of new roads, railways, and schools,

Defeated Ethiopians give the Fascist salute as invading Italian troops march into Aksum, Ethiopia.

the draining of marshlands, and the building of new cities, monuments, and infrastructure.

(4) **The last period of autarchy (or national self-sufficiency)**, which began early in the tenure of the regime but climaxed only in the late 1930s. The concept of autarchy, one of the themes of Fascist propaganda, pushed an image of Italy as an independent country struggling to restore its ancient prestige. In reality, the autarchy campaign benefited industrial corporations and won allegiance from the large landowners in the rural south of Italy, while adversely affecting other parts of the economy. While to a certain extent the autarchy program stimulated research (especially in the chemical, hydroelectric, and mechanical industries), it failed to achieve for Italy real national economic independence. In hindsight, the policy led to a shortage of raw materials that made Italy more and more dependent on the German economy.

The Lateran Pacts of 1929. When Mussolini came to power, he had to deal with a curious political situation that had existed for some half a century. Ever since the last Papal States (central Italian territories that the popes controlled from 756 to 1870) were finally wrested from the Catholic Church, the popes had proclaimed themselves "prisoners in the Vatican," refusing to recognize the validity of the new Italian state. To guarantee himself wide-ranging authority and popular support, Mussolini entered into negotiations with Pope Pius XI. Mussolini's interests in the matter were clear; the Vatican, for its part, saw in Fascism a barrier against communism, liberalism, and socialism. The Lateran Pacts, or Treaty of February 11, 1929, recognized the sovereign power of the pope over his own state—Vatican City. The Pacts also compensated the Church (to the tune of some $85 million) for state actions (loss of the Papal States), gave the clergy ample privileges, and protected Catholic structures throughout the country. In exchange, the Church publicly recognized the boundaries of the Italian nation and the establishment of Rome as its capital city. The Pacts furthermore designated Catholicism as the nation's official religion, awarding civil recognition to Catholic marriage and instituting the teaching of Catholic doctrine in public education (which would continue until 1985).

The Lateran Pacts compromised the secular nature of the nation and ran counter to the liberal tradition that had inspired the Italian government since the unification of the country in 1861. On one side, the agreement attributed ample privileges to the Church and, on the other side, it gave Fascism, which could now point to the support of the Church, considerable propagandist strength on both national and international levels. Pope Pius XI, three days after the ratification of the Lateran Pacts, identified Mussolini as a leader who had been sent by Providence.

Fascist propaganda and the Ethiopian campaign. Alongside the enforcement of censorship, Fascism developed an intensive campaign of propaganda that used for its purposes the most modern means of communication (the press, the radio, and, to a certain degree, the movie industry). The regime also sponsored a number of photographic and public expositions (the most famous were on the Fascist revolution, the processes of land reclamation, the minerals extracted on national soil, and sports).

Fascist propaganda centered mainly on portraying Mussolini (who adopted the title *Il Duce*, or "the leader") as the man who would return Italy to the splendor and prosperity it had enjoyed in antiquity. Propaganda newsreels, radio programs, and audiovisual documentaries (often shown during cinema performances) emphasized Fascist values and pushed the regime's central policies, notably its campaigns for a higher birth rate, the achievement of economic self-sufficiency, and the Italian expansionist policy. To encourage a strong sense of patriotism, the regime produced radio broadcasts of Mussolini's speeches, lessons on the history of Fascism, commentaries on the achievements of professional athletes, and coverage of public ceremonies.

After the national reform of education in 1923, schools and educational institutions began to promote the ancient splendor of Rome and to glorify Mussolini's regime. Beginning in 1931, all teachers and public officials were required to take a formal oath of loyalty to the regime.

Under the auspices of the regime, a number of Fascist and para-Fascist organizations disseminated ideology among the masses. Beginning in infancy, young Italians were organized into a series of gymnastic, cultural, and leisure organizations, such as the *Figli della Lupa* (Sons of the She-Wolf, for boys from 0-8 years of age) and the *Giovani Italiane* (Young Female Italians, for girls aged 13-18). University students were organized into the Fascist Groups of University Students (*GUF*). Other women's organizations, such as the *Massaie Rurali* (Rural Housewives), were created to reinforce the myth of the prosperous countryside. The welfare role of the state was emphasized through the promotion of additional agencies such as the *Opera Nazionale Maternità e Infanzia* (National Agency for Maternity and Infancy), which encouraged population growth, instituted merit fellowships for students, and promoted the building of seaside and mountain resorts for the children of the working classes. Newly organized after-work organizations (such as the *Dopolavoro*—a series of recreational clubs for working people) extended the Fascist practical and ideological control outside the workplace.

Fascist nationalist propaganda reached a climax around 1935 with Italy's military campaign against Ethiopia. Italy's expansionist policy was strongly advocated not only for international prestige, but also to stimulate industrial production and divert public attention from the internal problems of the country, above all the economic crisis. Propaganda presented the war as a crusade against barbarism and as a way to restore the prestige of ancient Rome. On October 2, 1935, Mussolini gave a famous speech calling on Italy to mobilize for war. The next day about 110,000 Italian soldiers began an invasion of Ethiopia from Italian Somaliland. Extremely violent, the war ended in May 1936, when the capital city, Addis Ababa, surrendered and Mussolini proclaimed Italy's King Victor Emmanuel III the "Emperor of Ethiopia." The move upset the more than 50 member countries of the League of Nations, prompting them to levy a series of economic and commercial sanctions against Italy. Many Italians were persuaded to believe the sanctions were an unjust penalty perpetrated against their country by foreign nations, above all the "plutocratic" (in Mussolini's terms) powers of Britain and France.

In terms of international politics, the Ethiopian war led to the alliance between Fascist Italy and Nazi Germany. After their joint support of the Spanish Civil War—in 1936 both Mussolini and Hitler sent troops to back the Fascist counterrevolutionary forces in Spain—a pact of friendship was signed between Italy and Germany. The pact, identified by Mussolini as the "Rome-Berlin axis," was transformed in May 1939 into the *Patto d'Acciaio* (Pact of Steel) military alliance, in which Germany and Italy pledged to support one another in the event of an international threat.

The persecution of opponents. The enactment of the Fascist Laws in 1925 entailed the establishment of a *Tribunale Speciale* (Special Tribunal) for the Defense of the State, whose members were chosen from among Fascist consuls and *squadristi* (squad members). This tribunal often worked in cooperation with a powerful branch of the police, OVRA (an acronym for *Organizzazione per* *la Vigilanza e la Repressione dell'Antifascismo,* or Organization for Vigilance and Repression of Anti-Fascism), which was devoted to the repression of anti-Fascist activity. With its assistance, the *Tribunale Speciale* arrested, imprisoned, and condemned hundreds of the regime's opponents, including Antonio Gramsci. On mere suspicion, opponents could be apprehended, tortured, imprisoned, and deported. They would be sent to remote Italian villages (as in the case of Carlo Levi, who, after his confinement in southern Italy, wrote the novel *Christ Stopped at Eboli*), or to secluded islands such as Ustica, Lipari, or Ponza. Many opponents of the regime were murdered, while over 10,000 left Italy, becoming part of a phenomenon known as *fuoriscitismo* ("political exile"). Some of the exiles organized a campaign against the Fascist regime from abroad. Apart from Benedetto Croce's *Manifesto of the Antifascist Intellectuals* (1925), only a few voices within Italy spoke publicly against Fascism. Nonetheless, the struggle of the regime's opponents continued surreptitiously within the country. Until the outbreak of World War II, in fact, thousands of anti-Fascists manifested their dissent in various forms, from small-scale sabotage to acts of propaganda, attempts on Mussolini's life, resistance to the authorities, or aid to fugitives trying to escape Italy. Anarchist organizations and the Communist Party, among other groups, continued their activities clandestinely. In retaliation, the Fascist militiamen beat, killed, or kidnapped hundreds of people.

Official justice institutions often operated secretly and arbitrarily, too. Between 1926 and 1929, for example, the Special Tribunal decided 4,805 cases. By the end of Fascism in 1943, 110,000 Italians had been registered as subversive, about 160,000 had been officially put under special police surveillance, and 17,000 had been confined. While capital punishment was enforced in only a very limited number of cases, the political prisoners of Fascism regularly faced conditions of brutal deprivation, strict isolation, and even torture in the course of their imprisonment. When these prisoners could communicate with outside society through letters, as in Gramsci's case, they had to contend with and, if necessary, find clever ways to circumvent the prison censors.

The imprisonment of Antonio Gramsci is a classic case of Fascist repression. He had by 1926 established himself as a Marxist thinker and a Communist Party leader who spread his ideas through action and writings. Among other predictions, Gramsci had speculated that the Fascist regime might evolve into a brutal dictatorship. He was quickly arrested after the institution of the Special Tribunal. First confined on the island of Ustica, he was subsequently sentenced to long-term imprisonment. Gramsci spent the rest of his life in various facilities (the prisons of Regina Coeli in Rome, San Vittore in Milan, the penitentiary of Turi in Apulia, near Bari). In solitary confinement for most of this time, despite progressive physical and mental deterioration, he produced an impressive array of writings, from personal letters to philosophical and literary notes. Gramsci's corpus of prison writings, besides expounding the thought of one of Italy's leading intellectuals, testifies to a relentless determination on the part of anti-Fascists to live, think, and write as honestly as possible despite totalitarian repression and violence.

The Letters in Focus

Contents summary. Antonio Gramsci did not intend to publish his letters, and these cannot be considered a conventional work of literature for several reasons. First, since outgoing messages from prisons were censored, Gramsci avoided discussing personal issues in detail or addressing political matters explicitly in the letters. Secondly, prisoners could write only on given days of the week and in very limited amounts of time. Consequently, Gramsci could not review or edit his letters, and much of his epistolary work seems to be a first draft. Finally, while he was a very prolific writer of essays, articles, and notes, as well as a tireless editor of newspapers and journals (such as *Ordine Nuovo* and *L'Unità*), Gramsci never published or collected his writings during his lifetime. The posthumous publication of his letters appears to be the product of an editorial effort on the part of scholars, friends, and comrades.

Written over ten years, the corpus of Gramsci's letters consists of about 480 documents. A chronological reading of the letters makes it possible to outline the different stages of his imprisonment.

The first days of imprisonment. Following his arrest on November 8, 1926, Gramsci spent 16 days in the Regina Coeli prison in Rome before being transferred to Palermo, Sicily. We have very few letters from this period.

In a letter addressed to his "dearest Mother" (Gramsci, *Letters from Prison*, vol. 1, p. 37) just a few days after the arrest, Gramsci declares his

In 1939 Mussolini and Aldolf Hitler (shown here in May 1940) signed a mutual-protection alliance, the *Patto d'Acciaio* (Pact of Steel).

determination to resist the adverse effects of imprisonment and isolation. "I'm tranquil and serene," Gramsci states, because "morally I was prepared for everything. Physically too I will try to overcome the difficulties that may await me and to keep my balance. You know my character and you know that at the bottom of it there is always a quantum of cheerful humor: this will help me live" (*Letters from Prison*, vol. 1, p. 37). Of course, Gramsci did not know at the time of the forthcoming hardships related to his long-term confinement in isolation, nor that he would ultimately die without ever seeing his loved ones again.

The confinement at Ustica. On December 7, 1926, Gramsci was transferred from Palermo to the island of Ustica, off the coast of Sicily. Here he spent six weeks in confinement with hundreds of other political and common prisoners. As Gramsci wrote after his arrival on the island, the total population of Ustica was "about 1,600 inhabitants, 600 of them detainees" (*Letters from Prison*, vol. 1, p. 49). There, Gramsci could write freely, but he did not send out many letters. In those he did send, he asked for books, medicines, toiletries, and other "small things that it is impossible to find here in Ustica" (*Letters from Prison*, vol. 1, p. 56). He was mainly moved in these messages to reassure his loved ones.

Imprisonment at San Vittore in Milan. On January 27, 1927, Gramsci was transferred from Ustica to the prison of San Vittore in Milan. Here he spent a year and a half waiting for evidence to be gathered against him. In Milan, Gramsci was relatively free to write. About 100 missives stem from this part of the detention.

In a famous letter dated March 19, 1927, and addressed to his sister-in-law, Tatiana ("Tania") Schucht, Gramsci states that he will continue his intellectual work to overcome feelings of loneliness and despair. Besides attesting to its author's tenacity, this document shows Gramsci's determination to carry out a systematic project of scholarly study in prison:

> My life still goes by always with the same monotony. Studying too is much more difficult than it might seem. I've received some books and I actually read a lot (more than a book a day, besides the newspapers), but this is not what I'm referring to, I'm talking about something else. I am obsessed (this is a phenomenon typical of people in jail, I think) by this idea: that I should do something *für ewig* [for eternity]. . . . In short, in keeping with a preestablished program, I would like to concentrate intensely and systematically on some subject that would absorb and provide a center to my inner life.
>
> (*Letters from Prison*, vol. 1, p. 83)

The same letter contains a first outline of the main themes Gramsci wanted to address in his scholarly work:

- An inquiry into the "Italian intellectuals, their origins, their grouping in accordance with cultural currents, and their various ways of thinking" (*Letters from Prison*, vol. 1, p. 83).
- A study of comparative linguistics (to repay a debt he felt he owed to the academic world, which he had abandoned to take up politics).
- Scholarly research on the theater of Luigi Pirandello and the transformation of Italian theatrical taste (see Pirandello's *Six Characters in Search of an Author*, also in *WLAIT 7: Italian Literature and Its Times*).
- A study of serial novels and popular taste in literature.

What these topics have in common, Gramsci states, is that they display "the creative spirit of the people in its diverse stages and degrees of development" (*Letters from Prison*, vol. 1, p. 84).

IN FAILING HEALTH, WITH A TRIUMPHANT SPIRIT

❧

"I'm four years older, I have many white hairs, I've lost my teeth, I no longer laugh with gusto as I used to, but I believe that I have become wiser and that I have enriched my experience of men and of things . . . as long as we want to live, as long as we have a taste for life and we still want to attain some goal, we succeed in withstanding all misfortunes and all illnesses."

To his mother 4 years after the arrest, on December 15, 1930. (*Letters from Prison*, vol. 1, p. 367)

A few months later, Gramsci started working on the first of his notebooks—a school exercise book, ruled, and marked with the prison stamp. By the end of his life, Gramsci completed over 30 notebooks containing brief notes, short essays, monographs, translations, and other fragments. In the end, he dealt not only with the topics he originally intended but with so much more, including Machiavelli's political treatise *The Prince,* as it might be read both in historical context and with respect to contemporary Italy (also in *WLAIT 7: Italian Literature and Its Times*). Gramsci's *Prison Notebooks*, edited and published after World War II, are now regarded not only as a masterpiece of political writing, but also as one of the major modern-day works in the study of contemporary interpretive thought.

The trial and the years in Turi. In May 1928, Gramsci was transferred from Milan to Rome in order to attend his trial. On May 28, the first day of the proceedings, Gramsci is reported to have turned to the judges and said: "You will lead Italy to ruin and it will be up to us Communists to save her" (*Letters from Prison*, vol. 1, p. 6). On June 4, 1928, at the end of the trial, the Special Tribunal sentenced Gramsci to twenty years, four months, and five days in prison.

A month later Gramsci was transferred to the Casa Penale of Turi, near Bari. Here, his physical condition started deteriorating dramatically. Between 1931 and 1933 he suffered from haemoptyses (the coughing up of blood), hallucinations, and ravings. Nevertheless, he managed during this time to write the major part of his *Notebooks* as well as approximately 300 letters. Due to prison censorship, he seldom wrote to his political comrades or other members of the Communist Party. Still, with the help of his wife's sister, Tania, he managed, to a certain degree, to participate in political and cultural debate.

Tania, in particular, served as an intermediary between Gramsci and Piero Sraffa, a world-renowned economist who had been Gramsci's friend since their student days in Turin. By arrangement, Tania hid Sraffa's messages in her own letters to the prisoner. In turn, when she received his responses, Tania transcribed and forwarded Gramsci's messages to Sraffa. In early 1932, at Sraffa's suggestion, Tania wrote Gramsci and pretended she had to produce a review of Benedetto Croce's influential work, *The History of Europe in the Nineteenth Century*. Gramsci responded with a series of six letters (dated April 18 and 25; May 2, 9 and 23; and June 6, 1932) that articulate briefly his own response to the work of Croce's—one of the major European philosophers of the time, commonly referred to as the founder of neoidealism—and express Gramsci's famous understanding of the historico-political concept of "hegemony." Briefly, "hegemony," as Gramsci uses it, means the system of ideological (as opposed to physical) control that a dominant group exercises throughout society. These six letters constitute a single message that the author was not able to complete in one session because he was allowed to write only a limited number of pages per week.

Sraffa's effort to smuggle out Gramsci's views did not pass unnoticed. The prison censor believed that Tania's request for help with writing a review of Croce's work masked an attempt to publish Gramsci's thoughts abroad. Gramsci suffered for it, undergoing interrogations and searches and experiencing in general a worsening of prison conditions.

The last phase: Civitavecchia and Rome. While Gramsci was being consumed by Pott's disease, pulmonary tuberculosis, hypertension, angina, and gout, an international movement arose on his behalf. French writer Romain Rolland and the Archbishop of Canterbury, among other major figures, made public statements and vehemently protested Gramsci's imprisonment. The pressure on the Italian government resulted in Gramsci's sentence being reduced.

In November 1933, Gramsci was transferred from Turi to Civitavecchia and then to a clinic in Formia, near Rome. Tatiana was permitted to come to aid him now, since his health had by this time worsened considerably. In August 1935 he was transferred to the Quisisana clinic in Rome, which was run by Swiss nuns. Here Gramsci could write freely, but his physical ailments made his pieces shorter and less regular. In one of his last messages to his son Delio, Gramsci minimizes the gravity of his situation. While asking for information about his son and giving him advice for the future, in this fragment Gramsci summarizes his own conception of history (which he had discussed extensively in the *Notebooks* and in other letters) and reiterates his understanding of man in general as a "historical formation" (*Letters from Prison*, vol. 1, p. 302). The letter to Delio is characterized by the profoundly loving tone of a father who addresses his son knowing that there is but a very slim chance of ever seeing him again:

> Dearest Delio,
> I am feeling a bit tired and cannot write a lot. Write to me always and tell me about everything that interests you in school. I think you like history just as I did when I was your age, because it deals with human beings. And everything that deals with people, as many people as possible, all the people in the world as they join together in society and work and struggle and better themselves, should please you more than any thing else. But is it like that? I embrace you. Papa.
>
> (*Letters from Prison*, vol. 2, pp. 383-84)

Gramsci died in Rome on April 27, 1937, only three days before his scheduled release.

Domination and hegemony. Gramsci is perhaps most famous for his development of the idea of *hegemony*, which he distinguishes from *domination*. According to Gramsci, *domination* refers to physical coercion or force while *hegemony* indi-

cates ideological control. It entails a consent that permeates social institutions (unions, schools, churches, and families) and collective thought (shared values and beliefs—e.g., what makes "common sense").

In Gramsci's view, when hegemony encourages sacrifice and deprivation for the sake of the system, it promotes political passivity and encourages the idea that people have no control

GRAMSCI'S CORRESPONDENTS

During his imprisonment Gramsci wrote to relatives and friends. The most important correspondents are:

- **Giuseppina "Peppina" Marcias Gramsci** (1861-1932). Gramsci's mother, a native Sardinian who died while her son was imprisoned. Remarkably, Antonio did not write any letters to his father.
- **Julca "Giulia" Schucht** (1896-1980). Gramsci's wife. Starting in the early 1920s, her health deteriorated and she suffered several nervous breakdowns (probably caused by a form of epilepsy), with her condition worsening after her husband's arrest. She spent most of her life, including the years of Gramsci's imprisonment, in Moscow.
- **Delio "Delka" Gramsci** and **Giuliano "Julik" Gramsci**. Sons of Antonio and Julca. Delio was born in Moscow in 1924. Giuliano was born in 1926, and his father never met him in person.
- **Tatiana "Tania" Schucht** (1887-1943). Sister of Julca. Besides writing extensively to Gramsci and transcribing his messages to other recipients, Tania visited Gramsci in prison and directly assisted him in the last phase of the imprisonment. She was present at his death.
- **Piero Sraffa** (1898-1983). World-famous economist and friend of Gramsci since their student years in Turin. He served as Professor of Economics at the Universities of Perugia, Milan, and Cagliari before being appointed lecturer at Cambridge University (1927-31) and then Fellow of Trinity College (1939-83). Sraffa authored a series of studies on David Ricardo and Karl Marx and wrote a famous letter, printed in the *Manchester Guardian* in October 1929, against Gramsci's imprisonment.
- Gramsci also sent letters to his siblings **Carlo**, **Grazietta**, and **Teresina Gramsci**, and to his former Roman landlady **Clara Passarge**. Other letters are addressed to Communist militants like **Virginio Borioni** (in prison with Gramsci in Rome) and **Giuseppe Berti** (confined in Ustica).

Gramsci died after a decade in prision. Nearly 60 years later, on April 25, 1994, students commemorate the end of Fascism in Italy with a large banner bearing his likeness.

over events. Political revolution in such an environment is impossible unless a crisis occurs to disrupt the ideological hegemony. It follows that socialist movements must create just such a crisis—must spread through society a "counter-hegemony" that will break the system's ideological bonds and penetrate the false world of established appearances. Only in this way can new, "liberated" ideas and values be established. So working people must unite, constitute themselves into a class (the proletariat), lead the nation, and eventually found a new government. In other words, they must engage in a struggle for hegemony under the auspices of the Communist Party (seen by Gramsci as an organized revolutionary avant-garde). The struggle, taught Gramsci, ought to be waged by way of a new politically engaged person, rather than the highly theoretical and highly specialized intellectual.

According to Gramsci, all those who have attained prominence in civil society should contribute to the creation of counter-hegemony. Intellectuals, in particular, should give voice to the needs and ideas of other, potentially revolutionary sectors of society (especially the working class and the peasantry) and in this way become "organic" agents in the development of civil consciousness.

Sources and literary context. The tradition of epistolary (or letter) writing is strong in the history of Italian literature. The letters of Saint Catherine of Siena (1347-80) were the first to be recognized for their literary merit; the epistolary texts of several other Italian writers (including Machiavelli and Galileo Galilei) were also widely published and studied alongside more conventional literary works. From the end of the eighteenth century, the epistolary genre assumed a primary importance in Italian culture, as indicated by the highly popular novel *The Last Letters of Jacopo Ortis* (also in *WLAIT 7: Italian Literature and Its Times*).

As we can infer from the *Letters* and the *Notebooks*, Gramsci had a wide knowledge of Italian and international literatures. His main literary models ranged (according to a letter sent to his son, Delio, in the summer of 1936) from Homer to Aeschylus, Dante, Shakespeare, Goethe, and Cervantes. Gramsci refers to Tolstoy as one of the few writers in the world "who has attained the greatest perfection in art and has aroused and continues to arouse torrents of emotion everywhere, even in the worst translations, even in the men and women who are brutalized by heavy toil and have an elementary culture." In the same document Gramsci admires Chekhov, calling him a "progressive" writer who "has contributed to the liquidation of the middle classes, the intellectuals, the petty bourgeois as the standard bearers of Russian history and its future" (*Letters from Prison*, vol. 2, p. 360).

Reception. The first Italian edition of the *Letters from Prison* was published by Giulio Einaudi in 1947—ten years after Gramsci's death and four years after the demise of the Fascist regime. The book consisted of a selection of 218 letters and met with an enthusiastic popular response. After having sold 12,000 copies in just a few months, the book was awarded the Premio Viareggio (one of Italy's highest literary awards) for nonfiction.

The Viareggio prize committee recognized the artistic value of the letters, finding in Gramsci "a lucid affirmer and witness" of the human condition (Repaci in Gramsci, *Letters from Prison*, vol. 1, p. 1). The most influential literary critics of the time likewise recognized the importance to Italian literature of Gramsci's published letters. Benedetto Croce reacted in 1947 with the observation that "as a man of thought Gramsci was one of us, one of those who in the first decades of this century in Italy devoted themselves to forming a philosophical and historical habit of mind adequate to the problems of the present" (Croce, p. 86). Other Italian critics, such as Carlo Bo and Italo Calvino, stressed the universality of Gramsci's testimony and spoke of the desire for life that courses through the text. Finally, in his introduction to the letters, Paolo Spriano sizes them up with a poetic flourish, dwelling on the collection's personal impact:

> Gramsci's letters constitute both a human and a literary monument. Taken together, they pace the rhythm of his captivity, and constitute a tragic tale that becomes gloomier and gloomier, to culminate in a sort of farewell to life in the 1936 notes to his far apart children.
>
> The reader enters a tunnel, and the light at its end gets dimmer and dimmer and eventually dies out.
>
> (Spriano in Gramsci, *Lettere dal Carcere*, p. xvii; trans. S. Ovan)

—Paolo Matteucci

For More Information

Boggs, Carl. *Gramsci's Marxism*. London: Pluto, 1976.

Chabod, Federico. *A History of Italian Fascism*. Trans. Muriel Grindrod. New York: H. Fertig, 1975.

Croce, Benedetto. Review of *Le lettere dal carcere*, by Antonio Gramsci. *Quaderni della Critica* 8 (July 1947): 86.

Dombroski, Robert. *Antonio Gramsci*. Boston: Twayne, 1989.

Fiori, Giuseppe. *Antonio Gramsci: Life of a Revolutionary*. Trans. Tom Nairn. New York: Schocken Books, 1973.

Fogu, Claudio. *The Historic Imaginary: Politics of History in Fascist Italy*. Buffalo: University of Toronto Press, 2003.

Gramsci, Antonio. *Lettere dal carcere*. Ed. Paolo Spriano. Torino: Einaudi, 1971.

————. *Letters from Prison*. Ed. Frank Rosengarten; trans. Raymond Rosenthal. 2 vols. New York: Columbia University Press, 1994.

————. *Selections from Cultural Writings*. Ed. David Forgacs and Geoffrey Nowell-Smith; trans. William Boelhower. Cambridge: Harvard University Press, 1985.

Repaci, Leonida. *Ricordo di Gramsci*. Roma: Macchia, 1948.

Sraffa, Piero. *Lettere a Tania per Gramsci*. Ed. Valentino Gerratana. Roma: Editori Riuniti, 1991.

Life of a Man

by

Giuseppe Ungaretti

Giuseppe Ungaretti was born February 8, 1888, in Alexandria, Egypt, of Italian immigrant parents. Surprisingly, in light of his future role as founder of modern Italian poetry, he was educated in French and did not travel to his parents' homeland until 1912, when he passed through on his way to Paris to study. In Paris he attended lectures by the French philosopher Henri Bergson and met the Spanish artist Pablo Picasso, the French poet Max Jacob, and Italy's Futurist writer Filippo Tommaso Marinetti. Artist-critic Ardengo Soffici invited Ungaretti to contribute to the new journal *Lacerba,* in which his first poems were published in 1915. Ungaretti returned to Italy at the onset of World War I, serving as a soldier on the Carso plateau from 1915 to 1918 and composing 33 poems that became the core of his first collection *The Joy of Shipwrecks* (partially published in 1916, updated and republished in 1921 and, as *Joy,* in 1931). He married Jeanne Dupoix and in 1921 moved to Rome, where he accepted a post in the French Press division of the foreign ministry, which he held until 1936. During these 15 years, he traveled as a newspaper correspondent, wrote articles, translated literary works, lectured on Italian literature, and produced his second book of poetry—*A Sense of Time* (1933). For the next half dozen years (1936-42), Ungaretti taught Italian literature at the University of São Paulo, Brazil. Forced to return to Italy when Brazil entered World War II on the side of the Allies, he was offered a post at the University of Rome. In

THE LITERARY WORK

A poetic corpus set in twentieth-century Italy; published in Italian (as *Vita d'un uomo*) from 1916-1970, in English in part beginning in 1958.

SYNOPSIS

Conceived as a diary of Ungaretti's inner life, the corpus consists of separate poetic collections that reflect spiritual transformations.

the wake of the war, Ungaretti published *Affliction* (1950), in which he mourned the deaths of his elder brother and nine-year-old son as well as Italy's losses in the internal struggle between Resistance fighters and Fascists (1943-45). More poetic collections followed: *The Promised Land* (1950), *A Cry and Landscapes* (1952), and *The Old Man's Notebook* (1960), which with *Poesie disperse,* or *Lost Poems* (1945), and some later poems, completes the corpus that would become *Life of a Man.* From its inception, Ungaretti conceived it as a sustained meditation on death, that is, on the moral strength it reveals, which alone can withstand the contradiction between metaphysical despair and sensual innocence. It was Ungaretti's ability to evoke this moral strength in the fleeting poetic word that for a whole generation made his name synonymous with poetry itself.

Giuseppe Ungaretti

Events in History at the
Time of the Poems

Modernity and avant-garde revolution. Italian futurism, launched in 1909 from Paris by Marinetti's **Futurist Manifesto** (also in *WLAIT 7: Italian Literature and Its Times*), quickly spread throughout Europe its call for artists to bury the past and celebrate experimentation, technological innovation, and the vast crowds of the modern city. The movement was reacting in part to Italy's perceived failure to produce an artistic rebirth to mirror its political unification during the wars of the Risorgimento (1859), or "reunification," which resulted in its becoming a unified political power for the first time since the fall of the Roman Empire in the fifth century. Futurism stepped in to effect a concomitant artistic rebirth, responding at the same time to a broader crisis over the role of the modern artist in Western capitalist societies. All over Europe, artists argued that modernity was not the shallow, materialistic "progress" championed by the bourgeoisie, but a revolutionary, anarchic force that would break down class divisions and social conventions. Indeed, the flourishing of "isms" in art at the time—from cubism and surrealism in France, to expressionism in Germany, and imagism in Great Britain—reflected the frenetic desire to create not only a new artistic form but also a new society that would validate it.

In Italy in particular, the younger generation sought to escape a heritage embodied in the flamboyant writing of Gabriele D'Annunzio (1863-1938), who achieved international success, it was said, by pandering to the bourgeois, though he also infused Italian verse with a renewed sensual fullness and a prescient sense of modernity's spiritual abyss (see D'Annunzio's **Child of Pleasure,** *also in WLAIT 7: Italian Literature and Its Times*). First the so-called crepuscular poets, with their ironic, subdued, everyday style, and then the Futurists, with their attack on all conventions, rejected the pessimistic view that, in his bombast and anguish, D'Annunzio signaled the final expulsion of art from modern industrial and scientific societies. There was, as Ungaretti later averred, much merit in the Futurists' call for a drastic change, especially their call for expressive forms to mirror an increasingly fragmented, chaotic, decentered world. Like the French avant-garde, the Futurists opposed naturalistic representation. They sought instead dynamic art forms to impose upon their audience some contemporary realities: the quintessentially modern phenomenon of impersonal violence; the awareness of distant experiences; and the loss of linear time as a result of increasing speed. Artists gave expression to these ideas in the Futurist *serata* (evening), a public performance including the display of paintings, the use of Intonarumori (machines built by the Futurists to make musical noise) or perhaps the blaring of avant-garde music, poetry recitations, harangues against the past and the political establishment, and mutual pelting of audience and performers with rotten fruit. Though Ungaretti never adhered to a particular avant-garde or Futurist group, he was shaped by their debates and drew from them a lifelong preoccupation with the conflict between individual freedom, on one hand, and the desire for new mythologies to heal modern alienation, on the other hand. Individual freedom for Ungaretti entailed both creative and existential freedom, that is, the freedom to question and perhaps not to find the ultimate meaning of life and death.

Overwhelmingly the avant-garde artists, Ungaretti among them, favored Italy's intervention in World War I: the war, for many, represented the final breakdown of traditional society, paving the way for a new world in which Italy would reinvent both art and the individual. More specifically, for the pro-war newspaper *Il Popolo d'Italia* (1914-43; The Italian People), founded by Benito Mussolini, the war would empower "the people" both politically and culturally—a claim to which Ungaretti, proud of his working-class origins, was very susceptible.

Mass death, estrangement, and mourning. For the Italians and for Europe in general, World War I turned out to be far more disruptive than anyone could have imagined. Individually the unprecedented number of deaths brought new and lasting psychological traumas. Socially the solidarity experienced on the battlefield seemed to disintegrate in postwar Italy in the face of partisan politics and a return to prewar social divisions.

The social divisions coalesced around at least three issues. The first issue was the result of the failure to deliver on a promise. At the height of the war the government pledged that soldiers would afterwards experience greater social justice and specifically new land allocations, which did not materialize. This led to the recurrent image of the victimized "peasant-soldier" who, deprived of land, could not fulfill his mission of re-fertilizing Italy, literally *and* spiritually. Second, Italy's defeat at Caporetto (October 24, 1917), a crushing military humiliation, led to almost as crushing an argument about who was to blame: while the head of Italy's military forces, Luigi Cadorna, was punitively replaced by Armando Diaz, the military simultaneously condemned ordinary soldiers for too often showing a lack of courage and deserting. Three years into peacetime, an investigative commission on Caporetto was still trying to exonerate those who had been unjustly shot as traitors. The third issue contributing to social disunity concerned the Treaty of Versailles (June 28, 1919), which, in the opinion of many Italians, gave credence only to a "mutilated victory" (as the popular expression went), since it did not award Italy control over the Austrian territories in Dalmatia (once controlled by Venice, Italy), or of the city of Fiume (formerly controlled by Italy). These areas had been at the center of the wartime campaign and in the postwar era would inspire bitter attacks against the liberal government, which was seen as having "betrayed" the territories' Italian populations. As one government after another fell in postwar Italy, Mussolini gained popularity, particularly with intellectuals and artists, largely because he promised to heal these rifts and (through an antibourgeois revolution) to restore Italy's territorial unity.

In addressing wartime trauma Mussolini's only rival was Gabriele D'Annunzio, who had also been vocal in interventionism and who, like Mussolini, returned from the war as a multi-decorated, wounded hero. In his postwar speeches, as well as in his main literary work of this period (*Nocturne,* partially published, 1916; final version, 1921), D'Annunzio's regard for the process of commemoration reflects his intuition that some ritual was necessary to facilitate the psychological reintegration of men whose worldviews had been shattered. Soldiers' "identification" with "the death of every comrade" needed expression (Leed, p. 211). D'Annunzio conjured an image of the northern front on the bare, rocky, pockmarked Carso Mountains as a type of hell. Meanwhile, French poet André Breton, whose own writings concentrated in part on mental disorders and dreams, was using free association to help psychiatric patients voice their experience of an alienation so radical no language or paradigm could contain it. Ungaretti would later reinvent D'Annunzio's image, portraying himself as a barren Carsic rock (Ungaretti, *A Major Selection,* p. 69). Also he later conceived poetry born from feelings of alienation that resembled those of Breton:

> A spell has been broken; men no longer have anything in common, except their delirious suffering, and even that separates and wounds them. . . . Who is still capable of knowing what art is, what life is, who is capable of introspection without experiencing the terror of yet another disappointment . . . ?
> (Ungaretti, *Correspondance,* p. 12)

Much of D'Annunzio's popularity came from asserting the primacy of the war experience over any distinction between Fascism and anti-Fascism. The stands the poet took on issues after the war, particularly his physical takeover of Fiume (1919-20), with the help of a band of irregulars, reflect a blurring of boundaries among the artistic, political, social, and religious spheres. This blurring occurred within the poetry, fiction, and political speeches he and others wrote: to give expression to collective mourning was at once a religious, highly individualistic act and a representative political act. A young poet at the time, Ungaretti would produce works (*The Buried Harbor* [1916] and its expansion *The Joy of Shipwrecks* [1919]) that provided an alternative rhetoric of mourning, which reacted to and borrowed from D'Annunzio, meanwhile helping modern Italian poetry supersede D'Annunzio's perspective.

Fascism and its rewritings. By 1922 disaffection and political instability were so great in Italy that Mussolini could organize a march on Rome by 30,000 Fascists (October 28) and thereby force the hand of King Victor Emmanuel. The king offered Mussolini the post of prime minister and the task of forming a government of national unity, both of which the future dictator accepted. Generally speaking, the rise to power of Fascism was accompanied by a growing desire for a return to order after the agitation and experimentation that had purportedly led to the First World War and continued thereafter. This desire for order reverberated in art, where the influential literary journal *La Ronda* (The Circle), in which Ungaretti published, championed the Italian classics as well as socially unengaged writing—writing as "pure style" separate from societal involvement. The return to order set the stage for Fascism's transformation into an ideology of permanent revolution, featuring a rhetoric of violence that gave vent to emotions but ultimately suppressed the possibility of any real change. Artists were encouraged to develop revolutionary aesthetics so long as they were divorced from individual moral commitment or social action: this was largely the direction taken, often unwittingly, by Futurism. Others retreated into introspective, alternatively nostalgic and bitterly pessimistic work. In the end, the Futurists, who in their second phase sought to reconcile the modern with the classical, would transform their initial celebration of technological change. They would develop it into a rhetorical ornament that did not disturb the social conservatism of the Fascist regime.

By 1924, Mussolini's charisma, combined with intimidation, ensured a win for Fascism of an absolute majority in parliament. A turning point came with the murder on June 10, 1924, of Giacomo Matteotti, who had spoken out passionately against the brutal Fascist methods. In 1925, Giovanni Gentile, at that time Fascism's official ideologue, wrote the "Manifesto of Fascist Intellectuals," which presented Fascism as the heir to the Italian Risorgimento, as evidenced by its capacity to unite Italy in a totalitarian and spiritual fashion: some 250 intellectuals signed it, including Ungaretti. Other intellectuals objected. Their leader, Benedetto Croce, responded with the "Manifesto of Anti-Fascist Intellectuals" (also 1925), signed by about 200 initially, and later by many more. It would be the last time such open criticism could be voiced. By 1926 the death penalty had been instituted for severe political crimes, and anti-Fascists were increasingly being sent into internal exile (*confino*) or imprisoned, sometimes never to reemerge. The 1929 Lateran Pacts, which sealed the alliance between Fascism and the Catholic Church, paved the way for imposing an ever tighter cultural consensus on citizens. In 1931 the government required all university professors to swear allegiance to Fas-

cism or lose their posts: they overwhelmingly complied, though by then many had already fled or been purged. Cultural life was all but immobilized by the "continual awareness of there being no way out" (Pavese in Cary, p. 21).

Resistance developed slowly because disenchantment with Fascism could only grow in isolation and secrecy. Intellectuals such as Ungaretti continued to support certain aspects of the regime, such as agricultural and other public projects. At the same time, major journals—such as the anti-Fascist *Solaria* (1926-36), in which Ungaretti published—adopted increasingly indirect, metaphoric ways to signal their awareness of Fascist violence. For example, writers devised an imaginary interview with a "foreigner," translated "non-Fascist" authors, or slyly transposed political issues into a seemingly apolitical domain, like literary criticism (Ungaretti engaged in the last two). Another avenue, albeit one that required caution, was the publication of works that might be construed as anti-Fascist in foreign journals such as Marguerite Caetani's Parisian *Commerce* (1924-32), in which Ungaretti was quite active.

Another pivotal juncture came in 1935, when Italy's colonial war in Ethiopia led to economic sanctions against Italy by the League of Nations and ultimately to Mussolini's turn toward Hitler's Germany. The alliance, signed in 1936 and sealed by Hitler's visit to Rome in 1938, brought the spread of racial laws in Italy in September of that same year. Deportations began, and Jews were no longer able to teach or publish in the country. Italy proceeded to fight a disastrous war alongside Germany. In July 1943, after the Americans had landed in Sicily, Fascism fell and Mussolini was arrested. A new Italian government signed an armistice with the Allies as they came to liberate south-central Italy, and the Nazis reacted. They rescued Mussolini and put him at the head of a so-called social republic (the Republic of Salò, 1943-45) in the Nazi-occupied North. Suddenly the country was split in two. The Fascists and Nazis became occupying forces, confronted not only by the Americans, who fought their way north, but also by Italian anti-Fascists, who began organizing a military resistance to the Republic of Salò, which precipitated a civil war in the North. On April 25, 1945, the insurrection of the internal resistance movement combined with a military push by the Allies finally brought Mussolini down and liberated the North. But there were grave consequences. The civil war had not only divided northern Italians; there had been political divisiveness in the resistance movement itself, among Catholics, liberals, and Communists (the majority). In the war's aftermath, all these groups angled for power, sometimes violently. American pressure ultimately ensured a conservative, Christian Democrat government in Italy, which was a blow to many of Italy's intellectuals, who at this point favored more radical, anti-Fascist parties.

In these years, a newly free press exposed both Fascist and Nazi violence, shocking Italians out of complacency and consent. Hence postwar Italy was shaped not only by the renewed psychological trauma of mass death, but also by a historical trauma that could be framed by a series of uncomfortable questions: How could so many Italians, and especially artists and thinkers, have supported such a repressive regime and, worst of all, the alliance with Nazi genocide? How strong and long-lived had the Resistance been? Why was social injustice as bad, if not worse, in postwar Italian society as before the war?

In literature and cinema, the neorealism movement developed in the 1950s and 1960s as a postwar answer to these questions. It was based on the fiction of writers who had participated in the Resistance (Italo Calvino, Carlo Cassola, Natalia Ginzburg, Primo Levi), and on documentary-like films about the war's end (by Roberto Rossellini, Vittorio De Sica, Luchino Visconti). To varying degrees, neorealist works shared two characteristics, stemming from their authors' desire to empower the individual against Fascist ideology: first, the works were committed to a narrative realism based on the accumulation of true-to-life details and the interplay of multiple points of view; second, they emphasized personal freedom in making moral choices, aiming to elicit compassion for the oppressed and disdain for political conformism. Neorealist works, in the infancy of the movement, suggested that few Italians had really supported the regime in their day-to-day lives or conscience, and that in their hearts Italians of all political stripes had joined in a resistance movement aimed exclusively at the Nazis and a few hardened Fascists. In this climate, the purging of intellectuals who had collaborated with the Fascist regime was driven as much by a need to condemn "the few" who were "really responsible" as by the need to uphold a worldview in which historical responsibility was clear-cut. Writers like D'Annunzio and Marinetti became pariahs (even though they were dead) not only because of their involvement with the regime, but also because their antirealistic styles came to be associated with a dangerous moral relativism. In contrast, Ungaretti, with his spare style, would survive the era of purges almost unscathed.

As neorealism evolved into new forms of experimentation from the 1970s onward, however,

UNGARETTI AND FASCISM

Ungaretti's support of Fascism remains an uncomfortable subject. Undoubtedly, like many intellectuals, he believed in its promise to reorganize the social classes and reestablish "the dream . . . that comes from the people" (Ungaretti, *Saggi e Interventi*, pp. 151, 153; trans. L. Wittman). From Ungaretti's vantage point, Fascism was revolutionary, antibourgeois (it seemed to reject material gain in favor of spiritual renewal), and progressive (as manifested in its great public works campaigns). This would explain why in 1919 he joined Mussolini's Fasci (Fascist Party), dedicated to Mussolini the poem "The People" in *The Joy of Shipwrecks,* and sought a preface by him for a 1923 edition of *The Buried Harbor* (a preface never included in subsequent editions). Yet, as Ungaretti repeatedly pointed out, he never received special favors from the regime and was in fact arrested more than once for complaining about it. He helped various friends escape arrest and, at great personal risk, sheltered a young Jewish woman around 1943-44. At liberation, in 1944, Ungaretti was suspended from his university post (on grounds that he got it from the Fascist regime without proper competition), was examined by three commissions, and (after suffering a heart attack) was reinstated in 1946 when the government left the decision to the university faculty alone.

Nonetheless, Francesca Petrocchi's publications of Ungaretti's letters to Mussolini (in 1987 and 1995), among other writings, give the lie to the notion that the poet's involvement with the regime was purely idealistic. He joined the party, as noted, wrote articles in the 1920s defending the Fascist restoration of order, and participated in the 1925 Congress of Fascist Intellectuals in Bologna. Twenty years later, on November 22, 1945, writing his French friend Jean Paulhan, who was about to risk his reputation by resisting the persecution of French writers who had collaborated with the Nazis, Ungaretti expounded on the unclear nature of political choices at the time: "I was very fond of Drieu [the French writer la Rochelle, who had just committed suicide after being threatened as a result of his collaboration], and I was truly saddened. It is difficult to know who is right and who is wrong, at a time when the world is in the middle of such a tragic change, which is far from having ended its cycle" (Ungaretti, *Correspondance*, p. 353).

the questions raised by the Fascist experience were revisited. Indeed, the undeniable support of many Italians for the regime (including intellectuals, and even Resistance icons such as Ignazio Silone) continues to be the subject of artistic as well as scholarly investigation. Ungaretti's politics were, in truth, precariously balanced between an extremely rigorous assertion of moral and spiritual conscience, on one hand, and, on the other, a sincere, if also convenient, belief in Fascism's "revolutionary" promises, particularly with regard to the creation of a more equitable Italian society. This ambivalent attitude was emblematic of a whole generation of intellectuals, in whom blindness toward Fascist oppression was furthered by a high-minded refusal to enter the fray of politics. From this perspective, Ungaretti's 1933 book of poetry, *A Sense of Time,* often read as a call for personal moral commitment, must also be read as a tragic witness to the powerlessness of the individual in the face of Fascism (and all modern forms of nationalism).

UNGARETTI ON STYLE AND WORLD WAR I

Ungaretti claimed the lack of rhyme, punctuation, and grammatically complete thoughts in his collection *Joy* was due to the war more than avant-garde experimentation: "War suddenly revealed the [new] language to me. That is, I had to speak quickly because time might turn out to be very short, and most tragically . . . quickly I had to express what I felt quickly with few words . . . and thus with words that had to acquire an extraordinary intensity of meaning."

(Ungaretti, *Saggi e Interventi,* p. 820; trans. L. Wittman)

His 1936 move to Brazil too must be seen as an escape and a defeat, not a rebellion. Fascism, his experience implies, stemmed not from the moral failure of the few, but from the moral crisis of the many, whose desire for absolute answers and uncompromising politics were fuelled in part by an inability to live with uncertainty about the future. In response, Ungaretti's postwar poems in *Life of a Man* move from individual powerlessness and an acknowledgment of inevitable errors to the search for a human commonness in suffering, and in joy, that might serve as an alternative to the homogenizing power of an uncompromising ideology. The merit of his work lies not in his own political choices, but rather

in his ability to lay bare the conflicts, uncertainties, and compromises inherent in individual moral struggle. Unlike the previous generations' pessimism and retreat from action, Ungaretti's verse urges us to engage in this struggle even though we cannot fully control its outcome.

The Poems in Focus

Contents summary. Ungaretti's *Life of a Man* is divided into three phases, according to the author's autobiographical writings. The first phase evokes the "horror of eternity" and the "familiarity with death" experienced in World War I (Ungaretti, *Saggi e Interventi,* p. 130; trans. L. Wittman); the second explores the unfolding of existential time, backward, from the perspective of death, as the poet seeks to rediscover an initial innocence through memory; the third discovers a sacred dimension in this struggle.

Phase One: *Joy.* The collection *Joy* begins with the section "The Last Ones," the final pre-World War I poems written by Ungaretti, which evoke his sense of isolation as a returning emigrant (with the help of the nothingness of the African desert). Throughout the collection, the images are stark and fragmented; the lines, grammatically incomplete and lacking in rhyme and punctuation. As he writes in "Insomnia," dated December 23, 1915,

> A whole night
> crushed against
> a massacred
> companion
> with his contorted
> mouth
> turned to the moonlight
> . . . .
> I wrote
> letters full of love
>
> (Ungaretti, *Tutte le Poesie,* p. 25;
> trans. L. Wittman)

Unlike his later poems, those in *Joy* stem from a single moment of intuition, as indicated by the precise date and time that usually accompany them.

"The Buried Harbor," *Joy*'s longest section, focuses on the "sentiment of participating in others' suffering" (Ungaretti, *Saggi e Interventi,* p. 821; trans. L. Wittman). Its central image is drawn from the original harbor of Alexandria, buried underwater and only lately discovered. For Ungaretti, it represented the subterranean source of poetic intuitions, uniquely individual yet reaching into a collective unconscious and expressed in word play (Italian terms with multiple meanings, inner rhymes, anagrams, acrostics, and puns).

In the section "Brothers" the meaning of the title word is radically transformed by its metaphorical description in the poem as a "shuddering . . . leaf" that expresses the "involuntary rebellion / of man present to his own / frailness." Before this metaphor, in the first two lines, *brothers* is used with fear in the question "What regiment are you from / brothers?"; at the end, constituting by itself the whole last line of the poem, it becomes a statement of existential unity (Ungaretti, *Selected Poems,* p. 31).

The next section, "Shipwrecks," opens with "The Joy of Shipwrecks," a poem in which the poet asserts the paradoxical discovery of the whole collection: moments of joy—when he feels his unity with creation (notwithstanding the horrors of war)—are reached only through shipwreck or suffering and are always temporary.

"Wanderer," a very short section written after Caporetto and before the war's end, characterizes wartime "wandering" as a permanent existential erring in search of "one minute of inchoate / life" (Ungaretti, *Selected Poems,* p. 67). In contrast to the opening of the collection, the final section is entitled "First Ones"; it prefigures the next phase's turn to memory to rediscover or at least to search for lost innocence.

Phase Two: *A Sense of Time.* This three-part collection meditates on the fleeting nature of poetic intuitions, corrupted as they are by time. Stylistically, the collection reflects a "return to order," which, for Ungaretti, took the form of a new emphasis on two elements. Stressed in this collection is the Italian poetic tradition behind specific words (e.g. *shipwreck,* derived from Giacomo Leopardi's famous 1819 poem "The Infinite"). Secondly the section stresses the hendecasyllable (the major verse of Italian lyric poetry, comparable to the iambic pentameter in English, which stresses the tenth syllable in an eleven-syllable line). There are complex ensembles of images in this section, in which memory struggles to redeem time: *D'altri diluvi una colomba ascolto.* For example, in the line "From within other floods to a dove I listen," the dove, an image of peace and the holy spirit, and in Italian poetry of maidenly innocence, is transformed into a more modern and indefinable salvation by its flight over "other" floods, which suggest the recent cataclysm of World War II ("A Dove," *Tutte le Poesie,* p. 113; trans. L. Wittman). These poems are dated only by their year, reflecting a longer maturation than those in the first collection.

The first part of *A Sense of Time* includes three sections, written during Ungaretti's first years in Rome, when he spent nights wandering in the Tivoli gardens; here the decay of the Roman countryside represents historical memory and civilization's decadence. Time is a "fleeting tremor," bringing us "concealed whispers" from the past (Ungaretti, *Selected Poems,* p. 83). The second part also consists of three sections—"Legends," "Hymns," and "Death Meditated": here time unfolds as the drama of the self exposed to its own nothingness, longing for its redemption into the eternal from the ephemeral. Individual memory now persecutes the poet by suggesting that no redemption from time's error is possible; time marches on erratically, unpredictably, moving away from an original pristine condition. The "Hymns" in particular mark a religious crisis, in which Ungaretti wonders whether he has fallen prey to a "servitude to words" that are nothing but "phantoms" and "dry leaves," because from man's hands there "issue endlessly only limits," so that to think of the "Eternal, / He has only blasphemies" (Ungaretti, *Selected Poems,* pp. 121, 127). Written between 1928 and 1932, these poems allude to Ungaretti's return to Catholicism by evoking his awareness of his distance from God. This collection closes with the poem "A sense of time," in which the poet hopes that the "distance" between ephemeral limits and eternal primordial innocence might be "open to [the] measure" of God's mystery, to having a sense of this mystery (Ungaretti, *A Major Selection,* p. 245). The last section of *A Sense of Time,* "Love," which focuses on aging and "perishing in [Ungaretti's] flesh itself," looks toward his later work. Unexpectedly the section celebrates the vitality of the very erring of memory with the cry, "Suffering, don't leave me, stay!" (Ungaretti, *Saggi e Interventi,* p. 826; trans. L. Wittman; "Greetings for his own birthday," *Selected Poems,* p. 147).

Phase Three: *Affliction, The Promised Land,* and more. Ungaretti's third phase alternates between moments of peace (brought on by the poet's learning to accept time as an inevitable yet temporary exile from the idea of the eternal) and moments of tumultuous suffering (brought on by perceiving this idea as an illusion and exile as a useless struggle against the void). In this spiritual torment, suffering is never placated by the momentary intuition or the echo of the eternal, which is, however, all that poetry can provide.

Spanning 1937 to 1946, *Affliction,* a collection inspired by tragedies of the 1930s and 1940s, divides into five sections. "I Have Lost Everything" consists of two poems that are outcries of petrified shock at the "obliterating nothingness" of the deaths of the poet's son and brother (Ungaretti, *Selected Poems,* p. 185). "Day by Day" is the dramatic unfolding of Ungaretti's mourning for his son in one 17-stanza poem, while "Time Is Silent" delves into the bittersweet recollection of his son's young innocence. "Toward a Pine" consists of a single poem with the same title, which envisions Ungaretti's return to Rome as a pilgrimage to a "soaring" pine that, among ruins "full of memories," still "reache[s] out" "undaunted" though "contorted" in "mortification" (Ungaretti, *Tutte le Poesie,* p. 219; trans. L. Wittman). "Rome Occupied" and "Memories" meditate on how the pain of the present overwhelms even those past moments that seemed happy (Ungaretti, *Tutte le Poesie,* p. 237).

The phase's remaining collections include *The Promised Land,* described as "fragments" of a goal that could not be fully reached (Ungaretti, *Tutte le Poesie,* p. 546; trans. L. Wittman). The collection begins with the immobile void of death in order to invoke (in Platonic terms) the turn away from the world of appearances toward a new dawn in which an ideal love is reborn. Three figures from Roman mythology represent, in turn, the poet's initial determination to face death serenely, as a passage into eternal innocence (like the hero Aeneas visiting the underworld); his inability to leave behind an autumnal yet golden sensual love (abandoned Dido in the throes of passion even after death); and finally his discovery that a serene death is the supreme illusion, the mistaken notion of having reached the impossible-to-reach promised land (shipwrecked Palinurus, Aeneas' helmsman, thinks he will find land but in fact continues to be borne by the waves even in death). This last phase—*A Cry and Landscapes* (again for his son, and about Rome)—includes some final collections and poems: *The Old Man's Notebook;* "Apocalypses"; "Proverbs"; *Dialogue;* and *New Ones.* All of them are subsumed under the sign of shipwreck, that is, of a forever unreachable promise of salvation. In the concluding poem, "The Petrified and the Velvet," the speaker is almost obliterated in the stony abstraction of death, but then suddenly awakened by a velvet gaze to long for a redemption. In the end, he calls out for mercy, shuddering at the deathly void that lies ahead.

Revelation and illusion. Ungaretti's poetry returns throughout the years to a critical question: since the aspiration toward eternity (or the pursuit of innocence) is founded on intuition and echo, is this aspiration merely an illusion? Or, as

a 1916 poem asks, "Closed off among things that die / (Even the starry sky will end) / Why do I long for God?" (Ungaretti, *Selected Poems,* p. 25). This question is Ungaretti's expression of a quintessentially modern quandary: Why is Western civilization still vitally concerned, through longing or even denial, with a "God," even as its culture increasingly lacks any vocabulary with which to discuss religious sentiment? Is this concern just nostalgic illusion?

Though Ungaretti eventually became a practicing Catholic, his faith was never dogmatic and always permeated by doubt: his poetry reflects this spiritual struggle. Ironically it enables him to reconcile what his predecessors could not, to achieve an acceptance of modernity's chaotic lack of meaning and to rebel against it without merely returning to older certainties.

For Ungaretti, to rebel against meaninglessness and defend existence necessarily involves facing death and the reality of non-existence. "O Night," which opens *A Sense of Time,* meditates on poetry's role in defining a new religious sentiment based not on articles of faith but rather on the more extreme claim that the ultimate meaning of death is an impenetrable mystery. "O Night" uses two different poetic images to illustrate Ungaretti's unique intertwining of hope and despair. The section speaks of "oceanic silences / celestial nests of illusion," alluding on the one hand to the belief that silence is celestial, that it is God's sublime silence, and fear is but an illusion, for human existence is ultimately one with the immense night (Ungaretti, *Tutte le poesie,* p. 103; trans. L. Wittman). On the other hand, in those same lines Ungaretti invokes the belief that the night sky and its sublimity is an "illusion" (like his predecessor Leopardi, who wrote "The Infinite," in which such silence leads to a shipwreck in which existence is annulled). While D'Annunzio and other writers of the preceding generation often turned away from such pessimistic irony and embraced some faith in God's sublime silence, Ungaretti's vision remains suspended between faith and pessimistic irony. Moreover, by envisioning nests, Ungaretti proposes a paradox: it can be nurturing rather than frightful not to know whether longing for God can reach any harbor. Within the "starry silence," "trees and the night" are born and live and move "from nests" (Ungaretti, *Selected Poems,* p. 151). Life in all its risky vitality is linked to a refusal to make assertions about God's existence.

Thus, Ungaretti expresses a modern anxiety through complex allusions that link his poems with one another and with tradition. Stylistic techniques such as ambiguity, oxymoron, and allusion make all certainties recede, opening us to the anguish of questions. Condensed in the Italian words *svelata alberatura*, the image of "trees like masts revealed," could also be read as "masts like trees revealed," which raises the question, Are these the dead remains of a shipwreck come back to life or are they living trees that are becoming ossified and sterile? Ungaretti's poetry refuses to give any answer, instead conveying the urgency of the question itself, acting on his belief that "the [poetic] word has a sacred value derived from technical difficulty itself" (Ungaretti, *Saggi e Interventi*, p. 762; trans. L. Wittman). The search for oxymoron and ambiguity, the very attempt to make language turn back upon itself, against its desire for clarity, is religious because through it we experience our distance from the mystery, our fallen-ness, our need for redemption.

Sources and literary context. Because Ungaretti's education was predominantly French, his initial inspiration came from the late-nineteenth-century French symbolist and decadent poets, mainly Charles Baudelaire, Jules Laforgue, and Stéphane Mallarmé, as well as the German philosopher Friedrich Nietzsche. Marking the final Romantic rebellion against bourgeois materialism, these poets were "outcasts," living in a time of "disorientation" that forced them to try ever more desperate physical and moral experiments to evade their "hallucinated" solitude (Ungaretti, *Saggi e Interventi*, pp. 22-23; trans. L. Wittman). Filtered first through avant-garde and Futurist writings, this experimentation gave rise to the modern poetic fragment, which mirrored a broken society and a shattered psyche by scattering the different elements of analogy across the page in brief lines or words surrounded by the white void of silence. Though all this experimentation influenced Ungaretti, he distanced himself from what he saw as Futurism's purely destructive value, subscribing to Henri Bergson's philosophy that intuition can briefly grasp how fragments are opposed to, yet caught in, the eternal flow of time.

The French symbolists thought Western civilization had reached its decadent phase, like the Roman Empire once did. In this environment, poetry was a form of music that ought to evoke a mood rather than a mental or moral reaction. The belief was that everything in the mind correlated to something in nature and that everything in nature correlated to something in the spirit world—hence the focus on the symbol. One line of Symbolist poetry (emblematized by Stéphane Mallarmé, 1842-98) aimed for a formal perfection seen as "decadent" in that coming at the end of Western tradition, it could concentrate the greatest ambiguity of meanings in single images and words. Another line of Symbolist poetry reached back to the French poet Charles Baudelaire (1821-67) and through his work to that of Michelangelo. In Baudelaire and Michelangelo,

---

"O NIGHT"

From dawn's widening anxiety
Trees like masts revealed.

Suffered awakenings.

Leaves, sister leaves,
I listen to your lament.

Autumns,
Dying sweetness.

O youth,
Just past is the hour of parting.

Upswept skies of youth,
Freely rushing.

And already I am desert.

Lost in this curving melancholy.

But night dispels distances.

Oceanic silences,
Celestial nests of illusion,

O night.

(Ungaretti, *Tutte le poesie*, p. 103; trans. L. Wittman)

Ungaretti saw the same "dramatic" confrontation "of heaven and hell," the same "precariousness," the same "horror of a world deprived of God," and (most emblematically in Michelangelo's sculpture the Milan *Pietà*, c. 1555-64) the same "horror" of "a body without a soul" (Ungaretti, *Saggi e Interventi*, p. 208; *Tutte le Poesie*, pp. 534-35; trans. L. Wittman). Rather than formal perfection and the mystery of the poetic word, such poetry emphasized a lacerating awareness of the immense abyss between man and God. Caught in a world of appearances understood as illusions, the poet can only hurl his cry against emptiness, turning from the shadows without yet seeing the night (let alone the dawn) ahead. It is in this last consideration that Ungaretti comes closest to

D'Annunzio but also proves most intent on bypassing him to invent a different tradition for modern Italian poetry. Most obviously, D'Annunzio's titanic pessimism gives way to a more existential mourning: like the leaves in "O Night," lost illusions still rustle in the distance, as the poet learns through irony to accept both their falseness and their beauty.

While little concrete detail is known about Ungaretti's piety, as he was a very private person, it is clear that his Catholicism was connected to the religious modernism that flourished before World War I. Open to the varieties of religious experience, its ideals were focused on compassion and the alleviation of suffering. Ungaretti situated the core of religious experience in the *noli me tangere* (the moment between the resurrection and the ascension, when Christ appears but cannot be touched). Invariably he emphasized not the Church as institution but the individual religious drama and the human solidarity it could foster. Moreover, Ungaretti's religious sentiment took inspiration from Plato in that it understood the world of existence as exile from the world of eternal forms. The philosophy of Bergson suggested that one might glimpse these forms through poetic intuitions, but also gave rise to the idea that eternal forms might be merely another illusion. The attempt to reconcile Plato and Bergson is yet another illustration of Ungaretti's intertwining of hope and despair, of horror at the abyss and ironic distancing.

Impact. Throughout the 1920s and 1930s, Ungaretti published extensively in journals in both France and Italy, acquiring a reputation as a leader in laying the foundation for a modern Italian poetry, one that would reinvent tradition. As the critic Alfredo Gargiulo wrote, "such purity . . . , which is undoubtedly the supreme aspiration of modern lyricism, can be found no where and in no one so much as in Ungaretti" (Gargiulo in Ungaretti, *Vita d'un uomo,* p. 7; trans. L. Wittman). By 1939-40, a number of major critics, from Gargiulo, to Carlo Bo, Gianfranco Contini, and Giuseppe De Rober-

tis, had acknowledged the complex existential dimension of Ungaretti's work. They also attributed to him, along with the poets Eugenio Montale and Umberto Saba, the invention of a new poetic movement, dubbed "hermeticism" because of its emphasis on formal beauty and penchant for oblique references to tradition. Though Ungaretti did not deny the "hermetic" quality of his work, he disassociated himself from the movement, insisting on the moral and metaphysical dimensions of his poetry. In retrospect it is clear that Ungaretti, as well as the younger Montale, demonstrated that formal perfection could embody a modern spiritual searching, paving the way for a new tradition of metaphysical or speculative poetry in Italy, one that dramatically puts the very edifice of metaphysics in question yet does not deny the power of religious longing.

—Laura Wittman

For More Information

Adamson, Walter L. *Avant-Garde Florence: From Modernism to Fascism.* Cambridge, Mass.: Harvard University Press, 1993.

Cambon, Glauco. *Giuseppe Ungaretti.* New York: Columbia University Press, 1967.

Cary, Joseph. *Three Modern Italian Poets: Saba, Ungaretti, Montale.* Chicago: University of Chicago Press, 1993.

Jones, Frederic J. *Giuseppe Ungaretti: Poet and Critic.* Edinburgh: Edinburgh University Press, 1977.

Leed, Eric J. *No Man's Land: Combat and Identity in World War I.* New York: Cambridge University Press, 1979.

Ungaretti, Giuseppe. *Correspondance Jean Paulhan / Giuseppe Ungaretti.* Paris: Gallimard, 1989.

———. *A Major Selection of the Poetry of Giuseppe Ungaretti.* Trans. Diego L. Bastianutti. Toronto: Exile Editions, 1997.

———. *Saggi e Interventi.* Milan: Mondadori, 1974.

———. *Selected Poems.* Trans. Andrew Frisardi. New York: Farrar, Straus and Giroux, 2002.

———. *Tutte le Poesie.* Milan: Mondadori, 1988.

———. *Vita d'un uomo: 106 poesie.* Milan: Mondadori, 1980.

Mirandolina, or
The Mistress of the Inn

by

Carlo Goldoni

An extraordinarily prolific playwright, Carlo Goldoni is considered the most significant Italian dramatist of the eighteenth century. The father of reform in Italy's comic theater, he was born in Venice on February 25, 1707, in his grandfather's mansion. Goldoni spent his childhood in a happy family circle governed by his mother while his father studied and practiced medicine in Rome. The boy later joined his father in Perugia, attending a Jesuit school before being sent to the School of the Dominican Father in Rimini to study philosophy and logic. Goldoni spent much of his time there reading Latin, Italian, and French plays. He went on to study law in Pavia, getting expelled but then finally earning his law degree at the University of Padua in 1731. He embarked on a legal career and began to pen tragicomedies and *commedia dell'arte* scenarios for Antonio Sacchi, one of the greatest comic actors of the day. Goldoni eventually quit the law and settled into a career as a playwright in Venice with his wife, Nicoletta. Almost single-handedly he would transform the improvised, stereotypical *commedia dell'arte* performances of his era into the scripted plays of the modern theater. He would also become the first modern, bourgeois intellectual no longer to depend upon a noble patron but rather, to earn his living entirely by writing. Enormously prolific, Goldoni wrote about 150 works, some in Italian, others in Venetian dialect and later in French. They range from comedies, to tragedies, tragicomedies, scenarios for *commedia dell'arte*, *intermezzi* for musical theater, *libretti* for *opera*

THE LITERARY WORK

A play in three acts set in Florence in the middle of the eighteenth century; first staged in Venice in 1753; published in Italian (as *La locandiera*) in 1753, in English in 1912.

SYNOPSIS

Admired and courted by the guests of her inn, the innkeeper Mirandolina charms a misogynist aristocrat, the Cavaliere of Ripafratta, who ends up falling in love with her but loses out to an unexpected rival.

buffa (comic opera), and musical farces. His finest plays were written in Venice in the first two phases of his career: at the Sant'Angelo Theater (1748-53), where he wrote *The Mistress of the Inn* (*La Locandiera*, 1753), and at the San Luca Theater (1753-62), where he composed such works as *The Boors* (*I rusteghi*, 1760), *The Superior Residence* (*La casa nova*, 1760), *Mr. Todero, the Grumper* (*Sior Todero Brontolon*, 1762), and *The Squabbles of Chioggia* (*Le baruffe chiozzotte*, 1762).

Annoyed by the competition among playwrights and by the controversy provoked by his reforms, Goldoni left Venice in 1762 for Paris, where he spent the remainder of his life. He continued working in theater, penning 24 *commedia dell'arte* scenarios, until he grew so disillusioned with the world of the theater that he became an Italian tutor for the royal princesses at Versailles.

Carlo Goldoni

In this late third phase of his career, Goldoni wrote in French, producing a few additional plays and his *Memoirs* (*Mémoires,* 1787), one of the most remarkable eighteenth-century autobiographies. In 1793, at the height of the French Revolution, Goldoni died poor and blind, his royal pension having been abolished by the revolutionaries. The very same day, unaware of his death, the National Convention (an assembly to decide France's future) reinstated his pension, voicing appreciation for the subtle, barbed criticism of the nobility that pervades many of his plays. One such play, *The Mistress of the Inn,* features the witty intrigues of a charming middle-class woman and relegates to the background, in ridiculous silhouette, men of a declining aristocracy.

Events in History at the Time of the Play

The splendid decline of the *Serenissima*. Though ostensibly set in Florence, *The Mistress of the Inn* depicts eighteenth-century Venetian society. Goldoni masked the true target of his irony and disguised the true setting of his work to avoid censorship by the city's aristocracy.

In the mid-eighteenth century, when the playwright wrote *The Mistress of the Inn,* the Republic of Venice could boast of a glorious history that spanned more than a thousand years. Elsewhere

in Europe, France and England were establishing themselves as superpowers, while the various Italian city-states lay fragmented largely under the rule of Spain and Austria. An exception, Venice continued to enjoy independence and a republican constitution, thanks to a shrewd decision to remain politically neutral in the European wars. But its golden age would soon dissolve entirely. As the center of trade between East and West, the *Serenissima* ("most serene"), as Venice was called, had reached its apogee as a maritime and imperial republic in the 1400s, thereafter suffering the slow, inexorable political and economic decline that afflicted it during Goldoni's day. In 1797, the city would lose its independence; betrayed by France's general Napoleon Bonaparte, it was ceded to the Austro-Hungarian Empire.

Though relegated to the margins of international trade and politics, eighteenth-century Venice occupied a pivotal place on the cultural and artistic horizon of Europe, equal to, if not surpassing, that of Paris and London. An obligatory stopover on the Grand Tour—the educational trip undertaken by young members of the European aristocracy—the city exuded a sophisticated, cosmopolitan atmosphere and foreigners flocked to the lagoon. In cafés such as the Florian in Piazza San Marco and salons such as those hosted by Isabella Teotochi Albrizzi and Giustina Renier Michiel (both famous locales for learned debate and polite conversation), Venice's elite discussed art, literature, and the new Enlightenment principles from France, such as reason and tolerance, equality and philosophical materialism. The Venetian publishing industry and book market were the most vibrant on the Italian peninsula. It was in Venice that all the literature coming from the rest of Europe was printed, translated, and distributed to various locations throughout Italy. Among the most important English novels that circulated in Venice were Jonathan Swift's *Gulliver's Travels,* Daniel Defoe's *Robinson Crusoe,* and Henry Fielding's *Tom Jones.*

No longer the dominant power in the politics of the Mediterranean, Venice turned to the cultivation of spectacle and pleasure, offering a life of unparalleled hedonism. There were sumptuous parades, public processions, and ceremonies, which transformed the city into something of an open theater. The annual Carnival before Lent brought galas, masquerades, and gambling into its streets and *palazzi* (buildings), fostering an atmosphere of gaiety and amusement. Theatrical and operatic productions flourished. Venice boasted five times as many theaters as Paris at the time. All social classes, including the working class, crowded the theaters during the three theatrical seasons of the year. Against this extraordinary urban background, the great libertines of the century staged their amorous intrigues in life and art. Among them were Mozart's librettist, Lorenzo da Ponte (1749-1830), author of the text for the opera *Don Giovanni*, and Giacomo Casanova (1725-98), author of **The Duel** (also in *WLAIT 7: Italian Literature and Its Times*) and a landmark autobiography. It was during this period that Venice experienced its grand moment in music, with such luminaries as Antonio Vivaldi (1678-1741), composer of *The Four Seasons* and more than 600 other concertos. The city also achieved heights in painting at the time. While Giambattista Tiepolo (1696-1770) painted his famous frescoed ceilings, Antonio Canaletto (1697-1768) and Francesco Guardi (1712-93) immortalized the lagoon in famous views that foreigners took home as souvenirs. At the same time, Pietro Longhi (1701-85), Goldoni's friend, painted interiors and intimate scenes of Venetian life with great realism. Like Goldoni's newly reformed dramas, Longhi's images provide glimpses into the daily rites, gestures, and habits not only of Italian nobles, but also of the bourgeois and working classes.

The reform of the theater. When Carlo Goldoni decided to commit himself to playwriting, the world of the stage in Venice (as in the other states of the Italian peninsula) was dominated by a very popular theatrical form known as the *commedia dell'arte*, in addition to the various genres of musical performances such as opera, *opera buffa* (comic opera), and *intermezzi* (brief entertainment provided between the acts of a play). By then, the *commedia dell'arte* had already grown stale and repetitive: often amounting to a vulgar farce, it was based on stereotyped comedy, obscene humor, and slapstick physicality. Inspired by the rationalism of the Enlightenment, Goldoni aimed to transform the obsolete *commedia dell'arte* theater, rejecting its obscenity and buffoonery, and injecting it with a greater sense of verisimilitude and naturalness. It was through the playwright's reforms, in fact, that principles of realism began to enter Italian literature and theater started to become a reflection of social reality. As he asserts in the preface to the first edition of his plays (*Commedie*, 1750), the "World" and "Theater"—contemporary reality and his experiential knowledge of theatrical production—are his only sources of inspiration.

Refashioning Italian drama, Goldoni forged innovations in the structure, content, and performance of a play. Most notably, the script was no longer improvised on the basis of generic rough drafts but written by the author in its entirety and memorized by the actors. Goldoni's *The Clever Woman* (*La donna di garbo,* 1743) was the first fully scripted comedy, making authorship more important than actorship. In Goldoni's comedies, language became truer to contemporary idiom, fresh and lively, with all its social and vernacular subtleties and nuances, rather than

---

SOCIETY IN EIGHTEENTH-CENTURY VENICE

An acute observer of his contemporary reality, Goldoni stages in his plays the complex social stratification of the Venice of the epoch, focusing on social boundaries and their permeability. In 1766, the city claimed a population of 137,000 inhabitants, who were divided into a rigid class system. The aristocracy, just one-fortieth of the population, was subdivided into *grandi* (the old nobility that governed the city), *quarantiotti* (minor nobility excluded from senatorial power), and *barnaboti* (impoverished nobility with no financial standing). Originally linked to commerce and imperial and mercantile expansion, the aristocracy had immobilized their capital in real estate investments and lived in idleness, largely causing the economic and political decline of the republic. The common class, known as the *popolo*, was subdivided into various economic strata: the most dynamic and prestigious sector, which threatened social stability, was that of the rich professionals and the merchant middle class (lawyers, doctors, factory owners, and individuals involved in manufacture, trade, and commerce). Further down the scale, the lower middle class included shopkeepers and innkeepers, while porters, servants, artisans, boatmen, lacemakers, silk-weavers, and laundresses comprised the *popolo minuto*. Finally there were the *marginali*, people perceived as marginal—the disabled, women without families, abandoned children, beggars—who were supported by charity.

---

stuffed with stereotyped jokes or obscene *lazzi* (jests), as in the *commedia dell'arte*. The stage and sets acquired new significance, shifting from the abstract, stylized backgrounds of traditional theater to fully historicized realistic scenery. Thus, for the first time *calli* and *campielli* (Venetian streets and squares) as well as the interiors of bourgeois, aristocratic, and even lower-class homes began to appear on the stage. Meanwhile, the performance was entrusted to entirely new figures; stock characters and masks symbolizing abstract virtues and vices (the custom in *commedia dell'arte*) were replaced by largely, though not completely, individualized characters. They were psychologically well developed yet representative of the different social classes that intermixed in

---

THE *COMMEDIA DELL'ARTE*

Performed by troupes of professional actors in cities across Europe, the *commedia dell'arte* or *commedia all'improvviso* flourished from the mid-sixteenth to the early eighteenth centuries. Originating in Renaissance Italy as a popular reaction to the *commedia erudita* (learned literary drama), the *commedia dell'arte* was a type of performance based purely on spectacle and diversion: a creative and exuberant mix of body language and acrobatics, improvised dialogue and verbal pungency, jokes and gags, pantomime and tricks, music and dances. Staged on a small platform, invariably representing a stylized street with a house front or marketplace, the performance was enacted by a gallery of stock characters often wearing masks and costumes: the old men (the greedy merchant Pantalone from Venice, the pedantic doctor from Bologna); the *zanni,* or male servants (the naïve Arlecchino, the cunning Brighella, both from the Bergamask countryside, and the Neapolitan Pulcinella); the charming and quick-witted *servetta,* or servant (Colombina or Franceschina); the young lovers; and the Captain (an unmasked character resembling a Spanish hidalgo, sometimes a hero, sometimes a villain). The production depended on a *canovaccio* (a skeletal outline of the plot); the rest was entrusted to the talents of the actors, who improvised standard situations and gags, basing their performances on a repertoire of *lazzi* (verbal and physical routines) and *tirate* (speeches and monologues). The most famous professional companies—the Gelosi (1571-1604), the Confidenti (1574-1639), the Uniti (1578-1640), and the Fedeli (1601-40)—traveled from the squares and courts of the Italian peninsula to Paris, Dresden, Lisbon, Warsaw, and St. Petersburg.

---

the republic's dynamic urban environments. In Goldoni, the city and theater became entwined and began to mirror each other. His theory of playwriting is literally enacted in the play *The*

Comic Theater (*Il teatro comico,* 1750), in which the actors themselves, preparing a play within the play, explain the rationale behind Goldoni's reforms.

The reform of drama proceeded at a gradual, cautious pace and for good reason. Goldoni's innovations met with success as well as disfavor: the actors did not want to memorize the texts; the public preferred to be entertained with the grossly comic, somewhat obscene gags of the *commedia dell'arte,* and theater managers feared losing their profits. Despite all these obstacles, Goldoni's innovations were indelible and enduring. His texts are counted among the ones that best exemplify the climate of the Enlightenment. Rationality, order, decorum, naturalness—the values privileged in Goldoni's plays—were the new philosophical and aesthetic tenets imposing themselves all over Europe, superseding the artifice, extravagance, and irrationality of the Baroque age. Goldoni's infusion of social critique into his works fits with Europe's burgeoning Enlightenment culture: his pen is ironic and cutting in its portrayal of the privileges and excesses of the aristocratic class; at the same time, it exalts and endorses the ethics and ideals of a newly ascendant social group, the merchants and bourgeoisie. *The Mistress of the Inn* is, in this regard, an exemplary text. However, in a later phase of his dramaturgy, Goldoni would expose the contradictions and flaws inherent in the middle class itself, ending his creative career in Venice with a dazzling portrayal of a working-class community of noisy fishermen and their squabbling wives.

Venetian women and the Enlightenment. While still a predominantly patriarchal society, eighteenth-century Venice offered women more freedom and independence than their predecessors as Enlightenment ideas spread throughout the city. In everyday life, women of the era were less likely to be subjected to cloistering than before, and, while arranged marriages remained common among the nobility, women of all social classes were increasingly able to dissolve their unhappy marriages. Venetian women also had a valid alternative to marriage or the convent: the option of lay spinsterhood. Some forms of sexual freedom and adultery—although not uncommon among the aristocracy even in earlier years—were tolerated with indulgence in the relatively uninhibited city. Venetian women also enjoyed an exceptional degree of economic power. Although noblewomen were subject to somewhat complicated laws, most daughters could inherit assets of all kinds from their fathers, as special emphasis was placed on wills, like the testament left by Mirandolina's father. Also, women's dowries remained their own property, and were restored to them if they were widowed, rather than being directly absorbed into their husbands' holdings. As a result, some Venetian women "were enabled—and obliged at the same time—to play a patriarchal role, dowering their daughters, sisters, and nieces, sometimes supporting their whole family, including their own husbands" (Ambrosini, p. 435). Literacy played an essential role in shaping a life of independence: an increasing number of women were taught to read and write, even among the lower social ranks, while in 1678 the noblewoman Elena Lucrezia Cornaro Piscopia became the first female to be granted a doctorate (at the University of Padova). Goldoni himself, in his 1743 play *The Clever Woman*, defended the right of women to be wise and highly educated against men who resisted this social development. Champions of the Enlightenment argued that educating women would serve society in good stead, a claim supported by living examples of Venetian women who worked as journalists (Elisabetta Caminer Turra, Gioseffa Cornoldi Caminer), as writers and critics (Luisa Bergalli, Isabella Teotochi Albrizzi, Giustina Renier Michiel, Elisabetta Mosconi Contarini), and as painters (Rosalba Carriera).

In keeping with these trends, female characters occupy a central place in Goldoni's theater and often embody the Enlightenment principle of rationality. Always spirited and vivacious, many of his female characters become the mediators of tensions between social classes and generations; often bearers of good sense and reason, they are seen as civilizing agents, a force that can temper the irrational impulses inherent in society and in men. The innkeeper Mirandolina, protagonist of *The Mistress of the Inn,* is one such protagonist; enigmatic in her own way, she evinces a sharp-tongued wit in the course of the play, and a sober intelligence in her final selection of a mate.

The Play in Focus

Plot summary. The play takes place at an inn in Florence (a stand-in for Venice), which Mirandolina, a charming young woman of intelligence and poise, has inherited from her father. Often the aristocratic patrons of the inn fall in love with her; at the play's end however, she chooses to marry the plebeian Fabrizio in keeping with her father's last wishes.

Act I begins with the rivalry between two guests, the Marquis of Forlimpopoli and the Count of Albafiorita, for the romantic conquest of the innkeeper. While the two aristocrats continue their ridiculous quarrel in the background, seeking unsuccessfully to seduce Mirandolina with gifts or with offers to protect her, a third character enters the inn, the Cavaliere (knight) of Ripafratta. A fierce misogynist, he derides his noble companions for their silly infatuation and treats Mirandolina with rude arrogance: "A female's upset you? A female's ruffled your feathers? A FEMALE! It's absurd! I'll never fall into that trap. Brrrr! Women! Never been in love with one. Never even liked one. You want my opinion? A woman's like a bad bout of flu: exhausting, and hard to shake off" (Goldoni, *Mirandolina*, p. 108). Irked by the gentleman's dismissive attitude and touched at the core of her feminine pride, the innkeeper—for her own amusement—decides to vindicate herself by making the Cavaliere fall in love with her. The act ends with a soliloquy that discloses her subtle plot: "I'm going to make that woman-hater love me if it's the last thing I do. I'm not giving up a pleasure like that easily. . . . Who can resist a woman, when she gets a chance to use her skills?" (*Mirandolina*, pp. 132-33).

In Act II, the innkeeper puts her artful strategy of conquest in motion. First with the excuse of offering him a gourmet tidbit, then with a precious wine from Burgundy, Mirandolina enters the Cavaliere's room. She finally wins his trust, managing to entice him with her charm and even agreeing with him when he slanders the female sex. Mirandolina meanwhile exposes two new guests—a pair of extravagant professional actresses masquerading as noblewomen—for who they truly are. They try to seduce the Cavaliere as well, but without success. Aware of his risky situation ("She's trying to destroy me. But she does it so beautifully, the little witch!" [*Mirandolina*, p. 147]), the Cavaliere decides to leave the inn, but he is hindered by the innkeeper, who first pretends to cry and then to collapse ("Women have all sort of methods for conquering men, but when in doubt—pass out" [*Mirandolina*, p. 157]). Mirandolina's fainting act seals the nobleman's defeat.

Act III opens with the innkeeper intent on ironing the linens. Now insensitive and pitiless, she stubbornly rejects the Cavaliere's offers of love ("Would you mind telling me why you're tormenting me like this? I love you" [*Mirandolina*, p. 167]), as well as the precious gift he offers her,

Painting of the Piazza San Marco in Venice, by Salomon Corrodi (1810–92).

a gold vial of lemon balm essence. Conquered and publicly humiliated, the Cavaliere loses his temper and begins raving. Mirandolina, realizing the risk of her own game ("I am starting to regret my little scheme. Oh, it was fun, getting him to chase after me like that—but things are out of control now" [*Mirandolina,* p. 177]), wisely decides to marry Fabrizio, a faithful and humble servant of her inn, thus fulfilling her father's wishes for her: "I've got a husband now: I shan't need admirers, or presents. I've always pleased myself, you see—sometimes at other people's expense. I've risked my reputation now and then. But not anymore" (*Mirandolina,* p. 187).

Staging social rivalry. The first exchange of retorts between the Marquis of Forlimpopoli and the Count of Albafiorita, which opens the text ("Marquesses before counts"; "This is an inn. My money's as good as yours"), is dense with symbolic significance (*Mirandolina,* p. 104). The exchange introduces the issue of differences between social classes in the eighteenth century. Not only a delightful inn where a woman-hater is defeated, the lodge is also, metaphorically, a microcosm of Venetian society: an open space in which various social groups intermingle, a stage where the rivalry between the aristocracy and the emerging merchant middle class is enacted. The characters of the Marquis and the Count embody two variants of Venetian aristocracy in the mid-

1700s, both subtly critiqued by Goldoni's barbed pen. On one hand, the Marquis represents the decline of the older nobility, which has lost its economic power and prestige; on the other hand, the Count exemplifies the more recently minted nobility, the aristocrats with more promising financial possibilities ("Economics is everything these days" [*Mirandolina,* p. 107]). While the Marquis believes that Mirandolina should submit to his courtly game because of an ancient privilege given to his class ("rank still counts for something"; "Blue blood. That's the only commodity of real value"), the Count plans to entrap her in dependence through his economic power ("We're both in love with Mirandolina. I'm trying to get her for cash. He's trying to get her on tick. Only he calls it nobility" [*Mirandolina,* pp. 105, 107]). In the competition between the two ethical and economic systems, the Marquis proves the loser: his money is scarce, his social prestige insignificant, and the presents he is able to offer Mirandolina are all too humble (a lace handkerchief, a light wine of poor quality) in comparison with the Count's ostentatious gifts (a gold necklace, diamond earrings). At the opposite end of the social scale is the humble servant Fabrizio, who wins Mirandolina in marriage: as a young peasant *inurbato* (migrant from the country to the city), he transgresses geographical and social boundaries. Through hard work and sacrifice, he achieves a marriage with a petit-bourgeois property owner, earning love (perhaps), upward social mobility, and economic power.

At the center of this dynamic microcosm stands the innkeeper, representative of an urban class of artisans and entrepreneurs. Beyond the splendid palaces of the nobility on the Grand Canal, mid-century Venice is full of shops, inns, and taverns where individuals like Mirandolina—artisans, hotel-keepers, dyers, glass-blowers, cobblers, gondoliers, vendors—produce wealth, commodities, and material goods. They also create a new morality, based on common sense, honesty, thrift, and hard work, in contrast to the arrogant world of the aristocracy, based on appearances and a lack of productivity. Mirandolina adheres to the new mercantile ethic, constant in her impeccably professional demeanor and her focus on the good of her business. The tools of her trade that surround her (sheets, table linens, food, wine, laundry) symbolize a productive bourgeois world, while her language (dominated by the verbs *fare,* to do; *sapere,* to know; *volere,* to want) demonstrates her willful entrepreneurial character. Her value system is based on pragmatism and prudence: ultimately she renounces the pleasures of the game of seduction and returns to her everyday duties, deciding wisely to marry the dependable Fabrizio, rather than yield to the noble Cavaliere. Her choice is both expedient and dutiful; as an obedient daughter, she fulfills her father's last wishes for her to marry the faithful servant. As a docile representative of an emerging social group, Mirandolina does not step over the confines of her proper position, which would threaten the stability of social hierarchies. As an honest woman herself, she instead marries a healthy, hard-working young man, making a match that contributes to the growth of her class and city. The ending—typical for Goldoni—moralizes and reassures.

It cannot escape the modern reader's attention, however, that under the tranquil surface of this play lies a subtly disquieting quality; by marrying the lowly waiter Fabrizio, Mirandolina continues to exert her social and economic power, as a wife and as mistress of the inn, maintaining for herself a margin of freedom ("Perhaps I should marry him! At least I'd be able to protect my interests—and keep my freedom" [*Mirandolina,* p. 177]). She in fact reverses the hierarchy of gender roles within the nuclear family, just as she earlier subverted social and sexual roles in her clever game of seduction, making three noblemen fall in love with her without surrendering herself to any one of them. Such an assertion of agency and sexual independence constitutes a remarkable achievement for an eighteenth-century fictional heroine.

Playing with gender. On closer inspection, the inn is a much more complex place than it seems to be. It is not just a mirror of Venetian society but also, metaphorically, a theater and a salon. It is the setting in which Mirandolina—mimicking the famous aristocratic *salonnières* (salon-holders) of her time—displays her wit and cunning as she engages her guests in a game of clever seduction. She is the rational individual of the age of Enlightenment and also, paradoxically, the actress, demonstrating a propensity for pretence, deception, and theatricality. In her careful game of seduction, she manipulates masculine and feminine gender roles, confusing the traits associated with them. At first, she feigns a feminine timidity and naiveté, entering the Cavaliere's room to bring him fine white linen from Flanders. Then, to win over the Cavaliere, she pretends to be different from other women ("Women. . . . But I shouldn't malign on my own sex"; "A toast: DOWN WITH WOMEN" [*Mirandolina,* p. 119, 139]). All feigning aside, she shows a tendency toward traditionally male attributes—freedom, independence, honesty ("Freedom is priceless" [*Mirandolina,* p. 119]). She even goes so far as to belittle emasculated men who stupidly fall in love with women ("Oh, come on sir—you are an intelligent man. Leave falling in love to fools like the count" [*Mirandolina,* p. 140]). The subtle stratagem succeeds and the Cavaliere believes Mirandolina's feigned sincerity: "Know what I like best? Her honesty. That's what I can't stand about women, you see—all that affectation. But in this case . . ." (*Mirandolina,* p. 136). Once the Cavaliere is reassured, she is ready to perform a game of exquisite femininity: she flatters him, she goes to his room to tempt him with delicate gourmet foods and rich wine from Burgundy. She cleverly transforms the everyday tools of her trade (sheets, wine, and food) into potent instruments of seduction, into aphrodisiac foods and magical love potions. Her performance of beguiling femininity is sealed with tears and fainting, a gesture of superb drama.

The final act presents all of the play's psychological elements and symbolic objects: Mirandolina, in the laundry room, intent on ironing, has renounced the pleasure of games and pretense. The servant Fabrizio, jealous, enters with the hot iron—a humble working tool and a symbol of the young peasant's sexual potency. The Cavaliere, raving by now, insists on (uselessly) giving a vial of lemon balm to a Mirandolina who grows colder and more disdainful by the minute. This precious object symbolizes the Cavaliere's defeat: he, like the other noblemen, wrongly expects to create a relationship of almost feudal dependence with the lady through a material object. But the gold flask of lemon balm, though precious, does not suit Mirandolina: traditionally used to revive a fainting lady, it is useless to her, an outmoded object that stands for a passive, frivolous notion of femininity. Thus, Mirandolina redefines herself apart from the cultural construction of gender. Finally, all the intrigue and Mirandolina's rejection of the passionate love that the Cavaliere offers her are a reflection of the tempered character that love acquired in Goldoni's day. She resists passion because she embodies the very spirit of the Enlightenment—an age in which love is only a gallant game, lacking any emotional depth or irrational complication.

Sources. One of Goldoni's most original creations, Mirandolina represents a highly sophisticated evolution of the *servitore* (servant). Departing from the comic and ridiculous representations of this character typically found in classical and Renaissance theater, the Venetian playwright invested the role with human dignity as well as the capacity for insight and social critique. The feminine version of the *servitore*, the *servetta* plays a pivotal role in Goldoni's theater, always shrewd and high-spirited, or steady and kind-hearted, often the agent of intrigue. If indeed, as Goldoni maintains, "the World" and "the Theater" are the two books upon which he fashioned his dramatic work, it is in these models that one should seek the inspiration for the protagonist of *La locandiera*. In many ways Mirandolina recalls one of the traditional characters of the *commedia dell'arte*, the artful servant or witty chambermaid (known as Corallina or Smeraldina). Goldoni's character also echoes the quick-witted servant-girl of Gian Battista Pergolesi's *opera buffa, Servant-girl as Mistress* (*La serva padrona*, 1733), in which the *servetta* succeeds in marrying her rich and foolish master. Goldoni's protagonist also has ties with a character seemingly very different from her: the libertine Don Giovanni. Originally created by the Spanish playwright Tirso de Molina in 1630, Don Giovanni became the protagonist of a renowned play by the French dramatist Molière (1622-73). The same character would become famous in theaters all over Europe at the end of the century, through Mozart's celebrated opera. Both Don Giovanni and Mirandolina, motivated by strong narcissistic tendencies, share the subtle art of seduction and a taste for the game of love, without becoming emotionally involved in its intricacies.

Beyond such theatrical exemplars, sources for the figure of Mirandolina can be found in a real historical woman. As Goldoni himself recounted, the character was patterned on the actress Maddalena Riffi Marliani of the Medebac Company who specialized in the role of the *servetta*: "Madame Marliani, who was lively, witty, and naturally artful, gave a new flight to my imagination, and encouraged me to labor in that species of comedy which requires a display of finesse and artifice" (Goldoni, *Memoirs,* p. 272). Goldoni revolutionized the structure of traditional theater for this actress, transforming the normally marginal role of the *servetta* into that of protagonist.

Finally Mirandolina is suggestive of the spirit and vivacity of groundbreaking Venetian women in the century of the Enlightenment. Like these women, she is a fascinating mixture of rationality, cleverness, grace, and allure.

Performance and reception. Staged during the Carnival of Venice in January 1753, *The Mistress of the Inn* was first published in Florence that same year. Goldoni himself paints a rosy picture of the play's reception in his *Memoirs:* "The success of this piece was so brilliant that it was not only placed on a level with, but even preferred to, everything which I had yet done" (*Memoirs,* p. 277). In reality, the production was abandoned after only four performances. Goldoni's assignment of the pivotal role to Marliani provoked "a storm of feminine rancor" behind the scenes, as well as the jealousy of the prima donna, Teodora Medebach (Chatfield-Taylor, p. 200). After its failure at the Italian Theater in Paris (under the title *Camille aubergiste,* 1764), the play was rediscovered only in the nineteenth century, when a company of Venetian actors performed it all over Europe. The triumphant revival of *The Mistress of the Inn* began with a Parisian production of 1830, starring the famous Italian actress Carolina Internari.

The name Carlo Goldoni appeared in the United States for the first time in an anthology of Italian drama, published in 1829 by Pietro Bachi for the students of Harvard University. In the place of *The Mistress of the Inn,* however, the editor published one of Goldoni's less significant works. He excused himself for this omission, fearing that Mirandolina's libertine and proto-feminist spirit would provoke a scandal in America's puritan atmosphere. The play was first produced in New York in 1896 (in Italian), starring one of the greatest Italian divas of all time, Eleonora Duse. The first translation, in 1912, was that of Merle Pierson for the Wisconsin Dramatic Society of Madison.

The play has been performed in a variety of ways and elicited a wide range of responses since its first production. Mirandolina is a famously ambiguous character, one who has been subject to divergent interpretations over several centuries. Attesting to this ambiguity are two seminal Italian stage productions of the mid-to-late twentieth century. The first, directed by Luchino Visconti, opened in 1952 at the International Theater Festival in Venice. In Marliani's original incarnation of her, Goldoni's heroine had been extraordinarily high-spirited. However, under Visconti's radically modern direction, Mirandolina was sober and spontaneous but showed no trace of her typical vivacity or coquetry. In 1972, by contrast, the director Mario Missiroli depicted Mirandolina as a petty lower-middle-class woman, selfish and greedy, oppressed by social and patriarchal conventions and so constrained to renounce true passion and marry the servant Fabrizio.

One of the most critically acclaimed of Goldoni's works, *The Mistress of the Inn* remains one of his best-loved and most commonly staged plays in Italy and abroad. The comedy is regularly performed across Europe and has been translated into more than 22 languages, including Chinese and Turkish. Mirandolina's famous ambiguity, alternately seductive and rational, is in no small part responsible for this popularity. A genuine *femme fatale*, the character continues to exercise her inescapable attraction, defying any stable or definitive interpretation.

—Flora Ghezzo

For More Information

Ambrosini, Federica. "Toward a Social History of Women in Venice: From the Renaissance to the Enlightenment." In *Venice Reconsidered: The History and Civilization of an Italian City-State, 1297-1797*. Ed. John Martin and Dennis Romano. Baltimore: The Johns Hopkins University Press, 2000.

Andrieux, Maurice. *Daily Life in Venice in the Time of Casanova*. Trans. Mary Fitton. New York: Praeger, 1969.

Chatfield-Taylor, H. C. *Goldoni: A Biography*. New York: Duffield, 1913.

Farrell, Joseph, ed. *Carlo Goldoni and Eighteenth-Century Theatre*. Lewiston, N.Y.: Edwin Mellen Press, 1997.

Fido, Franco. Introduction to *The Holiday Trilogy*, by Carlo Goldoni. Trans. Anthony Oldcorn. New York: Marsilio, 1992.

———. *Nuova guida a Goldoni: Teatro e società nel settecento*. Torino: Einaudi, 2000.

Goldoni, Carlo. *Memoirs of Carlo Goldoni Written by Himself*. Trans. John Black. New York: Alfred A. Knopf, 1926.

———. *Mirandolina*. In *The Venetian Twins*. Trans. Ranjit Bolt. Bristol: The Longdunn Press, 1993.

Günsberg, Maggie. "Artful Women: Morality and Materialism in Goldoni." In *Gender and the Italian Stage*. Cambridge: Cambridge University Press, 1997.

———. *Playing with Gender: The Comedies of Goldoni*. Leeds: Northern University Press, 2001.

Richards, Kenneth, and Laura Richards. *The Commedia dell'arte: A Documentary History*. Oxford: Basil Blackwell, 1990.

Steele, Eugene. *Carlo Goldoni. Life, Work and Times*. Ravenna: Longo Editore, 1981.

The Moon and the Bonfires

by

Cesare Pavese

Cesare Pavese was born in 1908 in the small village of Santo Stefano Belbo in the Langhe hills of lower Piedmont. He spent his childhood vacations there with the family at his parents' farm, the rest of the year with them in Turin. When Pavese was six, his father died from a brain tumor. The loss, along with his mother's coldness, contributed to his shyness around strangers and a preference for solitude. He developed a persistent sense of exile that found its counterpoint in the physical world when in 1935 the Fascist government exiled Pavese to Brancaleone, in Calabria, for ten months for anti-Fascist activities. Exile is a factor in his fiction; the protagonist of *The Moon and the Bonfires,* Eel, goes into self-imposed exile in America. Why does Pavese send Eel to the United States, a country he himself never visited? Pavese discovered an affinity for America and American literature at the University of Turin, where he wrote a thesis on Walt Whitman and acquired an impression of the country as a place of hard work, vitality, and progress, but also of alienation and isolation. His interest grew into a passion, as reflected in his career. For most of his adult life Pavese worked for the Turin publishing house Einaudi as an editor and translator, rendering American classics such as Herman Melville's *Moby Dick* into Italian and gaining a reputation as the pre-eminent Italian translator of American literature. He meanwhile produced a diverse body of writings in his brief life, from poetry (*Hard Labor* [1932], *Mania for Solitude* [1950]), to short stories (*The Beautiful Summer* [1940]), novels (*The Political Prisoner* [1938-9], *The House on the Hill* [1947-

THE LITERARY WORK

A novel set in Piedmont in northern Italy after the Second World War, with flashbacks to the prewar and war years; published in Italian (as *La luna e i falò*) in 1950, in English in 1952.

SYNOPSIS

After 20 years in the United States, Eel, a foundling, returns to the village of his childhood in the Langhe Hills on a journey of rediscovery.

8]), dialogues (*Dialogues with Leucò* [1947]), essays (*American Literature and Other Essays* [1930-1950]), and a diary (*The Business of Living*, published posthumously [1952]). *The Moon and the Bonfires* was his last novel. Four months after its release and successful reception, Pavese committed suicide by taking an overdose of sleeping pills. He had harbored suicidal tendencies since his youth, and an unhappy love affair with American film actress Constance Dowling was the final blow. A last literary gasp, this work features a man given to isolation searching for his roots in a familiar but transformed environment.

Events in History at the Time of the Novel

The Fascist period. *The Moon and the Bonfires* fictionalizes some of the experiences that took

Although Mussolini ruled as prime minister from 1922 to 1943, King Victor Emmanuel III remained head of state. Here, Fascists show their support of the royal family with a Fascist salute.

place in the Langhe hills during the Fascist regime and the partisan war of Resistance mounted against it. By this time, the regime had been in control of Italy for more than two decades. It came to power under Benito Mussolini in 1922, drawing support from veterans of the First World War and from the strong anti-socialist sentiment in the country. Slowly, Mussolini transformed Italy from a constitutional monarchy into a dictatorship (1925-29) with a nominal king. He did so through a mixed strategy of repression and the clever enlistment of his opponents in the regime and its concerns.

The Fascist government showed no mercy. Opposition leaders were eliminated by murder, imprisonment, or exile. Assassinations took the life of Socialist leader Giacomo Matteotti, as well as those of liberal anti-Fascists Giovanni Amendola and Piero Gobetti; imprisonment confined the communist Antonio Gramsci to lengthy incarceration (in his case, close to 11 years) and forced exile removed such leaders as Don Luigi Sturzo, founder of the Christian Democrat Party (see Gramsci's **Letters from Prison,** also in *WLAIT 7: Italian Literature and Its Times*).

Many of these anti-Fascist leaders lived in the city of Turin in Piedmont. The city became a center of communist and liberal opposition to the authoritarian regime. Even before the 1922 advent of

Fascism, Turin distinguished itself as a stronghold of working-class politics, the home of Antonio Gramsci, founder of the Italian Communist Party. Here Gramsci directed the political journal *L'ordine nuovo* (The New Order) and the Communist daily *L'Unità* (Unity), until he, too, was imprisoned. Turin was also a center of progressive liberalism: here, in the early 1920s, Piero Gobetti, a friend of Gramsci, organized a political movement around his own journals *La rivoluzione liberale* (The Liberal Revolution) and *Baretti* (a last name).

Though despotic and reactionary, the Fascist regime maintained a conciliatory approach to some degree, striving to obtain the consent of the masses. This approach was visible in its retirement, maternity, and childhood plans; its organization of leisure time and youth organizations; its teaching of fascist theorists in school; and its propagandistic use of radio, cinema, and the press. For a time, the approach met with some success and in 1934, in a referendum, 99.84 percent of Italian people expressed their trust in Mussolini's policy. Popular consent reached a climax in 1936 when the government proclaimed the establishment of an Italian empire, following an aggressive colonial policy in Africa. The Fascist government was supported by a large majority of the population; some prominent intellectuals—the scientist Guglielmo Marconi, for example—decided to set an example and to fight in the war in Africa for his country. Shortly thereafter, dissent against the regime spread, due largely to the growing subordination of Italy to Germany and the promulgation of racial laws against Italian Jews in 1938.

Italy during the Second World War. With Nazism coming to power in Germany in 1933, and Italy thoroughly under Fascist control, Mussolini turned his attention to foreign policy, launching a colonial campaign against Ethiopia. This policy won him global ill-will, isolating Italy from the international community, except for Germany. The two countries came together thereafter. By 1936 the stage was set for a "Pact of Steel," an alliance between Fascist Italy and Nazi Germany, which was quickly tested in the form of military assistance from the two dictators to the fascists who were fighting a civil war in Spain for control of that country (1936-39). Still, when the Second World War erupted in September 1939, Italy did not immediately enter the war. In June 1940, however, Mussolini's Italy finally entered the world war on the side of Nazi Germany.

The war swept everyone and everything into its fold. All the resources of the belligerent forces, human and material, were mobilized, involving average people in the fray in a myriad of ways. First, in Italy as elsewhere, women and the elderly went to work in factories and on farms to replace men who left to fight for Italy. This was the case at Fiat, the main Italian automobile factory in Turin. Second, both sides bombed important European cities, trying to cripple the industrial power of the adversaries, dealing blows to their economy and morale.

The night of June 12-13, 1940, Turin was bombed for the first time by British airplanes that struck many buildings near the center of the city, sending the community into shock. Sadly the shock would wear off; such bombings became habitual in 1942, as did the rationing of consumer goods. From the onset of the war until autumn 1942, the city suffered 14 bombings, always at night. Between November 1942 and August 1943, there were 12 terribly damaging raids. Residents finally evacuated the city; by July 1, 1943, 48 percent of the citizens had abandoned Turin, no doubt in some cases saving their lives by doing so. By war's end, more than 2,000 had died in Turin alone from the final bombings. Out of the ashes of this grim atmosphere arose Pavese's despondent novel.

Anti-Fascism and Resistance. Dissent spread in Italy following the disastrous results of wartime conflict. To express disagreement with the regime, workers staged repeated strikes in factories in the North, especially in Turin, Italy's main industrial center. The situation worsened when Anglo-American troops landed in Sicily on July 9 and 10, 1943, and started to conquer the peninsula. On July 25, the Grand Council of Fascism deposed Mussolini. The Italian king (Victor Emmanuel III) proceeded to arrest Mussolini and to make General Badoglio prime minister. During summer 1943, the new prime minister negotiated with the Allies to take Italy out of the war while the general populace and the army lived in limbo, uncertain of their destiny. Meanwhile, the Germans rescued Mussolini and put him at the head of Nazi-occupied northern Italy, allowing him and his Fascist followers to form the Republic of Salò there. The northern populace split between those who backed Mussolini (out of fear or genuine conviction), and those who resisted Mussolini, with arms or through other means.

The Resistance attracted diverse groups. In northern and central Italy, workers, peasants, students, intellectuals, and veterans of the dissolved Italian army joined the movement. They fought under the guidance of anti-Fascist parties, an umbrella term that included Catholics, liberals, and socialists but centered around the Communist Party, a well-organized group that benefited from years of underground experience. From an initial membership of 11,000 in winter 1943, the Resistance movement grew to 120,000-130,000 in 1944. By then, its followers had formed a real army, which took orders from the CLN (Comitato di Liberazione Nazionale—Committee of National Liberation).

Part of the population at large supported the Resistance, not only by supplying soldiers to fight the Nazi occupation army, but also in the countryside by furnishing hospitality and aid of all kinds to the partisans, or active members of the Resistance movement. While the various partisan groups shared the same goal—liberation of the national territory from the Fascist hold—they held a range of political views. The Badogliani (named after Pietro Badoglio) were planning a monarchic restoration after liberation, for example, while the socialist Matteotti (named after Giacomo Matteotti) and the communist "Garibaldi" brigades (named after Giuseppi Garibaldi) set out to achieve revolutionary social change. The Resistance involved two related but separate agendas: there were 1) fighting organizations bent on defeating the invaders and the Fascist government in northern Italy and 2) political movements concerned with laying the foundation and defining the nature of the future Italian state. This last task was mostly carried out by the intellectuals, many of whom endured hard times during the Fascist period.

The intellectual Resistance. Fascism drove many Italian intellectuals into voluntary exile. Others became fervent supporters of the Fascist regime because of a very clever ploy. The regime co-opted intellectuals to its side by leaving a great deal of room for them to participate in the game of defining exactly what Italian *Fascism* was. Players could take almost any position, from conservative, to middle-of-the-road, to revolutionary, as long as they thought of and called the position a *Fascist* one. So the intellectuals could think of themselves as Fascists, or, more exactly, as a Fascist elite, even if their politics differed greatly from other Fascists. In other words, the meaning of *fascist* was quite murky in Italy. Indeed little was black and white about Fascism there or the resistance to it (except for the black shirts worn by the para-military squads of the Fascist Party).

As in other dictatorships, the Fascist regime wiped out freedom of speech. Already in 1926 Mussolini created a "Special Court in Defense of the State" to prevent any intellectual or practical activity against the regime. Censorship spread, subjecting the press, theater, cinema, literature, and education to strict controls. In 1931, the regime forced university professors to take an oath swearing their allegiance to the Fascist Party and promising to indoctrinate their students accordingly. Most professors took the oath. But as the Fascists tightened their grip on every aspect of Italian life, intellectuals whose views conflicted with the regime's found it ever more difficult to write, teach, or otherwise work, so many emigrated. The writer Giuseppe Antonio Borghese and the physician Enrico Fermi moved to the United States. The Rosselli brothers (Nello and Carlo) left for Paris, where they organized a social-democratic struggle against Fascism, founding the group Justice and Freedom. Both brothers were assassinated.

Openly anti-Fascist intellectuals who remained in Italy were exiled to small villages far from the main cities, resigning themselves to a condition known as *al confino,* internal exile or confinement. Isolated, they were rendered harmless to the regime, or so went the thinking. Pavese suffered this fate, his exile in Calabria inspiring his novel *The Political Prisoner*, written between November 1938 and April 1939. Poets wrote introspective, ambiguous, and highly personal verse, seeking refuge in it from the intolerable aspects of surrounding society—the censorship

laws, repression, violence, and general lack of freedom. Examples of such poets are Eugenio Montale and Giuseppe Ungaretti (see Ungaretti's **Life of a Man,** also in *WLAIT 7: Italian Literature and Its Times*).

Not only was Turin the center of political opposition to Fascism, it was also the heart of the intellectual opposition. This status was due not only to the liberal and communistic leaders who had lived here (Gobetti and Gramsci), but also to the Einaudi Publishing House. Many of those associated with Einaudi were known anti-Fascists struggling for political and spiritual freedom. The police kept them under constant surveillance, and the publishing house itself fell afoul of the Fascist authorities. Early in 1934 Leone Ginzburg, a friend of Pavese and editor of the journal *La cultura* (The Culture), published by Einaudi, was arrested. Pavese applied for the vacant post and was appointed, in the hope that his non-partisan views might ease the pressure exerted on Einaudi by the Fascist administration.

Actually Pavese's position in the internal struggle against the Fascist regime is regarded as ambiguous. He was never directly involved in anti-Fascist political activities. Although he was brought to trial and consigned to internal exile in 1935, the reason was rather mundane. He was arrested because an anti-Fascist friend asked him to receive letters for her from a politically suspect correspondent, a Communist serving a jail term at the Regina Coeli prison in Rome. The police searched Pavese's house and found an incriminating letter. Pavese refused to reveal the name of the letter's recipient and was arrested.

Later, during the civil war, though some of his friends died in the struggle, Pavese did not fight. Instead he took refuge with his sister in Serralunga, a village near Monferrato, in Piedmont. Pavese spent most of his time here until the end of the war, giving private lessons in a convent school. Others judged his response as a failure to take anti-Fascist action at the crucial moment, and they resented him for this. He became a controversial figure in Italian literature and politics, as shown by debates on him in the press after his death (e.g., in an October 1953 issue of the Communist daily *L'Unità*).

Pavese is representative of those intellectuals who did not take direct political action but, after witnessing and meditating on the unfolding events, went on to take action in their own unique ways. So shocked was he by the suffering around him that he joined the Italian Communist Party after the war. Possibly the success

A group of Italian Resistance fighters after helping Allied troops find German snipers in Pistoia, Italy.

of the Resistance convinced him that activism could indeed change society and that writing could be an agent of such change. He may have come to feel that postwar Italy and Europe needed every possible effort, material and spiritual, to rebuild the badly ravaged areas. In the end, he took action of another sort, infusing events of the recent past in his novels.

The Novel in Focus

Plot summary. There is an interweaving of different time frames in *The Moon and the Bonfires*: present and past, events the main character witnesses and old memories. The narrator and main character, Eel, grew up in the Langhe Hills in Piedmont. After the Second World War, he returns from America to the village of his youth in a quest to reunite himself with his peasant roots and the landscape of his childhood. He is driven by an obscure desire to rediscover a sense of identity, to overcome a feeling of separation and estrangement both in himself and from the place that gave him his first consciousness of the world.

The narration unfolds in three parts. In the first part Eel revisits familiar places, hills, and farms, sometimes in the company of Nuto, his childhood friend. Narrator as well as main character, Eel recalls the time he spent working for a poor peasant couple at the Gaminellas' farm.

He was a foundling, a bastard taken in by the poor family out of a desperate desire for a government stipend. As his mind wanders into the past, Eel registers absences in the present: the loss of familiar landmarks; houses that have been burned down; hills leveled; rows of hazel cut; rye fields gone. He reaches the Gaminellas', where instead of his old employers, he finds Cinto Valino, a violent and rude peasant who lives with his son, mother, and sister-in-law. The individuals, then, have changed, but other elements of village life have remained constant.

> The slope from the field to the road was the same as ever. The same stain of copper sulfate around the trellis on the wall. The same rosemary bush at the corner of the house. And the smell, the smell of the house, of the bank, of rotten apples, of dry glass and rosemary.
> (Pavese, *The Moon and the Bonfires*, p. 24)

Focusing on Valino's poor undernourished son, Eel sees himself in younger years; the boy seems fated for a similar destiny, a life equally empty of meaningful attachments.

In the second part of the novel, details from the past surface in dialogues with Nuto. Eel spends this part on another farm, Mora, receiving no salary for his labor, only board. It is here that he meets Nuto, a farmhand like himself and his closest friend even in adulthood. Nuto is the clarinet player in the local band. He served as a partisan of sorts during the war, and has since become the village Marxist. He is full of resolve: "Nuto is Nuto, and knows better than I do what is right" (*The Moon and the Bonfires*, p. 21). Always rooted in one place, he never questions the basic tenets of his existence. He knows his own mind, observes Eel, crediting Nuto's activism to his immobility: "Something has also happened to the one who never moved, a destiny—that idea of his that things must be understood, made better, that the world is badly made and it's in everyone's interest to change it" (*The Moon and the Bonfires*, p. 36). Remaining in his birthplace, Nuto has assimilated the atavistic, or periodically recurring, nature of the place. The moon, he says, is something "you have to believe in whether you want it or not. Try to cut a pine during the full moon, the worms will eat it for you" (*The Moon and the Bonfires*, p. 44).

THE INTERPRETATION OF FIRE-FESTIVALS

Harking back to ancient times, the customs of kindling great bonfires, leaping over them, and driving cattle through or around them was nearly universal in Europe, as were processions or races with lit torches around fields, orchards, pastures, or even cattle stalls. Whether in the form of bonfires blazing at fixed points, or torches carried from place to place, or embers and ashes taken from a smoldering heap of fuel, the element of fire was thought to promote the growth of crops and the well-being of people or animals, either by promoting positive effects or by thwarting dangers from forces such as "thunder and lightning, conflagration, blight, mildew, vermin, sterility, disease, and not least of all witchcraft" (Frazer, p. 743).

Eel's memories carry him back to Sor Matteo. The well-to-do owner of the Mora, a rich farm, Sor Matteo had three beautiful daughters. The adolescent Eel idolized the girls, seeing them as the incarnation of an unattainable, disturbing femininity while he remained the ever-solitary adolescent.

For Eel, adolescence is a period of seclusion. Observing carts full of fairgoers on their way to summer gatherings, he would stay behind in his place at Mora, always "looking at the same vineyards and sky" (*The Moon and the Bonfires*, p. 91).

On evenings like that, a light, a bonfire seen on a distant hill, would make me cry out and roll on the ground because I was poor, because I was a boy, because I was nothing. I was almost happy when a thunderstorm, a real summer disaster, blew up and drenched their party. But now, just thinking about them, I was missing those times and wanting them back.

(*The Moon and the Bonfires*, p. 91)

Unfortunately Eel finds no succor in the past, and in the last part of the novel, its memories collide with a tragic present. At the present-day Gaminella farm, Valino burns and destroys the barn, murders his sister-in-law and mother, tries unsuccessfully to kill his son, sets the farm ablaze, and finally hangs himself. Happiness no longer even graces the Mora, where Eel idolized the beautiful sisters Silvia, Irene, and Santina. After a love affair with an older man, Silvia dies from an illegal abortion. Irene marries and takes off to lead a miserable life full of beatings by her husband. Santina, the youngest and most beautiful, becomes a prostitute of sorts, exchanging sex with Fascists for food and clothes. To survive and lead a decent life during the war, she aligns herself with the Fascists, but, feeling sympathy with the partisans, eventually joins them in the hills and fights courageously. Nevertheless she is suspect; the partisans decide Santina must be a spy. Doubting her sincerity, they shoot her and burn her body in a large bonfire. Nuto recalls: "Then we poured gasoline on her and lit it. By noon it was all ash. The mark was still there last year, like the bed of a bonfire" (*The Moon and the Bonfires*, p. 154).

An expatriate's homecoming. Eel uproots himself, travels, earns his fortune, and then returns to his small native patch of earth to reconnect with his past and find himself. He journeys overseas like the epic hero Ulysses (or Odysseus), who must gain "experience of the world and of the vices and the worth of men" before returning home to Ithaca (Dante Alighieri, p. 325). Eel also resembles another literary character, the cousin in a 1936 poem by Pavese, "The South Seas,"

My cousin talked this evening.
. . . You who live in Turin . . .
. . . When you live
a long way from home, make good, enjoy
   yourself
and then come back at forty, like me,
everything's new. The Langhe hills don't
   disappear.

(Pavese, *A Mania for Solitude*, p. 29)

At the start of the poem, the cousin leaves to spend 20 years wandering the globe, convinced that life at its fullest is to be found anywhere but home. Eel, likewise, leaves for America because he likes "to have one foot always on the gang-plank" (*The Moon and the Bonfires*, p. 6). Disenchanted, he returns. The United States bears little resemblance to the European myth of America as the "land of opportunity." He sees rootlessness, alienation, and restlessness in its inhabitants, dismissing the immigrants and native inhabitants alike as "all bastards" (*The Moon and the Bonfires*, p. 9). Eel relates only superficially to other people in America; nothing touches the deeper regions of his being. He is frightened by this different world:

> Even among themselves they didn't know each other. . . . A day would come when just to touch something, to make himself known, a man would strangle a woman, shoot her in her sleep, crack her head upon a monkey wrench.
>
> (*The Moon and the Bonfires*, p. 16)

Eel returns home to reconnect, hoping for relief. His hopes are grounded in notions of childhood popular in Pavese's day and earlier. Childhood is so important, as Pavese gleans from the eighteenth-century Italian philosopher Giovan Battista Vico (see **New Science,** also in *WLAIT 7: Italian Literature and Its Times*), because in a child's contact with the world, he or she creates images, myths, and symbols that form future meanings for things. Pavese adopts such ideas, working them into his fiction.

> From our earliest years, from our childhood, from all those moments of our first, essential contact with things and with the world which are liable to catch a man off guard with their immediate, emotional impact, from all the "first times," irreducible to rationality . . . there comes a giddy sensation, as if rising from a whirlpool or rushing in through a door thrown wide open—a promise of conscious awareness, an ecstatic presentiment.
>
> (Pavese in Thompson, p. 102)

After the "first, essential contact," images and places become unique, absolute, and mythical. In fact, events that happened there become singular, different from any others in the world, part of a non-temporal, non-spatial dimension, sanctuaries, legendary places of childhood. Returning to them is an attempt to search for those ecstatic instants, the original mythic moments of contact with the world to overcome alienation and solitude experienced in the city. This explains Eel's deep attachment to the places of his childhood.

However, Eel fails to reconnect. Pavese wrote in his diary about his own displacement on returning to his native land:

> Strange moment when (at twelve or thirteen) you left your country home, had your first glimpse of the world, and set out, buoyed up by fancies (adventures, cities, names, decisive rhythms, the unknown). You did not know you were starting a long journey that, through those cities, adventures, names, delights, and unknown worlds, would lead you to discover how rich in all the future was your moment of departure, the moment when, with more of the country in you than the world, you gave your backward glance. The world, the future now within you as your past, as experience, as skill in technique, and rich, everlasting mystery is found to be the childish you that, at the time, you made no effort to possess.
>
> (Pavese, *This Business of Living*, p. 247)

The answer for Eel, and Pavese, seems not to lie in reconnecting with the past: "I don't know," says Eel, "whether I will buy a bit of land . . . I don't think so; my days now are phone calls, shipments, city pavements" (*The Moon and the Bonfires*, p. 70). Though the country still has a strong effect on him, everything is the same yet changed. The bonfires still blaze, only now not to awaken the earth and assure rain and fertility but to reduce Santina to ashes and to burn down Valino's barn.

The implication is that, for Pavese at least, with the end of childhood came the dissolution of the mythic atmosphere of the past. In his poem "The South Seas" the cousin character claims "you don't lose the Langhe" (*A Mania for Solitude*, p. 29); he seems to succeed at reabsorbing himself in his native land. Eel, on the other hand, notes how the faces, voices, and hands that should have touched him, are no longer there. What remains is a village square the day after a fair, "a vineyard after the harvest" (*The Moon and the Bonfires*, p. 65). The two works suggest a sobering shift with respect to Pavese's emotional ties to home and an increasing sense of alienation that extends from the city to the village of his birth, expanding rather than contracting over time.

Sources and literary context. During the closing months of 1943 Pavese fled the massive bombings in Turin, returning, as noted, to the countryside of his childhood, hoping to recover "lost time." He thus draws on personal experience in depicting Eel's quest in the novel.

Pavese's debt to the Italian philosopher Giovan Battista Vico (1668-1744) has been described. In fact, Vico is but one of a host of thinkers that influenced the novelist. Around 1950 he edited a "Collection of Religious, Ethological, and Psychological Studies" for the Einaudi publishing house that encouraged him to find ritual meanings in the countryside. The novelist drew on this and other works by specific scholars of his day:

Hungarian classical scholar Károly Kerényi (1897–1973) Provided the idea of myth as a unique moment and of its repeatability (in works such as *The Role of Myth in Life* [1926]).

German essayist and novelist Thomas Mann (1875-1955) Informed Pavese's notions of the association between myth and poetry and of the return of events (in *Joseph and His Brothers* [1933-43]).

AMERICAN LITERATURE IN FASCIST ITALY

"Around 1930 . . . some young Italians discovered America in their books; a pensive and barbarian, happy and quarrelsome, fertile America, heavy with all the past of the world and at the same time young and innocent. For a few years these young people through their reading, translating, and writing were driven by a joy of discovery and of revolt that offended the official culture. . . . The [Fascist] regime tolerated this with a clenched jaw. . . . The flavor of scandal . . . that surrounded these new books and their subjects . . . [was] irresistible to a public whose sense had not yet been totally dulled by conformism. . . . One can frankly say that . . . the new mania helped fan and perpetuate the political opposition of the Italian "reading" public, even if it was vague and futile. For many, the meeting with [the renowned American writers] Caldwell, Steinbeck, Saroyan, even the old Lewis, provided a glimmer of freedom, the first suspicion that the culture of the entire world did not culminate in Fascism."

(Pavese, *La letteratura americana*, p. 173; trans. C. Villa)

Romanian historian Mircea Eliade (1907-86) Strengthened the notion of the idea of the return of events (in *The Myth of the Eternal Return* [1949]).

Austrian founder of psychoanalysis Sigmund Freud (1856-1939) Reinforced Pavese's idea of a deep connection between the myth and the psychology of the unconscious (in *Totem and Tabu* [1913]).

Swiss psychiatrist Carl Jung (1875-1961) Conceived of myth as being not about the world but about the mind, a symbolic production created by the "collective unconscious" (in *On the Psychology of the Unconscious* [1916]).

British anthropologist James Frazer (1854-1941) Provided information on the rites, beliefs, superstitions, and taboos of early and Christian cultures, and on fire festivals in Europe (in *The Golden Bough: A Study in Magic and Religion* [1922]).

Irish fiction writer James Joyce (1882-1941) Taught about spiritual renewal by plunging into the unconscious (in *A Portrait of an Artist as a Young Man* [1916], translated in 1934 by Pavese).

Pavese admired the realism of American writers such as Herman Melville (e.g., *Benito Cereno*) and Sherwood Anderson (*Dark Laughter*). He read and translated such works, impressed by the willingness of American writers to experiment with form and language to portray contemporary reality. Especially appealing to him was their focus on the alienation of the individual in a rapidly changing social environment. Influenced by them, Pavese set out to depict alienation in his own writings, setting himself in opposition to the Italian literary tradition, rich, as it was then, in surrealist, Futurist, and hermetic writings.

Events in History at the Time the Novel Was Written

Intellectuals and the postwar period. Pavese wrote *The Moon and the Bonfires* in 1950. At the time strong tensions coursed through Italy, along with strong hopes of participating in the country's reconstruction after its near disintegration after all the executions, deportations, hunger, racial persecution, and devastating bombings. The cultural debate was lively. On the one hand, intellectuals noted the demise of Italy's Fascist myths. On the other hand, they felt an urgent need to formulate a new culture, one that freed humanity from exploitation and misery.

In 1945, rising to the challenge, the novelist and editor Elio Vittorini founded the review *Il Politecnico* (The Polytechnic), which linked culture to social criticism, popular epic, and political commitment. This same goal was also adopted by the neorealist movement, an Italian literary and cinematic movement dedicated to portraying Italy's prewar poverty and postwar social problems. The neorealists focused on the victims of power, striving to depict their experiences with fidelity and perhaps even to influence reality. Among the neorealist novels were Elio Vittorini's *Men and Not Men* (1945), Vasco Pratolini's *Chronicle Of Poor Lovers* (1947), and Pavese's *The Moon and the Bonfires* (1950).

In literature as well as in politics, the close examination of the past focused in particular on the Resistance. After the war, conservatives, fueled by anti-Communist feelings, pointed to every killing that came to light as evidence that the Resistance was "a guerrilla war, illegality, bloodshed" (*The Moon and the Bonfires*, p. 55). At the other end of the spectrum, radicals tended to suppress evidence of unethical partisan behavior to preserve the myth of a united Resistance whose members operated in harmony against the evil Fascist invaders. Meanwhile, asserts Pavese's novel, "the man who really risked his neck [wouldn't] talk about it" (*The Moon and the Bonfires*, p. 56). Pavese mirrors the two extremes in his novel, which itself refuses to idealize the Resistance. *The Moon and the Bonfires* instead depicts the partisans as a complex group, one that has its own share of outsiders and draws members who join not for idealistic reasons, but to avoid conscription or city life: "You know how it was, a little of everything in the bands. People from all over Italy and abroad. Fools, too" (*The Moon and the Bonfires*, p. 57). Also the novel portrays the partisans as capable of unjust violence (the killing of Santina). Pavese thus writes a story that distances himself and the reader from the political extremes; also he sets the record straight.

Reception. When *The Moon and the Bonfires* was published, Pavese had just received the famous literary prize, Strega, for his trilogy *The Beautiful Summer* (*La bella estate*, 1949). His next novel was therefore received with great interest by Italy's critics and the reading public alike. Some well-known critics, such as Giuseppe De Robertis (in the review *Tempo*, June 1950), praised *The Moon and the Bonfires*, especially for its predominant theme of memory. For this reason, others compared Pavese to Marcel Proust. Not all the responses were positive. The Communists thought the novel ought to have a stronger connection to the ideals of the Party (since Pavese had joined it). In the newspaper *Il corriere della sera* (in the article "*Pavese decadente*," December 22, 1954), the famous Italian novelist Alberto Moravia found fault with Pavese's work. He charged Pavese with having been influenced by the German scholar Friedrich Nietzsche and his Italian disciple Gabriele D'Annunzio, who spoke of a mythic age

when man acted irrationally (see D'Annunzio's *Child of Pleasure,* also in *WLAIT 7: Italian Literature and Its Times*). Writers like Pavese, said Moravia, were using simple characters to analyze how such a man faced reality—and to poor effect. The practice resulted in lower-class characters expressing a cultivated writer's ideas in their own plain language. Pavese might have deflated this charge; he had rebuffed such critics before, pointing to the high value he placed on mirroring reality. But this time he committed suicide, and left the barbs dangling in postwar Italy—unanswered.

—Cristina Villa

For More Information

Alighieri, Dante. *Inferno.* Trans. John D. Sinclair. London: Oxford University Press, 1971.

Frazer, James George. *The Golden Bough. A Study in Magic and Religion.* New York: Macmillan, 1951.

Guj, Lisa. "The Migratory Journey of Eel: A Path to Hope in Post-War Italy." *Italian Quarterly* 27 (spring 1986): 37-44.

Lajolo, Davide. *An Absurd Vice: A Biography of Cesare Pavese.* Trans. Mario and Mark Pietralunga. New York: New Directions, 1983.

Merry, Bruce. "Artifice and Structure in *La luna e i falò.*" *Forum Italicum* 3 (September 1971): 351-52.

O'Healy, Aine. *Cesare Pavese.* Boston: Twayne, 1988.

Pavese, Cesare. *A Mania for Solitude. Selected Poems 1930-1950.* Trans. Margaret Crosland. London: Peter Owen, 1969.

———. *La letteratura americana e altri saggi.* Torino: Einaudi, 1951.

———. *The Moon and the Bonfires.* Trans. R. W. Flint. New York: New York Review Books, 2002.

———. *This Business of Living. Diary 1935-1950.* Trans. Alma E. Murch. London: Peter Owen, 1961.

Peitsch, Helmut, Charles Burdett, and Claire Gorrara, eds. *European Memories of the Second War.* New York: Berghahn, 1999.

Thompson, Doug. *Cesare Pavese, a Study of the Major Novels and Poems.* New York: Cambridge University Press, 1982.

Wilkinson, James D. *The Intellectual Resistance in Europe.* Cambridge, Mass.: Harvard University Press, 1981.

Moor Harlequin's 22 Misfortunes

by

Marco Martinelli

One of the most innovative contemporary Italian playwrights, Marco Martinelli is quickly changing the face of Italian theater. Born August 14, 1956, in Reggio Emilia, Martinelli has been involved in theater since 1977 as actor, director, and playwright. In 1983 Martinelli founded Teatro delle Albe, now known as Ravenna Teatro, along with his wife Ermanna Montanari, Luigi Dadina, and Marcella Nonni. Eight years later Martinelli became Artistic Director, a position he still holds today. He has written close to 20 plays, all produced and performed by Ravenna Teatro. One of twenty Italian theater companies the Italian government considers nationally important, the Ravenna Theater is an interethnic community-based theater committed to cross-cultural performance, a commitment best expressed in Martinelli's oft-quoted "manifesto": "Give me a theater that is tall and short, philosophy and laughs, tradition and the off-beat, feminine and masculine, white and black and yellow and red and even light blue" (Martinelli, "Prologo alle Albe"). Identified as "Afro-Romagnolo," the company is uniquely composed of artists from Romagna (the eastern half of the Italian region known as Emilia-Romagna) and Senegal (such as Mandiaye N'Diaye and Mor Awa Niang). Consistent with this makeup, Ravenna Teatro is particularly interested in the dialogue between the Senegalese and Romagnolo cultures. Martinelli locates his theatrical pieces in multicultural Italy, and specifically in an Italy that must confront the change in its society as a result of migration from countries Italy and other European countries once

---

THE LITERARY WORK

A play in three acts set in Milan in the late twentieth century; published in Italian (as *I ventidue infortuni di Mor Arlecchino*) in 1993, in English in 1997.

SYNOPSIS

The play updates an eighteenth-century scenario by Carlo Goldoni, transforming his familiar Harlequin character into an African immigrant who undergoes a series of mishaps while trying to return home to Senegal.

---

ruled as colonies. According to Martinelli, the new multicultural Italy is grounds for celebration, not resistance. Most of Martinelli's works take up this political and historical project. His repertoire includes early plays like *Ruh. Romagna più Africa uguale* (1988; Ruh: Romagna Plus Africa Equals); *Siamo asini o pedanti?* (1989; Are We Asses or Pedantics?); *Lunga vita all'albero* (1990; Long Live the Tree) as well as later ones like *Salmagundi* (2004). Martinelli is also well known for updating drama classics. His *All'inferno!* (1996; To Hell!) is based on Aristophanes' comedies; his *Sogno di una notte di mezza estate* (2002) reinterprets Shakespeare's *A Midsummer Night's Dream*. In this vein, *Moor Harlequin's 22 Misfortunes* mixes various forms of drama to explore migration, racism, and cross-cultural encounters in contemporary Italian society.

Events in History at the Time of the Play

Immigration and multiculturalism in late-twentieth-century Italy. While Italy has long been a country of emigration, in the last 25 years that status has quickly changed to one of immigration. In 1991, about when Martinelli's play was written, there were 700,000-800,000 immigrants in Italy. Twelve years later with 2.6 million immigrants currently living in the country, Italy is experiencing the fastest increase in migration in all of Europe (Ginsborg, p. 62; Caritas, p. 2). Why this sudden mass immigration to Italy? There are a few main reasons: delayed immigration from African nations, political developments in Eastern Europe and the former Soviet Union, and a dramatic improvement in the Italian economy. Whereas in the past hungry Italians had to leave their country to find enough work, now Italy attracts workers from abroad.

In the past few decades, immigrants to Italy have come increasingly from the "Global South"—that is, from Africa (Senegal, Eritrea, Somalia, Ethiopia, Morocco, Algeria, and Tunisia), Asia (Bangladesh, Pakistan, the Philippines), and parts of South America. There are also sizable numbers of immigrants from Eastern countries (Romania, Albania, Bosnia, Serbia, Poland, Russia, the Ukraine, and China). The overwhelming majority of immigrants in Italy in the past 20 years have come from non-European Union and non-North American countries (approximately 50 percent in 1991, and 85 percent in 2003). Many of these new immigrants came to Italy not directly from Africa but by way of Great Britain and France, countries that began turning away immigrants in the late 1980s. Others came from the recently dissolved Soviet Union and Yugoslavia. Immigrants from such areas form the new majority of newcomers to Italy. Both legally and informally, this new majority is commonly referred to as *extracomunitari*, or from "outside the European Common Market," a term that has taken on negative connotations. Since they have no right to live in Italy long-term without the coveted *permesso di soggiorno* (legal permission to stay), many are undocumented, or *clandestini* (clandestine). In 1991 it was estimated that Italy had roughly 400,000 undocumented immigrants, while that number is now estimated to have doubled (Ginsborg, p. 62).

Factors that "pushed" the immigrants to leave their native country are overcrowding and extreme poverty without hope of employment. Other reasons include war on home soil, as in Eritrea and Somalia. Of course, one of the largest reasons has been the dissolution of European colonies in Africa. When they were finally liberated, the locals, often Westernized during the colonial period, struggled to recover from decades of outside rule and exploitation. In such dire circumstances, migration to the country of a wealthier former colonizer (France, England, Italy), whose languages the Africans had at least some familiarity with, was an attractive option. In view of the fact that Britain and France have closed their borders, Italy receives not only from its own ex-colonies (Somalia, Eritrea, Libya, and Ethiopia), but from the ex-colonies of other European countries too.

In contemporary Italy, a climate of fear, and even panic, has taken hold of Italian society on account of all this sudden mass immigration; residents fear the loss of their jobs and the increase in crime in their neighborhoods. One example of this anxiety is a 1997 cartoon in *Il Giornale*, a conservative national Italian newspaper, showing "a white woman held tight by a big black man and facing another man with a fez, who was threatening her" (Riccio, p. 195). The next day *Il Manifesto*, another major paper, ran a similarly racist image of a black man raping a white woman. Yet, scholars protest that such anxiety on the part of the Italian public is not reflective of reality, but rather due to an image perpetuated by the Italian media and by the fact that the new immigrants from Africa and other parts of the Global South are immensely "visible" in a white, Catholic society. In 1992 immigrants were said to make up 15.4 percent of those held in police custody (Commissioni per le Politiche di Integrazione degli Immigrati). While certainly not small, this figure shows that immigrants are by no means responsible for the majority of the crimes in Italy.

Statistics show that these new immigrants are often themselves the victims of violence by Italian citizens. In 1997, a study by the University of Rome reported there were 374 total acts of violence against immigrants (one each day), 111 of which were fatal. One of the most sensational fatalities—prompting a moment of national reevaluation—was that of Jerry Essan Mazlo in 1991. A political refugee from South Africa and a temporary worker in the tomato fields in southern Italy, Mazlo was killed by local youths during a night raid on the immigrant camp where he was living. As one historian reports, his murder is typical of the anti-immigrant violence of the late 1980s and 1990s: "Immigrants' caravans were set alight in Florence, raids were organized on immigrant camps all round the country, countless beatings took place of foreign workers picked upon at random. Only the most serious cases reached the press, while a whole history of discrimination went by unchecked and unrecorded" (Ginsborg, p. 65).

Some say that the rise of xenophobia or "cultural anxiety" in Italy is due to the fact that immigration is occurring so rapidly while Italy is still not quite settled into a firm national identity. Unified only in 1861, Italy is a new country still very much divided by regional differences. This regional character is key to appreciating just how difficult it is for an immigrant from Senegal or Algeria to become part of a local Italian culture. Due to large differences in dialect and culture, it is already difficult for someone from one Italian region to be integrated in another region—how much more so then for an African to do the same? The emphasis on local culture in Italy in many ways privileges cultural "authenticity" and "purity." For example, many Italians pride themselves on being "one-hundred percent Venetian" or "pure Milanese." This sense of cultural, even local, purity is violently disrupted by the mass immigration. The result is a racism tied to the attachment to cultural purity, as shown, for example, by the policies of the ultra right political group Lega Nord. The party has adopted a racist stance not only with respect to non-European Union immigrants, but also to Italian southerners, defining itself as a completely separate culture, even a separate "race" (Foot, p. 221).

Still others argue that the current racism and cultural anxiety derives from the fact that Italy was simply unprepared for the arrival of peoples so different from themselves. Before this wave of immigration, Italy was "extraordinarily homogenous—in color of skin, religion, even increasingly in language" (Ginsborg, p. 64). Suddenly the nation must contend with racism in its midst as it attempts to deal with its new multicultural society.

The fate of Italy's new immigrants. How, in such an environment, has the immigrant from Africa or Pakistan or the Philippines fared? On one hand, some immigrants have managed to integrate themselves, become legalized, find work, and begin new lives in Italy. On the other hand, many endure isolation, powerlessness, marginalization, and exploitation. Generally *extracomunitari* immigrants live in almost total social segregation in Italy. Most reside on the outskirts of the city, and even those who work and are active in society, complain of the strict social barriers that exist between the *extracomunitaro* employee and the Italian employer.

Studies have shown that these new immigrants fare best—in terms of legal rights, job opportunities, and social acceptance—in the North in cities like Bologna and Milan. Such cities typically offer work in factories, whereas the South has consistently offered more casual piecework, such as picking tomatoes. A study of Senegalese immigration in Italy reports these immigrants' sense of being exploited because of their racial difference. "Blacks here," says one of these immigrants, "can only find work that breaks your back and mine is already broken, and other kinds of job like in service you are refused or underpaid" (Riccio, *Toubab,* p. 194). Other immigrants describe feeling forced to perform undocumented work or work they would never do at home (prostitution, street selling, or degrading manual labor). They likely live in immigrant camps, abandoned buildings, or overcrowded apartments. Adequate housing and food is a problem for many, as is the struggle to obtain legal status. While there were a few key years (1982; 1987-89; 1990-92) when the government granted undocumented immigrants permission to stay, obtaining the proper document (*permesso di soggiorno*) is still for many the major obstacle to finding work, or getting health care.

Solitude is another difficulty. Many of the immigrants, who are mostly men, come to Italy alone (in 1999, some 90 percent of Senegalese immigrants were men [Riccio in Grillo and Pratt, p. 180]). Leaving behind families, they plan to earn money, then return to their original homes. A number of immigrants manage to fulfill this dream, but most do not. Only 10 percent ever leave Italy, and many of them go not to their home country but elsewhere (Caritas, p. 3).

In Italy, though they may live alongside newcomers of similar background, the immigrants often complain of emotional hardships: intense nostalgia; racism due to their visibly different skin, hair, or clothing; the trauma of being anonymous or ignored members of society. The sense of invisibility and loneliness is perhaps best expressed by poet Gezim Hajdari from Albania: "I am a bell in a sea of silence and voices / a hermit closed in a Temple / no God hears my sounds / . . . When will this punishment end?" (Hajdari, p. 29).

The new "migration Literature" in Italy. The recent immigration explosion and multicultural composition of Italy has given birth to a new form of literature in Italian. Since 1990, immigrants to Italy from countries outside the United

States and Western Europe have been writing a growing number of literary works in Italian. Examples are the 1990 novels *Immigrato* (Immigrant) by Salah Methnani and *Io, venditore degli elefanti* (I Am an Elephant Salesman) by Pap Khouma. Another is the 1995 dramatic monologue *Ana de Jesús* by Cristiana Caldas Brito.

While some of the first works by immigrants were written with an Italian co-author for linguistic reasons, most authors now work alone and write directly in Italian. The early works tend to be autobiographical (even taking the form of diaries, like Khouma's work) and to focus mainly on major immigration issues like legal documentation, poverty, and housing problems. Fanning outward, more recent works have begun to experiment more with form, genre, and language and to venture into a wider range of themes. Also more women have joined the ranks of these new writers, reflecting the increase in female immigrants in Italy. Examples of these more recent works include Rosana Crispim da Costa's (Brazil) *Il mio corpo traduce molte lingue* (1998; My Body Translates Many Languages) and Gezim Hajdari's (Albania) *Antologia della pioggia* (2000; Anthology of the Rain). The question of how (or, for some, even if) all these works fit into the larger scheme of Italian literature is still hotly debated.

In the eyes of many, since these works are frequently written by the immigrant from an ex-Italian or ex-European colony and deal with race and nation, they fall into the tradition of postcolonial Italian literature. For example, Ribka Sibhatu's mulitgenre work *Aulò: Canto-poesia dall'Eritrea* (1993; Aulò: Song-Poetry from Eritrea) writes about her experience as an immigrant in the context of Eritrea's colonial history. Yet postcolonial literature is not reserved to the locals of ex-colonies, nor to authors of color. One well-known postcolonial novelist, Erminia Dell'Oro (*L'abbandono*, 1991; The Abandoning), although born and raised in Eritrea, is the granddaughter of an early Italian settler. In addition to authors from ex-colonies, the category widens to include postcolonial Italian authors born and living in Italy today, writers like Marco Martinelli, whose works explore issues derived from colonial history, such as racism and nationalism.

The Play in Focus

Plot summary. The first act takes place just outside Milan. It begins at Scapino's motel, introducing Lelio along with Angelica and Spinetta, his valet. All three are trying to get home to Mi-

lan, but have run out of money. Apparently Lelio was supposed to have gone to Venice to find his sister, Sapienza, whom he has never seen. She was sent at a young age by their father, Pantaloon, to live in Venice with her uncle, a wealthy widower. Now that the uncle has died, Sapienza has inherited his money, and Pantaloon has decided to bring her home to reap the economic rewards. But before reaching Venice to find his sister, Lelio becomes sidetracked; he meets and marries Angelica, a bar maid at Scapino's motel. Lelio must now face the problem of bringing home to his upper-class father the lower-class Angelica instead of his newly wealthy sister. He has a plan: he will pass off Angelica as Sapienza.

Meanwhile, in the background appears Moor Harlequin, an African immigrant on his way home to Senegal. He enters the motel after following the sound of music coming from inside. He finds an African musician, whom he greets in the Wolof language of Senegal, and begins to dance animatedly. He then is surprised to find that the hotel owner, Scapino, is a fellow Senegalese. He tells Scapino of his plans to return home to Senegal as Scapino takes in all five of his suitcases, loaded with presents for people there. Yet, when Harlequin tells him that he has no money, having spent it all on the gifts, Scapino, despite being his compatriot, throws him and his suitcases out of the motel. The truth is revealed later that Moor is really saving his money in order to impress those at home with the "fortune" he earned in Italy. Scapino's inhospitality marks the first of Moor's "22 misfortunes" on his way home (hence the play's title). In the course of the play, they will range from beatings and arrests to being set on fire (twice) and robbed. Angelica confesses to the valet Spinetta that she is nervous to meet her new father-in-law, Pantaloon. As she does so, Moor is mugged by a group of racist thieves who order him to "go back to Africa!" and proceed to steal all his suitcases (Martinelli, *Moor Harlequin's 22 Misfortunes*, p. 32). Lelio, taking pity on Moor, gives him his business card, promising that if Moor ever comes to Lelio's "big, red palazzo" in Milan, he will help him out (*Moor Harlequin's 22 Misfortunes,* p. 33). Scapino gets a hold of the card and makes plans to visit the Pantaloon family palace to collect the money Lelio owes him for his motel bill.

Act 2 finds Lelio and Angelica back in Pantaloon's decadent palace in the center of the city. With overwhelming enthusiasm, Pantaloon welcomes Angelica, whom he believes to be Sapienza, the daughter he has not seen for so long. The play takes a surprising turn when to Lelio's horror in a symbolic scene Pantaloon eats Angelica/Sapienza's hand. Moor arrives to the bloody scene and asks Lelio for money for the plane ride home to Senegal. Distraught after the tragedy, Lelio considers going with Moor back to Senegal. Yet, just in that moment the police arrive and arrest Moor, whom they take to be a thief in Pantaloon's home. We then learn that Pantaloon has promised Sapienza in marriage to Horatio, the son of a doctor, who promptly arrives with his father. At this point Angelica's true identity is revealed. Moor returns, having missed the plane after being detained by police. In the meantime, Lelio challenges Horatio to a duel for Angelica (a.k.a. Sapienza). As a last resort, Moor attempts to mug Horatio for money for the plane ticket, but is interrupted by Horatio's father, who violently flings Moor to the ground. Knocked unconscious, Moor misses his flight again. Moor gains consciousness and decides to hide in the fireplace from Horatio's father and Pantaloon. The act ends on a hilarious—if disturbing—note when Spinetta lights the fireplace and Moor comes out burnt and screaming.

Act 3 also takes place at the palace, but outside. It turns out that Pantaloon has decided to pay for Moor's ticket home in order to rid himself of his "troublesome" presence. Yet, after all this chaos and confusion, now Scapino also wants to go home to Senegal, despite his initial attachment to Italy. Finally, to everyone's surprise, the legitimate daughter, Sapienza, returns, and offers to marry the Doctor instead of Horatio. As she orders Moor to work at her wedding, his trip risks being canceled once again; he finally faints out of desperation as African drums beat in the background. The play ends just after the wedding takes place between Sapienza and the Doctor, and it is discovered to everyone's horror that once again Pantaloon has eaten his own kin—this time Sapienza!

The problems of *home* in postcolonial Italy. The struggle to define one's "home"—to comedic and even grotesque ends—is what binds the play's otherwise motley cast of characters. This struggle is at once responsible for the paranoia, anxiety, hysteria, confusion, misfortune, and even violence that dominate the meaningfully outrageous plot. Mainly, Moor Harlequin desperately attempts to return home to Senegal—despite the numerous misfortunes that he must undergo before doing so. The causes of his misfortunes are due not only to his own fixation on getting home whatever the obstacle, but even more to the setbacks presented by other characters.

These setbacks are intimately tied to the issues of migration, nationality, and racism in present-day Italy. As an immigrant from Senegal, Moor represents one of the many *extracomunitari*—immigrants from nations that are not part of the European Union—who have arrived in the last two decades. Yet, he is not from an ex-Italian colony, as one might expect, but from an ex-French colony. In the play he speaks French and Italian as well as Wolof, the language of Senegal. The question of where home is, if one judges by language, is clearly complex.

SUITCASES BULGING WITH MEANING

Moor packs some mammoth suitcases to carry back to Senegal. An extended metaphor of the absurd difficulty with which many immigrants must move between two homes, the suitcases symbolize the postcolonial migration experience. He aims to haul back just about all of Italy in his suitcases—"a camera, a VCR, a refrigerator, a washing machine, and a sewing machine" (*Moor Harlequin's 22 Misfortunes*, p. 28). The image of Moor and the stuffed suitcases evokes the stereotype of the *vu' cumprà*, a derogatory term for undocumented African immigrants in Italy, particularly Senegalese immigrants who earn a living as vendors of all types of products, from clothes, watches, and handbags, to tissues and lighters. The phrase *vu' cumprà* ("You want buy?") imitates the vendors' mix of broken Italian and French. The *vu' cumprà* often carry their wares in suitcases packed to the limit—hence Moor and his many suitcases. Mostly the vendors sell their wares in large cities and in the shore town Rimini, in Emilia Romagna, where the city of Ravenna (site of the Ravenna Teatro) is also located. The actor who first played Moor, Mor Awa Niang, worked as an undocumented vendor on the beaches of Rimini before joining Ravenna Teatro.

While Moor's homelessness points to his powerlessness, Pantaloon's grand palace, tellingly located near City Hall in "King's Court," suggests the "absolute power that he maintains over his family and servants" (Nasi in Martinelli, p. 95). Fiercely attached to his home (the actual structure as well as its symbolic value as an indication of his status), Pantaloon (as a kind of metaphor of the postcolonial Italian nation) makes desperate, even hysterical attempts to maintain social divisions. In one scene, disgusted to discover that "a moor" with a "burnt face" has been in his home, Pantaloon complains that if it were up to his son, "this house would be opened up to dogs and pigs" (*Moor Harlequin's 22 Misfortunes*, p. 47). It is suggested that the attitude is a pervasive one, characteristic of other classes too. In the play, Spinetta, Pantaloon's driver, remarks, "That black man is such a pain! But I would have to say that black people in general. . . ." Spinetta goes so far as to call Moor an "animal" (*Moor Harlequin's 22 Misfortunes*, pp. 25, 33). To Spinetta, the African immigrant is not just alien; he's subhuman. Even Moor himself makes racist assumptions. He is perplexed to discover that Scapino, a fellow African, owns the motel.

HARLEQUIN AND PANTALOON IN ITALIAN DRAMA

Harlequin and Pantaloon are two of many stock characters of the *commedia dell'arte* tradition, which enjoyed widespread popularity in Italy from the 1500s to the early 1700s. Acrobatic and dressed in a colorful mismatched costume, the traditional Harlequin of the *commedia dell'arte* is usually a jester, as well as a servant figure (sometimes a servant to Pantaloon) from Bergamo. While often clever and even knavish, Harlequin is usually the butt of his own and others' jokes. Moor's African-Italian costume and energetic dance scenes vividly recall the traditional Harlequin. Also, as in the *commedia dell'arte,* Martinelli's comedy takes place at Moor's expense. Pantaloon, on the other hand, is in traditional Italian comic theater an old, powerful, and wealthy shopkeeper or merchant. Business always comes before family for him. A figure of high status, he usually speaks with a pure Venetian accent. While Martinelli's Pantaloon is a lawyer from Milan, he echoes the power, wealth, and stress on local origins of the traditional Pantaloon.

Ironically it is Scapino who expresses most clearly the economic fears that go hand-in-hand with much of the racism in the play (and, by implication, in real life): "here among thieves, gypsies and immigrants, you just can't live anymore. Taxes go up and respectable people have to pay for everyone" (*Moor Harlequin's 22 Misfortunes*, p. 35). The action only underscores the economic fears. Some policemen arrest Moor, believing him to be a thief simply because he is an African in a white man's house. They operate on the strength of the general misconception that African immigrants are somehow "naturally" criminal, without consideration for the notion that someone may feel forced into desperate measures by dire economic straits. Moor finally does mug Horatio, and by doing so conforms to a role expected of the immigrant—that of criminal; he, however, has been forced into this role, suggests the play, by the injustices others have imposed on him.

One's home is related to one's identity in the play. A comical series of mistaken identities unfold as the plot progresses. Scapino is mistaken for a customer, not the owner of his hotel bar. Angelica is mistaken for Pantaloon's daughter. Ironically Pantaloon, who so strictly divides family from strangers, does not even recognize his own daughter. His devotion to home furthermore turns self-destructive, indicated quite literally in cannibalism. So bent is he on protecting it (and his social identity, which is tied to it) that he becomes "all-devouring," consuming even his own kin (*Moor Harlequin's 22 Misfortunes*, p. 39).

The inability to ascertain a person's identity counteracts the sense of belonging evoked by the idea of home. When Sapienza returns to meet her father, she presents legal proof of her identity. These legal documents point to the difficulties of ascertaining one's identity in the society of the play, as well as to the likelihood of Moor's own problems of legality as an *extracomunitario*. Lelio's identity is also unstable. At one point, he babbles in French, something he tends to do when he "gets confused" (*Moor Harlequin's 22 Misfortunes*, p. 32). Lelio grew up in France, so for him home is difficult to locate; periodically he even plays with his origins. In another case of mistaken identity, he at one point is identified as a leader of thieves, and he ponders the possibility: "Yes I could be he! . . . Why not? Another life . . . maybe born in another place . . . another father" (*Moor Harlequin's 22 Misfortunes*, p. 32). Later he jumps at the chance to leave Italy to go to Senegal with Moor. In both scenes he lightheartedly asks himself, "Why not?" Home, his reaction suggests, is not an absolute. It does not determine us; we determine it. In contrast, Moor Harlequin—much like Pantaloon—remains fiercely committed to one, absolute "home"; Moor tries at all costs to return to Senegal despite all the obstacles he faces. In sum, home, a source of anxiety in this play, is not the stable place many believe it to be. It is this anxiety that drives the comedy. Playfully it scrambles origins and evokes sheer mayhem regarding "home," a concept that is shown to be guarded to hysteri-

SEPARATED BY TWO CENTURIES, JOINED BY "MIGRATION"

Goldoni's Characters	Martinelli's Characters
Harlequin, drifter from Bergamo	Moor Harlequin, immigrant from Senegal
Pantaloon, wealthy father	Pantaloon, wealthy father and lawyer
Lelio, Pantaloon's son	Lelio, Pantaloon's son
Angélique, Venetian lady	Angelica, motel maid
Flaminia, Pantaloon's naïve daughter	Sapienza, Pantaloon's clever daughter
Scapin, the valet (servant)	Spinetta, a female valet (driver)
George, innkeeper	Scapino, Senegalese motel owner

cal proportions and often to destructive and violent ends.

Sources. The primary inspiration for Martinelli's work is Goldoni's eighteenth-century scenario *Les vingt deux infortunes de Arlequin* (1763; The 22 Misfortunes of Harlequin). Consisting of approximately 14 pages of rough notes about dialogue, setting, plot, and action, the scenario first existed in Italian in 1738 under the name *Le trentadue disgrazie di Arlecchino* (The Thirty-two Mishaps of Harlequin). The scenario tells the 22 tragic-comic travails of Harlequin, a wandering, poor foreigner from Bergamo on his way to Milan. His misfortunes are the result of some hilarious—if not disastrous—interactions with Pantaloon and his family. At an inn outside Milan, Harlequin meets Pantaloon's son, Lelio, on his way back from Venice, where he went to retrieve his sister. Instead he leaves her there and takes a new wife, Angelique. Back in Milan, he tries to pass her off as his sister and poor Harlequin attempts to get enough money to finally go home.

Martinelli describes his initial encounter with Goldoni's forgotten scenario: "When I ran into these seven or eight pages written by Goldoni I was struck by their contemporariness. As for the Harlequin, you just had to change the color of his skin and passport to transform him from eighteenth-century citizen of Bergamo [in Italy's Lombardy region] to an African at the end of the millennium" (Martinelli, *Moor Harlequin's 22 Misfortunes*, pp. 2-3). In an essay written with co-producer Michele Sambin of TamTeatromusica, Martinelli explains the similar economic situation of the two characters: "A hungry stranger like his predecessors; they [the Bergamesque harlequins] fled to Venice from the valleys of Bergamo searching for food and work. In rich Venice, the old Bergamesque servants toil as servants and porters. Today's Harlequins flee from the deserts of the South, and Venice is the rich Western world" (Martinelli and Sambin in Holm, p. 129). In Martinelli's piece, the eighteenth-century harlequin is transformed from a "foreigner" from Bergamo to a late-twentieth-century immigrant from another nation (Senegal), which is actually comparable, since in Goldoni's day, before the unification of Italy, the country was a patchwork of separate kingdoms and states that made Bergamo and Milan foreign to each other. Martinelli's piece reflects the transformation of Italy into a land where strong regionalism is sometimes overshadowed by a strong sense of nationalism that has been recently triggered by immigration. Goldoni's and Martinelli's characters are both wanderers, both laden with baggage, both miserably poor. The entrance of the main character in the earlier play resounds in the later one:

From Goldoni

Harlequin enters, dressed as a traveler and laden with baggage. He tells the audience that he's traveled the world round, serving one master, now another, but that it hasn't done him any good, since—despite his efforts—he was and still is so poor that his entire wealth consists of six *écus* [about 18 days' wages].

(Goldoni, p. 76)

From Martinelli

From the back of the stage, illuminated by the passing cars, enter[s] Moor Harlequin. Loaded down with suitcases. He is hitchhiking. No one stops.

(*Moor Harlequin's 22 Misfortunes*, p. 26)

The difference is that the travel is transnational, even transcontinental in the later play, and that Goldoni's social conflict—between "master" and "servant"—is reframed in Martinelli's day as a racial conflict.

The play retains some eighteenth-century elements, for example, Vivaldi's background tune "*Nisi Dominus*" and traditional costumes, including Venetian masks and capes. But it mixes these with modern-day African and Italian elements—jazz music and Senegalese percussion. Also the later play abandons Goldoni's happy ending (his Harlequin marries Pantaloon's maidservant as compensation for all his troubles). Martinelli's Moor Harlequin instead meets with a final misfortune.

Martinelli's work belongs to the tradition of postcolonial and/or intercultural theatrical pieces increasingly being produced all over Italy today. The theater companies that produce them include the Afro-Italian "Mascherenere" (Blackmasks) of Milan, "Palcoscenico d'Africa" (Africa's Stage) of Rome, and "La Cooperativa Teatro Laboratorio" (Theater Laboratory Cooperative) of Brescia. Martinelli and these theater groups are unique among postcolonial Italian authors in their use of comedy to draw attention to the tragic circumstances of migration. His sources of inspiration include the *commedia dell'arte,* the Italian improvisational drama popular from the 1500s through early 1700s. In fact, the *commedia dell'arte* was also the main source of Goldoni's scenario. In Martinelli's work are slapstick elements like "*lazzi* [physical jests and acrobatics], surprises, beatings with a stick" as well as the *comique de repetition,* or "comedy of repetition," as well as stock characters from the old tradition (Fido in Martinelli, p. 93). Using the same method as Goldoni, Martinelli—who believes in a "group theater" rather than one of single authors—wrote the play with specific actors in mind. Martinelli's play is also very much in the tradition of Italian political theater of the 1970s, though perhaps more physical than the political theater. It has been suggested that the work is indebted to that of Italian playwright Dario Fo, which sometimes mixes political satire with elements of the *commedia dell'arte,* the absurd, and surrealism. Martinelli's piece is almost certainly working in the tradition of the "theater of the absurd," shaped by playwrights such as Samuel Beckett, as demonstrated by the scenes of cannibalism in which Pantaloon eats first Angelica, then Sapienza. Martinelli himself has cited the general influence on his theater of another Italian writer, Pier Paolo Pasolini; comparing himself to Pasolini, Martinelli explains, "in my theater [too] the laughter is black" (Martinelli in Holm, p. 125).

Martinelli's play furthermore draws on postcolonial and postmodern notions in which home can be multiply located. It also belongs to the tradition in postcolonial drama of updating colonial issues in literary classics; another example is Aime Césaire's *A Tempest* (published in French in 1969; 1985 in English), a restaging of Shakespeare's *The Tempest.* Finally, the play moves outside Europe altogether as it incorporates elements of the Senegalese griot tradition of oral and migrant storytelling. Just as in griot, music and dance are central elements of Martinelli's play rather than minor accompaniments. Especially in keeping with the tradition is the use of Senegalese drums in the play. Also, Moor's story recalls the wandering nature of ancient *griots.* The actor who first played Moor, Mor Awa Niang, is in fact from a family of Senegalese griots.

Technically Martinelli is well-known for his emphasis on innovation, including experimentation with language. His theatrical pieces daringly mix Wolof with Italian and with the Romagnolo dialect, as well as with other languages. In fact, the term "play" does not quite capture his work given the way it fuses elements of traditional drama with music, dance, and methods such as non-verbal performance.

Performance and reception. The production of *Moor Harlequin's 22 Misfortunes* was a collaboration between Ravenna Teatro and TAM Teatromusica, an experimental theater founded in 1980 by Michele Sambin, Laurent Dupont, and Pierangela Allegro. Performed January 28, 1993, in Teatro Rasi, the home base of Ravenna Teatro, the original cast included two Senegalese actors (Mor Awa Niang as Mor Arlecchino and Mandiaye N'Diaye), two Italian/French actors (Luigi Dadina and Laurent Dupont), and two Italian actresses (Ermanna Montanari and Pierangela Allegro), in addition to Italian and Senegalese musicians.

Martinelli has received various awards for his work, including the prestigious Italian and European drama awards Premio Drammaturgia In/finita (1995; In/finita Playwriting Award); Premio Ubu (1996-97); Premio Hystrio for direction (1999), and the Golden Laurel at the International Theater Festival MESS in Sarajevo (2003). Declared "an adventurous voyage rich in surprises," *Moor Harlequin's 22 Misfortunes* was met at its debut with enthusiastic praise for its historical and political timeliness and artistic innovation (Libero, p. 12). In 1993 the piece was honored with the invitation to participate in the *Bicentario Goldiano,* the 200th anniversary of Goldoni's death. Critics agree that *Moor Harlequin's 22 Misfortunes* ranks as a major contribution to Italian theater. The play is considered a refreshing showcase of contemporary issues too often oversimplified or swept under the table in polite Italian society. Counted a success on multiple levels, the work has been heartily applauded as "a tale capable of capturing not only the heart but the mind" (Guermandi, p. 21).

—Rebecca Hopkins

For More Information

Caritas. *Immigrazione: Dossier Statistico 2004.* Rome: IDOS, 2004.

Commisione per le politiche di integrazione degli immigrati. "Secondo Reporto: Immigrazione e deviazione." Cestim Online, 2000. http://www.cestim.it.

Foot, John. "San Salvario, Turin: The Creation of a Dangerous Place 1990-99." In *Eldorado or Fortress? Migration in Southern Europe.* Ed. Russell King, Gabriella Lazaridis, and Charalambos Tsardanidis. New York: Palgrave Macmillan, 2000.

Ginsborg, Paul. *Italy and Its Discontents.* New York: Palgrave Macmillan, 2003.

Goldoni, Carlo. *Harlequin's 22 Misfortunes.* Trans. David Posner. *An African Harlequin In Milan: Marco Martinelli Performs Goldoni.* West Lafayette: Bordighera, 1997.

Guermandi, Andrea. "Il viaggio senza ritorno di Mor Arlecchino." *L'Unita,* February 3, 1993, 21.

Grillo, Ralph, and Jeff Pratt, eds. *The Politics of Recognizing Difference: Multiculturalism Italian Style.* Aldershot: Ashgate, 2002.

Hajdari, Gezim. "Sono una campana di mare." In *Memorie in valigia.* Ed. Alessandro Ramberti and Roberta Sangiorgi. Rome: Fara Editore, 1997.

Holm, Bent. "Harlequin's Black Laughter." In *An African Harlequin In Milan: Marco Martinelli Performs Goldoni.* West Lafayette, Ind.: Bordighera, 1997.

Libero, Luciana. "Arlecchino senegalese." *La Nazione,* January 12, 1994, 12.

Martinelli, Marco. *Moor Harlequin's 22 Misfortunes.* Trans. Wiley Feinstein. In *An African Harlequin in Milan: Marco Martinelli Performs Goldoni.* West Lafayette, Ind.: Bordighera, 1997.

———. "Prologo alle Albe" (Prologue to the Albe). Teatro delle Albe. 1994. http://www.Teatrodelle Albe.com.

Parati, Graziella, ed. *Mediterranean Crossroads: Migration Literature in Italy.* Madison: Fairleigh Dickinson University Press, 1999.

Riccio, Bruno. "Senegalese Transmigrants and the Construction of Immigration in Emilia-Romagna." PhD diss., University of Sussex, 2000.

———. "*Toubab* and *Vu Cumprà.* Italian Perceptions of Senegalese Transmigrants and the Senegalese Afro-Muslim Critique of Italian Society." In *The Politics of Recognizing Difference: Multiculturalism Italian Style.* Aldershot, Hampshire: Ashgate, 2002.

My Life

by

Benvenuto Cellini

A celebrated goldsmith, sculptor, and writer, Benvenuto Cellini (1500-71) memorialized his notorious life in one of the world's earliest surviving autobiographies. He was born November 3, 1500, in Florence to Giovanni Cellini and Elisabetta Granacci. His father, a musician and instrument maker, wanted his son to follow in his footsteps, and for years Cellini struggled between complying and heeding his own artistic ambitions. Finally at age 14, against his father's will, Cellini became apprenticed to a goldsmith. Within months he rivaled the most skilled goldsmiths in the field. Shortly thereafter, in 1516, Cellini experienced the first of many encounters with the law when he violently defended his brother in an attack. Thereafter, Cellini was three times accused of sodomy and twice penalized for the offense. He went to work in the studio of the well-known goldsmith, Ulivieri della Chiostra, in Pisa until Cellini killed a man and his legal troubles resurfaced. Convicted of the crime, Cellini fled to Rome to escape the death sentence. He remained there from 1519-40, working for Popes Clement VII and Paul II and for the cardinal in Ferrara, on medals, seals, coins, jewelry, chalices, and more. Cellini behaved brazenly in Rome too; here he was imprisoned on the false charge of stealing jewels from the papal coffers. He finally left to work in France (1540-45) at the court of King Francis I, where he won international fame for the pieces he produced, including a saltcellar adorned with an image of the Greek god Zeus. His tenure in France did not pass without incident; he became

THE LITERARY WORK

An autobiography set in Italy and France from 1500 to 1562; written from 1558-66; published in Italian (as *La Vita di Benvenuto Cellini*) in 1728, in English in 1771.

SYNOPSIS

Cellini recounts his adventures and artistic endeavors, as well as his relations with contemporaries. Endeavoring to reshape his image, he writes to explain his life's work as an artist and, in a violence- and sex-charged memoir, to justify his character and behaviors.

embroiled in sexual scrapes there and angered the king's mistress, Madame d'Étampes (Anne d'Heilly). Upon his return to Florence, Cellini began work for the Duke Cosimo de' Medici, producing the bronze statue *Perseus*, which took nearly a decade (1545-54) to complete and won renown as his masterpiece.

After his conviction for sodomy in 1557, Cellini's career as a sculptor faded and he concentrated on his writings—more than 100 sonnets, two art treatises (on goldsmithing and sculpture), his autobiography, which also took nearly a decade (1558-66) to complete, and more. Cellini ends his autobiography in 1562, the year he married Piera di Salvatore de' Parigi, a servant with whom he had five children (only three lived to adulthood). Having contracted syphilis earlier

Benvenuto Cellini (in foreground).

in life and in poor health during his final years, Cellini died at the age of 70, respected even by his enemies. He was buried as he himself directed, amid great fanfare in the Church of the Annunziata. The artist Giorgio Vasari (who hated and was duly hated by Cellini) wrote of him as a man of great spirit and veracity—bold, active, enterprising, formidable, as his autobiography indicates. Both his life story and efforts at self-promotion were in keeping with cultural practices of the day, particularly with respect to questions of honor. The ideal citizen of the Renaissance has been described as "knightly . . . still concerned with honour and reputation . . . [harboring] a highly developed concern with appearances; with matters of personal affront and vindication" (Anglo, p. 3). Passionate as a man and an artist, Cellini easily lives up to this definition.

Events in History at the Time of the Autobiography

Cellini and the concept of honor. Many literary works during the Renaissance defined contemporary standards of behavior. Francesco Guicciardini (*Ricordi,* 1512) explained how to be the perfect citizen, Baldassarre Castiglione (***The Book of the Courtier,*** 1528) how to be the perfect courtier, Niccolò Machiavelli (***The Prince,*** 1529) how to be the perfect prince, and Della Casa (*Galateo,* 1558) how to behave in general (both also in *WLAIT 7: Italian Literature and Its Times*). Cellini's autobiography attempts to explain one man's life and work as measured against contemporary standards. The autobiography has itself become a source from which later scholars glean some of those standards and is used as such in the discussion below.

In his lifetime, Cellini was accused of sodomy, murder, theft, counterfeiting, and slander. His autobiography, written while he was under house arrest for sodomy, provided a way for him to reestablish his honor and, from his point of view, set the record straight. The concept of honor and Cellini's defense of it is a recurring theme in the autobiography. Verbal assault—failing to address someone on the street properly, attacking a friend or relative, or insulting one's city—were considered as damaging as physical assaults. Duels and physical retribution served as ways to quickly resolve conflict and reestablish one's honor, as illustrated by an incident from the autobiography:

> A careless, swaggering young man . . . mockingly said many offensive things about the Florentine nation. . . . Quietly and without anybody seeing me, I came up to this fellow. . . . Confronting him, I asked if he was that impertinent man who was speaking ill of the Florentines. He immediately replied: 'I am that man.' Upon these words, I raised my hand and gave him a slap in the face, saying: 'And I am this man!'
>
> (Cellini, *My Life*, p. 40)

Some affronts were considered so grievous that they were regarded as criminal acts in sixteenth-century Florence, and in these cases violence was permissible in defense of honor. Cellini recalls how he vengefully murdered his brother's killer; the officers who came to arrest Cellini backed down when they heard why he committed the crime.

In the case of an artist, another way to exact retribution was to decline a commission. After Cellini gained a reputation, he was offered a job in England but did not go, in part because the man who invited him, Piero Torrigiani, attacked Michelangelo, the artist Cellini revered above all. Torrigiani described breaking Michelangelo's nose to Cellini, raising his ire: "These words generated so much hatred in me . . . that not only did I not have any desire to go to England . . . but I could not even bear to look at [Torrigiani]" (*My Life*, p. 21). Instead, Cellini went to Rome, where he quickly won fame and was ultimately named head of the papal mint. Here, as in Florence, his honor was again threatened, this time not by an insult but by an assault on the city in which he lived. On May 6, 1527, Rome was attacked and sacked by troops under the Holy Roman Emperor Charles V, ruler of large tracts of Europe. Charles fought many wars against King Francis I of France. In Rome, Pope Clement VII, in league with some of the other Italian states, declared himself in favor of France. Charles, considering this a hostile act, struck Rome; unexpectedly, on the night of May 5, 1527, his general, the Duke of Bourbon, arrived with an army 40,000 strong. The following morning a brutal assault took place. Clement's poorly armed troops had to retreat to Castel Sant'Angelo, a castle outside the Vatican. While the defenders stayed in the castle, Rome was looted and 40,000 were killed. Cellini, who fought in defense of Castel Sant'Angelo, claims to have defended it single-handedly, professing to have killed the Duke of Bourbon as he scaled the castle walls, for the sake not only of his land and leader, but also for his manhood.

More subtly, Cellini struggled with the honor given an artist by a patron. In Paris, King Francis I accorded Cellini high respect by giving him financial rewards and the utmost liberty to determine the particulars of a sculpture or other piece of commissioned artwork. By contrast, when Cellini returned to Italy he landed one of two salaried positions for artists given out by Cosimo de' Medici, the ruling Duke of Florence. Ultimately, Cellini lamented this return many times, feeling that Cosimo did not treat him with the respect he deserved. Both patrons gave him homes. But Cosimo did not pay Cellini as generously as Francis I had. Nor, Cellini thought, did his new patron give him enough leeway to make artistic decisions or show enough trust in the works he produced. Cellini attributes this behavior to Cosimo's ignorance about matters of art. Nevertheless, it was Cosimo who sponsored his *Perseus*, a sculpture that took nine years to produce and received much acclaim by fellow artists, who wrote sonnets to celebrate it and left them at the foot of the statue.

Male-male and male-female relations. Cellini's account of his numerous amorous relationships give us insight into prevailing attitudes during his day. While it is difficult to determine if his relationships are typical of the times or more typical of a man whose character is consistently self-indulgent, a number of texts indicate that at least some of his behaviors conform to social norms of the day. Other texts, however, suggest that

Cellini's attitudes are remnants of medieval concepts about women and that their status had in fact risen much higher by the late Renaissance. Noblemen and progressive thinkers began to educate their daughters, and a few women became notable poets (for example, Gaspara Stampa and Veronica Franco, both covered in *WLAIT 7: Italian Literature and Its Times*).

One perception that still held sway in Cellini's day was a highly negative image of women as materialistic and vain, jabbering and prattling, or downright evil. According to this view, women were not individuals but appendages; they existed to gratify the sexual, artistic, or social ambitions of a man. Such a mindset encouraged the rape of women in Cellini's era, as in earlier and later times.

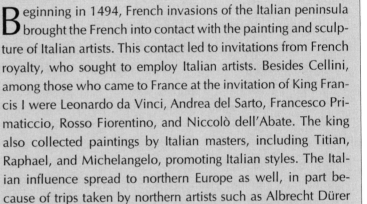

FROM THE ITALIAN TO THE EUROPEAN RENAISSANCE

Beginning in 1494, French invasions of the Italian peninsula brought the French into contact with the painting and sculpture of Italian artists. This contact led to invitations from French royalty, who sought to employ Italian artists. Besides Cellini, among those who came to France at the invitation of King Francis I were Leonardo da Vinci, Andrea del Sarto, Francesco Primaticcio, Rosso Fiorentino, and Niccolò dell'Abate. The king also collected paintings by Italian masters, including Titian, Raphael, and Michelangelo, promoting Italian styles. The Italian influence spread to northern Europe as well, in part because of trips taken by northern artists such as Albrecht Dürer and Pieter Brueghel (Pieter the Elder) to the Italian peninsula. The artists of the Italian peninsula found themselves in demand at courts as far-flung as those of the Ottoman Empire.

Cellini's sexual encounters include both females and males, especially young boys. In his day, sodomy was considered an unnatural sexual act but was commonly practiced nonetheless, and Cellini wrote openly about it. For a man to engage in sodomy with young men was something of a rite of passage. But a man who made a habit of it was frowned upon, especially when he did so with young boys.

The aggressor was always seen as the "man" in the relationship (Cellini's role). The passive recipient was sometimes considered a "woman," even a "wife." It was not unheard of for a man married to a woman to have affairs with young men and be considered a sodomite because of these affairs. Others, such as Michelangelo and Leonardo Da Vinci, showed exclusive homosexual love for men and even wrote poems for their lovers. Neither married, although both had platonic relationships with women.

Though it was often overlooked, sodomy carried some legal penalties. Standard punishment included mild fines or exile. In 1542, Cosimo de'

MEDICI RULE

The Medici family came to power in Florence at the end of the fourteenth century and their domination, though not continual, ended with the death of Cosimo III's grandson Gian Gastone in 1737. The family earned its fortune through banking, business, and marriages to influential families (one such match was the wedding in 1533 between 14-year-old Catherine de' Medici and Henry of Orleans, a son to the French king Francis I). Cosimo il Vecchio (*the old*) was the first Cosimo and is considered the founder of the family. He spent much of his wealth on charity, literature, and the arts, providing patronage to such luminaries as Brunelleschi, Donatello, and Alberti. Cosimo il Vecchio also promoted a resurgence of Greek and Latin classics, supporting their translations into the vernacular. He furthermore commissioned biographies of Dante, Petrarch, and Boccaccio. All this promoted a sense of Florentine identity, which strengthened the Medici family's popularity.

After the French invasion of Florence in 1494, the Medicis lost power until it was restored some years later by the Spanish. When the Spanish defeated the French, the Medicis were invited back to Florence and began to rule under Cosimo I. This is the Cosimo who controlled the city during Cellini's life and became his patron. Cosimo quickly proved an effective economic and military leader, as well as a strong promoter of arts and letters. He is remembered as a calm, efficient ruler who raised the status of his family. Cellini comments in the autobiography about Cosimo's lack of aesthetic and artistic knowledge. Interestingly, Cellini sculpted a bronze bust of Cosimo so realistic that it included a wart on his left cheek. Preferring the more perfect bust by Baccio Bandinelli, Cosimo sent off Cellini's to Elba Island and retained Bandinelli's for Florence.

Medici tightened the existing sodomy laws so that sodomy was regarded as a violent crime, one punishable by imprisonment and exile. Cellini's arrest for sodomy therefore led to a four-year

prison sentence, which he began to serve. After pleas to Cosimo, the duke finally agreed to let Cellini serve his sentence under house arrest. It was then, as noted, that Cellini began to write his autobiography and so justify his life. The image of "Cellini the sodomite under house arrest" was not the one he wanted to convey; it was antithetical to the manly, fearless, adventurous artist he claimed to be.

Apart from male sexual relations, male friendship and loyalty were highly valued in late Renaissance Italy. Cellini recounts his friendships as bonds of mutual admiration in which either party would go to any length to help his fellow, whether by forfeiting a coveted woman to him or defending him verbally or physically. As recounted in the *Vita*, his life story, Cellini forfeited his desire in one case for a Bolognese prostitute and in another for a pretty young woman out of loyalty to friends.

From apprentice to master. In Cellini's era, Italy had two training systems. One was the intellectual-based system in Latin at the university; the other, the manual-based system in vernacular Tuscan in artists' workshops. Artistic training involved five years as an apprentice and two years as a journeyman, or qualified worker for a master artist. Once an artist became a master himself, he generally got his own workshop, or *bottega,* which included a small group of men who produced a wide variety of objects in collaboration. While there were obvious differences in the two types of training—schooling and university-based Latin learning as opposed to apprenticeship and Italian-based learning—apprentices had to be literate to keep records, measure amounts, and draft bills. They also had to be learned enough to feature Latin subjects in their artwork. In any case, literacy was high in Renaissance Florence (about a third of its inhabitants could read and write in the fifteenth century [Gallucci, p. 10]), even though there was no proof of formal training for Florentine artists until the opening of an art academy (the Accademia del Disegno) in Florence in 1561. Painters and sculptors were still denigrated because of mid-sixteenth-century prejudices against manual labor, work that involved retail trade, and against artists themselves, who were often poor and lacked learning compared to intellectuals. To combat these prejudices, artists engaged in a great deal of self-promotion—to good effect. Their status began to rise in the Renaissance, thanks in no small part to their self-assertion through memoirs, about 100 of which have survived from Florence alone (Burke, p. 195). Artists became less like carpenters, more like intellectuals, and their writing of memoirs and treatises only enhanced this.

Compensation to the artists varied. Sometimes they received payment upon completion, sometimes in installments while a work was in progress. Assignments were parceled out by a patron, who might be a prince, guild, fraternity, committee, or merchant. Sometimes the patron commissioned a single work; sometimes he took an artist into his service on a more or less permanent basis, as Francis I and Cosimo I did with Cellini. Cosimo I had only two salaried artists at the Medici court in 1550, the other being Agnolo Bronzino. The duke gave Cellini a house, and the artist used its interior garden as his workshop. Despite his "permanent" employment by the duke, formal competitions for commissions sometimes occurred, and at the end of Cellini's career he lost out on a number of these.

The Autobiography in Focus

Contents overview. Cellini's autobiography is divided into three parts, an introduction and two books. The introduction begins with a sonnet and continues with a short paragraph in which Cellini explains that he chose to dictate rather than write the autobiography to save time. He nevertheless imitates language, style, and stories of great writers in an attempt to be classified as one himself. Book One covers Cellini the man, from 1500 to 1562, including details of his childhood, his personal and artistic relationships, and his work in Rome, in Paris, and again in Florence. Book Two focuses more on Cellini the artist, most notably giving a detailed account of his work on the Perseus. Overall the book is a brazen account of his life and artwork, in which he describes assaults and murders he commits without remorse or apology.

Book One. Cellini acknowledges his humble birth as a Florentine and admits to being well aware of the elevated status of those who write autobiographies. Elevating his status at the start, he lends luster to his birth by linking it to the illustriousness of Florence and of its founding by Julius Caesar. In explaining his family origins, Cellini confers glory onto a family ancestor, through whom he links himself to the great Caesar.

Cellini's description of his birth and infancy sets the stage for an explanation of why he figures among those destined to chronicle their lives. He compares himself to the legendary Hercules,

noting that, in the cradle, baby Hercules was already so strong he could strangle serpents. In Cellini's case, at age three the baby takes a poisonous scorpion in hand, showing a fearlessness that becomes a recurring trait in the life story.

When Cellini reaches the age of 13, his father insists that he dedicate himself to music, but Cellini has other ideas. Defying his father's will, he begins work as an apprentice for a Florentine goldsmith. Cellini ventures from Florence to Siena, Pisa, and Bologna to learn the craft, then back to Florence to study the art of Michelangelo. During this period, the cultural Renaissance begins to spread to other countries, whose courts vie for Italian artists. Cellini at this point rejects an opportunity to work at the court of Henry VIII in England.

Instead Cellini moves to Rome, where he spends two years in the employ of various masters. Professionally, Cellini experiences extraordinary artistic success in Rome. He fashions silver for cardinals, alters the setting of jewels for ladies, binds prayer books, even ornaments swords. Cellini recounts how, regardless of what he works on, he does so with absolute conscientiousness, manipulating each piece with a fresh mind. Cellini's success attracts the envy of other goldsmiths, leading to the first of his Roman quarrels. According to the autobiography, Gherardo Guasconti, a cousin of a goldsmith who had wronged Cellini, shoves a load of bricks at Cellini and laughs, which so enrages him that he knocks Guasconti out. The felled man's relatives turn on Cellini, who, knife in hand, threatens to kill at least one of them. At this point Guasconti takes the matter to court, whereupon Cellini marches into the man's home and stabs him, doing little harm, intending only to intimidate him.

Cellini shows a sense of entitlement that emerges from his description of such incidents. He presents himself as outside the realm of the average, corroborating this self-concept with the opinions of the pope and the king of France: "You should know that men like Benvenuto, unique in their profession, need not be subject to the law: especially not Benvenuto," observes Pope Paul III to a friend (*My Life*, p. 125). The thinking is that men like Cellini are so unique in their creative capacity they ought not be subject to common rules.

Still in Rome, Cellini fights duels, has love affairs, defends his shop against robbers, becomes enmeshed in stabbings, and survives deathly fevers. The uninhibited artist yields to every impulse, pursues every pleasure, laying claim to an

King Francis I of France visits the studio of Benvenuto Cellini in Rome.

animal compulsion towards beauty. He speaks of love affairs with men and women. In general, his recounting mirrors a corrupt yet resplendent side of life in Renaissance Italy, depicting it as a land in which violence and the pursuit of honor are pervasive.

Cellini travels to France on occasion. In 1538, back in Rome, he describes being falsely accused of theft by a servant and arrested by Pope Paul III for stealing gold and jewels. He is imprisoned, despite the lack of incriminating evidence and his pleas of innocence, in the Castel Sant'Angelo. Cellini details his confinement and his failed attempt to escape. On his knees, he prays, refusing to turn around when a captain and some 20 guards arrive, his brazen sense of defiance intact: "To this God who bears me up, the One who rules the heavens, I've turned my soul, my contemplation, and all my vital spirits; and to you I've turned exactly what belongs to you" (*My Life,* p. 205).

Book Two. The cardinal of Ferrara prevails upon the pope to free Cellini. Thereafter, the artist completes work on a fine chalice for the cardinal, then leaves Rome for France, where he spends five years (1540-45) in the service of King Francis I.

Cellini executes great works of art in France but encounters difficulties because of his ignorance of French habits, his pride, friction with the King's mistress, and his ungovernable temper. The details of two lawsuits provide a graphic picture of French courts of justice. Here again, Cellini recalls taking the law into his own hands. He claims to have extricated himself from a dangerous trial by screaming, then beating and kicking people and threatening attorneys with his sword. In another case, he is accused of sodomy with his own mistress, Caterina, but is not convicted.

Cellini finally returns to Florence, a decision he regrets, since King Francis was generous with him and, as Cellini saw it, was the only patron to ever treat him with the esteem he deserves. He recalls Francis's words, using them to add to the image of himself he tries through the life story to convey:

> "Since . . . this man . . . is . . . slow to ask, I want him to be provided for without saying another word about it: for men such as these, who are not used to asking for anything, are certain that their works ought to ask a great deal on their behalf; take care, therefore, to provide him with the first abbey that becomes vacant with revenues worth up to two thousand scudi."
> (*My Life,* p. 279)

Back in Florence, Cellini creates art for the duke in control of the city, Cosimo de' Medici. The artist portrays his patron as a cautious, small-minded, meddling Florentine, who loves to bargain, play tricks, and pretend to protect the arts without understanding his role as patron. Always short of money, Cosimo is surrounded by avaricious servants. He also has little faith in his own judgment as a connoisseur of art and so falls prey to the schemes of inferior artists.

It is during this period that Cellini sculpts *Perseus*, a statue of a legendary Greek hero. In Book Two there are long, detailed descriptions about this work and the many trials involved with its execution. Upon completing *Perseus*, Cellini congratulates himself. No man on earth, he raves, could have achieved as much, though he concedes that Michelangelo could have sculpted such a statue when he was younger. Cellini's *Perseus*, exposed to public view in the great square, meets with universal acclaim, as is reported in the autobiography. An invitation to work in Sicily follows, but Cellini refuses to quit the duke's service. Problems ensue, however, when Cosimo fails to value *Perseus* as Cellini does. Cellini enlists the help of a friend to entreat Cosimo to pay a fair amount, and the duke sends a rival sculptor, Baccio Bandinello, to examine and value the *Perseus* statue, planning to pay exactly what Bandinello says it is worth. This only leads to more trouble, until the duchess steps in to resolve the problem.

Cellini continues to work until he falls ill and is replaced at Cosimo's court by the artist Bartolommeo Ammanato. Thankfully Cellini recovers, but sadness follows. The Cardinal de' Medici dies, which fills Cellini with grief. At this point, the artist sets out for Pisa, and abruptly the autobiography ends.

Fortune during the Renaissance. Two millennia before the Renaissance, the Greek scholar Aristotle connected fortune to "external goods"—noble birth, wealth, power, friends, fine children, personal appearance, good luck and bad luck. He also tied fortune to chance, conceiving of the former as the power that distributes external goods among human beings in ways that affect their happiness. His explanations would enjoy renewed popularity during the Italian Renaissance. For two centuries, its writers produced texts wholly or partly devoted to a discussion of the role of fortune in man's life.

1354 *Remedies for Both Kinds of Fortune* by Francesco Petrarch (*De remediis utriusque fortunae*)

1396 *On Fate and Fortune* by Coluccio Salutati (*De Fato et fortuna*)

1448 *On the Vicissitudes of Fortune* by Poggio Bracciolini (*De Varietate fortunae*)

1529 *The Prince* by Niccolò Machiavelli (*Il Principe*)

Fortune surfaces repeatedly in Cellini's autobiography, and to some degree his attitude to fortune echoes Machiavelli in **The Prince** (also in *WLAIT 7: Italian Literature and Its Times*). Machiavelli believes that man can exercise his power to achieve at least a degree of control over fortune. As people shifted from a medieval preoccupation with God's role in man's fate, to a view concerned more with the power of man—his intellect, talent, and strength—fortune stopped being held responsible for all that happened. Human effort gained new importance. In keeping with this emphasis, Cellini suggests that a man's will can impact his fortune, at least to a degree. He believes himself to be persecuted by bad fortune in all he undertakes. Yet he struggles against it. Arriving in Venice one day, the sculptor decides to "fence" with her (fortune was traditionally conceived of as a woman, sometimes blindfolded to indicate her own ignorance with respect to why she distributes "external goods" as she does): "On . . . pondering upon the divers ways my cruel fortune took to torment me, yet at the same time feeling myself none the less sound in health and hearty, I made up my mind to fence with her according to my wont" (Cellini, *The Autobiography of Benvenuto Cellini*, p. 340).

Born under the sign of Scorpio, Cellini believed that his body was dominated by a devil that provoked him to behave as he did. He gave much credence to this explanation, blaming the stars and never taking responsibility for his actions. Others in the society of his day, from wise men to the unschooled, might easily have reacted the same way. The court astrologer was a familiar figure among Renaissance nobles and even around religious scholars. One real-life astrologer of Cellini's day, Luca Gaurico, had a particularly distinguished career, making a number of predictions that came true, forecasting in 1493, for example, that Giovanni de' Medici would become pope within 20 years (he indeed became pope as Leo X in 1513). Gaurico wrote a famous work, published in the vernacular in 1539 and after 1540 published and republished in Latin (*Tractatus astrologiae*). The work was a collection of aphorisms backed up by six books of horoscopes: 1) of towns and cities; 2) of popes and cardinals; 3) of kings and princes; 4) of great artists and scientists, including Michelangelo, whose fate, like that of others, is said to have been shaped by the stars; 5) of those who died violently; and 6) of monsters and the deformed. An appendix after each book "showed" how the predictions came true. As astrology spread, the practice of it fell under frequent attack. Treatises that railed against astrology in the sixteenth century gave rise to many defenses of the "art." So pundits of the day argued about how useful or damaging or misguided it was. Thus, while Cellini may have been self-serving when he blamed the stars for his behavior and fashioned an image of himself as an honorable man, he was indeed in tune with his times.

Sources and literary context. Virtue in the Renaissance meant the capacity to do important things. Cellini himself explains that he wrote his autobiography because any virtuous man ought to do so after a certain age: "All men of any condition who have done something of special worth . . . should . . . write in their own hands the story of their lives, but they should not begin . . . until they have passed the age of forty" (*My Life,* p. 5).

During the sixteenth and seventeenth centuries, a sense of progress and individualism inspired self-representation and the representation of others. Families, artists, individuals began to chronicle their lives by writing life histories. Among artists, many of the life stories were written by others. A notable set of collected biographies by Giorgio Vasari, *Lives of the Artists,* appeared in 1550, followed by a second, much expanded edition in 1568. Today the work remains one of the most important sources of information on the major artists of the age. Cellini was distinct in writing his own life story.

Much discussion has centered on the accuracy of information in Cellini's *Life.* Whether he seems a braggart, or even a liar, his accounts resound with sincerity. Studies have shown that he does not invent the facts and that his historical data is for the most part accurate. There are some inaccuracies, such as the reference to Julius Caesar when Cellini speaks of his heritage. He mentions a high-ranking captain of Caesar, Fiorino of Cellino, alleging that this captain played an essential role in the formation of Florence. Scholars dismiss this as false information and there are undoubtedly other inaccuracies, especially in excerpts entailing self-praise on Cellini's part. A number of inaccuracies may have crept in because Cellini dictated rather than wrote the manuscript. He employed two scribes, depending mostly on a 13-year-old boy with excellent handwriting. The writing style is thus a consequence of the fact that Cellini was speaking when its content was set down.

Cellini set out to be counted among the greatest of writers as well as greatest of artists. He thus employs language used in the vernacular literary tradition and in many instances imitates the language and writing styles of Dante, Petrarch, and Boccaccio. Most importantly, Cellini is devoted to describing truth as he sees it, fearlessly and without worrying about the consequences. His criticisms of his patron Cosimo de' Medici as ignorant in artistic matters is in keeping with his personality.

Publication and reception. To this day, it is not clear if Cellini ever corrected his manuscript. He is known to have asked Benedetto Varchi to correct it, but Varchi declined, thinking it better to leave it in its original form. In any case, 156 years passed before the work was published; Cellini intended but failed to have it published in his own lifetime. The first edition appeared in 1728. Some recent scholarship finds that "the lack of signs of true dictation in this manuscript, such as backtracking, restatements, or jumbled chronology, suggest that a text first dictated was subjected to later editing; perhaps this is a clean copy prepared for the printer and the actual first draft (or drafts) of the *Vita* was lost or destroyed" (Gallucci, p. 13).

Cellini's *Vita* has always had a varied readership, appealing to doctors, musicians, artists, historians, even scholars of crime. Two commentaries led the way for reviewers: that of Giuseppe Baretti in *La frusta letteraria* (*The Literary Whip,* 1763-65) and that of the great Romantic poet Johann Wolfgang von Goethe in his preface to the German translation of the autobiography. Baretti influenced those scholars who wanted to study the work from a textual point of view (its literary qualities, its language), in the belief that the language represented spoken Florentine. Goethe's interpretation, which focused heavily on Cellini's humor, was the basis for many scholars who proceeded to study the sculptor's character.

Like Goethe, Baretti considered the autobiography a unique document of Italian life in the 1500s. Baretti, however, criticized Cellini's manner of writing, calling it the product of one who speaks before he thinks. This view foreshadowed that of the early 1800s Romantics, who saw Cellini as a man governed entirely by instinct. In their eyes, he was the exemplary immoderate Italian who wavered between genius and insanity, a precursor to the hero of their own age. The concept of genius and immoderateness was taken up later in the 1800s by, among others, the Italian criminologist Cesare Lombroso, who considered a genius to be someone who was sick, who was to some degree pathological.

The modern critic tended to associate Cellini the writer with Cellini the artist. There was, according to this view, an excess in style in both media that gave way to mannerist art (a reaction against proportion rules of the classical style, favored in the high Renaissance, mannerism featured figures that were disproportionate and longer than usual). Today some critics see Cellini as a mannerist writer who was fully conscious of the style he employed. Some attribute his anarchy to a joyful spontaneity; others, to a lack of dexterity on his part.

One of the most all-encompassing descriptions of Cellini as a man and an artist comes from the English translator John Addington Symonds (1840-98). Symonds saw Cellini as the typical Italian of the 1500s. His "passions were the passions of his countrymen; his vices were the vices of his time; his eccentricity and energy and vital force were what the age idealized as virtù. Combining rare artistic gifts with a most violent temper and a most obstinate will, he paints himself at one time as a conscientious craftsman, at another as a desperate bravo. . . . . The mixture of these qualities . . . renders Cellini a most precious subject for the student of [the] Renaissance" (Symonds, p. 475). Scholars who followed him have concurred: "[La vita] describes the whole man . . . with marvelous truth and completeness. It does not spoil the impression when the reader often detects him bragging or lying; the stamp of a mighty, energetic, and thoroughly developed nature remains . . . a significant type of the modern spirit" (Burckhardt, p. 330).

—Elissa Tognozzi

For More Information

Allen, Don Cameron. *The Star-Crossed Renaissance.* New York: Octagon, 1966.

Anglo, Sydney. *Chivalry in the Renaissance.* Woodbridge, Suffolk: The Boydell Press, 1990.

Burckhardt, Jacob. *The Civilization of the Renaissance in Italy.* New York: Harper & Row, 1958.

Burke, Peter. *The Italian Renaissance: Culture and Society in Italy.* Princeton, N.J.: Princeton University Press, 1986.

Cellini, Benvenuto. *The Autobiography of Benvenuto Cellini.* Trans. John Addington Symonds. Garden City, K.S.: Doubleday, 1948.

———. *My Life.* Trans. Julia Conaway Bondanella and Peter Bondanella. New York: Oxford University Press, 2002.

Cochrane, Eric. *Italy 1530-1630.* London: Longman, 1988.

Gallucci, Margaret A. *Benvenuto Cellini: Sexuality, Masculinity, and Artistic Identity in Renaissance Italy.* New York: Palgrave Macmillan, 2003.

Hay, Denys, and John Law. *Italy in the Age of the Renaissance: 1380-1530.* London: Longman, 1989.

Marino, John A., ed. *Early Modern Italy, 1550-1796.* Oxford: Oxford University Press, 2002.

Symonds, John Addington. *The Renaissance in Italy.* London: Smith, Elder, 1877.

Tylus, Jane. *Writing and Vulnerability in the Late Renaissance.* Stanford: Stanford University Press, 1993.

Myrrha

by
Vittorio Alfieri

Born in Asti, Piedmont, in 1749, Vittorio Alfieri was the son of Count Antonio Amedeo Alfieri di Cortemilia and Monica Maillard di Tournon. Educated at the Royal Military Academy in Turin, Alfieri graduated with a Master of Arts degree in 1766. During most of the following decade, Alfieri traveled widely throughout Europe, visiting France, England, Holland, and Russia. At this time, he developed his longstanding political ideals, which included a hatred of absolutism and tyranny. He also improved upon his early education, reading the works of Dante, Petrarch, Machiavelli, Ariosto, and Tasso, and embarked upon a career as a playwright and poet. His first tragedy, *Cleopatra*, was produced in Turin in 1775 and, though he discounted the work, enjoyed immediate success. After a trip to Florence to absorb the dialect, which by then had become the basis for an Italian literary language, he painstakingly switched from writing in French (still popular among Piedmontese aristocrats) to writing in Italian. Alfieri identified increasingly with the Italian libertarian ideals, drafting two treatises expressing his political views—*Of Tyranny* and *The Prince and Letters*—circa 1777. Around this time, he voluntarily forfeited his property and rights as a Piedmont citizen in response to laws decreeing that citizens must obtain permission from the government censor to publish outside Piedmont's boundaries. Thereafter, Alfieri lived abroad, supporting himself on an annuity approximately equal to half his former revenues. An initial supporter of the French Revolution, Alfieri deplored its later excesses as tyrannical and departed France in 1792 to settle in Florence with his

---

THE LITERARY WORK

A tragic play set in Cyprus during an unspecified mythological time; published in Italian (as *Mirra*) in 1787-89, in English in 1876.

SYNOPSIS

A princess intends to marry a prince in order to hide her incestuous passion for her father, which precipitates a series of calamitous events.

---

longtime companion, Louise de Stolberg, Countess of Albany, from whom he experienced the pain of separation several times during their relationship and her marriage to Edward Stuart, pretender to the throne of England. The marriage ended with the death of her husband in 1788, at which point she settled in with Alfieri, who was in the midst of a productive period in his life. The 1780s saw him compose a host of tragic plays, including *Philip* (*Filippo*, 1783), *Agamemnon* (*Agamennone*, 1783), and, most notably, *Saul* (1783) and *Myrrha* (*Mirra*, 1784-86). Acclaimed as one of Alfieri's masterpieces, *Myrrha* quickly distinguished itself for its sensitive handling of a controversial and by then already age-old theme of father-daughter incest.

Events in History at the Time the Play Takes Place

Myrrha and literary tradition. When Alfieri began to write his tragedy, there were already

ITALIAN LITERATURE AND ITS TIMES

301

Vittorio Alfieri

several well-known versions of the Myrrha (sometimes called Smyrna) myth. The best known was probably the one told in Ovid's *Metamorphoses*, which was Alfieri's primary source. In Ovid's rendition of the story, Myrrha is the daughter of King Cinyras and Queen Cenchreis of Paphos, in Cyprus. Afflicted by a supernatural curse, Myrrha burns with an incestuous passion for her father, Cinyras, rejecting all suitors in order to remain with him. One night, the guilt-ridden daughter tries to hang herself, but her old nurse prevents the suicide and presses Myrrha to reveal her torment. The lovestruck young woman finally sobs that she envies her mother, who is blessed with such a husband as Cinyras. The horrified nurse recognizes the implications of this confession but promises to help her charge gain her heart's desire. While Queen Cenchreis is away from court to participate in a ritual honoring the harvest goddess Ceres, the nurse tells the king a young woman wishes to be his lover. Cinyras agrees to an assignation, and, under cover of darkness, the nurse brings Myrrha to her father, who unknowingly commits incest with her. After several nights, however, Cinyras becomes curious about his new lover's identity and lights a lamp while they are in bed together. Appalled to discover he has been sleeping with his own daughter, he draws his sword to kill her, but Myrrha flees the kingdom. Now pregnant by her father and indifferent to her own survival,

she wanders in the wilderness for nine months. Before giving birth, she prays to be removed from both life and death. Answering her prayers, the gods transform her into a myrrh tree that weeps fragrant tears. Its trunk splits open to deliver the baby, a beautiful boy called Adonis, who later becomes the beloved of the love goddess Venus and dies prematurely in a hunting accident.

Ovid was followed by other authors who tackled the Myrrha legend, from Italy's Dante Alighieri to France's Pierre Bersuire and Colard Mansion, to England's John Dryden, William Barksted, and Henry Austin. In Dante's *Inferno*, Myrrha appears with the damned, falsifying spirits in the eighth circle of Hell; Dante treats the character as wholly evil, describing her as "accursed" and "dishonored" (Dante in Simmonds, p. 62). However Bersuire and Mansion interpret Myrrha as "the blessed virgin who conceived through the father and was changed into myrrh, that is bitterness and into the fragrance of scent" (Bersuire and Mansion in Simmonds, p. 63). The reference here is to myrrh plant's resin, which has a bitter taste but a fragrant smell.

Unlike their medieval and Renaissance counterparts, seventeenth-century poets such as Barksted and Austin avoided drawing parallels between classical myth and Christian scripture. But Barksted's *Mirrha the Mother of Adonis* (1607) introduced some original touches: Myrrha's unlawful passion for her father is attributed to her rejection of Cupid's advances. She is associated with sin but more as a victim of dark forces than an evildoer. Henry Austin's *The Scourge of Venus* (1613) departed even more dramatically from Ovid by portraying Cinyras—usually Myrrha's dupe—as almost complicit in the incest. While in bed with his unknown lover, he seems to fantasize about such an affair: "Come kisse thy father, gentle daughter then, / And learn to sport thee in a wanton bed" (Austin in Simmonds, p. 68).

Whether Alfieri knew of the post-Ovid treatments of the Myrrha legend remains uncertain, but his rendition contributes to the evolution of the legend and character through time. Over the centuries, there seems to have been a gradual shift towards a more sympathetic view of Myrrha's plight. In keeping with this shift, Alfieri's tragedy departs from the original in several important respects, eliminating the Adonis subplot and changing Myrrha's experience. In Alfieri's version, her desire for her father goes unconsummated and, until the last moments of the play, unconfessed. The emphasis is not on the heroine's sin and punishment, but on her emotional struggle to overcome what she knows to be an unlawful passion and to spare her family from the knowledge of her sinful yearnings.

The goddess of love. Although he introduced some important changes in *Myrrha*, Alfieri retained the original legend's setting and social elements, including the worship of Venus. Originally a Roman goddess of nature and fertility, Venus had by then developed into the Roman equivalent of Aphrodite, Greek goddess of erotic love.

The island of Cyprus, in the northeastern end of the Mediterranean Sea, was Venus's principal cult center; the goddess figures largely in many Cypriot myths. In one important legend, related by Hesiod, Venus sprang fully formed from sea foam fertilized by the severed genitals of the sky god, Uranus, and came ashore at Cyprus. Represented as beautiful and passionate, she had love affairs not only with fellow gods but with mortals too, often bearing the latter children who became heroes—like Aeneas, legendary founder of Rome. She also bore several children to Mars, the god of war, including Cupid, himself a god of love.

Although Venus could be encouraging towards young lovers, she could also be ruthless and cruel to those who spurned her or to women whose beauty was compared to her own. In another famous myth, Venus charged her son Cupid to wound Psyche, a princess whose loveliness was causing many to neglect their worship of the love goddess. She directed Cupid to make the princess fall in love with someone unsuitable; instead, he wounded himself and became enamored of Psyche. After many trials and tribulations, frequently caused by Venus, Cupid and Psyche were married and the latter was granted immortality.

Venus also figures heavily in several versions of the Myrrha myth. Cenchreis, Myrrha's mother, is said to have boasted about her daughter's beauty, provoking Venus to afflict Myrrha with an incestuous passion for her own father, Cinyras. Alfieri employs this version of the myth in his tragedy, deflecting blame from Myrrha herself. In a pivotal scene, Queen Cenchreis confesses to her husband that she has twice offended Venus, first by withholding tribute, then by boasting that her daughter's beauty surpassed that of the goddess:

> Lo, from that day
> Henceforward, Myrrha lost her peace; her life,
> Her beauty, like frail wax before the fire,
> Slowly consumed; and nothing in our hands
> From that time seem'd to prosper.
> (Alfieri, *Myrrha*, p. 343)

Marriage in imperial Rome. The mythical setting of *Myrrha* complicates attempts to place its institutions within a definite historical context. However, since Alfieri was working from Ovid's *Metamorphoses*, a logical supposition is that Ovid (43 B.C.E.-c. 17 C.E.) had his own era in mind while composing his long narrative poem.

Ovid's lifespan coincides with the founding of imperial Rome and the reign of Augustus (27 B.C.E.-14 C.E.). During this period, marriages could be arranged, contracted, and dissolved with remarkable ease, especially among the upper classes. Parents of a prospective bride and groom could negotiate a match when their offspring were just children. Indeed, a Roman maiden from a wealthy, propertied family might be only ten years old when her marriage was contracted, and most Roman women were married by their early twenties. For the most part, the bride had little say in the matter: her father would arrange the match, perhaps after some consultation with her mother, and negotiations proceeded with the prospective groom or, if he himself was a child, with his older male relations.

 Myrrha

TREATMENTS OF THE MYRRHA MYTH THROUGH THE AGES

c. 470 B.C.E. Pindar's *Pythian Odes*
c. 1st century C.E. Hyginus's *Fables*
c. 8 C.E. Ovid's *Metamorphoses*, Book X
c. 100 C.E. Plutarch's *Parallel Lives of Greeks and Romans*
c. 100-200 C.E. Apollodorus's *Library*
c. 1307-21 Dante's *The Divine Comedy, The Inferno*, Canto XXX
c. 1342-50 Pierre Bersuire's *Ovidius moralizatus*
1484 Colard Mansion's French adaptation of Ovid's *Metamorphoses, La Bible des poetes, metamorphoze*
1607 William Barksted's *Mirrha the Mother of Adonis: Or Lustes Prodigies*
1613 Henry Austin's *The Scourge of Venus*
1700 Dryden's English translation of Ovid's "Cinyras and Myrrha" (from *Fables, Ancient and Modern*)
1787-89 Vittorio Alfieri's *Myrrha*

After marriage, the bride joined her husband's family; he acquired the legal control and jurisdiction over her that her father had previously held. At best, it was hoped that husband and wife would develop a strong bond based on mutual respect and affection and the birth of legitimate children, preferably sons. Indeed, procreation was regarded as the main purpose of

303

any marriage; husbands could divorce wives who disappointed them by proving infertile.

By contrast, the Myrrha of Ovid's poem and Alfieri's play has an unusual degree of freedom when it comes to marital choice. In *Metamorphoses*, Cinyras, "whom an abundance of worthy / suitors had left undecided," consults Myrrha as to which suitor she might prefer (Ovid, bk. 10, lines 438-39). Similarly Alfieri's Myrrha is also permitted to choose her prospective husband, as Queen Cenchreis reveals:

> The most illustrious, powerful potentates
> Of Greece and Asia, all in rivalry,
> From the wide-spreading rumor of her beauty,
> To Cyprus flock'd: and as respected us,
> She was the perfect mistress of her choice.
> (*Myrrha*, p. 318)

Moreover, when Myrrha appears discontented with her choice, her parents are willing to let her break off her betrothal, rather than see her unhappily married.

WOMEN AND MARRIAGE IN ALFIERI'S TIME

That Myrrha's parents would have taken into consideration her preferences for a spouse coincides with a rise in women's status in Alfieri's day. Also called the Age of Reason, the Enlightenment era gave rise to vigorous debate on education for women and on their potential for contributing to Italian society, as reflected in an article in the magazine *Il Caffè* (1764-66). The article, "Defence of Women" by Carlo Sebastiano Franci, advocated intellectual and moral instruction for women in order to maximize the contribution they could make to society. Although men produced articles and journals like these, the mid- to late-eighteenth century saw the introduction of the first Italian women's magazines (e.g., *Europa letteraria* (1768-73), which addressed cultural issues as well as fashion. Thus, the role of the ideal female was broadening in Alfieri's day, though her place as family caregiver and homemaker remained primary, and marital love continued to be defined in practical terms. The emotional bond between a wife and husband, though called "love," generally signified not a passionate bond but a mix of Christian charity, fidelity, and endurance.

The Play in Focus

Plot summary. The play opens with a conversation between Cenchreis, Queen of Cyprus, and Eurycleia, the faithful nurse of Cenchreis's daughter, the princess Myrrha. Now a young woman, Myrrha is soon to wed Pereus, prince of Epirus. Myrrha's behavior is causing her family concern: Eurycleia reports that her charge is suffering some great distress of mind that causes bouts of weeping and sleepless nights, during which Myrrha begs for death to release her from her torment. The nurse has been unable to convince Myrrha to speak of her malady. Cenchreis and Eurycleia suspect Myrrha does not love Pereus but are mystified because he is an estimable young man, whom Myrrha herself chose as her consort. Cenchreis bids Eurycleia to return to Myrrha's side and watch over her. The queen then speaks to her husband, Cinyras, who has also noticed their daughter's unhappiness. Both agree that their only beloved child should not be forced to marry against her will.

In the second act, Cinyras questions Pereus, his future son-in-law, regarding Myrrha's feelings about the upcoming marriage. Pereus confesses that while he is devoted to Myrrha, he is unsure that she returns his love. Her conduct confuses him; first, she wishes to hasten their wedding, then, just as abruptly, she wishes to postpone the ceremony. Nor does she offer a reason for her actions. Rather than make Myrrha unhappy, Pereus resolves to release her from their betrothal if she so wishes. Cinyras commends the young man's nobility and summons Myrrha to speak privately to her betrothed, then withdraws.

Alone with Myrrha, Pereus begs her to tell him how he has displeased her and promises to leave her sight if she dislikes him. Myrrha continues to vacillate. Finally, she insists that she will marry Pereus, on the condition that they depart Cyprus forever the day after the ceremony. The prince, still fearing he will be the cause of his beloved's destruction, urges her to break their betrothal.

Now alone, Myrrha encounters Eurycleia, who reveals that she has visited the temple of Venus to ask her pity on Myrrha. However, the goddess rejected Eurycleia's offering of incense and seemed to order her departure from the temple. In despair, Myrrha asks her nurse to help her commit suicide; shocked, Eurycleia refuses. A resigned Myrrha then declares that she will marry Pereus but that she expects to die of heartbreak soon after the wedding.

In act 3, Myrrha meets with her parents, who continue to express concern over her obvious misery. Myrrha admits that she suffers great anguish but still refuses to disclose the reason. She tells her parents that, while she does not love

Pereus as he loves her, she is aware of his many virtues and intends to fulfill her vows to him. She also reveals that she wishes to leave Cyprus permanently the day after the marriage. Indeed, she feels that her own salvation lies in her departure from her homeland. Although distraught at the prospect of parting from their daughter, Cinyras and Cenchreis finally consent to the departure. Myrrha then withdraws to prepare for her wedding.

Queen Cenchreis confesses to Cinyras that she feels responsible for Myrrha's condition. She reveals that some years earlier, intoxicated with her own happiness as a wife and mother, she withheld a tribute of incense intended for Venus and then boasted that Myrrha's beauty attracted more worshippers to Cyprus than Venus herself. Cenchreis fears that her own pride brought the wrath of Venus down upon her daughter's head. Cinyras reproaches his wife for her boast and for not telling him of her offense so that he could attempt to appease the goddess's anger. The king now believes that Myrrha's one hope of happiness depends upon her leaving Cyprus. He manages to convince the still-apprehensive Pereus that Myrrha does care for him and remains committed to their nuptials.

In act 4, Myrrha declares herself ready for the ceremony and tries to comfort Eurycleia, who laments her charge's imminent departure from Cyprus. Myrrha regrets that she cannot take Eurycleia with her but feels she must leave all reminders of her old life behind. Pereus enters and Myrrha assures him that she is ready to marry him and endeavor to be his loving wife.

The royal family and their subjects gather for the ceremony. The priests and choruses began to chant hymns, praising the betrothed pair and asking for Venus's blessings upon both, especially the bride. In the middle of their oration, however, Myrrha cries out that she sees the Furies all around her, and the ceremony breaks up in horror. Distressed by his bride's ravings and convinced that she abhors him, Pereus releases her from their contract and runs off. Cinyras dismisses the guests and berates his now-swooning daughter for her cruelty to Pereus, claiming that she has disgraced her parents.

Regaining consciousness, Myrrha finds her mother tending to her. She begs Cenchreis for a sword so that she may end her wretched life. When a horrified Cenchreis refuses to let her child destroy herself, Myrrha wildly accuses her mother of being the cause of all her woe by giving birth to her. Grief-stricken, Cenchreis offers

to escort her daughter to her quarters, all the while entreating Myrrha to confide in her.

Act 5 begins with Cinyras lamenting his discovery of Pereus's corpse: the prince has committed suicide in his grief over Myrrha. Cinyras is determined to discover the cause of his daughter's irrational behavior. When Myrrha enters, Cinyras informs her of Pereus's death and reproaches her for it, demanding that she explain herself. The king voices the belief that Myrrha secretly loves another and tells her that he will consent to her marrying that other man if she will simply reveal his identity. Horrified, Myrrha tries at first to deny her father's charge but admits at last, "I love, yes; since thou forcest me to say it; / I desperately love, and love in vain. / But, who's the object of that hopeless passion, / Nor thou, nor any one, shall ever know" (*Myrrha*, p. 361). Cinyras remains adamant, however, and continues to press her on the subject. Again, Myrrha tries to avoid answering, but finally breaks down and reveals her jealousy of Cenchreis and her incestuous passion for Cinyras himself: "O happy is my mother! . . . she, at least, / Press'd in thy arms . . . may breathe . . . her last sigh" (*Myrrha*, p. 362). No sooner has Cinyras realized the implications of this confession than Myrrha seizes his dagger and fatally stabs herself.

Full of pity and rage, Cinyras rejects Myrrha, reveals her guilty secret to a bewildered Cenchreis, and then drags his wife off, leaving their dying daughter alone with Eurycleia. With her last breaths, Myrrha reproaches her nurse for not killing her before she confessed her unnatural love to Cinyras, thereby increasing her guilt and her parents' anguish.

Forbidden passion. The challenge of how to portray Myrrha's incestuous desire for her father preoccupied Alfieri from the start. He had initially considered such a theme ill-suited to the heroic tragedies that were his preferred genre. In his memoirs, however, Alfieri writes, "I had read in Ovid's *Metamorphoses* the animated and sublime address of Myrrha to her nurse. It had melted me into tears and suddenly inspired me with the idea of a tragedy" (Alfieri, *Memoirs*, p. 238).

In adapting Ovid's story, Alfieri made significant changes. The most important of these were to the character of Myrrha herself. Describing his heroine as "much more unfortunate than culpable," Alfieri omitted the last part of the myth: Myrrha's seduction of Cinyras and the incestuous conception of Adonis (*Memoirs*, p. 238). Instead, Myrrha's unnatural love goes unconsummated and, for most of the play, undiscovered. For the entire first act, Myrrha remains offstage while her family discusses her unhappiness and speculates as to its cause. Moreover, on appearing, Myrrha continually refuses to reveal the cause of her suffering, wishing alternately to commit suicide or to marry and leave Cyprus forever.

"SUBLIME ADDRESS"

According to Alfieri's *Memoirs*, it was the "sublime address" of Ovid's Myrrha to her nurse that inspired him with the idea for his tragedy. In the following passages from *Metamorphoses*, a distraught Myrrha tries to avoid confessing her incestuous love for her father, but her nurse's pleas and her own passion finally compel her to reveal her terrible secret:

> Myrrha in frenzy leapt up / and threw herself onto the bed, pressing her face in the pillows: / "Leave me, I beg you," she said. "Avoid my wretched dishonor; / leave me or cease to ask me the cause of my sorrow: / what you attempt to uncover is sinful and wicked!" . . . She lifted her head with her eyes full of tears spilling over / onto the breast of her nurse and repeatedly tried to / speak out, but repeatedly stopped herself short of confession, / hiding her shame-colored face in the folds of her garments, / until she finally yielded, blurting her secret: / "O mother," she cried, "so fortunate you with your husband!" / and said no more but groaned.
>
> (Ovid, bk. 10, lines 495-99, 505-11)

Alfieri also expanded the roles of Myrrha's parents and invented the character of Pereus, a noble young prince whom Myrrha pledges to marry in the hope of overcoming her unlawful passion for her father. Additionally, the playwright chose not to make Myrrha's nurse, Eurycleia, a confidante and conspirator in Cinyras's seduction but to portray her as another helpless bystander to her charge's tragedy. He aims thus to "save the virtue of Eurycleia and prolong the innocence of Myrrha" (Introduction, *Myrrha*, p. 314). The result is a pathos that emerges in Myrrha's final rebuke: "When I asked it . . . of thee, . . . thou . . . O Eurycleia, . . . then . . . shouldest . . . have given to my hands . . . the sword: I had died . . . guiltless; . . . guilty . . . now . . . I die" (*Myrrha*, p. 364). Coaxed into confessing her dark secret, Myrrha commits suicide and dies in disgrace, rejected by all but Eurycleia.

The unsparing harshness of Alfieri's play recalls that of the classical tragedies, such as Sophocles' *Oedipus the King*, that were his major inspiration. Incest was a recurring theme in classical mythology; within the Olympic pantheon, the gods married their own siblings. However, mortals who committed incestuous acts, even unwittingly, were severely punished. Within ancient Greek and Roman society, incest was considered an unnatural abomination. In the following dialogue between two philosophers, Athenian and Megillus, the former condemns incest between siblings or, worse, between father and child.

> *Athenian:* The desire for this sort of pleasure [incest] is stifled by a few words?
> *Migillus:* What words do you mean?
> *Athenian:* The doctrine that "these acts are absolutely unholy, an abomination in the sight of the gods, and at that nothing is more revolting." We refrain from them because we never hear them spoken of in any other way. From the day of our birth each of us encounters a complete unanimity of opinion wherever we go; we find it not only in comedies but often in the high seriousness of tragedy too. . . . We watch these characters dying promptly by their own hand as a penalty for their crimes.
>
> (Lefkowitz and Fant, p. 49)

Sources and literary context. While the primary source of inspiration for Alfieri's *Myrrha* was Ovid's *Metamorphoses*, the playwright also had access to other versions of the myth, including those attributed to Apollodorus, Plutarch, and Hyginus. All three variants contend that Myrrha's mother offended Venus by boasting of her daughter's beauty, so Venus cursed Myrrha with forbidden love for her father. Alfieri further exculpates his Myrrha from blame by utilizing this element. Although the dramatist did not know how receptive audiences would be to a play that dealt with the theme of incest, he was pleased with his tragedy and thought it would show to great effect on the stage.

Alfieri's play evokes comparisons too with works by seventeenth-century playwrights, such as the French dramatists Pierre Corneille (1606-84) and Jean Racine (1639-99). In particular, Racine's *Phèdre* (1677) is similarly drawn from classical myth and also features a title character struggling against an unnatural passion: *Phèdre*, wife of Theseus, desires her stepson, Hippolytus. Alfieri's keen, probing exploration of his characters' psyches is considered unique for a playwright of the eighteenth century and has led some scholars and critics to classify him as a forerunner of the Romantic movement that would supplant Neoclassicism in the nineteenth century.

Events in History at the Time the Play Was Written

Between Neoclassicism and Romanticism. During the seventeenth and eighteenth century, most European nations were caught up in the Enlightenment, a philosophical movement emphasizing the ability of people to govern themselves and to reason independently of divine revelation. The precepts of the Enlightenment attracted a particularly strong following in France and England. Like their French and English counterparts, the Italian intellectual elite (aristocrats, upper clergy, artists, and scholars) participated in this movement. Some founded societies dedicated to the study of subjects like science and mathematics. Others published and circulated gazettes discussing the latest ideas and discoveries garnering attention throughout Europe. In the arts, many writers and painters adopted the simple, harmonious style and elevated subject matter found in the works of classical Greece and Rome.

As a dramatist of the late eighteenth century, Alfieri occupies an unusual position between these Neoclassicists and the Romantics who were to succeed them in the early 1800s. On one hand, the protagonists of Alfieri's plays tended to be heroic, larger than life figures, drawn from such sources as classical myth, the Bible, and contemporary history. As befitted the subjects of high tragedy, his heroes and heroines were caught up in life-altering situations and spoke in appropriately poetic language. On the other hand, Alfieri explored not only his characters' thought processes but also their individual emotional states, a trademark of the Romantics, who emphasized emotional spontaneity, subjective experience, and nature over reason, objective experience, and Neoclassical art.

Of all Alfieri's plays, *Myrrha* may best illustrate his anticipation of the Romantic sensibility. Drawn from classical myth, Alfieri's Myrrha is a princess famed for her beauty and virtue—a suitable tragic heroine, on the surface. But much of the play's "action" is internal, focusing upon Myrrha's moodiness, melancholy, and unspoken sorrows. When she is absent, the other characters discuss her emotional state; when she is present, she reveals her innermost feelings and subjective experience in a manner Franco Betti describes as "unthinkable in a classical context" (Betti, p. 86). On being questioned by her betrothed about her melancholy on the eve of their wedding, Myrrha thus defends herself: "pensiveness / is oft a second nature; ill could one / Who feels its potent sway, explain the cause" (*Myrrha*, p. 329).

Reception and impact. Early information about *Myrrha*'s production history tends to be sketchy. Apparently, the tragedy was performed in Alfieri's lifetime, with Madame Pollandi in the title role, and was accounted successful, despite its controversial subject matter. According to biographer Edward Copping, *Myrrha* was "taken up years afterwards by [the actress] La Marchionni at the suggestion of [the writer and literary patron] Madame de Staël" (Copping, p. 116). No less a personage than the British poet Lord Byron attended this 1819 production. Reportedly, Byron—who had himself touched on the subject of incest in his closet drama, *Manfred*—was so overcome by Alfieri's play that he fainted.

The work also influenced other important Romantic writers. Mary Wollstonecraft Shelley, at the request of her husband, Percy Shelley, worked on translating *Myrrha* in 1818. The following year, she wrote her novella, *Matilda*, which concerns a father's desire for his daughter. Told from Matilda's perspective, the novella includes a line of dialogue that applauds the play: "I thought *Myrrha* the best of Alfieri's tragedies" (Shelley in Bennett and Curran, p. 20). A couple of scholars make reference to the positive reception accorded the play in Shelley's England 30 years after it was written: "Taken at face value, it is no more than an innocent observation Mathilda 'chanced to say' . . . a reading supported by the fact that she is expressing a common literary preference of the day. On closer inspection, though, the remarks suggests her secret complicity with, even encouragement of, her father's passion" (Bennett and Curran, p. 68). In this version of the Myrrha myth, the father drowns himself, and by the story's end, his daughter is close to death. William Godwin, Mary Shelley's own father, though he appreciated aspects of the novella's style, viewed its content as "disgusting and detestable" (Godwin in Shelley, p. 3). *Matilda* would not be published until 1959. In fact, Spanish readers reacted much the same. The plot, said a poet (Manuel de Cabanyes) from Catalonia in Spain, "is as repulsive to the ordinary reader as a story could well be . . . the skill, however, with which the plot is worked up to the climax . . . so that the interest never once flags, is very considerable"; in Madrid and in Paris the play was performed successfully (Cabanyes in Peers, p. 130).

In his memoirs, printed posthumously in 1804, Alfieri wrote of the challenges he had faced while composing *Myrrha*: "I perceived that it was necessary to display, by action alone, what is related in Ovid, and that the heroine must execute her purpose without divulging it" (*Memoirs*, p. 238). Alfieri also realized how difficult it would be to preserve, over the course of five acts, "the terrible fluctuation of Myrrha's soul" (*Memoirs*, p. 238). Nonetheless, the challenge spurred him on; others, he said, would have "to decide how far I have succeeded in overcoming [this difficulty]" (*Memoirs*, p. 238). Certainly Alfieri gave Myrrha's story new poignancy and relevance for an impending literary age; as critic Franco Betti states rhetorically, "Who more than Myrrha foreshadows the typical heroine of Romantic literature?" (Betti, p. 86).

—Pamela S. Loy

For More Information

Alfieri, Vittorio. *Memoirs*. Oxford: Oxford University Press, 1961.

———. *Myrrha*. In *The Tragedies of Vittorio Alfieri*. Vol. 2. Trans. E. A. Bowring. London: G. Bell and Sons, 1876.

Bennett, Betty T., and Stuart Curran, eds. *Mary Shelley in Her Times*. Baltimore: Johns Hopkins University Press, 2000.

Betti, Franco. *Vittorio Alfieri*. Boston: Twayne, 1984.

Brand, Peter, and Lino Pertile, eds. *The Cambridge History of Italian Literature*. Cambridge: Cambridge University Press, 1999.

Copping, Edward. *Alfieri and Goldoni*. London: Addey, 1857.

Davis, John A., ed. *Italy in the Nineteenth Century*. Oxford: Oxford University Press, 2000.

Lefkowitz, Mary R., and Maureen B. Fant. *Women's Life in Greece and Rome*. Baltimore: Johns Hopkins University Press, 1992.

Ovid. *Metamorphoses*. Trans. Charles Martin. New York: W. W. Norton, 2004.

Peers, Allison E. "The Vogue of Alfieri in Spain." *Hispanic Review* 1, no. 2 (April 1933): 122-40.

Schoenberg, Thomas J., and Lawrence J. Trudeau, eds. *Nineteenth-Century Literature Criticism*. Vol. 101. Detroit: Gale Group, 2002.

Shelley, Mary. *Matilda. The Novels and Selected Works of Mary Shelley*. Vol. 2. Ed. Pamela Clemit. London: Pickering, 1996.

Simmonds, James D. *Milton Studies XIV*. Pittsburgh: University of Pittsburgh Press, 1980.

The Name of the Rose

by

Umberto Eco

Umberto Eco was born in 1932 in the Italian province of Piedmont. He began his academic career in the 1950s as a medieval scholar but soon became interested in the philosophy of language. Particularly fascinating to Eco were developments in semiology, or the science of signs and signifying systems, a field that draws on linguistics, literary studies, anthropology, and psychology, and concerns the basic structures and principles of human communication. As a result of his work in cultural journalism, especially after writing a book on aesthetics, *Opera aperta* (1962; The Open Work), Eco became associated with a network of contemporary Italian writers called "Gruppo 63," who encouraged formal experimentation and rejected the elegant novels produced by authors like Giuseppe Tomasi di Lampedusa (see **The Leopard**, also in *WLAIT 7: Italian Literature and Its Times*). Eco proceeded to write a series of scholarly books on semiotics and other subjects, after which he published *The Name of the Rose* to sudden national and international acclaim. Other works of fiction followed, including *Pendolo di Foucault* (1988; Foucault's Pendulum) and *Isola del giorni prima* (1994; The Island of the Day Before). Despite his success, he kept a foot in the academic world, continuing to work at the University of Bologna. Eco's vast readership in many countries testifies to his ability to convey complex ideas within a gripping narrative style—one of the defining qualities of *The Name of the Rose*.

THE LITERARY WORK

A murder mystery set in an abbey in northern Italy during the early fourteenth century; published in Italian (as *Il nome della rosa*) in 1980, in English in 1983.

SYNOPSIS

The elderly Adso recalls his week as a young novice to an English monk at a powerful Benedictine monastery. The monk, William of Baskerville, uncovers the motive for a series of mysterious deaths but is unable to prevent an imminent catastrophe.

Events in History at the Time the Novel Takes Place

The rise of the monasteries. Although we often think of the medieval period in European history—roughly, from the seventh to the fifteenth centuries—as a monolithic age marked by all-pervasive religious authority, by the absolutist rule of monarchs, and by lack of progress in science and the arts, the reality is different. From the twelfth century onward, Europe saw the growth of new centers of knowledge and education (universities and municipal schools of various kinds), and a struggle for more intellectual and political breathing-space on the part of many individuals and groups (scholars interpreting rediscovered works from classical antiquity, independent

Umberto Eco

religious orders challenging the bishops, civic assemblies in the growing commercial towns). Notwithstanding such cracks in the structure of medieval Europe, however, it largely remained an age in which people saw their lives governed by religious belief and in which piety and devotion were the universal standards in accordance with which the Christian was expected to live. The Church's constant warnings about eternal damnation and punishment in hell also played a role in securing the obedience of the faithful. An obsession with punishment in the afterlife led to a part-official, part-informal traffic in "indulgences" (time deducted from the sinner's sentence in Purgatory). Originating at the end of the eleventh century, with plenary indulgences dispensed by the pope to armies going on the Crusades, a vast and theologically unsound market in distributing indulgences to individuals had grown in all parts of Europe. Although Church authorities were often uneasy about the idea, the insatiable demand on the part of ordinary people for indulgences kept the business going.

From the papacy on down, the Christian hierarchy continued to defend the status of the Church as the final authority in intellectual, philosophical, and political conflicts. In 1302 Pope Boniface VIII issued one of the most uncompromising declarations ever delivered of the supreme authority and "comprehensiveness of the Christian church" when he denied that any secular ruler could challenge the papacy and claimed that outside the church there could be "no salvation or remission of sins" (Boniface in Swanson, p. 1). Despite the pope's absolutist theory, however, he knew as well as anyone that the relationship between the Church and the powerful monarchs of Europe had never been stable or uncomplicated. There had long been a division of interest between church and state in the West. Meanwhile, among themselves the secular rulers had fought savage wars for political control—despite the universal Christian ideal of brotherhood to which they all subscribed, at least in theory.

The roots of the tension between secular and religious power lie deep in the culture of the Germanic tribes that conquered what remained of the Roman Empire during the fourth and fifth centuries, and gradually assimilated to the Christian religion and remnants of the Graeco-Roman culture. Prior to this assimilation, the warrior ethic and crude sense of law and justice that dominated the Germanic peoples entailed a principle that kings and chieftains were often subject to election (or at least to being deposed for cowardice or incompetence) by tribal assemblies, and that nobody was above the tribal law. If this qualification of royal authority gave rise to a persistent political tension, it also inspired a flexibility that allowed various kinds of rule to develop in different parts of Europe. During the Dark Ages (named for the fact that very little is known about the period, which extends from about the sixth to the ninth century), a Romano-Germanic aristocracy dominated Western Europe. This aristocracy had little or no idea of enlightened government, while the Church often showed more interest in its property than in the welfare of the masses.

Out of this history grew an alternative type of Christian practice: monasticism. The concept of a refuge from the violence and corruption of the world, in which men devote their lives to prayer and sustain themselves through simple labor, was put into perhaps its most effective form by St. Benedict, who founded the Benedictine order of monks in the sixth century at Montecassino in Italy. The Benedictines were the first order to establish a chain of command, with the abbot in unquestioned authority. They touched off a movement that over time saw the founding of other monastic orders across Europe, such as the Cistercians in the eleventh century and the Dominicans in the thirteenth century. Many abbeys became centers for the study of Christian writers and texts from the classical literatures of Greece and Rome, helping to prepare the way for the European Renaissance. Over time the orders became increasingly influential in politics too, partaking in controversies despite the intention to withdraw from the struggles of the outside world.

Poverty as principle. By the twelfth century, feudalism, spreading from France, had created a new and multi-faceted power structure throughout much of Western Europe. More centralized than the old German warrior clans and the aristocracy that had emerged from them, feudal systems embodied a complex system of loyalties extending laterally to other nobles but also upward toward the king. The Church meanwhile came into closer contact with local government during the feudal era (roughly 1000 to 1450). Rural parishes, or Church districts, were formed, often in tandem with the consolidation and administration of large estates owned by a local lord. Meanwhile, towns and cities underwent a revitalization. A period of economic buoyancy set in around feudal Europe, whose growing urban centers extended their power and influence by setting up civic institutions and building cathedrals and schools, which incidentally competed with the established learning centers of the monasteries and abbeys.

After several centuries, the Benedictine monasteries in particular found themselves well adjusted to the feudal system. They were prosperous, often politically well-connected entities. Also they held a great deal of local power, since, until the growth of the medieval towns, they frequently provided the only means of education, medical assistance, and prudent economic management. Both the regular Church hierarchy and the established religious orders were about to be challenged, however. University scholars such as Peter Abelard (1079-1142) in Paris, France, and Roger Bacon (1214?-94) in Oxford, England, began to press beyond the established borders of philosophical and intellectual inquiry. Around the same time, a number of newly formed independent religious orders (among them, the Cistercians, Dominicans, and Franciscans) offered a return to the austerity and high ideals of an earlier period of Christianity. The most energetic and influential of these new orders, the Franciscans, followed the lead of their charismatic founder, St. Francis of Assisi (1181-1226), by traveling, preaching, helping the poor and the sick, and refusing all personal property or wealth for themselves or their order.

The pursuits and practices of the Franciscans amounted to a permanent accusation directed at both established orders such as the Benedictines and the wealthy bishops of the local church hierarchy. In the century after the founding of the order, the Franciscans found themselves inextricably involved in the complex politics of Europe and the shifting power struggles among three main camps: the pope, the various monarchies of Europe (including the constellation of German rulers known as the Holy Roman Empire), and an expanding urban middle class that was increasingly less willing to be subordinate to the local nobility. The Franciscans' principle of poverty—based on an interpretation of the New Testament in which Christ never sought or kept any wealth or property for himself—was a potential threat to the established order. The wealth of the Church, of the landowners, and of the new urban bourgeoisie contrasted sharply with the simple Franciscan ways and with the condition of misery and ignorance in which the lower classes of medieval Europe lived. It was not just the political implications of the Franciscan tenets that put the order into a quasi-hostile posture vis-à-vis the establishment, however; it was also the Franciscan vision of the faith as an ecstatic, mind-altering experience that contained its own authority and legitimacy. This shift in emphasis from a rational to a mystical experience of faith—that is from an observable, controllable experience to a private, ungovernable one—could also be seen as an implicit danger to the established order.

The Novel in Focus

Plot summary. *The Name of the Rose* opens with a preface by an unnamed narrator who tells the story of finding an old book in Paris in August 1968. Supposedly the book is a translation of a fourteenth-century Latin manuscript by a German monk, Adso of Melk. The narrator lost the book before completing a translation, he claims, but has since discovered an alternative version in a bookstore in Buenos Aires, Argentina. He then presents the story of Adso of Melk out of a sense of "sheer narrative pleasure" (Eco, *Name of the Rose*, p. 5). Before beginning, he notes that Adso's account is divided into seven days and further subdivided into the traditional liturgical hours by which the medieval monks lived: Matins, Lauds, Prime, Terce, Sext, Nones, Vespers, and Compline. The monastery's day began with Matins at roughly 2:30 to 3:00 A.M. in the morning and ended with Compline, at about 6:00 P.M. in the wintertime.

Adso introduces himself as a man who is presently "at the end of [his] poor sinner's life,

A MONASTERY FOR THE MIDDLE AGES

Prior to the fourth century, monks resided in solitude as hermits with no communal building in which they lived and prayed. It was in Egypt, during the fourth century, that Saint Pachomius introduced the organized monastery, but it was St. Benedict (died c. 547) of Nursia in central Italy who established the building standard for European monasteries. The monastery in *The Name of the Rose* would have resembled that standard, including most or all of the following parts:

- **Dormitories** Area for monks to sleep (including a staircase linked to the church for 3:00 A.M. prayers).
- **Church** Monks of the Middle Ages spent about a third of the day here devoted to prayer and song.
- **Cloister** Center of the monastery; contained cubbyholes for studying.
- **Warming house** Contained a large fireplace to warm the monks.
- **Lavatorium** Area for monks to wash themselves (monks were required to wash before entering the chapter house).
- **Chapter house** A chapter of the Rule of St. Benedict (a rulebook for monks written in 530 C.E. by St. Benedict) was read each day here and punishments were given out for misbehaving monks.
- **Infirmary hall** A place for monks to go if they felt ill; had its own chapel and kitchen attached to it.
- **Almonry building** Where the poor were received and helped—given leftover food and clothing.
- **Guest house** Lodged travelers, who stayed at no cost.
- **Watching chamber** An area to guard the monastery against theft (many monasteries contained a great amount of wealth).
- **School** To educate wealthy children.
- **Bakehouse and Brewhouse** Where servants would bake bread and brew ale.
- **Kitchen** A monk would prepare the food in this area—monks were allowed only one meal a day.
- **Refectory** Or dining hall, where monks ate in silence (speaking was forbidden).
- **Parlor** An area where monks could talk to one another.
- **Library** Held books for study.
- **Gate** Large entrance into the monastery.
- **Abbot's house** The abbot was the leader of the monks, and lived in a separate house containing his own chapel, bedroom, dining room, and kitchen.
- **Land and fields** Another form of worship included working in the fields.
- **Barn and stables** Where livestock was kept.
- **Cemetery** An area to bury the dead.

[his] hair now white" (*The Name of the Rose*, p. 11). At the time of the main narrative, he is probably 16 or 17. Adso's father has put him under the direction of an English Franciscan monk, William of Baskerville, to assist him in an important mission. Brother William is a tall, thin Englishman over 50 years old (a very aged man, in terms of the life expectancy of the Middle Ages), with reddish-yellow hair and freckles. He is an intellectual and scholar, in contrast to the uneducated Franciscans of Germany and Italy; he believes in scientific investigation and in de-

ducing facts from empirical evidence, and has studied at Oxford University under the great English Franciscan philosopher, Roger Bacon. Unusual as well in his approach to life, William evinces a dry humor and makes satirical observations in a manner that Adso has not experienced before. Adso develops great affection for the English monk but, like other characters in the story, sometimes has difficulty figuring out whether William is being serious or ironic.

Upon reaching the monastery, Adso and William are greeted by the abbot, Abo, who informs them of a delicate and unpleasant incident. A young monk, Adelmo of Otranto, has been found dead at the foot of one of the cliffs on which the Benedictine monastery is built. The abbot says that it is unclear whether it was suicide or murder. Because William has been an officer of the Inquisition (a tribunal to suppress deviation from the teachings of the Roman Catholic Church), the abbot wants him to investigate, but discreetly; William requests complete freedom of movement, but the abbot declares that the upper floor of the central building, containing the abbey's famous library, is out of bounds. William knows that the library is one of the largest in Christendom, with many rare, centuries-old manuscripts that must be protected.

Shortly after the interview with the abbot, William and Adso proceed to the monastery's kitchen, where they meet the strange, disfigured monk Salvatore. Appearing to be mentally slow, he speaks a garbled, disconnected combination of several languages: French, Italian, German, English, and Latin. He uses a word, *Penitenziagite,* that piques William's curiosity, but William fails to extract any useful information from him. As Salvatore leaves, in comes Ubertino of Casale, a monk with a colorful past and a reputation as a mystical thinker and visionary. Ubertino has been associated with the Spiritual Franciscans (a radical group on the fringe of the order) and is convinced that William is really a supporter of his; in fact, William does not quite trust Ubertino and considers his ideas to be wild and paradoxical.

Breaking the rules, William and Adso explore the "scriptorium," the abbey's library, which is shaped like a maze. They meet the librarian, Malachi of Hildesheim, and an old monk, Jorge of Burgos (the library has monks from all over Christian Europe working on its manuscripts). Now blind, Jorge is a grim figure who frightens the younger monks. He finds William, Adso, and Malachi looking at some fantastic drawings in the margin of a manuscript on which the deceased

Adelmo had been working. They are chuckling over the strange images when Jorge enters and attacks them for laughing, a reaction he disdains as boorish and unwarranted by scripture. Later that day, the abbey's glazier, Nicholas, is very impressed by William's reading glasses, a novelty in this era.

THE SPIRITUAL FRANCISCANS

In the early fourteenth century, shortly before the time when *The Name of the Rose* takes place, the radical group known as the Spiritual Franciscans was active in Italy and France. The Spirituals rejected considerable amounts of orthodox, church-approved theology, "claiming that their revelations had a gospel quality which superseded the controls exercised by the church" (Swanson, p. 179). Although monastic orders prided themselves on their independence, they were generally unwilling to upset the secular or ecclesiastical powers-that-be. The Franciscans were the most unconventional of the orders. The Spiritual Franciscans, more radical still than their Franciscan brothers, went even further. Linking belief, preaching, and way of life, their challenge to the authorities was both theological and social and was something of an embarrassment to the mainstream Franciscan order. Meanwhile, there was an obsession on the part of the Church with locating and condemning heresy, which apparently had more to do with the fear that a visionary, mystical Christianity could easily become a subversive force than with any measure of orthodoxy. The questionable motivation for the obsession with heresy surfaces in *The Name of the Rose,* in dialogues on the shifting, often fuzzy borderline between subjective, internal piety and external political agendas.

The following morning a second monk is found murdered. The victim is Venantius, a young monk who worked with the previously murdered Adelmo in the library. William questions Severinus, the monastery's medical expert and herbalist. Severinus admits that various substances can be healthful in small doses but dangerous and even fatal in large ones. Curious about how balanced Venantius's perception was in his final moments, William probes the herbalist regarding vision-inducing or mind-altering plant substances. William suggests to Adso that the monk Adelmo may have wandered around in a drugged or deranged state before taking his

Manuscript illumination of education in a monastery. From a facsimile of the Manesse (Manessa) Codex, German manuscript, 1305-1340.

own life. Hearing rumors of homosexual behavior among the monks, William comments that the present-day obsession with hell and punishment (most intense in Italy) is leading to an increase in immoral and self-destructive behavior.

William and the blind Jorge have another tense discussion in the library regarding humor and laughter. Once again Jorge argues that laughter is an impious act, noting that Christ never struck a comic pose in his parables. William disagrees, pointing out how effective humor can be in pointing up moral lessons. Shortly afterward, William hears more information from the young Swedish monk, Benno, confirming the stories of covert homosexual activities in the abbey, involving Adelmo, Venantius, and a third monk, Berengar.

The abbot shows William and Adso the rich treasure of the church, with its gold chalice and the plating and inlays surrounding the altar. William deliberately brings up the forthcoming meeting between various religious orders and the pope's envoys, in which the subject of voluntary poverty is to be discussed. Adso has only a fuzzy grasp of the real issues and their background, but knows that the principle of voluntary poverty—and whether or not the example of Christ demands that it be followed—has become a tense controversy in Europe, creating strange hostilities and alliances among the pope, the emperor, and different religious orders in the Church. There are major players involved, and William has taken on the delicate, and in some ways dangerous, task of being coordinator of their meeting in the abbey. This is his important mission.

William and Adso secretly enter the library at night and disturb someone who is attempting to remove manuscripts, including the one on which Adelmo and Venantius were working. William discovers writing in secret ink, but cannot understand the meaning behind the coded message (in Latin) *Secretum finis Africae*, or "the secret at the end of Africa." During their search of the mazelike library, Adso is overcome by at first blush what seem to be spirits emerging from the walls, and he collapses. William finds the fallen Adso and realizes that he has inhaled a poisonous or narcotic vapor probably from a chemical mixed in with the decorative inks to protect a particular manuscript. By early morning, they find the exit from the labyrinth with difficulty, and discover that Berengar has been missing for several hours. William discovers that his spectacles are missing, and asks the glazier, Nicholas, to try to make him a new pair.

William tries to explain the nature of heresy and revolutionary movements to Adso, arguing that society has created large and dangerous groups of outcasts who have no stake in the social order. They are ripe recruits for apocalyptic preachers who promise them justice and revenge, and the ecclesiastical and political leaders add to the problem by accusing anyone with an idea for reforming society of being a heretic. In William's view, oppression gives rise to a violent reaction among the poor, which in turn gives rise to "heresy." It is the violent reaction that instigates heresy and not heresy that instigates the violence. Meanwhile, afraid of social upheaval, the Church is quick to label anything unexpected or challenging as heresy. Adso struggles to assimilate these disturbing ideas to his previous beliefs about the universal embrace of the Church. He had thought of it until now as an institution that offers meaning to the lives of rich and poor alike, and condemns heresy only for genuine theological reasons.

Shortly thereafter, William hears from the abbot that the leader of the pope's delegation for the meeting at the monastery will be a man called Bernard Gui. Gui has a reputation for being the papal hatchet-man, a cool tactician who shows no mercy toward any presumed heresy that he discovers. Given that the question of voluntary poverty (whether the Church should own property of any kind) is the controversial issue that will be addressed, William believes that the unavoidable implication of this news is that the pope wants a confrontation with the religious orders rather than constructive diplomacy. The abbot worries that Gui might use the recent murders against him.

William and Adso attempt a speculative drawing of the library, based upon their experiences searching through and getting lost in it the previous night. They realize quickly that the structure of the library is a honeycomb of rooms built to a precise geometric system but turned into a disorienting maze by the deliberately unpredictable distribution of interconnected entrances—not every room has a way out as well as a way in.

Adso asks the kitchen aide, Salvatore, to prepare some food for him and William. Along with the food, Salvatore gives Adso an oil-lamp; however mentally slow he seems to be, apparently he knows that they want to explore the library. Later Adso questions Ubertino about the history of the radical preacher Fra [Friar] Dolcino, whose cry *"Penitenziagite"* (which Salvatore mutters at times) was an uneducated man's version of a longer Latin phrase meaning, "Repent, for the kingdom of heaven is at hand!" Fra Dolcino had begun to preach fanatically, encouraging his followers to attack and rob anyone who looked even modestly prosperous, and he eventually formed an army of wild followers who practiced sexual freedom and a type of primitive communal socialism. He and his cohorts—including a beautiful woman named Margaret—were eventually hunted down and executed.

His mind somewhat disturbed by thoughts of heresy and sensuality, Adso wanders back into the kitchen, where he has an unexpected encounter. He stumbles over a local peasant girl, about Adso's own age, who is hiding in a dark corner. They are both surprised and a little scared. They don't speak each other's language, but neither moves to go. Adso, a novice monk who has spent his young life so far in an entirely male environment, is confused and aroused by the physical presence of the exotic girl; she is wild-haired, barefoot, and clearly wearing nothing but a ragged and dirty dress. The girl begins to touch and caress him, and he cannot stop himself from responding in kind. They are both caught in a sudden wave of intense passion. To Adso's pleasure and astonishment (his narrative at this point continually shifts into Latin and biblical phraseology, as if he can't find the proper words) the peasant girl takes off her dress, removes some of Adso's clothing, and they make love.

After this encounter, he is overcome with remorse and blurts out the story to William. William hears his confession, and tells Adso that it was indeed wrong to give in to carnal desire, but that some things can't be helped and the experience will be good for him as a priest later in life, giving him more understanding about sins of the flesh than he otherwise would have had. William says that the girl was probably regularly giving sexual favors to someone in the monastery in return for scraps of food for her family. William closes the matter:

> "But I see you are still agitated, my poor Adso. . . . I have absolved you, but one never knows. Go and ask the Lord's confirmation." And he gave me a rather brisk slap on the head, perhaps as a show of paternal and virile affection. . . . Or perhaps (as I culpably thought at that moment) in a sort of good-natured envy, since he was a man who so thirsted for new and vital experiences.
>
> (*Name of the Rose*, p. 254)

Immediately after this, William and Adso discover the corpse of the missing monk Berengar, who has died by drowning.

William is bothered by a black substance on the dead man's fingers, a phenomenon he noticed on Venantius. Severinus the herbalist tells William a story of a rare, extremely poisonous substance that a monk had given him. After a storm, when several jars and containers in the infirmary were destroyed, Severinus noticed that the jar with the poison was missing. Questioning Salvatore in the kitchen, William extracts the admission that he and his superior, the head cook Remigio, were both involved with the rad-

ical Fra Dolcino. Remigio later admits his involvement, and confesses that both he and Salvatore shared the peasant girl in return for presents of food from the kitchens.

Representatives of the Franciscan friars begin to arrive at the abbey. They impress Adso as an eccentric bunch, obsessed with their own separate ideas rather than with larger issues.

Returning from their next trip to explore the library, William and Adso discover that Bernard Gui has captured the peasant girl and arrested Salvatore. He intends to try the girl as a witch. William warns Adso not to interfere, as he can do nothing except endanger himself. As the debate between the two teams begins, it becomes clear that the unity between the various orders, especially the Franciscans and the Dominicans, is fragile. They are unable to present a common front on the issue of voluntary poverty to Gui and the papal delegates.

William delivers a speech at the meeting in which he argues for the gradual development of elected civic assemblies as the governing bodies of the future. He suggests that the story of Genesis, in which Adam is free to give a name to all creatures, is a clear guide to the right to exercise legislative power. Bernard Gui asks William if he would be prepared to present his ideas directly to Pope John, but William says he must decline the offer because of his health. Guards burst in at that moment and inform Gui that the body of Severinus has been discovered on the floor of the infirmary.

Bernard Gui convenes a court of the Inquisition there in the abbey to try Remigio and the peasant girl. Salvatore testifies in his multi-lingual babble that both he and Remigio had been followers of Fra Dolcino. Remigio breaks down and confesses to lurid crimes and wild heresies as a member of Fra Dolcino's band, which pleases the papal representative since he can then point to Remigio as merely the extreme version of a type of revolutionary thinking shown by those who incline to the secular authority of the emperor rather than to the pope.

That night, William and Adso join the other monks to listen to a sermon by Jorge of Burgos. It is a terrifying performance by the old man, full of apocalyptic imagery and warnings. He accuses the monks of having allowed the sin of pride to grow among them, as a result of over-valuing the scholarly and intellectual work they do. He warns that the day of the Antichrist has come, and that the deaths in the abbey are a sign that the world is descending into a final chaos. After the sermon, Adso asks William if he thinks Bernard Gui will still be inclined to have the peasant girl burned as a witch. William admits sadly that he thinks Gui certainly will do so, and Adso is haunted by guilt; in fact, he admits to having remained obsessed by the memory of the girl: "This was the only earthly love of my life, and I could not, then or ever after, call that love by name" (*Name of the Rose*, p. 407).

The next day the body of the librarian, Malachi, is found. His fingers show the same traces of a black substance that have been seen on the other victims. Nicholas, the glazier, tells William and Adso a strange story he has heard in the monastery regarding the appointment of a librarian several decades earlier. William examines the library records and realizes that 40 years earlier some unidentified individual was running the library, but the person's handwriting disappears from the records, suggesting that he never became head librarian.

In an audience with the abbot, William tells him that the solution to the plague of murders involves a book that has been examined by several monks and is secreted in the "finis Africae," the inner core of the scriptorium labyrinth. William realizes that Adso has, by accident, solved the riddle of access to the secret room. They make their entry, and discover the individual who has been manipulating the events for so long and is guilty of the murders of the monks. He has dusted the manuscripts with the rare toxin stolen from the herbalist. William has known the truth for a while, at least intuitively, but it comes as a shock to Adso. William also knows what the perpetrator was trying to protect: it is a manuscript from classical Greece—believed to be lost forever—that could alter the culture of Christian Europe and bring about a structural shift, elevating comedy from its low position. The perpetrator defends his actions—the library is dangerous, he thinks. Its potential for subversion of religious faith is as great as its reputation for intellectual resources. The perpetrator tries to flee, and in the ensuing struggle knocks an oil lamp out of Adso's hand. The papers and manuscripts in the library catch fire. William and Adso save themselves, but—like the other monks—look on helplessly as the entire abbey is destroyed by fire. The fire burns for three days and nights. Nothing can be saved.

The monks and everyone else desert the ruins. Adso and William head north, crossing the Alps into Germany. In Munich they part, never to see each other again. As a final gift, William presents Adso with his spare pair of reading glasses, and Adso tells the reader he is wearing them now, many decades later, as he writes this account. Adso finishes his story, admitting that he does not really know what it means, or for whom he is writing it. He is an old man now, waiting only for the silence of death to descend upon him. His last sentence, written in Latin, says that "yesterday's rose endures in its name, and we hold bare names" (*The Name of the Rose*, p. 502). The name "rose" means something important to him from his past, but it's now merely an abstract signifier of a memory fraught with emotion, not a real presence.

Sins and desire. Adso's painful confusion—his oscillation between feelings of love and pangs of guilt and disgust after his encounter with the peasant girl in the abbey's kitchen—is the product of a host of beliefs concerning the medieval Church and sexual desire. The teaching of the Church, particularly the fifth-century bishop and philosopher St. Augustine, as well as older traditions from the classical period, tended to see the world of matter, the physical body, and human reproduction as lower down the chain of being than spirit and idea. However, there was no reason to believe, as one historian has put it, "that medieval clerics lacked the usual complement of hormonal tides" (Brundage, p. 298). These "tides," of course, rose in the clerics as in everyone else. Moreover, although Christian theology defined the soul as the non-gendered essence present in every human being, women were in fact regarded as spiritually weak, untrustworthy, and dangerous to the sincere believer because of their ability to inspire sexual attraction. Marriage was seen as a second-best choice after chastity, the highest badge of religious commitment, and sex for purposes other than reproduction was subject to ecclesiastical disapproval. But in the real world, such ideals were difficult if not impossible to monitor and maintain (typically a priest hearing confession would not interrogate a married couple to establish whether or not they had derived pleasure from sexual intercourse), and only the most egregious sexual transgressions were prosecuted in Church courts. In the more remote areas of Europe where central Church authority was far away, even the papal ban on married priests was often ignored as a strange and rather naïve regulation.

Adso, a well-meaning and conscientious young novice, about 16 years of age, is far from cynical or casual in his behavior. He believes that he must keep himself pure—and that what he has learned about women from books is all he needs to know to avoid temptation. He is not ignorant of the temptations of homosexual behavior among novices and monks in an all-male environment. He would have been aware of the various instructional texts on sinful behavior:

> One manual . . . alerts the priest to sixteen degrees of sexual transgression, ranging from unchaste kisses to bestiality. Among these masturbation, ranked twelfth, is presented as a more deadly sin than incest, ranked eleventh, for, it is reasoned, masturbation wastes semen altogether, while incest at least directs it toward its proper end.
>
> (Ozment, p. 218)

When Adso meets a real young woman his own age who seems to have no inhibitions regarding sex, he is unprepared for the experience. The hormonal tides of the medieval cleric sweep away all the theory that Adso has shored up against sexual temptation. He is then racked with remorse, and subject also to recurring thoughts and desires regarding the young woman, a combination that reduces him to psychic exhaustion.

William hears Adso's confession and discharges him into penance with a paternal slap on the head. He knows that Adso will be a more mature monk and a more understanding confessor if he has had at least one sexual experience of his own while young. What William may not realize is that, for Adso, the encounter with the peasant girl becomes a moment of beauty that he never forgets, and perhaps never could forget. The "Rose" of the title may—the novel never quite makes it clear—be the girl. It is even more likely, however, that the "Rose" is the *memory* of the girl, of the closeness of their encounter and, subsequently, the widening gulf between their two worlds. As an elderly monk, Adso struggles to name the most influential and poignant experience of his life—one that he comes close to admitting that he can neither completely describe nor fully understand. His struggle is an ironic reversal of the way the medieval Church tried to name each and every possible sexual transgression, even the most minor, while at the same time claiming that sex was nothing but an unimportant and primitive drive.

Sources and literary context. In his "Postscript," Eco claims that the origin of *The Name of the Rose* can be found partly in the vast library of odd and unused information on the Middle Ages that he had stored up over the years (*Name of the Rose*, pp. 509-10). Certainly the novel is rooted in a consistent study of the medieval pe-

riod and its culture, politics, and religious ideologies. But the matter goes even deeper, as Eco clearly admits, when he says that his problem was to write about the Middle Ages without looking as if he was taking himself too seriously. He invented Adso as a way of assuming the persona of a fairly well-educated but naïve and limited young man who was trying to relate matters that he often did not fully grasp. The young novice is the foil for William's ironic barbs and self-deprecating manner.

The novel, as the commentators in *The Key to The Name of the Rose* make clear, is full of "playful allusions to . . . Arthur Conan Doyle and Jorge Luis Borges" (Haft, White, and White, p. 27). The connection with Conan Doyle, originator of the detective Sherlock Holmes, is especially marked in the name William of Baskerville, echoing Sir Arthur Conan Doyle's novel *The Hound of the Baskervilles*. The blind librarian Jorge of Burgos is a humorous gesture in the direction of Borges, renowned author of unique multi-layered fictions and for many years director of the National Library of Argentina. Thus, while keeping the realistic narrative of fourteenth-century Italy intact, Eco's novel refers to later texts and individuals.

Eco turns a satirical light, in particular, on the relationship of the British to the continental European intellectual. This is reflected in the discomfort and tension provoked by William's constant desire to have some concrete validation of statements and claims by various individuals. His desire for this validation reflects a controversy in Eco's own day as a result of a newly popular concept—"deconstruction." Deconstruction was originally a philosophical proposition advanced in the 1960s by the French writer Jacques Derrida. He argued that the assumed structure of the universe in Western thinking, configured always by a central term such as "God," "science," or "civilization," had by his day been de-centered, or deconstructed. In Derrida's view, meaning does not derive from such a central presence but rather from language that imposes categories on a world, infusing it with meaning. Deconstruction quickly became a way of undermining the idea that books, poems, and other texts contain "meaning" in the sense of an independent, objective significance that the reader can elicit from the text. William's desire for concrete evidence and belief in objective "meaning" in the novel reflects the attitude of traditional literary critics, primarily in Great Britain and the United States, who regarded the deconstructionist wave of the 1970s and 1980s with skepticism and even hostility—seeing it as damaging to the status of literature. On the other hand, deconstructionists in Continental Europe and elsewhere rejected the traditional pragmatic insistence on objective meaning.

The novel satirizes the transnational intellectual controversy—in which Eco himself played an important role—that accompanied literary study of the late twentieth century (see, for example, the various essays by Eco and others in the collection *Interpretation and Over-interpretation*).

Events in History at the Time the Novel Was Written

Twentieth-century parallels. In 1973 the Italian communist leader Enrico Berlinguer advanced the idea of the "historic compromise." Broadly, the "compromise" was an argument that the two strongest political forces in Italy, the conservative Christian Democrats (DC) and the left-wing Italian Communist Party (PCI), would be forced one day to work together to save the nation from catastrophe brought about by an increasingly polarized society. Neither side would give up its ideology, but each would have to recognize that it could not get rid of the other. During the 1970s, as an economic downturn seemed to be reversing much of the prosperity and social advances of the post-World War II era, the Communist Party was expanding to the detriment of the Christian Democrats. It began to look as if the Communists were at the door of power. All that it required was the next government crisis to step inside.

The increasing respectability of the Communist Party had disadvantages, however. The more radical left, growing since the student movement and the anti-Vietnam War activism of the late 1960s and early 1970s, began to reject the party as a disguised conservative force no longer committed to revolution. Voicing their views in *La Lotta Continua* (The Struggle Goes On) and other newspapers, the new left gained adherents from independent workers' movements, environmental campaigns, feminist groups, and the like. The so-called "Red Brigades," a small, radical fringe of the new left, turned to violence.

Acts of urban terrorism increased in Italy during the 1970s. Bombings at rail terminals and other public facilities caused fatalities and introduced a strong note of paranoia into political discourse (encouraged by revelations of strange and ominous connections between the intelligence services and terrorist groups). In 1978, the year that Eco began writing *The Name of the Rose*, "the late twentieth-century terrorist era," as one scholar expresses it, "would reach a peak in Italy with approximately 3,000 incidents, including assassinations and kidnappings" (Wagner-Pacifici, p. 48). Indeed, as Eco tells us in his "Postscript," he began writing his novel in March of 1978. That same month the most sensational event in the national political drama took place: the kidnapping and eventual murder of the former Italian prime minister and senior Christian Democrat politician Aldo Moro. The heady mix of student movement politics, sexual liberation, pop culture, and violence achieved its apotheosis in the Red Brigades, who took the battle into the arena of the hated political and cultural establishment with a vengeance.

The figures of Salvatore, Ubertino, and even William himself in *The Name of the Rose* can be seen as projections backward in time from the Italy of the 1970s. The problems of visionary politics versus stability and rational change, intellectual exploration (the scholar) versus random, violent challenges to authority (the man of action), and erotic drives transformed into ideals of spiritual purity are recreated in the fourteenth-century setting in a way that raises haunting similarities between the two eras. The cold, manipulative skills of Bernard Gui, the self-absorbed passion and naïve idealism of Ubertino, and the activities of Fra Dolcino and his roving band of mystics and criminals offer clear parallels with the volatile and unpredictable politics of late 1970s Italy, in which radical groups declared their love for humanity yet committed multiple murders for political ends.

Reception. A novel that was at once a lovingly detailed re-creation of the Middle Ages, a psychological thriller, and a satire on current intellectual controversies, *The Name of the Rose* met with remarkable popular and critical success. General readers responded to the novel primarily as a tightly plotted, atmospheric thriller, while many reviewers showed an awareness of Eco's reputation as a scholar and critic and this consciousness flowed into their comments.

"*The Name of the Rose* is a mirrored-hallway," wrote one reviewer, "each strand of the tale is in some sense merely a reflection, a blind alley" ("J.S.," p. 76). Richard Ellman reviewed the novel for the *New York Review of Books*, commenting that it "succeeds in being amusing and ambitious at the same time. It can be regarded as a philosophical novel masked as a detective story, or as a detective story masked as a historical novel, or even better as a blend of all three" (Ellman, p. 11).

—Martin Griffin

For More Information

Barber, Richard. *The Penguin Guide to Medieval Europe.* Harmondsworth, Middlesex: Penguin Books, 1984.

Brundage, James A. "Sin, Crime, and the Pleasures of the Flesh: The Medieval Church Judges Sexual Offenses." In *The Medieval World.* Eds. Peter Linehan and Janet L. Nelson. New York: Routledge, 2001.

Coletti, Theresa. *Naming the Rose: Eco, Medieval Signs, and Modern Theory.* Ithaca, N.Y.: Cornell University Press, 1988.

Eco, Umberto. *The Name of the Rose.* Trans. William Weaver. San Diego: Harcourt Brace, 1994.

————, Richard Rorty, Jonathan Culler, and Christine Brooke-Rose. *Interpretation and Over-interpretation.* Cambridge: Cambridge University Press, 1992.

Ellman, Richard. Review of *The Name of the Rose,* by Umberto Eco. *New York Review of Books*, July 21, 1983, 11.

Haft, Adele J., Jane G. White, and Robert J. White. *The Key to* The Name of the Rose, *Including Translations of All Non-English Passages.* Harrington Park, N.J.: Ampersand, 1987.

Hollister, C. Warren. *Medieval Europe: A Short History.* New York: John Wiley & Sons, 1974.

"J. S." Review of *The Name of the Rose,* by Umberto Eco. *Harper's,* August 1983, 76.

Ozment, Steven. *The Age of Reform, 1250-1550: An Intellectual and Religious History of Late Medieval and Reformation Europe.* New Haven, Conn.: Yale University Press, 1980.

Swanson, R. N. *Religion and Devotion in Europe, c. 1215–c. 1515.* Cambridge: Cambridge University Press, 1995.

Wagner-Pacifici, Robin Erica. *The Moro Morality Play: Terrorism as Social Drama.* Chicago: University of Chicago Press, 1986.

The New Science of Giambattista Vico

by

Giambattista Vico

Giovanni Battista Vico (1668-1744), generally called Giambattista, was born in Naples, Italy, where he lived nearly all his life. His early education was unremarkable, but later, while working as a tutor, the young Vico spent a decade poring over classical literature, philosophy, and law, as well as Italian literature. In 1699 he married an uneducated friend from childhood named Teresa Destito, with whom he would have eight children. That same year, Vico was appointed professor of rhetoric at the University of Naples. Plagued always by poverty, he suffered his greatest disappointment in 1723, when he failed to secure advancement to a higher-paying job as law professor at the same university. Yet his professional frustration pushed him to begin composing the work now recognized as his masterpiece, the *New Science*. Vico traces this process in his *Autobiografia* (1725-28; Autobiography), a memoir of his intellectual development written just after the original *New Science* was published. Vico had earlier written *De antiquissima italorum sapientia* (1710; On the Most Ancient Wisdom of the Italians) and *De universi iuris uno principio et fine uno liber unus* (1720; On the One Principle and One End of Universal Law). In such works, he began to develop the ideas that would find their fullest expression in the *New Science*. These ideas emerged out of—and partly in reaction to—the scientific and philosophical revolution that permanently reshaped European thought at the beginning of the sixteenth century.

THE LITERARY WORK

An essay written in Italy in the 1720s to 1740s; revised and published in Italian (as *Principi di Scienza Nuova di Giambattista Vico d'Intorno alla Comune Natura delle Nazioni*) in 1744; in English in part in 1834, in full in 1948.

SYNOPSIS

A wide-ranging philosophical inquiry into the characteristics of history, Vico's essay follows in the wake of the scientific revolution. The essay argues that since humans make their past but do not make nature (the subject of science), history is ultimately more knowable than science.

Events in History at the Time of the Essay

Galileo, Newton, and the birth of modern science. In the first half of the sixteenth century, the Polish astronomer Nicolaus Copernicus (1473-1543) opened the door to modern science by suggesting that the earth revolves around the sun. In reviving this idea (introduced much earlier by ancient Greek scientists), Copernicus opposed the earth-centered picture of the universe long proclaimed by European religious authorities. Copernicus's theory found observational support in the pioneering work of Italian astronomer Galileo Galilei (1564-1642), who in

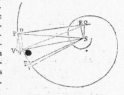

Page from *Philosphiae Naturalis Principia
Mathematica,* 1687, by Sir Isaac Newton.

1609 became the first to use the recently invented telescope to examine stars and planets in the night sky. Galileo also carried out the systematic investigations into the physics of falling objects that have won him recognition as the father of experimental physics.

After a century of intense activity by a number of scientists in various European countries, the scientific revolution begun by Copernicus and Galileo culminated during Vico's lifetime in the genius of the English physicist Isaac Newton (1642-1727). In 1687, when Vico was not yet twenty, Newton published his findings in a book, the *Philosophiae Naturalis Principia Mathematica* (Mathematical Principles of Natural Philosophy), usually called the *Principia.* By common consent the most influential scientific work ever published, the *Principia* lays out in precise mathematical detail the far-reaching discoveries Newton had made over several decades. Newton's great insight was that one of the forces that governs the movements of all physical bodies, big or small—from distant planets to falling objects on earth—is gravity. His laws of gravitation and motion explained the workings of the Copernican solar system by subjecting the orbits of the planets to mathematical analysis, and also explained Galileo's experimental observations with falling objects.

To express his findings, Newton invented a new mathematical language, the calculus, which could describe moving bodies such as planets or falling objects. Around the same time, the calculus was independently invented by German mathematician and philosopher Gottfried von Leibniz (1646-1716), who used a superior system of notation. Vico's *New Science* acknowledges the power of the advances made by Newton and Leibniz, referring to them as "the two foremost minds of our age" (Vico, *New Science,* p. 104).

Rationalism and empiricism in Enlightenment thought. In the seventeenth century, science still belonged to the larger discipline of philosophy. What we call science today went under the name "natural philosophy," which is how Newton used the phrase in the title of his great work. Earlier natural philosophers had already drawn attention to the deep connection between that discipline and mathematics. A half-century before Newton's work, for example, the French philosopher and mathematician René Descartes (1596-1650) published his *Discourse on Method* (1637). In this seminal work, Descartes argued that mathematics was the purest form of reason, that reason was the sole path to certain knowledge, and that such knowledge could only occur in philosophy. Accordingly, Descartes disparaged the study of history, as lacking the degree of verifiability necessary to be included among the branches of knowledge.

Taken together with the astonishing discoveries of the scientists, Descartes' ideas ultimately helped spark a reverence for the power of reason that dominated European culture in the eighteenth century, a period that soon came to be called the Enlightenment (otherwise known as the Age of Reason). At the beginning of the Enlightenment—often said to extend from the publication of Newton's *Principia* in 1687 to the French Revolution in 1789—Vico was a young man in Naples. Like others he spent time conversing about intellectual and cultural matters in the city's lively salons, where groups discussed the newest ideas. As he relates in the *Autobiography,* he discussed Descartes with his friends, and like most of them he began his intellectual life accepting the French philosopher's ideas.

By the end of the first decade of the eighteenth century, however, Vico had changed his earlier opinion. While he continued to accept that mathematics offered knowable truth, he did so not because he thought that this truth was unchanging and external to humanity (as Descartes did). Instead, Vico saw mathematics as a human creation, and so as knowable by humans. Vico likewise rejected Descartes' disparagement of history, arguing that history too is a human creation and therefore knowable to humans.

The idea that something can be fully understood only by its creator has been traced as far back as the fifth-century theologian St. Augustine. Vico seized on this concept, which in his book *On the Most Ancient Wisdom of the Italians* (1710), he expressed in Latin as *verum et factum reciprocantur* ("the true and the made are interchangeable"). Around this central idea, often called the *verum/factum* principle, Vico would spend the rest of his life carefully assembling his case in history's defense. That long effort resulted in the *New Science*, which can be seen, essentially, as Vico's impassioned answer to Descartes.

However, Vico was not the first to reject Cartesian rationalism, as Descartes' approach is called. Even before Descartes' works appeared, other philosophers had laid the foundations of an opposing position. In claiming reason as the sole path to knowledge, Descartes had insisted that all real knowledge can be attained by reason alone, without the aid of experience. A contrary argument, that true knowledge about the world springs primarily from actual experience of it, had already been articulated by the English philosopher Francis Bacon (1561-1626). Called *empiricism* (from the Greek word for "experience"), this tradition admitted an important role for reason but also stressed the value of observation and experiments in establishing scientific truths.

Bacon insisted that scientists must observe details before using reason to form general theories, a method he called induction (in contrast to deduction, making conclusions about details based on general theories). Isaac Newton subscribed to Bacon's ideas, as did his friend, the English philosopher John Locke (1632-1704), who elaborated his own influential interpretation of empiricism in his widely read *An Essay Concerning Human Understanding* (1690). Supported by such weighty figures, Bacon's approach also influenced other Enlightenment thinkers and acted to counterbalance Descartes' extreme rationalism. While rejecting Locke's version of empiricism, Vico exalted Bacon as one of his venerated "four authors." In the *New Science* he calls Bacon's inductive technique "the best ascertained method of philosophizing" (*New Science*, p. 67).

Changing views of history. Vico was not the first to defend the study of history against the hostile claims of rationalist thinkers such as Descartes. Indeed, one such defender was none other than Gottfried von Leibniz, himself an eminent rationalist, who worked in his later years as historian of the princely German house of Hanover. Leibniz's rationalistic approach to the study of history reflected a widespread attempt, starting in the seventeenth century, to legitimize it by making it more "scientific." This desire led to significant improvements in historical method, as historians, like scientists, grew convinced that their discipline should be governed by rational rules and principles designed to foster a critical spirit. For example, the French ecclesiastical historian Sébastien de Tillemont (1637-98) strove openly for a new objectivity, critically weighing the major sources from each period in his magisterial accounts of early Christianity and the Roman Empire.

NAPLES AND EPICUREANISM

During Vico's lifetime, the Kingdom of Naples was ruled first by the Spanish branch of the House of Habsburg (to 1707), then by the Austrian branch (to 1734), and then by an offshoot of the Spanish branch under Charles, son of Philip V of Bourbon. A 1738 peace treaty recognized Charles, who had driven out the Austrians, as king of a sovereign Naples. Pleased to be independent again, the kingdom enjoyed a vibrant, cultural atmosphere, invigorated by an unusual number of libraries, academies, and learned salons, or discussion centers. Some 40 bookstores graced the short Via di Biagio dei Libri, including a small store owned by Vico's father, a poor bookseller. Vico was born in the store's single room, where the family also lived.

Since ancient times, Naples had been known as a center of Epicureanism, an ancient Greek philosophy whose adherents upheld (among other ideas) the atomistic theory of matter, which held that the universe is made up of simple unchanging particles too small to be seen. Another common view of the Epicureans was that primitive humans lived in fear of nature and of the gods. In the seventeenth century, several leading Epicurean philosophers founded the well-known Academy of the Investigators in Naples, modeling it on such recently established scientific institutions as Britain's Royal Society and France's Academy of the Sciences. Espoused by other influential thinkers, like French scientist Pierre Gassendi (1592-1655), Epicureanism played a major role in shaping European intellectual attitudes of the eighteenth century, including Vico's.

This critical, rationalist spirit has continued to shape the writing of history up to the present day. In Vico's own day, it was represented most notably by the French author Voltaire (1694-1778; François Marie-Arouet), often called the Enlightenment's leading spirit. After making his reputation as a poet, Voltaire turned to history with his book *A History of Charles XII* (1731), showing how the Swedish king's militaristic arrogance had led to tragedy and ruin for his country. In the decades after Vico's death, the rationalistic tradition would be carried on by the greatest of Enlightenment historians, the English scholar Edward Gibbon (1737-94), who relied extensively on de Tillemont in researching his own masterpiece, *The Decline and Fall of the Roman Empire* (1776-88).

SKEPTICISM, SECULARISM, AND VICO'S PROVIDENCE

Having used reason to overturn the Church's view of the universe, the scientific revolution and the Enlightenment ushered in a new age of skeptical, secular values among European thinkers. Descartes' attack on history was reinforced during Vico's lifetime by the works of such philosophers as Pierre Bayle (1647-1706), whose radical skepticism towards historical sources cast further doubt on the very possibility of historical knowledge. Like many Enlightenment thinkers, Bayle was also a religious skeptic. In writings like his *Critical and Historical Dictionary* (1697), Bayle satirically attacked Christian dogma and popular superstition along with unfounded historical beliefs. Vico mentions Bayle twice in the *New Science*, both times to denounce Bayle for suggesting that human societies can exist without religion. A devout Catholic in a strongly Catholic society, Vico rejected the secular outlook, giving a central place to divine providence in the unfolding of history that he schematizes in the *New Science*.

These Enlightenment historians and many others who followed have shared a number of assumptions and values:

- They have tended to see human nature as unchanging and constant, assuming that people in one age and culture share the same basic values and attitudes of people in another.
- They have generally accepted the existence of certain absolute, timeless truths in areas like morality, politics, and culture, assuming that

reason is the best way of recognizing those truths.

- They often write history in such a way as to illustrate those truths, as a moralizing lesson in the proper conduct of human affairs.
- Accordingly, historians of this dominant tradition have frequently projected their own cultural attitudes onto the past. The historians have promoted values common to Enlightenment thought—secularism, tolerance, freedom, and learning—and placed them in opposition to religion, intolerance, fanaticism, and obscurantism.

In the *New Science*, Vico rejects the assumptions behind this approach to history. Just as importantly, he also rejects the historians' projection of their own rationalistic values onto the past (though not necessarily rejecting the values themselves). Far from merely trying to turn history *into* a science that reflects the rationalistic assumptions and values on which science is based, Vico aims instead to create an entirely new kind of discipline to stand *alongside* science. While incorporating some useful elements of the scientific method, Vico's "new science" will uphold assumptions and values all its own, ones based on imagination as much as reason.

The Essay in Focus

Contents summary. The five books of the *New Science* are titled as follows: "Book One: Establishment of Principles," "Book Two: Poetic Wisdom," "Book Three: Discovery of the True Homer," "Book Four: The Course the Nations Run," and "Book Five: The Recourse of Human Institutions Which the Nations Take When They Rise Again." An engraved allegorical frontispiece depicts Vico's main concepts in graphic form.

An introduction, "The Idea of the Work," explains the frontispiece in detail, then gives a summary of the book's thesis. By "studying the common nature of nations in the light of divine providence," Vico will uncover "the origins of divine and human institutions" and lay out a system to explain "the natural law" of human society (*New Science*, p. 20). According to Vico's system, after an initial stage of bestial savagery, civilizations pass through "three periods" of development:

- An "age of gods," in which people are dominated by religion and the fear of the supernatural
- An "age of heroes," in which societies divide themselves into "patricians" (ruling aristocrats) and "plebs" (lower-class subjects)

- An "age of men," in which emerging political equality helps give rise to "popular commonwealths" and "monarchies"

(*New Science*, p. 20)

The rest of the essay is devoted to filling out the background and details of this basic picture.

Book One introduces the assumptions and methods that will shape the ideas presented later. Vico begins with a complex "Chronological Table" of history, outlining "the world of the ancient nations" (as Vico sees it) with a separate column for each: Hebrews, Chaldeans, Scythians, Phoenicians, Egyptians, Greeks, and Romans (*New Science*, p. 29). Vico discusses each in turn. In the next section, Vico offers 114 "axioms," brief propositions whose truth he will assume as a given in his later arguments. (Here Vico is inspired by mathematics, which proceeds on the assumption of axiomatic propositions.)

Vico divides his axioms into two categories, general and particular. The general axioms (the first 22 axioms) comprise broad principles to be followed in the study of history. They define characteristics of humanity that Vico believes persist across time, and that many or most cultures have in common. Often cryptic and vague (like much of Vico's writing), they nevertheless contain many of his key ideas.

- **Number 2:** "Whenever men can form no idea of distant and unknown things, they judge them by what is familiar and at hand" (*New Science*, p. 60). Vico explains, for example, that historians in advanced cultures can mistakenly attribute to less advanced cultures the institutions and attributes of their own culture.
- **Number 3** ("the conceit of nations"): "Every nation . . . has had the same conceit that it before all other nations invented the comforts of human life and its remembered history goes back to the very beginning of the world" (*New Science*, p. 61). Every culture tends to glorify its own achievements and to hold its origins as uniquely ancient.
- **Number 4** ("the conceit of scholars"): "To this conceit of nations is added that of scholars, who will have it that what they know is as old as the world" (*New Science*, p. 61). Knowledge of the past is not an ever-dwindling body of traditions that either get passed on in an unbroken chain or lost forever, but something that can be discovered and increased through scholarly work.
- **Number 10:** "Philosophy contemplates reason, whence comes knowledge of the true; philology observes that of which

human choice is the author, whence comes consciousness of the certain" (*New Science*, p. 63). Certainty for Vico refers to a psychological state rather than to external reality. It comes from "authority," such as divine revelation or human testimony, which results in consciousness (*conscienza*) of certainty. By contrast, knowledge (or *scienza*) of truth, comes from reason (as applied to experience, Vico might have said, in agreement with Francis Bacon). By marrying philosophy with philology, Vico hopes to join *scienza* of the true with *conscienza* of the certain.

- **Number 13:** "Uniform ideas originating among entire peoples unknown to each other must have a common ground of truth" (*New Science*, p. 63). In explaining this axiom, Vico refers to "the natural laws of the gentes [peoples]," another important idea that comes up frequently in the *New Science*. This "natural law" amounts to the moral impulse common to humanity, as contrasted with the often sharply differing manmade laws ("laws of nations") found in various cultures. Historians had tried to trace ideas like "natural law" to one original parent culture from which they then spread to other cultures, but Vico argues that such ideas often originate separately among cultures that have no connection with one another.

- **Number 22:** "There must in the nature of human institutions be a mental language common to all nations . . ." (*New Science*, p. 67). To illustrate this "mental language," Vico states that many proverbs with identical messages exist in different forms in different languages.

Most of the remaining axioms are specific to particular cultures and types of cultures, though with characteristic inconsistency Vico includes some broader axioms (such as Number 36) with this latter group.

- **Number 24:** "The Hebrew nation was founded by the true God on the prohibition of the divination on which all the gentile nations arose" (*New Science*, p. 68).

- **Number 36:** "Imagination is more robust in proportion as reasoning power is weak" (*New Science*, p. 71).

- **Number 88:** "The aristocratic commonwealths keep the wealth within the order of the nobility, for wealth adds to the power of this order" (*New Science*, p. 83).

Two brief sections round off Book One. In the first, titled "Principles," Vico articulates the essay's central idea, the *verum/factum* principle:

> But in the night of thick darkness enveloping the earliest antiquity, so remote from ourselves, there shines the eternal and never failing light of a truth beyond all question: that the world of civil society has certainly been made by men, and that its principles are therefore to be found within the modifications of our own human mind.
>
> (*New Science*, p. 96)

These principles can further be found, he states, by seeing "what institutions all men agree and always have agreed" upon (*New Science*, p. 97). There are three such institutions, he says: religion, marriage, and solemn burial of the dead. These three institutions are thus Vico's "first three principles," and he identifies them as having originally lifted humanity from its "bestial" state (*New Science*, p. 97). In other words, for Vico the institutions of religion, marriage, and burial comprise a minimal definition of what it means to be human.

In the final section of Book One, titled "Method," Vico stresses the need for a monumental effort of imagination in recovering the past, which he says seems almost as remote from our understanding as the future. In each of the three sorts of ages, as well as in various cultures, people have thought and acted in ways that have dif-

fered sharply. Therefore, we cannot assume that people in the past acted or thought as we do. Only by applying our imaginations will we be able properly to use the best methods we have of entering the thinking of another age or culture. Those methods combine a variety of sources: "philosophic proofs" like legal history and theology, along with "philological proofs" like mythology, heroic verse, and etymology (*New Science*, p. 105).

Book Two ("Poetic Wisdom") comprises a long, difficult, and extremely detailed account of the first, religious stage of development that Vico believes all nations pass through after emerging from a primitive state. He calls it "poetic" because "the wisdom of the ancients was that of the theological poets, who without doubt were the first sages of the gentile world" (*New Science*, p. 112). Hence, the overall goal of Book Two is to "show clearly and distinctly how the founders of gentile humanity imagined the gods" (*New Science*, p. 112). (Vico holds Jewish history apart from the rest of humanity, as having been founded by direct divine intervention.) Vico traces the origins of primitive religions to "poetic metaphysics," arguing that these early religions were first sparked by the irrational fears that dominated early humanity's outlook (*New Science*, p. 116). Making frequent reference to Roman, Greek, and European history, Vico then goes on to describe at length the "poetic" languages, morals, economies, politics, physics, cosmography, astronomy, chronology, and finally geography that arose afterward.

Book Three ("Discovery of the True Homer") amounts to a sustained historical analysis of the *Iliad* and the *Odyssey*, the two epic poems conventionally ascribed to the ancient Greek poet Homer (c. 750 B.C.E.). Vico argues that, rather than being the creation of a single author, these heroic poems were in fact the accumulated results of generations of Greek poets working within a single tradition. As one leading Vico scholar suggests, Vico appears to include this discussion "primarily as a demonstration of the proper use of a body of historical evidence" in interpreting history (Pompa, *Vico: A Study of the "New Science,"* pp. 5-6).

Only in Book Four ("The Course the Nations Run") does Vico turn to the task of elaborating the "three periods" of human social development (age of gods, age of heroes, age of men) that he sketched in the introduction. Each of these periods is accompanied by its own distinctive outlook, and most of Book Four is devoted to breaking those outlooks down into specific ar-

Statue of Clio, the Muse of History.

eas. Accordingly, section headings cover "Three Kinds of Natures," "Three Kinds of Customs," and so on, including Natural Law, Governments, Languages, Characters (written symbols or letters), Jurisprudence (civil law), Authority, Reason, Judgments (criminal law), and Sects of Times (the general temper of the times). All of these triads, however, are "embraced by one general unity. This is the unity of the religion of a provident divinity, which is the unity of spirit that informs and gives life to this world of nations" (*New Science*, p. 335).

Among these triads are the three kinds of language that go with the three periods. For example, in the first period, the age of the gods, people used mute signs, which Vico calls a "divine mental language," since humanity "did not yet possess articulate speech" (*New Science*, p. 340). During the age of heroes, speech was poetic and militaristic. Articulate popular speech did not develop until the third age, the age of men. Governments, too, have evolved along similar lines, from theocracies (rule by priests), to aristocracies, to "human governments," which include both monarchies and popular commonwealths, and in which "all are accounted equal under the laws" (*New Science*, p. 339).

Book Five ("The Recourse of Human Institutions Which the Nations Take When They Rise Again") is relatively brief, but elaborates an important dimension of the schematic vision Vico has laid out so far. This is the concept of "recourse" (*ricorso* in Italian), by which the cycle of evolution is repeated over time. For example, after the ancient world went through its three stages, a new barbarism descended on Europe during the "Dark Age." Out of this evolved a new Christian religious age, a new feudal heroic age, and finally (beginning with the Renaissance) the modern human age of European civilization. Eventually this age too will decline, Vico suggests, and the cycle will start all over again. Finally, the conclusion restates the main points of the essay, closing with the assertion "that this Science carries inseparably with it the study of piety, and that he who is not pious is not truly wise" (*New Science*, p. 426).

Vico's use of etymology. In keeping with his emphasis on the importance of language, throughout the *New Science* (as in his earlier works) Vico uses etymology, or the study of word origins, to make historical points. Take, for example, the axiom, "The order of ideas must follow the order of institutions."

> This was the order of human institutions: first the forests, after that the huts, then the villages, next the cities, and finally the academies.
>
> (*New Science*, p. 78)

Vico goes on to give the Latin word for "law," *lex.* Like nearly all words in Latin, Vico asserts, its origins have to do with forests or countryside: originally, it must have meant a collection of acorns, since the Latin for "oak" is *ilex*, a similar word. From there *lex* came to mean "a collection of vegetables," hence the word *legumina*, a type of vegetable. "Finally, collecting letters, and mak-

ing, as it were, a sheaf of them for each word, was called *legere*, reading" (*New Science*, p. 78).

These connections are mostly wrong. In fact, despite his wide knowledge of Greek and Latin, most (though not all) of the word origins Vico proposes are incorrect. *Lex,* for example, has nothing to do with either *ilex* or *legumina*, although it is perhaps related to *legere* (modern authorities disagree on that point). Yet Vico correctly identifies the root of *legere* (to read) as meaning "to collect." Moreover, modern linguists see this same root in another word that originally meant "a thing that is collected," *lignum*, which is the Latin word for "wood" (as in "firewood"). So Vico appears to have been on the right track, even if he got most of the details wrong.

The practice of etymology goes back to the ancient Greeks (who were also usually wrong about word origins), and was popular among classically trained scholars of Vico's day. However, not until the nineteenth century did linguistic studies advance sufficiently for scholars to accurately make the sorts of connections between words that Vico attempts.

Yet, whether correct or incorrect, Vico's etymologies serve to underscore many of his key ideas, revealing in the process much about the steps he takes to arrive at those ideas. Other etymologies Vico proposes include *familia* (family) as being from *famuli* (servants)—this is correct; Greek *polemos* (war) as being from Greek *polis* (city)—this is incorrect; and *mutus* (mute) as being related to the Greek *mythos* (myth)—this is incorrect. In most cases Vico uses etymology to illustrate the basic idea he espouses in the axioms quoted above: that word histories reflect cultural evolution, and generally proceed from the concrete and commonplace to the abstract. Again, although Vico gets the details mostly wrong, modern scholars would agree with that idea. In this, Vico's etymological speculations resemble his work as a whole, which modern scholars have found to be remarkably insightful in its overall thrust, if often mistaken in detail.

Sources and literary context. The full title of Vico's work unmistakably echoes three great works of the scientific revolution: Bacon's *New Organon* (1620), Galileo's *Dialogues Concerning the Two New Sciences* (1638), and Newton's *Principia* (1687). Such scientific models aside, Vico used an extraordinarily wide variety of sources in composing the *New Science*, including ancient Greek and Roman authorities, Renaissance humanists, and Enlightenment thinkers. Many of these sources are clear, often because Vico mentions them by name either in the *New Science* itself or in his *Autobiography*. Others are less clear, and tracing them has occupied generations of scholars.

Vico's many Greek and Roman sources include the Greek epic poet Homer, the fourth century B.C.E. Greek philosopher Plato (the first of Vico's "four authors"), the weighty philosophical traditions known as Stoicism and Epicureanism, and the Latin writers Varro (116-27 B.C.E.), Lucretius (c. 94-55 B.C.E.), and Tacitus (c. 56-120 C.E., the second of Vico's "four authors"). From Varro, to whom Vico frequently refers, came the idea that history could be divided into three ages, those of the gods, of heroes, and of men, which by Vico's time was a literary commonplace. (Vico follows Varro in tracing this idea back to the ancient Egyptians.) From Lucretius, whose poem *On the Nature of Things* put Epicurean philosophy into darkly powerful epic verse, came a view of early humanity as bestial, savage, and dominated by fear of nature and of the gods. Lucretius was thought to have lived and taught in Naples. His poem, recently translated into Italian, was widely read and discussed by young intellectuals in the 1680s and 1690s, when Vico was a young man.

Closer to Vico's own time were the humanists, historians, philosophers, scientists, and legal scholars whose ideas he incorporated into his theories or reacted against. The last of Vico's "four authors," the Dutch legal scholar Hugo Grotius (1583-1645), had shown Vico how philosophy and philology could be united. Yet Vico ultimately rejected the belief of Grotius and others that nations were bound by "natural law," which was conceived as a rational, eternal, and overriding human nature. These natural-law theorists portrayed primitive peoples as entering into the sorts of sophisticated civil contracts discussed by recent European philosophers, an idea that Vico ridiculed. On the other hand, he developed a picture of primitive society that owed much to one of the natural-law theorists, the English philosopher Thomas Hobbes (1588-1679). In *Leviathan* (1651) and other writings Hobbes had portrayed such peoples as plagued by violence, savagery, and despair. Hobbes's fearful, irrational primitives, however, were afraid of each other, whereas Vico's—like those of Lucretius—were afraid of nature and of the gods (whom they saw in the awesome forces of nature).

Determining the origin of Vico's central idea, the *verum/factum* principle, has proved especially intriguing for Vico scholars. St. Augustine and later medieval writers had suggested that mak-

ing something can help one understand it better and that God has a privileged understanding of nature because He created it. This is different, however, from saying that only if one makes (or does) something can one truly understand it. The modern Italian philosopher Benedetto Croce (1866-1952), a major proponent of Vico's ideas in the twentieth century, traced that thought to the Spanish writer Francisco Sánchez (1523-1601), whom Vico is known to have read but who stated it quite casually. Other sources of inspiration have been suggested (including Thomas Hobbes), but it seems clear that Vico's emphasis on the importance of the *verum/factum* principle (if not the principle itself) was original to him.

VICO'S FOUR AUTHORS

In both the *Autobiography* and the *New Science*, Vico repeatedly mentions the "four authors whom he admired above all others":

- **Plato** (fifth-fourth century B.C.E), the Greek philosopher who Vico says contemplates "man as he should be"
- **Tacitus** (56-120 C.E.), the Roman historian who Vico says "contemplates man as he is"
- **Francis Bacon** (1561-1626), the English philosopher who Vico says "did justice to all the sciences"
- **Hugo Grotius** (1583-1645), the Dutch legal scholar who founded modern international law, and who Vico says "embraces in a system of universal law the whole of philosophy and philology" (Vico, *Autobiography*, pp. 138-39; 155)

Publication and impact. The first edition of the *New Science* was published in 1725, the second in 1730, and the third in 1744, just after Vico's death on the night of January 22 of that year. The second edition reflected significant alterations and expansion on the first, and Vico declared himself finally satisfied with the third *New Science*. While Vico's reputation was substantial both during and after his lifetime in Italy, outside of his own country, the *New Science* and its author were largely ignored until the nineteenth century. Within Italy itself, the *New Science* joined an already existing controversy over the idea that early humanity was primitive and wild, which countered Catholic doctrine. Supporting Vico's portrayal were the *ferini* (or "wilders") and against it were the *antiferini* ("antiwilders"). The controversy came to a head after Vico's death, between 1760 and 1780.

Vico's attempt to elevate imagination to a central role in the study of history kept him out of the mainstream of the rationalist thinking that prevailed in the years after his death. With the rise of the antirationalist Romantic movement at the end of the eighteenth century, the *New Science* was praised in passing by a few European thinkers, most notably the German Romantic poet Johann Wolfgang von Goethe (1749-1832). Given the book as if it were "a sacred treasure" when he visited Naples in 1787, Goethe found that it held prophecies "of the good and just that would or should hereafter be realized, based on serious contemplation of life and tradition" (Goethe in Vico, *Autobiography*, p. 68). Another German, the historian Johann Gottfried von Herder (1744-1803), already knew of Vico when he visited Naples two years later. It remains unclear whether Herder actually read the *New Science* before forming his own very similar ideas, but his works (e.g., *Ideas Toward the Philosophy of the History of Mankind*, 1784-87) would be decisive in the growing call for historians to use their imaginative powers in trying to grasp other civilizations.

Indeed, it is to Vico that scholars now trace the idea that distinct civilizations and cultures have existed in history, each with its own set of values and attitudes. To Vico as well goes credit for first recognizing the need for imagination in attempting to enter what has been called the "thought world" of another culture. That Vico has been given credit for these ideas is due largely to the efforts of the influential nineteenth-century French historian Jules Michelet (1798-1874), whose French translation of the *New Science* (1827) and enthusiastic support of its ideas brought Vico into the European intellectual mainstream for the first time. Since then, the *New Science* has influenced widely diverse writers and thinkers, from German political theorist Karl Marx (1818-83), the founder of communism, to Irish writer James Joyce (1882-1941), whose masterpiece *Finnegans Wake* (1939) begins with a reference to Vico's idea of historical recourse. In addition to revolutionizing the study of history, Vico has also been seen as a precursor of modern fields such as anthropology, sociology, and ethnology.

—Colin Wells

For More Information

Berlin, Isaiah. *Against the Current: Essays in the History of Ideas*. New York: Viking, 1980.

Burke, Peter. *Vico*. New York: Oxford University Press, 1985.

Collingwood, R. G. *The Idea of History*. Oxford: Oxford University Press, 1946.

Manuel, Frank E. *The Eighteenth Century Confronts the Gods*. New York: Atheneum, 1967.

Pompa, Leon. *Vico: A Study of the "New Science."* Cambridge: Cambridge University Press, 1975.

————, ed. *Vico: Selected Writings*. Cambridge: Cambridge University Press, 1982.

Stone, Harold Samuel. *Vico's Cultural History: The Production and Transmission of Ideas in Naples, 1685-1750*. New York: E. J. Brill, 1997.

Tagliacozzo, Giorgio, and Hayden V. White, eds. *Giambattista Vico: An International Symposium*. Baltimore: Johns Hopkins University Press, 1969.

Tagliacozzo, Giorgio, and Donald Phillip Verene, eds. *Giambattista Vico's Science of Humanity*. Baltimore: Johns Hopkins University Press, 1976.

Vico, Giambattista. *The Autobiography of Giambattista Vico*. Trans. Max Harold Fisch and Thomas Goddard Bergin. Ithaca: Cornell University Press, 1944.

————. *The New Science of Giambattista Vico*. Trans. Thomas Goddard Bergin and Max Harold Fisch. Ithaca: Cornell University Press, 1948.

Orlando Furioso
(The Frenzy of Orlando)

by

Lodovico Ariosto

odovico Ariosto (1474-1533) was a minor nobleman and courtier in the northern Italian duchy of Ferrara. His family's fortunes were made by their connection to his distant cousin Lippa degli Ariosti, mistress of Obizzo III d'Este, Marquis of Ferrara, who on her deathbed became his wife. Her son Alberto (legitimated by his father) was the great-grandfather of Ercole I, Duke of Ferrara when Lodovico was born. Lodovico's own father, Count Niccolo, served in many high offices during the duke's reign, which made it possible for Lodovico to enjoy a carefree youth. Lodovico's greatest concern seems to have been persuading his father to let him abandon an apprenticeship in law for the university and a degree in the humanities. His father relented but then died suddenly, leaving his oldest son, 26-year-old Lodovico, to fend for his four younger brothers and five sisters. Becoming chief bread-winner for the family, Lodovico, like his father, sought employment as a retainer in the Este household, first for the old duke and later for his third son, Ippolito. Twenty years later Ippolito's older brother, who by then had inherited the title of Duke Alfonso, took Lodovico into his service. Lodovico was thus in the thick of the affairs of the Este brothers for most of his life. His intellectual soulmate, however, was their sister Isabella (also born in 1474), who encouraged him in his literary endeavours and advised him to take up an unfinished chivalric epic poem—*Orlando Innamorato* (Roland in Love)—begun by another Ferrarese courtier, Matteo Maria Boiardo. Boiardo had died in 1494, before completing the poem,

> ### THE LITERARY WORK
>
> A chivalric epic poem set in France, England, Spain, and the Middle East during the reign of the Frankish king Charlemagne (r. 768-814); published in Italian in 1516 (revised 1521; revised and expanded 1532), in English in 1591.
>
> ### SYNOPSIS
>
> Roland (Orlando, in Italian), greatest peer in the realm of Charlemagne, deserts his post while Arab Muslims besiege Paris to pursue his beloved, Princess Angelica of Cathay.

which wove together popular legends of France's most famous knight. Named Roland (in Italian, Orlando), his adventures were a favorite subject of the oral storytellers who wandered northern Italy. Heeding Isabella's advice, Lodovico Ariosto wrote a sequel called *Orlando Furioso*. The sequel links love to madness; exploring obsession and the resulting betrayal of political alliances and personal friendships. The poem takes place seven centuries before it was written yet raises issues of great relevance to the troubled times in which Ariosto lived.

Events in History at the Time the Poem Takes Place

The matter of Britain and the matter of France. In 604 C.E., Pope Gregory I ("the Great")

Lodovico Ariosto

died in Rome after a reign of nearly 14 years. A prolific author, the pope was also an inspiring leader to the Christian community in Europe (at a time when Christianity had not yet completely triumphed over paganism). After he died, however, intellectual activity in this region drastically diminished. Hardly any written documents were produced on the Continent for nearly 200 years, until the coming of Charlemagne, monarch of the Franks, the Germanic people whose territory embraced most of modern-day France and Germany. Charlemagne gathered a group of intellectuals around him in the Germanic town of Aachen in the 790s and there resulted a brief flowering of manuscripts, which by modern standards was small. And even that brief flowering would fade under Charlemagne's successors, as invasions from the east (by Magyars and Avars) and from the north (by Vikings) took their toll. Not until the late eleventh or early twelfth century, roughly around the time of the crusades, would medieval Europe see a resurgence in record-keeping. In one respect, this hiatus may have been beneficial: it would have allowed folk legends to flourish. Two important cycles of tales that may stem back to such origins dominated the literary landscape by the crusades.

The first cycle, commonly known as "the matter of Britain," concerns events at the court of King Arthur and his queen Guinevere, focusing especially on his knights, members of the order of the Round Table. The chief of these knights, Lancelot, falls in love with Guinevere despite his friendship with Arthur, and their adulterous love sets in motion a train of events that culminates in an apocalyptic battle between Arthur and his nephew (some sources say bastard son) Mordred, in which Mordred is killed. Arthur, also mortally wounded, is borne off to the otherworldly isle of Avalon, to await a summons from the British when they have need of him at some future date.

Certain features became characteristic of the Arthur stories. Subsidiary tales, including the romance of Tristan and Iseult, were attached to the main narrative. These tales often parallel the episode of Lancelot and Guinevere in recounting an adulterous love in which desire goes forever unfulfilled; the affair refines the lovers' characters as it leads to suffering and tragedy. Out of these arose a new concept of love, "courtly love," which thus became associated with the "matter of Britain." The stories also use magic as a major impetus for plot development. Arthur is raised by the wizard Merlin, and his half-sister Morgana is a witch who, in some versions, seduces Arthur and tricks him into siring Mordred, her son. Moreover, the setting is generally marvelous, full of objects and creatures that violate lifelike characterization and realistic plot development.

The Arthur tales were first recounted in detail by Geoffrey of Monmouth in his Latin chronicle *Historia Regum Britaniae* (History of the British Kings), composed in the 1130s, when the Crusades were transforming European society. Taken by many of Geoffrey's contemporaries as true and unvarnished history, this chronicle inspired a whole series of literary works produced in the twelfth century, mainly in French by the somewhat shadowy figure known as Chrétien de Troyes. His romances (so-called because they were produced in the vernacular Romance languages, not Latin) became enormously popular throughout Europe, especially in northern Italy, where French was highly regarded and widely used among the ruling classes. A century before Ariosto's day, in the early 1400s, the Este family of Ferrara (Ariosto's future patrons) owned a copy of Tristan and Iseult as well as other romances set down by various writers (Gundersheimer, p. 87).

Parallel to the "matter of Britain" in medieval histories was the "matter of France." Unlike the Arthurean material, the matter of France comprises tales woven around the court of Charlemagne, a verifiable historical personage, and the tales contain no magical elements. Charlemagne reigned over the Frankish kingdom for nearly half a century (742-814). His grandfather, Charles Martel, had established the dynasty, and during his tenure had blocked the Arab advance northward from Spain (which the Arabs had begun to conquer in 711 C.E.) through his victory at the Battle of Poitiers in southern France. The Arab troops in Spain were few and thinly spread so it is unlikely that they viewed this military defeat as very important—at least it does not appear in any of the major Arab chronicles of the period. But in French annals, it was magnified into a major victory. Its glory was reflected onto Charles Martel's grandson, Charlemagne, who became the champion of Christianity against Islam for later generations, especially for the crusaders of the late eleventh and twelfth centuries. This image of Charlemagne as the most Christian king was enhanced by his being crowned Holy Roman Emperor on Christmas Day 800 C.E. The reality, though, shows him to be less militantly Christian than legend suggests. According to a reliable biography by his friend and clerk Einhard—*Vita Caroli Magna*—we know Charlemagne mostly fought not Muslims but pagan enemies to the east (the Saxons and Avars) and rival Christian dynasties to the south (the Lombards and dukes of Aquitaine).

One incident early in the king's reign involved him in the political struggles of the Arabs in the Iberian Peninsula. In 750 a new Arab dynasty, the Abbasids, displaced the former rulers of the Islamic empire, the Umayyads. In the aftermath of their takeover, the Abbasids hunted down all male members of the Umayyad clan, killing them to consolidate Abbasid rule. One of the Umayyads, Abd al-Rahman, managed to escape westward to North Africa, where he rallied his kinsmen around him. Together they invaded Spain and defeated the small army of the newly installed Abbasid governor there, taking control of cities in the southern part of the land. But in the northeast, close to the border with France, there remained some adherents of the Abbasids. In 777, one of these, the governor of Barcelona, Sulayman ibn Yaqdhan al-A'rabi, petitioned the newly enthroned Charlemagne for help. Charlemagne agreed. His father had already started establishing friendly ties with the Abbasids as fellow enemies of his rivals to the east, the Byzantines. In brief, the Franks, the Pope (the strongest authority in Italian lands), and the Abbasids banded together against the Byzantines in the East and the Umayyads in Spain.

Having amassed a large army, Charlemagne advanced southward to join the Arab governor Sulayman in the siege of the Umayyad-held city of Saragossa in Spain. His alliance with the Arab governor collapsed, however, after a period of inconclusive fighting. Charlemagne had begun a retreat when the historical incident transpired in which his lieutenant Roland supposedly distinguished himself. At the pass of Roncesvalles in the Pyrenees Mountains, the rearguard of Charlemagne's army was ambushed by raiders of the Basques; a people of the Iberian peninsula, they reneged on an earlier promise to let Charlemagne's troops pass unmolested. Einhard recounts the incident:

> The lightness of their armor and the nature of the battle ground stood the Gascons [Basques] in good stead on this occasion, whereas the Franks fought at a disadvantage in every respect, because of the weight of their armor and the unevenness of the ground. Eggihard, the King's steward; Anselm, Count Palatine; and Roland, Governor of the March of Brittany, with very many others, fell in this engagement. This ill turn could not be avenged for the nonce, because the enemy scattered so widely after carrying out their plan that not the least clue could be had to their whereabouts.
>
> (Einhard, p. 34)

This is the sole mention of the otherwise unknown Count Roland in the historical records of Charlemagne's reign.

SARACENS, MOORS, AND TURKS

Ariosto, following his sources, frequently refers to Orlando's Arab enemies as Saracens, Moors, or Turks. These words reflect different historical phases in the encounters between the West and the Muslim world. *Saracen* is a term derived from the Greek "Sarakenoi," the name of a tribe whom the Greeks encountered on the Arabian peninsula in classical times. *Moor* stems back to the Latin geographical term *Mauretania,* which the Romans used for northwestern Africa. *Mauri* or *Moors* became the term for the inhabitants of this region, who were ethnically mostly Berbers. The term *Turks* reflects the political and military reality of Ariosto's own time, when the major force in the Islamic world was the Ottoman Empire, whose ruling dynasty traced their ancestry back to nomadic Turkish tribes.

In the 1120s, in the midst of the Crusades, a Latin chronicle surfaced that gave a vastly expanded account of the story of Roland. This chronicle was supposedly written by a bishop named Turpin of Rheims who had accompanied Charlemagne into Spain, fought in the ambush, and witnessed Roland's death. Because it was composed several hundred years after Turpin's death and thus was not written by him, it has become known to posterity as the "Pseudo-Turpin."

In the Pseudo-Turpin, Charlemagne is summoned in a dream to enter Spain to save the shrine of St. James of Compostela from the "Saracen menace" (Smyser, p. 18). He remains three years in Galicia and northern Spain winning victory after victory and pacifying the country. After his return to France, Charlemagne hears that the African king Aigolandus has invaded the recently liberated territory. So, supported by his second-in-command, Duke Milo de Angulariis, he re-enters Spain where he meets the African king in a series of inconclusive battles. In one of the battles, Roland, the son of Duke Milo and Charlemagne's sister Bertha, defeats the Arab giant Ferractus in single combat. As a result of this battle, and other engagements recounted in the Pseudo-Turpin, the Franks emerge victorious and "nobody dares challenge [Charlemagne's] power in Spain" (Smyser, p. 36). On the way back to France, Charlemagne hears that two Arab kings who have pledged loyalty to him plan to rebel. He sends Count Ganelon to the Arabs with the order that they must accept baptism or pay tribute. But, accepting a bribe, Ganelon betrays his sovereign. He reveals the return route of the Frankish army; they will retreat through the pass at Roncesvalles, guarded by a small contingent of France's greatest knights under the command of Roland. The Arab kings, with a huge army in tow, sweep down upon the rearguard and massacre them. Roland, who survives the initial attack, hunts down one of the Arab kings and kills him, but is "gravely wounded" in the process (Smyser, p. 41). Only then does he blow his great ivory horn, summoning Charlemagne and the main army to the rescue. Charlemagne prepares to respond but is dissuaded by the traitorous Ganelon (who in later versions is Roland's stepfather and harbors a grudge against him), who dismisses the sound: "Roland is always blowing his horn without cause and . . . is probably merely hunting" (Smyser, p. 41).

Finally Bishop Turpin brings King Charlemagne news of the ambush. By the time the king does retrace his route and rush to the rescue, however, he finds Roland dead. Swearing revenge, Charlemagne pursues the Arabs to Saragossa and kills 4,000. He then hears of Ganelon's treachery and orders him to submit to judgement in an or-

deal by combat, which he loses. Following standard practice, Ganelon's arms and legs are tied to four horses that run in the four directions of the compass and Ganelon is torn to pieces.

As with the matter of Britain, the historical account of Roland's death gave rise to dozens of literary works, mostly in French, and all using the same material. Generically these stories were called the *chansons de geste* ("songs of heroic deeds"). The most famous of these today, *Chanson de Roland* (Song of Roland), was actually not well known in the Middle Ages or the Renaissance, having been deposited in an English monastery in the late 1200s. It would not be rediscovered until the mid-nineteenth century; by this time around 60 other *chansons de geste* had been catalogued in old manuscripts by scholars. These 60 or so chansons had been widely disseminated throughout Europe, spreading along with French cultural influence (which penetrated into England, Italy, Germany, and more). Whether historical or literary, the various versions share a key feature—the transformation of the actual episode, which saw Charlemagne form an alliance with the Arab Abbasids and his deputy Roland suffer death at the hands of Basque (Christian) fighters. In every version, the facts are rejected in favor of a story that features a crusading zeal against Muslims, elevates the role of religious issues, and mistakenly identifies Roland's killers as Arabs rather than Basques.

The Italian Roland. The story of Roland entered Italy very early, through French literary versions as well as the Pseudo-Turpin, perhaps by the mid-1100s. The major additions to the story that Ariosto would have known appear in *I Reali di Francia* (The Nobles of France), a prose chronicle by the Florentine writer Andrea Da Barberino (c. 1370-1431/3) that provided Orlando with an Italian childhood. In Andrea's version, King Charlemagne's second-in-command, Duke Milo, seduces Bertha, the king's sister, after entering her quarters disguised as a woman. When Charlemagne discovers their affair and imprisons them, the couple escapes to Italy, where Roland is born in a stable (like Jesus) and grows up in complete poverty. He is reunited with his uncle when the latter comes to Italy to be crowned Holy Roman Emperor. Roland and his parents are reconciled to Charlemagne, and the four return as a family to France. Thus, in adapting the Matter of France into the Italian milieu, Italian writers saw Roland—or Orlando as he was known to them— as peculiarly their own, a home-grown hero, rather than an alien figure imported from afar.

The Poem in Focus

Contents overview. *Orlando Furioso* is divided into 46 cantos, whose action has been described as a "crisscrossing of [various] narratives" (Ascoli, p. 7). But the poem does in fact exhibit a core architecture, with certain sections, or cantos, marking important transition points in the narrative. In Canto 23, exactly halfway through the poem, Orlando descends into madness after his discovery that Angelica loves another. Halfway between the beginning of the work and Canto 23, in Canto 12, the crisis of 23 is foreshadowed when Angelica meets her new love, the Saracen youth Medoro, and suddenly disappears from the action. Likewise, halfway between Canto 23 and the poem's end, in Canto 34, the English knight Astolfo visits the moon by way of the Earthly Paradise, where he recovers Orlando's lost wits, and takes them back to earth in a glass flask. Once Orlando is restored to sanity, he and Astolfo collaborate against the armies of Agramant, the Saracen leader. In the final canto, 46, they and the entire royal court witness the wedding of Bradamant and Ruggerio (in Italian, Ruggiero), founders of the Este dynasty.

The poem in detail. The first canto catapults the reader into the middle of the historical action, the Saracen siege of Paris. In a few informative stanzas, Ariosto fills in the background of the story presented in the poem his work is continuing, the *Innamorato*. Ariosto's poem reunites the characters left scattered at the end of the former poem. Orlando triumphantly returns Angelica, the superlatively beautiful princess of the central Asian land of Cathay, back to Charlemagne's control. At the outset of the *Innamorato*, Angelica had challenged all the knights around Paris (both Christian and Saracen) to defeat her champion and thus obtain her favor. Her purpose had been to incite discord among the soldiers in both armies while her father's troops seized as much territory as possible. Her champion was finally defeated, after which she led the French knights on a merry chase all over Europe. In the *Furioso*, Angelica again escapes from Charlemagne's custody, and all the knights abandon their military duties to collaborate, if only temporarily, in pursuing the elusive princess. This allows the poem to introduce the major male characters and focus on them one by one.

Next the poem introduces two new storylines, interweaving their exposition with the pursuit of the Princess of Cathay. The first set of stories concerns Charlemagne's decision to send Rinaldo, Or-

lando's friend and sometime rival, to England (home of the Arthurian legends) to seek help from the knights there. Rinaldo quickly becomes embroiled in the affairs of various pairs of noble lovers at the English and Scottish courts. The second set of stories concerns Bradamant, the Christian female warrior who is Rinaldo's sister. When *Orlando Furioso* opens, Bradamant has already fallen in love with Ruggerio, a rising star of the Saracen armies, whose ancestry on one side of the family harks back to Hector of Troy. Once Bradamant and Ruggerio overcome the obstacles that separate them, they will marry and go on to found the House of Este, the family of Ariosto's patrons.

This amalgam of stories about Bradamant and Ruggerio, supplemented by Rinaldo's encounters, rather than the more straightforward account of the battles between the forces of Charlemagne and Agramant, monopolizes the first third or so of the *Orlando Furioso*. In fact, only in Canto 14 does the confrontation between the armies begin in earnest.

The first two cantos follow Bradamant as she searches steadfastly for Ruggerio, distinguishing herself as the only one able to remain impervious to Angelica's charms. Unlike the male warriors, distracted by losing their tempers—and control of their horses—as they pursue the princess, Bradamant (contrary to a Renaissance stereotype of the woman as overemotional) is able to singlemindedly pursue her quest. But Bradamant herself is eventually led astray by the deceitful knight Pinabello, nephew of Ganelon. After getting them both lost in the mountains, he pushes her down the hole leading to Merlin's cave in an effort to dispose of her (end of Canto 2).

Meanwhile, Charlemagne has decided to send Rinaldo to England for help. Ariosto's reporting on the progress of Rinaldo's mission becomes a vehicle for introducing several pairs of lovers whose adventures recall the pattern set by the heroes and heroines of Arthurian romances. The most important of these is probably Zerbino, Prince of Scotland, and Isabella, Princess of Galicia (in Spain), a chaste pair of lovers whose story—ending in their deaths at the hands of Saracen warriors—forms a kind of tragic counterpoint to the more fortunate fates of Orlando and Angelica and especially of Bradamant and Ruggerio.

Next, the first third of the *Orlando Furioso* turns to Bradamant's lover, Ruggerio, concentrating on his rescue from the clutches first of his tutor, the magician Atlas, and later of the powerful enchantress Alcina, who seduces Ruggerio with her dazzling beauty, just as she once bewitched

A depiction of the death of Roland. Axe in hand, Roland fights off the enemy.

the English knight Astolfo. Freed by Ruggerio, Astolfo learns to handle the hippogriff, a fantastical creature, half-horse, half-bird, on which he will ascend (in Canto 34) to the Earthly Paradise and, aided by the Apostle John, retrieve a flask containing Orlando's wits, that is, his ability to reason.

The last two-thirds of the poem (roughly Cantos 14-45) pays greater attention to the siege of Paris than the earlier cantos. The English troops have already arrived in France to aid Charlemagne (Canto 10), and now (in Canto 14) the Saracen warriors, Agramant and his allies, send south for reinforcements. These troop movements and maneuverings on the battlefield are intercut with Astolfo's adventures in the Eastern Mediterranean as he flies far and wide on the hippogriff, landing in Damascus, where he rescues the French knight Grifon from false imprisonment and in the process encounters Ruggerio's sister, the warrior maiden Marfisa, who is seeking to recover her lost armor. The group returns to France, where Ruggerio's beloved Bradamant, mistaking the reason for the affection between Ruggerio and Marfisa, becomes wildly jealous and even tries to kill herself, which she finds impossible to accomplish, since she is at the time wearing a coat of mail (Canto 32). She then seeks refuge at the castle of Lord Tristram, where the applicants for shelter must either (if they are male) defeat all the other knights present in sin-

gle combat, or (if they are female) triumph over all the other women in a contest of beauty. Bradamant succeeds in both categories and elects to be admitted to the castle because of her prowess in battle. Following these adventures, she seeks the Saracen camp, intending to challenge Ruggerio to a fight, hoping that this will soothe her suffering from his unfaithfulness to her. But, in the midst of their combat, the voice of Ruggerio's tutor (Atlas) is heard, rising from his tomb to explain the truth about Ruggerio and Marfisa, and the misunderstanding is resolved. Marfisa and Bradamant become fast friends and depart for Charlemagne's camp (where Marfisa is baptized a Christian), while Ruggerio remains behind in support of the Saracen leader Agramant.

The last third of the poem focuses ever more narrowly on uniting the Saracen warrior Ruggerio and the Christian warrior maiden Bradamant in their foreordained dynastic marriage, without which the Este family will not come into being. Now this storyline is linked to the resolution of the conflict between Agramant and Charlemagne: the former proposes deciding the issues between them by single combat, and Ruggerio is chosen as his champion, to be opposed by the French peer Rinaldo, brother of Bradamant. Once the duel begins, Ruggerio is reluctant to injure his beloved's brother, and Agramant, seeing his champion losing, is persuaded to launch a general attack, which is defeated. The Saracen armies flee, and Ruggerio stays behind to protect the rear, ending up lost at sea when his ship overturns (Canto 41). In exchange for his life, he promises God he will become a Christian and makes good on the promise when he lands on an island and is baptized by a hermit there. Orlando and Rinaldo, reunited and magically cured of their passion for Angelica, rescue Ruggerio from the island and he promises to wed Bradamant. Her father, Amon, however, has betrothed her to the Byzantine emperor Leon. Elected King of the Bulgars (which makes him worthy of Bradamant's hand), Ruggerio defeats Leon and his forces in battle. Amon nevertheless refuses to dissolve the engagement and Ruggerio decides to kill himself, whereupon Leon renounces Bradamant and the path is opened for the lovers to be married, which they prepare to do in Canto 46. At the last minute Rodomont, a formidable Saracen warrior, interrupts the wedding feast and challenges Ruggerio to single combat, accusing him of abandoning his oath of fealty to his king. They fight, and the poem ends as abruptly as it began, with Ruggerio stabbing his enemy fatally in the heart.

Dipping into Arabic story—Canto 28. The Italians, with their long history of contact and trade with other cultures, were sharply attuned to the idea that new lessons could be learned from foreigners, and Ariosto, in his choice of material for the *Orlando Furioso*, was no exception to this trend. We find his tolerance and open-mindedness illustrated in many places in the poem, but nowhere more pointedly than in his recounting of the story that serves as the focal point for Canto 28. The tale, about the affairs in a minor Italian princedom very like Ariosto's Ferrara, is in fact an adaptation of the frame tale of the Arabic classic *The Arabian Nights*.

In Canto 27 the Saracen warrior Rodomont is rejected by his beloved Doralice for his rival Mandricardo. This rejection causes Rodomont to complain bitterly of the faithlessness of women, and in a rage he gallops away from camp. Southeast of Paris, heading for the Marseille coast, he stops at an inn in the Saone River Valley. Here, the innkeeper tells him a story in support of Rodomont's new guiding principle "that chaste women were never to be found, whether poor or of rank; and if one seemed more chaste than another, it was because she was smarter in hiding herself" (Ariosto, *Orlando Furioso*, 27.132).

The story consists of three separate, mutually reinforcing episodes. Fausto, a knight at the court of Astolfo, king of the Lombards, boasts that his brother Jocondo is the most beautiful man in the world. The king, naturally curious (because he had considered himself unsurpassed in beauty) commands Fausto to bring his brother to court, where all might judge the truth of his claim. Jocondo is reluctant to leave his young and beautiful wife, who loves him dearly, but finally agrees to go. Upon his departure, his tearful wife unfastens the pilgrim's cross around her neck and gives it to him "to wear . . . for love of her, so that every hour he might remember her" (*Orlando Furioso*, 28.16). But in the excitement of departure Jocondo forgets the cross. When he returns home to retrieve it, he finds his wife in the arms of one of his own servants. Although he contemplates killing them both, he masters his impulse and rides off as fast as he can.

His torment leaves its traces on his face and form and naturally the king has difficulty accepting Fausto's claim that this wretch should be considered more beautiful than any other man, especially himself. Jocondo spends most of his time wandering alone through Astolfo's palace, lamenting. One day, while the men are out hunting, he spies the queen having intercourse with a dwarf. The king, it seems, is an even worse cuckold than he. Drawing strength from this new knowledge, Jocondo's health improves immeasurably, and his beauty begins to return. The king notices the change and asks Jocondo the cause. Jocondo, fearing to tell this powerful ruler the truth, makes Astolfo swear not to harm him and then reveals all.

These two episodes parallel almost exactly the frame-tale of the *The Arabian Nights*. There, the king Shahzaman decides to visit his older brother Shahriyar, ruler of the neighboring kingdom. On the eve of his departure, he leaves and then returns to finds his wife in their bedchamber, in the embrace of a kitchen boy. Enraged, he kills them both, unlike Jocondo. But like Jocondo, he begins to waste away from grief and humiliation once he arrives at his brother's palace. When Shahriyar goes out hunting one day, Shahzaman spies his brother's wife and all her ladies cavorting in the palace gardens with a platoon of black slaves. The sight causes an improvement in his health, but he fears to reveal the cause, and he exacts an oath from Shahriyar identical to that which Jocondo demanded from Astolfo.

Up to this point in the narrative, the major difference between the two stories consists in the fact that Ariosto, in the first episode, has given the faithless wife at least a symbolic motivation for her betrayal. The night before they parted, she gave Jocondo a cross that she said was an emblem of their love. Jocondo forgot the cross, just, one might say, as he forgot his obligations to his wife in order to seek rewards and a potential position at court. If he undervalues her in such a way, is it such a surprise that she, in turn, deserts him for another? The story can thus be interpreted in a way that is more charitable to women than the original *The Arabian Nights* frame tale. Certainly Ariosto's version belies the innkeeper's claim (echoing Rodomont's prejudice) that women are naturally disloyal and treacherous to those they love.

ADULTERY AND DEATH AMONG THE ESTE

Among members of the court assembled at Ferrara, the initial audience for the *Orlando Furioso*, the recitation of Canto 28 probably aroused an ominous undercurrent of anxiety. In the reign of Alfonso's grandfather, Niccolo, an eerily similar incident had occurred within the Este family. Niccolo, a widower, took a second wife much younger than himself, named Parisina. She was something of an intellectual, fond of romances like that of Tristan and Iseult. Parisina fell in love with Niccolo's eldest son, Ugo. When their adultery was exposed, Niccolo executed the two young lovers. Thus, in bringing up a tale that dealt with the issue of faithful wives, Ariosto did something very daring in reminding the Este family of an uncomfortable episode in the not-too-distant past.

Ariosto will maintain his more charitable stance in the third episode of his tale, which diverges considerably from *The Arabian Nights*. In the Arabic version, the two kings travel the world, searching for a man who can actually enforce the faithfulness of his consort. After a humiliating encounter with a woman imprisoned by a jinni, or demon, who forces them to have sex with her while the jinni sleeps next to them, they ultimately decide there is no way to keep a woman faithful. So Shahriyar, upon returning to his kingdom, decides to take a new wife every evening and execute her in the morning. He is only interrupted in this disastrous course when his chief minister's daughter, Shahrazad, volunteers to marry her lord and tricks him into keeping her alive by telling him a story whose conclusion she will only reveal the following night. For a thousand and one nights,

Shahrazad keeps up this stratagem, until Shahriyar realizes she has been faithful to him all along and he loves her, along with the children she has borne with him in the interim. Before this ending, however, the tale seems to bear out the supposition that no woman will be true to her lover.

Ariosto follows a different path in *Orlando Furioso*. King Astolfo and Jocondo likewise wander the world. Growing weary of this, they both fall in love with Fiametta, the daughter of an innkeeper in Valencia, and then coerce her father "to give his daughter into their power" for a handsome sum (*Orlando Furioso*, 28.53). Next they hit upon the stratagem of having her always sleep between them so she cannot be unfaithful. But, unbeknownst to them, Fiametta has long been in love with Greco, a servant of her father. Greco follows her, and they devise a plan whereby he crawls up from the foot of the bed and they make love, while Jocondo and Astolfo both think her partner is the other one of them. When the deception is discovered, the king decides immediately that Fiametta's faithfulness to her first love should be rewarded and gives her in marriage to Greco along with a handsome dowry. The story, unlike *The Arabian Nights*, features a woman so steadfast that under duress she refuses to abandon her soul mate. At the conclusion of the episode, Ariosto further reinforces the lesson by having an old man in the audience say "'Those who have left their husbands have in most cases reason for it'" (*Orlando Furioso*, 28.81).

Sources and literary context. The most important source for the *Orlando Furioso* seems obviously to be the poem it continues, Matteo Maria Boiardo's *Orlando Innamorato*. Yet critical opinion remains curiously divided on this. Clearly, it is helpful to know something of the plot from the earlier poem. But Ariosto's work quickly establishes an independent identity, and—as generations of readers have proved, since the *Innamorato* became a book rarely read after the mid-fifteenth century—it is not necessary to know the first poem to enjoy the second.

Ariosto's sources far exceed *Orlando Innamorato*. He drew on many other works produced in northern Italy in the years preceding his birth, from Latin treatises to Italian folktales, as recounted by the great nineteenth-century Italian scholar Pio Rajna in his monumental catalogue of Ariosto's sources, *Le Fonti dell'Orlando Furioso* (The Sources of the *Orlando*). Of all the inspirations for the *Furioso*, none is perhaps less obvious from a casual reading of it, or more important than Virgil's epic *The Aeneid*.

Both stories concern the founding of a dynasty and city: in Virgil's case of Rome and its Caesars; in Ariosto's case, of the Este family and Ferrara. Virgil had begun his poem by announcing he would sing of "arms and the man" (*Aeneid*, 1:1). The *Aeneid* contains 12 books that divide neatly into two halves with Aeneas's descent into the underworld marking the transition from Part 1 to Part 2. Ariosto's poem too divides neatly in half, when Orlando goes mad in Canto 23. Ariosto's female warrior Bradamant owes something to a female warrior in Virgil's poem, Camilla (who, in turn, has her antecedents in Homer's Amazon queen Penthesilea). Other examples of the *Aeneid*'s influence on the *Furioso* occur in nearly every canto.

Events in History at the Time the Poem Was Written

Age of invasions. In 1494, when Ariosto was 20, King Charles VIII of France invaded northern Italy, shattering nearly half a century of relative calm and growing prosperity in that part of the Italian peninsula. Though Charles only temporarily occupied Naples and quickly withdrew, the military weakness of the Italian city-states had been revealed and for the next 35 or 40 years, virtually until the end of Ariosto's life, northern Italy was rent by a series of wars, battles, and intrigues among the European powers that caused this period of Italian history to be known as the "Age of Invasions." Ariosto was himself deeply involved in many of these events. The most notable was probably in the summer of 1512, the year of the battle of Ravenna (described in Cantos 14 and 15 of the *Furioso*). After this battle, Ariosto helped Duke Alfonso escape in disguise from imprisonment by Pope Julius in Rome (where they had been, incidentally, viewing the newly completed frescoes by Michelangelo in the Sistine Chapel). Though a party to these intrigues, Ariosto lamented them and the suffering they caused in the *Orlando Furioso,* implicitly contrasting the lofty ideals of medieval chivalry with the avarice and brutality of his own day. Most poignantly, at the start of Canto 34, he compares the outside forces gathering around Italy to a flock of harpies—evil creatures from Greek mythology with the bodies and faces of women, the wings of vultures, and eagles' claws, who attack and steal the food of unfortunate victims:

O foul Harpias, greedy, hunger-starved,
Whom wrath divine for just revenge hath sent
To blinded Italy, that hath deserved
For sins both old and late to be so shent

[broken up]
The sustenance that should for food have
   served,
For widows poor and orphans innocent,
These filthy monsters do consume and waste it,
Oft at one meal, before the owners taste it.

He doubtless guilty is of grievous sin
That first set open that long-closèd cave
From which all filth and greediness came in
To Italy and it infected have;
Then ended good, then did bad days begin,
And discord foul so far off all peace drave
That now in wars, in poverty and pain
It long hath tarried and shall long remain.
        (Ariosto in Gottfried, p. 275;
        Orlando Furioso, 34.1)

Elsewhere (particularly in Cantos 14, 15, 26 and 33), Ariosto praises his Este patrons for their victories as allies of the French invaders, but here he seems to step back and give voice to the same opinions traditionally ascribed to his predecessor Boiardo, who is said to have broken off the *Orlando Innamorato* in dismay over the invasion of Charles VIII, though the historical record is not entirely clear on this point.

Reception. When Ariosto published the final edition of the *Orlando Furioso* in 1532, he sent a copy to Isabella d'Este in Mantua. "Most excellent M. Lodovico," she responded, "your book . . . is in every respect most welcome by me . . . I can only expect to take new pleasure and delight in reading it" (Isabella d'Este in Beechers, p. 75). On the other hand, her brother, Ippolito, casually dismissed it: "Messer Lodovico, where ever did you pick up so much trash?" (Ippolito in Gardner, pp. 122-23). History has borne out Isabella's praise rather than Ippolito's disapproval. The *Furioso* became one of the first bestsellers in the Renaissance; scholars estimate that by 1601 more than 200,000 copies were in circulation (Ariosto, p. xi). Even more significantly, by the end of the sixteenth century, the *Furioso* was on the list of required texts for many schools. As one author of the day (1589) enthused, "if you find yourself in salons, if you enter academies, you never hear anything but Ariosto being read and recited. Indeed, why do I say courts and academies when in private homes, in country houses, even in hovels and huts one also finds the *Furioso* continually recited" (Javitch, p. 14). It even inspired a reworking of the same material on which Ariosto drew into another epic poem. This second epic, Torquato Tasso's **Jerusalem Delivered**, became a masterpiece in its own right (also in *WLAIT 7: Italian Literature and Its Times*). Nor was the

Furioso's popularity limited to Italy. Before the sixteenth century ended, more than 40 printings of translations appeared in Spanish, English, and French. In England, the poem became the chief source for the most influential epic of the age, Edmund Spenser's *Faerie Queen*.

—Terri DeYoung

For More Information

Ariosto, Lodovico. *Orlando Furioso: An English Translation with Introduction, Notes and Index,* 2 vols. Trans. Allan Gilbert. New York: S. F. Vanni, 1954.

Ascoli, Albert. *Ariosto's Bitter Harmony.* Princeton: Princeton University Press, 1987.

Beechers, Donald, Massimo Ciavolella, and Roberto Fedi, eds. *Ariosto Today: Contemporary Perspectives.* Toronto: University of Toronto Press, 2003.

Buckler, F. W. *Harunu'l-Rashid and Charles the Great.* Cambridge, Mass.: The Medieval Academy of America, 1931.

Einhard. *The Life of Charlemagne.* Trans. Sidney Painter. Ann Arbor: University of Michigan Press, 1960.

Gardner, Edmund G. *The King of Court Poets: A Study of the Life and Times of Lodovico Ariosto.* London: Archibald Constable, 1906.

Gottfried, Rudolf, ed. *Ariosto's Orlando Furioso: Selections from the Translation of Sir John Harington.* Bloomington: Indiana University Press, 1971.

Gundersheimer, Werner L. *Ferrara: The Style of a Renaissance Despotism.* Princeton: Princeton University Press, 1973.

Javitch, Daniel. *Proclaiming a Classic: The Canonization of* Orlando Furioso. Princeton: Princeton University Press, 1991.

Rajna, Pio. *Le Fonti Dell'Orlando Furioso: Ricerche e Studi.* Florence: G. C. Sansoni, 1900.

Smyser, H. M., ed. *Pseudo-Turpin.* Cambridge, Mass.: The Medieval Academy of America, 1937.

Virgil. *The Aeneid.* Ed. R. D. Williams. London: Macmillan, 1973.

The Path to the Spiders' Nests

by

Italo Calvino

Italo Calvino was born into a family of Italian scientists in Santiago de las Vegas, near Havana, Cuba, on October 15, 1923. In 1925 the Calvino family returned to San Remo, Italy, located in the Liguria region, near Italy's border with France. A lively, cosmopolitan city, San Remo sits on the Mediterranean Sea and remained Calvino's home for most of his youth. World War II broke out when he was living there; Calvino was only 15 at the time. A few years later, in 1943, Calvino joined the Resistance movement against the remains of Mussolini's Fascist government, which, with German backing, had founded the Republic of Salò in northern Italy. Calvino became a member of the "Brigata Garibaldi" (Garibaldi Brigade) operating in the Maritime Alps of Liguria, where his first novel, *The Path to the Spiders' Nests*, and some of the fiercest partisan-Fascist battles would take place. A year later Calvino joined the Partito Comunista Italiano (Italian Communist Party) and began work for several local newspapers. His first fictional work, *The Path to the Spiders' Nests* won the literary award "Premio Riccione," after which Calvino concentrated on critical writings. Calvino maintained his Communist affiliation for another decade, then left the party in 1957, disagreeing with its stance on the role of intellectuals in Italian society: "In the heated debate sparked by ideologues who desired the programmatic literature and art of socialist realism Calvino took his stand with those who believed that any form of constraint on the artist would ultimately result in propaganda" (Ricci, "Italo

THE LITERARY WORK

A novel set in Liguria, in northwest Italy in 1944; published in Italian (as *Il sentiero dei nidi di ragno*) in 1947, in English in 1957.

SYNOPSIS

A young orphan who joins the Italian Resistance against the occupying forces from Germany during World War II discovers some spiders' nests in which he hides a gun that he steals from a German soldier.

Calvino," p. 53). By 1965 Calvino had moved to Paris and joined the experimental group Ouvroir de Littérature Potentielle (Workshop of Potential Literature, or OuLiPo). Included among his works of the period are *I nostri antenati* (1960; *Our Ancestors*, 1980) and a new edition of *The Path to the Spiders' Nests* with an added preface, which many take to be a deep speculation on his own writing. Some memorable novels followed (*Se una notte d' inverno un viaggiatore* [1979; *If on a Winter's Night a Traveller*, 1981] and *Palomar* [1983; *Mr. Palomar*, 1985], whose title stems back to the name of an American observatory in the state of California). Calvino died in 1985, while writing some lectures to deliver at America's Harvard University (*Lezioni americane: Sei proposte per il prossimo millennio* [1988; *Six Memos for the Next Millennium*, 1988]). In his first novel, he sets out to rescue the subject of the Italian Resistance from formulaic rhetoric, treating it with

Italo Calvino

an originality of thought and style that recurs in future works, lacing his storytelling with imagination, humor, and a gritty sense of reality.

Events in History at the Time the Novel Takes Place

World War II and Italy—an overview. The events narrated in Calvino's novel take place during World War II, in the months following the Armistice of September 8, 1943. The truce was signed by Italy and the Allies (Great Britain, France, Russia, and the United States) after the overthrow of Fascist dictator Benito Mussolini and the king's appointment of Pietro Badoglio to head the government. Suddenly Italy found itself fighting the Germans for freedom. Its former ally had become a determined enemy.

Just four years earlier, Italy had signed the "Pact of Steel" (May 22, 1939), joining forces with Germany and entering World War II. On June 10, 1940, Italy declared war against France and Great Britain and sent troops to fight alongside the Germans. A series of defeats involving a great loss of life characterized Italy's participation in the war. In 1940 the attempt to invade Greece failed. In 1941 Italy was forced to forfeit the African colonies of Eritrea, Somalia, and Ethiopia. Italy also contributed 229,000 troops to Germany's disastrous attempt to invade the

former Soviet Union. Nearly 75,000 perished. A third of the troops, insufficiently equipped and inadequately trained, failed to return home in the spring of 1943.

Popular support for Mussolini and the Fascist Party dwindled. Between 1942 and 1943, the most important industrial cities of the North (Turin, Milan, and Genoa) saw strikes and anti-Fascist demonstrations, and the divide widened between the Fascist regime and a great part of the Italian population. "While since 1941," explains one historian, "there had been growing disquiet among Italians in view of the sacrifices forced upon them by the war, from 1942 there was more open opposition to the regime, which the authorities attempted to conceal" (Dunnage, p. 118).

When the Allied forces invaded Sicily on July 10, 1943, the condition of the Italian military had undeniably deteriorated and Mussolini's support even among members of his own government had significantly diminished. A few weeks later, on September 8, Field Marshal Badoglio, head of the military government, announced to the country that an armistice with the Allies had been signed. Fearing the retaliation of the German troops, Badoglio ordered the Italian army not to join the Allied forces in battle. But they were ordered to respond to any attack elsewhere in Italy.

In the months that followed, almost 600,000 Italian soldiers were deported by the Germans to labor camps or were employed by the key military-supply industries. The majority of these soldiers were by this time anti-Nazi, but 186,000 decided to join Germany's armed forces, and many of this group went on to join the SS, the Nazi special police, a black-uniformed elite corps of the Nazi Party that was operative in Italy as well as Germany. On the other hand, roughly 250,000 participated at one point or another in the Resistance movement, which was dedicated to extinguishing what it saw as the Nazi-Fascist menace in Italy. The partisans, the active members of the Resistance, mounted an effective campaign, but the cost was high: overall 35,000 partisans and 10,000 civilians were killed by the Nazi-Fascist forces (Dunnage, p. 131).

On April 25, 1945, the city of Genoa in Liguria became the first to be freed by the Resistance forces. Slowly the German troops retreated towards the North, beyond the Alps. As the Allies, led by General Mark W. Clark, advanced northward, the forces of the Italian Resistance fought to liberate northern Italy. On May 9, Germany admitted defeat in Rheims. World War II was over.

The Resistance movement. After the Armistice on September 8, 1943, King Vittorio Emanuele III fled from Rome with his newly appointed head of government, Pietro Badoglio, to seek refuge in the south of Italy, already under Allied control. On September 10, Rome, in chaos and without appropriate military defense, was invaded by German troops. A month later, on October 13, Italy officially split with Mussolini and declared war on Germany.

Italy was now divided into two. The Allied forces were waging war just south of Rome. Slowly they advanced toward the northern provinces where Resistance bands were locked in violent battle with Germany's Nazi forces (joined by Fascist troops that had remained loyal to Mussolini).

Resistance actions were conducted by partisan brigades, which formed immediately after the announcement of the Armistice. In Rome, anti-Fascist parties congregated to establish the CLN, or Comitato di Liberazione Nazionale (Committee of National Liberation), devoting themselves to the creation of a new democratic and progressive country. The task was no simple proposition: both in its formation and its operations, the Resistance movement was complex.

Over time the Comitato would function as a partisan high command that oversaw a coordinated effort, calling on everyday Italians to fight the oppressive Nazi-Fascist rule. In reply, immediately after September 8, partisan groups of different sizes formed in Liguria, Piedmont, Lombardia, Veneto, and the Apennine mountains of Emilia Romagna. The northern hills came alive with Resistance activity as one partisan band after another sprang into being. Regional CLNs were established, followed by even smaller CLNs at the provincial and village levels.

Resistance leaders soon realized that the strategy to follow should diverge from an orthodox military one. But there were different views on how best to conduct operations. Would it be wisest to attack the Nazi-Fascist forces by surprise or, as those closer to the Catholic Church said, to take a less aggressive stance and restrict the Resistance to counter-intelligence, sabotage, and the seizure of supplies and materiel. In the end, both approaches were employed.

The partisans themselves had mixed motives for joining the Resistance. Italian soldiers, adrift after the flight of the king and the cabinet, and civilians took up arms against the Nazi-Fascist forces in the North. But not all the partisans were virulent anti-Fascists. As Calvino explains in the preface he added in 1964, the motivation for siding with one foe or another sometimes had little to do with ideals:

> For many of my contemporaries it had been solely a question of luck which determined what side they should fight on; for many of them the sides suddenly changed over, so that soldiers of Mussolini's Fascist Republic became partisans and vice versa.
>
> (Calvino, Preface, *The Path to the Spiders' Nests*, p. 22)

Spies, traitors, ordinary villains, and opportunists joined the partisan bands, along with patriots. Calvino's cast of characters in *The Path to the Spiders' Nests* portrays this diversity, as well as the difficulties encountered by the partisan recruits. Especially at first, not all of the brigades were either well organized or sufficiently equipped, as this excerpt from the novel suggests:

> They [the partisans] might even be soldiers, a company of soldiers who had disappeared during a war many years ago and been wandering in the forests ever since without finding their way back, their uniforms in rags, their boots falling to pieces, their hair and their beards all matted, carrying weapons which now they only use to kill wild animals.
>
> (*The Path to the Spiders' Nests*, p. 95)

Thus, the partisans often stole equipment from the Nazi-Fascists—cannons, armored cars, machine guns, Tommy guns, rifles, pistols, mortars, hand grenades, ammunition.

The brigades conducted their menacing Resistance activities from September 1943 to May 1945. One source counts 85 active units altogether, responsible for 200 pitched battles and more than 5,000 surprise actions (Lewis, pp. 24-25). Beyond pilfering equipment, the partisan bands sabotaged railways, blew up bridges, destroyed power lines, and shot the enemy; in return, they were captured, tortured, and shot to death. In July 1944, for instance, the year Calvino's novel takes place, the Nazis captured a group of partisans (led by Eugenio Calo), forced them to dig a deep pit, then buried them in it up to their necks. Sticks of dynamites were placed by their heads to induce them to talk, but they wouldn't, so the Nazis lit the dynamite. By war's end, the partisans had killed 16,000 Nazi-Fascists, against the above-cited 45,000 partisan and civilian losses by enemy hands—or sticks of dynamite.

The roles of women and youth in the Resistance. Like the men, women became active in the Resistance for various reasons. Some had no choice but to join a brigade, especially those women who were at risk because people suspected them of having contacts with partisans. Such is the predicament of Giglia, wife to the partisan named Mancino in Calvino's novel. A woman in this type of fix might serve as a cook or seamstress for the brigade. But generally "women and men were concentrated in different sectors [of the Resistance movement] and often were organized separately" (Slaughter, p. 53).

THE GARIBALDI BRIGADE

Of all partisan units, the largest (close to 40 percent of all partisan membership) was the one to which Calvino belonged—Brigata Garibaldi (the Garibaldi Brigade). Other partisan units, the Gruppi di Azione Patriottica (GAP, or Groups of Patriotic Action) conducted actions in urban areas, while the Squadre di Azione Patriottica (SAP, or Patriotic Action Squads) focused on the countryside. Beyond the GAP and SAP, female rebels founded the Gruppi Difesa della Donna (GDD, or Women's Defense Groups), which was mostly devoted to supporting Resistance operations in practical ways (delivering messages and weapons, assisting medical personnel, distributing anti-Fascist literature). The Communist Party played a major role in resisting the Nazi-Fascist occupation. In the early days of the Resistance the Garibaldi Brigade and many others were formed by Communists.

The common denominator for these groups was secrecy, and their activities gave rise to heroes like the fictional Red Wolf in Calvino's novel. One real-life hero, Mario Fiorentini, conducted activities on behalf of the GAP, then associated himself with the U.S. Office of Strategic Services. Called Fringuello (finch/goldfinch), he parachuted into the northern mountains around the time Calvino's novel takes place. Fringuello carried out repeated liaison missions between the partisan brigades and military headquarters in Milan and Rome, at great risk to his own life and limb. The Fascists kept arresting him, but each time he escaped. In the summer of 1944, he managed to set up an intelligence network between army officials in Rome and the partisans in the provinces of Lombardy and Emilia Romagna as well as the novel's Liguria.

At first underestimated, women partisans became a mainstay of Resistance operations. Aside from collecting clothing and food for the rebels, women activists acquired medicine, joined medical staffs, distributed anti-Fascist literature, delivered messages and weapons, and helped the families of deportees and partisans. Studies indicate that 66 percent of the women involved with the Resistance were under 30 years old and mostly filled positions as factory workers, teachers, students, and clerks (Slaughter, p. 54). One of the most important roles played by the female partisan was that of *staffetta,* or courier. Couriers had the dangerous job of delivering important messages without being caught by the Nazi-Fascist police. Because of the delicate work, they were strictly selected on the basis of such criteria as ability to travel and connections to the anti-Fascist environment. A few women in the mountain brigades served as military commanders. Mostly, though, females took up traditional roles, albeit in a more public setting than the home. Over the course of the war, some 5,000 female partisans were ultimately arrested and/or tortured; more than half of these perished (Addis Saba, p. 48).

The male partisans showed some ambivalence about and prejudice against the women in their midst. Especially in the mountain brigades, women were regarded with suspicion. This mistrust is well depicted in Calvino's novel by Cousin, a partisan who gives the boy-protagonist a piece of advice: "Of course, behind all the stories with a bad ending there's always a woman, make no mistake about that. You're young, just listen what I tell you. War is all the fault of women" (*The Path to the Spiders' Nests*, p. 85).

Usually women were kept away from the partisan bands. The leaders of the brigades often preferred women to serve as a connection between the mountains and the urban areas. These women often carried their children with them during a mission, to provide a motherly image, which would diffuse any suspicion. Such women hid dynamite in their babies' carriages, or orders in their children's clothing, well aware of the danger. If the woman was arrested, their children often carried on the role of messenger. The Resistance thus often used children to deliver letters. Some young Italians also served as guides across the mountains, while others helped by performing daily chores for family members engaged in the Resistance. Additionally, children helped steal food, weapons, and clothing for the partisans.

The Novel in Focus

Plot summary. *The Path to the Spiders' Nests* takes place during the spring of 1944 in the Riviera di

Ponente, between a small sea town and the mountains just north of it, in western Liguria, near the French border.

Pin is a young boy in his early teens who lives with his only sister, Rina, also known as the Dark Girl of Long Alley, a prostitute whose clients include a German soldier. Pin's father, a sailor, abandoned his children after their mother died. An isolated youth, Pin has no friends. Other children and their mothers dislike him, which makes little difference to Pin. He far prefers the adult company at the local tavern where everyone seems to listen to his stories and the songs he sings. The regulars there call him "little monkey"; he wants very much to be accepted by them.

One day a man by the name of Michel asks Pin to steal the gun of the German soldier who visits his sister. Perform this deed, says Michel, and Pin will earn the right to become an official member of the group at the tavern. The boy takes the challenge very seriously. In order to steal the gun, he must wait for the German soldier to lie down with his sister. Pin is not new to sexuality, at least as an observer; after all, he shares a single room with his sister, the room in which she receives clients.

Pin steals the gun and runs to the tavern but finds no one there willing to listen to him. The men are discussing the possibility of organizing a group for patriotic action. With tears in his eyes, Pin runs away and hides the gun where spiders make their nests. On his way back, some German soldiers bring him in for questioning. His sister's German client has accused him. Pin meets Michel, who warns him not to reveal anything about the goings-on at the tavern. During the interrogation, Pin starts to scream; he is finally sent to jail. On his way out of the office, he learns that Michel has betrayed the brigade formed at the tavern. The Fascists offered Michel a salary, a black Fascist uniform, a weapon, and the right to search houses and hunt partisans, and he accepted the offer. The betrayal upsets Pin, not in itself but because it seems to him that he is "getting it wrong every time and never being able to foresee what grown-ups will do next" (*The Path to the Spiders' Nests*, p. 60).

In prison, Pin meets Red Wolf, a 16-year-old partisan with a reputation. Pin is thrilled. He has heard a lot about Red Wolf and wanted very much to meet him. Together they escape jail. Red Wolf praises the importance of the Communist propaganda. Pin is impressed by Red Wolf's self-confidence. They hide for a while until Red Wolf leaves and fails to return. At this point, left alone,

the young protagonist meets a huge man by the name of Cousin. Abandoned by his wife, Cousin believes that women only create problems. Together they reach an encampment of partisans who are anything but idealistic heroes driven by a thirst for democracy and freedom. Poverty, ignorance, and opportunism have prompted these men to join the group. Yet Pin is happy here; he sings for the partisans and helps their cook, Mancino. Mancino's wife Giglia has fled town because the townspeople grew suspicious of her. Now at the camp, with the task of also helping her husband cook, she flirts with the partisan leader, Dritto.

Two episodes drastically change the situation. A young arrogant partisan, Pelle, who boasts of all his experience with weapons and women, betrays the partisan band. Also, a fire starts because of an oversight by Dritto, the commander, while flirting with Giglia. Two Resistance commanders, Ferriera and Kim, join the brigade to assess who is responsible for the fire and also to plan the partisan action that the group will undertake the following day.

A German attack follows these events, and the brigade is dissolved by the central command. Pin is alone now. He goes back for his gun, the one he stole from the German soldier, but cannot find it. He discovers that Pelle found the gun and left it to Rina, his sister. Pin retrieves the gun and runs away with it. He meets Cousin again, who asks where Rina lives. Pin supplies the information, thinking Cousin is interested in his sister as just another client. The boy has no idea that Cousin intends to kill Rina, convinced that she is a Fascist spy. Cousin leaves and returns, after which "the big man and the child" walk off "into the night, amid the fireflies, holding each other by the hand" (*The Path to the Spiders' Nests*, p. 185).

A note about style. Despite the novel's edge of sharp realism, there is a tendency to experiment with literary genres and styles. Though an omniscient narrator tells the story, the narrator gives no background information; the reader discovers events together with Pin. Dialogue or interior monologue allows for shifting perspectives, even though there is a third-person narrator. After the escape from prison with Red Wolf, when Pin is alone, the novel dips into some interior monologue:

> The cherries are ripe at this season. Here's a tree, far from the house. Has it grown by magic? . . . When he has taken the edge off his hunger he . . . walks on again spitting out cherry-stones. Then he thinks the Fascists might follow the track. . . . But no one in all the world would be clever enough to think of a thing like that, no one except Red Wolf. Yes, if Pin leaves a trail of cherry-stones, Red Wolf will manage to find him.
>
> (*The Path to the Spiders' Nests*, p. 81)

As shown by the lines above, far from documentary style, the novel even blends a fairy-tale element into its depiction of reality: Pin, a lone child protagonist, gets lost in the woods and steals a gun, from his point of view, a sort of magical object. He also has to go through many trials—the stealing of the gun, the police-station episode, the prison, the escape from it, the crossing of the German lines, and the search for a friend. Similarly, detective-story elements are used to help describe the execution of the traitor Pelle—there is a man in a raincoat with his hand in his pockets and the narration quickens, building to a crescendo at the moment of Pelle's execution.

The Resistance—a selfless or selfish cause? In chapter 9, Dritto and his men are visited by Ferriera and Kim, the commander and the commis-

sar of the brigade. Ferriera is a working-class man whose sole purpose is the struggle to spread class consciousness. Kim, on the other hand, is a young medical student who "has an enormous interest in humanity; that is why he is a medical student, for he knows that the explanation of everything is to be found in the grinding, moving cells of the human body," not in philosophical suppositions (*The Path to the Spiders' Nests*, p. 132). Like Calvino himself, Kim is a middle-class intellectual. He seeks knowledge fostered by logic but also takes an interest in psychiatry, which allows him to ponder the irrational and unknown dimensions of human life.

Ferriera and Kim represent two different types: the partisan who believes in communist ideology aimed at creating class consciousness among workers, and the middle-class intellectual who acknowledges that the Resistance might not be attached to a lofty purpose for everyone involved. Through Kim and his philosophical digression on the various reasons Italians decided to join or fight the Resistance, Calvino provides a picture of Italian society at a moment in time. Workers, peasants, intellectuals, students, and foreign prisoners who escaped concentration camps joined partisan detachments. Some of these partisans fought against the Nazi-Fascist enemy who was burning down their houses. Others joined the Fascists or became spies for them. In any case, they mostly did not join to fight idealistically for the liberation of their country but rather because of their own interests. At this juncture in the war, with the Allies controlling the South and the Nazi-Fascist forces in central and northern Italy, people lost the ability to identify with their land. "Country" became limited to one's private sphere and to the struggle for the survival of that sphere.

By fall 1943, when the Resistance began, Italians were demoralized by the difficulties brought on by the war, the defeats they had suffered, the thousands of soldiers who lay dead or sat captive as prisoners of war, the bombing of their major cities, and the general economic distress. The introduction in 1941 of a controlled system of food distribution by means of ration cards distributed to the families—200 grams of bread per head per day—gave rise to a black market and the corruption of government inspectors. Basic services, such as electricity and water, were scarce, if they existed at all. Hospitals lacked proper medical supplies. Schools closed down. While men were fighting, women had to enter the work force and at the same time tend their families. Some women "found themselves ignoring moral principles in the desperate search for food," in other words, prostituting themselves for a meal (Dunnage, p. 120). Ironically, since Italian Fascism taught that the preeminent duty for a woman was motherhood, in 1923 Fascist law obliged all prostitutes to carry certification of vaginal examination. Also the Fascist government operated the *case chiuse* ("closed brothels"), the only legal venue for this kind of service, the intent being as much as possible to protect public morals and the notion of woman as a symbol of motherhood.

Sources and literary context. *The Path to the Spiders' Nests* was Calvino's contribution to post-World War II neorealist literature—literature that dealt with present-day subject matter, took place in clearly defined locations, and focused on segments of society that did not exercise sweeping power but that felt its effects. Everyday language became standard in this literature. Novelists integrated Italian dialects, including their vocabulary and rhythm, more consciously into the written language than ever before. The aim was to express the collective experience of the war as well as the Resistance (later referred to also as a civil war that Italy suffered while it was still enmeshed in the final phases of World War II).

Calvino clearly drew on his own experience in the Resistance to write the novel, sharing the need to do so with other writers of the era.

> The fact of having emerged from an experience—a war, a civil war—which had spared no one, established an immediacy of communication between the writer and his public: we were face to face, on equal terms, bursting with stories to tell; everyone had experienced their own drama, had lived a chaotic, exciting, adventurous existence; we took the words from each other's mouths. . . . During the partisan war, the adventures we had only just lived through were transformed and reshaped into stories told around the fire at night; they had already assumed a style, a language, a tone of bravado, which relished harrowing detail or horrific effects. The subject matter and language of some of my short stories, as well as some parts of this novel stem from this newly born oral tradition.
>
> (*The Path to the Spiders' Nests,* p. 8)

Calvino soon realized that reality could not be retold in a direct, didactic manner. It became a challenge for him to convey its complexity and its contradictions, a challenge that he met by making his protagonist a young boy rather than a man like himself and by making most of the other characters traitors, deserters, and liars.

Giovanni Verga's *I Malavoglia* (1881; *The House by the Medlar Tree,* 1890), Elio Vittorini's *Conversazioni in Sicilia* (1941; *Conversation in Sicily,* 1961) and Cesare Pavese's *Paesi tuoi* (1941; *The Harvesters,* 1961) are the texts that Calvino cites in his preface to the 1964 edition of *The Path to the Spiders' Nests.* These authors mark the starting point from where neorealist writers moved in order to investigate and represent reality (see **The House by the Medlar Tree,** also in WLAIT 7: *Italian Literature and Its Times*). Calvino diverged from traditional neorealist narrative strategies invoked by other writers at the time. Chronicles, diaries, and memoirs flourished in the postwar years. Unlike these works, Calvino's novel invokes fairytale-style discourse and adapts partisan stories from oral tradition. There is an effort to avoid an impersonal documentary style, promote critical inquiry, and conjure a realistic picture of the Resistance, not one burdened with postwar leftist rhetoric. In short, Calvino sought a personal yet legitimate way to represent the complexity of reality while avoiding the rote heroic celebration of the Resistance being generated around him. The result was *The Path to the Spiders' Nests.*

CALVINO ON NEOREALISM

"Neo-realism was not a school. (Let me try to be precise about these matters.) It was many voices combined, mostly voices from provinces, a many-sided revelation of the different Italys that existed. . . . The local settings were intended to give a flavour of authenticity to a fictional representation with which everyone the world over would be able to identify."

(Preface, *The Path to the Spiders' Nests,* p. 10)

Events in History at the Time the Novel Was Written

In search of a democratic renewal. In the postwar years, all the anti-Fascist political parties that championed freedom and democracy faced the practical challenge of Italy's political and economic reconstruction. On June 2, 1946, the nation held a referendum on whether the government should be a monarchy or a republic. At the same time, Italians voted for the delegates to the Constituent Assembly that would write a new constitution to take effect January 1, 1948. The country chose to be a republic, and the new Assembly was formed. The majority of its delegates belonged to the Christian Democrat Party (which arose from the alliance of a number of Catholic organizations), followed by smaller numbers of Socialist delegates and then Communist delegates. The Republic's first election, held in 1948, saw victory go to the Christian Democrats, who won 48.5 percent of the votes, the largest share in the nation.

Confronted by the rise of the Christian Democrats, activists in the Communist Party debated the role of intellectuals in post-war Italian society. In the end, these debates became an attempt to force intellectuals to contribute to its political objectives. The school of socialist realism, in the Soviet Union, taught that every form of art has to highlight and celebrate the working class and its struggle to survive. Andrei Zhadanov (1896-1948), a founder of this doctrine, was the theoretician whose dogmatic and rigorous ideas the Partito Comunista Italiano, or Italian Communist Party, decided to promote. Calvino never felt comfortable with the policy. Siding with those intellectuals who refused to serve the ideology of a political party by turning themselves into an instrument of political propaganda, he acted accordingly. The Communist Party's approach, which amounted to a censorial attitude, is precisely what Calvino was rejecting when he started writing *The Path to the Spider's Nests* in 1947.

The debate about the role of literature raged in many different political and literary journals of the day, one of them being Vittorini's *Il Politecnico* (The Polytechnic), which was dedicated to cultural regeneration—the title of Vittorini's first editorial was "For a New Culture." The journal, which insisted on its cultural independence from party politics, remained active from 1945 to 1947, and Calvino became one of its major contributors. In the interest of cultural renewal, Vittorini attributed great importance to keeping the Italian intelligentsia informed about European and American philosophical and literary trends. Vittorini and Pavese, either as editors or translators, were instrumental to the translation of many foreign literary texts, including works by T. S. Eliot, W. H. Auden, Bertolt Brecht, André Malraux, William Faulkner, Herman Melville, and Ernest Hemingway, to name only a few.

This led to a famous polemic exchange between Vittorini and Palmiro Togliatti, the leader of the Communist Party at the time, who saw Vittorini's support for innovative and experimental writing as a shift from the cultural policies of the party.

Reception. *The Path to the Spiders' Nests* received both positive and negative reviews. Critics fixed on its fusion of reality and imagination. Some applauded Calvino's original use of language, imagery, and style. Others faulted the story for placing undue emphasis on the individual situation, for using spoken language (in view of the great difference between spoken Italian and written literary Italian), and for failing to include a collective voice.

Positive reviews came from those who thought Calvino's first novel showcased his drive toward the investigation of the relationship between oneself and the reality into which one is plunged. The first positive review came from Pavese, who supported publication of the novel and would soon write a World War II novel of his own (see *The Moon and the Bonfires*, also in *WLAIT 7: Italian Literature and Its Times*). The review, published in the then Communist newspaper *L'Unità* on October 26, 1947, highlights the importance of the fairy-tale dimension in the book: "The astuteness of Calvino . . . was in the observation of the partisan life as if it were a fairy-tale of the woods, spectacular, many-colored, 'different'" (Pavese, p. 274; trans. M. L. Mosco).

Calvino's importance as a writer was clearly recognized in North America as well, even at this early stage in his literary career. In 1958, the year after the novel's release in English, Raymond Rosenthal referred in the *New York Times* to the fact that Italian critics were comparing *The Path to the Spiders' Nests* to the novels of Robert Louis Stevenson because of its magical evocation of adolescence (Rosenthal, p. 36).

—Maria Laura Mosco

For More Information

Addis Saba, Marina. *Le partigiane. Tutte le donne della Resistenza*. Milan: Mursia, 1998.

Bolongaro, Eugenio. *Italo Calvino and the Compass of Literature*. Toronto: University of Toronto Press, 2003.

Calvino, Italo. *The Path to the Spiders' Nests*. Trans. Archibald Colquhoun. London: Jonathan Cape, 1998.

Dunnage, Jonathan. *Twentieth Century Italy: A Social History*. London: Longman, 2002.

Lewis, Laurence. *Echoes of Resistance*. Tunbridge Wells, Kent: Costello, 1985.

Pavese, Cesare. "Il Sentiro dei nidi di ragno." In *La Letteratura Americana e altri saggi*. Turin: Einaudi, 1952.

Re, Lucia. *Calvino and the Age of Neorealism: Fables of Estrangement*. Stanford: Stanford University Press, 1990.

Ricci, Franco. "Italo Calvino." In *Dictionary of Literary Biography*. Vol. 196. Ed. Augustus Pallotta. Detroit: Gale, 1999.

————. *Painting with Words, Writing with Pictures*. Toronto: Toronto University Press, 2001.

Rosenthal, Raymond. "A Report on Literary Trends in Italy." *New York Times*, February 9, 1958, p. BR36.

Slaughter, Jane. *Women and the Italian Resistance. 1943-1945*. Denver, Colo.: Arden Press, 1997.

Wilhelm, Maria de Blasio. *The Other Italy: Italian Resistance in World War II*. New York: W. W. Norton, 1988.

Poems in Terza Rima

by

Veronica Franco

Veronica Franco was born in Venice in 1546 to a family of *cittadini originari*, native-born citizens of Venice who made up the city's middle class. Franco's mother, Paola Fracassa, had been a courtesan and probably passed her skills down to Veronica, who learned the profession by the mid-1560s. As a *cortigiana onesta* (honored courtesan), Franco made her living by providing company, conversation, and sexual favors to powerful and wealthy Venetian men as well as to foreign visitors. She was married to a doctor named Paolo Panizza in the early 1560s, but by 1564 she separated from him. Franco later bore six children (only three of whom survived) by different men. In 1575, a terrible outbreak of the bubonic plague struck Venice. When the outbreak finally ended in 1577, over a third of the city's inhabitants were dead. Thankfully Franco managed to escape infection, but she lost many of her valuable possessions due to theft during the plague years and found herself in serious financial straits thereafter. In 1580 Franco was accused by her son's tutor, Ridolfo Vanitelli, of casting magical spells and was brought to trial for this offense by the Venetian Inquisition. Although she was subsequently cleared of the charge, the trial may have irreparably damaged her reputation. Just two years later, she filed a tax report that indicated she was living in an area of Venice inhabited by the city's poorest prostitutes. Veronica Franco died in 1591 at the age of 45.

Franco enjoyed bouts of wealth and success in her short life. Along with her three brothers, she

THE LITERARY WORK

A collection of 25 poems, 18 by Franco and 7 by Marco Venier and/or an unidentified male author; set in Venice and Verona in the late sixteenth century; published in Italian in 1575, in English in 1998.

SYNOPSIS

Poems in Terza Rima, so named because of the meter in which the poems are composed, dramatizes Franco's professional and personal relationships with male patrons; also the poems celebrate her skills as a writer and as one of Venice's most celebrated courtesans.

was educated by a private tutor, a rare opportunity for Venetian girls at the time. Her literary career began to blossom in the 1570s, when she became involved with Domenico Venier's prestigious literary salon, where she must have met many of Venice's most important writers, artists, and intellectuals. Domenico Venier (1517-1582), a Venetian aristocrat and poet in his own right, was both patron and literary mentor to Franco. Her book of *Lettere familiari a diversi* (Familiar Letters to Various People), published in Venice in 1580, reveals the mutual respect the two poets had for each other. It was in Venier's salon that Franco first circulated the poems that would become part of the *Poems in Terza Rima*. The verse is written with a forthright eroticism and witty eloquence that sets it apart from the work of other women writers of Franco's day.

Events in History at the Time of the Poems

The hierarchy of prostitution in sixteenth-century Venice. In 1543, three years before Veronica Franco was born, the Venetian government passed a law that defined prostitutes (*meretrici*) as single or married women who lived apart from their husbands and engaged in "business (*comertio*) and intercourse (*praticha*) with one or more men" (*Leggi e memorie venete*, p. 108; trans. C. Quaintance). Thus, any woman who had sex with a man outside of marriage and who accepted money or gifts from that man was legally considered a prostitute. The distinction between a sixteenth-century Venetian prostitute (*meretrice*) and a courtesan (*cortigiana*) is blurry, since these two words, along with the more vulgar term for whore (*puttana*), were used interchangeably in literary and legal documents. Still, it is likely that the term *cortigiana*, which comes from the same root as *cortigiano* (male courtier) and thus implies a certain standard of elegance, was adopted by women who aspired to the heights of the profession.

The Venetian historian Guido Ruggiero identifies five to six different levels of prostitution in most major sixteenth-century Italian cities, including Venice (Ruggiero, *Binding Passions*, pp. 35-36). At the bottom of the heap were the many women who practiced their trade in the streets or in the city's many taverns and inns. Patronized mainly by men from the lower social classes, they were not registered with the Venetian government, meaning they did not pay taxes on their earnings. Next came the registered prostitutes who worked in large houses, or *bordelli*, which were often run by prominent families. Above these prostitutes were the third and fourth levels, including, respectively, both unregistered and registered women who worked outside the *bordelli* and usually had a procurer or procuress who arranged their encounters.

Above and beyond this last class were the *cortigiane oneste* (honored courtesans), an elite class of intellectual courtesans at the top of the hierarchy of prostitution, into which Veronica Franco fits. In Venice there was also a distinctly less-honored variety, the *cortigiane di lume* (lower-class courtesans). While the *cortigiana onesta* lived independently and often kept a household full of servants, most *cortigiane di lume* operated out of inns (generally in the "Castelletto," an area near the Rialto district).

The Venetian *cortigiana onesta*. The term *cortigiana onesta*, coined in the late fifteenth century, refers to a courtesan who was "'honored,' rather than 'honest,' that is, privileged, wealthy, recognized" (Jones and Rosenthal in Franco, *Poems in Terza Rima*, p. 3). Unlike the lowlier prostitutes, courtesans often lived in splendid palaces, kept numerous servants, and dressed in rich fabrics. But what really set them apart from common prostitutes was their intellectual, artistic, and literary prowess. Skilled in music and versed in classical as well as contemporary literature, courtesans such as Veronica Franco rubbed elbows with the cultural elite of Venice. Like her male counterpart, the courtier, the courtesan's livelihood depended on her ability to perform, with effortless grace, the roles expected of her by her noble patrons (mainly skilled conversationalist, companion, entertainer, and lover). Emulating the nobility in both manners and dress, courtesans and courtiers sought to ascend the social and economic ladder. The successful courtesan of Venice aligned herself with the nobility there, violating a boundary for respected women of the day by appearing in public. At the same time, the courtesan distanced herself from the vulgar world of the *bordello*. She projected a highly sophisticated public image, using it "to move beyond the domestic space of the family. . . . Mimicking the graces and donning the costumes of the noblewoman, she was able to differentiate herself from the *cortigiana di lume* and *meretrice* (Rosenthal, *The Honest Courtesan*, p. 68). Since the wealth earned by an honored courtesan gave her the means for splendid clothing, she dressed herself in ways that made it practically impossible to tell her apart from the women of the upper classes.

Prostitution and the law. Although prostitution remained legal throughout the 1500s, prostitutes were disciplined by society to an increasing degree over the century. In mid-1500s Venice, courtesans were subject to repeated legal attempts to control their dress, behavior, and freedom of movement. In 1543, and again in 1562, for example, courtesans were prohibited from wearing gold, silver, and silk in public, and in 1571, they were prohibited from attending church services on feast days.

The government's attempts to control the city's courtesans do not appear to have been very successful. In 1579, when Veronica Franco was 33, the Officers of Public Health complained that the prostitutes and courtesans in the city behaved very boldly despite recent efforts to punish them for their infractions. "They are incorrigible," said the officers, "and they disregard all of our laws and regulations" (Scarabello, p. 19; trans. C. Quaintance).

Yet even as it denounced prostitutes for their morally corrupt behavior, the Venetian government tolerated, and even profited from, prostitution. Like other registered prostitutes and courtesans, Veronica Franco paid a sizeable tax to the government, which in this manner gained financially from the trade. Also there were social reasons that might explain why the Venetian authorities did not simply outlaw the selling of sex. In a society where married noblewomen were kept under lock-and-key to preserve their chastity, people had few legal outlets for sexuality. A sixteenth-century English visitor to the city, Thomas Coryat, remarked that Venetians tolerated prostitution because without it "the chastity of their wives would be the sooner assaulted, and so consequently they should be capricornified [cuckolded] . . . were it not for these places of evacuation" (Coryat, vol. 1, pp. 402-03). In other words, prostitution was seen as a necessary evil: by providing an outlet for the libidos of young Venetian men, it protected noble daughters and wives. Prostitution was also seen as a deterrent to sodomy, which people of the day viewed as the most abominable of vices. Finally, authorities turned a blind eye to prostitution because it "eased the severe socioeconomic problems facing sixteenth-century Venetian society" (Rosenthal, *The Honest Courtesan*, p. 23). Legend has it that the prostitutes residing in Venice's most notorious red-light district were in fact encouraged to stand topless on the "Ponte delle Tette" (Bridge of Tits) to entice passersby. Despite the fact that the existence of this illicit sex trade was seen as necessary to the stability of the Venetian Republic, prostitutes—and especially courtesans, who were much more visible—faced many serious obstacles as they sought to enter the tightly knit ranks of Venetian high society.

Sixteenth-century courtesan satires. While honored courtesans were sometimes praised by their male contemporaries for their beauty, grace, and literary talent, they were also the subject of a host of satires and invectives that denounced them as venal, mercenary whores. Nowhere was this truer than in sixteenth-century Venice, where courtesans were plentiful and powerful. Even the most illustrious courtesans were victims of barbed literary attacks that sought to denigrate and demean them.

Invectives against courtesans began pouring from Venetian presses sometime after 1527, when the brilliant satirist Pietro Aretino (1492-1556) settled in Venice and published his scandalous

Sonetti lussuriosi (Lascivious Sonnets), a sequence of pornographic sonnets featuring some of Rome's most notorious courtesans. Aretino's most famous work on courtesans, however, is the *Ragionamenti* (Dialogues), also known as the *Sei giornate* (Six Days). First published in Venice between 1534 and 1536, the work is organized as six days of dialogue between various female characters. During the first three days, the experienced courtesan Nanna, who is trying to decide whether to make her daughter a courtesan, discusses with her friend Antonia the merits and perils of the

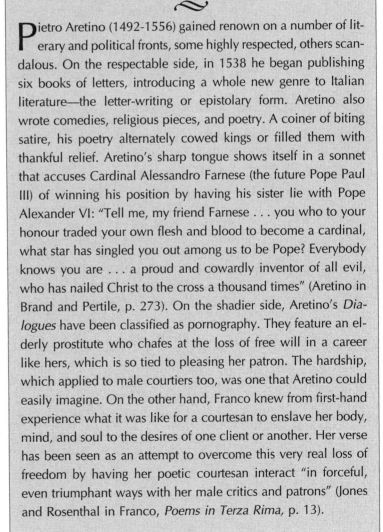

PIETRO ARETINO, FROM THE SACRED TO THE BANNED

Pietro Aretino (1492-1556) gained renown on a number of literary and political fronts, some highly respected, others scandalous. On the respectable side, in 1538 he began publishing six books of letters, introducing a whole new genre to Italian literature—the letter-writing or epistolary form. Aretino also wrote comedies, religious pieces, and poetry. A coiner of biting satire, his poetry alternately cowed kings or filled them with thankful relief. Aretino's sharp tongue shows itself in a sonnet that accuses Cardinal Alessandro Farnese (the future Pope Paul III) of winning his position by having his sister lie with Pope Alexander VI: "Tell me, my friend Farnese . . . you who to your honour traded your own flesh and blood to become a cardinal, what star has singled you out among us to be Pope? Everybody knows you are . . . a proud and cowardly inventor of all evil, who has nailed Christ to the cross a thousand times" (Aretino in Brand and Pertile, p. 273). On the shadier side, Aretino's *Dialogues* have been classified as pornography. They feature an elderly prostitute who chafes at the loss of free will in a career like hers, which is so tied to pleasing her patron. The hardship, which applied to male courtiers too, was one that Aretino could easily imagine. On the other hand, Franco knew from first-hand experience what it was like for a courtesan to enslave her body, mind, and soul to the desires of one client or another. Her verse has been seen as an attempt to overcome this very real loss of freedom by having her poetic courtesan interact "in forceful, even triumphant ways with her male critics and patrons" (Jones and Rosenthal in Franco, *Poems in Terza Rima,* p. 13).

three occupations available to women in the Renaissance: nun, wife, or prostitute. As the second part of the dialogue begins, Nanna teaches her daughter, Pippa, the art of courtesanry, and warns

Pietro Aretino. Engraving by Marcantonio Raimondi, after a painting by Titian of the early to mid-sixteenth century.

her of the dangers posed by men. On the last day, a new speaker, the "Midwife," explains how to be a procuress as the other women listen attentively.

Aretino's two obscene texts became archetypal for a circle of aspiring literary pornographers, including Niccolò Franco (1515-1570, no relation to Veronica), Anton Francesco Doni (1513-1574), and Lorenzo Venier (1510-1550), the elder brother of Veronica Franco's patron Domenico Venier. In 1531 Lorenzo Venier published a pair of risqué invectives targeting two of the most popular courtesans in the city. Venier's first poem, *La puttana errante* (The Wandering Whore), casts the courtesan Elena Ballerina as a sexually voracious whore who embarks on a quest to bed every man between Venice and Rome. As the poem concludes, the courtesan, racked with syphilis and crowned with lowly cabbage leaves, is hauled off amidst a jeering crowd to end her days on the Ponte Sisto, the infamous bridge in Rome where only the poorest prostitutes ply their trade. The satire, in effect, transforms the elegant courtesan into a low-class, disease-ridden prostitute.

On the other hand, *Il trentuno della Zaffetta* (The Zaffetta's Thirty-one) recounts in graphic detail the violent tale of the *trentuno*—a pseudonym for gang-rape—that a slighted lover inflicts upon Angela dal Moro, who falls victim to a procession of 80 peasants, fishermen, gondoliers, and other low-status males. In the final stanzas, the poet holds up Angela's misfortune as a warning to all courtesans who dare to refuse their noble lovers: "If some gentleman wants to screw you, think first about Angela and her dishonor. By saying yes, you will pay him homage, and this, my dear whores, is the road to success" (Venier, p. 63; trans. C. Quaintance). Whether this passage comes from some real historical account, as some scholars believe, is in one sense beside the point. The words accomplish what the rapes would have: the public humiliation of the courtesan.

The Poems in Focus

Contents overview. Franco's *Poems in Terza Rima* is dedicated to Gugliemo Gonzaga, the Duke of Mantua and a famous patron of musicians. The collection, which contains 25 poems, can be divided into two parts. The first section consists of 14 poems arranged in pairs: a poem from a male author is followed by a response from Franco, and vice versa. The second section consists of eleven *capitoli*, all by Franco and addressed to specific male authors. The collection ends with a long *capitolo* in praise of "Fumane," the country estate belonging to an important man of the Church, Marcantonio della Torre (1531-1591) of Verona.

All of the poems in Franco's collection are examples of the *capitolo in terza rima*, the preferred form for academic, satiric, and comic poetry in the first half of the sixteenth century. Modeled after Dante's **Divine Comedy,** the *capitolo in terza rima* consists of a series of *terzine* (sets of three lines of eleven syllables each) that follow the rhyme scheme *aba / bcb / cdc / . . .* and end with a single line that stands on its own and rhymes with the middle line of the preceding set: *aba / bcb / cdc / d.* Franco's choice of the *capitolo* is remarkable, since the difficult form was almost never used by other women writers of her era. In her *Poems in Terza Rima*, the *capitoli* exchanged between the female poet and the unidentified male author make up a poetic debate, or in literary terms, a *tenzone.*

Contents summary. *Capitoli 1-2.* By including poems from aristocratic male authors in her collection, Franco allies herself with one of Venice's most elite social and literary circles. The pair of poems that opens the collection not only sets the tone of poetic debate that pervades the entire book, but also presents Franco's literary persona to her readers. The first poem in the book is identified in later copies as being by an "incerto autore" (unidentified author), but in an earlier edition he is identified as Marco Venier (1537-1602), a distant relative of her patron Domenico Venier. Marco Venier, an important figure in Venetian politics, may well be the author of all of the poems now labeled "incerto autore."

As *Capitolo 1* begins, the poet-lover entreats "la signora Veronica Franco" to relieve the suffering caused by his unrequited love for her, presenting himself as the abject, yearning lover in the tradition of Petrarch (see Petrarch's **Canzoniere**, also in *WLAIT 7: Italian Literature and Its Times*). The poet presents the object of his love as a cruel lady who refuses to satisfy his desires: "But how ever can it be, in the tenderest part / of your body, that your fair, fine, white breast / can enclose a heart so hard and pitiless?" (Franco, *Poems in Terza Rima*, p. 51). Reminding his beloved that her beauty will not last forever, the poet insists that in order to become "eternal and divine on earth," she must replace her cruelty towards him with "pity for the man who loves [her]" (*Poems*, p. 53).

Even as it laments her resistance to love, Marco Venier's poem celebrates Franco both for her legendary beauty and for her skill as a writer: "And so among beauties you are famous for your learning, / and among learned women you are known for your beauty, / and in both you excel one group and the other" (*Poems*, p. 57). After praising the courtesan's literary talent, the poet cautions her not to let her intellectual pursuits take precedence over her skills in the arts of love. She will make her name eternal through the "gifts of Venus," he asserts, no less than through her writing. He ends the poem with a final plea for mercy, declaring that if she will do as he asks, she will be "without equal on earth" (*Poems*, p. 59).

Franco begins her response (*Capitolo 2*) by warning Venier that his words are not enough to make her believe that he truly loves her. What she requires instead is that he prove his love through action:

> Since I will not believe that I am loved,
> nor should I believe it or reward you
> for the pledge you have made me up to now,
> win my approval sir, with deeds.
>
> (*Poems*, p. 63)

She tempts him with a description of her erotic prowess, promising him erotic fulfillment on the condition that he demonstrate his love for her "through more than compliments" (*Poems*, p. 63). Insisting that "such an act doesn't suit my profession," Franco declares that she will not accept money as a sign of love (*Poems*, p. 65). She

proceeds to echo her earlier request, once again asking him to demonstrate his love in deeds instead of words. (Although the poem never makes this explicit, Franco may have hoped that Venier would collaborate on a literary project; the "deeds" were probably poems she asked him to contribute.) She sweetens her request with praise: "This will be no burden to you / for to your prowess any undertaking, / however difficult, comes with ease" (*Poems*, p. 67).

FIGHTING WITH WORDS—THE *TENZONE*

Inherited from the French region of Provence, the *tenzone* entered the Italian poetic tradition in the thirteenth century as a means for personal exchange and debate between two or more poets. The first author proposed the subject of the debate (often love, religion, or politics) and set the rhyme scheme, and the second author responded in like rhyme.

While early Italian poets mostly used the sonnet form to conduct their *tenzoni*, early-sixteenth-century satirists, such as Franceso Berni (1497/8-1535), adopted the *capitolo* form instead. In the hands of Berni and his followers, the *capitolo*, considered a highly sophisticated form because of the difficulties posed by its complicated rhyme scheme, was used as a verbal weapon against other writers and even political figures. In sixteenth-century Venetian literary circles, the *tenzone* turned into a *proposta/risposta* (challenge/response) exchange between two poets, which is the form it takes in Franco's *Poems in Terza Rima*.

The poem ends with a restatement of the original request and the promise of erotic reward, but only on Franco's terms:

> Let me see the [poetic?] works
> I've asked for from you,
> for then you'll enjoy my sweetness to the full;
> and I will also take pleasure in yours,
> in the way that mutual love allows,
> which provides delight free from all pain.
> I yearn and long to have a good reason
> to love you: decide what you think best,
> for every outcome depends on your will.
> I have no more to say; go in peace.
>
> (*Poems*, p. 71)

The poetic debate with Maffio Venier. That Franco's position in Venetian society was precarious is evident from the vicious literary attack waged upon her by Maffio Venier (1550-1586), the son of Lorenzo Venier and nephew of Domenico Venier. Sometime in the 1570s, Maffio wrote and circulated a series of three obscene poems in Venetian dialect targeting Franco, who was away from Venice at the time. The dialect poems are not included in *Poems in Terza Rima,* but they are an integral part of the poetic debate in Franco's book: several of her *capitoli* are indirect or direct responses to Maffio Venier's defamatory verse.

Capitoli 13-14. Franco initially believed that the poems attacking her were penned by one of her lovers (probably Marco Venier), as is demonstrated in *Capitolo 13.* Here Franco accuses a man with whom she has been intimately involved of betraying her. Her poem opens with an angry call to arms: "No more words! To deeds, to the battlefield, to arms! / For, resolved to die, I want to free myself from such merciless mistreatment" (*Poems,* p. 133). At the beginning of the poem, Franco adopts the language of military combat, challenging her opponent to a duel and threatening to rip his heart from his breast and his "deceiving tongue" from his mouth (*Poems,* p. 133). After having shed his blood, she continues, she may turn the knife on her own breast.

The violent language in the first part of the poem gives way to erotic imagery as the poet contemplates her bed, the locus of their amorous delights and the place "where I took you in my arms, and which still / preserves the imprint of our bodies, breast to breast" (*Poems,* p. 135). Proposing the bed as battleground, she invites her lover-adversary to lay down his weapons and join her in an erotic contest: "What if, all weapons laid aside, you took / the path opened to a love match in bed?" (*Poems,* p. 137).

The final episode of the poem invokes the ambiguous language that often attends a relationship charged with sexual desire. The woman speaker suggests that she wants to "die" with her opponent, yet her final words emphasize her refusal to accept the traditional position of womanly submission and her resolve to best her opponent in the erotic battle she proposes:

> Perhaps I would even follow you to bed,
> and, stretched out there in skirmishes with you,
> I would yield to you in no way at all.
>   To take revenge for your unfair attack,
> I'd fall upon you, and in daring combat,
> as you too caught fire defending yourself,
>   I would die with you, felled by the same
>   blow.
> . . . .
>   But hold firm, my strong, undaunted
>   heart,

and with that felon's final destruction,
avenge your thousand deaths with his one.
   Then end your agony with the same
      blade.

(*Poems,* p. 137)

In *Capitolo 14,* the male author seems unaware of the obscene verses directed against Franco. The first line of his poem both echoes Franco's challenge in *Capitolo 13* and reverses it, exhorting the courtesan to make peace with him: "No more war, but peace! and may the hate and rage, / and whatever disagreement has arisen between us / be transformed into twice as much love" (*Poems,* p. 139). Protesting his innocence, he suggests that another man could be to blame: "perhaps someone was offended / by our living together, so that he was quick / to scatter his poison over our sweetness" (*Poems,* p. 141). The male poet uses the language of military combat introduced by Franco in *Capitolo 13,* describing his beloved as a "fierce warrior," armed against him with the arrows of Love. In the final verses, he affirms both his position as abject, powerless lover and the erotic supremacy of the courtesan:

> As for myself, as long as you are satisfied,
> I grant you complete dominion over me,
> bound hand and foot, and legs and arms;
>   and I send you, in faith, carte blanche
> to have total sovereignty over my heart,
> so that no part of it does not belong to you.

(*Poems,* p. 147)

Capitolo 16. The poetic debate culminates in *Capitolo 16.* Here it is clear that Franco has realized that her attacker is not the man she accused in *Capitolo 14* (who was probably Marco Venier). Now the attacker is Maffio Venier. She never explicitly identifies her adversary in the poem, but she does describe him as a poet who prefers to write in dialect and she even refers to one of his more famous works (*Poems,* p. 167).

The first part of the *capitolo* contrasts Maffio Venier to the conventional image of the virtuous courtly knight, bound by duty to protect and defend the female sex. In the opening lines, Franco reprimands Venier for having broken one of the fundamental rules of knightly conduct: he assailed an unarmed opponent without warning. Even worse, she continues, the victim of his assault is a defenseless woman. In this first part of the poem, Franco emphasizes female weakness, describing women as "weak in body, and not only quite unfit / to injure others, but also far distant, through their timid hearts, from self-defense" (*Poems,* p. 161). The poet extends the notion of female weakness to herself; at the time of Venier's attack she was "defenseless, alone, off my guard, / fainthearted and never practiced in combat" (*Poems*, p. 161). There is an abrupt change of tone at line 31, however: though at first she "wondered whether [she] would survive" his vicious poems, the attack has become the catalyst for the courtesan's transformation from defenseless woman to female warrior:

> As if jolted awake from sweet sleep all
>   at once,
> I drew courage from the risk I'd avoided,
> though a woman, born to milder tasks;
>   and, blade in hand, I learned warrior's
>   skills,
> so that, by handling weapons, I learned
> that women by nature are no less agile than
>   men.
>   So, devoting all my effort to arms,
> I see myself now, thanks to heaven, at the
>   point where I no
> longer fear harm from anyone.
>   (*Poems*, pp. 162-163)

"Women by nature are no less agile than men," says the poet, deftly reversing her initial statement of the inability of women to defend themselves. She also comes to the defense of the entire female sex. When women are allowed to train in the arts of war, they will be able to prove they are men's equals: "When we women, too, have weapons and training, / we will be able to prove to all men that we have hands and feet and hearts like yours" (*Poems*, p. 163). Franco bolsters her arguments by stepping into the role of poet-speaker, who through her verse will serve as a model for feminist action: "And to prove to you that I speak the truth, / among so many women I will act first, / setting an example for them to follow" (*Poems*, p. 165).

Challenging her adversary to a duel, Franco underscores her own literary skills, declaring that she is ready to compete with him in any language or manner he chooses. Whether the language is Venetian dialect or Italian, whether the style is lofty or comic, makes no difference to her. She is equally skilled whatever the conditions. In fact, she has honed her talents precisely for the purpose of engaging in literary debate with him.

She then proceeds to break down Venier's dialect poem, "Verily Unique Whore," which he intended as a vulgar pun upon her given name, Veronica. Her analysis of how the enemy poet uses the words "unique" and "whore" turns his usage on its head. "Unique," she says, is correctly used only as "a term meant for most excellent things" (*Poems*, p. 169). Thus, when he calls her

a "verily unique whore," he is unwittingly paying tribute to her virtue: "without realizing it, you give me praise / for qualities based upon goodness and virtue" (*Poems*, p. 169). Likewise, his use of a positive adjective to modify *whore* turns the negative word into a positive term, and praises both Franco as an individual and her profession in general.

Franco ends the *capitolo* by reiterating her challenge and restating her literary prowess. If Venier refuses to respond to her, she will tell the world that he is afraid:

> So make ready now your paper and ink
> and tell me, this time, without further delay
> which weapons I must wield in combat with
>   you.
> . . . .
>   You may choose the language of every
>   day,
> or whatever other idiom you please,
> for I have had practice in them all;
>   and if you do not write me a response,
> I will say that you feel great fear of me,
> even though you think yourself so brave.
>   (*Poems*, p. 171)

Nothing personal? The exchanges between Franco and her male attackers reflect a growing hostility against courtesans that would persist throughout the sixteenth century and beyond. By the time Veronica Franco had risen to the heights of fame as a courtesan and writer, invective and satirical literature targeting the vices of courtesans was flourishing in the literary salons of Venice. Domenico Venier's salon, where Franco honed her literary skills and met many of the most famous writers in the city, was no exception. While Franco's experience in the salon was undoubtedly fundamental in furthering her literary career, her relationship with the men she met there was not always positive. Indeed, the literary attack waged on her by Maffio Venier suggests that her presence in the salon was not always welcome. In 1575 another visitor to the salon, the Paduan scholar Sperone Speroni (1500-1588), wrote a moralistic tract entitled *Orazione contra le cortegiane* (Oration Against Courtesans) that denounced courtesans as nothing more than prostitutes. In the preface, Speroni asserts that the tract, which gives examples of courtesans ruined by greed and *lussuria* (lascivious desire), aims to show such women the errors of their ways in hopes that they will leave the profession for a more honorable lifestyle.

In attacking the courtesan, these satires joined a centuries-old tradition of anti-female literature that harks back at least to the philosophical and medical theories of the ancient Greeks. Indeed, sixteenth-century satirists justified their literary attacks on specific courtesans by invoking long-standing misogynist stereotypes (all women are greedy, sexually voracious, and incapable of faithfulness, to name a few). Yet, though long-standing, these commonplaces were used in attacks tied to personal and social relations specific to sixteenth-century Venice.

A number of male poets may have had professional cause for their jealousy and insecurity, since they had to compete with upwardly mobile courtesan writers like Veronica Franco for the attention and resources of patrons. Indeed, the attention Franco received from her patron Domenico Venier may have been the catalyst for Maffio Venier's vicious literary attack. What is remarkable about Veronica Franco is that she was not silenced by Maffio's attempts to defame and dishonor her. Instead, she responded to Maffio's attack by urging him to compete with her in a poetic battle, turning the attack into an opportunity to bolster her public and literary persona.

Sources and literary context. The most important influence on Franco's literary production was her association with Domenico Venier's literary salon held at his private palace in the heart of Venice. Venier, born into one of Venice's most privileged noble families, was the most important literary mentor in the city and a poet and an editor in his own right. His salon was the major center for intellectual and literary exchange in Venice until his death in 1582. One of the group's preferred poetic forms was the *capitolo*, the form that Franco chose for her *Poems in Terza Rima*; in fact, some of its *capitoli* were probably exchanged in manuscript with members of the salon before the book's publication in 1575.

Although Domenico Venier is not explicitly named as one of the men with whom she converses in the *Poems in Terza Rima*, "his role as literary and moral counselor is often evoked in her verses," and *capitoli* 15, 18, and 23 are addressed to him (Rosenthal, *The Honest Courtesan*, p. 179). In *Capitolo* 18, for example, Franco asks an unnamed "Molto illustre signor" (Most illustrious sir), for help with revisions of a poem she is writing.

Venier's group of vernacular poets also translated and wrote commentary on the themes and images of ancient Roman elegy (love poetry), which figure prominently in Franco's *capitoli*. The group's work on the Latin elegies of the poets Catullus, Ovid, Propertius, and Tibullus probably provided the basis for Franco's adaptation of their verse. Franco adapted the ancient writers' laments on exile, infidelity, jealousy, and loss, transforming their male voices into a female voice (*Poems*, p. 7). One of the most important Latin sources for Franco's poetry is Ovid's *Heroides*, a collection of letters in which the male poet writes in the female voice. Through Ovid's pen, classical heroines such as Penelope, Dido, and Medea reproach the famous lovers who have abandoned them. Franco also drew many powerful poetic images from the myths collected in Ovid's *Metamorphoses*. In a number of her poems Franco describes the effects of her lover's cruelty, which has caused her to flee the city, by using notions drawn from ancient Latin elegies (the pain of love, the distant lover's constant weeping and sighing). Interestingly, while the Latin poets present themselves as victims of powerful, talkative, sexually assertive courtesans, faulting the women for such qualities, Franco's speaker revels in precisely those qualities.

Reception. Franco probably circulated her poems in manuscript form among writers associated with the Venier salon. However, since very few copies of the *Poems in Terza Rima* were actually printed, it is unlikely that her poems were widely read outside her circle during her lifetime. Domenico Venier's interest in her poetry—given his role as the most important literary patron in the city—attests to at least some recognition of Franco's literary talent while she was alive. So does the fact that she was asked to compile a collection of sonnets as a tribute to a slain military hero (Estore Martinengo). This recognition would grow in the centuries to come.

In 1726, the Venetian poet and editor Luisa Bergalli included two of Franco's *capitoli* (Poem 12, in praise of Venice, and Poem 24, in which Franco takes a man to task for having threatened to slash a woman's face) in an anthology (*Componimenti poetici delle più illustri rimatrici d'ogni secolo* [Poems by the Most Illustrious Women Writers from Every Century]). About 150 years later, the Venetian historian Giuseppe Tassini wrote the first full-length biography of Franco (1874). It would, however, be another hundred years before Franco's work began to be studied as literature in its own right. Scholars of the twentieth century tried to place it in the tradition of sixteenth-century Petrarchan love poetry or its opposing camp. One study even suggested that Franco's verse was a corrective to Petrarchan poetry (Adler, p. 215). Later, in the twentieth century, in her landmark literary biography *The Honest Courtesan* (1992), Margaret F. Rosenthal presented Franco's poetry as part of a project of self-fashioning by Franco to gain entry into elite social and literary circles. Considering the poet's remarkable achievement, Rosenthal observed how groundbreaking Franco was, especially in poetic debate. In her quarrels in verse with fellow Venetians, she at once "manipulate[d]" standard practice "to suit her own designs" and crossed "boundaries of private domesticity and public silence" that were typically placed on women in her day (Rosenthal, p. 197).

—Courtney K. Quaintance

For More Information

Adler, Sara Maria. "Veronica Franco's Petrarchan Terze Rima: Subverting the Master's Plan." *Italica* 65, no. 3 (1988): 213-33.

Brand, Peter, and Lino Pertile, eds. *The Cambridge History of Italian Literature.* Cambridge: Cambridge University Press, 1996.

Coryat, Thomas. *Coryat's Crudities.* Glascow: University of Glasgow Press, 1905.

Franco, Veronica. *Lettere dall'unica edizione del MDLXXX con Proemio e nota iconografica.* Naples: Ricciardi, 1949.

———. *Poems in Terza Rima.* In *Poems and Selected Letters.* Ed. Ann Rosalind Jones and Margaret F. Rosenthal. Chicago: The University of Chicago Press, 1998.

Lorenzi, Giovanni Batista, ed. *Leggi e memorie venete sulla prostituzione fino alla caduta della Repubblica.* Venice, 1870-1872.

Rosenthal, Margaret F. *The Honest Courtesan: Veronica Franco, Citizen and Writer in Sixteenth-Century Venice.* Chicago: University of Chicago Press, 1992.

———. "Veronica Franco's *Terze Rima*: The Venetian Courtesan's Defense." *Renaissance Quarterly* 42 (1989): 227-57.

Ruggiero, Guido. *Binding Passions: Tales of Magic, Marriage, and Power at the End of the Renaissance.* Oxford: Oxford University Press, 1993.

Scarabello, Giovanni. "Le 'signore' della repubblica." In *Il gioco dell'amore: le cortigiane di Venezia dal Trecento al Settecento.* Milan: Berenice, 1990.

Tassini, Giuseppe. *Veronica Franco: Celebre poetessa e cortigiana del secolo XVI.* Venice: Alfieri, 1969.

Venier, Lorenzo. *La Zaffetta.* Ed. Gino Raya. Catania: Libreria Tirelli, 1929.

The Poetry of Eugenio Montale

Born in Genova in 1896, Eugenio Montale began to study opera singing in 1915 for eight years, until the premature death of his teacher, the baritone Ernesto Sivori. He meanwhile (in 1916) started to write his first poems, which he described as musical in their inspiration. As a student at the University of Genova, Montale came into contact with the philosophy of Arthur Schopenhauer and Emile Boutroux, as well as with the music of Claude Debussy. Although Montale fought in the First World War in 1918, the experience did not shape his ongoing poetic production as much as would the advent of Fascism in 1922 or the Second World War. As the youngest son of a prosperous northern family, growing into adulthood during this era, Montale inherited a sense of futility, which nurtured his tendency to dabble in one thing and another (he studied opera and philosophy, worked for his father as an accountant, wrote poetry, painted, and worked as a journalist). It seemed to him that most life choices are at best awkward attempts at meaning. In 1926 he joined the Bemporad publishing house in Florence and quickly became a central figure in the Florentine literary world. Montale was increasingly recognized as a major voice in Italian poetry, his focus on isolation and the impossibility of communication resonating with the political disillusionment of his generation. In 1933 the poet began an intense love affair with the young Jewish-American scholar and writer Irma Brandeis, whom he considered following to the United States in 1938. Ultimately, how-

> ## THE LITERARY WORK
>
> Three collections of poetry, *Cuttlefish Bones*, *The Occasions*, and *The Storm, Etc.*, published in Italian in 1925, 1939, and 1956, respectively; in English in 1959, 1978, 1987, and 1992.
>
> ## SYNOPSIS
>
> Montale's poems reinvest with new meanings the medieval themes *amor de lonh* ("love from afar," tied to a sense of incompleteness and solitude) and *donna angelicata* ("angelic lady," guide to the lover-poet from beyond). In thoroughly modern terms, his poems reflect on alienation and the attempt to communicate with an elusive other.

ever, Montale remained in Italy and moved in with Drusilla Tanzi; their relationship would last until her death in 1963. In 1943-44 Montale sheltered a number of writer friends forced into hiding from the Fascist government, including the poet Umberto Saba and the novelist Carlo Levi.

After the war, Montale joined the liberal political party Partito d'Azione and began to write for Italy's leading daily, the Milanese *Il Corriere della Sera* (The Evening Courier), going on to become an editor for the paper. He also reinvented his poetic style in *Satura* (1962; Miscellany), *Diario del '71 e del '72* (1973; Diary of '71 and '72),

Eugenio Montale

and *Quaderno di Quattro Anni* (1977; Four Years' Notebook), describing these postwar collections as the reverse, more biting side of his earlier production. In 1975 Montale won the Nobel Prize for Literature, after which he continued to pursue his poetic and journalistic activities until his death in Milan in 1981. Focusing on the nothingness of his own self and of an inescapably chaotic world, Montale was in his later years self-consciously ironic about poetry's ability to communicate; this irony, however, is not without compassion for human solitude, and ultimately reflects Montale's lifelong commitment to a poetic enchantment that is as unstable, as precious, and as mortal as ourselves.

Events in History at the
Time of the Poems

Political and social disillusionment: the liberal era, Fascism, and its aftermath. As in the rest of Europe, Romanticism in Italy delved into the sublime solitude of a self confronted with the grandness of nature and the impossible realization of romantic love. Also as in other lands, Romanticism surfaced in Italy in the early nineteenth century, most intensely from about 1815 to 1827, a period of literary experimentation and debate in the still separate Italian states, which would unify only in 1861. Peculiar to Italy because of

this circumstance was the association of familiar Romantic themes with the longing for an as-yet-absent Italian nation, the achievement of a linguistic, social, and political identity that would give shape to, if not transcend, solitude.

Italy's political unification proved, however, to be a major disappointment in the 1860s, at least to the cultural elites. For them, unification failed to bridge the gap between industrialization in the North and poverty in the South, and between peasant and cosmopolitan identities. Furthermore, it did not resolve the conflict between an ideally cohesive Italian cultural tradition and the reality: religious skepticism, psychological fragmentation (connected to the rise of criminology and psychology), and the alienating force of modern capitalism and city life. During the liberal era, until the advent of Fascism in 1922, Italy's coalition governments fell at an alarming rate, reflecting these unresolved tensions.

Along with political unification came an intense anxiety about Italy's economic "backwardness," especially with respect to the major colonial powers of England and France. This worry led to a radical transformation of the northern landscape through the growth of industry and urbanization, and to ecological disaster in the South through harmful agricultural practices. The dominant trends of the era, in turn, led to a crisis in Italian local identity, which had been closely tied to native landscapes and established social structures, which in some parts of the country were still largely feudal. Until he was nearly 30, Montale retreated at times to his family home on the Ligurian shore in northwest Italy, depicted as a shelter from these changes, a garden paradise, though humble as an orchard or vegetable plot. The atmosphere was premodern, the social life, intimate, amounting to what Montale experienced as a vanishing world. It was a physical vestige of the past to which World War II (which destroyed his other childhood home, in Genova) would deal the last blow. The large majority of Italians lost one or more family members in World War I. As a soldier in this war, Montale witnessed mass death on an unprecedented scale. He seems to have experienced the Great War as a confirmation of the ceaseless chaotic violence of history, evoked recurrently in his poems. Consequently he reacted differently from the majority of Italians to Mussolini's takeover of power in the country during the March on Rome in 1922. While many Italians saw it as a necessary, if violent, redressing of the failures of Italian unification and of wartime uncertainties, Montale was part of a minority who saw the troubled prewar liberal era and Fascist totalitarianism as part of a flawed continuum. As an editor and writer in Florence in the 1920s and 1930s, he became part of a group of intellectuals (others include Carlo Emilio Gadda, Carlo Levi, Mario Praz, and Umberto Saba) who refused involvement in Fascism, at times militantly and dangerously (Levi was sentenced to internal exile for his political activities), and at times by disengaging from history's chaos and searching inward for their identity.

In the post-World War II era, after the fall of Fascism, Montale sided with Italian intellectuals who blamed the liberal era for the rise of Fascism in Italy. He also denounced the continuities between the Fascist leaders and the leaders of the Christian Democrat Party, which would govern Italy for more than 40 years after the war. For Montale, as for many dissenting left-wing Italians (and Europeans) from the 1940s through the 1960s, World War II became the very emblem for the rule of evil in the world and the bankrupt condition of Western civilization.

The crisis of individualism—Decadentism to Modernism. Decadence was a literary movement that began in France in the early 1880s. Named after the violent and dissolute period of the fall of the Roman Empire, the movement was shaped by a few writers (Joris-Karl Huysmans, Paul Bourget, and Jean Moréas). It denounced but also sought to complete the breakdown of Western ideologies, drawing parallels between a loss of faith in language to communicate, early psychology's discovery of a person's inherent internal conflicts, concepts of society as warring forces (Marxism and Anarchism), and skepticism about a higher religious or overarching spiritual order. In France, as in Italy, a dominant metaphor for this crisis was that of illness (of self, society, and the world). The Italian cultural movement of Decadentism, however, differed from that of its French partner, in particular because it saw in the many avant-garde movements that appeared at the turn of the century not a cure for but a deepening of decadence. In the eyes of the anti-Fascist intellectuals, the success of Fascism in Italy only reinforced this despondent view.

The foremost figure of Italian Decadentism was Gabriele D'Annunzio (1863-1938): in his novels, poems, and plays—but also in his nationalist speeches and symbolic World War I daredevil raids—he celebrated artifice. D'Annunzio championed the dandy, the "artist-superman" whose very life was a work of art, and the "superman-artist,"

a spiritual leader who could transform politics into a supreme aesthetic spectacle. For Montale and other writers of his generation, D'Annunzio became a father-like figure, despite the fact that his work showed a fundamental ambivalence. D'Annunzio's writings proposed art as the ultimate cure for the West's illness, yet essentially they also asserted that there could be no real cure. His 1919 takeover of the city of Fiume, which D'Annunzio accomplished with a band of disgruntled World War I veterans, became a symbol for Montale's generation. (The veterans were disgruntled because Italy, though a "winner" in the war suffered a "mutilated victory," losing territories in Dalmatia, where Fiume was located.) In December 1920 under international pressure, the Italian government bombed the city, ending the takeover and driving D'Annunzio into over 20 years of more-or-less voluntary solitude, in a home on Lake Garda.

There were artistic trends that tried to overcome the crisis in spirit and values reflected in Decadent art. Two responses emerged: first, from a collection of late-nineteenth-century poets known as the *I crepusculari* poets (from *crepuscolo*, or "sunset") and second, from the early-twentieth-century Futurist artists (see **The Founding and Manifesto of Futurism**, also in *WLAIT 7: Italian Literature and Its Times*). The crepuscular poets tried to focus on humble objects, people, and places tied to local and temporary contexts in the countryside, a strategy that enabled them to bypass the ideal of a modern art at one with social and political life. In contrast, Futurism found hope in the impersonal machine, the chaotic violence of modern city life, and the transforming capacity of war. Neither of these artistic responses solved the cultural crisis, however. A melancholy or sense of tacit loss surrounded the verse of the crepuscular poets, and Futurism's very reliance on the mechanical meant that it was just opposing an established order with another less visible, more abstract, but no less individually stifling order.

The main figures of what could be considered the Italian version of High Modernism (*Ermetismo*, or "Hermeticism") are Montale, Giuseppe Ungaretti, and Umberto Saba (see Ungaretti's **Life of a Man**, also in *WLAIT 7: Italian Literature and Its Times*). Though quite different from one another, the three have in common an overt desire no longer to overcome Decadentism's illness, but rather to face with courage the impossibility of a cure and the loss of any overarching, timeless, or externally objective truth. For Montale, the self is at once inescapably determined by the everyday and at the same time in search of an escape route, and the escape lies not in the discovery of an alternative order, but in the acceptance of disorder. The central image of *Cuttlefish Bones* is the self as a very small, pared-down, beautiful but useless debris buffeted by a history that is overarching but out of control:

> Oh, tumbled then
> like the cuttlefish bone by the waves,
> to vanish bit by bit;
>
> (Montale, *Eugenio Montale:*
> *Collected Poems*, p. 143)

Montale seeks acceptance of this self instead of a melancholy and crepuscular meditation on its vanishing.

The Poems in Focus

Contents summary. "Chrysalis" (from *Cuttlefish Bones*) focuses on the ephemeral quality of attempts at salvation. In "The hope of even seeing you again . . ." (from *The Occasions*), the poet discovers in a flash that on rare occasions reality offers up objects that recall the beloved and open at least a temporary possibility of communication. In "Iris" (from *The Storm, Etc.*), these elements come together. Montale finds in his absent lady's capacity for her own self-transcendence a relief from his personal conviction that truth can only be subjective, human, and possible but uncertain.

"Chrysalis." This poem interweaves the themes central to Montale's first collection, *Cuttlefish Bones*, focusing on passing traces of the absent lady, on the poet's experience of them as a sort of despairing or existential "limbo," and finally on his hope that the experience itself may be a form of communication that provides salvation. The poem opens with a wintery garden just barely awakened by "the breath of April," in which "quivers in the air" seem to beckon; in the second stanza, movement intensifies as the poet experiences "amazement" as well as "an undertow of memories" in which "time plummets," leading him to "reach / for this sunlit occurrence" from his "dark lookout" (Collected Poems, p. 115). This is not an ecstatic moment—the poet is constantly aware of his position in a darker present—but rather a reaching downward and inward into time past to invoke the presence of the lady. As is true for almost all of Montale's poems, the absent one—addressed mostly as "tu" (the singular "you"), but at times as "voi" (the plural and more formal "you")—is related to a specific person and real events, with an overlay of memories of other persons and events. Mon-

tale in his darker present cannot always separate one unique memory from another. In the third stanza, he compares the fleeting quality of "this sunlit occurrence" to the few essential moments of connection he has shared with another, stating finally that the mystery of life and joy lies only in such moments (Collected Poems, p. 115).

> You are my prey, who offer me
> one brief hour of human fervor.
> I don't want to waste an instant:
> this is my share, and nothing else has meaning;
> My wealth is this beating
> that moves in you and lifts
> your face to the sky; this slow
> staring around of eyes that can now see.
>
> (*Collected Poems*, pp. 115-17)

In the following two stanzas, an "opaque / shadow" envelops the moment and the memory, leaving the poet "in the bleak limbo of dissolved existences," in which even the signs of spring that seemed to beckon become "a barren secret" (*Collected Poems*, p. 117). The poet turns to the ocean, where "illusion can arise / and release its mists" so that there seems to appear "among the shoals" "in the hazy afternoon" "the bark of our salvation," which awaits, immobile, unable to give us direction (*Collected Poems*, p. 117). Finally, in the longest and last stanza, Montale at once expresses his desolation at how everything passes, how all is borne away by time, fixed in memory but unattainable, known through signs (like the bark) that offer no certain direction. At the same time, he opens himself to the hope that desolation itself conceals a truth, that in offering it to his absent lady, he might reach out to her joy:

> Ah chrysalis, how bitter
> is this nameless torture that envelops us
> and spirits us away—
> till not even our footprints last in the dust;
> and we'll go on, not having moved
> a single stone in the great wall;
> and maybe everything is fixed, is written,
> and we'll never see it come our way:
> freedom, the miracle,
> the act that wasn't pure necessity!
> . . . .
> the pact I want to make
> with destiny: to redeem
> your joy through my condemning.
> This is the hope that lives in my heart.
>
> (*Collected Poems*, pp. 117-19)

Ultimately the poem's title, referring to the cocooned pupa of the butterfly (in Ancient Greek the word is *psyche*, which also means soul), suggests that the lady's soul or personhood is not so much lost in shadow as it is enveloped and protected from the illusions of memory, so that, however prone to vanish, she remains potentially present.

"The hope of ever seeing you again . . ." Typical of Montale's second collection, *The Occasions,* this poem is mainly inspired, as is the whole collection, by the departure of Irma Brandeis, and Montale's intense experience of absence and separation. There is a distinctly medieval inspiration in the lady's disappearance behind a screen that is the world of appearances in which we are enmeshed. Also specific to this second collection is the poem's movement from memory toward the mystery of the objects that awakened it, which are made most palpably present at the end without revealing exactly how memory works. There is a disconcerting image of "jackals on a leash"; whether real or part of a whimsical shared moment, the image recalls for Montale an instant of connection with his lady so intensely personal that it must remain mostly unsaid. "Occasions," then, are moments in which memory simply is, in its vividness and power, beyond any possible explanation.

> The hope of even seeing you again
> was leaving me;
>
> and I asked myself if this which keeps me from
> all sense of you, this screen of images,
> is marked by death, or if, out of the past,
> but deformed and diminished, it entails
> some flash *of yours:*
>
> (under the arcades, at Modena,
> a servant in gold braid led
> two jackals on a leash).
>
> (*Collected Poems,* p. 197)

"Iris." In his third collection, *The Storm, Etc.,* Montale confronts most directly a struggle that is central to the Italian love lyric, giving it a uniquely modern interpretation. The struggle is one between the earthly temporal experience and transcendent absolutes, and it surfaces in "Iris." A poem again inspired by Irma Brandeis, "Iris" now links her absence to the poet's sense of God's withdrawal from the world. The first three stanzas (separated from the other four by ellipses denoting distance and a gap in understanding), evoke the Canadian landscape the poet imagines surrounding Irma Brandeis, superimposing upon it two symbolic interpretations. On the one hand, it is Saint Martin's day (November 1st), suggestive for Italians of Indian summer and the contrast of bright sunlight and "berries" with the oncoming cold (*Collected Poems,* p. 355). On the

other hand, the oxymoron of "icy fire" and the red "poppies" in the bleak white of winter recall "the bloodied Face [of Christ] on the shroud" and, most important, his double nature, at once human and divine (*Collected Poems,* p. 355). Hence the poet describes himself as a "poor dismayed Nestorian," referring to Nestorius, the patriarch of Constantinople who was banished to the desert for affirming that there existed in Jesus not one human and divine nature, but two separate ones, of which the human (compassion and suffering) was most important (*Collected Poems,* p. 574). The first part of the poem concludes with Montale's reassertion of concrete and historically situated suffering (World War II: "the shipwreck of my people [the Italians] / and yours [the Jews]"), within which the only "rosary," or trace of salvation, is his image of his beloved in her landscape, which radiates a light reminiscent of Christian salvation (*Collected Poems,* p. 355). In the second part of the poem, Montale contrasts the cruelty of the wildcat lynx with the coldness of a domestic cat, the "lovely tabby," which is "Syrian," a detail that alludes to the Near East and Irma Brandeis's origins (*Collected Poems,* p. 575). The lines can be read to mean that the cat and the lynx seem the same from the distance that separates her world from his, an almost transcendent distance, intimating that what divides humans from one another is not time and space but something more primordial. Finally in the last two stanzas, Montale evokes Irma Brandeis's own destiny as a Jew and an exile in search of a promised land, shaped by the common suffering of her people: distinct from Montale's own destiny, her life nonetheless embodies for him a compassion linked to Christ's humanity, the sign of an earthly salvation, a possible respite from human separation and separateness. Even though life has changed for both the poet and his beloved, and no concrete reunion is possible for them, they remain connected by his hope that through her work she may succeed in gaining the sense of self-transcendence that he cannot find.

> So that your work (which is a form
> of His) might flourish in other lights,
> Iris of Canaan, you deliquesced
> into that halo of mistletoe and holly
> which bears your heart into the night
> of the world, beyond the mirage
> of the desert flowers, your kin.
>
> If you appear, you bring me here again,
> under the pergola of barren vines
> by the landing on our river—and the ferry's
>   not returning,

the Indian summer sun dissolves, goes black.
But if you come back, you're not you,
your earthly history is changed,
you don't wait for the prow at the pier,

you watch for nothing: yesterday or tomorrow;

for His work (which is transforming
into yours) *has to continue.*
                    (*Collected Poems*, pp. 355-57)

The title of the poem, "Iride," which can be rendered as iris of the eye, iris as flower, rainbow,
and iridescence, suggests most of all the indeci-
pherable yet radiant light, ambiguously individual and transcendent, left by Montale's beloved
in her departure.

**Individual love, history, and contingent salva-
tion.** Montale's three main collections were written during the Fascist and post-World War II eras.
His poetry therefore reflects the double alienation
of a generation that experienced modernity not
only as the loss of local community and landscape
to industrialization, but also as the rise of totalitarian states that deprive the individual of freedom in its most basic sense: to shape one's
existence and search for meaning in life beyond
the restrictions of one particular ideology or another. In these years, his poems were known
mainly through a few small literary journals, including *Il Baretti*, edited by the anti-Fascist Piero
Gobetti, and *Solaria*, founded by Montale and
other dissident writers in Florence). Yet the poems were highly influential because of their sharp
critique of the present as a "barren limbo" in
which it was nonetheless urgent for the individual to experience love and to search for meaning
beyond the self. His reputation and his poetry's
focus on personal internal struggles allowed Montale to avoid Fascist censorship. As a defender of
human-centered values, he could appear to be relatively neutral politically, yet succeed under a totalitarian regime, in conveying to a generation of
aspiring writers the urgent need to respect the individual. In this context, Montale's poetry is an
unprecedented reinvention of the traditional love
lyric, on two levels. First, he reformulates an old
search to transcend the self that shows up in Italian literary works (such as Petrarch's *Secretum*),
into a modern question about what the search
means and whether it is truly possible to know
someone else. Second, he painfully acknowledges
how the forces of history infringe on any search
for self-transcendence, recognizing that even spiritual quests are shaped by material conditions. His
poetry sees in love a possible—but improbable
and ambiguous—salvation:

Maybe I'll find a face again:
[. . .]
I reach for it, and feel
another life becoming mine, encumbered
with a form that was taken from me;
and it's hair, not leaves, that winds
round my fingers like rings.

Then nothing more.
                    (*Collected Poems*, p. 139)

You know: I have to give you up again
and I can't. [. . .]
I'm after the lost sign, the single
pledge you graced me with.
                    And hell is certain.
                    (*Collected Poems*, p. 193)

In the **Divine Comedy**, Dante distinguishes
between sacred and profane love, and is guided
toward the end of his journey through the afterlife by the spirit of his beloved Beatrice, who
leads him to a final reunion with the divine
essence (also in *WLAIT 7: Italian Literature and
Its Times*). Montale implicitly questions Dante's
delineation of the category "profane" or "infernal" love. As Dante explains it, initially his love
for Beatrice was profane; later it was entirely spir-
itualized. Montale questions this clear-cut
distinction, insisting that from a modern, secular viewpoint, the sacred and profane stem from
the same source. His lady is therefore, at once
she who "burned with love / for Him who moved
her," meaning, an angelic guide, and "the ghost
of memory," a "phantom" who is perhaps an illusion or mere projection of desire (*Collected Poems*, pp. 377, 379, 5).

Sources and literary context. More than any
other Modernist poet, Montale draws on the tradition of the Italian and Provençal love lyric, re-
visiting some of its core elements, such as the
tension between sacred love and profane love,
the lover's tormented search for traces or tokens
of love from his lady, his lonely introspection,
and finally the disconnection between love and
history. The title of Montale's third collection,
The Storm, echoes Dante's *Inferno* 5, which includes the adulterous lovers Paolo and Francesca,
condemned to eternal uprootedness in an infernal gale ("bufera infernal," that is, storm), and to
endless regret for the "profane" love they briefly
shared. Drawing on the **"Dolce stil novo"** (Sweet
New Style) that preceded Dante's *Comedy*, and
on troubadour lyrics, Montale insists on the
painful ambivalence of signals given by the lady
and of the objects that are her emblems (also in
WLAIT 7: Italian Literature and Its Times). Hence

MONTALE'S COMPLEX LANGUAGE

Montale's use of language reflects his sense of complexity in life: hypothetical phrases, questions, and a constant return to contradiction and paradox are some of his standard practices. They are central to his sharp questioning of language's power to communicate and describe. One of his earliest statements to this effect is from *Cuttlefish Bones:*

> Don't ask us for the word to square
> our shapeless spirit on all sides,
> [. . .]
> This, today, is all we can tell you:
> what we are *not,* what we do *not* want.
>
> *(Collected Poems,* p. 39)

Montale draws on his experience in music, on French Symbolist poetry, and on medieval Italian poetry for this strategy of speaking negatively. The strategy tries first to achieve the allusiveness of music, in particular its moments of counterpoint and dissonance. Second is the impact of the French Symbolist poets, who associated their verse not only with music but also with beautiful but mysterious objects whose true essence or purpose remains hidden. Third, Montale is inspired by negative theology in the works of such early Italian poets as Guido Cavalcanti, whose systematic negation of all that has been previously asserted leads one to experience a "nothingness." This nothingness is ironically vaster and fuller than all the terms that fail to circumscribe it. These are the factors that help shape such poems as Montale's "The Garden" (ellipses ours):

> I don't know . . .
>
> . . . .
> I don't know if . . .
>
> . . . .
> I don't know if your muffled step,
>
> . . . .
> I don't know if your step that makes
> my veins throb . . .
>
> . . . .
> I don't know if the hand grazing my shoulder
>
> . . . .
> . . . If the power
> that drives the disk [LP, record] *already etched* were another
> surely your destiny conjoined with mine
> would show a single groove.
>
> *(Collected Poems,* pp. 363-65)

the ray of light radiating from the beloved's forehead and eyes (a typical image for love's action in medieval writings) is at once a "sign [that] was right" and "a glare that snares the eyes," a deceitful trap (*Collected Poems,* pp. 407, 43). Also for Montale, unlike the medieval poets, the emblems themselves constantly change in meaning, so there can be no victory or defeat in love, only uncertainty.

The poet's introspection here comes to the fore, as it did following Dante in love poetry written in the style of Petrarch's verse: the psychological effects of love become more important than the lady herself, and the self-absorbed poet struggles with his own *pensier* ("thought"; see Petrarch's *Canzoniere,* also in *WLAIT 7: Italian Literature and Its Times*). But whereas Petrarch's solitude leads to an understanding of the self as a meaningful microcosm of the world, in Montale solitude is never fully distinguishable from the idea that the self is all that has reality or that one can know in life. In such a context, thought and even poetry itself may be nothing more than empty self-pity:

> and the dark voice love dictates
> goes hoarse, becomes whining writing
> (Collected Poems, p. 77)

The traditions set for the love lyric underwent change in the nineteenth century, taking on a new form. The early-nineteenth-century Romantics saw unrealizable love, both for the beloved and for the nation (in the poetry of Ugo Foscolo, in particular), as an ennobling tragic passion. Later, this view was undercut by the Decadent Movement, whose members regarded such passion as an illness.

Affected by new disciplines like psychology, many of the twentieth-century reflections on love have explored the emptiness of desire. In contrast, Montale insists that passion's very failure can be productive. What elicits desire is, in his view, greater, more complex and more contradictory than what desire can grasp. Also, for Montale, one must take into account the events of history; its unpredictability is what makes all gestures such as love momentary and uncertain. Irma Brandeis, to whom the following lines are dedicated, was wrested away from Montale, as he saw it, by her Jewish American identity and the realities of World War II.

> the blind have failed to see
> the omen of your incandescent forehead,
> the line I've etched in blood there, cross and
>   chrism
> charm calamity vow farewell
> perdition and salvation;
> (Collected Poems, p. 393)

Aside from drawing on the Italian love lyric tradition, Montale's poetry was shaped by conversations with his contemporaries, in particular with the two Italian poets Giuseppe Ungaretti and Umberto Saba. To varying degrees, they all turned to the French Symbolists as a way to bridge the gap between Romanticism and the present in Italian poetry. Montale saw in the isolation of the poetic word and in the finiteness of objects a potentially enriching, if negative, experience of the connection he longed for, a longing for contact with the other that although unrealized was nevertheless real. Other influences on Montale were his conversations with the American-born Ezra Pound, from whom Montale gained his appreciation of the sense of infinite yearning and pain in the British poetry of Robert Browning. Returning to Italian influences, he undercuts this sense with an irony linked to the skepticism, self-deprecation, and idea of an "existence imagined but not achieved" apparent in the writing of Italo Svevo (Collected Poems, p. 471; see Zeno's Conscience, also in WLAIT 7: Italian Literature and Its Times). What was the impact of all these influences? In the end, Montale's poetry evolved less as a spiritual journey into the self than as a paring down of the self to make room for yearning.

Reception. For a small literary circle Montale's work came to represent an emphasis on individual freedom in contrast with Fascist repression. But it was only after World War II that he became a major player, both in Italy's postwar cultural renewal, as a journalist, and internationally, as a representative of that renewal. Montale's visits to the American-English writer T. S. Eliot in 1948 and to the French writer Albert Camus in 1953 are markers of his increasing international presence. Major studies of his work include West's Eugenio Montale, Poet on the Edge (1981), based in part on interviews with the poet, Cambon's Eugenio Montale's Poetry: a Dream in Reason's Presence (1982), as well as Biasin's Montale, Debussy, and Modernism (1989). Most important, Montale's first three collections appeared in Jonathan Galassi's translation in 1998. The fruit of many years of meditation on Montale, it is both lyrically successful and explanatory. Accompanying the poems is a thorough discussion that makes Montale's main works far more accessible to English-speaking audiences than the works of his Italian contemporaries. For Galassi, the import of Montale lies in his ability to confront in verses the "terrors and failings of the present" as well as "the great ruin of the past," yet at the same time convey a hint of faith "in his dream, in himself, in the essential power of poetry" (Collected Poems, pp. 426-27).

—Laura Wittman

For More Information

Becker, Jared. Eugenio Montale. Boston: Twayne Publishers, 1986.

Biasin, Gian-Paolo. Montale, Debussy, and Modernism. Princeton, N. J.: Princeton University Press, 1989.

Brook, Clodagh J. The Expression of the Inexpressible in Eugenio Montale's Poetry: Metaphor, Negation, and Silence. Oxford: Oxford University Press, 2002.

Cambon, Glauco. Eugenio Montale's Poetry: A Dream in Reason's Presence. Princeton, N. J.: Princeton University Press, 1982.

Cary, Joseph. *Three Modern Italian Poets: Saba, Ungaretti, Montale.* New York: New York University Press, 1993.

Huffman, Claire de C. L. *Montale and the Occasions of Poetry.* Princeton: Princeton University Press, 1983.

Montale, Eugenio. *Eugenio Montale: Collected Poems, 1920-1958.* Ed. and trans. Jonathan Galassi. New York: Farrar, Straus and Giroux, 1998.

Petrucciani, Mario. *La poetica dell'ermetismo italiano.* Torino: Loascher, 1955.

West, Rebecca J. *Eugenio Montale, Poet on the Edge.* Cambridge, Mass.: Harvard University Press, 1981.

The Prince

by

Niccolò Machiavelli

Niccolò Machiavelli was born in Florence on May 3, 1469, the year Lorenzo de' Medici began to rule the city. Niccolò's father was a notary/lawyer from a well-respected but not an overly wealthy family with noble origins and some landholdings in the Tuscan countryside. Machiavelli enjoyed an education suitable for a young man of his station—he was schooled in Latin but apparently not in Greek. Though interested in a career in government, he lost a bid to become secretary in the second chancellery (which prepared reports for Florentine leaders) under the rule of the Dominican friar Girolamo Savonarola, who had succeeded Lorenzo de' Medici in 1494. In 1498, when Savonarola fell from power, Machiavelli's fortunes improved. The Florentine Republic elected him secretary of the second chancellery, and he was also appointed secretary of the *10 of balìa,* which oversaw foreign relations. These postings and his diplomatic travels allowed Machiavelli to observe the military and political conditions in Florence and other Italian states. Of particular importance for *The Prince* was his view (1502-1503) of the ambitious military campaigns of Cesare Borgia, son of Pope Alexander VI. Borgia tried to carve out a permanent power base in central Italy, acting with a ruthless abandon that would serve as a model for Machiavelli when he wrote *The Prince.* Machiavelli also drew on his experiences as diplomatic envoy to the court of the king of France and to the Holy Roman Emperor in Germany (1498-1512). In 1512 Spanish troops allied with Cardinal Giovanni de' Medici sacked the nearby

THE LITERARY WORK

A political essay describing the Italian states in 1513; published in Italian (as *De Principatus*) in 1532, in English in 1640.

SYNOPSIS

After listing the types of territories governed by princes and explaining how to acquire and retain power, the treatise exhorts the rulers of Florence to liberate the regions of Italy from foreign rule.

city of Prato, provoking the fall of Machiavelli's employer—the Florentine Republic. The period of republican rule (1494-1512) ended, and Machiavelli lost his position. The Medici family, who had ruled Florence before the republican period, returned to power, followed by another period of republican rule (1527-1530). Finally, the troops of Charles V, the Holy Roman Emperor and Spanish monarch, besieged Florence, and it again returned to Medici rule, which led to its becoming a hereditary duchy (in 1532) with Alessandro de' Medici as duke. It was in this same year that Machiavelli published *The Prince.* Despite having written a short treatment in favor of Medici rule (*Ai Palleschi,* 1512), Machiavelli was imprisoned and, it seems, tortured for his alleged role in an anti-Medici plot in 1513. Later that year Giovanni de' Medici became the pope (as Leo X), and Machiavelli was released as part of

Niccolò Machiavelli

an amnesty. He tried in vain to regain his Florentine post by writing *De Principatus* (*The Prince*) and dedicating it to Lorenzo II de' Medici (1492-1519), Duke of Urbino.

Aside from his nonfiction works, Machiavelli wrote poetry and drama. He composed the raucous comedies *The Mandrake* (1518) and *The Clizia* (1525), both modeled on the comedy-of-errors type of play by classical authors. Closer to *The Prince* is his other political treatise, *The Discourses* (1513-19), a commentary on the historical writings of the ancient Roman historian Livy. In his political writings, Machiavelli attempts to address the weaknesses of republican Florence and the Italian states of his day by understanding the successes of ancient Rome. While *The Prince* can be seen as a handbook for autocrats, *The Discourses* can be thought of as a companion piece with political advice for republican institutions. It is in *The Prince* that Machiavelli provides a brutally realistic assessment of the uses of power that still resonates today.

Events in History at the Time of the Essay

Economic and political decline. During Machiavelli's youth, the Italian states reached the apex of a period of cultural and economic prosperity unparalleled since classical times. Florence had grown into a major financial and commercial center, as had Venice. The Papal States (centered in Rome) enjoyed widespread political influence, since Church authorities throughout Europe considered themselves subject to the Roman pope rather than to the rulers of their respective countries. Machiavelli's generation would witness the ebbing of this favorable position for the Italian states, however. Part of the urgency in works like *The Prince,* as in the histories of Machiavelli's friend Francesco Guicciardini (1483-1540), is a desire to understand the downturn in Italy's fortunes.

Machiavelli worked in the Florentine chancellery from 1498 until he went into forced retirement after the Medici restoration in 1512. During this period, the political map of the world changed to the disadvantage of the previously independent states of the Italian peninsula. In the fifteenth century, events to the east and to the west of the peninsula had repeatedly disfavored them. The Venetian republic had become increasingly vulnerable to incursions from the Ottoman Empire after the Turkish conquest of Constantinople in 1453. Moreover, explorations and discoveries achieved by other Europeans jeopardized the trading advantages enjoyed by the Italians. The Portuguese established routes around Africa, and the Spanish reached the Americas, developments that would later diminish Italy's geographic advantage in world trade. Italian merchants would eventually lose their middleman position between northern European markets and Far Eastern traders of spices and silks, though in Machiavelli's lifetime, Venice, for example, continued to engage in a vigorous spice trade. Meanwhile, the Roman Catholic Church lost some prestige because of the unsavory conduct of Pope Alexander VI and scandals caused by later popes who sold indulgences to finance the rich papal court in Rome. During his brief rule in Florence, the friar Girolamo Savonarola attempted a radical reform of the Roman Catholic Church, but he was burned at the stake in 1498. Attempts at religious reform would soon continue with renewed vigor, but these attempts would begin only after Machiavelli wrote *The Prince.*

In 1513, when Machiavelli finished the treatise, Italy was in the throes of the Italian Wars, which saw the monarchies of France and Spain fighting for military and political control over parts of the Italian peninsula. (The period is described by Guicciardini in his *History of Italy* [1561, 1564]). After the French king Charles VIII invaded the peninsula in 1494, it experienced increasing violence and political chaos; by comparison, the late fifteenth century was tranquil. In mid century, the Peace of Lodi (1454) had stabilized relations among the Italian states, whose pact endured so well that later observers looked back on the period (1454-94) as a golden age. These were the years of Machiavelli's boyhood. Florence was more politically independent at this stage than in his adult years, when persistent conflicts engulfed the Italian states and much of their peninsula. Also, before Charles VIII's 1494 invasion, rivalries for political control had ensued largely among Italian peninsular powers; now the peninsula was more internationally contested. The French invasion and subsequent struggles among France, Spain, the Papal States, and the Venetian Republic pointed to a fundamental weakness in the Italian states of the early 1500s: none had consolidated enough control of the peninsula to prevent Italy from becoming a battleground in the struggle between France and Spain to dominate Europe. It is during this troubled period in Italian history that Machiavelli served (1498-1512) in Florence's chancellery.

Cultural decline? The peninsula's political struggles gave rise to shifting alliances among Venice, France, the Papal States, Milan, and Spain, alliances that form a backdrop for *The Prince*. As noted, the treatise is to some degree an urgent call to rid the land of outsiders. Beyond this call, Machiavelli's works show a desire to understand and, if possible, correct the course of Italian history in his day, which Machiavelli expressed not only in his writings. Until his death in 1527, he tried to regain a political post in Florence. Strife meanwhile continued to plague the peninsula. The very year of his death, Spanish troops under the generals of Charles V, Holy Roman Emperor and king of Spain, sacked and brutally pillaged the holy city of Rome, one horrific episode in a cycle of warfare that spanned more than half a century (1494-1559).

As the Italian states lost political autonomy, the religious environment heated up too. In 1517 Martin Luther posted a list of grievances against the Catholic Church on the door of All Saints Church in Wittenberg, Germany, and thus began the religious revolt known as the Reformation. Luther's movement inspired a backlash by the Church hierarchy in Rome, which led to the Counter Reformation, a movement to block the loss of papal authority.

Meanwhile, Italy maintained its distinction as the artistic and intellectual heart of Europe. Italian artists and intellectuals forged ahead despite the troubles, continuing the rediscovery of classical Greek and Roman ideas, practices, and artifacts that had so far characterized their activities during the Renaissance. This rediscovery of classical models had gained momentum since the fourteenth century through the writings of poets such as Petrarch. And it had reached a pinnacle in the works of, for example, Michelangelo Buonarroti (1475-1564) and Leonardo Da Vinci (1452-1519), two artists who, like Machiavelli,

---

CESARE BORGIA

Cesare Borgia (1475-1507) was the natural son of Roderigo Borgia (1431-1503), who became pope, as Alexander VI, in 1492. Cesare was made an archbishop at 7 and a cardinal at 18 years of age. In 1498, Cesare Borgia took the title of Duke of Valentinois, bestowed on him by the French king Louis XII. Until the death of his father in 1503, Cesare Borgia led a ruthless and temporarily successful campaign of territorial expansion in central Italy. Machiavelli witnessed Borgia's use of deception and murder to increase his power (described in Chapter 7 of *The Prince*). Upon the death of his father, Cesare Borgia lost his position in the Papal States and was exiled to Spain, where he died in battle in 1507.

---

came from Florence. Treatises like *The Prince* were part of a literary trend influenced by the rediscovery of classical culture and history. Authors such as Machiavelli took advantage of the potential for a wider examination of history, including classical history, offered by the mass diffusion of written works after the invention of the printing press (c. 1450). In fact, *The Prince* belongs to a literary genre that developed during the Renaissance—the genre of guidebooks on specific subjects, from manners to scientific topics. Machiavelli's handbook for the ineffective, corrupt leaders of his day, *The Prince*, was just one of many advice books published in the period that offered counsel on numerous subjects, from polite manners (*Il Galateo* by Giovanni Della Casa) to the conduct of the courtier (**The Book of the Courtier** by Baldesar Castiglione, also *in WLAIT 7: Italian Literature and Its Times*). Of all these advice books, two proved remarkably influential throughout Europe: Castiglione's social guidebook for the professional courtier and Machiavelli's political counterpart, *The Prince*.

Francesco Guicciardini, Florentine diplomat and friend to Machiavelli.

The Essay in Focus

Contents summary. From the start, *The Prince* is a constant play between opposites. The title of the work and its 26 chapter headings are in the learned language of Latin, the accepted format for high discourse at the time. But the substance of each chapter is in Machiavelli's own Florentine dialect, the language of the people and everyday existence. *The Prince* opens with a dedication to Lorenzo II de' Medici, not the famous Lorenzo de' Medici, ruler and patron of the arts in Florence, who became known as Lorenzo the Magnificent, but his short-lived nephew, the Duke of Urbino. The themes Machiavelli introduces in this dedication set the tone for the work. Like a landscape painter, says the dedication, only one who views the lowly people from the heights of power, such as a prince, truly understands their motivations and passions. On the other hand, Machiavelli explains, his own ability to understand how power operates is due to his lowly vantage point. Observing princes from below, as one of the people, has allowed him to gain insight on the workings of power, much like a landscape painter can better observe a mountaintop if he paints from a valley bottom. The text after the dedication has often been divided by critics into four sections—defining principalities (chap-

ters 1-11), military organization (chapters 12-14), the personal attributes of a prince (chapters 15-23), and the summary (chapters 24-26).

Defining principalities. In the first section, Machiavelli discusses new principalities and the manner in which they may be acquired and maintained by a prince. He defines the various types of principalities, referring to Italian states of his day and warning that how best to treat a territory depends on whether it is accustomed to self-rule. According to Machiavelli, "hereditary principalities" are the easiest to maintain as long as their rulers are attentive to local tradition; he points to the style of rule in the duchy of Ferrara as an example. Machiavelli turns next to "mixed (composite) principalities," by which he means territories added or conquered by a hereditary prince, going into detail about how they can cause difficulties. It is easier, advises Machiavelli, to maintain a new territory when the previous ruling line has been eliminated and when there are few linguistic or cultural differences between the new territory and the ruling power that has just taken it over. Such difficulties, however, may be overcome if the prince plants colonists in the new territory or moves there himself. Machiavelli offers the positive example of the Roman conquest of Greece in classical times. He also offers the negative, recent example of attempts under French kings like Louis XII to attain the duchy of Milan and the failed efforts of the pope and Cesare Borgia to create a permanent power base throughout the Italian peninsula.

The text moves to the difficulties a prince may encounter when attempting to conquer a state that is used to authoritarian rule. Alexander the Great's conquest of Persia under the ruler Darius is one such instance. Bringing the discussion closer to his own day, Machiavelli contrasts France, then dominated by an active class of noblemen who operated from regional power bases, to absolutist Ottoman Turkey, an area dominated more completely by one power, the sultan. According to Machiavelli, an absolutist state like Turkey may be harder to conquer but is easier to maintain; a more fractured state like France, on the other hand, may be less difficult to conquer but harder to maintain because of the enduring influence of separate traditions in the different regions. How, then, does one break the hold of old laws and traditions? Machiavelli offers several solutions: a prince can destroy the conquered territory, reside in it himself, introduce his colonists into the area, or delegate power to an oligarchy there. Examples from antiquity include Rome's destruction of Carthage and Sparta's dominance over the defeated Athenians in Greece.

Next the essay turns to new principalities conquered not with one's own resources but with the fortune and arms of others. Machiavelli describes the cruel and tricky methods used to attain power by individuals like Cesare Borgia or like certain citizens of ancient Rome who attained the position of emperor by bribing armies. Presented are the different methods by which Borgia (in central Italy) and Francesco Sforza (in Milan) attempted to attain power. In the end, says Machiavelli, Borgia's downfall was the result of his own choices. A prince's personal capacity, his "virtue" in the face of unpredictable fortune is a deciding factor in his success or failure.

The essay turns next to the conquest of a principality through crime. Agathocles of Syracuse and Oliverotto da Fermo both resorted to trickery and rose to power through violent massacres. Machiavelli warns that such methods may be effective only in the short run. The prudent prince should try to attain power not by violence or wickedness but by cultivating the approval of the nobles or the people. Thereafter, he should strive to retain the support of the faction that backed him and should furthermore reach out to the opposition.

In conclusion, the first section returns to types of principalities, focusing largely on theocracies, or "Ecclesiastical principalities." It notes that a general respect for religious tradition gives them the advantage of stability, then provides some cautionary examples from recent Italian history of the ambitious conduct of popes Alexander VI, Julius II, and Leo X. The discussion next turns to the failed efforts of French monarchs like Charles VIII to conquer the Italian peninsula in Machiavelli's lifetime.

Military organization. The second section concentrates on a prince's possible military resources. Machiavelli outlines four categories: indigenous militias formed from a principality's own citizenry; mercenary militias consisting of troops whose only loyalty to the prince is financial; auxiliary militias, or troops supplied not by a prince's own people but by allies; and mixed militias, which are any combination of the other three. Disposing of one of these categories, Machiavelli blames the use of mercenary troops and their unpredictable leaders for the unhappy political condition of the Italian peninsula in his day. He offers historical precedents of victorious mercenary captains who turned around and dethroned the princes who hired them. In contrast to examples of unsuccessful Italian princes, Machiavelli proposes the military organization of the ancient Spartans or Romans as two possible models.

Machiavelli next takes up the topic of auxiliary, or additional armies a prince may have to use. Pope Julius II's use of Spanish troops and Florence's reliance on French troops serve as two cases in point. The victories of auxiliary troops may ultimately put the principality that called on them into the power of these troops. Returning to the subject of mercenary troops, Machiavelli discerns even greater danger from them and offers examples of leaders who wisely rejected their use (e.g., the biblical David or Cesare Borgia). Less successful were leaders of the later Roman Empire who became prey to the Germanic mercenaries it employed. The section concludes by declaring that a prince's primary duty is to prepare for war.

Princely attributes. Section 3 is devoted to the personal attributes a prince should possess. In this most celebrated and criticized section, the treatise elevates practical concerns over ethical ones. The ultimate goal of the prince, says the essay, is to maintain power. Turning to the subjects of "generosity and parsimony," "cruelty and compassion, whether it is better to be loved or feared" and "the loyalty of princes," Machiavelli examines princely behavior through a series of opposites. In considering the opposites and delivering advice, he lets short-run practical considerations take precedence over ethical ones:

> From this arises the question whether it is better to be loved more than feared, or feared more than loved. The reply is, that one ought to be both feared and loved, but as it is difficult for the two to go together, it is much safer to be feared than loved, if one of the two has to be wanting.
>
> (Machiavelli, *The Prince,* p. 61)

It is in this part of the text that Machiavelli makes statements commonly understood as "the ends justify the means." In fact, what the text says is "In judging the actions of men, and above all of princes, who cannot actually be called to judgment, one must consider the ends. The prince must do what is necessary to win and retain his state: the means will always be judged as honorable and praised by all, because the common people are always swayed by appearances" (Machiavelli, *Il Principe,* p. 168; trans. C. Celli).

Turning to the relationship between a prince and his subjects, the treatise considers how a prince avoids disdain and hatred. He must, above all, prevent his subjects from hating him, as shown by a catalogue of negative examples from history—the conspiracy-ridden leading families of Bologna, the emperors from the late Roman Empire, and the sultan of Turkey. The treatise advises the prince on how to gain esteem: one must concentrate on foreign affairs, undertaking great enterprises abroad, such as the consolidation of power by the Spanish monarch Ferdinand I. Within his own lands, a prince must act resolutely and take clear positions. He should not remain neutral. A prince ought furthermore to encourage the arts and the professions so that he may be identified with vibrant activities, and to this same end, should also promote spectacles and festivals for his subjects to enjoy.

What about the prince's aides? How does one sift out the true advisor from a bevy of flatterers? Distinguish, says Machiavelli, among those who can understand things on their own, those who need the help of others, and those incapable of understanding anything. He advises a prince to choose ministers who think more about the prince's interests than their own. Conversely it is the prince's duty to be concerned about the welfare of his ministers, for if he pays no heed to their well-being, they cannot be expected to work effectively in his interests.

Summary chapters. Machiavelli sums up the catchword concepts that he uses in previous chapters—*fortuna* (fortune) and *virtù* (virtue, or capability and know-how)—into a realistic and materialistic worldview whose objective is to rid Italy of foreign domination. First he considers why the Italian princes have lost authority to outsiders, listing the mistakes made by deposed Italian rulers. He factors in the power and unpredictability of fortune, a force above human activity that he compares to a river whose flooding can be tempered by preparing for the unforeseen, but never fully controlled.

In the final chapter, Machiavelli makes a stirring plea to Italian princes to rid Italy of "barbarian" foreign domination. He exhorts the Medici family to seize the moment and provide the regions of Italy with a stable source of native political and military leaders who operate according to the precepts laid out in his treatise. In closing, he cites Petrarch's poem "Italia mia" (My Italy), a hymn that calls for ridding the land of foreign oppressors in an earlier age, pointing to the glory of Italy's past as well as the hope for its future.

Of kings and commoners. Machiavelli's achievement lies not only in the ideas he makes bold to express, but also in the manner in which he expresses them. Machiavelli is critical of the Italian rulers of his day, whom he sees as responsible for foreign incursion in peninsular affairs. In his

view, the rulers failed to make ready for such an eventuality; they neglected to prepare for the caprices of fortune. Such foresight on behalf of the state, such virtue, in other words, is a quality Machiavelli finds lacking in his age, especially when compared to the republican era of ancient Rome. In his ideal republic, leaders should be so "imbued with *virtù* (as were the ancient Romans) that they would willingly sacrifice themselves for the state" (Brucker, p. 280). The criticism is forthright, certainly bold.

Along with virtue, fortune becomes a running theme in *The Prince*. At the end, in the chapter "How Much Fortune can Do in Human Affairs and How it may be Opposed," Machiavelli makes a final statement about the power of fortune as opposed to virtue. The statement, following a treatise full of learned examples, builds on an earlier earthy image of Fortune as a capricious woman with an equally earthy, commonsense metaphor about rivers and dams. In so doing, *The Prince* mixes a learned tone with popular expressions.

> I think it may be true that fortune is the ruler of half our actions, but that she allows the other half or thereabouts to be governed by us. I would compare her to an impetuous river that, when turbulent, inundates the plains, casts down trees and buildings, removes earth from this side and places it on the other; everyone flees before it, and everything yields to its fury without being able to oppose it; and yet . . . when it is quiet, men can make provision against it by dikes and banks, so that when it rises it will either go into a canal or its rush will not be so wild and dangerous. So it is with fortune, which shows her power where no measures have been taken to resist her, and directs her fury where she knows that no dykes or barriers have been made to hold her.
>
> (*The Prince*, p. 91)

There are other references to popular imagery in the treatise: it warns that men more easily forget the loss of a father than the loss of a patrimony; it refutes a common proverb invoked by rulers of the time—that whomsoever bases power on the people, bases it on mud. It invokes the metaphor of the lion and the fox as a description for understanding when and how a ruler ought to use power:

> A prince being thus obliged to know well how to act as a beast must imitate the fox and the lion, for the lion cannot protect himself from traps, and the fox cannot defend himself from wolves. One must therefore be a fox to recognize traps, and a lion to frighten wolves. Those that wish to be only lions do not

understand this. Therefore a prudent ruler ought not to keep faith when by so doing it would be against his interest, and when the reasons which made him bind himself no longer exist. If men were all good, this precept would not be a good one, but as they are bad, and would not observe their faith with you, so you are not bound to keep faith with them.

(*The Prince*, p. 64)

The recurrence of peasant-like maxims and proverbial wisdom is part of the play of opposites that characterizes *The Prince* and gives Machiavelli his universal appeal as a writer. These references show him to be well versed in both high culture and popular culture, particularly popular themes that evince a cynicism about human nature. Machiavelli's work is considered remarkable for its day, "not just for his bold questioning of received ideas but also for its prose, the vigour of which matched his plain speaking"; the style is largely "down to earth," drawing on familiar imagery and "echoing the everyday speech of the city" (Brand and Pertile, p. 191).

Sources and literary context. *The Prince* conveys the sense of urgency (even tragedy) that Machiavelli felt about the course of Italian history at the time. The work also arose from frustration over the interruption of his career in government after 1512. In his day, treatises like *The Prince* attempted to understand the world and form a learned basis for action. While Machiavelli's treatise spoke to princes, writing it was also a way for him to grapple with personal developments.

Using a mix of real-life experience and literary sources, Machiavelli approaches politics on the Italian peninsula from three vantage points: 1) his interpretation of ancient historical examples, from biblical figures to the Roman Empire; 2) events on the Italian peninsula in preceding generations and centuries; 3) his experience as an ambassador and valued member of the Florentine chancellery in the Florentine Republic until 1512. His literary sources included classical Greek and Roman works. Machiavelli has been credited with transcribing *De rerum natura*, a classical text offering a materialistic worldview. Written by the Latin philosopher Lucretius, it is often regarded as an influence on Machiavelli's later writings, including *The Prince*. Many of the historical examples in *The Prince* come from Machiavelli's earlier works. His *Descrizione del modo tenuto dal Duca Valentino nello ammazzare Vitellozzo Vitelli, Oliverotto da Fermo, il signor Pagolo e il duca di Gravina Orsini* (1503; Description of the manner in which the Duke of Valentinois murdered Vitellozzo Vitelli, Oliverotto da Fermo and Signor

Pagolo and the Duke Gravina Orsini) includes historical examples of attaining power through wickedness that reappear in *The Prince*. He first made holding onto power a higher priority than ethical concerns in the *Ghiribizzi* (1506). In his *Discorso dell'ordinare lo stato di Firenze alle armi* (1506; On the Manner of Organizing the Military of the State of Florence), Machiavelli anticipates many of his later ideas about military organization. His *Rapporto delle cose della Magna* (1507; Report from Germany) contains a description of German culture that reappears in *The Prince*.

MACHIAVELLI'S LIGHTER SIDE

Some of Machiavelli's letters reveal a light, earthy side to his character. A 1509 letter to Luigi Guicciardini describes an encounter with a laundress/prostitute, for example. Such letters, at times obscene and sarcastic, certainly do not conform to the rather austere image of Machiavelli suggested by the brutally realistic discussion of politics in *The Prince*. This side to his character is also evident in his comical plays and his 1516 satirical poem *L'asino* (The Ass), which spoofs Dante's *Divine Comedy*. In fact, in much of his corpus, Machiavelli seems to be a writer who has more in common with irreverent authors of his day (such as the French writer François Rabelais [1490-1553]) than with historians or political writers.

Machiavelli wrote various letters that provide insight into the events behind works like *The Prince*. A letter of September 1506 to Giovan Battista Soderini is often cited as a source of ideas that he later developed in *The Prince*. Another missive, dated December 10, 1513, and sent to Francesco Vettori, describes the composition of *The Prince*, listing many influences, from Machiavelli's daily contact with locals in a tavern to his time spent on ancient works:

> When evening comes, I return to my home, and I go into my study; and on the threshold, I take off my everyday clothes, which are covered with mud and mire, and I put on my regal and curial robes; and dressed in a more appropriate manner I enter into the ancient courts of ancient men and am welcomed by them kindly, and . . . there I am not ashamed to speak to them, to ask them the reasons for their actions; and they, in their humanity, answer me.
>
> (Machiavelli, *The Prince and the Discourses*, p. 69)

Others in Machiavelli's day were dispensing advice to the Medici rulers too, among them, his friend Francesco Guicciardini, who wrote *Come assicuare lo stato alla casa de' Medici* (1512; How to Ensure the State to the House of the Medici). Years later, in 1530, Guicciardini wrote another treatise (*Considerazioni intorno ai Discorsi del Machiavelli,* or Considerations on the Discourses of Machiavelli), in which he objected to his older friend's reliance on ancient Roman models and historical examples.

A PALACE FOR POETS AND PHILOSOPHERS

The Renaissance saw the formation of the intellectual circle around a nobleman or cultured merchant in his villa and gardens. Such a circle included professors, literary celebrities, clergymen, and at times women. Often the company attended Mass together, then partook of a light meal, including choice wines, fruits, and preserves from distant lands, followed by an hour of conversation. The topics varied, from the best form of government, to moneymaking, to the differences between men and women, the worth of the Italian language, and whether or not animals can reason. Introduced at the end of the fourteenth century, this sort of intellectual circle grew in popularity. In the late fifteenth century, the nobleman Bernardo Rucellai built a great palace surrounded by a garden that became the site for this type of circle. It was here that Machiavelli engaged in learned discourse and debate with other writers, philosophers, and political thinkers, sometimes reading them passages from his works: "Being unable," he explained, "to speak of the art of silk, or the art of wool, or of profits and losses, it befits me to speak of the state; I must speak of that or resign myself to silence" (Machiavelli in Lucas-Dubreton, p. 251).

Reception. Machiavelli presented *The Prince* to Lorenzo de' Medici in 1515, but the work was received coolly. Still *The Prince,* like other writings by Machiavelli, enjoyed a limited circulation among learned circles in Italy, especially among his fellow members of the Rucellai gardens cultural circle. The treatise was first printed in Rome in 1532 and was placed on the papal index of prohibited books in 1559. The work was banned because it made holding onto power a higher priority than ethical concerns. Its brutal honesty about politics furthermore offended both Protestant and Catholic readers. Despite this unhappy beginning, and perhaps in part because of its notoriety, *The Prince* eventually gained a wide and continuing readership and its influence has been immense.

Machiavelli's theories have become a point of reference for all subsequent political study. His theories about military organization entered into debates about the value of standing armies during the English revolution (1640), and his views have influenced thinking about the conception of the modern nation state. During the Italian struggle for unification in the mid-nineteenth century, Machiavelli was viewed by the Italian critic and historian Francesco De Sanctis as having reached a high point of nationalist sentiment, in particular because *The Prince* ends with a quote from Petrarch's poem "My Italy." Over the centuries since its release, Machiavelli's *The Prince* has been intimately studied by key leaders in world history. The elements that contributed to the making of *The Prince*—Machiavelli's personal history, the crisis in Italy during the Italian Wars, the influence of Renaissance classical culture, and Machiavelli's often earthy ability to invoke peasant proverbs and animal imagery—have made *The Prince* one of the few treatises from the Italian Renaissance that continues to enjoy universal recognition and appeal.

—Carlo Celli

For More Information

Brand, Peter, and Lino Pertile. *The Cambridge History of Italian Literature.* Cambridge: Cambridge University Press, 1996.

Brucker, Gene A. *Renaissance Florence.* Berkeley: University of California Press, 1969.

Guicciardini, Francesco. *The History of Italy.* Trans. Sidney Alexander. Princeton: Princeton University Press, 1984.

Lucas-Dubreton, J. *Daily Life in Florence in the Time of the Medici.* Trans. A. Lytton Sells. London: George Allen & Unwin, 1960.

Machiavelli, Niccolò. *Machiavelli and His Friends: Their Personal Correspondence.* Trans. and ed. James B. Atkinson and David Sices. Dekalb, Ill.: Northern Illinois University Press, 1996.

———. *The Portable Machiavelli.* Ed. and trans. Peter Bondanella and Mark Musa. New York: Viking Penguin, 1979.

———. *The Prince and the Discourses.* New York: Modern Library, 1950.

———. *Il principe.* Ed. Piero Melograni. Milan: Rizzoli, 1991.

Ridolfi, Roberto. *The Life of Niccolò Machiavelli.* London: Routledge and Kegan, 1963.

Viroli, Maurizio. *Niccolo's Smile.* New York: Farrar, Straus and Giroux, 2002.

Rime

by

Gaspara Stampa

Along with Vittoria Colonna, Veronica Franco, and Veronica Gambara, Gaspara Stampa is considered one of the most important female poets of the Italian Renaissance. Only fragments of Stampa's life have been sufficiently documented. She was born in the northern Italian city of Padua around 1523. The daughter of an impoverished Milanese family, Stampa was educated in the fine arts in the Republic of Venice. Becoming a skilled musician and *cantatrice* ("singer"), she performed regularly in the fashionable salons of the Venetian aristocracy. Venice at the time was famous for its love of luxury and pleasure, and Stampa quickly gained a reputation as a *virtuosa* (fifteenth- or sixteenth-century woman skilled in fine arts, especially the performance of music in salons). In 1548 Stampa fell in love with a Venetian count and began to document the turbulent "love story" in poetic form. Their different social standings doomed the relationship from the start, filling Stampa with despair. The result was poetry that elevates unrequited love to a new literary plane by redirecting the focus from the "beloved" to the complex female lover-poet. Stampa turns the spotlight on her emotional self, conveying the torments of frustration through some of the most musical poetry in Italian literature. Daring for her time, her work is highly intimate and awash with sexual innuendo. There is debate today as to whether or not she was an "honest courtesan"—that is, a woman adept at an array of fluctuating roles, from artist to entertainer, conversationalist, and, to a degree, prostitute. Her rise to acclaimed writer is a "Cinderella

THE LITERARY WORK

A collection of 311 poems set in Italy between 1548 and 1553; published in Italian (as *Rime di Madonna Gaspara Stampa*) in 1554, in English in 1994.

SYNOPSIS

From the viewpoint of a woman, the poems depict love as a phenomenon fraught with contradictions.

story" that has become the subject of poems, plays, short stories, and novels. At the heart of all the scrutiny lies Stampa's verse. Her only literary work, *Rime* is a collection of 311 poems. Together they form the largest, most varied *canzoniere* (poetic song book) in Italian literature, one that broke new ground by offering a female perspective on love in a male-dominated universe.

Events in History at the Time of the Poems

Venice in the sixteenth century. In the sixteenth century, Italy was home to five major cities that had grown into larger states—Milan, Florence, Venice, Naples, and the residence of the popes, Rome. None of them became strong enough to conquer and unify the entire peninsula. In contrast to France, Spain, and England, where different political and geopolitical circumstances made unifying monarchies possible in the sixteenth century, Italy would not form a unified nation for another 300 years. To settle territorial disputes and gain political hegemony, the states of Italy often asked powerful nations to intervene. Leagues were formed, treaties signed and broken, and alliances bought and sold. The major European powers gladly interfered, angling to expand their degree of direct rule over the peninsula. Through the turmoil of the century, Venice survived as an independent republic, but its fortunes had by then started to wane.

THE ITALIAN RENAISSANCE

The Renaissance—a philosophical, literary, and artistic revolution inspired by the rediscovery of the ancient Greek and Roman cultures—spread from Italy across Europe during the fourteenth to the sixteenth century. In the process, the movement revolutionized the worldview of an elite minority—the artists and intellectuals of European society. In an age dominated by the Church and the nobility, these artists and intellectuals began looking to classical texts (by Plato and others) as guides to living a fulfilled human life. Their enterprise is associated with the philosophical movement known as humanism, which promoted the idea that truth could be discovered by human effort. The Renaissance thinkers went so far as to reposition man as the driving force in society, discerning a unique capacity in every human being. In keeping with this view, the notion of self-expression gained momentum, changing the artists' and intellectuals' outlook on life.

Venice amassed an empire of its own in the early 1000s C.E. At its zenith, around 1400, this empire included an impressive range of territories. Along with large parts of northern Italy (Treviso, Padua, Vicenza, Verona, Brescia, and Bergamo), the Venetians controlled Friuli, the Istrian Peninsula and the Dalmatian coast, the Cyclades and Sporades islands, the shores of Thessaly, the Sea of Marmara and the Black Sea, and the islands of Crete and Cyprus. This empire gave the Venetians trading posts in the Adriatic (Gulf of Venice), Mediterranean, and Aegean seas, which made it possible for the Republic to monopolize trade routes from Europe to Asia Minor. During these golden years, Venice was the busiest trading center in Europe and one of the most prosperous metropolitan areas in the known world. The Venetian

government invested large amounts of its imperial income in the creation of magnificent monuments that testified to its economic and political success. At the government's behest, some of the most renowned artists of the period participated in the design, construction, and ornamentation of a host of luxurious public buildings and churches. In time, Venice itself became one of the first "tourist destinations." People throughout the Christian world admired the Republic's art.

By the early 1500s, however, the empire had already begun to decline. Two issues dominated Venice's political history for most of the century. In the West, the Venetians engaged in an ever-shifting alliance with rival European powers bent on consolidating the bitterly divided regions of Italy for their own gain so one rival or another could rule the entire area; in the East, the rapid rise of the powerful Ottoman Empire ultimately ended Venice's longstanding hegemony in the Mediterranean Sea. Harbor by harbor, island by island, the Venetian Empire lost its Eastern possessions to the expanding Ottomans, and age-old shipping routes turned dangerous and unreliable. In 1497-98, in a search to reach India by way of the Atlantic Ocean, the Portuguese discovered the Cape of Good Hope and a route around it to India. Thereafter, the Atlantic Ocean joined the Mediterranean Sea as a possible waterway for India-bound vessels, and the Venetian merchants began to lose their monopoly on trade with the East.

Meanwhile, Venice's political problems spun out of control in the West. Its presumptuous foreign policy so alienated the major European powers that they united in a military alliance against Venice. The alliance, called the League of Cambrai, clashed with the Venetian army in 1509, outside the village of Agnadello. The League dealt the Venetians such a decisive blow that it forced the Republic to sue for peace. In the ensuing negotiations, the victors mercilessly divided the Republic's colonies among themselves. The setback was temporary, though, for the League of Cambrai soon dissolved, and Venice gained new territory that mostly made up for its losses. Although the empire would never fully recover, it remained an important military power in the early 1500s and managed, through all the turmoil, to sustain a vibrant, often extravagant cultural life.

Culture in sixteenth-century Venice. In the early 1500s, the Republic of Venice became—and remained for the rest of the century—the undisputed intellectual center among the Italian city-states. During those years, more books were

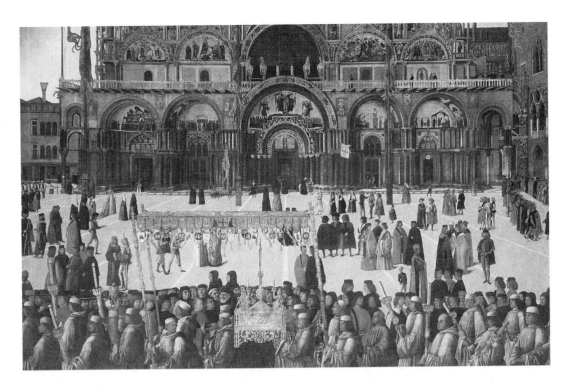

Detail of *Procession in St. Mark's Square,* tempera on canvas by Gentile Bellini, 1496. Though historians speak of the relatively lax moral atmosphere in sixteenth-century Venice, it remained solidly Catholic. Stampa herself wrote some religious poems.

published in Venice than in Milan, Rome, and Naples combined. Through the rapid spread of the newly invented printing press (c. 1450), both reading and writing became more accessible to the general public. Books were no longer the privilege of the ruling elite. With the help of mass production, their cost dropped and the middle classes began buying them. Venice became the publishing hub of all Europe, exporting books as far as northern Germany and Flanders. The first publications were mostly reproductions of existing literature, generally the Greek and Roman classics. By the turn of the 1500s, however, publishers were asking writers to edit or translate books and even to write them, which gave rise to a new form of patronage in Italy.

Among the arts in general, the sixteenth century marked the height of Venice's artistic grandeur. Architects like Jacopo Sansovino, Mauro Coducci, Andrea Palladio, and the Lombardo family defined Venice's lavish skyline. The Venetian school of painting (Vittore Carpaccio, Giovanni Bellini, Titian, Giorgione, Tintoretto, and Paolo Veronese) rose to European supremacy, challenged only by Florence's Michelangelo Buonarroti. In literature, the satirist Pietro Aretino, the "scourge of princes," settled and worked in Venice, along with Sperone Speroni, Benedetto

Varchi, and Giuseppe Betussi. Venice became the envy of all Europe for its relatively liberal atmosphere. Though still solidly Catholic, it offered greater intellectual freedom than any other eminent Italian state and was one of the few places that tolerated religious differences. Historians speak of sixteenth-century Venice as notably indifferent to the stricter moral prescriptions of Christianity. Art and sensuality were closely linked in the city of Venice. Upper-class Venetians avidly pursued sexual pleasures, the most refined among them seeking an ambience that fused sexuality and art. It seems to have been the demand for this sensual blend that led to a new phenomenon in Venetian artistic circles: the "honest" courtesan.

The honest courtesan. Scholars tend to divide courtesans in the Renaissance into two major types. The *cortigiane di lume o candela,* or "lower-class courtesans," worked and lived in a brothel and were forced into prostitution out of economic necessity. The *cortigiana onesta,* the "honest" or "honored" courtesan, developed physical as well as social and intellectual attributes that elevated her above the ordinary prostitute. Typically coming from a middle-class background, the *cortigiana onesta* was endowed with exceptional beauty, elegance, and grace. She did not bestow sexual favors on an hourly basis. Her clientele was strictly from the privileged classes, including nobles, artists, and intellectuals, and she normally offered her services to one individual for the duration of their "relationship." Typically she was an active member of the social circuit frequented by high society; often she was celebrated and popular—at least with men. The honest courtesan established a presence mainly in Rome and Venice, often commanding the respect of cardinals and kings as well as the native nobility. In Venice, she remained part of the social scene for more than a century (from about 1500 to the early 1600s), starting to lose her allure as a society figure by about the 1550s. Some of the honest courtesans were talented singers and musicians who held their own salons, where guests were entertained and became involved in subtle philosophical disputes. The honest courtesans were multitalented: they corresponded with contemporary male writers, artists, and intellectuals; participated in the ongoing literary debates; contributed to anthologies; and published their own poetry. In the highly competitive and male-dominated literary circles, these courtesans introduced a female point of view, "refashion[ing] literary conventions to serve the concerns of women who had been silenced by male authority" (Rosenthal, p. 56). It was in such an atmosphere that Gaspara Stampa conceived her remarkable verse, inspired by the main love affair of her life with the Italian nobleman Count Collaltino di Collalto.

The life of Gaspara Stampa. Gaspara's father, Bartolomeo Stampa, was an impoverished jewel merchant in Padua. He educated his son and two daughters at home. The three of them—Gaspara, Cassandra, and Baldassare—studied Greek, Latin, rhetoric, music, and literature. In 1531, when Gaspara's father died, her mother, Cecilia, decided to relocate to her native Venice. The children continued their studies, taking private lessons from Fortunio Spira, a renowned grammarian, who was friends with some of the most celebrated literati of the day. The two girls were also instructed by the famous French musician Perissone Cambio, who trained them in lute and in voice. From 1535 to 1540, the house of Cecilia Stampa served as a salon, or literary and musical center for young nobles, intellectuals, poets, and musicians, such as Francesco Sansovino, poet, editor, and close friend of Gaspara's brother, Baldassare. Other patrons of the salon included the poet Lodovico Domenichi (who wrote *rime petrarchesche*—Petrarchan verse), the poet and or-

ganist Girolamo Parabosco, the physician Ortensio Lando, and the scholars Sperone Speroni and Benedetto Varchi. The two Stampa sisters entertained the company with impressive musical performances of, among other works, the poems of Francesco Petrarch, which they sang while accompanying themselves on the lute (see Petrarch's *Canzoniere,* also in *WLAIT 7: Italian Literature and Its Times*). Gaspara's teacher, Cambio, a celebrated singer himself, called her a "heavenly siren," remarking that "No lady in the world loves music more than she, and none has a rarer degree of mastery over it" (Cambio in Stampa, *Selected Poems*, p. xiii). Parabosco, the organist, agreed: "What can I say about the angelic voice, which creates such sweet harmony whenever it strikes the air with its divine sounds . . . save that it infuses spirit and life into the coldest stones, making them weep from overpowering sweetness?" (Parabosco in Bassanese, p. 4).

Although not a noblewoman, Gaspara was admitted into the most renowned salons of Venetian high society. The salon of Domenico Venier, a Venetian aristocrat who suffered from paralysis, was the preferred gathering place for many of Venice's literati at the time. Interested greatly in poetry, they took a keen interest in the poetry of Petrarch, especially in the imitation of his verse as viewed by the century's leading literary expert, Pietro Bembo. It was in the Venier salon, at age 26, that Stampa met Count Collaltino di Collalto.

The Collaltos were a wealthy family, who traced their heritage back to an illustrious set of medieval ancestors, the Langobardi. It is in keeping with this heritage that the Collaltos settled on three estates near Treviso. Stampa emphasizes Collaltino's lofty social rank in many of her poems. She calls him by his title, "Count," and transfigures him metaphorically into a "high hill" that she, as a woman from an inferior class, must conquer. Even if he had wanted (which is doubtful, since he seemed more interested in the thrills of war than the melodrama of love), the Count would almost certainly not have married Gaspara Stampa. She was already past marriageable age, her dowry did not amount to enough to attract a landed aristocrat, and her participation in literary salons gave her a dubious reputation. Moreover, marriages in sixteenth-century Venice were a practical matter. People usually entered into them on the basis of political, economic, and social interests, not romantic affection. In upper-class society, the aim was to preserve and, if possible, increase a family's riches. Usually only the eldest son married so the wealth would not have to be split among various heirs and their wives. Hence there were many unmarried noblemen in sixteenth-century Venice. Even those who married seem to have been in no hurry to do so; most waited until their thirties. Meanwhile, female companionship was there for the taking. Not only a liberal city but also a tourist attraction, Venice offered natives and visitors alike a choice of thousands of prostitutes, courtesans, and concubines.

Stampa's on-again, off-again relationship with Collaltino began in her mid-twenties and lasted a few years, until their final breakup in 1550. The affair inspired most of the poems for which Stampa is best known. Shortly after their breakup, she entered into a new relationship with a Venetian named Bartolomeo Zen, whom she also speaks of, albeit with far less intensity, in her poetry. In her thirtieth year, the poetess grew ill and left Venice for the milder climate of Florence. She stayed into the following year. On April 23, 1554, two weeks after her return to Venice, the 31-year-old poetess died; three years later Collaltino married a woman of his own rank.

The Poems in Focus

Contents overview. Gaspara Stampa's *Rime* was first published posthumously in 1554, thanks to Cassandra Stampa, the poetess's younger sister (only three of Gaspara's poems were published during her lifetime). Since Stampa's original manuscript is lost, we cannot be sure of the order in which the poems were conceived or the order in which she herself intended to publish them. Present-day editions generally divide the material into two sections: "Rime d'Amore" (Love Poems) and "Rime Varie" (Miscellaneous Poems). In both parts, the poems are closely tied to specific events and individuals in Stampa's life. The incidents and individuals are arranged in chronological order, and there is a loose narrative thread. The "Love Poems" section contains 245 lyrical works: 218 sonnets, 19 madrigals, 5 capitoli, 2 sestinas, and one canzone. These poems are addressed to Count Collaltino di Collalto and to Stampa's later love interest, Bartolomeo Zen. The second section, "Miscellaneous Poems," contains 66 lyrical works: 62 sonnets, 2 capitoli, one canzone, and one dialogue in quatrains. Much less interrelated than the first section, "Miscellaneous Poems" includes a few poems written for special occasions, including some written on the death of a relative, Sister Angelica Paola de'Negri, Abbess of the Convent of San Paolo in Milan. Other poems in this section were composed for friends and other writers (in-cluding Girolamo Molin, Ortensio Lando, Domenico Venier, Sperone Speroni, Leonardo Emo, Luigi Alamanni, Trifon Gabriele, Giovanna d'Aragona, and Ippolita Mirtilla). The second section ends with several religious sonnets. In general, despite the work's loose narrative thread, *Rime* remains a collection of individual lyrical compositions; it was never intended to be read as a single narrative poem.

POPULAR FORMS OF LYRIC IN THE RENAISSANCE

Petrarchan sonnet Also known as the *Italian sonnet,* the Petrarchan sonnet was the most popular form among sixteenth-century lyric poets. Developed in the 1200s, it reached a pinnacle in the works of Francesco Petrarch (1304-74). The sonnet is a 14-line poem, made up of two quatrains (an octave) with the rhyme scheme *abbaabba,* followed by two tercets (a sestet), with one of several rhyme schemes, usually *cdecde* or *cdcdcd.* The meter is the 11-syllable line, called the Italian *hendecasyllable,* with irregular accents and pauses. Generally the octave presents the problem or thesis of the poem; the sestet resolves the problem.

Canzone A form of lyric that originated in Provençe, France, and was introduced into Italy by the poets of the Sicilian School in the thirteenth century. The canzone is a series of stanzas without a refrain; the form is written mostly in hendecasyllabic (11-syllable) lines with some heptasyllables (7-syllable lines).

Capitolo An Italian verse form that is either an imitation or a parody of Dante's *terza rima* (a series of tercets linked to one another by how they are constructed—the second line of each tercet rhymes with the first and third lines of the one that follows (in the pattern *aba bcb cdc*). Originally used to teach a moral, in the high Renaissance the form was used for satire.

Dialogue in quatrains A form in which speakers discuss a subject in verse. The quatrain, a stanza of four lines, normally rhymes. There are wide variations in rhyme scheme; some of the most common are *abab* (alternating, or cross-rhyme), *xbyb* (x and y represent unrhymed lines), *aabb* (opposed couplets), *abba* (envelope rhyme), or *aaxa* (near monorhyme).

The "Love Poems." Thematically the first of the "Love Poems" introduces the entire collection. In the style of Petrarch, Stampa sets the tone and defines her main topics in a prefatory sonnet.

The sonnet proclaims her interest in the complex relationships between love and pain, suffering and inspiration, aspiration and self-expression, art and fame. Like her master, Petrarch, Stampa addresses the reader directly with the same words that open *his* prefatory sonnet "Voi ch'ascoltate" (you who listen):

> O you who listen to these mournful verses,
> In these unhappy, in these somber accents . . .
> I hope to find among some well-born people,
>
> . . .
>
> Not only pardon for my tears, but glory,
> Because the reason for them is so lofty.
> I dare to hope some woman will exclaim:
> "Happy is she, she who has undergone
> For such a noble cause, sorrow so noble!"
>
> (Stampa, *Selected Poems*, p. 3)

The general mood is melancholic and nostalgic. There follows a set of 244 poems in which Stampa relives the emotional rollercoaster of her two major love affairs over a four-year period, first the relationship with Count Collaltino di Collalto and, after their breakup, with the second Venetian nobleman, Bartolomeo Zen.

As Stampa records in Poem 2, it was around Christmastime—the year was 1548—that she met and fell passionately in love with Collaltino di Collalto. The attraction was mutual, and their relationship started out happily (as Stampa points out in Poem 1, she wants to be envied for her "high fortune," "such great love," and "such a splendid lord"). This was true despite their different social standings and the occasional chilliness on the count's part (in Poem 4 Stampa observes that "the pale Moon / Made his heart colder than my warm desire" (*Selected Poems*, pp. 3, 9). Very early in the *Rime*, we learn about the social obstacles to Stampa's love for Collaltino: while the poetess is of "low" social status, her beloved belongs to the aristocracy as metaphorically expressed by his name, Collalto, "high hill." Throughout she will refer to him as "Count," addressing him in a way that highlights the inequality between them.

At first, Collaltino, who must have been flattered by Stampa's undivided attention, dedicated some sonnets of his own to her, though his poetry—some of which is published in Salza's critical edition of Stampa's *Rime*—was by no means a fitting match for Stampa's original verse. She in fact discourages him from continuing in this very vein, saying that he should leave it to her to celebrate him and not vice versa: "Why do you waste, my lord, paper and ink / In praising me?" (*Selected Poems*, p. 95).

In this early and brief phase of their relationship, the couple spends considerable time together, which fills Stampa with a happiness she records in Poem 17: "For my delights are such and so abundant / They cannot be contained in human heart, / While I enjoy the presence of those lights" (*Selected Poems*, p. 23). Much of her energy seems dedicated to trying to please her beloved Collaltino. She sings his praise and celebrates his many virtues: "So he alone among us should be perfect. / Saturn gave him his height of intellect; / Jupiter, love for all that's fair and noble; / Mars made all men beside him seem unwarlike"; he has "style" and "judgement," "beauty" and "grace"; he is a "gentleman with sweet expression," "young in years"; and "His hair is blond, and his complexion light, / He's tall in stature, with a manly chest" (*Selected Poems*, pp. 9, 23).

Despite her poetic compliments, Collaltino soon starts losing interest in Stampa. He often goes to his castle of San Salvatore on the banks of the Piave River, leaving her behind. In Poem 21, "Love . . . flies away"; in Poem 43, we learn that her beloved "flees" from her; and in Poem 47, Stampa waits in vain as "he shuts his ears against returning," "while he lives happily among his hills" (*Selected Poems*, p. 45). His behavior makes Stampa feel hurt and lonely. "Forever weeping," she is consigned to her "unhappy fate" (*Selected Poems*, p. 27). As early as Poem 5, she compares the fluctuation of their relationship to the changing of the seasons. In Poem 18, she likens her lover to the wandering sun: in Collaltino's presence, she feels "happiness and vigor," but when he departs, the sun sets and "leaves the earth to sink down in the west" (*Selected Poems*, p. 25). Her feelings are even more intense because she can never be sure he will return: "While my sun's brilliant dawning and return / To me is doubtful; certain is the parting" (*Selected Poems*, p. 25). References to unrequited love increase until they become a central theme in the collection "Count, where has fled so soon / The faithful love that once you swore to me?" (*Selected Poems*, p. 189).

As Collaltino spends more and more time away from her, Stampa's poetry takes on a sinister tone, bearing witness to a fast-growing internal struggle. The speaker of her verse complains about her lover's unfaithful nature, then shows a raging jealousy. She lives in constant "fear that another woman holds him" (*Selected Poems*, p. 51).

In 1549 Collaltino goes to France to fight under King Henry II: "O mighty valor of a courteous knight / Who carried off to France a loving heart" (*Selected Poems*, p. 75). Now in danger of losing his life in combat, he gives Stampa cause for new torment and distress: "Now hope is gone and grief remains alone, / Since, owing to my bitter, evil star, / You, my dear lord, took flight from me to France" (*Selected Poems*, p. 76). In his absence, Stampa awaits the count's return. When she finally learns that his arrival is imminent, she is overcome with joyful anticipation. "O blissful, dear, and sweetest of all news, / Message of joy, in which you promise me / That I'll see again the dear and happy / Lights . . ." (*Selected Poems*, p. 79). They spend a beatific night together, reconciled as poet and warrior, but not for long. Collaltino soon returns to France, where he remains until 1550. Although Stampa writes many letters, he responds only rarely, which causes her to suffer intense loneliness and jealousy. Her speaker sends off a desperate message to him in Poem 145: "Tell him my life is drawing near its sunset, / Unless in a few days—or, better, hours— / His rays appear to light my weary eyes" (*Selected Poems*, p. 115).

In 1551 Collaltino returns to Venice and sees Stampa, but they pass most of the time together quarreling; he torments her with demands, accusations, and threats of abandonment. This time Collaltino carries out his threats: he leaves, never to return. Stampa falls into a deep depression and goes off alone to recuperate. As the days pass, she slowly breaks free from his spell and accepts the suffering as a fair price to pay for her literary fame: "Since you, O Love, have given me back my freedom, / Keep me forever in this happy state, / So that my heart's my own, as once it was" (*Selected Poems*, p. 159).

Probably in 1551, a new lover, the Venetian patrician Bartolomeo, appears on the horizon. Not much is known about the specifics of this relationship, although judging from Stampa's poems, it is less intense and passionate than her previous affair. While the poetry inspired by her love for Collaltino is permeated with images of death, pessimism, and pain, the poems to Zen carry a brighter tone, centered more on spiritual love. In this phase, Stampa was keen to explore the relationship between "earthly" and "heavenly" love (between the love exchanged by humans and the love of God).

> He teaches us to love him and our neighbour too.
> Now if you must love, what better way is there than by loving me
> For I adore you and I've made a temple and mirror of your lovely face?
> Love then; and, by loving, keep Christ's pact.
> (Stampa in Bassanese, p. 120)

A few poems in the "Rime d'Amore" section deal with topics other than Stampa's love affairs, such as war, social issues, and reflections on the ideas of Plato. The opening verses of Poem 134 are an homage to the city of Venice as the seat of republican freedom. Praising the Venetian salon society "that enables her performances of passion and poetry," Stampa portrays Venice itself as a nurturing mother and "a space of freedom that allows even a female poet to raise herself proudly" (Smarr, p. 10). In Poem 248, she denounces the greed and violence of war and comments on the political situation of her time. Several condemn the political ideology that divides people into social ranks.

FLEXING HER POETIC MUSCLES?

Many scholars consider the poems in the *Rime Varie* an elaborate exercise in the art of writing. In the Renaissance it was fashionable to write just for writing's sake; most people in cultured society tried their literary luck, some in search of fame, some just for fun or prank, often in imitation of famed writers.

Section two—"Miscellaneous Poems." Most modern editions of Stampa's *Rime* are based on Abdelkader Salza's 1913 edition of Gaspara Stampa's and Veronica Franco's poetry. Salza arranged Stampa's miscellaneous poems in thematic blocks. One large section comprises all poems addressed to Stampa's friends: Domenico Venier, Sperone Speroni, and Giovanni Della Casa (Poems 246-295). Another, smaller section, which ends the book, contains the poems written in homage to a deceased nun, Angelica Paolo (Poems 296-303). This final section closes with eight religious sonnets (Poems 304-311).

In Poem 250 Stampa declines a friend's invitation to visit her birthplace, Padua. The poet uses this occasion to reminisce about her native town, striking a rather nostalgic tone: "Without me, lord, you went . . . where I was born, / Where the first light of heaven struck my eyes, / So sweet a place, none other is its equal" (*Selected Poems*, p. 197). In Poem 276 of the same section, Stampa repays in kind Leonardo Emo's praise of her in his verse: "Since I have been recorded in your poems, / Emo, and polished by your artist's file! . . . And if Apollo pours his gifts upon me, / I will go praising you and that high spring" (*Selected Poems*, p. 203).

Poem 298 belongs to the second thematic block, the collection of poems addressed to the nun Angelica Paolo, Stampa's relative and dear friend. Comparing the nun's life in a convent to that of most other women, Stampa finds a way to address urgent issues that her female contemporaries faced when married: the complaining husband, quarreling children, the torments that women underwent to look attractive: "Some strive to make their hair curly and blond, / Try every art, every ingenious trick / Which only drives their souls to the abyss. . . . One spoils her face with acids and bleaches, / Injuring in this way her own good health" (*Selected Poems*, pp. 207-213).

The nature of love. In one of Stampa's most famous and influential sonnets, "O night . . ." (Sonnet 104), she describes a night with Collaltino after he returns from the French battlefield. The poem testifies to her connection with the Renaissance spirit. The centerpiece of the sonnet is the surprisingly bold first tercet: it refers candidly to an erotic episode in Greek mythology. The god Zeus wants to spend the night with a mortal queen, Alcmena, and in order to gain access to her bed, disguises himself as her husband. To prolong the joyous experience, Zeus delays the arrival of morning, making the night twice as long as usual. Stampa's mythological allusion to the tale in her verse allows her to display her knowledge of ancient narratives and to share her uplifting sexual experience with the reader, a highly unconventional topic for a female poet. One of Stampa's greatest literary contributions to the poetry written in the style of Petrarch is her substitution of an unattainable, forever honored platonic love with sensual, flesh-and-blood relationships.

Another remarkable aspect in Sonnet 104 is the shift in focal point from the beloved to the lover. Throughout the sonnet, Stampa uses personal and possessive pronouns that highlight the speaker's own persona, either as lover or artist. There are eight instances of *I, me, my* and *mine*, compared to one *him,* and no *he* or *his.* The entire poem is addressed to the night, which Stampa personifies and has her speaker address in the second person singular, a voice usually reserved for the beloved or love itself. Stampa gives the night a starring role, focusing on the interaction between this natural force, this "You," and the lover, "I," while relegating the beloved to a supporting role.

"O night . . ."

O night, more glorious and more blest to me
Than are the brightest and most blissful days!
Night, worthy to be praised by the most
    brilliant
Of human minds, not only by my words.
You only were the faithful minister
Of all my joys: and all the bitterness
That had oppressed me you made sweet and
    dear,
Bringing back to my arms him who had
    bound me.
I only lacked the gift that was bestowed
On fortunate Alcmena, when you lingered
Far past the usual hour of dawn's return.
And yet I cannot say so much of you,
O shining night, but that song of mine
Will not be overwhelmed by what it sings.
          (*Selected Poems*, p. 85)

Sources and literary context. By liberating her lyrics from the tradition of featuring the beloved, Stampa renounces the fairly rigid, pre-formulated language of her predecessors in favor of a more sincere and spontaneous female voice. Yet her poetry is intimately tied to Italian literary tradition. At the outset, the speaker of the *Rime* identifies herself as a servant of love, in the manner of the Sicilian poets of the *dolce stil novo* ("Sweet New Style"), of Dante, and most notably, of Petrarch. By modeling her opening poem closely on the prefatory sonnet of Petrarch's *Canzoniere*, Stampa immediately places her *Rime* within the Petrarchan poetic tradition and its verse forms, especially the sonnet. In the Renaissance, the evoking of a familiar pattern was an integral part of the strategy of the sophisticated writer. Skillful imitation was not considered a fault, but an excellence. According to Bembo, the century's leading literary theorist, the current Italian writers should imitate the works of the *tre corone*, the three great writers of the fourteenth century: Dante Alighieri, Giovanni Boccaccio, and Francesco Petrarch.

Petrarch's *Canzoniere* was the standard model for amorous lyric poetry throughout Western Europe during the Renaissance. A collection of 366 lyric poems on various subjects with diverse metrical forms (sonnets, madrigals, *canzoni* ["songs"], and sestinas), Petrarch's corpus would remain extraordinarily influential throughout the century and beyond. That Stampa drew on Petrarch is evident in her frequent use of his sonnet form, her systematic borrowing of his vocabulary and rhymes, and her imitation of his style and rhetorical devices. But Stampa tailored his lyric standard to her own experiences, asserting her independence in her own prefatory sonnet. While Petrarch condemns his love as a youthful error, Stampa celebrates hers as a "noble cause" (*Selected Poems*, p. 3). Petrarch concedes that love has been futile, shameful, and frail and calls it an obstacle on his way to salvation, whereas Stampa accepts love as her destiny. Unlike Petrarch's opening lyrics, which conclude that human pleasures "are but brief dreams" and which preach repentance, the verses in Stampa's opening poem lack any religious connotation (Petrarch in Durling, p. 37). In Petrarch's prefatory sonnet, a man pursues a woman and laments his amorous defeat from the perspective of a devout Christian; Stampa, on the other hand, focuses on a tormented woman's yearning for redemption in the form of earthly fame and glory. Throughout her *Rime*, Stampa's speaker is *mesto* ("mournful," "unhappy") (*Selected Poems*, p. 3); most of the poems document her lover's lack of warmth and his indifference to her yearnings, loneliness, bereavement, jealousy, humiliation, and suffering. But instead of merely pitying herself, the speaker identifies the agony of unrequited love as a torturous but essential sentiment in the inventory of a writer: "O noble object, O bright object, O divine object, since even in tormenting me you are beneficial and produce fruit" (*Selected Poems*, p. xxxiii). As her love story approaches an unhappy ending, the fateful equation *pena-penna* (pain-pen) grows more and more prominent: the stronger is the pain, the stronger her pen. Ultimately the speaker recognizes pain as the primary source of her inspiration. The commemoration of amorous pain as the stimulus of the creative process is not only a prominent theme throughout her poetry but a significant new perspective in love poetry.

Publication and reception. Gaspara Stampa's lyrics circulated and were read in Venetian salons, and her madrigals were performed and sung during her lifetime. However, only three of her poems, all sonnets, were published while she was alive. They appeared in the anthology *Il sesto libro delle Rime di diversi eccellenti autori nuovamente raccolte e mandate in luce con un discorso di Girolamo Ruscelli* (The sixth book of the Rhymes of diverse excellent authors newly collected and published with an introduction by Girolamo Ruscelli, published in Venice by G. M. Bonelli in 1553). Six years later, the three sonnets were reprinted in another anthology. Finally in October 1554, the year of Stampa's death, her sister, most probably with Giorgio Benzone, compiled an entire collection of poems under the title *Rime di Madonna Gaspara Stampa (con gratia et privilegio) in Venezia—per Plinio Pietrasanta 1554* (Rhymes by Lady Gaspara Stampa—[with grace and distinction]—published in Venice by Plinio Pietrasanta in 1554).

After its initial publication, Stampa's *Rime* was forgotten for almost two centuries until one of Collaltino's descendants rescued her poetry from oblivion. In 1738 Count Antonio Rambaldo di Collalto commissioned Luisa Bergalli to reissue the text, this time with several illustrations (including portraits of Gaspara and Collaltino) and with poetry by Collaltino and Vinciguerra II di Collalto.

The second edition of Stampa's poems appeared in 1738 and was introduced by a biography written by Count Antonio Rambaldo, heir to the family title of the Collaltos. This unauthenticated biographical account of Stampa's life marks the beginning of romantic legend about her that endured for centuries. The *Rime* was read as autobiography, equating the speaker with the woman who wrote the poems. Rambaldo's account has since given rise to fictional recreations of Stampa's life in plays, stories, and novels.

In the twentieth century, the renowned critic Benedetto Croce minimized the importance of the *Rime*, describing it as nothing but a diary of Stampa's single greatest love. Yet Stampa's poetry impressed at least two twentieth-century poets. Italy's Gabriele D'Annunzio took his personal motto from a line by Stampa—"to live burning and not to feel the pain" (*Selected Poems*, p. xxv). For the German poet Rainer Maria Rilke, Stampa was inspirational in the language of transcendent love, that is, of love that soars above earthly emotion to become divine.

—Petra Wirth

For More Information

Bassanese, Fiora A. *Gaspara Stampa*. Boston: Twayne, 1982.

Durling, Robert M., ed. and trans. *Petrarch's Lyric Poems*. Cambridge, Mass.: Harvard University Press, 1976.

Jones, Ann Rosalind. "Feminine Pastoral as Heroic Martyrdom. Gaspara Stampa and Mary Wroth." In *The Currency of Eros: Women's Love Lyric in Europe, 1540-1620*. Bloomington: Indiana University Press, 1990.

Lane, Frederic C. *Venice, a Maritime Republic*. Baltimore: Johns Hopkins University Press, 1973.

Robin, Diana. "Courtesans, Celebrity, and Print Culture in Renaissance Venice: Tullia d'Aragona, Gaspara Stampa, and Veronica Franco." In *Italian*

Women and the City. Madison, N.J.: Fairleigh Dickinson University Press, 2003.

Rosenthal, Margaret F. "Courtesan." In *The Feminist Encyclopedia of Italian Literature*. Westport, Conn.: Greenwood Press, 1997.

Salza, Abdelkader. *Gaspara Stampa-Veronica Franco. Rime*. Bari, Italy: Laterza, 1913.

Smarr, Janet Levarie. "Introduction." In *Italian Women and the City*. Madison, N.J.: Fairleigh Dickinson University Press, 2003.

Stampa, Gaspara. *Rime*. Ed. Maria Bellonci. Milan: Rizzoli, 1976.

———. *Selected Poems*. Ed. and trans. Anna Laura Stortoni and Mary Prentice Lillie. New York: Italica Press, 1994.

Warnke, Frank. "Aphrodite's Priestess, Love's Martyr: Gaspara Stampa." In *Women Writers of the Renaissance and Reformation*. Athens: University of Georgia Press, 1987.

The Secret

by

Alba de Céspedes

Alba de Céspedes was born in Rome, Italy, in 1911 to an Italian mother and a Cuban father (serving as Cuban ambassador to Italy at the time). Although de Céspedes was raised to speak both Spanish and Italian, she wrote the majority of her literary works in her mother's native tongue. De Céspedes's passion for writing began with the poems she composed as a small child, which were the first products of a talent her father encouraged her to keep developing. Married at the age of 15 and a mother by 16, de Céspedes put her writing career on hold until her divorce at the age of 20. At 24, she published a collection of short stories and then returned to writing poetry. In the 1930s, while Italy was under the Fascist dictatorship of Benito Mussolini, de Céspedes participated in the Resistance—the anti-German, anti-Fascist struggle in Italy. The writer paid for her involvement in the Resistance. She was arrested and jailed for several days in 1935, and the Fascist government banned her 1938 novel, *There's No Turning Back* (*Nessuno torna indietro*). A few years later she became a commentator for the Resistance radio in Bari, Italy, taking turns with other partisans each evening to speak anonymously about liberating Italy from the grips of Fascism. In 1944, de Céspedes founded the partisan journal *Il Mercurio*, and later she collaborated on other journals, such as *Epoca* and *La Stampa*. Her post-World War II novels include politically and socially engaged works such as *Dalla parte di lei* (1949; The Best of Husbands); *Quaderno proibito* (1952; The Secret); *Prima e dopo* (1955; Between Then and Now) and *Il rimorso* (1962; Remorse). After years of personal

THE LITERARY WORK

A novel set in Rome, Italy, in 1952; published in Italian (as *Quaderno proibito*) in 1952, in English in 1957.

SYNOPSIS

While keeping a secret diary, Valeria unexpectedly discovers that she harbors a hidden discontent with her stifling social role as a working wife and mother in postwar Italy.

and literary social involvement in Italy, de Céspedes left the country to live in Paris, France, where she died in 1997. *The Secret* remains de Céspedes's most successful work. Although its widespread appeal stems from universal portraits of family life, the plot and characters are deeply rooted in the real-life experience of bourgeois women in postwar Italy.

Events in History at the Time of the Novel

Women under and against Italian Fascist rule. The role prescribed for Italian women under Fascism was directly affected by the ambitions of dictator Benito Mussolini, who set out to create a large labor and military force as well as an Italian empire (a burgeoning population would justify the colonization of lands abroad). In his determination to boost the Italian population, already at 40 million, Mussolini, or Il Duce ("the leader"), initiated various pro-childbirth policies. In 1926, all prostitutes were ordered off the streets and into regulated brothels in an attempt to discourage illicit sex and encourage sex for procreative purposes within the confines of marriage. In a further attempt to promote marriage and therefore procreation, the end of 1926 saw the introduction of a celibacy tax, to be paid by men who remained unmarried past the age of 26. The same year the Fascist government outlawed the display, possession, and sale of information about contraception and abortion. Mussolini's regime also called on the secret police to intervene in any suspected instance of birth-control use.

ALBA DE CÉSPEDES AND THE ITALIAN RESISTANCE

During World War II Alba de Céspedes was among the daring women who became active in the Italian Resistance, an experience carefully chronicled in the author's diaries. An entry on November 17, 1943, reveals her desire to be treated as an equal of her male companions:

> The news of a massacre at Sant'Agata has reached us. The Germans suddenly arrived at a farm where they rounded up the men, threw them against a haystack and they mowed/cut them down with a machine gun. All of the women were spared. This possibility of being saved due only to the fact of being a woman humiliates me profoundly. . . . I have decided that if they catch us I will scream furiously: 'down with Germany, long live Italy!' so they will not take pity on me.
>
> (De Céspedes in Carroli, "Alba de Céspedes Revisited," p. 55)

While serving as a female partisan, de Céspedes provided the voice of "Clorinda" for a Resistance radio station in Bari, sharing over the airwaves her desire for the liberation of Italy from Fascist rule. The writer adopted her radio pseudonym from the brazen female character in Torquato Tasso's epic poem *Jerusalem Delivered* (also in *WLAIT 7: Italian Literature and Its Times*). Tasso's Clorinda cross-dressed as a male warrior and, according to de Céspedes, the partisan women working for Radio Bari always wore men's trousers.

Mussolini offered both financial rewards and public recognition to enlarge the size of the family: 1928 saw the inauguration of tax breaks for families with children, and in 1933 Il Duce pro-

claimed December 24 to be Italy's official Mother's Day. The highlight of this new holiday was a parade in Rome featuring a procession of the women who had the highest number of live births in Italy's 90 provinces. In 1942 Mussolini took this pro-childbirth propaganda a step further when he started to award a gold medal to the most prolific mothers in the country. Through all of these legal and symbolic actions, the Fascist regime made clear the message that the only acceptable social function for women was that of mother, a submissive and self-sacrificing role limited strictly to the domestic sphere.

Yet at the same time Fascism gave Italian women their first sense of themselves as a political force. The regime organized women, in fact, mass organized them. By the Second World War, membership in the women's organization of the Fascist Party approached 3.2 million. Conditioned to accept, even promote the male-dominated, authoritarian nature of their society, they nevertheless gained civic experience. The women of Italy acquired a new gender consciousness, a sense of themselves as a political class. This new consciousness emerged not only because of their involvement in Fascist politics, but also because of their resistance to it. A number of anti-Fascist women were involved in clandestine efforts to help the Resistance movement that took shape following the fall of Mussolini in 1943. While there are no definite figures for the total number of women involved in the Resistance, Victoria de Grazia provides the following statistics: "Forty-six hundred women were arrested, tortured, and tried, 2,750 were deported to German concentration camps, and 623 were executed or killed in battle" (De Grazia, p. 274).

At the conclusion of the war, many of the surviving female Resistance fighters, who had actively participated in an important political cause, found it difficult to return to a limited social role, which confined them to the domestic sphere. Many of these women therefore took action to dislodge the limitations, becoming forerunners of the 1960s feminist movement by struggling for women's rights in the workplace and home. In 1944, partisan women in northern Italy joined with women in southern Italy to form the Unione donne italiane, or UDI (Italian Women's Union), an organization that would always remain fairly militant. The union aimed at protecting women's rights in the labor force, often by organizing strikes among female workers, and dedicated itself as well to more overarching goals, such as the promotion of peace and an end

Female assembly worker in an Olivetti typewriter factory.

to hunger and homelessness. Among other accomplishments, the UDI is largely responsible for the campaign for and eventual acquisition of female suffrage in Italy in 1945.

Women in postwar Italy: economic hard times. In 1945 Mussolini was captured, along with his mistress Clara Petacci, and executed by Italian partisans. Other major changes followed. World War II ended, and a 1946 popular election abolished the monarchy and declared Italy a republic. The nation ratified a new constitution, and in 1948, Alcide De Gasperi led his party, the Christian De-

mocrats (known as DC, for Democrazia Cristiana), to power. De Gasperi was confronted with an enormous economic challenge: damages to Italy from the Second World War exceeded 7,000 billion lire, or 20 percent of the nation's property. From the war's end in 1945 until 1947, Italy's economy faced a period of great instability, punctuated by uncontrolled inflation and skyrocketing unemployment. Although some relief came when in 1947 Italy entered a phase of relative financial stability, serious financial problems continued to plague the country, and its economy remained stagnant. The picture brightened with Italy's receipt of $1.5 billion from the United States (about $1.4 billion as a grant, the remainder as a loan) in 1948-52 under the Marshall Plan—the U.S. program of aid to European countries for postwar recovery.

While Europe entered a period of vigorous economic growth lasting for more than a decade (1950-63), the upward trend did not begin in Italy until 1958. Italy experienced its economic "miracle" in the 1960s, transforming in a blink of the eye from a country of peasants to a modern industrial nation, thanks, among other factors, to a cheap labor force and the formation of the European Common Market, which promoted free trade among member nations. With the help of a number of manufacturers, such as the automobile maker Fiat and the typewriter maker Olivetti, the Italian economy experienced an extraordinary boom between 1958 and 1963. Olivetti, for example, increased its production of typewriters fourfold within part of this period (1957-1961).

Having filled in for the drafted soldiers in virtually all fields of work during the Second World War, women continued to make up a large part of the Italian labor force during the postwar years. Article 37 of the 1947 constitution sanctioned equal pay for equal work, although in reality most women kept earning lower wages than their male counterparts. Also, the Christian Democrat Party still emphasized a subordinate role for women—despite their legally prescribed equality in the work force and their active role in the new economy. For example, Guido Gonella, a prominent member of the party, sanctioned inequality in the home, publicly declaring that women were "Equals in civil life, subordinates in family life" (Cutrufelli, p. 155; trans. V. Mirshak).

Women in postwar Italy: the constraints of the Roman Catholic Church. One of the most significant influences on gender issues in Italy has been the Catholic Church. Under the Fascist regime in 1929, the Lateran Treaty and Concordat had given the Church sovereignty over its territory (as Vatican City); these same agreements allowed for religious instruction in public schools, and recognized that Catholic marriages were subject to canon law. By forming a strong, centralized organization and directly involving lay people in its interests through the collaborative political group Catholic Action (Azione cattolica, or AC), the Church continued to wield political influence in the postwar period. In fact, many active members of the AC became key political players in the Christian Democrat government. The Italian people found in the stable structure of the Church a bastion of constancy during the tumultuous post-World War II years. Many also found in the Catholic Church a strong ally to counter the threat posed by atheistic Marxism, a threat that solidified the bond of cooperation between the DC and the Church and resulted in its gaining formidable control over everyday life in Italy. Due to its close cooperation with the DC, the Church influenced such issues as the use of contraception and cinematic production.

Pius XII, the pope from 1939 until his death in 1958, led the Catholic Church throughout this term of great sociopolitical influence. In 1946 Pius XII revealed his conservative stance towards women's liberation when he declared, "What is the woman if not the helper of the man?" (Cutrufelli, p. 149; trans. V. Mirshak). In addition to vehement opposition to abortion and birth control, he also guaranteed the prohibition of divorce, or in more religious terms, the indissolubility of marriage, an institution that remained under Church control during the postwar period.

During Pius XII's papacy, motherhood and virginity took precedence as the ultimate values to be associated with a woman. In 1947 the pope stressed the need to "rebuild" the Catholic family with the mother as the central figure and strongly discouraged women from working outside the home. In a further exaltation of motherhood, Pius XII revived the Marian cult and praised the Virgin Mother as the perfect model of a suffering and self-sacrificing maternal figure. In 1950 Pius XII effectively reinforced the value placed on an unmarried woman's virginity through the canonization of Maria Goretti, an 11-year-old peasant who had been murdered while resisting sexual molestation.

Thus, women of the Fascist and postwar periods faced numerous legal and social obstacles to an expansion of their roles in Italian society. Although the UDI (Italian Women's Union) had been working as early as the 1940s to obtain equality in the workplace and female participation in the legislative body, not until the 1960s would women confront more explosive issues, such as the legalization of divorce and abortion. With a conservative church and state at the helm, women's rights went through a slow but steady building phase in Italy from the close of World War II in 1945 to the early 1960s. It is hardly surprising, given this state of affairs, that the burgeoning of numerous Italian feminist collectives would be delayed until 1968, close to two decades after the release of de Céspedes's novel

The Secret. Inspired by a new left on the political scene at the time, these collectives were no doubt established by thousands of women for whom the years of Fascist and postwar oppression must have been a distant memory.

The Novel in Focus

Plot summary. The novel, written in diary form, opens with an entry describing how the protagonist, Valeria Cossati, comes to possess a sleek black notebook in which she begins to record the everyday events of her life. In Italian the title of the novel is *Quaderno proibito* ("forbidden notebook"), and the account of Valeria's purchase of the notebook at the shop of a tobacconist reveals the double meaning of this title. Valeria buys the notebook on a Sunday, a day on which, by law, a tobacconist can sell only tobacco and newspapers. On her way out, she has to walk past the policeman guarding the shop door with the notebook tucked under her coat. This deception foreshadows the intense secrecy that will surround Valeria's keeping of the diary throughout the novel. She intends to hide her writing from friends and family. Valeria feels guilty about her private inclinations and emotions; thus, the first entry in the diary begins with a confession, "I was wrong to buy this notebook, terribly wrong" (De Céspedes, *Secret*, p. 1).

As Valeria records everyday events, her discontent and frustration with her role as wife and mother begin to surface. The protagonist, who participated in the Resistance movement during the Second World War, feels keenly her lack of independence in postwar Italy. She is disturbed to realize that she does not even have any corner of the house to call her own. She seems even to have lost possession of her own name: she is simply "Baby" to her parents, "Mamma" to her husband and children. After her family laughs at the idea of her keeping a diary ("What would you write in it, Mamma?" [*Secret*, p. 7]), the troubled housewife becomes obsessed with finding new hiding places for it in their cramped apartment. Each new entry in the diary is accompanied by growing pangs of guilt; Valeria detests keeping a secret from her loved ones and regrets the time taken away from her never-ending housework.

Valeria's discontent in her marriage to Michele was unknown to her before she began to examine her subconscious through the writing process. Gradually this discontent becomes more pronounced as the novel unfolds. The couple married young and now that they are entering middle age, both husband and wife are doing some serious soul-searching. Surrounded by a world at war for the better part of their lives, from childhood to adulthood, Valeria and Michele are accustomed to living under the shadow of political and economic instability. As their children reach the age in which they become more demanding financially, the couple grow increasingly dissatisfied with their meager wages and their constant scrabbling to make ends meet. In fact, a sense of despair prevails in the novel when it comes to the economy and the effects of war: their son, Riccardo, is unable to attend a Christmas social because the family cannot afford to rent a dinner jacket; Valeria fears that their daughter, Mirella, will be "bought" by an older gentleman because Valeria and Michele are unable to spoil her with the material things the other girls her age flaunt;

TIMELINE: THE LIBERATION OF ITALIAN WOMEN

1910 Italian feminist groups create a common manifesto demanding female suffrage.

1931 Penal code mandates heavy penalties for illegal abortion, including two to five years in jail for anyone aiding and abetting it.

1944 Formation of the *Unione Donne Italiane* or *UDI* (Italian Women's Union), which fought for equal rights for women in the workplace.

1945 Female suffrage is granted in Italy.

1956 The Court of Cassation (highest judicial authority in Italy) rules that the husband does not have the right to exercise "corrective power" (that is, the use of domestic violence) over his wife.

1968 Numerous Italian feminist groups are formed. Law dictating the inequality of the sexes in adultery cases (sanctioning the imprisonment of women convicted of adultery) is declared unconstitutional.

1970 Divorce is legalized.

1978 Abortion is legalized.

---

the constant threat of a third world war hampers the family's economic hopes. Valeria's own mother continues to resent the loss of her aristocratic family's fortune during the First World War. Also her mother makes clear her disapproval of working women, so that while Valeria has come to enjoy her job in a bustling office setting, she again feels guilty about the pleasure and ends up constantly reminding herself that she is there by necessity, not by choice.

Meanwhile, Michele, hoping to acquire a more glamorous and liberating lifestyle than the one he experiences in his banking career, writes a screenplay. He manages to keep his writing a secret until the script is finished. Along with her children, Valeria only learns of the screenplay when Michele decides to show it to Clara, a progressive, highly independent family friend in the film business. The Cossatis become momentarily hopeful of putting an end to their economic woes when Clara suggests that she might find a buyer for the screenplay. Unhappily the script is rejected, which seals the family's position as part of the struggling working class in postwar Rome.

"WRITING IS A SIN"

An article summarizing a 1954 conference presentation by de Céspedes provides a glimpse into her ideas about placing social restrictions on women's writing:

"Writing is a sin," thus Alba De [sic] Céspedes has defined the attitude of a woman who pursues a literary vocation, in her conference held last Thursday night under the auspices of the Lyceum. . . . Writing for these women [i.e., the Brontë sisters and Austen] means stealing time from their families, their children, their homes. While men have the right to shut themselves in their studies, protected and undisturbed, women must work in secret, and keep a "forbidden notebook," like the protagonist in de Céspedes's latest novel. She [de Céspedes] too had the feeling she was doing something wrong when writing. Only with experience accumulated day by day, spurred on by a tenacious persistence, after long and hard readings, did Alba de Céspedes convince herself and everyone else . . . that she had the right to be a writer; in short, she was finally rid of her fear and guilt.

(Carroli, "Alba de Céspedes Revisited," p. 45)

In addition to her financial disappointments, Valeria is troubled by her 20-year-old daughter's relationship with a man in his thirties. The protagonist tries to sever Mirella's ties to the prominent lawyer Sandro Cantoni, but instead must face some harsh realities about her own life as a submissive housewife. "If you love me, how can you wish me a life like yours?" Mirella asks her mother (*Secret*, p. 34). The question highlights the stark distinction between the two women— one, a traditionalist who feels obligated to be the perfect wife and mother; the other, determined to establish a romantic relationship based on intelligent exchanges and mutual respect.

In contrast with the often-hostile relations between mother and daughter in the novel, Valeria reveals only sympathetic tenderness towards her son, Riccardo. Riccardo shares his mother's traditional mores, and she dotes on him as he works to finish his studies and fulfill his dream of finding success in Argentina. The young man resolves to make his fortune in life instead of repeating his father's mistake of "settling" for a steady but low-paying job. But despite the resolve, Riccardo's ambitious plans are shattered when he discovers that his girlfriend, Marina, is pregnant. Suddenly finding himself on the verge of marriage and fatherhood, he ends up accepting his own steady but low-paying position at the same bank where Michele works.

As Valeria, in writing her diary, takes ever greater notice of the distant friendliness that has become the foundation of her marriage, she begins to interpret the seemingly innocent gestures of her boss, Guido, for what they really are: romantic advances. Meeting alone together in their office on Saturdays, Valeria and Guido share their frustration with their respective lives outside the office and indulge in the fantasy of taking a clandestine trip for two to Venice. Guido makes Valeria feel younger and more attractive, restores a piece of her identity by calling her "Valeria" rather than addressing her as mother, daughter, or wife, and provides the listening ear that she fails to find at home.

Yet the unhappy woman ultimately realizes she does not have the courage to leave her husband and children or to abandon the traditional role of self-sacrificing wife and mother that she has so carefully cultivated over the years. Unwilling to let Riccardo's soon-to-be bride, Marina, take over as matriarch in the Cossati home, Valeria decides to return to her role as submissive wife, mother, and now grandmother as well. Consumed by the irrational fear that Marina will someday find her secret diary and reveal her subversive thoughts to the family, Valeria prepares to burn the notebook at the close of the novel. Even as she decides to destroy the diary, Valeria believes that Marina, upon returning to the house and smelling the faint odor of burning, will understand what has happened. The novel closes with this affirmation of the shared bond between women and their similar journeys of self-discovery:

[Marina will] understand, I'm certain, because every woman hides a black notebook, a secret diary, and every woman must destroy it. Now I wonder where I've been more sincere, in these pages or in my actions—actions that will leave behind an image of me like a beautiful portrait.

(Secret, p. 249)

The mother-daughter relationship in *The Secret*.

The Secret reveals the effects of the Fascist and then the conservative postwar political regimes on motherhood in Italy. Valeria's interactions with her own mother are limited to discussions about cooking, cleaning, and the rising price of produce. Her mother disapproves of her daughter having a job outside the home and worries that she is neglecting her duties as a wife and mother. While Valeria aspires to raise her daughter, Mirella, differently, aiming for their relationship to be a friendship, she is shocked to find herself attempting to reinforce in her daughter the traditional, oppressive ideals for females.

Valeria's insistence on denying the importance of Mirella's new job as a legal assistant, along with her refusal to accept the emotionally and intellectually fulfilling relationship Mirella shares with an older attorney, results in the breakdown of the mother-daughter relationship, recognized by the protagonist when she laments that her daughter views her as an enemy (Secret, p. 37). Valeria is devastated to realize that Mirella may have good reason to reject her traditional ideas. In a flash of self-awareness, Valeria discovers that she may in fact be harming her daughter by teaching her the female role imposed on women: "I felt she was trying to protect herself against my love, as if against something dangerous; I wondered if I'd have had the strength to do the same with my mother, and I knew I wouldn't" (Secret, p. 77). In other words, Valeria discovers that she has become for her daughter the same voice that she had grown up hearing in her own mother: a voice that reinforces the very patriarchal system that has been passed down from generation to generation, not only by the men who hold the power, but also by the women themselves.

The dangerous, cyclical nature of the oppression of women as a social construct passed from mother to daughter can be found in Italian women's writing dating as far back as the mid-1800s. One of the most striking examples is a novel by Neera (pseudonym of Anna Radius Zuccari) entitled *Teresa* (1886; also in *WLAIT 7: Italian Literature and Its Times*). In the novel, the primary model that the young protagonist, Teresa, has of femininity is her mother's entirely weak and passive character. In turn, Teresa grows into a submissive woman, bowing to her father's wishes and ending her relationship with Orlandi, the man she loves. It is only when both her parents have died and her younger siblings are out on their own that Teresa can bring herself to go to her lover. Sadly by this time, both Teresa's youth and Orlandi's health have faded, and Teresa seeks to fulfill for her partner more the role of caretaker than lover.

While *Teresa* addresses the issue of motherhood's role in the perpetuation of the patriarchal system, the novel suggests no real solution to the problem. In contrast, the protagonist of Sibilla Aleramo's 1906 novel, *A Woman* (also in *WLAIT 7: Italian Literature and Its Times*), definitively breaks the chain of female subordination. Like the maternal figure in *Teresa*, the protagonist's mother in *A Woman* is described as sad, tired, and entirely acquiescent. However, the protagonist of *A Woman* is driven by the desire to resist modeling herself on her mother's negative example. Instead, she makes the painful decision to leave her abusive husband and, in doing so, she is also forced to give up all rights to her young child. In the case of *A Woman*, the protagonist refuses to let her son see her submit to a tyrannical and oppressive marriage.

With the male-dominated Futurist movement of the 1910s and 1920s, women writers in Italy moved even further away from the ideal of motherhood. For example, in her 1918 novel *Un ventre di donna* (A Woman's Womb), Enif Robert creates a protagonist who is eager to have her uterus removed, thereby guaranteeing her sterility. Also, no reference is made to the protagonist's mother, nor does she think of her own child very often. Although the novel vacillates back and forth between repulsion and appreciation for the female body, the desire for complete equality between the sexes—a desire that effectively eliminates the maternal role—is a dominant theme.

With de Céspedes's *The Secret*, the institutionalization of motherhood appeared once again at the forefront of women's issues. The tortured relationship between Valeria and her daughter echoes the struggles already present in the works of Neera and Aleramo, as well as the conspicuous absence of the mother-child bond in Robert's novel. In writing her deepest thoughts and emotions in her diary, Valeria realizes that she is indeed guilty of attempting to perpetuate the traditional female role through her strained interaction with Mirella.

However, the historical place and time of *The Secret*, amidst the turmoil of change taking place in postwar Italy, make Valeria's situation different from the literary characters preceding her. Near the conclusion of the novel, Valeria discovers that she, as a woman of the postwar period, is not only living in a changing time, but she is also an integral part of the cultural transition taking place:

> I feel everything confusedly and can't talk about it to my mother or to Mirella, because neither of them would understand. They belong to two different worlds, one of which died [during the war] and the other of which was born from it. In me the two worlds clash, and I suffer. . . . [Mirella] doesn't realize that it's I, with my life torn between old reassuring traditions and new emergencies, who have set her free. It fell to me. I'm the bridge she profited from.
>
> (*Secret,* pp. 237-238)

Although *The Secret* concludes on a pessimistic note regarding the liberation of women as Valeria burns her secret diary, de Céspedes successfully injects the novel with hope that a true women's liberation is on the horizon for Italy. In fact, unlike the novels that precede it, *The Secret* features a female character poised to become a mother who passes on to her daughter not a meek and submissive role, but the strong conviction that women possess their own unique identities. Certainly Mirella is a remarkably lifelike representation of the numerous young women who came of age during the postwar period and continued on to become the key players in the Italian feminist movement of the 1960s.

Sources and literary context. Most of what is known about Alba de Céspedes's inspiration for the writing of *The Secret* comes from the comprehensive research and interview with the author conducted by Piera Carroli. Although de Céspedes once alluded to the fact that the idea for the narration of her most popular novel stemmed from a life experience, no specific autobiographical details are available. While her early experiences as a young wife and mother may have influenced her writing, at the time she composed *The Secret*, the educated, economically independent, and politically active de Céspedes was certainly leagues apart from her story's protagonist, Valeria. The author denies the claim of some critics that she identifies herself with one of the novel's most socially progressive characters, the screenwriter Clara, and declares instead that she finds herself in "all and none" of the novel's characters (Carroli, *Esperienza e narrazione,* p. 147; trans. V. Mirshak).

Although *The Secret* is written in diary form, traditionally the most acceptable style of women's literature in the historically male-dominated field of writing, Alba de Céspedes produced a literary work that exceeded the accomplishments of many other female and male writers of her period. With *The Secret*, de Céspedes set herself apart from other novelists who examined the feminine condition by delving into the conflicted psychological world of women and painstakingly detailing their daily lives as they were forced to confront the tumultuous cultural changes that characterized postwar Italy. According to Elisabetta Rasy, a leading figure of the 1970s feminist movement, de Céspedes effectively "rewrote" the psychological bourgeois novel in a feminine key (Rasy in Carroli, *Esperienza e narrazione,* p. 10). Recognizing the immense impact of *The Secret* and *Remorse* on women of the period, one scholar thinks it "highly probable that de Céspedes's novels were indeed instrumental in bringing about individual and social change" (Carroli, "Alba de Céspedes Revisited," p. 46).

Reception and impact. *The Secret*, like the de Céspedes novels before it, was initially dismissed by many critics as the product of a *scrittrice rosa*, or romance novelist, but shortly thereafter received high acclaim both in Italy and abroad. In fact, out of all of de Céspedes's publications, *The Secret* has enjoyed the most success worldwide. In a shining review for the *New York Times* in 1958 Frances Keene praised the Italian writer for the novel's verisimilitude: "Signora de Céspedes is one of the few distinguished women writers since Colette to grapple effectively with what it is to be a woman. Her brilliant handling of Valeria's moral Hegira places her in the forefront of contemporary novelists" (Keene in Carroli, "Alba de Céspedes Revisited," p. 38).

Despite much praise from abroad, *The Secret* was not well received by everyone in Italy. Many Catholics disapproved of the author's views regarding the absurdity of remaining faithful to a spouse whose affection was more like that of a sibling than a lover (Carroli, *Esperienza e narrazione,* p. 75). Also the novel "irritated some Italian males who still hold romantic and unreasonable notions about women's 'duties' and their 'place in the home'" (Murray in Carroli, "Alba de Céspedes Revisited," p. 52). But the 1953 article that discloses this last reaction also indicates that many Italians disagreed with it. Despite the critics, de Céspedes received hundreds of letters a day in fan mail and *The Secret* enjoyed vigorous sales in Italy. So while the novel encountered some negative feedback from Italians, it also struck a positive chord in many of its native readers.

—Valerie Mirshak

For More Information

Birnbaum, Lucia Chiavola. *Liberazione della donna: Feminism in Italy.* Middleton, Conn.: Wesleyan University Press, 1986.

Carroli, Piera. "Alba de Céspedes Revisited." *Writing Beyond Fascism: Cultural Resistance in the Life and Works of Alba de Céspedes.* Ed. Carole C. Gallucci and Ellen Nerenburg. Cranbury, N.J.: Associated University Presses, 2000.

———. *Esperienza e narrazione nella scrittura di Alba de Céspedes.* Ravenna, Italy: Longo Editore, 1993.

Cutrufelli, Maria Rosa, et al. *Il Novecento delle italiane: Una storia ancora da raccontare.* Rome, Italy: Editori riuniti, 2001.

De Céspedes, Alba. *The Secret.* Trans. Isabel Quigley. New York: Simon & Schuster, 1958.

De Grazia, Victoria. *How Fascism Ruled Women: Italy, 1922-1945.* Berkeley: University of California Press, 1992.

McCarthy, Patrick, ed. *Italy Since 1945.* New York: Oxford University Press, 2000.

Sassoon, Donald. *Contemporary Italy: Economy, Society and Politics Since 1945.* New York: Longman, 1997.

Smith, Denis Mack. *Mussolini: A Biography.* New York: Vintage Books, 1982.

The Silent Duchess

by

Dacia Maraini

THE LITERARY WORK

A historical novel set in eighteenth-century Sicily; published in Italian (as *La lunga vita di Marianna Ucrìa*) in 1990, in English in 1992.

SYNOPSIS

Raped by her uncle, who becomes her husband, Duchess Marianna Ucrìa loses not only her memory of the violence but also her voice; without speaking, she manages to recover it over the course of the novel.

Dacia Maraini (b. 1936) has helped spearhead a multifaceted quest for a new female literature that has characterized Italian culture since the early 1960s. The eldest daughter of Tuscan ethnologist Fosco Maraini and Sicilian painter Topazia Alliata, Dacia was born in Florence, Italy, but spent nine years of her childhood (1938-47) in Japan. Her anti-Fascist parents relocated there for her father's anthropological research and to escape Fascist oppression. When Japan sided with Germany and Italy in World War II, Maraini's parents refused to pledge allegiance to the Fascist government in Italy, as requested by the Japanese authorities, so from 1943 to 1946 the whole family was interned in a Japanese concentration camp. In interviews, in her poetry collection *Devour Me, Too* (*Mangiami pure*, 1978) and, most recently, in the memoir *The Ship to Kobe* (*La nave per Kobe*, 2001), Maraini depicts the trauma of war, imprisonment, and deprivation. She experienced a second, subtler loss of freedom when her family returned to her mother's native region of Sicily. At the age of 18, emerging from these experiences both "dumb" and "paralyzed," she moved to Rome, where she found part-time work as a journalist and studied literature (Maraini in Sumeli Weinberg, p. 68). In 1962 she married the painter Lucio Pozzi but divorced him four years later after losing an unborn son. Maraini continued to move in literary circles during this time, meeting such significant Italian authors as Alberto Moravia, who became her life partner for a decade (see Moravia's **The Conformist,** also

in *WLAIT 7: Italian Literature and Its Times*). Meanwhile, Maraini added to her body of work, which she has divided into three phases: 1) anti-conventional, disturbingly realistic novels (*La vacanza* [1962; The Holiday]); 2) overtly feminist works of the 1970s and 1980s (the novel *Donna in guerra* [1975; Women at War] and the theater piece *Dialogo di una prostituta con un suo cliente* [1978; Dialogue between a Prostitute and Her Patron]); and 3) works that situate women in history and in the literary canon (*The Silent Duchess* and the detective novel *Voci* [1995; Voices]). Through all three phases, Maraini attempts to recover women's identity by amplifying their muted voices. In *The Silent Duchess* she broadcasts the voice of a mutilated woman in eighteenth-century Sicily, making her story part of the movement for women's liberation two centuries later, in Maraini's own day.

Dacia Maraini

Events in History at the Time the Novel Takes Place

Eighteenth-century Sicily. A bridge between the European and African continents and a divider between the eastern and western Mediterranean regions, Sicily sits at a strategic position that has made it a coveted crossroads. It became subject to domination by a striking array of foreign powers and cultures. Always the most salient trait of Sicilian history, the island's changing status is wryly represented in *The Silent Duchess* by a display of foreign flags that the widow Marianna Ucrìa discovers in her mansion's basement, an array of alternatives kept on hand to welcome the ever-new invader.

Timeline of Sicilian History

3000 B.C.E.	The Sicans arrive from the Iberian Peninsula
700 B.C.E.	Greek colonization
210 B.C.E.	Sicily under Roman rule
493 C.E.	Invasion of the Goths
535	Domination of the Byzantines
827	Arrival of the Arabs; Arab rule begins in 903
1060	Beginning of the Norman Conquest
1130	Sicily becomes a Norman possession with the rest of southern Italy, known as The Kingdom of Sicily
1266	Charles of Anjou takes over rule of Sicily
1282	The Sicilian Vespers uprising against misrule by French leader Charles of Anjou; failed attempt to form an autonomous state
1302	Spanish (Aragonese) rule
1503	Sicily is ruled directly by the Spanish (Charles V)
1713	Sicily becomes a possession of Savoy
1720	Savoy trades Sicily for Sardinia; Sicily passes to Austria
1734	Sicily falls under Spanish rule again, under the Bourbons
1816	Sicily is reunited with southern Italy to form the Kingdom of the Two Sicilies under the Spanish Bourbons
1820-48	Sicilians participate in the revolts leading to the unification of Italy (Risorgimento)
1860	Sicilians play a crucial role in the success of Giuseppe Garibaldi's "Expedition of the Thousand" to liberate Sicily; Sicily joins the Kingdom of Italy (officially declared March 17, 1861)
1946	Sicily becomes an autonomous region of the Italian Republic; like four other Italian border regions, Sicily is granted special status that gives it political autonomy in certain matters

Despite all the changes, there was a stubborn stability to life on the island. Regardless of how many rulers came and went, Sicily's social structure remained obstinately fixed.

Sicilian upper-class society. The Sicilian aristocracy consisted of a small group of feudal landlords who owned large estates bequeathed to the first male descendent of the family. There was also a small wealthy middle class of merchants and artisans who lived in the main cities. But mostly the population consisted of poor peasants who toiled in the fields to feed themselves and sustain the opulent lifestyles of their landlords.

Sicily fell behind the times economically as well as socially. Northern Europe addressed the social and economic distress following the Thirty Years War (1618-48) with more efficient agricultural methods. In Piedmont (in northern Italy), enlightened rulers followed suit and tried to improve the taxation system too. But the landlords in Sicily resisted change. Many built sumptuous mansions in the country and held lavish celebrations or sallied forth in fashionable hunting parties. Rather than investing in old estates, the landlords bought new ones, becoming absentee owners who themselves lived in the city of Palermo to partake in the glamorous social life of the viceroy's court there. In the eighteenth century, more and more noblemen transferred the administration of their country estates to a mediator, or *gabellotto*, who paid the rent in advance to the distant landowner and often dealt brutally with the rural workers.

The Silent Duchess features a duke whose traits epitomize those of the Sicilian aristocracy— traits that are seen to be at the root of the island's decline: resignation, disillusionment, attachment to their class privileges, and denial of the social and economic changes in the rest of Europe that were subtly infiltrating their backward world. One of the most effective means of preserving the status quo was the Tribunal of the Inquisition. Organized to prevent deviation from the teachings of the Catholic Church, it allowed the conservative Sicilian aristocracy to collaborate with the Catholic Church and with the Spanish administration.

Aristocratic women in eighteenth-century Sicily. The silent duchess of the novel's title, Marianna Ucrìa, belongs to the class of aristocratic women of the eighteenth century. Generally speaking, European noblewomen of that time had limited access to education and new ideas. At best, in Roman Catholic areas such as Sicily, wealthy girls attended convent boarding schools, which charged costly tuitions. The aim was to educate good Christian mothers. Whether through home schooling or through the cloister, religious instruction, needlework, sewing, and, in the most fortunate cases, music, heavily outweighed the acquisition of reading, writing, and arithmetic skills. The development of intellectual independence and critical thinking would have been counter-productive to the societal status quo. It might have prevented women from accomplishing the only social mission they were allowed to fulfill—strengthening families' financial and social status through marriage and childbearing. To avoid fragmenting the large family estate into small parcels distributed among an aristocrat's children, only the first male heir inherited the estate, a practice known as "primogeniture." Female heirs were at a particular disadvantage. When the family was able to provide them with a generous dowry, they were often forced to marry noblemen who represented a good match in terms of wealth and possessions. Weddings within the same family—as between the novel's Marianna and her uncle—were no exception. The eighteenth-century aristocracy regarded marriage as a contract to consolidate the families' wealth and prestige. After the marriage, aristocratic women served to enhance the social role of the family: first they procreated male heirs; second they played an important part in the sumptuous celebrations that punctuated the aristocracy's social life at that time. It was for this reason that many were educated in music. Only one alternative existed for aristocratic women who wanted to escape marriage, or whose families could not afford a dowry—life in a convent. Feeling alienated from their bodies and emotions, women "often reacted to their reduced lives by becoming sick or dependent, or by taking

THE INQUISITION

In 1478, in response to a request from King Ferdinand and Queen Isabella, Pope Sixtus IV instituted the Inquisition, which aimed to root out Catholic converts who secretly practiced Judaism, or, later, Islam. Operating in Sicily from 1487 to the late 1700s, the Tribunal of the Spanish Inquisition erased its minority populations. All Jews were expelled by the mid-1700s. The King of Spain himself appointed the Inquisitors who, in turn, selected their collaborators from among the local noblemen. These "lay familiars" received legal and financial privileges for preserving religious and political orthodoxy. Apparently many of them exploited their role for selfish purposes. The trial summaries suggest that in Sicily "the Holy Office was frequently manipulated by local residents in order to revenge themselves on private enemies, and that perjured testimony to the Inquisition was far more common here than in Spain" (Monter, p. 182). Sicilians did not suffer such conduct without protest—the uprisings of 1511 and 1526 were prompted in large part by hatred for the court's familiars, but they continued to wield power.

Records suggest that in Sicily the Inquisition had to deal especially with public morality. The tribunal found that blasphemy, witchcraft, heterosexual and homosexual sodomy were practiced here with a "creativity" ascribed to the multicultural history of the island. The ultimate goal of the Holy Office was to quash freethinking by eliminating any deviation in religious behavior, scientific thought, or sexual practices. While the last victim burned at the stake in Sicily, Antonio Canzoneri, died in 1732, the tribunal continued to exercise tight control until 1782. At this point, a so-called man of the Enlightenment, the marquis Domenico Caracciolo, became viceroy of Sicily and finally saw to it that the Inquisition was suppressed and abolished by royal order. Most resistance before then was no doubt very secret and private, of the kind exhibited by Marianna Ucrìa in the novel.

drugs. To facilitate the smooth working of the patriarchal system, women were [furthermore] socialized to imprison other women" (Brooke in Marotti and Brooke, p. 194). That is, older women conditioned their daughters and nieces to accept their limits and obediently step into the prescribed roles. In the novel, all these elements surface in the problematic relationships between the Duchess Marianna Ucrìa and her mother, her daughters, and her servants.

According to the historian Denis Mack Smith, in spite of the general backwardness of Sicilian society, the eighteenth century witnessed a slight opening of Sicilian culture to the revolutionary ideas of the Enlightenment, the intellectual movement that celebrated reason and the power of the individual to improve the human condition. There were heralds of the new philosophy in nearby Naples and others brought their enthusiasm to Sicily from overseas—for example, the German poet and philosopher Johann Wolfgang von Goethe. The presence of such cultivated foreigners, along with private tutors and family librarians from Tuscany, England, and France, and the efforts of a few Sicilian and Neapolitan reformers began to shake the heretofore impenetrable religious and political establishment. Despite the severe penalties that still threatened in 1769, the traveler Patrick Brydone found in family libraries several English and French books and translations of works by Arthur Young, Alexander Pope, David Hume, John Locke, Voltaire, Denis Diderot, and Montesquieu. In the novel, the silent duchess is induced by her reading of Hume's *Treatise on Human Nature* to reconsider her whole life. Such ideas were perhaps more earthshaking in Sicily than almost anywhere else. Especially here the eighteenth century can be seen as "a moment of rupture, due to the emerging of new philosophical attitudes that bring about historical change" (Marotti in Blumenfeld, p. 167).

The Novel in Focus

Plot summary. The novel begins with a journey that takes the seven-year-old, deaf-mute Marianna Ucrìa and her beloved father, Duke Signoretto Ucrìa, from the country town of Bagheria to Palermo, Sicily's capital city. Duke Signoretto is on his way to perform his duties as a lay familiar; he will be preparing the young victim of an Inquisition trial, a 13-year-old bandit, for death by hanging on the main square of Palermo. The duke will force his daughter to witness the hanging, a spectacle that amounts to a cathartic

ritual and a warning to the public. After the cruel sight of the bandit's agony on the gallows, the duke urges Marianna to speak. The duke knows his daughter's silence to be the result of a violent trauma she herself has suffered and he hopes to restore her voice through a similarly traumatic experience. However, his hopes are dashed. Little Marianna not only has no voice; she has no memory of the violence done to her.

Seven years after the hanging of the young brigand, Marianna attends a traditional Sicilian puppet show that culminates with the execution of the protagonist. This time she faints. When she regains her senses, in her parents' bedroom, Marianna's mother informs her that she has to marry her uncle, Pietro Ucrìa di Campo Spagnolo. Marianna's written protests go unheeded. Her mother, herself a victim of the patriarchal society, had decided long ago to escape into the artificial paradise of opium and laudanum, and cannot change Marianna's fate. On the contrary, she urges her daughter to accept marriage as a contract that strengthens the family's wealth. Marianna thus becomes the 13-year-old wife of the elderly, melancholic, eccentric uncle who abused her when she was a child. His abuse, though she has no memory of it, is in fact the violence that prompted her to lose her voice.

The third-person narrative proceeds chronologically but is constantly interrupted by flashbacks, flash-forwards, interior monologues, and dreams. The action resumes four years later, when Marianna, pregnant with her third child, is supervising the building of the new family mansion in the country. "And now," wonders the narrator, "who is going to break the news to the Duke that it is another girl? . . . If it was a peasant woman the child would be given a little spoonful of poisoned water" (Maraini, *The Silent Duchess*, p. 36). At age 19, after bringing into life three girls, Marianna finally fulfills the expectations of her husband, family, and society by giving birth to her first son and her husband's male heir. Among the gifts that follow, she values especially one from her father: a precious writing outfit made of silver, gold, glass, and leather, complete with pen, notebook, and a small portable table that can hang from two gold chains attached to her belt.

This sophisticated present initiates continuous improvement in Marianna's writing and reading skills, which distinguish her from the other aristocratic women of her time. Her husband, a traditional nobleman, respects Marianna's intellectual needs without understanding them; "[f]or him, his wife is the child of a new century, incomprehensible" (*The Silent Duchess*, p. 49). In fact, however, the silent duchess is between centuries, a reflection of the old and the new. For instance, she does not object to receiving a human as a gift when her father brings her as a present a 12-year-old girl, the daughter of a man sentenced to death by the Inquisition, hoping Marianna will take better care of her than a convent for orphans would. Marianna goes on to make of this girl, Fila, a faithful servant and later her travel companion. In time Marianna gives birth to a fifth child, a son named Signoretto, whom she openly prefers to her other children. A warm, physical bond unites them, until Signoretto dies at the age of four from smallpox. Another few years pass before Marianna realizes she has given up her body to her children: "She has put into motherhood both her flesh and her feelings, adapting them, restricting them, renouncing them. . . . But how can one live without a body, as she has done for the past thirty years, without ending up mummified?" (*The Silent Duchess*, p. 80). After these nocturnal reflections, Marianna refuses for the first time to be intimate with her husband. Shortly thereafter, she refuses for the first time to appear in Palermo for an auto-da-fé, or the burning at the stake of heretics condemned by the Tribunal of the Holy Inquisition. A nun and a friar have been accused of heresy and have not repented of their alleged sins.

Marianna's maturation continues. A man she identifies simply as Grass, a British cosmopolitan friend of her son Mariano, has left her a handwritten copy of David Hume's *Treatise on Human Nature*. Grass's dedication reads: "To her who does not speak—may she accept with her generous mind a few thoughts that are close to me" (*The Silent Duchess*, p. 95). Marianna pours over Hume's musings on human nature, knowledge, truth, and religion. His experimental approach to all aspects of human existence inspires in him skepticism toward philosophic and religious dogmatism and profound tolerance of differences. Both skepticism and tolerance challenge Marianna's conservative education: "We speak not strictly and philosophically when we talk of the combat of passion and of reason. Reason is, and ought only to be the slave of the passions, and can never pretend to any other office than to serve and obey them"; Hume's conclusion is "the exact opposite to what she has been taught" (*The Silent Duchess*, p. 95).

After becoming acquainted with Hume's philosophy, Marianna expands her readings. In addition to the classics she finds in the family library, she orders an increasing number of modern for-

eign texts, including Milton's *Paradise Lost* as well as history and philosophy books. Marianna learns French and English, and fills her solitude with the rich imaginary life that those books nurture. One night she discovers that Fila has a younger brother, Saro, whom she has been hiding in fear of the duchess's reaction. What follows shows that her fears were groundless. The duchess and duke accept Saro as a servant. Not only is he very attractive; he is also a gifted young man with intellectual and practical abilities. Quickly he learns the good manners of aristocratic education, and acquires writing and reading skills in order to communicate with the duchess. One day, after the duke's death, Saro declares his love for her with a handwritten note: "I LOVE YOU" (*The Silent Duchess*, p. 153). The widowed duchess tries to resist the reciprocal attraction.

DAVID HUME (1711-76), PHILOSOPHER OF EXPERIENCE

~

A Scottish philosopher and historian, David Hume (1711-76) gained familiarity with Italy by studying the classics, Latin poetry, and vernacular Italian. His philosophical writings (e.g., *A Treatise of Human Nature* [1739-40] and *An Enquiry Concerning Human Understanding* [1748]) argue that the existence of the external world cannot be proven. Hume insists on the primacy of experience, arguing that one cannot go beyond it to determine original causes. All we have are our perceptions, which consist of impressions and ideas that spring from these impressions. Everything is grounded in these perceptions, including habits and customs, which are the products of repeated experiences. From experiences come our beliefs (which determine our moral decisions) and the idea of personal identity (the result of a succession of impressions, emotions, memories, and anticipations). Previous thinkers taught that the passions are irrational, animalistic elements threatening to overwhelm the rational self. In contrast, Hume regarded the passions as vital, legitimate parts of human nature, which he, of course, linked to human perceptions. His view, and its defiance of past views, helps explain his famous statement, cited in the novel, "Reason is and ought to be the slave of passions" (Hume in *The Silent Duchess*, p. 95).

Through her self-education, Marianna acquires a newly liberal outlook with regard to social and private issues. She becomes involved in the administration of her rural estates, seeks to establish some kind of social justice and human respect toward the underprivileged, and shows fresh understanding for the emotional needs of her daughters. To avoid being tempted by her attraction to him, she even provides Saro with a spouse of his age and social class, visiting her brother, an abbot in Palermo, to find the bride. The meeting between the two represents the second turning point in Marianna's maturation. Marianna's muteness has heightened her other senses, in particular her ability to read other people's thoughts, an aptitude that allows her to validate her obscure, dreamlike recollections of a remote past when she did have a voice. At the end of the meeting with her brother, Marianna writes him a message asking if she had ever talked in her childhood. Despite his peremptory denial, Marianna penetrates his memories:

> One evening they heard screams to make the flesh creep and Marianna with her legs all bloodstained being dragged away between their father and Raffaele Cuffa. Strange the absence of the women . . . yes . . . Uncle Pietro . . . had assaulted her and left her half-dead. . . . And then, afterwards, yes, afterwards, when Marianna was healed it was realized that she could no longer speak as if *zap*, he had cut out her tongue.
> (*The Silent Duchess*, pp. 186-87)

From this, Marianna comes to know what happened to her, and to realize that her own father knew, accepted, and even helped perpetuate the violence against her when he forced her as a young girl to marry her uncle.

Fila, meanwhile, has become fiercely jealous of Saro, his wife Peppinedda, and their newborn son. One night, possessed by madness, she stabs the three of them while asleep. The baby dies, Peppinedda goes home to her family to heal, and Fila is rushed to a mental hospital. While Marianna tends Saro's deep wounds, she finally accepts her desire and her body:

> How she came to find herself undressed beside Saro's naked body Marianna was unable to say. She knows it was very simple and that she felt no shame. She knows they were in each other's arms like two friendly bodies in harmony and that welcoming him inside her was like finding once more a part of her own body she had believed lost for ever.
> (*The Silent Duchess*, p. 210)

While this relationship hinges on a profound, harmonious synthesis of the senses, a different relationship of cultural affinities of the minds unfolds at this point between the 40-year-old duchess and the judge Giacomo Camalèo. In-strumental in saving Fila from execution for the attempted murder of Saro and his young family, Camalèo appreciates Marianna's vast learning. In the last of their intense epistolary exchanges on philosophy and society, Don Camalèo declares: "It is your disability that makes you unique" and proposes marriage (*The Silent Duchess*, pp. 230-31). However, Marianna has attained a sense of independence and a self-confidence that prevents her from limiting herself either to Saro and their fulfilling communion of the senses, or to judge Camaleo and their harmonious communion of the intellects.

Marianna and Fila, whom the duchess has rescued from the mental hospital, embark on a ship that will take them to Naples. They encounter the Roman excavations of Stabia and Herculaneum, the roughness of the Vesuvius volcano, the danger posed by bandits, and the amiable friendship of a theater company. With the actors, they continue their adventurous journey to Rome. There, Fila will eventually marry the proprietor of the inn where they stay. Marianna, on the other hand, chooses to continue her quest. The novel concludes with an image of her contemplating the Tiber River, with thoughts of "walk[ing] straight into the waters" (*The Silent Duchess*, p. 234). In the end, though she knows there are no final answers to the fundamental questions of life, "the will to resume her journey is stronger. Marianna fixes her gaze on the gurgling yellow water. She questions her silences. But the only answer she receives is another question. And it is mute" (*The Silent Duchess*, p. 235).

Journey and silence. The thread that weaves together the chapters of the novel, spanning 40 years of the first half of the eighteenth century, is the protagonist's journey toward self-discovery and expression that she undertakes in spite of, but also thanks to, her silence. The novel begins with a journey—from Bagheria to Palermo—and ends with an open-ended journey—from Palermo into an uncertain future of life experiences. While the first journey had been set up by Marianna's father, Duke Signoretto, to make her recover her voice through a violent experience, the last journey results from her decision to continue the process of learning and maturation that has defined her whole life. She defies convention in more than one way: while her first journey is dictated by her father and the conservative, patriarchal society for which he stands, her last journey is one of her own making in the company of her servant Fila. Subverting the societal rules of her day, she interacts with the underprivileged on a more natural and equal basis than before, becoming the protagonist of a novel of formation, or bildungsroman. Marianna's personal growth parallels a historical transition from the old to the new in Sicily, occurring in tandem with its shift away from feudal aristocratic rule and religious dogmatism to make room for a fledgling middle class and a measure of the skepticism and tolerance endemic to the Enlightenment. Examples of the new order include the suppression of the Inquisition in Sicily in 1782 and a 1789 edict that was designed to increase the number of small farms on the island by bringing new areas under cultivation (in the end, the edict would have no effect at all).

The Silent Duchess is a novel of formation with respect to the time it was written as well as the time it takes place. A militant feminist writer, Maraini chooses the past with the present in mind. Her novel strives to promote the maturation of her society by looking at history through the lens of a female victim of an earlier, patriarchal Sicily; at the same time, it strives to advance the growing cause of Italian feminism in Maraini's day. She sees in the eighteenth century the beginning of a "process of feminization of society" that is emerging more visibly in her own time (Marotti in Blumenfeld, p. 176).

Sources and literary context. Maraini, along with other Italian women writers (Elsa Morante, Anna Banti, and Mariarosa Cutrufelli, to name a few), attempts through literature "to rewrite woman's history from a personal and critical point of view" (Lazzaro-Weis in Marotti and Brooke, p. 44). In *The Silent Duchess*, the story's deep roots in the historical documentation of eighteenth-century Sicilian culture are crucial to the success of the undertaking. Maraini remarks in several interviews that she spent five years studying and researching the Sicilian past in local archives. While the historical research no doubt inspired realistic details, a personal experience inspired the development of her main character. At the end of her autobiography, *Bagheria* (1993), Maraini mentions her first encounter with her ancestor Duchess Marianna Ucrìa. Maraini, on a visit to the family's Villa Valguarnera in Bagheria, eyed a portrait of this mysterious noblewoman that mesmerized her: "She holds a sheet of paper in her hand, for writing was the only way she could express herself: she was called 'the dumb one'" (Maraini, *Bagheria*, p. 116). Entranced by the enigmatic smile in the portrait, Maraini felt compelled to unveil her ancestor's story and, at the same time, investigate her own past.

According to Maraini's autobiography, the evidence suggests that her ancestor had legendary writing skills, which were developed because of her disability. It is furthermore implied that she used these skills to defeat silence and violence. In doing so, she contributed to the formation of a literary female genealogy that harks back to ancient mythology. Maraini revisits several ancient myths (e.g., the myth of Philomela) while rewriting our perception of history through her novel.

THE INSPIRATIONAL PORTRAIT

"I am turned to stone, gazing at that portrait as if I recognized it from the deepest part of myself, as if I have been waiting for years to find myself face to face with this woman who has been dead for two centuries, and who holds between her fingers a small sheet of paper on which is written some part, lost and unknown, of my Sicilian past."

(Maraini, *Bagheria*, p. 119)

Events in History at the Time the Novel Was Written

Italian feminism and neo-feminism. *The Silent Duchess*, a historical novel, fictional autobiography, and bildungsroman, reflects the evolution of the twentieth-century Italian women's movement from feminism to neo-feminism. In Italy, feminism became a powerful political force in the late 1960s. Women had contributed substantially to the Italian labor market before and during the industrial development from the late nineteenth to the early twentieth century. Yet they experienced "a vast gulf between their contribution to the nation through work and the minimal rights accorded them by the state" (Wood and Farrell in Baranski, p. 143). Not until 1945, for example, were full voting rights extended to Italian women. One crucial reason for this delay was the deep polarization between a strong socialist movement and an increasingly powerful Fascist Party earlier in the century. Fascism, supported by traditional Catholicism, promulgated the patriarchal image of woman, relegating her to the roles of wife and mother whose primary mission was to bear and nurture children for the fatherland. The World War II experience helped displace this image, however. With their active participation in the Resistance movement against

Nazism and Fascism, Italian women paved the way for their more official recognition in postwar Italy.

After the birth of the Italian Republic by popular vote in 1946, Italian society was torn between the Christian Democratic Party (which exercised widespread influence through the Catholic Church) and strong Communist and Socialist parties. For the traditional leftist organizations, the fight for women's rights became secondary to class struggle, and the familiar patriarchal mentality still held sway. The leftists did, however, support women's rights to equal wages, divorce, and more.

PHILOMELA, A MYTHICAL FEMALE VOICE AGAINST SILENCE

According to Ovid's *Metamorphoses* (2-8 c.e.), King Tereus of Thrace (son to Ares, god of war) married Procne and fell in love with her sister Philomela. He savagely raped the sister, then cut off her tongue and imprisoned her to prevent her from revealing his crime; slyly she exposed him anyway, through her art:

And what shall Philomela do? A guard prevents her flight . . . speechless lips can give no token of her wrongs. But grief has sharp wits. . . . *She hangs a Thracian web on her loom, and skillfully weaving purple signs on a white background, she thus tells the story of her wrongs.*
(Ovid, Book VI, lines 572-78, emphasis added)

The two sisters later avenge themselves by killing Tereus's son and serving the corpse as a meal to Tereus. Before he can exact his own revenge, all three are transformed into birds, Philomela into the nightingale, the bird with the most beautiful voice (the Greek etymology of her name means "love for singing").

At the end of the 1960s, the women's movement entered a more independent phase in the drive for their liberation. Italy's political parties were experiencing a crisis at the time, due to a civil rights movement in the country and to the global context of the Vietnam War and the Cold War. These events promoted social awareness, to the advantage of the Italian students', workers', and women's movements. The women formed political and cultural associations that held "consciousness-raising sessions" (*sedute di autocoscienza*), during which women discussed their daily lives and attitudes toward women's liberation in Italy. The sessions pro-

moted individual and group-oriented growth. The continental and American feminist movements popularized a relevant motto—"The personal is political"—which stressed the importance of women's claiming more individual space for themselves in the family and of their subverting gender roles in private life to attain social justice and political recognition in public life. In this light, Marianna Ucrìa's silent defiance in the novel is a political as well as a personal statement, as shown in the progression of her awakening. A short while after she refuses to have sexual relations with her husband, she refuses to attend an auto-da-fé held by the Inquisition in Palermo.

In its first stage (1960s and 1970s), Italian feminism focused on equality in the family and society and achieved impressive gains—legalization of divorce in 1970 (confirmed by a referendum in 1974) and of abortion in 1978, along with legislation on equal treatment at work and home. The second stage of Italian feminism, neofeminism (1980s to the present), has focused on the importance of sexual difference in order to determine women's separate contributions to all areas of culture. This new focus has given rise to groups such as the Association of Italian Women Historians, founded in 1989, just a year before *The Silent Duchess* appeared. A central concern of feminist historiography has been the revision of research methods to encompass oral memory and traditions.

The new Italian woman has been depicted by writers as seeking to escape becoming totally enmeshed in pregnancy, birth, and child-rearing. "Her desire is to explore the world, read women's history, probe her own psychic heights and depths, pursue knowledge and seek self-mastery," goals with which the eighteenth-century duchess Marianna Ucrìa could readily identify (Amoia, pp. 85-86).

Reception. *The Silent Duchess* has enjoyed high acclaim since its first Italian edition in 1990. That same year the novel received one of Italy's most prestigious literary awards, the Campiello Prize. Translated into 15 different languages, Maraini's novel won praise in the United Kingdom (1992), and then in the United States (1998) as "a story of grace and endurance, not mere survival" (Harrison, p. BR8). Beyond its literary success, Maraini's novel has been adapted into a celebrated film (*Marianna Ucrìa,* 1997, directed by Roberto Faenza, starring the deaf-mute French actress Emanuelle Laborit). The focus on a female destiny that is at the same time historical and a-historical, particular and universal, private and political appears to have widespread appeal. Meanwhile, the language—both realistic and lyrical, to give voice to the heightened visual, olfactory, and tactile senses of the mute duchess—has prevented defensive reactions of the kind caused by the more aggressive tone in Maraini's more overtly feminist novels. In sum, critics in and out of Italy have saluted *The Silent Duchess* as one of the most intriguing and inspiring female historical, mythical, formation novels in contemporary Italian literature.

—Margherita Heyer-Caput

For More Information

Amoia, Alba. *No Mothers We!: Italian Women Writers and Their Revolt Against Maternity.* Lanham, Md.: University Press of America, 2000.

Baranski, Zygmunt G., and Rebecca J. West, eds. *The Cambridge Companion to Modern Italian Culture.* Cambridge: Cambridge University Press, 2001.

Blumenfeld, Rodica Diaconescu, and Ada Testaferri, eds. *The Pleasure of Writing: Critical Essays on Dacia Maraini.* West Lafayette, Ind.: Purdue University Press, 2000.

Duby, Georges, and Michelle Perrot, eds. *A History of Women in the West.* Vol. 3. Cambridge, Mass.: Belknap Press, 1993.

Harrison, Kathryn. "The Silence." Review of *The Silent Duchess,* by Dacia Maraini. *The New York Times Book Review,* December 13, 1998, BR8.

Mack Smith, Denis. *A History of Sicily.* New York: Viking, 1968.

Maraini, Dacia. *Bagheria.* Trans. Dick Kitto and Elspeth Spottiswood. London: Peter Owen, 1994.

———. *The Silent Duchess.* Trans. Dick Kitto and Elspeth Spottiswood. New York: The Feminist Press at the City University of New York, 1998.

Marotti, Maria Ornella, and Gabriella Brooke, eds. *Gendering Italian Fiction: Feminist Revisions of Italian History.* Madison, N.J.: Farleigh Dickinson University Press, 1999.

Monter, William. *Frontiers of Heresy: The Spanish Inquisition from the Basque Lands to Sicily.* Cambridge, Mass.: Cambridge University Press, 1990.

Ovid. *Metamorphoses.* Trans. Charles Martin. New York: W. W. Norton, 2004.

Sumeli Weinberg, Grazia. "An Interview with Dacia Maraini." *Tydskrif vir letterkunde* 27, no. 3 (1989): 64-72.

Six Characters in Search of an Author

by
Luigi Pirandello

orn in Sicily in 1867, Luigi Pirandello was the son of a prosperous sulfur merchant. The successful merchant initially sent his son to study commerce at the local technical institute, but Pirandello later transferred to an academic secondary school, where he distinguished himself in oratory and literature. As a young man, he studied at the universities of Palermo, Rome, and Bonn, receiving a degree in Romance philology in 1891. He went on to launch a literary career, publishing the collection of poems *Painful Joy* (*Mal giocondo*) in 1889 and his first novel, *The Outcast* (*L'esclusa*), in 1893. In 1894 Pirandello married Maria Antonietta Portulano, daughter of his father's business partner; the couple settled in Rome and had three children. Pirandello continued to write, publishing his first play, *If Not So, or Other People's Reason* (*Se non cosi, o La ragione degli altri*), in 1896. He began to achieve critical success in 1904 with the publication of his second novel, *The Late Mattia Pascal* (*Il fu Mattia Pascal*). That same year, however, Pirandello suffered financial disaster when a flood destroyed his family's sulfur mines; his wife suffered a nervous breakdown, a result at least in part of the financial disaster, from which she never fully recovered. She later had to be committed to an asylum. The pressure of Pirandello's personal and business woes resulted in a period of intense creativity between 1915 and 1922, during which he produced some of the works for which he is now most famous, such as the dramas *Henry IV* (*Enrico IV*) and *Six Characters in Search of an Author* (*Sei personaggi in cerca d'au-*

THE LITERARY WORK

A comic play set in a theater during an unspecified time; first performed and published in Italian (as *Sei personaggi in cerca d'autore*) in 1921; translated into English in 1922.

SYNOPSIS

Six fictional characters seeking to have their story put on the stage interrupt a director and a group of actors rehearsing a play.

---

tore). The latter premiered in 1921, startled its audiences with its unique handling of the themes of theatrical illusion and reality, and won Pirandello both notoriety and acclaim. To this day, *Six Characters in Search of an Author* is considered a watershed in modern drama. The following year, the success of Pirandello's *Henry IV* consolidated his reputation as one of Italy's foremost playwrights; he would go on to win global acclaim when he received the Nobel Prize in Literature in 1934.

Events in History at the Time of the Play

Italy and the First World War. After World War I broke out in 1914, Italy initially declared itself neutral. As the conflict continued, however, many influential Italians began to regret their country's neutrality and to wish that Italy had the

Luigi Pirandello

chance to acquire prestige and territory in the war. In 1915 the prime minister, Antonio Salandra, acting without the knowledge of the Italian parliament (which still favored neutrality), signed the secret Treaty of London, pledging to enter the war on the side of England and France, against Italy's former allies Austria and Germany. Presented with this fait accompli, parliament had no choice but to go along with this plan.

Entering the war in May 1915, Italy was unprepared for the conflict in several respects. Like the other participating nations, Italy underestimated the duration of the war, believing that it would end quickly. During the next three and a half years some 5 million Italians—many of them peasants from the poor South—were conscripted into the army; more than 600,000 were killed in the fighting at the Alpine foothills of Friuli and Trentino (Duggan, p. 191). Newly unified only in 1861, Italy had nationalists who believed the country incomplete until certain other areas were attached to it—Trentino, for example, then under Austrian control, had a population that was 97 percent Italian (Hamilton, p. 6). In the first month of the war, an invasion of Austria was launched, with most of the combat occurring along the River Isonzo and the Carso sector, which seriously inhibited the strategic plans of Italy's commanding officer Luigi Cadorna. Ultimately, some 200,000 Italian lives were lost in attacks designed to break through Austrian lines

(Killinger, p. 137). To make matters worse, Austrian forces broke through Italian lines to seize the plains around Venice. Although Italian troops retaliated by capturing Gorizia, their advance was halted, with neither side gaining an advantage.

In October 1917 Italian troops faced their most humiliating defeat yet at Caporetto, where a combined German and Austrian force drove them into a panicked retreat. The following year, however, Italian troops drove the Austrians back across the River Piave, capturing the village of Vittorio Veneto and much of the Trentino. A month later, Italy, along with its allies, accepted an armistice with Germany and the crumbling Austrian Empire. Optimistic, Italy hoped that its recent victory at Vittorio Veneto would be rewarded with a handsome territorial gain in the postwar negotiations; its disappointment in this matter contributed to the rise of Fascism in a now politically unstable and economically devastated country.

The rise of Fascism in Italy. The years following the First World War were difficult for Italy. The conflict had left more than half a million Italians dead and perhaps another half million injured, captured, or missing (Killinger, p. 139). The nation struggled with a devastated economy and an unstable government. Several republican administrations had collapsed during the war years, leaving political chaos in their wake and causing many to question the viability of the liberal state. Also, as noted, Italy was severely disappointed at the Paris Peace Conference in April 1919, when it did not receive the hoped-for territorial rewards. In the end, Italy was granted Trent, the South Tyrol, and Istria but denied Dalmatia and the port city of Fiume. Led by the prime minister Vittorio Emmanuele Orlando, the Italian delegation walked out of the conference in disgust. Nationalist newspapers and politicians declared that the war was "a mutilated victory" for Italy, in that it gained so much less than anticipated. Hostility towards the government increased after Francesco Saverio Nitti replaced Orlando as prime minister in June 1919 and adopted a conciliatory approach toward the Allies, for which he was branded "Cagoia" (vile coward) by the poet and political agitator Gabriele D'Annunzio (see **The Child of Pleasure**, also in WLAIT 7: Italian Literature and Its Times).

In September 1919 D'Annunzio staged a grandiose ploy of his own, marching into Fiume with several thousand followers, mainly students, veterans, and fervent nationalists. During his occupation of the city, D'Annunzio proclaimed himself its governor in absence of a sovereign or other ruling body. He also proposed a march on Rome, and suggested the use of several symbols—including black shirts, later adopted by the Fascists—to denote their new movement. The former prime minister, Giovanni Giolitti, returned to power in June 1920 and managed to oust D'Annunzio from Fiume six months later by calling in the navy. Nonetheless, many were to consider D'Annunzio's campaign a "dress rehearsal" for the Fascist regime—spearheaded by Benito Mussolini—that would seize control of the Italian government in the 1920s.

Shortly before, in March 1919, Benito Mussolini, once a Socialist Party member who advocated class revolution, formed the new Fascio di Cambattimento (Fighting Groups), including Socialists, Futurists, syndacalists, and *arditi* (special forces). The original Fascist platform was somewhat left-wing in its politics and economics, having been designed to appeal to middle-class loyalties as well as attract Italian workers to a nationalist-socialist agenda. But in the 1920s the platform became increasingly conservative, in response to the perceived threat of a Bolshevik-style revolution. The Fascists organized themselves into squads and began conducting violent attacks against the Socialists and their institutions, including Socialist Party offices, labor organizations, newspapers, and peasant leagues. Although these attacks cost a large share of the victims their lives, the police—many of whom sympathized with the Fascists—repeatedly ignored the violence. More right-wing extremists joined Mussolini's group, which, by late 1921, was a quarter million strong.

Matters came to a head in the following year. Having gained the support of the military, and received 19 percent of the vote in the 1921 national elections, Mussolini organized a march on Rome, during which Fascist operatives were supposed to seize control of rail lines and strategic public buildings, converge upon the capital, and drive the current government from power. The maneuver was successfully carried out on October 28, 1922, without firing a single shot. Acceding to demands of the "black shirts," the king invited Mussolini to form a government. For the next two decades Mussolini ruled Italy as prime minister and authoritarian dictator.

Given Pirandello's rejection of conservative forms in fiction and drama, his open support for the Fascist Party, which he joined in 1924, might seem puzzling at first. However, one should remember that as both a movement and an ideology Italian Fascism was far from straightforwardly conservative. In fact, Fascism presented and continued to propose itself as a cultural revolution that subscribed to the same anti-naturalist teachings that nourished Pirandello's writing. It should therefore not be surprising that Mussolini referred to Pirandello more than any other writer in interviews with the journalist Emil Ludwig in 1932, or that Mussolini had the government subsidize a theater—the Teatro d'Arte—run by the playwright. Conversely, literary scholar Renate Matthaei argues that Pirandello was perhaps less in sympathy with the Fascists' political intentions than he was both desirous of radical social change and a sense of group identification. Whatever his motives, Pirandello expressed, in a series of interviews, his unreserved loyalty for Mussolini and the new government, even advocating such anti-democratic policies as the abolition of freedom of the press and the dissolution of parliament.

Italian drama in the 1920s. During the early decades of the twentieth century, the theater in Italy was undergoing a radical transformation. In the late 1800s naturalistic dramas (like those of Henrik Ibsen and Gerhart Hauptman), sentimental melodramas (like the plays of the younger Alexandre Dumas), and elaborate spectacles had dominated the stage, and they continued to be performed in the early 1900s. However, another generation of Italian dramatists was emerging to give theater a bold new voice—many were influenced by the *commedia dell'arte*, a tradition of masked improvisational comedy that originated in Tuscany during the sixteenth century, then spread throughout Europe, enjoying popular appeal into the early eighteenth century. *Commedia dell'arte* featured ensemble acting, stock characters like Harlequin (a trickster) and Pantalone (a foolish old man), and stock situations, such as romantic triangles featuring young lovers, wily servants, and tyrannical fathers. The repertoire ranged from comedy and farce to parody and political satire, with the use of masks and the improvisation of stock situations remaining constant.

Up to the 1920s Italian playwrights such as Luigi Chiarelli, Luigi Antonelli, Rosso di San Secondo, and Enrico Cavacchioli regularly composed plays that parodied the conventions of the old-style sentimental theater. Chiarelli describes how the conservative and the experimental coexisted in the Italian theater of 1914:

> At that time it was impossible to go to the theater without encountering languishing, talkative descendants of [such characters as] Marguerite Gautier, or Rose Bernd, or lazy camp followers of Oswald or Cyrano. The public shed sentimental tears and left the theater depressed.

But the next evening it met again in large numbers to applaud a spicy little sketch such as *Le pillote d'Ercole*, in order to restore its moral and social balance.

(Chiarelli in Matthaei, pp. 21-22)

Perhaps the most startling theatrical innovation was the *grottesco* (grotesque) movement. Even more than the parodies, this movement set itself in opposition to the naturalistic and sentimental dramas, which tended to focus on such aspects

---

VERISMO: THE ITALIAN NATURALISM

Between the 1870s and 1890s, *verismo,* the Italian counterpart to French naturalism, dominated much of Italian literature. *Verismo* called for an impersonal style, language appropriate to the chosen subject, a detailed study of modern Italy from its lowest to highest classes, and a scientific reproduction of the social, economic, and geographical aspects of the chosen environment. Unlike French naturalism, however, *verismo* chose to emphasize stylistic over scientific aspects in literary works; *verismo* also concerned itself with provincial rather than urban life; and its political ideology was conservative rather than democratic. Although *verismo* was most prevalent in the Italian novel, it influenced other genres as well, including the drama. By the start of the twentieth century, theater audiences in Italy had become accustomed to naturalistic, "slice of life" dramas, whether "home-grown" or imported from France. Even during the 1920s the conservative Italian theater balked at more experimental plays, including those of Pirandello, himself a former practitioner of *verismo.* In *Six Characters in Search of an Author,* during a rehearsal of the play within the play (*The Rules of the Game*), Pirandello has the director complain, "What can I do if France can't produce any good theatre and we are reduced to putting on Pirandello plays which you have to be lucky to understand and which are written in a way never to please either critics or actors or public" (*Six Characters in Search of an Author,* p. 8).

---

of bourgeois life as money, love, and family. The *grottesco* playwrights, who became more vocal during the years of the First World War (1914-18), wished to free Italian theater from the constrictions of naturalism and open it up to "dreamscapes, parables, mystery, burlesque farce, visions, and fantasy" (Bassanese, p. 45). They also added satiric or absurd twists to stock situations and characters found in popular sentimental dramas, such as adulterous lovers, crimes of passion, business and family scandals, suicides, wastrel sons who fall into profligacy, and beautiful daughters who sacrifice their virtue to preserve their families. Luigi Chiarelli skewed several of those well-worn devices in his play *The Mask and the Face* (*La Maschera y il Volto,* 1914), in which a husband solemnly vows to his friends that he would kill his wife if she were guilty of adultery. When he discovers his wife's infidelity, he finds out he cannot carry out his vow and decides to send her away rather than kill her. He must then resort to ridiculous extremes to make it appear that he fulfilled his vendetta. The play becomes still more farcical when the "dead" wife returns from exile, desiring reconciliation, and the reunited spouses must flee the country in secret to escape the consequences of his charade. Significantly, *The Mask and the Face* was well received in Italy and abroad, suggesting that some theater audiences were ready for a new kind of drama.

Pirandello's own involvement with the theater dates back to the 1880s. As a student in Palermo, he had composed various plays in an experimental vein, including *Birds in the Sky* (*Gli uccelli dell'alto,* 1886) and *Rehearsing the Play* (*Provando la commedia,* 1887). During the 1890s, however, difficulties in staging his play *Epilogue* (*L'epilogo,* 1898; retitled *The Vise—La Morsa—*in 1908) soured Pirandello on the theater and he concentrated on fiction for a time, although he did not give up writing plays. *The Vise* and *Sicilian Limes* were both staged in 1910, but only a half-dozen years later, with the 1916 production of *Think It Over, Giacomino* (*Pensaci, Giacomino*) for the Sicilian dialect theater, would Pirandello become firmly established as a successful playwright.

While Pirandello's early plays show naturalist influences, especially in their evocation of Sicilian daily life, his work became increasingly innovative and experimental as he entered his second decade as a dramatist. During the war years, he discovered common artistic ground with the *grottesco* playwrights, especially their mingling of the comic with the tragic and their challenge to the sentimental theater of the bourgeois. *The Rules of the Game* (*Il giuoco delle parti,* 1918)—one of Pirandello's first plays written after the war—undercuts the potentially tragic elements of a failed marriage, a romantic triangle, and a duel by juxtaposing them against ironic scenes of the emotionally cold protagonist discussing philosophy and preparing his meals. In *Six Characters in Search of an Author,* Pirandello mounted a more direct attack upon the old-fashioned drama that had held sway in the Italian theater. In one scene, the stepdaughter accuses the director of wishing to soften the sordid reality of her incestuous near-encounter with the father into "a nice little messy sentimental romantic scene" to satisfy theatrical conventions (Pirandello, *Six Characters in Search of an Author*, p. 48). The play is likewise considered a critique of naturalism in the theater, the mechanical reproduction of reality rather than the reality itself.

The Play in Focus

Plot summary. While preparing to rehearse *The Rules of the Game*, a Pirandello play, a director and his troupe of actors are startled by the interruption of six fictional characters:

A 50-year-old man
A woman in widow's weeds
A beautiful 18-year-old girl
A 22-year-old man
A 14-year-old boy
A 4-year-old girl

The six characters announce that they are searching for an author to put their drama on the stage. Initially annoyed by their intrusion, the director eventually becomes interested enough to listen to the characters' story.

Although the characters have different interpretations of the events, the basic story emerges thus. Years ago, the older man and woman had married, and she had borne him a son, but the father, who had intellectual pretensions, soon became bored with his simple wife. Seeking to rid himself of her, he encouraged a love affair between his wife and his secretary, whose disposition more readily suited hers, then turned the pair out of the house. The legitimate son was sent away to the country to be reared among peasants. Oddly enough, however, after all this was accomplished, the father found himself lonely. He had been keeping track of his cast-off wife, who started a new family with her lover, bearing him three children. Of these three, the estranged husband took a special interest in the eldest daughter. He would follow her when she went to school and offer her little presents. On hearing of this, the mother became alarmed, distrusting her estranged husband's motives. Soon after, her new family secretly moved to another town, and the father lost all contact with them.

More years passed, the secretary died, and the mother and her children returned to their former town. Unbeknownst to her mother, to support

their destitute family, the eldest daughter went to work as a prostitute for Madam Pace, a dressmaker who was also a procuress. One day the father visited the establishment of Madam Pace in search of sexual satisfaction and was introduced to the young girl, whom he failed to recognize. The mother interrupted their impending liaison with the revelation that the young prostitute was the father's own stepdaughter. On learning of his wife's poverty, the father permitted her to return to their home with all her children. The resulting domestic situation proves wretched, however: the legitimate son is cold and aloof towards his mother, who tries desperately to win his affection; the neglected younger children eventually come to grief; and the elder stepdaughter runs away in the wake of a family tragedy, leaving the original trio (the father, mother, and son) intact but emotionally isolated from one another.

Now seeing the dramatic potential in the characters' story, the director decides he will try to adapt it to the stage. He calls for a short break and summons the six characters to talk with him privately in his office; the astonished actors speculate about this strange new development as they go offstage.

On their return to the stage, the director and the father immediately clash when the latter insists that no formal script is needed for their play and that he and the other characters will enact their own designated roles rather than relegate them to the actors. The stepdaughter echoes the father's demands, and the director decides to humor them for the moment since they are only rehearsing. He begins to question the father and stepdaughter about their encounter in Madame Pace's shop, then wonders who should play the dressmaker in that scene. The father assures the director that he need not worry about that detail and quickly borrows some hats and wraps from the actors to set up a quick facsimile of the dress shop. To everyone's amazement, Madame Pace suddenly appears, as though conjured by magic; outraged by the sight, the mother, who has been silent until now, berates the dressmaker and tears off her wig. Madame Pace refuses to play her part in the mother's presence and exits.

The father and stepdaughter proceed with the scene. As he tries to seduce her with soft words, the mother watches and suffers during this reenactment of a painful incident she has already endured. The director eventually halts the action and insists that the leading actors in his own company now play the scene. The brazen stepdaughter laughs at the leading lady's performance, and the father raises similar objections to the leading man's interpretation of his role. Both insist that they want to enact their own drama. Again the characters replace the actors, and the scene continues up to the point where the father suggests the stepdaughter undress and the mother enters and pulls her daughter away from her estranged husband. As the characters—especially the mother—relive the anguish and humiliation of that moment, the director declares with satisfaction that they have a promising ending for the play's first act.

As preparations for the second scene begin, the director, the father, and the stepdaughter argue about the sets, which should include a garden and the interior of a house. The father also becomes embroiled in another argument with the actors on the nature of illusion versus reality. When the director mockingly suggests that the six fictional characters are more real than the flesh-and-blood actors, he is shocked when the father confirms that suggestion. The actors' reality changes from day to day, unlike that of the characters: "Immutable reality—it should make you shudder to be near us!" (*Six Characters in Search of an Author*, p. 56). Moreover, the father continues, "When a character is born, he immediately assumes so much independence even from his own author, that he can be imagined by everybody in a number of other situations in which the author never thought of putting him, and sometimes he even acquires a meaning the author never dreamed of giving him!" (*Six Characters in Search of an Author*, p. 56). The father then reveals that he and his companions were the creations of an author who decided not to use them in his works, after all. The stepdaughter wistfully remembers how she, especially, tried to persuade the author to continue their story:

> I tried to tempt him many times while he was at his desk feeling melancholy around twilight or when he would abandon himself to his armchair, unable to decide whether or not to turn on the lights, allowing the shadows to invade the room, shadows that were swarming with our presence, coming to tempt him. . . . Ah, my life! What scenes, what scenes we proposed to him!
>
> (*Six Characters in Search of an Author*, p. 57)

Impatient with all this talk, the director demands a return to the action of the play.

The second act starts and the director places the two youngest children in the garden, as the characters suggest. Meanwhile, he tries to arrange a scene in the house between the mother and the legitimate son. Displeased, the son asks to be left

out of this scene, complains that he did not consent to have his story told, and refuses to participate in the drama. When the father tries to force him to play his part, the son upbraids him for wanting to flaunt the family's shame before the world and again refuses to become involved. Under questioning from the director, however, the son reluctantly reveals that he and his mother never had a conversation in the house. Instead, still pursued by her, he went for a walk in the garden and discovered, to his horror, that the little girl had drowned in the pool. Rushing to pull her out, the son saw the younger boy staring crazily at his dead sister. As the characters react to this tragedy, a shot rings out from behind the bushes: the boy has killed himself with a revolver.

Pandemonium erupts in the theater, as the two children are carried offstage to the loud lamentations of the mother. The director asks if the boy was wounded; the actors argue among themselves whether the child is really dead or whether the whole business was make-believe. The father asserts that everything that happened was real. Losing his patience and his temper, the director washes his hands of the play and the characters, complaining that he has wasted a whole day on them. In the complicated stage directions that follow this pronouncement, the actors disappear, the three members of the original family reappear on stage, and the stepdaughter runs out of the theatre, laughing raucously.

Plays within plays. The dramatic structure of *Six Characters in Search of an Author* remains one of its more compelling aspects. As numerous critics have pointed out, there are actually three dramas taking place on the stage: the interrupted rehearsal of Pirandello's *Il giuoco delle parti* (*The Rules of the Game*), a family drama that the six characters wish to see performed in its stead, and the frame play about the fictional sextet invading the theater and arguing with the director and troupe. All three components work together to provide a forum for Pirandello's own views of life and art.

First performed in Rome in 1918, *The Rules of the Game* depicts the ironic outcome of a triangle between Leone Gala, whose only passions are food and reason; Leone's estranged, volatile wife, Silia; and Guido Venanzi, Silia's long-term lover and Leone's erstwhile friend. Bitterly resenting her husband's cold detachment, Silia tries to destroy him by involving him in a quarrel with one of the city's deadliest duelists to defend her honor. Gala turns the tables on his wife and her lover by agreeing to the duel, then refusing to fight, which leaves Venanzi (as his second and as Silia's virtual husband) to take up the challenge instead. Ultimately, Venanzi dies at the hand of his more skilled opponent as Gala calmly sits down to breakfast. While the performance of *The Rules of the Game* in *Six Characters in Search of an Author* never reaches this point, stopping before the duel, the inclusion of the first play in the second is nonetheless significant. The first play itself deals with role-playing; the director explains as much to the leading man while describing the opening scene in which Leone Gala beats eggs and discusses Henri Bergson's philosophy, which holds that reality is an ever-changing, vital impulse whose nature cannot be adequately known by reason.

> Yes, sir, put [the chef's hat] on and beat the eggs. Do you think that this egg-beating business is simply that? If so, you're in trouble. You have to represent the shell of those eggs you are beating! Yes sir, the shell: that is to say, the empty form of reason, and your wife is instinct in a game of assigned roles, according to which you, who play your own role, purposely become the puppet of yourself.
>
> (*Six Characters in Search of an Author*, p. 9)

Although not quoted in *Six Characters in Search of an Author*, Gala's initial speech in *The Rules of the Game* contains these important sentiments:

> All that in our reality is fluid, living, mobile, dark, yes, I admit it, it escapes reason. . . . How it escapes reason, however, I cannot quite see, from the very fact that Signor Bergson can say it. How does he manage to say it? What makes him say it, if not reason? And so, it seems to me, it does not escape reason.
>
> (Pirandello in Bloom, p. 131)

One of the major conflicts in *Six Characters in Search of an Author* is the fluidity of life versus the fixity of reason, or rather, form.

That conflict takes on renewed urgency when the acting troupe attempts to adapt the six characters' turgid family drama for the stage. The characters, especially the father and stepdaughter, resist the imposition of artificial form (the scripted performances of the actors) upon the sordid family drama (deliberately reminiscent of the sentimental melodramas of the previous century) that is their entire existence. The father explains to the troupe, "What for you is an illusion that must be created, is for us, instead, our only reality" (*Six Characters in Search of an Author*, p. 54). And because their very being is invested in the unfinished drama, the more fully realized of the six characters experience real distress when they observe the actors playing *their* assigned

roles. This, in turn, generates a series of arguments between characters and actors regarding the nature of reality, the limits of art, and the ability of fictional characters to exist independently of their creator. Although the director of the troupe regards these discussions as an irritating distraction from his attempt to stage the characters' family drama, they are in fact the meat of Pirandello's play: the tenets of his theatrical theory delivered through the speeches of his six characters.

Throughout his career, Pirandello voiced ambiguity about the theater as a mode of artistic expression. In an 1899 article, "Spoken Action" ("L'azione parlata"), Pirandello wrote that descriptive narrative devices should be abolished on the stage and replaced by the characters' own dialogue and expressions, composed when the author has wholly immersed himself in his creation. According to this article, it is not the drama that makes the characters but the characters that make the drama. Two 1908 essays by Pirandello—"On Humor" ("L'umorismo") and "Illustrators, Authors, and Translators" ("Illustratori, attori e traduttori")—discuss, respectively, the humorist writer's practices of unmasking his characters, stripping away their illusions, and tackling the specific difficulties in transferring the writer's work to the stage. In the latter essay, especially, Pirandello expresses his reservations about the stage as a medium. From the outset, he contends, the writer and the actor are at cross-purposes; the former develops characters from a vast array of possibilities in his imagination, while the latter gives the characters material substance but cannot encompass everything a writer envisions with regard to those characters. The physical realization of the writer's imaginings is thus always incomplete and imperfect, although, at best, not displeasing. Pirandello also dismisses the actor's fitness to judge a play's quality: "The actor doesn't know how to recognize artistic merits in a play because he is only looking for a good part, and if he finds it the play is good and if not, it is bad" (Pirandello in Bloom, p. 50).

Even in 1922, with *Six Characters in Search of An Author* enjoying worldwide success, Pirandello continued to express his discomfort over the rehearsal and performance process, remarking in an interview: "When I've written a play, when it's finished, alive or dead, as it is, from my hands, when my part in the creation is finished, then the actors cut, fix, criticize. . . . If you were to be at the rehearsals of one of my works, you'd realize that for me it's tortuous" (Pirandello in Bloom, pp. 51-52). That very conflict unfolds in Pirandello's play, as the characters fight to preserve their story's sordid truth over the director's frantic protests that "all this cannot be done on stage" (*Six Characters in Search of an Author*, p. 49).

Pirandello's philosophy regarding the theater was intensely personal; among his Italian contemporaries, he was, in some respects, one of a kind. Although other *grottesco* playwrights mingled genres of tragedy, comedy, farce, and satire to produce similar results in their own works, none appeared to have explored the conflict between the nature of reality and the limits of art.

SIX CHARACTERS FROM THE PAGE TO THE STAGE

Having originally created his six characters for a novel, which he abandoned unfinished, Pirandello later described in a 1925 preface to his play how the characters "went on living on their own, choosing certain moments of the day to reappear before me in the solitude of my study and coming—now one, now the other, now two together—to tempt me" into finishing their story (Pirandello in Cole, p. 206). Finally, the playwright came up with an entirely different solution:

"Why not," I said to myself, "present this highly strange fact of an author who refuses to let some of his characters live though they have been born in his fantasy, and the fact that these characters, having by now life in their veins, do not resign themselves to remaining excluded from the world of art? They are detached from me; live on their own, have acquired voice and movement. . . . And so let them go where dramatic characters do go to have life: on a stage. And let us see what will happen."

(Pirandello in Cole, p. 207)

Pirandello's models in that area were in fact not dramatic, but philosophical; he relied especially upon the writings of Henri Bergson, the French philosopher. Yet if Pirandello had no peer within his own country, writers from other nations were turning out bold, innovative works at the same time. In Germany, a movement known as expressionism began just before the First World War (1914-18), reaching its zenith between 1910 and 1925. Expressionist writers and artists mounted a radical revolt against a tradition of realism; most of them exaggerated or distorted aspects of the outside world in their works and portrayed the individual as standing alone and afraid in an industrial society that was itself slowly disintegrating into chaos. For some critics, Pirandello's exploration of such themes as social alienation and emotional isolation prompts comparison with the expressionists, artists such as the painters Emil Nolde and Franz Marc and the writers Franz Kafka and Bertolt Brecht. Meanwhile, experimental movements of a similar nature began in Great Britain and America during the first two decades after World War I, which are often referred to as the modern period. Again, many intellectuals rejected traditional forms and subjects and began to experiment with new modes in art and literature. Poets like T. S. Eliot and Ezra Pound introduced innovative styles and verse forms, while the novelists James Joyce and Virginia Woolf attempted comparable feats in prose. Whatever their nationality or medium of expression, the concern for all these artists was, in Ezra Pound's famous phrase, to "make it new."

Sources and literary context. Pirandello's inspiration for some aspects of *Six Characters in Search of an Author* was partly autobiographical. The subplot of the father's forbidden attraction to his stepdaughter, for example, stemmed from a painful incident in the playwright's personal life. In 1917 Pirandello's wife, Antonietta—the victim of an irreversible nervous breakdown several years before—accused him of committing incest with their daughter, Lietta. Although the accusation was groundless, Lietta was horrified by her mother's venom and fled her parents' house, refusing to return. Two years later, Antonietta was committed to an asylum.

More significantly, Pirandello was at this time planning a novel centering on the tragedy enacted by the six characters. In 1917 he wrote to one of his sons:

Six Characters in Search of an Author; a novel to be written. Perhaps you understand. Six characters, taken up in a terrible drama, who come up close to me, to be composed in a novel, an obsession, and I don't want to know about it, and I say to them that it is useless and they don't matter to me, and that nothing any longer matters to me; and they who show me all of their wounds, I chase them away.

(Pirandello, p. xii)

Ultimately Pirandello reworked this projected novel into a play and cast himself as the unnamed author who had abandoned the characters he created. They were thus compelled to seek out someone else to realize their drama.

Along with his own experiences and writings, a variety of literary and dramatic materials shaped Pirandello's composition of drama. In the early years of his career, he immersed himself in philosophical, historical, literary, cultural, and even psychological studies. Several French thinkers proved especially influential; Alfred Binet, in *The Alterations of Personality (Les Alterations de la Personnalité,* 1892), introduced Pirandello to issues of consciousness and psychological relativism, a philosophy contesting the belief that all humans share a similar or potentially similar psychological reality. The writings of French philosopher Henri Bergson contributed to Pirandello's concept of "the fluidity, essential evanescence, and changeability of life and emotion" (Bassanese, p. 8). Dramatically, as noted, Pirandello owed a debt to the *grottesco* movement and the *commedia dell'arte,* the conventions of which can be detected in Pirandello's suggested stage directions for *Six Characters in Search of an Author.* He recommends, for example, that each of the six appear wearing masks denoting his or her particular emotional state, such as grief, remorse, and revenge.

While Pirandello described *Six Characters in Search of an Author* as a "comedy," the play has been associated not only with the theater of the grotesque but also with absurdism, which holds that the human condition is fundamentally senseless. The play has likewise been associated with humorism, a movement developed by Pirandello himself, which mingles elements of comedy and tragedy to produce a simultaneous awareness of both aspects of the human condition. That this play was dismissive of sentimental and naturalistic forms of theater has already been established. Pirandello was similarly dismissive of symbolism and allegory, writing in a 1925 preface to *Six Characters in Search of an Author:* "I hate symbolic art in which the presentation loses all spontaneous movement in order to become a machine . . . made for the demonstration of some moral truth. Spiritual need . . . cannot be satisfied . . . by such allegorical symbolism" (Pirandello in Cole, p. 206).

Reception. *Six Characters in Search of an Author* premiered in Rome on May 10, 1921, and caused immediate controversy. Not knowing how to react to the play's theatrical innovations, many members of the audience began to heckle the performance, whistling their derision and crying out "manicomio" (madhouse) and "buffone" (buffoon). Pirandello's supporters in the theater took exception to this so quarrels and even fights broke out on the spot. When Pirandello himself appeared onstage at the end of the play, he too was heckled. Later, a hostile crowd accosted the playwright while he was exiting the theater with his daughter and threw insults and coins at him as he got into a taxi. The general pandemonium caused by the play erupted into the streets surrounding the theater and lasted well into the night.

Four months later, Pirandello's play received a very different reception from audiences in Milan. By that time the text of *Six Characters in Search of an Author* had been published and critics had had the opportunity to read it. This time, the audience listened "in religious silence" throughout the performance and the play was accounted a

> ### STAGING PIRANDELLO
>
>
> Since its premiere in 1921, *Six Characters in Search of an Author* has been performed many times, and in different countries. Directors have chosen to interpret and stage Pirandello's play in a variety of ways. One famous early production was held at the Théâtre des Champs-Élysées in 1923; the director, Georges Pitoëff had the six characters flooded with a green light and lowered to the stage in an old scenery elevator for their grand entrance. Amazingly, the lift jammed just before reaching the boards and the characters had to climb down, one by one, onto the stage. Even without that unscripted bit of drama, the Pitoëff production proved to be a sensation with Parisian audiences. Another critically lauded production took place in Berlin, Germany, in 1924; Max Reinhardt, the director, chose to focus upon the tragic elements of the play. He also placed the figure of the director at the forefront; for example, the director kept his back to the audience at all times, while the six characters acted out their drama before him as if they were part of his particular vision. By contrast, Pirandello chose to de-emphasize the director and the acting troupe when he mounted his own production of the play—also held in Berlin—in 1925; in keeping with the title of the play, he concentrated upon the six characters instead, especially the father and stepdaughter. German audiences were taken aback by the openness and terseness of the Teatro d'Arte's production, not to mention its more comic tone; ironically, some German critics even dismissed Pirandello's staging as "primitive" and less profound than Reinhardt's had been (Matthaei, p. 95).

triumph (Giudice, p. 117). Indeed, *Six Characters in Search of an Author* went on to be a great success; between 1922 and 1927 it was performed not only in every major city in Europe but also in New York, Buenos Aires, and Tokyo.

—Pamela S. Loy

For More Information

Bassanese, Fiora A. *Understanding Luigi Pirandello*. Columbia: University of South Carolina Press, 1997.

Bentley, Eric. *The Pirandello Commentaries*. Evanston: Northwestern University Press, 1986.

Bloom, Harold, ed. *Modern Critical Views: Luigi Pirandello*. New York: Chelsea House, 1989.

Cole, Toby, ed. *Playwrights on Playwriting*. New York: Hill & Wang, 1960.

DiGaetani, John Louis, ed. *A Companion to Pirandello Studies*. New York: Greenwood Press, 1991.

Duggan, Christopher. *A Concise History of Italy*. Cambridge: Cambridge University Press, 1994.

Giudice, Gaspare. *Pirandello: A Biography*. London: Oxford University Press, 1975.

Hainsworth, Peter, and David Robey, eds. *The Oxford Companion to Italian Literature*. Oxford: Oxford University Press, 2002.

Hamilton, Alastair. *The Appeal of Fascism*. New York: Macmillan, 1971.

Killinger, Charles L. *The History of Italy*. Westport, Conn.: Greenwood Press, 2002.

Marker, Frederick J., and Christopher Innes. *Modernism in European Drama: Ibsen, Strindberg, Pirandello, Beckett*. Toronto: University of Toronto Press, 1998.

Matthaei, Renate. *Luigi Pirandello*. New York: Frederick Ungar, 1973.

Pirandello, Luigi. *Six Characters in Search of an Author and Other Plays*. Trans. Mark Musa. London: Penguin, 1995.

Starkie, Walter. *Luigi Pirandello*. Berkeley: University of California Press, 1965.

Stanzas on the Tournament

by

Angelo Poliziano

Angelo Poliziano was born Angelo Ambrogini in the Tuscan community of Montepulciano in 1454; later, he took his pen name from the Latinization of his birthplace (Mons Politianus). The eldest child of Benedetto Ambrogini, a supporter of the Medici family, Poliziano went to Florence after his father was murdered in a local vendetta in 1464. Poliziano soon distinguished himself in the study of Latin and Greek. In 1470 he began translating Homer's *Iliad* into Latin, dedicating part of the translation to Lorenzo de' Medici, ruler of Florence since the previous year. His scholarly prowess attracted Lorenzo's attention. By 1473 Poliziano was established in the Medici household as Lorenzo's protégé and companion; two years later, he had also become Lorenzo's secretary and the tutor of his son Piero. Poliziano continued to pursue his own literary career as well, composing scholarly essays in Latin (he would later become one of the foremost classical scholars of the Italian Renaissance). Poliziano also wrote light verse and occasional poems (penned in response to a public event or historical occasion), mostly in the Tuscan vernacular. Arguably the most famous of his occasional works was his *Stanze per la giostra* (Stanzas on the Tournament), the full title of which is *Stanze cominciate per la giostra del Magnifico Giuliano de' Medici* (Stanzas Begun for the Tournament of the Magnificent Giuliano de' Medici). This narrative poem in the Italian stanza form *ottava rima* celebrates the Florentine tournament of 1475 and the triumphs of its victor Giuliano de' Medici—Lorenzo's younger

THE LITERARY WORK

A narrative poem set in Florence during the 1470s; composed from 1475 to 1478; first published in Italian (as *Stanze per la giostra*) in 1494, in English in 1979.

SYNOPSIS

Through Cupid's stratagems, a Florentine youth who scorns women falls in love with a beautiful nymph and resolves to try his fighting skills against other men in hopes of winning her favor.

brother—and Giuliano's devotion to the beautiful Simonetta Cattaneo, in whose honor he fought. Translated into English only in the twentieth century, Poliziano's *Stanze* is at once an impressive tribute to one of Renaissance Italy's most powerful families and a celebration of the transcendent power of love.

Events in History at the Time of the Poem

Florence and the Medici. From the eleventh century onward, several Italian cities, including Florence, grew increasingly important and independent, achieving the status of self-governing communes. Initially, the landed aristocracy held most of the authority within the commune; however, during the thirteenth century, Florence

Stanzas on the Tournament

Angelo Poliziano

experienced a significant shift in power as the guilds, professional corporations based on trade interests, became a more dominant force in society. As the century progressed, the Florentine *popolo*—a term for the guildsmen and merchants, as opposed to the leading aristocrats—grew more numerous, more confident, and better organized. The *popolo* went on to seize power in the commune after 1266.

The government of the *popolo* relied on an executive board of magistrates, or priors, who were elected every two months to prevent anyone from holding power too long. All magistrates had to come from the guilds, which now controlled the city's administration. The aristocrats, who had formerly dominated Florentine political life, were barred from holding office. No more than 5 percent of the population was eligible to vote and less than one per cent could hold public office. By the late thirteenth century the number of guilds was fixed: there were six major guilds (importers of cloth, bankers, silk merchants, wool manufacturers, doctors and apothecaries, and lawyers and notaries) and fifteen minor guilds. Theoretically, all the guilds shared power; however, the major guilds came to assume the primary political role in the government. By the next century, the Florentine government had become an oligarchy of merchant families, whose wealth was derived from banking, trade, and textile manufacturing.

In 1434 the Medici—a powerful family of bankers—emerged from the guild movement and assumed control over Florence throughout most of the fifteenth century. No coup or revolution was necessary; the Medici used their enormous wealth and network of influential friends and associates to retain power in the city. Many Medici allies were themselves members of prominent Florentine families. Others were middle- and lower-class clients who were willing to fight for the Medici if necessary (which later proved to be the case during the Pazzi conspiracy in 1478). The Medici also encouraged political participation: under their administration, the voting franchise rose from five to twenty percent of the population.

Besides wealth and politics, the Medici also took a keen interest in arts and literature. Cosimo de' Medici, the de facto ruler from 1434 to 1464, imported precious manuscripts from Alexandria and Greece, hired some 45 copyists, and made translations of these treasures available to teachers and students. In 1439 he also encouraged the humanist movement by founding a Platonic Academy in Florence, to which he lured Eastern scholars and churchmen. Florentine intellectuals embraced this "new learning," which included the study of Greek literature and philosophy, and the more liberal, secular spirit the movement embodied. Cosimo's son Piero (r. 1464-69) and grandson Lorenzo (r. 1469-92) followed his example, helping to develop Florence as one of the intellectual and cultural capitals of Europe.

Arguably, Lorenzo—later to be known as "the Magnificent"—was the most famous of the Medici. Although he was not yet 20 when his father, Piero, died in 1469, the young Lorenzo had been groomed since childhood for his new position as virtual ruler of Florence. For the most part Lorenzo adhered to the political practices of his grandfather and father: he preserved the traditional communal legislative councils but prevented opponents of the Medici from gaining office. Likewise, he was an enthusiastic patron of the arts and numbered many philosophers, poets, and painters among his acquaintances. Poliziano himself was one of Lorenzo's protégés and friends, rescued from poverty and given a place in the Medici household after Lorenzo recognized the younger man's scholarly gifts. In the *Stanze*, Poliziano even pays grateful tribute to his patron:

> And you, well-born Laurel (Lorenzo), under whose shelter happy Florence rests in peace, fearing neither winds nor threats of heaven, nor irate Jove in his angriest countenance: receive

my humble voice, trembling and fearful, under the shade of your sacred trunk; o cause, o goal of all my desires, which draw life only from the fragrance of your leaves.

(Poliziano, *Stanze*, 1.4)

The Tournament of 1475. As Lorenzo became more established in his position as virtual ruler of Florence, his handsome younger brother Giuliano succeeded him as "prince of youth," a role that Lorenzo had filled when their father was still alive. In February 1469 Lorenzo had held a grand tournament, in which he competed on horses that had been presented to him as tokens of friendship from the King of Naples and the dukes of Milan and Ferrara. Resplendent in velvet and silk, wearing rubies and diamonds in his cap, Lorenzo rode to victory in the jousts; his triumph inspired *La Giostra* (*The Tournament*), a poem by Luigi Pulci. In due course, Giuliano held a tournament, which took place on January 28, 1475 and was deemed as magnificent as his brother's had been six years earlier. Lorenzo's longtime mistress Lucrezia Donati was the Queen of the Tournament, but Simonetta Cattaneo—recently married at the age of 16 to Marco Vespucci—was the tournament's "Queen of Beauty." At that time, the Genoa-born Simonetta was considered the most beautiful woman in Florence, and her gentle disposition further endeared her to the Florentine people. The exact nature of her relationship with Giuliano de' Medici has not been determined; some have identified her as Giuliano's mistress, while others have suggested that any relationship between the two was entirely platonic.

In any case, Giuliano apparently wore Simonetta's favor (a love token), along with a suit of silver armor rumored to have cost some 8,000 florins, when he took to the field for the jousts. Fighting in Simonetta's honor, Giuliano unseated all of his opponents and received the prize of the tournament. His looks and skill, as well as his Medici heritage, made his victory a popular result.

Poets and painters alike commemorated this tournament, which was accounted a great success. Three of Sandro Botticelli's major paintings—*The Birth of Venus, Mars and Venus,* and *Return of Spring*—derived some inspiration from the tournament; significantly, Lorenzo commissioned all three of those paintings. And just as Pulci had immortalized Lorenzo's triumph in the *Giostra* of 1469, so did Poliziano seek to perform a similar task for the *Giostra* of 1475. Indeed, *Stanze per la giostra* presents a mythologized version of the romance between Giuliano and Simonetta,

clearly intended to culminate in Giuliano's victory in the tournament.

Ironically, history ensured that Poliziano's poem would never be completed. In 1476, a year after the tournament, Simonetta fell ill and died, to the great grief of the city. Lorenzo thus recorded the tragedy in his *Commento*: "In our city, there died a lady who generally moved all the Florentine people to pity; it is no great marvel, for she was truly adorned with as much beauty and gentle kindness as any lady before her" (Medici in Poliziano, p. x). In Book II of his *Stanze*, Poliziano

managed to work around the sad fact of his heroine's death by transforming her into the goddess of Fortune, who was still destined to be the guiding force of the hero's life. In 1478, however, an even greater tragedy struck Florence when Giuliano was assassinated in the Pazzi conspiracy against the Medici. While the plot was ultimately foiled and Lorenzo retained control of Florence, the murder of the much-loved Giuliano plunged the city into mourning; thereafter, Poliziano abandoned his *Stanze*.

The Pazzi conspiracy. In 1478 Lorenzo de' Medici faced what historians consider the most serious challenge to his leadership of Florence. The so-called Pazzi conspiracy had its roots in several conflicts, including a burgeoning animosity between Lorenzo and Pope Sixtus IV, who was elected in 1471. Lorenzo had first incurred the pope's resentment in 1474 by preventing the Medici bank from advancing the pope funds to purchase Romagnol towns from their traditional overlords, a move that would have increased the temporal power of the popes within the Papal States. On discovering that Florence was trying to purchase the town of Imola—located between Bologna and Ravenna—Sixtus obtained sufficient sums from the Pazzi, a rival Florentine banking family, and bought Imola himself, making the town subject to papal authority. The Pazzi thus gained the lucrative privilege of handling the papal revenues, formerly managed by the Medici—an act calculated to enrage Lorenzo, who undertook measures to ruin the Pazzi firm. In an act of nepotism, Sixtus appointed his nephew Girolamo Riario to be governor of Imola.

Matters between the pope and Florence's de facto leader deteriorated further after Lorenzo arranged a triple alliance between Florence, Venice, and Milan to preserve peace in northern Italy and counter the threat posed by the augmented Papal States. Sixtus promptly teamed up with the Kingdom of Naples, exacerbating the friction between the northern and southern powers of Italy. Still seething over Lorenzo's new foreign policy, Sixtus appointed Francesco Salviati, an enemy of the Medici, to the archbishopric of Pisa, then a Florentine province, without consulting the Florentine government. Lorenzo ordered Pisa to exclude Salviati from its Church offices and managed to hinder the new appointee from assuming his post for three years.

The escalating tensions between Lorenzo and Sixtus came to a head in 1478. Several of Lorenzo's enemies, including Riario, Salviati, and Francesco Pazzi (nephew of Jacopo Pazzi, head of the Pazzi family), hatched a conspiracy to overthrow the Medici family by murdering Lorenzo and his younger brother, Giuliano. Sixtus too was drawn into this plot and while he did not sanction the assassination of the Medici brothers, he

did not discourage the conspirators from pursuing their ends.

Recruiting additional followers, the conspirators planned to kill the brothers during the celebration of High Mass in the cathedral of Santa Maria del Fiore on Sunday, April 26, 1478. At the moment of the Elevation of the Host, the assassins sprang upon their victims. Although Giuliano suffered a great blow to the head and dropped to the ground, his killers continued to hack at his body long after he had fallen. Lorenzo was wounded in the shoulder, but managed to fight off his enemies by using his sword and his cloak to defend himself. Lorenzo's friends surrounded him, helping him to break through the ring of his attackers and flee to the safety of the sacristy; one friend, Francesco Nori, was felled by a sword that had been thrust in Lorenzo's defense. Poliziano, who was among those in the sacristy with Lorenzo, described the scene thus:

> Having fled to the same place, I together with some other persons then got the bronze doors shut and so we held off Bandini [one of the assassins]. While we guarded the doors, some within feared for Lorenzo because of his wound and were anxious to do something about it. Antonio Rodolfo . . . sucked out the wound [in case there might be poison]. Lorenzo himself gave no thought to his own safety but kept asking how Giuliano was; he also made angry threats and lamented that his life had been endangered by people who had hardly any reason to attack him.
>
> (Poliziano in Watkins, p. 176)

Reinforcements loyal to the Medici eventually came to Lorenzo's aid and escorted him to the safety of his home, shielding him from the sight of Giuliano's body. On departing the church himself, however, Poliziano was distraught to see his patron's brother "lying in wretched state, covered with wounds, and hideous with blood. I was so weakened by the sight that I could hardly walk or control myself in my overwhelming grief, but some friends helped me to get home" (Poliziano in Watkins, p. 177). The contrast between the mutilated body and the dashing hero of Poliziano's *Stanze* could not have been more painful, and it is believed that the poet abandoned work on the poem thereafter.

Meanwhile, the conspirators were not meeting with the success they had anticipated. Riding through the streets, Jacopo Pazzi tried to rouse the people with cries of "Libertà!" (Liberty) only to be greeted with shouts of "Vivano le palle!" (Long live the balls—the emblem of the Medici family). Salviati, invading the Palazzo Vecchio with a hundred armed followers, received an equally hostile reception; the priors—loyal to the Medici—promptly put the archbishop and his cohorts under arrest. Once the news of the attack upon Lorenzo and Giuliano became known, the Florentine populace rose up in rage against the conspirators. A bloodthirsty mob dragged Francesco Pazzi, who had wounded his own leg while stabbing Giuliano, from his sickbed and hanged him before one of the windows in the Palazzo Vecchio. Archbishop Salviati met the same fate, and in his death agonies, he was seen to sink his teeth into Francesco's body, which was hanging beside him. His followers fared no better; the priors tossed several from the palazzo windows to the pavement below, some meeting their deaths in the fall, some being finished off by the crowd. Jacopo Pazzi, fleeing to the hills for safety, was eventually captured, dragged back to the city, tortured and hanged. Over the next few months, many more conspirators and suspected conspirators were apprehended and sentenced to death or imprisonment for their involvement in the plot.

Expressing outrage over Archbishop Salviati's fate, Pope Sixtus excommunicated Lorenzo and suspended all religious services throughout the Florentine dominions. At his suggestion, papal ally King Ferrante I of Naples sent an envoy to Florence demanding that Lorenzo either be delivered to the pope or banished. The Florentine government refused even to consider these conditions, and war subsequently broke out between Florence and the papacy in 1479. After Florence suffered several humiliating defeats in battle, Lorenzo carried out a bold political venture, sailing to Naples to conduct personal negotiations with Ferrante. During his stay, which lasted several months, Lorenzo attempted to persuade his host of the potential threat that the papacy posed not only to Florence but to Naples as well. Ferrante came to admire Lorenzo's courage and determination; ultimately, he signed a peace treaty with him, and Lorenzo returned to Florence in triumph in 1480.

Florence and the papacy were also eventually reconciled after a Turkish force invaded and captured the southern harbor-town of Otranto. Declaring that all Italians needed to band together to resist the infidels, Sixtus IV invited a body of Florentine commissioners to Rome, where he cleansed them—and by implication, all of Florence—of their sins and persuaded them to equip fifteen galleys against the Turks. There-

after, Lorenzo's authority and position were never seriously threatened again. The death of Giuliano, however, remained a lifelong sorrow for Lorenzo and the Florentines who had revered the young man.

EULOGY FOR GIULIANO

As one of the friends who had accompanied Lorenzo to the cathedral that fateful Sunday, Poliziano was in the position to offer an eyewitness account of the tragedy. While his resulting *Commentary on the Pazzi Conspiracy* may succeed better as pro-Medici propaganda than objective history, he nonetheless offers a moving tribute to the murdered Giuliano at the conclusion:

[Giuliano] was tall and sturdy, with a large chest. His arms were rounded and muscular, his joints strong and big, his stomach flat, his thighs powerful, his calves rather full. He had bright lively eyes, with excellent vision, and his face was rather dark, with thick, rich black hair worn long and combed straight back from the forehead. He was skilled at riding and at throwing, jumping and wrestling, and prodigiously fond of hunting. Of great courage and steadfastness, he fostered piety and good morals. He was accomplished in painting and music and every sort of refinement. He had some talent for poetry, and wrote some Tuscan verses which were wonderfully serious and edifying. And he always enjoyed reading amatory verse. He was both eloquent and prudent, but not at all showy; he loved wit and was himself quite witty. He hated liars and men who hold grudges. Moderate in his grooming, he was nonetheless amazingly elegant and attractive. He was very mild, very kind, very respectful of his brother, and of great strength and virtue. These virtues and others made him beloved by the people and his own family during his lifetime, and they rendered more painful and bitter to us all the memory of his loss.

(Poliziano in Watkins, p. 183)

The Poem in Focus

Plot summary. The poem opens, in the style of many epics, with invocations to the guiding spirit of the work: in this case, the god of love and Lorenzo de' Medici himself (here referred to as "Laurel," his poetic name in his literary circle). Afterwards, the narrator tells of Laurel's younger brother Julio (modeled on Giuliano de' Medici), a youth who excels in martial and intellectual activities but who scorns women and scoffs at lovers. Offended by Julio's mockery, Cupid decides to punish him by making him fall in love.

One morning, while Julio is out hunting, Cupid sets a white doe in his path. The young man gives chase and soon becomes separated from his companions; nonetheless, Julio pursues his quarry all the way into a forest clearing. There, the doe vanishes and Julio encounters a beautiful nymph; at this point Cupid fires an arrow into Julio's breast and he falls instantly in love. The nymph reveals to Julio that her name is Simonetta, that she is married, and that she lives in Florence. She then bids the youth farewell and departs.

Julio returns home safely, to the relief of his anxious retinue, but he is now a changed man, consumed by thoughts of his beloved Simonetta. Meanwhile, a triumphant Cupid flies back to his mother Venus's garden and palace, which Poliziano describes in lavish detail. Finding Venus upon a couch with her lover Mars, Cupid gleefully reports his wounding of the formerly scornful Julio.

Venus expresses approval of Cupid's activities. Mother and son then discuss the romantic fates of Laurel and Julio. Laurel—who has proven faithful to his mistress Lucrezia—is to be rewarded for his fidelity in love; Cupid will ensure that the haughty Lucrezia returns Laurel's devotion. Julio, however, will have to prove himself in arms to attain Simonetta's favor. Venus sends out her winged cherubs to wound the young men of Florence, inspiring them with thoughts of love and martial prowess. At Venus's bidding, Pasithea—one of the Graces—obtains a dream from the god of sleep. The dream is intended for Julio. While in the grip of his dream, Julio sees Simonetta, clad in armor, overpowering Cupid and binding him to an olive tree. Cupid, now appearing weak and vulnerable, exhorts Julio to save him and tells the young man that only "a triumphal palm" (*Stanze*, 2.31) will win him Simonetta. A vision of Glory, accompanied by Poetry and History, then descends, stripping Simonetta of her armor and bearing Julio himself off to the battlefield. Emerging victorious from his conflict, Julio discovers to his dismay that a dark cloud has enveloped Simonetta. She soon emerges in a radiant new form as Fortune, destined to "govern his life, and make them both eternal through fame" (*Stanze*, 2.34).

Dawn arrives and Julio awakens from his dream, "burning with love and a desire for glory" (*Stanze*, 2.39). Now eager to try his strength against the nobles of Florence, Julio prays to Minerva, Glory, and Cupid for victory in arms and love. The poem then ends before the great tournament takes place.

The triumph of love. Poliziano's conception of love as a redemptive force is derived from several influences. His translator David E. Quint observes that the writings of Dante, Petrarca (Petrarch), and Giovanni Boccaccio may have provided the most immediate source of inspiration because they embodied a familiar tenet of early Italian literature—that love transforms and ennobles the lover. One tale from Boccaccio's *Decameron*, in fact, describes the fate of a youth much like Poliziano's Julio, who undergoes a similar change when he falls in love:

> Because of the love which he bore Efigenia, not only did he change his harsh and rustic voice into a citizenly and mannerly one, but he became master of dance and song, and he became expert and bold in riding and martial skills, those of the sea as well as those of the land . . . he had not completed one quarter of a year before he became better graced and better mannered, with more individual virtues, than any other youth on the island of Cyprus.
>
> (Boccaccio in Quint, p. xv)

In the *Stanze*, Julio begins as a daring athletic youth, who excels at hunting, riding, and even composing poetry. However, he is also described as an "arrogant boy . . . always unkempt and hardened in aspect," who scorns women, lovers, and all the softer passions (*Stanze*, 1.10). Once struck by love, he undergoes a transformation that alters the pattern of his entire existence; his boyish self-sufficiency gives way to a willing subjection to and dependency upon his beloved. To win Simonetta's regard, he must leave the pastoral woodlands of his childhood and prove his worth among the young noblemen of Florence. The *Stanze* thus sets the stage for a tournament that will represent a triumph not only for the maturation of Julio but, as Cupid points out to Venus, for love itself:

> This, noble Mother, is my victory; this has been my toil and my sweat; for which our glory, our reputation, our ancient honor will rise above the heavens, for which your memory, Mother, and that of your son, Love, will never be erased; for which verses and lyrics will forever sing of our arrows, flames, bows, and quivers.
>
> (*Stanze*, 2.12)

Love as an ennobling, transcendent force was not solely a literary conceit. Indeed, the *Stanze* may also owe something to the writings of Poliziano's friend Marsilio Ficino, a philosopher who made a lifelong career out of translating the works of Plato and Plato's later followers—the Neoplatonists—into Italian. Ficino's best-known work may have been his *De amore* (c. 1459; Of Love), a commentary on Plato's *Symposium on Love*. Although *De Amore* was not printed until 1484, manuscript copies (in Italian and Latin) circulated privately among Ficino's acquaintances after its composition. Lorenzo de' Medici, who employed Ficino as a translator for the Medici family, requested an Italian translation of *De amore* for two of his friends. It is probable that Poliziano, also employed by the Medici household, encountered *De Amore* in manuscript.

The basic argument of Ficino's treatise presupposes (1) that all existence emanates from God to the physical world in a descending hierarchy, (2) that all living beings desire to return to their source (God), (3) that this desire is called love, and (4) that the quality of the source that arouses this desire is called beauty. The human soul is capable of earthly love, based upon the desire to procreate (descending), and of heavenly love, in which the soul aspires to higher levels of being in hopes of closer union with God (ascending): "Human love is therefore a good thing because in both its phases, descending and ascending, it is part of a natural cosmic process in which all creatures share" (Jayne in Ficino, p. 7).

Ficino's work enjoyed considerable popularity among his contemporaries. Lorenzo de' Medici used *De amore* in his commentary upon his own love poems, and the renowned scholar Mario Equicola accorded Ficino a place of honor when he compiled a history of treatises on love in 1495. *De amore* also inspired other efforts in a similar vein, most notably Leone Ebreo's *Dialogues of Love* (c. 1512) and Baldassare Castiglione's **The Book of The Courtier** (1528; also in *WLAIT 7: Italian Literature and Its Times*). It is unclear to what extent Poliziano agreed with Ficino's philosophy of love; it has been suggested that he seems less concerned than Ficino with the relations between man and God. However, in the *Stanze,* Poliziano does portray Julio ascending to a higher level of being as he abandons his rustic sports and the forest beasts for the world of human love and human endeavor. It is possible to see his progress as an ascent up the ladder of being: from the lowest level of matter (the woods) to higher levels of nature (the hunt), to active human life (interest in Simonetta), and finally to the supernatural realm (the Garden of Venus, inhabited by the goddess herself).

Sources and literary context. As the full title indicates—*Stanze Cominciate per la Giostra del Magnifico Giuliano de' Medici* (Stanzas Begun for the Tournament of the Magnificent Giuliano de' Medici)—a specific historical event inspired Poliziano's poem: namely, the Florentine tournament of 1475, won by Giuliano de' Medici. Poliziano drew his cast of characters from real life too, although he Latinized the names of Lorenzo and Giuliano to Laurel and Julio, respectively, and presented his tale as myth.

Transferring contemporary events and personages to a classical setting was a common practice among Renaissance court poets. Indeed, Poliziano's use of Greek and Roman mythology in his work was entirely consistent with his humanism. He also consciously echoed familiar classical and Italian texts, such as Ovid's *Ars Amatoria,* Claudian's *Epithalamium,* and Petrarch's **Canzoniere** (also in *WLAIT 7: Italian Literature and Its Times*). Poliziano's immediate audience would not have disapproved of these liberal borrowings from antiquity. Rather, many would have said that literary allusions enriched their understanding of the work. Quint explains how familiar a strategy it was:

> From his reading the Renaissance schoolboy compiled a personal *florilegium,* or notebook anthology, of catchy phrases, aphorisms, metaphors, and rhetorical figures from which he was to form his own speech and writing. . . . The true *doctus,* the learned man, exploiting a deep and wide erudition, could find the apposite classical allusion or model for any occasion. For Poliziano, literary imitation did not limit, but rather expanded the range of individual expression.
>
> (Quint, p. xiii)

Significantly, Poliziano did not adopt the long, classical epic form characteristic of Cicero, a Roman author whose style and diction many writers chose to emulate. Rather, Poliziano cultivated a brief, allusive poetic style, possibly similar to that used by Callimachus and Catullus to compose mini-epics, or epyllions.

As previously noted, Poliziano's models for the lyrical and erotic aspects of the *Stanze* probably included works by Dante, Boccaccio, and Petrarch, along with Ficino's *De Amore.* In the end, the multiplicity of literary sources helped Poliziano create a poem that managed to fuse the beauty and splendor of classical literature with the vigor and spontaneity of Italian vernacular poetry.

Reception and impact. While Poliziano's poem was not officially published until 1494, it may have circulated privately among his intimates in Lorenzo de' Medici's court circle. Lorenzo himself would most likely have been pleased by the poet's tribute to his younger brother.

THE *STANZE* VERSE

Writing in the vernacular Tuscan, Poliziano's *Stanze* uses *ottava rima*—an eight-line verse form with the rhyme scheme *abababcc*, conventionally used in narrative poetry. Poliziano's light, skillful application of this form inspired later Italian writers, including Lodovico Ariosto and Torquato Tasso (see **Orlando Furioso** and **Jerusalem Delivered,** also in *WLAIT 7: Italian Literature and Its Times*). Arguably, the most famous English practitioner was Lord Byron, who used *ottava rima* for his comic satire, *Don Juan* (1816-24). An example of Poliziano's handling of the octave, with a translation, follows:

> Le gloriose pompe e' fieri ludi
> della città che 'l freno allenta e stringe
> a' magnanimi Toschi, e i regni crudi
> di quella dea che 'l terzo ciel dipinge,
> e i premi degni alli onorati studi
> la mente audace a celebrar mi spinge,
> sí che i gran nomi e i fatti egregi e soli
> fortuna o morte o tempo non involi.

My daring mind urges me to celebrate the glorious pageants and the proud games of the city that bridles and gives rein to the magnanimous Tuscans, the cruel realms of the goddess who adorns the third heaven, and the rewards merited by honorable pursuits; in order that fortune, death, or time may not spoil great names and unique and eminent deeds.

(*Stanze*, 1.1)

The *Stanze* is often cited as the literary source for many of Sandro Botticelli's famous paintings. Indeed, Poliziano's lavishly detailed description of the birth of Venus (*Stanze*, 1.99-101) appears to have furnished the inspiration for Botticelli's painting of the same name:

> With lovely and happy gestures, a young woman with nonhuman countenance, is carried on a conch shell, wafted to shore by playful zephyrs; and it seems that heaven rejoices in her birth. . . . You could swear that the goddess had emerged from the waves, pressing her hair with her right hand, covering with the other her sweet mound of flesh; and where the strand was

imprinted with her sacred and divine step, it had clothed itself in flowers and grass; then with happy, more than mortal features, she was received in the bosom of the three nymphs and cloaked in a starry garment.

(*Stanze*, 1.99-101)

While Poliziano's poetry was admired in his lifetime, later generations of critics—such as those of post-Unification Italy in the late nineteenth century—tended to dismiss his and other poetic works of the Italian Renaissance. These critics acknowledged the classical influences and stylistic beauty of the poetry but paid little attention to its content. In his late-twentieth-century English translation, Quint strove for an effect that was both lyrical and literal, that conveyed not only the rich classical inheritance of the humanist poet but also his attempt to depict love as the means by which human potential is realized. Quint's effort was well received. One review called his translation "excellent, conveying the tone and content of the poetry in prose paragraphs which reflect the octave of the original . . . an outstanding contribution" (*Italica*). Another review spoke of the far-reaching effect the translation, released 500 years after the original, promised to have: "[Quint's] book cannot fail to cast new light on the Italian Renaissance in general, and on Poliziano in particular" (*Forum Italicum*). Finally, *Choice* magazine applauded Quint's translation as "rich, vibrant, and rhythmic, while at the same time accurate and natural. It captures the fragile and fugitive beauty of the original Italian verses, emulating the complex models of Latin and Greek literature" (*Choice* in Mooney, p. 1012).

—Pamela S. Loy

For More Information

Brucker, Gene Adam. *Florence, the Golden Age 1138-1737.* New York: Abbeville Press, 1983.

———. *Renaissance Florence.* Berkeley: University of California Press, 1969.

Everson, Jane, and Diego Zancani, eds. *Italy in Crisis, 1494.* Oxford: Legenda, 2000.

Ficino, Marsilio. *Commentary of Plato's Symposium on Love.* Trans. Sears Jayne. Dallas: Spring Publications, 1985.

Forum Italicum. "David Quint: The Stanze of Poliziano." Review of the *Stanze of Angelo Poliziano.* Penn State University Press. http://www.psupress.org/books/titles/0-271-00937-3.html.

Lucas-Dubretton, J. *Daily Life in Florence in the Time of the Medici.* Trans. A. Lytton Sells. New York: Macmillan, 1961.

Martines, Lauro. *April Blood: Florence and the Plot Against the Medici.* Oxford: Oxford University Press, 2003.

Mooney, Martha T., ed. *Book Review Digest.* Vol. 75. New York: H. W. Wilson, 1980.

Poliziano, Angelo. *The Stanze of Angelo Poliziano.* Trans. David Quint. Amherst: University of Massachusetts Press, 1979.

Quint, David. Introduction to *The Stanze of Poliziano,* by Angelo Poliziano. Amherst: University of Massachusetts Press, 1979.

Trexler, Richard. *Public Life in Renaissance Florence.* Ithaca: Cornell University Press, 1980.

Watkins, Renée Neu, ed. *Humanism & Liberty.* Columbia: University of South Carolina Press, 1978.

Stil Novo Poetry

by

Guido Guinizzelli and Guido Cavalcanti

The term *stil novo* designates a loosely organized group of late-thirteenth-century poets who shared an innovative treatment of love poetry. Outstanding among poets connected with this new style were Guido Guinizzelli and Guido Cavalcanti, the first of whom was approximately two decades older than the second.

Two men by the name of Guido Guinizzelli are mentioned in documents from Bologna around the mid-1200s, one belonging to the noble class, the other to a family of skilled laborers. Most probably, Guinizzelli the poet was born around 1240 to a family originally involved in craftsmanship and, later on, in the practice of law. Following in the footsteps of his father and grandfather, Guinizzelli pursued a commercial and judicial career. He was working as a consulting lawyer in the mid-1200s, and also writing poetry. At the time, Bologna and the major cities in the Romagna region, as well as nearby Tuscany, were rent by fierce political struggle between the Guelphs and the Ghibellines. Guinizzelli sided with the Ghibellines, supporters of the emperor. When they were defeated in 1274, he was sent from Bologna to Monselice, a small town in northern Italy. Never returning to Bologna, Guinizzelli died in exile around 1276.

Guido Cavalcanti, a poet on the opposite political side, led an even more eventful life than Guinizzelli. Probably born around 1250, Cavalcanti belonged to one of the most powerful Florentine families involved in the political struggle between the Guelphs and the Ghibellines. As a small child, he was banished from Florence af-

THE LITERARY WORKS

Two collections of love poems (22 by Guido Guinizzelli and 52 by Guido Cavalcanti) written in the late 1200s; transcribed in Italian in the mid-1300s; translated into English by Dante Gabriel Rossetti in 1861.

SYNOPSIS

The poems focus on love for a lady, the noble heart, and the superiority of the lady: Guinizzelli's lyrics introduce the concept of the noble heart; Cavalcanti's lyrics speak of the poet's deep suffering from love and internal struggle with conflicting emotions.

ter the Ghibelline victory of Montaperti in 1260; all families supporting the Guelphs were expelled from the city at the time, and their houses were razed to the ground. Six years later, among other far-reaching consequences, a Guelph victory in southern Italy allowed Cavalcanti to return to Florence. In 1267 Cavalcanti became engaged to a woman belonging to a family whose political views opposed his own; theirs was probably one of the engagements celebrated that year to bring about peace between warring factions. In the 1290s, his political faction itself split into smaller factions—the White Guelphs and the Black Guelphs. The first was aligned with the longtime rich and the drive to keep Florence independent, the second with the newly wealthy and the pope.

Guido Cavalcanti

Cavalcanti sided with the first, the White Guelphs, and their main representatives in Florence, the Cerchi family. They opposed the Donati, leaders of the Black Guelphs and a family personally hated by Cavalcanti. Nearly killed by Corso Donati, Cavalcanti attempted to murder him in return but also failed.

Cavalcanti took an active part in the political life of Florence, trying to help bring the continuous struggles to an end. He was barred, along with other noblemen, from public office in 1293-94 in accordance with the anti-aristocratic laws passed at the time. There was violent street-fighting following the assassination of the imprisoned Cerchi, which had an impact on political opponents like Cavalcanti. In June 1300, the priors (elected magistrates) of Florence, including the poet's former friend Dante, banished Cavalcanti, sending him into exile to Sarzana, in northern Italy. The banishment was revoked in July 1300, but Cavalcanti apparently contracted malaria and died that same year in August.

Though Guinizzelli and Cavalcanti led eventful political lives, their poems contain little autobiographical information. The bulk of their lyrics center instead on love. Some critics attribute this absence of politically charged verse to repression by the winning faction against anyone likely to publicize opposing views. Others ascribe the predominance of love in *stilnovist* poetry to the profound philosophical research and

debate in the thirteenth century at the universities of Paris and Bologna, following the introduction of newly translated works by Aristotle. Certainly this debate affected the way the poets wrote their love lyrics. Rejecting the mannered style of their predecessors, they developed a new type of poetry, with Guinizzelli distinguishing himself as its forerunner, Cavalcanti as its initiator in earnest. Guinizzelli introduces elements of this new style in the poem "Love Returns Always to a Noble Heart" (*Al cor gentil rempaira sempre amore*); Cavalcanti demonstrates it in full in "A Lady Beseeches Me and Therefore I Am Willing to Treat" (*Donna me prega,—per ch'eo voglio dire*).

Events in History at the Time of the Poems

From Frederick II to peninsular disharmony. Political and social unrest plagued the regions of Italy during the Middle Ages. In Sicily, the emperors of Germany attained a measure of power when one of their descendents, Henry VI, married Constance of Altavilla, heiress of the Norman dynasty that was then in control of the island. Henry's son, Fredrick II, firmly established his power throughout southern Italy, thanks to a feudal structure of imperial administrators and vassals that left very little freedom to the individual villages and towns. His obstacle to further expansion into central Italy was the Church, which had established a wide net of semi-independent territories that were loyal to the pope. Fierce animosity soon developed in the territories of Tuscany and the Romagna. On one side were the supporters of the pope (the Guelphs)—who opposed the Holy Roman Emperor and his policy of strict subjugation of local authorities; on the other side were supporters of the emperor (the Ghibellines), who objected to the papacy's assumption that it was entitled to extend its spiritual power into temporal matters, deeming its interference intolerable. Eventually, after two violent battles in central and southern Italy at Benevento (1266) and Tagliacozzo (1268), the Ghibellines were defeated and the last descendant of the German dynasty was killed. After the Ghibelline defeat, the Guelphs returned to power in Florence for good, but then split into two factions. Around 1300 they divided into the Black and White Guelphs, repeating the earlier division between supporters of the Pope and followers of the Holy Roman Emperor. There was by then also a poetic split, perhaps best understood as a progression from the Sicilian school of poetry that had gathered around Frederick II to a new style.

Emergence of the new style. Among the late-thirteenth-century writers who favored an innovative treatment of love poetry was Dante Alighieri, author of the *Commedia*, or ***The Divine Comedy*** (also in *WLAIT 7: Italian Literature and Its Times*). The term *stil novo* was in fact coined by Dante in *Purgatory* 24 (lines 55-57) of his *Divine Comedy*. Traveling through Purgatory, Dante meets the Tuscan poet Bonagiunta Orbicciani, a representative of the "old style," to whom Dante explains that he is one of the new poets who, without fanfare or rhetoric, expresses with fidelity the love in his heart. Enlightened by Dante's explanations, Bonagiunta understands the difference between the old school of poetry (represented by himself, the Tuscan poet Guittone d'Arezzo, and the Sicilian poet Giacomo da Lentini [alluded to by Dante as the Notary]). "My brother, now I see," Bonagiunta says to Dante, "the knot that held Guittone and the Notary and me back from the sweet new style I hear!" (Dante, *Purgatory* 24, lines 55-57). Guinizzelli's fame as the precursor of this *dolce stil novo,* or "sweet new style," rests on the fact that Dante himself, when he meets Guinizzelli soon after Bonagiunta in *Purgatory* 26, recognizes him as the one who influenced the new circle of poets. Dante praises him as "a father to me, and to those my betters, who have ever used the sweet and pleasant rhymes of love" (Dante, *Purgatory* 26, lines 97-99). Earlier, in *Purgatory* 11, Dante had established a kind of literary chronology within the *stil novo* movement by saying that the second Guido (Guido Cavalcanti) had outdone the poetic skills of the first (Guido Guinizzelli), and by foreseeing with veiled modesty the advent of a new poet (Dante himself) who would surpass them both: "Thus hath one Guido from the other snatch'd the letter'd prize: and he, perhaps, is born, who shall drive either from their nest" (Dante, *Purgatory* 11, lines 97-99). Other *stil novo* poets include Lapo Gianni, Gianni degli Alfani, Dino Frescobaldi, and Cino da Pistoia.

The new style and medieval philosophy. Both Guinizzelli and Cavalcanti wrote a few love poems that are openly erotic, but the image of the lady in their works is mainly one of physical insubstantiality. Normally she served a philosophical purpose, an emphasis in keeping with scholarly trends of the day. During the 1100s and 1200s there was a surge in the growth of urban centers in Italy, prompted by movement from the countryside to the city. Apart from causing economic and social changes, the shift to cities meant that new cultural institutions needed to be created to satisfy the needs of a burgeoning population. Fundamental among these institutions were universities, which gave rise to medieval philosophy, a discipline that took on a name born of its association with them—Scholasticism. Among other concerns, the Scholastics tried to reconcile rational and religious beliefs by explaining how human reason was related to faith and how the intellect could comprehend the idea of divine revelation. This philosophical quest generated renewed interest in Plato (427-347 B.C.E.) and, especially, Aristotle (384-322 B.C.E.).

From 500 to 800 C.E. philosophical speculation focused on Plato, whose beliefs could easily be related to some ideas of Christianity. The theory of One Supreme Being who regulates the whole universe, for instance, lent itself well to the Christian concepts of one and only one first cause, God the Creator, and the soul's immortality. Also, Plato's belief that the physical world must have a metaphysical source could be adapted to the Christian notion that the physical world is but an illusion of the senses, an image of a superior realm located in heaven. Plato's ideas led to interpretations that gave rise to a system of thought called Neoplatonism. Some *stilnovists,* like Guinizzelli and most notably Dante, echoed Platonism in their theories of love, considering the lady and the ideal beauty she represented as physical intermediaries between the sensible world and the higher, invisible realm of God.

Aristotle was the other Greek philosopher who stirred the curiosity of medieval thinkers, but not until the second period of Scholasticism (the 1200s). Until then Aristotle's works had not been available in Latin, the common language of medieval Europe. After the remarkable linguistic effort made in the twelfth century by the Archbishop of Toledo and his school of translators in Spain, the Aristotelian corpus became accessible in its Latin version to students and professors in schools and universities. Aristotle had written extensively about the intellect and the way it functions in relation to the senses. Some of the key concepts in Aristotle's works regarded the natural world and the way human beings apprehend it. Contrary to Plato, Aristotle believed that the explanation of physical phenomena is contained within the phenomena themselves, and is apprehended through the senses. Human knowledge, taught Aristotle, originates in the perception of sensible forms. Once the intellect has apprehended the sensible forms of the physical world, it can envision the essence of the physical forms. This process of abstraction is made possible by the existence of a potential and an actual intellect. In its potential stage, the intellect has the ability to apprehend abstract forms. When this ability is triggered by sensory perceptions, the intellect interprets the data received by the senses, developing from potentiality into act, thus becoming actual intellect. Aristotle illustrates this complex intellectual process through an example from the physical world. Just as colors—which are potentially visible—are actually perceived through light, so does the potential intellect turn into actual intellect when stimulated by sensory perceptions.

NATURAL WONDERS—LIGHT, STARS, AND LOVE

A philosophy of light developed in Italy and England during the twelfth and thirteenth centuries. According to this philosophy, just as light can be explained through mathematical rules, so can all physical events, since they are all made visible by light. Rules governing the phenomena of light can thus be used to explain the whole visible world. This idea found its way into Cavalcanti's "A Lady Beseeches Me," along with Aristotle's concept of the possible intellect. Explaining what brings love into existence, the poet says it is "formed, like the diaphanous, by light" and "finds its place and dwelling in the possible intellect" (Cavalcanti in Shaw, p. 98). That is, love is potentially there in the heart, and the woman brings it into existence, just as light brings into visible form the potential colors mentioned.

Aristotle maintained that the stars and the planets cause everything in the universe to move and change. In keeping with the way he understood the universe, the *stilnovists* believed that the lady was able to bring about change by stirring up emotions in the poet's noble heart. They also referred in their poetry to the planet Mars. Medieval astrologers associated Mars with evil influence. Thus, whoever was under its influence was in a state of mental disorder, a reference that found its way into poetry, becoming associated with the condition of the lover.

Another common strategy used by the *stilnovists* to describe a lady was a simile comparing her to the qualities of the sun, stars, or angels. In the poems of both Guinizzelli and Cavalcanti such similes are not just a strategy to conjure a visual image. Nor are they just an exterior way of praising the lady through flamboyant expression. Rather they are logically connected with the Aristotelian theory of change from potentiality into act.

Several medieval philosophers opposed Aristotle's ideas because they gave human reason a prevailing role, thereby minimizing the role of divine revelation. Nevertheless, many Aristotelian ideas were taken up and elaborated by the poets of the *stil novo*. Aristotle came up with a theory of change from potentiality into act, for instance; traces of this theory can be recognized in Guinizzelli's "I Think a Man Foolish, To Tell the Truth" (*Tegno de folle 'mpres,' a lo ver dire*), a poem about a lady whose appearance causes the countryside around her to turn into a luminous landscape. Her radiant beauty makes a potentially visibly joyous land become just that. This idea of transformation and movement implied the concept of creation as opposed to Plato's theory of fixed, eternal essences. The idea may also be a reflection in poetry of the fact that rapid social changes were occurring in the regions of Tuscany and the Romagna.

The Aristotelian theory of the possible and actual intellect preoccupied Cavalcanti, who, in his poem "A Lady Beseeches Me" (*Donna me prega*) elaborated on the chances of the intellect ever changing from potentiality into act when one is under the influence of physical love. In "Who Is It Who Comes, Whom Every Man Admires" (*Chi é questa che vèn, ch'ogn'om la mira*), he stresses the impossibility of attaining any knowledge in the lady's presence. When she appears, she creates turmoil in onlookers and prevents a man's senses from connecting calmly with his intellect in order to turn sensible images into a vision of the mind.

Guinizzelli's and Cavalcanti's poems center on the turmoil created by the lady's appearance and the effects of love on the poets' hearts and bodies. These effects are philosophical as well as lyrical. The lady is not only the source of poetic inspiration; she also becomes the image that the poet uses to illustrate his theory of knowledge.

Philosophy of the noble heart. One of the main tenets of the *stilnovists*, especially Guinizzelli, was that "love and the noble heart are concomitant co-creations, with the noble heart as natural abode for love" (Brand and Pertile, p. 20). This theory was based on the belief that love could be fully understood only by those who were endowed with honorable feelings, regardless of their lineage or social status. Although the theory of the noble heart was part of an established literary tradition, it is particularly associated with the climate of social mobility that characterized the main cities in the central regions of Tuscany and the Romagna in the thirteenth century. At that time, the political power of the aristocracy, traditionally hereditary, was being eroded by the rising merchant class, and a new idea of power based on merit was developing. The communal societies and their "democratic" values seem to have been the perfect cradle for the development of the theory of the noble heart, which held that what counted most was not who a man's ancestors were but the purity of his feelings. Such a theory would provide a fundamental premise that justified doing away with rigid social structures based on an aristocratic hierarchy. At the same time, a poem that celebrated this new theory would give expression to an individual soul. The idea of the noble heart, defined not by wealth or aristocratic title but by integrity of emotion, had much to do with the advent of the new style of poetry in the Italian states. In the words of one literary historian, the *stil novo* poets changed the very social basis of poetry, shifting it "from a feudal court with fixed, inherited values to an imaginary country: the community that joins them is a community of the noble heart and an aristocracy of the spirit" (Edwards, p. xxiii).

One cannot say with certainty that the theory of the noble heart was the expression of "democratic" values emanating from the communes (self-governing, semi-republican cities) in the 1200s. However, the vast literary and philosophical debate that the theory awakened indicates that scholars in those years were taking seriously the issue of knowledge, which entailed understanding love. It also suggests that to their minds knowledge was intimately tied to the inner workings of passions in a noble heart.

The Poems in Focus

Contents summary—"Love returns always to a noble heart." Guinizzelli's poetic production consists of 5 songs, 15 sonnets, and 2 fragments of songs. Their sequence of composition remains unknown. Most of his poems center on the superiority of the lady and the effects of love on the poet's heart. Primarily they do so through praise of the beautiful lady, who is compared to a star or an angel, and through vivid description of the deadly consequences of love on the poet. The lyrics depict him as struck by a thunderbolt, wounded by an arrow, or left like a dead body by Love's assault, a "brass statue / with no life or spirit flowing" (Guinizzelli, Poem 6 in *The Poetry of Guido Guinizzelli*, p. 33). Some of Guinizzelli's poems are influenced by earlier genres and styles, especially the image of the poet as the worshipper of the lady—a depiction that harks back to

the feudal obedience of a vassal to his lady. However, in his trademark poem, *Al cor gentil rempaira sempre amore* ("Love Returns Always to a Noble Heart"), Guinizzelli introduces into poetry a philosophical concept of love that was new in the vernacular language of Italy and was to be the main theme of some of the later *stilnovists*.

The poem begins with love returning to a noble heart, just as a bird going back to its natural setting, a forest. After the initial comparison, the verse proceeds with the typical progression of a philosophical demonstration—a thesis is put forward and then illustrated through examples. The thesis is that love and the noble heart are coexistent: "Nature did not make love before the noble heart, / Nor the noble heart before love (Poem 4 in *The Poetry of Guido Guinizzelli*, p. 21). Love is said to be joined with the noble heart just like the sun is tied to brightness, or heat is associated with fire. The second stanza explains that love descends into a noble heart through the action of the lady, drawing an analogy between two series of elements: a) the sun, a precious stone, and a star; b) nature, the noble heart, and the lady. Medieval thinkers taught that the sun, by purifying a precious stone, enables it to receive its special qualities from a star; in like manner, nature makes a heart noble and pure, which enables it to be infused with love from a lady. Through examples taken, once again, from the natural world, the third stanza stresses that love's true abode is the noble heart, and that love is incompatible with a base nature. Love rightfully dwells in the noble heart "like a diamond in a vein of ore," or like fire "on the tip of a candle" (Poem 4 in *The Poetry of Guido Guinizzelli*, p. 21).

After explaining the coexistent nature of love and the noble heart, and their necessary relationship, the poet goes on to expound the doctrine that derives from the premises in the first three stanzas: "No man should believe / That nobility exists outside of the heart / By right of lineage, / Unless he has a noble heart disposed to virtue" (Poem 4 in *The Poetry of Guido Guinizzelli*, p. 21). The fact that true nobility resides not in lineage but in a pure heart is unchangeable and corroborated again by nature, this time by the recurrence of unchangeable natural phenomena. No matter how long the sun shines on mud, dirt will remain dirt, while the sun will continue to shine, emanating the same heat. The fifth stanza establishes a subtle comparison between God and the lady. The angels, who are attracted to God, make the heavens turn by the intensity of their desire to be close to God, and by so doing they are able both to obey Him and to satisfy their own wishes. By the same token, just as God bestows perfect satisfaction on the angels who obey Him by keeping them near Him, so the lady should grant grace to her lover when his eyes shine with desire, which is always a desire to obey her. The sixth and last stanza is a somewhat humorous dialog between God and the poet. Picturing himself in the sight of the Almighty, the poet imagines God objecting to the blasphemous comparison made by the poet between the sacred love that is due Him and the profane love that the poet feels for his lady. "But," says the poet, "I shall say to Him, "She had the likeness / Of an angel from your kingdom. / It's not my fault if I fell in love with her" (Poem 4 in *The Poetry of Guido Guinizzelli*, p. 23).

Although no clear evolution can be established in Guinizzelli's production of poems, it is commonly agreed that the comparison of the lady to an angel belongs to the last stage in the thematic development of his poetry. This and other themes in his lyrics influenced poems by later *stilnovists*, such as Cavalcanti. Influential elements include the theme of praise of the lady, the imagery of light and the importance of what is seen, and the poet's preoccupation with his pain and suffering, as shown in the following lines:

> Your lovely greeting and the gentle gaze
> You give me when I meet you kill me:
> Love assaults me and still is unconcerned
> Whether he does me good or ill,
> For he shot an arrow through my heart's
>   center
> That cuts one part from the other and divides
>   the whole:

> I cannot speak since I burn in great pain
> Like a man who sees his own death.
>
> (Poem 6 in *The Poetry of
> Guido Guinizzelli*, p. 33)

Especially this last theme of death is characteristic of Cavalcanti's verse.

"A lady beseeches me, and therefore I am willing to treat." Like Guinizzelli's corpus, Cavalcanti's 52 poems are almost exclusively about love. His production consists of 36 sonnets, 11 ballads, 2 songs, 2 isolated stanzas, and one short, witty poem. Cavalcanti's early poems praise the lady (*Fresca rosa novella*—"Fresh new rose"), and a few realistic lyrics describe sensual love (*In un boschetto trova' pasturella*—"In a little wood I once found a young shepherdess" (Cavalcanti, Poem 46 in *Rime*, p. 156; trans. T. Serafini). Most of his later poems, however, portray love as a spirit that kills, as in *Voi, che per gli occhi miei passaste al core*—"You, who pierce my heart through my eyes" (Poem 13 in *Rime*, p. 93; trans. T. Serafini). Cavalcanti especially connects love to states of psychic dissolution and physical distress. Indeed, his recurring words are "sighs, sorrow, fear, dismay, battle, death" (*sospiri, dolor, temenza, sbigottimento, battaglia, morte*).

Love is a fleeting accident brought about by a physical stimulus on earth and not a permanent quality, the poet declares at the beginning of "A Lady Beseeches Me." In this first stanza Cavalcanti outlines the whole poem. He will give a philosophical and scientific explanation of where love dwells and who brings about its creation; what love's virtues and powers are; what its essence and its effects are; what pleasure it gives; and whether it is visible. Love, writes the poet in the second stanza, dwells in that part of the soul where memory is, and it originates from a darkness that comes from Mars (a planet, it was believed, that influences people adversely, befuddling the senses and hampering clear vision). As a passion of the senses, love is described by Cavalcanti as a darkness that obscures the intellect. Love comes from a form—an idea—that the mind abstracts from visual perceptions. This ideal form takes its place in the possible intellect (i.e., the part that receives all intelligible forms from the senses and, by interpreting them, develops into its counterpart, the active intellect). In the possible intellect, love is accompanied by no pain and no pleasure but by contemplation (since at this stage it is still connected with an idea of the mind and does not involve a physical transmutation due to passion). In this internal space, love is contained within itself and can "provide no kindred image" because it does not have a physical counterpart yet (Cavalcanti in Shaw, p. 98). The third stanza is about virtue and the power of love. Love is not a rational virtue aiming at the perfect good (a good guided by reason); rather, it is a sensitive virtue (aimed at gratifying the senses). As a consequence, whoever is affected by love only gains an incomplete knowledge (his discernment being defective because he is guided by the senses rather than by reason). Not only that, but love is often so powerful that it results in the death of the lover, who loses rational control over himself. In the next stanza the poet speaks about the essence and the effects of love in its actuality. In contrast with the earlier image of ideal love as a contemplation of beauty free of desire and suffering, when it passes from potentiality into act, love becomes a ceaseless yet fleeting desire. In its active incarnation, love exceeds the boundaries of natural balance. It is a conflict of emotions that turns laughter into tears, or disfigures the lover's face with fear. As in Guinizzelli's poem, love is normally a characteristic of a noble heart, but Cavalcanti's version does not subscribe to the Guinizzellian idea of a love that is partially satisfied in the presence of the lady. Here the lover sends out sighs, stares into empty space, is oblivious to his own safety, and can find no solace or gain any knowledge through love.

The last two verses of the fourth stanza "are a fling against the traditional convention of Provençal and Italian poets that Love is joy; that the lover finds happiness even in his bitterest trials; that Love is . . . the source of wisdom. . . . There is no truth in all that, says Guido: Love is acute pain, helpless misery, and confusion of thought, except at first, when it seems to promise happiness" (Shaw, p. 69). The pleasure that inspires love is based on affinity, declares the poet in the fifth stanza, because it comes from finding a lady of similar attitudes and inclinations. Although the lover can apparently tell from the lady's glance whether pleasure is near, love itself is invisible. Hard to see because of lack of color and secluded in the darkness that comes from Mars, love—a transient accident—makes it enormously risky to engage in amorous relationships, the poet seems to suggest. Nonetheless, from love alone "comes the true reward," Cavalcanti admits out of his own sad experience, speaking as "one, in all sincerity, who can be trusted" (Cavalcanti in Shaw, p. 101).

Deadly love. In Cavalcanti's verse, the lady around whom the poetry revolves is no longer a being who turns the country into a luminous landscape as in some of Guinizzelli's poems. In-

Manuscript folio from a book of poems written by Guido Cavalcanti, fourteenth century (Codice Chigiano 1, VIII. 305, fol. 56r; in the Biblioteca Apostolica Vaticana).

stead she takes on a destructive dimension, her glance splitting the poet's heart in four: *Perché non fuoro a me gli occhi miei spenti*—"Why were my eyes not ripped from my body" (Cavalcanti, Poem 12 in *Rime,* p. 92; trans. T. Serafini). Many of Cavalcanti's poems give voice to a personal drama of psychic fragmentation and speak of Death personified, appearing before the poet and tearing apart his heart (as in the earlier cited "You, who pierce my heart through my eyes"). For Cavalcanti, love is a battle and he, a victim. His love for the lady is debilitating; it breaks him into ailing pieces. The lady is fragmented in his verse by metonym, the substitution of the part for the whole, as in "her 'noble spirit' laughing and telling the lover that he must die"; likewise, the poet-lover is fragmented into suffering parts: "the eyes, the heart and soul, the tears, the 'grieving spirit'" (Harrison, p. 78). Love empties him of life, leaves him as speechless as a copper statue, as in *Tu m'hai sì piena di dolor la mente*—"You have filled my mind with so much grief" (Poem 8 in *Rime,* p. 83; trans. T. Serafini). So powerful is love that it results in the "death" of the lover, meaning he loses rational control over himself.

The idea of death in Cavalcanti's poetry takes on a remarkable bodily characterization, a development that owes much to the intertwining of natural science with philosophy in his day. During the thirteenth century, enthusiasm for Aristotle culminated in the study of the philosophical theories of one of his most prestigious commentators, the physician and philosopher Averroes (Latin name for the Arabic philosopher Ibn Rushd). Among others, Averroes proclaimed the existence of vital spirits, maintaining that they were moved by one organ only, the heart, and that they carried the vital faculties out to the limbs and back to the heart. If this back-and-forth movement perchance was interrupted, "a sudden and unforeseen death was brought about," cautioned physician Ugo of Siena, who subscribed to the teachings of Averroes (Corti, p. 11; trans. T. Serafini). The belief that such spirits were real bodily entities imbued Cavalcanti's representation of death. He infused it with frequent personifications of the spirits fleeing the heart, speaking to the flabbergasted soul of the lover, or addressing the personification of love itself. Through this convention, the standard metaphors of death and anguish in connection with love acquired a physiological dimension. They became tied to ideas of literal cessation of life and pain, distinguishing Cavalcanti's poetry in a way that made it truly innovative within the framework of thirteenth-century Italian lyrics.

Sources and literary context. In his sonnet 20a, Guinizzelli acknowledges that he is indebted to the poet Guittone of Arezzo, the most representative of a group of Tuscan poets who introduced into the regions of Tuscany and the Romagna the early lyrics of the Sicilian School (the poetic movement that flourished under Frederick II in the early thirteenth century). Guinizzelli even addresses Guittone as his artistic father in the sonnet, but it is difficult to ascertain if Guinizzelli's praise was sincere, or merely a way to tone down the innovative tendencies in his lyrics by paying formal homage to an established school of poetry. Whatever the motivations, Guinizzelli's sonnet indicates that he was well aware of the literary models of his day. In fact, both Guinizzelli's and Cavalcanti's verses can be tied not only to the poetry of Sicily but also to that of the non-Italian area of Provençe.

Provençal and Sicilian poetry offered the models for the theory of the noble heart, which they, in turn, derived from the famous twelfth-century treatise *De amore* (On Love) by Andreas Cappellanus. In his book Cappellanus makes it clear that behavior is the most important feature when one wants to acquire love, and stresses that "only goodness of character makes a man rejoice in true

nobility and shine forth" (Cappellanus in Edwards, p. xli). Guinizzelli also took concepts as well as metrical and rhyme schemes from Provençal and Sicilian models, as did Cavalcanti and the other *stilnovists*. The Provençal representation of love as a feudal relationship of service, for instance, is evident in Guinizzelli's and Cavalcanti's assertion of the superiority of the lady. Sicilian elements resonate in Guinizzelli's nature-based imagery—sun, stars, fire, iron, and magnets. However, Guinizzelli differs from Sicilian tradition by elevating the lady above her earthly connection with nature and above her worldly function as a sensual symbol bound to the physical plane. His lady is an intermediary between a man's idealized love for her and the yearning for God. Guinizzelli furthermore introduces through his poetry a new regard for the ability of love to pierce any "noble" heart, not just that of an aristocrat. In Cavalcanti's case, the poet swings Italian poetry more fully into a new direction. Earlier Sicilian and Tuscan poems portrayed the lady as an angel in a social milieu, or celebrated her angelic nature within a moral project of the poet's religious purification, as in Guittone's verses. Cavalcanti's lady, however, is devoid of any social or religious purpose. Instead she mediates between individual human experience and a higher philosophical truth. In this, Cavalcanti was probably influenced by the Scholastic debate on knowledge and the nature of love, and by works on the teachings of Averroes. Cavalcanti seems to have known the radical theories of Aristotle and Averroes elaborated in books like *Questio de felicitate* (On Happiness), written by the physician Giacomo of Pistoia and dedicated to Cavalcanti. In the poet's mind, the idea of perfect happiness was connected with rational control over human passions.

Reviews. The most eloquent and enthusiastic commentator on Guinizzelli's poetry was Dante. In his opinion Guinizzelli was a model of artistic composition. At a time when poets were experimenting with the developing Italian language and its metric potentials, Dante admired Guinizzelli's skill in versification: "Guinizzelli adopts the 'most splendid' (*superbius*) eleven-syllable line which affords the poem adequate duration and the necessary scope for richness in meaning, construction and vocabulary" (Dante in Edwards, p. xxvi). Guinizzelli's idea of the angelic lady would lead to the identification in Dante's poetry of earthly love with the love for God. The earthly love would find its most powerful manifestation in a worldly lady of idealized beauty.

While Dante praised Guinizzelli for his boldness, others objected to it. Guinizzelli faced bitter opposition from "old style" poets such as Guittone and Bonagiunta Orbicciani. Bonagiunta wrote a sizzling sonnet that criticized Guinizzelli for deviating from the usual "pleasant" ways of writing love lyric, complaining about his obscure language. Guittone wrote a sonnet that spoke of Guinizzelli's alleged abuse of metaphor and comparison (as in *S'eo tale fosse ch'io potesse stare*— "If I were the kind of man who could reproach" [*The Poetry of Guido Guinizzelli,* p. xxv]).

No doubt Guittone also engaged in literary debate with Cavalcanti, who wrote a harsh sonnet depicting Guittone as unable to write poetry that followed a logical process of reasoning. Apparently Cavalcanti showed a refusal to compromise in his writing, demonstrating a stubbornness that is in line with characterizations by contemporaries. The uncompromising nature of Cavalcanti's writing is in line with descriptions made by his contemporaries, who spoke of him as "touchy and irascible" or as "courteous and brave, but haughty, a loner and absorbed in study" (Villani and Compagni in Brand and Pertile, p. 22). His reputation as a natural philosopher probably influenced his reception as a poet. Remarkably Dante does not give Cavalcanti a role in *The Divine Comedy*, mentioning him there only indirectly. The exclusion has been ascribed by some critics to Dante's and Cavalcanti's differing philosophical views. Some speak of Cavalcanti's theories as rational and free from religious concerns, in contrast to Dante's deeply Christian ideas. The philosophical bent of Cavalcanti's poetry was heavily criticized by Guido Orlandi. In one of his sonnets, Orlandi disapproves of Cavalcanti's reasoning, calling it overly subtle. Among later commentators who appreciated Cavalcanti's philosophical erudition was Giovanni Boccaccio. He devotes one of the short stories in his **Decameron** to Cavalcanti (also in *WLAIT 7: Italian Literature and Its Times*). In the story, Cavalcanti outwits a group of ignorant rogues who are unable to understand the subtleties of his words (*Decameron*, 4.9).

—Tiziana Serafini

For More Information

Ardizzone, Maria Luisa. *Guido Cavalcanti: The Other Middle Ages.* Toronto: University of Toronto Press, 2002.

Boccaccio, Giovanni. *Decameron.* Ed. Vittore Branca. Milan: Arnoldo Mondadori Editore, 1985.

Brand, Peter, and Lino Pertile, eds. *The Cambridge History of Italian Literature.* Cambridge: Cambridge University Press, 1996.

Cavalcanti, Guido. *Rime.* Milan: BUR, 2001.

Corti, Maria. *Scritti su Cavalcanti e Dante.* Turin: Einaudi, 2003.

Dante Alighieri. *The Divine Comedy.* Trans. Charles S. Singleton. Princeton: Princeton University Press, 1970.

Guinizzelli, Guido. *The Poetry of Guido Guinizzelli.* Trans. Robert Edwards. New York: Garland, 1987.

———. *Rime.* Naples: Liguori, 1998.

Harrison, Robert Pogue. *The Body of Beatrice.* Baltimore: The Johns Hopkins University Press, 1988.

Pound, Ezra. *The Sonnets and Ballate of Guido Cavalcanti.* Boston: Small, Maynard, 1912.

Shaw, J. E. *Guido Cavalcanti's Theory of Love.* Toronto: University of Toronto Press, 1949.

Survival in
Auschwitz

by
Primo Levi

Primo Levi (1919-87), one of the foremost Holocaust writers of his time, was born, lived most his life, and died in Turin, Italy. Fascinated by chemistry at an early age, he worked as a chemist for much of his adult life. He meanwhile married, had two children, and began a writing career that led him to international prominence in later years. Even when he wrote about the Holocaust, three biographical factors intersected to influence Levi's perspective as an author: his belonging to the small Italian-Jewish community, his training in science and lengthy career as an industrial chemist, and his upbringing in twentieth-century Italy with its underlying classical culture. Explorations of the intersection of science and literature appear in many of his works, including his Holocaust writing. Although he came to prominence with autobiographical works about the Holocaust, he also achieved renown in Italy and abroad for his novels, short stories, science fiction, poetry, and essays. Prominent among them are *The Reawakening* (1963), *The Periodic Table* (1975), and *The Drowned and the Saved* (1986). Altogether they reveal a writer of unusual equanimity, clarity, and gracefulness, one who reflects forthrightly and sometimes with irony on the themes of good and evil, human justice, and the makeup of humankind. These themes coalesce in the original title of *Survival in Auschwitz*, *Se questo è un uomo*, ("If This Is a Man"). In this first memoir, and in subsequent works Levi explores what it means, on the psychological and ethical levels, to be a human being (*un uomo*) and how humans behave

THE LITERARY WORK

A Holocaust memoir set in Auschwitz between late 1943 and early 1945; published in Italian (as *Se questo è un uomo*) in 1947, in English in 1959 (as *If This Is a Man)* and in 1961 (as *Survival in Auschwitz*).

SYNOPSIS

Arrested as a partisan and a Jew in wartime Italy, Primo Levi is deported to the Auschwitz death camp in Poland, where he spends the next 11 months. His memoir of the period reflects on the meaning of humanity and presents vivid portraits of the various camp dwellers.

under difficult circumstances. He bases these explorations not only on skills of close observation related to his training as a scientist but also on grim firsthand experience as a victim of man's inhumanity to man.

Events in History at the Time of the Memoir

The Holocaust arrives to Italy. Fascist Italy and Nazi Germany were allies in World War II from May 22, 1939 (the signing of the Pact of Steel), until July 25, 1943 (Mussolini's ouster from power). A short two months later, on September 8, 1943, Italy unconditionally surrendered to the

Primo Levi

Anglo-American troops, who had invaded it from the south; at this point Italy effectively switched sides from the Axis Pact (Nazi Germany and Japan) to the Allied forces (Britain, the Soviet Union, and the United States). Nazi troops, which had been massed in central and northern Italy, overnight went from confederates to belligerents, with brutal implications for the country's Jews. At the same time, the partisan guerrilla war—mounted by Italian civilians against Nazi troops and Fascist diehards—swung into high gear. Italy was plunged into chaos, with the war now being fought on many fronts. Italian Jews immediately found themselves in danger as they never had been before; indeed, the roundup and murder of Jews on Italian soil began on September 16, 1943, and culminated in the deportation of more than 8,800 Jews from the Italian mainland and territories. Among them was Primo Levi.

The rise of Fascism and Italy's Jews. From 1922 until mid-1943, Italy was governed by Benito Mussolini and his Fascist regime. Seizing power in the 1922 "March on Rome," the charismatic Mussolini established a totalitarian state that would later be imitated by Germany (1933–45) and Spain (1939–75). Italian Fascism was based on the concepts of militarism and empire-building, economic corporatism, and the consolidation of power in the Fascist political party. Its leaders quashed political dissent, often through

the use of violence and terror. Cultural norms were imposed by the state—including jingoistic conceptions of language, art, and music—and family life was carefully regimented. The family, for example, was legally defined as a "social and political institution," allowing the state to intervene in matters such as family size and female education. To gain public support, the government sponsored public-works projects and propaganda campaigns. The appearance of order and alliances with the monarchy (from the ruling House of Savoy) and the papacy likewise fostered support.

Life for Italy's 35,000 Jews (0.9 percent of a total 1931 Italian population of 41 million) resembled that of other Italian citizens. Indeed, Italian Jews were highly visible and assimilated, present throughout the professions, and associated with both ends of the political spectrum: on the left, as dissenters and members of the anti-Fascist Resistance Movement, and on the right, as supporters of the Fascist Party, and even members of Mussolini's cabinet.

The tide began to turn for Italian Jewry in 1936, when Italy invaded Ethiopia and started to adopt racial categories that would enable the Italian government to classify its citizens by race. This same year Fascist Italy and Nazi Germany established the Rome-Berlin Axis, in which the two governments committed themselves to fighting Bolshevism in Europe and supporting Francisco Franco's rebellion against the democratic government of Spain. Nazi dictator Adolf Hitler had already promulgated racially based laws targeting the Jews, and Mussolini, as a consequence of his new alliance with Hitler, soon espoused the German leader's view that Jews—unlike "Aryan" Germans or Italians—belong to an inferior, non-Aryan "race" and therefore warrant discrimination. A series of Italian "Racial Laws" (based on Germany's Nuremburg Laws) were passed in 1938. They banned Jews from practicing most professions, from owning large businesses, and from attending public schools. In general, the laws restricted the movements of Italy's Jews, especially in relation to their contacts with non-Jewish Italians.

While the Italian populace was generally perplexed by the regulations afflicting their Jewish neighbors, few protests were registered. Most Italians of the day were preoccupied with the war effort—the new theaters of conflict in Albania and Greece, the establishment in 1939 of the Nazi-Fascist "Pact of Steel," and Italy's 1940 entry into World War II on the side of the Axis Powers and against the Allies. (The key provision in the "Pact of Steel" was for either signatory to come to the military aid of the other signatory in the event of war.)

The Italian Jews' 2,000-year history. In order to better understand the position of the Italian Jews (including Primo Levi) during the war years, in the Resistance, and in the Holocaust, it is important to briefly explore the history of the Jews in Italy. Much of this history comes to play in Levi's personal biography as well as in *Survival in Auschwitz*.

The Italian Jewish community is the oldest in Europe, dating back more than 2,100 years. It was initially a large, flourishing community, living mainly in southern Italy between Sicily and Rome. Its population had climbed as high as 120,000, becoming traders, shopkeepers, and small farmers. By the Middle Ages, its numbers had dwindled some and, through many vicissitudes, it had become well-established in southern society. This southern Italian Jewish community fell subject in 1492 to an order of expulsion from King Ferdinand of Spain that covered all the Italian territories then in his possession (roughly from Sicily to Naples). Jews were forced to move northward to Rome and its environs. For the first time, they began settling in large numbers in areas of northern Italy; meanwhile, Ferdinand's edict virtually eradicated all Jews from southern Italy (where their presence is sparse even today).

In 1555 the papal bull *Cum nimis absurdum*, issued by Pope Paul IV, required that all Jews move to self-contained (often walled-off) areas within the cities where they lived. All sizeable cities under papal influence eventually established Jewish quarters, or *ghettos*, a term that probably derives from *geto,* the Renaissance Venetian word for "iron foundry" (such a foundry stood by Venice's Jewish quarter). The papal bull ushered in the ghetto era in Italy, which persisted for more than 300 years, until the last Jewish ghetto (in Rome) was emancipated in 1870.

Although significant variation existed with respect to living conditions within the ghettos, they were generally deplorable. The inhabitants became subject to frequent outbreaks of disease and, especially in Rome and the Papal States, were generally reduced to pauperdom. The conditions decimated the Jewish population, to a low of 20,000 by the mid-1600s (Della Pergola, p. 56).

Abolition of the Jewish ghettos coincided in most cases with the Risorgimento ("revival" or "renewal"), a process lasting from 1848 to 1870 and culminating in the establishment of a unified Italy, the first federation since the fall of the Roman Empire in 476. The new Italian state, officially consolidated in 1870, was quick to extend full citizenship to all Italians, including Jews—a policy that promptly won over the Italian Jews and fostered an enduring sense of allegiance to the state. This allegiance partly accounts, in later years, for Jewish support from some quarters for the Fascist government. Jews like Primo Levi's grandparents, capitalized on their newfound freedom and equal rights to enter various domains: the universities, professions previously closed to them (like law and medicine), the military, and politics. Or they established their own businesses (Levi's paternal grandfather was a civil engineer, while his maternal grandfather was a cloth merchant). Many Italian Jews served with distinction in World War I, including Levi's father, Cesare.

Primo Levi: family life, education, and Resistance activities. Cesare Levi (1878-1941) was an electrical engineer and his wife, Ester (1895-1991)—Primo Levi's mother—was a housewife. They lived in a stylish apartment in the center of Turin, the capital of Piedmont in northern Italy. The family (Primo had a younger sister, Anna Maria) was highly assimilated and steeped in Italian classical culture. Levi himself attended a classical high school, where he studied works by Dante Alighieri, Ludovico Ariosto, Giacomo Leopardi, Alessandro Manzoni, and other canonical authors, as well as Greek and Latin literature. Many of these authors would be referenced in *Survival in Auschwitz* and in Levi's subsequent writings. Even more passionate about science than he was about literature, Levi pursued a chemistry degree at the University of Turin, completing it in 1941. At that time, the Racial Laws had been in effect for three years, complicating his search for a thesis advisor and requiring the annotation "of the Jewish race" after his name on his diploma.

Levi took up employment as an industrial chemist in the Lombardy region, first in Lanza and then in Milan. In 1942, with Italy at war on the side of Nazi Germany and the Allies about to land in Sicily, Levi, together with a group of Turinese friends, made contact with the Resistance and joined the clandestine *Partito d'Azione* (Action Party). They became partisans, bent on defeating the Italian Fascist-Nazi war effort. In July 1943 Mussolini was ousted from power as leader of Italy by his own party but, with Nazi connivance, managed to flee north where he set up a rump government, the Italian Social Republic.

Meanwhile, Field Marshall Pietro Badoglio governed the country as a whole; Badoglio dissolved the Fascist Party and, on October 13, 1943, declared war on Nazi Germany, Italy's erstwhile ally. Levi and his friends at this point joined a partisan cell centered in the mountains, in the northern Val d'Aosta Alps. Completely unprepared and ill-equipped, they were arrested on December 13, 1943. The authorities had Levi deported to a holding camp in Carpi-Fossoli (near Modena) run by Republican (Fascist) guards and, from there, in February 1944—once the camp was turned over to Nazi guards—to Auschwitz. *Survival in Auschwitz* begins on the eve of Levi's deportation and covers the next 11 months of his life, from February 22, 1944, until Auschwitz was liberated, on January 27, 1945.

Auschwitz: anatomy of a concentration camp. Auschwitz, a complex of three main camps plus smaller satellite camps, was located near Cracow, Poland. It was the largest of the Nazi concentration camps, and the most infamous of the six camps devoted to extermination. Nearly all of the roughly 8,800 Jews deported from Italy and the Italian territories were sent directly from Italy to Auschwitz; afterwards, some, like Primo Levi, were assigned to smaller camps within the Auschwitz complex or to independent concentration camps (like Flossenberg, Gross-Rosen, etc.).

Auschwitz I was established in 1940 as a penal camp, though even then it featured a gas chamber and crematorium (used to kill prisoners and then incinerate their bodies to dispose of them). Auschwitz I became infamous for the torturous pseudo-medical experiments conducted on inmates (often children) by Dr. Josef Mengele. Auschwitz II, also called Auschwitz-Birkenau or just Birkenau, was the largest subdivision and included sections for women, men, Roma (Gypsies), and families deported from the Theresienstadt ghetto in Czechoslovakia. Most of the mass murder by gassing (with Zyklon B gas) was carried out in Auschwitz-Birkenau's four large gas chambers.

Trains arrived nearly daily at Auschwitz I and II, carrying Jews and other prisoners from those European countries that had fallen to the Nazi invasion (Poland, Hungary, Czechoslovakia, France, Italy, and others). Prisoners were either sent to the camp to be used as slave labor or sent directly to the gas chambers to be killed. When the camp was overcrowded, whole transports of Jews were sent directly to the gas chambers. Of the roughly 1.3 million people deported to Auschwitz, "[a]t least 1.1 million Jews were killed [there]. Other victims included between 70,000

and 75,000 Poles, 21,000 Roma, and about 15,000 Soviet prisoners of war" ("Auschwitz"). Of the roughly 8,800 Jews deported from Italy and its territories to Nazi *lagers* [camps], [only] about 1,000 (or 12 percent) survived; the survival rate for Italian Jews in Auschwitz was half that, 6 percent (Picciotto Fargion, pp. 25-26; Gutman, p. 1801). The number in Primo Levi's company who survived was about half again as large; of the 650 Italian Jews deported along with Levi in his transport, just 23 (or 3.5 percent) survived.

Primo Levi was tattooed, initiated, and given a chemistry exam, which he passed. Afterward, he was assigned to Auschwitz III, or Buna (also called Monowitz), an outlying camp where German manufacturer I. G. Farben managed a synthetic rubber plant. Levi credited his survival to a series of lucky circumstances: first among them was his knowledge of his captors' language, German (part of the standard Italian university chemistry curriculum of the day) and his chemistry expertise (which eventually got him removed from manual labor and assigned to lab work). He also credited his survival to the material assistance provided by Lorenzo Perrone, a non-Jewish Italian "civilian laborer," who provided an extra daily ration of soup; to his friendship with Alberto Dalla Volta; and to the fact that he neither became seriously ill nor suffered a serious beating during his imprisonment. Of Lorenzo in particular he writes, "Thanks to Lorenzo, I managed not to forget that I myself was a man" (Levi, *Survival in Auschwitz*, p. 122).

Levi was still alive to greet the liberating Russian Army troops in January 1945 and was evacuated by them back to a Soviet DP (deported persons) camp. After several months of enforced idleness, Levi became impatient to return to Turin and began a five-month labyrinthine and picaresque journey through White Russia, the Ukraine, Romania, Hungary, and Austria. He traveled either alone or with occasional companions, on foot, by truck, and by train, arriving home in Italy on October 19, 1945 (the trip was the subject of his second book, *The Reawakening*). In Turin, amid a difficult readjustment to peacetime Italy and life after Auschwitz, Levi took up residence in his family's apartment, found work as an industrial chemist in a Turin paint factory, became engaged to his future wife, Lucia Morpurgo, and began transforming his memories and the few notes he took with him from Auschwitz into his first book, *Survival in Auschwitz*.

The Memoir in Focus

Content summary. *Survival in Auschwitz* comprises an author's preface, a poetic epigraph by Levi, and 17 short chapters, ranging in length from 4 to 22 pages. The author's preface is notable for three points: it opens with an homage to the "good fortune" that allowed Levi to be deported to Auschwitz late in the war, thus increasing his chances of survival (rarely do similar Holocaust memoirs include such preeminent paeans to luck). The preface goes on to state Levi's objective in writing: not to "formulate new accusations" but "rather, to furnish documentation for a quiet study of certain aspects of the human mind" (*Survival in Auschwitz*, p. 9). In conclusion Levi avows that "none of the facts are invented" (*Survival in Auschwitz*, p. 10). (That Levi felt compelled to add this assurance testifies to the skepticism with which many Holocaust survivors' stories were greeted in the immediate aftermath of World War II.)

The oft-studied poetic epigraph to *Survival in Auschwitz* (called "Shema" when published in Levi's *Collected Poems*, 1988, but here untitled) is one of Levi's very first writings upon returning to Turin. Composed on January 10, 1946, it evokes in its title ("Hear!" in Hebrew), its structure, and its lexicon the central prayer of Judaism (also called the Shema, found in Deuteronomy 6:4-9), an affirmation of the centrality of God. Levi alters the prayer to admonish his readers to "[m]editate that this [the Holocaust] came about" and warns them to repeat his message about the destruction of man in the Holocaust, lest harm befall them and their children abandon them (*Survival in Auschwitz*, p. 11). The original title of *Survival in Auschwitz* comes from the poem's fifth verse (*Considerate se questo è un uomo*; "Consider if this is a man").

The first chapter, "The Journey," opens with the details of Levi's capture by Fascist militiamen on December 13, 1943. The author immediately asserts the "justice" of his subsequent fate, Auschwitz included, in that it is in line with the *lager* doctrine he is about to learn: "he who errs, pays." Once captured, Levi prefers to offer up that he is a Jew rather than admit to being a partisan: the latter would lead to torture or death, while the former earns him a trip to the Carpi-Fossoli holding camp. Soon, Nazi SS officers (Nazi Germany's special police force) take over the running of the camp from the Italian Fascists and the inmates are told to prepare for deportation. In watching a group of devout Libyan Jews at prayer, Levi for the first time feels a direct connection to his ancient Jewish roots. On the other hand, when an SS officer refers to the Jewish prisoners as "pieces," he realizes the horrible metamorphosis that awaits him. Levi describes the transit to Auschwitz, the deaths along the way, and the incomprehensible, frantic scene as prisoners are separated into the able-bodied (who enter the camp) and the invalids (who are sent to the gas chambers). He almost expects to hear Charon—the ferryman to Hell in Dante's *Inferno*—shout, "Woe unto you, wicked spirits!" (Dante, *Inferno* 3.84).

Though a sign on the Auschwitz gates reads "Arbeit Macht Frei" (work gives freedom), Levi instead feels that he has reached bottom (thus, the title of the next chapter, "On the Bottom"). "This is hell," he writes (*Survival in Auschwitz*, p. 22). Levi and his campmates are shaved and tattooed (Levi would keep his tattoo, 174517, his whole life, as a reminder of Auschwitz). A veteran prisoner explains that they are in Monowitz in High Silesia, Poland, and that they will be expected to work. The showers suddenly burst on, followed by four SS officers shouting orders and throwing them ragged clothing and broken clogs. Levi feels transformed into one of the "phantoms" that he had glimpsed just the day before inside the camp. He meditates that "for the first time we became aware that our language lacks words to express this offence, the demolition of a man. . . . We had reached the bottom. It is not possible to sink lower than this" (*Survival in Auschwitz*, p. 26).

A cacophony of new words accosts him: *häftling* (prisoner), *kapo* (inmate overseer), *kommando* (work detail), and so forth. Their special meanings will become clear over time—to Levi and to the reader. One striking characteristic of this memoir is its linguistic heterogeneity: Levi uses a wealth of *lager*-specific terms (sometimes called *Lagerjargon*) as well as snippets of phrases in the languages heard at Auschwitz (German, Polish, Hungarian, Yiddish, French, and others). By doing so, he conveys not just the physical but also the cultural impact of the *lager*.

That the memoir manages to deliver a narrative punch in a foreign idiom becomes clear at the beginning of his internment. Thirsty, Levi reaches for an icicle, only to have a guard snatch it from him. "*Warum?*"—Why?—he asks. "*Hier ist kein warum* (there is no why here)" comes the reply (*Survival in Auschwitz*, p. 29). The incomprehensibility and injustice of the concentration-camp system resound in the reply, gnawing at

Levi, the rational scientist. To stave off the demolition of the soul he recognizes in some inmates, he sets out to document and, perhaps, determine the "why" of the Holocaust. Primarily he aims to investigate human nature in the crucible of Auschwitz: what makes a man a man; how can he retain his humanity; how and under what circumstances does he lose it? Levi starts by describing the absurd Nazi rituals and the inmates' work assignments. He reveals, sadly, that the few Italian prisoners—scattered among Auschwitz's many barracks—soon cease their Sunday evening get-togethers because "it was so tiring to walk those few steps and then, meeting each other, to remember and to think. It was better not to think" (*Survival in Auschwitz*, p. 37).

Levi's "initiation" into camp life includes awareness of the perpetual linguistic Babel of the camp, where "bread," for example, is alternately referred to as "pane-Brot-Broit-chleb-pain-lechem-keny`er" (*Survival in Auschwitz*, p. 39). Fights, he learns, are the norm, and ironically in the shadows of crematoria prisoners are exhorted to wash their hands before eating. Levi meets a certain Steinlauf, who eloquently confides that he insists on maintaining personal hygiene, not for reasons of cleanliness *per se* but to resist becoming animal-like. Levi rejects such deliberately conceived practice and belief, asking, "would it not be better to acknowledge one's lack of a system?" (*Survival in Auschwitz*, p. 41). His portrait of Steinlauf is just the first in what will be a series of vivid portraits along the lines of medieval *exampla* (sketches used to point to a moral). Another intense portrait profiles Null Achtzehn, a man with no name other than his number "Zero Eighteen": "as if everyone was aware that only man is worthy of a name, and that Null Achtzehn was no longer a man" (*Survival in Auschwitz*, p. 42). Levi often finds himself working alongside this shell of a man.

One day, while carrying dangerously heavy loads from the train to a storehouse, Levi injures his foot, precipitating a trip to the *ka-be* (*krankenbau*, or infirmary). His destination is fraught with peril, since both disease and "selections" (for the gas chamber) are rife in the infirmary; making matters worse, foot injuries (which imply an inability to work) are often the first step in the chain of events that leads to the crematorium. Indeed, a *ka-be* inmate pitilessly tells Levi, "*Du Jude, kaputt. Du schnell Krematorium fertig* (You Jew, finished. You soon ready for crematorium)" (*Survival in Auschwitz*, p. 49). Miraculously, Levi emerges healed from the *ka-be,* but not before

experiencing the particular "limbo" it represents or, in conversations with longer-term prisoners, revealing that he still naively *disbelieves* (even after weeks in the camp) in the existence of selections, gassings, and crematoriums. Perhaps, suggests Levi, the "missing" inmates have been transferred to other camps? "He does not want to understand," the older prisoners irritably conclude (*Survival in Auschwitz*, p. 53).

During the winter of 1944, Levi befriends Alberto Dalla Volta, which turns out to be a real boon, since, contrary to *lager* ethos of each man for himself, the two decide to divide any material gains (extra soup or items to barter). Both come out the stronger for the arrangement. As the fall days become shorter, the prisoners get more time to sleep. Levi is tormented by a recurring dream, simple in its structure, but devastating (and prescient) in its content: his sister (Anna Paola), his friends, and many others listen to him telling his story of Auschwitz—the hunger, the lice-control, the beatings, and the rest. Levi feels intense pleasure in being home among friends and having so much to recount, then notices that his listeners are completely indifferent. His own sister gets up and walks away without a word. At this point Levi feels intense grief and awakens. (The dream foreshadows the real-life indifference that greeted Italian Holocaust survivors on their return to Italy. A meager group—less than 800—they were totally overshadowed by the hundreds of thousands of returning solders and partisans, and their stories remained untold for many years.)

Regulating the rhythm of sleeping and dreams is the harsh reality of work. One day Levi finds himself carrying 175-pound sleepers—structural parts—back and forth through a field of soft mud; another time his work squad must transport cast-iron supports; yet another time, push wagons and break stones. Although Levi was later to write about work as ennobling man (in *The Monkey's Wrench* [1978]), here work portends maiming, injuries, beatings, and exhaustion. Indeed the rations given to Auschwitz inmates are not calculated for long-term survival and the inmates are literally worked to death. Levi writes, "The Lager *is* hunger: we ourselves are hunger, living hunger" (*Survival in Auschwitz*, p. 74). A "good day" (in the chapter of the same name) means a day when his *kommando* "organizes" an extra 11 gallons of soup. "What more could one want?" Levi asks sardonically but also sincerely. He describes sitting down to eat with the German verb *fressen*, "the way of eating of

Railroad tracks leading up to the Nazi concentration camp Auschwitz-Birkenau in Poland.

animals," not *essen*, "the human way of eating" (*Survival in Auschwitz*, p. 76).

If the concentration camps were a "Germanic social organism," as Levi contends, then they also included a range of types, with two at their extremes, the "drowned" and the "saved," the title of a chapter (*Survival in Auschwitz*, pp. 83, 87). The drowned are represented by the *muselmänner*, "the weak, the inept, those doomed to selection," like Null Achtzen. The saved are represented by the *kleine Nummer* ("low numbers," or camp veterans—referring to their low tattoo numbers), the *organisators*, *kombinators*, and *lagerältesteren* (prisoner-directors)—all the various kinds of *prominenten* (prominent persons) in the camp. Levi's memoir reaches a conclusion about the *prominenten*, or, more generally, about human nature:

> If one offers a position of privilege to a few individuals in a state of slavery, exacting in exchange the betrayal of a natural solidarity with their comrades, there will certainly be someone who will accept. He will be withdrawn from the common law and will become untouchable; the more power that he is given, the more he will be consequently hateful and hated.
>
> (*Survival in Auschwitz*, p. 91)

In the chapter "The Drowned and the Saved," the memoir offers a rogue's gallery of such hateful individuals, beginning with Schepschel, a petty *kombinator* who didn't hesitate to condemn one of his partners in crime to a flogging in order to gain favor with the *blockältester* (block director). There is also Alfred L., an erstwhile industrialist who, in the camp, coldly uses his former prestige to advance in the camp hierarchy. Two portraits stand out in particular. Elias Lindzin is a dwarf of prodigious strength, cast-iron stomach, exceptional capacity for work, and a hair-trigger temper. He is both admired and feared. With regard to Levi's inquiry into who is a "man," he writes, "We can now ask who is this man Elias. If he is a madman, incomprehensible and para-human. . . . Or if he is perhaps a product of the camp itself, what we will all become if we do not die in the camp, and if the camp itself does not end first. . . . In the Lager, Elias prospers and is triumphant" (*Survival in Auschwitz*, pp. 97-98). Another who triumphs in the camp is Henri. Unlike Elias's brute strength, Henri has as his weapon his civilized façade and capacities for "organization, pity and theft" (*Survival in Auschwitz*, p. 98). He can be warm when he calculates that warmth is needed and evinces compassion from the *kapos* whenever he can. Levi reserves his harshest judgment for Henri, writing, "I know that Henri is living today. I would give much to know his life as a free man, but I do not want to see him again" (*Survival in Auschwitz*, p. 100).

Thus, the first nine chapters of the memoir are dedicated to narrating the literal and epistemological demands of the *lager*, and to Levi's process of acculturation. The chapters concern themselves especially with his acculturation as an Italian Sephardic Jew in a primarily Eastern European and Ashkenazi populace (Ashkenazi and Sephardi being the two main ethnic branches of world Jewry), relaying the process of acculturation as a voyage downwards towards "the bottom." Subsequently Levi's fortunes change when he is removed from outdoor manual labor to indoor lab work in support of Buna's synthetic rubber production (Levi comments on the bitter irony that despite hundreds of thousands of deaths in the name of this elusive goal, no synthetic rubber was ever produced there).

The pages devoted to Levi's chemical examination (in chapter 10) are some of the most densely packed in the book. The author conveys, with restraint and an eye for detail, the absurdity of interrogating half-starving, demoralized Auschwitz inmates in German on the finer points of chemical reactions. Levi struggles to recall his university learning and is momentarily euphoric when he realizes that his exam may have gone well. His status as prisoner is brutally recalled, however, when a guard named Alex escorts Levi back to his barracks. His hand dirty with some grease, Alex wipes it on Levi's shoulder as if he were nothing but a rag. "[H]e would be amazed, the poor brute Alex," Levi writes, "if someone told him that today, on the basis of this action, I judge him . . . and the innumerable others like him, big and small, in Auschwitz and everywhere" (*Survival in Auschwitz*, p. 108).

As the summer and fall of 1944 approach, so do rumors that the Allies are nearing Auschwitz and the war will soon be over. However, October comes and so does the now-infamous, massive Auschwitz "selection" of that same month, decreed to relieve overcrowding. Levi is spared, as is a prisoner named Kuhn. Praying aloud, Kuhn thanks God "because he has not been chosen," heedless of poor Beppo the Greek in the bunk next to him, a 20-year-old lad who knows he will be gassed the next day (*Survival in Auschwitz*, p. 129). Levi is irate at Kuhn's arrogance and insensitivity. He calls his prayer an "abomination" and says, "If I [were] God, I would spit at Kuhn's prayer" (*Survival in Auschwitz*, p. 130).

Levi spends the winter of '44-45 sheltered in the chemistry lab. After what he has been through, it hardly seems like working. He also participates in the camp black market, stealing and selling soap and gasoline. Working side by side with non-Jewish Polish and Ukrainian women, a strange thing happens: he becomes aware as if for the first time of how distant he is from them, how close he has come to the "bottom," and another side of him—the non-camp side—painfully begins to come out of hibernation. When in January 1945 Levi hears the advancing Russian troops in the distance, he has ever so slightly emerged from a cocoon of brutalizing survival instincts.

Just before liberation, the SS abandon Auschwitz, leaving the sickest prisoners behind (including Levi, who had come down with a providential case of scarlet fever). They take along about 66,000 prisoners (including Levi's friend Alberto) on what is to become a death march (more than 15,000 will perish on the way) (Laquer, p. 44). In the days before January 27, when the Soviets arrive at Auschwitz, Levi and two other abandoned *men* (meaning, in Levi's connotation, humane individuals)—Charles and Arthur—forge bonds of friendship, care for the sick in their hospital ward, and reawaken long-dormant feelings of altruism and concern. Bitterness mixes with joy in the end:

> It is man who kills, man who creates or suffers injustice; it is no longer man who, having lost all restraint, shares his bed with a corpse. Whoever waits for his neighbor to die in order to take his piece of bread is, albeit guiltless, further from the model of thinking man than the most primitive pygmy or the most vicious sadist. Part of our existence lies in the feelings of those near to us. This is why the experience of someone who has lived for days during which man was merely a thing in the eyes of man is non-human. We three were for the most part immune from it, and we owe each other mutual gratitude.
>
> (*Survival in Auschwitz*, pp. 171-72)

Survival in Auschwitz ends with the words "Arthur has reached his family happily and Charles has taken up his teacher's profession again; we have exchanged long letters and I hope to see him again one day" (*Survival in Auschwitz*, p. 173).

From Dante's *Divine Comedy* to the Holocaust. An extraordinary chapter of *Survival in Auschwitz* has drawn attention from scholars and readers alike because of its rich layers of meaning, luminously spare writing (just over six pages long), and illuminating reference to a classic of world literature, Dante's ***Divine Comedy*** (1310-14; also in *WLAIT 7: Italian Literature and Its Times*). As Levi does elsewhere, he lets Dante speak in his stead; Dante's description of Hell stands in for a description of the incomprehensible world of Auschwitz.

"The Canto of Ulysses" chapter begins with Levi's work detail cleaning the inside of an underground oil tank. Working alongside Levi is Jean (Jean Samuel), the *pikolo* (messenger-clerk) of the detail, a well-liked 17-year-old from Alsace who is fluent in French and German but not Italian. Though Jean is a *prominent*, he and Levi have become friends. That day Jean uses his power to have Levi accompany him on *essenholen* (ration retrieval) duty—carrying the daily vats of soup. This is a prize assignment indeed since it means "a pleasant walk there without a load, and the ever-welcome chance of going near the kitchens" (*Survival in Auschwitz*, p. 111). Along the way Jean mentions his desire to learn Italian and Levi agrees to teach him, surprising even himself with his choice of text, Canto 26 of Dante's *Inferno* from the *Divine Comedy*: "The Canto of Ulysses. Who knows how or why it comes into my mind. . . . If Jean is intelligent, he will understand. He *will* understand—today I feel capable of so much" (*Survival in Auschwitz*, p. 112).

In the *Divine Comedy* Dante considered Ulysses a noble sinner—an ancient hero to be revered poetically but, as a pre-Christian, to be condemned theologically. He is placed in the eighth *bolgia* (circle) of Hell, along with the "evil counsellors" "who have used their high mental gifts for guile" (Sinclair in Dante, p. 329). As a Jewish author, Levi is less interested in Dante's reasons for condemning Ulysses than in the Greek warrior's high mental gifts. He is particularly drawn to Ulysses' brashness, daring, and thirst for knowledge. Levi too seeks to know his world—in his case, a brutal concentration-camp world. Ulysses' reckless attempt to burst beyond the Strait of Gibraltar—the ancient Greek boundary of the end of the known world—has its parallel in Levi's own incessant philosophical questioning. And if, in the end, the Greek's ship is smashed to bits and Levi is answered "there is no why here," each remains persuaded that the quest for knowledge is central to human experience.

It is under the aegis of enlightenment that Levi begins his Italian lesson with Jean. Translating bits of the Ulysses canto helps Levi to comprehend and convey his own situation in the Nazi *lager*. The autobiographical often intersects with the allegorical, as the Polish Carpathian Mountains outside Auschwitz recall the Italian Alps outside Turin, and in turn Dante's Mountain of Purgatory—"a mountain, grey / With distance" (Dante in *Survival in Auschwitz*, p. 114).

At the same time, harking back to a central text of Italian literature, the *Divine Comedy* (and through it to Homer's *Odyssey*, one of the oldest texts of the Western world), Levi reaffirms the value of civilization in a cosmos from which it is notably absent. Through Dante, Levi defines man as a creature of culture and knowledge, as well as order and justice. Ulysses exhorts his crew to "Think of your breed; for brutish ignorance / Your mettle was not made; you were made men, / To follow after knowledge and excellence" (Dante in *Survival in Auschwitz*, p. 113). For Levi, the exhortation validates the mind's potential to soar beyond its confines—even the confines of Auschwitz. The fact that Levi's Dante adventure takes place within the context of his friendship with Jean gives the adventure added significance; it is the rare instance of human solidarity (with Alberto, Lorenzo, Charles, Arthur, and Jean) that sustains him in camp and that constitutes a form of resistance against the Nazi plan to destroy man.

Canto 26 ends with a whirlwind rising up and striking Ulysses' ship. "And three times round she went in roaring smother / With all the waters; at the fourth the poop / Rose, and the prow went down, as pleased Another" (Dante in *Survival in Auschwitz*, p. 114). In the *Inferno* Ulysses and his men are sunk, as ordained from on high (by God, or "Another"). Levi's chapter ends on a similar note. He quotes these lines from Dante, just after telling Jean he regrets that he cannot recall the preceding rhyme. Significantly, they include the verse "We rejoiced, but soon our joy was turned to grief" (Dante, *Inferno* 26.134). Levi too rejoices at remembering most of the canto, sharing it with Jean, and enjoying the momentary mental escape it affords him from Auschwitz, but his joy becomes grief shortly thereafter. In the soup line, Jean informs him of the day's soup: "*Choux et navets. Kaposzta és rèpak*" (cabbages and turnips). Levi replies by invoking the line from Dante's *Inferno*, "'And over our heads the hollow seas closed up'" (*Survival in Auschwitz*, p. 115). His words reverberate with the disillusionment of a man fully back in Auschwitz but who, by his very act of quotation, still clings to the life raft of literature.

Sources and literary context. Upon his return from Auschwitz in October 1945, Levi found an Italy in ruins after a disastrous ground and aerial war fought within its borders by the Allied and Axis powers, and an equally wrenching civil war fought between the remains of the Fascist militia and the partisan irregulars. It was in this climate that Primo Levi found work outside Turin in the Duco-Montecatini paint factory and began his memoir. The seed for the memoir came from stories he told to whomever would listen upon his return to Italy, most immediately the people at the factory, where he also lived and drafted his manuscript: "I wrote *Survival in Auschwitz* without giving [style] a second thought: at night, in the lab, on the train, wherever I happened to find myself" (Sodi, "An Interview with Primo Levi," p. 366). At night and on weekends, he wrote feverishly, finishing the first draft in several months.

FROM MOUTH TO HAND: GENESIS OF A MEMOIR

"Well, when I had just come back from the camp, . . . I had an impelling need to tell this story to whomever at all! I had just gotten a job as a chemist in a little paint factory near Turin, and the workers there considered me something of a harmless kook because . . . I told my story to anyone and everyone, at the drop of a hat, from the plant manager to the yardman, even if they had other things to do. . . . And then I would type into the night (because I also lived in the factory). I typed every night, and this was considered even crazier!"

(Levi in Sodi, "An Interview with Primo Levi," p. 356)

Levi acknowledged a mix of literary models for *Survival in Auschwitz*, ranging from the *Divine Comedy* to his weekly lab reports. He admitted in a 1985 interview, "I've constructed a sort of legend around that book, that I wrote it without a plan, that I wrote it on impulse, that I wrote it without reflecting at all." In actual fact, he went on to observe, "writing is never spontaneous" (Levi in Belpoliti, p. 4). His memoir, he realized, is actually full of literature: "When the time came . . . to write this book, and I did have a pathological need to write it, I found inside myself a whole 'programme.' And it was that literature I'd studied more or less unwillingly, the Dante I'd had to do in high school, the Italian classics and so forth" (Levi in Belpoliti, p. 4).

Beyond helping initiate a flow of Holocaust memoirs, *Survival in Auschwitz* follows in the tradition of such nonfiction works of Italian literature as Italian patriot Silvio Pellico's memoirs of his prison years, *Le mie prigioni* (1832; My Prisons); novelist and man of letters Alessandro Manzoni's *Storia della colonna infame* (1840-42; History of the Column of Infamy), a reconstruction of the Milan plague of 1629 with particular emphasis on its moral ramifications; and author

and partisan Emilio Lussu's *Un anno sull'altipiano* (1938; A Year on the High Plains), an evocation of his experiences as a soldier in World War I. After Levi's memoir came other Italian first-hand accounts of the Holocaust, such as Liana Millu's *Il fumo di Birkenau* (1947; Smoke over Birkenau), Giuliana Tedeschi's *C'e' un punto sulla terra* (1988; There Is a Place on Earth [first published in 1947 as *Questo povero corpo*, or This Poor Body]), and Bruno Piazza's *Perche' gli altri dimenticano* (1956; Because the Others Forget).

Publication and reception. Levi first brought his manuscript to the Turin publishing house of Einaudi in 1947. Its editor-in-chief, Giulio Einaudi, rejected the manuscript on the recommendation of Levi's friend and fellow Turinese Jew, Natalia Ginzburg (herself an author of distinction) in the belief that the time was not yet ripe for a Holocaust memoir. Indeed the publishing market was then flooded with memoirs of the great suffering endured by Italian troops. With over 200,000 Italians returning from World War II, there was a ready-made audience for such works, eclipsing the interest that a memoir by an Italian Jewish concentration-camp survivor might have. On a global level, the word "Holocaust" had not yet entered into the world's vocabulary and another decade would pass before systematic studies of the Holocaust were undertaken.

Levi persisted, nevertheless, finding a company that published his manuscript in 1948—De Silva publishing house, owned by former-partisan-turned-editor Franco Antonicelli. The work received favorable reviews in five Italian newspapers, including a review on May 6 in *L'Unità* (Unity) by Italo Calvino, who would go on to become Italy's most influential postwar author (see **The Path to the Spiders' Nests**, also in *WLAIT 7: Italian Literature and Its Times*). Nonetheless, few of Levi's initial readers came from outside Turin. De Silva printed 2,500 copies of the memoir and sold 1,400. The remainder, stocked in a Florence warehouse, was destroyed in a 1966 flood.

After De Silva declined to publish a second edition, Levi returned to Einaudi, in the wake of a popular 1955 Turin exhibit on deportation. This time Einaudi said "yes" and brought out a new, slightly longer edition in 1958. The first Einaudi press run of 2,000 copies sold out and a second was called for; *Survival in Auschwitz* has never been out of print since. In 1959 English translations appeared in Great Britain and the United States; two years later a German edition—which Levi personally oversaw—appeared. Other translations followed. In 1976 *Survival in Auschwitz* was adopted into the national middle-school curriculum in Italy and a special version annotated by Levi was published. By 1995 nearly 1.5 million copies had been published in Italy, and sales abroad continue to be strong.

Levi was not alive to witness the extent of his work's success. On April 11, 1987, he died in his apartment building in Turin. The death was ruled a suicide, but some friends and scholars continue to argue that it was instead accidental.

Over the past 50 years, *Survival in Auschwitz* has emerged as one of the preeminent works of Holocaust narrative published in any language, and Primo Levi as one of the world's most compelling thinkers on the Holocaust. In the words of the American critic Irving Howe, Levi's is "the voice of a man struggling to retrieve the sense of what it means in the twentieth century to be, or become, a *mensh* [Yiddish for "man," used to signify a decent person]"; "How," the critic wonders, "would you say that in Italian?" (Howe in Levi, p. 16).

—Risa Sodi

For More Information

Belpoliti, Marco, and Robert Gordon, eds. *The Voice of Memory: Interviews, 1961-87.* Trans. Robert Gordon. Cambridge: Polity, 2001.

Dante Alighieri. *Inferno.* In *The Divine Comedy.* Trans. John D. Sinclair. London: Oxford University Press, 1971.

Della Pergola, Sergio. *Anatomia dell'ebraismo italiano: Caratteristiche demografiche, economiche, sociali, religiose e politiche di una minoranza.* Assisi/Rome: Beniamino Carucci Editore, 1976.

Gutman, Israel, ed. *Encyclopedia of the Holocaust.* New York: Macmillan, 1990.

Hughes, H. Stuart. *Prisoners of Hope: The Silver Age of the Italian Jews, 1924-1974.* Cambridge, Mass.: Harvard University Press, 1983.

Laquer, Walter, ed. *The Holocaust Encyclopedia.* New Haven: Yale University Press, 2001.

Levi, Primo. *If Not Now, When?* Trans. William Weaver. New York: Summit, 1982.

———. *Survival in Auschwitz* and *The Reawakening.* Trans. Stuart Woolf. New York: Summit, 1985.

Picciotto Fargion, Liliana. *Il libro della memoria: Gli ebrei deportati dall'Italia 1943-1945.* Milan: Mursia editore, 1991.

Sodi, Risa. *A Dante of Our Time: Primo Levi and Auschwitz.* New York: Peter Lang, 1990.

———. "An Interview with Primo Levi." *Partisan Review,* Summer 1987, 355-66.

Thomson, Ian. *Primo Levi.* London: Hutchinson, 2002.

United States Holocaust Memorial Museum Holocaust Learning Center. "Auschwitz." http://www.ushmm.org/wlc/en/index.php.

Teresa

by

Neera

Anna Zuccari was born in 1846 in Milan to a middle-class family. A defining moment in her young life came at the age of 10 when her mother died. Although Anna loved and admired her father, it was partially because of this loss that she characterized her childhood as isolated, dreary, and emotionally deprived. With no mother or sisters and few friends, she spent most of her time alone and had little contact with the outside world. Her only salvation was her imagination, which she nourished by reading literature and writing stories. But even these activities, which can be considered her education, she pursued on her own, since formal education beyond the lower grades was not a realistic option for most girls at that time. In 1871 Anna married Adolfo Radius, a lawyer, and together they had two children. She began to write professionally, adopting the pseudonym "Neera." Despite a modest and relatively secluded adult life, Neera became one of the most popular and productive female writers of her day. A novelist, short-story writer, and essayist, she participated in Milan's lively literary and art world and corresponded with major authors of the era (such as Luigi Capuana, Giovanni Verga, and Antonio Fogazzaro). Neera's first novels, published in the 1870s, focused mainly on the subjects of adulterous women and their punishments or on virtuous women and their rewards. Her later novels, corresponding thematically to her nonfiction writing, concentrate on moral questions. In between these two phases came *Teresa*, Neera's most famous and what is commonly thought of

---

> ## THE LITERARY WORK
>
> A novel set in northern Italy in the late nineteenth century; published in Italian (as *Teresa*) in 1886, in English in 1998.
>
> ## SYNOPSIS
>
> As Teresa comes of age in a traditional, provincial middle-class family, she endures many emotional hardships in order to conform to her father's rigid ideas about her future.

---

as her finest work, in which she experiments with elements of *verismo*, a type of literary realism influenced by French naturalism. In *Teresa* and the two other novels that comprise this phase, *Lydia* (1886) and *L'indomani* (1890; The Next Day), Neera explores the social factors that led to oppressive conditions for the late-nineteenth-century woman in provincial Italy and her limited options for coping with them.

Events in History at the Time the Novel Takes Place

The legacy of the Risorgimento: literacy and education. The long process of transforming Italy from a disparate group of separate territories governed by foreign rulers into a single, unified nation (known as the Risorgimento, or Unification) came to a close in 1870. It ended when Rome was incorporated and declared the country's capital city, but in truth the event marked a beginning more than an end. Once Italy was politically unified, politicians had to embark on the job of creating an economically, socially, and culturally cohesive nation. There were many problems to address: a huge national debt; a lack of transportation and industry; an unfair system of taxation that weighed heavily on the lower class; a hopelessly poor standard of living (particularly, but not exclusively, among the rural peasantry); and a resistance to assimilating to a set of standardized customs on the part of regions that had spoken their own languages and cultivated their own unique traditions for hundreds of years.

Hoping to alleviate the new nation's problems, the government promoted education and literacy by pushing strongly to give the lower and middle classes better access to education. The Casati Law of 1859 extended the right to a primary education not only to boys but also to girls, requiring both groups to attend two years of elementary school so they would at least learn to read and write. While the law was not always enforced, it, and similar mandates, resulted in a surge in the number of literate people among the general Italian population between 1870 and 1900 (although the incidence of illiteracy among women was still higher than among men). In other words, there was a much larger reading public, which, in turn, required a greater quantity of reading materials. To meet the need, publishers produced more novels and introduced more political and cultural magazines. Newspapers emerged too, in the major cities.

These new literary resources contributed to a marked decline in what some saw as Italy's insular unawareness of cultural developments outside its own land. While men benefited more than women from this cultural expansion, in this period Italy also saw the rise of various publications run by women and devoted to women's issues in the new Italy. For example, *La donna* (Woman), founded in 1868 by Gualberta Beccari, whose father was active in the wars for independence, gave voice to the whole range of thought by women activists. In *Teresa*, Neera depicts the big city and its dynamic culture using two young male characters, Teresa's brother and her would-be fiancé, Orlandi, through whom Teresa lives vicariously. The boys' higher education and Orlandi's participation in journalism in Milan highlight the deprivation she suffers because of her gender and location. While in Milan and other Italian cities, women were beginning to attend universities, work outside the home, and even become doc-

tors, those in the still very traditional provinces (like Teresa) were less fortunate.

Milan in particular was a relatively progressive place for Italian women in the late nineteenth century, and women who hailed from the city played a central role in the Italian feminist movement. Traditionally the city had exhibited less oppressive thought about women's social roles than other areas, which contributed to the fact that already at this time women constituted a significant part of the workforce in that city. In fact, the census of 1881 tells us that 54 percent of girls over nine years old and 73 percent of young women between 15 and 20 in Milan had jobs outside the home (Buttafuoco, p. 37). Typically they worked in factories, as seamstresses, launderesses and as office assistants, and often they held managerial positions as well. Of course, women of the lower classes had been working for a living for quite some time; it was the bold entry of middle-class women into the workforce around this time that constituted an important advancement in the struggle for women's independence.

One factor that contributed to the phenomenon of middle-class women's obtaining jobs that would allow them to support themselves (although their salaries were still far lower than those of their male counterparts) was access to education. Such access was more readily available in the cosmopolitan cities of the North than in the South or the rural areas of the provinces. Italian universities began accepting women in 1874, although some professors refused to allow them into their classrooms. Slowly the progress continued. Just three years before the novel takes place, in 1883, secondary schools for boys opened their classrooms to women. Such legal victories, however, provided opportunities, not mandates. It remained up to a girl's family to decide whether or not she should be allowed to benefit from these advances, and widespread acceptance of them was a slow process. In the mid-1880s, when the novel takes place, it was very unlikely that a provincial family would send a young woman, who could be used to work at home, away to be educated or to work in the big city.

Women and the Risorgimento. Despite the fact that after the Unification more girls could expect to be taught to read and write, their education in post-Unification Italy was not exactly designed to emancipate them from their established roles of dutiful wife and mother. In fact, a girl's education was often aimed at instilling conservative values in her so that she could better play her part in strengthening the family unit and passing on a strong moral education to her children. To be sure, there were attempts during this time to gain rights and legal protections for women: bills "proposed (and defeated) to . . . reform the patriarchal character of Italian family law"; Anna Maria Mozzoni's formation of the League Promoting Women's Interests; and Mozzoni's 1870 translation of English writer John Stuart Mill's *The Subjection of Women*, which warns society of the dangers in *not* allowing women more opportunity (Sbragia, p. 298). Beyond all these efforts, there were even literary studies like Neera's *Teresa*. They paled, however, against the conditioning of women into traditional roles. All over the country, not only in the provinces but in the cities as well, women were constantly faced with the backlash of cultural conservatism. In certain regions, such as Lombardy (of which Milan is the capital), some women enjoyed more rights under previous governments than under the "liberal" administration of unified Italy. Many women had experienced a degree of respect and autonomy in the public sphere during the Unification movement, when they worked on every level alongside men to free their country from foreign rulers. This advance was only temporary, though.

The infant country's central government enacted the New Code of 1865, conferring all familial authority onto husbands and fathers. Article 131 concisely stated that "The husband is the head of the household and the husband-wife relationship must be founded on the wife's recognition of her husband's authority" (Graziosi, p. 9; trans. A. Boylan). This codification of male dominance gave men the sole control over all family finances, including their wives' dowries and any other of their personal possessions, and it prevented women from having guardianship of their children. Also the code explicitly stated that women could not vote nor hold any public offices. Along with the code, lawyers' groups also successfully banned women from practicing law, which would have allowed them to challenge the same civil codes and perhaps reverse their denial of equal rights. Noted feminist Anna Maria Mozzoni (1837–1920) wrote that "since the unification of Italy we have gained a point or two in the code," but also lamented that "the senate, the nobility, the clergy, the queen [Margherita Teresa, wife of Umberto I]—who is very devout, very aristocratic and not very intelligent—hesitate at every reform measure" (Mozzoni in Stanton, pp. 447-48). The New Code had afforded women a few rights—like men, they were recognized as adults upon turning 21; they were allowed to write their own wills

and to inherit property under certain circumstances, such as if they were widowed; and they could enter into certain kinds of financial contracts, still regulated, of course, by their husbands. But Mozzoni condemned the code in general for driving women back "into the home, into solitude and into silence" (Mozzoni in Graziosi, p. 11). She saw the huge amount of work that lay ahead.

LA MAESTRA

There was one widely accepted profession for women in late-nineteenth-century Italy: that of teacher, or *maestra*. The occupation even came to be seen as a patriotic duty. Often it required young women to travel from the relatively well-off North to the impoverished South or to rural areas as part of an official attempt to bridge the gap between the country's economically disparate regions. In Neera's novel, Teresa's youngest sister, Ida, follows this path. From the start, the novel distinguishes Ida from her marriage-hungry sisters by establishing her superior intelligence and motivation. She seems unaffected by romance or marriage. This, coupled with the fact that she is her father's favorite, earns her the privilege of attending a special teachers' training school. The privilege allows her to escape Teresa's sad fate as well as the hollow life of her other sisters, who married because they had to conform to the social requirements of their time. But teaching, though it offered a woman a degree of self-sufficiency and freedom perhaps from a domineering family, was far from an ideal option. Young female teachers often had to contend with inferior schoolhouses, classrooms, and materials, as well as suspicious townspeople who showed hostility to outsiders. Of course, male teachers confronted the same obstacles, but the females earned only a fraction of the salary paid to their male counterparts.

Women's relegation to the domestic sphere was a social reality in Italy when Neera wrote *Teresa*. In the mid-to-late nineteenth century, women—particularly middle-class women—were given the all-important task of preserving the family unit, which, it was theorized, required them to stay out of the public sphere. Society prescribed this limitation in the belief that men have a natural ability to function rationally while women succumb to their emotions. In the words of one scholar, conservatives feared that women's ability to feel would, "if not held in check by

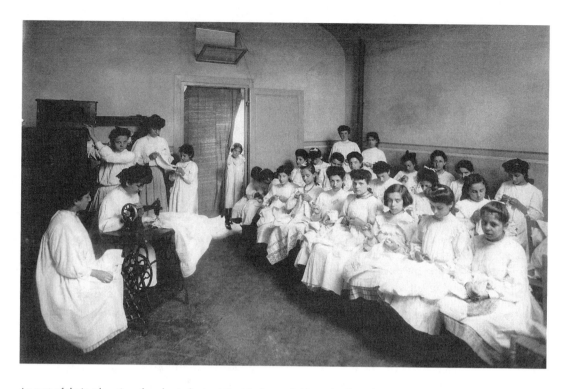

As part of their education, female students at the Via Santo Spirito school in Florence, Italy, attend sewing class c. 1910.

reason and masculine authority, and channeled towards the domestic and respectable feelings of spousal and maternal love, degenerate into unruly passion" (Re in Ascoli, p. 172). Many saw the unchecked female will as an imminent threat to the very fabric of society. With this in mind, there was "profound opposition to women's learning anything that may have taken their minds beyond the walls of the family home" during this period (Re in Ascoli, p. 165).

The official word of the Catholic Church was also working against women who aspired to obtain an existence outside the four walls of the home. In 1891 Pope Leo XIII published the *Rerum Novarum* on capital and labor, a papal letter aimed at establishing just relationships between employers and employees, widely distributed at a time when socialists were engaged in a furious battle for workers' rights and unrest was spreading through Italy. While in some parts the *Rerum Novarum* seems to be an invective from the Church against greed and mistreatment of workers, it also communicates a message of obedience and domesticity in relation to women. In paragraph 43 the Pope declares that women "are not suited for certain occupations; a woman is by nature fitted for home-work, and it is that which is best adapted at once to preserve her modesty and to promote the good bringing up of children and the well-being of the family" (Pope Leo XIII).

The role of science. Society in the second half of the nineteenth century greatly valued scientific progress. Scientists and intellectuals credited improvements in health, hygiene, transportation, and many other facets of the general standard of living to the theories of positivism (deems the only valid knowledge to be facts one can verify through the senses) and empiricism (relies solely on experience to verify knowledge). The two theories were based on the idea that observation and sensory experience constituted the foundation of the scientific method and that by observing the minute and the detailed, general patterns could be distinguished. It was a strategy that intellectuals of the day began to apply not only to scientific questions, but also to the social sciences and the arts. At the same time, in the medical and scientific world, there was also a great interest in deviant behavior and mental illness, particularly among women. Cesare Lombroso—an important figure in Milanese intellectual circles, who won renown as the founder of criminal anthropology (the study of the criminal mind) in Europe—was one of many scientists and intellectuals engaged in the study of abnormal female behavior, including hysteria. In his highly regarded view, hysteria resulted from a natural female proclivity. Because of the importance placed on science by many writers and theorists of literary movements, scientific and pseudo-scientific views of this kind filtered into the arts. The commingling of the two disciplines is evidenced by the fact that Neera and Lombroso frequented some of the same circles and actually collaborated on a nonfiction work, *Dizionario d'igiene per le famiglie* (1881; Dictionary of Hygiene for Families).

By the late nineteenth century the positivist trend had affected society as a whole. It had very distinct ramifications for women when used in ongoing debate about whether gender roles were biologically or socially determined. There was a tendency to enlist the new scientific methods to prove the biological, and thus, society reasoned, the inherent general inferiority of the female species. Texts like Darwin's *Descent of Man* (1871) and Lombroso's *La donna delinquente: La prostituta e la donna normale* (1893; *Criminal Women: The Prostitute and the Normal Woman*), purposefully or not, relegated women to an inferior intellectual status. This, in turn, led to their relegation to inferior social and economic positions, all in the name of biological science.

In the literary sphere, the emphasis on objective observation allowed authors to frankly portray the depressing and unjust conditions of daily life for the poor and oppressed without adhering to a certain political ideology. This was particularly important for female authors in that they could let "the facts" speak for themselves and point to these social ills as the underlying reasons for hysteria, physical weakness, and intellectual inferiority among women, all conditions traditionally attributed to their biology. The women writers observed conditions in a detached manner, distancing themselves from their subject and turning a critical eye on the social structures that led to female oppression and its mental and physical consequences. It was the strategy Neera invoked to write *Teresa:*

> For the first and only time in her career as a writer, Neera dares to study the dilemma of her heroines from the point of view of its relation to past conditioning: these women are not victims of their passions, they are victims of their upbringings. For the first and only time her characters acquire, if not great psychological depth as individuals, certainly well-documented case histories.
>
> (Kroha, p. 77)

The era gave rise to a preoccupation with hysterical women and an interest in the social roots of psychological distress in women. Reflected in Neera's fiction, the interest was shared by her friend Luigi Capuana, the main theorist of *verismo* (although another writer, Giovanni Verga, achieved renown as the style's most successful writer and most faithful interpreter). Capuana's style was heavily influenced by empirical science and the French naturalists. To fit strictly into the genre, a work had to be impersonal, use language suitable to the subject with an emphasis on dialogue rather than narration, contribute to the study of social class, invoke a scientific-style examination of the social environment, and subscribe to the positivist and naturalist view of the environment as a causative agent. Capuana

LA ZITELLA AND THE ECONOMICS OF MARRIAGE

If marriage and childbearing conferred the desired social status on women in late-nineteenth-century Italy, and were perceived as intimately connected to the survival of the Italian nation, then it is logical that the unmarried woman would be an outcast. Some even regarded her as a threat. In her defense, many women authors wrote about *la zitella* (the spinster) and the cruel treatment she received. Neera, in particular, was concerned about the fate of *la zitella*, an issue she addressed not only in novels like *Teresa* but also in various nonfiction essays. Neera laments the destiny of unmarried women: "This, after all, is the great injustice: society that deprives women of their natural rights whenever they have been unable to find a husband, makes fun of them if they remain spinsters, calling them mean, envious, sensual" (Neera in Pacifici, p. 57).

was also particularly interested in studying the causes and symptoms of mental illness. One of his best-known novels, *Giacinta* (1879), which he dedicated to Emile Zola, deals with a girl who grows up in a materially comfortable but affectionless upper-class family. She has deep psychological problems due to a traumatic childhood, including having been raped, and a complete inability to communicate with her distant, unmaternal, and promiscuous mother. The novel is a study of her inescapable descent into rebellion, then madness, and finally self-destruction as a result of her upbringing and a lack of emotional fulfillment. In a flashback that foreshadows the troubles of Giacinta's adult life, Capuana describes her tragic childhood:

> And the little girl, who didn't feel loved by anyone, often closed herself off in an out-of-the-way room; and in that storeroom—among cast-off gadgets, broken frames, her father's old hats,

slippers, empty bottles, chairs that could no longer stand up, falling-apart boxes filled with papers and books with creased pages—she easily found a way to make a racket without her mother even giving her a second thought.

(Capuana, p. 34; trans. A. Boylan)

Italian *verismo,* or naturalism, differed from the French variety in that the Italians focused more on style than on the scientific parts of the story and often highlighted peasants in the provinces rather than workers in a city. Moreover, the fiction frequently conveyed not a liberal but a conservative political outlook on the part of the writers. A similar concern for scientific observation of the social environment and female madness can be seen in the visual arts of the time, for example in Telemaco Signorini's painting *The Ward of the Madwomen at San Bonifazio in Florence* (1865-70).

MADNESS AND HYSTERIA

The late nineteenth century has been called "the golden age" of hysteria. In Italy, Cesare Lombroso's work on the subject, which led to his description of hysteria as "the exaggeration of womanhood," influenced a myriad of Italian writers to treat the theme during this time (Lombroso in Mazzoni, p. 157). Clinically speaking, hysteria is a psychological condition that produces physical symptoms for which there seems to be no organic cause. It is generally thought that the possible symptoms, ranging from paralysis, to respiratory problems, to intestinal distress, are defense mechanisms that transfer mental anguish to the physical body. While oftentimes hysteria and its close relation, madness, have been used to make the case for feminine weakness, in literature about women these conditions sometimes serve in an opposite capacity as a result of, and at the same time a refusal to, conform to patriarchal oppression. In *Teresa,* not only the title character's slip into hysterical behavior but also Calliope, the town madwoman, constantly reminds readers of the danger of not conforming to the social norms for women; in Calliope's case, the offenses are a past blighted by uninhibited sexuality and a generally defiant spirit.

The Novel in Focus

Plot summary. The narrative deals primarily with the inner thoughts and motivations of its protagonist, Teresa Caccia, a young girl growing up in a small town in Lombardy in northern Italy. Most of the action occurs in the Caccia family's middle-class home.

The novel opens in the midst of a winter flood on the banks of the Po River in northern Italy. Rising waters are threatening a small town, and the townsmen are frantically monitoring the danger. Through this crisis, Neera introduces a whole range of characters whose conversations reveal important clues about the town's rigid social, political, and religious hierarchy. Two men emerge who will later become the dominating (and opposing) forces in the heroine's life. Signor Caccia, the tax collector (and Teresa's father), is a stiff, pretentious man who enters bearing bad news of death and destruction in nearby towns. Orlandi, the dashing, heroic, unruly youth who will become Teresa's all-consuming love interest, materializes out of the dark in a boat upon the raging river, carrying a baby he bravely rescues from certain death.

While Chapter 1 features a dangerous exterior world inhabited principally by men, Chapter 2 introduces readers to the interior world of the home, the family, and the female. As the waters rise outside, Signor Caccia's wife, Signora Soave, is about to deliver her fifth child. It is after Signora Soave's exclamation, "If only it's a boy!" that the novel expresses its central question: "But what can girls, poor things, look forward to in this world?" (Neera, *Teresa,* p. 12). The novel first introduces Teresa during her mother's frightful labor. Fifteen years old, she has just been taken out of school to embark on her domestic education at the side of her sickly mother. Now that Signora Soave is ill, the family expects Teresa to assume her mother's homemaking duties; so begins her journey into womanhood.

Teresa sacrifices her own life to meet the needs of her brother, her sisters, and her parents, and her father reinforces her self-sacrifice with vehement statements regarding a woman's character and her proper place in the world. At one point, he rages at his wife: "It's obvious you have not the slightest inkling about life. You're just a silly woman good for nothing but idle chatter . . . we have a male heir, the family's mainstay! It's for him we must make sacrifices. . . . The male carries the Caccia name and honor" (*Teresa,* pp. 135-36). For four years Teresa endures an essentially affectionless existence, the monotony of which is broken only once, by an exciting and pivotal visit to her aunt in a neighboring village.

In her aunt's village Teresa gets her first taste of love. She attends a dance where the local postman's son sweeps her off her feet. The experience leaves her confused, weak, and extremely lovesick. Her vacation ends abruptly when her aunt and uncle realize what has happened. Teresa returns home, but not without a new awareness of her sensual self; she is still the virginal, innocent young girl she had been before, but she now has an awareness of emotions that lie beyond her affections for her family. Teresa's subsequent discovery of romance novels and a trip to the opera serve only to enhance her confusing new emotions. She begins to close herself off from the outside world, preferring to retreat into her amorous (but chaste) fantasies rather than to live in the dreary reality of her daily existence.

Out of pity for the young daydreamer, Teresa's good friend and neighbor, the judge's wife, tries to discourage her unrealistic desires. She explains how the institution of marriage functions, describing it as a union based not on love but on material exchange and social considerations, encouraging Teresa to forget her passionate ideas lest she end up an old maid. But Teresa refuses to accept such an unsentimental philosophy. To cheer Teresa up, the judge's wife articulates an opinion about men previously expressed by Teresa's aunt Rosa, which recurs as a subtext throughout the novel: "Look, if you only knew . . . if only I could tell you how worthless they are" (*Teresa*, p. 68).

A small diversion in Teresa's monotonous life occurs when her brother, Carlino, who has been studying at the university, returns home for a visit. Sharing his experiences, he gives Teresa a glimpse of the world outside her secluded life in the family home and provincial village. She takes keen interest in stories about one of his friends, the notorious and handsome Orlandi. Taking advantage of an unusual opportunity to get out of the house, Teresa accompanies Carlino and Signora Letizia, Orlandi's aunt, on a walk in the countryside. It is during this excursion that she comes face to face with the by-now legendary young man, Orlandi himself, who takes an immediate liking to Teresa.

After this initial meeting, Teresa thinks of Orlandi constantly. She relishes the vague, luxurious emotions experienced in connection with the infatuation. One day Orlandi slips her a letter asking her to meet him at her window in the middle of the night. Teresa agonizes over whether to comply, torn between the compulsion to meet Orlandi and her ingrained sense of propriety. She sleepwalks through the day and evening, dis-

playing what the novel calls consummate female behavior: "And so all alone in the low kitchen, intent on everyday chores, the girl was deceived by an infinitude of hope, docilely bound to her chains, learning the great female virtue of self-control, the profound female aptitude of hiding anguish behind a smile" (*Teresa*, p. 98).

Teresa finally decides to meet Orlandi, and he vows his undying love. He promises to write while away at the university and they begin a passionate courtship, facilitated by the discreet postman. At this point Teresa's world undergoes a major shift. Her love for Orlandi replaces her affection for her family; he becomes the center of her existence. On the surface, Teresa is still the dutiful daughter, but privately she takes delight in her secret joy. Meanwhile, Orlandi, though still enjoying a carefree, pleasure-filled life in the big city, begins to devote more time to his studies in anticipation of marrying Teresa. Teresa's close friend, the judge's wife, tries yet again to inject some practicality into Teresa's fantasies by discouraging her interest in the flighty yet charming young man, but Teresa remains unconvinced. Meanwhile, the townspeople begin to gossip about the budding affair between Teresa and Orlandi, still completely unknown to Teresa's parents.

After several years of secret courtship, Orlandi finally asks Signor Caccia for Teresa's hand. He is vehemently rebuffed. Signor Caccia reveals that he does not intend to spend the family's money (completely reserved for Carlino's education) on a dowry for Teresa. Since Orlandi does not have a stable job yet (thus making a dowry essential for the couple's survival), he vows to secure one and then return.

The conversation with Orlandi leaves Signor Caccia in a rage, incensed that Teresa put his and his family's honor so deeply in jeopardy by carrying on the illicit affair. On the other hand, Teresa, despite her father's wrath and her own sadness, refuses to give up on the possibility of one day marrying Orlandi. She declares her intention to wait as long as it takes. Her mother, resigned and affectionate, becomes a wellspring of sympathy.

Despite his own good intentions and sincere feelings for Teresa, Orlandi does not have a well-thought-out plan. He abandons his chosen profession, the law, and indulges his new interest in politics and journalism, which requires him to move to Milan. His letters to Teresa become less frequent as his life grows more decadent. Teresa, on the other hand, remains ardently attached to her dreams of love and happiness with him.

Upon learning that the correspondence between his daughter and Orlandi has continued and the whole town knows it, Signor Caccia lashes out at Teresa. He impresses upon her the fact that she has ruined the family and the reputations of her sisters. Suddenly Teresa's secret joy metamorphoses into humiliation and sorrow. The townspeople gossip and openly ridicule her. As her days grow even more monotonous, she floats through them like a zombie.

Teresa's "mute but profound" sorrow is briefly interrupted by a surprise visit from Orlandi when Signor Caccia forces Teresa to accompany her twin sisters to a masquerade ball for Carnival (*Teresa*, p. 157). As she reluctantly dances with a dull young man with marriage designs on her sister, Orlandi breaks in and proposes another secret meeting. Again Teresa vacillates between disobeying her father and the desire to be loved. She eventually gives in to desire.

This time Orlandi makes an extremely bold request. He asks Teresa to run away with him. When it becomes clear that she will not oblige him, he realizes the futility of the relationship and definitively pulls away. Teresa remains steadfast, nonetheless. She vows to love him always no matter what her destiny.

Several years pass during which Teresa's two younger sisters marry, her brother graduates from law school and finds a job in southern Italy, and her youngest sister is allowed to attend teacher-training school. Meanwhile, Teresa slips ever more deeply into spinsterhood. She starts to take on the nervous ailments of her mother and even falls victim to hysterical seizures. Hatred, bitterness, and disgust for men and society take root and start to grow inside her. The only source of sustenance for her seems to be Orlandi's letters, which he continues to write out of guilt. His life, too, grows unhappy. Failing to obtain a steady job, he lives from day to day as a freelance writer, lonely and poor.

When Signora Soave dies, "Teresina realize[s] her greatest comfort, most unconditional source of love, [is] gone" (*Teresa*, p. 184). Teresa's physical and mental condition worsens with the loss until she degenerates into a full-fledged hysteric. More and more, she is bothered by the disparity between her pure love for Orlandi and the incomplete glimpses she catches at what might be impure love in the same romance novels she once read for escape. She herself suffers from a total lack of affection.

Signor Caccia's life does not end with the dignity and power that he had hoped. His health deteriorates to the point where he is crippled and Teresa becomes responsible for washing, dressing, and feeding him. After he dies, Teresa receives a letter from Orlandi telling her of his own destitute condition and loss of health. The next day she decides to go to him. When questioned by the judge's wife as to what she should tell people who ask after her, Teresa replies, "Well, you can tell those zealous people I've paid my whole life for this moment of freedom. That price is high enough, don't you agree?" (*Teresa*, p. 199). The novel ends with the judge's wife watching as Teresa's train for Milan gradually pulls away from the station and out of sight.

The ambiguous ending. Interestingly, Teresa chooses to love and wants to marry Orlandi regardless of the fact that he is destined for an unconventional life and that his "refusal to assume manly responsibilities . . . creates disorder in a society structured around uniformity" (Finucci, p. 231). In this way Teresa shows her implicit and intuitive rejection of the established social structure (as well as her tendency toward romantic idealism). Yet it is precisely in Neera's analysis of the consequences that arise from this rejection that she brings us to see what little power women like Teresa have over their own lives. The novel "contains a merciless in-depth analysis of the factors which contribute to deny Teresa any real possibility of choice in life—patriarchal family, the precedence accorded to male offspring in matters of education, the subtle messages transmitted to her from her earliest years as to what constitutes femininity" (Kroha, p. 78). The novel's ending confirms this observation with finality, in that even in the unconventional step she takes of going to the now broken Orlandi, she sacrifices herself for the sake of a man and places herself once again in the role of caretaker.

While Neera offers Teresa an option beyond the fate of the other two doomed women in the novel—Calliope, the extreme example of nonconformity who ends up a madwoman and ridiculed outcast, or Teresa's own mother, whose conformity is so complete she becomes a nonperson—at the same time she seems to be asking readers to reflect on just how different an alternative it actually is. Neera's readers begin to wonder what Teresa's life would have been like if she had had the opportunities for education afforded the novel's truly unique female character, her younger sister Ida, who was never concerned about marriage or other social restrictions and who had no burden of housework or childcare saddled on her.

Ida represents hope for a new generation, even if her job as a *maestra* might be at times less than ideal. Indeed, in real life, there was cause for hope. Many women were engaged in the struggle to gain legal and social equality. The already mentioned Anna Maria Mozzoni, regarded as the founder of Italian feminism, was particularly active in Milan during the second half of the nineteenth century. She came from an upper-class family that, despite financial troubles, was dedicated to providing her with an education beyond the two years required by the state. From an early age, Mozzoni took up the struggle for women's rights, mainly from a legal perspective, but bringing to the cause a highly informed philosophical background as well.

In 1864, at age 27, Mozzoni wrote *La donna e i suoi rapporti sociali in occasione della revisione del codice italiano* (Woman and Her Social Relationships on the Occasion of the Revision of the Italian Civil Code), which served as a critique of the conservative and exclusive nature of Italian family law. She believed that equality under the law in education and in the workplace were the pillars of female emancipation, and that a woman needed to have a place in public life rather than be confined within the four walls of her father's or husband's home. In addition to publishing numerous pamphlets and articles promoting women's rights, she worked determinedly for women's suffrage, which, although she almost secured it, would not be fully adopted in Italy until 1945. On the educational front, she wanted to prepare young women to be citizens of a modern nation; she proposed a higher education for girls and fought to include subjects like foreign languages, science, and a survey of the historical conditions of women in different countries. She became involved too in projects such as creating daycare centers for the children of women workers who would otherwise have to stay home to tend their sons and daughters.

Meanwhile, other women formed networks and published journals. In addition to the more liberal *La donna*, there were the Catholic-centered, "emancipationist" periodicals such as Olimpia Saccati's *La missione della donna* (Women's Mission), and others like the slightly more radical *La Cornelia* (a woman's name), founded by the Neopolitan aristocrat Aurelia Cimino Folliero in 1872. Reaching more and more women with their message of emancipation, early activists also had a degree of legal success: in 1890 a law was passed allowing women to participate in public administration, which, in turn, gave them a chance to represent their interests at political meetings (Graziosi, p. 63).

Teresa, then, takes place during the early stages of a slow but steady struggle that began to transform the experience of many women in Italian society but that would also encounter many setbacks along the way.

Sources and literary context. Neera was writing during the heyday of the novel in Italy. Realism was the dominant genre of the period, and it gave rise to the subcategory of naturalism, which aimed for a scientifically accurate rendering of life, even in its ugliness and disharmony. *Teresa,* more than any other of Neera's fictional works, shows the influence of Italy's unique brand of naturalism, *verismo.* In some ways a reaction against Romanticism, *verismo* had as its most important goal the objective, impersonal analysis of the daily realities of the poor, downtrodden, and oppressed. Verist writers were interested in identifying the laws, particularly economic, that govern human society and in presenting them in such a way that the facts speak for themselves. Since one of *verismo*'s principal concerns was the fate of the weaker members of society, women often played important parts in verist novels.

While Neera never exclusively embraced one style in particular, Luigi Capuana is often credited with inspiring her to experiment with his particular brand of *verismo,* although his exact influence on her writing is still unknown. Certainly Neera incorporated some aspects of verismo into *Teresa,* given that it portrays the harsh realities of women caught in impossible social situations and exploited by the economics of marriage. But, like many women writers of the time, she does not follow the verist philosophy to the letter, drawing upon other genres as well to create a sort of hybrid form that, while it doesn't fit neatly into the realist canon, suits her purposes better. For example, she periodically abandons the detached narrator's voice and inserts her own observations into the novel.

The work, in its hybrid form, was a powerful communicative tool in the struggle to improve women's lives in Neera's Italy. In general in Italy, "the novel in this period became for the first time . . . the most influential and widely disseminated medium in which women spoke about women" (Re in Ascoli, p. 176). Neera formed a key part of this vanguard, most notably with her novel *Teresa.*

Although Neera's life experience was not as repressive as Teresa's and her book is clearly not an autobiography, there are some similarities. In the author's memoirs and other autobiographical essays, she wrote with regret about her emotionally solitary childhood and her lack of access to an education, two factors that contribute in the novel to Teresa's frustration and her prison-like environment. According to one scholar, Neera went so far as to attribute her literary career to this deprivation: "My brothers had their studies, walks, friends, and then they were at university for many years. They got to laugh sometimes. Me, never. . . . Immobile . . . completely silent, the only resource I had was to flee through the ever-open door of my imagination" (Neera in Kroha, p. 71).

NEERA ON WOMEN'S WORK AND FEMALE IDENTITY

Neera can be described as "a writer with two faces" (Zecchi, p. 90). On the one hand, she wrote compassionate and condemning words about women's inferior position in her society; on the other hand, she objected to the official feminist movement. This ambivalence likely stemmed from her faith as a Catholic, which would account for her resistance to any movement intertwined, as the early Italian feminist movement was, with socialism. Neera was also opposed to rejecting femininity, a stance promoted by feminists like Anna Maria Mozzoni. Neera took up another position altogether, championing women's rights by calling attention to their specifically feminine biology, "different but not inferior, and in some instances, as in the case of motherhood, even superior to that of men" (Zecchi, p. 90). In her group of essays, *Le idee di una donna* (1903; The Ideas of a Woman), Neera writes:

> Promoting laws for women's work is certainly an excellent thing, but something that is not directly connected to the happiness of women themselves. Since woman's essential need harmoniously meets the purpose for which she was created, these laws will be of benefit, but will always come after the law of love, from which she is distanced by having to compete with men for a career and by her material participation in public life . . . . Neither inferior, nor superior, nor equal, but different and equivalent. Since this is my judgment with regard to the two sexes, I ask myself why woman should be required to take on, in addition to her own role, the role of a man, while one does not ask men to take on women's duties. There is no reason, not emotional, not scientific, not economic, that justifies such an inversion of rights and duties, because, compared to men's work, if the inimitable and invaluable work of motherhood is sufficient for female dignity, scientific and economic judgment have for a long time proclaimed the advantage of the division of labor.
>
> (Neera in Croce, pp. 816-17; trans. A. Boylan)

Reception. Neera was one of a handful of female writers taken seriously by male contemporaries. In fact, a major issue of the period, of direct consequence to Neera, was the rise in popularity of women writers and the subsequent backlash against them. On the one hand, Italian women writers, because they were excluded from a narrow literary canon skewed heavily towards poetry and the classical, had an advantage over male authors, who produced these traditional types of literature for an elite group of intellectuals. While few women were steeped in the classical tradition like their male counterparts, they found themselves more in tune with the sensibilities of mass culture. Women furthermore made ideal writers in view of the largely female Italian readership at the time. Often self-taught like Neera, women writers found favor with an Italian publishing industry that was determined to benefit from the public's rising demand for readable books.

Yet there was a downside to the new demand and the female writers who set out to meet it. Many male authors felt threatened by the fact that literature had been opened up to women, seeing this shift as an attack on established social norms for the different sexes. Some launched a counterattack, claiming that although women authors enjoyed success among the female public, their writing could never be considered true art since women lacked the capacity of originality and reflection, two activities that were supposedly performable only by the male mind.

In response to undeniably talented female writers, such as Neera, Matilde Serao, and Grazia Deledda, a large share of the male establishment stereotyped them as manly, unnatural women. They were not, in the eyes of this establishment, true females. The alternatives posed by male society—that the woman writer was either inferior or unwomanly—put female authors in a very delicate and uncomfortable situation. Possibly in response to these negative characterizations, in addition to her novels, Neera wrote what could be considered anti-feminist essays; she discouraged women from becoming writers, even as she portrayed their repressed lives with such insight.

Although Neera faced adversity as a woman writer, she had the support of two very important literary figures of her time, Luigi Capuana and Benedetto Croce, even though they too would eventually participate in the backlash against women writers. Her works were generally well received, thanks in part to this support. In his role as critic, Capuana published several essays on Neera's work, most notably in his *Studi sulla let-*

teratura contemporanea (1882; Studies in Contemporary Literature) and *Gli "ismi" contemporanei* (1898; Contemporary "isms"). Croce, a seminal influence in literary criticism and aesthetics during the first half of the twentieth century, wrote significant essays on Neera from 1905 on and also edited a definitive edition of Neera's works, including *Teresa*, which was published in 1942. In his view, it is the most balanced and precise novel Neera wrote. This estimation echoes and prefigures others that resemble it. In a 1901 article in the influential journal *Nuova antologia* (New Anthology), Guido Menasci refers to the critical consensus that *Teresa* is Neera's "masterpiece" and lauds the "intimate naturalness" and "beautiful simplicity" of her style (Menasci, p. 270; trans. A. Boylan). Seventy-five years later, Luigi Baldacci, the critic who reintroduced a mostly forgotten *Teresa* to contemporary readers, would in retrospect applaud the work as, "one of the finest novels of the last two decades of the last century" (Baldacci in Kroha, p. 67).

—Amy Boylan

For More Information

Ascoli, Albert Russell, and Krystyn Von Henneberg Buttafuoco, eds. *Making and Remaking Italy, The Cultivation of National Identity around the Risorgimento*. Oxford: Berg, 2001.

Buttafuoco, Annarita. *Questioni di cittadinanza, donne e diritti sociali nell'Italia liberale*. Siena: Protagon Editori Toscani, 1995.

Capuana, Luigi. *Giacinta*. Milan: Treves, 1931.

Croce, Benedetto. "Neera." In *La letteratura della nuova Italia, Saggi critici*. Vol. 3. Bari: Laterza, 1964.

Finucci, Valeria. "Between Acquiescence and Madness: Neera's Teresa." *Stanford Italian Review* 7, nos. 1-2 (1987): 217-39.

Graziosi, Mariolina. *La donna e la storia, identità di genere e identità collettiva nell'Italia liberale e fascista*. Naples: Liguori Editore, 2000.

Kroha, Lucienne. *The Woman Writer in Late-Nineteenth-Century Italy, Gender and the Formation of Literary Identity*. Lewiston: Edwin Mellen Press, 1992.

Mazzoni, Cristina. "Hysteria." In *The Feminist Encyclopedia of Italian Literature*. Westport, Conn.: Greenwood Press, 1997.

Menasci, Guido. "Neera." In *Nuova antologia* 95 (September 1901): 263-78.

Neera. *Teresa*. Trans. Martha King. Evanston: Northwestern University Press, 1998.

Pacifici, Sergio. *The Modern Italian Novel: From Capuana to Tozzi*. Vol. 2. Carbondale: Southern Illinois University Press, 1973.

Pope Leo XIII. "*Rerum Novarum*: Encyclical Letter on Capital and Labor." The Vatican: The Holy See. May 15, 1891. http://www.vatican.va/index.htm.

Sbragia, Albert. "Risorgimento." In *The Feminist Encyclopedia of Italian Literature*. Westport, Conn.: Greenwood Press, 1997.

Stanton, Theodore. *The Woman Question in Europe: A Series of Original Essays*. New York: G. P. Putnam & Sons, 1884.

Zecchi, Barbara. "Feminism: Nineteenth Century." In *The Feminist Encyclopedia of Italian Literature*. Westport, Conn.: Greenwood Press, 1997.

The Travels of Marco Polo

by
Marco Polo

Born in 1254 in Venice, Italy, Marco Polo was the son of a prosperous merchant family. At the age of 17, young Marco accompanied his father, Nicolo, and his uncle, Maffeo, on a three-year journey to China that took the travelers through Persia, Afghanistan, and other countries. In 1275 the three Polos were warmly received at the imperial court of the Mongol warlord Kublai Khan in China. Marco, in particular, became a favorite with the Great Khan, who employed the young man on public missions that sent him to various parts of the empire. The Polos remained in China 17 years. Returning to Venice in 1295, they resumed their business as merchants there. In 1298 Marco Polo became involved in a sea battle between the rival Venetian and Genoese fleets; the Venetians suffered defeat and Marco was taken prisoner. While captive, he dictated the stories of his travels to Rustigielo, a fellow prisoner and a scribe from Pisa. *Divisament du Monde*, more familiarly known to Western readers as *The Travels of Marco Polo*, circulated after Marco's release in 1299 and became an instant success. Impressing even those who doubted its veracity, the travel narrative charmed believers and skeptics alike with its detailed accounts of life in the Far East.

Events in History at the Time of the Travel Narrative

The rise of Venice. Although Polo's contemporaries sometimes referred to him as "Marco the Venetian," he writes little of his native Venice in

---

> ### THE LITERARY WORK
>
> A travel narrative set primarily in China and Southeast Asia, spanning the years 1260 to 1295; first published in Franco-Italian (as *Divisament du Monde*; Description of the World) in 1299; in English in 1579.
>
> ### SYNOPSIS
>
> A Venetian merchant journeys to the Far East, enters the service of Kublai Khan of China, and describes the places he visits or hears of while he is away.

---

his famous book. By his day the city had grown into a maritime power, gaining a reputation that paved the way for such trading expeditions as the Polos'. Venice conducted a sweeping intercontinental trade, stretching from the English Channel to the Black Sea at the European-Asian border and beyond. The republic was well-situated for such far-reaching trade. Located on a lagoon at the head of the Adriatic Sea and flanked to the east and west by the Byzantine Empire and Lombardy, respectively, Venice thrived as a port of exchange. It came by its status through efforts of its own, subduing pirates to win control of the Adriatic Sea, securing trading privileges in several Mediterranean seaports, and serving as a major port of embarkation for the Crusades to Palestine. In the thirteenth and fourteenth centuries, Venice's phenomenal commercial expansion earned it the

Marco Polo

rivalry of Genoa, another Italian maritime republic, and a long struggle for regional dominance ensued. Venice continued to grow, amassing a colonial empire that included Crete, the Ionian Islands, and more. In 1204 Enrico Dandolo, the doge (chief magistrate) of Venice, became a leader of the Fourth Crusade, which conquered Constantinople. Venice subsequently gained possession of three-eighths of Constantinople itself, including the port facilities. From Constantinople such costly goods as silk, dyes, furs, pepper, cotton, peacock-feathers, slaves, and timber were exported to Venice, whose merchants turned around and traded them to places across Europe. Inevitably, thousands of Venetians, perhaps most notably merchants, flocked to Constantinople in hopes of making their fortunes, including the Polos. It was from Constantinople that the Polo brothers first decided to venture east, intending to conduct trade in jewels within the Mongol realm of the "Golden Horde," that is, the western territories of Asia, encompassing the steppe lands and Russian principalities. Wars between Mongol chiefs in the region impeded the Polos' return to Venice, leading ultimately to their journey to China (called Cathay) and the court of Kublai Khan.

Western perceptions of the East. Before the Polos' expedition, Europeans knew little of China or the continent of Asia. What they did know was based on ancient maps, writings, and oral literature, including age-old myths and legends. Most Europeans associated Asia with stories of Alexander the Great, who fought Darius of Persia and conquered part of northern India in the fourth century B.C.E. According to one legend, Alexander locked two giants—Gog and Magog—behind iron gates in a bronze wall across the Caucasus Mountains. Other legends spoke of Alexander encountering monstrous races in the East—the Cynocephali (dog-headed men); the Blemmyae, who had faces on their breasts; and the Sciopods, each of whom had one giant foot that it used as a sunshade. Along with fantastic races, the Europeans believed fantastic beasts inhabited the region, too—unicorns, griffins, dragons, and manticores (with the body of a lion and the face of a man), as well as less sensational creatures, such as camels and elephants.

During the twelfth century, the visit to Rome of a man claiming to be "Patriarch John of India" further shaped the European vision of Asia as a land of exotic marvels. Although "Patriarch John" may have been an imposter perpetrating an elaborate hoax (who he really was remains unknown), he apparently delivered a lecture on the Indian city of Hulna, which he claimed was a Christian city. His lecture enthralled the papal curia, or Church administrators. Another influential development in this century was the appearance of the anonymous *Letter of Prester John* (1165), which likewise captivated Europeans. It was supposedly written by a different John, a Christian priest and ruler of the East. The letter describes the magnificence of his palace; the prosperity of his kingdom, a land of milk, honey, and precious stones; and the moral purity of his capital city. Beyond these marvels, the kingdom of the legendary Prester John was said to contain fire-dwelling salamanders and numerous fountains of youth. From this letter, written a century before Marco Polo's book, the notion spread that an entire Christian kingdom existed in the Far East. Modern scholars still debate the authenticity and authorship of the *Letter of Prester John* and theorize that it should be interpreted as a dream vision or utopian fantasy—or an elaborate hoax. But twelfth-century readers had no such scruples about taking the letter at its word. They interpreted it literally, believing that indeed there was a powerful Christian king in the Orient, who reigned over a realm of unimaginable wealth and exotic wonders.

Travelers along the Silk Road. Trade between China and the West began centuries before the Polos made their expedition. Most transactions took place via the Silk Road, a caravan route consisting of interlinked roads along which merchants exchanged goods—including silk, spices, jade, and gold. Numerous branches of the main Silk Roads extended into such places as Korea, Japan, and the Philippines. Actually, there were three main branches of the route:

1) The northern Silk Road, in use after 138 B.C.E., started at the ancient Chinese capital city of Chang'an (now called Xi'an). From there the road crossed the Yellow River and passed through the Gobi Desert and present-day Uzbekistan, Iran, and Iraq, before meeting the western boundary of the Roman Empire.

2) The southern Silk Road was actually a sea route that began at the ports of Xuwen and Hepu in South China, passed through the Malacca Strait, and ended in Burma or the Huangchi Kingdom of southern India.

3) A third Silk Road began in Chengdu in Sichuan Province and ran through Yunnan Province, Burma, India, Afghanistan, and Russia, before joining the northern Silk Road at Mary, a city in Turkmenistan.

In Polo's lifetime, the Mongols controlled the Silk Road, while Middle Eastern, Far Eastern, and European merchants traded profitably along its lengths. The road was a cultural as well as a commercial institution, allowing the exchange not only of material goods but also of ideas, traditions, languages, and religious practices.

Christian missionaries, hoping to establish their faith more securely in the predominantly Islamic East, traveled along the Silk Road. In 1245 Pope Innocent IV dispatched a party of envoys, led by Franciscan friar Giovanni di Plano Carpini on just such an errand. Starting from Lyons, France, Fra Giovanni and his party journeyed first to the realm of the Golden Horde on the Volga, then across the Altai Mountains to Karakorum, Mongolia (the capital of the Mongol world), where they delivered papal letters to the Great Khan Güyük. Ultimately, Güyük rejected Christian doctrine and demanded the Pope's personal appearance and submission at his court, though he permitted the envoys to depart in peace. After his return, Fra Giovanni recorded his observations on the Mongols, their customs, and their land in his *Historia Mongolorum*, which became an important source of information and was widely copied. In 1253 the Franciscan friar William of Rubruck obtained the permission of King Louis IX of France to travel to Karakorum as a missionary. Although cordially received at the court of Möngke Khan, William failed to convince the ruler or his subjects that Christianity was superior to other faiths. Like Fra Giovanni, William also kept a record of his travels in the Mongol territories (translated from Latin as *The Journey of William of Rubruck to the Eastern Parts of the World, 1253-1255*).

Not all journeys to the East were so short-lived or had such little impact. A Dominican friar known as David of Ashby apparently visited and stayed at the Mongol court sometime between 1260 and 1274; in 1291, the Franciscan friar Giovanni da Montecorvino, who had been active in Armenia and Iran from the 1270s, traveled as far as Peking, China, eventually building the first Christian cathedral there in 1305. Some Western merchants traveling the Silk Road even chose to settle in the East. By the seventh century B.C.E., an estimated 200,000 Persians, Arabs, Indians, Malays, and others were living in the port city of Canton (Guangzhou), while further north, merchants from Arabia, Persia, Syria, India, Italy, and Morocco were engaged in extensive business relations with the Chinese (Stockwell, p. 16). There is evidence to suggest the possible existence of an Italian community in southern China—specifically, the tombstones of Domenico Vilioni and his unmarried daughter Catherine, who both died and were buried at Yangchow in the early 1300s. The Vilioni had been well known in Venice as a merchant family apparently involved in the commerce of Asia for many years.

Thus, Marco Polo, his father, and uncle were not the first European merchants—nor even the first Italian merchants—to venture along the Silk Road or enter China, though few of their contemporaries apparently journeyed as far as Kublai Khan's domain. On the other hand, of all the travelers to the East, Marco seems to have composed the most extensive written record of his journeys; it was his book that was to impart a lasting impression of the exotic East upon the curious West.

The Mongol Conquest. Polo devotes several chapters of his book to a somewhat inaccurate history of the Mongols (to whom he refers as Tartars), a nomadic people dwelling among the steppes of eastern Asia who ruled China between 1211 and 1368. While most of the Mongol khans remained nomads at heart and devoted their time to conquest, they also established a strong centralized power structure and implemented a universal code of law (the Yasa), which became the institutional foundation for the Mongol Empire.

In 1206 the Mongols became united under the leadership of one man: Chingghis (Genghis) Khan ("Universal Ruler"). Backed by a highly disciplined army that he himself organized and trained, Genghis Khan embarked upon a series of triumphant military campaigns. Polo erroneously identifies the year of Genghis's ascent to power as 1187, then freely interweaves fantasy with history by relating how Genghis defeated the legendary King Prester John, an incident entirely made up. Genghis's actual exploits, however, were as remarkable as anything in Polo's book. In the 1210s he captured the Xi Xia kingdom and city of Yanjing in China, then turned west to annex Bokhara and Samarkand.

When Genghis Khan died in 1226, his heirs carried on his work, extending Mongol control over the north and west. The issue of succession proved a recurring problem within Genghis Khan's family. Again Polo errs by describing the imperial succession thus: "To Chinghis Khan succeeded Cuy Kaan; the third was Batuy Kaan, the fourth Alacou Kaan, the fifth Mongou Kaan, the sixth Kublai Kaan" (Polo, *The Travels of Marco Polo*, p. 75). In fact, Genghis chose his third son, Ögödei, as his immediate heir, and Ögödei's son Güyük succeeded his father. At this point, complications developed. Sorghaghtani Beki, the Nestorian Christian wife of Genghis's fourth son, Tolui, was an intelligent, ambitious woman who intended that at least one of her four sons would one day rule the empire. To that end, she cultivated the support of Muslims, Buddhists, Taoists, and other religious groups, as well as that of several Mongol nobles. In 1251 her eldest son Möngke became Great Khan after the sudden death of Güyük, who was rumored to have been poisoned.

Like his grandfather and uncle, Möngke Khan sought to expand his domain, launching conquests of Persia and South China. He died, however, in 1259 before his conquest of South China could be completed, and his younger brother Kublai succeeded him, officially in 1260. By that time, the Mongolian Empire controlled two-thirds of Eurasia, encompassing all of present-day China, Mongolia, Iran, Iraq, Afghanistan, and Korea. The governing of so enormous a kingdom required an effective and capable leader; Kublai proved equal to the task.

The reign of Kublai Khan. The first two volumes of Polo's book deal extensively with the wealth, majesty, and military prowess of Kublai Khan. While the account is certainly colorful, it is not entirely accurate or sufficiently complete. Polo offers lavish descriptions of Kublai's palaces and court entertainments and touts his victories in battle over his kinsmen. He dwells less upon the khan's formidable administrative skills, which were vital to the maintenance of the empire.

In fact, Kublai distinguished himself as a warrior and as an administrator. As was expected of a Mongol ruler, he expanded his empire, completing the conquest of South China in 1279 and launching successful campaigns to subdue Annam (northern Vietnam), Champa (southern Vietnam), Burma, and Kampuchea (Cambodia), then compelling these areas to accept Mongol sovereignty. During his brother Möngke's reign, Kublai had proved an efficient governor of the Chinese territories granted to him. Recognizing that effective administration required more skills than his people at the moment had, Kublai employed Chinese—as well as non-Chinese—officials and advisers in his administration. This policy, which he continued to invoke, earned him the allegiance of many of his Chinese subjects, though some still resented the Mongols as intruders in their country. Ironically, many conservative Mongols also came to resent Kublai for his adoption of various Chinese customs and institutions.

Within Kublai Khan's empire, the Mongols occupied the top of the social pyramid, followed successively by the *semu ren* (Western and Central Asians), the *han ren* (northern Chinese), and the *nan ren* (southern Chinese). This social pyramid did not preclude Kublai Khan from invoking the practices of the lower social groups. He retained many features of Chinese government, including a civilian administration and a traditional division between the civil, military, and censorial branches of government. Along with Mongol and Chinese functionaries, Kublai employed educated foreigners in his court. The Polos became the first European additions to an administration that also employed Tibetans, Armenians, Arabs, Persians, and Turks. Kublai had established his imperial city of Khanbalik (now called Beijing) as a true world capital, populated by scholars, physicians, merchants, and clerics from Middle Eastern, Asian, African, and European nations. To an impressionable young man like Marco Polo, the opportunities for advancement must have seemed limitless.

In his account, Polo praises Kublai Khan as a wise and beneficent ruler who, by virtue of the size of his realm, the number of his subjects, and the revenue he accrues, "surpasses every sovereign that has heretofore been or that now is in the world" (*Travels*, p. 97). Indeed, Polo finds virtually no fault with the khan, although history has documented that Kublai had his share of flaws. Certainly, he could be extravagant; his military expeditions, the construction of his new imperial capital at Khanbalik, and his decision to issue paper currency placed heavy burdens on the treasury and led to financial woes. In the last years of his reign, Kublai suffered these financial woes as well as personal losses, especially the deaths of his favorite wife and their son, whom he had designated as his heir. When Kublai Khan died in 1294, he was a broken man, despite all he had achieved.

While in his prime, Kublai invigorated China's economy, improving the postal relay system, extending the Grand Canal from Hangzhou in the south to the capital, Khanbalik, and stimulating trade with Europe by opening his court to foreign visitors like Polo and by encouraging commerce along the Silk Road. His merchant fleet developed markets from India to Malaysia and the Persian Gulf.

Kublai also made significant cultural contributions by introducing new intellectual elements into Chinese society. Having conquered much of the Middle East, he encouraged its Persian astronomers and physicians to introduce their ideas and theories to the Chinese. It was in this same spirit that he began his long association with the Polos—two of the first Europeans he encountered. In part, no doubt, because of his own Christian heritage (on his mother's side), their religion claimed his attention. He had a mission for the Polos: though Kublai himself evinced no desire to convert to Christianity, he wanted them to have the Pope send 100 Christian scholars to his court to argue the merits of their faith.

The Travel Narrative in Focus

Plot summary. Although *The Travels of Marco Polo* purports to be autobiographical, the work focuses more on the places that Polo, his father, and uncle visit on their journey eastward. The narrative shifts back and forth between first-person, and, more often, third-person. Polo emphasizes the natives' diet, religion, and social practices in each region. He also shows a keen interest in the various wares produced and sold in a region, from carpets and silks to furs. Divided into four volumes, Polo's travel narrative opens with a lengthy prologue.

The prologue. Polo's book begins with a grandiose promise to reveal all the marvels of the East, as told by "Marco Polo, a wise and learned citizen of Venice, who states distinctly what things he saw and what things he heard from others" (*Travels*, p. 3). Asserting that no man has ever seen as much, the prologue explains that while impris-

oned by the Genoese, Polo dictated the story of his travels to his fellow inmate Rustigielo of Pisa.

The prologue then explains that the brothers Nicolo and Maffeo Polo take a first trip to the East in 1260. From Constantinople, they venture into the realm of the Tartars, where they encounter a Tartar ambassador who invites them to accompany him to the court of the Great Khan (Kublai), emperor of China. After a year-long journey, the Polos arrive at the imperial court at Shangdu (called Xanadu by Westerners and poets) and receive a gracious welcome from Kublai Khan. The khan questions them about their Christian faith, then sends them on a special mission as his ambassadors to the pope. The Polos are to request that the pope send to the khan's court "a hundred men of learning" to argue the merits of Christianity. The khan also requests that, on their return to China, the Polos bring him some of the holy oil from the lamp above Christ's sepulcher in Jerusalem.

Consenting to the mission, the Polos depart China, reaching Acre, the Crusader stronghold in Palestine, in 1269. Pope Clement has died, however, and there is a long delay in electing a new pope. Returning to Venice, the Polos discover that Nicolo's wife has also died. His son, Marco, is now 15 years old. In 1271 the Polos decide to resume their mission for the khan and to take Marco with them. On learning that Gregory X has been appointed pope, the Polos relay to him the khan's request for missionaries; the new pope decides to send only two friars, both of whom quickly abandon the Polos' expedition once they hear of the hardships and dangers involved. More than three years later, the Polos once again reach the khan's court.

Accepting the Polos' gift of the holy oil and explanation of the friars' defection from the mission, the khan receives the Venetians as warmly as before. The great ruler takes a particular fancy to Marco, now in his early twenties. For the next 17 years, the Polos remain in China as the khan's honored guests. Marco adopts the manners of the Tartars and becomes the khan's emissary. Knowing that the khan "took a pleasure in hearing accounts of whatever was new to him respecting the customs and manners of people, and the peculiar circumstances of distant countries," the young man records what he sees and hears on his missions for the khan (*Travels*, p. 12).

In 1292, fearing that the aging khan's death will leave them vulnerable to the enmity of jealous courtiers, the Polos head homeward. They reach Venice safely in 1295, laden with riches from their journeys.

Illustration of Marco Polo arriving in China.

Book 1. Unlike the prologue, the subsequent volumes of *The Travels of Marco Polo* do not possess a sustained narrative. Rather, each relates Polo's observations of the regions he visits or hears about during his missions for the khan. In Book 1, Marco gives an account of the Polos' journey from Lower Armenia to the Court of the Great Khan at Shangdu. He begins by describing Lesser and Greater Armenia, noting the terrain, the religious practices, and the goods each people has to sell. He also describes the countries of the Middle East, especially Persia, Iraq, and Asia Minor. Polo dwells upon local myths and legends, re-

ferring to Alexander the Great and the iron gates he supposedly constructed in a bronze wall imprisoning two giants and to a notorious Old Man of the Mountain, who recruited young men as assassins, ensuring their obedience with drugs and promises of paradise on earth.

Polo continues westward towards Cathay (China) via Badakshan, the Pamir, Kashmir, Samarkand, Khotan, Lop, and finally the Great Desert (later known as the Gobi). Reaching the heartland of the Tartars, he gives a detailed, if not wholly accurate, account of one man: Chinghis (Genghis) Khan ("Universal Ruler"), and of his defeat of the powerful prince Unc Can (also known as Prester John). According to Polo, Genghis routed the army of Prester John, who perished in the battle, then married his daughter and founded a dynasty. Directly descended from Chingghis, Kublai was the sixth and current Great Khan. Book 1 concludes with Polo's introductory account of Kublai Khan's world, mentioning Kublai's summer palace of Shandu (Shangdu), his stable of 10,000 snow-white horses and mares, and his court astrologers, who claim to prevent—by magic—the rain from falling upon the palace.

Book 2. The second and longest volume of Polo's books deals extensively with Kublai Khan, recounting his reputation as a warrior, his domestic life (four wives, 47 sons, and a plethora of concubines), his splendid winter palace at Taidu, the festivals held on his birthday and at the New Year, and the khan's great hunting parties.

Polo dwells less extensively on the administrative matters in the khan's government. He does, however, mention the circulation of paper money, the planting of trees along roadsides, the black stones dug out of the ground in Cathay and used for fuel, the relay postal system by which couriers on horseback carry messages through the provinces, and the khan's almsgiving to the poor.

In later chapters, Polo describes a journey to the western provinces: in Thebeth (Tibet) musk is produced from local animals and salt is used as currency; the province of Karazan features huge crocodiles; fathers in the province of Kardandan suckle infants themselves after mothers give birth; the city of Mien, in Burma, has two pyramidal towers, one of gold, one of silver, that mark the tomb of a great monarch of the past; and the province of Bangala (Benghal) is rich in cotton, spices, and many kinds of drugs. In Bangala, says Polo, eunuchs serve as slaves, especially to guard women.

Book 2 also explores Mangi, or South China, which Kublai Khan reportedly invaded and annexed in 1268. The book describes other provincial cities in the region: Yan-Gui, of which Marco Polo was supposedly governor for three years; Sa-yan-fu, which the Polos reportedly helped the khan to annex by building a catapult that crushed the city's walls and buildings; and Kin-sai, a beautiful, prosperous town with a canal system and 12,000 bridges. Traveling onward, Polo journeys to the kingdom of Kon-Cha, which boasts huge tigers, people who eat human flesh, and fowls allegedly covered with black hair instead of feathers (Polo admits to not having seen the birds himself). This second volume closes with descriptions of a few cities: Un-Guen, where sugar is manufactured; Zai-tun, a prosperous port; and Tin-Gui, famous for its fine porcelain.

Book 3. This volume deals mainly with India, which Polo divides into Greater, Lesser, and Middle India. Book 3 also contains the only Western references to Japan (called Zipangu) before the sixteenth century. After a detailed description of Chinese junks, Polo relies on hearsay to discuss Japan. He mentions the wealth of Japan—"they have gold in the greatest abundance, its sources being inexhaustible"—and Kublai Khan's failed attempts to annex the island (*Travels*, p. 219). Polo goes on to mention other islands in the Japanese archipelago—Java, Sumatra, and the Andaman Isles, for instance. (Significantly, Polo never visited Japan and, although cartographers and future explorers were intrigued by his information, much of it has been dismissed as inaccurate.)

Polo follows up his account of Japan with accounts of Zeilon (Ceylon), 10 of the 13 kingdoms of "Greater India," and the western Indian Ocean. He gives detailed information about Maabar (a province of Greater India), mingling facts about the natives' religious rites and daily lives with fables and stories of, for example, miracles at the shrine of St. Thomas the Apostle. Polo goes on to mention more regions: the Isles of Men and Women, Socotra (an island near Yemen in the Indian Ocean), Abyssinia (Middle India), Zanzibar, and Madagascar. He concludes Book 3 by announcing his intent to speak next of northern regions he has so far neglected.

Book 4. The last and shortest volume of Polo's book begins with a lengthy account of the hostility between Kublai Khan and his nephew, Kaidu, who ruled Great Turkey in Central Asia. On several occasions, uncle and nephew went to war against each other, and many lives were lost. Ultimately, Kublai Khan's forces prevailed and Kaidu and his army retreated to Samarkand in Great Turkey. After discussing other conflicts among the eastern Tartars, Polo mentions a few northern regions in Tartar territory, chiefly Russia. The volume concludes somewhat abruptly, after an account of the wars between Tartar lords of the west. Given the strife, Polo's departure from China is timely indeed. He notes as much, adding piously, "I believe it was God's pleasure that we should get back in order that people might learn about the things that the world contains. Thanks be to God! Amen! Amen!" (*Travels*, p. 295).

What the account leaves out. While Polo's book has been an object of fascinated study for centuries, the author remains a shadowy figure within its pages. Moreover, it is often difficult to separate Polo's narrative from that of his collaborator, Rustigielo. At times Polo is referred to in the first-person, at other times in the third-person as "Messer Marco." Little is known of Polo's childhood and rearing; despite the autobiographical slant of his work, he reveals no details of his life before he was old enough to accompany his father and uncle on their second journey to China. Even his career and accomplishments in China are expressed in the most general terms. According to the book, he adapted quickly to Mongol ways, acquired reading and writing proficiency in four languages, and undertook several missions at Kublai Khan's behest that took him to various parts of the Mongol Empire.

MAPS AND MARCO POLO

The *Catalan Mappamundi* (c. 1450-60), based on the *Catalan Atlas* produced 70 to 80 years before, shows Marco Polo's influence on early cartography. The names of the Chinese towns located between the Yangtze and Huang He rivers are taken from Polo, as are the annotations pertaining to them. The northeast region of China is labeled "Chataio" (Cathay) and shows the capital of "Canbalech" (another spelling for Kublai Khan's new imperial city, Khanbalik). Quinsai (Kin-sai, in Polo's book) is also plotted on the map, near the coast, and Polo's detail about the town having 12,000 bridges has been included. Another map, by Henricus Martellus Germanicus (c. 1489-90), mentions the position of Zipangu (Japan) in relation to other cities and countries, though Zipangu itself is not shown. Finally, Martin Behaim's Terrestrial Globe (c. 1492) makes the first explicit reference to Marco Polo as a source for mapping; the globe shows "Thebeth," the kingdoms of Cathay and Mangi, and even Zipangu, which is plotted at 25 degrees east of China.

On his return from China, Marco Polo was 41 years old and, like his father and uncle, unrecognizable to his Venetian neighbors, who had thought the Polos long dead. According to an account by Giambattista Ramusio—written centuries after the fact—the trio was shabbily dressed and spoke their native Venetian haltingly, with Tartar accents. Only after the Polos displayed the rich raiment and jewels acquired on their travels

to the East were the doubts regarding their identities quelled. It is said that, in addition to goods, Marco may have brought back a Mongol slave, Pietro, who was ultimately granted his freedom in Marco's will.

Factual details of the Polos' later years are sparse. They reestablished themselves as Venetian merchants and purchased a palace in the quarter of San Giovanni Crisostomo. While serving in a war between Venice and Genoa, Marco was, as noted, imprisoned by the Genoese for a year, during which he wrote his famous book. Later, he married a Venetian woman, Donata Badoer, and they had three daughters. He was often called upon to relate the story of his travels to incredulous friends and neighbors, who nicknamed his house "the court of the millions" and Marco himself "Marco of the Millions," a reference perhaps to his purported wealth or to his numerous tales of the East (*Il Milione* [The Million] was also an alternate title of Polo's book). After Marco's death, a comic figure representing "Marco of the Millions" is said to have become a staple of the Venetian carnival. Dressed as a clown, this figure perpetrated gross exaggerations to entertain the crowds, a backhanded tribute to the deceased Marco. In England, the phrase "It's a Marco Polo" would become synonymous with telling a falsehood.

Fact or fiction? Marco Polo was fully aware of the legends that had sprung up about the East; indeed, he refers to the tales of Alexander the Great and Prester John in the first volume of his book. However, he also debunks a number of myths in the course of his account: "Of the salamander under the form of the serpent, supposed to exist in fire," reports Polo, "I could never discover any traces in the eastern regions" (*Travels*, p. 69).

Even without the trappings of legend, the sights Polo records seemed incredible enough to his contemporaries. Yet modern historians have confirmed some of the more fantastic elements. For example, Polo mentions a substance that "when woven into cloth, and thrown into the fire . . . remains incombustible"; this is clearly asbestos (*Travels*, p. 68). He mentions black stones used as fuel in China, which have since been identified as coal. Coconuts, which Polo terms "Indian nuts," are likewise accurately described: they are "the size of a man's head, containing an edible substance that is sweet and pleasant to the taste and white as milk. . . . [and] filled with liquor clear as water" (*Travels*, p. 230). And the "couvade"—the practice of a father nursing his newborn baby as though he, rather than the mother, had given birth—has been observed in India, Borneo, Siam, Africa, and parts of South America. On the other hand, like Polo's contemporaries, historians have questioned how truthful Polo is: why doesn't he, they wonder, refer to what would become the Great Wall of China (begun centuries before the Polos' expedition), tea drinking, or the binding of women's feet? They also point to the lack of evidence supporting Polo's claim that he was governor of Yan-Gui. As for his claim that he participated in the siege of Sa-yan-fu, this, say modern historians, is impossible since it was captured in 1273, two years before Polo arrived in China. Such discrepancies have fueled a theory that Polo never went to China, but compiled his book from Persian and Arabic sources. Opponents of this theory contend that much of what would become the Great Wall was not standing in the thirteenth century, that "tea-culture" had not yet reached North and Central China, where Marco mostly resided, and that foot-binding was at that time limited to upper-class ladies, who would have been confined to their houses and so rarely observed by outsiders (Larner, p. 59). Moreover, the Polos' whereabouts for 24 years has not been otherwise explained, nor has a plausible motive for lying about their whereabouts been offered. Finally there are all the exotic possessions that Marco acquired. One needs to keep in mind that Polo's book admits to being a mix of eyewitness testimony and hearsay and that it constitutes a milestone in travel narratives. However spurious or unreliable parts of Polo's narrative may be, his account remains one of the first Western descriptions of life in the East.

Sources and literary context. Polo's book is supposedly based on his own experiences of what he witnessed or heard. While a prisoner of the Genoese, Polo reportedly sent for his travel notebooks before dictating his reminiscences to his fellow prisoner Rustigielo.

The Travels of Marco Polo is among the earliest of all accounts of foreign travel and is unquestionably the most detailed European account of life in continental Asia, eclipsing even that of the missionaries Fra Giovanni di Plano Carpini and William of Rubruck. As a merchant, Polo naturally expressed more interest than they in Eastern trade, but he also recorded far more, including the climate, diet, and religious practices of Eastern peoples.

Impact. *The Travels of Marco Polo* was a popular success from its first appearance in 1299, remaining in continual circulation during the author's lifetime. Over the next 25 years, Polo's book, originally written in French or Franco-Italian, was translated into several languages and dialects, including Tuscan, Venetian, Latin, and German. Polo enjoyed increased fame as a result; he was even consulted on geographical matters by learned men like Pietro d'Abano, professor of the University of Padua. In his *Conciliator differentiarum philosophorum* (1310), d'Abano described Polo as "the most extensive traveler and the most diligent inquirer whom I have ever known" (d'Abano in Larner, p. 44). Polo's reputation soon extended beyond his native Venice; in 1307 Thibaud de Chepoix, Vicar General to Charles de Valois (Latin emperor of Constantinople), requested a copy of Polo's book from the author himself.

Christopher Columbus used his own copy of *The Travels of Marco Polo* as a guidebook, making notes in the margins and underlining passages about precious gems and other riches. Indeed, it was towards the China of Polo's description that Columbus set sail in 1492, carrying letters addressed to the Great Khan by the Spanish monarchs Ferdinand and Isabella.

Polo's book had its detractors, the skeptics who doubted the veracity of his information. Polo rebuffed them with a few simple words. He was on his deathbed when some friends who feared for his salvation entreated him to retract some of the more fantastical elements in his book. Instead Polo simply replied, "I have not told half of what I saw" (*Travels*, p. 313).

—Pamela S. Loy

For More Information

Critchley, John. *Marco Polo's Book.* Aldershot, U.K.: Variorum, 1992.

Dramer, Kim. *Kublai Khan.* New York: Chelsea House, 1990.

Larner, John. *Marco Polo and the Discovery of the World.* New Haven: Yale University Press, 1999.

Lister, R. P. *Marco Polo's Travels in Xanadu with Kublai Khan.* London: Gordon & Cremonesi, 1976.

Martines, Lauro. *Power and Imagination: City-States in Renaissance Italy.* New York: Alfred A. Knopf, 1979.

Nicolle, David. *The Mongol Warlords.* New York: Firebird, 1990.

Phillips, J. R. S. *The Medieval Expansion of Europe.* Oxford: Oxford University Press, 1988.

Polo, Marco. *The Travels of Marco Polo.* Trans. Manuel Komroff and William Marsden. New York: Modern Library, 2001.

Roberts, J. A. G. *A Concise History of China.* Cambridge: Harvard University Press, 1999.

Stockwell, Foster. *Westerners in China.* Jefferson, N.C.: McFarland, 2003.

Weatherford, Jack. *Genghis Khan and the Making of the Modern World.* New York: Crown, 2004.

Wood, Frances. *Did Marco Polo go to China?* London: Secker & Warburg, 1995.

We Won't Pay! We Won't Pay!

by

Dario Fo

Playwright, actor, political activist, and Nobel laureate, Dario Fo (1926-present) distinguished himself in the latter twentieth century as one of Italy's most renowned and iconoclastic playwrights. Fo was born in San Giano in the northern part of Lombardy to Felice Fo, a railroad employee, and Pina Rota, the daughter of a peasant family that labored in northern Italy's rice paddies. In 1940, the Fos decided to send their intellectually promising son to study art at the Liceo Brera (Brera High School), part of the famed Accademia Brera (Brera Academy) in Milan. Although the Second World War temporarily interrupted his studies, Fo finally enrolled in the Accademia Brera and the Istituto Politecnico (Polytechnical Institute), where he studied art and architecture, respectively. In 1949 Fo abandoned formal study to concentrate on the stage, which led to his performing a series of monologues entitled *Poer Nano* (Poor Lad) at the Odeon Theater in Milan in 1952. Two years later he married the actress Franca Rame, and in 1958 the two founded their own theater company, La Campagnia Fo-Rame (The Fo-Rame Company). This move launched the first phase of Fo's career, dubbed by most critics as "the bourgeois period." During this phase (1959-68), Fo wrote such noteworthy plays as *Archangels Don't Play Pinball* (*Gli arcangeli non giocano a flipper*, 1959), *He Had Two Pistols and White and Black Eyes* (*Aveva due pistole con gli occhi bianchi e neri*, 1960), and *Isabella Three Caravels and a Con-Man* (*Isabella, tre caravelle e un cacciballe*, 1963). The year

THE LITERARY WORK

A farce set in 1970s Italy; first performed in Italian (as *Non si paga! Non si paga!*) in Milan in 1974, in English in Great Britain in 1978.

SYNOPSIS

A working-class housewife combats Italy's astronomical cost of living by joining other frustrated women in looting the local market.

1968 marked the beginning of Fo's next or "revolutionary phase," in which he started to write and perform theater for a working-class audience. To this period belong several of his most well-known works: *Funny Mystery* (*Mistero Buffo*, 1969), *Tie Me Up and I'll Still Smash Everything* (*Legami pure che tanto io spacco tutto lo stesso*, 1969), *Accidental Death of an Anarchist* (*Morte accidentale di un anarchico*, 1970), and *We Won't Pay! We Won't Pay!* In 1977, Fo switched gears yet again to embark on what many label as his "feminist phase," which includes *Elizabeth: Almost By Chance a Woman* (*Quasi per caso una donna: Elisabetta*, 1984). In some respects, *We Won't Pay! We Won't Pay!*, a farce that addresses pressing social issues as seen by female characters, is the knot that joins these last two phases. The play reflects a period of social and political upheaval that involved workers and women, and that drastically altered the shape of Italian society in the 1970s.

Dario Fo

Events in History at the Time of the Play

Unrest in the Italian factory. From 1968 to the early 1970s, the Italian factory became the setting of intense labor disputes, many of which stemmed from grievances about poor working conditions and low pay. Unrest erupted on March 7, 1968, when La Confederazione Generale Italiana dei Lavoratori (CGIL; The Italian General Workers' Confederation) called a general strike over pension reform. This particular act of protest took place just as parliament was preparing to debate the issue, which had been looming in the background ever since late 1967. The strike represented a watershed moment in Italy's labor history, as it not only signaled a fierce act of protest against the country's center-left government, but also demonstrated a degree of unity among workers and competing unions that had never been seen before in Italy (Lumley, *States of Emergency*, p. 170). While the general strike raged in the spring of 1968, workers in many of Italy's largest factories began organizing shop-floor rebellions in protest against their employers. In April, textile workers at Valdagno in the Veneto region demonstrated by dismantling a statue of business leader Gaetano Marzotto on display in the town square, while wildcat strikes broke out at Montedison's plant in Porto Marghera in July of 1968.

Although relations between labor and management proved tenuous in many Italian factories during 1968, the situation at most of these locations paled in comparison to that at the Pirelli rubber factory in Milan. In February, the management of Pirelli signed a national contract for the rubber sector, of which the bulk of the factory's workers disapproved. Discontent over the contract led to complaints regarding other unresolved issues, such as inadequate pay, production speed, and unpleasant working conditions. As a result of these grievances, a state of "permanent conflict" (*conflittualita permanente*) took hold at Pirelli (Lumley, *States of Emergency*, p. 183). Disaffected Pirelli workers began coordinating an independent rank-and-file organization dubbed Il Comitato Unitario di Base (CUB; Unitary Base Committee) to make their voices heard. They also implemented output-reduction strikes, slowing production, which cost the management exorbitant sums of money. This practice of self-reduction represented a new kind of workplace disobedience, which Pirelli workers used alongside more traditional methods, such as lightning strikes and work stoppages. Later, in the mid-1970s, Italian consumers would implement a variation of self-reduction to combat rising inflation. But for now, the self-reduction strategy remained tied to the workplace, where it pointed to ever worsening relations between labor and management. In the coming months, this tension between worker and employer would spiral out of control nationwide.

The hot autumn: a season of discontent. By the autumn of 1969, the workers' movement had not only taken root in factories across the nation, it had also infected other sectors of Italian society. During that fateful autumn, the contract for engineering workers came up for renewal. This, coupled with the tumultuous labor disputes of the past several months, led many to forecast momentous conflicts between labor and management. In its September 21st edition, the newspaper *24 ore* (24 Hours), itself closely linked to industrial interests in Milan, coined the term "autunno caldo" (Hot Autumn) to refer to the mood sweeping through the country during this conflict-ridden period. As Robert Lumley observes, this label may have been used to demonize protesting workers and their supporters: "Without undue forcing, this particular metaphor can be seen as part of a genre in which industrial action, demonstrations and riots were described as 'volcanic explosions,' 'sicknesses' and 'abnormalities,' metaphors which proliferated in the conservative press during subsequent events" (Lumley, *States of Emergency*, p. 208).

Events in 1969 at the Fiat automotive plant in Turin best illustrate the types of conflicts that characterized the hot autumn. Disturbances began erupting at Fiat in the spring of 1969; however, it was not until September of that year that the situation grew truly untenable. When Fiat workers demanded a pay raise, management responded by suspending some 7,000 employees as punishment for alleged insubordination. Italy's unions struck back by moving up the deadline for renewal of the engineering contract, which prompted a national demonstration of workers in that sector on September 25, 1969. Meanwhile, in Milan, the situation was scarcely any better. A massive strike over questions of union rights, such as the recognition of elected delegates, the need for a factory council, and mass meetings during work hours, paralyzed the Pirelli rubber factory. In the midst of these escalating tensions, Italy's unions still hoped to win important concessions from management regarding the disputed engineering contract.

In the summer of 1969, the unions began drawing up a list of demands that needed to be met in the new contract: pay raises; a 40-hour week to be implemented over the course of three years; parity between manual and clerical workers; and union rights within the factory (Lumley, *States of Emergency*, p. 220). Interestingly enough, however, the formal demands identified by the unions did not always correspond to the concessions workers themselves hoped to win. An inquiry into working conditions for female employees at the Borletti factory showed their complaints to be mainly about the piece-rate and grading systems, and about work-related illnesses. Migrant workers and workers in so-called unskilled sectors of production often shared many of these frustrations; however, the formal demands put forth by the unions did not reflect these issues. The methods of protest invoked by workers in factories revealed the existence of this basic discrepancy between their interests and those of the unions that represented them.

Workers decorated their factories with graffiti and revolutionary posters; they also organized marches throughout Italian cities, sometimes on an almost daily basis. Between November and December of 1969 rising tensions escalated into violent conflicts. The first of these outbursts occurred on November 6 during a demonstration in Corso Sempione in Milan against the RAI's (Radiotelevisione Italiana) coverage of industrial

conflicts. Several engineering workers were arrested and subsequently jailed as a result of this demonstration, which led sympathetic protesters to picket local police stations. An even more dangerous situation took place just twelve days later during another demonstration in via Larga, which resulted in a standoff between protestors and police that left a young officer, Antonio Annarumma, dead. A bomb-blast on December 12, 1969, rocked Piazza Fontana, also located in Milan, leading to the deaths of twelve people. In the wake of these tragic events, Italy's conservative press pointed the finger of blame at the unions and their protesting membership. However, despite the conservative press's best efforts, Italians did not universally line up to denounce the workers' movement. In fact, distrust of the Italian government grew as word began to spread that the Piazza Fontana bombing might in fact have been the work of militant fascists operating alongside allies within the government.

As Italy moved into the next decade, this atmosphere of distrust and conflict continued to plague the nation. The battle for improved working conditions spread to other facets of the workforce, such as public-sector workers like teachers, white-collar workers, and technicians. In 1972, the metalworkers' contract came up for renewal, which led to a brief resurgence in militant labor protest in early 1973. Employers broke off contract negotiations in an attempt to stymie the unions, but this method failed to obtain the desired result, and instead led to the two-day occupation of the Fiat plant in Mirafiori. Management quickly resumed negotiations, which led to the signing of a new metalworkers' contract later that year. The implementation of this contract ranked as a triumph for Italy's trade unions. Although the workers' movement of this period may have experienced many such triumphs, it also faced certain hardships. As the 1970s dawned, a future of economic instability, terrorism, and growing social awareness awaited Italian society.

A time of economic uncertainty. In the early 1970s the industrialized world was beset with economic difficulties, which would in one form or another, shape both international relations and domestic policy for many nations well into the 1980s. Italy was no exception.

Economic hardship began for many nations at this time with the oil crisis that took shape in the fall of 1973, when the Organization of Petroleum Exporting Countries (OPEC) voted to increase the price of crude oil. In the wake of this decision, oil prices soared throughout the industrialized

We Won't Pay! We Won't Pay!

world. The effects of the oil crisis reverberated through many facets of society: industry increased prices, which led to a downturn in profits, while the consumer saw a surge in energy costs. The Italian economy fared especially poorly in this tenuous climate; Italy lacked sufficient domestic energy resources, which made the country especially reliant on imported oil. As a result, soaring oil prices crippled the nation's economy. At the same time, Italy suffered from a rather weak government and a history of labor unrest, which complicated an already difficult economic situation. One historian observes that for much of the decade, Italy's economy followed a "stop-go" pattern of development (Ginsborg, p. 352). From 1972-73, the economy experienced a slight upsurge, followed the next year by a paralyzing recession. The economy rebounded in 1976, only to falter again a year later in 1977.

SLOGANS OF THE REVOLUTION

Agnelli, Pirelli—ladri gemelli (Agnelli, Pirelli [the two industry leaders]—thieves the pair of them)

Siamo-stanchi-di pagare-tutti-vizi-dei padroni (We are tired of paying for all the bosses' vices)

Tutto il potere-agli operai (All power to the workers)

Lo stato dei padroni-si abbatte e non si cambia (The bosses' state is for smashing, not changing)

Cosa volete? Tutto. Quando? Subito. (What do you want? Everything. When do you want it? Now)

Inconsistency was just one of many economic problems facing the country at this time. Throughout the 1970s, Italy held the dubious distinction of having the highest rate of inflation of any Western nation. Inflation reached a record high in 1974, and failed to significantly decline thereafter throughout the rest of the decade. Soaring prices proved to be a special hardship for the Italian consumer. The consumer, however, faced other, perhaps more serious dilemmas; not only prices but also unemployment began to rise.

In order to conform to International Monetary Fund regulations, the Bank of Italy introduced deflationary policies during the early 1970s, and it severely limited the money supply. These measures sparked a business recession that forced some factories to close their doors and led others to fire some workers. As a result, indus-

trial production floundered and unemployment reached astronomical heights in the country.

Italian citizens reacted to surging prices and rising unemployment by implementing their own brand of self-reduction in 1974. Consumers began paying only what they believed to be a fair price for goods and services, rather then abiding by the prices set by distributors. In some cases, consumers simply refused to pay anything at all.

The rise of terrorism. Some Italian citizens grew tired of waiting for the nation's unions and its government to improve the lives of the working class. A number of these disgruntled individuals organized terrorist groups, which aimed to effect change through armed conflict. One of Italy's most notorious terrorist organizations, the Red Brigades, was founded as early as October 20, 1970. "They described themselves as 'autonomous workers' organizations' prepared to fight the employers" by means of violent, armed struggle if necessary (Ginsborg, p. 361).

For the most part, the founding members of the Red Brigades came from working- or lower-middle-class families. Most of the activists had been students who previously participated in nonviolent left-wing groups, such as the FGCI, or Communist Party youth movement. Many of their early actions focused on two Milanese factories: Pirelli, and Sit Siemens. In the beginning, the Red Brigades limited their activity to vandalism and occasional beatings. This began to change on April 18, 1974, when the terrorists kidnapped a Genoese judge, Mario Sossi, and held him hostage for some 35 days. This bold act earned the group national attention and inspired a police crackdown on terrorist organizations throughout Italy. The police uncovered hideouts, made a number of high-profile arrests, and in some extreme cases engaged in shootouts with terrorists who refused to be taken alive. By 1976, nearly all the members of the Red Brigade's so-called executive committee had been either captured or killed; however, the organization would remain active even after losing its founding members.

Another terrorist group, led by publishing magnate Giangiacomo Feltrinelli, also surfaced in the early 1970s. Feltrinelli christened his group the Gruppo di Azione Patigiana (GAP; Partisan Action Group). However, the GAP was largely unsuccessful in attracting the same attention as the Red Brigades. As for Feltrinelli, he accidentally blew himself up in 1972, while attempting to plant a bomb at Segrate factory near Milan.

Feminism. While the rise of terrorism represented an extreme reaction to the social, economic, and political climate of 1970s Italy, it was not the only significant movement to grow out of this period: the late 1960s and 1970s also witnessed the resurgence of feminism.

On December 1, 1966, Il Gruppo Demistificazione Autoritarismo (Demystification of Patriarchal Authoritarianism), or DEMAU, issued its manifesto. This document, entitled *Manifesto programmatico del gruppo De Mau* (Programmatic Manifesto of the DEMAU Group) identified an apparent conflict between women and society: in the 1960s, many people viewed women, or more precisely the question of women's rights, as a problem for society. However, according to DEMAU, if this is the case, then it must follow that society is in turn a problem for women (The Milan Women's Bookstore Collective, p. 35). This refreshing perspective placed women in the position of subject, rather then object, for the first time, and in this respect, proved innovative. The DEMAU group went on to study women's relationship to the family, concentrating on the ways in which the family subordinated and dominated women. The DEMAU group did not last very long. By 1968, it had lost nearly half its members, many of whom chose to join male groups addressing questions of workers rights; however, DEMAU proved instrumental in raising questions about women's role within the family, and in a larger context, within society as a whole.

DEMAU paved the way for the birth of several other important feminist groups in the early 1970s. In Rome and Milan in 1970, Rivolta Femminile (Feminine Revolt) circulated its own manifesto, along with a landmark essay by noted feminist writer Carla Lonzi, entitled "Spuntiamo Su Hegel" ("We Spit on Hegel"). In its manifesto, Rivolta Femminile denounced marriage, unpaid domestic labor, and male control over female sexuality. While Rivolta Femminile was publishing this influential document, other feminist organizations were also cropping up throughout Italy. Il Movimento de Liberazione della Donna (MLD; Women's Liberation Movement) appeared in 1970, while Lotta Femminista (Feminist Struggle) came into being in 1971. Lotta Femminista spearheaded the "wages for housework" campaign, which held that women (and men) should receive financial compensation from the Italian government for domestic work. In its own manifesto, MLD made demands pursuant to four key issues: the right for women to control their bodies (legalization of abortion, availability of free contraceptives); the elimination of gender stereotypes in schools and workplaces and the

dismantlement of myths associated with women (the myth of the ideal wife or mother); the elimination of economic exploitation (through the institution of public daycare), and legal equalities. While the various feminist groups focused on different aspects of the women's question, one nagging issue seemed to unite all the organizations: the debate over abortion.

Beginning in the early 1970s, Il Centro Italiano di Serilizzazione e Aborto (CISA; The Italian Center for Sterilization and Abortion), in tandem with the Women's Liberation Movement, launched a campaign in support of a woman's right to choose an abortion. In 1975, mass demonstrations in favor of abortion attracted some 25,000 participants, while just one year later the number rose to 100,000 (Lumley, *States of Emergency,* p. 321). Women also collected signatures to force a referendum on the issue, and in some cases even engaged in a practice known as *autodenuncia* (self-incrimination), wherein women procured illegal abortions and then turned themselves in to the authorities. By 1978, this action paid off: parliament passed a law legalizing abortion that year. However, the victory came at a high price for feminist activists. The law stipulated that women must consult with a doctor or social worker prior to obtaining an abortion, and also instituted a seven-day waiting period. Additionally, the law mandated that women under 18 seek parental consent prior to the procedure. Finally, doctors could object to performing abortions on moral grounds. Although all these stipulations irritated many feminist groups, the debate surrounding the issue galvanized action on other women's issues, such as rape and domestic violence. Thus, the battle over abortion affected women in multiple ways.

The Play in Focus

Plot summary. The farce unfolds in an anonymous Italian city during the chaos of inflation and unemployment that characterized 1970s Italy. As the play begins, we meet Antonia, a working-class woman struggling to manage her household amidst rising prices. In the play's first scene, Antonia returns from the market, carrying a veritable cornucopia of food, accompanied by her loyal friend Margherita. When Margherita demands to know how Antonia managed to afford so much food, the heroine relates the story of a madcap self-reduction strike at the local market:

Antonia: This morning I had to go grocery shopping, but I didn't know how I could buy anything, because I didn't have any money. So I walked into the supermarket, and I see a crowd of women. They're all raising hell because the prices are higher than they were just the day before. The manager's trying to calm them down. "Well, there's nothing I can do about it," he said. "The distributors set the prices, and they've decided to raise them." "They decided? With whose permission?" "With nobody's permission. It's the free market. Free competition." "Free competition against who? Against us? And we're supposed to give in? . . . While they fire our husbands . . . and keep raising prices . . ." So I yelled, "You're the thieves!" . . . And then I hid, because I was really scared.

(Fo, *We Won't Pay! We Won't Pay!*, pp. 9-10)

One of the disgruntled shoppers proclaims that the women will pay what they wish, and if the manager doesn't like it, then they won't pay anything at all. As the women begin helping themselves to groceries, the police arrive clad in riot gear to subdue them. The women, however, remain undaunted and calmly exit the store, bags in hand.

Although Antonia relates this adventure to Margherita beaming with pride, her joy is quickly tempered when Margherita asks how Antonia plans to explain the presence of so much food to her husband, Giovanni, who is a devout member of the Communist Party:

Antonia: Yeah . . . maybe it's a bit much. The problem is, he's a man. You know how men are. They can't see the big picture. He's a law and order freak. Who knows what kind of tantrum he'll throw! "How could you do such a thing?" he'll say. "My father built a good life for his children by following the rules. I follow rules. We're poor, but we're honest!" He doesn't know that I've spent everything, that there's nothing left to pay the gas, the electric or the rent. . . . I don't even know how many months behind we are.

(*We Won't Pay! We Won't Pay!*, pp. 11-12)

In order to conceal her crime from Giovanni, Antonia gives some of the purloined food to Margherita, who hides it under her coat to keep him from seeing it. However, an observant Giovanni notices Margherita's sudden "weight gain," and questions his wife about it. Antonia, lying, replies that Margherita is pregnant. Confused, Giovanni wonders how her pregnancy progressed so quickly and why her husband doesn't seem to know about it. A fast-thinking Antonia says Margherita hasn't told her husband because she stopped taking the birth-control pill in order to follow papal doctrine.

Later on, Antonia departs to visit Margherita, leaving a famished Giovanni to eat cat food in her absence. While Giovanni is waiting for his wife, a policeman arrives to inform him that the authorities are systematically searching area homes for goods stolen from the local market earlier that day. When Giovanni expresses his outrage at the looting that took place at the market, the officer surprises him by revealing he in fact sympathizes with the women:

Sergeant: Sure they were . . . they couldn't put up with all this for much longer: You might not believe me, but sometimes it disgusts me to be a policeman . . . to have to rob people of their dignity. And for who . . . for the politicians and slumlords who steal them blind and leave them homeless and hungry.

(*We Won't Pay! We Won't Pay!*, p. 21)

Later on, Margherita and Antonia return to the apartment. A state trooper arrives to search the residence yet again, but this officer is not as sympathetic as his colleague. In an effort to rid themselves of him, Margherita feigns labor. This, however, only complicates matters when the state trooper insists that Margherita go to the hospital in an awaiting ambulance. Margherita and Antonia reluctantly elect to follow the trooper's advice, leaving Giovanni alone once again in the semi-deserted apartment. As Giovanni awaits the return of Antonia and Margherita, Luigi, Margherita's husband, arrives in search of his wife. Luigi explains that he left work early on a work stoppage and arrived home to find the doors open and his wife missing. Giovanni quickly breaks the news of Margherita's alleged pregnancy to a stunned Luigi. Together, the two men decide to go in search of their wives. In the true tradition of farce, Margherita and Antonia return home shortly after their husbands depart, having managed to evade the forced trip to the hospital. Antonia decides to hide her pilfered goods in her father-in-law's shed, so she stuffs them under her coat to create the illusion of pregnancy, and prepares to head out.

Meanwhile, as Giovanni and Luigi frantically prowl the streets in search of their wives, they stumble upon sacks of coffee, which apparently fell from a truck. Unable to resist the temptation, they help themselves to some of it and prepare to make their escape, just as the ubiquitous state trooper arrives. The bumbling duo stumbles off, managing to evade capture, while the state trooper heads back towards Antonia and Giovanni's apartment. Once he tricks the two women into letting him in, the trooper attempts to intimidate Antonia and Margherita so that they will admit to being in possession of stolen goods. However, the eternally crafty Antonia turns the tables on him; when the lights go out because of her failure to pay the power bill, she convinces the trooper he is going blind. In an attempt to escort him out of the darkened apartment, she hits him in the head rendering him unconscious. Believing that she killed him, Antonia tries to resuscitate the unconscious trooper by pumping oxygen from Giovanni's welding equipment into him. However, Antonia succeeds only in bloating the trooper's stomach, thus once again creating the illusion of pregnancy.

Amidst all this chaos, Giovanni and Luigi somehow find their way home, wanting to know how it is that Margherita is no longer pregnant, but Antonia apparently is. After attempting to string together a series of convincing fibs, Antonia finally confesses to her part in the self-reduction strike:

> Antonia: Let him kill me! Go ahead. I'm sick of this lousy life! And I'm fed up with your sermonizing . . . about law and order, and how you follow the rules, rules, rules . . . with such pride. Bullshit! You swallow your pride every day. And then when other people try to find a little dignity by breaking free of the rules you call them looters, bums, terrorists. Terrorism . . . Terrorism is being held hostage by a minimum-wage job. But you don't want to know how things really are.
>
> (*We Won't Pay! We Won't Pay!*, p. 63)

Much to Antonia's astonishment, Giovanni actually agrees with her impassioned speech; the events of the past several hours have made him see the motivation behind Antonia's recent actions. The four go to the window to see an angry mob chasing away the police; as the play ends Giovanni turns to address the audience: "Desperation's funny isn't it?" he asks (*We Won't Pay! We Won't Pay!*, p. 65). This question cuts to the very heart of *We Won't Pay! We Won't Pay!*, a play that finds humor in desperate times.

Political humor in Italy. Dario Fo's work belongs to a broader trend in Italian history of the 1960s and 1970s: the tendency to confront political and social issues through humor. During the time of Fo's writing, Italian cinema, and in some instances even newspapers, had begun to view political and social problems through the lens of satire.

In 1962 Pietro Germi directed the famed comedy *Divorzio all'italiana* ("Divorce Italian Style"), which provided a satirical glimpse into gender re-

lations in southern Italy while simultaneously tackling the politically loaded issue of divorce. During the ensuing two decades, several other comic films also examined political and social questions pertinent to the times. Lina Wertmuller's 1971 work *La seduzione di Mimì* ("The Seduction of Mimì") presents the story of a Sicilian man who opts to look for work in Turin after losing his job for voting for a Communist candidate against a Mafia-backed opponent. Franco Brusati's 1973 film *Pane e Cioccolato* ("Bread and Chocolate") addresses the plight of southern Italian emigrants. The 1974 motion picture *C'eravamo tanto amati* ("We All Loved Each Other So Much") takes a humorous look at the politics of post-war Italy by following the ongoing friendship of three veterans who each take turns falling in love with the same woman. As the preceding examples make clear, political humor infected the cinema in the 1960s and 1970s. However, filmmakers were not the only artists using humor to confront challenging political issues.

Political cartoons also gained in importance following the upheaval of 1968. In the 1950s, stringent censorship laws, coupled with an underdeveloped mass media, made the political cartoon next to impossible to realize. Throughout much of the 1960s the fledgling nature of Italy's mass-media outlets rendered it difficult for artists to find suitable showcases for their work. However, after 1968 cartoons became a prolific means of subverting the establishment and voicing discontent over numerous hot-button issues. From the late 1960s onwards, most political cartoonists identified themselves with left-wing politics; that notwithstanding, many, such as Alfredo Chiappori, found employment at mainstream newspapers and magazines (Lumley, "The Political Cartoon," p. 266).

The plays that belong to Fo's revolutionary period, which were more overtly political in content than the works he penned during the bourgeois phase of his career, fit nicely into this culture of comedy.

Sources and literary context. Although several important theatrical figures and traditions play a part in shaping Fo's play, perhaps the greatest inspiration for *We Won't Pay! We Won't Pay!* remains the events that actually took place in Italy in 1974.

Critics, and Fo himself, identify a number of other overarching influences. The first is the *commedia dell'arte*. A theatrical tradition dating back to the 1500s, *commedia dell'arte* featured Harlequin, a clownish figure often governed by his

insatiable appetites. Appetite is very much at issue in *We Won't Pay! We Won't Pay!*, which one
scholar even classifies as a "comedy of hunger":

> Hunger is a recurring theme in the comedies of
> Dario Fo. His characters are not just hungry for
> food. They are hungry for dignity, hungry for
> justice, hungry for love. The protagonists of *We
> Won't Pay! We Won't Pay* are driven by their
> collective hungers to break free from the con-
> straints in which their poverty has confined
> them.
>
> (Jenkins, "The Comedy of Hunger," p. iv)

Fo also held in high regard several other theatrical traditions, such as vaudeville and bedroom farce. He once defined *We Won't Pay! We
Won't Pay!* as a kind of *pochade,* or one-act French
farce; a play in two acts, Fo's work fails to adhere perfectly to the *pochade,* but it no doubt borrows heavily from the tradition of French farce.
The French playwrights Feydeau and Labiche influenced Fo a great deal, as did clowns, circus
performers, and especially the Neapolitan theatrical tradition. Other influences include *giullari*
and *fabulatori.* Although literally translated as
"jugglers" in English, the *giullari* were theatrical
performers in medieval Italy. They often recited
one-man shows in streets or town squares. Fo
encountered many *fabulatori* (storytellers) during
his childhood. Often they were fishermen who
recounted elaborate folktales in a theatrical manner. However, of all Fo's most cherished dramatic
mentors, the fifteenth-century actor Ruzzante
ranks the highest.

Ruzzante, whose real name was Angelo Beolco,
lived from approximately 1495 to 1542. He probably came originally from the northeastern region
of Veneto. In Ruzzante's work, Fo identified what
he terms a "theater of situation," which in his estimation lay at the heart of popular or working-
class theater (Farrell, "Fo and Ruzzante," p. 84).
In this theater of situation, class conflict and any
situations that result therefrom, determine character behavior. The reader or spectator of Fo's *We
Won't Pay! We Won't Pay!* may immediately recognize such a technique. For the most part, the
backgrounds of the characters remain unknown
to us, and their behavior during the course of the
play depends entirely on the situations with
which they are confronted. Fo also adapted from
Ruzzante the technique of allowing characters to
speak directly to the audience, as Giovanni does
at the end of *We Won't Pay! We Won't Pay!* (Farrell, "Fo and Ruzzante," p. 91).

Reception. Just a few short months after the staging of Fo's play, Italian citizens actually did

begin implementing self-reduction in stores
throughout the country. In fact, when several
women were tried for stealing food from stores
following the play's 1974 debut, prosecuting attorneys attempted to implicate the playwright
himself. Fortunately for Fo, the judge in this particular case did not agree with the prosecutors'
assessment of Fo's perceived role in the incident.

Prosecutors were not the only ones to react
unfavorably to Fo's play. The response to *We
Won't Pay! We Won't Pay!* proved rather mixed
following the play's Italian debut. Many critics
found it difficult to reconcile the work's political message with its farcical structure. Critic
Lanfranco Binni even went so far as to label *We
Won't Pay! We Won't Pay!* as didactic. While many
critics focused on the play's apparent advocacy
of self-reduction, few noticed its feminist under-
tones, or subtle satire of the Communist Party,
reflected in the character of Giovanni. In the
years since *We Won't Pay! We Won't Pay!* critics
have in fact begun to appreciate the work's larger
significance with respect to the burgeoning feminist movement, going so far as to label the play
Fo's first real feminist creation.

Despite the mixed reception in Italy following its initial premiere, *We Won't Pay! We Won't
Pay!* remains one of Fo's most popular works
abroad, having been performed in over 30 countries. Giovanni's parting question to the audience regarding desperation perhaps explains
the resonance of this particular work throughout the world.

—Sarah Annunziato

For More Information

Behan, Tom. *Dario Fo: Revolutionary Theatre.* Lon-
don: Pluto, 2000.
Farrell, Joseph. *Dario Fo and Franca Rame: Harle-
quins of the Revolution.* London: Methuen, 2001.
———. "Fo and Ruzzante: Debts and Obligations."
In *Dario Fo: Stage Text and Tradition.* Ed. Joseph
Farrell and Antonio Scuderi. Carbondale, Ill:
Southern Illinois University Press, 2000.
Fo, Dario. *We Won't Pay! We Won't Pay! and Other
Plays. The Collected Plays of Dario Fo.* Vol. 1. Ed.
Franca Rame. Trans. Ron Jenkins. New York:
Theatre Communications Group, 2001.
Ginsborg, Paul. *A History of Contemporary Italy: So-
ciety and Politics, 1943-1988.* New York: Palgrave
MacMillan, 2003.
Jenkins, Ron. "The Comedy of Hunger." In *We
Won't Pay! We Won't Pay! and Other Plays. The
Collected Plays of Dario Fo.* Vol. 1. Ed. Franca
Rame. Trans. Ron Jenkins. New York: Theatre
Communications Group, 2001.

Lumley, Robert. "The Political Cartoon." In *Italian Cultural Studies: An Introduction*. Ed. David Forgacs and Robert Lumley. Oxford: Oxford University Press, 1996.

———. *States of Emergency: Cultures of Revolt in Italy from 1968-1978*. London: Verso, 1990.

The Milan Women's Bookstore Collective. *Sexual Difference: A Theory of Social-Symbolic Practice*. Bloomington: Indiana University Press, 1990.

Mitchell, Tony. *Dario Fo: People's Court Jester*. London: Methuen, 1986.

We Won't Pay! We Won't Pay!

A Woman

by

Sibilla Aleramo

Journalist, poet, and novelist Sibilla Aleramo (1876-1969) distinguished herself as a leading proponent of women's rights in turn-of-the-twentieth-century Italy with the publication of her first novel, *A Woman*. Born Rina Faccio in Alessandria, Aleramo changed her name in 1906 at the urging of her lover, the poet Giovanni Cena. The daughter of Ernestina Cottimo and Ambrogio Faccio, Aleramo was formally educated only through elementary school, at which time her father relocated his family to the provincial southern town of Porto Marche Civitanova, where the young woman was no longer able to attend school. Aleramo nevertheless developed a passion for literature and writing, which prompted her to contribute articles to various newspapers and magazines. In 1899, Aleramo received an offer to direct *L'Italia femminile* (Women's Italy), a Milan-based magazine. This new position put her in contact with many intellectual luminaries of the era, such as Giovanni Cena, who would eventually wield a major influence over her early literary career. The publication of *A Woman* transformed Aleramo from a struggling writer to an internationally acclaimed author. Thirteen years would elapse before Aleramo published another novel, *Il Passaggio* (1919; The Passage), which received a tepid reaction from the Italian press, despite earning much praise abroad, in particular in France. In 1921, Aleramo followed up *Il Passaggio* with two new books, *Momenti* (Moments), a volume of poetry, and *Andando e Stando* (Going and Staying), a collection of prose works. Another novel, *Trasfigurazione* (Transfig-

THE LITERARY WORK

An autobiographical novel set in Milan and a southern Italian village around 1900; published in Italian (as *Una donna*) in 1906, in English in 1908.

SYNOPSIS

A first-person narrative, the novel centers on a young woman forced into an unhappy and abusive marriage, and powerless under early-twentieth-century Italian law to defend herself against her husband's transgressions.

uration), appeared in 1922, followed five years later by a third, *Amo, Dunque Sono* (I Love, Therefore I Am). Aleramo published her final novel, *Il Frustino* (The Riding Crop), in 1932. Out of all of Aleramo's works, *A Woman* remains by far the most acclaimed. Appearing at a time when feminism was just beginning to take root in Italy, *A Woman* quickly became synonymous with the women's rights movement.

Events in History at the Time of the Novel

The angel in Italy's house. The Italian states of the nineteenth century struggled hard to shake off foreign rule and to unite for the first time in more than a thousand years, since the collapse of the Roman Empire in the West. They succeeded in the 1860s, thanks largely to the combined efforts of Victor Emmanuel, Camillo Cavour, and Giuseppe Garibaldi. After founding the Kingdom of Italy under Victor Emmanuel in 1861, the activists set about forging a new society, but one that consigned women to familiar roles. Although an earlier patriot, Giuseppe Mazzini, had a radically different vision of the roles women would play in a united Italy, the one finally prescribed fell into line with the conception of women in other European societies. In Italy, as

---

THE NEW ITALIAN WOMAN—A PATRIOT'S VISION, ABORTED

In February of 1849, Giuseppe Mazzini, a patriot with a dream of Italian unity, founded the Roman republic. Mazzini wasted no time in attempting to incorporate women in his plans for the new Italy. A forward-thinking visionary, he considered women the political and social equal of men. But Mazzini would not have a chance to put his beliefs into practice because his newly minted Roman republic was short lived. The French king Louis Napoleon came to the aid of the pope in Rome, sending in troops that quashed the fledgling republic on July 2, 1849. A month later Austrian forces repressed a republic that had been founded in Venice. In the wake of these defeats, Mazzini fled Italy. A decade later, when unification finally ensued, the Italy that began to emerge differed widely from the one Mazzini had envisioned, in which women were to fill both political and maternal roles. Under King Victor Emanuel, this ideal was replaced by another—*maternità illustri* (illustrious motherhood)—which exalted motherhood as the highest female goal, diverging radically from Mazzini's original plan.

---

elsewhere, women were mostly confined to the role of dutiful mother and wife. Middle-class women lived sheltered lives; except when attending school, they rarely left home alone. At the start of the twentieth century, there were few women who pursued higher education or a profession. Those who did not marry still had only one other acceptable choice: life in a religious order or convent. The working daughters of laborers and peasants were less confined, but even they were kept under close watch. Female laborers worked in separate shops from men, often in silence under the gaze of nuns. So strict were the mills and factories in this regard that

peasants had few qualms about sending their daughters away to work.

Italian women were conditioned to pursue domesticity and motherhood; the emphasis on domestic life reinforced the concept of the *angelo del focolare,* or angel of the house, the model that women were to emulate. The angel of the house never soiled herself with sexual desires. Nor did she engage in intellectual pursuits, and she remained steadfastly faithful and submissive to her husband. Her unending struggle to preserve and defend her chastity simultaneously preserved and defended her husband's honor, and by extension, that of the entire family. Nineteenth-century Italian society repeatedly exalted motherhood and wifehood as every woman's ideal states of being. Society demanded total, selfless dedication from a mother to her offspring and from a wife to her husband. Women who refused to enter into marriage, motherhood, or the religious life were regarded as rebels; their actions, it was thought, threatened to unravel the very fabric of Italian society.

Unsurprisingly, during the nineteenth and early twentieth century a considerable body of literature reinforcing the stereotype of the angel of the house appeared. Not only did such literature exalt motherhood and domesticity as the highest goals of womankind; it also castigated those who turned away from these goals. (Ironically the criticism of these female "transgressors" often came from women writers of the day.) This literary perception of the proper place of Italian women predominated in 1906, when Aleramo's book first appeared.

Italian women and the workforce. The role of women in the Italian workforce changed following unification, largely because of the rapidly shifting political climate. In the post-unification days, the new citizens founded several political movements that attracted members of the Italian workforce. Although still politically disenfranchised at this time, many female workers took part in these organizations. Established in 1892, the Socialist Party made significant inroads with factory workers and agricultural laborers, threatening the Catholic Church's hold on the Italian populace. The Party wasted no time recruiting workers for its so-called "red" labor unions; the Church countered with unions of its own, often referred to as "white" (Meyer, p. 12). These Church-based unions appealed especially to female workers, who joined them in record numbers. The white unions, following the Church's agenda, tried to prevent women workers from becoming members of the Socialist Party. However, they led to an unanticipated consequence: some of the white unions broke away to form independent groups and the Church found itself struggling to reassert control over them. In the end, the participation of women in these white unions was extremely significant. With them, "a process of indefinite potential for women's sense of identity had begun" (Meyer, p. 13). In the second half of the nineteenth century the white unions gave rise to an important branch of the early Italian feminist movement, that of the Christian feminists.

The struggle for suffrage. Aleramo's *A Woman* appeared around 40 years after the Italian unification of 1861. Unification brought the question of women's rights to the fore by opening the workforce to women and raising the issue of women's suffrage. Shortly after the unification of the Italian states in 1861, Italy's new parliament issued a bill that barred women from voting in national elections. Despite this early setback, some individual members of parliament came out in support of voting rights for women. One of these members, Salvatore Morelli, introduced a bill to grant women's suffrage in 1867. Despite Morelli's best efforts, the bill failed and women were once again denied the vote in the newly unified Italy. This continued rejection only encouraged politically active women to campaign more stridently for voting rights.

The Socialist Party included female workers and important feminists, such as Anna Kuliscioff and Anna Maria Mozzoni. But since its constituency in the late nineteenth century consisted mainly of male workers, the leadership chose to cater to its masculine majority. The decision to focus on the interests of male workers lessened the socialists' attention to questions of interest to women, such as suffrage. Mozzoni, her Socialist ties aside, continued to lead the way (later she would gain renown as the first Italian feminist).

The 1890s saw working women, some of them lower-middle-class, launch a struggle for female emancipation. These female workers—factory hands, teachers, and clerks—followed Mozzoni's lead. But soon the middle-class activists turned away from her radical stance. Instead of demanding recognition as equal citizens based on natural human rights, they argued for this recognition because, as mothers, they were vital to the social order.

Despite such feminist leaders as Kuliscioff and Mozzoni, the Socialist Party began to see women voters as a potential threat: much of the female population lived in the South, whose constituents tended to vote in favor of the Church's political agenda, which usually conflicted with that of the Socialists. The fear was that should women gain the vote, they would only boost the ranks of the opposition in this region.

Kuliscioff and Mozzoni nevertheless encouraged debate over suffrage. In 1901 Giovanni Giolitti became prime minister of Italy. He soon took steps to dramatically expand male suffrage but ignored the question of voting rights for women, not because of any strong conviction but because of his political agenda. During his tenure as prime minister, Giolitti entered into deals with Catholic leaders and expanded male suffrage, in part to draw the country's Catholic voters into the ranks of the electorate. He also wanted to encourage Catholics to participate in the Liberal Party and to discourage the Vatican from attempting to form a new opposition party. Since many staunch Catholics were against women's suffrage, Giolitti ignored the question to appease them.

The growth of the Italian women's movement and the committed writer. Late-nineteenth and early-twentieth-century Italian law reflected the prevailing beliefs about women. The law afforded women no rights whatsoever in the governing of their families and little means of escape from a disastrous marriage. Although divorce was out of the question at the time of the novel, legal separation could be obtained, but only with the husband's approval. Moreover, in the event of separation, Italian law automatically granted custody of any minor children to the father. Also married women could only inherit money or property with their husband's permission; hence a separated woman might find it difficult to obtain any material possessions that were willed to her. Along with women's growing participation in the workforce and their struggle for suffrage, the drive for legal reform sparked the development of an Italian feminist movement that would confront all these pressing questions.

Unsurprisingly the women's movement in late-nineteenth- and early-twentieth-century Italy was not a monolithic institution. Two opposing currents emerged in the first decade of the 1900s: a Catholic, Christian women's movement and a secular variety. The first current, the so-called Christian feminists, consisted mainly of activists from the Church's white labor unions. The early Christian feminists concentrated on service to the community and opposed socialism and concerns of the secular movement, such as the push for women to attain the vote. The secular branch of feminism frequently consisted of members of the Italian bourgeoisie. Focusing on the struggle for equal rights with men, the secular activists championed pertinent causes such as suffrage. A tense relationship, spurred on by fundamental differences in ideology, existed between these competing branches of the women's movement. Yet both types of activism made profound contributions to Italian society of the day.

The Christian feminist movement produced many influential thinkers and activists. Elena da Persico directed the women's magazine *L'Azione Muliebre* (Woman's Action), which briefly employed Adelaide Coari, who in 1904 founded the women's journal *Pensiero e Azione* (Thought and Action) to discuss issues facing young female workers. Dora Melegari explored the nature of the Italian feminist movement itself, examining how Italian women were viewed abroad and attempting to explain why feminism developed much later in Italy than in other nations.

IMPORTANT DATES IN THE EARLY FEMINIST MOVEMENT

1861 Parliament passes a bill blocking women's suffrage.

1864 Anna Maria Mozzoni publishes *Woman and Her Social Relationships.*

1868 *La Donna* is founded in Venice.

1892 The Socialist Party is founded.

1897 L'Associazione Nazionale delle Donne (National Association of Women) is founded in Milan.

1899 Fascio Femminile Demoratico Cristiano (Women's Christian Democratic Party) organizes its journal in Milan.

1899 L'Unione Femminile Nazionale (The National Women's Union) is founded in Milan.

1903 Il Consiglio Nazionale delle Donne (The National Council of Women) is founded in Rome.

While the Christian activists were engaged in these enterprises, their anticlerical counterparts were busy making contributions of their own. In 1864 Anna Maria Mozzoni published her first book, entitled *Woman and Her Social Relationships,* which began to delineate her trademark philosophies of feminism and women's rights. Addressing her book to young, middle-class women, Mozzoni urged them to forgo restrictive traditions for new horizons. In subsequent writing, she would offer the women's movements

underway in the United States and other parts of Europe as models for Italian activists. Mozzoni advocated improving women's status in Italy by reforming the educational system. She sought to create an educated female middle class, charged with achieving social and political change for Italian women everywhere. While Mozzoni pitched her views, Kuliscioff kept promoting women's suffrage, with limited success.

In the meantime, in 1868, *La Donna* (Woman), one of Italy's first women's magazines, began publication in Venice. The magazine featured a variety of articles by authors all over Italy and included items on women's movements in other countries. Although the publication of *La Donna* continued only until 1891, it did a great deal to facilitate awareness on issues of central importance to women in Italy.

For her part, Sibilla Aleramo participated in the burgeoning women's movement by making regular contributions to women's journals, such as *Vita Moderna* (Modern Life), an achievement she incorporates in *A Woman*, when she describes her character's initial efforts to pen articles for women's publications. At the dawn of the twentieth century, Sibilla Aleramo was poised to add her voice to the growing chorus of those demanding a better life for Italian women and in a more dramatic way than she had ever done before, with the publication of her novel.

The Novel in Focus

Plot summary. Structurally *A Woman* adheres to a strict tripartite division. Part One consists of nine chapters, which document the protagonist's adolescence, marriage, and entrance into motherhood. The ten chapters that comprise Part Two chronicle her growing marital difficulties, blossoming career as a writer, and efforts to separate from her husband. The last part—just three chapters—focuses squarely on the psychological forces that motivate the young woman to finally abandon the conjugal home and her son.

The novel, a first-person narrative, opens with a description of the unnamed heroine's long-since-abandoned youth: "I had an active, carefree childhood. If I try to live it again in my memory, rekindle it in my conscious mind, I always fail. I see the child I was at six, at ten years old, but it is as if I am dreaming her" (Aleramo, *A Woman*, p. 3). In the course of the novel, the young woman will undergo a radical process of transformation; having moved from independent, carefree child to abused wife, she ultimately circles back to independence once again.

The protagonist's story begins in earnest when her father, an employee at his brother-in-law's business, returns home and announces that he has just quit his job. Soon enough, he receives an offer to head a chemical plant in southern Italy, so he swiftly relocates his family from Milan to this new locale. The change signals a major transformation in the young heroine's life; now 12 years old and always an intellectually active child, she finds her studies stunted by the backward educational system in her new southern environment. No longer able to attend school, the young adolescent goes to work in her father's factory and becomes a sort of confidante and business associate to him. The time spent with her father is no hardship for her. She completely identifies with him and rejects her mother's domestic life: "The servants must have told hair-raising stories about me. I was never seen with a needle in my hand, was rarely at home, and showed no interest in helping with the housework" (*A Woman*, p. 17). Apparently the narrator rejects typical female roles in the household. The family as a whole meanwhile faces a difficult cultural transition because of its move from wealthy northern Italy to the seemingly narrow-minded South. The father especially finds the townspeople to be backward and corrupt. He looks down upon them with an air of contempt, and they return the sentiment.

Amidst all this radical change, the protagonist's mother begins fighting a losing battle against depression that culminates in a suicide attempt. The heroine relates how her mother's brush with death shakes the family to its very core, particularly her father, who continues to distance himself from his loved ones.

As the protagonist watches her mother gradually slip into madness and her beloved father become increasingly aloof, she faces physical and psychological transformations of her own. Rapidly developing into an attractive young woman, she garners the attention of a male coworker some ten years her senior. Eventually this newfound friend informs the heroine that local gossip suggests her father has been carrying on an affair with another woman. The news is devastating to the young woman, who responds by spending more time with her would-be suitor. Their relationship takes a profoundly disturbing turn when he rapes her one day in their office, thereby plunging her into a dangerous identity crisis, which causes her to ask the question, "Did this man own me?" (*A Woman*, p. 36). After the rape, Sibilla and her attacker make plans to wed.

Her father at first objects to the marriage on the grounds that Sibilla is too young to become a wife. But in a few months he relents, allowing Sibilla to marry her rapist at the age of 16.

Although the new bride leaves her parents' home, she continues to be plagued by her family's problems. Her mother descends ever more deeply into madness, until the family must place her in an asylum. Her father continues to neglect his younger offspring and, scornful of his eldest daughter's marriage, has very little contact with her despite their earlier closeness when they worked together at his factory. As she faces the pain of her own mother's madness, the heroine is forced to consider how she feels about motherhood for the first time when she suffers a miscarriage. A successful pregnancy follows, and she gives birth to a son. Her son's appearance corresponds to the figurative birth of her writing career—the heroine begins documenting her child's growth in a journal.

Unfortunately all is not well for the young mother—a scandal erupts when she is falsely accused of having an affair with a male friend. Although she has not betrayed her husband, the accusations send him into a rage that leads him to verbally and physically assault her. After receiving a particularly savage beating at his hands, she attempts suicide by ingesting poison and is saved by a local doctor.

The protagonist's failed suicide attempt signals the beginning of a new life for her, albeit one still dominated by her husband. Although shaken by his wife's desperate actions, the husband refuses to trust her. He begins locking her away in their home by day while he goes to work in her father's factory.

Emotionally and physically fragile following her suicide attempt, the protagonist receives a book from her father, which gives her a new lease on life. At this point her husband begins encouraging her to write, albeit only to confess her sins. But the young woman has other ambitions; she begins penning articles for various journals, including one in which she uses the word *feminism* for the first time. The narrator's writing soon becomes the main source of financial support for her and her husband, who, after an argument with her father, loses his job at the factory. They relocate to Rome, where the young writer takes a job working for a women's journal, *Mulier* (Woman), which brings her into contact with intellectuals for the first time. Thanks to these new acquaintances, and her ongoing writing career, she begins to consider the possibility of legally separating from her husband. Despite her best efforts to convince him, her husband remains opposed to such a separation. Although her marriage becomes more tolerable following the move to Rome, she is terrified when her husband receives an offer to return to their former home to become director of the factory. One by one, her colleagues at the magazine advise her not to follow her husband back, but she is torn over the likelihood of losing her son. When she finds a letter written many years earlier by her mother to her grandparents, the situation becomes even more pressing. The letter reveals that before losing her mind, the mother also grappled with the decision to leave

---

FINDING THEIR VOICES: INVENTING WOMEN'S LITERATURE

The unnamed protagonist of *A Woman* draws an important conclusion: most female authors of her era are producing pale imitations of literary works already penned long ago by men:

> I thought them mere parodies of male literary fashion, written by women even more vain and stupid than the society dolls whose "modern style" apartments we featured in our magazine. Didn't they know that the literary world was already overcrowded? When would these "intellectual" women realize that they could only justify a place in it by producing books which had a strong character of their own?
>
> (*A Woman*, pp. 137-38)

At the time of Aleramo's writing, works written by men continued to dominate the literary world; Aleramo believed that these texts presented an idealized image of women, which reinforced the stereotypical roles prescribed for females in traditional Italian society. She identified a willingness on the part of other female writers to imitate the idealized models set forth by established male writers. In Aleramo's estimation, a style of writing unique to women had yet to be fashioned: men defined the linguistic forms for literary works while women simply imitated them, adopting a language not their own (Wood, p. 84). In Aleramo's estimation, women writers could learn to manipulate the male discourse, but this achievement would be at the expense of developing distinctly female forms of expression, which for this author had yet to be invented (Wood, p. 84).

---

her husband and children; in this missive, Sibilla's mother reveals the depth of her unhappiness as a woman trapped in a loveless marriage. To avoid losing her mind, explains the letter, she must leave

her husband, and by extension her children as well. She struggles with leaving her children and the effect her departure will have on them. Reading these revelations at this point in her own life, Sibilla realizes that her mother erred by staying with her family. Her mother's breakdown occurred years after she wrote the letter, but clearly she lost her mind because of the abuse and oppression suffered at the hands of her husband:

> "I have to leave . . . I'm going mad here . . . he doesn't love me any more. . . . And I am so unhappy that I no longer even love my children . . . I have to leave them, I have to leave . . . I'm sorry for my children, but perhaps this will be better for them."
>
> (*A Woman*, p. 192)

After enduring more physical abuse from her husband, and realizing that he may have exposed her to venereal disease, the heroine makes the difficult decision to leave both him and her son. At the close of the novel she relates that a year has passed since she last saw her little boy, and it is this separation that convinces her of the need to write about her troubles, so that one day he may understand his mother's actions.

The Southern Question. Without a doubt, one of the most crucial turning points in the life of Aleramo's heroine occurs when she relocates from Milan to southern Italy. The move signals a radical shift in culture, as it transports her from an urban northern setting to an economically and socially underdeveloped southern town. Although Aleramo herself moved with her family to the southern town of Porto Marche Civitanova, in her novel she takes great care to never name the protagonist's new home, referring to it only as a southern village.

Aleramo's anonymous heroine receives her first culture shock in her new environment when she learns that her education will be cut short:

> I was twelve. In our village (dignified by the locals to the status of town) there was only an elementary school. A schoolmaster was brought in to give me lessons, but was quickly dismissed because he was unable to teach me more than I already knew.
>
> (*A Woman*, p. 14)

Women especially are affected by the town's meager educational resources. The men of the town are of two types: peasants, fishermen, and workers employed primarily in her father's factory, and middle-class "professional men" (*A Woman*, p. 20). Middle-class men managed to establish careers despite the town's lack of educational resources, while here, as elsewhere in Italy, women had far fewer options at their disposal. Thus, the women found themselves consigned to lives spent caring for a home and family: "Cooking, religion, and the lazy, rough and ready care of children was their entire life" (*A Woman*, p. 49).

The protagonist frowns upon the southern Italian way of life, and is especially critical of the women. The heroine concentrates most of her disdain for southern women on her mother-in-law and sister-in-law, whose child-rearing techniques and superstitious tendencies she condemns as "barbaric practices" (*A Woman*, p. 59). Aleramo's young narrator relates that her mother-in-law reacts unfavorably to her insistence that they refrain from adorning her son's crib with amulets or other talismans, as was often customary in southern Italy during this era.

The author reveals her own bias against southern Italy through her protagonist's rather condescending sentiments. Although Aleramo sought to improve the condition of women in early-twentieth-century Italy, she did not concern herself with rural women of the impoverished South. Aleramo believed it was most critical to liberate middle-class women from the domination of their fathers and husbands, and that this liberation would lead to the emancipation of women throughout the country (Wood, p. 82). Like many northerners of this era, she regarded the South as a backward region, an attitude tied to one of Italy's most pressing social issues of the day: the "Southern Question."

The "Southern Question" refers to the issues facing the provinces south of Rome, where poverty, economic and industrial underdevelopment, organized crime, and patriarchal gender roles were rife. The Southern Question gave rise to deeply entrenched stereotypes of southerners as superstitious, corrupt, and undisciplined. While North-South divergences had plagued literary Italy for some time, they crystallized into a North-versus-South debate in the decades after Unification, especially from 1870 into the 1890s. Northerners came to attribute the South's lack of economic prosperity to the inherent defects of its residents rather than to "objective economic and political conditions" (Gramsci, p. 71). This stereotype was promoted by sociologists such as Alfredo Niceforo and even reinforced (perhaps unwittingly) by novelists like Aleramo in their writings.

Sources and literary context. Aleramo began formulating her famous novel in a series of diary entries written as early as 1901. Just one year later, she would start writing *A Woman* at the urging of Giovanni Cena (Drake, p. xiv). While he supported Aleramo's work to a great extent, his was not the strongest influence on the young author. It is fair to say that Aleramo's past played the greatest role in stimulating her to compose *A Woman*. Although the novel only refers to characters by the titles that delineate their social relationship to the protagonist (e.g., mother, father, husband, etc.) and is vague about dates and locations, the details of Aleramo's life make it clear that her own personal experiences inspired the story. In her preface to the Italian edition, Maria Corti lists aspects of the novel that correspond to events in Aleramo's life:

- The father's decision to relocate his family to the South
- The young girl's employment in her father's factory
- The mother's depression
- The physical violence the young girl suffers at the hands of her future husband
- The protagonist's abusive marriage
- The miscarriage
- The birth of the protagonist's son
- The heroine's decision to leave her husband and son

(Corti, p. ix)

Also Aleramo, like the heroine, attempted suicide following a severe bout of depression. Her exposure to other works of art was influential too. During her recovery, she read *L'Europa giovane* (Young Europe) by sociologist Guglielmo Ferrero, a work often credited with igniting her interest in issues such as feminism. Prior to separating from her husband, Aleramo also saw Henrik Ibsen's *A Doll's House*, a late-nineteenth-century play that culminates in the heroine's shocking decision to leave her husband and three young children to make a better life for herself. *A Woman* has a similar ending.

Despite these obvious autobiographical influences, Aleramo stopped short of labeling *A Woman* an autobiography. What rendered her work a novel in Aleramo's eyes was not what the book shared with its readers, but what *A Woman* failed to reveal. Prior to leaving her husband in 1902, Aleramo had engaged in an extra-marital affair, which is not chronicled in her novel. In addition, after moving out of her husband's house, Aleramo took up residence with Cena in Rome, another detail not included in *A Woman*. It was Cena who convinced Aleramo to eliminate all traces of her affairs from the final version of her novel, to strengthen *A Woman's* ultimate condemnation of women's plight in contemporary

Italy (Drake, p. xv). In the end, Aleramo did not want to write an autobiography but a story about a woman who resembled many others.

However one might classify it, the publication of *A Woman* constituted a major development in Italian literature. Although many people were already advocating political and social reforms to improve women's condition at the time of Aleramo's writing, very few female authors dealt with these concerns in their works. In this respect, *A Woman* signals a critical turning point in Italian literature by women, a shift away from a group of writers like those whom Aleramo's protagonist criticizes during her years of work at *Mulier* to another group that focused on liberating Italian women. The works of the former did not question women's traditional role in society, nor did they display any interest in creating a unique style of writing. The popular nineteenth-century author Neera stands out as an important example of some of these tendencies. In her most famous novel, *Teresa* (also in *WLAIT 7: Italian Literature and Its Times*), Neera vividly describes the tedious life her heroine leads enslaved as caretaker for her father and younger siblings. However, Neera does not advocate liberating her from the traditional societal roles that imprison her in an unsatisfying life, as Aleramo does in *A Woman*. Aleramo proved to be a pivotal writer in this regard. Those who followed her shared her interest in criticizing some of the obstacles that oppressed women, and discouraged them from imitating male authors at the expense of creating a new type of women's literature. In short, Aleramo's novel laid the groundwork for the new type of women's fiction for which her heroine yearned.

Reception. Following its 1906 publication, *A Woman* achieved much success both at home and abroad. Numerous Italian critics pondered the question of genre when reviewing Aleramo's novel. In fact, many early reviewers were as puzzled by the autobiographical question as Aleramo herself may have been. Additionally Italian critics saw in *A Woman* a very modern literary achievement and were fascinated by its depiction of the heroine's relationships with different members of her family. However, reaction in Italy was mixed, to say the least; many critics attacked the heroine's decision to forsake her marriage and leave her son behind. Virginia Olper Monis harshly criticized the heroine's drastic action, pointing out that in the end the child left behind became an innocent victim. She also insisted that Aleramo's *A Woman* not be viewed as an exam-

ple for intelligent women to follow (Grimaldi Morosoff, p. 12). Additional female reviewers found particular fault with the novel on account of other elements in the plot, such as the heroine's anger towards her husband for infecting her with venereal disease:

> But the straw that broke Sibilla's back is the illness [the venereal disease] which her husband contracts when his wife is absent for some weeks. A malicious argument, because if all wives were to abandon their husbands made ill by human weakness it is plain to all how many hearths would remain deserted.
>
> (Gropollo in Wood, p. 81)

Other critics reacted favorably to Aleramo's novel, regarding it a triumph in the cause of women's rights. Far from selfishness, the heroine's final decision to leave home was seen by Adolfo Sassi as an act of sacrifice to the greater goal of women's emancipation (Grimaldi Morosoff, p. 11). Gina Lombroso applauded the generational bond established in the work: "The drama . . . is not so much between this man and this woman but the struggle which the woman carries on with her own mother" (Lombroso in Wood, p. 81). The famed playwright Luigi Pirandello praised the novel's aesthetic qualities, calling it a "serious" and "profound" work (Pirandello in Grimaldi Morosoff, p. 12; trans. S. Annunziato).

If Italian critics did not quite know what to make of Aleramo's novel, foreign reviewers had few doubts about *A Woman*. The German press praised the novel heartily, and other translations appeared in English, French, Spanish, Swedish, Polish, and Russian. French reviewers were perhaps kinder to *A Woman* than any other foreign audience. Published in 1908, the French translation was met with glowing reviews from critics who acknowledged Aleramo's young protagonist as "the most complete female character in Italian literature" (Drake, p. vi).

—Sarah Annunziato

For More Information

Aleramo, Sibilla. *A Woman*. Trans. Rosalind Delmar. Berkeley: University of California Press, 1980.

Amoia, Alba. *No Mothers We: Italian Women Writers and Their Revolt Against Maternity*. Lanham, Md.: University Press of America, 2000.

Beales, Derek, and Eugenio F. Biagini. *The Risorgimento and the Unification of Italy*. London: Longman, 2002.

Corti, Maria. Foreward to *Una Donna*, by Sibilla Alermo. Milan: Feltrinelli, 1998.

Drake, Richard. Introduction to *A Woman*, by Sibilla Alermo. Berkeley: University of California Press, 1980.

Gramsci, Antonio. *Selections from the Prison Notebooks*. Trans. Quintin Hoare and Geoffrey Nowell Smith. New York: International Publishers, 1971.

Grimaldi Morosoff, Anna. *Transfigurations: The Autobiographical Novels of Sibilla Aleramo*. New York: Peter Lang, 1999.

Meyer, Donald B. *Sex and Power: The Rise of Women in America, Russia, Sweden, and Italy*. Middletown, Conn.: Wesleyan University Press, 1987.

Riall, Lucy. *The Italian Risorgimento: State, Society, and National Unification*. London: Routledge, 1994.

Schneider, Jane. "The Dynamics of Neo-Orientalism in Italy (1848-1995)." Introduction to *Italy's "Southern Question": Orientalism in One Country*. Ed. Jane Schneider. Oxford: Berg, 1998.

Wood, Sharon. *Italian Women's Writing 1860-1994*. London: Athlone, 1995.

Zeno's Conscience

by

Italo Svevo

I talo Svevo, whose real name was Ettore Aron Schmitz, was born in 1861 in Trieste to Jewish parents of mixed backgrounds. His mother, Allegra Moravia, belonged to an Italian Jewish family. His father, Francesco Schmitz, a German Jew also born in Trieste, had by then managed to establish himself as a successful businessman. Schmitz had a comfortable childhood. At the age of 11 he was sent to an academy near Würzburg, Germany, where, for the next five years he studied business and commerce and improved his command of the German and French languages. Upon returning to Trieste, he enrolled at the Istituto Revoltella, the local business school for higher education, and during his tenure there read French, German, and Italian literary works in their original languages, and English and Russian texts in translation. Trieste had a very fine theater, which Schmitz attended regularly.

He began to write short literary reviews for the local paper, *L'Indipendente* (The Independent), as well as some short stories and plays. His relatively carefree lifestyle ended in 1880, however; his father's business failed, and Schmitz felt compelled to take a job as a clerk at Unionbank, a Viennese bank with a branch in Trieste. Although very unhappy in it, he kept the job for the next 20 years while continuing to write. In 1892 Schmitz self-published his first novel, *Una Vita* (A Life), the tale of an inept bank clerk with literary aspirations. Here for the first time Ettore Schmitz used the pseudonym Italo Svevo, meaning "Italian Swabian (or German)," to underline his mixed heritage. In 1896, after a short but in-

THE LITERARY WORK

An ironic novel set in Trieste c. 1900–1915; published in Italian (as *La coscienza di Zeno*) in 1923, in English in 1930.

SYNOPSIS

In the form of a personal diary, the novel narrates the adventures and comic misadventures of a Triestine businessman, Zeno Cosini: his failed attempt to quit smoking, the death of his father, his marriage, his unsuccessful business endeavors, and his problematic interaction with psychoanalysis.

tense affair with a local working-class woman, Schmitz married Livia Veneziani, the daughter of his first cousin (a successful industrialist), with whom he had his only child, Letizia. His family did not deter him from his literary pursuits, but critical response did. In 1898, again at his own expense, Svevo published his second novel, *Senilità* (Enrico's Carnival), and, embittered by the few unfavorable reviews, decided to abandon a literary career. His wife recalled him saying, "Write one must. What one needn't do is publish" (Svevo in Veneziani, p. 35).

In 1899 Svevo began work at his in-laws' factory (manufacturing naval and submarine paint). Because his new job took him to England intermittently, he decided to take English lessons at the Berlitz school in Trieste. It was here that in 1906, he met Irish writer James Joyce, a teacher at the school. The two developed a friendship based on mutual admiration. Joyce read *Senilità* with pleasure and encouraged Schmitz to keep writing. In the next decade Svevo became interested in the recently published works of Sigmund Freud and continued to draft short stories and plays. He began his masterpiece, *La coscienza di Zeno* (Zeno's Conscience), in 1919 and yet again published it at his own expense in 1923. Schmitz died after a car accident just five years later, in September 1928.

The masterpiece he left behind does for Trieste what Joyce's works do for Dublin, and Franz Kafka's do for Prague. Trieste becomes a virtual character, a symbolic city reflective of the complex cultural and political identity of its inhabitants at the turn of the twentieth century.

Events in History at the Time of the Novel

Trieste—historical background. A small, independent, vulnerable settlement after the fall of the Roman Empire, in 1382 Trieste placed itself under the protection of the Holy Roman Empire for fear of being conquered by the nearby rich and powerful Republic of Venice. Until the eighteenth century it remained an insignificant fishing town; even the imperialistic Habsburg dynasty of Europe had little interest in this small outpost. Things changed in the eighteenth century when, thanks to a 1749 decree by Archduchess Maria Teresa, the city of Trieste acquired the privileges and exemptions of a free port (one through which merchandise can be moved without paying duties) for goods entering and leaving the Austro-Hungarian Empire. The effect was monumental; Trieste grew from an economically insignificant border-town into the main port of the Empire. It became a productive, financially powerful city devoted principally to commerce: during the nineteenth century Trieste housed a very active stock exchange as well as insurance companies and shipping agencies. The Austro-Hungarian policy of religious tolerance and the possibility of economic mobility made the city appealing to a great many immigrants from Europe and the Middle East. By the mid-nineteenth century, the city population included not only Italians but also Slavs, Germans, Austrians, Eastern European Jews, Greeks, and Turks; Trieste attained a multiethnic, multicultural quality, which by century's end was one of its most distinct characteristics.

Despite the privileged position that came from being part of the Austro-Hungarian Empire, most Italian Triestines subscribed to the Italian nationalist movement that saw Trieste and its surroundings as *terre irredente*, or "unredeemed lands," that ought to be annexed to Italy. Part of their motivation in so thinking was that the population's heterogeneity presented something of a threat; Trieste's rise in status brought with it a large proletarian class, composed mostly of Slovenes, who abandoned the surrounding countryside to try to improve their economic conditions in the city. The ever-increasing number of Slovenes who moved to Trieste to offer cheap labor (between 1864 and 1909 the city's population doubled, increasing from 112,000 to 224,000) threatened the Italian Triestines, who feared becoming a minority in a city they considered Italian. Theirs was a complicated nationalism, though; they could not accept without reservations the Italian nationalist movement, being perfectly aware that their economic power depended upon belonging to the Austro-Hungarian Empire. Pulled by conflicting national, ethnic, and economic interests, the city became, for turn-of-the-twentieth-century Triestine authors, an emblem of the crisis of the modern man and woman. They had to learn to live in a world that was becoming more and more fragmented, in which no single set of beliefs was enough to deal with the complexities of life.

The cultural and political ambivalence came to an abrupt end at the onset of World War I, when Italy joined France, Russia, and Britain against Germany and Austro-Hungary. Many Italian Triestines, although they were Austrian citizens, escaped to Italy to join the Italian army and fight as Italian soldiers against the Empire. With the defeat of the Austro-Hungarian Empire in 1918, Trieste and the surrounding Adriatic coast became part of Italy, and the unique cosmopolitan atmosphere that had characterized the city soon disappeared. There was an intensely nationalistic atmosphere in the immediate aftermath of the war that swept the city into its fold (and would lead Italy in a few years to embrace the Fascist regime).

Literary Trieste and its philosophical influences. Because of its unique cosmopolitan environment, early-twentieth-century Trieste produced what Claudio Magris later called "the great Triestine generation" (Magris, p. 293). To this generation belonged, among others, the writers Scipio Slataper, Umberto Saba, and Carlo Michelstaedter, all of whom were interested in the irresolvable conflicts of modern civilization that were so visible in their city (e.g., nationalism versus internationalism, urban versus rural life). In his critical essays for the famous literary and cultural journal *La Voce* (The Voice; based in Florence), Slataper analyzes Trieste's cultural and political heterogeneity, and in his fragmentary autobiography *Il mio Carso* (My Karst) portrays the city's complex urban environment. The poetry of Umberto Saba (1883-1957) is inspired by the lively, tormented atmosphere of his port town. In 1910 Carlo Michelstaedter (1887-1910), a young philosopher from the nearby town of Gorizia, wrote the treatise *Le persuasione e la rettorica* (Persuasion and Rhetoric), and then killed himself. The text examines the impossibility of living an authentic life in a world whose relationships are dictated by pure appearance and rhetoric. Although the three authors wrote at more or less the same time, and, in the cases of Slataper and Michelstaedter, even attended the same university in Florence, they did not collaborate with one another. This is readily apparent from Slataper's articles for *La Voce*, in which he dismisses Trieste's cultural and literary assets: he strongly criticizes Saba's poems while ignoring the existence of Svevo's first two novels. Yet, while not a homogenous group, all three were reacting to the same literary practice, aestheticism, promoted by Gabriele D'Annunzio, one of the most emulated writers in Italy at the time. The movement celebrated art for art's sake, divorcing it from any ethical aim, seeing it as existing only for the purpose of its own beauty. The Triestine authors took issue with this artistic detachment, and the difference showed in their writing.

In opposition to the refined language, elegant imageries, and aristocratic settings that characterized D'Annunzio's novels *Il Piacere* (1889; **Child of Pleasure,** also in *WLAIT 7: Italian Literature and Its Times*) and *L'Innocente* (1892; *The Intruder*), the Triestine authors offered a prosaic style that originated from the bourgeois setting in which they lived. Their reading and assimilation of the theories of German philosopher Friedrich Nietzsche (1844-1900) is particularly telling. Although it is indisputable that Nietzsche was a major influence on D'Annunzio, as on many Triestine authors, his philosophy was filtered differently on either side of the border. The authors writing in Trieste at this time recognized Nietzsche "to be an extremely lucid and unmasking—certainly not emphatic or vitalistic—spokesman for the discontent of civilization" (Magris, p. 294). D'Annunzio and other Italian intellectuals seized on a comparatively small aspect of Nietzsche's philosophy, his concept of the "superman," de-veloping it into a stereotypical image of strength and power. Meanwhile, the Triestine writers focused on a prominent part of the philosophy, Nietzsche's notion that all values "are *relative* to a particular framework, an outlook, a culture, a time and place," that it is impossible to get at separate truths unfettered by conditions or perspectives (Solomon and Higgins, p. 37). It was this unveiling of the relativity of any system of values that preoccupied the writers of Trieste.

IMPORTANT DATES IN TRIESTE'S HISTORY

C. 60 B.C.E. Trieste is the Roman colony of Tergeste

1000s Trieste becomes independent commune

1100s-1200s Series of armed conflicts with Venice

1382 Trieste accepts the protection of Leopold III of Austria

1719 Trieste is declared a free port

1749 Archduchess Maria Teresa implements the rule that Trieste is a free port and extends tax exemptions beyond the port to the entire city.

1797-1813 Intermittent occupation by Napoleonic army

1861 Italy becomes a nation-state

1878 Political demonstrations in Trieste against the occupation of Bosnia-Herzegovina by Austro-Hungarian troops; many Triestines in the Austro-Hungarian army desert, form irredentist organizations committed to an expanded Italy, including not-yet-acquired border territories such as Trieste

1882 Emperor Franz Joseph visits Trieste to celebrate the 500th anniversary of Austrian power; Guglielmo Oberdan, a young Triestine irredentist found with two bombs he planned to use against the emperor, is sentenced to death

1914 Assassination of Archduke Franz Ferdinand, heir to the Austrian throne, by Serbian nationalists; beginning of World War I

1915 Italy enters the war against Austria and Germany and after some devastating losses, emerges a victor in 1918

1919 Trieste becomes part of the Kingdom of Italy

From psychoanalysis to sex. Because of its geographical position, Trieste became a hub of cultural dissemination between northern Europe and Italy. Sigmund Freud's psychoanalytical theories

Sigmund Freud, whose writings had an important influence on Italo Svevo.

(late 1890s) and Otto Weininger's controversial study *Sex and Character* (1903) both entered Italy through Trieste. "Whilst in Italy Freud's ideas met with considerable opposition, both in their scientific and cultural implications, in Trieste they took root with relative ease, on account of the particular social and political configuration of the city" (Bosinelli in McCourt, p. 227). It is no surprise that in a city as diverse and connected to the Austro-Hungarian Empire as Trieste, psychoanalysis would find fertile soil.

The most eminent psychoanalytical authority in the city was Freud's student Edoardo Weiss, a Triestine who practiced there until 1931. The Triestine intellectual class was generally intrigued by these new theories; Weiss could count among his patients the poet Umberto Saba and the critic Bobi Bazlen. Svevo, however, remained skeptical about psychoanalysis, in part because he saw the negative effects it had on his brother-in-law, who, in 1910, after suffering a serious nervous breakdown, was sent to Vienna to be analyzed by Freud himself. Not only did analysis not help the young man, but as Svevo liked to recall: "He returned from the cure destroyed, as lacking in will power as before, but with his feebleness aggravated by the conviction that, being as he was, he could not behave otherwise. It was he who convinced me how dangerous it was to explain to a man how he is made" (Svevo in Veneziani, p. 75).

Still, while Svevo never embraced psychoanalysis as a possible cure, he recognized its value "as a method of looking at the world" and maintained a profound curiosity about it; many of the lapses and neuroses presented in his novel are influenced by Freud's theories (Furbank, p. 107). According to Svevo, his first encounter with Freud's studies occurred in 1908. By this time Freud had already published some of his most important works: *The Interpretation of Dreams* (1900), *The Psychopathology of Everyday Life* (1901), *Jokes and Their Relation to the Unconscious* (1901), and *Delusions and Dreams in Jensen's "Gradiva"* (1907). Svevo was attracted by Freud's theories of the unconscious, the sexual origination of neuroses, and the meaningfulness of dreams, but what he found especially compelling was the Austrian analyst's use of writers and artists to expound his theories. *Delusions and Dreams in Jensen's "Gradiva,"* for instance, invokes a story by German writer Wilhelm Jensen about an archeologist who is enthralled with the marble relief of a woman walking. Freud uses the archeologist's obsession with and recurrent dreams about the effigy to explain the relationship between dreams and reality. "[A] great man our Freud, but more for novelists than for invalids," wrote Svevo in 1927 to Italian author Valerio Jahier (Svevo in Gatt-Rutter, p. 247).

The other intellectual widely read in Trieste at the time was also an Austrian, Otto Weininger, whose anti-feminist and anti-Semitic views made his philosophical treatise, *Sex and Character*, highly controversial among Triestine intellectuals, who could read his work in the original even before it was translated into Italian in 1912. The fact that Weininger committed suicide at age 23, shortly after publishing the work, only made him even more appealing to Triestine intellectuals. As with Freud, Svevo maintained a detached irony towards Weininger's theories. Although he quotes Weininger in his novel, and Weininger's concerns about masculinity and genius are present in his text, he presents them with amused irony.

In *Zeno's Conscience*, Svevo infuses contemporary philosophical/cultural concerns as well as the political complexities peculiar to Trieste into his story. He does so by having his initially confused protagonist learn to navigate a world that is becoming ever more labyrinthine. It is a disoriented, disorienting place, in which a traditional, rigid perspective that attempts to categorize every human and artistic expression in terms of absolute opposites (health versus illness, masculinity versus femininity, nationalism versus internationalism) is being replaced by a more ironic, ambiguous way of perceiving reality.

The Novel in Focus

Plot summary. The novel is introduced by a comical preface, in which a psychoanalyst, Doctor S., states that he is publishing an autobiography written by his patient, Zeno Cosini, as part of his treatment. The doctor is doing so without the patient's consent, in revenge for Cosini having "suspended treatment just when things were going well, denying me the fruit of my long and painstaking analysis of these memories" (Svevo, *Zeno's Conscience*, p. 3). With regret, the doctor concludes that if Cosini had continued with the analysis, he would now be able to discuss and learn from "the many truths and the many lies he has assembled here" (*Zeno's Conscience*, p. 3).

This preface introduces us to the frame of the plot: the aged Zeno Cosini decides to undergo psychoanalysis, seeking a cure for what he considers his various diseases (his inability to quit smoking, his inability to see life as a coherent whole, his constant desire to cheat on his wife, and so forth). The doctor tells him to write down his memories, and Zeno grudgingly complies, although he is uncertain if what he is writing really happened or if he is inventing it. These inconsistent memories form the novel itself. The various entries in Zeno's journal follow a thematic rather than linear narrative pattern; the same period of time is revisited in different chapters, giving the novel a circular, disorienting pattern that captures Zeno's own perception of his life: "For me, time is not that inconceivable thing that never stops. For me, and only for me, it retraces its steps" (*Zeno's Conscience*, p. 14).

The events of the novel can be summarized as follows: Zeno Cosini is born into a rich bourgeois family and spends a carefree youth studying at the university. His innate laziness and indecisiveness make him constantly change his field of study—from chemistry, to law, and then back to chemistry—without ever finishing his degree. The same indecisiveness is visible in his inability to quit smoking despite many attempts, some of which are comical. In the most outlandish, he becomes obsessed with dates, which he writes all over the walls of his room, in the belief that, if the date is significant enough, such as the "ninth day of the ninth month of 1899" or "first day of the first month of 1901," he will be able to give up smoking (*Zeno's Conscience*, p. 13). The only result is that when the walls are completely covered with dates he moves into a different apartment: "Probably I left that room precisely because it had become the graveyard of my good intentions and I believed it no longer possible to conceive any further such intentions in that tomb of so many old ones" (*Zeno's Conscience*, p. 12).

Needless to say, Zeno's odd character worries his father, an old-fashioned businessman who believes his son is crazy. As a consequence, the old Cosini arranges it so that his son will never have executive powers within his firm, and makes Mr. Olivi, his faithful manager, the sole administrator. This slap in the face is coupled with a real one: just before dying the old Cosini raises his hand and then lets it fall against his son's cheek. Was his last intention to chastise Zeno or was it just a freak accident? This question will haunt Zeno for the rest of his life.

FAMOUS CITIZENS

~

Because of its cosmopolitan aura and its beautiful Adriatic setting, Trieste attracted some prominent intellectual figures. In 1911 the poet Rainer Maria Rilke (1875-1926) was a guest of the Princess von Thurn und Taxis at the Duino Castle, not far from Trieste, and it was here that he was inspired to write his most famous collection of poems, *The Duino Elegies* (1923). The Irish writer James Joyce (1882-1941) made Trieste his home for about a decade, from approximately 1904 until the beginning of World War I, and then returned for another short period in 1919. *Dubliners* (1914) was finished in Trieste, and here he also wrote *A Portrait of the Artist as a Young Man* (1916) and conceived his modernist masterpiece, *Ulysses* (1922). (Some critics suggest that Svevo himself was the model for *Ulysses'* hero, Leopold Bloom.) Finally, Sigmund Freud lived in Trieste for a short time when, as a medical student, he worked at the city's marine biology laboratory.

Left with a generous monthly salary, and very little to do, Zeno becomes more and more obsessed with his idiosyncratic neuroses and his attempts to cure them: "Disease is a conviction, and I was born with that conviction" (*Zeno's Conscience*, p. 14).

Legally barred from working in his own firm, Zeno, who still has some aspirations of becoming a respectful businessman, spends his idle days at the stock exchange, where he soon befriends an older investor, Giovanni Malfenti.

Amused by Zeno's inexperience and inertia, Malfenti takes the young man under his wing and teaches him some tricks of the trade. However, he never takes Zeno seriously; indeed, when Zeno, excited by this new activity, proposes to get rid of Olivi and to manage his father's business himself, Malfenti firmly opposes Zeno.

OTTO WEININGER'S *SEX AND CHARACTER*

~

In his long treatise Weininger sets out to define the differences between the sexes. He posits an "ideal man" and an "ideal woman" (similar to the platonic ideals). While "man" is capable of abstracting a coherent whole from the multiplicity of existence, he says, "woman" (and she shares this with the Jew) is wholly defined by her sexuality: "The female, moreover, is completely occupied and content with sexual matters, whilst the male is interested in much else, in war and sports, in social affairs, and feasting, in philosophy and art" (Weininger, p. 89). This obsession distracts women from the higher spiritual and intellectual achievements of humankind, which can be accomplished only by men. Thus, only men can ever achieve a level of genius: "genius declares itself to be a kind of higher masculinity, and thus the female cannot be possessed of genius" (Weininger, p. 111). For Weininger the end of the nineteenth century is the most degenerate period ever experienced by humankind because the Jewish and feminine elements prevail over the masculine; absorbed in the sensual multiplicity of the world, people have lost their sense of unity, their wholeness: "Our age is not only the most Jewish but the most feminine. It is a time when . . . genius is supposed to be a form of madness; a time with no great artists and no great philosophers; a time without originality and yet with the most foolish craving for originality" (Weininger, pp. 329-30).

Soon Zeno is introduced to Malfenti's wife and four daughters. Zeno decides that, in order to be cured from his various pathologies, he should find a wife, and in this way become a respectable patriarch. He immediately falls in love with the beautiful and serious Ada, but she rejects him. He then proposes to the other sisters (all in the course of a single evening) and finally contracts to marry the homely Augusta, the least attractive of the Malfenti girls. Shortly afterwards, Ada marries Guido Spaier, who seems blessed with the healthy attributes that Zeno lacks. He is good-looking,

well-spoken, and self-assured. Also he plays violin and, most importantly, has a business degree; in fact, he is in charge of his own business.

The two marriages play out quite differently. Zeno's marriage turns out to be a happy one. Augusta is a very devoted wife, and she is able to laugh at Zeno's many oddities, while Zeno admires her matter-of-fact attitude towards life: "She knew all the things that could drive me to despair, but in her hands these things changed their nature. Just because the earth rotates, you don't have to get seasick! Quite the contrary! The earth turned, but all other things stayed in their proper place" (*Zeno's Conscience*, p. 157). With her concrete approach to reality, Augusta comes to represent the health that Zeno lacks; he even believes that, through Augusta, he will finally become a healthy man. This, of course, does not happen, so Zeno keeps turning to the medical community. Throughout the story we are introduced to different doctors, who attempt unsuccessfully to cure Zeno's various ticks and ailments.

Augusta soon becomes a mother, but the children interest Zeno very little, and not much is said about them. In spite of his happiness at home, he is unable to remain faithful to his wife. He soon meets a young singer, Carla, who becomes his mistress. Although he feels terrible for cheating on Augusta, and is many times on the verge of confessing his adultery, he finds himself unable to leave the young woman and rationalizes the affair by stating that his sense of guilt towards Augusta makes him love her even more. The affair ends when Carla marries her music teacher. In the meantime Guido invites (or at least so we are told) Zeno to become his partner, and the two brothers-in-law start working together. Zeno accepts the partnership not only in order to keep himself busy, but also because in this way he can be close to Ada, for whom he still has some feelings, although he denies them. Soon he realizes that Guido is not as smart a businessman as he has led the Malfenti family to believe. His "health" is just a façade: he loses money quickly; he is indiscreet about his love affair with his beautiful and incompetent secretary; and he is unable to complete even the simplest business transaction. Ada, aware of what is going on, suffers miserably. She is soon diagnosed with a thyroid ailment and must be sent to a clinic for long periods of time. Uncertain about what to do, Ada, who now sees in Zeno the perfect husband, begs him to keep an eye on her husband and help him reestablish his business. The old patriarch, Malfenti, who is too sick to take charge of the situation, soon dies.

At this point, as the rest of the family sees it, Zeno becomes the man in charge. Moved by Ada's plea, he sets out to restructure the business. Guido, in an attempt to regain a large amount of capital, plays the stock market with disastrous results. Not knowing what to do, he feigns a suicide (an expedient he used before to get some money from Ada), but this time he takes too much poison and dies. Although Zeno knows of Guido's plan, he does not say anything. Instead he tries to get the money back by playing the stock market himself. In 50 frantic hours at the stock exchange Zeno is indeed able to recuperate most of the losses. However, he is late for Guido's funeral, and once he makes it to the cemetery, he follows the wrong procession. Ada interprets Zeno's absence as a clear sign of Zeno's hatred for her late husband, and in the moment when Zeno thought that he would be thanked for helping restore the family's capital, he is instead accused of being responsible for Guido's death.

This ends the bulk of Zeno's memories. The last chapter, "Psychoanalysis," is added a year later, after six months of psychoanalysis. In this chapter Zeno states that he is disappointed with the psychoanalytical method, which has made him feel much worse, despite the doctor's assurance that he has been cured. He also complains that the doctor is paying too much attention to his confessions. At the end of the novel Zeno reveals how misleading his writing is, how innately deceptive, because instead of his local Triestine dialect he has written in Tuscan Italian, which he has not mastered as well:

> [T]he doctor puts too much faith also in those damned confessions of mine, which he won't return to me so I can revise them. Good heavens! He studied only medicine and therefore doesn't know what it means to write in Italian for those of us who speak the dialect and can't write it. A confession in writing is always a lie. With our every Tuscan word, we lie! If he knew how, by predilection, we recount all the things for which we have the words at hand, and how we avoid those things that would oblige us to turn to the dictionary!
> (Zeno's Conscience, p. 404)

The best proof that Zeno is not healed is that his attraction to much younger women still afflicts him, as he points out after an innocent encounter with a young peasant girl.

After having dismissed the doctor's cure, Zeno turns his attention to the events that are shaking the world at this time. It is May 1915 (the time Italy joined France and England against Austria and Germany in the First World War), and Zeno remembers finding himself in the midst of the war. He and his family are on vacation in their house in Italy, not far from Trieste, and one fine morning Zeno decides to go out for a long walk before his usual morning coffee. Without realizing it, he crosses the border into Austria, but when he tries to get back to the Italian side, Austro-Hungarian soldiers will not let him cross over. After a few unfortunate attempts to return to his family, he decides that there is nothing else for him to do but take the train all the way to Trieste, still yearning for his coffee. Once in Trieste, for the first time in his life he must take care of his own affairs because Olivi, an Italian, has fled with his family. Zeno starts to buy and sell all sorts of goods, making an incredible profit. The frantic economic activity in the midst of the conflict makes him realize that indeed he is healthy. What he had been trying to cure was life itself, and unlike other illnesses, life is always fatal: "It doesn't tolerate therapies" (Zeno's Conscience, p. 435).

In the novel's final paragraph Zeno comments on the human condition. Looking at the devastation around him, he recognizes that man's attempt to use various mechanical devices to improve on life is in fact responsible for its decline. In apocalyptic terms he concludes by stating that perhaps an enormous explosion will free the earth from all of its parasites and sickness.

The obsession with health. Throughout the novel Zeno searches for a sense of health. By the end of the story he considers Dr. S., his psychoanalyst, no more than a charlatan and is also disappointed with Dr. Paoli, a physician who has tried for years to cure him. Finally Zeno decides that true health does not exist and that it is futile and ridiculous to spend one's life pursuing it. Zeno's realization reflects the crisis of modern man, who would like to believe in absolute truths (here represented by the idea of health) but must admit that in the contemporary world this is impossible. Compared to his father-in-law Malfenti, and even Guido, Zeno appears weak and inept—but he is the only male figure in the novel who survives and prospers. Svevo here is demonstrating how in his day the old, solid, patriarchal society with its traditional world view must be replaced by a more complex interpretation of existence that allows for contradictions and multiplicity. Instead of seeing life as a coherent organic whole, late-nineteenth-century society must be open to unpredictability and fragmentation. This becomes clear at the end of the novel when Zeno starts buying wares as everyone is selling them.

Observing the devastation of World War I, Zeno concludes that man's attempt to use machinery to improve life has only made things worse. Above, the unburied dead of the Italian army litter the battlefield on the Carso Plateau.

Having become conscious of the variability of reality, he accepts the flexibility of the economic market and purposely decides to invest his money not in gold, but in any type of merchandise whose price can fluctuate constantly. Metaphorically, Zeno's investment practice corresponds to his realization that every experience and situation is relative. Zeno's decision to be a buyer of "any goods" signifies his acceptance of any event as potentially positive and valuable (*Zeno's Conscience*, p. 434). Commerce is the perfect cure for Zeno, not because it leads him to a comprehensive vision of himself or the reality around him, but because it validates his understanding and acceptance of the fluctuation of all seemingly fixed values. By embracing the fluidity of the economic world, Zeno also reevaluates the concept of illness, insofar as inconsistency is considered a disease in turn-of-the-twentieth-century Europe. Thus, Svevo, like other Italian writers in Trieste, begins to disseminate through fiction the concept (from Nietzsche) that adjustment to life in post-World War I Italy calls for a fresh approach, a new philosophical outlook, one that embraces the validity of relative perspectives.

Sources and literary context. With his usual irony, Svevo points out in one of his essays just how deceptive his use of philosophical ideas really is; novelists, he says, "have the habit of playing with philosophic ideas, without really being in a position to expound them. We falsify them, but we also humanize them" (Svevo in Furbank, p. 178). Still, it is possible to detect the profound influence that the ideas of Schopenhauer, Weininger, and Freud had on Svevo. He first read Arthur Schopenhauer's *The World as Will and Representation* in 1885. More than Schopenhauer's pessimism, what interested Svevo was the position that life is an illusory facade. Embracing this and other Schopenhauer ideas enabled Svevo to identify beneath one's conscious motives and rationalizations "the unconscious motives and the hidden egoism which is always working away in secret" (Gatt-Rutter, p. 69). One of the best examples of Svevo's use of Freud's theory of the unconscious occurs when Zeno misses Guido's funeral. Although Zeno keeps telling us he considered Guido a friend, the fact that "by mistake" he follows the wrong funeral suggests that he indeed hates him, as Ada suggests. The importance that dreams acquire in Freud's theories is reflected early in the novel by descriptions of Zeno's dreams. The third obvious influence is Weininger's anti-feminine and anti-Semitic philosophy, which is questioned by our "feminine"-style hero, whose success at the end of the novel depends on his embracing his sickness. Against Weininger, Svevo, as suggested, favors the view of Nietzsche that existence does not add up to a coherent whole but must be embraced in all its peculiar, fragmented parts.

The name Zeno, as well as the character's inability to see time as a linear procession of events, might have been inspired by the ancient Greek philosopher Zeno of Elea, whose paradoxes argued against the very existence of motion, or by Zino Zini, a contemporary of Svevo, whose 1914 *The Two-Fold Mask of the Universe: A Philosophy of Time and Space* (1914) argues that the concept of linear time is illusory.

While the extended use of psychoanalysis is Svevo's own creation, the use of a journal narrative was used before by Luigi Piranello in *The Late Mattia Pascal* (*Il fu Mattia Pascal*, 1904). Both writers are interested in similar issues: the lack of a precise identity and the ways a person deals with reality. But while for Pirandello's characters, the individual perceives his or her lack of an unequivocal identity as a crisis, for Svevo this lack is a part of existence that must be embraced and can, in fact, lead to interesting and positive outcomes.

In Svevo's day, first-person and autobiographical narrative was particularly popular with the *vociani*, a group of young writers who worked for the Florence-based journal *La Voce*. Svevo's text, however, differs greatly from those proposed by the *vociani*. Whereas they made extensive use of expressionistic fragments and were mainly interested in art that communicated their ethical concerns, Svevo was more interested in emphasizing the deceptive role of language.

Svevo's association with James Joyce influenced him greatly. As Svevo's wife recalls, the two writers' weekly English lessons "had nothing to do with grammar; the pair of them talked of literature and touched on a hundred other subjects" (Veneziani, p. 66). Both wanted to find a style that would allow them to reflect on the inner workings of the individual mind.

Finally, there are strong autobiographical elements in the novel. The constant smoking, the inability to play the violin, and the authoritarian father are all parts of Svevo's life. Malfenti recalls Svevo's father-in-law, while his brother-in-law, Giuseppe Oberti, inspired the character of Guido.

Reception. *La coscienza di Zeno* was published in 1923 to very little interest. The few reviews that appeared in Italian papers were mixed: Silvio Benco, a famous Triestine critic, showed some reservations, deeming the style of the novel to be syntactically flawed. A brief summary and comment on the novel in Milan's *Corriere della Sera* newspaper described it as "a somewhat ramshackle and fragmentary novel, perhaps overprolix, but not without psychological interest" (Caprin in Gatt-Rutter, p. 318). Concerned that his latest novel would suffer the same destiny as his first two, Svevo sent James Joyce a copy of the book. The Irish author, who by this time was famous and could count among his friends authors of the caliber of André Gide, Paul Valéry, Ezra Pound, and T. S. Eliot, did not hesitate to help his Triestine friend by introducing the novel to his literary circle. In 1925 Joyce arranged a dinner in Paris with Svevo and the French literary critics Valéry Larbaud and Benjamin

---

ZENO'S NEW PERCEPTION OF ILLNESS

"Naturally I am not ingenuous, and I forgive the doctor for seeing life itself as a manifestation of sickness. Life does resemble sickness a bit, as it proceeds by crises and lyses, and has daily improvements and setbacks. Unlike other sicknesses, life is always fatal. It doesn't tolerate therapies. It would be like stopping holes that we have in our bodies, believing them wounds. We would die of strangulation the moment we were treated."

(*Zeno's Conscience*, p. 435)

Cremieux, who later that year wrote an influential article that hailed Svevo as the Italian Marcel Proust. Cremieux's article was translated into Italian and published in the Milanese *Fiera letteraria* (Literary Fair) in February 1926. In the meantime, the young poet Eugenio Montale heard the name of Svevo for the first time in Paris, where Svevo was held to be one of the most interesting figures of contemporary Italian narrative. Back in Italy Montale bought and read all three novels and, impressed by them, wrote an article for the literary journal *L'Esame* (The Exam) that praised Svevo's innovative style, pointing out how the circular structure of the novel on Zeno reflected the madness of the contemporary world. Montale especially admired Svevo's desire to represent "that dark subterranean zone of *coscienza* [conscience] where the appearances that are most readily taken for granted wobble and blur" (Montale in Gatt-Rutter, p. 330). After the publication of these reviews and articles Svevo was finally recognized as an important literary figure, both in Italy and abroad. All his novels were republished and soon appeared in French, English, and German.

—Elena Coda

For More Information

Cary, Joseph. *A Ghost in Trieste*. Chicago: University of Chicago Press, 1993.

Furbank, P. N. *Italo Svevo: The Man and the Writer*. London: Secker and Warburg, 1966.

Gatt-Rutter, John. *Italo Svevo: A Double Life*. Oxford: Clarendon Press, 1988.

Lebowitz, Naomi. *Italo Svevo*. New Brunswick: Rutgers University Press, 1978.

Magris, Claudio. "Things Near and Far: Nietzsche and the Great Triestine Generation." *Stanford Italian Review* 6, nos. 1-2 (1986): 293-99.

McCourt, John. *The Years of Bloom*. Dublin: The Lilliput Press, 2000.

Minghelli, Giuliana. *In the Shadow of the Mammoth: Italo Svevo and the Emergence of Modernism*. Toronto: University of Toronto Press, 2002.

Moloney, Brian. *Italo Svevo: A Critical Introduction*. Edinburgh: Edinburgh University Press, 1974.

Solomon, Robert C., and Kathleen M. Higgins. *What Nietzsche Really Said*. New York: Schocken, 2000.

Svevo, Italo. *Zeno's Conscience*. Trans. William Weaver. New York: Alfred A. Knopf, 2001.

Veneziani Svevo, Livia. *Memoir of Italo Svevo*. Marlboro, Vt.: The Marlboro Press, 1989.

Weininger, Otto. *Sex and Character*. New York: Putnam, 1907.

Index